Collins

English-Portuguese
Português-Inglês
Dictionary

Collins

HarperCollins Publishers
Westerhill Road
Bishopbriggs
Glasgow
G64 2QT
Great Britain

Fifth Edition 2010

Reprint 10 9 8 7 6 5 4 3 2 1 0

© HarperCollins Publishers 1992, 1995,
2001, 2006, 2010

ISBN 978-0-00-733152-9

Collins® is a registered trademark of
HarperCollins Publishers Limited

www.collinslanguage.com

A catalogue record for this book is
available from the British Library

Disal S.A.
Av. Marquês de São Vicente 182
Barra Funda
01139-000 São Paulo
Brazil

www.disal.com.br

Segunda edição 2010

ISBN 978-0-00-785953-5

Typeset by Wordcraft, Glasgow

Printed in Italy by LEGO Spa,
Lavis (Trento)

Acknowledgements
We would like to thank those authors and
publishers who kindly gave permission for
copyright material to be used in the Collins
Word Web. We would also like to thank
Times Newspapers Ltd for providing
valuable data.

Entered words that we have reason to
believe constitute trademarks have been
designated as such. However, neither the
presence nor absence of such designation
should be regarded as affecting the legal
status of any trademark.

When you buy a Collins dictionary
or thesaurus and register on
www.collinslanguage.com for the free
online and digital services, you will not be
charged by HarperCollins for access to
Collins free Online Dictionary content or
Collins free Online Thesaurus content on
that website. However, your operator's
charges for using the internet on your
computer will apply. Costs vary from
operator to operator. HarperCollins is not
responsible for any charges levied by online
service providers for accessing Collins free
Online Dictionary or Collins free Online
Thesaurus on www.collinslanguage.com
using these services.

HarperCollins does not warrant
that the functions contained in
www.collinslanguage.com content will
be uninterrupted or error free, that
defects will be corrected, or that
www.collinslanguage.com or the server
that makes it available are free of viruses
or bugs. HarperCollins is not responsible
for any access difficulties that may be
experienced due to problems with network,
web, online or mobile phone connections.

ÍNDICE

CONTENTS

MANAGING EDITOR/EDITORA-CHEFE
Gaëlle Amiot-Cadey

EDITORIAL COORDINATION/
COORDENAÇÃO EDITORIAL
Susie Beattie

CONTRIBUTORS/COLABORADORES
John Whitlam
Helen Newstead
Vitoria Davies
Mike Harland
Jane Horwood
Lígia Xavier
Gerard Breslin
Laura Neves
Emma McDade

SERIES EDITOR/DIRETOR DA COLEÇÃO
Rob Scriven

William Collins' dream of knowledge for all began with the publication of his first book in 1819. A self-educated mill worker, he not only enriched millions of lives, but also founded a flourishing publishing house. Today, staying true to this spirit, Collins books are packed with inspiration, innovation, and practical expertise. They place you at the centre of a world of possibility and give you exactly what you need to explore it.

Language is the key to this exploration, and at the heart of Collins Dictionaries is language as it is really used. New words, phrases, and meanings spring up every day, and all of them are captured and analysed by the Collins Word Web. Constantly updated, and with over 2.5 billion entries, this living language resource is unique to our dictionaries.

Words are tools for life. And a Collins Dictionary makes them work for you.

Collins. Do more

INTRODUÇÃO

Ficamos felizes com a sua decisão de comprar o Dicionário Inglês-Português Collins e esperamos que este lhe seja útil na escola, em casa, de férias ou no trabalho.

Esta introdução fornece algumas sugestões de como utilizar da melhor maneira possível o seu dicionário – não somente a partir da ampla lista de palavras mas também a partir das informações fornecidas em cada verbete. Este dicionário visa ajudá-lo a ler e a entender o inglês moderno assim como a exprimir-se corretamente.

No início do Dicionário Collins aparecem as abreviaturas utilizadas, e a ilustração dos sons através de símbolos fonéticos. Você encontrará, a seguir, quadros com verbos portugueses e verbos irregulares ingleses, seguidos por uma seção com números, horas e datas. E, por fim, o novo guia para viajantes fornece centenas de frases úteis que visam lhe dar ajuda prática em situações cotidianas durante uma viagem.

COMO UTILIZAR O DICIONÁRIO COLLINS

Um grande número de informações pode ser encontrado neste dicionário. Vários tipos e tamanhos de letras, símbolos, abreviaturas e parênteses foram utilizados. As convenções e símbolos usados são explicados nas seções seguintes.

VERBETES

As palavras que você procurar no dicionário – os verbetes – estão em ordem alfabética. Eles estão impressos em cor para uma rápida identificação. As palavras que aparecem no topo de cada página indicam o primeiro verbete (se for nas páginas pares) ou o último verbete (se for nas páginas ímpares) da página em questão. Informações sobre a utilização ou forma de certos verbetes são dadas entre parênteses e, em geral, aparecem em forma abreviada e em itálico (p. ex. *(fam), (Com)*).

Quando for apropriado, palavras derivadas aparecem agrupadas no mesmo verbete (**abade, abadia; produce, producer**) num formato ligeiramente menor do que o verbete.

As expressões comuns nas quais o verbete aparece estão impressas em um tamanho diferente de negrito romano. O símbolo '~' usado nas expressões representa o verbete principal no começo de cada parágrafo. Por exemplo, na entrada '**cold**', a expressão '**to be ~**' equivale a '**to be cold**'.

SIGNIFICADOS

A tradução para o verbete aparece em letra normal e quando há mais de um significado ou utilização, estes estão separados por um ponto e vírgula. Frequentemente, você encontrará outras palavras em itálico e entre parênteses antes da tradução, sugerindo contextos nos quais o verbete pode aparecer (p. ex. **rough** *(voice)* ou *(weather)*), ou fornecendo sinônimos (p. ex. **rough** *(violent)*).

PALAVRAS-CHAVE

Atenção especial foi dada a certas palavras em inglês e em português considerados 'palavras-chave' em cada língua. Elas podem, por exemplo, ser usadas com muita frequência ou ter muitos tipos de utilização (p. ex. **be, get**). Verbetes destacados com números ajuda a distinguir as

categorias gramaticais e diferentes significados.
Informações complementares são fornecidas entre
parênteses e em itálico na língua relevante para o usuário.

As categorias gramaticais são dadas em itálico e abreviadas
após a ortografia fonética do verbete (p. ex. *vt, adj, vi*).

Os adjetivos aparecem em ambos os gêneros quando forem
diferentes (**interno, -a**). Esta distinção também é feita
quando os adjetivos têm uma forma irregular no feminino
ou no plural (p. ex. **ateu, atéia**). As formas irregulares de
substantivos feminino ou plural também são indicadas
(p. ex. **child** (*pl* **~ren**)).

INTRODUCTION

We are delighted you have decided to buy the Collins Portuguese Dictionary and hope you will enjoy and benefit from using it at school, at home, on holiday or at work.

This introduction gives you a few tips on how to get the most out of your dictionary – not simply from its comprehensive wordlist but also from the information provided in each entry. This will help you to read and understand modern Portuguese, as well as communicate and express yourself in the language.

The Collins Portuguese Dictionary begins by listing the abbreviations used in the text and illustrating the sounds shown by the phonetic symbols. Next you will find Portuguese verb tables and English irregular verbs followed by a section on numbers, time, and dates. Finally, the new Phrasefinder supplement gives you hundreds of useful phrases which are intended to give you practical help in everyday situations when travelling.

USING YOUR COLLINS DICTIONARY
A wealth of information is presented in the dictionary, using various typefaces, sizes of type, symbols, abbreviations and brackets. The conventions and symbols used are explained in the following sections.

HEADWORDS
The words you look up in the dictionary – 'headwords' – are listed alphabetically. They are printed in colour for rapid identification. The headwords appearing at the top of each page indicate the first (if it appears on a left-hand page)

and last word (if it appears on a right-hand page) dealt with on the page in question.

Information about the usage or form of certain headwords is given in brackets after the phonetic spelling. This usually appears in abbreviated form and in italics. (e.g. (*fam*), (*Comm*)).

Where appropriate, words related to headwords are grouped in the same entry (**abade, abadia; produce, producer**) in a slightly smaller bold type than the headword. Common expressions in which the headword appears are shown in a different size of bold roman type. The swung dash, ~, represents the main headword at the start of each entry. For example, in the entry for '**caminho**', the phrase '**pôr-se a ~**' should be read '**pôr-se a caminho**'.

PHONETIC SPELLINGS

The phonetic spelling of each headword (indicating its pronunciation) is given in square brackets immediately after the headword (e.g. **grande** ['grãdʒi]). A list of these spellings is given on page xv.

MEANINGS

Headword translations are given in ordinary type and, where more than one meaning or usage exists, they are separated by a semicolon. You will often find other words in italics in brackets before the translations. These offer suggested contexts in which the headword might appear (e.g. **intenso** (*emoção*)) or provide synonyms (e.g. **cândido** (*inocente*)).

Special status is given to certain Portuguese and English words which are considered as 'key' words in each language. They may, for example, occur very frequently or have several types of usage (e.g. **bem, ficar**). A combination of lozenges and numbers helps you to distinguish different parts of speech and different meanings. Further helpful information is provided in brackets and in italics in the relevant language for the user.

GRAMMATICAL INFORMATION
Parts of speech are given in abbreviated form in italics after the phonetic spellings of headwords (e.g. *vt, adj, prep*).

Genders of Portuguese nouns are indicated as follows: *m* for a masculine and *f* for a feminine noun. Feminine and irregular plural forms of nouns are also shown next to the headword (**inglês, -esa; material** (*pl* **-ais**)). Adjectives are given in both masculine and feminine forms where these forms are different (**comilão, -lona**).

The gender of the Portuguese translation also appears in *italics* immediately following the key element of the translation, except where there is a regular masculine singular noun ending in 'o', or a regular feminine singular noun ending in 'a'.

ABREVIATURAS

ABBREVIATIONS

abreviatura	*ab(b)r*	abbreviation
adjetivo	*adj*	adjective
administração	*Admin*	administration
advérbio, locução adverbial	*adv*	adverb, adverbial phrase
aeronáutica	*Aer*	flying, air travel
agricultura	*Agr*	agriculture
anatomia	*Anat*	anatomy
arquitetura	*Arq, Arch*	architecture
artigo definido	*art def*	definite article
artigo indefinido	*art indef*	indefinite article
uso atributivo do substantivo	*atr*	compound element
automobilismo	*Aut(o)*	the motor car and motoring
auxiliar	*aux*	auxiliary
aeronáutica	*Aviat*	flying, air travel
biologia	*Bio*	biology
botânica, flores	*Bot*	botany
português do Brasil	BR	Brazilian Portuguese
inglês britânico	*Brit*	British English
química	*Chem*	chemistry
linguagem coloquial (!chulo)	*col(!)*	colloquial (offensive!)
comércio, finanças, bancos	*Com(m)*	commerce, finance, banking
comparativo	*compar*	comparative
computação	*Comput*	computing
conjunção	*conj*	conjunction
construção	*Constr*	building
uso atributivo do substantivo	*cpd*	compound element
cozinha	*Culin*	cookery
artigo definido	*def art*	definite article
economia	*Econ*	economics
educação, escola e universidade	*Educ*	schooling, schools and universities
eletricidade, eletrônica	*Elet, Elec*	electricity, electronics
especialmente	*esp*	especially
exclamação	*excl*	exclamation
feminino	*f*	feminine
ferrovia	*Ferro*	railways
uso figurado	*fig*	figurative use
física	*Fís*	physics
fotografia	*Foto*	photography

ABREVIATURAS

Português	Abrev.	English
(verbo inglês) do qual a partícula é inseparável	fus	(phrasal verb) where the particle is inseparable
geralmente	gen	generally
geografia, geologia	Geo	geography, geology
geralmente	ger	generally
impessoal	impess, impers	impersonal
artigo indefinido	indef art	indefinite article
linguagem coloquial (!chulo)	inf(!)	colloquial (offensive!)
infinitivo	infin	infinitive
invariável	inv	invariable
irregular	irreg	irregular
jurídico	Jur	law
gramática, linguística	Ling	grammar, linguistics
masculino	m	masculine
matemática	Mat(h)	mathematics
medicina	Med	medicine
ou masculino ou feminino, dependendo do sexo da pessoa	m/f	masculine/feminine
militar, exército	Mil	military matters
música	Mús, Mus	music
substantivo	n	noun
navegação, náutica	Náut, Naut	sailing, navigation
adjetivo ou substantivo numérico	num	numeral adjective or noun
	o.s.	oneself
pejorativo	pej	pejorative
fotografia	Phot	photography
física	Phys	physics
fisiologia	Physio	physiology
plural	pl	plural
política	Pol	politics
particípio passado	pp	past participle
preposição	prep	preposition
pronome	pron	pronoun
português de Portugal	PT	European Portuguese
pretérito	pt	past tense
química	Quím	chemistry
religião e cultos	Rel	religion, church services
	sb	somebody
educação, escola e universidade	Sch	schooling, schools and universities
singular	sg	singular

ABREVIATURAS

ABBREVIATIONS

	sth	something
sujeito (gramatical)	*su(b)j*	(grammatical) subject
subjuntivo, conjuntivo	*sub(jun)*	subjunctive
superlativo	*superl*	superlative
também	*tb*	also
técnica, tecnologia	*Tec(h)*	technical term, technology
telecomunicações	*Tel*	telecommunications
tipografia, imprensa	*Tip*	typography, printing
televisão	*TV*	television
tipografia, imprensa	*Typ*	typography, printing
inglês americano	*US*	American English
ver	*V*	see
verbo	*vb*	verb
verbo intransitivo	*vi*	intransitive verb
verbo reflexivo	*vr*	reflexive verb
verbo transitivo	*vt*	transitive verb
zoologia	*Zool*	zoology
marca registrada	®	registered trademark
equivalente cultural	≈	cultural equivalent

PORTUGUESE PRONUNCIATION

The rules given below refer to Brazilian Portuguese.

CONSONANTS

c	[k]	café	c before a, o, u is pronounced as in cat
ce, ci	[s]	cego	c before e or i, as in receive
ç	[s]	raça	ç is pronounced as in receive
ch	[ʃ]	chave	ch is pronounced as in shock
d	[d]	data	as in English EXCEPT
de, di	[dʒ]	difícil cidade	d before an i sound or final unstressed e is pronounced as in judge
g	[g]	gado	g before a, o, u as in gap
ge, gi	[ʒ]	gíria	g before e or i, as s in leisure
h		humano	h is always silent in Portuguese
j	[ʒ]	jogo	j is pronounced as s in leisure
l	[l]	limpo, janela	as in English EXCEPT
	[w]	falta, total	l after a vowel tends to become w
lh	[ʎ]	trabalho	lh is pronounced like the lli in million
m	[m]	animal, massa	as in English EXCEPT
	[ãw]	cantam	m at the end of a syllable preceded by a
	[ĩ]	sim	vowel nasalizes the preceding vowel
n	[n]	nadar, penal	as in English EXCEPT
	[ã]	cansar	n at the end of a syllable, preceded by a
	[ẽ]	alento	vowel and followed by a consonant, nasalizes the preceding vowel
nh	[˜]	tamanho	nh is pronounced like the ni in onion
q	[k]	queijo	qu before i or e is usually pronounced as in kick
q	[kw]	quanto cinquenta	qu before a or o, and sometimes before e or i, is pronounced as in queen
-r-	[r]	compra	r preceded by a consonant (except n) and followed by a vowel is pronounced with a single trill
r-, -r-	[h]	rato, arpão	inital r, r followed by a consonant and
rr	[h]	borracha	rr are pronounced like h in house
-r	[r]	pintar, dizer	word-final r can sometimes be heard as a single trill, but usually it is not pronounced at all in colloquial speech
s-	[s]	sol escada livros	as in English EXCEPT

-s-	[z]	mesa	intervocalic s and s before b, d, g, l, m, n,
		rasgar,	r, and v, as in rose
		desmaio	
-ss-	[s]	nosso	double s is always pronounced as in boss
t	[t]	todo	as in English EXCEPT
te, ti	[tʃ]	amante	t followed by an i sound or final
		tipo	unstressed e is pronounced as ch in cheer
x-	[ʃ]	xarope	initial x is pronounced like sh in ship
-x-	[s]	exceto	x before a consonant is pronounced
		explorar	like s in sail
ex-	[z]	exame	x in the prefix ex before a vowel is pronounced as z in squeeze
-x-	[ʃ]	relaxar	x in any other position may be
	[ks]	fixo	pronounced as in ship, axe or sail
	[s]	auxiliar	
z	[z]	zangar	as in English
		cartaz	

b, f, k, p, v, w are pronounced as in English.

VOWELS

a, á, à, â	[a]	mata	a is normally pronounced as in father
ã	[ã]	irmã	ã is pronounced approximately as in sung
e	[e]	vejo	unstressed (except final) e is pronounced like e in they, stressed e is pronounced either as in they or as in bet
-e	[i]	fome	final e is pronounced as in money
é	[ε]	miséria	é is pronounced as in bet
ê	[e]	pêlo	ê is pronounced as in they
i	[i]	vida	i is pronounced as in mean
o	[o]	locomotiva	unstressed (except final) o is pronounced as in local;
	[ɔ]	loja	stressed o is pronounced either as in
	[o]	globo	local or as in rock
-o	[u]	livro	final o is pronounced as in foot
ó	[ɔ]	óleo	ó is pronounced as in rock
ô	[o]	colônia	ô is pronounced as in local
u	[u]	luva	u is pronounced as in rule
	[w]	linguiça	it is usually silent as in gue, gui, que, qui
		frequente	but in some words it is pronounced as a w sound in this position

xvi

DIPHTHONGS

ãe	[ãj]	mãe	nasalized, approximately as in fl*y*ing
ai	[aj]	vai	as is r*i*de
ao, au	[aw]	aos, auxílio	as is sh*ou*t
ão	[ãw]	vão	nasalized, approximately as in r*ou*nd
ei	[ej]	feira	as is th*ey*
eu	[ew]	deusa	both elements pronounced
oi	[oj]	boi	as is t*oy*
ou	[o]	cenoura	as is l*o*cal
õe	[õj]	aviões	nasalized, approximately as in 'b*oi*ng!'

STRESS

The rules of stress in Portuguese are as follows:

(a)   when a word ends in *a, e, o, m* (except *im, um* and their plural
        forms) or *s*, the second last syllable is stressed;
        cama*ra*da; cama*ra*das
        *par*te; *par*tem

(b)   when a word ends in *i, u, im* (and plural), *um* (and plural), *n* or a
        consonant other than *m* or *s*, the stress falls on the last syllable:
        ven*di*, al*gum*, al*guns*, fa*lar*

(c)   when the rules set out in (a) and (b) are not applicable, an
        acute or circumflex accent appears over the stressed vowel:
        *ó*tica, *â*nimo, in*glês*

In the phonetic transcription, the symbol [¹] precedes the syllable
on which the stress falls.

PRONÚNCIA INGLESA

VOGAIS

	Exemplo Inglês	Explicação
[a:]	father	Entre o *a* de *padre* e o *o* de *nó*; como em *fada*
[ʌ]	but, come	Aproximadamente como o primeiro *a* de *cama*
[æ]	man, cat	Som entre o *a* de *lá* e o *e* de *pé*
[ə]	father, ago	Som parecido com o *e* final pronunciado em Portugal
[ə:]	bird, heard	Entre o *e* aberto e o *o* fechado
[ɛ]	get, bed	Como em *pé*
[ɪ]	it, big	Mais breve do que em *si*
[i:]	tea, see	Como em *fino*
[ɔ]	hot, wash	Como em *pó*
[ɔ:]	saw, all	Como o *o* de *porte*
[u]	put, book	Som breve e mais fechado do que em *burro*
[u:]	too, you	Som aberto como em *juro*

DITONGOS

	Exemplo Inglês	Explicação
[aɪ]	fly, high	Como em *baile*
[au]	how, house	Como em *causa*
[ɛə]	there, bear	Como o *e* de *aeroporto*
[eɪ]	day, obey	Como o *ei* de *lei*
[ɪə]	here, hear	Como *ia* de *companhia*
[əu]	go, note	[ə] seguido de um *u* breve
[ɔɪ]	boy, oil	Como em *boia*
[uə]	poor, sure	Como *ua* em *sua*

CONSOANTES

	Exemplo Inglês	Explicação
[d]	mended	Como em *dado*, an*d*ar
[g]	get, big	Como em *grande*
[dʒ]	gin, judge	Como em i*d*ade
[˜]	sing	Como em *cinco*
[h]	house, he	*h* aspirado
[j]	young, yes	Como em *iogurte*
[k]	come, mock	Como em *cama*
[r]	red, tread	*r* como em *para*, mas pronunciado no céu da boca
[s]	sand, yes	Como em *sala*
[z]	rose, zebra	Como em *zebra*

[ʃ]	she, machine	Como em *ch*apéu
[tʃ]	chin, rich	Como *t* em *t*imbre
[w]	water, which	Como o *u* em á*gu*a
[ʒ]	vision	Como em *j*á
[θ]	think, myth	Sem equivalente, aproximadamente como um *s* pronunciado entre os dentes
[ð]	this, the	Sem equivalente, aproximadamente como um *z* pronunciado entre os dentes

b, f, l, m, n, p, t, v pronunciam-se como em português.

O sinal [*] indica que o r final escrito pronuncia-se apenas em inglês britânico, exceto quando a palavra seguinte começa por uma vogal. O sinal [¹] indica a sílaba acentuada.

EUROPEAN PORTUGUESE SPELLING

In 2009, a spelling reform was introduced in all the Portuguese-speaking countries with the aim of eliminating the differences which existed between Brazilian and European Portuguese spelling. The following table summarizes these differences, which you will come across in texts written before the 2009 reform:

Description	Brazilian spelling pre-2009	European Portuguese spelling pre-2009	Universal spelling post-2009
The combinations -gue-, -gui-, -que-, -qui- when u is pronounced	With trema, e.g. lingüiça, freqüente etc.	Without trema, e.g. linguiça, frequente etc.	Without trema, e.g. linguiça, frequente etc.
Stressed -ei- and -oi- in penultimate syllables	With acute accent, e.g. idéia, heróico	Without acute accent, e.g. ideia, heroico	Without acute accent, e.g. ideia, heroico
Stressed o followed by unstressed o	First o has circumflex accent, e.g vôo, abençôo	No written accent, e.g. voo, abençoo	No written accent, e.g. voo, abençoo
First person plural preterite tense of -ar verbs	Without accent, e.g. amamos, jogamos	With acute accent, e.g. amámos, jogámos	Without accent, e.g. amamos, jogamos
comum + mente	comumente	comummente	comumente
com + nós	conosco	connosco	conosco
(h)úmido and derivatives	úmido, umidade	húmido, humidade	úmido, umidade
Latin consonant group -ct-	Simplified to -c-/-ç- or -t-, e.g. acionar, ação, ator	Silent -c- retained, e.g. accionar, acção, actor	Simplified spelling, e.g. acionar, ação, ator
Latin consonant group -pt-	Simplified to -ç- or -t-, e.g. exceção, ótimo	Silent -p- retained, e.g. excepção, óptimo	Simplified spelling, e.g. exceção, ótimo
Months of the year	e.g. janeiro, dezembro	e.g. Janeiro, Dezembro	e.g. janeiro, dezembro

One important difference between Brazilian and Portuguese spelling which still applies even after the reform is that, when a written accent is required on stressed e and o before m or n, Brazilian uses the circumflex while European uses the acute accent, reflecting the difference in the way the sounds are pronounced, e.g. tênis (BR), ténis (PT); econômico (BR), económico (PT). In addition, there are cases where two different spellings are permitted in European Portuguese to reflect two possible pronunciations, e.g. súdito/súbdito, sutil/subtil, anistia/amnistia.

English – Portuguese

Inglês – Português

A, a [eɪ] *n* A, a *m*; (*Mus*) lá *m*

KEYWORD

a [eɪ, ə] *indef art* (*before vowel or silent h: an*) **1** um(a); **a book/girl/mirror** um livro/uma menina/um espelho; **an apple** uma maçã; **she's a doctor** ela é médica
2 (*instead of the number "one"*) um(a); **a year ago** há um ano, um ano atrás; **a hundred/thousand** *etc* **pounds** cem/mil *etc* libras
3 (*in expressing ratios, prices etc*): **3 a day/week** 3 por dia/semana; **10 km an hour** 10 km por hora; **30p a kilo** 30p o quilo

aback [ə'bæk] *adv*: **to be taken ~** ficar surpreendido, sobressaltar-se
abandon [ə'bændən] *vt* abandonar ▷ *n*: **with ~** com desenfreio

---

abbey ['æbɪ] *n* abadia, mosteiro
abbreviation *n* abreviatura
abdomen ['æbdəmən] *n* abdômen *m*
abduct [æb'dʌkt] *vt* sequestrar
ability [ə'bɪlɪtɪ] *n* habilidade *f*, capacidade *f*; (*talent*) talento
able ['eɪbl] *adj* capaz; (*skilled*) hábil, competente; **to be ~ to do sth** poder fazer algo
abnormal [æb'nɔːməl] *adj* anormal
aboard [ə'bɔːd] *adv* a bordo ▷ *prep* a bordo de
abolish [ə'bɔlɪʃ] *vt* abolir
aborigine [æbə'rɪdʒɪnɪ] *n* aborígene *m/f*
abort [ə'bɔːt] *vt* (*Med*) abortar; (*plan*) cancelar; **abortion** *n* aborto; **to have an abortion** fazer um aborto

KEYWORD

about [ə'baut] *adv approximately*) aproximadamente; **it takes about 10 hours** leva ou menos 10 horas; **it's just about finished** está quase terminado
2 (*referring to place*) por toda parte, por todo lado; **to run/walk** *etc* **about** correr/andar *etc* por todos os lados
3: **to be about to do sth** estar a ponto de fazer algo
▷ *prep* **1** (*relating to*) acerca de, sobre; **what is it about?** do que se trata?, é sobre o quê?; **what** *or* **how about doing this?** que tal se fizermos isso?
2 (*place*) em redor de, por

above [ə'bʌv] *adv* em *or* por cima, acima ▷ *prep* acima de, por cima de; **costing ~ £10** que custa mais de £10; **~ all** sobretudo

abroad [ə'brɔːd] *adv* (*be abroad*) no estrangeiro; (*go abroad*) ao estrangeiro

abrupt [ə'brʌpt] *adj* (*sudden*) brusco; (*curt*) ríspido

abscess ['æbsɪs] *n* abscesso (*BR*), abcesso (*PT*)

absence ['æbsəns] *n* ausência

absent ['æbsənt] *adj* ausente; **absent-minded** *adj* distraído

absolute ['æbsəluːt] *adj* absoluto; **absolutely** [æbsə'luːtlɪ] *adv* absolutamente

absorb [əb'zɔːb] *vt* absorver; (*group, business*) incorporar; (*changes*) assimilar; (*information*) digerir; **absorbent cotton** (*US*) *n* algodão *m* hidrófilo

abstain [əb'steɪn] *vi*: **to ~ (from)** abster-se (de)

abstract ['æbstrækt] *adj* abstrato

absurd [əb'sɜːd] *adj* absurdo

abuse [*n* ə'bjuːs, *vt* ə'bjuːz] *n* (*insults*) insultos *mpl*; (*misuse*) abuso; (*ill-treatment*) maus-tratos *mpl* ▷ *vt* insultar; maltratar; abusar; **abusive** [ə'bjuːsɪv] *adj* ofensivo

abysmal [ə'bɪzməl] *adj* (*ignorance*) profundo, total; (*very bad*) péssimo

academic [ækə'dɛmɪk] *adj* acadêmico; (*pej: issue*) teórico ▷ *n* universitário(-a)

academy [ə'kædəmɪ] *n* (*learned body*) academia; **~ of music** conservatório

accelerate [æk'sɛləreɪt] *vt, vi* acelerar; **accelerator** *n* acelerador *m*

accent ['æksɛnt] *n* (*written*) acento; (*pronunciation*) sotaque *m*; (*fig: emphasis*) ênfase *f*

accept [ək'sɛpt] *vt* aceitar; (*responsibility*) assumir;

acceptable *adj* (*offer*) bem-vindo; (*risk*) aceitável; **acceptance** *n* aceitação *f*

access ['æksɛs] *n* acesso; **accessible** [æk'sɛsəbl] *adj* acessível; (*available*) disponível

accessory [æk'sɛsərɪ] *n* acessório; (*Law*): **~ to** cúmplice *m/f* de

accident ['æksɪdənt] *n* acidente *m*; (*chance*) casualidade *f*; **by ~** (*unintentionally*) sem querer; (*by coincidence*) por acaso; **accidental** [æksɪ'dɛntl] *adj* acidental; **accidentally** [æksɪ'dɛntəlɪ] *adv* sem querer; **Accident and Emergency Department** *n* (*Brit*) pronto-socorro

acclaim [ə'kleɪm] *n* aclamação *f*

accommodate [ə'kɔmədeɪt] *vt* alojar; (*subj: car, hotel, etc*) acomodar; (*oblige, help*) comprazer a; **accommodation** [əkɔmə'deɪʃən] *n* alojamento; **accommodations** (*US*) *npl* = **accommodation**

accompany [ə'kʌmpənɪ] *vt* acompanhar

accomplice [ə'kʌmplɪs] *n* cúmplice *m/f*

accomplish [ə'kʌmplɪʃ] *vt* (*task*) concluir; (*goal*) alcançar; **accomplishment** *n* realização *f*

accord [ə'kɔːd] *n* tratado ▷ *vt* conceder; **of his own ~** por sua iniciativa; **accordance** [ə'kɔːdəns] *n*: **in accordance with** de acordo com; **according to** segundo; (*in accordance with*) conforme; **accordingly** *adv* por conseguinte; (*appropriately*) do modo devido

account [ə'kaunt] *n* conta; (*report*) relato; **accounts** *npl* (*books, department*) contabilidade *f*; **of no ~** sem importância; **on ~** por conta;

on no ~ de modo nenhum; **on ~ of** por causa de; **to take into ~, take ~ of** levar em conta; **account for** vt fus (explain) explicar; (represent) representar; **accountant** n contador(a) m/f (BR), contabilista m/f (PT); **account number** n número de conta

accumulate [ə'kju:mjuleɪt] vt acumular ▷ vi acumular-se

accuracy ['ækjurəsɪ] n exatidão f, precisão f

accurate ['ækjurɪt] adj (description) correto; (person, device) preciso; **accurately** adv com precisão

accusation [ækju'zeɪʃən] n acusação f; (instance) incriminação f

accuse [ə'kju:z] vt: **to ~ sb (of sth)** acusar alguém (de algo); **accused** n: **the accused** o/a acusado/a

ace [eɪs] n ás m

ache [eɪk] n dor f ▷ vi (yearn): **to ~ to do sth** ansiar por fazer algo; **my head ~s** dói-me a cabeça

achieve [ə'tʃi:v] vt alcançar; (victory, success) obter; **achievement** n realização f; (success) proeza

acid ['æsɪd] adj, n ácido

acknowledge [ək'nɔlɪdʒ] vt (fact) reconhecer; (also: **~ receipt of**) acusar o recebimento de (BR) or a recepção de (PT); **acknowledgement** n notificação f de recebimento

acne ['æknɪ] n acne f

acorn ['eɪkɔ:n] n bolota

acoustic [ə'ku:stɪk] adj acústico

acquire [ə'kwaɪər] vt adquirir

acquit [ə'kwɪt] vt absolver; **to ~ o.s. well** desempenhar-se bem

acre ['eɪkər] n acre m (= 4047m²)

across [ə'krɔs] prep (on the other side of) no outro lado de; (crosswise)

através de ▷ adv: **to walk ~ (the road)** atravessar (a rua); **the lake is 12 km ~** o lago tem 12 km de largura; **~ from** em frente de

acrylic [ə'krɪlɪk] adj acrílico ▷ n acrílico

act [ækt] n ação f; (Theatre) ato; (in show) número; (Law) lei f ▷ vi tomar ação; (behave, have effect) agir; (Theatre) representar; (pretend) fingir ▷ vt (part) representar; **in the ~ of** no ato de; **to ~ as** servir de; **acting** adj interino ▷ n: **to do some acting** fazer teatro

action ['ækʃən] n ação f; (Mil) batalha, combate m; (Law) ação judicial; **out of ~** (person) fora de combate; (thing) com defeito; **to take ~** tomar atitude; **action replay** n (TV) replay m

activate ['æktɪveɪt] vt acionar

active ['æktɪv] adj ativo; (volcano) em atividade; **actively** adv ativamente; **activity** [æk'tɪvɪtɪ] n atividade f

actor ['æktər] n ator m

actress ['æktrɪs] n atriz f

actual ['æktjuəl] adj real; **actually** adv realmente; (in fact) na verdade; (even) mesmo

acute [ə'kju:t] adj agudo; (person) perspicaz

ad [æd] n abbr = **advertisement**

A.D. adv abbr (= Anno Domini) d.C.

adamant ['ædəmənt] adj inflexível

adapt [ə'dæpt] vt adaptar ▷ vi: **to ~ (to)** adaptar-se (a)

add [æd] vt acrescentar; (figures: also: **~ up**) somar ▷ vi: **to ~ to** aumentar

addict ['ædɪkt] n viciado(-a); **drug ~** toxicômano(-a); **addicted** [ə'dɪktɪd] adj: **to be/become**

addicted to ser/ficar viciado em;
addiction n dependência;
addictive adj que causa
dependência
addition [ə'dɪʃən] n adição f; (thing
added) acréscimo; **in ~** além disso;
in ~ to além de; **additional** adj
adicional
additive ['ædɪtɪv] n aditivo
address [ə'drɛs] n endereço;
(speech) discurso ▷ vt (letter)
endereçar; (speak to) dirigir-se a,
dirigir a palavra a; **to ~ (o.s. to)**
enfocar
adequate ['ædɪkwɪt] adj (enough)
suficiente; (satisfactory)
satisfatório
adhere [əd'hɪər] vi: **to ~ to** aderir a;
(abide by) ater-se a
adhesive [əd'hi:zɪv] n adesivo
adjective ['ædʒɛktɪv] n adjetivo
adjoining [ə'dʒɔɪnɪŋ] adj adjacente
adjourn [ə'dʒə:n] vt (session)
suspender ▷ vi encerrar a sessão;
(go) deslocar-se
adjust [ə'dʒʌst] vt (change) ajustar;
(clothes) arrumar; (machine) regular
▷ vi: **to ~ (to)** adaptar-se (a);
adjustment n ajuste m; (of engine)
regulagem f; (of prices, wages)
reajuste m; (of person) adaptação f
administer [əd'mɪnɪstər] vt
administrar; (justice) aplicar;
(drug) ministrar; **administration**
[ədmɪnɪs'treɪʃən] n administração
f; (US: government) governo;
administrative [əd'mɪnɪstrətɪv]
adj administrativo
admiral ['ædmərəl] n almirante m
admire [əd'maɪər] vt (respect)
respeitar; (appreciate) admirar;
admission [əd'mɪʃən] n
(admittance) entrada; (fee)
ingresso; (confession) confissão f

admit [əd'mɪt] vt admitir; (accept)
aceitar; (confess) confessar **admit
to** vt fus confessar; **admittance** n
entrada; **admittedly** adv
evidentemente
adolescent [ædəu'lɛsnt] adj, n
adolescente m/f
adopt [ə'dɔpt] vt adotar; **adopted**
adj adotivo; **adoption** n adoção f
adore [ə'dɔ:r] vt adorar
Adriatic [eɪdrɪ'ætɪk], **Adriatic Sea**
n (mar m) Adriático
adrift [ə'drɪft] adv à deriva
ADSL n abbr (= asymmetric digital
subscriber line) ADSL m
adult ['ædʌlt] n adulto(-a) ▷ adj
adulto; (literature, education) para
adultos
adultery [ə'dʌltərɪ] n adultério
advance [əd'vɑ:ns] n avanço;
(money) adiantamento ▷ adj
antecipado ▷ vt (money) adiantar
▷ vi (move forward) avançar;
(progress) progredir; **in ~** com
antecedência; **to make ~s to sb**
fazer propostas a alguém;
advanced adj adiantado
advantage [əd'vɑ:ntɪdʒ] n
vantagem f; (supremacy)
supremacia, vantagem f; **to take ~
of** aproveitar-se de
adventure [əd'vɛntʃər] n aventura
adverb ['ædvə:b] n advérbio
adverse ['ædvə:s] adj (effect)
contrário; (weather, publicity)
desfavorável
advert ['ædvə:t] n abbr
= **advertisement**
advertise ['ædvətaɪz] vi anunciar
▷ vt (event, job) anunciar; (product)
fazer a propaganda de; **to ~ for**
(staff) procurar; **advertisement**
[əd'və:tɪsmənt] n (classified)
anúncio; (display, TV) propaganda,

anúncio; **advertising** n
publicidade f
advice [əd'vaɪs] n conselhos mpl;
(notification) aviso; **piece of ~**
conselho; **to take legal ~**
consultar um advogado
advise [əd'vaɪz] vt aconselhar;
(inform): **to ~ sb of sth** avisar
alguém de algo; **to ~ sb against
sth** desaconselhar algo a alguém;
to ~ sb against doing sth
aconselhar alguém a não fazer
algo; **advisory** adj consultivo; **in
an advisory capacity** na
qualidade de assessor(a) or
consultor(a)
advocate [vt ˈædvəkeɪt, n ˈædvəkɪt]
vt defender; (recommend) advogar
▷ n advogado(-a); (supporter)
defensor(a) m/f
Aegean [iː'dʒiːən] n: **the ~ (Sea)** o
(mar) Egeu
aerial [ˈɛərɪəl] n antena ▷ adj aéreo
aerobics [ɛə'rəʊbɪks] n ginástica
aeroplane [ˈɛərəpleɪn] (Brit) n
avião m
aerosol [ˈɛərəsɒl] n aerossol m
affair [ə'fɛər] n (matter) assunto;
(business) negócio; (question)
questão f; (also: **love ~**) caso
affect [ə'fɛkt] vt afetar; (move)
comover; **affected** adj afetado
affection [ə'fɛkʃən] n afeto, afeição
f; **affectionate** adj afetuoso
afflict [ə'flɪkt] vt afligir
affluent [ˈæfluənt] adj rico; **the ~
society** a sociedade de abundância
afford [ə'fɔːd] vt (provide) fornecer;
(goods etc) ter dinheiro suficiente
para; (permit o.s.): **I can't ~ the
time** não tenho tempo;
affordable adj acessível
afraid [ə'freɪd] adj assustado; **to be
~ of/to** ter medo de; **I am ~ that**

lamento que; **I'm ~ so/not** receio
que sim/não
Africa [ˈæfrɪkə] n África; **African**
adj, n africano(-a)
after [ˈɑːftər] prep depois de ▷ adv
depois ▷ conj depois que; **a
quarter ~ two** (US) duas e quinze;
what are you ~? o que você quer?;
who are you ~? quem procura?;
~ having done tendo feito; **to ask
~ sb** perguntar por alguém; **~ all**
afinal (de contas); **~ you!** passe
primeiro!; **aftermath** n
consequências fpl; **afternoon** n
tarde f; **after-shave, after-shave
lotion** n loção f após-barba;
aftersun [ˈɑːftəsʌn] n loção f
pós-sol; **afterwards** adv depois
again [ə'gɛn] adv (once more) outra
vez; (repeatedly) de novo; **to do sth
~** voltar a fazer algo; **~ and ~**
repetidas vezes
against [ə'gɛnst] prep contra;
(compared to) em contraste com
age [eɪdʒ] n idade f; (period) época
▷ vt, vi envelhecer; **he's 20 years
of ~** ele tem 20 anos de idade; **to
come of ~** atingir a maioridade;
it's been ~s since I saw him faz
muito tempo que eu não o vejo;
aged [ˈeɪdʒɪd] adj idoso ▷ npl: **the
aged** os idosos; **age group** n faixa
etária; **age limit** n idade f
mínima/máxima
agency [ˈeɪdʒənsɪ] n agência;
(government body) órgão m
agenda [ə'dʒɛndə] n ordem f do dia
agent [ˈeɪdʒənt] n agente m/f
aggravate [ˈægrəveɪt] vt agravar;
(annoy) irritar
aggressive [ə'grɛsɪv] adj agressivo
AGM n abbr (= annual general
meeting) AGO f
ago [ə'gəʊ] adv: **2 days ~** há 2 dias

(atrás); **not long ~** há pouco tempo; **how long ~?** há quanto tempo?

agony ['ægənɪ] n (pain) dor f; **to be in ~** sofrer dores terríveis

agree [ə'griː] vt combinar ▷ vi (correspond) corresponder; **to ~ (with)** concordar (com); **to ~ to do** aceitar fazer; **to ~ to sth** consentir algo; **to ~ that** concordar or admitir que; **agreeable** adj agradável; (willing) disposto; **agreed** adj combinado; **agreement** n acordo; (Comm) contrato; **in agreement** de acordo

agricultural [ægrɪ'kʌltʃərəl] adj (of crops) agrícola; (of crops and cattle) agropecuário

agriculture ['ægrɪkʌltʃər] n (of crops) agricultura; (of crops and cattle) agropecuária

ahead [ə'hɛd] adv adiante; **go right** or **straight ~** siga em frente; **go ~!** (fig) vá em frente!; **~ of** na frente de

aid [eɪd] n ajuda ▷ vt ajudar; **in ~ of** em benefício de; **to ~ and abet** (Law) ser cúmplice de

AIDS [eɪdz] n abbr (= acquired immune deficiency syndrome) AIDS f (BR), SIDA f (PT)

aim [eɪm] vt: **to ~ sth (at)** apontar algo (para); (missile, remark) dirigir algo (a) ▷ vi (also: **take ~**) apontar ▷ n (skill) pontaria; (objective) objetivo; **to ~ at** mirar; **to ~ to do** pretender fazer

ain't [eɪnt] (inf) = **am not**; **aren't**; **isn't**

air [ɛər] n ar m; (appearance) aparência, aspecto ▷ vt arejar; (grievances, ideas) discutir ▷ cpd aéreo; **to throw sth into the ~** jogar algo para cima; **by ~** (travel) de avião; **to be on the ~** (Radio, TV)

estar no ar; **air bed** ['ɛəbɛd] (Brit) n colchão m de ar; **air conditioning** n ar-condicionado; **aircraft** n inv aeronave f; **airfield** n campo de aviação; **Air Force** n Força Aérea, Aeronáutica; **air hostess** (Brit) n aeromoça (BR), hospedeira (PT); **airline** n linha aérea; **airliner** n avião m de passageiros; **airmail** n: **by airmail** por via aérea; **airplane** (US) n avião m; **airport** n aeroporto; **airsick** adj: **to be airsick** enjoar-se (no avião); **airtight** adj hermético; **airy** adj (room) arejado; (manner) leviano

aisle [aɪl] n (of church) nave f; (of theatre etc) corredor m

ajar [ə'dʒɑːr] adj entreaberto

alarm [ə'lɑːm] n alarme m; (anxiety) inquietação f ▷ vt alarmar; **alarm clock** n despertador m

album ['ælbəm] n (for stamps etc) álbum m; (record) elepê m

alcohol ['ælkəhɔl] n álcool m; **alcohol-free** adj sem álcool; **alcoholic** [ælkə'hɔlɪk] adj alcoólico ▷ n alcoólatra m/f

ale [eɪl] n cerveja

alert [ə'ləːt] adj atento; (to danger, opportunity) alerta ▷ n alerta m ▷ vt: **to ~ sb (to sth)** alertar alguém (de or sobre algo); **to be on the ~** estar alerta; (Mil) ficar de prontidão

Algarve [æl'gɑːv] n: **the ~** o Algarve

algebra ['ældʒɪbrə] n álgebra

Algeria [æl'dʒɪərɪə] n Argélia

alias ['eɪlɪəs] adv também chamado ▷ n (of criminal) alcunha; (of writer) pseudônimo

alibi ['ælɪbaɪ] n álibi m

alien ['eɪlɪən] n estrangeiro(-a); (from space) alienígena m/f ▷ adj: **~ to** alheio a

alight [ə'laɪt] *adj* em chamas; (*eyes*) aceso; (*expression*) intento ▷ *vi* (*passenger*) descer (de um veículo); (*bird*) pousar

alike [ə'laɪk] *adj* semelhante ▷ *adv* similarmente, igualmente; **to look ~** parecer-se

alive [ə'laɪv] *adj* vivo; (*lively*) alegre

 KEYWORD

all [ɔ:l] *adj* (*singular*) todo(-a); (*plural*) todos(-as); **all day/night** o dia inteiro/a noite inteira; **all five came** todos os cinco vieram; **all the books/food** todos os livros/ toda a comida
▷ *pron* 1 tudo; **all of us/the boys went** todos nós fomos/todos os meninos foram; **is that all?** é só isso?; (*in shop*) mais alguma coisa? 2 (*in phrases*): **above all** sobretudo; **after all** afinal (de contas); **not at all** (*in answer to question*) em absoluto, absolutamente não; **I'm not at all tired** não estou nada cansado; **anything at all will do** qualquer coisa serve; **all in all** ao todo
▷ *adv* todo, completamente; **all alone** completamente só; **it's not as hard as all that** não é tão difícil assim; **all the more** ainda mais; **all the better** tanto melhor, melhor ainda; **all but** quase; **the score is 2 all** o jogo está empatado em 2 a 2

allegiance [ə'li:dʒəns] *n* lealdade *f*

allergic [ə'lə:dʒɪk] *adj*: **~ (to)** alérgico(a)

allergy ['ælədʒɪ] *n* alergia

alleviate [ə'li:vɪeɪt] *vt* (*pain*) aliviar; (*difficulty*) minorar

alley ['ælɪ] *n* viela

alliance [ə'laɪəns] *n* aliança

all-in (*Brit*) *adj, adv* (*charge*) tudo incluído

allocate ['æləkeɪt] *vt* destinar

allot [ə'lɔt] *vt*: **to ~ to** designar para

all-out *adj* (*effort etc*) máximo ▷ *adv*: **all out** com toda a força

allow [ə'lau] *vt* permitir; (*claim, goal*) admitir; (*sum, time estimated*) calcular; (*concede*): **to ~ that** reconhecer que; **to ~ sb to do** permitir a alguém fazer **allow for** *vt fus* levar em conta; **allowance** [ə'lauəns] *n* ajuda de custo; (*welfare, payment*) pensão *f*, auxílio; (*Tax*) abatimento; **to make allowances for** levar em consideração

all right *adv* (*well*) bem; (*correctly*) corretamente; (*as answer*) está bem!

ally [*n* 'ælaɪ, *vt* ə'laɪ] *n* aliado ▷ *vt*: **to ~ o.s. with** aliar-se com

almighty [ɔ:l'maɪtɪ] *adj* onipotente; (*row etc*) maior

almond ['ɑ:mənd] *n* amêndoa

almost ['ɔ:lməust] *adv* quase

alone [ə'ləun] *adj* só, sozinho ▷ *adv* só, somente; **to leave sb ~** deixar alguém em paz; **to leave sth ~** não tocar em algo; **let ~ ...** sem falar em ...

along [ə'lɔŋ] *prep* por, ao longo de ▷ *adv*: **is he coming ~?** ele vem conosco?; **he was hopping/ limping ~** ele ia pulando/ coxeando; **~ with** junto com; **all ~** o tempo tudo; **alongside** *prep* ao lado de ▷ *adv* encostado

aloof [ə'lu:f] *adj* afastado, altivo ▷ *adv*: **to stand ~** afastar-se

aloud [ə'laud] *adv* em voz alta

alphabet ['ælfəbɛt] *n* alfabeto

Alps [ælps] *npl*: **the ~** os Alpes

already [ɔːlˈrɛdɪ] *adv* já

alright [ˈɔːlˈraɪt] (*Brit*) *adv* = **all right**

also [ˈɔːlsəu] *adv* também; (*moreover*) além disso

altar [ˈɔltəʳ] *n* altar *m*

alter [ˈɔltəʳ] *vt* alterar ▷ *vi* modificar-se

alternate [*adj* ɔlˈtəːnɪt, *vi* ˈɔltəːneɪt] *adj* alternado; (*US: alternative*) alternativo ▷ *vi*: **to ~ with** alternar-se (com)

alternative [ɔlˈtəːnətɪv] *adj* alternativo ▷ *n* alternativa; **alternatively** *adv*: **alternatively one could ...** por outro lado se podia ...

although [ɔːlˈðəu] *conj* embora; (*given that*) se bem que

altitude [ˈæltɪtjuːd] *n* altitude *f*

altogether [ɔːltəˈgɛðəʳ] *adv* totalmente; (*on the whole*) no total

aluminium [æljuˈmɪnɪəm] (*Brit*) *n* alumínio

aluminum [əˈluːmɪnəm] (*US*) *n* = **aluminium**

always [ˈɔːlweɪz] *adv* sempre

Alzheimer's [ˈæltshaɪməz], **Alzheimer's disease** *n* mal *m* de Alzheimer

am [æm] *vb see* **be**

a.m. *adv abbr* (= *ante meridiem*) da manhã

amateur [ˈæmətəʳ] *adj, n* amador(a) *m/f*

amaze [əˈmeɪz] *vt* pasmar; **to be ~d (at)** espantar-se (de *or* com); **amazement** *n* pasmo, espanto; **amazing** *adj* surpreendente; (*fantastic*) fantástico

Amazon [ˈæməzən] *n* Amazonas *m*

ambassador [æmˈbæsədəʳ] *n* embaixador/embaixatriz *m/f*

amber [ˈæmbəʳ] *n* âmbar *m*; **at ~**

(*Brit: Aut*) em amarelo

ambiguous [æmˈbɪgjuəs] *adj* ambíguo

ambition [æmˈbɪʃən] *n* ambição *f*; **ambitious** *adj* ambicioso

ambulance [ˈæmbjuləns] *n* ambulância

ambush [ˈæmbuʃ] *n* emboscada ▷ *vt* emboscar

amend [əˈmɛnd] *vt* emendar; **to make ~s (for)** compensar

America [əˈmɛrɪkə] *n* (*continent*) América; (*USA*) Estados Unidos *mpl*; **American** *adj* americano; (*from USA*) norte-americano, estadunidense ▷ *n* americano(-a); (*from USA*) norte-americano(-a)

amicable [ˈæmɪkəbl] *adj* amigável

ammunition [æmjuˈnɪʃən] *n* munição *f*

among [əˈmʌŋ], **amongst** [əˈmʌŋst] *prep* entre, no meio de

amount [əˈmaunt] *n* quantidade *f*; (*of money etc*) quantia ▷ *vi*: **to ~ to** (*total*) montar a; (*be same as*) equivaler a, significar

amp [æmp], **ampère** [ˈæmpɛəʳ] *n* ampère *m*

ample [ˈæmpl] *adj* amplo; (*abundant*) abundante; (*enough*) suficiente

amplifier [ˈæmplɪfaɪəʳ] *n* amplificador *m*

amuse [əˈmjuːz] *vt* divertir; (*distract*) distrair; **amusement** *n* diversão *f*; (*pleasure*) divertimento; (*pastime*) passatempo; **amusement park** *n* parque *m* de diversões

an [æn, ən, n] *indef art see* **a**

anaesthetic [ænɪsˈθɛtɪk], (*US*) **anesthetic** *n* anestésico

analyse [ˈænəlaɪz], (*US*) **analyze** *vt* analisar; **analysis** [əˈnæləsɪs] (*pl*

analyses) n análise f; **analyst** ['ænəlɪst] n analista m/f; (psychoanalyst) psicanalista m/f

analyze ['ænəlaɪz] (US) vt = **analyse**

anarchy ['ænəkɪ] n anarquia

anatomy [ə'nætəmɪ] n anatomia

ancestor ['ænsɪstər] n antepassado

anchor ['æŋkər] n âncora ▷ vi (also: **to drop ~**) ancorar, fundear ▷ vt (fig): **to ~ sth to** firmar algo em; **to weigh ~** levantar âncoras

anchovy ['æntʃəvɪ] n enchova

ancient ['eɪnʃənt] adj antigo; (person, car) velho

and [ænd] conj e; **~ so on** e assim por diante; **try ~ come** tente vir; **he talked ~ talked** ele falou sem parar; **better ~ better** cada vez melhor

Andes ['ændi:z] npl: **the ~** os Andes

angel ['eɪndʒəl] n anjo

anger ['æŋgər] n raiva

angina [æn'dʒaɪnə] n angina (de peito)

angle ['æŋgl] n ângulo; (viewpoint): **from their ~** do ponto de vista deles

Anglican ['æŋglɪkən] adj, n anglicano(-a)

angling ['æŋglɪŋ] n pesca à vara (BR) or à linha (PT)

angry ['æŋgrɪ] adj zangado; **to be ~ with sb/at sth** estar zangado com alguém/algo; **to get ~** zangar-se

anguish ['æŋgwɪʃ] n (physical) dor f, sofrimento; (mental) angústia

animal ['ænɪməl] n animal m, bicho ▷ adj animal

aniseed ['ænɪsi:d] n erva-doce f, anis f

ankle ['æŋkl] n tornozelo

annex [n 'æneks, vt ə'neks] n (Brit: building) anexo ▷ vt anexar

anniversary [ænɪ'və:sərɪ] n aniversário

announce [ə'nauns] vt anunciar; **announcement** n anúncio; (official) comunicação f; (in letter etc) aviso; **announcer** n (Radio, TV) locutor(a) m/f

annoy [ə'nɔɪ] vt aborrecer; **don't get ~ed!** não se aborreça!; **annoying** adj irritante

annual ['ænjuəl] adj anual ▷ n (Bot) anual f; (book) anuário

anonymous [ə'nɔnɪməs] adj anônimo

anorak ['ænəræk] n anoraque m (BR), anorak m (PT)

another [ə'nʌðər] adj: **~ book** (one more) outro livro, mais um livro; (a different one) um outro livro, um livro diferente ▷ pron outro; see also **one**

answer ['ɑ:nsər] n resposta; (to problem) solução f ▷ vi responder ▷ vt (reply to) responder a; (problem) resolver; **in ~ to your letter** em resposta or respondendo à sua carta; **to ~ the phone** atender o telefone; **to ~ the bell** or **the door** atender à porta **answer back** vi replicar, retrucar **answer for** vt fus responder por, responsabilizar-se por **answer to** vt fus (description) corresponder a; **answering machine** n secretária eletrônica; **answerphone** n (esp Brit) secretária eletrônica

ant [ænt] n formiga

Antarctic [ænt'ɑ:ktɪk] n: **the ~** o Antártico

antenatal ['æntɪ'neɪtl] adj pré-natal

anthem ['ænθəm] n: **national ~** hino nacional

anticipate [æn'tɪsɪpeɪt] vt prever;

(*expect*) esperar; (*look forward to*) aguardar, esperar; **anticipation** *n* expectativa; (*eagerness*) entusiasmo

anticlimax [æntɪˈklaɪmæks] *n* desapontamento

anticlockwise [æntɪˈklɔkwaɪz] (*Brit*) *adv* em sentido anti-horário

antics [ˈæntɪks] *npl* bobices *fpl*; (*of child*) travessuras *fpl*

antifreeze [ˈæntɪfriːz] *n* anticongelante *m*

antihistamine [æntɪˈhɪstəmiːn] *n* anti-histamínico

antique [ænˈtiːk] *n* antiguidade *f* ▷ *adj* antigo; **antique shop** *n* loja de antiguidades

antiseptic [æntɪˈsɛptɪk] *n* antisséptico

antisocial [æntɪˈsəuʃəl] *adj* antissocial

antivirus [ˈæntɪˈvaɪərəs] *adj* antivírus *m inv*; **~ software** software antivírus

antlers [ˈæntləz] *npl* esgalhos *mpl*, chifres *mpl*

anxiety [æŋˈzaɪətɪ] *n* (*worry*) inquietude *f*; (*eagerness*) ânsia; (*Med*) ansiedade *f*; **~ to do** ânsia de fazer

anxious [ˈæŋkʃəs] *adj* (*worried*) preocupado; (*worrying*) angustiante; (*keen*) ansioso; **~ to do/for sth** ansioso para fazer/por algo; **to be ~ that** desejar que

 KEYWORD

any [ˈɛnɪ] *adj* **1** (*in questions etc*) algum(a); **have you any butter/children?** você tem manteiga/filhos?; **if there are any tickets left** se houver alguns bilhetes sobrando

2 (*with negative*) nenhum(a); **I haven't any money/books** não tenho dinheiro/livros

3 (*no matter which*) qualquer; **choose any book you like** escolha qualquer livro que quiser

4 (*in phrases*): **in any case** em todo o caso; **any day now** qualquer dia desses; **at any moment** a qualquer momento; **at any rate** de qualquer modo; **any time** a qualquer momento; (*whenever*) quando quer que seja

▷ *pron* **1** (*in questions etc*) algum(a); **have you got any?** tem algum?

2 (*with negative*) nenhum(a); **I haven't any (of them)** não tenho nenhum (deles)

3 (*no matter which one(s)*): **take any of those books (you like)** leve qualquer um desses livros (que você quiser)

▷ *adv* **1** (*in questions etc*) algo; **do you want any more soup/sandwiches?** quer mais sopa/sanduíches?; **are you feeling any better?** você está se sentindo melhor?

2 (*with negative*) nada; **I can't hear him any more** não consigo mais ouvi-lo

anybody [ˈɛnɪbɔdɪ] *pron* qualquer um, qualquer pessoa; (*in interrogative sentences*) alguém

anyhow [ˈɛnɪhau] *adv* (*at any rate*) de qualquer modo, de qualquer maneira; **I shall go ~** eu irei de qualquer jeito; **do it ~ you like** faça do jeito que você quiser; **she leaves things just ~** ela deixa as coisas de qualquer maneira

anyone [ˈɛnɪwʌn] *pron* (*in questions etc*) alguém; (*with negative*) ninguém; (*no matter who*) quem quer que seja; **can you see ~?** você pode ver alguém?; **if ~ should phone ...** se alguém telefonar; **~ could do it** qualquer um(a) poderia fazer isso

anything ['ɛnɪθɪŋ] *pron* (*in questions etc*) alguma coisa; (*with negative*) nada; (*no matter what*) qualquer coisa; **can you see ~?** você pode ver alguma coisa?

anyway ['ɛnɪweɪ] *adv* (*at any rate*) de qualquer modo; (*besides*) além disso; **I shall go ~** eu irei de qualquer jeito

anywhere ['ɛnɪwɛə'] *adv* (*in questions etc*) em algum lugar; (*with negative*) em parte nenhuma; (*no matter where*) não importa onde, onde quer que seja; **can you see him ~?** você pode vê-lo em algum lugar?; **I can't see him ~** não o vejo em parte nenhuma; **~ in the world** em qualquer lugar do mundo

apart [ə'pɑːt] *adv* à parte, à distância; (*separately*) separado; **10 miles ~** a uma distância de 10 milhas um do outro; **to take ~** desmontar; **~ from** além de, à parte de

apartment [ə'pɑːtmənt] (*US*) *n* apartamento

ape [eɪp] *n* macaco ▷ *vt* macaquear, imitar

aperitif [ə'pɛrɪtɪv] *n* aperitivo

aperture ['æpətʃjʊə'] *n* orifício; (*Phot*) abertura

APEX ['eɪpɛks] *n* (= *advance passenger excursion*) tarifa aérea com desconto por compra antecipada

apologize [ə'pɔlədʒaɪz] *vi*: **to ~ (for sth to sb)** desculpar-se *or* pedir desculpas (por *or* de algo a alguém); **apology** *n* desculpas *fpl*

apostrophe [ə'pɔstrəfɪ] *n* apóstrofo

appalling [ə'pɔːlɪŋ] *adj* (*shocking*) chocante; (*awful*) terrível

apparatus [æpə'reɪtəs] *n* aparelho; (*in gym*) aparelhos *mpl*; (*organization*) aparato

apparent [ə'pærənt] *adj* aparente; (*obvious*) claro, patente; **apparently** *adv* aparentemente, pelo(s) visto(s)

appeal [ə'piːl] *vi* (*Law*) apelar, recorrer ▷ *n* (*Law*) recurso, apelação *f*; (*request*) pedido; (*plea*) súplica; (*charm*) atração *f*; **to ~ (to sb) for** suplicar (a alguém); **to ~ to** atrair; **to ~ to sb for mercy** pedir misericórdia a alguém; **appealing** *adj* atraente

appear [ə'pɪə'] *vi* aparecer; (*Law*) apresentar-se, comparecer; (*publication*) ser publicado; (*seem*) parecer; **to ~ in "Hamlet"** trabalhar em "Hamlet"; **to ~ on TV** (*person, news item*) sair na televisão; (*programme*) passar na televisão; **appearance** *n* aparecimento; (*presence*) comparecimento; (*look, aspect*) aparência

appendicitis [əpɛndɪ'saɪtɪs] *n* apendicite *f*

appendix [ə'pɛndɪks] (*pl* **appendices**) *n* apêndice *m*

appetite ['æpɪtaɪt] *n* apetite *m*; (*fig*) desejo

appetizer ['æpɪtaɪzə'] *n* (*food*) tira-gosto; (*drink*) aperitivo

applaud [ə'plɔːd] *vi* aplaudir ▷ *vt* aplaudir; (*praise*) admirar; **applause** *n* aplausos *mpl*

apple ['æpl] *n* maçã *f*

appliance [ə'plaɪəns] *n* aparelho; **electrical** *or* **domestic ~s** eletrodomésticos *mpl*

applicant ['æplɪkənt] *n*: **~ (for)** (*for*

post) candidato(-a) (a); (*Admin: for benefit etc*) requerente *m/f* (de)

application [æplɪˈkeɪʃən] *n* aplicação *f*; (*for a job, a grant etc*) candidatura, requerimento; (*hard work*) empenho; **application form** *n* (formulário de) requerimento

apply [əˈplaɪ] *vt* (*paint etc*) usar; (*law etc*) pôr em prática ▷ *vi*: **to ~ to** (*be suitable for*) ser aplicável a; (*be relevant to*) valer para; (*ask*) pedir; **to ~ for** (*permit, grant*) solicitar, pedir; (*job*) candidatar-se a; **to ~ o.s. to** aplicar-se a, dedicar-se a

appoint [əˈpɔɪnt] *vt* (*to post*) nomear; **appointment** *n* (*engagement*) encontro, compromisso; (*at doctor's etc*) hora marcada; (*act*) nomeação *f*; (*post*) cargo; **to make an appointment (with sb)** marcar um encontro (com alguém)

appraisal [əˈpreɪzl] *n* avaliação *f*

appreciate [əˈpriːʃɪeɪt] *vt* (*like*) apreciar, estimar; (*be grateful for*) agradecer; (*understand*) compreender ▷ *vi* (*Comm*) valorizar-se; **appreciation** *n* apreciação *f*, estima; (*understanding*) compreensão *f*; (*gratitude*) agradecimento; (*Comm*) valorização *f*

apprehensive [æprɪˈhɛnsɪv] *adj* apreensivo, receoso

apprentice [əˈprɛntɪs] *n* aprendiz *m/f*

approach [əˈprəʊtʃ] *vi* aproximar-se ▷ *vt* aproximar-se de; (*ask, apply to*) dirigir-se a; (*subject, passer-by*) abordar ▷ *n* aproximação *f*; (*access*) acesso; (*to problem, situation*) enfoque *m*

appropriate [*adj* əˈprəʊprɪɪt, *vt* əˈprəʊprɪeɪt] *adj* (*apt*) apropriado; (*relevant*) adequado ▷ *vt* apropriar-se de

approval [əˈpruːvəl] *n* aprovação *f*; **on ~** (*Comm*) a contento

approve [əˈpruːv] *vt* (*publication, product*) autorizar; (*motion, decision*) aprovar **approve of** *vt fus* aprovar

approximate [əˈprɔksɪmɪt] *adj* aproximado; **approximately** *adv* aproximadamente

apricot [ˈeɪprɪkɔt] *n* damasco

April [ˈeɪprəl] *n* abril *m*

apron [ˈeɪprən] *n* avental *m*

apt [æpt] *adj* (*suitable*) adequado; (*appropriate*) apropriado; (*likely*): **~ to do** sujeito a fazer

Aquarius [əˈkwɛərɪəs] *n* Aquário

Arab [ˈærəb] *adj, n* árabe *m/f*

Arabian [əˈreɪbɪən] *adj* árabe

Arabic [ˈærəbɪk] *adj* árabe; (*numerals*) arábico ▷ *n* (*Ling*) árabe *m*

arbitrary [ˈɑːbɪtrərɪ] *adj* arbitrário

arbitration [ɑːbɪˈtreɪʃən] *n* arbitragem *f*

arcade [ɑːˈkeɪd] *n* arcos *mpl*; (*passage with shops*) galeria

arch [ɑːtʃ] *n* arco; (*of foot*) curvatura ▷ *vt* arquear, curvar

archaeology [ɑːkɪˈɔlədʒɪ], (*US*) **archeology** *n* arqueologia

archbishop [ɑːtʃˈbɪʃəp] *n* arcebispo

archeology [ɑːkɪˈɔlədʒɪ] (*US*) **= archaeology**

architect [ˈɑːkɪtɛkt] *n* arquiteto(-a); **architecture** *n* arquitetura

Arctic [ˈɑːktɪk] *adj* ártico ▷ *n*: **the ~** o Ártico

are [ɑːʳ] *vb see* **be**

area [ˈɛərɪə] *n* (*zone*) zona, região *f*; (*part of place*) região; (*in room, of knowledge, experience*) área; (*Mat*) superfície f, extensão f

area code (US) n (Tel) (código) DDD (BR), indicativo (PT)

aren't [ɑ:nt] = **are not**

Argentina [ɑ:dʒən'ti:nə] n Argentina

arguably ['ɑ:gjuəblɪ] adv possivelmente

argue ['ɑ:gju:] vi (quarrel) discutir; (reason) argumentar; **to ~ that** sustentar que

argument ['ɑ:gjumənt] n (reasons) argumento; (quarrel) briga, discussão f

Aries ['εərɪz] n Áries m

arise [ə'raɪz] (pt **arose**, pp **arisen**) vi (emerge) surgir

arithmetic [ə'rɪθmətɪk] n aritmética

arm [ɑ:m] n braço; (of clothing) manga; (of organization etc) divisão f ▷ vt armar; **arms** npl (weapons) armas fpl; (Heraldry) brasão m; **~ in ~** de braços dados

armchair n poltrona

armed adj armado

armour ['ɑ:məʳ], (US) **armor** n armadura

armpit ['ɑ:mpɪt] n sovaco

armrest ['ɑ:mrɛst] n braço (de poltrona)

army ['ɑ:mɪ] n exército

aroma [ə'rəumə] n aroma; **aromatherapy** n aromaterapia

arose [ə'rəuz] pt of **arise**

around [ə'raund] adv em volta; (in the area) perto ▷ prep em volta de; (near) perto de; (fig: about) cerca de

arouse [ə'rauz] vt despertar; (anger) provocar

arrange [ə'reɪndʒ] vt (organize) organizar; (put in order) arrumar ▷ vi: **to ~ to do sth** combinar em or ficar de fazer algo; **arrangement**

n (agreement) acordo; (order, layout) disposição f; **arrangements** npl (plans) planos mpl; (preparations) preparativos mpl; **home deliveries by arrangement** entregas a domicílio por convênio; **I'll make all the necessary arrangements** eu vou tomar todas as providências necessárias

array [ə'reɪ] n: **~ of** variedade f de

arrears [ə'rɪəz] npl atrasos mpl; **to be in ~ with one's rent** estar atrasado com o aluguel

arrest [ə'rɛst] vt prender, deter; (sb's attention) chamar, prender ▷ n detenção f, prisão f; **under ~** preso

arrival [ə'raɪvəl] n chegada; **new ~** recém-chegado; (baby) recém-nascido

arrive [ə'raɪv] vi chegar

arrogant ['ærəgənt] adj arrogante

arrow ['ærəu] n flecha; (sign) seta

arse [ɑ:s] (Brit: inf!) n cu m (!)

arson ['ɑ:sn] n incêndio premeditado

art [ɑ:t] n arte f; (skill) habilidade f, jeito; **Arts** npl (Sch) letras fpl

artery ['ɑ:tərɪ] n (Med) artéria; (fig) estrada principal

art gallery n museu m de belas artes; (small, private) galeria de arte

arthritis [ɑ:'θraɪtɪs] n artrite f

artichoke ['ɑ:tɪtʃəuk] n (globe artichoke) alcachofra; (also: **Jerusalem ~**) topinambo

article ['ɑ:tɪkl] n artigo; **articles** npl (Brit: Law: training) contrato de aprendizagem; **~s of clothing** peças fpl de vestuário

articulate [adj ɑ:'tɪkjulɪt, vt ɑ:'tɪkjuleɪt] adj (speech) bem articulado; (writing) bem escrito; (person) eloquente ▷ vt expressar

artificial [ɑ:tɪ'fɪʃəl] adj artificial;

(*person, manner*) afetado
artist ['ɑːtɪst] *n* artista *m/f*; (*Mus*)
intérprete *m/f*; **artistic** [ɑːˈtɪstɪk]
adj artístico
art school *n* ≈ escola de artes

KEYWORD

as [æz, əz] *conj* **1** (*referring to time*)
quando; **as the years went by** no
decorrer dos anos; **he came in as I
was leaving** ele chegou quando eu
estava saindo; **as from tomorrow**
a partir de amanhã
2 (*in comparisons*) tão ... como,
tanto(s) ... como; **as big as** tão
grande como; **twice as big as** duas
vezes maior que; **as much/many
as** tanto/tantos como; **as much
money/many books as** tanto
dinheiro quanto/tantos livros
quanto; **as soon as** logo que,
assim que
3 (*since, because*) como
4 (*referring to manner, way*) como;
do as you wish faça como quiser
5 (*concerning*): **as for** *or* **to that**
quanto a isso
6: **as if** *or* **though** como se; **he
looked as if he was ill** ele parecia
doente
▷ *prep* (*in the capacity of*): **he works
as a driver** ele trabalha como
motorista; **he gave it to me as a
present** ele me deu isso de
presente; *see also* **long; such; well**

a.s.a.p. *abbr* = **as soon as possible**
asbestos [æzˈbɛstəs] *n* asbesto,
amianto
ash [æʃ] *n* cinza; (*tree, wood*) freixo
ashamed [əˈʃeɪmd] *adj*
envergonhado; **to be ~ of** ter
vergonha de

ashore [əˈʃɔːʳ] *adv* em terra; **to go ~**
descer à terra, desembarcar
ashtray ['æʃtreɪ] *n* cinzeiro
Asia ['eɪʃə] *n* Ásia; **Asian** *adj, n*
asiático(-a)
aside [əˈsaɪd] *adv* à parte, de lado
▷ *n* aparte *m*
ask [ɑːsk] *vt* perguntar; (*invite*)
convidar; **to ~ sb sth** perguntar
algo a alguém; **to ~ sb to do sth**
pedir para alguém fazer algo; **to ~
(sb) a question** fazer uma
pergunta (a alguém); **to ~ sb out
to dinner** convidar alguém para
jantar **ask after** *vt fus* perguntar
por **ask for** *vt fus* pedir; **it's just
~ing for it** *or* **trouble** é procurar
encrenca
asleep [əˈsliːp] *adj* dormindo; **to
fall ~** dormir, adormecer
asparagus [əsˈpærəgəs] *n* aspargo
(*BR*), espargo (*PT*)
aspect ['æspɛkt] *n* aspecto;
(*direction in which a building etc faces*)
direção *f*
aspire [əsˈpaɪəʳ] *vi*: **to ~ to** aspirar a
aspirin ['æsprɪn] *n* aspirina
ass [æs] *n* jumento, burro; (*inf*)
imbecil *m/f*; (*US: inf!*) cu *m* (!)
assassinate [əˈsæsɪneɪt] *vt*
assassinar
assault [əˈsɔːlt] *n* assalto ▷ *vt*
assaltar, atacar; (*sexually*) agredir,
violar
assemble [əˈsɛmbl] *vt* (*people*)
reunir; (*objects*) juntar; (*Tech*)
montar ▷ *vi* reunir-se
assembly [əˈsɛmblɪ] *n* reunião *f*;
(*institution*) assembleia
assert [əˈsəːt] *vt* afirmar
assess [əˈsɛs] *vt* avaliar;
assessment *n* avaliação *f*
asset ['æsɛt] *n* vantagem *f*, trunfo;
assets *npl* (*property, funds*) bens *mpl*

assign [əˈsaɪn] vt (date) fixar; **to ~ (to)** (task) designar (a); (resources) destinar (a); **assignment** n tarefa

assist [əˈsɪst] vt ajudar; **assistance** n ajuda, auxílio; **assistant** n assistente m/f, auxiliar m/f; (Brit: also: **shop assistant**) vendedor(a) m/f

associate [adj əˈsəʊʃɪɪt, vt, vi əˈsəʊʃɪeɪt] adj associado; (professor, director etc) adjunto ▷ n sócio(-a) ▷ vi: **to ~ with sb** associar-se com alguém ▷ vt associar; **association** n associação f; (link) ligação f

assorted [əˈsɔːtɪd] adj sortido

assortment [əˈsɔːtmənt] n (of shapes, colours) sortimento; (of books, people) variedade f

assume [əˈsjuːm] vt (suppose) supor, presumir; (responsibilities etc) assumir; (attitude, name) adotar, tomar; **assumption** [əˈsʌmpʃən] n suposição f, presunção f

assurance [əˈʃuərəns] n garantia; (confidence) confiança; (insurance) seguro

assure [əˈʃuəʳ] vt assegurar; (guarantee) garantir

asthma [ˈæsmə] n asma

astonish [əˈstɒnɪʃ] vt assombrar, espantar; **astonishment** n assombro, espanto

astound [əˈstaund] vt pasmar, estarrecer

astray [əˈstreɪ] adv: **to go ~** extraviar-se; **to lead ~** desencaminhar

astrology [əsˈtrɒlədʒɪ] n astrologia

astronaut [ˈæstrənɔːt] n astronauta m/f

astronomy [əsˈtrɒnəmɪ] n astronomia

asylum [əˈsaɪləm] n (refuge) asilo; (hospital) manicômio; **asylum seeker** [-siːkəʳ] n solicitante m/f de asilo

○ KEYWORD

at [æt] prep **1** (referring to position) em; (referring to direction) a; **at the top** em cima; **at home/school** em casa/na escola; **to look at sth** olhar para algo
2 (referring to time): **at 4 o'clock** às quatro horas; **at night** à noite; **at Christmas** no Natal; **at times** às vezes
3 (referring to rates, speed etc): **at £1 a kilo** a uma libra o quilo; **two at a time** de dois em dois
4 (referring to manner): **at a stroke** de um golpe; **at peace** em paz
5 (referring to activity): **to be at work** estar no trabalho; **to play at cowboys** brincar de mocinho
6 (referring to cause): **to be shocked/ surprised/annoyed at sth** ficar chocado/surpreso/chateado com algo; **I went at his suggestion** eu fui por causa da sugestão dele
▷ n (symbol @) arroba

ate [eɪt] pt of **eat**

atheist [ˈeɪθɪɪst] n ateu/ateia m/f

Athens [ˈæθɪnz] n Atenas

athlete [ˈæθliːt] n atleta m/f; **athletic** [æθˈlɛtɪk] adj atlético; **athletics** n atletismo

Atlantic [ətˈlæntɪk] adj atlântico ▷ n: **the ~ (Ocean)** o (oceano) Atlântico

atlas [ˈætləs] n atlas m inv

ATM abbr (= automated teller machine) caixa eletrônico m

atmosphere [ˈætməsfɪəʳ] n atmosfera; (fig) ambiente m

atom ['ætəm] n átomo; **atomic**
[ə'tɔmɪk] adj atômico

attach [ə'tætʃ] vt prender;
(document, letter) juntar, anexar;
(importance etc) dar; **to be ~ed to
sb/sth** (like) ter afeição por
alguém/algo; **to ~ a file to an
email** anexar um arquivo a um
e-mail

attachment [ə'tætʃmənt] n (tool)
acessório; (to email) anexo; (love):
~ **(to)** afeição f (por)

attack [ə'tæk] vt atacar; (subj:
criminal) assaltar; (task etc)
empreender ▷ n ataque m; (on sb's
life) atentado; **heart ~** ataque
cardíaco or de coração

attain [ə'teɪn] vt (also: ~ **to**:
happiness, results) alcançar, atingir;
(: knowledge) obter

attempt [ə'tɛmpt] n tentativa ▷ vt
tentar; **to make an ~ on sb's life**
atentar contra a vida de alguém

attend [ə'tɛnd] vt (lectures) assistir
a; (school) cursar; (church) ir a;
(course) fazer; (patient) tratar
attend to vt fus (matter)
encarregar-se de; (needs, customer)
atender a; (patient) tratar de;
attendance n comparecimento;
(people present) assistência;
attendant n servidor(a) m/f ▷ adj
concomitante

attention [ə'tɛnʃən] n atenção f;
(care) cuidados mpl ▷ excl (Mil)
sentido!; **for the ~ of ...** (Admin)
atenção ...

attic ['ætɪk] n sótão m

attitude ['ætɪtjuːd] n atitude f

attorney [ə'tɜːnɪ] n (US: lawyer)
advogado(-a)

attract [ə'trækt] vt atrair, chamar;
attraction n atração f; **attractive**
adj atraente; (idea, offer)

interessante

attribute [n 'ætrɪbjuːt, vt ə'trɪbjuːt]
n atributo ▷ vt: **to ~ sth to** atribuir
algo a

aubergine ['əubəʒiːn] n beringela

auction ['ɔːkʃən] n (also: **sale by ~**)
leilão m ▷ vt leiloar

audience ['ɔːdɪəns] n (in theatre,
concert etc) plateia; (of writer,
magazine) público

audit ['ɔːdɪt] vt fazer a auditoria de

audition [ɔː'dɪʃən] n audição f

August ['ɔːgəst] n agosto

aunt [ɑːnt] n tia; **auntie** n titia;
aunty n titia

au pair ['əu'pɛəʳ] n (also: ~ **girl**) au
pair f

Australia [ɔs'treɪlɪə] n Austrália;
Australian adj, n australiano(-a)

Austria ['ɔstrɪə] n Áustria;
Austrian adj, n austríaco(-a)

authentic [ɔː'θɛntɪk] adj autêntico

author ['ɔːθə] n autor(a) m/f

authority [ɔː'θɔrɪtɪ] n autoridade f;
(government body) jurisdição f;
(permission) autorização f; **the
authorities** npl (ruling body) as
autoridades

authorize ['ɔːθəraɪz] vt autorizar

auto ['ɔːtəu] (US) n carro,
automóvel m

autobiography [ɔːtəbaɪ'ɔgrəfɪ] n
autobiografia

autograph ['ɔːtəgrɑːf] n autógrafo
▷ vt (photo etc) autografar

automatic [ɔːtə'mætɪk] adj
automático ▷ n (gun) pistola
automática; (washing machine)
máquina de lavar roupa
automática; (car) carro
automático

automobile ['ɔːtəməbiːl] (US) n
carro, automóvel m

autonomy [ɔː'tɔnəmɪ] n

autonomia

autumn ['ɔːtəm] *n* outono

auxiliary [ɔːgˈzɪlɪərɪ] *adj, n* auxiliar *m/f*

available [əˈveɪləbl] *adj* disponível; (*time*) livre

avalanche [ˈævəlɑːnʃ] *n* avalanche *f*

Ave. *abbr* (= *avenue*) Av., Avda.

avenue [ˈævənjuː] *n* avenida; (*drive*) caminho; (*means*) solução *f*

average [ˈævərɪdʒ] *n* média ▷ *adj* (*mean*) médio; (*ordinary*) regular ▷ *vt* alcançar uma média de; **on ~** em média; **average out** *vi*: **to ~ out at** dar uma média de

avert [əˈvɜːt] *vt* prevenir; (*blow, one's eyes*) desviar

avocado [ævəˈkɑːdəu] *n* (*Brit: also:* **~ pear**) abacate *m*

avoid [əˈvɔɪd] *vt* evitar

await [əˈweɪt] *vt* esperar, aguardar

awake [əˈweɪk] (*pt* **awoke**, *pp* **awoken**) *adj* acordado ▷ *vt, vi* despertar, acordar; **~ to** atento a

award [əˈwɔːd] *n* prêmio, condecoração *f*; (*Law: damages*) sentença; (*act*) concessão *f* ▷ *vt* outorgar, conceder; (*damages*) determinar o pagamento de

aware [əˈwɛəʳ] *adj*: **~ of** (*conscious*) consciente de; (*informed*) informado de *or* sobre; **to become ~ of** reparar em, saber de; **awareness** *n* consciência

away [əˈweɪ] *adv* fora; (*faraway*) muito longe; **two kilometres ~ a** dois quilômetros de distância; **the holiday was two weeks ~** faltavam duas semanas para as férias; **he's ~ for a week** está ausente uma semana; **to take ~** levar; **to work/pedal** *etc* **~** trabalhar/pedalar *etc* sem parar; **to fade ~** (*colour*) desbotar;

(*enthusiasm, sound*) diminuir

awe [ɔː] *n* temor *m* respeitoso

awful [ˈɔːfəl] *adj* terrível, horrível; (*quantity*): **an ~ lot of** um monte de; **awfully** *adv* (*very*) muito

awkward [ˈɔːkwəd] *adj* (*person, movement*) desajeitado; (*shape*) incômodo; (*problem*) difícil; (*situation*) embaraçoso, delicado

awoke [əˈwəuk] *pt of* **awake**; **awoken** [əˈwəukən] *pp of* **awake**

axe [æks], (*US*) **ax** *n* machado ▷ *vt* (*project etc*) abandonar; (*jobs*) reduzir

axle [ˈæksl] *n* (*also:* **~ tree**: *Aut*) eixo

b

B, b [biː] *n* B, b *m*

baby ['beɪbɪ] *n* neném *m/f*, nenê *m/f*; bebê *m/f*; (*US: inf*) querido(-a); **baby carriage** (*US*) *n* carrinho de bebê; **baby food** *n* papinha de bebê; **baby-sit** *irreg vi* tomar conta da(s) criança(s); **baby-sitter** *n* baby-sitter *m/f*; **baby wipe** *n* lenço umedecido

bachelor ['bætʃələʳ] *n* solteiro; **B~ of Arts/Science** ≈ bacharel *m* em Letras/Ciências

back [bæk] *n* (*of person*) costas *fpl*; (*of animal*) lombo; (*of hand*) dorso; (*of car, train*) parte *f* traseira; (*of house*) fundos *mpl*; (*of chair*) encosto; (*of page*) verso; (*of book*) lombada; (*of crowd*) fundo; (*Football*) zagueiro (*BR*), defesa *m* (*PT*) ▷ *vt* (*candidate: also:* **~ up**) apoiar; (*horse: at races*) apostar em; (*car*) dar ré com ▷ *vi* (*car etc: also:* **~ up**) dar ré (*BR*), fazer marcha atrás (*PT*) ▷ *cpd* (*payment*) atrasado; (*Aut: seats, wheels*) de trás ▷ *adv* (*not forward*) para trás; (*returned*): **he's ~** ele voltou; (*restitution*): **throw the ball ~** devolva a bola; (*again*): **he called ~** chamou de novo; **he ran ~** voltou correndo **back down** *vi* desistir **back out** *vi* (*of promise*) voltar atrás, recuar **back up** *vt* (*support*) apoiar; (*Comput*) fazer um backup de; **backache** *n* dor *f* nas costas; **backbone** *n* coluna vertebral; (*fig*) esteio; **backfire** *vi* (*Aut*) engasgar; (*plan*) sair pela culatra; **background** *n* fundo; (*of events*) antecedentes *mpl*; (*basic knowledge*) bases *fpl*; (*experience*) conhecimentos *mpl*, experiência; **family background** antecedentes *mpl* familiares; **backing** *n* (*fig*) apoio; **backlog** *n*: **backlog of work** atrasos *mpl*; **backpack** *n* mochila; **back pay** *n* salário atrasado; **backstage** *adv* nos bastidores; **backstroke** *n* nado de costas; **backup** *adj* (*train, plane*) reserva *inv*; (*Comput*) de backup ▷ *n* (*support*) apoio; (*Comput: also:* **backup file**) backup *m*; **backward** *adj* (*movement*) para trás; (*person, country*) atrasado; **backwards** *adv* (*move, go*) para trás; (*read a list*) às avessas; (*fall*) de costas; **backyard** *n* quintal *m*

bacon ['beɪkən] *n* toucinho, bacon *m*

bacteria [bæk'tɪərɪə] *npl* bactérias *fpl*

bad [bæd] *adj* mau/má, ruim; (*child*) levado; (*mistake, injury*) grave; (*meat, food*) estragado; **his ~ leg** sua perna machucada; **to go ~** estragar-se

badge [bædʒ] n (of school etc) emblema m; (policeman's) crachá m

badger ['bædʒər] n texugo

badly ['bædlɪ] adv mal; **~ wounded** gravemente ferido; **he needs it ~** faz-lhe grande falta; **to be ~ off (for money)** estar com pouco dinheiro

badminton ['bædmɪntən] n badminton m

bad-tempered adj mal humorado; (temporary) de mau humor

bag [bæg] n saco, bolsa; (handbag) bolsa; (satchel, shopping bag) sacola; (case) mala; **~s of ...** (inf: lots of) ... de sobra; **baggage** n bagagem f; **baggage allowance** n franquia de bagagem; **baggy** adj folgado, largo; **bagpipes** npl gaita de foles

bail [beɪl] n (payment) fiança; (release) liberdade f sob fiança ▷ vt (prisoner: gen: grant bail to) libertar sob fiança; (boat: also: **~ out**) baldear a água de; **on ~** sob fiança **bail out** vt (prisoner) afiançar

bait [beɪt] n isca, engodo; (for criminal etc) atrativo, chamariz m ▷ vt iscar, cevar; (person) apoquentar

bake [beɪk] vt cozinhar ao forno; (Tech: clay etc) cozer ▷ vi assar; **baked beans** npl feijão m cozido com molho de tomate; **baked potato** n batata assada com a casca; **baker** n padeiro(-a); **bakery** n (for bread) padaria; (for cakes) confeitaria; **baking** n (act) cozimento; (batch) fornada; **baking powder** n fermento em pó

balance ['bæləns] n equilíbrio; (scales) balança; (Comm) balanço; (remainder) resto, saldo ▷ vt equilibrar; (budget) nivelar; (account) fazer o balanço de; **~ of trade/payments** balança comercial/balanço de pagamentos; **balanced** adj (report) objetivo; (personality, diet) equilibrado; **balance sheet** n balanço geral

balcony ['bælkənɪ] n varanda; (closed) galeria; (in theatre) balcão m

bald [bɔːld] adj calvo, careca; (tyre) careca

ball [bɔːl] n bola; (of wool, string) novelo; (dance) baile m; **to play ~ with sb** jogar bola com alguém; (fig) fazer o jogo de alguém

ballerina [bælə'riːnə] n bailarina

ballet ['bæleɪ] n balé m; **ballet dancer** n bailarino(-a)

balloon [bə'luːn] n balão m

ballot ['bælət] n votação f

ballpoint ['bɔːlpɔɪnt], **ballpoint pen** n (caneta) esferográfica

ban [bæn] n proibição f, interdição f; (suspension, exclusion) exclusão f ▷ vt proibir, interditar; (exclude) excluir

banana [bə'nɑːnə] n banana

band [bænd] n (group) orquestra; (Mil) banda; (strip) faixa, cinta; **band together** vi juntar-se, associar-se

bandage ['bændɪdʒ] n atadura (BR), ligadura (PT) ▷ vt enfaixar

B & B n abbr = **bed and breakfast**

bang [bæŋ] n estalo; (of door) estrondo; (of gun, exhaust) explosão f; (blow) pancada ▷ excl bum!, bumba! ▷ vt bater com força; (door) fechar com violência ▷ vi produzir estrondo; (door) bater; (fireworks) soltar

bangs [bæŋz] (US) npl (fringe) franja

banish ['bænɪʃ] vt banir

banister ['bænɪstər] n, **banisters**

['bænɪstəz] *npl* corrimão *m*
bank [bæŋk] *n* banco; (*of river, lake*) margem *f*; (*of earth*) rampa, ladeira ▷ *vi* (*Aviat*) ladear-se **bank on** *vt fus* contar com, apostar em; **bank account** *n* conta bancária; **bank card** *n* cartão *m* de garantia de cheques; **banker** *n* banqueiro(-a); **Bank holiday** (*Brit*) *n* feriado nacional; **banking** *n* transações *fpl* bancárias; **banknote** *n* nota (bancária)
bankrupt ['bæŋkrʌpt] *adj* falido, quebrado; **to go ~** falir
bank statement *n* extrato bancário
banner ['bænər] *n* faixa
baptism ['bæptɪzəm] *n* batismo
bar [bɑːr] *n* barra; (*rod*) vara; (*of window etc*) grade *f*; (*fig: hindrance*) obstáculo; (*prohibition*) impedimento; (*pub*) bar *m*; (*counter: in pub*) balcão *m* ▷ *vt* (*road*) obstruir; (*person*) excluir; (*activity*) proibir ▷ *prep*: **~ none** sem exceção; **behind ~s** (*prisoner*) atrás das grades; **the B~** (*Law*) a advocacia
barbaric [bɑːˈbærɪk] *adj* bárbaro
barbecue ['bɑːbɪkjuː] *n* churrasco
barbed wire ['bɑːbd-] *n* arame *m* farpado
barber ['bɑːbər] *n* barbeiro, cabeleireiro
bar code *n* código de barras
bare [bɛər] *adj* despido; (*head*) descoberto; (*trees, vegetation*) sem vegetação; (*minimum*) básico ▷ *vt* mostrar; **barefoot** *adj, adv* descalço; **barely** *adv* apenas, mal
bargain ['bɑːgɪn] *n* negócio; (*agreement*) acordo; (*good buy*) pechincha ▷ *vi* (*haggle*) regatear; (*negotiate*): **to ~ (with sb)**

pechinchar (com alguém); **into the ~** ainda por cima **bargain for** *vt fus*: **he got more than he ~ed for** ele conseguiu mais do que pediu
barge [bɑːdʒ] *n* barcaça **barge in** *vi* irromper
bark [bɑːk] *n* (*of tree*) casca; (*of dog*) latido ▷ *vi* latir
barley ['bɑːlɪ] *n* cevada
barmaid ['bɑːmeɪd] *n* garçonete *f* (*BR*), empregada (de bar) (*PT*)
barman ['bɑːmən] *irreg n* garçom *m* (*BR*), empregado (de bar) (*PT*)
barn [bɑːn] *n* celeiro
barometer [bəˈrɔmɪtər] *n* barômetro
baron ['bærən] *n* barão *m*; (*of press, industry*) magnata *m*; **baroness** ['bærənɪs] *n* baronesa
barracks ['bærəks] *npl* quartel *m*, caserna
barrage ['bærɑːʒ] *n* (*Mil*) fogo de barragem; (*dam*) barragem *f*; (*fig*): **a ~ of questions** uma saraivada de perguntas
barrel ['bærəl] *n* barril *m*; (*of gun*) cano
barren ['bærən] *adj* (*land*) árido
barricade [bærɪˈkeɪd] *n* barricada
barrier ['bærɪər] *n* barreira; (*fig: to progress etc*) obstáculo
barrister ['bærɪstər] (*Brit*) *n* advogado(-a), causídico(-a)
barrow ['bærəu] *n* (*wheelbarrow*) carrinho (de mão)
bartender ['bɑːtɛndər] (*US*) *n* garçom *m* (*BR*), empregado (de bar) (*PT*)
base [beɪs] *n* base *f* ▷ *vt* (*opinion, belief*): **to ~ sth on** basear or fundamentar algo em ▷ *adj* (*thoughts*) sujo; **baseball** *n* beisebol *m*
basement ['beɪsmənt] *n* porão *m*
bases[1] ['beɪsɪz] *npl of* **base**

bases² ['beɪsiːz] npl of **basis**

bash [bæʃ] (inf) vt (with fist) dar soco or murro em; (with object) bater em

basic ['beɪsɪk] adj básico; (facilities) mínimo; **basically** adv basicamente; (really) no fundo; **basics** npl: **the basics** o essencial

basin ['beɪsn] n bacia; (also: **wash~**) pia

basis ['beɪsɪs] (pl **bases**) n base f; **on a part-time ~** num esquema de meio-expediente; **on a trial ~** em experiência

basket ['bɑːskɪt] n cesto; (with handle) cesta; **basketball** n basquete(bol) m

bass [beɪs] n (Mus) baixo

bastard ['bɑːstəd] n bastardo(-a); (inf!) filho da puta m (!)

bat [bæt] n (Zool) morcego; (for ball games) bastão m; (Brit: for table tennis) raquete f ▷ vt: **he didn't ~ an eyelid** ele nem pestanejou

batch [bætʃ] n (of bread) fornada; (of papers) monte m

bath [bɑːθ] n banho; (bathtub) banheira ▷ vt banhar; **to have a ~** tomar banho (de banheira); see also **baths**

bathe [beɪð] vi banhar-se; (US: have a bath) tomar um banho ▷ vt (wound) lavar; **bathing** n banho; **bathing costume**, (US) **bathing suit** n (woman's) maiô m (BR), fato de banho (PT)

bathrobe ['bɑːθrəʊb] n roupão m de banho

bathroom ['bɑːθrʊm] n banheiro (BR), casa de banho (PT)

baths [bɑːθs] npl banhos mpl públicos

baton ['bætən] n (Mus) batuta; (Athletics) bastão m; (truncheon) cassetete m

batter ['bætəʳ] vt espancar; (subj: wind, rain) castigar ▷ n massa (mole); **battered** ['bætəd] adj (hat, pan) amassado, surrado

battery ['bætərɪ] n bateria; (of torch) pilha

battle ['bætl] n batalha; (fig) luta ▷ vi lutar; **battlefield** n campo de batalha

bay [beɪ] n (Geo) baía; **to hold sb at ~** manter alguém a distância

bazaar [bə'zɑːʳ] n bazar m

BBC n abbr (= British Broadcasting Corporation) companhia britânica de rádio e televisão

B.C. adv abbr (= before Christ) a.C. ▷ abbr (Canada) = **British Columbia**

 KEYWORD

be [biː] (pt **was** or **were**, pp **been**) aux vb **1** (with present participle: forming continuous tense) estar; **what are you doing?** o que você está fazendo? (BR) or a fazer (PT)?; **it is raining** está chovendo (BR) or a chover (PT); **I've been waiting for you for hours** há horas que eu espero por você

2 (with pp: forming passives): **to be killed** ser morto; **the box had been opened** a caixa tinha sido aberta; **the thief was nowhere to be seen** tinha sumido o ladrão

3 (in tag questions): **it was fun, wasn't it?** foi divertido, não foi?; **she's back again, is she?** ela voltou novamente, é?

4 (+ to + infin): **the house is to be sold** a casa está para ser vendida; **you're to be congratulated for all your work** você devia ser cumprimentado pelo seu trabalho;

he's not to open it ele não pode abrir isso

▷ *vb + complement* **1** (*gen*): **I'm English** sou inglês; **I'm tired** estou cansado; **2 and 2 are 4** dois e dois são quatro; **be careful!** tome cuidado!; **be quiet!** fique quieto!, fique calado!; **be good!** seja bonzinho!

2 (*of health*) estar; **how are you?** como está?

3 (*of age*): **how old are you?** quantos anos você tem?; **I'm twenty (years old)** tenho vinte anos **4** (*cost*) ser; **how much was the meal?** quanto foi a refeição?; **that'll be £5.75, please** são £5.75, por favor

▷ *vi* **1** (*exist, occur etc*) existir, haver; **the best singer that ever was** o maior cantor de todos os tempos; **is there a God?** Deus existe?; **be that as it may ...** de qualquer forma ...; **so be it** que seja assim **2** (*referring to place*) estar; **I won't be here tomorrow** eu não estarei aqui amanhã; **Edinburgh is in Scotland** Edinburgo é or fica na Escócia

3 (*referring to movement*) ir; **where have you been?** onde você foi?; **I've been in the garden** estava no quintal

▷ *impers vb* **1** (*referring to time*) ser; **it's 8 o'clock** são 8 horas; **it's the 28th of April** é 28 de abril

2 (*referring to distance*) ficar; **it's 10 km to the village** o lugarejo fica a 10 km de distância

3 (*referring to the weather*) estar; **it's too hot/cold** está quente/frio demais

4 (*emphatic*): **it's only me** sou eu!; **it was Maria who paid the bill** foi Maria quem pagou a conta

beach [biːtʃ] *n* praia ▷ *vt* puxar para a terra *or* praia, encalhar

beacon ['biːkən] *n* (*lighthouse*) farol *m*; (*marker*) baliza

bead [biːd] *n* (*of necklace*) conta; (*of sweat*) gota

beak [biːk] *n* bico

beam [biːm] *n* (*Arch*) viga; (*of light*) raio ▷ *vi* (*smile*) sorrir

bean [biːn] *n* feijão *m*; (*of coffee*) grão *m*; **runner/broad ~** vagem *f*/fava

bear [bɛəʳ] (*pt* **bore**, *pp* **borne**) *n* urso ▷ *vt* (*carry, support*) arcar com; (*tolerate*) suportar ▷ *vi*: **to ~ right/left** virar à direita/à esquerda **bear out** *vt* (*theory, suspicion*) confirmar, corroborar **bear up** *vi* aguentar, resistir

beard [bɪəd] *n* barba

bearing ['bɛərɪŋ] *n* porte *m*, comportamento; (*connection*) relação *f*; **bearings** *npl* (*also*: **ball ~s**) rolimã *m*; **to take a ~** fazer marcação

beast [biːst] *n* bicho; (*inf*) fera

beat [biːt] (*pt* **beat**, *pp* **beaten**) *n* (*of heart*) batida; (*Mus*) ritmo, compasso; (*of policeman*) ronda ▷ *vt* (*hit*) bater em; (*eggs*) bater; (*defeat*) vencer, derrotar ▷ *vi* (*heart*) bater; **to ~ it** (*inf*) cair fora; **off the ~en track** fora de mão **beat off** *vt* repelir **beat up** *vt* (*inf: person*) espancar; (*eggs*) bater; **beating** *n* (*thrashing*) surra

beautiful ['bjuːtɪful] *adj* belo, lindo, formoso

beauty ['bjuːtɪ] *n* beleza; (*person*) beldade *f*, beleza

beaver ['biːvəʳ] *n* castor *m*

because [bɪ'kɔz] *conj* porque; **~ of** por causa de

beckon ['bɛkən] *vt* (*also*: **~ to**)

chamar com sinais, acenar para
become [bɪ'kʌm] (*irreg: like* **come**)
vi (+ n) virar, fazer-se, tornar-se;
(+ adj) tornar-se, ficar
bed [bɛd] n cama; (*of flowers*)
canteiro; (*of coal, clay*) camada,
base f; (*of sea, lake*) fundo; (*of river*)
leito; **to go to ~** ir dormir,
deitar(-se); **bed and breakfast** n
(*place*) pensão f; (*terms*) cama e café
da manhã (BR) or pequeno almoço
(PT); **bedclothes** npl roupa de
cama; **bedding** n roupa de cama;
bedroom n quarto, dormitório;
bedside n: **at sb's bedside** à
cabeceira de alguém ▷ cpd (*book*,
lamp) de cabeceira; **bedsit**
['bɛdsɪt], **bedsitter** ['bɛdsɪtə'ʳ]
(*Brit*) n conjugado; *ver nota*

● **BEDSIT**
●
● Um **bedsit** é um quarto
● mobiliado cujo aluguel inclui uso
● de cozinha e banheiro comuns.
● Esse sistema de alojamento é
● muito comum na Grã-Bretanha
● entre estudantes, jovens
● profissionais liberais etc.

bedspread ['bɛdsprɛd] n colcha
bedtime ['bɛdtaɪm] n hora de ir
para cama
bee [biː] n abelha
beech [biːtʃ] n faia
beef [biːf] n carne f de vaca; **roast ~**
rosbife m; **beefburger** n
hambúrguer m
been [biːn] pp of **be**
beer [bɪəʳ] n cerveja
beetle ['biːtl] n besouro
beetroot ['biːtruːt] (*Brit*) n
beterraba
before [bɪ'fɔːʳ] prep (*of time*) antes

de; (*of space*) diante de ▷ conj antes
que ▷ adv antes, anteriormente; à
frente, na dianteira; **~ going** antes
de ir; **the week ~** a semana
anterior; **I've never seen it ~**
nunca vi isso antes; **beforehand**
adv antes
beg [bɛg] vi mendigar, pedir esmola
▷ vt (*also:* **~ for**) mendigar; **to ~ sb
to do sth** implorar a alguém para
fazer algo; *see also* **pardon**
began [bɪ'gæn] pt of **begin**
beggar ['bɛgəʳ] n mendigo(-a)
begin [bɪ'gɪn] (*pt* **began**, *pp* **begun**)
vt, vi começar, iniciar; **to ~ doing** or
to do sth começar a fazer algo;
beginner n principiante m/f;
beginning n início, começo
behalf [bɪ'hɑːf] n: **on** or **in** (US) **~ of**
(*as representative of*) em nome de;
(*for benefit of*) no interesse de
behave [bɪ'heɪv] vi comportar-se;
(*well: also:* **~ o.s.**) comportar-se
(bem); **behaviour**, (US) **behavior**
n comportamento
behind [bɪ'haɪnd] prep atrás de
▷ adv atrás; (*move*) para trás ▷ n
traseiro; **to be ~ (schedule) with
sth** estar atrasado or com atraso
em algo; **~ the scenes** nos
bastidores
beige [beɪʒ] adj bege
Beijing [beɪ'ʒɪŋ] n Pequim
being ['biːɪŋ] n (*state*) existência;
(*entity*) ser m
belated [bɪ'leɪtɪd] adj atrasado
belch [bɛltʃ] vi arrotar ▷ vt (*also:*
~ out: *smoke etc*) vomitar
Belgian ['bɛldʒən] adj, n belga m/f
Belgium ['bɛldʒəm] n Bélgica
belief [bɪ'liːf] n (*opinion*) opinião f;
(*trust, faith*) fé f
believe [bɪ'liːv] vt: **to ~ sth/sb**
acreditar algo/em alguém ▷ vi:

to ~ in (*God, ghosts*) crer em; (*method, person*) acreditar em; **believer** *n* (*Rel*) crente *m/f*, fiel *m/f*

bell [bɛl] *n* sino; (*small, doorbell*) campainha

bellow ['bɛləʊ] *vi* mugir; (*person*) bramar

bell pepper *n* (*esp US*) pimentão *m*

belly ['bɛlɪ] *n* barriga, ventre *m*

belong [bɪ'lɒŋ] *vi*: **to ~ to** pertencer a; (*club etc*) ser sócio de; **the book ~s here** o livro fica guardado aqui; **belongings** *npl* pertences *mpl*

beloved [bɪ'lʌvɪd] *adj* querido, amado

below [bɪ'ləʊ] *prep* (*beneath*) embaixo de; (*lower than, less than*) abaixo de ▷ *adv* em baixo; **see ~** ver abaixo

belt [bɛlt] *n* cinto; (*of land*) faixa; (*Tech*) correia ▷ *vt* (*thrash*) surrar; **beltway** (*US*) *n* via circular

bemused [bɪ'mju:zd] *adj* bestificado, estupidificado

bench [bɛntʃ] *n* banco; (*work bench*) bancada (de carpinteiro); (*Brit: Pol*) assento num Parlamento; **the B~** (*Law*) o tribunal; (*people*) os magistrados, o corpo de magistrados

bend [bɛnd] (*pt* **bent**, *pp* **bent**) *vt* (*leg, arm*) dobrar; (*pipe*) curvar ▷ *vi* dobrar-se, inclinar-se ▷ *n* curva; (*in pipe*) curvatura **bend down** *vi* abaixar-se **bend over** *vi* debruçar-se

beneath [bɪ'ni:θ] *prep* abaixo de; (*unworthy of*) indigno de ▷ *adv* em baixo

beneficial [bɛnɪ'fɪʃəl] *adj*: **~ (to)** benéfico (a)

benefit ['bɛnɪfɪt] *n* benefício, vantagem *f*; (*money*) subsídio, auxílio ▷ *vt* beneficiar ▷ *vi*: **to ~**

from sth beneficiar-se de algo

benign [bɪ'naɪn] *adj* (*person, smile*) afável, bondoso; (*Med*) benigno

bent [bɛnt] *pt, pp of* **bend** ▷ *n* inclinação *f* ▷ *adj*: **to be ~ on** estar empenhado em

bereaved [bɪ'ri:vd] *npl*: **the ~** os enlutados

beret ['bɛreɪ] *n* boina

Berlin [bə:'lɪn] *n* Berlim

berry ['bɛrɪ] *n* baga

berth [bə:θ] *n* (*bed*) beliche *m*; (*cabin*) cabine *f*; (*on train*) leito; (*for ship*) ancoradouro ▷ *vi* (*in harbour*) atracar, encostar-se; (*at anchor*) ancorar

beside [bɪ'saɪd] *prep* (*next to*) junto de, ao lado de, ao pé de; **to be ~ o.s. (with anger)** estar fora de si; **that's ~ the point** isso não tem nada a ver

besides [bɪ'saɪdz] *adv* além disso ▷ *prep* (*as well as*) além de

best [bɛst] *adj* melhor ▷ *adv* (o) melhor; **the ~ part of** (*quantity*) a maior parte de; **at ~** na melhor das hipóteses; **to make the ~ of sth** tirar o maior partido possível de algo; **to do one's ~** fazer o possível; **to the ~ of my knowledge** que eu saiba; **to the ~ of my ability** o melhor que eu puder; **best-before date** *n* validade *f*; **best man** *n* padrinho de casamento

bet [bɛt] (*pt, pp* **bet** *or* **betted**) *n* aposta ▷ *vt, vi*: **to ~ (on)** apostar (em)

betray [bɪ'treɪ] *vt* trair; (*denounce*) delatar

better ['bɛtəʳ] *adj, adv* melhor ▷ *vt* melhorar; (*go above*) superar ▷ *n*: **to get the ~ of sb** vencer alguém; **you had ~ do it** é melhor você fazer isso; **he thought ~ of it**

pensou melhor, mudou de opinião; **to get ~** melhorar; **you'd be ~ off this way** seria melhor para você assim

betting ['bɛtɪŋ] n jogo; **betting shop** (*Brit*) agência de apostas

between [bɪ'twi:n] *prep* no meio de, entre ▷ *adv* no meio

beverage ['bɛvərɪdʒ] n bebida

beware [bɪ'wɛəʳ] *vi*: **to ~ (of)** precaver-se (de), ter cuidado (com); **"~ of the dog"** "cuidado com o cachorro"

bewildered [bɪ'wɪldəd] *adj* atordoado; (*confused*) confuso

beyond [bɪ'jɔnd] *prep* (*in space, exceeding*) além de; (*exceeding*) acima de, fora de; (*date*) mais tarde que; (*above*) acima de ▷ *adv* além; (*in time*) mais longe, mais adiante; **~ doubt** fora de qualquer dúvida; **to be ~ repair** não ter conserto

bias ['baɪəs] n parcialidade

bib [bɪb] n babadouro, babador m

Bible ['baɪbl] n Bíblia

bicycle ['baɪsɪkl] n bicicleta

bid [bɪd] (*pt* **bade** *or* **bid**, *pp* **bidden** *or* **bid**) n oferta; (*at auction*) lance m; (*attempt*) tentativa ▷ *vi* fazer lance ▷ *vt* oferecer; **to ~ sb good day** dar bom dia a alguém

big [bɪg] *adj* grande; (*bulky*) volumoso; **~ brother/sister** irmão(-irmã) mais velho/a

bigheaded ['bɪg'hɛdɪd] *adj* convencido

bike [baɪk] n bicicleta

bikini [bɪ'ki:nɪ] n biquíni m

bilingual [baɪ'lɪŋgwəl] *adj* bilíngue

bill [bɪl] n conta; (*invoice*) fatura; (*Pol*) projeto de lei; (*US: banknote*) bilhete m, nota; (*in restaurant*) conta, notinha; (*notice*) cartaz m; (*of bird*) bico; **to fit** *or* **fill the ~** (*fig*)

servir; **billboard** n quadro para cartazes

billfold ['bɪlfəuld] (*US*) n carteira

billiards ['bɪlɪədz] n bilhar m

billion ['bɪlɪən] n (*Brit*) trilhão m; (*US*) bilhão m

bin [bɪn] n caixa; (*Brit: also*: **dust~**; **litter ~**) lata de lixo

bind [baɪnd] (*pt, pp* **bound**) *vt* atar, amarrar; (*oblige*) obrigar; (*book*) encadernar ▷ n (*inf*) saco

binge [bɪndʒ] (*inf*) n: **to go on a ~** tomar uma bebedeira

bingo ['bɪngəu] n bingo

binoculars [bɪ'nɔkjuləz] *npl* binóculo

bio ... [baɪəu] *prefix* bio ...; **biochemistry** n bioquímica; **biography** n biografia; **biology** n biologia; **biometric** *adj* biométrico

birch [bə:tʃ] n bétula

bird [bə:d] n ave f, pássaro; (*Brit: inf: girl*) gatinha; **bird flu** n gripe f aviária

birth [bə:θ] n nascimento; **to give ~ to** dar à luz, parir; **birth certificate** n certidão f de nascimento; **birth control** n controle m de natalidade; (*methods*) métodos *mpl* anticoncepcionais; **birthday** n aniversário (*BR*), dia m de anos (*PT*) ▷ *cpd* de aniversário; *see also* **happy**

biscuit ['bɪskɪt] n (*Brit*) bolacha, biscoito; (*US*) pão m doce

bishop ['bɪʃəp] n bispo

bit [bɪt] *pt of* **bite** ▷ n pedaço, bocado; (*of horse*) freio; (*Comput*) bit m; **a ~ of** (*a little*) um pouco de; **~ by ~** pouco a pouco

bitch [bɪtʃ] n (*dog*) cadela, cachorra; (*inf!*) cadela (!), vagabunda (!)

bite [baɪt] (pt **bit**, pp **bitten**) vt, vi morder; (insect etc) picar ▷ n (insect bite) picada; (mouthful) bocado; **to ~ one's nails** roer as unhas; **let's have a ~ (to eat)** (inf) vamos fazer uma boquinha

bitter ['bɪtəʳ] adj amargo; (wind, criticism) cortante, penetrante ▷ n (Brit: beer) cerveja amarga

black [blæk] adj preto; (humour) negro ▷ n (colour) cor f preta; (person): **B~** negro(-a) ▷ vt (Brit: Industry) boicotar; **to give sb a ~ eye** esmurrar alguém e deixá-lo de olho roxo; **~ and blue** contuso, contundido; **to be in the ~** (in credit) estar com saldo credor; **blackberry** n amora(-preta) (BR), amora silvestre (PT); **blackbird** n melro; **blackboard** n quadro(-negro); **black coffee** n café m preto; **blackcurrant** n groselha negra; **blackmail** n chantagem f ▷ vt fazer chantagem a; **black market** n mercado or câmbio negro; **blackout** n blecaute m; (fainting) desmaio; (of radio signal) desvanecimento; **Black Sea** n: **the Black Sea** o mar Negro

bladder ['blædəʳ] n bexiga

blade [bleɪd] n lâmina; (of oar, rotor) pá f; **a ~ of grass** uma folha de relva

blame [bleɪm] n culpa ▷ vt: **to ~ sb for sth** culpar alguém por algo; **to be to ~** ter a culpa

bland [blænd] adj (taste) brando

blank [blæŋk] adj em branco; (look) sem expressão ▷ n (of memory): **to go ~** dar um branco; (on form) espaço em branco; (cartridge) bala de festim

blanket ['blæŋkɪt] n cobertor m

blast [blɑːst] n (of wind) rajada; (of explosive) explosão f ▷ vt fazer voar

blatant ['bleɪtənt] adj descarado

blaze [bleɪz] n (fire) fogo; (in building etc) incêndio; (fig: of colour) esplendor m; (: of glory, publicity) explosão f ▷ vi (fire) arder; (guns) descarregar; (eyes) brilhar ▷ vt: **to ~ a trail** (fig) abrir (um) caminho

blazer ['bleɪzəʳ] n casaco esportivo, blazer m

bleach [bliːtʃ] n (also: **household ~**) água sanitária ▷ vt (linen) branquear

bleak [bliːk] adj (countryside) desolado; (prospect) desanimador(a), sombrio; (weather) ruim

bleed [bliːd] (pt, pp **bled**) vi sangrar

blemish ['blemɪʃ] n mancha; (on reputation) mácula

blend [blend] n mistura ▷ vt misturar ▷ vi (colours etc: also: **~ in**) combinar-se, misturar-se; **blender** n liquidificador m

bless [bles] (pt, pp **blessed**) vt abençoar; **~ you!** (after sneeze) saúde!; **blessing** n bênção f; (godsend) graça, dádiva; (approval) aprovação f

blew [bluː] pt of **blow**

blind [blaɪnd] adj cego ▷ n (for window) persiana; (also: **Venetian ~**) veneziana ▷ vt cegar; (dazzle) deslumbrar; **the blind** npl (blind people) os cegos; **blind alley** n beco sem saída m; **blindfold** n venda ▷ adj, adv com os olhos vendados, às cegas ▷ vt vendar os olhos a

blink [blɪŋk] vi piscar

bliss [blɪs] n felicidade f

blister ['blɪstəʳ] n (on skin) bolha; (in paint, rubber) empola ▷ vi empolar-se

blizzard ['blɪzəd] n nevasca
bloated ['bləʊtɪd] adj (swollen) inchado; (full) empanturrado
blob [blɔb] n (drop) gota; (indistinct shape) ponto
block [blɔk] n (of wood) bloco; (of stone) laje f; (in pipes) entupimento; (of buildings) quarteirão m ▷ vt obstruir, bloquear; (progress) impedir; **~ of flats** (Brit) prédio (de apartamentos); **mental ~** bloqueio; **blockade** [blɔ'keɪd] n bloqueio; **blockage** n obstrução f; **blockbuster** ['blɔkbʌstər] n grande sucesso
blog ['blɔg] n blog m
blogger ['blɔgər] n (inf: person) blogueiro(-a)
bloke [bləʊk] (Brit: inf) n cara m (BR), gajo (PT)
blond, blonde [blɔnd] adj, n louro(-a)
blood [blʌd] n sangue m; **blood donor** n doador(a) m/f de sangue; **blood group** n grupo sanguíneo; **blood poisoning** n toxemia; **blood pressure** n pressão f arterial or sanguínea; **bloodshed** n matança, carnificina; **bloodshot** adj (eyes) injetado; **bloodstream** n corrente f sanguínea; **blood test** n exame m de sangue; **blood vessel** n vaso sanguíneo; **bloody** adj sangrento; (nose) ensanguentado; (Brit: inf!): **this bloody ...** essa droga de ..., esse maldito ...; **bloody strong/good** forte/bom pra burro (inf)
bloom [blu:m] n flor f ▷ vi florescer
blossom ['blɔsəm] n flor f ▷ vi florescer; (fig): **to ~ into** (fig) tornar-se
blot [blɔt] n borrão m; (fig) mancha ▷ vt borrar **blot out** vt (view)

tapar; (memory) apagar
blouse [blauz] n blusa
blow [bləʊ] (pt **blew**, pp **blown**) n golpe m; (punch) soco ▷ vi soprar ▷ vt (subj: wind) soprar; (instrument) tocar; (fuse) queimar; **to ~ one's nose** assoar o nariz **blow away** vt levar, arrancar ▷ vi ser levado pelo vento **blow down** vt derrubar **blow off** vt levar **blow out** vt (candle) apagar **blow over** vi passar **blow up** vi explodir ▷ vt explodir; (tyre) encher; (Phot) ampliar; **blow-dry** n escova; **blow-out** n (of tyre) furo
blue [blu:] adj azul; (depressed) deprimido; **blues** n (Mus): **the ~s** o blues; **out of the ~** (fig) de estalo, inesperadamente; **bluebell** n campainha
bluff [blʌf] vi blefar ▷ n blefe m; **to call sb's ~** pagar para ver alguém
blunder ['blʌndər] n gafe f ▷ vi cometer or fazer uma gafe
blunt [blʌnt] adj (knife) cego; (pencil) rombudo; (person) franco, direto
blur [blə:r] n borrão m ▷ vt (vision) embaçar
blush [blʌʃ] vi corar, ruborizar-se ▷ n rubor m, vermelhidão f
board [bɔ:d] n tábua; (blackboard) quadro; (notice board) quadro de avisos; (for chess etc) tabuleiro; (committee) junta, conselho; (in firm) diretoria, conselho administrativo; (Naut, Aviat): **on ~** a bordo ▷ vt embarcar em; **full ~** (Brit) pensão f completa; **half ~** (Brit) meia-pensão f; **~ and lodging** casa e comida; **to go by the ~** ficar abandonado, dançar (inf) **board up** vt entabuar; **boarding card** n = **boarding pass**; **boarding pass**

(*Brit*) *n* (*Aviat, Naut*) cartão *m* de embarque; **boarding school** *n* internato

boast ['bəʊst] *vi*: **to ~ (about** *or* **of)** gabar-se (de), jactar-se (de)

boat [bəʊt] *n* barco *m*; (*ship*) navio

bob [bɒb] *vi* balouçar-se **bob up** *vi* aparecer, surgir

body ['bɒdɪ] *n* corpo; (*corpse*) cadáver *m*; (*of car*) carroceria; (*fig: group*) grupo; (: *organization*) organização *f*; (*quantity*) conjunto; (*of wine*) corpo; **body-building** *n* musculação *f*; **bodyguard** *n* guarda-costas *m inv*; **bodywork** *n* lataria

bog [bɒg] *n* pântano, atoleiro ▷ *vt*: **to get ~ged down (in)** (*fig*) atolar-se (em)

bogus ['bəʊgəs] *adj* falso

boil [bɔɪl] *vt* ferver; (*eggs*) cozinhar ▷ *vi* ferver ▷ *n* (*Med*) furúnculo; **to come to the** (*Brit*) *or* **a** (*US*) **~** começar a ferver **boil down to** *vt fus* (*fig*) reduzir-se a **boil over** *vi* transbordar; **boiled egg** *n* ovo cozido; **boiled potatoes** *npl* batatas *fpl* cozidas; **boiler** *n* caldeira; (*for central heating*) boiler *m*; **boiling point** *n* ponto de ebulição

bold [bəʊld] *adj* corajoso; (*pej*) atrevido, insolente; (*outline, colour*) forte

Bolivia [bə'lɪvɪə] *n* Bolívia

bollard ['bɒləd] *n* (*Brit: Aut*) poste *m* de sinalização

bolt [bəʊlt] *n* (*lock*) trinco, ferrolho; (*with nut*) parafuso, cavilha ▷ *adv*: **~ upright** direito como um fuso ▷ *vt* (*door*) fechar a ferrolho, trancar; (*food*) engolir às pressas ▷ *vi* fugir; (*horse*) disparar

bomb [bɒm] *n* bomba ▷ *vt*

bombardear; **bomb scare** *n* ameaça de bomba

bond [bɒnd] *n* (*binding promise*) compromisso; (*link*) vínculo, laço; (*Finance*) obrigação *f*; (*Comm*): **in ~** (*goods*) retido sob caução na alfândega

bone [bəʊn] *n* osso; (*of fish*) espinha ▷ *vt* desossar; tirar as espinhas de

bonfire ['bɒnfaɪər] *n* fogueira

bonnet ['bɒnɪt] *n* toucado; (*Brit: of car*) capô *m*

bonus ['bəʊnəs] *n* (*payment*) bônus *m*; (*fig*) gratificação *f*

boo [buː] *vt* vaiar ▷ *excl* ruuh!, bu!

book [bʊk] *n* livro; (*of stamps, tickets*) talão *m* ▷ *vt* reservar; (*driver*) autuar; (*football player*) mostrar o cartão amarelo a; **books** *npl* (*Comm*) contas *fpl*, contabilidade *f*; **bookcase** *n* estante *f* (para livros); **booking office** (*Brit*) *n* (*Rail, Theatre*) bilheteria (*BR*), bilheteira (*PT*); **book-keeping** *n* escrituração *f*, contabilidade *f*; **booklet** *n* livrinho, brochura; **bookmark** *n* (*for book*) marcador *m* de livro; (*Comput*) favorito, bookmark *m*; **bookshop, bookstore** *n* livraria

bookstore *n* = **bookshop**

boom [buːm] *n* (*noise*) barulho, estrondo; (*in sales etc*) aumento rápido ▷ *vi* retumbar; (*business*) tomar surto

boost [buːst] *n* estímulo ▷ *vt* estimular

boot [buːt] *n* bota; (*for football*) chuteira; (*Brit: of car*) porta-malas *m* (*BR*), porta-bagagem *m* (*PT*) ▷ *vt* (*Comput*) iniciar; **to ~ ...** (*in addition*) ainda por cima ...

booth [buːð] *n* (*at fair*) barraca;

(telephone booth, voting booth) cabine f

booze [buːz] (inf) n bebida alcoólica

border [ˈbɔːdə^r] n margem f; (for flowers) borda; (of a country) fronteira; (on cloth etc) debrum m, remate m ▷ vt (also: ~ **on**) limitar-se com **border on** vt fus (fig) chegar às raias de; **borderline** n fronteira

bore [bɔː^r] pt of **bear** ▷ vt (hole) abrir; (well) cavar; (person) aborrecer ▷ n (person) chato(-a), maçante m/f; (of gun) calibre m; **to be ~d to tears** or **~d to death** or **~d stiff** estar muito entediado; **boredom** n tédio, aborrecimento; **boring** adj chato, maçante

born [bɔːn] adj: **to be ~** nascer

borne [bɔːn] pp of **bear**

borough [ˈbʌrə] n município

borrow [ˈbɔrəu] vt: **to ~ sth (from sb)** pedir algo emprestado a alguém

bosom [ˈbuzəm] n peito

boss [bɔs] n (employer) patrão(-troa) m/f ▷ vt (also: ~ **about**; ~ **around**) mandar em; **bossy** adj mandão(-dona)

both [bəuθ] adj, pron ambos(-as), os dois/as duas ▷ adv: ~ **A and B** tanto A como B; ~ **of us went**, **we ~ went** nós dois fomos, ambos fomos

bother [ˈbɔðə^r] vt (worry) preocupar; (disturb) atrapalhar ▷ vi (also: ~ **o.s.**) preocupar-se ▷ n preocupação f; (nuisance) amolação f, inconveniente m

bottle [ˈbɔtl] n garrafa; (of perfume, medicine) frasco; (baby's) mamadeira (BR), biberão m (PT) ▷ vt engarrafar **bottle up** vt conter, refrear; **bottle bank** n

depósito de vidro para reciclagem, vidrão m (PT); **bottle-opener** n abridor m (de garrafas) (BR), abre-garrafas m inv (PT)

bottom [ˈbɔtəm] n fundo; (buttocks) traseiro; (of page, list) pé m; (of class) nível m mais baixo ▷ adj (low) inferior, mais baixo; (last) último

bought [bɔːt] pt, pp of **buy**

boulder [ˈbəuldə^r] n pedregulho, matacão m

bounce [bauns] vi saltar, quicar; (cheque) ser devolvido (por insuficiência de fundos) ▷ vt fazer saltar ▷ n (rebound) salto; **bouncer** (inf) n leão de chácara m

bound [baund] pt, pp of **bind** ▷ n (leap) pulo, salto; (gen pl: limit) limite m ▷ vi (leap) pular, saltar ▷ vt (border) demarcar ▷ adj: ~ **by** limitado por; **to be ~ to do sth** (obliged) ter a obrigação de fazer algo; (likely) na certa ir fazer algo; ~ **for** com destino a

boundary [ˈbaundrɪ] n limite m, fronteira

bout [baut] n (of malaria etc) ataque m; (of activity) explosão f; (Boxing etc) combate m

bow[1] [bəu] n (knot) laço; (weapon, Mus) arco

bow[2] [bau] n (of the body) reverência; (of the head) inclinação f; (Naut: also: ~**s**) proa ▷ vi curvar-se, fazer uma reverência; (yield): **to ~ to** or **before** ceder ante, submeter-se a

bowels [ˈbauəlz] npl intestinos mpl, tripas fpl; (fig) entranhas fpl

bowl [bəul] n tigela; (ball) bola ▷ vi (Cricket) arremessar a bola

bowler [ˈbəulə^r] n (Cricket) lançador m (da bola); (Brit: also: ~ **hat**) chapéu-coco m

bowling ['bəʊlɪŋ] n (game) boliche m; **bowling alley** n boliche m; **bowling green** n gramado (BR) or relvado (PT) para jogo de bolas

bowls [bəʊlz] n jogo de bolas

bow tie ['bəʊ-] n gravata-borboleta

box [bɒks] n caixa; (Theatre) camarote m ▷ vt encaixotar; (Sport) boxear contra ▷ vi (Sport) boxear; **boxer** n (person) boxeador m, pugilista m; **boxer shorts** npl cueca samba-canção; **boxing** n (Sport) boxe m, pugilismo; **Boxing Day** (Brit) n Dia de Santo Estêvão (26 de dezembro); **box office** n bilheteria (BR), bilheteira (PT)

boy [bɔɪ] n (young) menino, garoto; (older) moço, rapaz m; (son) filho

boycott ['bɔɪkɒt] n boicote m, boicotagem f ▷ vt boicotar

boyfriend ['bɔɪfrɛnd] n namorado

bra [brɑ:] n sutiã m (BR), soutien m (PT)

brace [breɪs] n (on teeth) aparelho; (tool) arco de pua ▷ vt retesar; **braces** npl (Brit) suspensórios mpl; **to ~ o.s.** (for weight, fig) preparar-se

bracelet ['breɪslɪt] n pulseira

bracket ['brækɪt] n (Tech) suporte m; (group) classe f, categoria; (range) faixa; (also: **round ~**) parêntese m ▷ vt pôr entre parênteses; (fig) agrupar

brag [bræg] vi gabar-se, contar vantagem

braid [breɪd] n (trimming) galão m; (of hair) trança

brain [breɪn] n cérebro; **brains** npl (Culin) miolos mpl; (intelligence) inteligência, miolos

braise [breɪz] vt assar na panela

brake [breɪk] n freio (BR), travão m (PT) ▷ vt, vi frear (BR), travar (PT)

bran [bræn] n farelo

branch [brɑ:ntʃ] n ramo, galho; (Comm) sucursal f, filial f **branch out** vi (fig) diversificar suas atividades; **to ~ out into** estender suas atividades a

brand [brænd] n marca; (fig: type) tipo ▷ vt (cattle) marcar com ferro quente; **brand-new** adj novo em folha, novinho

brandy ['brændɪ] n conhaque m

brash [bræʃ] adj (forward) descarado

brass [brɑ:s] n latão m; **the ~** (Mus) os metais; **brass band** n banda de música

brat [bræt] (pej) n pirralho(-a), fedelho(-a)

brave [breɪv] adj valente, corajoso ▷ vt (face up to) desafiar; **bravery** n coragem f, bravura

Brazil [brə'zɪl] n Brasil m; **Brazilian** adj, n brasileiro(-a)

breach [bri:tʃ] vt abrir brecha em ▷ n (gap) brecha; (breaking): **~ of contract** inadimplência (BR), inadimplemento (PT)

bread [brɛd] n pão m; **breadbin** (Brit) n caixa de pão; **breadbox** (US) n caixa de pão; **breadcrumbs** npl migalhas fpl; (Culin) farinha de rosca

breadth [brɛtθ] n largura; (fig) amplitude f

break [breɪk] (pt **broke**, pp **broken**) vt quebrar (BR), partir (PT); (promise) quebrar; (law) violar, transgredir; (record) bater ▷ vi quebrar-se, partir-se; (storm) estourar; (weather) mudar; (dawn) amanhecer; (story, news) revelar ▷ n (gap) abertura; (fracture) fratura; (rest) descanso; (interval) intervalo; (at school) recreio; (chance) oportunidade f; **to ~ the**

news to sb dar a notícia a alguém;
to ~ even sair sem ganhar nem
perder; **to ~ free** or **loose** soltar-se;
to ~ open (*door etc*) arrombar
break down vt (*figures, data*)
analisar ▷ vi (*machine, Aut*)
enguiçar, pifar (*inf*); (*Med*) sofrer
uma crise nervosa; (*person: cry*)
desatar a chorar; (*talks*) fracassar
break in vt (*horse etc*) domar ▷ vi
(*burglar*) forçar uma entrada;
(*interrupt*) interromper **break into**
vt fus (*house*) arrombar **break off** vi
(*speaker*) parar-se, deter-se;
(*branch*) partir **break out** vi (*war*)
estourar; (*prisoner*) libertar-se; **to ~
out in spots/a rash** aparecer
coberto de manchas/brotoejas
break up vi (*ship*) partir-se;
(*partnership*) acabar; (*marriage*)
desmanchar-se; **you're ~ing up**
sua voz está falhando ▷ vt (*rocks*)
partir; (*biscuit etc*) quebrar;
(*journey*) romper; (*fight*) intervir
em; **breakdown** n (*Aut*) enguiço,
avaria; (*in communications*)
interrupção f; (*of marriage*)
fracasso, término; (*Med: also:*
nervous breakdown)
esgotamento nervoso; (*of figures*)
discriminação f, desdobramento
breakfast ['brɛkfəst] n café m da
manhã (*BR*), pequeno almoço (*PT*)
break-in n roubo com
arrombamento
breakthrough ['breɪkθruː] n (*fig*)
avanço, novo progresso
breast [brɛst] n (*of woman*) peito,
seio; (*chest, meat*) peito;
breast-feed (*irreg: like* **feed**) vt, vi
amamentar; **breaststroke** n nado
de peito
breath [brɛθ] n fôlego, respiração f;
out of ~ ofegante, sem fôlego

breathe [briːð] vt, vi respirar
breathe in vt, vi inspirar **breathe
out** vt, vi expirar; **breathing** n
respiração f
breathless ['brɛθlɪs] adj sem fôlego
breed [briːd] (*pt, pp* **bred**) vt
(*animals*) criar; (*plants*) multiplicar
▷ vi acasalar-se ▷ n raça
breeze [briːz] n brisa, aragem f;
breezy adj (*person*)
despreocupado, animado;
(*weather*) ventoso
brew [bruː] vt (*tea*) fazer; (*beer*)
fermentar ▷ vi (*storm, fig*)
armar-se; **brewery** n cervejaria
bribe [braɪb] n suborno ▷ vt
subornar; **bribery** n suborno
brick [brɪk] n tijolo; **bricklayer** n
pedreiro
bride [braɪd] n noiva; **bridegroom**
n noivo; **bridesmaid** n dama de
honra
bridge [brɪdʒ] n ponte f; (*Naut*)
ponte de comando; (*Cards*) bridge
m; (*of nose*) cavalete m ▷ vt transpor
bridle ['braɪdl] n cabeçada, freio
brief [briːf] adj breve ▷ n (*Law*)
causa; (*task*) tarefa ▷ vt (*inform*)
informar; **briefs** npl (*for men*) cueca
(*BR*), cuecas fpl (*PT*); (*for women*)
calcinha (*BR*), cuecas fpl (*PT*);
briefcase n pasta; **briefly** adv
(*glance*) rapidamente; (*say*) em
poucas palavras
bright [braɪt] adj claro, brilhante;
(*weather*) resplendecente; (*person:
clever*) inteligente; (*: lively*) alegre,
animado; (*colour*) vivo; (*future*)
promissor(a), favorável
brilliant ['brɪljənt] adj brilhante;
(*inf: great*) sensacional
brim [brɪm] n borda; (*of hat*) aba
brine [braɪn] n (*Culin*) salmoura
bring [brɪŋ] (*pt, pp* **brought**) vt

b

trazer **bring about** vt ocasionar, produzir **bring back** vt restabelecer; (return) devolver **bring down** vt (price) abaixar; (government, plane) derrubar **bring forward** vt adiantar **bring off** vt (task, plan) levar a cabo **bring out** vt (object) tirar; (meaning) salientar; (new product, book) lançar **bring round** vt fazer voltar a si **bring up** vt (person) educar, criar; (carry up) subir; (question) introduzir; (food) vomitar

brisk [brɪsk] adj vigoroso; (tone, person) enérgico; (trade, business) ativo

bristle ['brɪsl] n (of animal) pelo rijo; (of beard) pelo de barba curta; (of brush) cerda ▷ vi (in anger) encolerizar-se

Britain ['brɪtən] n (also: **Great ~**) Grã-Bretanha

British ['brɪtɪʃ] adj britânico ▷ npl: **the ~** os britânicos; **British Isles** npl: **the British Isles** as ilhas Britânicas

Briton ['brɪtən] n britânico(-a)

brittle ['brɪtl] adj quebradiço, frágil

broad [brɔːd] adj (street, range) amplo; (shoulders, smile) largo; (distinction, outline) geral; (accent) carregado; **in ~ daylight** em plena luz do dia; **broadband** n banda larga; **broadcast** (pt, pp **broadcast**) n transmissão f ▷ vt, vi transmitir; **broaden** vt alargar ▷ vi alargar-se; **to broaden one's mind** abrir os horizontes; **broadly** adv em geral; **broad-minded** adj tolerante, liberal

broccoli ['brɔkəlɪ] n brócolis mpl (BR), brócolos mpl (PT)

brochure ['brəʊʃjuə'] n folheto, brochura

broke [brəʊk] pt of **break** ▷ adj (inf) sem um vintém, duro; (: company): **to go ~** quebrar

broken ['brəʊkən] pp of **break** ▷ adj quebrado; **in ~ English** num inglês mascavado

broker ['brəʊkə'] n corretor(a) m/f

bronchitis [brɔŋ'kaɪtɪs] n bronquite f

bronze [brɔnz] n bronze m

brooch [brəʊtʃ] n broche m

brood [bruːd] n ninhada ▷ vi (person) cismar, remoer

broom [brum] n vassoura; (Bot) giesta-das-vassouras

Bros. abbr (Comm: = brothers) Irmãos

broth [brɔθ] n caldo

brothel ['brɔθl] n bordel m

brother ['brʌðə'] n irmão m; **brother-in-law** n cunhado

brought [brɔːt] pt, pp of **bring**

brow [brau] n (forehead) fronte f, testa; (eyebrow) sobrancelha; (of hill) cimo, cume m

brown [braun] adj marrom (BR), castanho (PT); (hair) castanho; (tanned) bronzeado, moreno ▷ n (colour) cor f marrom (BR) or castanha (PT) ▷ vt (Culin) dourar; **brown bread** n pão m integral; **Brownie** n (also: **Brownie Guide**) fadinha de bandeirante; **brown sugar** n açúcar m mascavo

browse [brauz] vi (in shop) dar uma olhada; **to ~ through a book** folhear um livro; **browser** n (Comput) browser m

bruise [bruːz] n hematoma m, contusão f ▷ vt machucar

brunette [bruːˈnɛt] n morena

brush [brʌʃ] n escova; (for painting, shaving etc) pincel m; (quarrel) bate-boca m ▷ vt varrer; (groom) escovar; (also: **~ against**) tocar ao passar, roçar **brush aside** vt afastar, não fazer caso de **brush up** vt retocar, revisar

Brussels ['brʌslz] n Bruxelas; **Brussels sprout** n couve-de-bruxelas f

brutal ['bruːtl] adj brutal

bubble ['bʌbl] n bolha (BR), borbulha (PT) ▷ vi borbulhar; **bubble bath** n banho de espuma; **bubble gum** n chiclete m (de bola) (BR), pastilha elástica (PT)

buck [bʌk] n (rabbit) macho; (deer) cervo; (US: inf) dólar m ▷ vi corcovear; **to pass the ~** fazer o jogo de empurra **buck up** vi (cheer up) animar-se, cobrar ânimo

bucket ['bʌkɪt] n balde m

buckle ['bʌkl] n fivela ▷ vt afivelar ▷ vi torcer-se, cambar-se

bud [bʌd] n broto; (of flower) botão m ▷ vi brotar, desabrochar

Buddhism ['budɪzəm] n budismo

buddy ['bʌdɪ] (US) n camarada m, companheiro

budge [bʌdʒ] vt mover ▷ vi mexer-se

budgerigar ['bʌdʒərɪgɑː'] n periquito

budget ['bʌdʒɪt] n orçamento ▷ vi: **to ~ for sth** incluir algo no orçamento

budgie ['bʌdʒɪ] n = **budgerigar**

buff [bʌf] adj (colour) cor de camurça ▷ n (inf: enthusiast) aficionado(-a)

buffalo ['bʌfələu] (pl **buffalo** or **buffaloes**) n (Brit) búfalo; (US: bison) bisão m

buffer ['bʌfə'] n para-choque m; (Comput) buffer m

buffet¹ ['bufeɪ] (Brit) n (in station) bar m; (food) bufê m

buffet² ['bʌfɪt] vt fustigar

buffet car (Brit) n vagão-restaurante m

bug [bʌg] n (esp US: insect) bicho; (fig: germ) micróbio; (spy device) microfone m oculto, escuta clandestina; (Comput: of program) erro; (: of equipment) defeito ▷ vt (inf: annoy) apoquentar, incomodar; (room) colocar microfones em; (phone) grampear

build [bɪld] (pt, pp **built**) n (of person) talhe m, estatura ▷ vt construir, edificar **build up** vt acumular; **builder** n construtor(a) m/f, empreiteiro(-a); **building** n construção f; (residential, offices) edifício, prédio; **building society** (Brit) n sociedade f de crédito imobiliário, financiadora

built [bɪlt] pt, pp of **build** ▷ adj: **~-in** (cupboard) embutido

bulb [bʌlb] n (Bot) bulbo; (Elec) lâmpada

Bulgaria [bʌl'gɛərɪə] n Bulgária

bulge [bʌldʒ] n bojo, saliência ▷ vi inchar-se; (pocket etc) fazer bojo

bulk [bʌlk] n volume m; **in ~** (Comm) a granel; **the ~ of** a maior parte de; **bulky** adj volumoso

bull [bul] n touro

bulldozer ['buldəuzə'] n buldôzer m, escavadora

bullet ['bulɪt] n bala

bulletin ['bulɪtɪn] n noticiário; (journal) boletim m

bullfight ['bulfaɪt] n tourada; **bullfighter** n toureiro; **bullfighting** n tauromaquia

bully ['bulɪ] n fanfarrão m, valentão m ▷ vt intimidar, tiranizar

bum [bʌm] n (inf: backside) bumbum m; (esp US: tramp) vagabundo(-a), vadio(-a)

bumblebee ['bʌmblbiː] n mamangaba

bump [bʌmp] n (*in car*) batida; (*jolt*) sacudida; (*on head*) galo; (*on road*) elevação f ▷ vt bater contra, dar encontrão em ▷ vi dar sacudidas **bump into** vt fus chocar-se com or contra, colidir com; (*inf: person*) dar com, topar com; **bumper** n (*Brit*) para-choque m ▷ adj: **bumper crop/harvest** supersafra; **bumpy** adj (*road*) acidentado, cheio de altos e baixos

bun [bʌn] n pão m doce (*BR*), pãozinho (*PT*); (*in hair*) coque m

bunch [bʌntʃ] n (*of flowers*) ramo; (*of keys*) molho; (*of bananas, grapes*) cacho; (*of people*) grupo; **bunches** npl (*in hair*) cachos mpl

bundle ['bʌndl] n trouxa, embrulho; (*of sticks*) feixe m; (*of papers*) maço ▷ vt (*also:* **~ up**) embrulhar, atar; (*put*): **to ~ sth/sb into** meter or enfiar algo/alguém correndo em

bungalow ['bʌŋgələu] n bangalô m, chalé m

bunion ['bʌnjən] n joanete m

bunk [bʌŋk] n beliche m; **bunk beds** npl beliche m, cama-beliche f

bunker ['bʌŋkəʳ] n (*coal store*) carvoeira; (*Mil*) abrigo, casamata; (*Golf*) bunker m

buoy [bɔɪ] n boia **buoy up** vt (*fig*) animar; **buoyant** adj flutuante; (*person*) alegre; (*Comm: market*) animado

burden ['bə:dn] n responsabilidade f, fardo; (*load*) carga ▷ vt sobrecarregar; (*trouble*): **to be a ~ to sb** ser um estorvo para alguém

bureau [bjuə'rəu] n (pl **bureaux**) n (*Brit: desk*) secretária, escrivaninha; (*US: chest of drawers*) cômoda; (*office*) escritório, agência

bureaucracy [bjuə'rɔkrəsɪ] n burocracia

burglar ['bə:gləʳ] n ladrão/ladrona m/f; **burglar alarm** n alarma de roubo; **burglary** n roubo

burial ['bɛrɪəl] n enterro

burn [bə:n] (pt, pp **burned** or **burnt**) vt queimar; (*house*) incendiar ▷ vi queimar-se, arder; (*sting*) arder, picar ▷ n queimadura **burn down** vt incendiar; **burning** adj ardente; (*hot: sand etc*) abrasador(a); (*ambition*) grande

burrow ['bʌrəu] n toca, lura ▷ vi fazer uma toca, cavar; (*rummage*) esquadrinhar

burst [bə:st] (pt, pp **burst**) vt arrebentar; (*banks etc*) romper ▷ vi estourar; (*tyre*) furar ▷ n rajada; **to ~ into flames** incendiar-se de repente; **to ~ into tears** desatar a chorar; **to ~ out laughing** cair na gargalhada; **to be ~ing with** (*subj: room, container*) estar abarrotado de; (*: emotion*) estar tomado de; **a ~ of energy/speed/enthusiasm** uma explosão de energia/ velocidade/entusiasmo **burst into** vt fus (*room etc*) irromper em

bury ['bɛrɪ] vt enterrar; (*at funeral*) sepultar; **to ~ one's head in one's hands** cobrir o rosto com as mãos; **to ~ one's head in the sand** (*fig*) bancar avestruz; **to ~ the hatchet** (*fig*) fazer as pazes

bus [bʌs] n ônibus m inv (*BR*), autocarro (*PT*); **bus conductor** n cobrador(a) m/f de ônibus

bush [buʃ] n arbusto, mata; (*scrubland*) sertão m; **to beat about the ~** ser evasivo

business ['bɪznɪs] n negócio; (*trading*) comércio, negócios mpl; (*firm*) empresa; (*occupation*) profissão f; **to be away on ~** estar fora a negócios; **it's my ~ to ...**

encarrego-me de ...; **it's none of my ~** eu não tenho nada com isto; **he means ~** fala a sério; **business class** n (on plane) classe f executiva; **businesslike** adj eficiente, metódico; **businessman** irreg n homem m de negócios; **business trip** n viagem f de negócios; **businesswoman** ['bıznıswumən] irreg n mulher f de negócios

busker ['bʌskər] (Brit) n artista m/f de rua

bust [bʌst] n (Anat) busto ▷ adj (inf: broken) quebrado; **to go ~** falir

busy ['bızı] adj (person) ocupado, atarefado; (shop, street) animado, movimentado; (US: Tel) ocupado (BR), impedido (PT) ▷ vt: **to ~ o.s. with** ocupar-se em or de

 KEYWORD

but [bʌt] conj **1** (yet) mas, porém; **he's tired but Paul isn't** ele está cansado mas Paul não; **the trip was enjoyable but tiring** a viagem foi agradável porém cansativa

2 (however) mas; **I'd love to come, but I'm busy** eu adoraria vir, mas estou ocupado

3 (showing disagreement, surprise etc) mas; **but that's far too expensive!** mas isso é caro demais! ▷ prep (apart from, except) exceto, menos; **he was/we've had nothing but trouble** ele só deu problema/nós só tivemos problema; **no-one but him** só ele, ninguém a não ser ele; **but for** sem, se não fosse; **(I'll do) anything but that** (eu faria) qualquer coisa menos isso ▷ adv (just, only) apenas; **had I but known** se eu soubesse; **I can but**

try a única coisa que eu posso fazer é tentar; **all but finished** quase acabado

butcher ['butʃər] n açougueiro (BR), homem m do talho (PT) ▷ vt (prisoners etc) chacinar, massacrar; (cattle etc for meat) abater e carnear; **butcher's, butcher's shop** n açougue m (BR), talho (PT)

butler ['bʌtlər] n mordomo

butt [bʌt] n (cask) tonel m; (of gun) coronha; (of cigarette) toco (BR), ponta (PT); (Brit: fig: target) alvo ▷ vt (subj: goat) marrar; (: person) dar uma cabeçada em **butt in** vi (interrupt) interromper

butter ['bʌtər] n manteiga ▷ vt untar com manteiga

butterfly ['bʌtəflaı] n borboleta; (Swimming: also: **~ stroke**) nado borboleta

buttocks ['bʌtəks] npl nádegas fpl

button ['bʌtn] n botão m; (US: badge) emblema m ▷ vt (also: **~ up**) abotoar ▷ vi ter botões

buy [baı] (pt, pp bought) vt comprar ▷ n compra; **to ~ sb sth/sth from sb** comprar algo para alguém/algo a alguém; **to ~ sb a drink** pagar um drinque para alguém; **buyer** n comprador(a) m/f

buzz [bʌz] n zumbido; (inf: phone call): **to give sb a ~** dar uma ligada para alguém ▷ vi zumbir; **buzzer** n cigarra, vibrador m

 KEYWORD

by [baı] prep **1** (referring to cause, agent) por, de; **killed by lightning** morto por um raio; **a painting by Picasso** um quadro de Picasso **2** (referring to method, manner, means) de, com; **by bus/car/train** de ônibus/carro/trem; **to pay by cheque** pagar com cheque; **by moonlight/candlelight** sob o luar/à luz de vela; **by saving hard, he ...** economizando muito, ele ... **3** (*via, through*) por, via; **we came by Dover** viemos por *or* via Dover **4** (*close to*) perto de, ao pé de; **a holiday by the sea** férias à beira-mar; **she sat by his bed** ela sentou-se ao lado de seu leito **5** (*past*) por; **she rushed by me** ela passou por mim correndo **6** (*not later than*): **by 4 o'clock** antes das quatro; **by this time tomorrow** esta mesma hora amanhã; **by the time I got here it was too late** quando eu cheguei aqui, já era tarde demais **7** (*during*): **by daylight** durante o dia **8** (*amount*) por; **by the kilometre** por quilômetro **9** (*Math, measure*) por; **it's broader by a metre** tem um metro a mais de largura **10** (*according to*) segundo, de acordo com; **it's all right by me** por mim tudo bem **11**: **(all) by oneself** *etc* (completamente) só, sozinho; **he did it (all) by himself** ele fez tudo sozinho **12**: **by the way** a propósito ▷ *adv* **1** *see* **go**; **pass** *etc* **2**: **by and by** logo, mais tarde; **by and large** em geral

bye [ˈbaɪ], **bye-bye** [ˈbaɪˈbaɪ] *excl* até logo (*BR*), tchau (*BR*), adeus (*PT*)
bypass [ˈbaɪpɑːs] *n* via secundária, desvio; (*Med*) ponte *f* de safena ▷ *vt* evitar
byte [baɪt] *n* (*Comput*) byte *m*

C

C, c [siː] *n* C, c *m*; (*Mus*) dó *m*
cab [kæb] *n* táxi *m*; (*of truck etc*) boleia; (*of train*) cabina de maquinista
cabaret [ˈkæbəreɪ] *n* cabaré *m*
cabbage [ˈkæbɪdʒ] *n* repolho (*BR*), couve *f* (*PT*)
cabin [ˈkæbɪn] *n* cabana; (*on ship*) camarote *m*; (*on plane*) cabina de passageiros; **cabin crew** *n* (*Aviat*) tripulação *f*
cabinet [ˈkæbɪnɪt] *n* (*Pol*) gabinete *m*; (*furniture*) armário; (*also:* **display ~**) armário com vitrina
cable [ˈkeɪbl] *n* cabo; (*telegram*) cabograma *m* ▷ *vt* enviar cabograma para; **cable television** *n* televisão *f* a cabo
cactus [ˈkæktəs] (*pl* **cacti**) *n* cacto
café [ˈkæfeɪ] *n* café *m*
cage [keɪdʒ] *n* (*bird cage*) gaiola; (*for large animals*) jaula; (*of lift*) cabina

cagoule [kə'gu:l] n casaco de náilon

Cairo ['kaɪərəu] n o Cairo

cake [keɪk] n (large) bolo; (small) doce m, bolinho; **cake of soap** n sabonete m

calculate ['kælkjuleɪt] vt calcular; (estimate) avaliar; **calculation** n cálculo; **calculator** n calculador m

calendar ['kæləndər] n calendário; **calendar month** n mês m civil; **calendar year** n ano civil

calf [kɑ:f] (pl **calves**) n (of cow) bezerro, vitela; (of other animals) cria; (also: ~**skin**) pele f or couro de bezerro; (Anat) barriga da perna

calibre ['kælɪbər], (US) **caliber** n (of person) capacidade f, calibre m

call [kɔ:l] vt chamar; (label) qualificar, descrever; (Tel) telefonar a, ligar para; (witness) citar; (meeting, strike) convocar ▷ vi chamar; (shout) gritar; (Tel) telefonar; (visit: also: ~ **in**; ~ **round**) dar um pulo ▷ n (shout, announcement) chamada; (also: **telephone ~**) chamada, telefonema m; (of bird) canto; **to be ~ed** chamar-se; **on ~** de plantão **call back** vi (return) voltar, passar de novo; (Tel) ligar de volta **call for** vt fus (demand) requerer, exigir; (fetch) ir buscar **call off** vt (cancel) cancelar **call on** vt fus (visit) visitar; (appeal to) pedir **call out** vi gritar, bradar **call up** vt (Mil) chamar às fileiras; (Tel) ligar para; **call box** (Brit) n cabine f telefônica; **call centre** n (Brit: Tel) central f de chamadas; **caller** n visita m/f; (Tel) chamador(a) m/f

callous ['kæləs] adj cruel, insensível

calm [kɑ:m] adj calmo; (peaceful) tranquilo; (weather) estável ▷ n calma ▷ vt acalmar; (fears, grief) abrandar **calm down** vt acalmar, tranquilizar ▷ vi acalmar-se

calorie ['kælərɪ] n caloria

calves [kɑ:vz] npl of **calf**

Cambodia [kæm'bəudjə] n Camboja

camcorder ['kæmkɔ:dər] n filmadora, máquina de filmar

came [keɪm] pt of **come**

camel ['kæməl] n camelo

camera ['kæmərə] n máquina fotográfica; (Cinema, TV) câmera; **in ~** (Law) em câmara; **camera phone** n celular m com câmera

camouflage ['kæməflɑ:ʒ] n camuflagem f ▷ vt camuflar

camp [kæmp] n campo, acampamento; (Mil) acampamento; (for prisoners) campo; (faction) facção f ▷ vi acampar ▷ adj afeminado

campaign [kæm'peɪn] n (Mil, Pol etc) campanha ▷ vi fazer campanha

camper ['kæmpər] n campista m/f; (vehicle) reboque m

camping ['kæmpɪŋ] n camping m (BR), campismo (PT); **to go ~** acampar

campsite ['kæmpsaɪt] n camping m (BR), parque m de campismo (PT)

campus ['kæmpəs] n campus m, cidade f universitária

can[1] [kæn] n lata ▷ vt enlatar

 KEYWORD

can[2] [kæn] (negative **can't**, **cannot**, conditional **could**) aux vb 1 (be able to) poder; **you can do it if you try** se você tentar, você consegue fazê-lo; **I'll help you all I can** ajudarei você em tudo que eu puder; **she couldn't sleep that night** ela não conseguiu dormir aquela noite; **can you hear me?** você está me ouvindo? **2** (*know how to*) saber; **I can swim** sei nadar; **can you speak Portuguese?** você fala português? **3** (*may*): **could I have a word with you?** será que eu podia falar com você? **4** (*expressing disbelief, puzzlement*): **it CAN'T be true!** não pode ser verdade!; **what CAN he want?** o que é que ele quer? **5** (*expressing possibility, suggestion etc*): **he could be in the library** ele talvez esteja na biblioteca; **they could have forgotten** eles podiam ter esquecido

Canada ['kænədə] n Canadá m; **Canadian** [kə'neɪdɪən] adj, n canadense m/f
canal [kə'næl] n canal m
canary [kə'nɛərɪ] n canário
cancel ['kænsəl] vt cancelar; (*contract*) anular; (*cross out*) riscar, invalidar; **cancellation** [kænsə'leɪʃən] n cancelamento
cancer ['kænsəʳ] n câncer m (BR), cancro (PT); **C~** (*Astrology*) Câncer
candidate ['kændɪdeɪt] n candidato(-a)
candle ['kændl] n vela; (*in church*) círio; **candlestick** n (*plain*) castiçal m; (*bigger, ornate*) candelabro, lustre m
candy ['kændɪ] n (*also:* **sugar ~**) açúcar m cristalizado; (*US*) bala (BR), rebuçado (PT)
cane [keɪn] n (*Bot*) cana; (*stick*) bengala ▷ vt (*Brit: Sch*) castigar (com bengala)
canister ['kænɪstəʳ] n lata

cannabis ['kænəbɪs] n maconha
canned [kænd] adj (*food*) em lata, enlatado
cannon ['kænən] (*pl* **cannons**) n canhão m
cannot ['kænɔt] = **can not**
canoe [kə'nuː] n canoa
can't [kɑːnt] = **can not**
canteen [kæn'tiːn] n cantina; (*Brit: of cutlery*) jogo (de talheres)
canter ['kæntəʳ] vi ir a meio galope
canvas ['kænvəs] n (*material*) lona; (*for painting*) tela; (*Naut*) velas fpl
canvass ['kænvəs] vi (*Pol*): **to ~ for** fazer campanha por ▷ vt sondar
canyon ['kænjən] n canhão m, garganta, desfiladeiro
cap [kæp] n gorro; (*of pen, bottle*) tampa; (*contraceptive: also:* **Dutch ~**) diafragma m; (*for toy gun*) cartucho ▷ vt (*outdo*) superar; (*put limit on*) limitar
capable ['keɪpəbl] adj (*of sth*) capaz; (*competent*) competente, hábil
capacity [kə'pæsɪtɪ] n capacidade f; (*of stadium etc*) lotação f; (*role*) condição f, posição f
cape [keɪp] n capa; (*Geo*) cabo
caper ['keɪpəʳ] n (*Culin: gen pl*) alcaparra; (*prank*) travessura
capital ['kæpɪtl] n (*also:* **~ city**) capital f; (*money*) capital m; (*also:* **~ letter**) maiúscula; **capitalism** n capitalismo; **capitalist** adj, n capitalista m/f; **capital punishment** n pena de morte
Capitol ['kæpɪtl] n *ver nota*

- **CAPITOL**
-
- O Capitólio (**Capitol**) é a sede do
- Congresso dos Estados Unidos,
- localizado no monte Capitólio
- (*Capitol Hill*), em Washington.

Capricorn ['kæprɪkɔːn] *n* Capricórnio

capsize [kæp'saɪz] *vt, vi* emborcar, virar

capsule ['kæpsjuːl] *n* cápsula

captain ['kæptɪn] *n* capitão *m*

caption ['kæpʃən] *n* legenda

capture ['kæptʃəʳ] *vt* prender, aprisionar; (*person*) capturar; (*place*) tomar; (*attention*) atrair, chamar ▷ *n* captura; (*of place*) tomada

car [kɑːʳ] *n* carro, automóvel *m*; (*Rail*) vagão *m*

caramel ['kærəməl] *n* (*sweet*) caramelo; (*burnt sugar*) caramelado

caravan ['kærəvæn] *n* reboque *m* (*BR*), trailer *m* (*BR*), rulote *f* (*PT*); (*in desert*) caravana

carbohydrate [kɑːbəʊ'haɪdreɪt] *n* hidrato de carbono; (*food*) carboidrato

carbon ['kɑːbən] *n* carbono; **carbon dioxide** *n* dióxido de carbono; **carbon footprint** *n* pegada *f* de carbono; **carbon monoxide** [-mə'nɔksaɪd] *n* monóxido de carbono

carburettor [kɑːbju'rɛtəʳ], (*US*) **carburetor** *n* carburador *m*

card [kɑːd] *n* (*also*: **playing ~**) carta; (*visiting card, postcard etc*) cartão *m*; (*thin cardboard*) cartolina; **cardboard** *n* cartão *m*, papelão *m*

cardigan ['kɑːdɪgən] *n* casaco de lã, cardigã *m*

cardinal ['kɑːdɪnl] *adj* cardeal; (*Math*) cardinal ▷ *n* (*Rel*) cardeal *m*

care [kɛəʳ] *n* cuidado *m*; (*worry*) preocupação *f*; (*charge*) encargo, custódia ▷ *vi*: **to ~ about** (*person, animal*) preocupar-se com; (*thing, idea*) ter interesse em; **~ of** (*on*

letter) aos cuidados de; **in sb's ~** a cargo de alguém; **to take ~ (to do)** cuidar-se *or* ter o cuidado (de fazer); **to take ~ of** (*person*) cuidar de; (*situation*) encarregar-se de; **I don't ~** não me importa; **I couldn't ~ less** não dou a mínima **care for** *vt fus* cuidar de; (*like*) gostar de

career [kə'rɪəʳ] *n* carreira ▷ *vi* (*also*: **~ along**) correr a toda velocidade

carefree ['kɛəfriː] *adj* despreocupado

careful ['kɛəful] *adj* (*thorough*) cuidadoso; (*cautious*) cauteloso; **(be) ~!** tenha cuidado!; **carefully** *adv* cuidadosamente; cautelosamente

careless ['kɛəlɪs] *adj* descuidado; (*heedless*) desatento

carer ['kɛərəʳ] *n* (*professional*) acompanhante *m/f*; (*unpaid*) cuidador(a) *m/f*

caretaker ['kɛəteɪkəʳ] *n* zelador(a) *m/f*

car-ferry *n* barca para carros (*BR*), barco de passagem (*PT*)

cargo ['kɑːgəʊ] (*pl* **cargoes**) *n* carga

car hire (*Brit*) *n* aluguel *m* (*BR*) *or* aluguer *m* (*PT*) de carros

Caribbean [kærɪ'biːən] *n*: **the ~ (Sea)** o Caribe

caring ['kɛərɪŋ] *adj* (*person*) bondoso; (*society*) humanitário

carnation [kɑː'neɪʃən] *n* cravo

carnival ['kɑːnɪvəl] *n* carnaval *m*; (*US: funfair*) parque *m* de diversões

carol ['kærəl] *n*: **(Christmas) ~** cântico de Natal

car park (*Brit*) *n* estacionamento

carpenter ['kɑːpɪntəʳ] *n* carpinteiro

carpet ['kɑːpɪt] *n* tapete *m* ▷ *vt* atapetar

carriage ['kærɪdʒ] *n* carruagem *f*;

(*Brit: Rail*) vagão m; (*of goods*) transporte m; (*: cost*) porte m; **carriageway** (*Brit*) n (*part of road*) pista

carrier ['kærɪəʳ] n transportador(a) m/f; (*company*) empresa de transportes, transportadora; (*Med*) portador(a) m/f; **carrier bag** (*Brit*) n saco, sacola

carrot ['kærət] n cenoura

carry ['kærɪ] vt levar; (*transport*) transportar; (*involve: responsibilities etc*) implicar ▷ vi (*sound*) projetar-se; **to get carried away** (*fig*) exagerar **carry on** vi seguir, continuar ▷ vt prosseguir, continuar **carry out** vt (*orders*) cumprir; (*investigation*) levar a cabo, realizar

cart [kɑːt] n carroça, carreta ▷ vt transportar (em carroça)

carton ['kɑːtən] n (*box*) caixa (de papelão); (*of yogurt*) pote m; (*of milk*) caixa; (*packet*) pacote m

cartoon [kɑː'tuːn] n (*drawing*) desenho; (*Brit: comic strip*) história em quadrinhos (*BR*), banda desenhada (*PT*); (*film*) desenho animado

cartridge ['kɑːtrɪdʒ] n cartucho; (*of record player*) cápsula

carve [kɑːv] vt (*meat*) trinchar; (*wood, stone*) cinzelar, esculpir; (*initials, design*) gravar **carve up** dividir, repartir; **carving** n (*object*) escultura; (*design*) talha, entalhe m

case [keɪs] n caso; (*for spectacles etc*) estojo; (*Law*) causa; (*Brit: also:* **suit~**) mala; (*of wine etc*) caixa; **in ~ (of)** em caso (de); **in any ~** em todo o caso; **just in ~** conj se por acaso ▷ adv por via das dúvidas

cash [kæʃ] n dinheiro (em espécie) ▷ vt descontar; **to pay (in) ~** pagar em dinheiro; **~ on delivery** pagamento contra entrega; **cash card** (*Brit*) n cartão m de saque; **cash desk** (*Brit*) n caixa; **cash dispenser** n caixa automática *or* eletrônica

cashew [kæ'ʃuː] n (*also:* **~ nut**) castanha de caju

cashier [kæ'ʃɪəʳ] n caixa m/f

cash point n caixa m eletrônico

cash register n caixa registradora

casino [kə'siːnəu] n cassino

casket ['kɑːskɪt] n cofre m, porta-joias m inv; (*US: coffin*) caixão m

casserole ['kæsərəul] n panela de ir ao forno; (*food*) ensopado (*BR*) no forno, guisado (*PT*) no forno

cassette [kæ'set] n fita-cassete f; **cassette player** n toca-fitas m inv

cast [kɑːst] (*pt, pp* **cast**) vt (*throw*) lançar, atirar; (*Theatre*): **to ~ sb as Hamlet** dar a alguém o papel de Hamlet ▷ n (*Theatre*) elenco; (*also:* **plaster ~**) gesso; **to ~ one's vote** votar **cast off** vi (*Naut*) soltar o cabo; (*Knitting*) rematar os pontos **cast on** vi montar os pontos

caster sugar ['kɑːstəʳ-] (*Brit*) n acuçar m branco refinado

castle ['kɑːsl] n castelo; (*Chess*) torre f

casual ['kæʒjul] adj (*by chance*) fortuito; (*work etc*) eventual; (*unconcerned*) despreocupado; (*clothes etc*) descontraído, informal

casualty ['kæʒjultɪ] n ferido(-a); (*dead*) morto(-a); (*of situation*) vítima; (*department*) pronto-socorro

cat [kæt] n gato

catalogue ['kætələg], (*US*) **catalog** n catálogo ▷ vt catalogar

catarrh [kə'tɑːʳ] n catarro

catastrophe [kə'tæstrəfɪ] *n*
catástrofe *f*

catch [kætʃ] (*pt, pp* **caught**) *vt*
pegar (*BR*), apanhar (*PT*); (*fish*)
pescar; (*arrest*) prender, deter;
(*person: by surprise*) flagrar,
surpreender; (*attention*) atrair;
(*hear*) ouvir; (*also:* **~ up**) alcançar
▷ *vi* (*fire*) pegar; (*in branches etc*)
ficar preso, prender-se ▷ *n* (*fish etc*)
pesca; (*game*) manha, armadilha;
(*of lock*) trinco, lingueta; **to ~ fire**
pegar fogo; (*building*) incendiar-se;
to ~ sight of avistar **catch on** *vi*
(*understand*) entender (*BR*),
perceber (*PT*); (*grow popular*) pegar
catch up *vi* equiparar-se ▷ *vt* (*also:*
~ up with) alcançar; **catching** *adj*
(*Med*) contagioso

category ['kætɪgərɪ] *n* categoria

cater ['keɪtər] *vi* preparar comida
cater for *vt fus* (*needs*) atender a;
(*consumers*) satisfazer

caterpillar ['kætəpɪlər] *n* lagarta

cathedral [kə'θiːdrəl] *n* catedral *f*

catholic ['kæθəlɪk] *adj* eclético;
Catholic *adj, n* (*Rel*) católico(-a)

cattle ['kætl] *npl* gado

caught [kɔːt] *pt, pp of* **catch**

cauliflower ['kɔlɪflauər] *n*
couve-flor *f*

cause [kɔːz] *n* causa; (*reason*)
motivo, razão *f* ▷ *vt* causar,
provocar

caution ['kɔːʃən] *n* cautela,
prudência; (*warning*) aviso ▷ *vt*
acautelar, avisar

cautious ['kɔːʃəs] *adj* cauteloso,
prudente, precavido

cave [keɪv] *n* caverna, gruta **cave
in** *vi* ceder

cc *abbr* (= *cubic centimetre*) cc; (*on
letter etc*) = **carbon copy**

CD *n abbr* = **compact disc**; CD

burner, CD writer *n* gravador *m*
de CD; **CD-ROM** *n abbr* (= *compact
disc read-only memory*) CD-ROM *m*

cease [siːs] *vt, vi* cessar; **ceasefire**
n cessar-fogo *m*

cedar ['siːdər] *n* cedro

ceiling ['siːlɪŋ] *n* (*also fig*) teto

celebrate ['sɛlɪbreɪt] *vt* celebrar
▷ *vi* celebrar; (*birthday, anniversary
etc*) festejar; (*Rel: mass*) rezar;
celebration [sɛlɪ'breɪʃən] *n* (*party*)
festa

celery ['sɛlərɪ] *n* aipo

cell [sɛl] *n* cela; (*Bio*) célula; (*Elec*)
pilha, elemento

cellar ['sɛlər] *n* porão *m*; (*for wine*)
adega

cellphone ['sɛlfəun] *n* (telefone)
celular *m* (*BR*), telemóvel *m* (*PT*)

cement [sə'mɛnt] *n* cimento

cemetery ['sɛmɪtrɪ] *n* cemitério

censor ['sɛnsər] *n* censor(a) *m/f* ▷ *vt*
censurar; **censorship** *n* censura

census ['sɛnsəs] *n* censo

cent [sɛnt] *n* cêntimo; *see also* **per**

centenary [sɛn'tiːnərɪ] *n*
centenário

center ['sɛntər] (*US*) = **centre**

centigrade ['sɛntɪgreɪd] *adj*
centígrado

centimetre ['sɛntɪmiːtər], (*US*)
centimeter *n* centímetro

central ['sɛntrəl] *adj* central;
Central America *n* América
Central; **central heating** *n*
aquecimento central

centre ['sɛntər], (*US*) **center** *n*
centro; (*of room, circle etc*) meio ▷ *vt*
centrar

century ['sɛntjurɪ] *n* século; **20th ~**
século vinte

ceramic [sɪ'ræmɪk] *adj* cerâmico

cereal ['siːrɪəl] *n* cereal *m*

ceremony ['sɛrɪmənɪ] *n* cerimônia;

(*ritual*) rito; **to stand on ~** fazer cerimônia

certain ['sɜːtən] *adj* (*sure*) seguro; (*person*): **a ~ Mr Smith** um certo Sr. Smith; (*particular*): **~ days/places** certos dias/lugares; (*some*): **a ~ coldness/pleasure** uma certa frieza/um certo prazer; **for ~** com certeza; **certainly** *adv* certamente, com certeza; **certainty** *n* certeza

certificate [sə'tɪfɪkɪt] *n* certidão *f*

certify ['sɜːtɪfaɪ] *vt* certificar

cf. *abbr* (= *compare*) cf

CFC *n abbr* (= *chlorofluorocarbon*) CFC *m*

chain [tʃeɪn] *n* corrente *f*; (*of islands*) grupo; (*of mountains*) cordilheira; (*of shops*) cadeia; (*of events*) série *f* ▷ *vt* (*also*: **~ up**) acorrentar

chair [tʃɛəʳ] *n* cadeira; (*armchair*) poltrona; (*of university*) cátedra; (*of meeting*) presidência, mesa ▷ *vt* (*meeting*) presidir; **chairlift** *n* teleférico; **chairman** *irreg n* presidente *m*

chalk [tʃɔːk] *n* (*Geo*) greda; (*for writing*) giz *m*

challenge ['tʃælɪndʒ] *n* desafio ▷ *vt* desafiar; (*statement, right*) disputar, contestar; **challenging** *adj* desafiante; (*tone*) de desafio

chamber ['tʃeɪmbəʳ] *n* câmara; (*Brit: Law: gen pl*) sala de audiências; **chambermaid** *n* arrumadeira (*BR*), empregada (*PT*); **chamber of commerce** *n* câmara de comércio

champagne [ʃæm'peɪn] *n* champanhe *m or f*

champion ['tʃæmpɪən] *n* campeão(-peã) *m/f*; (*of cause*) defensor(a) *m/f*; **championship** *n* campeonato

chance [tʃɑːns] *n* (*opportunity*) oportunidade, ocasião *f*; (*likelihood*) chance *f*; (*risk*) risco ▷ *vt* arriscar ▷ *adj* fortuito, casual; **to take a ~** arriscar-se; **by ~** por acaso; **to ~ it** arriscar-se

chancellor ['tʃɑːnsələʳ] *n* chanceler *m*; **C~ of the Exchequer** (*Brit*) Ministro da Economia (Fazenda e Planejamento)

chandelier [ʃændə'lɪəʳ] *n* lustre *m*

change [tʃeɪndʒ] *vt* (*alter*) mudar; (*wheel, bulb, money*) trocar; (*replace*) substituir; (*clothes, house*) mudar de, trocar de; (*nappy*) mudar, trocar; (*transform*): **to ~ sb into** transformar alguém em ▷ *vi* mudar(-se); (*change clothes*) trocar-se; (*trains*) fazer baldeação (*BR*), mudar (*PT*); (*be transformed*): **to ~ into** transformar-se em ▷ *n* mudança; (*exchange*) troca; (*difference*) diferença; (*of clothes*) muda; (*coins*) trocado; **to ~ gear** (*Aut*) trocar de marcha; **to ~ one's mind** mudar de ideia; **for a ~** para variar; **changeable** *adj* (*weather*) instável; (*mood*) inconstante

channel ['tʃænl] *n* canal *m*; (*of river*) leito; (*groove*) ranhura; (*fig: medium*) meio, via ▷ *vt*: **to ~ (into)** canalizar (para); **the (English) C~** o Canal da Mancha

chant [tʃɑːnt] *n* canto; (*Rel*) cântico ▷ *vt* cantar; (*word, slogan*) entoar

chaos ['keɪɔs] *n* caos *m*

chap [tʃæp] *n* (*Brit: inf: man*) sujeito (*BR*), tipo (*PT*)

chapel ['tʃæpəl] *n* capela

chapter ['tʃæptəʳ] *n* capítulo

character ['kærɪktəʳ] *n* caráter *m*; (*in novel, film*) personagem *m/f*; (*letter*) letra; **characteristic**

[kærɪktə'rɪstɪk] adj característico

charcoal ['tʃɑːkəul] n carvão m de lenha; (Art) carvão m

charge [tʃɑːdʒ] n (Law) encargo, acusação f; (fee) preço, custo; (responsibility) encargo ▷ vt (battery) carregar; (Mil) atacar; (customer) cobrar dinheiro de; (Law): **to ~ sb (with)** acusar alguém (de) ▷ vi precipitar-se; **charges** npl: **bank ~s** taxas fpl bancárias; **to reverse the ~s** (Brit: Tel) ligar a cobrar; **how much do you ~?** quanto você cobra?; **to ~ an expense (up) to sb's account** pôr a despesa na conta de alguém; **to take ~ of** encarregar-se de, tomar conta de; **to be in ~ of** estar a cargo de or encarregado de; **charge card** n cartão m de crédito (emitido por uma loja)

charity ['tʃærɪtɪ] n caridade f; (organization) obra de caridade; (kindness) compaixão f; (money, gifts) donativo

charm [tʃɑːm] n (quality) charme m; (talisman) amuleto; (on bracelet) berloque m ▷ vt encantar, deliciar; **charming** adj encantador(a)

chart [tʃɑːt] n (graph) gráfico; (diagram) diagrama m; (map) carta de navegação ▷ vt traçar; **charts** npl (hit parade) paradas fpl (de sucesso)

charter ['tʃɑːtə²] vt fretar ▷ n (document) carta, alvará m; **chartered accountant** (Brit) n perito-contador m/perita-contadora f; **charter flight** n voo charter or fretado

chase [tʃeɪs] vt perseguir; (also: ~ **away**) enxotar ▷ n perseguição f, caça

chat [tʃæt] vi (also: **have a ~**) conversar, bater papo (BR), cavaquear (PT) ▷ n conversa, bate-papo m (BR), cavaqueira (PT); **chatroom** n sala f de bate-papo; **chat show** (Brit) n programa m de entrevistas

chatter ['tʃætə²] vi (person) tagarelar; (animal) emitir sons; (teeth) tiritar ▷ n tagarelice f; emissão f de sons; (of birds) chilro

chauvinist ['ʃəuvɪnɪst] n (also: **male ~**) machista m; (nationalist) chauvinista m/f

cheap [tʃiːp] adj barato; (poor quality) barato, de pouca qualidade; (behaviour) vulgar; (joke) de mau gosto ▷ adv barato; **cheaply** adv barato, por baixo preço

cheat [tʃiːt] vi trapacear; (at cards) roubar (BR), fazer batota (PT); (in exam) colar (BR), cabular (PT) ▷ n fraude f; (person) trapaceiro(-a); **to ~ sb out of sth** defraudar alguém de algo

check [tʃɛk] vt (examine) controlar; (facts) verificar; (halt) conter, impedir; (restrain) parar, refrear ▷ n controle m, inspeção f; (curb) freio; (US: bill) conta; (pattern: gen pl) xadrez m; (US) = **cheque** ▷ adj (pattern, cloth) xadrez inv **check in** vi (in hotel) registrar-se; (in airport) apresentar-se ▷ vt (luggage) entregar **check out** vi pagar a conta e sair **check up** vi: **to ~ up on sth** verificar algo; **to ~ up on sb** investigar alguém; **checkers** (US) n (jogo de) damas fpl; **check-in, check-in desk** n check-in m; **checking account** (US) n conta corrente; **checkout** n caixa; **checkpoint** n (ponto de) controle m; **checkroom** (US) n depósito de bagagem; **checkup** n (Med) check-up m

cheek [tʃiːk] n bochecha; (impudence) folga, descaramento; **cheekbone** n maçã f do rosto; **cheeky** adj insolente, descarado

cheer [tʃɪəʳ] vt dar vivas a, aplaudir; (gladden) alegrar, animar ▷ vi gritar com entusiasmo ▷ n (gen pl) gritos mpl de entusiasmo; **cheers** npl (of crowd) aplausos mpl; **~s!** saúde! **cheer up** vi animar-se, alegrar-se ▷ vt alegrar, animar; **cheerful** adj alegre; **cheerio** (Brit) excl tchau (BR), adeus (PT); **cheerleader** ['tʃɪəliːdəʳ] n animador(a) de torcida m/f

cheese [tʃiːz] n queijo

chef [ʃɛf] n cozinheiro-chefe/ cozinheira-chefe m/f

chemical ['kɛmɪkəl] adj químico ▷ n produto químico

chemist ['kɛmɪst] n (Brit: pharmacist) farmacêutico(-a); (scientist) químico(-a); **chemistry** n química; **chemist's, chemist's shop** (Brit) n farmácia

cheque [tʃɛk] (Brit) n cheque m; **chequebook** n talão m (BR) or livro (PT) de cheques; **cheque card** (Brit) n cartão m (de garantia) de cheques

cherry ['tʃɛrɪ] n cereja; (also: **~ tree**) cerejeira

chess [tʃɛs] n xadrez m

chest [tʃɛst] n (Anat) peito; (box) caixa, cofre m

chestnut ['tʃɛsnʌt] n castanha

chest of drawers n cômoda

chew [tʃuː] vt mastigar; **chewing gum** n chiclete m (BR), pastilha elástica (PT)

chic [ʃik] adj elegante

chick [tʃik] n pinto; (inf: girl) broto

chicken ['tʃikɪn] n galinha; (food) galinha, frango; (inf: coward) covarde m/f, galinha **chicken out** (inf) vi agalinhar-se; **chickenpox** n catapora (BR), varicela (PT)

chief [tʃiːf] n (of tribe) cacique m, morubixaba m; (of organization) chefe m/f ▷ adj principal; **chiefly** adv principalmente

child [tʃaɪld] (pl **children**) n criança; (offspring) filho(-a); **childbirth** n parto; **childhood** n infância; **childish** adj infantil; **child minder** (Brit) n cuidadora de crianças; **children** ['tʃɪldrən] npl of **child**

Chile ['tʃɪlɪ] n Chile m

chill [tʃɪl] n frio, friagem f; (Med) resfriamento ▷ vt (Culin) semi-congelar; (person) congelar

chilli ['tʃɪlɪ], (US) **chili** n pimentão m picante

chilly ['tʃɪlɪ] adj frio; (person) friorento

chimpanzee [tʃɪmpæn'ziː] n chimpanzé m

chin [tʃɪn] n queixo

China ['tʃaɪnə] n China

china ['tʃaɪnə] n porcelana; (crockery) louça fina

Chinese [tʃaɪ'niːz] adj chinês(-esa) ▷ n inv chinês(-esa) m/f; (Ling) chinês m

chip [tʃɪp] n (gen pl: Culin) batata frita; (: US: also: **potato ~**) batatinha frita; (of wood) lasca; (of glass, stone) lasca, pedaço; (Comput: also: **micro~**) chip m ▷ vt (cup, plate) lascar **chip in** (inf) vi interromper; (contribute) compartilhar as despesas

chiropodist [kɪ'rɔpədɪst] (Brit) n pedicuro(-a)

chisel ['tʃɪzl] n (for wood) formão m;

(*for stone*) cinzel m
chives [tʃaɪvz] npl cebolinha
chocolate ['tʃɔklɪt] n chocolate m
choice [tʃɔɪs] n (*selection*) seleção f;
(*option*) escolha; (*preference*)
preferência ▷ adj seleto,
escolhido
choir ['kwaɪəʳ] n coro
choke [tʃəuk] vi sufocar-se; (*on
food*) engasgar ▷ vt estrangular;
(*block*) obstruir ▷ n (*Aut*) afogador
m (*BR*), ar m (*PT*)
cholesterol [kə'lɛstərɔl] n
colesterol m
choose [tʃuːz] (*pt* **chose**, *pp* **chosen**)
vt escolher; **to ~ to do** optar por
fazer
chop [tʃɔp] vt (*wood*) cortar, talhar;
(*Culin: also:* **~ up**) cortar em
pedaços; (*meat*) picar ▷ n golpe m;
(*Culin*) costeleta; **chops** npl (*inf:
jaws*) beiços mpl
chopsticks ['tʃɔpstɪks] npl
pauzinhos mpl, palitos mpl
chord [kɔːd] n (*Mus*) acorde m
chore [tʃɔːʳ] n tarefa; (*routine task*)
trabalho de rotina
chorus ['kɔːrəs] n (*group*) coro;
(*song*) coral m; (*refrain*) estribilho
chose [tʃəuz] pt of **choose**; **chosen**
pp of **choose**
Christ [kraɪst] n Cristo
christen ['krɪsn] vt batizar;
(*nickname*) apelidar
Christian ['krɪstɪən] adj, n
cristão(-tã) m/f; **Christianity**
[krɪstɪ'ænɪtɪ] n cristianismo;
Christian name n prenome m,
nome m de batismo
Christmas ['krɪsməs] n Natal m;
Happy or **Merry ~!** Feliz Natal!;
Christmas card n cartão m de
Natal; **Christmas cracker** n ver
nota

● **CHRISTMAS CRACKER**
●
● Um cilindro de papelão que ao
● ser aberto faz estourar uma
● bombinha. Contém um presente
● surpresa e um chapéu de papel
● que cada convidado coloca na
● cabeça durante a ceia de Natal.

Christmas: **Christmas Day** n dia
m de Natal; **Christmas Eve** n
véspera de Natal; **Christmas tree**
n árvore f de Natal
chronic ['krɔnɪk] adj crônico; (*fig:
drunkenness*) inveterado
chubby ['tʃʌbɪ] adj roliço, gorducho
chuck [tʃʌk] vt jogar (*BR*), deitar
(*PT*); (*Brit: also:* **~ up, ~ in**: *job*)
largar; (: *person*) acabar com **chuck
out** vt (*thing*) jogar (*BR*) or deitar
(*PT*) fora; (*person*) expulsar
chuckle ['tʃʌkl] vi rir
chum [tʃʌm] n camarada m/f
church [tʃəːtʃ] n igreja; **churchyard**
n adro, cemitério
churn [tʃəːn] n (*for butter*) batedeira;
(*also:* **milk ~**) lata, vasilha **churn
out** vt produzir em série
chute [ʃuːt] n rampa; (*also:* **rubbish
~**) despejador m
CIA (*US*) n abbr (= *Central Intelligence
Agency*) CIA f
CID (*Brit*) n abbr = **Criminal
Investigation Department**
cider ['saɪdəʳ] n sidra
cigar [sɪ'gɑːʳ] n charuto
cigarette [sɪgə'rɛt] n cigarro
cinema ['sɪnəmə] n cinema m
cinnamon ['sɪnəmən] n canela
circle ['səːkl] n círculo; (*in cinema*)
balcão m ▷ vi dar voltas ▷ vt
(*surround*) rodear, cercar; (*move
round*) dar a volta de
circuit ['səːkɪt] n circuito; (*tour, lap*)

volta; (*track*) pista
circular ['sə:kjuləʳ] *adj* circular ▷ *n* (carta) circular *f*
circulate ['sə:kjuleɪt] *vt*, *vi* circular; **circulation** [sə:kju'leɪʃən] *n* circulação *f*; (*of newspaper, book etc*) tiragem *f*
circumstances ['sə:kəmstənsɪz] *npl* circunstâncias *fpl*; (*conditions*) condições *fpl*; (*financial condition*) situação *f* econômica
circus ['sə:kəs] *n* circo
citizen ['sɪtɪzn] *n* (*of country*) cidadão(-dã) *m/f*; (*of town*) habitante *m/f*; **citizenship** *n* cidadania
city ['sɪtɪ] *n* cidade *f*; **the C~** centro financeiro de Londres
civic ['sɪvɪk] *adj* cívico, municipal
civil ['sɪvɪl] *adj* civil; (*polite*) delicado, cortês; **civilian** [sɪ'vɪliən] *adj*, *n* civil *m/f*
civilized ['sɪvɪlaɪzd] *adj* civilizado
civil servant *n* funcionário(-a) público(-a)
Civil Service *n* administração *f* pública
civil war *n* guerra civil
claim [kleɪm] *vt* exigir, reclamar; (*rights etc*) reivindicar; (*responsibility*) assumir; (*assert*): **to ~ that/to be** afirmar que/ser ▷ *vi* (*for insurance*) reclamar ▷ *n* reclamação *f*; (*assertion*) afirmação *f*; (*wage claim etc*) reivindicação *f*
clam [klæm] *n* molusco
clamp [klæmp] *n* grampo ▷ *vt* prender **clamp down on** *vt fus* reprimir
clan [klæn] *n* clã *m*
clap [klæp] *vi* bater palmas, aplaudir
clarinet [klærɪ'nɛt] *n* clarinete *m*
clarity ['klærɪtɪ] *n* clareza

clash [klæʃ] *n* (*fight*) confronto; (*disagreement*) desavença; (*of beliefs*) divergência; (*of colours, styles*) choque *m*; (*of dates*) coincidência ▷ *vi* (*gangs, beliefs*) chocar-se; (*disagree*) entrar em conflito, ter uma desavença; (*colours*) não combinar; (*dates, events*) coincidir; (*weapons, cymbals etc*) ressoar
clasp [klɑ:sp] *n* fecho; (*embrace*) abraço ▷ *vt* prender; (*embrace*) abraçar
class [klɑ:s] *n* classe *f*; (*lesson*) aula; (*type*) tipo ▷ *vt* classificar
classic ['klæsɪk] *adj* clássico ▷ *n* clássico; **classical** *adj* clássico
classmate ['klæsmeɪt] *n* colega *m/f* de aula
classroom ['klæsrum] *n* sala de aula
clatter ['klætəʳ] *n* ruído, barulho; (*of hooves*) tropel *m* ▷ *vi* fazer barulho or ruído
clause [klɔ:z] *n* cláusula; (*Ling*) oração *f*
claw [klɔ:] *n* (*of animal*) pata; (*of bird of prey*) garra; (*of lobster*) pinça **claw at** *vt fus* arranhar; (*tear*) rasgar
clay [kleɪ] *n* argila
clean [kli:n] *adj* limpo ▷ *vt* limpar; (*hands, face etc*) lavar **clean out** *vt* limpar **clean up** *vt* limpar, assear; **cleaner** *n* faxineiro(-a); (*product*) limpador(a) *m*; **cleaner's** *n* (*also:* **dry cleaner's**) tinturaria; **cleaning** *n* limpeza
clear [klɪəʳ] *adj* claro; (*footprint, photograph*) nétido; (*obvious*) evidente; (*glass, water*) transparente; (*road, way*) limpo, livre; (*conscience*) tranquilo; (*skin*) macio ▷ *vt* (*space*) abrir; (*room*)

esvaziar; (*Law: suspect*) absolver; (*fence, wall*) saltar, transpor; (*cheque*) compensar ▷ vi (*weather*) abrir; (*sky*) clarear; (*fog etc*) dissipar-se ▷ adv: **~ of** a salvo de; **to ~ the table** tirar a mesa **clear up** vt limpar; (*mystery*) resolver, esclarecer; **clearance** n remoção f; (*permission*) permissão f; **clear-cut** adj bem definido, nítido; **clearing** n (*in wood*) clareira; **clearly** adv distintamente; (*obviously*) claramente; (*coherently*) coerentemente; **clearway** (*Brit*) n estrada onde não se pode estacionar

clench [klɛntʃ] vt apertar, cerrar; (*teeth*) trincar

clerk [klɑːk, (*US*) kləːrk] n auxiliar m/f de escritório; (*US: sales person*) balconista m/f

clever ['klɛvəᶜ] adj inteligente; (*deft, crafty*) hábil; (*device, arrangement*) engenhoso

click [klɪk] vt (*tongue*) estalar; (*heels*) bater; (*Comput*) clicar em ▷ vi (*make sound*) estalar; (*Comput*) clicar

client ['klaɪənt] n cliente m/f

cliff [klɪf] n penhasco

climate ['klaɪmɪt] n clima m; **climate change** n mudanças fpl climáticas

climax ['klaɪmæks] n clímax m, ponto culminante; (*sexual*) clímax

climb [klaɪm] vi subir; (*plant*) trepar; (*plane*) ganhar altitude; (*prices etc*) escalar ▷ vt (*stairs*) subir; (*tree*) trepar em; (*hill*) escalar ▷ n subida; (*of prices etc*) escalada; **climber** n alpinista m/f; (*plant*) trepadeira; **climbing** n alpinismo

clinch [klɪntʃ] vt (*deal*) fechar; (*argument*) decidir, resolver

cling [klɪŋ] (*pt, pp* **clung**) vi: **to ~ to**

pegar-se a, aderir a; (*support, idea*) agarrar-se a; (*clothes*) ajustar-se a

Clingfilm® ['klɪŋfɪlm] n papel m filme

clinic ['klɪnɪk] n clínica

clip [klɪp] n (*for hair*) grampo (*BR*), gancho (*PT*); (*also:* **paper ~**) mola, clipe m; (*TV, Cinema*) clipe ▷ vt (*cut*) aparar; (*papers*) grampear

cloak [kləuk] n capa, manto ▷ vt (*fig*) encobrir; **cloakroom** n vestiário; (*Brit: WC*) sanitários mpl (*BR*), lavatórios mpl (*PT*)

clock [klɔk] n relógio **clock in** (*Brit*) vi assinar o ponto na entrada **clock off** (*Brit*) vi assinar o ponto na saída **clock on** (*Brit*) vi ≈ clock in **clock out** (*Brit*) vi ≈ clock off; **clockwise** adv em sentido horário; **clockwork** n mecanismo de relógio ▷ adj de corda

clog [klɔg] n tamanco ▷ vt entupir ▷ vi (*also:* **~ up**) entupir-se

close [adj, adv kləus, vb, n kləuz] adj próximo; (*friend*) íntimo; (*examination*) minucioso; (*watch*) atento; (*contest*) apertado; (*weather*) abafado ▷ adv perto; **~ to** perto de ▷ vt fechar; (*end*) encerrar ▷ vi fechar; (*end*) concluir-se, terminar-se ▷ n (*end*) fim m, conclusão f, terminação f; **~ by, ~ at hand** perto, pertinho; **to have a ~ shave** (*fig*) livrar-se por um triz **close down** vi fechar definitivamente; **closed** adj fechado

closely ['kləuslɪ] adv (*watch*) de perto; **we are ~ related** somos parentes próximos

closet ['klɔzɪt] n (*cupboard*) armário

close-up [kləus-] n close m, close-up m

closure ['kləuʒəᶜ] n fechamento

clot [klɔt] n (gen: blood clot) coágulo; (inf: idiot) imbecil m/f ⊳ vi coagular-se

cloth [klɔθ] n (material) tecido, fazenda; (rag) pano

clothes [kləuðz] npl roupa

clothing ['kləuðɪŋ] n = **clothes**

cloud [klaud] n nuvem f; **cloudy** adj nublado; (liquid) turvo

clove [kləuv] n cravo; **clove of garlic** n dente m de alho

clown [klaun] n palhaço ⊳ vi (also: ~ **about**; ~ **around**) fazer palhaçadas

club [klʌb] n (society) clube m; (weapon) cacete m; (also: **golf ~**) taco ⊳ vt esbordoar ⊳ vi: **to ~ together** cotizar-se; **clubs** npl (Cards) paus mpl

clue [kluː] n indício, pista; (in crossword) definição f; **I haven't a ~** não faço ideia

clumsy ['klʌmzɪ] adj (person) desajeitado; (movement) deselegante, mal-feito; (attempt) inábil

clung [klʌŋ] pt, pp of **cling**

cluster ['klʌstəʳ] n grupo; (of flowers) ramo ⊳ vi agrupar-se, apinhar-se

clutch [klʌtʃ] n (grip, grasp) garra; (Aut) embreagem f (BR), embraiagem f (PT) ⊳ vt empunhar, pegar em

Co. abbr = **county**; (= company) Cia.

c/o abbr (= care of) a/c

coach [kəutʃ] n (bus) ônibus m (BR), autocarro (PT); (horse-drawn) carruagem f, coche m; (of train) vagão m; (Sport) treinador(a) m/f, instrutor(a) m/f; (tutor) professor(a) m/f particular ⊳ vt (Sport) treinar; (student) preparar, ensinar; **coach station** (Brit) n

rodoviária; **coach trip** n passeio de ônibus (BR) or autocarro (PT)

coal [kəul] n carvão m

coalition [kəuə'lɪʃən] n coalizão f

coarse [kɔːs] adj grosso, áspero; (vulgar) grosseiro, ordinário

coast [kəust] n costa, litoral m ⊳ vi (Aut) ir em ponto morto; **coastal** adj costeiro; **coastguard** n (service) guarda costeira; (person) guarda-costeira m/f; **coastline** n litoral m

coat [kəut] n (overcoat) sobretudo; (of animal) pelo; (of paint) demão f, camada ⊳ vt cobrir, revestir; **coat hanger** n cabide m; **coating** n camada

coax [kəuks] vt persuadir com meiguice

cobweb ['kɔbwɛb] n teia de aranha

cocaine [kə'keɪn] n cocaína

cock [kɔk] n (rooster) galo; (male bird) macho ⊳ vt (gun) engatilhar; **cockerel** n frango, galo pequeno

cockney ['kɔknɪ] n londrino(-a) (nativo dos bairros populares do leste de Londres)

cockpit ['kɔkpɪt] n (in aircraft) cabina

cockroach ['kɔkrəutʃ] n barata

cocktail ['kɔkteɪl] n coquetel m (BR), cocktail m (PT)

cocoa ['kəukəu] n cacau m; (drink) chocolate m

coconut ['kəukənʌt] n coco

cod [kɔd] n inv bacalhau m

code [kəud] n cifra; (dialling code, post code) código; **code of practice** n deontologia

coffee ['kɔfɪ] n café m; **coffee bar** (Brit) n café m, lanchonete f; **coffee bean** n grão m de café; **coffeepot** n cafeteira; **coffee table** n mesinha de centro

coffin ['kɔfɪn] n caixão m
coil [kɔɪl] n rolo; (Elec) bobina; (contraceptive) DIU m ▷ vt enrolar
coin [kɔɪn] n moeda ▷ vt (word) cunhar, criar
coincide [kəʊɪn'saɪd] vi coincidir; **coincidence** [kəʊ'ɪnsɪdəns] n coincidência
coke [kəʊk] n (coal) coque m
colander ['kɔləndə'] n coador m, passador m
cold [kəʊld] adj frio ▷ n frio; (Med) resfriado (BR), constipação f (PT); **it's ~** está frio; **to be** or **feel ~** (person) estar com frio; (object) estar frio; **to catch ~** pegar friagem; **to catch a ~** ficar resfriado; **in ~ blood** a sangue frio; **cold sore** n herpes m labial
coleslaw ['kəʊlslɔ:] n salada de repolho cru
collapse [kə'læps] vi cair, tombar; (building) desabar; (Med) desmaiar ▷ n desabamento, desmoronamento; (of government) queda; (Med) colapso
collar ['kɔlə'] n (of shirt) colarinho; (of coat etc) gola; (for dog) coleira; (Tech) aro, colar m; **collarbone** n clavícula
colleague ['kɔli:g] n colega m/f
collect [kə'lɛkt] vt (as a hobby) colecionar; (gather) recolher; (wages, debts) cobrar; (donations, subscriptions) colher; (mail) coletar; (Brit: call for) (ir) buscar ▷ vi (people) reunir-se ▷ adv: **to call ~** (US: Tel) ligar a cobrar; **collection** n coleção f; (of people) grupo; (of donations) arrecadação f; (of post, for charity) coleta; (of writings) coletânea; **collector** n colecionador(a) m/f; (of taxes etc) cobrador(a) m/f

college ['kɔlɪdʒ] n (of university) faculdade f; (of technology, agriculture) escola profissionalizante

collide [kə'laɪd] vi: **to ~ (with)** colidir (com)
collision [kə'lɪʒən] n colisão f
Colombia [kə'lɔmbɪə] n Colômbia
colon ['kəʊlən] n (sign) dois pontos; (Med) cólon m
colonel ['kə:nl] n coronel m
colony ['kɔlənɪ] n colônia
colour ['kʌlə'], (US) **color** n cor f ▷ vt colorir; (with crayons) colorir, pintar; (dye) tingir; (fig: account) falsear ▷ vi (blush) corar; **colours** npl (of party, club) cores fpl; **in ~** (photograph etc) a cores **colour in** vt (drawing) colorir; **colour-blind** adj daltônico; **coloured** adj colorido; (person) de cor; **colour film** n filme m a cores; **colourful** adj colorido; (account) vívido; (personality) vivo, animado; **colouring** n colorido; (complexion) tez f; (in food) colorante m; **colour television** n televisão f a cores
column ['kɔləm] n coluna; (of smoke) faixa; (of people) fila
coma ['kəʊmə] n coma m

comb [kəum] *n* pente *m*; (*ornamental*) crista ▷ *vt* pentear; (*area*) vasculhar

combat ['kɔmbæt] *n* combate *m* ▷ *vt* combater

combination [kɔmbɪ'neɪʃən] *n* combinação *f*; (*of safe*) segredo

combine [*vt, vi* kəm'baɪn, *n* 'kɔmbaɪn] *vt* combinar; (*qualities*) reunir ▷ *vi* combinar-se ▷ *n* (*Econ*) associação *f*

 KEYWORD

come [kʌm] (*pt* **came**, *pp* **come**) *vi* 1 (*movement towards*) vir; **come with me** vem comigo; **to come running** vir correndo
2 (*arrive*) chegar; **she's come here to work** ela veio aqui para trabalhar; **to come home** chegar em casa
3 (*reach*): **to come to** chegar a; **the bill came to £40** a conta deu £40; **her hair came to her waist** o cabelo dela batia na cintura
4 (*occur*): **an idea came to me** uma ideia me ocorreu
5 (*be, become*) ficar; **to come loose/undone** soltar-se/desfazer-se; **I've come to like him** passei a gostar dele

come about *vi* suceder, acontecer
come across *vt fus* (*person*) topar com; (*thing*) encontrar
come away *vi* (*leave*) ir-se embora; (*become detached*) desprender-se, soltar-se
come back *vi* (*return*) voltar
come by *vt fus* (*acquire*) conseguir
come down *vi* (*price*) baixar; (*tree*) cair; (*building*) desmoronar-se
come forward *vi* apresentar-se
come from *vt fus* (*subj: person*) ser de; (*: thing*) originar-se de
come in *vi* entrar; (*on deal etc*) participar; (*be involved*) estar envolvido
come in for *vt fus* (*criticism etc*) receber
come into *vt fus* (*money*) herdar; (*fashion*) ser; (*be involved*) estar envolvido em
come off *vi* (*button*) desprender-se, soltar-se; (*attempt*) dar certo
come on *vi* (*pupil, work, project*) avançar; (*lights, electricity*) ser ligado; **come on!** vamos!, vai!
come out *vi* (*fact*) vir à tona; (*book*) ser publicado; (*stain, sun*) sair
come round *vi* voltar a si
come to *vi* voltar a si
come up *vi* (*sun*) nascer; (*problem, subject*) surgir; (*event*) acontecer
come up against *vt fus* (*resistance, difficulties*) enfrentar, esbarrar em
come upon *vt fus* (*find*) encontrar, achar
come up with *vt fus* (*idea*) propor, sugerir; (*money*) contribuir

comedian [kə'miːdɪən] *n* cômico, humorista *m*

comedy ['kɔmɪdɪ] *n* comédia

comfort ['kʌmfət] *n* (*well-being*) bem-estar *m*; (*relief*) alívio ▷ *vt* consolar, confortar; **comforts** *npl* (*of home etc*) conforto

comfortable *adj* confortável; (*financially*) tranquilo; (*walk, climb etc*) fácil

comic ['kɔmɪk] *adj* (*also*: ~**al**) cômico ▷ *n* (*person*) humorista *m/f*; (*Brit: magazine*) revista em quadrinhos (*BR*), revista de banda desenhada (*PT*), gibi *m* (*BR: inf*)

comma ['kɔmə] *n* vírgula

command [kə'mɑːnd] *n* ordem *f*,

mandado; (*control*) controle *m*; (*Mil: authority*) comando; (*mastery*) domínio ⊳ *vt* mandar; **commander** *n* (*Mil*) comandante *m/f*

commemorate [kə'mɛmǝreɪt] *vt* (*with monument*) comemorar; (*with celebration*) celebrar

commence [kə'mɛns] *vt, vi* começar, iniciar

commend [kə'mɛnd] *vt* elogiar, louvar; (*recommend*) recomendar

comment ['kɔmɛnt] *n* comentário ⊳ *vi* comentar; **to ~ on sth** comentar algo; **"no ~"** "sem comentário"; **commentary** ['kɔmǝntǝrɪ] *n* comentário; **commentator** ['kɔmǝnteɪtǝʳ] *n* comentarista *m/f*

commerce ['kɔmǝːs] *n* comércio

commercial [kə'mǝːʃǝl] *adj* comercial ⊳ *n* anúncio, comercial *m*

commission [kə'mɪʃǝn] *n* comissão *f*; (*order for work of art etc*) empreitada, encomenda ⊳ *vt* (*work of art*) encomendar; **out of ~** com defeito; **commissioner** *n* comissário(-a)

commit [kə'mɪt] *vt* cometer; (*money, resources*) alocar; (*to sb's care*) entregar; **to ~ o.s. (to do)** comprometer-se (a fazer); **to ~ suicide** suicidar-se; **commitment** *n* compromisso; (*political etc*) engajamento; (*undertaking*) promessa

committee [kə'mɪtɪ] *n* comitê *m*

commodity [kə'mɔdɪtɪ] *n* mercadoria

common ['kɔmǝn] *adj* comum; (*vulgar*) ordinário, vulgar ⊳ *n* área verde aberta ao público; **Commons** *npl* (*Brit: Pol*): **the (House of) C~s**

a Câmara dos Comuns; **to have sth in ~ (with sb)** ter algo em comum (com alguém); **commonly** *adv* geralmente; **commonplace** *adj* vulgar; **common sense** *n* bom senso; **Commonwealth** *n*: **the Commonwealth** a Comunidade Britânica

communal ['kɔmjuːnl] *adj* comun

commune [*n* 'kɔmjuːn, *vi* kə'mjuːn] *n* (*group*) comuna ⊳ *vi*: **to ~ with** comunicar-se com

communicate [kə'mjuːnɪkeɪt] *vt* comunicar ⊳ *vi*: **to ~ (with)** comunicar-se (com);

communication [kǝmjuːnɪ'keɪʃǝn] *n* comunicação *f*; (*letter, call*) mensagem *f*

communion [kə'mjuːnɪǝn] *n* (*also*: **Holy C~**) comunhão *f*

communism ['kɔmjunɪzǝm] *n* comunismo; **communist** *adj, n* comunista *m/f*

community [kə'mjuːnɪtɪ] *n* comunidade *f*; **community centre** *n* centro social

commute [kə'mjuːt] *vi* viajar diariamente ⊳ *vt* comutar; **commuter** *n* viajante *m/f* habitual

compact [*adj* kəm'pækt, *n* 'kɔmpækt] *adj* compacto ⊳ *n* (*also*: **powder ~**) estojo; **compact disc** *n* disco laser; **compact disc player** *n* som cd *m*

companion [kəm'pænɪǝn] *n* companheiro(-a)

company ['kʌmpǝnɪ] *n* companhia; (*Comm*) sociedade *f*, companhia; **to keep sb ~** fazer companhia a alguém

comparative [kəm'pærǝtɪv] *adj* (*study*) comparativo; (*peace, safety*) relativo; **comparatively** *adj* relativamente

compare [kəm'pɛəʳ] vt comparar;
to ~ (to/with) comparar (a/com)
▷ vi: **to ~ with** comparar-se com;
comparison [kəm'pærɪsn] n
comparação f

compartment [kəm'pɑːtmənt] n
compartimento; (of wallet)
divisão f

compass ['kʌmpəs] n bússola;
compasses npl compasso

compassion [kəm'pæʃən] n
compaixão f

compatible [kəm'pætɪbl] adj
compatível

compel [kəm'pɛl] vt obrigar

compensate ['kɔmpənseɪt] vt
indenizar ▷ vi: **to ~ for** compensar;
compensation [kɔmpən'seɪʃən] n
compensação f; (damages)
indenização f

compete [kəm'piːt] vi (take part)
competir; (vie): **to ~ (with)**
competir (com), fazer competição
(com)

competent ['kɔmpɪtənt] adj
competente

competition [kɔmpɪ'tɪʃən] n
(contest) concurso; (Econ)
concorrência; (rivalry)
competição f

competitive [kəm'pɛtɪtɪv] adj
competitivo; (person)
competidor(a)

competitor [kəm'pɛtɪtəʳ] n (rival)
competidor(a) m/f; (participant,
Econ) concorrente m/f

complain [kəm'pleɪn] vi
queixar-se; **to ~ of** (pain) queixar-se
de; **complaint** n (objection)
objeção f; (criticism) queixa; (Med)
achaque m, doença

complement ['kɔmplɪmənt] n
complemento; (esp ship's crew)

tripulação f ▷ vt complementar

complete [kəm'pliːt] adj completo;
(finished) acabado ▷ vt (finish:
building, task) acabar; (: set, group)
completar; (: a form) preencher;
completely adv completamente;
completion n conclusão f,
término; (of contract etc)
realização f

complex ['kɔmplɛks] adj complexo
▷ n complexo; (of buildings)
conjunto

complexion [kəm'plɛkʃən] n (of
face) cor f, tez f

complicate ['kɔmplɪkeɪt] vt
complicar; **complicated** adj
complicado; **complication**
[kɔmplɪ'keɪʃən] n problema m;
(Med) complicação f

compliment [n 'kɔmplɪmənt, vt
'kɔmplɪmɛnt] n (praise) elogio ▷ vt
elogiar; **compliments** npl
cumprimentos mpl; **to pay sb a ~**
elogiar alguém; **complimentary**
[kɔmplɪ'mɛntərɪ] adj lisonjeiro;
(free) gratuito

comply [kəm'plaɪ] vi: **to ~ with**
cumprir com

component [kəm'pəunənt] adj
componente ▷ n (part) peça

compose [kəm'pəuz] vt compor;
to be ~d of compor-se de; **to ~ o.s.**
tranquilizar-se; **composer** n
(Mus) compositor(a) m/f;
composition [kɔmpə'zɪʃən] n
composição f

compound ['kɔmpaund] n (Chem,
Ling) composto; (enclosure) recinto
▷ adj composto

comprehensive [kɔmprɪ'hɛnsɪv]
adj abrangente; (Insurance) total;
comprehensive school (Brit) n
escola secundária de amplo programa;
ver nota

COMPREHENSIVE SCHOOL

Criadas na década de 1960 pelo governo trabalhista da época, as **comprehensive schools** são estabelecimentos de ensino secundário polivalentes concebidos para acolher todos os alunos sem distinção e lhes oferecer oportunidades iguais, em oposição ao sistema seletivo das *grammar schools*. A maioria dos estudantes britânicos frequenta atualmente uma **comprehensive school**, mas as *grammar schools* não desapareceram de todo.

compress [*vt* kəm'prɛs, *n* 'kɔmprɛs] *vt* comprimir; (*text, information etc*) reduzir ▷ *n* (*Med*) compressa

comprise [kəm'praɪz] *vt* (*also*: **be ~d of**) compreender, constar de; (*constitute*) constituir

compromise ['kɔmprəmaɪz] *n* meio-termo ▷ *vt* comprometer ▷ *vi* chegar a um meio-termo

compulsive [kəm'pʌlsɪv] *adj* compulsório

compulsory [kəm'pʌlsərɪ] *adj* obrigatório; (*retirement*) compulsório

computer [kəm'pju:təʳ] *n* computador *m*; **computer game** *n* game *m*; **computerize** *vt* informatizar, computadorizar; **computing** *n* computação *f*; (*science*) informática

conceal [kən'si:l] *vt* ocultar; (*information*) omitir

conceited [kən'si:tɪd] *adj* vaidoso

conceive [kən'si:v] *vt* conceber ▷ *vi* conceber, engravidar

concentrate ['kɔnsəntreɪt] *vi* concentrar-se ▷ *vt* concentrar; **concentration** *n* concentração *f*

concept ['kɔnsɛpt] *n* conceito

concern [kən'sə:n] *n* (*Comm*) empresa; (*anxiety*) preocupação *f* ▷ *vt* preocupar; (*involve*) envolver; (*relate to*) dizer respeito a; **to be ~ed (about)** preocupar-se (com); **concerning** *prep* sobre, a respeito de, acerca de

concert ['kɔnsət] *n* concerto

concession [kən'sɛʃən] *n* concessão *f*; **tax ~** redução no imposto

conclude [kən'klu:d] *vt* (*finish*) acabar, concluir; (*treaty etc*) firmar; (*agreement*) chegar a; (*decide*) decidir

conclusion [kən'klu:ʒən] *n* conclusão *f*

concrete ['kɔnkri:t] *n* concreto (BR), betão *m* (PT) ▷ *adj* concreto

concussion [kən'kʌʃən] *n* (*Med*) concussão *f* cerebral

condemn [kən'dɛm] *vt* denunciar; (*prisoner, building*) condenar

condensation [kɔndɛn'seɪʃən] *n* condensação *f*

condense [kən'dɛns] *vi* condensar-se ▷ *vt* condensar

condition [kən'dɪʃən] *n* condição *f*; (*Med: illness*) doença ▷ *vt* condicionar; **conditions** *npl* (*circumstances*) circunstâncias *fpl*; **on ~ that** com a condição (de) que; **conditioner** *n* (*for hair*) condicionador *m*; (*for fabrics*) amaciante *m*

condom ['kɔndɔm] *n* preservativo, camisinha

condominium [kɔndə'mɪnɪəm] (*US*) *n* (*building*) edifício

condone [kən'dəun] *vt* admitir, aceitar

conduct [n 'kɔndʌkt, vt, vi kən'dʌkt]
n conduta, comportamento ▷ vt
(*research etc*) fazer; (*heat, electricity*)
conduzir; (*Mus*) reger; **to ~ o.s.**
comportar-se; **conducted tour** n
viagem f organizada; **conductor** n
(*of orchestra*) regente m/f; (*on bus*)
cobrador(a) m/f; (*US: Rail*)
revisor(a) m/f; (*Elec*) condutor m
cone [kəun] n cone m; (*Bot*) pinha;
(*for ice-cream*) casquinha
confectionery [kən'fɛkʃnərɪ] n
(*sweets*) balas fpl; (*sweetmeats*)
doces mpl
confer [kən'fə:ʳ] vt: **to ~ on**
outorgar a ▷ vi conferenciar
conference ['kɔnfərns] n
congresso
confess [kən'fɛs] vt confessar ▷ vi
(*admit*) admitir; **confession** n
admissão f; (*Rel*) confissão f
confide [kən'faɪd] vi: **to ~ in** confiar
em, fiar-se em
confidence ['kɔnfɪdns] n
confiança, fé f; (*faith*) fé f; (*secret*)
confidência; **in ~** em confidência;
confident adj confiante, convicto;
(*positive*) seguro; **confidential**
[kɔnfɪ'dɛnʃəl] adj confidencial
confine [kən'faɪn] vt (*shut up*)
encarcerar; (*limit*): **to ~ (to)**
confinar (a); **confined** adj (*space*)
reduzido
confirm [kən'fə:m] vt confirmar;
confirmation [kɔnfə'meɪʃən] n
confirmação f; (*Rel*) crisma
confiscate ['kɔnfɪskeɪt] vt
confiscar
conflict [n 'kɔnflɪkt, vi kən'flɪkt] n
(*disagreement*) divergência; (*of
interests, loyalties*) conflito;
(*fighting*) combate m ▷ vi estar em
conflito; (*opinions*) divergir
conform [kən'fɔ:m] vi

conformar-se; **to ~ to** ajustar-se a,
acomodar-se a
confront [kən'frʌnt] vt (*problems*)
enfrentar; (*enemy, danger*)
defrontar-se com; **confrontation**
[kɔnfrən'teɪʃən] n confrontação f
confuse [kən'fju:z] vt (*perplex*)
desconcertar; (*mix up*) confundir,
misturar; (*complicate*) complicar;
confused adj confuso; **confusing**
adj confuso; **confusion** [kə
n'fju:ʒən] n (*mix-up*)
mal-entendido; (*perplexity*)
perplexidade f; (*disorder*) confusão f
congestion [kən'dʒɛstʃən] n (*Med*)
congestão f; (*traffic*)
congestionamento
congratulate [kən'grætjuleɪt] vt
parabenizar; **congratulations**
[kəngrætju'leɪʃənz] npl parabéns
mpl
congress ['kɔngrɛs] n congresso;
(*US*): **C~** Congresso

> ● **CONGRESS**
> ●
> ● O Congresso é o Parlamento dos
> ● Estados Unidos. Consiste na
> ● *House of Representatives* e no
> ● Senado *Senate*. Os
> ● representantes e senadores são
> ● eleitos por sufrágio universal
> ● direto. O Congresso se reúne no
> ● *Capitol*, em Washington.

congressman (*US*) *irreg* n deputado
conjure ['kʌndʒəʳ] vi fazer truques
conjure up vt (*ghost, spirit*) fazer
aparecer, invocar; (*memories*)
evocar
connect [kə'nɛkt] vt (*Elec, Tel*) ligar;
(*fig: associate*) associar; (*join*): **to ~
sth (to)** juntar or unir algo (a) ▷ vi:
to ~ with (*train*) conectar com; **to**

be ~ed with estar relacionado com; **I'm trying to ~ you** (Tel) estou tentando completar a ligação; **connecting flight** n conexão f; **connection** n ligação f; (Elec, Rail) conexão f; (Tel) ligação f

conquer ['kɔŋkə'] vt conquistar; (enemy) vencer; (feelings) superar; **conquest** ['kɔŋkwɛst] n conquista

conscience ['kɔnʃəns] n consciência

conscientious [kɔnʃɪ'ɛnʃəs] adj consciencioso

conscious ['kɔnʃəs] adj: **~ (of)** consciente (de); (deliberate) intencional; **consciousness** n consciência; **to lose/regain consciousness** perder/recuperar os sentidos

consent [kən'sɛnt] n consentimento ▷ vi: **to ~ to** consentir em

consequence ['kɔnsɪkwəns] n consequência; (significance): **of ~** de importância; **consequently** adv por conseguinte

conservation [kɔnsə'veɪʃən] n conservação f; (of the environment) preservação f

conservative [kən'sə:vətɪv] adj conservador(a); (cautious) moderado; (Brit: Pol): **C~** conservador(a) ▷ n (Brit: Pol) conservador(a) m/f

conservatory [kən'sə:vətrɪ] n (Mus) conservatório; (greenhouse) estufa

consider [kən'sɪdə'] vt considerar; (take into account) levar em consideração; (study) estudar, examinar; **to ~ doing sth** pensar em fazer algo

considerable [kən'sɪdərəbl] adj considerável; (sum) importante

considerate [kən'sɪdərɪt] adj atencioso; **consideration** [kənsɪdə'reɪʃən] n consideração f; (deliberation) deliberação f; (factor) fator m

considering [kən'sɪdərɪŋ] prep em vista de

consist [kən'sɪst] vi: **to ~ of** (comprise) consistir em

consistency [kən'sɪstənsɪ] n coerência; (thickness) consistência

consistent [kən'sɪstənt] adj (person) coerente, estável; (argument, idea) sólido

consolation [kɔnsə'leɪʃən] n conforto

console [vt kən'səul, n 'kɔnsəul] vt confortar ▷ n consolo

consonant ['kɔnsənənt] n consoante f

conspicuous [kən'spɪkjuəs] adj conspícuo

conspiracy [kən'spɪrəsɪ] n conspiração f, trama

constable ['kʌnstəbl] (Brit) n policial m/f (BR), polícia m/f (PT); **chief ~** chefe m/f de polícia

constant ['kɔnstənt] adj constante

constipated ['kɔnstɪpeɪtəd] adj com prisão de ventre

constipation [kɔnstɪ'peɪʃən] n prisão f de ventre

constituency [kən'stɪtjuənsɪ] n (Pol) distrito eleitoral; (people) eleitorado

constitution [kɔnstɪ'tju:ʃən] n constituição f; (health) compleição f

constraint [kən'streɪnt] n coação f, pressão f; (restriction) limitação f

construct [kən'strʌkt] vt construir; **construction** n construção f; (structure) estrutura

consul ['kɔnsl] n cônsul m/f;

consulate ['kɔnsjulɪt] *n*
consulado

consult [kən'sʌlt] *vt* consultar;
consultant *n* (*Med*) (médico(-a))
especialista *m/f*; (*other specialist*)
assessor(a) *m/f*, consultor(a) *m/f*;
consulting room (*Brit*) *n*
consultório

consume [kən'sju:m] *vt* (*eat*)
comer; (*drink*) beber; (*fire etc*,
Comm) consumir; **consumer** *n*
consumidor(a) *m/f*

consumption [kən'sʌmpʃən] *n*
consumo

cont. *abbr* = **continued**

contact ['kɔntækt] *n* contato ▷ *vt*
entrar *or* pôr-se em contato com;
contact lenses *npl* lentes *fpl* de
contato

contagious [kən'teɪdʒəs] *adj*
contagioso; (*fig: laughter etc*)
contagiante

contain [kən'teɪn] *vt* conter; **to ~
o.s.** conter-se; **container** *n*
recipiente *m*; (*for shipping etc*)
container *m*, cofre *m* de carga

contaminate [kən'tæmɪneɪt] *vt*
contaminar

cont'd *abbr* = **continued**

contemplate ['kɔntəmpleɪt] *vt*
(*idea*) considerar; (*person, painting
etc*) contemplar

contemporary [kən'tɛmpərərɪ]
adj contemporâneo; (*design etc*)
moderno ▷ *n* contemporâneo(-a)

contempt [kən'tɛmpt] *n* desprezo;
contempt of court *n* (*Law*)
desacato à autoridade do tribunal

contend [kən'tɛnd] *vt* (*assert*): **to ~
that** afirmar que ▷ *vi*: **to ~ with**
(*struggle*) lutar com; (*difficulty*)
enfrentar; (*compete*): **to ~ for**
competir por

content [*adj, vt* kən'tɛnt, *n*
'kɔntɛnt] *adj* (*happy*) contente;
(*satisfied*) satisfeito ▷ *vt* contentar,
satisfazer ▷ *n* conteúdo; (*fat
content, moisture content etc*)
quantidade *f*; **contents** *npl* (*of
packet, book*) conteúdo; **contented**
adj contente, satisfeito

contest [*n* 'kɔntɛst, *vt* kən'tɛst] *n*
contenda; (*competition*) concurso
▷ *vt* (*legal case*) defender; (*Pol*) ser
candidato a; (*competition*) disputar;
(*statement, decision*) contestar;
contestant [kən'tɛstənt] *n*
competidor(a) *m/f*; (*in fight*)
adversário(-a)

context ['kɔntɛkst] *n* contexto

continent ['kɔntɪnənt] *n*
continente *m*; **the C~** (*Brit*) o
continente europeu; **continental**
[kɔntɪ'nɛntl] *adj* continental;
continental quilt (*Brit*) *n*
edredom *m* (*BR*), edredão *m* (*PT*)

continual [kən'tɪnjuəl] *adj*
contínuo

continue [kən'tɪnju:] *vi* prosseguir,
continuar ▷ *vt* continuar; (*start
again*) recomeçar, retomar;
continuous [kən'tɪnjuəs] *adj*
contínuo

contour ['kɔntuər] *n* contorno;
(*also: ~ line*) curva de nível

contraceptive [kɔntrə'sɛptɪv] *adj*
anticoncepcional ▷ *n*
anticoncepcional *f*

contract [*n, cpd* 'kɔntrækt, *vt, vi*
kən'trækt] *n* contrato ▷ *cpd* (*work*)
de empreitada ▷ *vi* (*become smaller*)
contrair-se, encolher-se; (*Comm*):
to ~ to do sth comprometer-se por
contrato a fazer algo ▷ *vt* contrair

contradict [kɔntrə'dɪkt] *vt*
contradizer, desmentir

contrary¹ ['kɔntrərɪ] *adj* contrário
▷ *n* contrário; **on the ~** muito pelo

contrário; **unless you hear to the ~** salvo aviso contrário

contrary² [kən'trɛərɪ] adj teimoso

contrast [n 'kɒntrɑːst, vt kən'trɑːst] n contraste m ▷ vt comparar; **in ~ to** or **with** em contraste com, ao contrário de

contribute [kən'trɪbjuːt] vt contribuir ▷ vi dar; **to ~ to** (charity) contribuir para; (newspaper) escrever para; (discussion) participar de; **contribution** [kɒntrɪ'bjuːʃən] n (donation) doação f; (Brit: for social security) contribuição f; (to debate) intervenção f; (to journal) colaboração f; **contributor** [kən'trɪbjutəʳ] n (to newspaper) colaborador(a) m/f

control [kən'trəul] vt controlar; (machinery) regular; (temper) dominar ▷ n controle m; (of car) direção f (BR), condução f (PT); (check) freio, controle; **controls** npl (of vehicle) comandos mpl; (on radio, television etc) controle; **to be in ~ of** ter o controle de; (in charge of) ser responsável por

controversial [kɒntrə'vɜːʃl] adj controvertido, polêmico

controversy ['kɒntrəvɜːsɪ] n controvérsia, polêmica

convenience [kən'viːnɪəns] n (easiness) facilidade f; (suitability) conveniência; (advantage) vantagem f, conveniência; **at your ~** quando lhe convier; **all modern ~s**, **all mod cons** (Brit) com todos os confortos

convenient [kən'viːnɪənt] adj conveniente

convent ['kɒnvənt] n convento

convention [kən'vɛnʃən] n (custom) costume m; (agreement) convenção f; (meeting) assembleia; **conventional** adj convencional

conversation [kɒnvə'seɪʃən] n conversação f, conversa

convert [vt kən'vɜːt, n 'kɒnvɜːt] vt converter ▷ n convertido(-a); **convertible** [kən'vɜːtəbl] n conversível m

convey [kən'veɪ] vt transportar, levar; (thanks) expressar; (information) passar; **conveyor belt** n correia transportadora

convict [vt kən'vɪkt, n 'kɒnvɪkt] vt condenar ▷ n presidiário(-a); **conviction** n condenação f; (belief) convicção f; (certainty) certeza

convince [kən'vɪns] vt (assure) assegurar; (persuade) convencer; **convincing** adj convincente

cook [kuk] vt cozinhar; (meal) preparar ▷ vi cozinhar ▷ n cozinheiro(-a); **cookbook** n livro de receitas; **cooker** n fogão m; **cookery** n culinária; **cookery book** (Brit) n = **cookbook**; **cookie** (US) n bolacha, biscoito; **cooking** n cozinha

cool [kuːl] adj fresco; (calm) calmo; (unfriendly) frio ▷ vt resfriar ▷ vi esfriar

cop [kɒp] (inf) n policial m/f (BR), polícia m/f (PT), tira m (inf)

cope [kəup] vi: **to ~ with** poder com, arcar com; (problem) estar à altura de

copper ['kɒpəʳ] n (metal) cobre m; (Brit: inf: policeman/woman) policial m/f (BR), polícia m/f (PT); **coppers** npl (coins) moedas fpl de pouco valor

copy ['kɒpɪ] n cópia, duplicata; (of book etc) exemplar m ▷ vt copiar; (imitate) imitar; **copyright** n

direitos *mpl* autorais, copirraite *m*
coral ['kɔrəl] *n* coral *m*
cord [kɔːd] *n* corda; (*Elec*) fio, cabo; (*fabric*) veludo cotelê
corduroy ['kɔːdərɔɪ] *n* veludo cotelê
core [kɔːʳ] *n* centro; (*of fruit*) caroço; (*of problem*) âmago ▷ *vt* descaroçar
cork [kɔːk] *n* rolha; (*tree*) cortiça; **corkscrew** *n* saca-rolhas *m inv*
corn [kɔːn] *n* (*Brit*) trigo; (*US: maize*) milho; (*on foot*) calo; **~ on the cob** (*Culin*) espiga de milho
corned beef ['kɔːnd-] *n* carne *f* de boi enlatada
corner ['kɔːnəʳ] *n* (*outside*) esquina; (*inside*) canto; (*in road*) curva; (*Football etc*) córner *m* ▷ *vt* (*trap*) encurralar; (*Comm*) açambarcar, monopolizar ▷ *vi* fazer uma curva
cornflakes ['kɔːnfleɪks] *npl* flocos *mpl* de milho
cornflour ['kɔːnflauəʳ] (*Brit*) *n* farinha de milho, maisena®
cornstarch ['kɔːnstɑːtʃ] (*US*) *n* = **cornflour**
Cornwall ['kɔːnwəl] *n* Cornualha
coronary ['kɔrənərɪ] *n*: **~ (thrombosis)** trombose *f* (coronária)
coronation [kɔrə'neɪʃən] *n* coroação *f*
coroner ['kɔrənəʳ] *n* magistrado que investiga mortes suspeitas
corporal ['kɔːpərl] *n* cabo ▷ *adj*: **~ punishment** castigo corporal
corporate ['kɔːpərɪt] *adj* (*finance*) corporativo; (*action*) coletivo; (*image*) da empresa
corporation [kɔːpə'reɪʃən] *n* (*of town*) município, junta; (*Comm*) sociedade *f*
corps [kɔːʳ] (*pl* **corps** [kɔːz]) *n* (*Mil*) unidade *f*; (*diplomatic*) corpo; **the**

press ~ a imprensa
corpse [kɔːps] *n* cadáver *m*
correct [kə'rɛkt] *adj* exato; (*proper*) correto ▷ *vt* corrigir; **correction** *n* correção *f*
correspond [kɔrɪs'pɔnd] *vi* (*write*): **to ~ (with)** corresponder-se (com); (*be equal to*): **to ~ to** corresponder a; (*be in accordance*): **to ~ (with)** corresponder (a); **correspondence** *n* correspondência; **correspondent** *n* correspondente *m/f*
corridor ['kɔrɪdɔːʳ] *n* corredor *m*
corrode [kə'rəud] *vt* corroer ▷ *vi* corroer-se
corrupt [kə'rʌpt] *adj* corrupto; (*Comput*) corrupto, danificado ▷ *vt* corromper; **corruption** *n* corrupção *f*
Corsica ['kɔːsɪkə] *n* Córsega
cosmetic [kɔz'mɛtɪk] *n* cosmético ▷ *adj* (*fig*) simbólico, superficial
cost [kɔst] (*pt, pp* **cost**) *n* (*price*) preço ▷ *vt* custar; **costs** *npl* (*Comm*) custos *mpl*; (*Law*) custas *fpl*; **at all ~s** custe o que custar
co-star [kəu-] *n* coestrela *m/f*
Costa Rica ['kɔstə'riːkə] *n* Costa Rica
costly ['kɔstlɪ] *adj* caro
costume ['kɔstjuːm] *n* traje *m*; (*Brit: also:* **swimming ~**: *woman's*) maiô *m* (*BR*), fato de banho (*PT*); (: *man's*) calção *m* (de banho) (*BR*), calções *mpl* de banho (*PT*)
cosy ['kəuzɪ], (*US*) **cozy** *adj* aconchegante; (*life*) confortável
cot [kɔt] *n* (*Brit*) cama (de criança), berço; (*US*) cama de lona
cottage ['kɔtɪdʒ] *n* casa de campo; **cottage cheese** *n* queijo tipo cottage (*BR*), queijo creme (*PT*)
cotton ['kɔtn] *n* algodão *m*; (*thread*)

fio, linha **cotton on** (*inf*) *vi*: **to ~ on (to sth)** sacar (algo); **cotton bud** (*Brit*) *n* cotonete® *m*; **cotton candy** (*US*) *n* algodão *m* doce; **cotton wool** (*Brit*) *n* algodão *m* (hidrófilo)

couch [kautʃ] *n* sofá *m*; (*doctor's*) cama; (*psychiatrist's*) divã *m*

cough [kɔf] *vi* tossir ▷ *n* tosse *f*

could [kud] *pt, conditional of* **can²**

couldn't ['kudnt] = **could not**

council ['kaunsl] *n* conselho; **city** *or* **town ~** câmara municipal; **council estate** (*Brit*) *n* conjunto habitacional; **council house** (*Brit*) *n* casa popular; **councillor** *n* vereador(a) *m/f*

counsellor ['kaunsələʳ], (*US*) **counselor** *n* conselheiro(-a); (*US*: *Law*) advogado(-a)

count [kaunt] *vt* contar; (*include*) incluir ▷ *vi* contar ▷ *n* (*of votes etc*) contagem *f*; (*of pollen, alcohol*) nível *m*; (*nobleman*) conde *m* **count on** *vt fus* contar com; **countdown** *n* contagem *f* regressiva

counter ['kauntəʳ] *n* (*in shop*) balcão *m*; (*in post office etc*) guichê *m*; (*in games*) ficha ▷ *vt* contrariar ▷ *adv*: **~ to** ao contrário de

counterfeit ['kauntəfɪt] *n* falsificação *f* ▷ *vt* falsificar ▷ *adj* falso, falsificado

counterpart ['kauntəpɑːt] *n* (*opposite number*) homólogo(-a); (*equivalent*) equivalente *m/f*

countess ['kauntɪs] *n* condessa

countless ['kauntlɪs] *adj* inumerável

country ['kʌntrɪ] *n* país *m*; (*nation*) nação *f*; (*native land*) terra; (*as opposed to town*) campo; (*region*) região *f*, terra; **countryside** *n* campo

county ['kauntɪ] *n* condado

coup [kuː] *n* golpe *m* de mestre; (*also*: **~ d'état**) golpe de (estado)

couple ['kʌpl] *n* (*of things, people*) par *m*; (*married couple, courting couple*) casal *m*; **a ~ of** um par de; (*a few*) alguns/algumas

coupon ['kuːpɔn] *n* cupom *m* (*BR*), cupão *m* (*PT*); (*voucher*) vale *m*

courage ['kʌrɪdʒ] *n* coragem *f*

courier ['kurɪəʳ] *n* correio; (*for tourists*) guia *m/f*, agente *m/f* de turismo

course [kɔːs] *n* (*direction*) direção *f*; (*process*) desenvolvimento; (*of river*, *Sch*) curso; (*of ship*) rumo; (*Golf*) campo; (*part of meal*) prato; **of ~** naturalmente; (*certainly*) certamente; **of ~!** claro!, lógico!

court [kɔːt] *n* (*royal*) corte *f*; (*Law*) tribunal *m*; (*Tennis etc*) quadra ▷ *vt* (*woman*) cortejar, namorar; **to take to ~** demandar, levar a julgamento

courtesy ['kəːtəsɪ] *n* cortesia; **(by) ~ of** com permissão de

court-house (*US*) *n* palácio de justiça

courtroom ['kɔːtrum] *n* sala de tribunal

courtyard ['kɔːtjɑːd] *n* pátio

cousin ['kʌzn] *n* primo(-a) *m/f*; **first ~** primo(-mã) irmão(-a)

cover ['kʌvəʳ] *vt* cobrir; (*with lid*) tampar; (*chairs etc*) revestir; (*distance*) percorrer; (*include*) abranger; (*protect*) abrigar; (*issues*) tratar ▷ *n* (*lid*) tampa; (*for chair etc*) capa; (*for bed*) cobertor *m*; (*of book*, *magazine*) capa; (*shelter*) abrigo; (*Insurance*) cobertura; **to take ~** abrigar-se; **under ~** (*indoors*) abrigado; **under separate ~** (*Comm*) em separado **cover up** *vi*: **to ~ up for sb** cobrir alguém;

coverage n cobertura; **cover charge** n couvert m

cover-up n encobrimento (dos fatos)

cow [kau] n vaca ▷ vt intimidar

coward ['kauəd] n covarde m/f; **cowardly** adj covarde

cowboy ['kaubɔɪ] n vaqueiro

cozy ['kəuzi] (US) adj = **cosy**

crab [kræb] n caranguejo

crack [kræk] n rachadura; (gap) brecha; (noise) estalo; (drug) crack m ▷ vt quebrar; (nut) partir, descascar; (wall) rachar; (whip etc) estalar; (joke) soltar; (mystery) resolver; (code) decifrar ▷ adj (expert) de primeira classe **crack down on** vt fus (crime) ser linha dura com **crack up** vi (Psych) sofrer um colapso nervoso; **cracker** n (biscuit) biscoito; (Christmas cracker) busca-pé-surpresa m

crackle ['krækl] vi crepitar

cradle ['kreɪdl] n berço

craft [krɑːft] n (skill) arte f; (trade) ofício; (boat) barco; **craftsman** irreg n artífice m, artesão m; **craftsmanship** n acabamento

cram [kræm] vt (fill): **to ~ sth with** encher or abarrotar algo de; (put): **to ~ sth into** enfiar algo em ▷ vi (for exams) estudar na última hora

cramp [kræmp] n (Med) cãibra; **cramped** adj apertado, confinado

cranberry ['krænbəri] n oxicoco

crane [kreɪn] n (Tech) guindaste m; (bird) grou m

crash [kræʃ] n (noise) estrondo; (of car) batida; (of plane) desastre m de avião; (Comm) falência, quebra; (Stock Exchange) craque m ▷ vt (car) bater com; (plane) jogar ▷ vi (car) bater; (plane) cair; (two cars) colidir, bater; (Comm) falir, quebrar; **crash course** n curso intensivo

crate [kreɪt] n caixote m; (for bottles) engradado

crave [kreɪv] vt, vi: **to ~ for** ansiar por

crawl [krɔːl] vi arrastar-se; (child) engatinhar; (insect) andar; (vehicle) andar a passo de tartaruga ▷ n (Swimming) crawl m

crayfish ['kreɪfɪʃ] n inv (freshwater) camarão-d'água-doce m; (saltwater) lagostim m

crayon ['kreɪən] n lápis m de cera, crayon m

craze [kreɪz] n (fashion) moda

crazy ['kreɪzi] adj louco, maluco, doido

creak [kriːk] vi ranger

cream [kriːm] n (of milk) nata; (artificial, cosmetic) creme m; (élite): **the ~ of** a fina flor de ▷ adj (colour) creme inv; **cream cheese** n ricota (BR), queijo creme (PT); **creamy** adj (colour) creme inv; (taste) cremoso

crease [kriːs] n (fold) dobra, vinco; (in trousers) vinco; (wrinkle) ruga ▷ vt (wrinkle) amassar, amarrotar ▷ vi amassar-se, amarrotar-se

create [kriː'eɪt] vt criar; (produce) produzir

creature ['kriːtʃər] n (animal) animal m, bicho; (living thing) criatura

credit ['krɛdɪt] n crédito; (merit) mérito ▷ vt (also: **give ~ to**) acreditar; (Comm) creditar; **credits** npl (Cinema, TV) crédito; **to ~ sb with sth** (fig) atribuir algo a alguém; **to be in ~** ter fundos; **credit card** n cartão m de crédito; **credit crunch** n contração f do crédito

creek [kri:k] n enseada; (US) riacho
creep [kri:p] (pt, pp **crept**) vi
(animal) rastejar; (person)
deslizar(-se)
cremate [krɪ'meɪt] vt cremar;
crematorium (pl **crematoria**) n
crematório
crept [krɛpt] pt, pp of **creep**
crescent ['krɛsnt] n meia-lua;
(street) rua semicircular
cress [krɛs] n agrião m
crest [krɛst] n (of bird) crista; (of hill)
cimo, topo; (of coat of arms) timbre m
crew [kru:] n (of ship etc) tripulação
f; (Cinema) equipe f
crib [krɪb] n manjedoira, presépio;
(US: cot) berço ▷ vt (inf) colar
cricket ['krɪkɪt] n (insect) grilo;
(game) criquete m, cricket m
crime [kraɪm] n (no pl: illegal
activities) crime m; (offence) delito;
(fig) pecado, maldade f; **criminal**
['krɪmɪnl] n criminoso ▷ adj
criminal; (morally wrong) imoral
crimson ['krɪmzn] adj carmesim inv
cringe [krɪndʒ] vi encolher-se
cripple ['krɪpl] n aleijado(-a) ▷ vt
aleijar
crisis ['kraɪsɪs] (pl **crises**) n crise f
crisp [krɪsp] adj fresco; (bacon etc)
torrado; (manner) seco; **crisps**
(Brit) npl batatinhas fpl fritas;
crispy adj crocante
criterion [kraɪ'tɪərɪən] (pl **criteria**)
n critério
critic ['krɪtɪk] n crítico(-a); **critical**
adj crítico; (illness) grave; **to be
critical of sth/sb** criticar algo/
alguém; **criticism** ['krɪtɪsɪzm] n
crítica; **criticize** ['krɪtɪsaɪz] vt
criticar
Croatia [krəʊ'eɪʃə] n Croácia
crockery ['krɔkərɪ] n louça
crocodile ['krɔkədaɪl] n crocodilo

crocus ['krəʊkəs] n açafrão-da-
primavera m
crook [kruk] n (inf: criminal)
vigarista m/f; (of shepherd) cajado;
crooked ['krukɪd] adj torto;
(dishonest) desonesto
crop [krɔp] n (produce) colheita;
(amount produced) safra; (riding
crop) chicotinho ▷ vt cortar **crop
up** vi surgir
cross [krɔs] n cruz f; (hybrid)
cruzamento ▷ vt cruzar; (street etc)
atravessar; (thwart) contrariar
▷ adj zangado, mal-humorado
cross out vt riscar **cross over** vi
atravessar; **crossing** n (sea
passage) travessia; (also:
pedestrian crossing) faixa (para
pedestres) (BR), passadeira (PT);
crossroads n cruzamento;
crosswalk (US) n faixa (para
pedestres) (BR), passadeira (PT);
crossword n palavras fpl cruzadas
crouch [krautʃ] vi agachar-se
crow [krəʊ] n (bird) corvo; (of cock)
canto, cocoricó m ▷ vi (cock)
cantar, cocoricar
crowd [kraud] n multidão f ▷ vt
(fill) apinhar ▷ vi (gather)
amontoar-se; (cram): **to ~ in**
apinhar-se; **crowded** adj (full)
lotado; (densely populated)
superlotado
crown [kraun] n coroa; (of head,
hill) topo ▷ vt coroar; (fig) rematar;
crown jewels npl joias fpl reais
crucial ['kru:ʃl] adj (decision) vital;
(vote) decisivo
crucifix ['kru:sɪfɪks] n crucifixo
crude [kru:d] adj (materials) bruto;
(fig: basic) tosco; (: vulgar) grosseiro
cruel ['kruəl] adj cruel
cruise [kru:z] n cruzeiro ▷ vi (ship)
fazer um cruzeiro; (car): **to ~ at ...**

km/h ir a ... km por hora

crumb [krʌm] n (of bread) migalha; (of cake) farelo

crumble ['krʌmbl] vt esfarelar ▷ vi (building) desmoronar-se; (plaster, earth) esfacelar-se; (fig) desintegrar-se

crumpet ['krʌmpɪt] n bolo leve

crumple ['krʌmpl] vt (paper) amassar; (material) amarrotar

crunch [krʌntʃ] vt (food etc) mastigar; (underfoot) esmagar ▷ n (fig): **the ~** o momento decisivo; **crunchy** adj crocante

crush [krʌʃ] n (crowd) aglomeração f; (love): **to have a ~ on sb** ter um rabicho por alguém; (drink): **lemon ~** limonada ▷ vt (press) esmagar; (squeeze) espremer; (paper) amassar; (cloth) enrugar; (army, opposition) aniquilar; (hopes) destruir; (person) arrasar

crust [krʌst] n (of bread) casca; (of snow, earth) crosta

crutch [krʌtʃ] n muleta

cry [kraɪ] vi chorar; (shout: also: **~ out**) gritar ▷ n grito; (of bird) pio; (of animal) voz f **cry off** vi desistir

crystal ['krɪstl] n cristal m

cub [kʌb] n filhote m; (also: **~ scout**) lobinho

Cuba ['kju:bə] n Cuba

cube [kju:b] n cubo ▷ vt (Math) elevar ao cubo; **cubic** adj cúbico

cubicle ['kju:bɪkl] n cubículo

cuckoo ['kuku:] n cuco

cucumber ['kju:kʌmbəʳ] n pepino

cuddle ['kʌdl] vt abraçar ▷ vi abraçar-se

cue [kju:] n (Snooker) taco; (Theatre etc) deixa

cuff [kʌf] n (of shirt, coat etc) punho; (US: on trousers) bainha; (blow) bofetada; **off the ~** de improviso

cul-de-sac ['kʌldəsæk] n beco sem saída

cull [kʌl] vt (story, idea) escolher, selecionar ▷ n matança seletiva

culminate ['kʌlmɪneɪt] vi: **to ~ in** terminar em

culprit ['kʌlprɪt] n culpado(-a)

cult [kʌlt] n culto

cultivate ['kʌltɪveɪt] vt cultivar

cultural ['kʌltʃərəl] adj cultural

culture ['kʌltʃəʳ] n cultura

cunning ['kʌnɪŋ] n astúcia ▷ adj astuto, malandro; (device, idea) engenhoso

cup [kʌp] n xícara (BR), chávena (PT); (prize, of bra) taça

cupboard ['kʌbəd] n armário

curator [kjuəˈreɪtəʳ] n diretor(a) m/f

curb [kə:b] vt refrear ▷ n freio; (US) = **kerb**

curdle ['kə:dl] vi coalhar

cure [kjuəʳ] vt curar ▷ n tratamento, cura

curfew ['kə:fju:] n toque m de recolher

curious ['kjuərɪəs] adj curioso; (nosy) abelhudo; (unusual) estranho

curl [kə:l] n (of hair) cacho ▷ vt (loosely) frisar; (tightly) encrespar ▷ vi (hair) encaracolar **curl up** vi encaracolar-se; **curler** n rolo, bobe m; **curly** adj cacheado, crespo

currant ['kʌrnt] n passa de corinto; (blackcurrant, redcurrant) groselha

currency ['kʌrnsɪ] n moeda; **to gain ~** (fig) consagrar-se

current ['kʌrnt] n corrente f ▷ adj corrente; (present) atual; **current account** (Brit) n conta corrente; **current affairs** npl atualidades fpl; **currently** adv atualmente

curriculum [kəˈrɪkjuləm] (pl

curriculums or **curricula**) n
programa m de estudos;
curriculum vitae n currículo
curry ['kʌrɪ] n caril m ▷ vt: **to ~
favour with** captar simpatia de
curse [kə:s] vi xingar (*BR*),
praguejar (*PT*) ▷ vt (*swear at*) xingar
(*BR*); (*bemoan*) amaldiçoar ▷ n
maldição f; (*swearword*) palavrão m
(*BR*), baixo calão m (*PT*); (*problem*)
castigo
cursor ['kə:sə'] n (*Comput*) cursor m
curt [kə:t] adj seco, brusco
curtain ['kə:tn] n cortina; (*Theatre*)
pano
curve [kə:v] n curva ▷ vi
encurvar-se, torcer-se; (*road*) fazer
(uma) curva
cushion ['kuʃən] n almofada ▷ vt
amortecer
custard ['kʌstəd] n nata, creme m
custody ['kʌstədɪ] n custódia; **to
take into ~** deter
custom ['kʌstəm] n (*tradition*)
tradição f; (*convention*) costume m;
(*habit*) hábito; (*Comm*) clientela;
customer n cliente m/f;
customized adj (*car etc*) feito sob
encomenda
customs ['kʌstəmz] npl alfândega;
customs officer n inspetor(a) m/f
da alfândega, aduaneiro(-a)
cut [kʌt] (*pt, pp* **cut**) vt cortar;
(*reduce*) reduzir ▷ vi cortar ▷ n
corte m; (*in spending*) redução f; (*of
garment*) tacho **cut down** vt (*tree*)
derrubar; (*reduce*) reduzir **cut off**
vt (*piece, Tel*) cortar; (*person, village*)
isolar; (*supply*) suspender **cut out**
vt (*shape*) recortar; (*activity etc*)
suprimir; (*remove*) remover **cut up**
vt cortar em pedaços
cute [kju:t] adj bonitinho
cutlery ['kʌtlərɪ] n talheres mpl

cutlet ['kʌtlɪt] n costeleta
cut-price, (*US*) **cut-rate** adj a preço
reduzido
cutting adj cortante ▷ n (*Brit: from
newspaper*) recorte m; (*from plant*)
muda
CV n abbr = **curriculum vitae**
cybercafé ['saɪbəkæfeɪ] n
cibercafé m
cyberspace ['saɪbəspeɪs] n
ciberespaço
cycle ['saɪkl] n ciclo; (*bicycle*)
bicicleta ▷ vi andar de bicicleta
cycling ['saɪklɪŋ] n ciclismo
cyclist ['saɪklɪst] n ciclista m/f
cylinder ['sɪlɪndə'] n cilindro; (*of
gas*) bujão m
Cyprus ['saɪprəs] n Chipre f
cyst [sɪst] n cisto; **cystitis** n
cistite f
czar [zɑ:'] n czar m
Czech [tʃɛk] adj tcheco ▷ n
tcheco(-a); (*Ling*) tcheco; **Czech
Republic** n: **the Czech Republic**
a República Tcheca

d

D (US) abbr (Pol) = **democrat(ic)**

dab [dæb] vt (eyes, wound) tocar (de leve); (paint, cream) aplicar de leve

dad [dæd] (inf) n papai m

daddy ['dædɪ] n = **dad**

daffodil ['dæfədɪl] n narciso-dos-prados m

daft [dɑːft] adj bobo, besta

dagger ['dægəʳ] n punhal m, adaga

daily ['deɪlɪ] adj diário ▷ n (paper) jornal m, diário ▷ adv diariamente

dairy ['dɛərɪ] n leiteria

daisy ['deɪzɪ] n margarida

dam [dæm] n represa, barragem f ▷ vt represar

damage ['dæmɪdʒ] n (harm) prejuízo; (dents etc) avaria ▷ vt danificar; (harm) prejudicar; **damages** npl (Law) indenização f por perdas e danos

damn [dæm] vt condenar; (curse) maldizer ▷ n (inf): **I don't give a ~** não dou a mínima, estou me lixando ▷ adj (inf: also: **~ed**) danado, maldito; **~ (it)!** (que) droga!

damp [dæmp] adj úmido ▷ n umidade f ▷ vt (also: **~en**: cloth, rag) umedecer; (: enthusiasm etc) jogar água fria em

dance [dɑːns] n dança; (party etc) baile m ▷ vi dançar; **dancer** n dançarino(-a); (professional) bailarino(-a); **dancing** n dança

dandelion ['dændɪlaɪən] n dente-de-leão m

dandruff ['dændrəf] n caspa

Dane [deɪn] n dinamarquês(-esa) m/f

danger ['deɪndʒəʳ] n perigo; (risk) risco; "**~!**" (on sign) "perigo!"; **to be in ~ of** correr o risco de; **in ~** em perigo; **dangerous** ['deɪndʒərəs] adj perigoso

dangle ['dæŋgl] vt balançar ▷ vi pender balançando

Danish ['deɪnɪʃ] adj dinamarquês(-esa) ▷ n (Ling) dinamarquês m

dare [dɛəʳ] vt: **to ~ sb to do sth** desafiar alguém a fazer algo ▷ vi: **to ~ (to) do sth** atrever-se a fazer algo, ousar fazer algo; **I ~ say** (I suppose) acho provável que; **daring** adj audacioso; (bold) ousado ▷ n coragem f, destemor m

dark [dɑːk] adj escuro; (complexion) moreno ▷ n escuro; **in the ~ about** (fig) no escuro sobre; **after ~** depois de escurecer; **darken** vt escurecer; (colour) fazer mais escuro ▷ vi escurecer(-se); **darkness** n escuridão f; **darkroom** n câmara escura

darling ['dɑːlɪŋ] adj, n querido(-a)

dart [dɑːt] n dardo; (in sewing) alinhavo ▷ vi precipitar-se; **to ~**

away/along ir-se/seguir precipitadamente; **darts** n (*game*) jogo de dardos

dash [dæʃ] n (*sign*) hífen m; (: *long*) travessão m; (*small quantity*) pontinha ▷ vt arremessar; (*hopes*) frustrar ▷ vi precipitar-se, correr **dash away** vi sair apressado **dash off** vi = **dash away**

dashboard ['dæʃbɔːd] n painel m de instrumentos

data ['deɪtə] npl dados mpl; **database** n banco de dados; **data processing** n processamento de dados

date [deɪt] n data; (*with friend*) encontro; (*fruit*) tâmara ▷ vt datar; (*person*) namorar; **to ~** até agora; **out of ~** desatualizado; **up to ~** moderno; **dated** ['deɪtɪd] adj antiquado

daughter ['dɔːtəʳ] n filha; **daughter-in-law** (pl **daughters-in-law**) n nora

daunting ['dɔːntɪŋ] adj desanimador(a)

dawn [dɔːn] n alvorada, amanhecer m; (*of period, situation*) surgimento, início ▷ vi (*day*) amanhecer; (*fig*): **it ~ed on him that ...** começou a perceber que ...

day [deɪ] n dia m; (*working day*) jornada, dia útil; **the ~ before/after** a véspera/o dia seguinte; **the ~ before yesterday** anteontem; **the ~ after tomorrow** depois de amanhã; **by ~** de dia; **day-care centre** ['deɪkeə-] n (*for elderly etc*) centro de convivência; (*for children*) creche f; **daydream** vi devanear; **daylight** n luz f (do dia); **day return** (*Brit*) n bilhete m de ida e volta no mesmo dia; **daytime** n dia m; **day-to-day** adj cotidiano

dazzle ['dæzl] vt (*bewitch*) deslumbrar; (*blind*) ofuscar

dead [dɛd] adj morto; (*numb*) dormente; (*telephone*) cortado; (*Elec*) sem corrente ▷ adv completamente; (*exactly*) absolutamente ▷ npl: **the ~** os mortos; **to shoot sb ~** matar alguém a tiro; **~ tired** morto de cansado; **to stop ~** estacar; **dead end** n beco sem saída; **deadline** n prazo final; **deadly** adj mortal, fatal; (*weapon*) mortífero

deaf [dɛf] adj surdo; **deafen** vt ensurdecer

deal [diːl] n (pt, pp **dealt**) n (*agreement*) acordo ▷ vt (*cards, blows*) dar; **a good** or **great ~ (of)** bastante, muito **deal in** vt fus (*Comm*) negociar em or com **deal with** vt fus (*people*) tratar com; (*problem*) ocupar-se de; (*subject*) tratar de; **dealer** n negociante m/f; **dealings** npl transações fpl

dean [diːn] n (*Rel*) decano; (*Sch: Brit*) reitor(a) m/f; (: *US*) orientador(a) m/f de estudos

dear [dɪəʳ] adj querido, caro; (*expensive*) caro ▷ n: **my ~** meu querido/minha querida ▷ excl: **~ me!** ai, meu Deus!; **D~ Sir/Madam** (*in letter*) Prezado Senhor/Prezada Senhora (*BR*), Exmo. Senhor/Exma. Senhora (*PT*); **D~ Mr/Mrs X** Prezado Sr. X/Prezada Sra. X; **dearly** adv (*love*) ternamente; (*pay*) caro

death [dɛθ] n morte f; (*Admin*) óbito; **death penalty** n pena de morte

debate [dɪ'beɪt] n debate m ▷ vt debater

debit ['dɛbɪt] n débito ▷ vt: **to ~ a sum to sb** or **to sb's account** lançar uma quantia ao débito de alguém or à conta de alguém; see also **direct debit**; **debit card** n cartão m de débito

debt [dɛt] n dívida; (state) endividiamento; **to be in ~** ter dívidas, estar endividado

decade ['dɛkeɪd] n década

decaffeinated [dɪ'kæfɪneɪtɪd] adj descafeinado

decay [dɪ'keɪ] n ruína; (also: **tooth ~**) cárie f ▷ vi (rot) apodrecer-se

deceased [dɪ'si:st] n: **the ~** o falecido/a falecida

deceit [dɪ'si:t] n engano; (duplicity) fraude f

deceive [dɪ'si:v] vt enganar

December [dɪ'sɛmbə^r] n dezembro

decent ['di:sənt] adj (proper) decente; (kind, honest) honesto, amável

deception [dɪ'sɛpʃən] n engano; (deceitful act) fraude f; **deceptive** adj enganador(a)

decide [dɪ'saɪd] vt (person) convencer; (question, argument) resolver ▷ vi decidir; **to ~ on sth** decidir-se por algo

decimal ['dɛsɪməl] adj decimal ▷ n decimal m

decision [dɪ'sɪʒən] n (choice) escolha; (act of choosing) decisão f; (decisiveness) resolução f

decisive [dɪ'saɪsɪv] adj (action) decisivo; (person) decidido

deck [dɛk] n (Naut) convés m; (of bus): **top ~** andar m de cima; (of cards) baralho; **record/cassette ~** toca-discos m inv/toca-fitas m inv

declare [dɪ'klɛə^r] vt (intention) revelar; (result) divulgar; (income, at customs) declarar

decline [dɪ'klaɪn] n declínio; (lessening) diminuição f, baixa ▷ vt recusar ▷ vi diminuir

decorate ['dɛkəreɪt] vt (paint) pintar; (paper) decorar com papel; **decoration** [dɛkə'reɪʃən] n enfeite m; (act) decoração f; (medal) condecoração f; **decorator** n (painter) pintor(a) m/f

decrease [n 'di:kri:s, vt, vi di:'kri:s] n: **~ (in)** diminuição f (de) ▷ vt reduzir ▷ vi diminuir

decree [dɪ'kri:] n decreto

dedicate ['dɛdɪkeɪt] vt dedicar; **dedication** [dɛdɪ'keɪʃən] n dedicação f; (in book) dedicatória; (on radio) mensagem f

deduce [dɪ'dju:s] vt deduzir

deduct [dɪ'dʌkt] vt deduzir; **deduction** n (deducting) redução f; (amount) subtração f; (deducing) dedução f

deed [di:d] n feito, título; (Law) escritura, título

deep [di:p] adj profundo; (voice) baixo, grave; (breath) fundo; (colour) forte, carregado ▷ adv: **the spectators stood 20 ~** havia 20 fileiras de espectadores; **to be 4 metres ~** ter 4 metros de profundidade; **deepen** vt aprofundar ▷ vi aumentar

deer [dɪə^r] n inv veado, cervo

default [dɪ'fɔ:lt] n (Comput) default m, padrão m; **by ~** (win) por desistência

defeat [dɪ'fi:t] n derrota; (failure) malogro ▷ vt derrotar, vencer

defect [n 'di:fɛkt, vi dɪ'fɛkt] n defeito ▷ vi: **to ~ to the enemy** desertar para se juntar ao inimigo; **defective** [dɪ'fɛktɪv] adj defeituoso

defence [dɪ'fɛns], (US) **defense** n defesa

defend [dɪ'fɛnd] vt defender; (Law) contestar; **defendant** n acusado(-a); (*in civil case*) réu/ré *m/f*; **defender** *n* defensor(a) *m/f*; (*Sport*) defesa

defer [dɪ'fəːʳ] *vt* (*postpone*) adiar

defiance [dɪ'faɪəns] *n* desafio, rebeldia; **in ~ of** a despeito de

defiant [dɪ'faɪənt] *adj* desafiador(a)

deficiency [dɪ'fɪʃənsɪ] *n* (*lack*) deficiência, falta; (*defect*) defeito

deficit ['dɛfɪsɪt] *n* déficit *m*

define [dɪ'faɪn] *vt* definir

definite ['dɛfɪnɪt] *adj* (*fixed*) definitivo; (*clear, obvious*) claro, categórico; (*certain*) certo; **he was ~ about it** ele foi categórico; **definitely** *adv* sem dúvida

deflate [diː'fleɪt] *vt* esvaziar

deflect [dɪ'flɛkt] *vt* desviar

defraud [dɪ'frɔːd] *vt*: **to ~ sb (of sth)** trapacear alguém (por causa de algo)

defrost [diː'frɔst] *vt* descongelar

defuse [diː'fjuːz] *vt* tirar o estopim *or* a espoleta de; (*situation*) neutralizar

defy [dɪ'faɪ] *vt* desafiar; (*resist*) opor-se a

degree [dɪ'griː] *n* grau *m*; (*Sch*) diploma *m*, título; **in maths** formatura em matemática; **by ~s** (*gradually*) pouco a pouco; **to some ~**, **to a certain ~** até certo ponto

dehydrated [diːhaɪ'dreɪtɪd] *adj* desidratado; (*milk*) em pó

delay [dɪ'leɪ] *vt* (*decision etc*) retardar, atrasar; (*train, person*) atrasar ▷ *vi* hesitar ▷ *n* demora; (*postponement*) adiamento; **to be ~ed** estar atrasado; **without ~** sem demora *or* atraso

delegate [*n* 'dɛlɪgɪt, *vt* 'dɛlɪgeɪt] *n* delegado(-a) ▷ *vt* (*person*) autorizar; (*task*) delegar

delete [dɪ'liːt] *vt* eliminar, riscar;

(*Comput*) deletar, excluir

deliberate [*adj* dɪ'lɪbərɪt, *vi* dɪ'lɪbəreɪt] *adj* (*intentional*) intencional; (*slow*) pausado, lento ▷ *vi* considerar; **deliberately** [dɪ'lɪbərɪtlɪ] *adv* (*on purpose*) de propósito

delicacy ['dɛlɪkəsɪ] *n* delicadeza; (*of problem*) dificuldade *f*; (*choice food*) iguaria

delicate ['dɛlɪkɪt] *adj* delicado; (*health*) frágil

delicatessen [dɛlɪkə'tɛsn] *n* delicatessen *f*

delicious [dɪ'lɪʃəs] *adj* delicioso; (*food*) saboroso

delight [dɪ'laɪt] *n* prazer *m*, deleite *m*; (*person*) encanto; (*experience*) delícia ▷ *vt* encantar, deleitar; **to take (a) ~ in** deleitar-se com; **delighted** *adj*: **delighted (at or with sth)** encantado (com algo); **delightful** *adj* encantador(a), delicioso

delinquent [dɪ'lɪŋkwənt] *adj, n* delinquente *m/f*

deliver [dɪ'lɪvəʳ] *vt* (*distribute*) distribuir; (*hand over*) entregar; (*message*) comunicar; (*speech*) proferir; (*Med*) partejar; **delivery** *n* distribuição *f*; (*of speaker*) enunciação *f*; (*Med*) parto; **to take delivery of** receber

delusion [dɪ'luːʒən] *n* ilusão *f*

demand [dɪ'mɑːnd] *vt* exigir; (*rights*) reivindicar, reclamar ▷ *n* exigência; (*claim*) reivindicação *f*; (*Econ*) procura; **to be in ~** estar em demanda; **on ~** à vista; **demanding** *adj* (*boss*) exigente; (*work*) absorvente

demise [dɪ'maɪz] *n* falecimento

demo ['dɛməu] (*inf*) *n abbr* (= *demonstration*) passeata

democracy [dɪˈmɔkrəsɪ] n democracia; **democrat** [ˈdɛmɘkræt] n democrata m/f; **democratic** [dɛmɘˈkrætɪk] adj democrático

demolish [dɪˈmɔlɪʃ] vt demolir, derrubar; (argument) refutar, contestar

demonstrate [ˈdɛmɘnstreɪt] vt demonstrar ▷ vi: **to ~ (for/ against)** manifestar-se (a favor de/contra); **demonstration** [dɛmɘnˈstreɪʃən] n (Pol) manifestação f; (: march) passeata; (proof) demonstração f; (exhibition) exibição f; **demonstrator** n manifestante m/f

demote [dɪˈmɘut] vt rebaixar de posto

den [dɛn] n (of animal) covil m; (of thieves) antro, esconderijo; (room) aposento privado, cantinho

denial [dɪˈnaɪəl] n refutação f; (refusal) negativa

denim [ˈdɛnɪm] n brim m, zuarte m; **denims** npl jeans m (BR), jeans mpl (PT)

Denmark [ˈdɛnmɑːk] n Dinamarca

denomination [dɪnɔmɪˈneɪʃən] n valor m, denominação f; (Rel) confissão f, seita

denounce [dɪˈnauns] vt denunciar

dense [dɛns] adj denso, espesso; (inf: stupid) estúpido, bronco

density [ˈdɛnsɪtɪ] n densidade f

dent [dɛnt] n amolgadura, depressão f ▷ vt amolgar, dentar

dental [ˈdɛntl] adj (treatment) dentário; (hygiene) dental; **dental floss** [-flɔs] n fio dental

dentist [ˈdɛntɪst] n dentista m/f

dentures [ˈdɛntʃəz] npl dentadura

deny [dɪˈnaɪ] vt negar; (refuse) recusar

deodorant [diːˈɘudərənt] n desodorante m (BR), desodorizante m (PT)

depart [dɪˈpɑːt] vi ir-se, partir; (train etc) sair; **to ~ from** (fig: differ from) afastar-se de

department [dɪˈpɑːtmənt] n (Sch) departamento; (Comm) seção f; (Pol) repartição f; **department store** n magazine m (BR), grande armazém m (PT)

departure [dɪˈpɑːtʃəʳ] n partida, ida; (of train etc) saída; (of employee) saída; **a new ~** uma nova orientação; **departure lounge** n sala de embarque

depend [dɪˈpɛnd] vi: **to ~ (up)on** depender de; (rely on) contar com; **it ~s** depende; **~ing on the result ...** dependendo do resultado ...; **dependant** n dependente m/f; **dependent** adj: **to be dependent (on)** depender (de), ser dependente (de) ▷ n = **dependant**

depict [dɪˈpɪkt] vt (in picture) retratar, representar; (describe) descrever

deport [dɪˈpɔːt] vt deportar

deposit [dɪˈpɔzɪt] n (Comm, Geo) depósito; (Chem) sedimento; (of ore, oil) jazida; (down payment) sinal m ▷ vt depositar; (luggage) guardar; **deposit account** n conta de depósito a prazo

depot [ˈdɛpɘu] n (storehouse) depósito, armazém m; (for vehicles) garagem f, parque m; (US) estação f

depress [dɪˈprɛs] vt deprimir; (press down) apertar; **depressed** adj deprimido; (area, market, trade) em depressão; **depressing** adj deprimente; **depression** n depressão f; (hollow) achatamento

deprive [dɪˈpraɪv] vt: **to ~ sb of**

privar alguém de; **deprived** adj carente

depth [dɛpθ] n profundidade f; (of feeling) intensidade f; **in the ~s of despair** no auge do desespero; **to be out of one's ~** (Brit: swimmer) estar sem pé; (fig) estar voando

deputy ['dɛpjutɪ] adj: **~ chairman** vice-presidente(-a) m/f ▷ n (assistant) ajunto, suplente m/f; (Pol: MP) deputado(-a)

derail [dɪ'reɪl] vt: **to be ~ed** descarrilhar

derelict ['dɛrɪlɪkt] adj abandonado

derive [dɪ'raɪv] vt: **to ~ (from)** obter or tirar (de) ▷ vi: **to ~ from** derivar-se de

descend [dɪ'sɛnd] vt, vi descer; **to ~ from** descer de; **to ~ to** descambar em; **descent** n descida; (origin) descendência

describe [dɪs'kraɪb] vt descrever; **description** [dɪs'krɪpʃən] n descrição f; (sort) classe f, espécie f

desert [n 'dɛzət, vt, vi dɪ'zə:t] n deserto ▷ vt (place) desertar; (partner, family) abandonar ▷ vi (Mil) desertar

deserve [dɪ'zə:v] vt merecer

design [dɪ'zaɪn] n (sketch) desenho, esboço; (layout, shape) plano, projeto; (pattern) desenho, padrão m; (art) design m; (intention) propósito, intenção f ▷ vt (plan) projetar

designer [dɪ'zaɪnə^r] n (Art) artista m/f gráfico(-a); (Tech) desenhista m/f, projetista m/f; (fashion designer) estilista m/f

desire [dɪ'zaɪə^r] n anseio; (sexual) desejo ▷ vt querer, desejar, cobiçar

desk [dɛsk] n (in office) mesa, secretária; (for pupil) carteira f; (at airport) balcão m; (in hotel)

recepção f; (Brit: in shop, restaurant) caixa

despair [dɪs'pɛə^r] n desesperança ▷ vi: **to ~ of** desesperar-se de

despatch [dɪs'pætʃ] n, vt = **dispatch**

desperate ['dɛspərɪt] adj desesperado; (situation) desesperador(a); **to be ~ for sth/ to do** estar louco por algo/para fazer; **desperately** adv desesperadamente; (very: unhappy) terrívelmente; (: ill) gravemente; **desperation** [dɛspə'reɪʃən] n desespero, desesperança; **in (sheer) desperation** desesperado

despise [dɪs'paɪz] vt desprezar

despite [dɪs'paɪt] prep apesar de, a despeito de

dessert [dɪ'zə:t] n sobremesa

destination [dɛstɪ'neɪʃən] n destino

destined ['dɛstɪnd] adj: **to be ~ to do sth** estar destinado a fazer algo; **~ for** com destino a

destiny ['dɛstɪnɪ] n destino

destroy [dɪs'trɔɪ] vt destruir; (animal) sacrificar; **destruction** n destruição f

detach [dɪ'tætʃ] vt separar; (unstick) desprender; **detached** adj (attitude) imparcial, objetivo; (house) independente, isolado

detail ['di:teɪl] n detalhe m; (trifle) bobagem f ▷ vt detalhar; **in ~** pormenorizado, em detalhe

detain [dɪ'teɪn] vt deter; (in captivity) prender; (in hospital) hospitalizar

detect [dɪ'tɛkt] vt perceber; (Med, Police) identificar; (Mil, Radar, Tech) detectar; **detection** n descoberta; **detective** n detetive m/f; **detective story** n romance m policial

detention [dɪ'tɛnʃən] n detenção f,
prisão f; (Sch) castigo
deter [dɪ'təː'] vt (discourage)
desanimar; (dissuade) dissuadir
detergent [dɪ'təːdʒənt] n
detergente m
deteriorate [dɪ'tɪərɪəreɪt] vi
deteriorar-se
determine [dɪ'təːmɪn] vt
descobrir; (limits etc) demarcar;
determined adj (person) resoluto;
determined to do decidido a fazer
detour ['diːtuə'] n desvio
detract [dɪ'trækt] vi: **to ~ from**
diminuir
detrimental [dɛtrɪ'mɛntl] adj:
~ (to) prejudicial (a)
develop [dɪ'vɛləp] vt desenvolver;
(Phot) revelar; (disease) contrair;
(resources) explotar ▷ vi (advance)
progredir; (evolve) evoluir;
(appear) aparecer; **development**
[dɪ'vɛləpmənt] n desenvolvimento;
(advance) progresso; (of land)
urbanização f
device [dɪ'vaɪs] n aparelho,
dispositivo
devil ['dɛvl] n diabo
devious ['diːvɪəs] adj (person)
malandro, esperto
devise [dɪ'vaɪz] vt (plan) criar;
(machine) inventar
devote [dɪ'vəut] vt: **to ~ sth to**
dedicar algo a; **devoted** [dɪ'vəutɪd]
adj (friendship) leal; (partner) fiel; **to
be devoted to** estar devotado a;
the book is devoted to politics o
livro trata de política; **devotion** n
devoção f; (to duty) dedicação f
devour [dɪ'vauə'] vt devorar
devout [dɪ'vaut] adj devoto
dew [djuː] n orvalho
diabetes [daɪə'biːtiːz] n diabete f
diagnosis [daɪəg'nəusɪs] (pl

diagnoses) n diagnóstico
diagonal [daɪ'ægənl] adj diagonal
▷ n diagonal f
diagram ['daɪəgræm] n diagrama
m, esquema m
dial ['daɪəl] n disco ▷ vt (number)
discar (BR), marcar (PT)
dial code (US) n = **dialling code**
dialect ['daɪəlɛkt] n dialeto
dialling code ['daɪəlɪŋ-] (Brit) n
código de discagem
dialling tone ['daɪəlɪŋ-] (Brit) n
sinal m de discagem (BR) or de
marcar (PT)
dialogue ['daɪəlɔg], (US) **dialog** n
diálogo; (conversation) conversa
diameter [daɪ'æmɪtə'] n diâmetro
diamond ['daɪəmənd] n diamante
m; (shape) losango, rombo;
diamonds npl (Cards) ouros mpl
diarrhoea [daɪə'rɪːə], (US)
diarrhea n diarreia
diary ['daɪərɪ] n (daily account)
diário; (engagements book) agenda
dice [daɪs] n inv dado ▷ vt (Culin)
cortar em cubos
dictate [dɪk'teɪt] vt ditar;
dictation n ditado
dictator [dɪk'teɪtə'] n ditador(a) m/f
dictionary ['dɪkʃənrɪ] n dicionário
did [dɪd] pt of **do**
didn't ['dɪdnt] = **did not**
die [daɪ] n, vi morrer; (fig: fade)
murchar; **to be dying for sth/to
do sth** estar louco por algo/para
fazer algo **die away** vi (sound,
light) extinguir-se lentamente **die
down** vi (fire) apagar-se; (wind)
abrandar; (excitement) diminuir **die
out** vi desaparecer
diesel ['diːzl] n diesel m; (also:
~ fuel, ~ oil) óleo diesel
diet ['daɪət] n dieta; (restricted food)
regime m ▷ vi (also: **be on a ~**) estar

de dieta, fazer regime

differ ['dɪfər] vi (be different): **to ~ from sth** ser diferente de algo, diferenciar-se de algo; (disagree): **to ~ (about)** discordar (sobre); **difference** n diferença; (disagreement) divergência; **different** adj diferente; **differentiate** [dɪfə'rɛnʃɪeɪt] vi: **to differentiate (between)** distinguir (entre)

difficult ['dɪfɪkəlt] adj difícil; **difficulty** n dificuldade f

dig [dɪg] (pt, pp **dug**) vt cavar ▷ n (prod) pontada; (archaeological) escavação f; (remark) alfinetada; **to ~ one's nails into** cravar as unhas em **dig into** vt fus (savings) gastar **dig up** vt (plant) arrancar; (information) trazer à tona

digest [vt daɪ'dʒɛst, n 'daɪdʒɛst] vt (food) digerir; (facts) assimilar ▷ n sumário; **digestion** [dɪ'dʒɛstʃən] n digestão f

digit ['dɪdʒɪt] n (Math) dígito; (finger) dedo; **digital** adj digital; **digital camera** n câmara digital **digital TV** n televisão f digital

dignified ['dɪgnɪfaɪd] adj digno

dignity ['dɪgnɪtɪ] n dignidade f

dilemma [daɪ'lɛmə] n dilema m

dilute [daɪ'luːt] vt diluir

dim [dɪm] adj fraco; (outline) indistinto; (room) escuro; (inf: person) burro ▷ vt diminuir; (US: Aut) baixar

dime [daɪm] (US) n (moeda de) dez centavos

dimension [dɪ'mɛnʃən] n dimensão f; (measurement) medida; (also: ~s: scale, size) tamanho

diminish [dɪ'mɪnɪʃ] vi diminuir

din [dɪn] n zoeira

dine [daɪn] vi jantar; **diner** n comensal m/f; (US: eating place) lanchonete f

dinghy ['dɪŋgɪ] n dingue m, bote m; **rubber ~** bote de borracha

dingy ['dɪndʒɪ] adj (room) sombrio, lúgubre; (clothes, curtains etc) sujo

dining car ['daɪnɪŋ-] (Brit) n (Rail) vagão-restaurante m

dining room ['daɪnɪŋ-] n sala de jantar

dinner ['dɪnər] n (evening meal) jantar m; (lunch) almoço; (banquet) banquete m; **dinner jacket** n smoking m; **dinner party** n jantar m; **dinner time** n (midday) hora de almoçar; (evening) hora de jantar

dip [dɪp] n (slope) inclinação f; (in sea) mergulho; (Culin) pasta para servir com salgadinhos ▷ vt (in water) mergulhar; (ladle etc) meter; (Brit: Aut: lights) baixar ▷ vi descer subitamente

diploma [dɪ'pləumə] n diploma m

diplomat ['dɪpləmæt] n diplomata m/f

dipstick ['dɪpstɪk] n (Aut) vareta medidora

dire [daɪər] adj terrível

direct [daɪ'rɛkt] adj direto; (route) reto; (manner) franco, sincero ▷ vt dirigir; (order): **to ~ sb to do sth** ordenar alguém para fazer algo ▷ adv direto; **can you ~ me to ...?** pode me indicar o caminho a ...?; **direction** [dɪ'rɛkʃən] n (way) indicação f; (TV, Radio, Cinema) direção f; **directions** npl (instructions) instruções fpl; **directions for use** modo de usar; **directly** adv diretamente; (at once) imediatamente; **director** n diretor(a) m/f

directory [dɪ'rɛktərɪ] n (Tel) lista (telefônica); (Comm) anuário comercial; (Comput) diretório;

directory enquiries, (*US*)
directory assistance n (serviço
de) informações *fpl*
dirt [dəːt] n sujeira (*BR*), sujidade
(*PT*); **dirty** adj sujo; (*joke*)
indecente ▷ vt sujar
disability [dɪsə'bɪlɪtɪ] n
incapacidade *f*
disabled [dɪs'eɪbld] adj deficiente
▷ npl: **the ~** os deficientes
disadvantage [dɪsəd'vɑːntɪdʒ] n
desvantagem *f*; (*prejudice*)
inconveniente *m*
disagree [dɪsə'griː] vi (*differ*) diferir;
(*be against, think otherwise*): **to ~
(with)** não concordar (com),
discordar (de); **disagreeable** adj
desagradável; **disagreement** n
desacordo; (*quarrel*) desavença
disappear [dɪsə'pɪəʳ] vi
desaparecer, sumir; (*custom etc*)
acabar; **disappearance** n
desaparecimento, desaparição *f*
disappoint [dɪsə'pɔɪnt] vt
decepcionar; **disappointed** adj
decepcionado; **disappointment** n
decepção *f*; (*cause*)
desapontamento
disapproval [dɪsə'pruːvəl] n
desaprovação *f*
disapprove [dɪsə'pruːv] vi: **to ~ of**
desaprovar
disarmament n desarmamento
disaster [dɪ'zɑːstəʳ] n (*accident*)
desastre *m*; (*natural*) catástrofe *f*
disbelief [dɪsbə'liːf] n
incredulidade *f*
disc [dɪsk] n disco; (*Comput*) = **disk**
discard [dɪs'kɑːd] vt (*old things*)
desfazer-se de; (*fig*) descartar
discharge [vt dɪs'tʃɑːdʒ, n
'dɪstʃɑːdʒ] vt (*duties*) cumprir,
desempenhar; (*patient*) dar alta a;
(*employee*) despedir; (*soldier*) dar

baixa em, dispensar; (*defendant*)
pôr em liberdade; (*waste etc*)
descarregar, despejar ▷ n (*Elec*)
descarga; (*dismissal*) despedida; (*of
duty*) desempenho; (*of debt*)
quitação *f*; (*from hospital*) alta;
(*from army*) baixa; (*Law*) absolvição
f; (*Med*) secreção *f*
discipline ['dɪsɪplɪn] n disciplina
▷ vt disciplinar; (*punish*) punir
disc jockey n (*on radio*) radialista
m/f; (*in discotheque*)
discotecário(-a)
disclose [dɪs'kləuz] vt revelar
disco ['dɪskəu] n abbr
= **discotheque**
discomfort [dɪs'kʌmfət] n (*unease*)
inquietação *f*; (*physical*)
desconforto
disconnect [dɪskə'nɛkt] vt
desligar; (*pipe, tap*) desmembrar
discontent [dɪskən'tɛnt] n
descontentamento
discontinue [dɪskən'tɪnjuː] vt
interromper; (*payments*)
suspender; **"~d"** (*Comm*) "fora de
linha"
discotheque ['dɪskəutɛk] n
discoteca
discount [n 'dɪskaunt, vt
dɪs'kaunt] n desconto ▷ vt
descontar; (*idea*) ignorar
discourage [dɪs'kʌrɪdʒ] vt
(*dishearten*) desanimar; (*advise
against*): **to ~ sth/sb from doing**
desaconselhar algo/alguém a fazer
discover [dɪs'kʌvəʳ] vt descobrir;
(*missing person*) encontrar;
(*mistake*) achar; **discovery** n
descoberta
discredit [dɪs'krɛdɪt] vt
desacreditar; (*claim*) desmerecer
discreet [dɪ'skriːt] adj discreto;
(*careful*) cauteloso

discrepancy [dɪ'skrɛpənsɪ] n diferença

discretion [dɪ'skrɛʃən] n discrição f; **at the ~ of** ao arbérito de

discriminate [dɪ'skrɪmɪneɪt] vi: **to ~ between** fazer distinção entre; **to ~ against** discriminar contra; **discrimination** [dɪskrɪmɪ'neɪʃən] n (discernment) discernimento; (bias) discriminação f

discuss [dɪ'skʌs] vt discutir; (analyse) analisar; **discussion** n discussão f; (debate) debate m

disease [dɪ'ziːz] n doença

disembark [dɪsɪm'bɑːk] vt, vi desembarcar

disgrace [dɪs'greɪs] n ignomínia; (shame) desonra ▷ vt (family) envergonhar; (name, country) desonrar; **disgraceful** adj vergonhoso; (behaviour) escandaloso

disgruntled [dɪs'grʌntld] adj descontente

disguise [dɪs'gaɪz] n disfarce m ▷ vt: **to ~ o.s. (as)** disfarçar-se (de); **in ~** disfarçado

disgust [dɪs'gʌst] n repugnância ▷ vt repugnar a, dar nojo em; **disgusting** adj repugnante; (unacceptable) inaceitável

dish [dɪʃ] n prato; (serving dish) travessa; **to do** or **wash the ~es** lavar os pratos or a louça **dish out** vt repartir **dish up** vt servir; **dishcloth** n pano de prato or de louça

dishonest [dɪs'ɒnɪst] adj (person) desonesto; (means) fraudulento

dishwasher ['dɪʃwɒʃəʳ] n máquina de lavar louça or pratos

disillusion [dɪsɪ'luːʒən] vt desiludir

disinfectant [dɪsɪn'fɛktənt] n desinfetante m

disintegrate [dɪs'ɪntɪgreɪt] vi desintegrar-se

disk [dɪsk] n (Comput) disco; (removable) disquete m; **disk drive** n unidade f de disco; **diskette** [dɪs'kɛt] (US) n (Comput) disquete m

dislike [dɪs'laɪk] n desagrado ▷ vt antipatizar com, não gostar de

dislocate ['dɪsləkeɪt] vt deslocar

disloyal [dɪs'lɔɪəl] adj desleal

dismal ['dɪzml] adj (depressing) deprimente; (very bad) horrível

dismantle [dɪs'mæntl] vt desmontar, desmantelar

dismay [dɪs'meɪ] n consternação f ▷ vt consternar

dismiss [dɪs'mɪs] vt (worker) despedir; (pupils) dispensar; (soldiers) dar baixa a; (Law, possibility) rejeitar; **dismissal** n demissão f; **disobedient** adj desobediente

disobey [dɪsə'beɪ] vt desobedecer a; (rules) transgredir

disorder [dɪs'ɔːdəʳ] n desordem f; (rioting) distúrbios mpl, tumulto; (Med) distúrbio

disown [dɪs'əun] vt repudiar; (child) rejeitar

dispatch [dɪs'pætʃ] vt (send: parcel etc) expedir; (: messenger) enviar ▷ n (sending) remessa, urgência; (Press) comunicado; (Mil) parte f

dispel [dɪs'pɛl] vt dissipar

dispense [dɪs'pɛns] vt (medicine) preparar (e vender) **dispense with** vt fus prescindir de; **dispenser** n (device) distribuidor m automático

disperse [dɪs'pəːs] vt espalhar; (crowd) dispersar ▷ vi dispersar-se

display [dɪs'pleɪ] n (in shop) mostra; (exhibition) exposição f; (Comput: information) apresentação f visual; (: device) display m; (of feeling) manifestação f ▷ vt mostrar; (*ostentatiously*) ostentar

displease [dɪs'pliːz] vt (*offend*) ofender; (*annoy*) aborrecer

disposable [dɪs'pəuzəbl] adj descartável; (*income*) disponível

disposal [dɪs'pəuzl] n (*of rubbish*) destruição f; (*of property etc*) venda, traspasse m; **at sb's ~** à disposição de alguém; **disposition** [dɪspə'zɪʃən] n disposição f; (*temperament*) índole f

dispute [dɪs'pjuːt] n (*domestic*) briga; (*also*: **industrial ~**) conflito, disputa ▷ vt disputar; (*question*) questionar

disqualify [dɪs'kwɔlɪfaɪ] vt (*Sport*) desclassificar; **to ~ sb for sth/ from doing sth** desqualificar alguém para algo/de fazer algo

disregard [dɪsrɪ'gɑːd] vt ignorar

disrupt [dɪs'rʌpt] vt (*plans*) desfazer; (*conversation, proceedings*) perturbar, interromper

dissect [dɪ'sɛkt] vt dissecar

dissent [dɪ'sɛnt] n dissensão f

dissertation [dɪsə'teɪʃən] n (*also*: *Sch*) dissertação f, tese f

dissolve [dɪ'zɔlv] vt dissolver ▷ vi dissolver-se; **to ~ in(to) tears** debulhar-se em lágrimas

distance ['dɪstns] n distância; **in the ~** ao longe

distant ['dɪstnt] adj distante; (*manner*) afastado, reservado

distil [dɪs'tɪl], (*US*) **distill** vt destilar; **distillery** n destilaria

distinct [dɪs'tɪŋkt] adj distinto; (*clear*) claro; (*unmistakable*) nítido; **as ~ from** em oposição a; **distinction** n diferença; (*honour*) honra; (*in exam*) distinção f

distinguish [dɪs'tɪŋgwɪʃ] vt (*differentiate*) diferenciar; (*identify*) identificar; **to ~ o.s.** distinguir-se; **distinguished** adj (*eminent*) eminente; (*in appearance*) distinto

distort [dɪs'tɔːt] vt distorcer

distract [dɪs'trækt] vt distrair; (*attention*) desviar; **distracted** adj distraído; (*anxious*) aturdido; **distraction** n distração f; (*confusion*) aturdimento, perplexidade f; (*amusement*) divertimento

distraught [dɪs'trɔːt] adj desesperado

distress [dɪs'trɛs] n angústia ▷ vt afligir; **distressing** adj angustiante

distribute [dɪs'trɪbjuːt] vt distribuir; (*share out*) repartir, dividir; **distribution** [dɪstrɪ'bjuːʃən] n distribuição f; (*of profits etc*) repartição f; **distributor** n (*Aut*) distribuidor m; (*Comm*) distribuidor(a) m/f

district ['dɪstrɪkt] n (*of country*) região f; (*of town*) zona; (*Admin*) distrito; **district attorney** (*US*) n promotor(a) m/f público(-a)

distrust [dɪs'trʌst] n desconfiança ▷ vt desconfiar de

disturb [dɪs'təːb] vt (*disorganize*) perturbar; (*upset*) incomodar; (*interrupt*) atrapalhar; **disturbance** n (*upheaval*) convulsão f; (*political, violent*) distúrbio; (*of mind*) transtorno; **disturbed** adj perturbado; (*child*) infeliz; **to be mentally/ emotionally disturbed** ter problemas psicológicos/ emocionais; **disturbing** adj perturbador(a)

ditch [dɪtʃ] n fosso; (*irrigation ditch*) rego ▷ vt (*inf: partner*) abandonar; (: *car, plan etc*) desfazer-se de

ditto ['dɪtəu] *adv* idem
dive [daɪv] *n* (*from board*) salto; (*underwater, of submarine*) mergulho ▷ *vi* mergulhar; **to ~ into** (*bag, drawer etc*) enfiar a mão em; (*shop, car etc*) enfiar-se em; **diver** *n* mergulhador(a) *m/f*
diversion [daɪ'vəːʃən] *n* (*Brit: Aut*) desvio; (*distraction, Mil*) diversão *f*; (*of funds*) desvio
divert [daɪ'vəːt] *vt* desviar
divide [dɪ'vaɪd] *vt* (*Math*) dividir; (*separate*) separar; (*share out*) repartir ▷ *vi* dividir-se; (*road*) bifurcar-se; **divided highway** (*US*) *n* pista dupla
divine [dɪ'vaɪn] *adj* (*also fig*) divino
diving ['daɪvɪŋ] *n* salto; (*underwater*) mergulho; **diving board** *n* trampolim *m*
division [dɪ'vɪʒən] *n* divisão *f*; (*sharing out*) repartição *f*; (*disagreement*) discórdia; (*Football*) grupo
divorce [dɪ'vɔːs] *n* divórcio ▷ *vt* divorciar-se de; (*dissociate*) dissociar; **divorced** *adj* divorciado; **divorcee** *n* divorciado(-a)
DIY *n abbr* = **do-it-yourself**
dizzy ['dɪzɪ] *adj* tonto
DJ *n abbr* = **disc jockey**

 KEYWORD

do [duː] (*pt* **did**, *pp* **done**) *aux vb* **1** (*in negative constructions*): **I don't understand** eu não compreendo **2** (*to form questions*): **didn't you know?** você não sabia?; **what do you think?** o que você acha? **3** (*for emphasis, in polite expressions*): **she does seem rather late** ela está muito atrasada; **do sit down/ help yourself** sente-se/sirva-se;

do take care! tome cuidado!
4 (*used to avoid repeating vb*): **she swims better than I do** ela nada melhor que eu; **do you agree? — yes, I do/no, I don't** você concorda? — sim, concordo/ não, não concordo; **she lives in Glasgow — so do I** ela mora em Glasgow — eu também; **who broke it? — I did** quem quebrou isso? — (fui) eu
5 (*in question tags*): **you like him, don't you?** você gosta dele, não é?; **he laughed, didn't he?** ele riu, não foi?
▷ *vt* **1** (*gen: carry out, perform etc*) fazer; **what are you doing tonight?** o que você vai fazer hoje à noite?; **to do the washing-up/ cooking** lavar a louça/cozinhar; **to do one's teeth/nails** escovar os dentes/fazer as unhas; **to do one's hair** (*comb*) pentear-se; (*style*) fazer um penteado; **we're doing Othello at school** (*studying*) nós estamos estudando Otelo na escola; (*performing*) nós vamos encenar Otelo na escola
2 (*Aut etc*): **the car was doing 190** o carro andava a 190 por hora; **we've done 200 km already** já percorremos 200 km; **he can do 190 km/h in that car** ele consegue chegar a 190 km/h naquele carro
▷ *vi* **1** (*act, behave*) fazer; **do as I do** faça como eu faço
2 (*get on, fare*) ir; **how do you do?** como você está indo?
3 (*suit*) servir; **will it do?** serve?
4 (*be sufficient*) bastar; **will £10 do?** £10 dá?; **that'll do** é suficiente; **that'll do!** (*in annoyance*) basta!, chega!; **to make do (with)** contentar-se (com) ▷ *n* (*inf: party*

etc) festa; **it was rather a do** foi uma festança
do away with *vt fus* (*kill*) matar; (*law etc*) abolir; (*withdraw*) retirar
do up *vt* (*laces*) atar; (*zip*) fechar; (*dress, skirt*) abotoar; (*renovate: room, house*) arrumar, renovar
do with *vt fus* (*be connected*) ter a ver com; (*need*): **I could do with a drink/some help** eu bem que gostaria de tomar alguma coisa/eu bem que precisaria de uma ajuda; **what has it got to do with you?** o que é que isso tem a ver com você?
do without *vi*: **if you're late for tea then you'll do without** se você chegar atrasado ficará sem almoço
▷ *vt fus* passar sem

dock [dɔk] *n* (*Naut*) doca; (*Law*) banco (dos réus) ▷ *vi* (*Naut: enter dock*) atracar; (*Space*) unir-se no espaço; **docks** *npl* docas *fpl*
doctor ['dɔktəʳ] *n* médico(-a); (*PhD etc*) doutor(a) *m/f* ▷ *vt* (*drink etc*) falsificar
document ['dɔkjumənt] *n* documento; **documentary** [dɔkju'mɛntərɪ] *adj* documental ▷ *n* documentário
dodge [dɔdʒ] *n* (*trick*) trapaça ▷ *vt* esquivar-se de, evitar; (*tax*) sonegar; (*blow*) furtar-se a
does [dʌz] *vb see* **do**
doesn't ['dʌznt] = **does not**
dog [dɔg] *n* cachorro, cão *m* ▷ *vt* (*subj: person*) seguir; (: *bad luck*) perseguir; **doggy bag** ['dɔgɪ-] *n* quentinha
do-it-yourself *n* sistema *m* faça-você-mesmo
dole [dəul] (*Brit*) *n* (*payment*) subsídio de desemprego; **on the ~**

desempregado **dole out** *vt* distribuir
doll [dɔl] *n* boneca; (*US: inf: woman*) gatinha
dollar ['dɔləʳ] *n* dólar *m*
dolphin ['dɔlfɪn] *n* golfinho
dome [dəum] *n* (*Arch*) cúpula
domestic [də'mɛstɪk] *adj* doméstico; (*national*) nacional
dominate ['dɔmɪneɪt] *vt* dominar
domino ['dɔmɪnəu] (*pl* **dominoes**) *n* peça de dominó; **dominoes** *n* (*game*) dominó *m*
donate [də'neɪt] *vt* doar
done [dʌn] *pp of* **do**
donkey ['dɔŋkɪ] *n* burro
donor ['dəunəʳ] *n* doador(a) *m/f*; **donor card** *n* cartão *m* de doador
don't [dəunt] = **do not**
doodle ['du:dl] *vi* rabiscar
doom [du:m] *n* (*fate*) destino ▷ *vt*: **to be ~ed to failure** estar destinado *or* fadado ao fracasso
door [dɔ:ʳ] *n* porta; **doorbell** *n* campainha; **doorstep** *n* degrau da porta, soleira; **doorway** *n* vão *m* da porta, entrada
dope [dəup] *n* (*inf: person*) imbecil *m/f*; (: *drugs*) maconha ▷ *vt* (*horse etc*) dopar
dormitory ['dɔ:mɪtrɪ] *n* dormitório; (*US*) residência universitária
dose [dəus] *n* dose *f*
dot [dɔt] *n* ponto; (*speck*) pontinho ▷ *vt*: **~ted with** salpicado de; **on the ~** em ponto
dotcom [dɔt'kɔm] *n* empresa pontocom
double ['dʌbl] *adj* duplo ▷ *adv* (*twice*): **to cost ~ (sth)** custar o dobro (de algo) ▷ *n* (*person*) duplo(-a) ▷ *vt* dobrar ▷ *vi* dobrar; **at the ~** (*Brit*), **on the ~** em passo acelerado; **double bass** *n*

contrabaixo; **double bed** n cama de casal; **double-click** vi (Comput) clicar duas vezes; **double-decker** [dʌbl'dɛkə^r] n ônibus m (BR) or autocarro (PT) de dois andares; **double room** n quarto de casal

doubt [daut] n dúvida ▷ vt duvidar; (suspect) desconfiar de; **to ~ that ...** duvidar que ...; **doubtful** adj duvidoso; **doubtless** adv sem dúvida

dough [dəu] n massa; **doughnut**, (US) **donut** n sonho (BR), bola de Berlim (PT)

dove [dʌv] n pomba

down [daun] n (feathers) penugem f ▷ adv (downwards) para baixo; (on the ground) por terra ▷ prep por, abaixo ▷ vt (inf: drink) tomar de um gole só; **~ with X!** abaixo X!; **down-and-out** n (tramp) vagabundo(-a); **downfall** n queda, ruína; **downhill** adv para baixo ▷ n (Ski: also: **downhill race**) descida; **to go downhill** descer, ir morro abaixo; (fig: business) degringolar

Downing Street ['daunɪŋ-] (Brit) n ver nota

DOWNING STREET

Downing Street é a rua de Westminster (Londres) onde estão localizadas as residências oficiais do Primeiro-ministro (número 10) e do Ministro da Fazenda (número 11). O termo **Downing Street** é frequentemente utilizado para designar o governo britânico.

down: download ['daunləud] vt (Comput) baixar, fazer o download

de; **downloadable** adj (Comput) baixável; **downright** adj (lie) patente; (refusal) categórico; **downstairs** adv (below) lá em baixo; (direction) para baixo; **down-to-earth** adj prático, realista; **downtown** adv no centro da cidade; **down under** adv na Austrália (or Nova Zelândia); **downward** ['daunwəd] adj, adv para baixo; **downwards** adv = **downward**

doze [dəuz] vi dormitar **doze off** vi cochilar

dozen ['dʌzn] n dúzia; **a ~ books** uma dúzia de livros; **~s of times** milhares de vezes

drab [dræb] adj sombrio

draft [drɑːft] n (first copy) rascunho; (Pol: of bill) projeto de lei; (bank draft) saque m, letra; (US: call-up) recrutamento ▷ vt (plan) esboçar; (speech, letter) rascunhar; see also **draught**

drag [dræg] vt arrastar; (river) dragar ▷ vi arrastar-se ▷ n (inf) chatice f (BR), maçada (PT); (women's clothing): **in ~** em travesti **drag on** vi arrastar-se

dragon ['drægən] n dragão m

dragonfly ['drægənflaɪ] n libélula

drain [dreɪn] n bueiro; (source of loss) sorvedouro ▷ vt drenar; (vegetables) coar ▷ vi (water) escorrer, escoar-se; **drainage** n (act) drenagem f; (system) esgoto; **drainpipe** n cano de esgoto

drama ['drɑːmə] n (art) teatro; (play, event) drama m; **dramatic** [drə'mætɪk] adj dramático; (theatrical) teatral

drank [dræŋk] pt of **drink**

drape [dreɪp] vt ornar, cobrir

drastic ['dræstɪk] adj drástico

draught [drɑːft], (US) **draft** n (of
air) corrente f; (Naut) calado; (beer)
chope m; **on ~** (beer) de barril;
draughts (Brit) n (jogo de) damas
fpl

draw [drɔː] (pt **drew**, pp **drawn**) vt
desenhar; (cart) puxar; (curtain)
fechar; (gun) sacar; (attract) atrair;
(money) tirar; (: from bank) sacar ▷ vi
empatar ▷ n empate m; (lottery)
sorteio; **to ~ near** aproximar-se
draw out vt (money) sacar **draw
up** vi (stop) parar(-se) ▷ vt (chair
etc) aproximar; (document) redigir;
drawback n inconveniente m,
desvantagem f; **drawer** n gaveta;
drawing n desenho; **drawing pin**
(Brit) n tachinha (BR), pionés m
(PT); **drawing room** n sala de
visitas

drawn [drɔːn] pp of **draw**

dread [drɛd] n medo, pavor m ▷ vt
temer, recear, ter medo de;
dreadful adj terrível

dream [driːm] (pt, pp **dreamed** or
dreamt) n sonho ▷ vt, vi sonhar

dreary ['drɪərɪ] adj (talk, time)
monótono; (weather) sombrio

drench [drɛntʃ] vt encharcar

dress [drɛs] n vestido; (no pl:
clothing) traje m ▷ vt vestir;
(wound) fazer curativo em ▷ vi
vestir-se; **to get ~ed** vestir-se
dress up vi vestir-se com
elegância; (in fancy dress)
fantasiar-se; **dress circle** (Brit) n
balcão m nobre; **dresser** n (Brit:
cupboard) aparador m; (US: chest of
drawers) cômoda de espelho;
dressing n (Med) curativo; (Culin)
molho; **dressing gown** (Brit) n
roupão m; (woman's) peignoir m;
dressing room n (Theatre)
camarim m; (Sport) vestiário;

dressing table n penteadeira
(BR), toucador m (PT); **dressmaker**
n costureiro(-a)

drew [druː] pt of **draw**

dribble ['drɪbl] vi (baby) babar ▷ vt
(ball) driblar

dried [draɪd] adj seco; (eggs, milk)
em pó

drier ['draɪəʳ] n = **dryer**

drift [drɪft] n (of current etc) força;
(of snow, sand etc) monte m;
(meaning) sentido ▷ vi (boat)
derivar; (sand, snow) amontoar-se

drill [drɪl] n furadeira; (bit, of
dentist) broca; (for mining etc) broca,
furadeira; (Mil) exercícios mpl
militares ▷ vt furar, brocar; (Mil)
exercitar ▷ vi (for oil) perfurar

drink [drɪŋk] (pt **drank**, pp **drunk**) n
bebida ▷ vt, vi beber; **a ~ of water**
um copo d'água; **drinker** n
bebedor(a) m/f; **drinking water** n
água potável

drip [drɪp] n gotejar m; (one drip)
gota, pingo; (Med) gota a gota m
▷ vi gotejar, pingar

drive [draɪv] (pt **drove**, pp **driven**) n
passeio (de automóvel); (journey)
trajeto, percurso; (also: **~way**)
entrada; (energy) energia, vigor m;
(campaign) campanha; (Comput)
drive m ▷ vt (car) dirigir (BR), guiar
(PT); (push) empurrar; (Tech: motor)
acionar; (nail): **to ~ sth into** cravar
algo em ▷ vi (Aut: at controls) dirigir
(BR), guiar (PT); (: travel) ir de carro;
left-/right-hand ~ direção à
esquerda/direita; **to ~ sb mad**
deixar alguém louco

driver ['draɪvəʳ] n motorista m/f;
(Rail) maquinista m; **driver's
license** (US) n carteira de motorista
(BR), carta de condução (PT)

driveway ['draɪvweɪ] n entrada

driving ['draɪvɪŋ] n direção f (BR), condução f (PT); **driving instructor** n instrutor(a) m/f de autoescola (BR) or de condução (PT); **driving licence** (Brit) n carteira de motorista (BR), carta de condução (PT); **driving test** n exame m de motorista

drizzle ['drɪzl] n chuvisco

droop [dru:p] vi pender

drop [drɔp] n (of water) gota; (lessening) diminuição f; (fall: distance) declive m ▷ vt (allow to fall) deixar cair; (voice, eyes, price) baixar; (set down from car) deixar (saltar/ descer); (omit) omitir ▷ vi cair; (wind) parar; **drops** npl (Med) gotas fpl **drop off** vi (sleep) cochilar ▷ vt (passenger) deixar **drop out** vi (withdraw) retirar-se; **drop-out** n pessoa que abandona o trabalho, os estudos etc

drought [draut] n seca

drove [drəuv] pt of **drive**

drown [draun] vt afogar; (also: ~ out: sound) encobrir ▷ vi afogar-se

drowsy ['drauzɪ] adj sonolento

drug [drʌg] n remédio, medicamento; (narcotic) droga ▷ vt drogar; **to be on ~s** (an addict) estar viciado em drogas; (Med) estar sob medicação; **drug addict** n toxicômano(-a); **druggist** (US) n farmacêutico(-a); **drugstore** (US) n drogaria

drum [drʌm] n tambor m; (for oil, petrol) tambor, barril m; **drums** npl (kit) bateria; **drummer** n baterista m/f

drunk [drʌŋk] pp of **drink** ▷ adj bêbado ▷ n (also: **~ard**) bêbado(-a); **drunken** adj (laughter) de bêbado; (party) com muita bebida; (person) bêbado

dry [draɪ] adj seco; (day) sem chuva; (humour) irônico ▷ vt secar, enxugar; (tears) limpar ▷ vi secar; **dry up** vi secar completamente; **dry-cleaner's** n tinturaria; **dryer** n secador m; (also: **spin-dryer**) secadora

DSS (Brit) n abbr (= Department of Social Security) ≈ INAMPS m

DTP n abbr (= desktop publishing) DTP m

dual ['djuəl] adj dual, duplo; **dual carriageway** (Brit) n pista dupla

dubious ['dju:bɪəs] adj duvidoso; (reputation, company) suspeitoso

duck [dʌk] n pato ▷ vi abaixar-se repentinamente

due [dju:] adj (proper) devido; (expected) esperado ▷ n: **to give sb his** (or **her**) **~** ser justo com alguém ▷ adv: **~ north** exatamente ao norte; **dues** npl (for club, union) quota; (in harbour) direitos mpl; **in ~ course** no devido tempo; (eventually) no final; **~ to** devido a

duet [dju:'ɛt] n dueto

dug [dʌg] pt, pp of **dig**

duke [dju:k] n duque m

dull [dʌl] adj (light) sombrio; (intelligence, wit) lento; (boring) enfadonho; (sound, pain) surdo; (weather, day) nublado, carregado ▷ vt (pain, grief) aliviar; (mind, senses) entorpecer

dumb [dʌm] adj mudo; (pej: stupid) estúpido

dummy ['dʌmɪ] n (tailor's model) manequim m; (mock-up) modelo; (Brit: for baby) chupeta ▷ adj falso

dump [dʌmp] n (also: **rubbish ~**) depósito m; (inf: place) chiqueiro ▷ vt (put down) depositar, descarregar; (get rid of) desfazer-se de

dumpling ['dʌmplɪŋ] n bolinho cozido

dungarees [dʌŋgə'riːz] *npl*
macacão *m* (BR), fato macaco (PT)

dungeon ['dʌndʒən] *n* calabouço

duplex ['djuːplɛks] (US) *n* casa
geminada; (*also*: **~ apartment**)
duplex *m*

duplicate [*n* 'djuːplɪkət, *vt*
'djuːplɪkeɪt] *n* (*of document*)
duplicata; (*of key*) cópia ▷ *vt*
duplicar; (*photocopy*) multigrafar;
(*repeat*) reproduzir

durable ['djuərəbl] *adj* durável;
(*clothes, metal*) resistente

during ['djuərɪŋ] *prep* durante

dusk [dʌsk] *n* crepúsculo, anoitecer *m*

dust [dʌst] *n* pó *m*, poeira ▷ *vt*
(*furniture*) tirar o pó de; (*cake etc*): **to ~
with** polvilhar com; **dustbin** *n* (*Brit*)
lata de lixo; **duster** *n* pano de pó;
dustman (*Brit*) *irreg n* lixeiro, gari *m*
(*BR: inf*); **dusty** *adj* empoeirado

Dutch [dʌtʃ] *adj* holandês(-esa) ▷ *n*
(*Ling*) holandês *m* ▷ *adv*: **let's go ~**
(*inf*) cada um paga o seu, vamos
rachar; **the Dutch** *npl* (*people*) os
holandeses; **Dutchman** *irreg n*
holandês *m*; **Dutchwoman** *irreg n*
holandesa

duty ['djuːtɪ] *n* dever *m*; (*tax*) taxa;
on ~ de serviço; **off ~** de folga;
duty-free *adj* livre de impostos

duvet ['duːveɪ] (*Brit*) *n* edredom *m*
(BR), edredão *m* (PT)

DVD *n abbr* (= *digital versatile or video
disc*) DVD *m*; **DVD burner** *n*
gravador *m* de DVD; **DVD player** *n*
DVD player *m*; **DVD writer** *n*
gravador *m* de DVD

dwarf [dwɔːf] (*pl* **dwarves**) *n* anão/
anã *m/f* ▷ *vt* anicar

dwindle ['dwɪndl] *vi* diminuir

dye [daɪ] *n* tintura, tinta ▷ *vt* tingir

dynamite ['daɪnəmaɪt] *n* dinamite *f*

dyslexia [dɪs'lɛksɪə] *n* dislexia

each [iːtʃ] *adj* cada *inv* ▷ *pron* cada
um(a); **~ other** um ao outro; **they
hate ~ other** (eles) se odeiam,
cada um de nós

eager ['iːgəʳ] *adj* ávido; **to be ~ to
do sth** ansiar por fazer algo; **to be
~ for** ansiar por

eagle ['iːgl] *n* águia

ear [ɪəʳ] *n* (*external*) orelha; (*inner,
fig*) ouvido; (*of corn*) espiga;
earache *n* dor *f* de ouvidos;
eardrum *n* tímpano

earl [əːl] *n* conde *m*

earlier ['əːlɪəʳ] *adj* mais adiantado;
(*edition etc*) anterior ▷ *adv* mais
cedo

early ['əːlɪ] *adv* cedo; (*before time*)
com antecedência ▷ *adj* (*sooner
than expected*) prematuro; (*reply*)
pronto; (*Christians, settlers*)
primeiro; (*man*) primitivo; (*life,
work*) juvenil; **in the ~** *or* **~ in the**

spring/19th century no princípio da primavera/do século dezenove
earmark ['ɪəmɑːk] vt: **to ~ sth for** reservar or destinar algo para
earn [əːn] vt ganhar; (*Comm: interest*) render; (*praise, reward*) merecer
earnest ['əːnɪst] adj (*wish*) intenso; (*manner*) sério; **in ~** a sério
earnings ['əːnɪŋz] npl (*personal*) vencimentos mpl, salário, ordenado; (*of company*) lucro
earphones npl fones mpl de ouvido
earring n brinco
earth [əːθ] n terra; (*Brit: Elec*) fio terra ▷ vt (*Brit: Elec*) ligar à terra; **earthquake** n terremoto (*BR*), terramoto (*PT*)
ease [iːz] n facilidade f; (*relaxed state*) sossego ▷ vt facilitar; (*pain, tension*) aliviar; (*help pass*): **to ~ sth in/out** meter/tirar algo com cuidado; **at ~!** (*Mil*) descansar!
ease off vi acalmar-se; (*wind*) baixar; (*rain*) moderar-se **ease up** vi = **ease off**
easily ['iːzɪlɪ] adv facilmente, fácil (*inf*)
east [iːst] n leste m ▷ adj (*region*) leste; (*wind*) do leste ▷ adv para o leste; **the E~** o Oriente; (*Pol*) o leste
Easter ['iːstəʳ] n Páscoa; **Easter egg** n ovo de Páscoa
eastern ['iːstən] adj do leste, oriental
easy ['iːzɪ] adj fácil; (*comfortable*) folgado, cômodo; (*relaxed*) natural, complacente; (*victim, prey*) desprotegido ▷ adv: **to take it** or **things ~** (*not worry*) levar as coisas com calma; (*go slowly*) ir devagar; (*rest*) descansar; **easy-going** adj pacato, fácil
eat [iːt] (*pt* **ate**, *pp* **eaten**) vt, vi

comer **eat away** vt corroer **eat away at** vt fus corroer **eat into** vt fus = **eat away at**
eavesdrop ['iːvzdrɔp] vi: **to ~ (on)** escutar às escondidas
eccentric [ɪk'sɛntrɪk] adj, n excêntrico(-a)
echo ['ɛkəu] (*pl* **echoes**) n eco ▷ vt ecoar, repetir ▷ vi ressoar, repetir
eclipse [ɪ'klɪps] n eclipse m
eco-friendly [iːkəu'frɛndlɪ] adj ecológico
ecological [iːkə'lɔdʒɪkəl] adj ecológico
ecology [ɪ'kɔlədʒɪ] n ecologia
e-commerce n abbr (= *electronic commerce*) comércio eletrônico
economic [iːkə'nɔmɪk] adj econômico; (*business etc*) rentável; **economical** adj econômico; **economics** n economia ▷ npl aspectos mpl econômicos
economize [ɪ'kɔnəmaɪz] vi economizar, fazer economias
economy [ɪ'kɔnəmɪ] n economia; **economy class** n (*Aviat*) classe f econômica
ecstasy ['ɛkstəsɪ] n êxtase m; **ecstatic** [ɛks'tætɪk] adj extasiado
eczema ['ɛksɪmə] n eczema m
edge [ɛdʒ] n (*of knife etc*) fio; (*of table, chair etc*) borda; (*of lake etc*) margem f ▷ vt (*trim*) embainhar; **on ~** (*fig*) = **edgy**; **to ~ away from** afastar-se pouco a pouco de; **edgy** adj nervoso, inquieto
edible ['ɛdɪbl] adj comestível
Edinburgh ['ɛdɪnbərə] n Edimburgo
edit ['ɛdɪt] vt (*be editor of*) dirigir; (*cut*) cortar, redigir; (*Comput, TV*) editar; (*Cinema*) montar; **edition** [ɪ'dɪʃən] n edição f; **editor** n redator(a) m/f; (*of newspaper*) diretor(a) m/f; (*of book*)

e

organizador(a) *m/f* da edição;
editorial [ɛdɪˈtɔːrɪəl] *adj* editorial
educate [ˈɛdjukeɪt] *vt* educar
education [ɛdjuˈkeɪʃən] *n*
educação *f*; (*schooling*) ensino;
(*science*) pedagogia; **educational**
adj (*policy, experience*) educacional;
(*toy etc*) educativo
eel [iːl] *n* enguia
eerie [ˈɪərɪ] *adj* (*strange*) estranho;
(*mysterious*) misterioso
effect [ɪˈfɛkt] *n* efeito ▷ *vt* (*repairs*)
fazer; (*savings*) efetuar; **to take ~**
(*law*) entrar em vigor; (*drug*) fazer
efeito; **in ~** na realidade; **effective**
[ɪˈfɛktɪv] *adj* eficaz; (*actual*) efetivo
efficiency [ɪˈfɪʃənsɪ] *n* eficiência
efficient [ɪˈfɪʃənt] *adj* eficiente;
(*machine*) rentável
effort [ˈɛfət] *n* esforço; **effortless**
adj fácil
e.g. *adv abbr* (= *exempli gratia*) p. ex.
egg [ɛg] *n* ovo; **hard-boiled/
soft-boiled ~** ovo duro/mole **egg
on** *vt* incitar; **eggcup** *n* oveiro;
eggplant (*esp US*) *n* beringela;
eggshell *n* casca de ovo
ego [ˈiːgəu] *n* ego
Egypt [ˈiːdʒɪpt] *n* Egito; **Egyptian**
[ɪˈdʒɪpʃən] *adj, n* egípcio(-a)
eight [eɪt] *num* oito; **eighteen**
[ˈeɪtiːn] *num* dezoito; **eighteenth**
num décimo oitavo; **eighth** [eɪtθ]
num oitavo; **eightieth** [ˈeɪtɪɪθ]
num octogésimo; **eighty** [ˈeɪtɪ]
num oitenta
Eire [ˈɛərə] *n* (República da) Irlanda
either [ˈaɪðə'] *adj* (*one or other*) um
ou outro; (*each*) cada; (*both*)
ambos ▷ *pron*: **~ (of them)**
qualquer (dos dois) ▷ *adv*: **no,
I don't ~** eu também não ▷ *conj*:
~ yes or no ou sim ou não
eject [ɪˈdʒɛkt] *vt* expulsar

elaborate [*adj* ɪˈlæbərɪt, *vt, vi*
ɪˈlæbəreɪt] *adj* complicado ▷ *vt*
(*expand*) expandir; (*refine*)
aperfeiçoar ▷ *vi*: **to ~ on**
acrescentar detalhes a
elastic [ɪˈlæstɪk] *adj* elástico;
(*adaptable*) flexível, adaptável ▷ *n*
elástico; **elastic band** (*Brit*) *n*
elástico
elbow [ˈɛlbəu] *n* cotovelo
elder [ˈɛldə'] *adj* mais velho ▷ *n*
(*tree*) sabugueiro; (*person*) o/a mais
velho(-a); **elderly** *adj* idoso, de
idade ▷ *npl*: **the elderly** as pessoas
de idade, os idosos
eldest [ˈɛldɪst] *adj* mais velho ▷ *n*
o(-a) mais velho(-a)
elect [ɪˈlɛkt] *vt* eleger ▷ *adj*: **the
president ~** o presidente eleito;
to ~ to do (*choose*) optar por fazer;
election *n* (*voting*) votação *f*;
(*installation*) eleição *f*; **electorate**
n eleitorado
electric [ɪˈlɛktrɪk] *adj* elétrico;
electrical *adj* elétrico; **electric
fire** *n* aquecedor *m* elétrico
electrician [ɪlɛkˈtrɪʃən] *n*
eletricista *m/f*
electricity [ɪlɛkˈtrɪsɪtɪ] *n*
eletricidade *f*
electrify [ɪˈlɛktrɪfaɪ] *vt* (*fence, Rail*)
eletrificar; (*audience*) eletrizar
electronic [ɪlɛkˈtrɔnɪk] *adj*
eletrônico; **electronic mail** *n*
correio eletrônico; **electronics** *n*
eletrônica
elegant [ˈɛlɪgənt] *adj* (*person,
building*) elegante; (*idea*) refinado
element [ˈɛlɪmənt] *n* elemento;
elementary [ɛlɪˈmɛntərɪ] *adj*
(*gen*) elementar; (*primitive*)
rudimentar; (*school, education*)
primário; **elementary school** (*US*)
n ver nota

- ● ELEMENTARY SCHOOL
- ●
- ● Nos Estados Unidos e no Canadá,
- ● uma **elementary school**
- ● (também chamada de *grade*
- ● *school* ou *grammar school* nos
- ● Estados Unidos) é uma escola
- ● pública onde os alunos passam
- ● de seis a oito dos primeiros anos
- ● escolares.

elephant ['ɛlɪfənt] *n* elefante *m*
elevator ['ɛlɪveɪtə'] (*US*) *n* elevador
m
eleven [ɪ'lɛvn] *num* onze; **eleventh**
num décimo-primeiro
eligible ['ɛlɪdʒəbl] *adj* elegível,
apto; **to be ~ for sth** (*job etc*) ter
qualificações para algo
elm [ɛlm] *n* olmo
eloquent ['ɛləkwənt] *adj*
eloquente
El Salvador [el'sælvədɔː'] *n* El
Salvador
else [ɛls] *adv* outro, mais;
something ~ outra coisa; **nobody
~ spoke** ninguém mais falou;
elsewhere *adv* (*be*) em outro lugar
(*BR*), noutro sítio (*PT*); (*go*) para
outro lugar (*BR*), a outro sítio (*PT*)
elusive [ɪ'luːsɪv] *adj* esquivo;
(*quality*) indescritível
email ['iːmeɪl] *n* e-mail *m*, correio
eletrônico ▷ *vt* (*person*) enviar um
e-mail a; **email account** *n* conta
de e-mail, conta de correio
eletrônico; **email address** *n*
e-mail *m*, endereço eletrônico
embark [ɪm'bɑːk] *vi* embarcar ▷ *vt*
embarcar; **to ~ on** (*fig*)
empreender, começar
embarrass [ɪm'bærəs] *vt*
(*politician*) embaraçar; (*emotionally*)
constranger; **embarrassed** *adj*

descomfortável; **embarrassing**
adj embaraçoso,
constrangedor(a);
embarrassment *n* embaraço,
constrangimento
embassy ['ɛmbəsɪ] *n* embaixada
embrace [ɪm'breɪs] *vt* abraçar, dar
um abraço em; (*include*) abarcar,
abranger ▷ *vi* abraçar-se ▷ *n*
abraço
embroider [ɪm'brɔɪdə'] *vt* bordar;
embroidery *n* bordado
emerald ['ɛmərəld] *n* esmeralda
emerge [ɪ'məːdʒ] *vi* sair; (*from
sleep*) acordar; (*fact, idea*) emergir
emergency [ɪ'məːdʒənsɪ] *n*
emergência; **in an ~** em caso de
urgência; **emergency exit** *n* saída
de emergência; **emergency
landing** *n* aterrissagem *f* forçada
(*BR*), aterragem *f* forçosa (*PT*)
emigrate ['ɛmɪgreɪt] *vi* emigrar
eminent ['ɛmɪnənt] *adj* eminente
emit [ɪ'mɪt] *vt* (*smoke*) soltar; (*smell*)
exalar; (*sound*) produzir
emoticon [ɪ'məutɪkən] *n* (*Comput*)
emoticon *m*
emotion [ɪ'məuʃən] *n* emoção *f*;
emotional *adj* (*needs, exhaustion*)
emocional; (*person*) sentimental,
emotivo; (*scene*) comovente; (*tone*)
emocionante
emperor ['ɛmpərə'] *n* imperador *m*
emphasis ['ɛmfəsɪs] (*pl* **emphases**)
n ênfase *f*
emphasize ['ɛmfəsaɪz] *vt* (*word,
point*) enfatizar, acentuar; (*feature*)
salientar
empire ['ɛmpaɪə'] *n* império
employ [ɪm'plɔɪ] *vt* empregar;
(*tool*) utilizar; **employee** *n*
empregado(-a); **employer** *n*
empregador(a) *m/f*, patrão(-troa)
m/f; **employment** *n* (*gen*)

e

emprego; (*work*) trabalho

empress ['ɛmprɪs] *n* imperatriz *f*

emptiness ['ɛmptɪnɪs] *n* vazio, vácuo

empty ['ɛmptɪ] *adj* vazio; (*place*) deserto; (*house*) desocupado; (*threat*) vão/vã ▷ *n, vt* esvaziar; (*place*) evacuar ▷ *vi* esvaziar-se; (*place*) ficar deserto; **empty-handed** *adj* de mãos vazias

emulsion [ɪ'mʌlʃən] *n* emulsão *f*; (*also:* **~ paint**) tinta plástica

enable [ɪ'neɪbl] *vt:* **to ~ sb to do sth** (*allow*) permitir que alguém faça algo; (*prepare*) capacitar alguém para fazer algo

enamel [ɪ'næməl] *n* esmalte *m*

enclose [ɪn'kləuz] *vt* (*land*) cercar; (*with letter etc*) anexar (*BR*), enviar junto (*PT*); **please find ~d** segue junto

enclosure [ɪn'kləuʒə^r] *n* cercado

encore [ɔŋ'kɔː^r] *excl* bis!, outra! ▷ *n* bis *m*

encounter [ɪn'kauntə^r] *n* encontro ▷ *vt* encontrar, topar com; (*difficulty*) enfrentar

encourage [ɪn'kʌrɪdʒ] *vt* (*activity*) encorajar; (*growth*) estimular; (*person*): **to ~ sb to do sth** animar alguém a fazer algo; **encouragement** *n* estímulo

encyclopaedia, encyclopedia [ɛnsaɪkləu'piːdɪə] *n* enciclopédia

end [ɛnd] *n* fim *m*; (*of table, line, rope etc*) ponta; (*of street, town*) final *m* ▷ *vt* acabar, terminar; (*also:* **bring to an ~, put an ~ to**) acabar com, pôr fim a ▷ *vi* terminar, acabar; **in the ~** ao fim, por fim, finalmente; **on ~** na ponta; **to stand on ~** (*hair*) arrepiar-se; **for hours on ~** por horas a fio **end up** *vi:* **to ~ up in** terminar em; (*place*) ir parar em

endanger [ɪn'deɪndʒə^r] *vt* pôr em perigo

endearing [ɪn'dɪərɪŋ] *adj* simpático, atrativo

endeavour [ɪn'dɛvə^r], (*US*) **endeavor** *n* esforço; (*attempt*) tentativa ▷ *vi:* **to ~ to do** esforçar-se para fazer; (*try*) tentar fazer

ending ['ɛndɪŋ] *n* fim *m*, conclusão *f*; (*of book*) desenlace *m*; (*Ling*) terminação *f*

endless ['ɛndlɪs] *adj* interminável; (*possibilities*) infinito

endorse [ɪn'dɔːs] *vt* (*cheque*) endossar; (*approve*) aprovar; **endorsement** *n* (*Brit: on driving licence*) descrição *f* das multas; (*approval*) aval *m*

endure [ɪn'djuə^r] *vt* (*bear*) aguentar, suportar ▷ *vi* (*last*) durar

enemy ['ɛnəmɪ] *adj, n* inimigo(-a)

energy ['ɛnədʒɪ] *n* energia

enforce [ɪn'fɔːs] *vt* (*Law*) fazer cumprir

engage [ɪn'geɪdʒ] *vt* (*attention*) chamar; (*interest*) atrair; (*lawyer*) contratar; (*clutch*) engrenar ▷ *vi* engrenar; **to ~ in** dedicar-se a, ocupar-se com; **to ~ sb in conversation** travar conversa com alguém; **engaged** *adj* (*Brit: phone*) ocupado (*BR*), impedido (*PT*); (: *toilet*) ocupado; (*betrothed*) noivo; **to get engaged** ficar noivo; **engaged tone** (*Brit*) *n* (*Tel*) sinal *m* de ocupado (*BR*) or de impedido (*PT*); **engagement** *n* encontro; (*booking*) contrato; (*to marry*) noivado; **engagement ring** *n* aliança de noivado

engine ['ɛndʒɪn] *n* (*Aut*) motor *m*; (*Rail*) locomotiva

engineer [ɛndʒɪ'nɪə^r] *n*

engenheiro(-a); (US: Rail)
maquinista *m/f*; (Brit: for repairs)
técnico(-a); **engineering** *n*
engenharia

England ['ɪŋglənd] *n* Inglaterra

English ['ɪŋglɪʃ] *adj* inglês(-esa) ▷ *n*
(Ling) inglês *m*; **the English** *npl*
(people) os ingleses; **English
Channel** *n*: **the English Channel**
o Canal da Mancha

engraving [ɪn'greɪvɪŋ] *n* gravura

enhance [ɪn'hɑːns] *vt* (gen)
ressaltar, salientar; (beauty)
realçar; (position) melhorar; (add
to) aumentar

enjoy [ɪn'dʒɔɪ] *vt* gostar de; (health,
privilege) desfrutar de; **to ~ o.s.**
divertir-se; **enjoyable** *adj*
agradável; **enjoyment** *n* prazer *m*

enlarge [ɪn'lɑːdʒ] *vt* aumentar;
(Phot) ampliar ▷ *vi*: **to ~ on**
(subject) desenvolver, estender-se
sobre

enlist [ɪn'lɪst] *vt* alistar; (support)
conseguir, aliciar ▷ *vi* alistar-se

enormous [ɪ'nɔːməs] *adj* enorme

enough [ɪ'nʌf] *adj*: **~ time/books**
tempo suficiente/livros suficientes
▷ *pron*: **have you got ~?** você tem
o suficiente? ▷ *adv*: **big ~**
suficientemente grande; **~!** basta!,
chega!; **that's ~, thanks** chega,
obrigado; **I've had ~ of him** estou
farto dele; **which, funnily** or
oddly ~ ... o que, por estranho que
pareça ...

enquire [ɪn'kwaɪəʳ] *vt, vi* = **inquire**

enrage [ɪn'reɪdʒ] *vt* enfurecer,
enraivecer

enrol [ɪn'rəʊl], (US) **enroll** *vt*
inscrever; (Sch) matricular ▷ *vi*
inscrever-se; matricular-se;
enrolment *n* inscrição *f*; (Sch)
matrícula

ensure [ɪn'ʃuəʳ] *vt* assegurar

entail [ɪn'teɪl] *vt* implicar

enter ['ɛntəʳ] *vt* entrar em; (club)
ficar or fazer-se sócio de; (army)
alistar-se em; (competition)
inscrever-se em; (sb for a
competition) inscrever; (write down)
completar; (Comput) digitar ▷ *vi*
entrar **enter for** *vt fus* inscrever-se
em **enter into** *vt fus* estabelecer;
(plans) fazer parte de; (debate,
negotiations) entrar em; (agreement)
chegar a, firmar

enterprise ['ɛntəpraɪz] *n* empresa;
(undertaking) empreendimento;
(initiative) iniciativa; **enterprising**
adj empreendedor(a)

entertain [ɛntə'teɪn] *vt* divertir,
entreter; (guest) receber (em casa);
(idea, plan) estudar; **entertainer** *n*
artista *m/f*; **entertaining** *adj*
divertido; **entertainment** *n*
(amusement) entretenimento,
diversão *f*; (show) espetáculo

enthusiasm [ɪn'θuːzɪæzəm] *n*
entusiasmo

enthusiast [ɪn'θuːzɪæst] *n*
entusiasta *m/f*; **enthusiastic**
[ɪnθuːzɪ'æstɪk] *adj* entusiasmado;
to be enthusiastic about
entusiasmar-se por

entire [ɪn'taɪəʳ] *adj* inteiro;
entirely *adv* totalmente,
completamente

entitle [ɪn'taɪtl] *vt*: **to ~ sb to sth**
dar a alguém direito a algo;
entitled [ɪn'taɪtld] *adj* (book etc)
intitulado; **to be entitled to sth/
to do sth** ter direito a algo/de fazer
algo

entrance [*n* 'ɛntrəns, *vt* ɪn'trɑːns]
n entrada; (arrival) chegada ▷ *vt*
encantar, fascinar; **to gain ~ to**
(university etc) ser admitido em;

entrance examination n exame m de admissão; **entrance fee** n joia

entrant ['ɛntrənt] n participante m/f; (Brit: in exam) candidato(-a)

entrepreneur [ɔntrəprə'nəːr] n empresário(-a)

entrust [ɪn'trʌst] vt: **to ~ sth to sb** confiar algo a alguém

entry ['ɛntrɪ] n entrada; (in register) registro, assentamento; (in account) lançamento; (in dictionary) verbete m; **"no ~"** "entrada proibida"; (Aut) "contramão" (BR), "entrada proibida" (PT); **entry phone** (Brit) n interfone m (em apartamento)

envelope ['ɛnvələup] n envelope m

envious ['ɛnvɪəs] adj invejoso; (look) de inveja

environment [ɪn'vaɪərnmənt] n meio ambiente m; **environmental** [ɪnvaɪərn'mɛntl] adj ambiental

envisage [ɪn'vɪzɪdʒ] vt prever

envoy ['ɛnvɔɪ] n enviado(-a)

envy ['ɛnvɪ] n inveja ▷ vt ter inveja de; **to ~ sb sth** invejar alguém por algo, cobiçar algo de alguém

epic ['ɛpɪk] n epopeia ▷ adj épico

epidemic [ɛpɪ'dɛmɪk] n epidemia

epilepsy ['ɛpɪlɛpsɪ] n epilepsia

episode ['ɛpɪsəud] n episódio

equal ['iːkwl] adj igual; (treatment) equitativo, equivalente ▷ n igual m/f ▷ vt ser igual a; **to be ~ to** (task) estar à altura de; **equality** [iː'kwɔlɪtɪ] n igualdade f; **equalize** vi igualar; (Sport) empatar; **equally** adv igualmente; (share etc) por igual

equator [ɪ'kweɪtər] n equador m

equip [ɪ'kwɪp] vt equipar; (person) prover, munir; **to be well ~ped** estar bem preparado or equipado;

equipment n equipamento; (machines etc) equipamentos mpl, aparelhagem f

equivalent [ɪ'kwɪvəlnt] adj equivalente ▷ n equivalente m

era ['ɪərə] n era, época

erase [ɪ'reɪz] vt apagar; **eraser** n borracha (de apagar)

erect [ɪ'rɛkt] adj (posture) ereto; (tail, ears) levantado ▷ vt erigir, levantar; (assemble) montar; **erection** n construção f; (assembly) montagem f; (Physio) ereção f

erode [ɪ'rəud] vt (Geo) causar erosão em; (confidence) minar

erotic [ɪ'rɔtɪk] adj erótico

errand ['ɛrnd] n recado, mensagem f

erratic [ɪ'rætɪk] adj imprevisível

error ['ɛrər] n erro

erupt [ɪ'rʌpt] vi entrar em erupção; (fig) explodir, estourar; **eruption** n erupção f; (fig) explosão f

escalate ['ɛskəleɪt] vi intensificar-se

escalator ['ɛskəleɪtər] n escada rolante

escape [ɪ'skeɪp] n fuga; (of gas) escapatória ▷ vi escapar; (flee) fugir, evadir-se; (leak) vazar, escapar ▷ vt fugir de; (elude): **his name ~s me** o nome dele me foge a memória; **to ~ from** (place) escapar de; (person) escapulir de

escort [n 'ɛskɔːt, vt ɪ'skɔːt] n acompanhante m/f; (Mil, Naut) escolta ▷ vt acompanhar

especially [ɪ'spɛʃlɪ] adv (above all) sobretudo; (particularly) em particular

espionage ['ɛspɪɑːʒ] n espionagem f

essay ['ɛseɪ] n ensaio

essence [ˈɛsns] n essência
essential [ɪˈsɛnʃl] adj (necessary) indispensável; (basic) essencial ▷ n elemento essencial
establish [ɪˈstæblɪʃ] vt estabelecer; (facts) verificar; (proof) demonstrar; (reputation) firmar; **establishment** n estabelecimento; **the Establishment** a classe dirigente
estate [ɪˈsteɪt] n (land) fazenda (BR), propriedade f (PT); (Law) herança; (Pol) estado; (Brit: also: **housing ~**) conjunto habitacional; **estate agent** (Brit) n corretor(a) m/f de imóveis (BR), agente m/f imobiliário(-a) (PT); **estate car** (Brit) n perua (BR), canadiana (PT)
estimate [n ˈɛstɪmət, vb ˈɛstɪmeɪt] n (assessment) avaliação f; (calculation) cálculo; (Comm) orçamento ▷ vt estimar, avaliar, calcular
etc. (= et cetera) etc.
eternal [ɪˈtəːnl] adj eterno
eternity [ɪˈtəːnɪtɪ] n eternidade f
ethical [ˈɛθɪkl] adj ético
ethics [ˈɛθɪks] n ética ▷ npl moral f
Ethiopia [iːθɪˈəʊpɪə] n Etiópia
ethnic [ˈɛθnɪk] adj étnico; (culture) folclórico
e-ticket [ˈiːtɪkɪt] n bilhete m eletrônico
etiquette [ˈɛtɪkɛt] n etiqueta
EU n abbr (= European Union) UE f
euro [ˈjʊərəʊ] n (currency) euro m
Europe [ˈjʊərəp] n Europa; **European** [jʊərəˈpiːən] adj, n europeu(-peia); **European Union** n: **the European Union** a União Europeia
evacuate [ɪˈvækjueɪt] vt evacuar
evade [ɪˈveɪd] vt (person) evitar; (question, duties) esquivar-se de; (tax) sonegar

evaporate [ɪˈvæpəreɪt] vi evaporar-se
eve [iːv] n: **on the ~ of** na véspera de
even [ˈiːvn] adj (level) plano; (smooth) liso; (equal, Sport) igual; (number) par ▷ adv até, mesmo; **~ if** mesmo que; **~ though** mesmo que, embora; **~ more** ainda mais; **~ so** mesmo assim; **not ~** nem; **to get ~ with sb** ficar quite com alguém **even out** vi nivelar-se
evening [ˈiːvnɪŋ] n (early) tarde f; (late) noite f; (event) noitada; **in the ~** à noite; **evening class** n aula noturna
event [ɪˈvɛnt] n acontecimento; (Sport) prova; **in the ~ of** no caso de; **eventful** adj cheio de acontecimentos; (game etc) cheio de emoção, agitado
eventual [ɪˈvɛntʃuəl] adj final; **eventually** adv finalmente; (in time) por fim
ever [ˈɛvər] adv (always) sempre; (at any time) em qualquer momento; (in question): **why ~ not?** por que não, ora?; **the best ~** o melhor que já se viu; **have you ~ seen it?** você alguma vez já viu isto?; **better than ~** melhor que nunca; **~ since** adv desde então ▷ conj depois que; **evergreen** n sempre-verde f

 KEYWORD

every [ˈɛvrɪ] adj **1** (each) cada; **every one of them** cada um deles; **every shop in the town was closed** todas as lojas da cidade estavam fechadas
2 (all possible) todo(-a); **I have every confidence in her** tenho absoluta confiança nela; **we wish**

you every success desejamo-lhe o maior sucesso; **he's every bit as clever as his brother** ele é tão inteligente quanto o irmão **3** (*showing recurrence*) todo(-a); **every other car had been broken into** cada dois carros foram arrombados; **she visits me every other/third day** ele me visita cada dois/três dias; **every now and then** de vez em quando

everybody ['ɛvrɪbɔdɪ] *pron* todos, todo mundo (*BR*), toda a gente (*PT*)

everyday ['ɛvrɪdeɪ] *adj* (*daily*) diário; (*usual*) corrente; (*common*) comum

everyone ['ɛvrɪwʌn] *pron* = **everybody**

everything ['ɛvrɪθɪŋ] *pron* tudo

everywhere ['ɛvrɪwɛəʳ] *adv* (*be*) em todo lugar (*BR*), em toda a parte (*PT*); (*go*) a todo lugar (*BR*), a toda a parte (*PT*); (*wherever*): **~ you go you meet ...** aonde quer que se vá, encontra-se ...

evict [ɪ'vɪkt] *vt* despejar

evidence ['ɛvɪdəns] *n* (*proof*) prova(s) *f(pl)*; (*of witness*) testemunho, depoimento; (*indication*) sinal *m*; **to give ~** testemunhar, prestar depoimento

evident ['ɛvɪdənt] *adj* evidente; **evidently** *adv* evidentemente; (*apparently*) aparentemente

evil ['iːvl] *adj* mau/má ▷ *n* mal *m*, maldade *f*

evoke [ɪ'vəuk] *vt* evocar

evolution [iːvə'luːʃən] *n* evolução *f*; (*development*) desenvolvimento

evolve [ɪ'vɔlv] *vt* desenvolver ▷ *vi* desenvolver-se

exact [ɪg'zækt] *adj* exato; (*person*) meticuloso ▷ *vt*: **to ~ sth (from)** exigir algo (de); **exactly** *adv* exatamente; (*indicating agreement*) isso mesmo

exaggerate [ɪg'zædʒəreɪt] *vt, vi* exagerar; **exaggeration** [ɪgzædʒə'reɪʃən] *n* exagero

exam [ɪg'zæm] *n abbr* = **examination**

examination [ɪgzæmɪ'neɪʃən] *n* exame *m*; (*inquiry*) investigação *f*

examine [ɪg'zæmɪn] *vt* examinar; (*inspect*) inspecionar; **examiner** *n* examinador(a) *m/f*

example [ɪg'zɑːmpl] *n* exemplo; **for ~** por exemplo

excavate ['ɛkskəveɪt] *vt* escavar

exceed [ɪk'siːd] *vt* exceder; (*number*) ser superior a; (*speed limit*) ultrapassar; (*limits*) ir além de; (*powers*) exceder-se em; (*hopes*) superar; **exceedingly** *adv* extremamente

excellent ['ɛksələnt] *adj* excelente

except [ɪk'sɛpt] *prep* (*also*: **~ for, ~ing**) exceto, a não ser ▷ *vt*: **to ~ sb from** excluir alguém de; **~ if/when** a menos que, a não ser que; **exception** *n* exceção *f*; **to take exception to** ressentir-se de

excerpt ['ɛksəːpt] *n* trecho

excess [ɪk'sɛs] *n* excesso; **excess baggage** *n* excesso de bagagem; **excessive** *adj* excessivo

exchange [ɪks'tʃeɪndʒ] *n* troca; (*of teachers, students*) intercâmbio; (*also*: **telephone ~**) estação *f* telefônica (*BR*), central *f* telefónica (*PT*) ▷ *vt*: **to ~ (for)** trocar (por); **exchange rate** *n* (taxa de) câmbio

excite [ɪk'saɪt] *vt* excitar; **to get ~d** entusiasmar-se; **excitement** *n* emoções *fpl*; (*agitation*) agitação *f*; **exciting** *adj* emocionante, empolgante

exclaim [ɪkˈskleɪm] *vi* exclamar;
exclamation [ɛksklǝˈmeɪʃǝn] *n*
exclamação *f*; **exclamation mark**
n ponto de exclamação

exclude [ɪkˈskluːd] *vt* excluir

exclusive [ɪkˈskluːsɪv] *adj*
exclusivo; **~ of tax** sem incluir os
impostos

excruciating [ɪkˈskruːʃɪeɪtɪŋ] *adj*
doloroso, martirizante

excursion [ɪkˈskǝːʃǝn] *n* excursão *f*

excuse [*n* ɪkˈskjuːs, *vt* ɪkˈskjuːz] *n*
desculpa ▷ *vt* desculpar, perdoar;
to ~ sb from doing sth dispensar
alguém de fazer algo; **~ me!**
desculpe!; **if you will ~ me ...** com
a sua licença ...

execute [ˈɛksɪkjuːt] *vt* (*plan*)
realizar; (*order*) cumprir; (*person*,
movement) executar; **execution** *n*
realização *f*; (*killing*) execução *f*

executive [ɪgˈzɛkjutɪv] *n* (*Comm*,
Pol) executivo(a) ▷ *adj* executivo

exempt [ɪgˈzɛmpt] *adj*: **~ from**
isento de ▷ *vt*: **to ~ sb from**
dispensar *or* isentar alguém de

exercise [ˈɛksǝsaɪz] *n* exercício ▷ *vt*
exercer; (*right*) valer-se de; (*dog*)
levar para passear ▷ *vi* (*also*: **to
take ~**) fazer exercício; **exercise
book** *n* caderno

exert [ɪgˈzǝːt] *vt* exercer; **to ~ o.s.**
esforçar-se, empenhar-se;
exertion *n* esforço

exhale [ɛksˈheɪl] *vt*, *vi* expirar

exhaust [ɪgˈzɔːst] *n* (*Aut*: *also*:
~ pipe) escape *m*, exaustor *m*;
(*fumes*) escapamento (de gás) ▷ *vt*
esgotar; **exhaustion** *n* exaustão *f*

exhibit [ɪgˈzɪbɪt] *n* (*Art*) obra
exposta; (*Law*) objeto exposto ▷ *vt*
(*courage etc*) manifestar, mostrar;
(*quality*, *emotion*) demonstrar;
(*paintings*) expor; **exhibition**

[ɛksɪˈbɪʃǝn] *n* exposição *f*

exhilarating [ɪgˈzɪlǝreɪtɪŋ] *adj*
estimulante, tônico

exile [ˈɛksaɪl] *n* exílio; (*person*)
exilado(-a) ▷ *vt* desterrar, exilar

exist [ɪgˈzɪst] *vi* existir; (*live*) viver;
existence *n* existência; (*life*) vida;
existing *adj* atual

exit [ˈɛksɪt] *n* saída ▷ *vi* (*Comput*,
Theatre) sair

exotic [ɪgˈzɔtɪk] *adj* exótico

expand [ɪkˈspænd] *vt* aumentar
▷ *vi* aumentar; (*trade, gas etc*)
expandir-se; (*metal*) dilatar-se

expansion [ɪkˈspænʃǝn] *n* (*of town*)
desenvolvimento; (*of trade*)
expansão *f*; (*of population*)
aumento

expect [ɪkˈspɛkt] *vt* esperar;
(*suppose*) supor; (*require*) exigir ▷ *vi*:
to be ~ing estar grávida;
expectation *n* esperança; (*belief*)
expectativa

expedition [ɛkspǝˈdɪʃǝn] *n*
expedição *f*

expel [ɪkˈspɛl] *vt* expelir; (*from
place, school*) expulsar

expense [ɪkˈspɛns] *n* gasto,
despesa; (*expenditure*) despesas *fpl*;
expenses *npl* (*costs*) despesas *fpl*;
at the ~ of à custa de; **expense
account** *n* relatório de despesas

expensive [ɪkˈspɛnsɪv] *adj* caro

experience [ɪkˈspɪǝrɪǝns] *n*
experiência ▷ *vt* (*situation*)
enfrentar; (*feeling*) sentir;
experienced *adj* experiente

experiment [ɪkˈspɛrɪmǝnt] *n*
experimento, experiência ▷ *vi*:
to ~ (with/on) fazer experiências
(com/em)

expert [ˈɛkspǝːt] *adj* hábil, perito
▷ *n* especialista *m/f*; **expertise**
[ɛkspǝːˈtiːz] *n* perícia

expire [ɪk'spaɪəʳ] vi expirar; (run out) vencer; **expiry** n expiração f, vencimento

explain [ɪk'spleɪn] vt explicar; (clarify) esclarecer **explain away** vt justificar

explicit [ɪk'splɪsɪt] adj explícito

explode [ɪk'spləud] vi estourar, explodir

exploit [n 'ɛksplɔɪt, vt ɪk'splɔɪt] n façanha ▷ vt explorar; **exploitation** [ɛksplɔɪ'teɪʃən] n exploração f

explore [ɪk'splɔːʳ] vt explorar; (fig) examinar, pesquisar; **explorer** n explorador(a) m/f

explosion [ɪk'spləuʒən] n explosão f

explosive [ɪk'spləusɪv] adj explosivo ▷ n explosivo

export [vt ɛk'spɔːt, n, cpd 'ɛkspɔːt] vt exportar ▷ n exportação f ▷ cpd de exportação; **exporter** n exportador(a) m/f

expose [ɪk'spəuz] vt expor; (unmask) desmascarar; **exposed** adj (house etc) desabrigado

exposure [ɪk'spəuʒəʳ] n exposição f; (publicity) publicidade f; (Phot) revelação f; **to die from ~** (Med) morrer de frio

express [ɪk'sprɛs] adj expresso, explícito; (Brit: letter etc) urgente ▷ n rápido ▷ vt exprimir, expressar; (quantity) representar; **expression** n expressão f; **expressway** (US) n rodovia (BR), autoestrada (PT)

extend [ɪk'stɛnd] vt (visit, street) prolongar; (building) aumentar; (offer) fazer; (hand) estender

extension [ɪk'stɛnʃən] n (Elec) extensão f; (building) acréscimo, expansão f; (of rights) ampliação f; (Tel) ramal m (BR), extensão f (PT);

(of deadline, campaign) prolongamento, prorrogação f

extensive [ɪk'stɛnsɪv] adj extenso; (damage) considerável; (broad) vasto, amplo

extent [ɪk'stɛnt] n (breadth) extensão f; (of damage etc) dimensão f; (scope) alcance m; **to some** or **to a certain ~** até certo ponto

exterior [ɛk'stɪərɪəʳ] adj externo ▷ n exterior m; (appearance) aspecto

external [ɛk'stə:nl] adj externo

extinct [ɪk'stɪŋkt] adj extinto

extinguish [ɪk'stɪŋgwɪʃ] vt extinguir

extra ['ɛkstrə] adj adicional ▷ adv adicionalmente ▷ n (surcharge) extra m, suplemento; (Cinema, Theatre) figurante m/f

extract [vt ɪk'strækt, n 'ɛkstrækt] vt tirar, extrair; (tooth) arrancar; (mineral) extrair; (money) extorquir; (promise) conseguir, obter ▷ n extrato

extradite ['ɛkstrədaɪt] vt (from country) extraditar; (to country) obter a extradição de

extraordinary [ɪk'strɔ:dnrɪ] adj extraordinário; (odd) estranho

extravagance [ɪk'strævəgəns] n extravagância; (no pl: spending) esbanjamento

extravagant [ɪk'strævəgənt] adj (lavish) extravagante; (wasteful) gastador(a), esbanjador(a)

extreme [ɪk'stri:m] adj extremo ▷ n extremo; **extremely** adv muito, extremamente

extrovert ['ɛkstrəvə:t] n extrovertido(-a)

eye [aɪ] n olho; (of needle) buraco ▷ vt olhar, observar; **to keep an ~**

on vigiar, ficar de olho em;
eyebrow *n* sobrancelha;
eyedrops *npl* gotas *fpl* para os
olhos; **eyelash** *n* cílio; **eyelid** *n*
pálpebra; **eyeliner** *n* delineador
m; **eye shadow** *n* sombra de
olhos; **eyesight** *n* vista, visão *f*

F, f [ɛf] *n* F, f *m*; (*Mus*) fá *m*
fabric ['fæbrɪk] *n* tecido, pano
face [feɪs] *n* cara, rosto; (*grimace*)
careta; (*of clock*) mostrador *m*;
(*side, surface*) superfície *f*; (*of
building*) frente *f*, fachada ▷ *vt*
(*facts, problem*) enfrentar;
(*particular direction*) dar para; **~
down** de bruços; (*card*) virado para
baixo; **to lose ~** perder o prestígio;
to save ~ salvar as aparências; **to
make** *or* **pull a ~** fazer careta; **in
the ~ of** diante de, à vista de; **on
the ~ of it** a julgar pelas
aparências, à primeira vista **face
up to** *vt fus* enfrentar; **face cloth**
(*Brit*) *n* pano de rosto; **face pack**
(*Brit*) *n* máscara facial
facilities [fə'sɪlɪtɪz] *npl* facilidades
fpl, instalações *fpl*; **credit ~** crediário
fact [fækt] *n* fato; **in ~** realmente,
na verdade

factor ['fæktə'] n fator m
factory ['fæktərɪ] n fábrica
factual ['fæktjuəl] adj real, fatual
faculty ['fækəltɪ] n faculdade f; (US) corpo docente
fad [fæd] (inf) n mania, modismo
fade [feɪd] vi desbotar; (sound, hope) desvanecer-se; (light) apagar-se; (flower) murchar
fag [fæg] (inf) n cigarro
fail [feɪl] vt (candidate) reprovar; (exam) não passar em, ser reprovado em; (subj: leader) fracassar; (: courage) carecer; (: memory) falhar ▷ vi fracassar; (engine, brakes, voice) falhar; **to ~ to do sth** deixar de fazer algo; (be unable) não conseguir fazer algo; **without ~** sem falta; **failing** n defeito ▷ prep na or à falta de; **failing that** senão; **failure** n fracasso; (mechanical etc) falha
faint [feɪnt] adj fraco; (recollection) vago; (mark) indistinto; (smell, trace) leve ▷ n desmaio ▷ vi desmaiar; **to feel ~** sentir tonteira
fair [fɛə'] adj justo; (hair) louro; (complexion) branco; (weather) bom; (good enough) razoável; (sizeable) considerável ▷ adv: **to play ~** fazer jogo limpo ▷ n (also: **trade ~**) feira; (Brit: funfair) parque m de diversões; **fairly** adv (justly) com justiça; (quite) bastante
fairy ['fɛərɪ] n fada
faith [feɪθ] n fé f; (trust) confiança; (denomination) seita; **faithful** adj fiel; (account) exato; **faithfully** adv fielmente; **yours faithfully** (Brit: in letters) atenciosamente
fake [feɪk] n (painting etc) falsificação f; (person) impostor(a) m/f ▷ adj falso ▷ vt fingir; (painting etc) falsificar

falcon ['fɔːlkən] n falcão m
fall [fɔːl] (pt **fell**, pp **fallen**) n queda; (US: autumn) outono ▷ vi cair; (price) baixar; **falls** npl (waterfall) cascata, queda d'água; **to ~ flat** cair de cara no chão; (plan) falhar; (joke) não agradar **fall back** vi retroceder **fall back on** vt fus recorrer a **fall behind** vi ficar para trás **fall down** vi (person) cair; (building) desabar **fall for** vt fus (trick) cair em; (person) enamorar-se de **fall in** vi ruir; (Mil) alinhar-se **fall off** vi cair; (diminish) declinar, diminuir **fall out** vi cair; (friends etc) brigar **fall through** vi (plan, project) furar
fallout ['fɔːlaut] n chuva radioativa
false [fɔːls] adj falso; **false teeth** (Brit) npl dentadura postiça
fame [feɪm] n fama
familiar [fə'mɪlɪə'] adj (well-known) conhecido; (tone) familiar, íntimo; **to be ~ with** (subject) estar familiarizado com
family ['fæmɪlɪ] n família
famine ['fæmɪn] n fome f
famous ['feɪməs] adj famoso, célebre
fan [fæn] n (hand-held) leque m; (Elec) ventilador m; (person) fã, fan (PT) ▷ vt abanar; (fire, quarrel) atiçar **fan out** vi espalhar-se
fanatic [fə'nætɪk] n fanático(-a)
fan belt n correia do ventilador (BR) or da ventoinha (PT)
fan club n fã-clube m
fancy ['fænsɪ] n capricho; (imagination) imaginação f; (fantasy) fantasia ▷ adj ornamental; (luxury) luxuoso ▷ vt desejar, querer; (imagine) imaginar; (think) acreditar, achar; **to take a ~ to** tomar gosto por; **he fancies her**

(*inf*) ele está a fim dela; **fancy dress** *n* fantasia

fantastic [fæn'tæstɪk] *adj* fantástico

fantasy ['fæntəsɪ] *n* (*dream*) sonho; (*unreality*) fantasia; (*imagination*) imaginação *f*

far [fɑːʳ] *adj* (*distant*) distante ▷ *adv* (*also*: **~ away, ~ off**) longe; **the ~ side/end** o lado de lá/a outra ponta; **~ better** muito melhor; **~ from** longe de; **by ~** de longe; **go as ~ as the farm** vá até a (*BR*) or à (*PT*) fazenda; **as ~ as I know** que eu saiba; **how ~?** até onde?; (*fig*) até que ponto?

farce [fɑːs] *n* farsa

fare [fɛəʳ] *n* (*on trains, buses*) preço (da passagem); (*in taxi: cost*) tarifa; (*food*) comida; **half/full ~** meia/inteira passagem

Far East *n*: **the ~** o Extremo Oriente

farewell [fɛə'wɛl] *excl* adeus ▷ *n* despedida

farm [fɑːm] *n* fazenda (*BR*), quinta (*PT*) ▷ *vt* cultivar; **farmer** *n* fazendeiro(-a), agricultor *m*; **farmhouse** *n* casa da fazenda (*BR*) or da quinta (*PT*); **farming** *n* agricultura; (*tilling*) cultura; (*of animals*) criação *f*; **farmyard** *n* curral *m*

far-reaching [-'riːtʃɪŋ] *adj* de grande alcance, abrangente

fart [fɑːt] (*inf!*) *vi* soltar um peido (!), peidar (!)

farther ['fɑːðəʳ] *adv* mais longe ▷ *adj* mais distante, mais afastado

farthest ['fɑːðɪst] *superl of* **far**

fascinate ['fæsɪneɪt] *vt* fascinar

fashion ['fæʃən] *n* moda; (*fashion industry*) indústria da moda; (*manner*) maneira ▷ *vt* modelar, dar feitio a; **in ~** na moda; **fashionable** *adj* da moda, elegante; **fashion show** *n* desfile *m* de modas

fast [fɑːst] *adj* rápido; (*dye, colour*) firme, permanente; (*clock*): **to be ~** estar adiantado ▷ *adv* rápido, rapidamente, depressa; (*stuck, held*) firmemente ▷ *n* jejum *m* ▷ *vi* jejuar; **~ asleep** dormindo profundamente

fasten ['fɑːsn] *vt* fixar, prender; (*coat*) fechar; (*belt*) apertar ▷ *vi* prender-se, fixar-se

fast food *n* fast food *f*

fat [fæt] *adj* gordo; (*book*) grosso; (*wallet*) recheado; (*profit*) grande ▷ *n* gordura; (*lard*) banha, gordura

fatal ['feɪtl] *adj* fatal; (*injury*) mortal

fate [feɪt] *n* destino; (*of person*) sorte *f*

father ['fɑːðəʳ] *n* pai *m*; **father-in-law** *n* sogro

fatigue [fə'tiːg] *n* fadiga, cansaço

fatty ['fætɪ] *adj* (*food*) gorduroso ▷ *n* (*inf*) gorducho(-a)

fault [fɔːlt] *n* (*blame*) culpa; (*defect*) defeito; (*Geo*) falha; (*Tennis*) falta, bola fora ▷ *vt* criticar; **to find ~ with** criticar, queixar-se de; **at ~** culpado; **faulty** *adj* defeituoso

favour ['feɪvəʳ], (*US*) **favor** *n* favor *m* ▷ *vt* favorecer; (*assist*) auxiliar; **to do sb a ~** fazer favor a alguém; **to find ~ with** cair nas boas graças de; **in ~ of** em favor de; **favourite** ['feɪvərɪt] *adj* predileto ▷ *n* favorito(-a)

fawn [fɔːn] *n* cervo novo, cervato ▷ *adj* (*also*: **~-coloured**) castanho-claro *inv* ▷ *vi*: **to ~ (up)on** bajular

fax [fæks] *n* fax *m*, fac-símile *m* ▷ *vt* enviar por fax or fac-símile

FBI *n abbr* (= *Federal Bureau of Investigation*) FBI *m*

fear [fɪə^r] n medo ▷ vt ter medo de, temer; **for ~ of** com medo de; **fearful** adj medonho, temível; (cowardly) medroso; (awful) terrível

feasible ['fi:zəbl] adj viável

feast [fi:st] n banquete m; (Rel: also: **~ day**) festa ▷ vi banquetear-se

feat [fi:t] n façanha, feito

feather ['fɛðə^r] n pena, pluma

feature ['fi:tʃə^r] n característica; (article) reportagem f ▷ vt (subj: film) apresentar ▷ vi figurar; **features** npl (of face) feições fpl; **feature film** n longa-metragem m

February ['fɛbruəri] n fevereiro

fed [fɛd] pt, pp of **feed**

federal ['fɛdərəl] adj federal

fed up adj: **to be ~** estar (de saco) cheio (BR), estar farto (PT)

fee [fi:] n taxa (BR), propina (PT); (of school) matrícula; (of doctor, lawyer) honorários mpl

feeble ['fi:bl] adj fraco; (attempt) ineficaz

feed [fi:d] (pt, pp **fed**) n (of baby) alimento infantil; (of animal) ração f; (on printer) mecanismo alimentador ▷ vt alimentar; (baby) amamentar; (animal) dar de comer a; (data, information): **to ~ into** introduzir em **feed on** vt fus alimentar-se de; **feedback** ['fi:dbæk] n reação f

feel [fi:l] (pt, pp **felt**) n sensação f; (sense of touch) tato; (impression) impressão f ▷ vt tocar, apalpar; (anger, pain etc) sentir; (think, believe) achar, acreditar; **to ~ hungry/cold** estar com fome/frio (BR), ter fome/frio (PT); **to ~ lonely/better** sentir-se só/ melhor; **I don't ~ well** não estou me sentindo bem; **it ~s soft** é macio; **to ~ like** querer; **to ~ about** or **around** tatear; **feeling** n sensação f; (emotion) sentimento; (impression) impressão f

feet [fi:t] npl of **foot**

fell [fɛl] pt of **fall** ▷ vt (tree) lançar por terra, derrubar

fellow ['fɛləu] n camarada m/f; (inf: man) cara m (BR), tipo (PT); (of learned society) membro ▷ cpd: **~ students** colegas m/fpl de curso; **fellowship** n amizade f; (grant) bolsa de estudo; (society) associação f

felony ['fɛləni] n crime m

felt [fɛlt] pt, pp of **feel** ▷ n feltro

female ['fi:meil] n (pej: woman) mulher f; (Zool) fêmea ▷ adj fêmeo(-a); (sex, character) feminino; (vote etc) das mulheres; (child etc) do sexo feminino

feminine ['fɛminin] adj feminino

feminist ['fɛminist] n feminista m/f

fence [fɛns] n cerca ▷ vt (also: **~ in**) cercar ▷ vi esgrimir; **fencing** n (sport) esgrima

fend [fɛnd] vi: **to ~ for o.s.** defender-se, virar-se **fend off** vt defender-se de

ferment [vi fə'mɛnt, n 'fə:mɛnt] vi fermentar ▷ n (fig) agitação f

fern [fə:n] n samambaia (BR), feto (PT)

ferocious [fə'rəuʃəs] adj feroz

ferret ['fɛrit] n furão m **ferret out** vt (information) desenterrar, descobrir

ferry ['fɛri] n (small) barco (de travessia); (large: also: **~boat**) balsa ▷ vt transportar

fertile ['fə:tail] adj fértil; (Bio) fecundo; **fertilizer** ['fə:tilaizə^r] n adubo, fertilizante m

festival ['fɛstivəl] n (Rel) festa; (Art, Mus) festival m

festive ['fɛstɪv] *adj* festivo; **the ~ season** (*Brit: Christmas*) a época do Natal

fetch [fɛtʃ] *vt* ir buscar, trazer; (*sell for*) alcançar

fête [feɪt] *n* festa

feud [fjuːd] *n* disputa, rixa

fever ['fiːvəʳ] *n* febre *f*; **feverish** *adj* febril

few [fjuː] *adj, pron* poucos(-as); **a ~ ...** alguns/algumas ...; **fewer** ['fjuːəʳ] *adj* menos; **fewest** ['fjuːɪst] *adj* o menor número de

fib [fɪb] *n* lorota

fickle ['fɪkl] *adj* inconstante; (*weather*) instável

fiction ['fɪkʃən] *n* ficção *f*; **fictional** *adj* de ficção

fiddle ['fɪdl] *n* (*Mus*) violino; (*swindle*) trapaça ▷ *vt* (*Brit: accounts*) falsificar **fiddle with** *vt fus* brincar com

fidget ['fɪdʒɪt] *vi* estar irrequieto, mexer-se

field [fiːld] *n* campo; (*fig*) área, esfera, especialidade *f*; (*Comm*) liderar

fierce [fɪəs] *adj* feroz; (*wind, attack*) violento; (*heat*) intenso

fifteen [fɪf'tiːn] *num* quinze

fifth [fɪfθ] *num* quinto

fifty ['fɪftɪ] *num* cinquenta; **fifty-fifty** *adv*: **to share** or **go fifty-fifty with sb** dividir meio a meio com alguém, rachar com alguém ▷ *adj*: **to have a fifty-fifty chance** ter 50% de chance

fig [fɪg] *n* figo

fight [faɪt] (*pt, pp* **fought**) *n* briga; (*Mil*) combate *m*; (*struggle: against illness etc*) luta ▷ *vt* lutar contra; (*cancer, alcoholism*) combater; (*election*) competir ▷ *vi* brigar, bater-se

figure ['fɪgəʳ] *n* (*Drawing, Math*) figura, desenho; (*number, cipher*) número, cifra; (*outline*) forma; (*person*) personagem *m* ▷ *vt* (*esp US*) imaginar ▷ *vi* figurar **figure out** *vt* compreender

file [faɪl] *n* (*tool*) lixa; (*dossier*) dossiê *m*, pasta; (*folder*) pasta; (*Comput*) arquivo; (*row*) fila, coluna ▷ *vt* (*wood, nails*) lixar; (*papers*) arquivar; (*Law: claim*) apresentar, dar entrada em ▷ *vi*: **to ~ in/out** entrar/sair em fila

fill [fɪl] *vt* encher; (*vacancy*) preencher; (*need*) satisfazer ▷ *n*: **to eat one's ~** encher-se or fartar-se de comer **fill in** *vt* (*form*) preencher; (*hole*) tapar; (*time*) encher **fill up** *vt* encher ▷ *vi* (*Aut*) abastecer o carro

fillet ['fɪlɪt] *n* filete *m*, filé *m*; **fillet steak** *n* filé *m*

filling ['fɪlɪŋ] *n* (*Culin*) recheio; (*for tooth*) obturação *f* (*BR*), chumbo (*PT*); **filling station** *n* posto de gasolina

film [fɪlm] *n* filme *m*; (*of liquid etc*) camada fina, veu *m* ▷ *vt* rodar, filmar ▷ *vi* filmar; **film star** *n* astro/estrela do cinema

filter ['fɪltəʳ] *n* filtro ▷ *vt* filtrar

filth [fɪlθ] *n* sujeira (*BR*), sujidade *f* (*PT*); **filthy** *adj* sujo; (*language*) indecente, obsceno

fin [fɪn] *n* barbatana

final ['faɪnl] *adj* final, último; (*definitive*) definitivo ▷ *n* (*Sport*) final *f*; **finals** *npl* (*Sch*) exames *mpl* finais; **finale** [fɪ'nɑːlɪ] *n* final *m*; **finalize** *vt* concluir, completar; **finally** *adv* finalmente, por fim

finance [faɪ'næns] *n* fundos *mpl*; (*money management*) finanças *fpl* ▷ *vt* financiar; **finances** *npl* (*personal finances*) finanças; **financial** [faɪ'nænʃəl] *adj* financeiro

find [faɪnd] (*pt, pp* **found**) *vt* encontrar, achar; (*discover*) descobrir ▷ *n* achado, descoberta; **to ~ sb guilty** (*Law*) declarar alguém culpado **find out** *vt* descobrir; (*person*) desmascarar ▷ *vi*: **to ~ out about** (*by chance*) saber de; **findings** *npl* (*Law*) veredito, decisão *f*; (*of report*) constatações *fpl*

fine [faɪn] *adj* fino; (*excellent*) excelente ▷ *adv* muito bem ▷ *n* (*Law*) multa ▷ *vt* (*Law*) multar; **to be ~** (*person*) estar bem; (*weather*) estar bom; **fine arts** *npl* belas artes *fpl*

finger ['fɪŋgə^r] *n* dedo ▷ *vt* manusear; **fingernail** *n* unha; **fingerprint** *n* impressão *f* digital; **fingertip** *n* ponta do dedo

finish ['fɪnɪʃ] *n* fim *m*; (*Sport*) chegada; (*on wood etc*) acabamento ▷ *vt, vi* terminar, acabar; **to ~ doing sth** terminar de fazer algo; **to ~ third** chegar no terceiro lugar **finish off** *vt* terminar; (*kill*) liquidar **finish up** *vt* acabar ▷ *vi* ir parar

Finland ['fɪnlənd] *n* Finlândia

Finn [fɪn] *n* finlandês(-esa) *m/f*; **Finnish** *adj* finlandês(-esa) ▷ *n* (*Ling*) finlandês *m*

fir [fə:^{r}] *n* abeto

fire ['faɪə^r] *n* fogo; (*accidental*) incêndio; (*gas fire, electric fire*) aquecedor *m* ▷ *vt* (*gun*) disparar; (*arrow*) atirar; (*interest*) estimular; (*dismiss*) despedir ▷ *vi* disparar; **on ~** em chamas; **fire alarm** *n* alarme *m* de incêndio; **firearm** *n* arma de fogo; **fire brigade** *n* (corpo de

bombeiros *mpl*; **fire engine** *n* carro de bombeiro; **fire escape** *n* escada de incêndio; **fire extinguisher** *n* extintor *m* de incêndio; **fireman** *irreg n* bombeiro; **fireplace** *n* lareira; **fire station** *n* posto de bombeiros; **firewall** *n* (*Comput*) firewall *m*; **firewood** *n* lenha; **fireworks** *npl* fogos *mpl* de artifício

firm [fə:m] *adj* firme ▷ *n* firma

first [fə:st] *adj* primeiro ▷ *adv* (*before others*) primeiro; (*when listing reasons etc*) em primeiro lugar ▷ *n* (*in race*) primeiro(-a); (*Aut*) primeira; (*Brit: Sch*) menção *f* honrosa; **at ~** no início; **~ of all** antes de tudo, antes de mais nada; **first aid** *n* primeiros socorros *mpl*; **first-aid kit** *n* estojo de primeiros socorros; **first-class** *adj* de primeira classe; **first-hand** *adj* de primeira mão; **first lady** (*US*) *n* primeira dama; **firstly** *adv* primeiramente, em primeiro lugar; **first name** *n* primeiro nome *m*; **first-rate** *adj* de primeira categoria

fish [fɪʃ] *n inv* peixe *m* ▷ *vt, vi* pescar; **to go ~ing** ir pescar; **fisherman** *irreg n* pescador *m*; **fishing boat** *n* barco de pesca; **fishing line** *n* linha de pesca; **fishmonger** ['fɪʃmʌŋgə^r] *n* peixeiro(-a); **fishmonger's (shop)** peixaria; **fishy** (*inf*) *adj* (*tale*) suspeito

fist [fɪst] *n* punho

fit [fɪt] *adj* em (boa) forma; (*suitable*) adequado, apropriado ▷ *vt* (*subj: clothes*) caber em; (*put in, attach*) colocar; (*equip*) equipar ▷ *vi* (*clothes*) servir; (*parts*) ajustar-se; (*in space, gap*) caber ▷ *n* (*Med*) ataque *m*; **~ to** bom para; **~ for**

adequado para; **a ~ of anger/ pride** um acesso de raiva/orgulho; **by ~s and starts** espasmodicamente **fit in** vi encaixar-se; (person) dar-se bem (com todos); **fitness** n (Med) saúde f, boa forma; **fitted kitchen** (Brit) n cozinha planejada; **fitting** adj apropriado ▷ n (of dress) prova; **fittings** npl (in building) instalações fpl, acessórios mpl

five [faɪv] num cinco; **fiver** (inf) n (Brit) nota de cinco libras; (US) nota de cinco dólares

fix [fɪks] vt (secure) fixar, colocar; (arrange) arranjar; (mend) consertar; (meal, drink) preparar ▷ n: **to be in a ~** estar em apuros **fix up** vt (meeting) marcar; **to ~ sb up with sth** arranjar algo para alguém; **fixed** adj (prices, smile) fixo; **fixture** n (furniture) móvel m fixo; (Sport) desafio, encontro

fizzy ['fɪzɪ] adj com gás, gasoso

flag [flæg] n bandeira; (for signalling) bandeirola; (flagstone) laje f ▷ vi acabar-se, descair **flag down** vt: **to ~ sb down** fazer sinais a alguém para que pare

flagpole ['flægpəul] n mastro de bandeira

flair [flɛəʳ] n (talent) talento; (style) habilidade f

flake [fleɪk] n (of rust, paint) lasca; (of snow, soap powder) floco ▷ vi (also: **~ off**) lascar, descamar-se

flamboyant [flæm'bɔɪənt] adj (dress) espalhafatoso; (person) extravagante

flame [fleɪm] n chama

flammable ['flæməbl] adj inflamável

flan [flæn] (Brit) n torta

flannel ['flænl] n (Brit: also: **face ~**)

pano de rosto; (fabric) flanela; **flannels** npl calça (BR) or calças fpl (PT) de flanela

flap [flæp] n (of pocket, table) aba; (of envelope) dobra ▷ vt (arms) oscilar; (wings) bater ▷ vi (sail, flag) ondular; (inf: also: **be in a ~**) estar atarantado

flare [flɛəʳ] n fogacho, chama; (Mil) foguete m sinalizador; (in skirt etc) folga **flare up** vi chamejar; (fig: person) encolerizar-se; (: violence) irromper

flash [flæʃ] n (of lightning) clarão m; (also: **news ~**) notícias fpl de última hora; (Phot) flash m ▷ vt piscar; (news, message) transmitir; (look, smile) brilhar ▷ vi brilhar; (light on ambulance, eyes etc) piscar; **in a ~** num instante; **to ~ by** or **past** passar como um raio; **flashlight** n lanterna de bolso

flat [flæt] adj plano; (battery) descarregado; (tyre) vazio; (beer) choco; (denial) categórico; (Mus) abemolado; (: voice) desafinado; (rate) único; (fee) fixo ▷ n (Brit: apartment) apartamento; (Mus) bemol m; (Aut) pneu m furado; **~ out** (work) a toque de caixa; **flatten** vt (also: **flatten out**) aplanar; (demolish) arrasar

flatter ['flætəʳ] vt lisonjear; **flattering** adj lisonjeiro; (clothes etc) favorecedor(a)

flaunt [flɔːnt] vt ostentar, pavonear

flavour ['fleɪvəʳ], (US) **flavor** n sabor m ▷ vt condimentar, aromatizar; **strawberry-~ed** com sabor de morango

flaw [flɔː] n defeito; (in character) falha; **flawless** adj impecável

flea [fliː] n pulga

flee [fliː] (pt, pp **fled**) vt fugir de ▷ vi fugir

fleece [fliːs] n tosão m; (coat) velo; (wool) lã f ▷ vt (inf) espoliar

fleet [fliːt] n (gen, of lorries etc) frota; (of ships) esquadra

fleeting ['fliːtɪŋ] adj fugaz

Flemish ['flɛmɪʃ] adj flamengo ▷ n

flesh [flɛʃ] n carne f; (of fruit) polpa

flew [fluː] pt of **fly**

flex [flɛks] n fio ▷ vt (muscles) flexionar; **flexible** adj flexível

flick [flɪk] n pancada leve; (with finger) peteleco, piparote m; (with whip) chicotada ▷ vt dar um peteleco; (switch) apertar **flick through** vt fus folhear

flicker ['flɪkəʳ] vi tremular; (eyelids) tremer

flight [flaɪt] n voo m; (escape) fuga; (of steps) lance m; **flight attendant** (US) n comissário(-a) de bordo

flimsy ['flɪmzɪ] adj (thin) delgado, franzino; (weak) débil; (excuse) fraco

flinch [flɪntʃ] vi encolher-se; **to ~ from sth/from doing sth** vacilar diante de algo/em fazer algo

fling [flɪŋ] (pt, pp **flung**) vt lançar

flint [flɪnt] n pederneira; (in lighter) pedra

flip-flops ['flɪpflɔps] (esp Brit) npl chinelo (de dedo)

flipper ['flɪpəʳ] n (of animal) nadadeira; (for swimmer) pé-de-pato, nadadeira

flirt [fləːt] vi flertar ▷ n namorador(a) m/f, paquerador(a) m/f

float [fləut] n boia; (in procession) carro alegórico; (sum of money) caixa ▷ vi flutuar; (swimmer) boiar

flock [flɔk] n rebanho; (of birds)

bando ▷ vi: **to ~ to** afluir a

flood [flʌd] n enchente f, inundação f ▷ vt inundar, alagar ▷ vi (place) alagar; (people, goods): **to ~ into** inundar; **flooding** n inundação f; **floodlight** n refletor m, holofote m

floor [flɔːʳ] n chão m; (storey) andar m; (of sea) fundo ▷ vt (fig: confuse) confundir, pasmar; **ground ~** (Brit) or **first ~** (US) andar térreo (BR), rés-do-chão (PT); **first ~** (Brit) or **second ~** (US) primeiro andar; **floorboard** n tábua de assoalho; **floor show** n show m

flop [flɔp] n fracasso ▷ vi fracassar; (into chair etc) cair pesadamente

floppy ['flɔpɪ] adj frouxo, mole ▷ n (also: **~ disk**) disquete m

florist ['flɔrɪst] n florista m/f; **florist's, florist's shop** n floricultura

flour ['flauəʳ] n farinha

flourish ['flʌrɪʃ] vi florescer ▷ vt brandir, menear ▷ n: **with a ~** con gestos floreados

flow [fləu] n fluxo; (of river, Elec) corrente f; (of blood) circulação f ▷ vi correr; (traffic) fluir; (blood, Elec) circular; (clothes, hair) ondular

flower ['flauəʳ] n flor f ▷ vi florescer, florir; **flower bed** n canteiro; **flowerpot** n vaso

flown [fləun] pp of **fly**

flu [fluː] n gripe f

fluctuate ['flʌktjueɪt] vi flutuar; (temperature) variar

fluent ['fluːənt] adj fluente; **he speaks ~ French, he's ~ in French** ele fala francês fluentemente

fluff [flʌf] n felpa, penugem f; **fluffy** adj macio, fofo

fluid ['fluːɪd] adj fluido ▷ n fluido

fluke [fluːk] (inf) n sorte f

flung [flʌŋ] pt, pp of **fling**

fluoride ['fluəraɪd] n fluoreto

flurry ['flʌrɪ] n (of snow) lufada; **~ of activity/excitement** muita atividade/animação

flush [flʌʃ] n (on face) rubor m ▷ vt lavar com água ▷ vi ruborizar-se ▷ adj: **~ with** rente com; **to ~ the toilet** dar descarga **flush out** vt levantar

flute [flu:t] n flauta

flutter ['flʌtəʳ] n agitação f; (of wings) bater m ▷ vi esvoaçar

fly [flaɪ] (pt **flew**, pp **flown**) n mosca; (on trousers: also: **flies**) braguilha ▷ vt (plane) pilotar; (passengers, cargo) transportar (de avião); (distances) percorrer ▷ vi voar; (passengers) ir de avião; (escape) fugir; (flag) hastear-se **fly away** vi voar **fly off** vi = **fly away**; **flying** n aviação f ▷ adj: **flying visit** visita de médico; **with flying colours** brilhantemente; **flying saucer** n disco voador; **flyover** (Brit) n viaduto

foal [fəul] n potro

foam [fəum] n espuma ▷ vi espumar; **foam rubber** n espuma de borracha

focus ['fəukəs] (pl **focuses**) n foco ▷ vt enfocar ▷ vi: **to ~ on** enfocar, focalizar; **in/out of ~** em foco/fora de foco

fog [fɔg] n nevoeiro; **foggy** adj nevoento

foil [fɔɪl] vt frustrar ▷ n folha metálica; (also: **kitchen ~**) folha or papel m de alumínio; (complement) contraste m, complemento; (Fencing) florete m

fold [fəuld] n dobra, vinco, prega; (of skin) ruga; (Agr) redil m, curral m ▷ vt dobrar; **to ~ one's arms** cruzar os braços **fold up** vi dobrar;

(business) abrir falência ▷ vt dobrar; **folder** n pasta; **folding** adj dobrável

folk [fəuk] npl gente f ▷ cpd popular, folclórico; **folks** npl (family) família, parentes mpl; **folklore** ['fəuklɔ:ʳ] n folclore m

follow ['fɔləu] vt seguir ▷ vi seguir; (result) resultar; **I don't quite ~ you** não consigo acompanhar o seu raciocínio; **to ~ suit** fazer o mesmo **follow up** vt (letter) responder a; (offer) levar adiante; (case) acompanhar; **follower** n seguidor(a) m/f; **following** adj seguinte ▷ n adeptos mpl

fond [fɔnd] adj carinhoso; (hopes) absurdo, descabido; **to be ~ of** gostar de

food [fu:d] n comida; **food mixer** n batedeira; **food poisoning** n intoxicação f alimentar; **food processor** n multiprocessador m de cozinha

fool [fu:l] n tolo(-a); (Culin) purê m de frutas com creme ▷ vt enganar ▷ vi (gen: fool around) brincar; **foolish** adj burro; (careless) imprudente; **foolproof** adj infalível

foot [fut] (pl **feet**) n pé m; (of animal) pata; (measure) pé (304 mm; 12 inches) ▷ vt (bill) pagar; **on ~** a pé; **footage** n (Cinema: length) ≈ metragem f; (: material) sequências fpl; **football** n bola; (game: Brit) futebol m; (: US) futebol norte-americano; **footballer** n jogador m de futebol; **football player** n jogador m de futebol; **footbridge** n passarela; **foothold** n apoio para o pé; **footing** n (fig) posição f; **to lose one's footing** escorregar; **footnote** n nota ao pé

da página, nota de rodapé;
footpath n caminho, atalho;
footprint n pegada; **footstep** n
passo; **footwear** n calçados mpl

 KEYWORD

for [fɔːʳ] prep **1** (indicating destination,
direction) para; **he went for the
paper** foi pegar o jornal; **is this for
me?** é para mim?; **it's time for
lunch** é hora de almoçar
2 (indicating purpose) para; **what's
it for?** para quê serve?; **to pray for
peace** orar pela paz
3 (on behalf of, representing) por; **he
works for the government/a
local firm** ele trabalha para o
governo/uma firma local; **G for
George** G de George
4 (because of) por; **for this reason**
por esta razão; **for fear of being
criticized** com medo de ser
criticado
5 (with regard to) para; **it's cold for
July** está frio para julho
6 (in exchange for) por; **it was sold
for £5** foi vendido por £5
7 (in favour of) a favor de; **are you
for or against us?** você está a
favor de ou contra nós?; **I'm all for
it** concordo plenamente, tem todo
o meu apoio; **vote for X** vote em X
8 (referring to distance): **there are
roadworks for 5 km** há obras na
estrada por 5 quilômetros; **we
walked for miles** andamos
quilômetros
9 (referring to time): **she will be
away for a month** ela ficará fora
um mês; **I have known her for
years** eu a conheço há anos; **can
you do it for tomorrow?** você
pode fazer isso para amanhã?

10 (with infinite clause): **it is not for
me to decide** não cabe a mim
decidir; **it would be best for you
to leave** seria melhor que você
fosse embora; **there is still time
for you to do it** ainda há tempo
para você fazer isso; **for this to be
possible ...** para que isso seja
possível ...
11 (in spite of) apesar de
▷ conj (since, as: rather formal) pois,
porque

forbid [fə'bɪd] (pt **forbad(e)**, pp
forbidden) vt proibir; **to ~ sb to
do sth** proibir alguém de fazer algo
force [fɔːs] n força ▷ vt forçar; **the
Forces** npl (Brit) as Forças
Armadas; **in ~** em vigor; **forceful**
adj enérgico, vigoroso
ford [fɔːd] n vau m
fore [fɔːʳ] n: **to come to the ~**
salientar-se
forearm ['fɔːrɑːm] n antebraço
forecast ['fɔːkɑːst] (irreg: like **cast**)
n previsão f; (also: **weather ~**)
previsão do tempo ▷ vt
prognosticar, prever
forefinger ['fɔːfɪŋgəʳ] n (dedo)
indicador m
foreground ['fɔːgraund] n
primeiro plano
forehead ['fɔrɪd] n testa
foreign ['fɔrɪn] adj estrangeiro;
(trade) exterior; **foreigner** n
estrangeiro(-a); **foreign
exchange** n câmbio; **Foreign
Office** (Brit) n Ministério das
Relações Exteriores
foreman ['fɔːmən] irreg n capataz
m; (in construction) contramestre
m, primeiro jurado
foremost ['fɔːməust] adj principal
▷ adv: **first and ~** antes de mais nada

forensic [fə'rɛnsɪk] *adj* forense;
~ **medicine** medicina legal
foresee [fɔː'siː] (*irreg: like* **see**) *vt*
prever; **foreseeable** *adj* previsível
forest ['fɔrɪst] *n* floresta
forestry ['fɔrɪstrɪ] *n* silvicultura
forever [fə'rɛvəʳ] *adv* para sempre
foreword ['fɔːwəd] *n* prefácio
forfeit ['fɔːfɪt] *vt* perder (direito a)
forgave [fə'geɪv] *pt of* **forgive**
forge [fɔːdʒ] *n* ferraria ▷ *vt*
falsificar; (*metal*) forjar **forge
ahead** *vi* avançar
constantemente; **forger** *n*
falsificador(a) *m/f*; **forgery** *n*
falsificação *f*
forget [fə'gɛt] (*pt* **forgot**, *pp*
forgotten) *vt, vi* esquecer;
forgetful *adj* esquecido
forgive [fə'gɪv] (*pt* **forgave**, *pp*
forgiven) *vt* perdoar; **to ~ sb for
sth** perdoar algo a alguém, perdoar
alguém de algo
fork [fɔːk] *n* (*for eating*) garfo; (*for
gardening*) forquilha; (*of roads etc*)
bifurcação *f* ▷ *vi* bifurcar-se **fork
out** (*inf*) *vt* (*pay*) desembolsar,
morrer em
forlorn [fə'lɔːn] *adj* desolado;
(*attempt*) desesperado; (*hope*)
último
form [fɔːm] *n* forma; (*type*) tipo;
(*Sch*) série *f*; (*questionnaire*)
formulário ▷ *vt* formar;
(*organization*) criar; **to ~ a queue**
(*Brit*) fazer fila; **in top ~** em plena
forma
formal ['fɔːməl] *adj* (*offer, receipt*)
oficial; (*person etc*) cerimonioso;
(*occasion, education*) formal; (*dress*)
a rigor (*BR*), de cerimônia (*PT*);
(*garden*) simétrico
format ['fɔːmæt] *n* formato ▷ *vt*
(*Comput*) formatar

former ['fɔːməʳ] *adj* anterior;
(*earlier*) antigo; **the ~ ... the latter
...** aquele ... este ...; **formerly** *adv*
anteriormente
formidable ['fɔːmɪdəbl] *adj*
terrível, temível
formula ['fɔːmjulə] (*pl* **formulas** *or*
formulae) *n* fórmula
fort [fɔːt] *n* forte *m*
fortify ['fɔːtɪfaɪ] *vt* (*city*) fortificar;
(*person*) fortalecer
fortnight ['fɔːtnaɪt] (*Brit*) *n*
quinzena, quinze dias *mpl*;
fortnightly *adj* quinzenal ▷ *adv*
quinzenalmente
fortunate ['fɔːtʃənɪt] *adj* (*event*)
feliz; (*person*): **to be ~** ter sorte; **it is
~ that ...** é uma sorte que ...;
fortunately *adv* felizmente
fortune ['fɔːtʃən] *n* sorte *f*; (*wealth*)
fortuna; **fortune-teller** *n*
adivinho(-a)
forty ['fɔːtɪ] *num* quarenta
forward ['fɔːwəd] *adj* (*movement*)
para a frente; (*position*) avançado;
(*not shy*) imodesto, presunçoso ▷ *n*
(*Sport*) atacante *m* ▷ *vt* (*letter*)
remeter; (*goods, parcel*) expedir;
(*career*) promover; (*plans*) ativar;
to move ~ avançar; ~ **planning**
planejamento para o futuro;
forwards *adv* para a frente;
forward slash *n* barra
foster ['fɔstəʳ] *vt* tutelar; (*activity*)
promover; **foster child** *irreg n*
tutelado(-a)
fought [fɔːt] *pt, pp of* **fight**
foul [faul] *adj* horrível; (*language*)
obsceno ▷ *n* (*Sport*) falta ▷ *vt* sujar;
foul play *n* (*Law*) crime *m*
found [faund] *pt, pp of* **find** ▷ *vt*
(*establish*) fundar; **foundation**
[faun'deɪʃən] *n* (*act*) fundação *f*;
(*base*) base *f*; (*also*: **foundation**

cream) creme *m* base;
foundations *npl* (*of building*)
alicerces *mpl*
founder ['faʊndə^r] *n* fundador(a)
m/f ▷ *vi* naufragar
fountain ['faʊntɪn] *n* chafariz *m*;
fountain pen *n* caneta-tinteiro *f*
four [fɔː^r] *num* quatro; **on all ~s** de
quatro; **four-letter word** *n*
palavrão *m*; **fourteen** *num*
catorze; *see also* **five**; **fourth** *num*
quarto
fowl [faʊl] *n* ave *f* (doméstica)
fox [fɔks] *n* raposa ▷ *vt* deixar
perplexo
foyer ['fɔɪeɪ] *n* saguão *m*
fraction ['frækʃən] *n* fração *f*
fracture ['fræktʃə^r] *n* fratura ▷ *vt*
fraturar
fragile ['frædʒaɪl] *adj* frágil
fragment ['frægmənt] *n*
fragmento
frail [freɪl] *adj* (*person*) fraco;
(*structure*) frágil
frame [freɪm] *n* (*of building*)
estrutura; (*body*) corpo; (*of picture,
door*) moldura; (*of spectacles: also:*
~s) armação *f*, aro ▷ *vt* (*picture*)
emoldurar; **framework** *n*
armação *f*
France [frɑːns] *n* França
frank [fræŋk] *adj* franco ▷ *vt* (*letter*)
franquear; **frankly** *adv*
francamente; (*candidly*)
abertamente
frantic ['fræntɪk] *adj* frenético;
(*person*) fora de si
fraud [frɔːd] *n* fraude *f*; (*person*)
impostor(a) *m/f*
fraught [frɔːt] *adj* tenso; **~ with**
repleto de
fray [freɪ] *n* combate *m*, luta ▷ *vi*
esfiapar-se; **tempers were ~ed**
estavam com os nervos em

frangalhos
freak [friːk] *n* (*person*) anormal *m/f*;
(*event*) anomalia
freckle ['frɛkl] *n* sarda
free [friː] *adj* livre; (*seat*)
desocupada; (*costing nothing*)
gratis, gratuito ▷ *vt* pôr em
liberdade; (*jammed object*) soltar;
~ (of charge) grátis, de graça;
freedom *n* liberdade *f*; **freelance**
adj freelance; **freely** *adv*
livremente; **free-range** *n* (*egg*)
caseiro; **freeway** (*US*) *n* via
expressa; **free will** *n* livre arbítrio;
of one's own free will por sua
própria vontade
freeze [friːz] (*pt* **froze**, *pp* **frozen**) *vi*
gelar(-se), congelar-se ▷ *vt*
congelar ▷ *n* geada; (*on arms,
wages*) congelamento; **freezer** *n*
congelador *m*, freezer *m* (*BR*);
freezing *adj*: **freezing (cold)**
(*weather*) glacial; (*water*) gelado;
3 degrees below freezing 3 graus
abaixo de zero; **freezing point** *n*
ponto de congelamento
freight [freɪt] *n* (*goods*) carga;
(*money charged*) frete *m*; **freight
train** (*US*) *n* trem *m* de carga
French [frɛntʃ] *adj* francês(-esa)
▷ *n* (*Ling*) francês *m*; **the French**
npl os franceses; **French bean**
(*Brit*) *n* feijão *m* comum; **French
fried potatoes** *npl* batatas *fpl*
fritas; **Frenchman** *irreg n* francês
m; **Frenchwoman** *irreg n* francesa
frenzy ['frɛnzɪ] *n* frenesi *m*
frequent [*adj* 'friːkwənt, *vt*
frɪ'kwɛnt] *adj* frequente ▷ *vt*
frequentar; **frequently** *adv*
frequentemente, a miúdo
fresh [frɛʃ] *adj* fresco; (*new*) novo;
(*cheeky*) atrevido; **freshen** *vi* (*wind,
air*) tornar-se mais forte **freshen**

up vi (person) lavar-se, refrescar-se;
freshly adv recentemente, há pouco

fret [frɛt] vi afligir-se

friction ['frɪkʃən] n fricção f; (between people) atrito

Friday ['fraɪdɪ] n sexta-feira f

fridge [frɪdʒ] n geladeira (BR), frigorífico (PT)

fried [fraɪd] adj frito; **~ egg** ovo estrelado or frito

friend [frɛnd] n amigo(-a); **friendly** adj simpático ▷ n (also: **friendly match**) amistoso; **friendship** n amizade f

fries [fraɪz] (esp US) npl = **French fried potatoes**

fright [fraɪt] n terror m; (scare) pavor m; **to take ~** assustar-se; **frighten** vt assustar; **frightened** adj: **to be frightened of** ter medo de; **frightening** adj assustador(a); **frightful** adj terrível, horrível

frill [frɪl] n babado

fringe [frɪndʒ] n franja; (on shawl etc) beira, orla; (edge: of forest etc) margem f

fritter ['frɪtəʳ] n bolinho frito **fritter away** vt desperdiçar

frivolous ['frɪvələs] adj frívolo; (activity) fútil

fro [frəu] adj see **to**

frock [frɔk] n vestido

frog [frɔg] n rã f; **frogman** irreg n homem-rã m

KEYWORD

from [frɔm] prep **1** (indicating starting place) de; **where do you come from?** de onde você é?; **we flew from London to Glasgow** fomos de avião de Londres para Glasgow; **to escape from sth/sb** escapar de algo/alguém
2 (indicating origin etc) de; **a letter/telephone call from my sister** uma carta/um telefonema da minha irmã; **tell him from me that ...** diga a ele que da minha parte ...; **to drink from the bottle** beber na garrafa
3 (indicating time): **from one o'clock to** or **until** or **till two** da uma hora até às duas; **from January (on)** a partir de janeiro
4 (indicating distance) de; **we're still a long way from home** ainda estamos muito longe de casa
5 (indicating price, number etc) de; **prices range from £10 to £50** os preços vão de £10 a £50
6 (indicating difference) de; **he can't tell red from green** ele não pode diferenciar vermelho do verde
7 (because of/on the basis of): **from what he says** pelo que ele diz; **to act from conviction** agir por convicção; **weak from hunger** fraco de fome

front [frʌnt] n frente f; (of vehicle) parte f dianteira; (of house) fachada; (also: **sea ~**) orla marítima ▷ adj da frente; **in ~ (of)** em frente (de); **front door** n porta principal; **frontier** ['frʌntɪəʳ] n fronteira; **front page** n primeira página

frost [frɔst] n geada; (also: **hoar~**) gelo; **frostbite** n ulceração f produzida pelo frio; **frosty** adj (window) coberto de geada; (welcome) glacial

froth [frɔθ] n espuma

frown [fraun] vi franzir as sobrancelhas, amarrar a cara

froze [frəuz] pt of **freeze**

frozen ['frəuzn] *pp of* **freeze**
fruit [fru:t] *n inv* fruta; *(fig)* fruto;
  fruit juice *n* suco *(BR)* or sumo *(PT)*
  de frutas; **fruit machine** *(Brit)* n
  caça-níqueis *m inv* *(BR)*, máquina
  de jogo *(PT)*; **fruit salad** *n* salada
  de frutas
frustrate [frʌs'treit] *vt* frustrar
fry [frai] *(pt, pp* **fried)** *vt* fritar; *see*
  also **small**; **frying pan** *n* frigideira
fudge [fʌdʒ] *n (Culin)* ≈ doce *m* de
  leite
fuel [fjuəl] *n (gen, for heating)*
  combustível *m*; *(for propelling)*
  carburante *m*; **fuel tank** *n*
  depósito de combustível
fulfil [ful'fil], *(US)* **fulfill** *vt*
  (function) cumprir; *(condition)*
  satisfazer; *(wish, desire)* realizar
full [ful] *adj* cheio; *(use, volume)*
  máximo; *(complete)* completo;
  (information) detalhado; *(price)*
  integral; *(skirt)* folgado ▷ *adv*: **~**
  well perfeitamente; **I'm ~ (up)**
  estou satisfeito; **~ employment**
  pleno emprego; **a ~ two hours**
  duas horas completas; **at ~ speed**
  a toda a velocidade; **in ~**
  integralmente; **full stop** *n* ponto
  (final); **full-time** *adj (work)* de
  tempo completo or integral; **fully**
  adv completamente; *(at least)*:
  fully as big as pelo menos tão
  grande como
fumble ['fʌmbl] *vi* atrapalhar-se;
  fumble with *vt fus* atrapalhar-se
  com
fume [fju:m] *vi* fumegar; *(be angry)*
  estar com raiva; **fumes** *npl* gases
  mpl
fun [fʌn] *n* divertimento; **to have ~**
  divertir-se; **for ~** de brincadeira;
  to make ~ of fazer troça de,
  zombar de

function ['fʌŋkʃən] *n* função *f*;
  (reception, dinner) recepção *f* ▷ *vi*
  funcionar
fund [fʌnd] *n* fundo; *(source, store)*
  fonte *f*; **funds** *npl (money)* fundos
  mpl
fundamental [fʌndə'mɛntl] *adj*
  fundamental
funeral ['fju:nərəl] *n (burial)*
  enterro
funfair ['fʌnfɛəʳ] *(Brit)* n parque *m*
  de diversões
fungus ['fʌŋgəs] *(pl* **fungi)** *n* fungo;
  (mould) bolor *m*, mofo
funnel ['fʌnl] *n* funil *m*; *(of ship)*
  chaminé *m*
funny ['fʌni] *adj* engraçado,
  divertido; *(strange)* esquisito,
  estranho
fur [fə:ʳ] *n* pele *f*; *(Brit: in kettle etc)*
  depósito, crosta
furious ['fjuəriəs] *adj* furioso;
  (effort) incrível
furnish ['fə:niʃ] *vt* mobiliar *(BR)*,
  mobilar *(PT)*; *(supply)*: **to ~ sb with**
  sth fornecer algo a alguém;
  furnishings *npl* mobília
furniture ['fə:nitʃəʳ] *n* mobília,
  móveis *mpl*; **piece of ~** móvel *m*
furry ['fə:ri] *adj* peludo
further ['fə:ðəʳ] *adj* novo, adicional
  ▷ *adv* mais longe; *(more)* mais;
  (moreover) além disso ▷ *vt*
  promover; **further education**
  (Brit) n educação *f* superior;
  furthermore *adv* além disso
furthest ['fə:ðist] *superl of* **far**
fury ['fjuəri] *n* fúria
fuse [fju:z] *n* fusível *m*; *(for bomb*
  etc) espoleta, mecha ▷ *vt* fundir;
  (fig) unir ▷ *vi* fundir-se;
  unir-se; **to ~ the lights** *(Brit: Elec)*
  queimar as luzes; **fuse box** *n* caixa
  de fusíveis

fuss [fʌs] *n* estardalhaço; (*complaining*) escândalo; **to make a ~** criar caso; **to make a ~ of sb** paparicar alguém; **fussy** *adj* (*person*) exigente; (*dress, style*) espalhafatoso

future ['fjuːtʃəʳ] *adj* futuro ▷ *n* futuro; **in (the) ~** no futuro

fuze [fjuːz] (*US*) = **fuse**

fuzzy ['fʌzɪ] *adj* (*Phot*) indistinto; (*hair*) frisado, encrespado

g

G, g [dʒiː] *n* (*Mus*) sol *m*

gadget ['gædʒɪt] *n* aparelho, engenhoca

Gaelic ['geɪlɪk] *adj* gaélico(-a) ▷ *n* (*Ling*) gaélico

gag [gæg] *n* (*on mouth*) mordaça; (*joke*) piada ▷ *vt* amordaçar

gain [geɪn] *n* ganho; (*profit*) lucro ▷ *vt* ganhar ▷ *vi* (*watch*) adiantar-se; (*benefit*): **to ~ from sth** tirar proveito de algo; **to ~ on sb** aproximar-se de alguém; **to ~ 3lbs (in weight)** engordar 3 libras

gal. *abbr* = **gallon**

gale [geɪl] *n* ventania; **~ force 10** vento de força 10

gallery ['gælərɪ] *n* (*in theatre etc*) galeria; (*also*: **art ~**: *public*) museu *m*; (: *private*) galeria (de arte)

gallon ['gæln] *n* galão *m* (*Brit* = 4.5 *litros*, *US* = 3.8 *litros*)

gallop ['gæləp] *n* galope *m* ▷ *vi*

galopar

gallstone ['gɔ:lstəun] n cálculo biliar

gamble ['gæmbl] n risco ▷ vt, vi jogar, arriscar; **gambler** n jogador(a) m/f; **gambling** n jogo

game [geɪm] n jogo; (match) partida; (esp Tennis) jogada; (strategy) plano, esquema m; (Hunting) caça ▷ adj (willing): **to be ~ for anything** topar qualquer parada; **big ~** caça grossa; **game show** n game show m

gang [gæŋ] n bando, grupo; (of criminals) gangue f; (of workmen) turma ▷ vi: **to ~ up on sb** conspirar contra alguém

gangster ['gæŋstəʳ] n gângster m, bandido

gap [gæp] n brecha, fenda; (in trees, traffic) abertura; (in time) intervalo; (difference): **~ (between)** diferença (entre)

gape [geɪp] vi (person) estar or ficar boquiaberto; (hole) abrir-se

garage ['gærɑ:ʒ] n garagem f; (for car repairs) oficina (mecânica)

garbage ['gɑ:bɪdʒ] n (US) lixo; (inf: nonsense) disparates mpl; **garbage can** (US) n lata de lixo; **garbage collector** (US) n lixeiro(-a)

garden ['gɑ:dn] n jardim m; **gardens** npl (public park) jardim público, parque m; **gardener** n jardineiro(-a); **gardening** n jardinagem f

garlic ['gɑ:lɪk] n alho

garment ['gɑ:mənt] n peça de roupa

garrison ['gærɪsn] n guarnição f

gas [gæs] n gás m; (US: gasoline) gasolina ▷ vt asfixiar com gás; **gas cooker** (Brit) n fogão m a gás; **gas cylinder** n bujão m de gás; **gas**

fire (Brit) n aquecedor m a gás

gasket ['gæskɪt] n (Aut) junta, gaxeta

gasoline ['gæsəli:n] (US) n gasolina

gasp [gɑ:sp] n arfada ▷ vi arfar **gasp out** vt dizer com voz entrecortada

gas station (US) n posto de gasolina

gate [geɪt] n portão m; **gate-crash** ['geɪtkræʃ] (Brit) vt entrar de penetra em; **gateway** n portão m, passagem f

gather ['gæðəʳ] vt colher; (assemble) reunir; (Sewing) franzir; (understand) compreender ▷ vi reunir-se; **to ~ speed** acelerar(-se); **gathering** n reunião f, assembleia

gauge [geɪdʒ] n (instrument) medidor m ▷ vt (fig: sb's capabilities, character) avaliar

gave [geɪv] pt of **give**

gay [geɪ] adj (homosexual) gay; (old-fashioned: cheerful) alegre; (colour) vistoso; (music) vivo

gaze [geɪz] n olhar m fixo ▷ vi: **to ~ at sth** fitar algo

GB abbr = **Great Britain**

gear [gɪəʳ] n equipamento; (Tech) engrenagem f; (Aut) velocidade f, marcha (BR), mudança (PT) ▷ vt (fig: adapt): **to ~ sth to** preparar algo para; **top** (Brit) or **high** (US)/ **low ~** quinta/primeira (marcha); **in ~** engrenado

geese [gi:s] npl of **goose**

gel [dʒɛl] n gel m

gem [dʒɛm] n joia, gema

Gemini ['dʒɛmɪnaɪ] n Gêminis m, Gêmeos mpl

gender ['dʒɛndəʳ] n gênero

general ['dʒɛnərl] n general m ▷ adj geral; **in ~** em geral; **general anaesthetic** n anestesia geral;

generally adv geralmente;
general practitioner n clínico(-a)
geral
generate ['dʒɛnəreɪt] vt gerar;
generator n gerador m
generous ['dʒɛnərəs] adj generoso;
(measure etc) abundante
genetically [dʒɪ'nɛtɪklɪ] adv: ~
modified (food etc) transgênico
Geneva [dʒɪ'niːvə] n Genebra
genitals ['dʒɛnɪtlz] npl órgãos mpl
genitais
genius ['dʒiːnɪəs] n gênio
gentle ['dʒɛntl] adj (touch, breeze)
leve, suave; (landscape) suave;
(animal) manso
gentleman ['dʒɛntlmən] irreg n
senhor m; (referring to social
position) fidalgo; (well-bred man)
cavalheiro
gently ['dʒɛntlɪ] adv suavemente
gents [dʒɛnts] n banheiro de
homens (BR), casa de banho dos
homens (PT)
genuine ['dʒɛnjuɪn] adj autêntico;
(person) sincero
geography [dʒɪ'ɔgrəfɪ] n geografia
geology [dʒɪ'ɔlədʒɪ] n geologia
geometry [dʒɪ'ɔmətrɪ] n
geometria
geranium [dʒɪ'reɪnjəm] n gerânio
geriatric [dʒɛrɪ'ætrɪk] adj geriátrico
germ [dʒəːm] n micróbio, bacilo
German ['dʒəːmən] adj
alemão(-mã) ▷ n alemão(-mã) m/f;
(Ling) alemão m; **German measles**
n rubéola
Germany ['dʒəːmənɪ] n Alemanha
gesture ['dʒɛstjəʳ] n gesto

KEYWORD

get [gɛt] (pt, pp **got**) ((US) pp **gotten**)
vi **1** (become, be) ficar, tornar-se; **to
get old/tired/cold** envelhecer/
cansar-se/resfriar-se; **to get
annoyed/bored** aborrecer-se/
amuar-se; **to get drunk**
embebedar-se; **to get dirty**
sujar-se; **to get killed/married** ser
morto/casar-se; **when do I get
paid?** quando eu recebo?, quando
eu vou ser pago?; **it's getting late**
está ficando tarde
2 (go): **to get to/from** ir para/de;
to get home chegar em casa
3 (begin) começar a; **to get to
know sb** começar a conhecer
alguém; **let's get going** or **started**
vamos lá!
▷ modal aux vb: **you've got to do it**
você tem que fazê-lo
▷ vt **1**: **to get sth done** (do) fazer
algo; (have done) mandar fazer
algo; **to get one's hair cut** cortar
o cabelo; **to get the car going** or
to go fazer o carro andar; **to get sb
to do sth** convencer alguém a
fazer algo; **to get sth/sb ready**
preparar algo/arrumar alguém
2 (obtain) ter; (find) achar; (fetch)
buscar; **to get sth for sb** arranjar
algo para alguém; (fetch) ir buscar
algo para alguém; **get me Mr
Harris, please** (Tel) pode chamar o
Sr Harris, por favor; **can I get you a
drink?** você está servido?
3 (receive: present, letter) receber;
(acquire: reputation, prize) ganhar
4 (catch) agarrar; (hit: target etc)
pegar; **to get sb by the arm/
throat** agarrar alguém pelo braço/
pela garganta; **get him!** pega ele!
5 (take, move) levar; **to get sth to
sb** levar algo para alguém; **I can't
get it in/out/through** não
consigo enfiá-lo/tirá-lo/passá-lo;
do you think we'll get it through

g

the door? você acha que conseguiremos passar isto na porta? **6** (*plane, bus etc*) pegar, tomar; **where do I get the train to Birmingham?** onde eu pego o trem para Birmingham?
7 (*understand*) entender; (*hear*) ouvir; **I've got it** entendi; **I don't get your meaning** não entendo o que você quer dizer
8 (*have, possess*): **to have got** ter
get about *vi* (*news*) espalhar-se
get along *vi* (*agree*) entender-se; (*depart*) ir embora; (*manage*) = **get by**
get around = **get round**
get at *vt fus* (*attack, criticize*) atacar; (*reach*) alcançar; **what are you getting at?** o que você está querendo dizer?
get away *vi* (*leave*) partir; (*escape*) escapar
get away with *vt fus* conseguir fazer impunemente
get back *vi* (*return*) regressar, voltar ▷ *vt* receber de volta, recobrar
get by *vi* (*pass*) passar; (*manage*) virar-se
get down *vi* descer ▷ *vt fus* abaixar ▷ *vt* (*object*) abaixar, descer; (*depress: person*) deprimir
get down to *vt fus* (*work*) pôr-se a (fazer)
get in *vi* entrar; (*train*) chegar; (*arrive home*) voltar para casa
get into *vt fus* entrar em; (*vehicle*) subir em; (*clothes*) pôr, vestir, enfiar; **to get into bed/a rage** meter-se na cama/ficar com raiva
get off *vi* (*from train etc*) saltar (*BR*), descer (*PT*); (*depart*) sair; (*escape*) escapar ▷ *vt* (*remove: clothes, stain*) tirar; (*send off*) mandar ▷ *vt fus* (*train, bus*) saltar de (*BR*), sair de (*PT*)

get on *vi* (*at exam etc*): **how are you getting on?** como vai?; (*agree*): **to get on (with)** entender-se (com) ▷ *vt fus* (*train etc*) subir em (*BR*), subir para (*PT*); (*horse*) montar em
get out *vi* (*of place, vehicle*) sair ▷ *vt* (*take out*) tirar
get out of *vt fus* (*duty etc*) escapar de
get over *vt fus* (*illness*) restabelecer-se de
get round *vt fus* rodear; (*fig: person*) convencer
get through *vi* (*Tel*) completar a ligação
get through to *vt fus* (*Tel*) comunicar-se com
get together *vi* (*people*) reunir-se ▷ *vt* reunir
get up *vi* levantar-se ▷ *vt fus* levantar
get up to *vt fus* (*reach*) chegar a; (*Brit: prank etc*) fazer

getaway ['gɛtəweɪ] *n* fuga, escape *m*
ghastly ['gɑːstlɪ] *adj* horrível; (*building*) medonho; (*appearance*) horripilante; (*pale*) pálido
ghost [gəust] *n* fantasma *m*
giant ['dʒaɪənt] *n* gigante *m* ▷ *adj* gigantesco, gigante
gift [gɪft] *n* presente *m*, dádiva; (*ability*) dom *m*, talento; **gifted** *adj* bem-dotado; **gift shop**, (*US*) **gift store** *n* loja de presentes
gigantic [dʒaɪ'gæntɪk] *adj* gigantesco
giggle ['gɪgl] *vi* dar risadinha boba
gills [gɪlz] *npl* (*of fish*) guelras *fpl*, brânquias *fpl*
gilt [gɪlt] *adj* dourado ▷ *n* dourado
gimmick ['gɪmɪk] *n* truque *m or* macete *m* (publicitário)
gin [dʒɪn] *n* gim *m*, genebra

ginger ['dʒɪndʒəʳ] n gengibre m

gipsy ['dʒɪpsɪ] n cigano

giraffe [dʒɪ'rɑːf] n girafa

girl [gəːl] n (small) menina (BR), rapariga (PT); (young woman) jovem f, moça; (daughter) filha; **girlfriend** n (of girl) amiga; (of boy) namorada; **Girl Guide** (Brit) n bandeirante f

gist [dʒɪst] n essencial m

○ KEYWORD

give [gɪv] (pt **gave**, pp **given**) vt
1 (hand over) dar; **to give sb sth, give sth to sb** dar algo a alguém
2 (used with n to replace a vb): **to give a cry/sigh/push** etc dar um grito/suspiro/empurrão etc; **to give a speech/a lecture** fazer um discurso/uma palestra
3 (tell, deliver: news, advice, message etc) dar; **to give the right/wrong answer** dar a resposta certa/errada
4 (supply, provide: opportunity, surprise, job etc) dar; (bestow: title, honour, right) conceder; **the sun gives warmth and light** o sol fornece calor e luz
5 (dedicate: time, one's life/attention) dedicar; **she gave it all her attention** ela dedicou toda sua atenção a isto
6 (organize): **to give a party/dinner** etc dar uma festa/jantar etc
▷ vi **1** (also: **give way**: break, collapse) dar folga; **his legs gave beneath him** suas pernas bambearam; **the roof/floor gave as I stepped on it** o telhado/chão desabou quando eu pisei nele
2 (stretch: fabric) dar de si

give away vt (money, opportunity) dar; (secret, information) revelar

give back vt devolver

give in vi (yield) ceder ▷ vt (essay etc) entregar

give off vt (heat, smoke) soltar

give out vt (distribute) distribuir; (make known) divulgar

give up vi (surrender) desistir, dar-se por vencido ▷ vt (job, boyfriend, habit) renunciar a; (idea, hope) abandonar; **to give up smoking** deixar de fumar; **to give o.s. up** entregar-se

give way vi (yield) ceder; (break, collapse: rope) arrebentar; (: ladder) quebrar; (Brit: Aut) dar a preferência (BR), dar prioridade (PT)

glacier ['glæsɪəʳ] n glaciar m, geleira

glad [glæd] adj contente

gladly ['glædlɪ] adv com muito prazer

glamorous ['glæmərəs] adj encantador(a), glamuroso

glamour ['glæməʳ] n encanto, glamour m

glance [glɑːns] n relance m, vista de olhos ▷ vi: **to ~ at** olhar (de relance) **glance off** vt fus (bullet) ricochetear em

gland [glænd] n glândula

glare [glɛəʳ] n (of anger) olhar m furioso; (of light) luminosidade f; (of publicity) foco ▷ vi brilhar; **to ~ at** olhar furiosamente para; **glaring** adj (mistake) notório

glass [glɑːs] n vidro, cristal m; (for drinking) copo; **glasses** npl (spectacles) óculos mpl

glaze [gleɪz] vt (door) envidraçar; (pottery) vitrificar ▷ n verniz m

gleam [gliːm] vi brilhar

glide [glaɪd] vi deslizar; (Aviat: birds) planar; **glider** n (Aviat)

g

planador *m*

glimmer ['glɪmər] *n* luz *f* trêmula; (*of interest, hope*) lampejo

glimpse [glɪmps] *n* vista rápida, vislumbre *m* ▷ *vt* vislumbrar, ver de relance

glint [glɪnt] *vi* cintilar

glisten ['glɪsn] *vi* brilhar

glitter ['glɪtər] *vi* reluzir, brilhar

global ['gləʊbl] *adj* mundial; **globalization** [gləʊbəlaɪ'zeɪʃən] *n* globalização *f*; **global warming** *n* aquecimento global

globe [gləʊb] *n* globo, esfera

gloom [gluːm] *n* escuridão *f*; (*sadness*) tristeza; **gloomy** *adj* escuro; (*sad*) triste

glorious ['glɔːrɪəs] *adj* (*weather*) magnífico; (*future*) glorioso

glory ['glɔːrɪ] *n* glória

gloss [glɒs] *n* (*shine*) brilho; (*also: ~ paint*) pintura brilhante, esmalte *m* **gloss over** *vt fus* encobrir

glossary ['glɒsərɪ] *n* glossário

glossy ['glɒsɪ] *adj* lustroso

glove [glʌv] *n* luva

glow [gləʊ] *vi* (*shine*) brilhar; (*fire*) arder

glucose ['gluːkəʊs] *n* glicose *f*

glue [gluː] *n* cola ▷ *vt* colar

GM *adj abbr* (= *genetically modified*) geneticamente modificado

gnaw [nɔː] *vt* roer

 KEYWORD

go [gəʊ] (*pt* **went**, *pp* **gone**, *pl* **goes**) *vi* **1** ir; (*travel, move*) viajar; **a car went by** um carro passou; **he has gone to Aberdeen** ele foi para Aberdeen

2 (*depart*) sair, ir embora

3 (*attend*) ir; **she went to university in Rio** ela fez universidade no Rio; **he goes to the local church** ele frequenta a igreja local

4 (*take part in an activity*) ir; **to go for a walk** ir passear

5 (*work*) funcionar; **the bell went just then** a campainha acabou de tocar

6 (*become*): **to go pale/mouldy** ficar pálido/mofado

7 (*be sold*): **to go for £10** ser vendido por £10

8 (*fit, suit*): **to go with** acompanhar, combinar com

9 (*be about to, intend to*): **he's going to do it** ele vai fazê-lo; **are you going to come?** você vem?

10 (*time*) passar

11 (*event, activity*) ser; **how did it go?** como foi?

12 (*be given*): **the job is to go to someone else** o emprego vai ser dado para outra pessoa

13 (*break*) romper-se; **the fuse went** o fusível queimou; **the leg of the chair went** a perna da cadeira quebrou

14 (*be placed*): **where does this cup go?** onde é que põe esta xícara?; **the milk goes in the fridge** pode guardar o leite na geladeira ▷ *n* **1** (*try*): **to have a go (at)** tentar **2** (*turn*) vez *f* **3** (*move*): **to be on the go** ter muito para fazer

go about *vi* (*also*: **go around**: *rumour*) espalhar-se ▷ *vt fus*: **how do I go about this?** como é que eu faço isto?

go ahead *vi* (*make progress*) progredir; (*get going*) ir em frente

go along *vi* ir ▷ *vt fus* ladear; **to go along with** concordar com

go away *vi* (*leave*) ir-se, ir embora

go back vi (return) voltar; (go again) ir de novo

go back on vt fus (promise) faltar com

go by vi (years, time) passar ▷ vt fus (book, rule) guiar-se por

go down vi (descend) descer, baixar; (ship) afundar; (sun) pôr-se ▷ vt fus (stairs, ladder) descer

go for vt fus (fetch) ir buscar; (like) gostar de; (attack) atacar

go in vi (enter) entrar

go in for vt fus (competition) inscrever-se em; (like) gostar de

go into vt fus (enter) entrar em; (investigate) investigar; (embark on) embarcar em

go off vi (leave) ir-se; (food) estragar, apodrecer; (bomb, gun) explodir; (event) realizar-se ▷ vt fus (person, place, food etc) deixar de gostar de

go on vi (continue) seguir, continuar; (happen) acontecer, ocorrer

go out vi sair; (for entertainment): **are you going out tonight?** você vai sair hoje à noite?; (couple): **they went out for 3 years** eles namoraram durante 3 anos; (fire, light) apagar-se

go over vi (ship) soçobrar ▷ vt fus (check) revisar

go round vi (news, rumour) circular

go through vt fus (town etc) atravessar; (search through) vasculhar; (examine) percorrer de cabo a rabo

go up vi (ascend) subir; (price, level) aumentar

go without vt fus passar sem

go-ahead adj empreendedor(a) ▷ n luz f verde

goal [gəul] n meta, alvo; (Sport) gol m (BR), golo (PT); **goalkeeper** n goleiro(-a) (BR), guarda-redes m/f inv (PT)

goat [gəut] n cabra

gobble ['gɔbl] vt (also: **~ down, ~ up**) engolir rapidamente, devorar

god [gɔd] n deus m; **G~** Deus; **godchild** n afilhado(-a); **goddess** n deusa; **godfather** n padrinho; **godmother** n madrinha

goggles ['gɔglz] npl óculos mpl de proteção

going ['gəuɪŋ] n (conditions) estado do terreno ▷ adj: **the ~ rate** tarifa corrente or em vigor

gold [gəuld] n ouro ▷ adj de ouro; **golden** adj (made of gold) de ouro; (gold in colour) dourado; **goldfish** n inv peixe-dourado m; **gold-plated** adj plaquê inv

golf [gɔlf] n golfe m; **golf ball** n bola de golfe; (on typewriter) esfera; **golf club** n clube m de golfe; (stick) taco; **golf course** n campo de golfe; **golfer** n jogador(a) m/f de golfe, golfista m/f

gone [gɔn] pp of **go**

gong [gɔŋ] n gongo

good [gud] adj bom/boa; (kind) bom, bondoso; (well-behaved) educado ▷ n bem m; **goods** npl (Comm) mercadorias fpl; **~!** bom!; **to be ~ at** ser bom em; **to be ~ for** servir para; **it's ~ for you** faz-lhe bem; **a ~ deal (of)** muito; **a ~ many** muitos; **to make ~** reparar; **it's no ~ complaining** não adianta se queixar; **for ~** para sempre, definitivamente; **~ morning/ afternoon!** bom dia/boa tarde!; **~ evening!** boa noite!; **~ night!** boa noite!; **goodbye** excl até logo (BR), adeus (PT); **to say goodbye**

despedir-se; **Good Friday** n Sexta-Feira Santa; **good-looking** adj bonito; **good-natured** adj (person) de bom gênio; (pet) de boa índole; **goodwill** n boa vontade f

Google® ['gugl] vi, vt pesquisar no Google®

goose [gu:s] (pl **geese**) n ganso

gooseberry ['guzbərı] n groselha; **to play ~** (Brit) ficar de vela

gorge [gɔ:dʒ] n desfiladeiro ▷ vt: **to ~ o.s. (on)** empanturrar-se (de)

gorgeous ['gɔ:dʒəs] adj magnífico, maravilhoso; (person) lindo

gorilla [gə'rılə] n gorila m

gosh [gɔʃ] (inf) excl puxa

gospel ['gɔspl] n evangelho

gossip ['gɔsıp] n (scandal) fofocas fpl (BR), mexericos mpl (PT); (chat) conversa; (scandalmonger) fofoqueiro(-a) (BR), mexeriqueiro(-a) (PT) ▷ vi (chat) bater (um) papo (BR), cavaquear (PT)

got [gɔt] pt, pp of **get**

gotten ['gɔtn] (US) pp of **get**

govern ['gʌvən] vt governar; (event) controlar

government ['gʌvnmənt] n governo

governor ['gʌvənər] n governador(a) m/f; (of school, hospital, jail) diretor(a) m/f

gown [gaun] n vestido; (of teacher, judge) toga

GP n abbr (Med) = **general practitioner**

grab [græb] vt agarrar ▷ vi: **to ~ at** tentar agarrar

grace [greıs] n (Rel) graça; (gracefulness) elegância, fineza ▷ vt (honour) honrar; (adorn) adornar; **5 days' ~** um prazo de 5 dias; **graceful** adj elegante, gracioso;

gracious ['greıʃəs] adj gracioso, afável

grade [greıd] n (quality) classe f, qualidade f; (degree) grau m; (US: Sch) série f, classe ▷ vt classificar; **grade crossing** (US) n passagem f de nível; **grade school** (US) n escola primária

gradient ['greıdıənt] n declive m

gradual ['grædjuəl] adj gradual, gradativo; **gradually** adv gradualmente, gradativamente, pouco a pouco

graduate [n 'grædjuıt, vi 'grædjueıt] n graduado, licenciado; (US) diplomado do colégio ▷ vi formar-se, licenciar-se; **graduation** [grædju'eıʃən] n formatura

graffiti [grə'fi:tı] n, npl pichações fpl

graft [grɑ:ft] n (Agr, Med) enxerto; (Brit: inf) trabalho pesado; (bribery) suborno ▷ vt enxertar

grain [greın] n grão m; (no pl: cereals) cereais mpl; (in wood) veio, fibra

gram [græm] n grama m

grammar ['græmər] n gramática; **grammar school** n (Brit) ≈ liceo

gramme [græm] n = **gram**

gran [græn] (Brit: inf) n vó f

grand [grænd] adj grandioso; (inf: wonderful) ótimo; **granddad** n vovô m; **granddaughter** n neta; **grandfather** n avô m; **grandma** ['grænmɑ:] n avó f, vovó f; **grandmother** n avó f; **grandpa** ['grænpɑ:] n = **granddad**; **grandparents** npl avós mpl; **grand piano** n piano de cauda; **grandson** n neto

granite ['grænıt] n granito

granny ['grænı] (inf) n avó f, vovó f

ejballNalaphegenral

grant [grɑːnt] vt (concede) conceder; (a request etc) anuir a; (admit) admitir ▷ n (Sch) bolsa; (Admin) subvenção f, subsídio; **to take sth for ~ed** dar algo por certo

grape [greɪp] n uva

grapefruit ['greɪpfruːt] n toranja, grapefruit m (BR)

graph [grɑːf] n gráfico; **graphic** ['græfɪk] adj gráfico; **graphics** n (art) artes fpl gráficas ▷ npl (drawings) desenhos mpl

grasp [grɑːsp] vt agarrar, segurar; (understand) compreender, entender ▷ n mão f; (understanding) compreensão f

grass [grɑːs] n grama (BR), relva (PT); **grasshopper** n gafanhoto

grate [greɪt] n (fireplace) lareira ▷ vi ranger ▷ vt (Culin) ralar

grateful ['greɪtful] adj agradecido, grato

grater ['greɪtəʳ] n ralador m

gratitude ['grætɪtjuːd] n agradecimento

grave [greɪv] n cova, sepultura ▷ adj sério; (mistake) grave

gravestone ['greɪvstəun] n lápide f

graveyard ['greɪvjɑːd] n cemitério

gravity ['grævɪtɪ] n (Phys) gravidade f; (seriousness) seriedade f, gravidade f

gravy ['greɪvɪ] n molho (de carne)

gray [greɪ] (US) adj = **grey**

graze [greɪz] vi pastar ▷ vt (touch lightly) roçar; (scrape) raspar ▷ n (Med) esfoladura, arranhadura

grease [griːs] n (fat) gordura; (lubricant) graxa, lubrificante m ▷ vt (dish) untar; (brakes etc) lubrificar, engraxar; **greasy** adj gordurento, gorduroso; (skin, hair) oleoso

great [greɪt] adj grande; (inf) genial; (pain, heat) forte; (important) importante; **Great Britain** n Grã-Bretanha

● **GREAT BRITAIN**
●
● A Grã-Bretanha, **Great Britain**
● ou **Britain** em inglês, designa a
● maior das ilhas britânicas e,
● portanto, engloba a Escócia e o
● País de Gales. Junto com a
● Irlanda, a ilha de Man e as ilhas
● Anglo-normandas, a
● Grã-Bretanha forma as ilhas
● Britânicas, ou British Isles. Reino
● Unido, em inglês United Kingdom
● ou UK, é o nome oficial da
● entidade política que
● compreende a Grã-Bretanha e a
● Irlanda do Norte.

great: **great-grandfather** n bisavô m; **great-grandmother** n bisavó f; **greatly** adv imensamente, muito

Greece [griːs] n Grécia

greed [griːd] n (also: **~iness**) avidez f, cobiça; **greedy** adj avarento; (for food) guloso

Greek [griːk] adj grego ▷ n grego(-a); (Ling) grego

green [griːn] adj verde; (inexperienced) inexperiente, ingênuo ▷ n verde m; (stretch of grass) gramado (BR), relvado (PT); (on golf course) green m; **greens** npl (vegetables) verduras fpl; **greenhouse** n estufa; **greenhouse effect** n: **the greenhouse effect** o efeito estufa; **greenhouse gas** n gás m de efeito estufa

Greenland ['griːnlənd] n Groenlândia

greet [griːt] vt acolher; (news)

receber; **greeting** n acolhimento; **greeting card, greetings card** n cartão m comemorativo

grew [gru:] pt of **grow**

grey [greɪ], (US) **gray** adj cinzento; (dismal) sombrio; **grey-haired** adj grisalho; **greyhound** n galgo

grid [grɪd] n grade f; (Elec) rede f; **gridlock** n (traffic jam) paralisia do trânsito

grief [gri:f] n dor f, pesar m

grievance ['gri:vəns] n motivo de queixa, agravo

grieve [gri:v] vi sofrer ▷ vt dar pena a, afligir; **to ~ for** chorar por

grill [grɪl] n (on cooker) grelha; (also: **mixed ~**) prato de grelhados ▷ vt (Brit) grelhar; (question) interrogar cerradamente

grille [grɪl] n grade f; (Aut) grelha

grim [grɪm] adj desagradável; (unattractive) feio; (stern) severo

grime [graɪm] n sujeira (BR), sujidade f (PT)

grin [grɪn] n sorriso largo ▷ vi: **to ~ (at)** dar um sorriso largo (para)

grind [graɪnd] (pt, pp **ground**) vt triturar; (coffee, pepper etc) moer; (make sharp) afiar; (US: meat) picar ▷ n (work) trabalho (repetitivo e maçante)

grip [grɪp] n (of hands) aperto; (handle) punho; (of tyre, shoe) aderência; (holdall) valise f ▷ vt agarrar; (attention) prender; **to come** or **get to ~s with** arcar com

gripping ['grɪpɪŋ] adj absorvente, emocionante

grit [grɪt] n areia, grão m de areia; (courage) coragem f ▷ vt (road) pôr areia em; **to ~ one's teeth** cerrar os dentes

groan [grəun] n gemido ▷ vi gemer

grocer ['grəusər] n dono(-a) de

mercearia; **grocer's, grocer's shop** n mercearia; **grocery** n mercearia; **groceries** npl comestíveis mpl

groin [grɔɪn] n virilha

groom [gru:m] n cavalariço; (also: **bride~**) noivo ▷ vt (horse) tratar; (fig): **to ~ sb for sth** preparar alguém para algo; **well-~ed** bem-posto

groove [gru:v] n ranhura, entalhe m

grope [grəup] vi: **to ~ for** procurar às cegas

gross [grəus] adj (flagrant) grave; (vulgar) vulgar; (: building) de mau-gosto; (Comm) bruto

ground [graund] pt, pp of **grind** ▷ n terra, chão m; (Sport) campo; (land) terreno; (reason: gen pl) motivo, razão f; (US: also: **~wire**) (ligação f à) terra, fio-terra m ▷ vt (plane) manter em terra; (US: Elec) ligar à terra; **grounds** npl (of coffee etc) borra; (gardens etc) jardins mpl, parque m; **on the ~** no chão; **to the ~** por terra; **groundsheet** (Brit) n capa impermeável; **groundwork** n base f, preparação f

group [gru:p] n grupo; (also: **pop ~**) conjunto ▷ vt (also: **~ together**) agrupar ▷ vi (also: **~ together**) agrupar-se

grouse [graus] n inv (bird) tetraz m, galo-silvestre m ▷ vi (complain) queixar-se, resmungar

grovel ['grɔvl] vi (fig): **to ~ (before)** abaixar-se (diante de)

grow [grəu] (pt **grew**, pp **grown**) vi crescer; (increase) aumentar; (develop): **to ~ (out of/from)** originar-se ▷ vt plantar, cultivar; (beard) deixar crescer; **to ~ rich/ weak** enriquecer(-se)/

enfraquecer-se **grow up** vi crescer, fazer-se homem/mulher

growl [graul] vi rosnar

grown [grəun] pp of **grow**

grown-up n adulto(-a), pessoa mais velha

growth [grəuθ] n crescimento; (increase) aumento; (Med) abcesso, tumor m

grub [grʌb] n larva, lagarta; (inf: food) comida, rango (BR)

grubby ['grʌbɪ] adj encardido

grudge [grʌdʒ] n motivo de rancor ▷ vt: **to ~ sb sth** dar algo a alguém de má vontade, invejar algo a alguém; **to bear sb a ~ for sth** guardar rancor de alguém por algo

gruelling ['gruəlɪŋ], (US) **grueling** adj duro, árduo

gruesome ['gru:səm] adj horrível

grumble ['grʌmbl] vi resmungar, bufar

grumpy ['grʌmpɪ] adj rabugento

grunt [grʌnt] vi grunhir

guarantee [gærən'ti:] n garantia ▷ vt garantir

guard [gɑːd] n guarda; (one person) guarda m; (Brit: Rail) guarda-freio; (on machine) dispositivo de segurança; (also: **fire~**) guarda-fogo ▷ vt (protect): **to ~ (against)** proteger (contra); (prisoner) vigiar; **to be on one's ~** estar prevenido **guard against** vt fus prevenir-se contra; **guardian** n protetor(a) m/f; (of minor) tutor(a) m/f

Guatemala [gwɔtə'mɑːlə] n Guatemala

guerrilla [gə'rɪlə] n guerrilheiro(-a)

guess [gɛs] vt, vi (estimate) avaliar, conjeturar; (correct answer) adivinhar; (US) achar, supor ▷ n suposição f, conjetura; **to take** or

have a ~ adivinhar, chutar (inf)

guest [gɛst] n convidado(-a); (in hotel) hóspede m/f

guidance ['gaɪdəns] n conselhos mpl

guide [gaɪd] n (person) guia m/f; (book, fig) guia m; (Brit: also: **girl ~**) escoteira ▷ vt guiar; **guidebook** n guia m; **guide dog** n cão m de guia; **guided tour** n visita guiada; **guidelines** npl (advice) orientação f

guilt [gɪlt] n culpa; **guilty** adj culpado

guinea pig ['gɪnɪpɪg] n porquinho-da-índia m, cobaia; (fig) cobaia

guitar [gɪ'tɑːr] n violão m

gulf [gʌlf] n golfo; (abyss: also fig) abismo

gull [gʌl] n gaivota

gulp [gʌlp] vi engolir em seco ▷ vt (also: **~ down**) engolir

gum [gʌm] n (Anat) gengiva; (glue) goma; (also: **~ drop**) bala de goma; (also: **chewing-~**) chiclete m (BR), pastilha elástica (PT) ▷ vt colar

gun [gʌn] n (gen) arma (de fogo); (revolver) revólver m; (small) pistola; (rifle) espingarda; (cannon) canhão m; **gunfire** n tiroteio; **gunman** irreg n pistoleiro; **gunpoint** n: **at gunpoint** sob a ameaça de uma arma; **gunpowder** n pólvora; **gunshot** n tiro (de arma de fogo)

gust [gʌst] n (of wind) rajada

gut [gʌt] n intestino, tripa; **guts** npl (Anat) entranhas fpl, (inf: courage) coragem f, raça (inf)

gutter ['gʌtər] n (of roof) calha; (in street) sarjeta

guy [gaɪ] n (also: **~rope**) corda; (inf: man) cara m (BR), tipo (PT); **Guy Fawkes' Night** n ver nota

g

● GUY FAWKES' NIGHT
●
● A **Guy Fawkes' Night**, também
● chamada de *bonfire night*, é a
● ocasião em que se comemora o
● fracasso da conspiração (a
● *Gunpowder Plot*) contra James I e
● o Parlamento, em 5 de novembro
● de 1605. Um dos conspiradores,
● Guy Fawkes, foi surpreendido no
● porão do Parlamento quando
● estava prestes a atear fogo a
● explosivos. Todo ano, no dia 5 de
● novembro, as crianças preparam
● antecipadamente um boneco de
● Guy Fawkes e pedem às pessoas
● que passam na rua *a penny for the*
● *Guy* (uma moedinha para o Guy),
● com o qual compram fogos de
● artifício.

gym [dʒɪm] *n* (*also*: **gymnasium**)
ginásio; (*also*: **gymnastics**)
ginástica
gymnast [ˈdʒɪmnæst] *n* ginasta
m/f
gymnastics [dʒɪmˈnæstɪks] *n*
ginástica
gynaecologist [gaɪnɪˈkɔlədʒɪst],
(*US*) **gynecologist** *n*
ginecologista *m/f*
gypsy [ˈdʒɪpsɪ] *n* = **gipsy**

H, h [eɪtʃ] *n* H, h *m*
haberdashery [ˈhæbəˈdæʃərɪ] (*Brit*)
n armarinho
habit [ˈhæbɪt] *n* hábito, costume *m*;
(*addiction*) vício; (*Rel*) hábito
hack [hæk] *vt* (*cut*) cortar; (*chop*)
talhar ▷ *n* (*pej*: *writer*)
escrevinhador(a) *m/f*; **hacker** *n*
(*Comput*) hacker *m*
had [hæd] *pt, pp of* **have**
haddock [ˈhædək] (*pl* **haddocks** *or*
haddock) *n* hadoque *m* (*BR*),
eglefim *m* (*PT*)
hadn't [ˈhædnt] = **had not**
haemorrhage [ˈhɛmərɪdʒ], (*US*)
hemorrhage *n* hemorragia
haemorrhoids [ˈhɛmərɔɪdz], (*US*)
hemorrhoids *npl* hemorróidas
fpl
haggle [ˈhægl] *vi* pechinchar,
regatear
hail [heɪl] *n* granizo; (*of objects*)

chuva; (*of criticism*) torrente *f*
▷ *vt* (*greet*) cumprimentar,
saudar; (*call*) chamar ▷ *vi* chover
granizo; **hailstone** *n* pedra de
granizo

hair [hɛəʳ] *n* (*of human*) cabelo; (*of
animal, on legs*) pelo; **to do one's ~**
pentear-se; **hairbrush** *n* escova de
cabelo; **haircut** *n* corte *m* de
cabelo; **hairdo** *n* penteado;
hairdresser *n* cabeleireiro(-a);
hairdresser's *n* cabeleireiro; **hair
dryer** *n* secador *m* de cabelo; **hair
gel** *n* gel *m* para o cabelo; **hair
spray** *n* laquê *m* (*BR*), laca (*PT*);
hairstyle *n* penteado; **hairy** *adj*
cabeludo, peludo; (*inf: situation*)
perigoso

hake [heɪk] (*pl* **hakes** *or* **hake**) *n*
abrótea

half [hɑːf] (*pl* **halves**) *n* metade *f*
▷ *adj* meio ▷ *adv* meio, pela
metade; **~ a pound** meia libra;
two and a ~ dois e meio; **~ a dozen**
meia-dúzia; **to cut sth in ~** cortar
algo ao meio; **~ asleep/empty/
closed** meio adormecido/vazio/
fechado; **half-hearted** *adj*
irresoluto, indiferente; **half-hour**
n meia hora; **half-price** *adj, adv*
pela metade do preço; **half term**
(*Brit*) *n* (*Sch*) dias de folga no meio do
semestre; **half-time** *n* meio tempo;
halfway *adv* a meio caminho;
(*in time*) no meio

hall [hɔːl] *n* (*for concerts*) sala;
(*entrance way*) hall *m*, entrada

hallmark ['hɔːlmɑːk] *n* (*also fig*)
marca

hall of residence (*Brit*) (*pl* **halls of
residence**) *n* residência
universitária

Hallowe'en ['hæləu'iːn] *n* Dia *m*
das Bruxas (*31 de outubro*)

● **HALLOWE'EN**
●
● Segundo a tradição, **Hallowe'en**
● é a noite dos fantasmas e dos
● bruxos. Na Escócia e nos Estados
● Unidos, sobretudo (bem menos
● na Inglaterra), as crianças, para
● festejar o **Hallowe'en**, se
● fantasiam e batem de porta em
● porta pedindo prendas
● (chocolates, maçãs etc).

hallway ['hɔːlweɪ] *n* hall *m*, entrada

halo ['heɪləu] *n* (*of saint etc*) auréola

halt [hɔːlt] *n* parada (*BR*), paragem
f (*PT*) ▷ *vi* parar ▷ *vt* deter; (*process*)
interromper

halve [hɑːv] *vt* (*divide*) dividir ao
meio; (*reduce by half*) reduzir à
metade

halves [hɑːvz] *npl of* **half**

ham [hæm] *n* presunto, fiambre *m*
(*PT*)

hamburger ['hæmbəːgəʳ] *n*
hambúrguer *m*

hammer ['hæməʳ] *n* martelo ▷ *vt*
martelar ▷ *vi* (*on door*) bater
insistentemente

hammock ['hæmək] *n* rede *f*

hamper ['hæmpəʳ] *vt* dificultar,
atrapalhar ▷ *n* cesto

hamster ['hæmstəʳ] *n* hamster *m*

hand [hænd] *n* mão *f*; (*of clock*)
ponteiro; (*writing*) letra; (*of cards*)
cartas *fpl*; (*worker*) trabalhador *m*
▷ *vt* dar, passar; **to give** *or* **lend sb
a ~** dar uma mãozinha a alguém,
dar uma ajuda a alguém; **at ~** à
mão, disponível; **in ~** livre;
(*situation*) sob controle; **to be on ~**
(*person*) estar disponível;
(*emergency services*) estar num
estado de prontidão; **on the
one ~ ..., on the other ~ ...** por um

lado ..., por outro (lado) ... **hand in** vt entregar **hand out** vt distribuir **hand over** vt entregar; (powers etc) transmitir; **handbag** n bolsa; **handbook** n manual m; **handbrake** n freio (BR) or travão m (PT) de mão; **handcuffs** npl algemas fpl; **handful** n punhado; (of people) grupo

handicap ['hændɪkæp] n (Med) incapacidade f; (disadvantage) desvantagem f; (Sport) handicap m ▷ vt prejudicar; **mentally/physically ~ped** deficiente mental/físico

handkerchief ['hæŋkətʃɪf] n lenço

handle ['hændl] n (of door etc) maçaneta; (of cup etc) asa; (of knife etc) cabo; (for winding) manivela ▷ vt manusear; (deal with) tratar de; (treat: people) lidar com; **"~ with care"** "cuidado - frágil"; **to fly off the ~** perder as estribeiras; **handlebar** n, **handlebars** ['hɑ:ndlbɑ:z] npl guidom m (BR), guidão m (PT)

handmade ['hændmeɪd] adj feito a mão

handout ['hændaut] n (money, food) doação f; (leaflet) folheto; (at lecture) apostila

hands-free kit ['hændzfri:-] n viva-voz m

handsome ['hænsəm] adj bonito, elegante; (profit) considerável

handwriting ['hændraɪtɪŋ] n letra, caligrafia

handy ['hændɪ] adj (close at hand) à mão; (useful) útil; (skilful) habilidoso, hábil

hang [hæŋ] (pt, pp **hung**) vt pendurar; (criminal: pt, pp **hanged**) enforcar ▷ vi estar pendurado; (hair, drapery) cair ▷ n (inf): **to get**

the ~ of (doing) sth pegar o jeito de (fazer) algo **hang about** vi vadiar, vagabundear **hang around** vi = **hang about hang on** vi (wait) esperar **hang up** vt (coat) pendurar ▷ vi (Tel) desligar; **to ~ up on sb** bater o telefone na cara de alguém

hanger ['hæŋəʳ] n cabide m

hang-gliding n voo livre

hangover ['hæŋəuvəʳ] n ressaca

happen ['hæpən] vi acontecer; **as it ~s ...** acontece que ...

happily ['hæpɪlɪ] adv (luckily) felizmente; (cheerfully) alegremente

happiness ['hæpɪnɪs] n felicidade f

happy ['hæpɪ] adj feliz; (cheerful) contente; **to be ~ (with)** estar contente (com); **to be ~ to do** (willing) estar disposto a fazer; **~ birthday!** feliz aniversário

harass ['hærəs] vt importunar; **harassment** n perseguição f

harbour ['hɑ:bəʳ], (US) **harbor** n porto ▷ vt (hope etc) abrigar; (hide) esconder

hard [hɑ:d] adj duro; (difficult) difícil; (work) árduo; (person) severo, cruel; (facts) verdadeiro ▷ adv (work) muito, diligentemente; (think, try) seriamente; **to look ~ at** olhar firme or fixamente para; **no ~ feelings!** sem ressentimentos!; **to be ~ of hearing** ser surdo; **to be ~ done by** ser tratado injustamente; **hardback** n livro de capa dura; **hard disk** n (Comput) disco rígido; **harden** vt endurecer; (steel) temperar; (fig) tornar insensível ▷ vi endurecer-se

hardly ['hɑ:dlɪ] adv (scarcely) apenas; (no sooner) mal; **~ ever**

quase nunca
hardship ['hɑːdʃɪp] n privação f
hard shoulder n acostamento
(BR), berma (PT)
hardware ['hɑːdwɛəʳ] n ferragens
fpl; (Comput) hardware m
hard-working adj trabalhador(a);
(student) aplicado
hardy ['hɑːdɪ] adj forte; (plant)
resistente
hare [hɛəʳ] n lebre f
harm [hɑːm] n mal m; (damage)
dano ▷ vt (person) fazer mal a,
prejudicar; (thing) danificar; **out of
~'s way** a salvo; **harmful** adj
prejudicial, nocivo; **harmless** adj
inofensivo
harmony ['hɑːmənɪ] n harmonia
harness ['hɑːnɪs] n (for horse)
arreios mpl; (for child) correia;
(safety harness) correia de
segurança ▷ vt (horse) arrear, pôr
arreios em; (resources) aproveitar
harp [hɑːp] n harpa ▷ vi: **to ~ on
about** bater sempre na mesma
tecla sobre
harsh [hɑːʃ] adj (life) duro; (sound)
desarmonioso
harvest ['hɑːvɪst] n colheita ▷ vt
colher
has [hæz] vb see **have**
hasn't ['hæznt] = **has not**
hassle ['hæsl] (inf) n complicação f
haste [heɪst] n pressa; **hasten**
['heɪsn] vt acelerar ▷ vi: **to hasten
to do sth** apressar-se em fazer
algo; **hastily** adv depressa; **hasty**
adj apressado; (rash) precipitado
hat [hæt] n chapéu m
hatch [hætʃ] n (Naut: also: **~way**)
escotilha; (also: **service ~**)
comunicação f entre a cozinha e a
sala de jantar ▷ vi sair do ovo,
chocar

hate [heɪt] vt odiar, detestar ▷ n
ódio; **hatred** ['heɪtrɪd] n ódio
haul [hɔːl] vt puxar ▷ n (of fish)
redada; (of stolen goods etc)
pilhagem f, presa
haunt [hɔːnt] vt (subj: ghost)
assombrar; (: problem, memory)
perseguir ▷ n reduto; (haunted
house) casa mal-assombrada

 KEYWORD

have [hæv] (pt, pp **had**) aux vb **1** (gen)
ter; **to have arrived/gone/
eaten/slept** ter chegado/ido/
comido/dormido; **he has been
kind/promoted** ele foi bondoso/
promovido; **having finished** or
when he had finished, **he left**
quando ele terminou, foi embora
2 (in tag questions): **you've done it,
haven't you?** você fez isto, não
foi?; **he hasn't done it, has he?**
ele não fez isto, fez?
3 (in short questions and answers):
**you've made a mistake — no I
haven't/so I have** você fez um
erro — não, eu não fiz/sim, eu fiz;
**I've been there before, have
you?** eu já estive lá, e você?
▷ modal aux vb (be obliged): **to have
(got) to do sth** ter que fazer algo;
I haven't got or **I don't have to
wear glasses** eu não preciso usar
óculos
▷ vt **1** (possess) ter; **he has (got)
blue eyes/dark hair** ele tem olhos
azuis/cabelo escuro
2 (referring to meals etc): **to have
breakfast** tomar café (BR), tomar
o pequeno almoço (PT); **to have
lunch/dinner** almoçar/jantar; **to
have a drink/a cigarette** tomar
um drinque/fumar um cigarro

3 (*receive, obtain etc*): **may I have your address?** pode me dar seu endereço?; **you can have it for 5 pounds** você pode levá-lo por 5 libras; **to have a baby** dar à luz (*BR*), ter um nenê *or* bebê (*PT*)
4 (*maintain, allow*): **he will have it that he is right** ele vai insistir que ele está certo; **I won't have it/this nonsense!** não vou aguentar isso/este absurdo!; **we can't have that** não podemos permitir isto
5: **to have sth done** mandar fazer algo; **to have one's hair cut** ir cortar o cabelo; **to have sb do sth** mandar alguém fazer algo
6 (*experience, suffer*): **to have a cold/flu** estar resfriado (*BR*) *or* constipado (*PT*)/com gripe; **she had her bag stolen/her arm broken** ela teve sua bolsa roubada/ela quebrou o braço; **to have an operation** fazer uma operação
7 (+ *n: take, hold etc*): **to have a swim/walk/bath/rest** ir nadar/passear/tomar um banho/descansar; **let's have a look** vamos dar uma olhada; **to have a party** fazer uma festa
8 (*inf: dupe*): **he's been had** ele comprou gato por lebre
have out *vt*: **to have it out with sb** (*settle a problem*) explicar-se com alguém

haven ['heɪvn] *n* porto; (*fig*) abrigo, refúgio
haven't ['hævnt] = **have not**
havoc ['hævək] *n* destruição *f*; **to play ~ with** (*fig*) estragar
hawk [hɔːk] *n* falcão *m*
hay [heɪ] *n* feno; **hay fever** *n* febre *f* do feno; **haystack** *n* palheiro

hazard ['hæzəd] *n* perigo, risco ▷ *vt* aventurar, arriscar; **hazard warning lights** *npl* (*Aut*) pisca-alerta *m*
haze [heɪz] *n* névoa
hazelnut ['heɪzlnʌt] *n* avelã *f*
hazy ['heɪzɪ] *adj* nublado; (*idea*) confuso
he [hiː] *pron* ele; **he who ...** quem ..., aquele que ...
head [hɛd] *n* cabeça; (*of table*) cabeceira; (*of queue*) frente *f*; (*of organization*) chefe *m/f*; (*of school*) diretor(a) *m/f* ▷ *vt* (*list*) encabeçar; (*group*) liderar; **~s or tails** cara ou coroa; **~ first** de cabeça; **~ over heels** de pernas para o ar; **~ over heels in love** apaixonadíssimo; **to ~ the ball** cabecear a bola **head for** *vt fus* dirigir-se a; (*disaster*) estar procurando; **headache** *n* dor *f* de cabeça; **heading** *n* título, cabeçalho; **headlamp** (*Brit*) *n* = **headlight**; **headlight** *n* farol *m*; **headline** *n* manchete *f*; **head office** *n* matriz *f*; **headphones** *npl* fones *mpl* de ouvido; **headquarters** *npl* sede *f*; (*Mil*) quartel *m* general; **headroom** *n* (*in car*) espaço (para a cabeça); (*under bridge*) vão *m* livre; **headscarf** *irreg n* lenço de cabeça
heal [hiːl] *vt* curar ▷ *vi* cicatrizar
health [hɛlθ] *n* saúde *f*; **good ~!** saúde!; **healthy** *adj* (*person*) saudável; (*air, walk*) sadio; (*economy*) próspero, forte
heap [hiːp] *n* pilha, montão *m* ▷ *vt* (*plate*) encher; **~s (of)** (*inf*) um monte (de)
hear [hɪəʳ] (*pt, pp* **heard**) *vt* ouvir; (*listen to*) escutar; (*news*) saber; **to ~ about** ouvir falar de; **to ~ from sb** ter notícias de alguém; **hearing**

n (sense) audição f; (Law) audiência; **hearing aid** n aparelho para a surdez

hearse [həːs] n carro fúnebre

heart [haːt] n coração m; (of problem, city) centro; **hearts** npl (Cards) copas fpl; **to lose/take ~** perder o ânimo/criar coragem; **at ~** no fundo; **by ~** (learn, know) de cor; **heart attack** n ataque m de coração; **heartbeat** n batida do coração; **heartbroken** adj: **to be heartbroken** estar inconsolável; **heartburn** n azia

hearty ['haːtɪ] adj (person) energético; (laugh) animado; (appetite) bom/boa; (welcome) sincero; (dislike) absoluto

heat [hiːt] n calor m; (excitement) ardor m; (Sport: also: **qualifying ~**) (prova) eliminatória ▷ vt esquentar; (room, house) aquecer **heat up** vi aquecer-se, esquentar ▷ vt esquentar; **heated** adj aquecido; (fig) acalorado; **heater** n aquecedor m

heather ['hɛðəʳ] n urze f

heating ['hiːtɪŋ] n aquecimento, calefação f

heaven ['hɛvn] n céu m, paraíso; **heavenly** adj celestial; (Rel) divino

heavily ['hɛvɪlɪ] adv pesadamente; (drink, smoke) excessivamente; (sleep, depend) profundamente

heavy ['hɛvɪ] adj pesado; (work) duro; (responsibility) grande; (rain, meal) forte; (drinker, smoker) inveterado; (weather) carregado

Hebrew ['hiːbruː] adj hebreu/hebreia ▷ n (Ling) hebraico

Hebrides ['hɛbrɪdiːz] npl: **the ~** as (ilhas) Hébridas

hectic ['hɛktɪk] adj agitado

he'd [hiːd] = **he would**; **he had**

hedge [hɛdʒ] n cerca viva, sebe f ▷ vi dar evasivas ▷ vt: **to ~ one's bets** (fig) resguardar-se

hedgehog ['hɛdʒhɔg] n ouriço

heed [hiːd] vt (also: **take ~ of**) prestar atenção a

heel [hiːl] n (of shoe) salto; (of foot) calcanhar m ▷ vt (shoe) pôr salto em

hefty ['hɛftɪ] adj (person) robusto; (parcel) pesado; (profit) alto

height [haɪt] n (of person) estatura; (of building, tree) altura; (of plane) altitude f; (high ground) monte m; (fig: of power) auge m; (: of luxury) máximo; (: of stupidity) cúmulo; **heighten** vt elevar; (fig) aumentar

heir [ɛəʳ] n herdeiro; **heiress** n herdeira

held [hɛld] pt, pp of **hold**

helicopter ['hɛlɪkɔptəʳ] n helicóptero

hell [hɛl] n inferno; **~!** (inf) droga!

he'll [hiːl] = **he will**; **he shall**

hello [hə'ləu] excl oi! (BR), olá! (PT); (surprise) ora essa!

helmet ['hɛlmɪt] n capacete m

help [hɛlp] n ajuda; (charwoman) faxineira ▷ vt ajudar; **~!** socorro!; **~ yourself** sirva-se; **he can't ~ it** não tem culpa; **helper** n ajudante m/f; **helpful** adj prestativo; (advice) útil; **helping** n porção f; **helpless** adj (incapable) incapaz; (defenceless) indefeso

hem [hɛm] n bainha ▷ vt embainhar **hem in** vt cercar, encurralar

hemorrhage ['hɛmərɪdʒ] (US) n = **haemorrhage**

hemorrhoids ['hɛmərɔɪdz] (US) npl = **haemorrhoids**

hen [hɛn] n galinha; (female bird) fêmea

hence [hɛns] *adv* daí, portanto;
2 years ~ daqui a 2 anos

her [hə:ʳ] *pron* (*direct*) a; (*indirect*)
lhe; (*stressed, after prep*) ela ▷ *adj*
seu/sua, dela; *see also* **me**; **my**

herb [hə:b] *n* erva

herd [hə:d] *n* rebanho

here [hɪəʳ] *adv* aqui; (*at this point*)
nesse ponto; **~ is/are** aqui está/estão;
~ he/she is! aqui está ele/ela!

heritage ['hɛrɪtɪdʒ] *n* patrimônio

hernia ['hə:nɪə] *n* hérnia

hero ['hɪərəʊ] (*pl* **heroes**) *n* herói *m*;
(*of book, film*) protagonista *m*

heroin ['hɛrəʊɪn] *n* heroína

heroine ['hɛrəʊɪn] *n* heroína; (*of
book, film*) protagonista

heron ['hɛrən] *n* garça

herring ['hɛrɪŋ] (*pl* **herrings** or
herring) *n* arenque *m*

hers [hə:z] *pron* (o) seu/(a) sua,
(o/a) dela; *see also* **mine**

herself [hə:'sɛlf] *pron* (*reflexive*) se;
(*emphatic*) ela mesma; (*after prep*) si
(mesma); *see also* **oneself**

he's [hi:z] = **he is**; **he has**

hesitant ['hɛzɪtənt] *adj* hesitante,
indeciso

hesitate ['hɛzɪteɪt] *vi* hesitar;
hesitation [hɛzɪ'teɪʃən] *n*
hesitação *f*, indecisão *f*

heterosexual ['hɛtərəʊ'sɛksjuəl]
adj heterossexual

heyday ['heɪdeɪ] *n*: **the ~ of** o auge
or apogeu de

hi [haɪ] *excl* oi!

hibernate ['haɪbəneɪt] *vi* hibernar

hiccup ['hɪkʌp] *vi* soluçar ▷ *npl*: **~s**
soluço; **to have (the) ~s** estar com
soluço

hide [haɪd] (*pt* **hid**, *pp* **hidden**) *n*
(*skin*) pele *f* ▷ *vt* esconder, ocultar;
(*view*) obscurecer ▷ *vi*: **to ~ (from**
sb) esconder-se or ocultar-se (de
alguém)

hideous ['hɪdɪəs] *adj* horrível

hiding ['haɪdɪŋ] *n* (*beating*) surra; **to**
be in ~ (*concealed*) estar escondido

hi-fi ['haɪfaɪ] *n* alta-fidelidade *f*;
(*system*) som *m* ▷ *adj* de
alta-fidelidade

high [haɪ] *adj* alto; (*number*)
grande; (*price*) alto, elevado; (*wind*)
forte; (*voice*) agudo; (*opinion*)
ótimo; (*principles*) nobre ▷ *adv*
alto, a grande altura; **it is 20 m ~**
tem 20 m de altura; **~ in the air** nas
alturas; **highchair** *n* cadeira alta
(para criança); **higher education**
n ensino superior; **high jump** *n*
(*Sport*) salto em altura; **highlands**
npl: **the Highlands** (*in Scotland*) a
Alta Escócia; **highlight** *n* (*fig*)
ponto alto; (*in hair*) mecha ▷ *vt*
realçar, ressaltar; **highly** *adv*:
highly paid muito bem pago; **to**
speak highly of falar
elogiosamente de; **high-rise** *adj*
alto; **high school** *n* (*Brit*) escola
secundária; (*US*) científico

● **HIGH SCHOOL**
●
● Uma **high school** é um
● estabelecimento de ensino
● secundário. Nos Estados Unidos,
● existem a *Junior High School*, que
● equivale aproximadamente aos
● dois últimos anos do primeiro
● grau, e a *Senior High School*, que
● corresponde ao segundo grau.
● Na Grã-Bretanha, esse termo às
● vezes é utilizado para as escolas
● secundárias.

high street (*Brit*) *n* rua principal

highway (*US*) *n* estrada; (*main road*)

rodovia

hijack ['haɪdʒæk] *vt* sequestrar; **hijacker** *n* sequestrador(a) *m/f* (de avião)

hike [haɪk] *vi* caminhar ▷ *n* caminhada, excursão *f* a pé; **hiker** *n* caminhante *m/f*, andarilho(-a)

hilarious [hɪ'lɛərɪəs] *adj* hilariante

hill [hɪl] *n* colina; (*high*) montanha; (*slope*) ladeira, rampa; **hillside** *n* vertente *f*; **hilly** *adj* montanhoso

him [hɪm] *pron* (*direct*) o; (*indirect*) lhe; (*stressed, after prep*) ele; *see also* **me**; **himself** *pron* (*reflexive*) se; (*emphatic*) ele mesmo; (*after prep*) si (mesmo); *see also* **oneself**

hinder ['hɪndə'] *vt* retardar

hindsight ['haɪndsaɪt] *n*: **with (the benefit of) ~** em retrospecto

Hindu ['hɪnduː] *adj* hindu

hinge [hɪndʒ] *n* dobradiça ▷ *vi* (*fig*): **to ~ on** depender de

hint [hɪnt] *n* (*suggestion*) indireta; (*advice*) dica; (*sign*) sinal *m* ▷ *vt*: **to ~ that** insinuar que ▷ *vi*: **to ~ at** fazer alusão a

hip [hɪp] *n* quadril *m*

hippopotamus [hɪpə'pɔtəməs] (*pl* **hippopotamuses** *or* **hippopotami**) *n* hipopótamo

hire ['haɪə'] *vt* (*Brit: car, equipment*) alugar; (*worker*) contratar ▷ *n* aluguel *m*; **for ~** aluga-se; (*taxi*) livre; **hire purchase** (*Brit*) *n* compra a prazo

his [hɪz] *pron* (o) seu/(a) sua, (o/a) dele ▷ *adj* seu/sua, dele; *see also* **my**; **mine**

hiss [hɪs] *vi* (*snake, fat*) assoviar; (*gas*) silvar; (*boo*) vaiar

historic [hɪ'stɔrɪk], **historical** [hɪ'stɔrɪkl] *adj* histórico

history ['hɪstərɪ] *n* história

hit [hɪt] (*pt, pp* **hit**) *vt* bater em;

(*target*) acertar, alcançar; (*car*) bater em, colidir com; (*fig: affect*) atingir ▷ *n* golpe *m*; (*success*) sucesso; (*internet visit*) visita; **to ~ it off with sb** dar-se bem com alguém

hitch [hɪtʃ] *vt* (*fasten*) atar, amarrar; (*also:* **~ up**) levantar ▷ *n* (*difficulty*) dificuldade *f*; **to ~ a lift** pegar carona (*BR*), arranjar uma boleia (*PT*)

hitch-hike *vi* pegar carona (*BR*), andar à boleia (*PT*); **hitch-hiker** *n* carona *m/f* (*BR*), viajante *m/f* à boleia (*PT*)

hi-tech *adj* tecnologicamente avançado ▷ *n* alta tecnologia

HIV *abbr*: **~-negative/-positive** HIV negativo/positivo

hive [haɪv] *n* colmeia *f*; **hive off** (*inf*) *vt* transferir

hoard [hɔːd] *n* provisão *f*; (*of money*) tesouro ▷ *vt* acumular

hoarse [hɔːs] *adj* rouco

hoax [həuks] *n* trote *m*

hob [hɔb] *n* parte de cima do fogão

hobble ['hɔbl] *vi* coxear

hobby ['hɔbɪ] *n* hobby *m*, passatempo predileto

hobo ['həubəu] (*US*) *n* vagabundo

hockey ['hɔkɪ] *n* hóquei *m*

hog [hɔg] *n* porco ▷ *vt* (*fig*) monopolizar; **to go the whole ~** ir até o fim

hoist [hɔɪst] *vt* içar

hold [həuld] (*pt, pp* **held**) *vt* segurar; (*contain*) conter; (*have*) ter; (*record etc: meeting*) realizar; (*detain*) deter; (*consider*): **to ~ sb responsible (for sth)** responsabilizar alguém (por algo) ▷ *vi* (*withstand pressure*) resistir; (*be valid*) ser válido ▷ *n* (*fig*) influência, domínio; (*of ship*) porão *m*; (*of* *plane*) compartimento para cargo; **~ the line!** (*Tel*) não desligue!; **to ~ one's own** (*fig*) virar-se, sair-se bem; **to catch** *or* **get (a) ~ of** agarrar, pegar **hold back** *vt* reter; (*secret*) manter, guardar **hold down** *vt* (*person*) segurar; (*job*) manter **hold off** *vt* (*enemy*) afastar, repelir **hold on** *vi* agarrar-se; (*wait*) esperar; **~ on!** espera aí!; (*Tel*) não desligue! **hold on to** *vt fus* agarrar-se a; (*keep*) guardar, ficar com **hold out** *vt* estender ▷ *vi* (*resist*) resistir **hold up** *vt* (*raise*) levantar; (*support*) apoiar; (*delay*) atrasar; (*rob*) assaltar; **holdall** (*Brit*) *n* bolsa de viagem; **holder** *n* (*of ticket*) portador(a) *m/f*; (*of record*) detentor(a) *m/f*; (*of office, title etc*) titular *m/f*; **hold-up** *n* (*robbery*) assalto; (*delay*) demora; (*Brit: in traffic*) engarrafamento

hole [həʊl] *n* buraco; (*small: in sock etc*) furo ▷ *vt* esburacar

holiday ['hɔlədɪ] *n* (*Brit: vacation*) férias *fpl*; (*day off*) dia *m* de folga; (*public holiday*) feriado; **to be on ~** estar de férias; **holiday camp** (*Brit*) *n* colônia de férias; **holiday-maker** (*Brit*) *n* pessoa (que está) de férias; **holiday resort** *n* local *m* de férias

Holland ['hɔlənd] *n* Holanda

hollow ['hɔləʊ] *adj* oco, vazio; (*cheeks*) côncavo; (*eyes*) fundo; (*sound*) surdo; (*laugh, claim*) falso ▷ *n* (*in ground*) cavidade *f*, depressão *f* ▷ *vt*: **to ~ out** escavar

holly ['hɔlɪ] *n* azevinho

holy ['həʊlɪ] *adj* sagrado; (*person*) santo, bento

home [həʊm] *n* casa, lar *m*; (*country*) pátria; (*institution*) asilo ▷ *cpd* caseiro, doméstico; (*Econ,*

Pol) nacional, interno; (*Sport: team*) de casa; (: *game*) no próprio campo ▷ *adv* (*direction*) para casa; (*right in: nail etc*) até o fundo; **at ~** em casa; **make yourself at ~** fique à vontade; **home address** *n* endereço residencial; **homeland** *n* terra (natal); **homeless** *adj* sem casa, desabrigado; **homely** *adj* (*simple*) simples *inv*; **home-made** *adj* caseiro; **Home Office** (*Brit*) *n* Ministério do Interior; **home page** *n* (*Comput*) página inicial; **Home Secretary** (*Brit*) *n* Ministro(a) do Interior; **homesick** *adj*: **to be homesick** estar com saudades (do lar); **home town** *n* cidade *f* natal; **homework** *n* dever *m* de casa

homoeopathic [həʊmɪə'pæθɪk], (*US*) **homeopathic** *adj* homeopático

homosexual [hɔməʊ'sɛksjuəl] *adj*, *n* homossexual *m/f*

Honduras [hɔn'djuərəs] *n* Honduras *m* (*no article*)

honest ['ɔnɪst] *adj* (*truthful*) franco; (*trustworthy*) honesto; (*sincere*) sincero; **honestly** *adv* honestamente; **honesty** *n* honestidade *f*, sinceridade *f*

honey ['hʌnɪ] *n* mel *m*; **honeymoon** *n* lua-de-mel *f*; (*trip*) viagem *f* de lua-de-mel

honorary ['ɔnərərɪ] *adj* (*unpaid*) não remunerado; (*duty, title*) honorário

honour ['ɔnəʳ], (*US*) **honor** *vt* honrar ▷ *n* honra; **honourable** *adj* honrado

hood [hʊd] *n* capuz *m*; (*of cooker*) tampa; (*Brit: Aut*) capota; (*US: Aut*) capô *m*

hoof [huːf] (*pl* **hooves**) *n* casco, pata

hook [huk] n gancho; (on dress) colchete m; (for fishing) anzol m ▷ vt prender com gancho (or colchete); (fish) fisgar

hooligan ['hu:lɪgən] n desordeiro(-a), bagunceiro(-a)

hoop [hu:p] n arco

hooray [hu:'reɪ] excl = **hurrah**

hoot [hu:t] vi (Aut) buzinar; (siren) tocar; (owl) piar

hooves [hu:vz] npl of **hoof**

hop [hɔp] vi saltar, pular; (on one foot) pular num pé só

hope [həup] vt, vi esperar ▷ n esperança; **I ~ so/not** espero que sim/não; **hopeful** adj (person) otimista, esperançoso; (situation) promissor(a); **hopefully** adv esperançosamente; **hopefully, they'll come back** é de esperar or esperamos que voltem; **hopeless** adj desesperado, irremediável; (useless) inútil

horizon [hə'raɪzn] n horizonte m; **horizontal** [hɔrɪ'zɔntl] adj horizontal

horn [hɔ:n] n corno, chifre m; (material) chifre m; (Mus) trompa; (Aut) buzina

horoscope ['hɔrəskəup] n horóscopo

horrendous [hə'rɛndəs] adj horrendo

horrible ['hɔrɪbl] adj horrível; (terrifying) terrível

horrid ['hɔrɪd] adj horrível

horror ['hɔrər] n horror m; **horror film** n filme m de terror

horse [hɔ:s] n cavalo; **horseback: on horseback** adj, adv a cavalo; **horse chestnut** n castanha-da-índia; **horsepower** n cavalo-vapor m; **horse-racing** n corridas fpl de cavalo, turfe m

hose [həuz] n (also: **~pipe**) mangueira

hospital ['hɔspɪtl] n hospital m

hospitality [hɔspɪ'tælɪtɪ] n hospitalidade f

host [həust] n anfitrião m; (TV, Radio) apresentador(a) m/f; (Rel) hóstia; (large number): **a ~ of** uma multidão de

hostage ['hɔstɪdʒ] n refém m/f

hostel ['hɔstl] n albergue m, abrigo; (also: **youth ~**) albergue da juventude

hostess ['həustɪs] n anfitriã f; (Brit: air hostess) aeromoça (BR), hospedeira de bordo (PT); (TV, Radio) apresentadora

hostile ['hɔstaɪl] adj hostil

hostility [hɔ'stɪlɪtɪ] n hostilidade f

hot [hɔt] adj quente; (as opposed to only warm) muito quente; (spicy) picante; (fierce) ardente; **to be ~** (person) estar com calor; (thing, weather) estar quente; **hot dog** n cachorro-quente m

hotel [həu'tɛl] n hotel m

hotspot ['hɔtspɔt] n (Comput: also: **wireless ~**) hotspot m (local público com acesso à Internet sem fio)

hound [haund] vt acossar, perseguir ▷ n cão m de caça, sabujo

hour ['auər] n hora; **hourly** adj de hora em hora; (rate) por hora

house [n haus, vt hauz] n (gen, firm) casa; (Pol) câmara; (Theatre) assistência, lotação f ▷ vt (person) alojar; (collection) abrigar; **on the ~** (fig) por conta da casa; **household** n família; (house) casa; **housekeeper** n governanta; **housekeeping** n (work) trabalhos mpl domésticos; (money) economia doméstica; **housewife** irreg n dona de casa; **housework** n

trabalhos *mpl* domésticos;
housing *n* (*provision*) alojamento;
(*houses*) residências *fpl*; **housing
development** *n* conjunto
residencial; **housing estate** (*Brit*)
n = **housing development**
hover ['hɔvər] *vi* pairar; **hovercraft**
n aerobarco

 KEYWORD

how [hau] *adv* **1** (*in what way*) como;
how was the film? que tal o filme?;
how are you? como vai?
2 (*to what degree*) quanto; **how
much milk/many people?**
quanto de leite/quantas pessoas?;
how long have you been here?
há quanto tempo você está aqui?;
how old are you? quantos anos
você tem?; **how tall is he?** qual é a
altura dele?; **how lovely/awful!**
que ótimo/terrível!

however [hau'ɛvər] *adv* de
qualquer modo; (+ *adj*) por mais ...
que; (*in questions*) como ▷ *conj* no
entanto, contudo
howl [haul] *vi* uivar
H.P. (*Brit*) *n abbr* = **hire purchase**
h.p. *abbr* (*Aut*: = *horsepower*) CV
HQ *n abbr* (= *headquarters*) QG *m*
HTML *n abbr* (= *Hypertext Mark-up
Language*) HTML *f*
huddle ['hʌdl] *vi*: **to ~ together**
aconchegar-se
huff [hʌf] *n*: **in a ~** com raiva
hug [hʌg] *vt* abraçar; (*thing*)
agarrar, prender
huge [hju:dʒ] *adj* enorme, imenso
hull [hʌl] *n* (*of ship*) casco
hum [hʌm] *vt* cantarolar ▷ *vi*
cantarolar; (*insect, machine etc*)
zumbir

human ['hju:mən] *adj* humano ▷ *n*
(*also:* **~ being**) ser *m* humano
humane [hju:'mein] *adj* humano
humanitarian [hju:mænı'tɛərıən]
adj humanitário
humanity [hju:'mænıtı] *n*
humanidade *f*
human rights *npl* direitos *mpl*
humanos
humble ['hʌmbl] *adj* humilde ▷ *vt*
humilhar
humid ['hju:mıd] *adj* úmido
humiliate [hju:'mılıeıt] *vt*
humilhar
humorous ['hju:mərəs] *adj*
humorístico; (*person*) engraçado
humour ['hju:mə'], (*US*) **humor** *n*
humorismo, senso de humor;
(*mood*) humor *m* ▷ *vt* fazer a
vontade de
hump [hʌmp] *n* (*in ground*) elevação
f; (*camel's*) corcova, giba;
(*deformity*) corcunda
hunch [hʌntʃ] *n* (*premonition*)
pressentimento, palpite *m*
hundred ['hʌndrəd] *num* cem;
(*before lower numbers*) cento; **~s of
people** centenas de pessoas;
hundredth *num* centésimo
hung [hʌŋ] *pt, pp of* **hang**
Hungary ['hʌŋgərı] *n* Hungria
hunger ['hʌŋgə'] *n* fome *f* ▷ *vi*: **to ~
for** (*desire*) desejar ardentemente
hungry ['hʌŋgrı] *adj* faminto,
esfomeado; (*keen*): **~ for** (*fig*) ávido
de, ansioso por; **to be ~** estar com
fome
hunt [hʌnt] *vt* buscar, perseguir;
(*Sport*) caçar ▷ *vi* caçar ▷ *n* caça,
caçada; **hunter** *n* caçador(a) *m/f*;
hunting *n* caça
hurdle ['hə:dl] *n* (*Sport*) barreira;
(*fig*) obstáculo
hurl [hə:l] *vt* arremessar, lançar;

(*abuse*) gritar

hurrah [hu'rɑ:] *excl* oba!, viva!

hurray [hu'reɪ] *excl* = **hurrah**

hurricane ['hʌrɪkən] *n* furacão *m*

hurry ['hʌrɪ] *n* pressa ▷ *vi* (*also:* ~ **up**) apressar-se ▷ *vt* (*also:* ~ **up**: *person*) apressar; (: *work*) acelerar; **to be in a ~** estar com pressa

hurt [hə:t] (*pt, pp* **hurt**) *vt* machucar; (*injure*) ferir; (*fig*) magoar ▷ *vi* doer

husband ['hʌzbənd] *n* marido, esposo

hush [hʌʃ] *n* silêncio, quietude *f* ▷ *vt* silenciar, fazer calar; ~! silêncio!, psiu! **hush up** *vt* abafar, encobrir

husky ['hʌskɪ] *adj* rouco ▷ *n* cão *m* esquimó

hut [hʌt] *n* cabana, choupana; (*shed*) alpendre *m*

hyacinth ['haɪəsɪnθ] *n* jacinto

hydrofoil ['haɪdrəfɔɪl] *n* hidrofoil *m*, aliscafo

hydrogen ['haɪdrədʒən] *n* hidrogênio

hygiene ['haɪdʒi:n] *n* higiene *f*

hymn [hɪm] *n* hino

hype [haɪp] (*inf*) *n* tititi *m*, falatório *m*

hyperlink ['haɪpəlɪŋk] *n* hiperlink *m*

hypermarket ['haɪpəmɑ:kɪt] (*Brit*) *n* hipermercado

hyphen ['haɪfn] *n* hífen *m*

hypnotize ['hɪpnətaɪz] *vt* hipnotizar

hypocrite ['hɪpəkrɪt] *n* hipócrita *m/f*; **hypocritical** *adj* hipócrita

hysterical [hɪ'stɛrɪkl] *adj* histérico; (*funny*) hilariante; **hysterics** *npl* (*nervous*) crise *f* histérica; (*laughter*) ataque *m* de riso; **to be in** *or* **have hysterics** ter uma crise histérica

---

I [aɪ] *pron* eu ▷ *abbr* (= *island, isle*) I

ice [aɪs] *n* gelo; (*ice cream*) sorvete *m* ▷ *vt* (*cake*) cobrir com glacê ▷ *vi* (*also:* ~ **over,** ~ **up**) gelar; **iceberg** *n* iceberg *m*; **ice cream** *n* sorvete *m* (*BR*), gelado (*PT*); **ice cube** *n* pedra de gelo; **ice hockey** *n* hóquei *m* sobre o gelo

Iceland ['aɪslənd] *n* Islândia

ice lolly (*Brit*) *n* picolé *m*

ice rink *n* pista de gelo, rinque *m*

icing ['aɪsɪŋ] *n* (*Culin*) glacê *m*; **icing sugar** (*Brit*) *n* açúcar *m* glacê

icon ['aɪkɔn] *n* (*gen, Comput*) ícone *m*

icy ['aɪsɪ] *adj* gelado

I'd [aɪd] = **I would**; **I had**

idea [aɪ'dɪə] *n* ideia

ideal [aɪ'dɪəl] *n* ideal *m* ▷ *adj* ideal

identical [aɪ'dɛntɪkl] *adj* idêntico

identification [aɪdɛntɪfɪ'keɪʃən] *n* identificação *f*; **means of ~** documentos pessoais

identify [aɪ'dɛntɪfaɪ] vt
identificar
identity [aɪ'dɛntɪtɪ] n identidade f;
identity card n carteira de
identidade
idiom ['ɪdɪəm] n expressão f
idiomática; (style of speaking)
idioma m, linguagem f
idiot ['ɪdɪət] n idiota m/f
idle ['aɪdl] adj ocioso; (lazy)
preguiçoso; (unemployed)
desempregado; (pointless) inútil,
vão(-vã) ▷ vi (machine) funcionar
com a transmissão desligada
  idle away vt: **to ~ away the time**
  perder or desperdiçar tempo
idol ['aɪdl] n ídolo
i.e. abbr (= id est) i.e., isto é

 KEYWORD

if [ɪf] conj **1** (conditional use) se;
  if necessary se necessário;
  if I were you se eu fôsse você
  2 (whenever) quando
  3 (although): **(even) if** mesmo que
  4 (whether) se
  5: **if so/not** sendo assim/do
  contrário; **if only** se pelo menos;
  see also **as**

ignition [ɪg'nɪʃən] n (Aut) ignição f;
  to switch on/off the ~ ligar/
  desligar o motor
ignorant ['ɪgnərənt] adj ignorante;
  to be ~ of ignorar
ignore [ɪg'nɔːʳ] vt (person) não fazer
  caso de; (fact) não levar em
  consideração, ignorar
I'll [aɪl] = **I will**; **I shall**
ill [ɪl] adj doente; (harmful: effects)
  nocivo ▷ n mal m ▷ adv: **to speak/
  think ~ of sb** falar/pensar mal de
  alguém; **to take** or **be taken ~**

ficar doente
illegal [ɪ'liːgl] adj ilegal
illegible [ɪ'lɛdʒɪbl] adj ilegível
illegitimate [ɪlɪ'dʒɪtɪmət] adj
  ilegítimo
illiterate [ɪ'lɪtərət] adj analfabeto
illness ['ɪlnɪs] n doença
illuminate [ɪ'luːmɪneɪt] vt
  iluminar, clarear
illusion [ɪ'luːʒən] n ilusão f
illustrate ['ɪləstreɪt] vt ilustrar;
  (point) exemplificar; **illustration**
  [ɪlə'streɪʃən] n ilustração f;
  (example) exemplo; (explanation)
  esclarecimento
I'm [aɪm] = **I am**
image ['ɪmɪdʒ] n imagem f
imaginary [ɪ'mædʒɪnərɪ] adj
  imaginário
imagination [ɪmædʒɪ'neɪʃən] n
  imaginação f; (inventiveness)
  inventividade f
imagine [ɪ'mædʒɪn] vt imaginar
imbalance [ɪm'bæləns] n
  desigualdade f
imitate ['ɪmɪteɪt] vt imitar;
  imitation [ɪmɪ'teɪʃən] n imitação
  f; (copy) cópia; (mimicry) mímica
immaculate [ɪ'mækjulət] adj
  impecável; (Rel) imaculado
immature [ɪmə'tjuəʳ] adj imaturo;
  (fruit) verde
immediate [ɪ'miːdɪət] adj
  imediato; (pressing) urgente,
  premente; (neighbourhood, family)
  próximo; **immediately** adv
  imediatamente; **immediately
  next to** bem junto a
immense [ɪ'mɛns] adj imenso;
  (importance) enorme
immerse [ɪ'məːs] vt submergir;
  to be ~d in (fig) estar absorto em
immigrant ['ɪmɪgrənt] n imigrante
  m/f

immigration [ɪmɪ'greɪʃən] *n*
imigração *f*

imminent ['ɪmɪnənt] *adj* iminente

immoral [ɪ'mɔrl] *adj* imoral

immortal [ɪ'mɔːtl] *adj* imortal

immune [ɪ'mjuːn] *adj*: **~ to** imune
a, imunizado contra; **immune
system** *n* sistema *m* imunológico

impact ['ɪmpækt] *n* impacto (*BR*),
impacte *m* (*PT*)

impair [ɪm'peəʳ] *vt* prejudicar

impartial [ɪm'pɑːʃl] *adj* imparcial

impatience [ɪm'peɪʃəns] *n*
impaciência

impatient [ɪm'peɪʃənt] *adj*
impaciente; **to get** *or* **grow ~**
impacientar-se

impeccable [ɪm'pɛkəbl] *adj*
impecável

impending [ɪm'pɛndɪŋ] *adj*
iminente, próximo

imperative [ɪm'pɛrətɪv] *adj* (*tone*)
imperioso, obrigatório; (*necessary*)
indispensável ▷ *n* (*Ling*) imperativo

imperfect [ɪm'pəːfɪkt] *adj*
imperfeito; (*goods etc*) defeituoso
▷ *n* (*Ling: also:* **~ tense**) imperfeito

imperial [ɪm'pɪərɪəl] *adj* imperial

impersonal [ɪm'pəːsənl] *adj*
impessoal

impersonate [ɪm'pəːsəneɪt] *vt*
fazer-se passar por, personificar;
(*Theatre*) imitar

implement [*n* 'ɪmplɪmənt, *vt*
'ɪmplɪmɛnt] *n* instrumento,
ferramenta; (*for cooking*) utensílio
▷ *vt* efetivar

implicit [ɪm'plɪsɪt] *adj* implícito;
(*complete*) absoluto

imply [ɪm'plaɪ] *vt* (*mean*) significar;
(*hint*) dar a entender que

impolite [ɪmpə'laɪt] *adj* indelicado,
mal-educado

import [*vt* ɪm'pɔːt, *n, cpd* 'ɪmpɔːt] *vt*
importar ▷ *n* importação *f*;
(*article*) mercadoria importada

importance [ɪm'pɔːtəns] *n*
importância

important [ɪm'pɔːtənt] *adj*
importante; **it's not ~** não tem
importância, não importa

impose [ɪm'pəuz] *vt* impor ▷ *vi*:
to ~ on sb abusar de alguém;
imposing *adj* imponente

impossible [ɪm'pɔsɪbl] *adj*
impossível; (*situation*) inviável;
(*person*) insuportável

impotent ['ɪmpətənt] *adj*
impotente

impoverished [ɪm'pɔvərɪʃt] *adj*
empobrecido; (*land*) esgotado

impractical [ɪm'præktɪkl] *adj*
pouco prático

impress [ɪm'prɛs] *vt* impressionar;
(*mark*) imprimir; **to ~ sth on sb**
inculcar algo em alguém

impression [ɪm'prɛʃən] *n*
impressão *f*; **to be under the ~
that** estar com a impressão de
que

impressive [ɪm'prɛsɪv] *adj*
impressionante

imprison [ɪm'prɪzn] *vt* encarcerar

improbable [ɪm'prɔbəbl] *adj*
improvável; (*story*) inverossímil
(*BR*), inverosímil (*PT*)

improper [ɪm'prɔpəʳ] *adj*
(*unsuitable*) impróprio; (*dishonest*)
desonesto

improve [ɪm'pruːv] *vt* melhorar
▷ *vi* melhorar; (*pupils*) progredir;
improvement *n* melhora,
progresso

improvise ['ɪmprəvaɪz] *vt, vi*
improvisar

impulse ['ɪmpʌls] *n* impulso,
ímpeto; (*Elec*) impulso; **to act on ~**
agir sem pensar *or* num impulso

KEYWORD

in [ɪn] *prep* **1** (*indicating place, position*) em; **in the house/garden** na casa/no jardim; **I have the money in my hand** estou com o dinheiro na mão; **in here/there** aqui dentro/lá dentro
2 (*with place names: of town, country, region*) em; **in London** em Londres; **in England/Japan/Canada/the United States** na Inglaterra/no Japão/no Canadá/nos Estados Unidos; **in Rio** no Rio
3 (*indicating time: during*) em; **in spring/autumn** na primavera/no outono; **in 1988** em 1988; **in May** em maio; **I'll see you in July** até julho; **in the morning** de manhã; **at 4 o'clock in the afternoon** às 4 da tarde
4 (*indicating time: in the space of*) em; **I did it in 3 hours/days** fiz isto em 3 horas/dias; **in 2 weeks, in 2 weeks' time** daqui a 2 semanas
5 (*indicating manner etc*) **in a loud/soft voice** em voz alta/numa voz suave; **written in pencil/ink** escrito a lápis/à caneta; **in English/Portuguese** em inglês/português; **the boy in the blue shirt** o menino de camisa azul
6 (*indicating circumstances*): **in the sun** ao *or* sob o sol; **in the rain** na chuva; **a rise in prices** um aumento nos preços
7 (*indicating mood, state*): **in tears** aos prantos; **in anger/despair** com raiva/desesperado; **in good condition** em boas condições
8 (*with ratios, numbers*): **1 in 10** 1 em 10, 1 em cada 10; **20 pence in the pound** vinte pênis numa libra; **they lined up in twos** eles se alinharam dois a dois
9 (*referring to people, works*) em
10 (*indicating profession etc*): **to be in teaching/publishing** ser professor/trabalhar numa editora
11 (*after superl*): **the best pupil in the class** o melhor aluno da classe; **the biggest/smallest in Europe** o maior/menor na Europa
12 (*with present participle*): **in saying this** ao dizer isto
▷ *adv*: **to be in** (*person: at home*) estar em casa; (: *at work*) estar no trabalho; (*fashion*) estar na moda; (*ship, plane, train*): **it's in** chegou; **is he in?** ele está?; **to ask sb in** convidar alguém para entrar; **to run/limp** *etc* **in** entrar correndo/mancando *etc*
▷ *n*: **the ins and outs** (*of proposal, situation etc*) os cantos e recantos, os pormenores

in. *abbr* = **inch(es)**
inability [ɪnə'bɪlɪtɪ] *n*: **~ (to do)** incapacidade *f* (de fazer)
inaccurate [ɪn'ækjurət] *adj* inexato, impreciso
inadequate [ɪn'ædɪkwət] *adj* insuficiente; (*person*) impróprio
inadvertently [ɪnəd'və:tntlɪ] *adv* inadvertidamente, sem querer
inappropriate [ɪnə'prəuprɪət] *adj* inadequado; (*word, expression*) impróprio
incapable [ɪn'keɪpəbl] *adj* incapaz
incense [*n* 'ɪnsɛns, *vt* ɪn'sɛns] *n* incenso ▷ *vt* (*anger*) exasperar, enraivecer
incentive [ɪn'sɛntɪv] *n* incentivo
inch [ɪntʃ] *n* polegada (= 25 mm; 12 in a foot); **to be within an ~ of** estar a um passo de; **he didn't give an ~** ele não cedeu nem um milímetro

inch forward vi avançar palmo a palmo

incident ['ɪnsɪdnt] n incidente m, evento

inclination [ɪnklɪ'neɪʃən] n (tendency) tendência; (disposition) inclinação f

incline [n 'ɪnklaɪn, vt, vi ɪn'klaɪn] n inclinação f, ladeira ▷ vt curvar, inclinar ▷ vi inclinar-se; **to be ~d to** tender a, ser propenso a

include [ɪn'klu:d] vt incluir

including [ɪn'klu:dɪŋ] prep inclusive

inclusive [ɪn'klu:sɪv] adj incluído, incluso; **~ of** incluindo

income ['ɪŋkʌm] n (earnings) renda, rendimentos mpl; (unearned) renda; **income tax** n imposto de renda (BR), imposto complementar (PT)

incoming ['ɪnkʌmɪŋ] adj (flight, passenger) de chegada; (mail) de entrada; (government, tenant) novo

incompetent [ɪn'kɔmpɪtənt] adj incompetente

incomplete [ɪnkəm'pli:t] adj incompleto; (unfinished) por terminar

inconsistent [ɪnkən'sɪstnt] adj inconsistente; **~ with** incompatível com

inconvenience [ɪnkən'vi:njəns] n (quality) inconveniência; (problem) inconveniente m ▷ vt incomodar

inconvenient [ɪnkən'vi:njənt] adj inconveniente, incômodo; (time, place) inoportuno

incorporate [ɪn'kɔ:pəreɪt] vt incorporar; (contain) compreender

incorrect [ɪnkə'rɛkt] adj incorreto

increase [n 'ɪnkri:s, vi, vt ɪn'kri:s] n aumento ▷ vi, vt aumentar

incredible [ɪn'krɛdɪbl] adj inacreditável; (enormous) incrível

incur [ɪn'kə:ʳ] vt incorrer em; (expenses) contrair

indecent [ɪn'di:snt] adj indecente

indeed [ɪn'di:d] adv de fato; (certainly) certamente; (furthermore) aliás; **yes ~!** claro que sim!

indefinitely [ɪn'dɛfɪnɪtlɪ] adv indefinidamente

independence [ɪndɪ'pɛndns] n independência; **Independence Day** n ver nota

> **INDEPENDENCE DAY**
>
> O dia da Independência
> **Independence Day** é a festa
> nacional dos Estados Unidos.
> Todo dia 4 de julho os
> americanos comemoram a
> adoção, em 1776, da declaração
> de Independência escrita por
> Thomas Jefferson que
> proclamava a separação das 13
> colônias americanas da
> Grã-Bretanha.

independent [ɪndɪ'pɛndnt] adj independente; (inquiry) imparcial

index ['ɪndɛks] n (pl **indexes**) (in book) índice m; (in library etc) catálogo; (pl **indices**: ratio, sign) índice m, expoente m

India ['ɪndɪə] n Índia; **Indian** adj, n (from India) indiano(-a); (American, Brazilian) índio(-a)

indicate ['ɪndɪkeɪt] vt (show) sugerir; (point to) indicar; **indication** [ɪndɪ'keɪʃən] n indício, sinal m; **indicative** [ɪn'dɪkətɪv] adj indicativo ▷ n (Ling) indicativo; **to be indicative of sth** ser sintomático de algo; **indicator** n indicador m; (Aut) pisca-pisca m

indices ['ɪndɪsiːz] *npl of* **index**
indifferent [ɪn'dɪfrənt] *adj*
indiferente; (*quality*) medíocre
indigenous [ɪn'dɪdʒɪnəs] *adj*
indígena, nativo
indigestion [ɪndɪ'dʒɛstʃən] *n*
indigestão *f*
indignant [ɪn'dɪgnənt] *adj*: **to be ~
about sth/with sb** estar
indignado com algo/alguém,
indignar-se de algo/alguém
indirect [ɪndɪ'rɛkt] *adj* indireto
individual [ɪndɪ'vɪdjuəl] *n* indivíduo
▷ *adj* individual; (*personal*) pessoal;
(*characteristic*) particular
Indonesia [ɪndə'niːzɪə] *n* Indonésia
indoor ['ɪndɔːr] *adj* (*inner*) interno,
interior; (*inside*) dentro de casa;
(*swimming pool*) coberto; (*games,
sport*) de salão; **indoors** *adv* em
lugar fechado
induce [ɪn'djuːs] *vt* (*Med*) induzir;
(*bring about*) causar, produzir
indulge [ɪn'dʌldʒ] *vt* (*desire*)
satisfazer; (*whim*) condescender
com; (*person*) comprazer; (*child*)
fazer a vontade de ▷ *vi*: **to ~ in**
entregar-se a, satisfazer-se com;
indulgent *adj* indulgente
industrial [ɪn'dʌstrɪəl] *adj*
industrial
industry ['ɪndəstrɪ] *n* indústria;
(*diligence*) aplicação *f*, diligência
inefficient [ɪnɪ'fɪʃənt] *adj*
ineficiente
inequality [ɪnɪ'kwɔlɪtɪ] *n*
desigualdade *f*
inevitable [ɪn'ɛvɪtəbl] *adj*
inevitável; **inevitably** *adv*
inevitavelmente
inexpensive [ɪnɪk'spɛnsɪv] *adj*
barato, econômico
inexperienced [ɪnɪk'spɪərɪənst]
adj inexperiente

infamous ['ɪnfəməs] *adj* infame,
abominável
infant ['ɪnfənt] *n* (*baby*) bebê *m*;
(*young child*) criança
infant school (*Brit*) *n* pré-escola
infect [ɪn'fɛkt] *vt* (*person*)
contagiar; (*food*) contaminar;
infection *n* infecção *f*; **infectious**
adj contagioso; (*fig*) infeccioso
infer [ɪn'fəːr] *vt* deduzir, inferir
inferior [ɪn'fɪərɪər] *adj* inferior;
(*goods*) de qualidade inferior ▷ *n*
inferior *m/f*; (*in rank*) subalterno(-a)
infertile [ɪn'fəːtaɪl] *adj* infértil;
(*person, animal*) estéril
infinite ['ɪnfɪnɪt] *adj* infinito
infirmary [ɪn'fəːmərɪ] *n*
enfermaria, hospital *m*
inflamed [ɪn'fleɪmd] *adj* inflamado
inflammation [ɪnflə'meɪʃən] *n*
inflamação *f*
inflatable [ɪn'fleɪtəbl] *adj* inflável
inflate [ɪn'fleɪt] *vt* (*tyre, balloon*)
inflar, encher; (*price*) inflar;
inflation *n* (*Econ*) inflação *f*
inflict [ɪn'flɪkt] *vt*: **to ~ sth on sb**
infligir algo em alguém
influence ['ɪnfluəns] *n* influência
▷ *vt* influir em, influenciar; **under
the ~ of alcohol** sob o efeito do
álcool; **influential** [ɪnflu'ɛnʃl] *adj*
influente
influenza [ɪnflu'ɛnzə] *n* gripe *f*
inform [ɪn'fɔːm] *vt*: **to ~ sb of sth**
informar alguém de algo ▷ *vi*: **to ~
on sb** delatar alguém
informal [ɪn'fɔːml] *adj* informal;
(*visit, discussion*) extraoficial
information [ɪnfə'meɪʃən] *n*
informação *f*, informações *fpl*;
(*knowledge*) conhecimento; **a piece
of ~** uma informação
informative [ɪn'fɔːmətɪv] *adj*
informativo

infuriating [ɪnˈfjuərɪeɪtɪŋ] adj de dar raiva, enfurecedor(a)

ingenious [ɪnˈdʒiːnjəs] adj engenhoso

ingredient [ɪnˈgriːdɪənt] n ingrediente m; (of situation) fator m

inhabit [ɪnˈhæbɪt] vt habitar; **inhabitant** n habitante m/f

inhale [ɪnˈheɪl] vt inalar ▷ vi (in smoking) tragar

inherent [ɪnˈhɪərənt] adj: ~ **in** or **to** inerente a

inherit [ɪnˈhɛrɪt] vt herdar; **inheritance** n herança

inhibit [ɪnˈhɪbɪt] vt inibir; **inhibition** [ɪnhɪˈbɪʃən] n inibição f

initial [ɪˈnɪʃl] adj inicial ▷ n inicial f ▷ vt marcar com iniciais; **initials** npl (of name) iniciais fpl; **initially** adv inicialmente, no início

initiate [ɪˈnɪʃɪeɪt] vt (start) iniciar, começar; (person) iniciar; **to ~ sb into a secret** revelar um segredo a alguém; **to ~ proceedings against sb** (Law) abrir um processo contra alguém

initiative [ɪˈnɪʃətɪv] n iniciativa

inject [ɪnˈdʒɛkt] vt (liquid, fig: money) injetar; (person) dar uma injeção em; **injection** n injeção f

injure [ˈɪndʒəʳ] vt ferir; (reputation etc) prejudicar; (offend) ofender; **injured** adj ferido; (feelings) ofendido, magoado; **injury** n ferida

injustice [ɪnˈdʒʌstɪs] n injustiça

ink [ɪŋk] n tinta

inland [adj ˈɪnlənd, adv ɪnˈlænd] adj interior, interno ▷ adv para o interior; **Inland Revenue** (Brit) n ≈ fisco, ≈ receita federal (BR)

inmate [ˈɪnmeɪt] n (in prison) presidiário(-a); (in asylum) internado(-a)

inn [ɪn] n hospedaria, taberna

inner [ˈɪnəʳ] adj (place) interno; (feeling) interior; **inner city** n aglomeração f urbana, metrópole f

innocent [ˈɪnəsnt] adj inocente

in-patient n paciente m/f interno(-a)

input [ˈɪnput] n entrada; (resources) investimento

inquest [ˈɪnkwɛst] n inquérito judicial

inquire [ɪnˈkwaɪəʳ] vi pedir informação ▷ vt perguntar **inquire into** vt fus investigar, indagar; **inquiry** n pergunta; (Law) investigação f, inquérito

ins. abbr = **inches**

insane [ɪnˈseɪn] adj louco, doido; (Med) demente, insano; **insanity** [ɪnˈsænɪtɪ] n loucura; (Med) insanidade f, demência

inscrutable [ɪnˈskruːtəbl] adj inescrutável, impenetrável

insect [ˈɪnsɛkt] n inseto

insecure [ɪnsɪˈkjuəʳ] adj inseguro

insensitive [ɪnˈsɛnsɪtɪv] adj insensível

insert [ɪnˈsəːt] vt (between things) intercalar; (into sth) introduzir, inserir

inside [ˈɪnˈsaɪd] n interior m ▷ adj interior, interno ▷ adv (be) dentro; (go) para dentro ▷ prep dentro de; (of time): ~ **10 minutes** em menos de 10 minutos; **insides** npl (inf) entranhas fpl; **inside out** adv às avessas; (know) muito bem; **to turn sth inside out** virar algo pelo avesso

insight [ˈɪnsaɪt] n insight m

insignificant [ɪnsɪgˈnɪfɪknt] adj insignificante

insincere [ɪnsɪnˈsɪəʳ] adj insincero

insist [ɪnˈsɪst] vi insistir; **to ~ on**

doing insistir em fazer; **to ~ that** insistir que; (*claim*) cismar que; **insistent** *adj* insistente, pertinaz; (*continual*) persistente

insomnia [ɪn'sɔmnɪə] *n* insônia

inspect [ɪn'spɛkt] *vt* inspecionar; (*building*) vistoriar; (*Brit: tickets*) fiscalizar; (*troops*) passar revista em; **inspection** *n* inspeção *f*; (*of building*) vistoria; (*Brit: of tickets*) fiscalização *f*; **inspector** *n* inspetor(a) *m/f*; (*Brit: on buses, trains*) fiscal *m*

inspire [ɪn'spaɪər] *vt* inspirar

install [ɪn'stɔːl] *vt* instalar; (*official*) nomear; **installation** [ɪnstə'leɪʃən] *n* instalação *f*

installment [ɪn'stɔːlmənt] (*US*) *n* = **instalment**

instalment [ɪn'stɔːlmənt] *n* (*of money*) prestação *f*; (*of story*) fascículo; (*of TV serial etc*) capítulo; **in ~s** (*pay*) a prestações; (*receive*) em várias vezes

instance ['ɪnstəns] *n* exemplo; **for ~** por exemplo; **in the first ~** em primeiro lugar

instant ['ɪnstənt] *n* instante *m*, momento ▷ *adj* imediato; (*coffee*) instantâneo; **instantly** *adv* imediatamente; **instant messaging** *n* sistema *m* de mensagens instantâneas

instead [ɪn'stɛd] *adv* em vez disso; **~ of** em vez de, em lugar de

instinct ['ɪnstɪŋkt] *n* instinto

institute ['ɪnstɪtjuːt] *n* instituto; (*professional body*) associação *f* ▷ *vt* (*inquiry*) começar, iniciar; (*proceedings*) instituir, estabelecer

institution [ɪnstɪ'tjuːʃən] *n* instituição *f*; (*organization*) instituto; (*Med: home*) asilo; (*asylum*) manicômio; (*custom*) costume *m*

instruct [ɪn'strʌkt] *vt*: **to ~ sb in sth** instruir alguém em *or* sobre algo; **to ~ sb to do sth** dar instruções a alguém para fazer algo; **instruction** *n* (*teaching*) instrução *f*; **instructions** *npl* ordens *fpl*; **instructions (for use)** modo de usar; **instructor** *n* instrutor(a) *m/f*

instrument ['ɪnstrumənt] *n* instrumento

insufficient [ɪnsə'fɪʃənt] *adj* insuficiente

insulate ['ɪnsjuleɪt] *vt* isolar; (*protect*) segregar; **insulation** [ɪnsju'leɪʃən] *n* isolamento

insulin ['ɪnsjulɪn] *n* insulina

insult [*n* 'ɪnsʌlt, *vt* ɪn'sʌlt] *n* ofensa ▷ *vt* insultar, ofender

insurance [ɪn'ʃuərəns] *n* seguro; **fire/life ~** seguro contra incêndio/de vida

insure [ɪn'ʃuər] *vt* segurar

intact [ɪn'tækt] *adj* intacto, íntegro; (*unharmed*) ileso, são e salvo

intake ['ɪnteɪk] *n* (*of food*) quantidade f ingerida; (*Brit: Sch*): **an ~ 200 a year** 200 matriculados por ano

integral ['ɪntɪgrəl] *adj* (*part*) integrante, essencial

integrate ['ɪntɪgreɪt] *vt* integrar ▷ *vi* integrar-se

intellect ['ɪntəlɛkt] *n* intelecto; **intellectual** [ɪntə'lɛktjuəl] *adj*, *n* intelectual *m/f*

intelligence [ɪn'tɛlɪdʒəns] *n* inteligência; (*Mil etc*) informações *fpl*

intelligent [ɪn'tɛlɪdʒənt] *adj* inteligente

intend [ɪn'tɛnd] *vt* (*gift etc*): **to ~**

sth for destinar algo a; **to ~ to do
sth** tencionar or pretender fazer
algo; (plan) planejar fazer algo
intense [ɪn'tɛns] adj intenso;
(person) muito emotivo
intensive [ɪn'tɛnsɪv] adj intensivo;
intensive care unit n unidade f de
tratamento intensivo
intent [ɪn'tɛnt] n intenção f ▷ adj:
to be ~ on doing sth estar
resolvido a fazer algo; **to all ~s and
purposes** para todos os efeitos
intention [ɪn'tɛnʃən] n intenção f,
propósito; **intentional** adj
intencional, propositado
interact [ɪntər'ækt] vi interagir;
interactive [ɪntər'æktɪv] adj
interativo
interchange ['ɪntətʃeɪndʒ] n
intercâmbio; (exchange) troca,
permuta; (on motorway) trevo
intercourse ['ɪntəkɔːs] n: **sexual ~**
relações fpl sexuais
interest ['ɪntrɪst] n interesse m;
(Comm: sum of money) juros mpl; (: in
company) participação f ▷ vt
interessar; **to be ~ed in**
interessar-se por, estar interessado
em; **interesting** adj interessante
interface ['ɪntəfeɪs] n (Comput)
interface f
interfere [ɪntə'fɪər] vi: **to ~ in**
interferir or intrometer-se em; **to ~
with** (objects) mexer em; (hinder)
impedir; (plans) interferir em
interference [ɪntə'fɪərəns] n
intromissão f; (Radio, TV)
interferência
interior [ɪn'tɪərɪər] n interior m
▷ adj interno; (ministry) do interior
intermediate [ɪntə'miːdɪət] adj
intermediário
intermission [ɪntə'mɪʃən] n
intervalo

intern [vt ɪn'təːn, n 'ɪntəːn] vt
internar ▷ n (US) médico-interno/
médica-interna
internal [ɪn'təːnl] adj interno
international [ɪntə'næʃənl] adj
internacional ▷ n (Brit: Sport: game)
jogo internacional
Internet ['ɪntənɛt] n: **the ~** a
Internet; **Internet café** n
cibercafé m; **Internet Service
Provider** n provedor de acesso à
Internet; **Internet user** n
internauta m/f
interpret [ɪn'təːprɪt] vt interpretar;
(translate) traduzir ▷ vi interpretar;
interpreter n intérprete m/f
interrogate [ɪn'tɛrəuɡeɪt] vt
interrogar; **interrogation**
[ɪntɛrə'ɡeɪʃən] n interrogatório
interrupt [ɪntə'rʌpt] vt, vi
interromper; **interruption** n
interrupção f
interval ['ɪntəvl] n intervalo
intervene [ɪntə'viːn] vi intervir;
(event) ocorrer; (time) decorrer
interview ['ɪntəvjuː] n entrevista
▷ vt entrevistar; **interviewer** n
entrevistador(a) m/f
intimate [adj 'ɪntɪmət, vt 'ɪntɪmeɪt]
adj íntimo; (knowledge) profundo
▷ vt insinuar, sugerir

⭕ KEYWORD

into ['ɪntu] prep em **1** (indicating
motion or direction) em; **come into
the house/garden** venha para
dentro/o jardim; **research into
cancer** pesquisa sobre o câncer;
he worked late into the night
ele trabalhou até altas horas
2 (indicating change of condition,
result): **she burst into tears** ela
desatou a chorar; **he was shocked**

into silence ele ficou mudo de choque; **into 3 pieces/French** em 3 pedaços/para o francês

intolerant [ɪnˈtɔlərənt] *adj*: ~ **(of)** intolerante (com *or* para com)
intranet [ˈɪntrənet] *n* intranet *f*
intricate [ˈɪntrɪkət] *adj* complexo, complicado
intrigue [ɪnˈtriːg] *n* intriga ▷ *vt* intrigar; **intriguing** *adj* intrigante
introduce [ɪntrəˈdjuːs] *vt* introduzir; **to ~ sb (to sb)** apresentar alguém (a alguém); **to ~ sb to** (*pastime, technique*) iniciar alguém em; **introduction** *n* introdução *f*; (*of person*) apresentação *f*; **introductory** *adj* introdutório
intrude [ɪnˈtruːd] *vi*: **to ~ (on** *or* **into)** intrometer-se (em); **intruder** *n* intruso(-a)
inundate [ˈɪnʌndeɪt] *vt*: **to ~ with** inundar de
invade [ɪnˈveɪd] *vt* invadir
invalid [*n* ˈɪnvəlɪd, *adj* ɪnˈvælɪd] *n* inválido(-a) ▷ *adj* inválido, nulo
invaluable [ɪnˈvæljuəbl] *adj* valioso, inestimável
invariably [ɪnˈvɛərɪəblɪ] *adv* invariavelmente
invent [ɪnˈvɛnt] *vt* inventar; **invention** *n* invenção *f*; (*inventiveness*) engenho; (*lie*) ficção *f*, mentira; **inventor** *n* inventor(a) *m/f*
inventory [ˈɪnvəntrɪ] *n* inventário, relação *f*
invest [ɪnˈvɛst] *vt* investir ▷ *vi*: **to ~ in** investir em; (*acquire*) comprar
investigate [ɪnˈvɛstɪgeɪt] *vt* investigar; **investigation** [ɪnvɛstɪˈgeɪʃən] *n* investigação *f*
investment [ɪnˈvɛstmənt] *n*

investimento
invisible [ɪnˈvɪzɪbl] *adj* invisível
invitation [ɪnvɪˈteɪʃən] *n* convite *m*
invite [ɪnˈvaɪt] *vt* convidar; (*opinions etc*) solicitar; **inviting** *adj* convidativo
invoice [ˈɪnvɔɪs] *n* fatura ▷ *vt* faturar
involve [ɪnˈvɔlv] *vt* (*entail*) implicar; (*require*) exigir; **to ~ sb (in)** envolver alguém (em); **involved** *adj* (*complex*) complexo; **to be/get involved in sth** estar/ficar envolvido em algo; **involvement** *n* envolvimento
inward [ˈɪnwəd] *adj* (*movement*) interior, interno; (*thought, feeling*) íntimo ▷ *adv* para dentro; **inwards** *adv* para dentro
iPod® [ˈaɪpɔd] *n* iPod® *m*
IQ *n abbr* (= *intelligence quotient*) QI *m*
IRA *n abbr* (= *Irish Republican Army*) IRA *m*
Iran [ɪˈrɑːn] *n* Irã *m* (*BR*), Irão *m* (*PT*)
Iraq [ɪˈrɑːk] *n* Iraque *m*
Ireland [ˈaɪələnd] *n* Irlanda
iris [ˈaɪrɪs] (*pl* **irises**) *n* íris *f*
Irish [ˈaɪrɪʃ] *adj* irlandês(-esa); **the Irish** *npl* os irlandeses; **Irishman** *irreg n* irlandês *m*; **Irish Sea** *n*: **the Irish Sea** o mar da Irlanda; **Irishwoman** *irreg n* irlandesa
iron [ˈaɪən] *n* ferro; (*for clothes*) ferro de passar roupa ▷ *adj* de ferro ▷ *vt* (*clothes*) passar **iron out** *vt* (*problem*) resolver
ironic [aɪˈrɔnɪk], **ironical** [aɪˈrɔnɪkl] *adj* irônico
ironing [ˈaɪənɪŋ] *n* (*activity*) passar roupa; (*clothes*) roupa passada; **ironing board** *n* tábua de passar roupa
irony [ˈaɪrənɪ] *n* ironia
irrational [ɪˈræʃənl] *adj* irracional

irregular [ı'rɛgjulə^r] *adj* irregular;
(*surface*) desigual

irrelevant [ı'rɛləvənt] *adj*
irrelevante

irresistible [ırı'zıstıbl] *adj*
irresistível

irresponsible [ırı'spɒnsıbl] *adj*
irresponsável

irrigation [ırı'geıʃən] *n* irrigação *f*

irritate ['ırıteıt] *vt* irritar;
irritating *adj* irritante; **irritation**
[ırı'teıʃən] *n* irritação *f*

is [ız] *vb see* **be**

Islam ['ızlɑ:m] *n* islamismo

island ['aılənd] *n* ilha; **islander** *n*
ilhéu/ilhoa *m/f*

isle [aıl] *n* ilhota, ilha

isn't ['ıznt] = **is not**

ISP *n abbr* (= *Internet Service Provider*)
ISP *m*

Israel ['ızreıl] *n* Israel; **Israeli**
[ız'reılı] *adj, n* israelense *m/f*

issue ['ıʃu:] *n* questão *f*, tema *m*;
(*of book*) edição *f*; (*of stamps*)
emissão *f* ▷ *vt* (*rations, equipment*)
distribuir; (*orders*) dar; **at ~** em
debate; **to take ~ with sb (over
sth)** discordar de alguém (sobre
algo); **to make an ~ of sth** criar
caso com algo

KEYWORD

it [ıt] *pron* **1** (*specific: subject*) ele/ela;
(*: direct object*) o/a; (*: indirect object*)
lhe; **it's on the table** está em cima
da mesa; **I can't find it** não
consigo achá-lo; **give it to me**
dê-mo; **about/from it** sobre/de
isto; **did you go to it?** (*party,
concert etc*) você foi?
2 (*impers*) isto, isso; (*after prep*) ele,
ela; **it's raining** está chovendo (*BR*)
or a chover (*PT*); **it's six o'clock/**

the 10th of August são seis horas/
hoje é (dia) 10 de agosto; **who is it?
— it's me** quem é? — sou eu

Italian [ı'tæljən] *adj* italiano ▷ *n*
italiano(-a); (*Ling*) italiano

italics [ı'tælıks] *npl* itálico

Italy ['ıtəlı] *n* Itália

itch [ıtʃ] *n* comichão *f*, coceira ▷ *vi*
(*person*) estar com *or* sentir
comichão *or* coceira; (*part of body*)
comichar, coçar; **I'm ~ing to do
something** estou louco para fazer
algo; **itchy** *adj* que coça; **to be
itchy** = **to itch**

it'd ['ıtd] = **it would**; **it had**

item ['aıtəm] *n* item *m*; (*on agenda*)
assunto; (*in programme*) número;
(*also*: **news ~**) notícia

itinerary [aı'tınərərı] *n* itinerário

it'll ['ıtl] = **it will**; **it shall**

its [ıts] *adj* seu/sua, dele/dela
▷ *pron* o seu/a sua, o dele/a dela

it's [ıts] = **it is**; **it has**

itself [ıt'sɛlf] *pron* (*reflexive*) si
mesmo(-a); (*emphatic*) ele mesmo/
ela mesma

ITV (*Brit*) *n abbr* (= *Independent
Television*) canal de televisão comercial

I've [aıv] = **I have**

ivory ['aıvərı] *n* marfim *m*

ivy ['aıvı] *n* hera

J, j [dʒeɪ] n J, j m

jab [dʒæb] vt cutucar ▷ n cotovelada, murro; (Med: inf) injeção f; **to ~ sth into sth** cravar algo em algo

jack [dʒæk] n (Aut) macaco; (Cards) valete m **jack up** vt (Aut) levantar com macaco

jacket ['dʒækɪt] n jaqueta, casaco curto, forro; (of book) sobrecapa

jackpot ['dʒækpɔt] n bolada, sorte f grande

jagged ['dʒægɪd] adj dentado, denteado

jail [dʒeɪl] n prisão f, cadeia ▷ vt encarcerar

jam [dʒæm] n geleia; (also: **traffic ~**) engarrafamento; (inf) apuro ▷ vt obstruir, atravancar; (mechanism) emperrar; (Radio) bloquear, interferir ▷ vi (mechanism, drawer etc) emperrar; **to ~ sth into sth** forçar algo dentro de algo

Jamaica [dʒə'meɪkə] n Jamaica

janitor ['dʒænɪtər] n zelador m

January ['dʒænjuəri] n janeiro

Japan [dʒə'pæn] n Japão m; **Japanese** [dʒæpə'niːz] adj japonês(-esa) ▷ n inv japonês(-esa) m/f; (Ling) japonês m

jar [dʒɑːr] n jarro ▷ vi (sound) ranger, chiar; (colours) destoar

jargon ['dʒɑːgən] n jargão m

javelin ['dʒævlɪn] n dardo de arremesso

jaw [dʒɔː] n mandíbula, maxilar m

jazz [dʒæz] n jazz m **jazz up** vt animar, avivar

jealous ['dʒɛləs] adj ciumento; **jealousy** n ciúmes mpl

jeans [dʒiːnz] npl jeans m (BR), jeans mpl (PT)

jelly ['dʒɛlɪ] n (jam) geleia; **jellyfish** ['dʒɛlɪfɪʃ] n inv água-viva

jerk [dʒəːk] n solavanco, sacudida; (wrench) puxão m; (inf: idiot) babaca m ▷ vt sacudir ▷ vi dar um solavanco

jersey ['dʒəːzɪ] n suéter m (BR), camisola (PT); (fabric) jérsei m, malha

Jesus ['dʒiːzəs] n Jesus m (Cristo)

jet [dʒɛt] n (of gas, liquid) jato; (Aviat) (avião m a) jato; (stone) azeviche m; **jet lag** n cansaço devido à diferença de fuso horário

jetty ['dʒɛtɪ] n quebra-mar m, cais m

Jew [dʒuː] n judeu(-dia) m/f

jewel ['dʒuːəl] n joia; **jeweller**, (US) **jeweler** n joalheiro(-a); **jewellery**, (US) **jewelry** n joias fpl, pedrarias fpl

Jewish ['dʒuːɪʃ] adj judeu/judia

jigsaw ['dʒɪgsɔː] n (also: **~ puzzle**) quebra-cabeça m

job [dʒɔb] n trabalho; (task) tarefa;

(*duty*) dever m; (*post*) emprego; **it's not my ~** não faz parte das minhas funções; **it's a good ~ that ...** ainda bem que ...; **just the ~!** justo o que queria!; **jobless** *adj* desempregado

jockey ['dʒɔkɪ] *n* jóquei *m* ▷ *vi*: **to ~ for position** manobrar para conseguir uma posição

jog [dʒɔg] *vt* empurrar, sacudir ▷ *vi* fazer jogging *or* cooper **jog along** *vi* ir levando; **jogging** *n* jogging *m*

join [dʒɔɪn] *vt* (*things*) juntar, unir; (*queue*) entrar em; (*become member of*) associar-se a; (*meet*) encontrar-se com; (*accompany*) juntar-se a ▷ *vi* (*roads, rivers*) confluir ▷ *n* junção *f* **join in** *vi* participar ▷ *vt fus* participar em **join up** *vi* unir-se; (*Mil*) alistar-se

joint [dʒɔɪnt] *n* (*Tech*) junta, união *f*; (*wood*) encaixe *m*; (*Anat*) articulação *f*; (*Brit: Culin*) quarto; (*inf: place*) espelunca; (: *marijuana cigarette*) baseado ▷ *adj* comum; (*combined*) conjunto; (*committee*) misto

joke [dʒəuk] *n* piada; (*also*: **practical ~**) brincadeira, peça ▷ *vi* brincar; **to play a ~ on** pregar uma peça em; **joker** *n* (*Cards*) curingão *m*

jolly ['dʒɔlɪ] *adj* (*merry*) alegre; (*enjoyable*) divertido ▷ *adv* (*Brit: inf*) muito, extremamente

jolt [dʒəult] *n* (*shake*) sacudida, solavanco; (*shock*) susto ▷ *vt* sacudir; (*emotionally*) abalar

Jordan ['dʒɔːdən] *n* Jordânia; (*river*) Jordão *m*

journal ['dʒəːnl] *n* jornal *m*; (*magazine*) revista; (*diary*) diário; **journalism** *n* jornalismo; **journalist** *n* jornalista *m/f*

journey ['dʒəːnɪ] *n* viagem *f*; (*distance covered*) trajeto

joy [dʒɔɪ] *n* alegria

judge [dʒʌdʒ] *n* juiz/juíza *m/f*; (*in competition*) árbitro; (*fig: expert*) especialista *m/f*, conhecedor(a) *m/f* ▷ *vt* julgar; (*competition*) arbitrar; (*estimate*) avaliar; (*consider*) considerar

judo ['dʒuːdəu] *n* judô *m*

jug [dʒʌg] *n* jarro

juggle ['dʒʌgl] *vi* fazer malabarismos; **juggler** *n* malabarista *m/f*

juice [dʒuːs] *n* suco (*BR*), sumo (*PT*); **juicy** *adj* suculento

July [dʒuːˈlaɪ] *n* julho

jumble ['dʒʌmbl] *n* confusão *f*, mixórdia ▷ *vt* (*also*: **~ up**: *mix up*) misturar; **jumble sale** (*Brit*) *n* bazar *m*; *ver nota*

- **JUMBLE SALE**

- As **jumble sales** têm lugar
- dentro de igrejas, salões de festa
- e escolas, onde são vendidos
- diversos tipos de mercadorias,
- em geral baratas e sobretudo de
- segunda mão, a fim de coletar
- dinheiro para uma obra de
- caridade, uma escola ou uma
- igreja.

jump [dʒʌmp] *vi* saltar, pular; (*start*) sobressaltar-se; (*increase*) disparar ▷ *vt* pular, saltar ▷ *n* pulo, salto; (*increase*) alta; (*fence*) obstáculo; **to ~ the queue** (*Brit*) furar a fila (*BR*), pôr-se à frente (*PT*)

jumper ['dʒʌmpəʳ] *n* (*Brit: pullover*) suéter *m* (*BR*), camisola (*PT*); (*US: pinafore dress*) avental *m*; **jumper cables** (*US*) *npl* = **jump leads**

jump leads, (*US*) **jumper cables**
  npl cabos *mpl* para ligar a bateria
Jun. *abbr* = **junior**
junction ['dʒʌŋkʃən] (*Brit*) *n* (*of
  roads*) cruzamento; (*Rail*)
  entroncamento
June [dʒuːn] *n* junho
jungle ['dʒʌŋgl] *n* selva, mato
junior ['dʒuːnɪəʳ] *adj* (*in age*) mais
  novo *or* moço; (*position*) subalterno
  ▷ *n* jovem *m/f*
junk [dʒʌŋk] *n* (*cheap goods*)
  tranqueira, velharias *fpl*; (*rubbish*)
  lixo; **junk food** *n* comida pronta de
  baixo valor nutritivo; **junk mail** *n*
  correspondência não-solicitada
jury ['dʒuərɪ] *n* júri *m*
just [dʒʌst] *adj* justo ▷ *adv* (*exactly*)
  justamente, exatamente; (*only*)
  apenas, somente; **he's ~ done it/
  left** ele acabou (*BR*) *or* acaba (*PT*) de
  fazê-lo/ir; **~ right** perfeito; **~ two
  o'clock** duas (horas) em ponto;
  she's ~ as clever as you ela é tão
  inteligente como você; **~ as well
  that ...** ainda bem que ...; **~ as he
  was leaving** no momento em que
  ele saía; **~ before/enough** justo
  antes/o suficiente; **~ here** bem
  aqui; **he ~ missed** falhou por
  pouco; **~ listen** escute aqui!
justice ['dʒʌstɪs] *n* justiça; (*US:
  judge*) juiz/juíza *m/f*; **to do ~ to** (*fig*)
  apreciar devidamente
justify ['dʒʌstɪfaɪ] *vt* justificar
jut [dʒʌt] *vi* (*also:* **~ out**) sobressair
juvenile ['dʒuːvənaɪl] *adj* juvenil;
  (*court*) de menores; (*books*) para
  adolescentes ▷ *n* menor *m/f* de
  idade

K, k [keɪ] *n* K, k *m*
K *abbr* (= *kilobyte*) K ▷ *n abbr* (= *one
  thousand*) mil
kangaroo [kæŋgəˈruː] *n* canguru *m*
karate [kəˈrɑːtɪ] *n* karatê *m*
kebab [kəˈbæb] *n* churrasquinho,
  espetinho
keen [kiːn] *adj* (*interest, desire*)
  grande, vivo; (*eye, intelligence*)
  penetrante; (*competition*) acirrado,
  intenso; (*edge*) afiado; (*eager*)
  entusiasmado; **to be ~ to do** *or* **on
  doing sth** sentir muita vontade de
  fazer algo; **to be ~ on sth/sb**
  gostar de algo/alguém
keep [kiːp] (*pt, pp* **kept**) *vt* ficar
  com; (*house etc*) cuidar; (*detain*)
  deter; (*shop etc*) tomar conta de;
  (*preserve*) conservar; (*family etc*)
  manter; (*promise*) cumprir;
  (*chickens, bees etc*) criar; (*prevent*):
  to ~ sb from doing sth impedir

alguém de fazer algo ▷ vi (food) conservar-se; (remain) ficar ▷ n (of castle) torre f de menagem; (food etc): **to earn one's ~** ganhar a vida; (inf): **for ~s** para sempre; **to ~ doing sth** continuar fazendo algo; **to ~ sb happy** manter alguém satisfeito; **to ~ a place tidy** manter um lugar limpo **keep on** vi: **to ~ on doing** continuar fazendo **keep out** vt impedir de entrar; **"~ out"** "entrada proibida" **keep up** vt manter ▷ vi não atrasar-se, acompanhar; **to ~ up with** (pace) acompanhar; (level) manter-se ao nível de; **keeper** n guarda m, guardião(-diã) m/f

kennel ['kɛnl] n casa de cachorro; **kennels** n (establishment) canil m

kerb [kə:b] (Brit) n meio-fio (BR), borda do passeio (PT)

kettle ['kɛtl] n chaleira

key [ki:] n chave f; (Mus) clave f; (of piano, typewriter) tecla ▷ cpd (issue etc) chave ▷ vt (also: **~ in**) digitar; **keyboard** n teclado; **keyhole** n buraco da fechadura; **keyring** n chaveiro

khaki ['kɑːkɪ] adj cáqui

kick [kɪk] vt dar um pontapé em; (ball) chutar; (inf: habit) conseguir superar ▷ vi (horse) dar coices ▷ n (from person) pontapé m; (from animal) coice m, patada; (to ball) chute m; (inf: thrill): **he does it for ~s** faz isso para curtir **kick off** vi (Sport) dar o chute inicial

kid [kɪd] n (inf: child) criança; (animal) cabrito; (leather) pelica ▷ vi (inf) brincar

kidnap ['kɪdnæp] vt sequestrar

kidney ['kɪdnɪ] n rim m

kill [kɪl] vt matar; (murder) assassinar ▷ n ato de matar; **killer** n assassino(-a); **killing** n assassinato; **to make a killing** (inf) faturar uma boa nota

kiln [kɪln] n forno

kilo ['ki:ləu] n quilo; **kilobyte** n kilobyte m; **kilogram, kilogramme** n quilograma m; **kilometre**, (US) **kilometer** n quilômetro; **kilowatt** n quilowatt m

kilt [kɪlt] n saiote m escocês

kin [kɪn] n see **next-of-kin**

kind [kaɪnd] adj (friendly) gentil; (generous) generoso; (good) bom/ boa, bondoso, amável ▷ n espécie f, classe f; (species) gênero; **in ~** (Comm) em espécie

kindergarten ['kɪndəgɑːtn] n jardim m de infância

kindly ['kaɪndlɪ] adj (good) bom/ boa, bondoso; (gentle) gentil, carinhoso ▷ adv bondosamente, amavelmente; **will you ~ ...** você pode fazer o favor de ...

kindness ['kaɪndnɪs] n bondade f, gentileza

king [kɪŋ] n rei m; **kingdom** n reino; **kingfisher** n martim-pescador m

kiosk ['ki:ɔsk] n banca (BR), quiosque m (PT); (Brit: also: **telephone ~**) cabine f

kipper ['kɪpər] n tipo de arenque defumado

kiss [kɪs] n beijo ▷ vt beijar; **to ~ (each other)** beijar-se; **kiss of life** (Brit) n respiração f boca-a-boca

kit [kɪt] n (for sport etc) kit m; (equipment) equipamento; (set of tools etc) caixa de ferramentas; (for assembly) kit m para montar

kitchen ['kɪtʃɪn] n cozinha

kite [kaɪt] n (toy) papagaio, pipa

kitten ['kɪtn] n gatinho

k

kitty ['kɪtɪ] *n* fundo comum, vaquinha

km *abbr* (= *kilometre*) km

knack [næk] *n*: **there's a ~ (to it)** tem um jeito

knee [ni:] *n* joelho; **kneecap** *n* rótula

kneel [ni:l] (*pt, pp* **knelt**) *vi* (*also:* **~ down**) ajoelhar-se

knew [nju:] *pt of* **know**

knickers ['nɪkəz] (*Brit*) *npl* calcinha (*BR*), cuecas *fpl* (*PT*)

knife [naɪf] (*pl* **knives**) *n* faca ▷ *vt* esfaquear

knight [naɪt] *n* cavaleiro; (*Chess*) cavalo

knit [nɪt] *vt* tricotar; (*brows*) franzir ▷ *vi* tricotar (*BR*), fazer malha (*PT*); (*bones*) consolidar-se; **knitting** *n* ato de tricotar, tricô (*BR*), malha (*PT*); **knitting needle** *n* agulha de tricô (*BR*) *or* de malha (*PT*); **knitwear** *n* roupa de malha

knives [naɪvz] *npl of* **knife**

knob [nɔb] *n* (*of door*) maçaneta; (*of stick*) castão *m*; (*on radio, TV etc*) botão *m*

knock [nɔk] *vt* bater em; (*bump into*) colidir com; (*inf*) criticar, malhar ▷ *n* pancada, golpe *m*; (*on door*) batida ▷ *vi*: **to ~ at** *or* **on the door** bater à porta **knock down** *vt* derrubar; (*pedestrian*) atropelar **knock off** *vi* (*inf: finish*) terminar ▷ *vt* (*inf: steal*) abafar; (*from price*): **to ~ off £10** dar um desconto de £10 **knock out** *vt* pôr nocaute, nocautear; (*defeat*) eliminar **knock over** *vt* derrubar; (*pedestrian*) atropelar

knot [nɔt] *n* nó *m* ▷ *vt* dar nó em

know [nəu] (*pt* **knew**, *pp* **known**) *vt* saber; (*person, author, place*) conhecer ▷ *vi*: **to ~ about** *or* **of sth** saber de algo; **to ~ how to swim** saber nadar; **know-how** *n* know-how *m*, experiência; **knowingly** *adv* (*purposely*) de propósito; (*spitefully*) maliciosamente

knowledge ['nɔlɪdʒ] *n* conhecimento; (*range of learning*) saber *m*, conhecimentos *mpl*; **knowledgeable** *adj* entendido, versado

knuckle ['nʌkl] *n* nó *m*

Koran [kɔ'rɑ:n] *n*: **the ~** o Alcorão

Korea [kə'rɪə] *n* Coreia

kosher ['kəuʃə*] *adj* kosher *inv*

Kosovo ['kɒsəvəu] *n* Kosovo *m*

L *abbr* (Brit: Aut: = learner) (condutor(a) *m/f*) aprendiz *m/f*

lab [læb] *n abbr* = **laboratory**

label ['leɪbl] *n* etiqueta, rótulo ▷ *vt* etiquetar, rotular

labor ['leɪbə'] (*US*) = **labour**

laboratory [lə'bɔrətərɪ] *n* laboratório

labour ['leɪbə'], (*US*) **labor** *n* trabalho; (*work force*) mão-de-obra *f*; (*Med*): **to be in ~** estar em trabalho de parto ▷ *vi*: **to ~ (at)** trabalhar (em) ▷ *vt* insistir em; **the L~ Party** (*Brit*) o Partido Trabalhista; **labourer** *n* operário; **farm labourer** trabalhador *m* rural, peão *m*

lace [leɪs] *n* renda; (*of shoe etc*) cadarço ▷ *vt* (*shoe*) amarrar

lack [læk] *n* falta ▷ *vt* (*money, confidence*) faltar; (*intelligence*) carecer de; **through** *or* **for ~ of** por falta de; **to be ~ing** faltar; **to be ~ing in** carecer de

lacquer ['lækə'] *n* laca; (*hair*) fixador *m*

lad [læd] *n* menino, rapaz *m*, moço

ladder ['lædə'] *n* escada *f* de mão; (*Brit: in tights*) defeito (em forma de escada)

ladle ['leɪdl] *n* concha (de sopa)

lady ['leɪdɪ] *n* senhora; (*distinguished, noble*) dama; (*in address*): **ladies and gentlemen, ...** senhoras e senhores, ...; **young ~** senhorita; **"ladies' (toilets)"** "senhoras"; **ladybird**, (*US*) **ladybug** *n* joaninha

lag [læg] *n* atraso, retardamento ▷ *vi* (*also*: **~ behind**) ficar para trás ▷ *vt* (*pipes*) revestir com isolante térmico

lager ['lɑ:gə'] *n cerveja leve e clara*

lagoon [lə'gu:n] *n* lagoa

laid [leɪd] *pt, pp of* **lay**

lain [leɪn] *pp of* **lie**

lake [leɪk] *n* lago

lamb [læm] *n* cordeiro

lame [leɪm] *adj* coxo, manco; (*excuse, argument*) pouco convincente, fraco

lament [lə'mɛnt] *n* lamento, queixa ▷ *vt* lamentar-se de

lamp [læmp] *n* lâmpada; **lamppost** (*Brit*) *n* poste *m*; **lampshade** *n* abajur *m*, quebra-luz *m*

land [lænd] *n* terra; (*country*) país *m*; (*piece of land*) terreno; (*estate*) terras *fpl*, propriedades *fpl* ▷ *vi* (*from ship*) desembarcar; (*Aviat*) pousar, aterrissar (*BR*), aterrar (*PT*); (*fig: arrive unexpectedly*) cair, terminar ▷ *vt* desembarcar; **to ~ sb with sth** (*inf*) sobrecarregar alguém com algo **land up** *vi*: **to ~**

up in/at ir parar em; **landing** n (Aviat) pouso, aterrissagem f(BR), aterragem f(PT); (of staircase) patamar m; **landlady** n senhoria; (of pub) dona, proprietária; **landlord** n senhorio, locador m; (of pub etc) dono, proprietário; **landmark** n lugar m conhecido; (fig) marco; **landowner** n latifundiário(-a)

landscape ['lændskeɪp] n paisagem f

landslide ['lændslaɪd] n (Geo) desmoronamento, desabamento; (fig: Pol) vitória esmagadora

lane [leɪn] n caminho, estrada estreita; (Aut) pista; (in race) raia

language ['læŋgwɪdʒ] n língua; (way one speaks, Comput, style) linguagem f; **bad ~** palavrões mpl; **language laboratory** n laboratório de línguas; **language school** n escola de línguas

lantern ['læntn] n lanterna

lap [læp] n (of track) volta; (of person) colo ⊳ vt (also: **~ up**) lamber ⊳ vi (waves) marulhar **lap up** vt (fig) receber com sofreguidão

lapel [lə'pɛl] n lapela

lapse [læps] n lapso; (bad behaviour) deslize m ⊳ vi (law) prescrever; **to ~ into bad habits** adquirir maus hábitos

laptop ['læptɔp], **laptop computer** n laptop m

lard [lɑːd] n banha de porco

larder ['lɑːdəʳ] n despensa

large [lɑːdʒ] adj grande; **at ~** (free) em liberdade; (generally) em geral; **largely** adv em grande parte; (introducing reason) principalmente; **large-scale** adj (map) em grande escala; (fig) importante, de grande alcance

lark [lɑːk] n (bird) cotovia; (joke) brincadeira, peça **lark about** vi divertir-se, brincar

laryngitis [lærɪn'dʒaɪtɪs] n laringite f

laser ['leɪzəʳ] n laser m; **laser printer** n impressora a laser

lash [læʃ] n (blow) chicotada; (also: **eye~**) pestana, cílio ⊳ vt chicotear, açoitar; (subj: rain, wind) castigar; (tie) atar **lash out** vi: **to ~ out (at sb)** atacar (alguém) violentamente; **to ~ out at** or **against sb** (criticize) atacer alguém verbalmente

lass [læs] (Brit) n moça

last [lɑːst] adj último; (final) derradeiro ⊳ adv em último lugar ⊳ vi durar; (continue) continuar; **~ week** na semana passada; **~ night** ontem à noite; **at ~** finalmente; **~ but one** penúltimo; **lastly** adv por fim, por último; (finally) finalmente; **last-minute** adj de última hora

latch [lætʃ] n trinco, fecho, tranca

late [leɪt] adj (not on time) atrasado; (far on in day etc) tardio; (former) antigo, ex-, anterior; (dead) falecido ⊳ adv tarde; (behind time, schedule) atrasado; **of ~** recentemente; **in ~ May** no final de maio; **latecomer** n retardatário(-a); **lately** adv ultimamente; **later** adj (date etc) posterior; (version etc) mais recente ⊳ adv mais tarde, depois; **later on** mais tarde; **latest** adj último; **at the latest** no mais tardar

lather ['lɑːðəʳ] n espuma (de sabão) ⊳ vt ensaboar

Latin ['lætɪn] n (Ling) latim m ⊳ adj latino; **Latin America** n América Latina; **Latin American** adj, n

latino-americano(-a)
latitude ['lætɪtjuːd] n latitude f
latter ['lætə^r] adj último; (of two)
segundo ▷ n: **the ~** o último, este
laugh [lɑːf] n riso, risada ▷ vi rir, dar
risada (or gargalhada); **(to do sth)
for a ~** (fazer algo) só de curtição
laugh at vt fus rir de **laugh off** vt
disfarçar sorrindo; **laughter** n
riso, risada
launch [lɔːntʃ] n (boat) lancha;
(Comm, of rocket etc) lançamento
▷ vt lançar **launch into** vt fus
lançar-se a
laundry ['lɔːndrɪ] n lavanderia;
(clothes) roupa para lavar
lava ['lɑːvə] n lava
lavatory ['lævətərɪ] n privada (BR),
casa de banho (PT)
lavender ['lævəndə^r] n lavanda
lavish ['lævɪʃ] adj (amount)
generoso; (person): **~ with** pródigo
em, generoso com ▷ vt: **to ~ sth
on sb** encher or cobrir alguém de
algo
law [lɔː] n lei f; (rule) regra; (Sch)
direito; **lawful** adj legal, lícito
lawn [lɔːn] n gramado (BR), relvado
(PT); **lawnmower** n cortador m de
grama (BR) or relva (PT)
lawsuit ['lɔːsuːt] n ação f judicial,
processo
lawyer ['lɔːjə^r] n advogado(-a); (for
sales, wills etc) notário(-a),
tabelião(-liã) m/f
lax [læks] adj (discipline) relaxado;
(person) negligente
laxative ['læksətɪv] n laxante m
lay [leɪ] (pt, pp **laid**) pt of **lie** ▷ adj
leigo ▷ vt colocar; (eggs, table) pôr
lay aside vt pôr de lado **lay by** vt
= **lay aside lay down** vt depositar;
(rules etc) impor, estabelecer; **to ~
down the law** (pej) impor regras;

to ~ down one's life sacrificar
voluntariamenta a vida **lay off** vt
(workers) demitir **lay on** vt (meal,
entertainment) prover **lay out** vt
(spread out) dispor em ordem;
lay-by (Brit) n acostamento
layer ['leɪə^r] n camada
layman ['leɪmən] irreg n leigo
layout ['leɪaut] n (of garden,
building) desenho; (of piece of
writing) leiaute m
lazy ['leɪzɪ] adj preguiçoso;
(movement) lento
lb. abbr (weight) = **pound**
lead¹ [liːd] (pt, pp **led**) n (front
position) dianteira; (Sport)
liderança; (fig) vantagem f; (clue)
pista; (Elec) fio; (for dog) correia; (in
play, film) papel m principal ▷ vt
levar; (be leader of) chefiar; (start,
guide: activity) encabeçar ▷ vi
encabeçar; **to be in the ~** (Sport: in
race) estar na frente; (: in match)
estar ganhando; **to ~ the way**
assumir a direção **lead away** vt
levar **lead back** vt levar de volta
lead on vt (tease) provocar **lead to**
vt fus levar a, conduzir a **lead up to**
vt fus conduzir a
lead² [lɛd] n chumbo; (in pencil)
grafite f
leader ['liːdə^r] n líder m/f;
leadership n liderança; (quality)
poder m de liderança
lead-free [lɛd-] adj sem chumbo
leading ['liːdɪŋ] adj principal; (role)
de destaque; (first, front) primeiro,
dianteiro
lead singer [liːd-] n cantor(a) m/f
leaf [liːf] (pl **leaves**) n folha ▷ vi: **to
~ through** (book) folhear; **to turn
over a new ~** mudar de vida, partir
para outra (inf)
leaflet ['liːflɪt] n folheto

league [li:g] n liga; **to be in ~ with** estar de comum acordo com

leak [li:k] n (of liquid, gas) escape m, vazamento; (hole) buraco, rombo; (in roof) goteira; (fig: of information) vazamento ▷ vi (ship) fazer água; (shoe) deixar entrar água; (roof) gotejar; (pipe, container, liquid) vazar; (gas) escapar ▷ vt (news) vazar

lean [li:n] (pt, pp **leaned** or **leant**) adj magro ▷ vt: **to ~ sth on** encostar or apoiar algo em ▷ vi inclinar-se; **to ~ against** encostar-se or apoiar-se contra; **to ~ on** encostar-se or apoiar-se em

lean back vi inclinar-se para trás

lean forward vi inclinar-se para frente **lean out** vi: **to ~ out (of)** inclinar-se para fora (de) **lean over** vi debruçar-se ▷ vt fus debruçar-se sobre

leap [li:p] (pt, pp **leaped** or **leapt**) n salto, pulo ▷ vi saltar; **leap year** n ano bissexto

learn [lə:n] (pt, pp **learned** or **learnt**) vt aprender; (by heart) decorar ▷ vi aprender; **to ~ about sth** (Sch: hear, read) saber de algo; **learner** n principiante m/f; (Brit: also: **learner driver**) aprendiz m/f de motorista

lease [li:s] n arrendamento ▷ vt arrendar

leash [li:ʃ] n correia

least [li:st] adj: **the ~** + n o/a menor; (smallest amount of) a menor quantidade de ▷ adv: **the ~** + adj o/a menos; **at ~** pelo menos; **not in the ~** de maneira nenhuma

leather ['lɛðəʳ] n couro

leave [li:v] (pt, pp **left**) vt deixar; (go away from) abandonar ▷ vi ir-se, sair; (train) sair ▷ n licença; **to ~** **sth to sb** deixar algo para alguém; **to be left** sobrar **leave behind** vt deixar para trás; (forget) esquecer **leave out** vt omitir

leaves [li:vz] npl of **leaf**

Lebanon ['lɛbənən] n Líbano

lecture ['lɛktʃəʳ] n conferência, palestra; (Sch) aula ▷ vi dar aulas, lecionar ▷ vt (scold) passar um sermão em; **lecturer** n (Brit: at university) professor(a) m/f

led [lɛd] pt, pp of **lead**

ledge [lɛdʒ] n (of window) peitoril m; (of mountain) saliência, proeminência

leek [li:k] n alho-poró m

left [lɛft] pt, pp of **leave** ▷ adj esquerdo ▷ n esquerda ▷ adv à esquerda; **on the ~** à esquerda; **to the ~** para a esquerda; **the L~** (Pol) a Esquerda; **left-handed** adj canhoto; **left-luggage**, **left-luggage office** (Brit) n depósito de bagagem

left-wing adj (Pol) de esquerda, esquerdista

leg [lɛg] n perna; (of animal) pata; (Culin: of meat) perna; (of journey) etapa; **lst/2nd ~** (Sport) primeiro/segundo turno

legacy ['lɛgəsɪ] n legado; (fig) herança

legal ['li:gl] adj legal

legend ['lɛdʒənd] n lenda; (person) mito

leggings ['lɛgɪŋz] npl legging f

legislation [lɛdʒɪsˈleɪʃən] n legislação f

legitimate [lɪˈdʒɪtɪmət] adj legítimo

leisure ['lɛʒəʳ] n lazer m; **at ~** desocupado, livre

lemon ['lɛmən] n limão(-galego) m; **lemonade** [lɛməˈneɪd] n limonada; **lemon tea** n chá m de limão

lend [lɛnd] (pt, pp **lent**) vt: **to ~ sth to sb** emprestar algo a alguém

length [lɛŋθ] n comprimento, extensão f; (amount of time) duração f; **at ~** (at last) finalmente, afinal; (lengthily) por extenso; **lengthen** vt encompridar, alongar ▷ vi encompridar-se; **lengthways** adv longitudinalmente, ao comprido; **lengthy** adj comprido, longo; (meeting) prolongado

lens [lɛnz] n (of spectacles) lente f; (of camera) objetiva

Lent [lɛnt] n Quaresma

lent [lɛnt] pt, pp of **lend**

lentil ['lɛntl] n lentilha

Leo ['liːəu] n Leão m

leotard ['liːətɑːd] n collant m

lesbian ['lɛzbɪən] n lésbica

less [lɛs] adj, pron, adv menos ▷ prep: **~ tax/10% discount** menos imposto/10% de desconto; **~ than ever** menos do que nunca; **~ and ~** cada vez menos; **the ~ he works ...** quanto menos trabalha ...

lessen ['lɛsn] vi diminuir, minguar ▷ vt diminuir, reduzir

lesser ['lɛsə'] adj menor; **to a ~ extent** or **degree** nem tanto

lesson ['lɛsn] n aula; (example, warning) lição f; **to teach sb a ~** (fig) dar uma lição em alguém

let [lɛt] (pt, pp **let**) vt (allow) deixar; (Brit: lease) alugar; **to ~ sb know sth** avisar alguém de algo; **~'s go!** vamos!; **"to ~"** "aluga-se" **let down** vt (tyre) esvaziar; (disappoint) desapontar **let go** vt, vi soltar **let in** vt deixar entrar; (visitor etc) fazer entrar **let off** vt (culprit) perdoar; (firework etc) soltar **let on** vi revelar **let out** vt deixar sair;

(scream) soltar **let up** vi cessar, afrouxar

lethal ['liːθl] adj letal

letter ['lɛtə'] n (of alphabet) letra; (correspondence) carta; **letterbox** (Brit) n caixa do correio

lettuce ['lɛtɪs] n alface f

leukaemia [luːˈkiːmɪə], (US) **leukemia** n leucemia

level ['lɛvl] adj (flat) plano ▷ adv no mesmo nível ▷ n nível m; (height) altura ▷ vt aplanar; **"A" ~s** npl (Brit) ≈ vestibular m; **"O" ~s** npl (Brit) provas prestadas no final do ensino fundamental; **to be ~ with** estar no mesmo nível que; **on the ~** em nível; (fig: honest) sincero **level off** vi (prices etc) estabilizar-se **level out** vi, vt = **level off**; **level crossing** (Brit) n passagem f de nível

lever ['liːvə'] n alavanca; (fig) estratagema m; **leverage** n força de uma alavanca; (fig: influence) influência

liability [laɪəˈbɪlətɪ] n responsabilidade f; (handicap) desvantagem f; **liabilities** npl (Comm) exigibilidades fpl, obrigações fpl

liable ['laɪəbl] adj (subject): **~ to** sujeito a; (responsible): **~ for** responsável por; (likely): **~ to do** capaz de fazer

liaise [liːˈeɪz] vi: **to ~ (with)** cooperar (com)

liar ['laɪə'] n mentiroso(-a)

libel ['laɪbl] n difamação f ▷ vt caluniar, difamar

liberal ['lɪbərl] adj liberal; (generous) generoso

liberation n liberação f, libertação f

liberty ['lɪbətɪ] n liberdade f; (criminal): **to be at ~** estar livre; **to**

be at ~ to do ser livre de fazer
Libra ['li:brə] *n* Libra, Balança
librarian [laɪ'brɛərɪən] *n*
  bibliotecário(-a)
library ['laɪbrərɪ] *n* biblioteca
Libya ['lɪbɪə] *n* Líbia
licence ['laɪsns], (*US*) **license** *n*
  (*gen, Comm*) licença; (*Aut*) carta de
  motorista (*BR*), carta de condução
  (*PT*)
license ['laɪsns] *n* (*US*) = **licence**
  ▷ *vt* autorizar, dar licença a;
  licensed *adj* (*car*) autorizado
  oficialmente; (*for alcohol*)
  autorizado para vender bebidas
  alcoólicas; **license plate** (*US*) *n*
  (*Aut*) placa (de identificação) (*do
  carro*)
lick [lɪk] *vt* lamber; (*inf: defeat*)
  arrasar, surrar; **to ~ one's lips** (*also
  fig*) lamber os beiços
lid [lɪd] *n* tampa; (*eyelid*) pálpebra
lie [laɪ] *vi* (*pt* **lay**, *pp* **lain**) (*act*)
  deitar-se; (*state*) estar deitado;
  (*object: be situated*) estar, encontrar-
  se; (*fig: problem, cause*) residir; (*in
  race, league*) ocupar; (*pt, pt* **lied**) (*tell
  lies*) mentir ▷ *n* mentira; **to ~ low**
  (*fig*) esconder-se **lie about** *vi*
  (*things*) estar espalhado; (*people*)
  vadiar **lie around** *vi* = **lie about**;
  lie-in (*Brit*) *n*: **to have a lie-in**
  dormir até tarde
lieutenant [lɛf'tɛnənt, (*US*)
  luː'tɛnənt] *n* (*Mil*) tenente *m*
life [laɪf] (*pl* **lives**) *n* vida; **to come
  to ~** animar-se; **lifeboat** *n* barco
  salva-vidas; **lifeguard** *n*
  salva-vidas *m/f*; **life jacket** *n*
  colete *m* salva-vidas; **lifelike** *adj*
  natural; (*realistic*) realista; **life
  preserver** (*US*) *n* = **lifebelt**; **life
  jacket**; **life sentence** *n* pena de
  prisão perpétua; **lifetime** *n* vida

lift [lɪft] *vt* levantar ▷ *vi* (*fog*)
  dispersar-se, dissipar-se ▷ *n* (*Brit:
  elevator*) elevador *m*; **to give sb a ~**
  (*Brit*) dar uma carona para alguém
  (*BR*), dar uma boleia a alguém (*PT*);
  lift-off *n* decolagem *f*
light [laɪt] (*pt, pp* **lit**) *n* luz *f*; (*Aut:
  headlight*) farol *m*; (: *rear light*) luz
  traseira; (*for cigarette etc*): **have
  you got a ~?** tem fogo? ▷ *vt*
  acender; (*room*) iluminar ▷ *adj*
  (*colour, room*) claro; (*not heavy, also
  fig*) leve; (*rain, traffic*) fraco;
  (*movement, action*) delicado; **lights**
  npl (*Aut*) sinal *m* de trânsito; **to
  come to ~** vir à tona; **in the ~ of** à
  luz de **light up** *vi* iluminar-se ▷ *vt*
  iluminar; **light bulb** *n* lâmpada;
  lighten *vt* tornar mais leve;
  lighter *n* (*also:* **cigarette lighter**)
  isqueiro, acendedor *m*;
  light-hearted *adj* alegre,
  despreocupado; **lighthouse** *n*
  farol *m*; **lighting** *n* iluminação *f*;
  lightly *adv* ligeiramente; **to get
  off lightly** conseguir se safar, livrar
  a cara (*inf*)
lightning ['laɪtnɪŋ] *n* relâmpago,
  raio
lightweight *adj* (*suit*) leve; (*Boxing*)
  peso-leve
like [laɪk] *vt* gostar de ▷ *prep* como;
  (*such as*) tal qual ▷ *adj* parecido,
  semelhante ▷ *n*: **the ~** coisas *fpl*
  parecidas; **his ~s and dislikes** seus
  gostos e aversões; **I would ~**, **I'd ~**
  (eu) gostaria de; **to be** *or* **look ~ sb/
  sth** parecer-se com alguém/algo,
  parecer alguém/algo; **do it ~ this**
  faça isso assim; **it is nothing ~ ...**
  não se parece nada com ...;
  likeable *adj* simpático, agradável
likelihood ['laɪklɪhud] *n*
  probabilidade *f*

likely ['laɪklɪ] *adj* provável; **he's ~ to leave** é provável que ele se vá; **not ~!** (*inf*) nem morto!

likewise ['laɪkwaɪz] *adv* igualmente; **to do ~** fazer o mesmo

liking ['laɪkɪŋ] *n* afeição *f*, simpatia; **to be to sb's ~** ser ao gosto de alguém

lilac ['laɪlək] *n* lilás *m*

lily ['lɪlɪ] *n* lírio, açucena

limb [lɪm] *n* membro

limbo ['lɪmbəʊ] *n*: **to be in ~** (*fig*) viver na expectativa

lime [laɪm] *n* (*tree*) limeira; (*fruit*) limão *m*; (*also*: **~ juice**) suco (*BR*) or sumo (*PT*) de limão; (*Geo*) cal *f*

limelight ['laɪmlaɪt] *n*: **to be in the ~** ser o centro das atenções

limestone ['laɪmstəʊn] *n* pedra calcária

limit ['lɪmɪt] *n* limite *m* ▷ *vt* limitar; **limited** *adj* limitado; **to be limited to** limitar-se a

limp [lɪmp] *n*: **to have a ~** mancar, ser coxo ▷ *vi* mancar ▷ *adj* frouxo

line [laɪn] *n* linha; (*rope*) corda; (*wire*) fio; (*row*) fila, fileira; (*on face*) ruga ▷ *vt* (*road, room*) encarreirar; (*container, clothing*): **to ~ sth (with)** forrar algo (de); **to ~ the streets** ladear as ruas; **in ~ with** de acordo com **line up** *vi* enfileirar-se ▷ *vt* enfileirar; (*set up, have ready*) preparar, arranjar

linen ['lɪnɪn] *n* artigos de cama e mesa; (*cloth*) linho

liner ['laɪnəʳ] *n* navio de linha regular; (*also*: **bin ~**) saco para lata de lixo

linger ['lɪŋɡəʳ] *vi* demorar-se, retardar-se; (*smell, tradition*) persistir

lining ['laɪnɪŋ] *n* forro; (*Anat*) parede *f*

link [lɪŋk] *n* (*of a chain*) elo; (*connection*) conexão *f* ▷ *vt* vincular, unir; (*associate*): **to ~ with** or **to** unir a; **links** *npl* (*Golf*) campo de golfe **link up** *vt* acoplar ▷ *vi* unir-se

lion ['laɪən] *n* leão *m*; **lioness** *n* leoa

lip [lɪp] *n* lábio; **lipread** *irreg vi* ler os lábios; **lip salve** *n* pomada para os lábios; **lipstick** *n* batom *m*

liqueur [lɪ'kjʊəʳ] *n* licor *m*

liquid ['lɪkwɪd] *adj* líquido ▷ *n* líquido

liquor ['lɪkəʳ] *n* licor *m*, bebida alcoólica; **liquor store** (*US*) *n* loja que vende bebidas alcoólicas

Lisbon ['lɪzbən] *n* Lisboa

lisp [lɪsp] *n* ceceio ▷ *vi* cecear, falar com a língua presa

list [lɪst] *n* lista ▷ *vt* (*write down*) fazer uma lista or relação de; (*enumerate*) enumerar

listen ['lɪsn] *vi* escutar, ouvir; **to ~ to** escutar; **listener** *n* ouvinte *m/f*

lit [lɪt] *pt, pp of* **light**

liter ['li:təʳ] (*US*) *n* = **litre**

literacy ['lɪtərəsɪ] *n* capacidade *f* de ler e escrever, alfabetização *f*

literal ['lɪtərl] *adj* literal

literary ['lɪtərərɪ] *adj* literário

literate ['lɪtərət] *adj* alfabetizado, instruído; (*educated*) culto, letrado

literature ['lɪtərɪtʃəʳ] *n* literatura; (*brochures etc*) folhetos *mpl*

litre ['li:təʳ], (*US*) **liter** *n* litro

litter ['lɪtəʳ] *n* (*rubbish*) lixo; (*young animals*) ninhada; **litter bin** (*Brit*) *n* lata de lixo

little ['lɪtl] *adj* (*small*) pequeno; (*not much*) pouco; **~ house** casinha ▷ *adv* pouco; **a ~** um pouco (de); **for a ~ while** por um instante; **as ~ as**

possible o menos possível; **~ by ~** pouco a pouco

live [*vi, vt* lɪv, *adj* laɪv] *vi* viver; *(reside)* morar ▷ *adj* vivo; *(wire)* eletrizado; *(broadcast)* ao vivo; *(shell)* carregado; **~ ammunition** munição de guerra **live down** *vt* redimir **live on** *vt fus* viver de, alimentar-se de; **to ~ on £50 a week** viver com £50 por semana **live together** *vi* viver juntos **live up to** *vt fus (fulfil)* cumprir

livelihood ['laɪvlɪhud] *n* meio de vida, subsistência

lively ['laɪvlɪ] *adj* vivo

liven up ['laɪvn-] *vt* animar ▷ *vi* animar-se

liver ['lɪvə'] *n* fígado

lives [laɪvz] *npl of* **life**

living ['lɪvɪŋ] *adj* vivo ▷ *n*: **to earn** *or* **make a ~** ganhar a vida; **living room** *n* sala de estar

lizard ['lɪzəd] *n* lagarto

load [ləud] *n* carga; *(weight)* peso ▷ *vt (gen, Comput)* carregar; **a ~ of**, **~s of** *(fig)* um monte de, uma porção de; **loaded** *adj (question, word)* intencionado; *(inf: rich)* cheio da nota; *(vehicle)*: **to be loaded with** estar carregado de

loaf [ləuf] *(pl* **loaves**) *n* pão-de-forma *m*

loan [ləun] *n* empréstimo ▷ *vt* emprestar; **on ~** emprestado

loathe [ləuð] *vt* detestar, odiar

loaves [ləuvz] *npl of* **loaf**

lobby ['lɒbɪ] *n* vestíbulo, saguão *m*; *(Pol: pressure group)* grupo de pressão, lobby *m* ▷ *vt* pressionar

lobster ['lɒbstə'] *n* lagostim *m*; *(large)* lagosta

local ['ləukl] *adj* local ▷ *n (pub)* bar *m* (local); **the locals** *npl (local inhabitants)* os moradores locais;

local anaesthetic *n* anestesia local

locate [ləu'keɪt] *vt (find)* localizar, situar; *(situate)*: **to be ~d in** estar localizado em

location [ləu'keɪʃən] *n* local *m*, posição *f*; **on ~** *(Cinema)* em externas

loch [lɒx] *n* lago

lock [lɒk] *n (of door, box)* fechadura; *(of canal)* eclusa; *(of hair)* anel *m*, mecha ▷ *vt (with key)* trancar ▷ *vi (door etc)* fechar-se à chave; *(wheels)* travar-se **lock in** *vt* trancar dentro **lock out** *vt* trancar do lado de fora **lock up** *vt (criminal, mental patient)* prender; *(house)* trancar ▷ *vi* fechar tudo

locker ['lɒkə'] *n* compartimento com chave; **locker-room** *(US)* *n (Sport)* vestiário

locksmith ['lɒksmɪθ] *n* serralheiro(-a)

lodge [lɒdʒ] *n* casa do guarda, guarita; *(hunting lodge)* pavilhão *m* de caça ▷ *vi (person)*: **to ~ (with)** alojar-se (na casa de) ▷ *vt (complaint)* apresentar; **lodger** *n* inquilino(-a), hóspede *m/f*

loft [lɒft] *n* sótão *m*

log [lɒg] *n (of wood)* tora; *(book)* = **logbook** ▷ *vt* registrar; **logbook** *n (Naut)* diário de bordo; *(Aviat)* diário de voo; *(of car)* documentação *f* (do carro)

logic ['lɒdʒɪk] *n* lógica; **logical** *adj* lógico

login ['lɒgɪn] *n (Comput)* login *m*

lollipop ['lɒlɪpɒp] *n* pirulito *(BR)*, chupa-chupa *m (PT)* **lollipop lady** *(Brit)* *n* mulher que ajuda as crianças a atravessarem a rua **lollipop man** *(Brit)* *n* homem que ajuda as crianças a atravessarem a rua; *ver nota*

● LOLLIPOP MEN/LADIES

Lollipop men/ladies são as pessoas que ajudam as crianças a atravessar a rua nas proximidades das escolas na hora da entrada e da saída. São facilmente localizados graças a suas longas capas brancas e à placa redonda com a qual pedem aos motoristas que parem. São chamados assim por causa da forma circular da placa, que lembra um pirulito (*lollipop*).

lolly ['lɔlɪ] *n* (*inf*: *ice*) picolé *m*; (: *lollipop*) pirulito
London ['lʌndən] *n* Londres; **Londoner** *n* londrino(-a)
lone [ləun] *adj* (*person*) solitário; (*thing*) único
loneliness ['ləunlɪnɪs] *n* solidão *f*, isolamento
lonely ['ləunlɪ] *adj* (*person*) só; (*place*, *childhood*) solitário, isolado
long [lɔŋ] *adj* longo; (*road*, *hair*, *table*) comprido ▷ *adv* muito tempo ▷ *vi*: **to ~ for sth** ansiar *or* suspirar por algo; **how ~ is the street?** qual é a extensão da rua?; **how ~ is the lesson?** quanto dura a lição?; **all night ~** a noite inteira; **he no ~er comes** ele não vem mais; **~ before/after** muito antes/depois; **before ~** (+ *future*) dentro de pouco; (+ *past*) pouco tempo depois; **at ~ last** por fim, no final; **so** *or* **as ~ as** contanto que; **long-distance** *adj* (*travel*) de longa distância; (*call*) interurbano; **longing** *n* desejo, anseio
longitude ['lɔŋɡɪtju:d] *n* longitude *f*
long: **long jump** *n* salto em distância; **long-sighted** *adj* presbita; **long-standing** *adj* de muito tempo; **long-term** *adj* a longo prazo
loo [lu:] (*Brit*: *inf*) *n* banheiro (*BR*), casa de banho (*PT*)
look [luk] *vi* olhar; (*seem*) parecer; (*building etc*): **to ~ south/(out) onto the sea** dar para o sul/o mar ▷ *n* olhar *m*; (*glance*) olhada, vista de olhos; (*appearance*) aparência, aspecto; **looks** *npl* (*good looks*) físico, aparência; **~ (here)!** (*annoyance*) escuta aqui!; **~!** (*surprise*) olha! **look after** *vt fus* cuidar de; (*deal with*) lidar com **look at** *vt fus* olhar (para); (*read quickly*) ler rapidamente; (*consider*) considerar **look back** *vi*: **to ~ back on** (*remember*) recordar, rever **look down on** *vt fus* (*fig*) desdenhar, desprezar **look for** *vt fus* procurar **look forward to** *vt fus* aguardar com prazer, ansiar por; (*in letter*): **we ~ forward to hearing from you** no aguardo de suas notícias **look into** *vt fus* investigar **look on** *vi* assistir **look out** *vi* (*beware*): **to ~ out (for)** tomar cuidado (com) **look out for** *vt fus* (*await*) esperar **look round** *vi* virar a cabeça, voltar-se **look through** *vt fus* (*papers*, *book*) examinar **look to** *vt fus* (*rely on*) contar com **look up** *vi* levantar os olhos; (*improve*) melhorar ▷ *vt* (*word*) procurar
loop [lu:p] *n* laço ▷ *vt*: **to ~ sth round sth** prender algo em torno de algo
loose [lu:s] *adj* solto; (*not tight*) frouxo ▷ *n*: **to be on the ~** estar solto; **loosely** *adv* frouxamente, folgadamente; **loosen** *vt* (*free*) soltar; (*slacken*) afrouxar

loot [luːt] n saque m, despojo ▷ vt
saquear, pilhar
lord [lɔːd] n senhor m; **L~ Smith**
Lord Smith; **the L~** (Rel) o Senhor;
good L~! Deus meu!; **the (House
of) L~s** (Brit) a Câmara dos Lordes
lorry ['lɒrɪ] (Brit) n caminhão m (BR),
camião m (PT); **lorry driver** (Brit) n
caminhoneiro (BR), camionista m/f
(PT)
lose [luːz] (pt, pp **lost**) vt, vi perder;
to ~ (time) (clock) atrasar-se; **loser**
n perdedor(a) m/f; (inf: failure)
derrotado(-a), fracassado(-a)
loss [lɒs] n perda; (Comm): **to make
a ~** sair com prejuízo; **heavy ~es**
(Mil) grandes perdas; **to be at a ~**
estar perplexo
lost [lɒst] pt, pp of **lose** ▷ adj
perdido; **~ and found** (US) (seção f
de) perdidos e achados mpl; **lost
property** (Brit) n (objetos mpl)
perdidos e achados mpl
lot [lɒt] n (set of things) porção f; (at
auctions) lote m; **the ~** tudo,
todos(-as); **a ~** muito, bastante; **a ~
of**, **~s of** muito(s); **I read a ~** leio
bastante; **to draw ~s** tirar à sorte
lotion ['ləʊʃən] n loção f
lottery ['lɒtərɪ] n loteria
loud [laʊd] adj (voice) alto; (shout)
forte; (noise) barulhento; (support,
condemnation) veemente; (gaudy)
berrante ▷ adv alto; **out ~** em voz
alta; **loudly** adv ruidosamente;
(aloud) em voz alta; **loudspeaker** n
alto-falante m
lounge [laʊndʒ] n sala de estar f;
(of airport) salão m; (Brit: also: **~
bar**) bar m social ▷ vi recostar-se,
espreguiçar-se **lounge about** vi
ficar à-toa **lounge around** vi
= **lounge about**
lousy ['laʊzɪ] (inf) adj ruim,

péssimo; (ill): **to feel ~** sentir-se mal
love [lʌv] n amor m ▷ vt amar; (like
a lot) adorar; **to ~ to do** adorar
fazer; **~ (from) Anne** (on letter) um
abraço or um beijo, Anne; **I ~ you** eu
te amo; **I ~ coffee** adoro o café; **"15
~"** (Tennis) "15 a zero"; **to be in ~
with** estar apaixonado por; **to fall
in ~ with** apaixonar-se por; **to
make ~** fazer amor; **love affair** n
aventura (amorosa), caso (de
amor); **love life** n vida sentimental
lovely ['lʌvlɪ] adj (delightful)
encantador(a), delicioso; (beautiful)
lindo, belo; (holiday,
surprise) muito agradável,
maravilhoso
lover ['lʌvəʳ] n amante m/f
loving ['lʌvɪŋ] adj carinhoso,
afetuoso; (actions) dedicado
low [ləʊ] adj baixo; (depressed)
deprimido; (ill) doente ▷ adv baixo
▷ n (Meteorology) área de baixa
pressão; **to be ~ on** (supplies) ter
pouco; **to reach a new ~ or an
all-time ~** cair para o seu nível mais
baixo; **low-alcohol** adj de baixo
teor alcoólico; **low-calorie** adj de
baixo teor calórico; **lower** adj mais
baixo; (less important) inferior ▷ vt
abaixar; (reduce) reduzir, diminuir;
low-fat adj magro
loyal ['lɔɪəl] adj leal; **loyalty** n
lealdade f
loyalty card n (Brit) cartão m de
fidelidade
L-plates ['ɛlpleɪts] (Brit) npl placas
fpl de aprendiz de motorista

● **L-PLATES**

● As **L-plates** são placas
● quadradas com um "L" vermelho
● que são colocadas na parte de

trás do carro para mostrar que a pessoa ao volante ainda não tem carteira de motorista. Até a obtenção da carteira, o motorista aprendiz possui uma permissão provisória e não tem direito de dirigir sem um motorista qualificado ao lado. Os motoristas aprendizes não podem dirigir em estradas mesmo que estejam acompanhados.

Ltd (Brit) abbr (= limited (liability) company) SA

luck [lʌk] n sorte f; **bad ~** azar m; **good ~!** boa sorte!; **bad** or **hard** or **tough ~!** que azar!; **luckily** adv por sorte, felizmente; **lucky** adj (person) sortudo; (situation) afortunado; (object) de sorte

ludicrous ['lu:dɪkrəs] adj ridículo

luggage ['lʌgɪdʒ] n bagagem f; **luggage rack** n porta-bagagem m, bagageiro

lukewarm ['lu:kwɔ:m] adj morno, tépido; (fig) indiferente

lull [lʌl] n pausa, interrupção f ▷ vt: **to ~ sb to sleep** acalentar alguém; **to be ~ed into a false sense of security** ser acalmado com uma falsa sensação de segurança

lullaby ['lʌləbaɪ] n canção f de ninar

lumber ['lʌmbər] n (junk) trastes mpl velhos; (wood) madeira serrada, tábua ▷ vt: **to ~ sb with sth/sb** empurrar algo/alguém para cima de alguém

luminous ['lu:mɪnəs] adj luminoso

lump [lʌmp] n torrão m; (fragment) pedaço m; (on body) galo, caroço; (also: **sugar ~**) cubo de açúcar ▷ vt: **to ~ together** amontoar; **lump sum** n montante m único; **lumpy**

adj encaroçado

lunatic ['lu:nətɪk] adj louco(-a)

lunch [lʌntʃ] n almoço; **lunch break, lunch hour** n hora do almoço

lung [lʌŋ] n pulmão m

lure [luər] n isca ▷ vt atrair, seduzir

lurk [lə:k] vi (hide) esconder-se; (wait) estar à espreita

lush [lʌʃ] adj exuberante

lust [lʌst] n luxúria; (greed) cobiça **lust after** vt fus cobiçar **lust for** vt fus = **lust after**

Luxembourg ['lʌksəmbə:g] n Luxemburgo

luxurious [lʌg'zjuəriəs] adj luxuoso

luxury ['lʌkʃəri] n luxo ▷ cpd de luxo

lying ['laɪɪŋ] n mentira(s) f(pl) ▷ adj mentiroso, falso

lyrics ['lɪrɪks] npl (of song) letra

M.A. abbr (Sch) = **Master of Arts**
mac [mæk] (Brit) n capa
impermeável
macaroni [mækə'rəʊnɪ] n
macarrão m
machine [mə'ʃiːn] n máquina ▷ vt
(dress etc) costurar à máquina;
(Tech) usinar; **machine gun** n
metralhadora; **machinery** n
maquinaria; (fig) máquina
mackerel ['mækrl] n inv cavala
mackintosh ['mækɪntɔʃ] (Brit) n
capa impermeável
mad [mæd] adj louco; (foolish) tolo;
(angry) furioso, brabo; (keen): **to be
~ about** ser louco por
madam ['mædəm] n senhora,
madame f
made [meɪd] pt, pp of **make**;
made-to-measure (Brit) adj feito
sob medida; **made-up** ['meɪdʌp]
adj (story) inventado

madly ['mædlɪ] adv loucamente;
~ in love louco de amor
madman ['mædmən] irreg n louco
madness ['mædnɪs] n loucura;
(foolishness) tolice f
magazine [mægə'ziːn] n (Press)
revista; (Radio, TV) programa m de
atualidades
maggot ['mægət] n larva de inseto
magic ['mædʒɪk] n magia, mágica
▷ adj mágico; **magical** adj
mágico; **magician** [mə'dʒɪʃən] n
mago(-a); (entertainer) mágico(-a)
magistrate ['mædʒɪstreɪt] n
magistrado(-a), juiz/juíza m/f
magnet ['mægnɪt] n ímã m;
magnetic [mæg'nɛtɪk] adj
magnético
magnificent [mæg'nɪfɪsnt] adj
magnífico
magnify ['mægnɪfaɪ] vt aumentar;
magnifying glass n lupa, lente f
de aumento
magpie ['mægpaɪ] n pega
mahogany [mə'hɔgənɪ] n mogno,
acaju m
maid [meɪd] n empregada; **old ~**
(pej) solteirona
maiden name n nome m de
solteira
mail [meɪl] n correio; (letters)
cartas fpl ▷ vt pôr no correio;
mailbox n (US) caixa do correio;
mailing list n lista de clientes,
mailing list m
main [meɪn] adj principal ▷ n (pipe)
cano or esgoto principal; **the
mains** npl (Elec, gas, water) a rede;
in the ~ na maior parte; **mainland**
n: **the mainland** o continente;
mainly adv principalmente; **main
road** n estrada principal;
mainstream n corrente f principal
maintain [meɪn'teɪn] vt manter;

(*keep up*) conservar (em bom estado); (*affirm*) sustentar, afirmar; **maintenance** ['meɪntənəns] *n* manutenção *f*; (*alimony*) alimentos *mpl*, pensão *f* alimentícia

maize [meɪz] *n* milho

majesty ['mædʒɪstɪ] *n* majestade *f*

major ['meɪdʒəʳ] *n* (*Mil*) major *m* ▷ *adj* (*main*) principal; (*considerable*) importante; (*Mus*) maior

Majorca [mə'jɔːkə] *n* Maiorca

majority [mə'dʒɔrɪtɪ] *n* maioria

make [meɪk] (*pt, pp* **made**) *vt* fazer; (*manufacture*) fabricar, produzir; (*cause to be*): **to ~ sb sad** entristecer alguém, fazer alguém ficar triste; (*force*): **to ~ sb do sth** fazer com que alguém faça algo; (*equal*): **2 and 2 ~ 4** dois e dois são quatro ▷ *n* marca; **to ~ a profit/loss** ter um lucro/uma perda; **to ~ it** (*arrive*) chegar; (*succeed*) ter sucesso; **what time do you ~ it?** que horas você tem?; **to ~ do with** contentar-se com **make for** *vt fus* (*place*) dirigir-se a **make out** *vt* (*decipher*) decifrar; (*understand*) compreender; (*see*) divisar, avistar; (*form, cheque*) preencher **make up** *vt* (*constitute*) constituir; (*invent*) inventar; (*parcel*) embrulhar ▷ *vi* reconciliar-se; (*with cosmetics*) maquilar-se (*BR*), maquilhar-se (*PT*) **make up for** *vt fus* compensar; **maker** *n* (*of film, programme*) criador *m*; (*manufacturer*) fabricante *m/f*; **makeshift** *adj* provisório; **make-up** *n* maquilagem *f* (*BR*), maquilhagem *f* (*PT*)

malaria [mə'leərɪə] *n* malária

Malaysia [mə'leɪzɪə] *n* Malaísia (*BR*), Malásia (*PT*)

male [meɪl] *n* macho ▷ *adj* masculino; (*child etc*) do sexo masculino

malignant [mə'lɪgnənt] *adj* (*Med*) maligno

mall [mɔːl] *n* (*also*: **shopping ~**) shopping *m*

mallet ['mælɪt] *n* maço, marreta

malt [mɔːlt] *n* malte *m*

Malta ['mɔːltə] *n* Malta

mammal ['mæml] *n* mamífero

mammoth ['mæməθ] *n* mamute *m* ▷ *adj* gigantesco, imenso

man [mæn] (*pl* **men**) *n* homem *m* ▷ *vt* (*Naut*) tripular; (*Mil*) guarnecer; (*machine*) operar; **an old ~** um velho; **~ and wife** marido e mulher

manage ['mænɪdʒ] *vi* arranjar-se, virar-se ▷ *vt* (*be in charge of*) dirigir, administrar; (*business*) gerenciar; (*ship, person*) controlar; **manageable** *adj* manejável; (*task etc*) viável; **management** *n* administração *f*, direção *f*, gerência; **manager** *n* gerente *m/f*; (*Sport*) técnico(-a); **manageress** [mænɪdʒə'rɛs] *n* gerente *f*; **managerial** [mænə'dʒɪərɪəl] *adj* administrativo, gerencial; **managing director** *n* diretor(a) *m/f*, diretor-gerente/ diretora-gerente *m/f*

mandarin ['mændərɪn] *n* (*also*: **~ orange**) tangerina; (*person*) mandarim *m*

mandatory ['mændətərɪ] *adj* obrigatório

mane [meɪn] *n* (*of horse*) crina; (*of lion*) juba

maneuver [mə'nuːvəʳ] (*US*) = **manoeuvre**

mango ['mæŋgəu] (*pl* **mangoes**) *n* manga

manhole ['mænhəul] *n* poço de inspeção

manhood ['mænhud] *n* (*age*) idade *f* adulta; (*masculinity*) virilidade *f*

m

mania ['meɪnɪə] n mania; **maniac** ['meɪnɪæk] n maníaco(-a); (fig) louco(-a)

manic ['mænɪk] adj maníaco

manicure ['mænɪkjuəʳ] n manicure f (BR), manicura (PT)

manifest ['mænɪfɛst] vt manifestar, mostrar ▷ adj manifesto, evidente

manipulate [mə'nɪpjuleɪt] vt manipular

mankind [mæn'kaɪnd] n humanidade f, raça humana

man-made adj sintético, artificial

manner ['mænəʳ] n modo, maneira; (behaviour) conduta, comportamento; (type): **manners** npl (conduct) boas maneiras fpl, educação f; **bad ~s** falta de educação; **all ~ of** todo tipo de; **all ~ of things** todos os tipos de coisa

manoeuvre [mə'nu:vəʳ], (US) **maneuver** vt manobrar; (manipulate) manipular ▷ vi manobrar ▷ n manobra

manpower ['mænpauəʳ] n potencial m humano, mão-de-obra f

mansion ['mænʃən] n mansão f, palacete m

manslaughter ['mænslɔ:təʳ] n homicídio involuntário

mantelpiece ['mæntlpi:s] n consolo da lareira

manual ['mænjuəl] adj manual ▷ n manual m

manufacture [mænju'fæktʃəʳ] vt manufaturar, fabricar ▷ n fabricação f; **manufacturer** n fabricante m/f

manure [mə'njuəʳ] n estrume m, adubo

manuscript ['mænjuskrɪpt] n manuscrito

many ['mɛnɪ] adj, pron muitos(-as);

a great ~ muitíssimos; **~ a time** muitas vezes

map [mæp] n mapa m **map out** vt traçar

maple ['meɪpl] n bordo

mar [mɑ:ʳ] vt estragar

marathon ['mærəθən] n maratona

marble ['mɑ:bl] n mármore m; (toy) bola de gude

March [mɑ:tʃ] n março

march [mɑ:tʃ] vi marchar; (demonstrators) desfilar ▷ n marcha, passeata

mare [mɛəʳ] n égua

margarine [mɑ:dʒə'ri:n] n margarina

margin ['mɑ:dʒɪn] n margem f; **marginal** adj marginal; **marginal seat** (Pol) cadeira ganha por pequena maioria

marigold ['mærɪɡəuld] n malmequer m

marijuana [mærɪ'wɑ:nə] n maconha

marine [mə'ri:n] adj marinho; (engineer) naval ▷ n fuzileiro naval

marital ['mærɪtl] adj matrimonial, marital; **~ status** estado civil

marjoram ['mɑ:dʒərəm] n manjerona

mark [mɑ:k] n marca, sinal m; (imprint) impressão f; (stain) mancha; (Brit: Sch) nota; (currency) marco ▷ vt marcar; (stain) manchar; (indicate) indicar; (commemorate) comemorar; (Brit: Sch) dar nota em; (: correct) corrigir; **to ~ time** marcar passo; **marker** n (sign) marcador m, marca; (bookmark) marcador

market ['mɑ:kɪt] n mercado ▷ vt (Comm) comercializar; **marketing** n marketing m; **marketplace** n mercado; **market research** n pesquisa de mercado

marmalade ['mɑːməleɪd] n geleia de laranja

maroon [mə'ruːn] vt: **to be ~ed** ficar abandonado (numa ilha) ▷ adj vinho inv

marquee [mɑː'kiː] n toldo, tenda

marriage ['mærɪdʒ] n casamento

married ['mærɪd] adj casado; (life, love) conjugal

marrow ['mærəʊ] n medula; (vegetable) abóbora

marry ['mærɪ] vt casar(-se) com; (subj: father, priest etc) casar, unir ▷ vi (also: **get married**) casar(-se)

Mars [mɑːz] n Marte m

marsh [mɑːʃ] n pântano; (salt marsh) marisma

marshal ['mɑːʃl] n (Mil: also: **field ~**) marechal m; (at sports meeting etc) oficial m ▷ vt (thoughts, support) organizar; (soldiers) formar

martyr ['mɑːtər] n mártir m/f

marvel ['mɑːvl] n maravilha ▷ vi: **to ~ (at)** maravilhar-se (de or com); **marvellous**, (US) **marvelous** adj maravilhoso

Marxist ['mɑːksɪst] adj, n marxista m/f

mascara [mæs'kɑːrə] n rímel m

masculine ['mæskjulɪn] adj masculino

mash [mæʃ] vt (Culin) fazer um purê de; (crush) amassar

mask [mɑːsk] n máscara ▷ vt (face) encobrir; (feelings) esconder, ocultar

mason ['meɪsn] n (also: **stone ~**) pedreiro(-a); (also: **free~**) maçom m; **masonry** n alvenaria

mass [mæs] n quantidade f; (people) multidão f; (Phys) massa; (Rel) missa; (great quantity) montão m ▷ cpd de massa ▷ vi reunir-se; (Mil) concentrar-se; **the masses** npl (ordinary people) as massas; **~es**

of (inf) montes de

massacre ['mæsəkər] n massacre m, carnificina

massage ['mæsɑːʒ] n massagem f

massive ['mæsɪv] adj (large) enorme; (support) massivo

mass media npl meios mpl de comunicação de massa, mídia

mast [mɑːst] n (Naut) mastro; (Radio etc) antena

master ['mɑːstər] n mestre m; (fig: of situation) dono; (in secondary school) professor m; (title for boys): **M~ X** o menino X ▷ vt controlar; (learn) conhecer a fundo; **mastermind** n (fig) cabeça ▷ vt dirigir, planejar; **masterpiece** n obra-prima

mat [mæt] n esteira; (also: **door~**) capacho; (also: **table ~**) descanso

match [mætʃ] n fósforo; (game) jogo, partida; (equal) igual m/f ▷ vt (also: **~ up**) casar, emparelhar; (go well with) combinar com; (equal) igualar; (correspond to) corresponder a ▷ vi combinar; (couple) formar um bom casal; **matchbox** n caixa de fósforos; **matching** adj que combina (com)

mate [meɪt] n (inf) colega m/f; (assistant) ajudante m/f; (animal) macho/fêmea; (in merchant navy) imediato ▷ vi acasalar-se

material [mə'tɪərɪəl] n (substance) matéria; (equipment) material m; (cloth) pano, tecido; (data) dados mpl ▷ adj material; **materials** npl (equipment) material

maternal [mə'təːnl] adj maternal

maternity [mə'təːnɪtɪ] n maternidade f

mathematical [mæθə'mætɪkl] adj matemático

mathematics [mæθə'mætɪks] n

matemática
maths [mæθs], (US) **math** n
matemática
matron ['meɪtrən] n (in hospital)
enfermeira-chefe f; (in school)
inspetora
matter ['mætə\] n questão f,
assunto; (Phys) matéria;
(substance) substância; (reading
matter etc) material m; (Med: pus)
pus m ▷ vi importar; **matters** npl
(affairs) questões fpl; **it doesn't ~**
não importa; (I don't mind) tanto
faz; **what's the ~?** o que (é que)
há?, qual é o problema?; **no ~ what**
aconteça o que acontecer; **as a ~ of
course** por rotina; **as a ~ of fact** na
realidade, de fato
mattress ['mætrɪs] n colchão m
mature [mə'tjuə\] adj maduro;
(cheese, wine) amadurecido ▷ vi
amadurecer
maul [mɔːl] vt machucar, maltratar
mauve [məuv] adj cor de malva inv
maximum ['mæksɪməm] (pl
maxima or **maximums**) adj
máximo ▷ n máximo
May [meɪ] n maio
may [meɪ] (conditional **might**) aux vb
(indicating possibility): **he ~ come**
pode ser que ele venha, é capaz de
vir; (be allowed to): **~ I smoke?**
posso fumar?; (wishes): **~ God
bless you!** que Deus lhe abençoe
maybe ['meɪbiː] adv talvez; **~ not**
talvez não
mayhem ['meɪhɛm] n caos m
mayonnaise [meɪə'neɪz] n
maionese f
mayor [mɛə\] n prefeito (BR),
presidente m do município (PT);
mayoress n prefeita (BR),
presidenta do município (PT)
maze [meɪz] n labirinto

 KEYWORD

me [miː] pron **1** (direct) me; **he heard
me** ele me ouviu; **it's me** sou eu
2 (indirect) me; **he gave me the
money** ele me deu o dinheiro; **give
it to me** dá isso para mim
3 (stressed, after prep) mim; **with me**
comigo; **without me** sem mim

meadow ['mɛdəu] n prado,
campina
meagre ['miːgə\], (US) **meager** adj
escasso
meal [miːl] n refeição f; (flour)
farinha; **mealtime** n hora da
refeição
mean [miːn] (pt, pp **meant**) adj
(with money) sovina, avarento,
pão-duro inv (BR); (unkind)
mesquinho; (shabby) malcuidado,
dilapidado; (average) médio ▷ vt
(signify) significar, querer dizer;
(refer to): **I thought you ~t her** eu
pensei que você estivesse se
referindo a ela; (intend): **to ~ to do
sth** pretender or tencionar fazer
algo ▷ n meio, meio termo; **means**
npl (way, money) meio; **by ~s of** por
meio de, mediante; **by all ~s!** claro
que sim!, pois não; **do you ~ it?**
você está falando sério?
meaning ['miːnɪŋ] n sentido,
significado; **meaningful** adj
significativo; (relationship) sério;
meaningless adj sem sentido
meant [mɛnt] pt, pp of **mean**
meantime ['miːntaɪm] adv (also:
in the ~) entretanto, enquanto
isso
meanwhile ['miːnwaɪl] adv
= **meantime**
measles ['miːzlz] n sarampo
measure ['mɛʒə\] vt, vi medir

▷ n medida; (*ruler: also*: **tape ~**) fita métrica

measurement ['mɛʒəmənt] n medida; **measurements** npl (*size*) medidas fpl

meat [miːt] n carne f; **cold ~s** (*Brit*) frios; **meatball** n almôndega

Mecca ['mɛkə] n Meca; (*fig*): **a ~ (for)** a meca (de)

mechanic [mɪ'kænɪk] n mecânico; **mechanical** adj mecânico

mechanism ['mɛkənɪzəm] n mecanismo

medal ['mɛdl] n medalha

meddle ['mɛdl] vi: **to ~ in** meter-se em, intrometer-se em; **to ~ with sth** mexer em algo

media ['miːdɪə] npl meios mpl de comunicação, mídia

mediaeval [mɛdɪ'iːvl] adj = **medieval**

mediate ['miːdɪeɪt] vi mediar

medical ['mɛdɪkl] adj médico ▷ n (*examination*) exame m médico

medication [mɛdɪ'keɪʃən] n medicação f

medicine ['mɛdsɪn] n medicina; (*drug*) remédio, medicamento

medieval [mɛdɪ'iːvl] adj medieval

mediocre [miːdɪ'əʊkəʳ] adj medíocre

meditate ['mɛdɪteɪt] vi meditar

Mediterranean [mɛdɪtə'reɪnɪən] adj mediterrâneo; **the ~ (Sea)** o (mar) Mediterrâneo

medium ['miːdɪəm] (*pl* **media** or **mediums**) adj médio ▷ n (*means*) meio; (*pl* **mediums**: *person*) médium m/f

meek [miːk] adj manso, dócil

meet [miːt] (*pt, pp* **met**) vt encontrar; (*accidentally*) topar com, dar de cara com; (*by arrangement*) encontrar-se com, ir ao encontro de; (*for the first time*) conhecer; (*go and fetch*) ir buscar; (*opponent, problem*) enfrentar; (*obligations*) cumprir; (*need*) satisfazer ▷ vi encontrar-se; (*for talks*) reunir-se; (*join*) unir-se; (*get to know*) conhecer-se **meet with** vt fus reunir-se com; (*difficulty*) encontrar; **meeting** n encontro; (*session: of club, Comm*) reunião f; (*assembly*) assembleia; (*Sport*) corrida

megabyte ['mɛgəbaɪt] n (*Comput*) megabyte m

megaphone ['mɛgəfəʊn] n megafone m

megapixel ['mɛgəpɪksl] n megapixel m

melancholy ['mɛlənkəlɪ] n melancolia ▷ adj melancólico

melody ['mɛlədɪ] n melodia

melon ['mɛlən] n melão m

melt [mɛlt] vi (*metal*) fundir-se; (*snow*) derreter ▷ vt derreter **melt down** vt fundir

member ['mɛmbəʳ] n membro(-a); (*of club*) sócio(-a); (*Anat*) membro; **M~ of Parliament** (*Brit*) deputado(-a); **membership** n (*state*) adesão f; (*members*) número de sócios; **membership card** n carteira de sócio

memento [mə'mɛntəʊ] n lembrança

memo ['mɛməʊ] n memorando, nota

memorandum [mɛmə'rændəm] (*pl* **memoranda**) n memorando

memorial [mɪ'mɔːrɪəl] n monumento comemorativo ▷ adj comemorativo; **Memorial Day** (*US*) n ver nota

- **MEMORIAL DAY**

- **Memorial Day** é um feriado nos
- Estados Unidos, a última
- segunda-feira de maio na maior
- parte dos estados, em memória
- aos soldados americanos mortos
- em combate.

memorize ['mɛmǝraɪz] *vt* decorar,
aprender de cor
memory ['mɛmǝrɪ] *n* memória;
(*recollection*) lembrança; **memory
stick** *n* (*Comput: flash pen*) pen
drive *m*; (*card*) cartão *m* de
memória
men [mɛn] *npl of* **man**
menace ['mɛnǝs] *n* ameaça;
(*nuisance*) droga ▷ *vt* ameaçar
mend [mɛnd] *vt* consertar, reparar;
(*darn*) remendar ▷ *n*: **to be on the
~** estar melhorando
meningitis [mɛnɪn'dʒaɪtɪs] *n*
meningite *f*
menopause ['mɛnǝupɔːz] *n*
menopausa
menstruation [mɛnstru'eɪʃǝn] *n*
menstruação *f*
mental ['mɛntl] *adj* mental;
mentality [mɛn'tælɪtɪ] *n*
mentalidade *f*
mention ['mɛnʃǝn] *n* menção *f* ▷ *vt*
(*speak of*) falar de; **don't ~ it!** não
tem de quê!, de nada!
menu ['mɛnjuː] *n* (*set menu*,
Comput) menu *m*; (*printed*) cardápio
(*BR*), ementa (*PT*)
MEP *n abbr* = **Member of the
European Parliament**
mercenary ['mǝːsɪnǝrɪ] *adj*
mercenário ▷ *n* mercenário
merchandise ['mǝːtʃǝndaɪz] *n*
mercadorias *fpl*
merchant ['mǝːtʃǝnt] *n*

comerciante *m/f*
merciless ['mǝːsɪlɪs] *adj*
desumano, inclemente
mercury ['mǝːkjurɪ] *n* mercúrio
mercy ['mǝːsɪ] *n* piedade *f*; (*Rel*)
misericórdia; **at the ~ of** à mercê de
mere [mɪǝʳ] *adj* mero, simples *inv*;
merely *adv* simplesmente,
somente, apenas
merge [mǝːdʒ] *vt* unir ▷ *vi* unir-se;
(*Comm*) fundir-se; **merger** *n* fusão *f*
meringue [mǝ'ræŋ] *n* suspiro,
merengue *m*
merit ['mɛrɪt] *n* mérito; (*advantage*)
vantagem *f* ▷ *vt* merecer
mermaid ['mǝːmeɪd] *n* sereia
merry ['mɛrɪ] *adj* alegre; **M~
Christmas!** Feliz Natal!;
merry-go-round *n* carrossel *m*
mesh [mɛʃ] *n* malha
mess [mɛs] *n* confusão *f*; (*in room*)
bagunça; (*Mil*) rancho; **to be in a ~**
ser uma bagunça, estar numa
bagunça **mess about** (*inf*) *vi*
perder tempo; (*pass the time*) vadiar
mess about with (*inf*) *vt fus* mexer
com **mess around** (*inf*) *vi* = **mess
about mess up** *vt* (*spoil*) estragar;
(*dirty*) sujar
message ['mɛsɪdʒ] *n* recado,
mensagem *f*
messenger ['mɛsɪndʒǝʳ] *n*
mensageiro(-a)
messy ['mɛsɪ] *adj* (*dirty*) sujo;
(*untidy*) desarrumado
met [mɛt] *pt, pp of* **meet**
metal ['mɛtl] *n* metal *m*
meteorology [miːtɪǝ'rɔlǝdʒɪ] *n*
meteorologia
meter ['miːtǝʳ] *n* (*instrument*)
medidor *m*; (*also*: **parking ~**)
parcômetro; (*US: unit*) = **metre**
method ['mɛθǝd] *n* método;
methodical [mɪ'θɔdɪkl] *adj*

metódico

metre ['miːtər], (US) **meter** n
metro

metric ['mɛtrɪk] adj métrico

metropolitan [mɛtrə'pɔlɪtən] adj
metropolitano

Mexico ['mɛksɪkəʊ] n México

mice [maɪs] npl of **mouse**

micro... [maɪkrəʊ] prefix micro;
microchip n microchip m;
microphone n microfone m;
microscope n microscópio;
microwave n (also: **microwave
oven**) micro-ondas m inv

mid [mɪd] adj: **in ~ May** em meados
de maio; **in ~ afternoon** no meio
da tarde; **in ~ air** em pleno ar;
midday n meio-dia m

middle ['mɪdl] n meio; (waist)
cintura ▷ adj meio; (quantity, size)
médio, mediano; **middle-aged** adj
de meia-idade; **Middle Ages** npl:
the Middle Ages a Idade Média;
Middle East n: **the Middle East** o
Oriente Médio; **middle name** n
segundo nome m

midge [mɪdʒ] n mosquito

midget ['mɪdʒɪt] n anão(-anã) m/f

midnight ['mɪdnaɪt] n meia-noite f

midst [mɪdst] n: **in the ~ of** no
meio de, entre

midsummer [mɪd'sʌmər] n: **a ~
day** um dia em pleno verão

midway [mɪd'weɪ] adj, adv: **~
(between)** no meio do caminho
(entre)

midweek [mɪd'wiːk] adv no meio
da semana

midwife ['mɪdwaɪf] (pl **midwives**)
n parteira

might [maɪt] vb see **may** ▷ n poder
m, força; **mighty** adj poderoso,
forte

migraine ['miːgreɪn] n enxaqueca

migrant ['maɪgrənt] adj
migratório; (worker) emigrante

migrate [maɪ'greɪt] vi emigrar;
(birds) arribar

mike [maɪk] n abbr = **microphone**

mild [maɪld] adj (character) pacífico;
(climate) temperado; (taste) suave;
(illness) leve, benigno; (interest)
pequeno

mile [maɪl] n milha (1609 m);
mileage n número de milhas;
(Aut) ≈ quilometragem f;
milestone ['maɪlstəʊn] n marco
miliário

military ['mɪlɪtərɪ] adj militar

milk [mɪlk] n leite m ▷ vt (cow)
ordenhar; (fig) explorar, chupar;
milk chocolate n chocolate m de
leite; **milkman** irreg n leiteiro;
milky adj leitoso

mill [mɪl] n (windmill etc) moinho;
(coffee mill) moedor m de café;
(factory) moinho, engenho ▷ vt
moer ▷ vi (also: **~ about**)
aglomerar-se, remoinhar

millimetre, (US) **millimeter** n
milímetro

million ['mɪljən] n milhão m; **a ~
times** um milhão de vezes;
millionaire n milionário(-a);
millionth num milionésimo

mime [maɪm] n mimo; (actor)
mímico(-a), comediante m/f ▷ vt
imitar ▷ vi fazer mímica

mimic ['mɪmɪk] n mímico(-a),
imitador(a) m/f ▷ vt imitar,
parodiar

min. abbr (= minute, minimum) min

mince [mɪns] vt moer ▷ vi (in
walking) andar com afetação ▷ n
(Brit: Culin) carne f moída;
mincemeat n recheio de sebo e
frutas picadas; (US: meat) carne f
moída; **mince pie** n pastel com

m

recheio de sebo e frutas picadas

mind [maɪnd] n mente f; (intellect) intelecto; (opinion): **to my ~** a meu ver; (sanity): **to be out of one's ~** estar fora de si ▷ vt (attend to, look after) tomar conta de, cuidar de; (be careful of) ter cuidado com; (object to): **I don't ~ the noise** o barulho não me incomoda; **it is on my ~** não me sai da cabeça; **to keep** or **bear sth in ~** levar algo em consideração, não esquecer-se de algo; **to make up one's ~** decidir-se; **I don't ~** (it doesn't worry me) eu nem ligo; (it's all the same to me) para mim tanto faz; **~ you, ...** se bem que ...; **never ~!** não faz mal, não importa!; (don't worry) não se preocupe!; **"~ the step"** "cuidado com o degrau"; **mindless** adj (violence, crime) insensato; (job) monótono

mine¹ [maɪn] pron o meu/a minha; **a friend of ~** um amigo meu

mine² [maɪn] n mina ▷ vt (coal) extrair, explorar; (ship, beach) minar

miner ['maɪnər] n mineiro

mineral ['mɪnərəl] adj mineral ▷ n mineral m; **minerals** npl (Brit: soft drinks) refrigerantes mpl; **mineral water** n água mineral

mingle ['mɪŋgl] vi: **to ~ with** misturar-se com

miniature ['mɪnətʃər] adj em miniatura ▷ n miniatura

minibus ['mɪnɪbʌs] n micro-ônibus m

minimal ['mɪnɪml] adj mínimo

minimum ['mɪnɪməm] (pl **minima**) adj mínimo ▷ n mínimo

mining ['maɪnɪŋ] n exploração f de minas

miniskirt ['mɪnɪskəːt] n minissaia

minister ['mɪnɪstər] n (Brit: Pol) ministro(-a); (Rel) pastor m ▷ vi: **to ~ to sb** prestar assistência a alguém; **to ~ to sb's needs** atender às necessidades de alguém

ministry ['mɪnɪstrɪ] n (Brit: Pol) ministério; (Rel): **to go into the ~** ingressar no sacerdócio

minor ['maɪnər] adj menor; (unimportant) de pouca importância; (Mus) menor ▷ n (Law) menor m/f de idade

minority [maɪ'nɔrɪtɪ] n minoria

mint [mɪnt] n (plant) hortelã f; (sweet) bala de hortelã ▷ vt (coins) cunhar; **the (Royal) M~** (Brit) or **the (US) M~** (US) ≈ a Casa da Moeda; **in ~ condition** em perfeito estado

minus ['maɪnəs] n (also: **~ sign**) sinal m de subtração ▷ prep menos

minute¹ [maɪ'njuːt] adj miúdo, diminuto; (search) minucioso

minute² ['mɪnɪt] n minuto; **minutes** npl (of meeting) atas fpl; **at the last ~** no último momento

miracle ['mɪrəkl] n milagre m

mirage ['mɪrɑːʒ] n miragem f

mirror ['mɪrər] n espelho; (in car) retrovisor m

misbehave [mɪsbɪ'heɪv] vi comportar-se mal

miscarriage ['mɪskærɪdʒ] n (Med) aborto (espontâneo); (failure): **~ of justice** erro judicial

miscellaneous [mɪsɪ'leɪnɪəs] adj (items, expenses) diverso; (selection) variado

mischief ['mɪstʃɪf] n (naughtiness) travessura; (fun) diabrura; (maliciousness) malícia; **mischievous** ['mɪstʃɪvəs] adj (naughty) travesso; (playful) traquino

misconception [mɪskən'sɛpʃən] n concepção f errada, conceito errado

misconduct [mɪs'kɔndʌkt] n comportamento impróprio; **professional ~** má conduta profissional

miser ['maɪzəʳ] n avaro(-a), sovina m/f

miserable ['mɪzərəbl] adj triste; (wretched) miserável; (weather, person) deprimente; (contemptible: offer) desprezível; (: failure) humilhante

misery ['mɪzərɪ] n (unhappiness) tristeza; (wretchedness) miséria

misfortune [mɪs'fɔːtʃən] n desgraça, infortúnio

misguided [mɪs'gaɪdɪd] adj enganado

mishap ['mɪshæp] n desgraça, contratempo

misinterpret [mɪsɪn'təːprɪt] vt interpretar mal

misjudge [mɪs'dʒʌdʒ] vt fazer um juízo errado de, julgar mal

mislay [mɪs'leɪ] irreg vt extraviar, perder

mislead [mɪs'liːd] irreg vt induzir em erro, enganar; **misleading** adj enganoso, errôneo

misplace [mɪs'pleɪs] vt extraviar, perder

misprint ['mɪsprɪnt] n erro tipográfico

Miss [mɪs] n Senhorita (BR), a menina (PT)

miss [mɪs] vt (train, class, opportunity) perder; (fail to hit) errar, não acertar em; (fail to see): **you can't ~ it** é impossível não ver; (regret the absence of): **I ~ him** sinto a falta dele ▷ vi falhar ▷ n (shot) tiro perdido or errado **miss out** (Brit) vt

omitir

missile ['mɪsaɪl] n míssil m; (object thrown) projétil m

missing ['mɪsɪŋ] adj (pupil) ausente; (thing) perdido; (removed) que está faltando; (Mil) desaparecido; **to be ~** estar desaparecido; **to go ~** desaparecer

mission ['mɪʃən] n missão f; (official representatives) delegação f

mist [mɪst] n (light) neblina; (heavy) névoa; (at sea) bruma ▷ vi (eyes: also: ~ over) enevoar-se; (Brit: also: ~ over, ~ up: windows) embaçar

mistake [mɪs'teɪk] irreg n erro, engano ▷ vt entender or interpretar mal; **by ~** por engano; **to make a ~** fazer um erro; **to ~ A for B** confundir A com B; **mistaken** pp of **mistake** ▷ adj errado; **to be mistaken** enganar-se, equivocar-se

mister ['mɪstəʳ] (inf) n senhor m; see **Mr**

mistletoe ['mɪsltəʊ] n visco

mistook [mɪs'tʊk] pt of **mistake**

mistress ['mɪstrɪs] n (lover) amante f; (of house) dona (da casa); (Brit: in school) professora, mestra; (of situation) dona; see **Mrs**

mistrust [mɪs'trʌst] vt desconfiar de

misty ['mɪstɪ] adj (day) nublado; (glasses etc) embaçado

misunderstand [mɪsʌndə'stænd] irreg vt, vi entender or interpretar mal; **misunderstanding** n mal-entendido; (disagreement) desentendimento

misuse [n mɪs'juːs, vt mɪs'juːz] n uso impróprio; (of power) abuso; (of funds) desvio ▷ vt abusar de; desviar

mix [mɪks] vt misturar; (combine)

combinar ▷ vi (people) entrosar-se ▷ n mistura; (combination) combinação f **mix up** vt (confuse: things) misturar; (: people) confundir; **mixed** adj misto; **mixed-up** adj confuso; **mixer** n (for food) batedeira; (person) pessoa sociável; **mixture** n mistura; (Med) preparado; **mix-up** n trapalhada, confusão f

mm abbr (= millimetre) mm

moan [məun] n gemido ▷ vi gemer; (inf: complain): **to ~ (about)** queixar-se (de), bufar (sobre) (inf)

moat [məut] n fosso

mob [mɔb] n multidão f ▷ vt cercar

mobile ['məubaıl] adj móvel ▷ n móvel m; **mobile phone** n telefone m celular (BR), telemóvel m (PT)

mock [mɔk] vt ridicularizar; (laugh at) zombar de, gozar de ▷ adj falso, fingido; (exam, battle) simulado; **mockery** n zombaria; **to make a mockery of sth** ridicularizar algo

mode [məud] n modo; (of transport) meio

model ['mɔdl] n modelo; (Arch) maqueta; (person: for fashion, Art) modelo m/f ▷ adj exemplar ▷ vt modelar; **to ~ o.s. on** mirar-se em ▷ vi servir de modelo; (in fashion) trabalhar como modelo

modem ['məudɛm] n modem m

moderate [adj, n 'mɔdərət, vi, vt 'mɔdəreıt] adj, n moderado(-a) ▷ vi moderar-se, acalmar-se ▷ vt moderar

modern ['mɔdən] adj moderno; **modernize** vt modernizar, atualizar

modest ['mɔdıst] adj modesto; **modesty** n modéstia

modify ['mɔdıfaı] vt modificar

moist [mɔıst] adj úmido (BR),

húmido (PT), molhado; **moisture** n umidade f (BR), humidade f (PT); **moisturizer** n creme m hidratante

mole [məul] n (animal) toupeira; (spot) sinal m, lunar m; (fig) espião(-piã) m/f

molest [mə'lɛst] vt molestar; (attack sexually) atacar sexualmente

molten ['məultən] adj fundido; (lava) liquefeito

mom [mɔm] (US) n = **mum**

moment ['məumənt] n momento; **at the ~** neste momento; **momentary** adj momentâneo; **momentous** [məu'mɛntəs] adj importantíssimo

momentum [məu'mɛntəm] n momento; (fig) ímpeto; **to gather ~** ganhar ímpeto

mommy ['mɔmı] (US) n = **mummy**

Monaco ['mɔnəkəu] n Mônaco (no article)

monarch ['mɔnək] n monarca m/f; **monarchy** n monarquia

monastery ['mɔnəstərı] n mosteiro, convento

Monday ['mʌndı] n segunda-feira

monetary ['mʌnıtərı] adj monetário

money ['mʌnı] n dinheiro; (currency) moeda; **to make ~** ganhar dinheiro; **money order** n vale m (postal)

mongrel ['mʌŋgrəl] n (dog) vira-lata m

monitor ['mɔnıtər] n (Comput) monitor m ▷ vt (heartbeat, pulse) controlar; (broadcasts, progress) monitorar

monk [mʌŋk] n monge m

monkey ['mʌŋkı] n macaco

monopoly [mə'nɔpəlı] n monopólio

monotonous [mə'nɔtənəs] *adj* monótono

monsoon [mɔn'suːn] *n* monção *f*

monster ['mɔnstər] *n* monstro

month [mʌnθ] *n* mês *m*; **monthly** *adj* mensal ▷ *adv* mensalmente

monument ['mɔnjumənt] *n* monumento

mood [muːd] *n* humor *m*; *(of crowd)* atmosfera; **to be in a good/bad ~** estar de bom/mau humor; **moody** *adj (variable)* caprichoso, de veneta; *(sullen)* rabugento

moon [muːn] *n* lua; **moonlight** *n* luar *m* ▷ *vi* ter dois empregos, ter um bico

moor [muər] *n* charneca ▷ *vt (ship)* amarrar ▷ *vi* fundear, atracar

moose [muːs] *n inv* alce *m*

mop [mɔp] *n* esfregão *m*; *(for dishes)* esponja com cabeça; *(of hair)* grenha ▷ *vt* esfregar **mop up** *vt* limpar

mope [məup] *vi* estar *or* andar deprimido *or* desanimado

moped ['məupɛd] *n* moto *f* pequena *(BR)*, motorizada *(PT)*

moral ['mɔrl] *adj* moral ▷ *n* moral *f*; **morals** *npl (principles)* moralidade *f*, costumes *mpl*

morale [mɔ'rɑːl] *n* moral *f*, estado de espírito

morality [mə'rælɪtɪ] *n* moralidade *f*; *(correctness)* retidão *f*, probidade *f*

○ KEYWORD

more [mɔːr] *adj* **1** *(greater in number etc)* mais; **more people/work/ letters than we expected** mais pessoas/trabalho/cartas do que esperávamos

2 *(additional)* mais; **do you want (some) more tea?** você quer mais chá?; **I have no** *or* **I don't have any more money** não tenho mais dinheiro

▷ *pron* **1** *(greater amount)* mais; **more than 10** mais de 10; **it cost more than we expected** custou mais do que esperávamos

2 *(further or additional)* mais; **is there any more?** tem ainda mais?; **there's no more** não tem mais

▷ *adv* mais; **more dangerous/ difficult** *etc* **than** mais perigoso/ difícil *etc* do que; **more easily/ economically/quickly (than)** mais fácil/econômico/rápido (do que); **more and more** cada vez mais; **more or less** mais ou menos; **more than ever** mais do que nunca

moreover [mɔː'rəuvər] *adv* além do mais, além disso

morning ['mɔːnɪŋ] *n* manhã *f*; *(early morning)* madrugada ▷ *cpd* da manhã; **in the ~** de manhã; **7 o'clock in the ~** (as) 7 da manhã; **morning sickness** *n* náusea matinal

Morocco [mə'rɔkəu] *n* Marrocos *m*

moron ['mɔːrɔn] *(inf) n* débil mental *m/f*, idiota *m/f*

Morse [mɔːs] *n (also: ~ code)* código Morse

mortar ['mɔːtər] *n (cannon)* morteiro; *(Constr)* argamassa; *(dish)* pilão *m*, almofariz *m*

mortgage ['mɔːgɪdʒ] *n* hipoteca ▷ *vt* hipotecar

mortuary ['mɔːtjuərɪ] *n* necrotério

mosaic [məu'zeɪɪk] *n* mosaico

Moscow ['mɔskəu] *n* Moscou *(BR)*, Moscovo *(PT)*

Moslem ['mɔzləm] *adj, n* = **Muslim**

mosque [mɔsk] *n* mesquita

mosquito [mɔs'ki:təʊ] (*pl* **mosquitoes**) *n* mosquito
moss [mɔs] *n* musgo

 KEYWORD

most [məʊst] *adj* **1** (*almost all: people, things etc*) a maior parte de, a maioria de; **most people** a maioria das pessoas **2** (*largest, greatest: interest*) máximo; (*money*): **who has (the) most money?** quem é que tem mais dinheiro?; **he derived the most pleasure from her visit** ele teve o maior prazer em recebê-la ▷ *pron* (*greatest quantity, number*) a maior parte, a maioria; **most of it/them** a maioria dele/deles; **most of the money** a maior parte do dinheiro; **do the most you can** faça o máximo que você puder; **I saw the most** vi mais; **to make the most of sth** aproveitar algo ao máximo; **at the (very) most** quando muito, no máximo ▷ *adv* (+ *vb*) o mais; (+ *adj*): **the most intelligent/expensive** etc o mais inteligente/caro etc; (+ *adv: carefully, easily etc*) o mais; (*very: polite, interesting etc*) muito; **a most interesting book** um livro interessantíssimo

mostly ['məʊstlɪ] *adv* principalmente, na maior parte
MOT (*Brit*) *n abbr* (= *Ministry of Transport*): **the ~ (test)** vistoria anual dos veículos automotores
motel [məʊ'tɛl] *n* motel *m*
moth [mɔθ] *n* mariposa; (*clothes moth*) traça
mother ['mʌðəʳ] *n* mãe *f* ▷ *adj* materno ▷ *vt* (*care for*) cuidar de

(como uma mãe); **motherhood** *n* maternidade *f*; **mother-in-law** *n* sogra; **mother-of-pearl** *n* madrepérola; **mother-to-be** *n* futura mamãe *f*; **mother tongue** *n* língua materna
motion ['məʊʃən] *n* movimento; (*gesture*) gesto, sinal *m*; (*at meeting*) moção *f* ▷ *vt, vi*: **to ~ (to) sb to do sth** fazer sinal a alguém para que faça algo; **motionless** *adj* imóvel; **motion picture** *n* filme *m* (cinematográfico)
motive ['məʊtɪv] *n* motivo
motor ['məʊtəʳ] *n* motor *m*; (*Brit: inf: vehicle*) carro, automóvel *m* ▷ *cpd* (*industry*) de automóvel; **motorbike** *n* moto(cicleta) *f*, motoca (*inf*); **motorboat** *n* barco a motor; **motorcar** (*Brit*) *n* carro, automóvel *m*; **motorcycle** *n* motocicleta; **motorist** *n* motorista *m/f*; **motor racing** (*Brit*) *n* corrida de carros, automobilismo; **motorway** (*Brit*) *n* rodovia (*BR*), autoestrada (*PT*)
motto ['mɔtəʊ] (*pl* **mottoes**) *n* lema *m*
mound [maʊnd] *n* (*of earth*) monte *m*; (*of blankets, leaves etc*) pilha, montanha
mount [maʊnt] *n* monte *m* ▷ *vt* (*horse etc*) montar em, subir a; (*stairs*) subir; (*exhibition*) montar; (*picture*) emoldurar ▷ *vi* (*increase*) aumentar **mount up** *vi* aumentar
mountain ['maʊntɪn] *n* montanha ▷ *cpd* de montanha; **mountain bike** *n* mountain bike *f*; **mountaineer** [maʊntɪ'nɪəʳ] *n* alpinista *m/f*, montanhista *m/f*; **mountaineering** *n* alpinismo; **mountainous** *adj* montanhoso
mourn [mɔ:n] *vt* chorar, lamentar

▷ vi: **to ~ for** chorar or lamentar a morte de; **mourning** n luto; **(to be) in mourning** (estar) de luto

mouse [maus] (pl **mice**) n camundongo (BR), rato (PT); (Comput) mouse m; **mouse mat, mouse pad** n (Comput) mouse pad m

mousse [mu:s] n musse f; (for hair) mousse f

moustache [məsˈtɑ:ʃ], (US) **mustache** n bigode m

mouth [mauθ] n boca; (of cave, hole) entrada; (of river) desembocadura; **mouthful** n bocado; **mouth organ** n gaita; **mouthwash** n colutório

move [mu:v] n movimento; (in game) lance m, jogada; (: turn to play) turno, vez f; (of house, job) mudança ▷ vt (change position of) mudar; (: in game) jogar; (emotionally) comover; (Pol: resolution etc) propor ▷ vi mexer-se, mover-se; (traffic) circular; (also: ~ house) mudar-se; (develop: situation) desenvolver; **to ~ sb to do sth** convencer alguém a fazer algo; **to get a ~ on** se apressar-se **move about** vi (fidget) mexer-se; (travel) deslocar-se **move along** vi avançar **move around** vi = **move about move away** vi afastar-se **move back** vi voltar **move forward** vi avançar **move in** vi (to a house) instalar-se (numa casa) **move on** vi ir andando **move out** vi sair (de uma casa) **move over** vi afastar-se **move up** vi ser promovido

movement [ˈmuːvmənt] n movimento; (gesture) gesto; (of goods) transporte m; (in attitude, policy) mudança

movie [ˈmuːvɪ] n filme m; **to go to the ~s** ir ao cinema

moving [ˈmuːvɪŋ] adj (emotional) comovente; (that moves) móvel

mow [məu] (pt **mowed**, pp **mowed** or **mown**) vt (grass) cortar; (corn) ceifar **mow down** vt (massacre) chacinar; **mower** n ceifeira; (also: **lawnmower**) cortador m de grama (BR) or de relva (PT)

Mozambique [məuzəmˈbiːk] n Moçambique m (no article)

MP n abbr = **Member of Parliament**

MP3 player n tocador m de MP3

mph abbr = **miles per hour**

Mr [ˈmɪstəʳ], (US) **Mr.** n: **Mr Smith** (o) Sr. Smith

Mrs [ˈmɪsɪz], (US) **Mrs.** n: **~ Smith** (a) Sra. Smith

Ms [mɪz], (US) **Ms.** n (= Miss or Mrs): **Ms X** (a) Sa X

● **Ms**
●
●
● **Ms** é um título utilizado em
● lugar de Mrs (senhora) ou de
● Miss (senhorita) para evitar a
● distinção tradicional entre
● mulheres casadas e solteiras.
● É aceito, portanto, como o
● equivalente de Mr (senhor) para
● os homens. Muitas vezes
● reprovado por ter surgido como
● manifestação de um feminismo
● exacerbado, é uma forma de
● tratamento muito comum hoje
● em dia.

MSc n abbr = **Master of Science**

◯ KEYWORD

much [mʌtʃ] adj muito; **how much money/time do you need?** quanto dinheiro/tempo você precisa?; **he's done so much work for the charity** ele trabalhou muito para a obra de caridade; **as much as** tanto como ▷ *pron* muito; **much has been gained from our discussions** nossas discussões foram muito proveitosas; **how much does it cost? — too much** quanto custa isso? — caro demais ▷ *adv* **1** (*greatly, a great deal*) muito; **thank you very much** muito obrigado(-a); **we are very much looking forward to your visit** estamos aguardando a sua visita com muita ansiedade; **he is very much the gentleman/politician** ele é muito cavalheiro/político; **as much as** tanto como; **as much as you** tanto quanto você **2** (*by far*) de longe; **I'm much better now** estou bem melhor agora **3** (*almost*) quase; **how are you feeling? — much the same** como você está (se sentindo)? — do mesmo jeito

muck [mʌk] *n* (*dirt*) sujeira (*BR*), sujidade *f* (*PT*) **muck about** (*inf*) *vi* fazer besteiras **muck around** *vi* = **muck about muck up** (*inf*) *vt* estragar
mud [mʌd] *n* lama
muddle ['mʌdl] *n* confusão *f*, bagunça; (*mix-up*) trapalhada ▷ *vt* (*also*: ~ **up**: *person, story*) confundir; (: *things*) misturar **muddle through** *vi* virar-se
muddy ['mʌdɪ] *adj* (*road*) lamacento
mudguard ['mʌdgɑ:d] *n* para-lama *m*
muesli ['mju:zlɪ] *n* muesli *m*
muffin ['mʌfɪn] *n* bolinho redondo e chato
mug [mʌg] *n* (*cup*) caneca; (: *for*

beer) caneco, canecão; (*inf: face*) careta; (: *fool*) bobo(-a) ▷ *vt* (*assault*) assaltar; **mugging** *n* assalto
muggy ['mʌgɪ] *adj* abafado
mule [mju:l] *n* mula
multimedia [mʌltɪ'mi:dɪə] *adj* multimídia
multiple ['mʌltɪpl] *adj* múltiplo ▷ *n* múltiplo; **multiple sclerosis** [-sklɪ'rəusɪs] *n* esclerose *f* múltipla
multiply ['mʌltɪplaɪ] *vt* multiplicar ▷ *vi* multiplicar-se
multistorey ['mʌltɪ'stɔ:rɪ] (*Brit*) *adj* de vários andares
mum [mʌm] *n* (*Brit: inf*) mamãe *f* ▷ *adj*: **to keep ~** ficar calado
mumble ['mʌmbl] *vt, vi* resmungar, murmurar
mummy ['mʌmɪ] *n* (*Brit: mother*) mamãe *f*; (*embalmed*) múmia
mumps [mʌmps] *n* caxumba
municipal [mju:'nɪsɪpl] *adj* municipal
murder ['mə:də^r] *n* assassinato ▷ *vt* assassinar; **murderer** *n* assassino
murky ['mə:kɪ] *adj* escuro; (*water*) turvo
murmur ['mə:mə^r] *n* murmúrio ▷ *vt, vi* murmurar
muscle ['mʌsl] *n* músculo; (*fig: strength*) força (muscular) **muscle in** *vi* imiscuir-se, impor-se; **muscular** ['mʌskjulə^r] *adj* muscular; (*person*) musculoso
museum [mju:'zɪəm] *n* museu *m*
mushroom ['mʌʃrum] *n* cogumelo ▷ *vi* crescer da noite para o dia, pipocar
music ['mju:zɪk] *n* música; **musical** *adj* musical; (*harmonious*) melodioso ▷ *n* musical *m*; **musician** [mju:'zɪʃən] *n* músico(-a)
Muslim ['mʌzlɪm] *adj, n* muçulmano(-a)

mussel ['mʌsl] n mexilhão m
must [mʌst] aux vb (obligation):
I ~ do it tenho que or devo fazer
isso; (probability): **he ~ be there
by now** ele já deve estar lá;
(suggestion, invitation): **you ~ come
and see me soon** você tem que vir
me ver em breve; (indicating sth
unwelcome): **why ~ he behave so
badly?** por que ele tem que se
comportar tão mal? ▷ n
necessidade f; **it's a ~** é
imprescindível
mustache ['mʌstæʃ] (US) n
= **moustache**
mustard ['mʌstəd] n mostarda
mustn't ['mʌsnt] = **must not**
mute [mju:t] adj, n mudo(-a)
mutiny ['mju:tɪnɪ] n motim m,
rebelião f
mutter ['mʌtər] vt, vi resmungar,
murmurar
mutton ['mʌtn] n carne f de carneiro
mutual ['mju:tʃuəl] adj mútuo;
(shared) comum
muzzle ['mʌzl] n (of animal)
focinho; (guard: for dog) focinheira;
(of gun) boca ▷ vt pôr focinheira em
my [maɪ] adj meu/minha; **this is
my house/car/brother** esta é a
minha casa/meu carro/meu
irmão; **I've washed my hair/cut
my finger** lavei meu cabelo/cortei
meu dedo
myself [maɪ'sɛlf] pron (reflexive) me;
(emphatic) eu mesmo; (after prep)
mim mesmo; see also **oneself**
mysterious [mɪs'tɪərɪəs] adj
misterioso
mystery ['mɪstərɪ] n mistério
mystify ['mɪstɪfaɪ] vt mistificar
myth [mɪθ] n mito; **mythology**
[mɪ'θɒlədʒɪ] n mitologia

nag [næg] vt ralhar, apoquentar
nail [neɪl] n (human) unha; (metal)
prego ▷ vt pregar; **to ~ sb down
to a date/price** conseguir que
alguém se defina sobre a data/o
preço; **nailbrush** n escova de
unhas; **nailfile** n lixa de unhas;
nail polish n esmalte m (BR) or
verniz m (PT) de unhas; **nail polish
remover** n removedor m de
esmalte (BR) or verniz (PT); **nail
scissors** npl tesourinha de unhas;
nail varnish (Brit) n = **nail polish**
naïve [naɪ'i:v] adj ingênuo
naked ['neɪkɪd] adj nu(a)
name [neɪm] n nome m; (surname)
sobrenome m; (reputation)
reputação f, fama ▷ vt (child)
pôr nome em; (criminal) apontar;
(price) fixar; (date) marcar; **what's
your ~?** qual é o seu nome?, como
(você) se chama?; **by ~** de nome;

in the ~ of em nome de; **namely** *adv* a saber, isto é
nanny ['nænɪ] *n* babá *f*
nap [næp] *n* (*sleep*) soneca ▷ *vi*: **to be caught ~ping** ser pego de surpresa
napkin ['næpkɪn] *n* (*also*: **table ~**) guardanapo
nappy ['næpɪ] *n* (*Brit*) fralda
narrative ['nærətɪv] *n* narrativa
narrow ['nærəʊ] *adj* estreito; (*fig: majority*) pequeno; (: *ideas*) tacanho ▷ *vi* (*road*) estreitar-se; (*difference*) diminuir; **to have a ~ escape** escapar por um triz; **to ~ sth down to** restringir *or* reduzir algo a; **narrowly** *adv* (*miss*) por pouco; **narrow-minded** *adj* de visão limitada, bitolado
nasty ['nɑ:stɪ] *adj* (*remark*) desagradável; (: *person*) mau, ruim; (*malicious*) maldoso; (*rude*) grosseiro, obsceno; (*taste, smell*) repugnante, asqueroso; (*wound, disease etc*) grave, sério
nation ['neɪʃən] *n* nação *f*
national ['næʃənl] *adj, n* nacional *m/f*; **national anthem** *n* hino nacional; **National Health Service** (*Brit*) *n* serviço nacional de saúde; **nationality** [næʃə'nælɪtɪ] *n* nacionalidade *f*; **nationalize** *vt* nacionalizar; **national park** *n* parque *m* nacional; **National Trust** (*Brit*) *n ver nota*

● **NATIONAL TRUST**
●
● O **National Trust** é uma
● instituição independente, sem
● fins lucrativos, cuja missão é
● proteger e valorizar os
● monumentos e a paisagem da
● Grã-Bretanha devido a seu

● interesse histórico ou beleza
● natural.

nationwide ['neɪʃənwaɪd] *adj* de âmbito *or* a nível nacional ▷ *adv* em todo o país
native ['neɪtɪv] *n* natural *m/f*, nativo(-a); (*in colonies*) indígena *m/f*, nativo(-a) ▷ *adj* (*indigenous*) indígena; (*of one's birth*) natal; (*language*) materno; (*innate*) inato, natural; **a ~ speaker of Portuguese** uma pessoa de língua (materna) portuguesa
NATO ['neɪtəʊ] *n abbr* (= *North Atlantic Treaty Organization*) OTAN *f*
natural ['nætʃrəl] *adj* natural; **naturally** *adv* naturalmente; (*of course*) claro, evidentemente
nature ['neɪtʃəʳ] *n* natureza; (*character*) caráter *m*, índole *f*
naughty ['nɔ:tɪ] *adj* travesso, levado
nausea ['nɔ:sɪə] *n* náusea
naval ['neɪvl] *adj* naval
nave [neɪv] *n* nave *f*
navel ['neɪvl] *n* umbigo
navigate ['nævɪgeɪt] *vi* navegar; (*Aut*) ler o mapa; **navigation** [nævɪ'geɪʃən] *n* (*action*) navegação *f*; (*science*) náutica
navy ['neɪvɪ] *n* marinha (de guerra)
Nazi ['nɑ:tsɪ] *n* nazista *m/f* (*BR*), nazi *m/f* (*PT*)
NB *abbr* (= *nota bene*) NB
near [nɪəʳ] *adj* (*place*) vizinho; (*time*) próximo; (*relation*) íntimo ▷ *adv* perto ▷ *prep* (*also*: **~ to**: *space*) perto de; (: *time*) perto de, quase ▷ *vt* aproximar-se de; **nearby** [nɪə'baɪ] *adj* próximo, vizinho ▷ *adv* à mão, perto; **nearly** *adv* quase; **I nearly fell** quase que caí; **near-sighted** *adj* míope

neat [ni:t] *adj* (*place*) arrumado, em ordem; (*person*) asseado, arrumado; (*work*) caprichado; (*plan*) engenhoso, bem bolado; (*spirits*) puro; **neatly** *adv* caprichosamente, com capricho; (*skilfully*) habilmente

necessarily ['nɛsɪsrɪlɪ] *adv* necessariamente

necessary ['nɛsɪsrɪ] *adj* necessário

necessity [nɪ'sɛsɪtɪ] *n* (*thing needed*) necessidade *f*, requisito; (*compelling circumstances*) necessidade; **necessities** *npl* (*essentials*) artigos *mpl* de primeira necessidade

neck [nɛk] *n* (*Anat*) pescoço; (*of garment*) gola; (*of bottle*) gargalo ▷ *vi* (*inf*) ficar de agarramento; **~ and ~** emparelhados

necklace ['nɛklɪs] *n* colar *m*

necktie ['nɛktaɪ] (*esp US*) *n* gravata

need [ni:d] *n* (*lack*) falta, carência; (*necessity*) necessidade *f*; (*thing needed*) requisito, necessidade ▷ *vt* precisar de; **I ~ to do it** preciso fazê-lo

needle ['ni:dl] *n* agulha ▷ *vt* (*inf*) provocar, alfinetar

needless ['ni:dlɪs] *adj* inútil, desnecessário; **~ to say ...** desnecessário dizer que ...

needlework ['ni:dlwə:k] *n* costura

needn't ['ni:dnt] = **need not**

needy ['ni:dɪ] *adj* necessitado, carente

negative ['nɛɡətɪv] *adj* negativo ▷ *n* (*Phot*) negativo; (*Ling*) negativa

neglect [nɪ'ɡlɛkt] *vt* (*one's duty*) negligenciar, não cumprir com; (*child*) descuidar, esquecer-se de ▷ *n* (*of child*) descuido, desatenção *f*; (*of house etc*) abandono; (*of duty*) negligência

negotiate [nɪ'ɡəʊʃieɪt] *vi* negociar ▷ *vt* (*treaty, transaction*) negociar; (*obstacle*) contornar; (*bend in road*) fazer; **negotiation** [nɪɡəʊʃi'eɪʃən] *n* negociação *f*

neighbour ['neɪbər], (*US*) **neighbor** *n* vizinho(-a); **neighbourhood** *n* (*place*) vizinhança, bairro; (*people*) vizinhos *mpl*; **neighbouring** *adj* vizinho

neither ['naɪðər] *conj*: **I didn't move and ~ did he** não me movi nem ele ▷ *adj, pron* nenhum (dos dois), nem um nem outro ▷ *adv*: **~ good nor bad** nem bom nem mau; **~ story is true** nenhuma das estórias é verdade

neon ['ni:ɔn] *n* neônio, néon *m*

nephew ['nɛvju:] *n* sobrinho

nerve [nə:v] *n* (*Anat*) nervo; (*courage*) coragem *f*; (*impudence*) descaramento, atrevimento; **to have a fit of ~s** ter uma crise nervosa

nervous ['nə:vəs] *adj* (*Anat*) nervoso; (*anxious*) apreensivo; (*timid*) tímido, acanhado; **nervous breakdown** *n* esgotamento nervoso

nest [nɛst] *vi* aninhar-se ▷ *n* (*of bird*) ninho; (*of wasp*) vespeiro

net [nɛt] *n* rede *f*; (*fabric*) filó *m* ▷ *adj* (*Comm*) líquido ▷ *vt* pegar na rede; (*money: subj: person*) faturar; (: *deal, sale*) render; **the N~** (*Internet*) a Rede; **netball** *n* espécie de basquetebol

Netherlands ['nɛðələndz] *npl*: **the ~** os Países Baixos

nett [nɛt] *adj* = **net**

nettle ['nɛtl] *n* urtiga

network ['nɛtwə:k] *n* rede *f*; **there's no ~ coverage here** (*Tel*) aqui não tem cobertura

n

neurotic [njuə'rɒtɪk] *adj, n* neurótico(-a)

neuter ['nju:tər] *adj* neutro ▷ *vt* (*cat etc*) castrar, capar

neutral ['nju:trəl] *adj* neutro ▷ *n* (*Aut*) ponto morto

never ['nɛvər] *adv* nunca; *see also* **mind**; **never-ending** *adj* sem fim, interminável; **nevertheless** *adv* todavia, contudo

new [nju:] *adj* novo; **New Age** *n* esoterismo; **newborn** *adj* recém-nascido; **newcomer** *n* recém-chegado(-a), novato(-a); **newly** *adv* recém, novamente

news [nju:z] *n* notícias *fpl*; (*Radio, TV*) noticiário; **a piece of ~** uma notícia; **newsagent** (*Brit*) *n* jornaleiro(-a); **newscaster** *n* locutor(a) *m/f*; **newsletter** *n* boletim *m* informativo; **newspaper** *n* jornal *m*; **newsreader** *n* = **newscaster**

newt [nju:t] *n* tritão *m*

New Year *n* ano novo; **New Year's Day** *n* dia *m* de ano novo; **New Year's Eve** *n* véspera de ano novo

New Zealand [-'zi:lənd] *n* Nova Zelândia; **New Zealander** *n* neozelandês(-esa) *m/f*

next [nɛkst] *adj* (*in space*) próximo, vizinho; (*in time*) seguinte, próximo ▷ *adv* depois; depois, logo; **~ time** na próxima vez; **~ year** o ano que vem; **~ to** ao lado de; **~ to nothing** quase nada; **next door** *adv* na casa do lado ▷ *adj* vizinho; **next-of-kin** *n* parentes *mpl* mais próximos

NHS (*Brit*) *n abbr* = **National Health Service**

nibble ['nɪbl] *vt* mordiscar, beliscar

Nicaragua [nɪkə'ræɡjuə] *n* Nicarágua

nice [naɪs] *adj* (*likeable*) simpático; (*kind*) amável, atencioso; (*pleasant*) agradável; (*attractive*) bonito; **nicely** *adv* agradavelmente, bem

nick [nɪk] *n* (*wound*) corte *m*; (*cut, indentation*) entalhe *m*, incisão *f* ▷ *vt* (*inf: steal*) furtar; **in the ~ of time** na hora H, em cima da hora

nickel ['nɪkl] *n* níquel *m*; (*US*) moeda de 5 centavos

nickname ['nɪkneɪm] *n* apelido (*BR*), alcunha (*PT*) ▷ *vt* apelidar de (*BR*), alcunhar de (*PT*)

niece [ni:s] *n* sobrinha

Nigeria [naɪ'dʒɪərɪə] *n* Nigéria

night [naɪt] *n* noite *f*; **at** *or* **by ~** à *or* de noite; **the ~ before last** anteontem à noite; **nightclub** *n* boate *f*; **nightlife** ['naɪtlaɪf] *n* vida noturna; **nightly** ['naɪtlɪ] *adj* noturno, de noite ▷ *adv* todas as noites, cada noite; **nightmare** ['naɪtmɛər] *n* pesadelo; **night-time** *n* noite *f*

nil [nɪl] *n* nada; (*Brit: Sport*) zero

nine [naɪn] *num* nove; **nineteen** [naɪn'ti:n] *num* dezenove (*BR*), dezanove (*PT*); **nineteenth** [naɪn'ti:nθ] *num* décimo nono; **ninetieth** ['naɪntɪɪθ] *num* nonagésimo; **ninety** ['naɪntɪ] *num* noventa; **ninth** [naɪnθ] *num* nono

nip [nɪp] *vt* (*pinch*) beliscar; (*bite*) morder

nipple ['nɪpl] *n* (*Anat*) bico do seio, mamilo

nitrogen ['naɪtrədʒən] *n* nitrogênio

 KEYWORD

no [nəu] (*pl* **noes**) *adv* (*opposite of "yes"*) não; **are you coming? — no (I'm not)** você vem? — não (não vou)

▷ *adj* (*not any*) nenhum(a), não ... algum(a); **I have no more money/ time/books** não tenho mais dinheiro/tempo/livros; **"no entry"** "entrada proibida"; **"no smoking"** "é proibido fumar"
▷ *n* não *m*, negativa

nobility [nəʊˈbɪlɪtɪ] *n* nobreza
noble [ˈnəʊbl] *adj* (*person*) nobre; (*title*) de nobreza
nobody [ˈnəʊbədɪ] *pron* ninguém
nod [nɒd] *vi* (*greeting*) cumprimentar com a cabeça; (*in agreement*) acenar (que sim) com a cabeça; (*doze*) cochilar, dormitar
▷ *vt*: **to ~ one's head** inclinar a cabeça ▷ *n* inclinação *f* da cabeça
nod off *vi* cochilar
noise [nɔɪz] *n* barulho; **noisy** *adj* barulhento
nominate [ˈnɒmɪneɪt] *vt* (*propose*) propor; (*appoint*) nomear; **nominee** [nɒmɪˈniː] *n* pessoa nomeada, candidato(-a)
none [nʌn] *pron* (*person*) ninguém; (*thing*) nenhum(a), nada; **~ of you** nenhum de vocês; **I've ~ left** não tenho mais
nonetheless [nʌnðəˈlɛs] *adv* no entanto, apesar disso, contudo
non-fiction *n* literatura de não-ficção
nonsense [ˈnɒnsəns] *n* disparate *m*, besteira, absurdo; **~!** bobagem!, que nada!
non-smoker *n* não-fumante *m/f*
non-stick *adj* tefal®, não-aderente
noodles [ˈnuːdlz] *npl* talharim *m*
noon [nuːn] *n* meio-dia *m*
no-one *pron* = **nobody**
nor [nɔːʳ] *conj* = **neither** ▷ *adv* see **neither**
norm [nɔːm] *n* (*convention*) norma;

(*requirement*) regra
normal [ˈnɔːml] *adj* normal
north [nɔːθ] *n* norte *m* ▷ *adj* do norte, setentrional ▷ *adv* ao or para o norte; **North America** *n* América do Norte; **north-east** *n* nordeste *m*; **northern** [ˈnɔːðən] *adj* do norte, setentrional; **Northern Ireland** *n* Irlanda do Norte; **North Pole** *n*: **the North Pole** o Pólo Norte; **North Sea** *n*: **the North Sea** o Mar do Norte; **north-west** *n* noroeste *m*
Norway [ˈnɔːweɪ] *n* Noruega; **Norwegian** [nɔːˈwiːdʒən] *adj* norueguês(-esa) ▷ *n* norueguês(-esa) *m/f*; (*Ling*) norueguês *m*
nose [nəʊz] *n* (*Anat*) nariz *m*; (*Zool*) focinho; (*sense of smell: of person*) olfato; (: *of animal*) faro **nose about** *vi* bisbilhotar **nose around** *vi* = **nose about**; **nosebleed** *n* hemorragia nasal; **nosey** (*inf*) *adj* = **nosy**
nostalgia [nɒsˈtældʒɪə] *n* nostalgia
nostril [ˈnɒstrɪl] *n* narina
nosy [ˈnəʊzɪ] (*inf*) *adj* intrometido, abelhudo
not [nɒt] *adv* não; **he is ~** or **isn't here** ele não está aqui; **it's too late, isn't it?** é muito tarde, não?; **he asked me ~ to do it** ele me pediu para não fazer isto; **~ yet/ now** ainda/agora não; see also **all**; **only**
notably [ˈnəʊtəblɪ] *adv* (*particularly*) particularmente; (*markedly*) notavelmente
notch [nɒtʃ] *n* (*in wood*) entalhe *m*; (*in blade*) corte *m*
note [nəʊt] *n* (*Mus, banknote*) nota; (*letter*) nota, bilhete *m*; (*record*) nota, anotação *f*; (*tone*) tom *m* ▷ *vt*

n

(*observe*) observar, reparar em; (*also*: **~ down**) anotar, tomar nota de; **notebook** n caderno; **notepad** n bloco de anotações; **notepaper** n papel m de carta

nothing ['nʌθɪŋ] n nada; (*zero*) zero; **he does ~** ele não faz nada; **~ new/much** nada de novo/de mais; **for ~** de graça, grátis; (*in vain*) à toa, por nada

notice ['nəʊtɪs] n (*sign*) aviso, anúncio; (*warning*) aviso; (*of leaving or losing job*) aviso prévio ▷ vt reparar em, notar; **at short ~** de repente, em cima da hora; **until further ~** até nova ordem; **to hand in** or **give one's ~** demitir, pedir a demissão; **to take ~ of** prestar atenção a, fazer caso de; **to bring sth to sb's ~** levar algo ao conhecimento de alguém; **noticeable** adj evidente, visível; **notice board** (*Brit*) n quadro de avisos

notify ['nəʊtɪfaɪ] vt: **to ~ sb of sth** avisar alguém de algo

notion ['nəʊʃən] n noção f, ideia

nought [nɔːt] n zero

noun [naun] n substantivo

nourish ['nʌrɪʃ] vt nutrir, alimentar; (*fig*) fomentar, alentar; **nourishment** n alimento, nutrimento

novel ['nɔvl] n romance m ▷ adj novo, recente; **novelist** n romancista m/f; **novelty** n novidade f

November [nəʊ'vɛmbəʳ] n novembro

now [nau] adv agora; (*these days*) atualmente, hoje em dia ▷ conj: **~ (that)** agora que; **right ~** agora mesmo; **by ~** já; **just ~** agora; **~ and then**, **~ and again** de vez em

quando; **from ~ on** de agora em diante; **nowadays** adv hoje em dia

nowhere ['nəʊwɛəʳ] adv (*go*) a lugar nenhum; (*be*) em nenhum lugar

nozzle ['nɔzl] n bocal m

nuclear ['njuːklɪəʳ] adj nuclear

nucleus ['njuːklɪəs] n (*pl* **nuclei**) n núcleo

nude [njuːd] adj nu(a) ▷ n (*Art*) nu m; **in the ~** nu, pelado

nudge [nʌdʒ] vt acotovelar, cutucar (*BR*)

nudist ['njuːdɪst] n nudista m/f

nuisance ['njuːsns] n amolação f, aborrecimento; (*person*) chato; **what a ~!** que saco! (*BR*), que chatice! (*PT*)

numb [nʌm] adj dormente; **~ with cold** duro de frio; **~ with fear** paralisado de medo

number ['nʌmbəʳ] n número; (*numeral*) algarismo ▷ vt (*pages etc*) numerar; (*amount to*) montar a; **a ~ of** vários, muitos; **to be ~ed among** figurar entre; **they were ten in ~** eram em número de dez; **number plate** (*Brit*) n placa (do carro)

numerous ['njuːmərəs] adj numeroso

nun [nʌn] n freira

nurse [nəːs] n enfermeiro(-a); (*also*: **~maid**) ama-seca, babá f ▷ vt (*patient*) cuidar de, tratar de

nursery ['nəːsərɪ] n (*institution*) creche f; (*room*) quarto das crianças; (*for plants*) viveiro; **nursery rhyme** n poesia infantil; **nursery school** n escola maternal

nursing ['nəːsɪŋ] n (*profession*) enfermagem f; (*care*) cuidado, assistência; **nursing home** n sanatório, clínica de repouso

nut [nʌt] *n* (*Tech*) porca; (*Bot*) noz *f*
nutmeg ['nʌtmɛg] *n* noz-moscada
nutritious [njuː'trɪʃəs] *adj* nutritivo
nuts [nʌts] (*inf*) *adj*: **he's ~** ele é
doido
nylon ['naɪlɔn] *n* náilon *m* (*BR*),
nylon *m* (*PT*) ▷ *adj* de náilon *or*
nylon

oak [əuk] *n* carvalho ▷ *adj* de
carvalho
OAP (*Brit*) *n abbr* = **old-age
pensioner**
oar [ɔːʳ] *n* remo
oasis [əu'eɪsɪs] (*pl* **oases**) *n* oásis *m
inv*
oath [əuθ] *n* juramento; (*swear
word*) palavrão *m*
oatmeal ['əutmiːl] *n* farinha *or*
mingau *m* de aveia
oats [əuts] *n* aveia
obedient [ə'biːdɪənt] *adj* obediente
obey [ə'beɪ] *vt* obedecer a;
(*instructions, regulations*) cumprir
obituary [ə'bɪtjuərɪ] *n* necrológio
object [*n* 'ɔbdʒɪkt, *vi* əb'dʒɛkt] *n*
objeto; (*purpose*) objetivo ▷ *vi*: **to ~
to** (*attitude*) desaprovar, objetar a;
(*proposal*) opor-se a; **I ~!** protesto!;
he ~ed that ... ele objetou que ...;
expense is no ~ o preço não é

problema; **objection** [əb'dʒɛkʃən]
n objeção f; **I have no objection to
...** não tenho nada contra ...;
objective n objetivo
obligation [ɔblɪ'geɪʃən] n
obrigação f; **without ~** sem
compromisso
obligatory [ə'blɪgətərɪ] adj
obrigatório
oblige [ə'blaɪdʒ] vt (do a favour for)
obsequiar, fazer um favor a; (force)
obrigar, forçar; **to be ~d to sb for
doing sth** ficar agradecido por
alguém fazer algo
oblong ['ɔblɔŋ] adj oblongo,
retangular ▷ n retângulo
obnoxious [əb'nɔkʃəs] adj odioso,
detestável; (smell) enjoativo
oboe ['əubəu] n oboé m
obscene [əb'si:n] adj obsceno
obscure [əb'skjuəʳ] adj obscuro,
desconhecido; (difficult to
understand) pouco claro ▷ vt
ocultar, escurecer; (hide: sun etc)
esconder
observant [əb'zɑ:vnt] adj
observador(a)
observation [ɔbzɑ'veɪʃən] n
observação f; (Med) exame m
observatory [əb'zɑ:vətrɪ] n
observatório
observe [əb'zɑ:v] vt observar; (rule)
cumprir; **observer** n
observador(a) m/f
obsess [əb'sɛs] vt obsedar, obcecar
obsolete ['ɔbsəli:t] adj obsoleto
obstacle ['ɔbstəkl] n obstáculo;
(hindrance) estorvo, impedimento
obstinate ['ɔbstɪnɪt] adj obstinado
obstruct [əb'strʌkt] vt obstruir;
(block: hinder) estorvar
obtain [əb'teɪn] vt obter; (achieve)
conseguir
obvious ['ɔbvɪəs] adj óbvio;

obviously adv evidentemente;
obviously not! (é)claro que não!
occasion [ə'keɪʒən] n ocasião f;
(event) acontecimento;
occasional adj de vez em quando;
occasionally adv de vez em quando
occupation [ɔkju'peɪʃən] n
ocupação f; (job) profissão f
occupy ['ɔkjupaɪ] vt ocupar;
(house) morar em; **to ~ o.s. in
doing** ocupar-se de fazer
occur [ə'kəːʳ] vi ocorrer;
(phenomenon) acontecer; **to ~ to sb**
ocorrer a alguém; **occurrence** n
ocorrência, acontecimento;
(existence) existência
ocean ['əuʃən] n oceano
o'clock [ə'klɔk] adv: **it is 5 ~** são
cinco horas
October [ɔk'təubəʳ] n outubro
octopus ['ɔktəpəs] n polvo
odd [ɔd] adj (strange) estranho,
esquisito; (number) ímpar; (sock
etc) desemparelhado; **60-~** 60 e
tantos; **at ~ times** às vezes, de vez
em quando; **to be the ~ one out**
ficar sobrando, ser a exceção;
oddly adv curiosamente; see also
enough; **odds** npl (in betting)
pontos mpl de vantagem; **it makes
no odds** dá no mesmo; **at odds**
brigados(-as), de mal
odour ['əudəʳ], (US) **odor** n odor m,
cheiro; (unpleasant) fedor m

 KEYWORD

of [ɔv, əv] prep **1** (gen) de; **a friend of
ours** um amigo nosso; **a boy of 10**
um menino de 10 anos; **that was
very kind of you** foi muito gentil
da sua parte
2 (expressing quantity, amount, dates
etc) de; **how much of this do you**

need? de quanto você precisa?; **3 of them** 3 deles; **3 of us went** 3 de nós foram; **the 5th of July** dia 5 de julho 3 (*from, out of*) de; **made of wood** feito de madeira

 KEYWORD

off [ɔf] *adv* **1** (*distance, time*): **it's a long way off** fica bem longe; **the game is 3 days off** o jogo é daqui a 3 dias

2 (*departure*): **I'm off** estou de partida; **to go off to Paris/Italy** ir para Paris/a Itália; **I must be off** devo ir-me

3 (*removal*): **to take off one's hat/ coat/clothes** tirar o chapéu/o casaco/a roupa; **the button came off** o botão caiu; **10% off** (*Comm*) 10% de abatimento *or* desconto

4 (*not at work*): **to have a day off** tirar um dia de folga; (: *sick*): **to be off sick** estar ausente por motivo de saúde

▷ *adj* **1** (*not turned on: machine, water, gas*) desligado; (: *light*) apagado; (: *tap*) fechado

2 (*cancelled*) cancelado

3 (*Brit: not fresh: food*) passado; (: *milk*) talhado, anulado

4: **on the off chance** (*just in case*) ao acaso; **today I had an off day** (*not as good as usual*) hoje não foi o meu dia

▷ *prep* **1** (*indicating motion, removal, etc*) de; **the button came off my coat** o botão do meu casaco caiu

2 (*distant from*) de; **5 km off (the road)** a 5 km (da estrada); **off the coast** em frente à costa

3: **to be off meat** (*no longer eat it*) não comer mais carne; (*no longer like it*) enjoar de carne

offence [ə'fɛns], (*US*) **offense** *n* (*crime*) delito; **to take ~ at** ofender-se com, melindrar-se com

offend [ə'fɛnd] *vt* ofender; **offender** *n* delinquente *m/f*

offensive [ə'fɛnsɪv] *adj* (*weapon, remark*) ofensivo; (*smell etc*) repugnante ▷ *n* (*Mil*) ofensiva

offer ['ɔfə^r] *n* oferta; (*proposal*) proposta ▷ *vt* oferecer; (*opportunity*) proporcionar; **"on ~"** (*Comm*) "em oferta"

office ['ɔfɪs] *n* (*place*) escritório; (*room*) gabinete *m*; (*position*) cargo, função *f*; **to take ~** tomar posse; **doctor's ~** (*US*) consultório; **office block**, (*US*) **office building** *n* conjunto de escritórios

officer ['ɔfɪsə^r] *n* (*Mil etc*) oficial *m/f*; (*of organization*) diretor(a) *m/f*; (*also*: **police ~**) agente *m/f* policial *or* de polícia

office worker *n* empregado(-a) *or* funcionário(-a) de escritório

official [ə'fɪʃl] *adj* oficial ▷ *n* oficial *m/f*; (*civil servant*) funcionário(-a) público(-a)

off-licence (*Brit*) *n* loja de bebidas alcoólicas

● **OFF-LICENCE**
●
● Uma loja **off-licence** vende
● bebidas alcóolicas (para viagem)
● nos horários em que os pubs
● estão fechados. Nesses
● estabelecimentos também se
● pode comprar bebidas
● não-alcoólicas, cigarros,
● batatas fritas, balas,
● chocolates etc.

off: **off line** *adj, adv* (*Comput*) off-line; **off-peak** *adj* (*heating etc*)

de período de pouco consumo;
(*ticket, train*) de período de pouco
movimento; **off-putting** (*Brit*) *adj*
desconcertante; **off-season** *adj*,
adv fora de estação *or* temporada
offset ['ɔfsɛt] *irreg vt* compensar,
contrabalançar
offshore [ɔf'ʃɔːʳ] *adj* (*breeze*) de
terra; (*fishing*) costeiro; **~ oilfield**
campo petrolífero ao largo
offside ['ɔf'saɪd] *adj* (*Sport*)
impedido; (*Aut*) do lado do
motorista
offspring ['ɔfsprɪŋ] *n*
descendência, prole *f*
often ['ɔfn] *adv* muitas vezes,
frequentemente; **how ~ do you
go?** com que frequência você vai?
oil [ɔɪl] *n* (*Culin*) azeite *m*;
(*petroleum*) petróleo; (*for heating*)
óleo ▷ *vt* (*machine*) lubrificar; **oil
painting** *n* pintura a óleo; **oil rig** *n*
torre *f* de perfuração; **oil slick** *n*
mancha de óleo; **oil tanker** *n*
(*ship*) petroleiro; (*truck*)
carro-tanque *m* de petróleo; **oil
well** *n* poço petrolífero; **oily** *adj*
oleoso; (*food*) gorduroso
ointment ['ɔɪntmənt] *n* pomada
O.K. ['əu'keɪ] *excl* está bem, está
bom, tá (bem *or* bom) (*inf*) ▷ *adj*
bom; (*correct*) certo ▷ *vt* aprovar
old [əuld] *adj* velho; (*former*) antigo,
anterior; **how ~ are you?** quantos
anos você tem?; **he's 10 years ~** ele
tem 10 anos; **~er brother** irmão
mais velho; **old age** *n* velhice *f*;
old-age pensioner (*Brit*) *n*
aposentado(-a) (*BR*),
reformado(-a) (*PT*); **old-fashioned**
adj fora de moda; (*person*)
antiquado; (*values*) obsoleto,
retrógrado
olive ['ɔlɪv] *n* (*fruit*) azeitona; (*tree*)

oliveira ▷ *adj* (*also:* **~-green**)
verde-oliva *inv*; **olive oil** *n* azeite *m*
de oliva
Olympic [əu'lɪmpɪk] *adj* olímpico
omelet, omelette ['ɔmlɪt] *n*
omelete *f* (*BR*), omeleta (*PT*)
omen ['əumən] *n* presságio,
agouro
ominous ['ɔmɪnəs] *adj*
preocupante
omit [əu'mɪt] *vt* omitir

 KEYWORD

on [ɔn] *prep* **1** (*indicating position*)
sobre, em (cima de); **on the wall**
na parede; **on the left** à esquerda
2 (*indicating means, method,
condition etc*): **on foot** a pé; **on the
train/plane** no trem/avião; **on
the telephone/radio** no telefone/
rádio; **on television** na televisão;
to be on drugs (*addicted*) ser
viciado em drogas; (*Med*) estar sob
medicação; **to be on holiday/
business** estar de férias/a negócio
3 (*referring to time*): **on Friday** na
sexta-feira; **a week on Friday** sem
ser esta sexta-feira, a outra; **on
arrival** ao chegar; **on seeing this**
ao ver isto
4 (*about, concerning*) sobre
▷ *adv* **1** (*referring to dress*): **to have
one's coat on** estar de casaco;
what's she got on? o que ela está
usando?; **she put her boots on** ela
calçou as botas; **he put his
gloves/hat on** ele colocou as
luvas/o chapéu
2: **screw the lid on tightly**
atarraxar bem a tampa
3 (*further, continuously*): **to walk/
drive on** continuar andando/
dirigindo; **to go on** continuar (em

frente); **to read on** continuar a ler ▷ *adj* **1** (*functioning, in operation: machine*) em funcionamento; (*light*) aceso; (*radio*) ligado; (*tap*) aberto; (*brakes: of car etc*): **to be on** estar freado; (*meeting*): **is the meeting still on?** (*in progress*) a reunião ainda está sendo realizada?; (*not cancelled*) ainda vai haver reunião?; **there's a good film on at the cinema** tem um bom filme passando no cinema **2**: **that's not on!** (*inf: of behaviour*) isso não se faz!

once [wʌns] *adv* uma vez; (*formerly*) outrora ▷ *conj* depois que; **~ he had left/it was done** depois que ele saiu/foi feito; **at ~** imediatamente; (*simultaneously*) de uma vez, ao mesmo tempo; **~ more** mais uma vez; **~ and for all** uma vez por todas; **~ upon a time** era uma vez **oncoming** [ˈɒnkʌmɪŋ] *adj* (*traffic*) que vem de frente

KEYWORD

one [wʌn] *num* um(a); **one hundred and fifty** cento e cinquenta; **one by one** um por um ▷ *adj* **1** (*sole*) único; **the one book which ...** o único livro que ... **2** (*same*) mesmo; **they came in the one car** eles vieram no mesmo carro ▷ *pron* **1** um(a); **this one** este/esta; **that one** esse/essa, aquele/ aquela; **I've already got one/a red one** eu já tenho um/um vermelho **2**: **one another** um ao outro; **do you two ever see one another?** vocês dois se veem de vez em quando?

3 (*impers*): **one never knows** nunca se sabe; **to cut one's finger** cortar o dedo; **one needs to eat** é preciso comer

oneself [wʌnˈsɛlf] *pron* (*reflexive*) se; (*after prep, emphatic*) si (mesmo(-a)); **by ~** sozinho(-a); **to hurt ~** ferir-se; **to keep sth for ~** guardar algo para si mesmo; **to talk to ~** falar consigo mesmo **one-sided** *adj* parcial **one-way** *adj* (*street, traffic*) de mão única (BR), de sentido único (PT) **ongoing** [ˈɒngəʊɪŋ] *adj* (*project*) em andamento; (*situation*) existente **onion** [ˈʌnjən] *n* cebola **on line** *adj, adv* (*Comput*) on-line, online **onlooker** [ˈɒnlʊkəʳ] *n* espectador(a) *m/f* **only** [ˈəʊnlɪ] *adv* somente, apenas ▷ *adj* único, só ▷ *conj* só que, porém; **an ~ child** um filho único; **not ~ ... but also ...** não só ... mas também ...
onset [ˈɒnsɛt] *n* começo
onto [ˈɒntʊ] *prep* = **on to**
onward [ˈɒnwəd], **onwards** [ˈɒnwədz] *adv* (*move*) para diante, para a frente; **from this time ~(s)** de (ag)ora em diante
ooze [uːz] *vi* ressumar, filtrar-se
opaque [əʊˈpeɪk] *adj* opaco, fosco
open [ˈəʊpn] *adj* aberto; (*car*) descoberto; (*road*) livre; (*fig: frank*) aberto, franco; (*meeting*) aberto, sem restrições ▷ *vt* abrir ▷ *vi* abrir(-se); (*book etc*) começar; **in the ~ (air)** ao ar livre **open on to** *vt fus* (*subj: room, door*) dar para **open up** *vt* abrir; (*blocked road*) desobstruir ▷ *vi* (*Comm*) abrir; **opening** *adj* de abertura ▷ *n*

o

abertura; (*start*) início;
(*opportunity*) oportunidade *f*;
openly *adv* abertamente;
open-minded *adj* aberto,
imparcial; **open-necked** *adj*
aberto no colo; **open-plan** *adj*
sem paredes divisórias; **Open
University** (*Brit*) *n* ver nota

● **OPEN UNIVERSITY**
●
● Fundada em 1969, a **Open
● University** oferece um tipo de
● ensino que compreende cursos
● (alguns blocos da programação
● da TV e do rádio são reservados
● para esse fim), deveres que são
● enviados pelo aluno ao diretor ou
● diretora de estudos e uma estada
● obrigatória em uma
● universidade de verão. É preciso
● cumprir um certo número de
● unidades ao longo de um período
● determinado e obter a média em
● um certo número delas para
● receber o diploma almejado.

opera ['ɔpərə] *n* ópera
operate ['ɔpəreɪt] *vt* fazer
funcionar, pôr em funcionamento
▷ *vi* funcionar; (*Med*): **to ~ on sb**
operar alguém
operation [ɔpə'reɪʃən] *n* operação
f; (*of machine*) funcionamento;
to be in ~ (*system*) estar em vigor
operator ['ɔpəreɪtər] *n* (*of machine*)
operador(a) *m/f*, manipulador(a)
m/f; (*Tel*) telefonista *m/f*
opinion [ə'pɪnɪən] *n* opinião *f*; **in
my ~** na minha opinião, a meu ver
opponent [ə'pəunənt] *n* oponente
m/f; (*Mil*, *Sport*) adversário(-a)
opportunity [ɔpə'tjuːnɪtɪ] *n*
oportunidade *f*; **to take the ~ of**

doing aproveitar a oportunidade
para fazer
oppose [ə'pəuz] *vt* opor-se a; **to be
~d to sth** opor-se a algo, estar
contra algo; **as ~d to** em oposição a
opposite ['ɔpəzɪt] *adj* oposto;
(*house etc*) em frente ▷ *adv* (lá) em
frente ▷ *prep* em frente de,
defronte de ▷ *n* oposto, contrário
opposition [ɔpə'zɪʃən] *n* oposição *f*
opt [ɔpt] *vi*: **to ~ for** optar por; **to ~
to do** optar por fazer; **to ~ out of
doing sth** optar por não fazer algo
optician [ɔp'tɪʃən] *n* oculista *m/f*
optimist ['ɔptɪmɪst] *n* otimista *m/f*;
optimistic [ɔptɪ'mɪstɪk] *adj*
otimista
option ['ɔpʃən] *n* opção *f*; **optional**
adj opcional, facultativo
or [ɔːʳ] *conj* ou; (*with negative*): **he
hasn't seen or heard anything**
ele não viu nem ouviu nada; **or else**
senão
oral ['ɔːrəl] *adj* oral ▷ *n* prova *f* oral
orange ['ɔrɪndʒ] *n* (*fruit*) laranja
▷ *adj* cor de laranja *inv*, alaranjado
orbit ['ɔːbɪt] *n* órbita ▷ *vt* orbitar
orchard ['ɔːtʃəd] *n* pomar *m*
orchestra ['ɔːkɪstrə] *n* orquestra;
(*US*: *seating*) plateia
orchid ['ɔːkɪd] *n* orquídea
ordeal [ɔː'diːl] *n* experiência
penosa, provação *f*
order ['ɔːdər] *n* ordem *f*; (*Comm*)
encomenda; **good** ~ bom estado
▷ *vt* (*also*: **put in ~**) pôr em ordem,
arrumar; (*in restaurant*) pedir;
(*Comm*) encomendar; (*command*)
mandar, ordenar; **in (working) ~**
em bom estado; **in ~ to do/that**
para fazer/que (+ *sub*); **on ~** (*Comm*)
encomendado; **out of ~** com
defeito, enguiçado; **order form** *n*
impresso para encomendas;

orderly n (Mil) ordenança m; (Med) servente m/f ▷ adj (room) arrumado, ordenado; (person) metódico

ordinary ['ɔ:dnrɪ] adj comum, usual; (pej) ordinário, medíocre; **out of the ~** fora do comum, extraordinário

ore [ɔ:ʳ] n minério

organ ['ɔ:gən] n órgão m; **organic** [ɔ:'gænɪk] adj orgânico

organization [ɔ:gənaɪ'zeɪʃən] n organização f

organize ['ɔ:gənaɪz] vt organizar

orgasm ['ɔ:gæzəm] n orgasmo

origin ['ɔrɪdʒɪn] n origem f

original [ə'rɪdʒɪnl] adj original ▷ n original m

originate [ə'rɪdʒɪneɪt] vi: **to ~ from** originar-se de, surgir de; **to ~ in** ter origem em

Orkney ['ɔ:knɪ] n (also: **the ~ Islands**; **the ~s**) as ilhas Órcadas

ornament ['ɔ:nəmənt] n ornamento; (on dress) enfeite m; **ornamental** [ɔ:nə'mɛntl] adj decorativo, ornamental

ornate [ɔ:'neɪt] adj enfeitado, requintado

orphan ['ɔ:fn] n órfão/órfã m/f

orthopaedic [ɔ:θə'pi:dɪk], (US) **orthopedic** adj ortopédico

ostrich ['ɔstrɪtʃ] n avestruz m/f

other ['ʌðəʳ] adj outro ▷ pron: **the ~ (one)** o outro/a outra ▷ adv (usually in negatives): **~ than** (apart from) além de; (anything but) exceto; **~s** (other people) outros; **otherwise** adv (in a different way) de outra maneira; (apart from that) além disso ▷ conj (if not) senão

otter ['ɔtəʳ] n lontra

ouch [autʃ] excl ai!

ought [ɔ:t] (pt **ought**) aux vb: **I ~ to do it** eu deveria fazê-lo; **he ~ to win** (probability) ele deve ganhar

ounce [auns] n onça (= 28.35g)

our ['auəʳ] adj nosso; see also **my**; **ours** pron (o) nosso/(a) nossa etc; see also **mine**; **ourselves** [auə'sɛlvz] pron pl (reflexive, after prep) nós; (emphatic) nós mesmos(-as); see also **oneself**

oust [aust] vt expulsar

 KEYWORD

out [aut] adv **1** (not in) fora; **(to stand) out in the rain/snow** (estar em pé) na chuva/neve; **out loud** em voz alta

2 (not at home, absent) fora (de casa); **Mr Green is out at the moment** Sr. Green não está no momento; **to have a day/night out** passar o dia fora/sair à noite

3 (indicating distance): **the boat was 10 km out** o barco estava a 10 km da costa

4 (Sport): **the ball is/has gone out** a bola caiu fora; **out!** (Tennis etc) fora!

▷ adj **1**: **to be out** (unconscious) estar inconsciente; (out of game) estar fora; (out of fashion) estar fora de moda

2 (have appeared: news, secret) do conhecimento público; (: flowers): **the flowers are out** as flores desabrocharam

3 (extinguished: light, fire) apagado; **before the week was out** (finished) antes da semana acabar

4: **to be out to do sth** (intend) pretender fazer algo; **to be out in one's calculations** (wrong) enganar-se nos cálculos ▷ prep: **out of 1** (outside, beyond): **out of**

fora de; **to go out of the house**
sair da casa; **to look out of the
window** olhar pela janela
2 (*cause, motive*) por
3 (*origin*): **to drink sth out of a cup**
beber algo na xícara
4 (*from among*): **1 out of every 3
smokers** 1 entre 3 fumantes
5 (*without*) sem; **to be out of milk/
sugar/petrol** etc não ter leite/
açúcar/gasolina etc

outback ['autbæk] n (*in Australia*):
the ~ o interior
outbreak ['autbreɪk] n (*of war*)
deflagração f; (*of disease*) surto;
(*of violence etc*) explosão f
outburst ['autbɑːst] n explosão f
outcast ['autkɑːst] n pária m/f
outcome ['autkʌm] n resultado
outcry ['autkraɪ] n clamor m (de
protesto)
outdated [aut'deɪtɪd] adj
antiquado, fora de moda
outdoor [aut'dɔːʳ] adj ao ar livre;
(*clothes*) de sair; **outdoors** adv ao
ar livre
outer ['autəʳ] adj exterior, externo;
outer space n espaço (exterior)
outfit ['autfɪt] n roupa, traje m
outgoing ['autgəuɪŋ] adj de saída;
(*character*) extrovertido, sociável;
outgoings (*Brit*) npl despesas fpl
outing ['autɪŋ] n excursão f
outlaw ['autlɔː] n fora-da-lei m/f
▷ vt (*person*) declarar fora da lei;
(*practice*) declarar ilegal
outlay ['autleɪ] n despesas fpl
outlet ['autlɛt] n saída, escape m;
(*of pipe*) desague m, escoadouro;
(*US: Elec*) tomada; (*also*: **retail ~**)
posto de venda
outline ['autlaɪn] n (*shape*)
contorno, perfil m; (*of plan*)

traçado; (*sketch*) esboço, linhas fpl
gerais ▷ vt (*theory, plan*) traçar,
delinear
outlook ['autluk] n (*attitude*) ponto
de vista; (*fig: prospects*) perspectiva;
(*: for weather*) previsão f
outnumber [aut'nʌmbəʳ] vt
exceder em número
out-of-date adj (*passport, ticket*)
sem validade; (*clothes*) fora de
moda
out-of-the-way adj remoto,
afastado
outpatient ['autpeɪʃənt] n
paciente m/f externo(-a) or de
ambulatório
outpost ['autpəust] n posto
avançado
output ['autput] n (volume m de)
produção f; (*Comput*) saída ▷ vt
(*Comput*) dar saída em
outrage ['autreɪdʒ] n escândalo;
(*atrocity*) atrocidade f ▷ vt ultrajar;
outrageous [aut'reɪdʒəs] adj
ultrajante, escandaloso
outright [adv aut'raɪt, adj 'autraɪt]
adv (*kill, win*) completamente; (*ask,
refuse*) abertamente ▷ adj
completo; franco
outset ['autsɛt] n início, princípio
outside [aut'saɪd] n exterior m
▷ adj exterior, externo ▷ adv (lá)
fora ▷ prep fora de; (*beyond*) além
(dos limites) de; **at the ~** (*fig*) no
máximo; **outsider** n (*stranger*)
estranho(-a), forasteiro(-a)
outsize ['autsaɪz] adj (*clothes*) de
tamanho extra-grande or especial
outskirts ['autskəːts] npl arredores
mpl, subúrbios mpl
outspoken [aut'spəukən] adj
franco, sem rodeios
outstanding [aut'stændɪŋ] adj
excepcional; (*work, debt*) pendente

outward ['autwəd] adj externo; (journey) de ida; **outwards** (esp Brit) adv para fora

outweigh [aut'weɪ] vt ter mais valor do que

oval ['əuvl] adj ovalado ▷ n oval m; **Oval Office** n ver nota

○ **OVAL OFFICE**
●
● O Salão Oval (**Oval Office**) é o
● escritório particular do
● presidente dos Estados Unidos
● na Casa Branca, assim chamado
● devido a sua forma oval. Por
● extensão, o termo se refere à
● presidência em si.

ovary ['əuvərɪ] n ovário
oven ['ʌvn] n forno

 KEYWORD

over ['əuvəʳ] adv **1** (across: walk, jump, fly etc) por cima; **to cross over to the other side of the road** atravessar para o outro lado da rua; **over here** por aqui, cá; **over there** por ali, lá; **to ask sb over** (to one's home) convidar alguém
2: **to fall over** cair; **to knock over** derrubar; **to turn over** virar; **to bend over** curvar-se, debruçar-se
3 (finished): **to be over** estar acabado
4 (excessively: clever, rich, fat etc) muito, demais; **she's not over intelligent** ela não é superdotada
5 (remaining: money, food etc): **there are 3 over** tem 3 sobrando/ sobraram 3
6: **all over** (everywhere) por todos os lados; **over and over (again)** repetidamente
▷ prep **1** (on top of) sobre; (above) acima de
2 (on the other side of) no outro lado de; **he jumped over the wall** ele pulou o muro
3 (more than) mais de; **over and above** além de
4 (during) durante

overall n, adj ['əuvərɔ:l, adv əuvər'ɔ:l] adj (length) total; (study) global ▷ adv (view) globalmente; (measure, paint) totalmente; **overalls** npl macacão m (BR), (fato) macaco (PT)

overboard ['əuvəbɔ:d] adv (Naut) ao mar

overcast ['əuvəkɑ:st] adj nublado, fechado

overcharge [əuvə'tʃɑ:dʒ] vt: **to ~ sb** cobrar em excesso a alguém

overcoat ['əuvəkəut] n sobretudo

overcome [əuvə'kʌm] irreg vt vencer, dominar; (difficulty) superar

overcrowded [əuvə'kraudɪd] adj superlotado

overdo [əuvə'du:] irreg vt exagerar; (overcook) cozinhar demais; **to ~ it** (work too hard) exceder-se

overdose ['əuvədəus] n overdose f, dose f excessiva

overdraft ['əuvədrɑ:ft] n saldo negativo

overdrawn [əuvə'drɔ:n] adj (account) sem fundos, a descoberto

overdue [əuvə'dju:] adj atrasado; (change) tardio

overestimate [əuvər'ɛstɪmeɪt] vt sobrestimar

overflow [vi əuvə'fləu, n 'əuvəfləu] vi transbordar ▷ n (also: **~ pipe**) tubo de descarga, ladrão m

overgrown [əuvə'grəun] adj (garden) coberto de vegetação

overhaul [vt əuvə'hɔ:l, n 'əuvəhɔ:l] vt revisar ▷ n revisão f

overhead [adv əuvə'hɛd, adj, n 'əuvəhɛd] adv por cima, em cima; (in the sky) no céu ▷ adj (lighting) superior; (railway) suspenso ▷ n (US) = **overheads**; **overheads** npl (expenses) despesas fpl gerais

overhear [əuvə'hɪəʳ] irreg vt ouvir por acaso

overheat [əuvə'hi:t] vi (engine) aquecer demais

overland ['əuvəlænd] adj, adv por terra

overlap [əuvə'læp] vi (edges) sobrepor-se em parte; (fig) coincidir

overload [əuvə'ləud] vt sobrecarregar

overlook [əuvə'luk] vt (have view on) dar para; (miss) omitir; (forgive) fazer vista grossa a

overnight [adv əuvə'naɪt, adj 'əuvənaɪt] adv durante a noite; (fig) da noite para o dia ▷ adj de uma (or de) noite; **to stay ~** passar a noite, pernoitar

overpass ['əuvəpɑːs] (esp US) n viaduto

overpower [əuvə'pauəʳ] vt dominar, subjugar; (fig) assolar

overrule [əuvə'ru:l] vt (decision) anular; (claim) indeferir

overrun [əuvə'rʌn] irreg vt (country etc) invadir; (time limit) ultrapassar, exceder

overseas [əuvə'si:z] adv (abroad) no estrangeiro, no exterior ▷ adj (trade) exterior; (visitor) estrangeiro

overshadow [əuvə'ʃædəu] vt ofuscar

oversight ['əuvəsaɪt] n descuido

oversleep [əuvə'sli:p] irreg vi dormir além da hora

overt [əu'və:t] adj aberto, indissimulado

overtake [əuvə'teɪk] irreg vt ultrapassar

overthrow [əuvə'θrəu] irreg vt (government) derrubar

overtime ['əuvətaɪm] n horas fpl extras

overturn [əuvə'tə:n] vt virar; (system) derrubar; (decision) anular ▷ vi capotar

overweight [əuvə'weɪt] adj acima do peso

overwhelm [əuvə'wɛlm] vt esmagar, assolar; **overwhelming** adj (victory, defeat) esmagador(a); (heat) sufocante; (desire) irresistível

owe [əu] vt: **to ~ sb sth**, **to ~ sth to sb** dever algo a alguém; **owing to** prep devido a, por causa de

owl [aul] n coruja

own [əun] adj próprio ▷ vt possuir, ter; **a room of my ~** meu próprio quarto; **to get one's ~ back** ir à forra; **on one's ~** sozinho **own up** vi: **to ~ up to sth** confessar algo; **owner** n dono(-a), proprietário(-a); **ownership** n posse f

ox [ɔks] (pl **oxen**) n boi m

oxygen ['ɔksɪdʒən] n oxigênio

oyster ['ɔɪstəʳ] n ostra

oz. abbr = **ounce(s)**

ozone ['əuzəun] n ozônio

p

p [piː] *abbr* (= *page*) p; (*Brit*) = **penny**; **pence**

p.a. *abbr* (= *per annum*) por ano

pace [peɪs] *n* passo; (*speed*) velocidade *f* ▷ *vi*: **to ~ up and down** andar de um lado para o outro; **to keep ~ with** acompanhar o passo de; **pacemaker** *n* (*Med*) marcapasso *m*

pacific [pə'sɪfɪk] *n*: **the Pacific (Ocean)** o (Oceano) Pacífico

pack [pæk] *n* pacote *m*, embrulho; (*US: of cigarettes*) maço; (*of hounds*) matilha; (*of thieves etc*) bando, quadrilha; (*of cards*) baralho; (*backpack*) mochila ▷ *vt* encher; (*in suitcase etc*) arrumar (na mala); (*cram*): **to ~ into** entupir de, entulhar com ▷ *vi*: **to ~ (one's bags)** fazer as malas; **~ it in!** para com isso! **pack off** *vt* (*person*) despedir

package ['pækɪdʒ] *n* pacote *m*; (*bulky*) embrulho, fardo; (*also*: **~ deal**) pacote; **package tour** (*Brit*) *n* excursão f organizada

packed lunch [pækt-] (*Brit*) *n* merenda

packet ['pækɪt] *n* pacote *m*; (*of cigarettes*) maço; (*of washing powder etc*) caixa

packing ['pækɪŋ] *n* embalagem *f*; (*act*) empacotamento

pad [pæd] *n* (*of paper*) bloco; (*to prevent friction*) acolchoado; (*inf: home*) casa ▷ *vt* acolchoar, enchumaçar

paddle ['pædl] *n* remo curto; (*US: for table tennis*) raquete *f* ▷ *vt* remar ▷ *vi* patinhar; **paddling pool** (*Brit*) *n* lago de recreação

paddock ['pædək] *n* cercado; (*at race course*) paddock *m*

padlock ['pædlɔk] *n* cadeado

paedophile, (*US*) **pedophile** ['piːdəʊfaɪl] *n* pedófilo(-a)

page [peɪdʒ] *n* página; (*also*: **~ boy**) mensageiro ▷ *vt* mandar chamar

pager ['peɪdʒər] *n* bip *m*

paid [peɪd] *pt*, *pp of* **pay** ▷ *adj* (*work*) remunerado; (*holiday*) pago; (*official*) assalariado; **to put ~ to** (*Brit*) acabar com

pain [peɪn] *n* dor *f*; **to be in ~** sofrer *or* sentir dor; **to take ~s to do sth** dar-se ao trabalho de fazer algo; **painful** *adj* doloroso; (*laborious*) penoso; (*unpleasant*) desagradável; **painkiller** *n* analgésico; **painstaking** ['peɪnzteɪkɪŋ] *adj* (*work*) esmerado; (*person*) meticuloso

paint [peɪnt] *n* pintura ▷ *vt* pintar; **paintbrush** *n* (*artist's*) pincel *m*; (*decorator's*) broxa; **painter** *n* pintor(a) *m/f*; **painting** *n* pintura;

(*picture*) tela, quadro

pair [pɛə'] *n* par *m*; **a ~ of scissors** uma tesoura; **a ~ of trousers** uma calça (*BR*), umas calças (*PT*)

pajamas [pɪ'dʒɑːməz] (*US*) *npl* pijama *m*

Pakistan [pɑːkɪ'stɑːn] *n* Paquistão *m*; **Pakistani** *adj, n* paquistanês(-esa) *m/f*

pal [pæl] (*inf*) *n* camarada *m/f*, colega *m/f*

palace ['pæləs] *n* palácio

pale [peɪl] *adj* pálido; (*colour*) claro; (*light*) fraco ▷ *vi* empalidecer ▷ *n*: **to be beyond the ~** passar dos limites

Palestine ['pælɪstaɪn] *n* Palestina; **Palestinian** [pælɪs'tɪnɪən] *adj, n* palestino(-a)

palm [pɑːm] *n* (*hand, leaf*) palma; (*also*: **~ tree**) palmeira ▷ *vt*: **to ~ sth off on sb** (*inf*) impingir algo a alguém

pamper ['pæmpə'] *vt* paparicar, mimar

pamphlet ['pæmflət] *n* panfleto

pan [pæn] *n* (*also*: **sauce~**) panela (*BR*), caçarola (*PT*); (*also*: **frying ~**) frigideira

Panama ['pænəmɑː] *n* Panamá *m*

pancake ['pænkeɪk] *n* panqueca

panda ['pændə] *n* panda *m/f*

pane [peɪn] *n* vidraça, vidro

panel ['pænl] *n* (*of wood, Radio, TV*) painel *m*

panic ['pænɪk] *n* pânico ▷ *vi* entrar em pânico

pansy ['pænzɪ] *n* (*Bot*) amor-perfeito; (*inf: pej*) bicha (*BR*), maricas *m* (*PT*)

pant [pænt] *vi* arquejar, ofegar

panther ['pænθə'] *n* pantera

panties ['pæntɪz] *npl* calcinha (*BR*), cuecas *fpl* (*PT*)

pantomime ['pæntəmaɪm] (*Brit*) *n* pantomima; *ver nota*

⊜ **PANTOMIME**
⊜
⊜ Uma **pantomime**, também
⊜ chamada simplesmente de
⊜ *panto*, é um gênero de comédia
⊜ em que o personagem principal
⊜ em geral é um rapaz e na qual há
⊜ sempre uma **dame**, isto é, uma
⊜ mulher idosa representada por
⊜ um homem, e um vilão. Na maior
⊜ parte das vezes, a história é
⊜ baseada em um conto de fadas,
⊜ como "A gata borralheira" ou "O
⊜ gato de botas", e a plateia é
⊜ encorajada a participar
⊜ prevenindo os heróis dos perigos
⊜ que estão por vir. Esse tipo de
⊜ espetáculo, voltado sobretudo
⊜ para as crianças, visa também ao
⊜ público adulto por meio de
⊜ diversas brincadeiras que fazem
⊜ alusão aos fatos atuais.

pants [pænts] *npl* (*Brit: underwear: woman's*) calcinha (*BR*), cuecas *fpl* (*PT*); (: *man's*) cueca (*BR*), cuecas (*PT*); (*US: trousers*) calça (*BR*), calças *fpl* (*PT*)

paper ['peɪpə'] *n* papel *m*; (*also*: **news~**) jornal *m*; (*also*: **wall~**) papel de parede; (*study, article*) artigo, dissertação *f*; (*exam*) exame *m*, prova ▷ *adj* de papel ▷ *vt* (*room*) revestir (com papel de parede); **papers** *npl* (*also*: **identity ~s**) documentos *mpl*; **paperback** *n* livro de capa mole; **paper bag** *n* saco de papel; **paper clip** *n* clipe *m*; **paperwork** *n* trabalho burocrático; (*pej*) papelada

par [pɑː'] *n* paridade *f*, igualdade *f*;

(*Golf*) média *f*; **on a ~ with** em pé de igualdade com

parachute ['pærəʃuːt] *n* para-quedas *m inv*

parade [pə'reɪd] *n* desfile *m* ▷ *vt* (*show off*) exibir ▷ *vi* (*Mil*) passar revista

paradise ['pærədaɪs] *n* paraíso

paraffin ['pærəfɪn] (*Brit*) *n*: **~ (oil)** querosene *m*

paragraph ['pærəgrɑːf] *n* parágrafo

Paraguay ['pærəgwaɪ] *n* Paraguai *m*

parallel ['pærəlɛl] *adj* (*lines etc*) paralelo; (*fig*) correspondente ▷ *n* paralela; correspondência

paralysis [pə'rælɪsɪs] (*pl* **paralyses**) *n* paralisia

paranoid ['pærənɔɪd] *adj* paranoico

parcel ['pɑːsl] *n* pacote *m* ▷ *vt* (*also:* **~ up**) embrulhar, empacotar

pardon ['pɑːdn] *n* (*Law*) indulto ▷ *vt* perdoar; **~ me!, I beg your ~** (*apologizing*) desculpe(-me); (**I beg your) ~?** (*Brit*), **~ me?** (*US*) (*not hearing*) como?, como disse?

parent ['pɛərənt] *n* (*father*) pai *m*; (*mother*) mãe *f*; **parents** *npl* (*mother and father*) pais *mpl*

Paris ['pærɪs] *n* Paris

parish ['pærɪʃ] *n* paróquia, freguesia

park [pɑːk] *n* parque *m* ▷ *vt, vi* estacionar

parking ['pɑːkɪŋ] *n* estacionamento; **"no ~"** "estacionamento proibido"; **parking lot** (*US*) *n* (parque *m* de) estacionamento; **parking meter** *n* parquímetro; **parking ticket** *n* multa por estacionamento proibido

parliament ['pɑːləmənt] (*Brit*) *n* parlamento

parole [pə'rəul] *n*: **on ~** em liberdade condicional, sob promessa

parrot ['pærət] *n* papagaio

parsley ['pɑːslɪ] *n* salsa

parsnip ['pɑːsnɪp] *n* cherivia, pastinaga

parson ['pɑːsn] *n* padre *m*, clérigo; (*in Church of England*) pastor *m*

part [pɑːt] *n* parte *f*; (*of machine*) peça; (*Theatre etc*) papel *m*; (*of serial*) capítulo; (*US: in hair*) risca, repartido ▷ *adv* = **partly** ▷ *vt* dividir; (*hair*) repartir ▷ *vi* (*people*) separar-se; (*crowd*) dispersar-se; **to take ~ in** participar de, tomar parte em; **to take sb's ~** defender alguém; **for my ~** pela minha parte; **for the most ~** na maior parte; **to take sth in good ~** não se ofender com algo **part with** *vt fus* ceder, entregar; (*money*) pagar

partial ['pɑːʃl] *adj* parcial; **to be ~ to** gostar de, ser apreciador(a) de

participate [pɑː'tɪsɪpeɪt] *vi*: **to ~ in** participar de

particle ['pɑːtɪkl] *n* partícula; (*of dust*) grão *m*

particular [pə'tɪkjulər] *adj* (*special*) especial; (*specific*) específico; (*fussy*) exigente, minucioso; **in ~** em particular; **particularly** *adv* em particular, especialmente; **particulars** *npl* detalhes *mpl*; (*personal details*) dados *mpl* pessoais

parting ['pɑːtɪŋ] *n* (*act*) separação *f*; (*farewell*) despedida; (*Brit: in hair*) risca, repartido ▷ *adj* de despedida; **~ shot** (*fig*) flecha de parto

partition [pɑː'tɪʃən] *n* (*Pol*) divisão *f*; (*wall*) tabique *m*, divisória

partly ['pɑːtlɪ] *adv* em parte

partner ['pɑːtnə^r] n (Comm) sócio(-a); (Sport) parceiro(-a); (at dance) par m; (spouse) cônjuge m/f; **partnership** n associação f, parceria; (Comm) sociedade f

partridge ['pɑːtrɪdʒ] n perdiz f

part-time adj, adv de meio expediente

party ['pɑːtɪ] n (Pol) partido; (celebration) festa; (group) grupo; (Law) parte f interessada, litigante m/f ▷ cpd (Pol) do partido, partidário

pass [pɑːs] vt passar; (exam) passar em; (place) passar por; (overtake, surpass) ultrapassar; (approve) aprovar ▷ vi passar; (Sch) ser aprovado, passar ▷ n (permit) passe m; (membership card) carteira; (in mountains) desfiladeiro; (Sport) passe m; (Sch): **to get a ~ in** ser aprovado em; **to make a ~ at sb** tomar liberdade com alguém **pass away** vi falecer **pass by** vi passar ▷ vt passar por cima de **pass for** vt fus passar por **pass on** vt (news, illness) transmitir; (object) passar para **pass out** vi desmaiar **pass up** vt deixar passar; **passable** adj (road) transitável; (work) aceitável

passage ['pæsɪdʒ] n (also: **~way**: indoors) corredor m; (: outdoors) passagem f; (Anat) via; (act of passing) trânsito; (in book) trecho; (by boat) travessia; (Mechanics, Med) conduto

passenger ['pæsɪndʒə^r] n passageiro(-a)

passer-by ['pɑːsə^r-] (pl **passers-by**) n transeunte m/f

passion ['pæʃən] n paixão f; **passionate** adj apaixonado; **passion fruit** n maracujá m

passive ['pæsɪv] adj passivo

passport ['pɑːspɔːt] n passaporte m

password ['pɑːswəːd] n senha

past [pɑːst] prep (in front of) por; (beyond) mais além de; (later than) depois de ▷ adj passado; (president etc) ex-, anterior ▷ n passado; **he's ~ forty** ele tem mais de quarenta anos; **ten/quarter ~ four** quatro e dez/quinze; **for the ~ few/3 days** nos últimos/3 dias

pasta ['pæstə] n massa

paste [peɪst] n pasta; (glue) grude m, cola ▷ vt grudar; **tomato ~** massa de tomate

pasteurized ['pæstəraɪzd] adj pasteurizado

pastime ['pɑːstaɪm] n passatempo

pastry ['peɪstrɪ] n massa; (cake) bolo

pasture ['pɑːstʃə^r] n pasto

pasty [n 'pæstɪ, adj 'peɪstɪ] n empadão m de carne ▷ adj (complexion) pálido

pat [pæt] vt dar palmadinhas em; (dog etc) fazer festa em

patch [pætʃ] n retalho; (eye patch) tapa-olho m; (area) área pequena; (mend) remendo ▷ vt remendar; **(to go through) a bad ~** (passar por) um mau pedaço **patch up** vt consertar provisoriamente; (quarrel) resolver; **patchy** adj (colour) desigual; (information) incompleto

pâté ['pæteɪ] n patê m

patent ['peɪtnt] n patente f ▷ vt patentear ▷ adj patente, evidente

paternal [pə'təːnl] adj paternal; (relation) paterno

path [pɑːθ] n caminho; (trail, track) trilha, senda; (trajectory) trajetória

pathetic [pə'θetɪk] adj (pitiful)

patético, digno de pena; (*very bad*) péssimo

pathway ['pɑːθweɪ] n caminho, trilha

patience ['peɪʃns] n paciência

patient ['peɪʃnt] adj, n paciente m/f

patio ['pætɪəu] n pátio

patrol [pə'trəul] n patrulha ▷ vt patrulhar; **patrol car** n carro de patrulha

patron ['peɪtrən] n (*customer*) cliente m/f, freguês(-esa) m/f; (*of charity*) benfeitor(a) m/f; **~ of the arts** mecenas m

pattern ['pætən] n (*Sewing*) molde m; (*design*) desenho

pause [pɔːz] n pausa ▷ vi fazer uma pausa

pave [peɪv] vt pavimentar; **to ~ the way for** preparar o terreno para

pavement ['peɪvmənt] n (*Brit*) calçada (*BR*), passeio (*PT*)

pavilion [pə'vɪlɪən] n (*Sport*) barraca

paving ['peɪvɪŋ] n pavimento, calçamento

paw [pɔː] n pata; (*of cat*) garra

pawn [pɔːn] n (*Chess*) peão m; (*fig*) títere m ▷ vt empenhar; **pawnbroker** n agiota m/f

pay [peɪ] (*pt, pp* **paid**) n salário; (*of manual worker*) paga ▷ vt pagar; (*debt*) liquidar, saldar; (*visit*) fazer ▷ vi valer a pena, render; **to ~ attention (to)** prestar atenção (a); **to ~ one's respects to sb** fazer uma visita de cortesia a alguém

pay back vt (*money*) devolver; (*person*) pagar **pay for** vt fus pagar a; (*fig*) recompensar **pay in** vt depositar **pay off** vt (*debts*) saldar, liquidar; (*creditor*) pagar, reembolsar ▷ vi (*plan, patience*) valer a pena **pay up** vt pagar;

payable adj pagável; (*cheque*): **payable to** nominal em favor de; **payment** n pagamento; **monthly payment** pagamento mensal; **pay packet** (*Brit*) n envelope m de pagamento; **pay phone** n telefone m público; **payroll** n folha de pagamento; **pay television** n televisão f por assinatura

PC n abbr (= *personal computer*) PC m

PDA n abbr (= *personal digital assistant*) PDA m (*assistente digital pessoal*)

pea [piː] n ervilha

peace [piːs] n paz f; (*calm*) tranquilidade f, quietude f; **peaceful** adj (*person*) tranquilo, pacífico; (*place, time*) tranquilo, sossegado

peach [piːtʃ] n pêssego

peacock ['piːkɔk] n pavão m

peak [piːk] n (*of mountain: top*) cume m; (*of cap*) pala, viseira; (*fig*) apogeu m

peanut ['piːnʌt] n amendoim m; **peanut butter** n manteiga de amendoim

pear [pɛəʳ] n pera

pearl [pəːl] n pérola

peasant ['pɛznt] n camponês(-esa) m/f

peat [piːt] n turfa

pebble ['pɛbl] n seixo, calhau m

peck [pɛk] vt (*also*: **~ at**) bicar, dar bicadas em ▷ n bicada; (*kiss*) beijoca; **peckish** (*Brit: inf*) adj: **I feel peckish** estou a fim de comer alguma coisa

peculiar [pɪ'kjuːlɪəʳ] adj (*strange*) estranho, esquisito; (*belonging to*): **~ to** próprio de

pedal ['pɛdl] n pedal m ▷ vi pedalar

pedestrian [pɪ'dɛstrɪən] n pedestre m/f (*BR*), peão m (*PT*) ▷ adj

P

(fig) prosaico; **pedestrian crossing** *(Brit)* n passagem *f* para pedestres *(BR)*, passadeira *(PT)*

pedigree ['pɛdɪgri:] n raça; *(fig)* genealogia ▷ *cpd (animal)* de raça

pedophile ['pi:dəufaɪl] *(US)* n = **paedophile**

pee [pi:] *(inf)* vi fazer xixi, mijar

peek [pi:k] vi: **to ~ at** espiar, espreitar

peel [pi:l] n casca ▷ vt descascar ▷ vi *(paint, skin)* descascar; *(wallpaper)* desprender-se

peep [pi:p] n *(Brit: look)* espiadela; *(sound)* pio ▷ vi espreitar **peep out** *(Brit)* vi mostrar-se, surgir

peer [pɪəʳ] vi: **to ~ at** perscrutar, fitar ▷ n *(noble)* par *m/f*; *(equal)* igual *m/f*; *(contemporary)* contemporâneo(-a)

peg [pɛg] n *(for coat etc)* cabide *m*; *(Brit: also:* **clothes ~**) pregador *m*

pelican ['pɛlɪkən] n pelicano

pelt [pɛlt] vt: **to ~ sb with sth** atirar algo em alguém ▷ vi *(rain: also:* ~ **down**) chover a cântaros; *(inf: run)* correr ▷ n pele *f* (não curtida)

pelvis ['pɛlvɪs] n pelvis *f*, bacia

pen [pɛn] n caneta; *(for sheep etc)* redil *m*, cercado

penalty ['pɛnltɪ] n pena, penalidade *f*; *(fine)* multa; *(Sport)* punição *f*

pence [pɛns] *(Brit)* npl of **penny**

pencil ['pɛnsl] n lápis *m*; **pencil case** n lapiseira, porta-lápis *m inv*; **pencil sharpener** n apontador *m* (de lápis) *(BR)*, apara-lápis *m inv* *(PT)*

pendant ['pɛndnt] n pingente *m*

pending ['pɛndɪŋ] prep até ▷ adj pendente

penetrate ['pɛnɪtreɪt] vt penetrar

penfriend ['pɛnfrɛnd] *(Brit)* n amigo(-a) por correspondência

penguin ['pɛŋgwɪn] n pinguim *m*

peninsula [pə'nɪnsjulə] n península

penis ['pi:nɪs] n pênis *m*

penitentiary [pɛnɪ'tɛnʃərɪ] *(US)* n penitenciária, presídio

penknife ['pɛnnaɪf] *irreg* n canivete *m*

penniless ['pɛnɪlɪs] adj sem dinheiro, sem um tostão

penny ['pɛnɪ] *(pl* **pennies** or *(Brit)* **pence**) n pêni *m*; *(US)* cêntimo

penpal ['pɛnpæl] n amigo(-a) por correspondência

pension ['pɛnʃən] n pensão *f*; *(old-age pension)* aposentadoria; **pensioner** *(Brit)* n aposentado(-a) *(BR)*, reformado(-a) *(PT)*

Pentagon ['pɛntəgən] n: **the ~** o Pentágono; *ver nota*

- **PENTAGON**
-
- O Pentágono **Pentagon** é o
- nome dado aos escritórios do
- Ministério da Defesa americano,
- localizados em Arlington, no
- estado da Virgínia, por causa da
- forma pentagonal do edifício
- onde se encontram. Por
- extensão, o termo é utilizado
- também para se referir ao
- ministério.

penthouse ['pɛnthaus] n cobertura

people ['pi:pl] npl gente *f*, pessoas *fpl*; *(inhabitants)* habitantes *m/fpl*; *(citizens)* povo; *(Pol)*: **the ~** o povo ▷ n *(nation, race)* povo; **several ~ came** vieram várias pessoas; **~ say that ...** dizem que ...

pepper ['pɛpəʳ] n pimenta; *(vegetable)* pimentão *m* ▷ vt apimentar; (*fig*): **to ~ with** salpicar de; **peppermint** n (*sweet*) bala de hortelã

per [pəːˀ] *prep* por

perceive [pə'siːv] *vt* perceber; (*notice*) notar; (*realize*) compreender

per cent n por cento

percentage [pə'sɛntɪdʒ] n porcentagem f, percentagem f

perch [pəːtʃ] (*pl* **perches**) n (*for bird*) poleiro; (*fish*) perca ▷ *vi*: **to ~ (on)** (*bird*) empoleirar-se (em); (*person*) encarapitar-se (em)

perfect [*adj, n* 'pəːfɪkt, *vt* pə'fɛkt] *adj* perfeito; (*utter*) completo ▷ *n* (*also*: **~ tense**) perfeito ▷ *vt* aperfeiçoar; **perfectly** *adv* perfeitamente

perform [pə'fɔːm] *vt* (*carry out*) realizar, fazer; (*piece of music*) interpretar ▷ *vi* (*well, badly*) interpretar; **performance** n desempenho; (*of play, by artist*) atuação f; (*of car*) performance f; **performer** n (*actor*) artista m/f, ator/atriz m/f; (*Mus*) intérprete m/f

perfume ['pəːfjuːm] n perfume m

perhaps [pə'hæps] *adv* talvez

perimeter [pə'rɪmɪtəˀ] n perímetro

period ['pɪərɪəd] n período; (*Sch*) aula; (*full stop*) ponto final; (*Med*) menstruação f, regra ▷ *adj* (*costume, furniture*) da época

perish ['pɛrɪʃ] *vi* perecer; (*decay*) deteriorar-se

perjury ['pəːdʒərɪ] n (*Law*) perjúrio, falso testemunho

perk [pəːk] (*inf*) n mordomia, regalia **perk up** *vi* (*cheer up*) animar-se

perm [pəːm] n permanente f

permanent ['pəːmənənt] *adj* permanente

permission [pə'mɪʃən] n permissão f; (*authorization*) autorização f

permit [*n* 'pəːmɪt, *vt* pə'mɪt] n licença; (*to enter*) passe m ▷ *vt* permitir; (*authorize*) autorizar

perplex [pə'plɛks] *vt* deixar perplexo

persecute ['pəːsɪkjuːt] *vt* perseguir

persevere [pəːsɪ'vɪəˀ] *vi* perseverar

Persian ['pəːʃən] *adj* persa ▷ *n* (*Ling*) persa m; **the (~) Gulf** o golfo Pérsico

persist [pə'sɪst] *vi*: **to ~ (in doing sth)** persistir (em fazer algo); **persistent** [pə'sɪstənt] *adj* persistente; (*determined*) teimoso

person ['pəːsn] n pessoa; **in ~** em pessoa; **personal** *adj* pessoal; (*private*) particular; (*visit*) em pessoa, pessoal; **personal assistant** n secretário(-a) particular; **personal computer** n computador m pessoal; **personality** [pəːsə'nælɪtɪ] n personalidade f; **personal organizer** n agenda

personnel [pəːsə'nɛl] n pessoal m

perspective [pə'spɛktɪv] n perspectiva

perspiration [pəːspɪ'reɪʃən] n transpiração f

persuade [pə'sweɪd] *vt*: **to ~ sb to do sth** persuadir alguém a fazer algo

Peru [pə'ruː] n Peru m

pervert [*n* 'pəːvəːt, *vt* pə'vəːt] n pervertido(-a) ▷ *vt* perverter, corromper; (*truth*) distorcer

pessimist ['pɛsɪmɪst] n pessimista m/f; **pessimistic** [pɛsɪ'mɪstɪk] *adj* pessimista

pest [pɛst] n (*animal*) praga; (*fig*) peste f

P

pester ['pɛstə^r] vt incomodar
pet [pɛt] n animal m de estimação
▷ cpd predileto ▷ vt acariciar ▷ vi
(inf) acariciar-se; **teacher's ~**
(favourite) preferido(-a) do
professor
petal ['pɛtl] n pétala
petite [pə'tiːt] adj delicado, mignon
petition [pə'tɪʃən] n petição f; (list
of signatures) abaixo-assinado
petrified ['pɛtrɪfaɪd] adj (fig)
petrificado, paralisado
petrol ['pɛtrəl] (Brit) n gasolina;
two/four-star ~ gasolina comum/
premium
petroleum [pə'trəulɪəm] n
petróleo
petrol: **petrol pump** (Brit) n bomba
de gasolina; **petrol station** (Brit) n
posto (BR) or bomba (PT) de
gasolina; **petrol tank** (Brit) n
tanque m de gasolina
petticoat ['pɛtɪkəut] n anágua
petty ['pɛtɪ] adj (mean) mesquinho;
(unimportant) insignificante
pew [pjuː] n banco (de igreja)
pewter ['pjuːtə^r] n peltre m
phantom ['fæntəm] n fantasma m
pharmacy ['fɑːməsɪ] n farmácia
phase [feɪz] n fase f ▷ vt: **to ~ in/
out** introduzir/retirar por etapas
PhD n abbr = **Doctor of Philosophy**
pheasant ['fɛznt] n faisão m
phenomenon [fə'nɔmɪnən] (pl
phenomena) n fenômeno
philosophical [fɪlə'sɔfɪkl] adj
filosófico; (fig) calmo, sereno
philosophy [fɪ'lɔsəfɪ] n filosofia
phishing ['fɪʃɪŋ] n phishing m; **~
attack** golpe m de phishing
phobia ['fəubjə] n fobia
phone [fəun] n telefone m ▷ vt
telefonar para, ligar para; **to be on
the ~** ter telefone; (be calling) estar

no telefone **phone back** vt, vi ligar
de volta **phone up** vt telefonar
para ▷ vi telefonar; **phone book** n
lista telefônica; **phone box** (Brit) n
cabine f telefônica; **phone call** n
telefonema m, ligação f; **phone
card** n cartão m telefônico; **phone
number** n número de telefone
phonetics [fə'nɛtɪks] n fonética
phoney ['fəunɪ] adj falso; (person)
fingido
photo ['fəutəu] n foto f
photo... ['fəutəu] prefix foto...;
photocopier n fotocopiadora f;
photocopy n fotocópia, xerox® m
▷ vt fotocopiar, xerocar
photograph ['fəutəgrɑːf] n
fotografia ▷ vt fotografar;
photographer [fə'tɔgrəfə^r] n
fotógrafo(-a); **photography**
[fə'tɔgrəfɪ] n fotografia
phrase [freɪz] n frase f ▷ vt
expressar; **phrase book** n livro de
expressões idiomáticas (para
turistas)
physical ['fɪzɪkl] adj físico
physician [fɪ'zɪʃən] n médico(-a)
physics ['fɪzɪks] n física
physiotherapy [fɪzɪəu'θɛrəpɪ] n
fisioterapia
physique [fɪ'ziːk] n físico
pianist ['piːənɪst] n pianista m/f
piano [pɪ'ænəu] n piano
pick [pɪk] n (tool: also: **~axe**)
picareta ▷ vt (select) escolher,
selecionar; (gather) colher;
(remove) tirar; (lock) forçar; **take
your ~** escolha o que quiser; **the ~
of** o melhor de; **to ~ one's nose**
colocar o dedo no nariz; **to ~ one's
teeth** palitar os dentes; **to ~ a
quarrel** or **a fight with sb** comprar
uma briga com alguém **pick at** vt
fus (food) beliscar **pick on** vt fus

(*person: criticize*) criticar; (: *treat badly*) azucrinar, aporrinhar **pick out** vt escolher; (*distinguish*) distinguir **pick up** vi (*improve*) melhorar ▷ vt (*from floor, Aut*) apanhar; (*Police*) prender; (*collect*) buscar; (*for sexual encounter*) paquerar; (*learn*) aprender; (*Radio, TV, Tel*) pegar; **to ~ up speed** acelerar; **to ~ o.s. up** levantar-se **pickle** ['pɪkl] n (*also*: **~s**: *as condiment*) picles mpl; (*fig: mess*) apuro ▷ vt (*in vinegar*) conservar em vinagre; (*in salt*) conservar em sal e água

pickpocket ['pɪkpɔkɪt] n batedor(a) m/f de carteira (BR), carteirista m/f (PT)

picnic ['pɪknɪk] n piquenique m

picture ['pɪktʃə^r] n quadro; (*painting*) pintura; (*drawing*) desenho; (*etching*) água-forte f; (*photograph*) foto(grafia) f; (*TV*) imagem f; (*film*) filme m; (*fig: description*) descrição f; (: *situation*) conjuntura ▷ vt imaginar-se; **the pictures** npl (*Brit: inf*) o cinema; **picture messaging** n serviço de mensagens multimídia

pie [paɪ] n (*vegetable*) pastelão m; (*fruit*) torta; (*meat*) empadão m

piece [piːs] n pedaço; (*portion*) fatia; (*item*): **a ~ of clothing/ furniture/advice** uma roupa/um móvel/um conselho ▷ vt: **to ~ together** juntar; **to take to ~s** desmontar

pie chart n gráfico de setores

pier [pɪə^r] n cais m; (*jetty*) embarcadouro, molhe f

pierce [pɪəs] vt furar, perfurar

pig [pɪg] n porco; (*fig*) porcalhão(-lhona) m/f; (*pej: unkind person*) grosseiro(-a); (: *greedy person*) ganancioso(-a)

pigeon ['pɪdʒən] n pombo

piggy bank ['pɪgɪ-] n cofre em forma de porquinho

pigsty ['pɪgstaɪ] n chiqueiro

pigtail ['pɪgteɪl] n rabo-de-cavalo, trança

pike [paɪk] (*pl inv or* **pikes**) n (*fish*) lúcio

pilchard ['pɪltʃəd] n sardinha

pile [paɪl] n (*heap*) monte m; (*of carpet*) pelo; (*of cloth*) lado felpudo ▷ vt (*also*: **~ up**) empilhar ▷ vi (*also*: **~ up**: *objects*) empilhar-se; (: *problems, work*) acumular-se **pile into** vt fus (*car*) apinhar-se

piles [paɪlz] npl hemorróidas fpl

pile-up n (*Aut*) engavetamento

pilgrim ['pɪlgrɪm] n peregrino(-a)

pill [pɪl] n pílula; **the ~** a pílula

pillar ['pɪlə^r] n pilar m; **pillar box** (*Brit*) n caixa coletora (do correio) (BR), marco do correio (PT)

pillow ['pɪləu] n travesseiro (BR), almofada (PT); **pillowcase** n fronha

pilot ['paɪlət] n piloto(-a) ▷ cpd (*scheme etc*) piloto inv ▷ vt pilotar; **pilot light** n piloto

pimple ['pɪmpl] n espinha

PIN n abbr (= *personal identification number*) senha

pin [pɪn] n alfinete m ▷ vt alfinetar; **~s and needles** comichão f, sensação f de formigamento; **to ~ sth on sb** (*fig*) culpar alguém de algo **pin down** vt (*fig*): **to ~ sb down** conseguir que alguém se defina or tome atitude

pinafore ['pɪnəfɔː^r] n (*also*: **~ dress**) avental m

pinch [pɪntʃ] n (*of salt etc*) pitada ▷ vt beliscar; (*inf: steal*) afanar; **at a ~** em último caso

p

pine [paɪn] n pinho ▷ vi: **to ~ for** ansiar por **pine away** vi consumir-se, definhar

pineapple ['paɪnæpl] n abacaxi m (BR), ananás m (PT)

pink [pɪŋk] adj cor de rosa inv ▷ n (colour) cor f de rosa; (Bot) cravo, cravina

pinpoint ['pɪnpɔɪnt] vt (discover) descobrir; (explain) identificar; (locate) localizar com precisão

pint [paɪnt] n quartilho (Brit = 568cc, US = 473cc)

pioneer [paɪə'nɪər] n pioneiro(-a)

pious ['paɪəs] adj pio, devoto

pip [pɪp] n (seed) caroço, semente f; **the pips** npl (Brit: time signal on radio) ≈ o toque de seis segundos

pipe [paɪp] n cano; (for smoking) cachimbo ▷ vt canalizar, encanar; **pipes** npl (also: **bag~s**) gaita de foles **pipe down** (inf) vi calar o bico, meter a viola no saco; **pipeline** n (for oil) oleoduto; (for gas) gaseoduto

pirate ['paɪərət] n pirata m ▷ vt piratear

Pisces ['paɪsiːz] n Pisces m, Peixes mpl

piss [pɪs] (inf!) vi mijar; **pissed** (inf!) adj (drunk) bêbado, de porre

pistol ['pɪstl] n pistola

piston ['pɪstən] n pistão m, êmbolo

pit [pɪt] n cova, fossa; (quarry, hole in surface of sth) buraco; (also: **coal ~**) mina de carvão ▷ vt: **to ~ one's wits against sb** competir em conhecimento or inteligência contra alguém; **pits** npl (Aut) box m

pitch [pɪtʃ] n (Mus) tom m; (fig: degree) intensidade f; (Brit: Sport) campo; (tar) piche m, breu m ▷ vt (throw) arremessar, lançar; (tent) armar ▷ vi (fall forwards) cair (para

frente); **pitch-black** adj escuro como o breu

pitfall ['pɪtfɔːl] n perigo (imprevisto), armadilha

pitiful ['pɪtɪful] adj comovente, tocante

pity ['pɪtɪ] n compaixão f, piedade f ▷ vt ter pena de, compadecer-se de

pixel ['pɪksl] n pixel m

pizza ['piːtsə] n pizza

placard ['plækɑːd] n placar m; (in march etc) cartaz m

place [pleɪs] n lugar m; (rank, position) posição f; (post) posto; (role) papel m; (home): **at/to his ~** na/para a casa dele ▷ vt pôr, colocar; (identify) identificar, situar; **to take ~** realizar-se; (occur) ocorrer; **out of ~** (not suitable) fora de lugar, deslocado; **in the first ~** em primeiro lugar; **to change ~s with sb** trocar de lugar com alguém, encomendar algo a alguém; **to be ~d** (in race, exam) classificar-se

plague [pleɪg] n (Med) peste f; (fig) praga ▷ vt atormentar, importunar

plaice [pleɪs] n inv solha

plain [pleɪn] adj (unpatterned) liso; (clear) claro, evidente; (simple) simples inv, despretensioso; (not handsome) sem atrativos ▷ adv claramente, com franqueza ▷ n planície f, campina; **plain chocolate** n chocolate m amargo; **plainly** adv claramente, obviamente; (hear, see) facilmente; (state) francamente

plaintiff ['pleɪntɪf] n querelante m/f, queixoso(-a)

plait [plæt] n trança, dobra

plan [plæn] n plano; (scheme) projeto; (schedule) programa m ▷ vt

planejar (BR), planear (PT) ▷ vi
fazer planos; **to ~ to do** pretender
fazer
plane [pleɪn] n (Aviat) avião m;
(also: **~ tree**) plátano; (fig: level)
nivel m; (tool) plaina; (Math) plano
planet ['plænɪt] n planeta m
plank [plæŋk] n tábua
planning ['plænɪŋ] n
planejamento (BR), planeamento
(PT); **family ~** planejamento or
planeamento familiar
plant [plɑːnt] n planta; (machinery)
maquinaria; (factory) usina, fábrica
▷ vt plantar; (field) semear; (bomb)
colocar, pôr
plaster ['plɑːstər] n (for walls)
reboco; (also: **~ of Paris**) gesso;
(Brit: also: **sticking ~**) esparadrapo,
band-aid m ▷ vt rebocar; (cover):
to ~ with encher or cobrir de
plastic ['plæstɪk] n plástico ▷ adj
de plástico; **plastic bag** n sacola
de plástico; **plastic surgery** n
cirurgia plástica
plate [pleɪt] n prato; (Phot, on door,
dental) chapa; (in book) gravura;
gold/silver ~ placa de ouro/prata
plateau ['plætəʊ] n (pl **plateaus** or
plateaux) n planalto
platform ['plætfɔːm] n (Rail)
plataforma (BR), cais m (PT); (at
meeting) tribuna; (raised structure:
for landing etc) plataforma; (Brit: of
bus) plataforma; (Pol) programa m
partidário
platinum ['plætɪnəm] n platina
plausible ['plɔːzɪbl] adj plausível;
(person) convincente
play [pleɪ] n (Theatre) obra, peça
▷ vt jogar; (team, opponent) jogar
contra; (instrument, music, record)
tocar; (role) fazer o papel de ▷ vi
(music) tocar; (frolic) brincar; **to ~**

safe não se arriscar, não correr
riscos **play down** vt minimizar
play up vi (person) dar trabalho;
(TV, car) estar com defeito; **player**
n jogador(a) m/f; (Theatre) ator/
atriz m/f; (Mus) músico(-a);
playful adj brincalhão(-lhona);
playground n (in park) playground
m; (in school) pátio de recreio;
playgroup n espécie de jardim de
infância; **playing card** n carta de
baralho; **playing field** n campo de
esportes (BR) or jogos (PT);
playtime n (Sch) recreio;
playwright n dramaturgo(-a)
plea [pliː] n (request) apelo, petição
f; (Law) defesa
plead [pliːd] vt (Law) defender,
advogar; (give as excuse) alegar ▷ vi
(Law) declarar-se; (beg): **to ~ with**
sb suplicar or rogar a alguém
pleasant ['plɛznt] adj agradável;
(person) simpático
please [pliːz] excl por favor ▷ vt
agradar a, dar prazer a ▷ vi
agradar, dar prazer; (think fit): **do**
as you ~ faça o que or como quiser;
~ yourself! (inf) como você quiser!,
você que sabe!; **pleased** adj
(happy): **pleased (with)** satisfeito
(com); **pleased to meet you**
prazer (em conhecê-lo)
pleasure ['plɛʒər] n prazer m; **"it's a**
~" "não tem de quê"
pleat [pliːt] n prega
pledge [plɛdʒ] n (promise) promessa
▷ vt prometer; **to ~ support for sb**
empenhar-se a apoiar alguém
plentiful ['plɛntɪful] adj
abundante
plenty ['plɛntɪ] n: **~ of** (food, money)
bastante; (jobs, people) muitos(-as)
pliers ['plaɪəz] npl alicate m
plod [plɔd] vi caminhar

pesadamente; (*fig*) trabalhar laboriosamente

plonk [plɔŋk] (*inf*) *n* (*Brit: wine*) zurrapa ▷ *vt*: **to ~ sth down** deixar cair algo (pesadamente)

plot [plɔt] *n* (*scheme*) conspiração *f*, complô *m*; (*of story, play*) enredo, trama; (*of land*) lote *m* ▷ *vt* (*conspire*) tramar, planejar (*BR*), planear (*PT*); (*Aviat, Naut, Math*) plotar ▷ *vi* conspirar; **a vegetable ~** (*Brit*) uma horta

plough [plau], (*US*) **plow** *n* arado ▷ *vt* arar; **to ~ money into** investir dinheiro em **plough through** *vt fus* abrir caminho por; **ploughman's lunch** (*Brit*) *n* lanche de pão, queijo e picles

ploy [plɔɪ] *n* estratagema *m*

pls *abbr* (= *please*) por favor

pluck [plʌk] *vt* (*fruit*) colher; (*musical instrument*) dedilhar; (*bird*) depenar ▷ *n* coragem *f*, puxão *m*; **to ~ one's eyebrows** fazer as sobrancelhas; **to ~ up courage** criar coragem

plug [plʌg] *n* (*Elec*) tomada (*BR*), ficha (*PT*); (*in sink*) tampa; (*Aut: also:* **spark(ing) ~**) vela (de ignição) ▷ *vt* (*hole*) tapar; (*inf: advertise*) fazer propaganda de **plug in** *vt* (*Elec*) ligar

plum [plʌm] *n* (*fruit*) ameixa ▷ *cpd* (*inf*): **a ~ job** um emprego joia

plumber ['plʌməʳ] *n* bombeiro(-a) (*BR*), encanador(a) *m/f* (*BR*), canalizador(a) *m/f* (*PT*)

plumbing ['plʌmɪŋ] *n* (*trade*) ofício de encanador; (*piping*) encanamento

plummet ['plʌmɪt] *vi*: **to ~ (down)** (*bird, aircraft*) cair rapidamente; (*price*) baixar rapidamente

plump [plʌmp] *adj* roliço,

rechonchudo ▷ *vi*: **to ~ for** (*inf: choose*) escolher, optar por **plump up** *vt* (*cushion*) afofar

plunge [plʌndʒ] *n* (*dive*) salto; (*fig*) queda ▷ *vt* (*hand, knife*) enfiar, meter ▷ *vi* (*fall, fig*) cair; (*dive*) mergulhar; **to take the ~** topar a parada

plural ['pluərl] *adj* plural ▷ *n* plural *m*

plus [plʌs] *n* (*also:* **~ sign**) sinal *m* de adição ▷ *prep* mais; **ten/twenty ~** dez/vinte e tantos

ply [plaɪ] *n* (*of wool*) fio ▷ *vt* (*a trade*) exercer ▷ *vi* (*ship*) ir e vir; **to ~ sb with drink/questions** bombardear alguém com bebidas/perguntas; **plywood** *n* madeira compensada

p.m. *adv abbr* (= *post meridiem*) da tarde, da noite

PMT *n abbr* (= *premenstrual tension*) TPM *f*, tensão *f* pré-menstrual

pneumatic drill *n* perfuratriz *f*

poach [pəutʃ] *vt* (*cook: fish*) escaldar; (: *eggs*) fazer pochê (*BR*), escalfar (*PT*); (*steal*) furtar ▷ *vi* caçar (*or* pescar) em propriedade alheia

pocket ['pɔkɪt] *n* bolso; (*fig: small area*) pedaço ▷ *vt* meter no bolso; (*steal*) embolsar; **to be out of ~** (*Brit*) ter prejuízo; **pocketbook** (*US*) *n* carteira; **pocket money** *n* dinheiro para despesas miúdas; (*for child*) mesada

pod [pɔd] *n* vagem *f*

podcast [pɔdka:st] *n* podcast *m*; **podcasting** [pɔdka:stɪŋ] *n* podcasting *m*

podiatrist [pɔ'di:ətrɪst] (*US*) *n* pedicuro(-a)

poem ['pəʊɪm] *n* poema *m*

poet ['pəʊɪt] *n* poeta/poetisa *m/f*;

poetic [pəʊ'ɛtɪk] *adj* poético;
poetry ['pəʊɪtrɪ] *n* poesia

point [pɔɪnt] *n* ponto; (*of needle,
knife etc*) ponta; (*purpose*) finalidade
f; (*significant part*) ponto principal;
(*position, place*) lugar *m*, posição *f*;
(*moment*) momento; (*stage*)
estágio; (*Elec: also:* **power ~**)
tomada; (*also:* **decimal ~**): **2 ~ 3
(2.3)** dois vírgula três ▷ *vt* mostrar;
(*gun etc*): **to ~ sth at sb** apontar
algo para alguém ▷ *vi:* **points** *npl*
(*Aut*) platinado, contato; (*Rail*)
agulhas *fpl*; **to ~ at** apontar para;
to be on the ~ of doing sth estar
prestes a *or* a ponto de fazer algo;
to make a ~ of fazer questão de,
insistir em; **to get the ~** perceber;
to miss the ~ compreender mal; **to
come to the ~** ir ao assunto;
there's no ~ (in doing) não há
razão (para fazer); **~ of view** ponto
de vista **point out** *vt* (*in debate etc*)
ressaltar **point to** *vt fus* (*fig*)
indicar; **point-blank** *adv*
categoricamente; (*also:* **at
point-blank range**) à
queima-roupa; **pointed** *adj* (*stick
etc*) pontudo; (*remark*) mordaz;
pointer *n* (*on chart*) indicador *m*;
(*on machine*) ponteiro; (*fig*) dica;
pointless *adj* (*useless*) inútil;
(*senseless*) sem sentido

poison ['pɔɪzn] *n* veneno ▷ *vt*
envenenar; **poisonous** *adj*
venenoso; (*fumes etc*) tóxico

poke [pəʊk] *vt* cutucar; (*put*): **to ~
sth in(to)** enfiar *or* meter algo em
poke about *vi* escarafunchar,
espionar

poker ['pəʊkə'] *n* atiçador *m* (de
brasas); (*Cards*) pôquer *m*

Poland ['pəʊlənd] *n* Polônia

polar ['pəʊlə'] *adj* polar; **polar bear**
n urso polar

Pole [pəʊl] *n* polonês(-esa) *m/f*

pole [pəʊl] *n* vara; (*Geo*) polo;
(*telegraph pole*) poste *m*; (*flagpole*)
mastro; **pole bean** (*US*) *n*
feijão-trepador *m*; **pole vault** *n*
salto com vara

police [pə'li:s] *n* polícia ▷ *vt*
policiar; **police car** *n*
rádio-patrulha *f*; **policeman** *irreg n*
policial *m* (*BR*), polícia *m* (*PT*);
police station *n* delegacia (de
polícia) (*BR*), esquadra (*PT*);
policewoman *irreg n* policial *f*
(feminina) (*BR*), mulher *f* polícia (*PT*)

policy ['pɔlɪsɪ] *n* política; (*also:
insurance ~*) apólice *f*

polio ['pəʊlɪəʊ] *n* polio(mielite) *f*

Polish ['pəʊlɪʃ] *adj* polonês(-esa)
▷ *n* (*Ling*) polonês *m*

polish ['pɔlɪʃ] *n* (*for shoes*) graxa; (*for
floor*) cera (para encerar); (*shine*)
brilho; (*fig*) refinamento, requinte
m ▷ *vt* (*shoes*) engraxar; (*make
shiny*) lustrar, dar brilho a **polish
off** *vt* (*work*) dar os arremates a;
(*food*) raspar

polite [pə'laɪt] *adj* educado;
politeness *n* gentileza, cortesia

political [pə'lɪtɪkl] *adj* político

politician [pɔlɪ'tɪʃən] *n* político(-a)

politics ['pɔlɪtɪks] *n, npl* política

poll [pəʊl] *n* (*votes*) votação *f*; (*also:
opinion ~*) pesquisa, sondagem *f*
▷ *vt* (*votes*) receber, obter

pollen ['pɔlən] *n* pólen *m*

pollute [pə'lu:t] *vt* poluir;
pollution *n* poluição *f*

polyester [pɔlɪ'ɛstə'] *n* poliéster *m*

polystyrene [pɔlɪ'staɪri:n] *n*
isopor® *m*

polythene ['pɔlɪθi:n] *n* politeno

pomegranate ['pɔmɪgrænɪt] *n*
romã *f*

p

pond [pɔnd] n (natural) lago pequeno; (artificial) tanque m

ponder ['pɔndəʳ] vt, vi ponderar, meditar (sobre)

pony ['pəunɪ] n pônei m; **ponytail** n rabo-de-cavalo; **pony trekking** (Brit) n excursão f em pônei

poodle ['puːdl] n cão-d'água m

pool [puːl] n (puddle) poça, charco; (pond) lago; (also: **swimming ~**) piscina; (fig: of light) feixe m; (: of liquid) poça; (Sport) sinuca ▷ vt juntar; **pools** npl (football pools) loteria esportiva (BR), totobola (PT); **typing** (Brit) or **secretary** (US) ~ seção f de datilografia

poor [puəʳ] adj pobre; (bad) inferior, mau ▷ npl: **the ~** os pobres; **~ in** (resources etc) deficiente em; **poorly** adj adoentado, indisposto ▷ adv mal

pop [pɔp] n (sound) estalo, estouro; (Mus) pop m; (US: inf: father) papai m; (inf: fizzy drink) bebida gasosa ▷ vt: **to ~ sth into/onto** etc (put) pôr em/sobre etc ▷ vi estourar; (cork) saltar **pop in** vi dar um pulo **pop out** vi dar uma saída **pop up** vi surgir, aparecer inesperadamente; **popcorn** n pipoca

pope [pəup] n papa m

poplar ['pɔplər] n álamo, choupo

poppy ['pɔpɪ] n papoula

popular ['pɔpjulər] adj popular; (person) querido

population [pɔpju'leɪʃən] n população f

porcelain ['pɔːslɪn] n porcelana

porch [pɔːtʃ] n pórtico; (US: verandah) varanda

pore [pɔːʳ] n poro ▷ vi: **to ~ over** examinar minuciosamente

pork [pɔːk] n carne f de porco

pornography [pɔː'nɔgrəfɪ] n pornografia

porridge ['pɔrɪdʒ] n mingau m (de aveia)

port [pɔːt] n (harbour) porto; (Naut: left side) bombordo; (wine) vinho do Porto; **~ of call** porto de escala

portable ['pɔːtəbl] adj portátil

porter ['pɔːtəʳ] n (for luggage) carregador m; (doorkeeper) porteiro

portfolio [pɔːt'fəulɪəu] n (case) pasta; (Pol) pasta ministerial; (Finance) carteira de ações ou títulos; (of artist) pasta, portfólio

portion ['pɔːʃən] n porção f, quinhão m; (of food) ração f

portrait ['pɔːtreɪt] n retrato

portray [pɔː'treɪ] vt retratar; (act) interpretar

Portugal ['pɔːtjugl] n Portugal m (no article)

Portuguese [pɔːtju'giːz] adj português(-esa) ▷ n inv português(-esa) m/f; (Ling) português m

pose [pəuz] n postura, pose f ▷ vi (pretend): **to ~ as** fazer-se passar por ▷ vt (question) fazer; (problem) causar; **to ~ for** (painting) posar para

posh [pɔʃ] (inf) adj fino, chique; (upper-class) de classe alta

position [pə'zɪʃən] n posição f; (job) cargo; (situation) situação f ▷ vt colocar, situar

positive ['pɔzɪtɪv] adj positivo; (certain) certo; (definite) definitivo

possess [pə'zɛs] vt possuir; **possession** n posse f, possessão f; **possessions** npl (belongings) pertences mpl; **to take possession of sth** tomar posse de algo

possibility [pɔsɪ'bɪlɪtɪ] n possibilidade f; (of sth happening) probabilidade f

possible ['pɔsɪbl] adj possível;
possibly adv pode ser, talvez;
(surprise): **what could they
possibly want with me?** o que
eles podem querer comigo?;
(emphasizing effort): **they did
everything they possibly could**
eles fizeram tudo o que podiam; **I
cannot possibly go** não posso ir
de jeito nenhum

post [pəust] n (Brit: mail) correio;
(job) cargo, posto; (pole) poste m;
(Mil) nomeação f ▷ vt (Brit: send by
post) pôr no correio; (: appoint): **to ~
to** destinar a; **postage** n porte m,
franquia; **postal order** n vale m
postal; **postbox** (Brit) n caixa de
correio; **postcard** n cartão m
postal; **postcode** (Brit) n código
postal, ≈ CEP m (BR)

poster ['pəustər] n cartaz m; (as
decoration) pôster m

postman ['pəustmən] irreg n
carteiro

postmark ['pəustmɑ:k] n carimbo
do correio

post office n (building) agência do
correio, correio; (organization)
≈ Empresa Nacional dos Correios e
Telégrafos (BR), ≈ Correios,
Telégrafos e Telefones (PT)

postpone [pəs'pəun] vt adiar

posture ['pɔstʃər] n postura; (fig)
atitude f

pot [pɔt] n (for cooking) panela; (for
flowers) vaso; (container) pote m;
(teapot) bule m; (inf: marijuana)
maconha ▷ vt (plant) plantar em
vaso; **to go to ~** (inf) arruinar-se,
degringolar

potato [pə'teɪtəu] (pl **potatoes**) n
batata; **potato peeler** n
descascador m de batatas

potent ['pəutnt] adj poderoso;
(drink) forte; (man) potente

potential [pə'tɛnʃl] adj potencial
▷ n potencial m

pothole ['pɔthəul] n (in road)
buraco; (Brit: underground)
caldeirão m, cova

potter ['pɔtər] n (artistic) ceramista
m/f; (artisan) oleiro(-a) ▷ vi (Brit):
to ~ around, ~ about ocupar-se
com pequenos trabalhos; **pottery**
n cerâmica; (factory) olaria

potty ['pɔtɪ] adj (inf: mad) maluco,
doido ▷ n penico

pouch [pautʃ] n (Zool) bolsa; (for
tobacco) tabaqueira

poultry ['pəultrɪ] n aves fpl
domésticas; (meat) carne f de aves
domésticas

pounce [pauns] vi: **to ~ on**
lançar-se sobre; (person) agarrar
em; (fig: mistake etc) apontar

pound [paund] n libra (weight =
453g, 16 ounces; money = 100 pence)
▷ vt (beat) socar, esmurrar; (crush)
triturar ▷ vi (heart) bater

pour [pɔ:r] vt despejar; (drink) servir
▷ vi correr, jorrar **pour away** vt
esvaziar, decantar **pour in** vi
(people) entrar numa enxurrada;
(information) chegar numa
enxurrada **pour off** vt esvaziar,
decantar **pour out** vi (people) sair
aos borbotões ▷ vt (drink) servir;
(fig) extravasar; **pouring** ['pɔ:rɪŋ]
adj: **pouring rain** chuva torrencial

pout [paut] vi fazer beicinho or
biquinho

poverty ['pɔvətɪ] n pobreza,
miséria

powder ['paudər] n pó m; (face
powder) pó-de-arroz m ▷ vt (face)
empoar, passar pó em; **powdered
milk** n leite m em pó

power ['pauə^r] n poder m; (of explosion, engine) força, potência; (ability, Pol) poder; (electricity) força; **to be in ~** estar no poder; **power cut** (Brit) n corte m de energia, blecaute m (BR); **powerful** adj poderoso; (engine) potente; (body) vigoroso; (blow) violento; (argument) convincente; (emotion) intenso; **powerless** adj impotente; **power point** (Brit) n tomada; **power station** n central f elétrica

PR n abbr = **public relations**

practical ['præktɪkl] adj prático; **practical joke** n brincadeira, peça

practice ['præktɪs] n (habit, Rel) costume m, hábito; (exercise) prática; (of profession) exercício; (training) treinamento; (Med) consultório; (Law) escritório ▷ vt, vi (US) = **practise**; **in ~** na prática; **out of ~** destreinado

practise ['præktɪs], (US) **practice** vt praticar; (profession) exercer; (sport) treinar ▷ vi (doctor) ter consultório; (lawyer) ter escritório; (train) treinar, praticar

practitioner [præk'tɪʃənə^r] n (Med) médico(-a)

prairie ['prɛərɪ] n campina, pradaria

praise [preɪz] n louvor m; (admiration) elogio ▷ vt elogiar, louvar

pram [præm] (Brit) n carrinho de bebê

prank [præŋk] n travessura, peça

prawn [prɔːn] n pitu m; (small) camarão m

pray [preɪ] vi: **to ~ for/that** rezar por/para que; **prayer** [prɛə^r] n (activity) reza; (words) oração f, prece f

preach [priːtʃ] vt pregar ▷ vi pregar; (pej) catequizar

precede [prɪ'siːd] vt preceder

precedent ['prɛsɪdənt] n precedente m

preceding [prɪ'siːdɪŋ] adj anterior

precinct ['priːsɪŋkt] n (US: district) distrito policial; **precincts** npl (of large building) arredores mpl; **pedestrian ~** (Brit) zona para pedestres (BR) or peões (PT); **shopping ~** (Brit) zona comercial

precious ['prɛʃəs] adj precioso

precise [prɪ'saɪs] adj exato, preciso; (plans) detalhado

predecessor ['priːdɪsɛsə^r] n predecessor(a) m/f, antepassado(-a)

predicament [prɪ'dɪkəmənt] n situação f difícil, apuro

predict [prɪ'dɪkt] vt prever, predizer, prognosticar; **predictable** adj previsível

predominantly [prɪ'dɔmɪnəntlɪ] adv predominantemente, na maioria

preface ['prɛfəs] n prefácio

prefect ['priːfɛkt] n (Brit: Sch) monitor(a) m/f, tutor(a) m/f; (in Brazil) prefeito(-a)

prefer [prɪ'fəː^r] vt preferir; **preferably** ['prɛfrəblɪ] adv de preferência

prefix ['priːfɪks] n prefixo

pregnancy ['prɛgnənsɪ] n gravidez f; (animal) prenhez f

pregnant ['prɛgnənt] adj grávida; (animal) prenha

prehistoric [priːhɪs'tɔrɪk] adj pré-histórico

prejudice ['prɛdʒudɪs] n preconceito; **prejudiced** adj (person) preconceituoso

premature ['prɛmətʃuə^r] adj

prematuro

première ['prɛmɪɛəʳ] n estreia

premium ['priːmɪəm] n prêmio; **to be at a ~** ser caro

premonition [prɛmə'nɪʃən] n presságio, pressentimento

preoccupied [priː'ɔkjupaɪd] adj (worried) preocupado

prepaid [priː'peɪd] adj com porte pago

preparation [prɛpə'reɪʃən] n preparação f; **preparations** npl (arrangements) preparativos mpl

prepare [prɪ'pɛəʳ] vt preparar ▷ vi: **to ~ for** preparar-se or aprontar-se para; **~d to** disposto a; **~d for** pronto para

preposition [prɛpə'zɪʃən] n preposição f

prerequisite [priː'rɛkwɪzɪt] n pré-requisito, condição f prévia

prescribe [prɪ'skraɪb] vt prescrever; (Med) receitar

prescription [prɪ'skrɪpʃən] n receita

presence ['prɛzns] n presença; (spirit) espectro

present [adj, n 'prɛznt, vt prɪ'zɛnt] adj presente; (current) atual ▷ n presente m; (actuality): **the ~** o presente ▷ vt (give) entregar algo a alguém; (describe) descrever; **at ~** no momento, agora; **to give sb a ~** presentear alguém; **presentation** [prɛzn'teɪʃən] n apresentação f; (ceremony) entrega; (of plan etc) exposição f; **present-day** adj atual, de hoje; **presenter** n apresentador(a) m/f; **presently** adv (soon after) logo depois; (soon) logo, em breve; (now) atualmente

preservative [prɪ'zɜːvətɪv] n conservante m

preserve [prɪ'zɜːv] vt (situation) conservar, manter; (building, manuscript) preservar; (food) pôr em conserva ▷ n (often pl: jam) geleia; (: fruit) compota, conserva

president ['prɛzɪdənt] n presidente(-a) m/f; **presidential** [prɛzɪ'dɛnʃl] adj presidencial

press [prɛs] n (printer's) imprensa, prelo; (newspapers) imprensa; (of switch) pressão f ▷ vt apertar; (clothes: iron) passar; (put pressure on: person) pressionar; (insist): **to ~ sth on sb** insistir para que alguém aceite algo ▷ vi (squeeze) apertar; (pressurize): **to ~ for** pressionar por; **we are ~ed for time/money** estamos com pouco tempo/ dinheiro **press on** vi continuar; **pressing** adj urgente; **press stud** (Brit) n botão m de pressão; **press-up** (Brit) n flexão f

pressure ['prɛʃəʳ] n pressão f; **to put ~ on sb (to do sth)** pressionar alguém (a fazer algo); **pressure cooker** n panela de pressão

prestige [prɛs'tiːʒ] n prestígio

presume [prɪ'zjuːm] vt supor

pretence [prɪ'tɛns], (US) **pretense** n pretensão f; **under false ~s** por meios fraudulentos

pretend [prɪ'tɛnd] vt, vi fingir

pretense [prɪ'tɛns] (US) n = **pretence**

pretty ['prɪtɪ] adj bonito ▷ adv (quite) bastante

prevail [prɪ'veɪl] vi triunfar; (be current) imperar

prevalent ['prɛvələnt] adj (common) predominante

prevent [prɪ'vɛnt] vt impedir

preview ['priːvjuː] n pré-estreia

previous ['priːvɪəs] adj (earlier) anterior; **previously** adv (before) previamente; (*in the past*) anteriormente

prey [preɪ] *n* presa ▷ *vi*: **to ~ on** (*feed on*) alimentar-se de; **it was ~ing on his mind** preocupava-o, atormentava-o

price [praɪs] *n* preço ▷ *vt* fixar o preço de; **priceless** *adj* inestimável; (*inf: amusing*) impagável

prick [prɪk] *n* picada ▷ *vt* picar; (*make hole in*) furar; **to ~ up one's ears** aguçar os ouvidos

pride [praɪd] *n* orgulho; (*pej*) soberba ▷ *vt*: **to ~ o.s. on** orgulhar-se de

priest [priːst] *n* (*Christian*) padre *m*; (*non-Christian*) sacerdote *m*

primarily ['praɪmərɪlɪ] *adv* principalmente

primary ['praɪmərɪ] *adj* primário; (*first in importance*) principal ▷ *n* (*US: election*) eleição *f* primária; **primary school** (*Brit*) *n* escola primária; *ver nota*

prime [praɪm] *adj* primeiro, principal; (*excellent*) de primeira ▷ *vt* (*wood*) imprimir; (*fig*) preparar ▷ *n*: **in the ~ of life** na primavera da vida; **~ example** exemplo típico; **prime minister** *n* primeiro-ministro/primeira-ministra

primitive ['prɪmɪtɪv] *adj* primitivo;

(*crude*) rudimentar

primrose ['prɪmrəuz] *n* prímula, primavera

prince [prɪns] *n* príncipe *m*

princess [prɪn'sɛs] *n* princesa

principal ['prɪnsɪpl] *adj* principal ▷ *n* (*of school, college*) diretor(a) *m/f*

principle ['prɪnsɪpl] *n* princípio; **in ~** em princípio; **on ~** por princípio

print [prɪnt] *n* (*letters*) letra de forma; (*fabric*) estampado; (*Art*) estampa, gravura; (*Phot*) cópia; (*footprint*) pegada; (*fingerprint*) impressão *f* digital ▷ *vt* imprimir; (*write in capitals*) escrever em letra de imprensa; **out of ~** esgotado; **printer** *n* (*person*) impressor(a) *m/f*; (*firm*) gráfica; (*machine*) impressora; **printout** *n* (*Comput*) cópia impressa

prior ['praɪəʳ] *adj* anterior, prévio; (*more important*) prioritário; **~ to doing** antes de fazer

priority [praɪ'ɔrɪtɪ] *n* prioridade *f*

prison ['prɪzn] *n* prisão *f* ▷ *cpd* carcerário; **prisoner** *n* (*in prison*) preso(-a), presidiário(-a); (*under arrest*) detido(-a)

privacy ['prɪvəsɪ] *n* isolamento, solidão *f*, privacidade *f*

private ['praɪvɪt] *adj* privado; (*personal*) particular; (*confidential*) confidencial, reservado; (*personal: belongings*) pessoal; (: *thoughts, plans*) secreto, íntimo; (*place*) isolado; (*quiet: person*) reservado; (*intimate*) íntimo ▷ *n* soldado raso; **"~"** (*on envelope*) "confidencial"; (*on door*) "privativo"; **in ~** em particular; **privatize** *vt* privatizar

privilege ['prɪvɪlɪdʒ] *n* privilégio

prize [praɪz] *n* prêmio ▷ *adj* de primeira classe ▷ *vt* valorizar; **prizewinner** *n* premiado(-a)

pro [prəu] n (Sport) profissional m/f
▷ prep a favor de; **the ~s and cons**
os prós e os contras

probability [prɔbə'bɪlɪtɪ] n
probabilidade f

probable ['prɔbəbl] adj provável;
(plausible) verossímil

probation [prə'beɪʃən] n: **on ~**
(employee) em estágio probatório;
(Law) em liberdade condicional

probe [prəub] n (Med, Space) sonda;
(enquiry) pesquisa ▷ vt investigar,
esquadrinhar

problem ['prɔbləm] n problema m

procedure [prə'siːdʒər] n
procedimento; (method) método,
processo

proceed [prə'siːd] vi (do afterwards):
to ~ to do sth passar a fazer algo;
(continue): **to ~ (with)** continuar or
prosseguir (com); (activity, event)
continuar; (go) ir em direção a,
dirigir-se a; **proceedings** npl
evento, acontecimento; **proceeds**
['prəusiːdz] npl produto,
proventos mpl

process ['prəusɛs] n processo ▷ vt
processar; **procession** [prə'sɛʃən]
n desfile m, procissão f; **funeral
procession** cortejo fúnebre

proclaim [prə'kleɪm] vt anunciar

prod [prɔd] vt empurrar; (with
finger, stick) cutucar ▷ n empurrão
m; cotovelada; espetada

produce [n 'prɔdjuːs, vt prə'djuːs] n
(Agr) produtos mpl agrícolas ▷ vt
produzir; (cause) provocar;
(evidence, argument) apresentar,
mostrar; (show) apresentar, exibir;
(Theatre) pôr em cena or em cartaz;
producer n (Theatre) diretor(a)
m/f; (Agr, Cinema, of record)
produtor(a) m/f; (country) produtor
m

product ['prɔdʌkt] n produto

production [prə'dʌkʃən] n
produção f; (of electricity) geração f;
(Theatre) encenação f

profession [prə'fɛʃən] n profissão f;
(people) classe f; **professional** n
profissional m/f ▷ adj profissional;
(work) de profissional

professor [prə'fɛsər] n (Brit)
catedrático(-a); (US, Canada)
professor(a) m/f

profile ['prəufaɪl] n perfil m

profit ['prɔfɪt] n (Comm) lucro ▷ vi:
to ~ by or **from** (benefit)
aproveitar-se de, tirar proveito de;
profitable adj (Econ) lucrativo,
rendoso

profound [prə'faund] adj profundo

programme ['prəugræm], (US)
program n programa m ▷ vt
programar; **programming**, (US)
programing n programação f

progress [n 'prəugrɛs, vi prə'grɛs] n
progresso ▷ vi progredir, avançar;
in ~ em andamento; **progressive**
[prə'grɛsɪv] adj progressivo;
(person) progressista

prohibit [prə'hɪbɪt] vt proibir

project [n prɔdʒɛkt, vt, vi prə'dʒɛkt]
n projeto; (Sch: research) pesquisa
▷ vt projetar; (figure) estimar ▷ vi
(stick out) ressaltar, sobressair

projection [prə'dʒɛkʃən] n
projeção f; (overhang) saliência

projector [prə'dʒɛktər] n projetor m

prolong [prə'lɔŋ] vt prolongar

prom [prɔm] n abbr = **promenade**;
promenade concert; (US: ball)
baile m de estudantes

promenade [prɔmə'nɑːd] n (by sea)
passeio (à orla marítima);
promenade concert (Brit) n
concerto (de música clássica); ver
nota

p

prominent ['prɔmɪnənt] adj
(standing out) proeminente;
(important) eminente, notório
promise ['prɔmɪs] n promessa;
(hope) esperança ▷ vt, vi prometer;
promising adj promissor(a),
prometedor(a)
promote [prə'məut] vt promover;
(product) promover, fazer
propaganda de; **promotion** n
promoção f
prompt [prɔmpt] adj pronto,
rápido ▷ adv (exactly) em ponto,
pontualmente ▷ n (Comput) sinal m
de orientação, prompt m ▷ vt (urge)
incitar, impelir; (cause) provocar,
ocasionar; **to ~ sb to do sth** induzir
alguém a fazer algo, ele não
hesitou em aceitar; **promptly** adv
imediatamente; (exactly)
pontualmente

prone [prəun] adj (lying) de bruços;
~ to propenso a, predisposto a
pronoun ['prəunaun] n pronome m
pronounce [prə'nauns] vt
pronunciar; (verdict, opinion)
declarar
pronunciation [prənʌnsɪ'eɪʃən] n
pronúncia
proof [pruːf] n prova ▷ adj: **~
against** à prova de
prop [prɔp] n suporte m, escora;
(fig) amparo, apoio ▷ vt (also: **~ up**)
apoiar, escorar; (lean): **to ~ sth
against** apoiar algo contra
propaganda [prɔpə'gændə] n
propaganda
proper ['prɔpər] adj (correct)
correto; (socially acceptable)
respeitável, digno; (authentic)
genuíno, autêntico; (referring to
place): **the village ~** a cidadezinha
propriamente dita; **properly** adv
(eat, study) bem; (behave)
decentemente
property ['prɔpətɪ] n propriedade f;
(goods) posses fpl, bens mpl;
(buildings) imóveis mpl
prophet ['prɔfɪt] n profeta m/f
proportion [prə'pɔːʃən] n
proporção f; **proportional** adj
proporcional
proposal [prə'pəuzl] n proposta;
(of marriage) pedido
propose [prə'pəuz] vt propor;
(toast) erguer ▷ vi propor
casamento; **to ~ to do** propor-se
fazer
proposition [prɔpə'zɪʃən] n
proposta, proposição f; (offer)
oferta
proprietor [prə'praɪətər] n
proprietário(-a), dono(-a)
prose [prəuz] n prosa
prosecute ['prɔsɪkjuːt] vt

processar; **prosecution**
[prɔsɪ'kju:ʃən] n acusação f;
(accusing side) autor m da demanda
prospect [n 'prɔspɛkt, vt, vi
prə'spɛkt] n (chance) probabilidade
f; (outlook, potential) perspectiva
▷ vi: **to ~ (for)** prospectar (por);
prospects npl (for work etc)
perspectivas fpl
prospectus [prə'spɛktəs] n
prospecto, programa m
prostitute ['prɔstɪtju:t] n
prostituta; **male ~** prostituto
protect [prə'tɛkt] vt proteger;
protection n proteção f;
protective adj protetor(a)
protein ['prəuti:n] n proteína
protest [n 'prəutɛst, vi, vt prə'tɛst]
n protesto ▷ vi protestar ▷ vt
insistir
Protestant ['prɔtɪstənt] adj, n
protestante m/f
protester [prə'tɛstər] n
manifestante m/f
proud [praud] adj orgulhoso; (pej)
vaidoso, soberbo
prove [pru:v] vt comprovar ▷ vi: **to
~ (to be) correct** etc vir a ser
correto etc; **to ~ o.s.** mostrar seu
valor
proverb ['prɔvə:b] n provérbio
provide [prə'vaɪd] vt fornecer,
proporcionar; **to ~ sb with sth**
fornecer alguém de algo, fornecer
algo a alguém **provide for** vt fus
(person) prover à subsistência de
providing [prə'vaɪdɪŋ] conj: **~
(that)** contanto que (+ sub)
province ['prɔvɪns] n província;
(fig) esfera; **provincial** [prə'vɪnʃəl]
adj provincial; (pej) provinciano
provision [prə'vɪʒən] n (supplying)
abastecimento; (in contract)
cláusula, condição f; **provisions**

npl (food) mantimentos mpl;
provisional adj provisório,
interino; (agreement, licence)
provisório
provocative [prə'vɔkətɪv] adj
provocante; (sexually) excitante
provoke [prə'vəuk] vt provocar;
(cause) causar
prowl [praul] vi (also: **~ about, ~
around**) rondar, andar à espreita
▷ n: **on the ~** de ronda, rondando
proxy ['prɔksɪ] n: **by ~** por
procuração
prudent ['pru:dənt] adj prudente
prune [pru:n] n ameixa seca ▷ vt
podar
pry [praɪ] vi: **to ~ (into)**
intrometer-se (em)
PS n abbr (= postscript) PS m
pseudonym ['sju:dənɪm] n
pseudônimo
psychiatrist [saɪ'kaɪətrɪst] n
psiquiatra m/f
psychic ['saɪkɪk] adj psíquico; (also:
~al: person) sensível a forças
psíquicas
psychologist [saɪ'kɔlədʒɪst] n
psicólogo(-a)
psychology [saɪ'kɔlədʒɪ] n
psicologia
PTO abbr (= please turn over) v.v., vire
pub [pʌb] n abbr (= public house) pub
m, bar m, botequim m; ver nota

p

> **PUB**
>
> Um **pub** geralmente consiste em
> duas salas: uma (the lounge) é
> bastante confortável, com
> poltronas e bancos estofados,
> enquanto a outra ("the public
> bar") é simplesmente um bar
> onde a consumação é em geral
> mais barata. O ("the public bar") é

muitas vezes também um salão
de jogos, dos quais os mais
comuns são os dardos, dominó e
bilhar. Atualmente muitos pubs
servem refeições, sobretudo na
hora do almoço, e essa é a única
hora em que a entrada de
crianças é permitida, desde que
estejam acompanhadas por
adultos. Em geral os pubs
funcionam das 11 às 23 horas,
mas isso pode variar de acordo
com sua permissão de
funcionamento; alguns pubs
fecham à tarde.

public ['pʌblɪk] *adj* público ▷ *n*
público; **in ~** em público; **to make
~** tornar público; **public
convenience** (*Brit*) *n* banheiro
público; **public holiday** *n* feriado;
public house (*Brit*) *n* pub *m*, bar *m*,
taberna
publicity [pʌb'lɪsɪtɪ] *n* publicidade *f*
publicize ['pʌblɪsaɪz] *vt* divulgar
public: **public school** *n* (*Brit*) escola
particular; (*US*) escola pública;
public transport, (*US*) **public
transportation** *n* transporte *m*
coletivo
publish ['pʌblɪʃ] *vt* publicar;
publisher *n* editor(a) *m/f*;
(*company*) editora; **publishing** *n* a
indústria editorial
pudding ['pʊdɪŋ] *n* (*Brit*: *dessert*)
sobremesa; (*cake*) pudim *m*, doce
m; **black** (*Brit*) **or blood** (*US*) **~**
morcela
puddle ['pʌdl] *n* poça
puff [pʌf] *n* sopro; (*of cigarette*)
baforada; (*of air, smoke*) lufada ▷ *vt*:
to ~ one's pipe tirar baforadas do
cachimbo ▷ *vi* (*pant*) arquejar **puff
out** *vt* (*cheeks*) encher; **puff

pastry, (*US*) **puff paste** *n* massa
folhada
pull [pʊl] *n* (*tug*): **to give sth a ~** dar
um puxão em algo ▷ *vt* puxar;
(*trigger*) apertar; (*curtain, blind*)
fechar ▷ *vi* puxar, dar um puxão;
to ~ to pieces picar em pedacinhos;
to ~ one's punches não usar toda
a força; **to ~ one's weight** fazer a
sua parte; **to ~ o.s. together**
recompor-se; **to ~ sb's leg** (*fig*)
brincar com alguém, sacanear
alguém (*inf*) **pull apart** *vt* (*break*)
romper **pull down** *vt* (*building*)
demolir, derrubar **pull in** *vi* (*Aut*: *at
the kerb*) encostar; (*Rail*) chegar (na
plataforma) **pull off** *vt* tirar; (*fig*:
deal etc) acertar **pull out** *vi* (*Aut*:
from kerb) sair; (*Rail*) partir ▷ *vt*
tirar, arrancar, dar uma fechada em
alguém **pull over** *vi* (*Aut*) encostar
pull through *vi* (*Med*) sobreviver
pull up *vi* (*stop*) deter-se, parar
▷ *vt* levantar; (*uproot*) desarraigar,
arrancar
pulley ['pʊlɪ] *n* roldana
pullover ['pʊləʊvəʳ] *n* pulôver *m*
pulp [pʌlp] *n* (*of fruit*) polpa
pulse [pʌls] *n* (*Anat*) pulso; (*of
music, engine*) cadência; (*Bot*)
legume *m*
pump [pʌmp] *n* bomba; (*shoe*)
sapatilha (de dança) ▷ *vt* bombear
pump up *vt* encher
pumpkin ['pʌmpkɪn] *n* abóbora
pun [pʌn] *n* jogo de palavras,
trocadilho
punch [pʌntʃ] *n* (*blow*) soco, murro;
(*tool*) punção *m*; (*drink*) ponche *m*
▷ *vt* (*hit*): **to ~ sb/sth** esmurrar or
socar alguém/algo
punctual ['pʌŋktjuəl] *adj* pontual
punish ['pʌnɪʃ] *vt* punir, castigar;
punishment *n* castigo, punição *f*

punk [pʌŋk] n (also: **~ rocker**) punk m/f; (also: **~ rock**) punk m; (US: inf: hoodlum) pinta-brava m

pupil ['pjuːpl] n aluno(-a); (of eye) pupila

puppet ['pʌpɪt] n marionete f, títere m; (fig) fantoche m

puppy ['pʌpɪ] n cachorrinho (BR), cachorro (PT)

purchase ['pəːtʃɪs] n compra ▷ vt comprar

pure [pjuəʳ] adj puro

purple ['pəːpl] adj roxo, purpúreo

purpose ['pəːpəs] n propósito, objetivo; **on ~** de propósito

purse [pəːs] n (Brit) carteira; (US) bolsa ▷ vt enrugar, franzir

pursue [pəˈsjuː] vt perseguir; (fig: activity) exercer; (: interest, plan) dedicar-se a; (: result) lutar por

pursuit [pəˈsjuːt] n perseguição f; (fig) busca

push [pʊʃ] n empurrão m; (of button) aperto ▷ vt empurrar; (button) apertar; (promote) promover ▷ vi empurrar; (press) apertar; (fig): **to ~ for** reivindicar **push aside** vt afastar com a mão **push off** (inf) vi dar o fora **push on** vi prosseguir **push through** vi abrir caminho ▷ vt (measure) forçar a aceitação de **push up** vt forçar a alta de; **pushchair** (Brit) n carrinho; **pusher** n (also: **drug pusher**) traficante m/f; **push-up** (US) n flexão f

put [pʊt] (pt, pp **put**) vt pôr, colocar; (put into) meter; (person: in institution etc) internar; (say) dizer, expressar; (case) expor; (question) fazer; (estimate) avaliar, calcular; (write, type etc) colocar, eu gostaria de colocar que ... **put about** vt (rumour) espalhar **put across** vt

(ideas) comunicar **put away** vt guardar **put back** vt (replace) repor; (postpone) adiar; (delay) atrasar **put by** vt (money etc) poupar, pôr de lado **put down** vt pôr em; (animal) sacrificar; (in writing) anotar, inscrever; (revolt etc) sufocar; (attribute: to put sth down to) atribuir algo a **put forward** vt apresentar, propor **put in** vt (application, complaint) apresentar; (time, effort) investir, gastar **put off** vt adiar, protelar; (discourage) desanimar **put on** vt (clothes, make-up, dinner) pôr; (light) acender; (play) encenar; (weight) ganhar; (brake) aplicar; (record, video, kettle) ligar; (accent, manner) assumir **put out** vt (take out) colocar fora; (fire, cigarette, light) apagar; (one's hand) estender; (inf: person): **to be ~ out** estar aborrecido **put through** vt (call) transferir; (plan) aprovar **put up** vt (raise) levantar, erguer; (hang) prender; (build) construir, edificar; (tent) armar; (increase) aumentar; (accommodate) hospedar **put up with** vt fus suportar, aguentar

puzzle ['pʌzl] n charada; (jigsaw) quebra-cabeça m; (also: **crossword ~**) palavras cruzadas fpl; (mystery) mistério ▷ vt desconcertar, confundir ▷ vi: **to ~ over sth** tentar entender algo; **puzzling** adj intrigante, confuso

pyjamas [pɪˈdʒɑːməz], (US) **pajamas** npl pijama m or f

pylon ['paɪlən] n pilono, poste m, torre f

pyramid ['pɪrəmɪd] n pirâmide f

Pyrenees [pɪrəˈniːz] npl: **the ~** os Pirineus

P

quack [kwæk] n grasnido; (pej: doctor) curandeiro(-a), charlatão(-tã) m/f

quaint [kweɪnt] adj (ideas) curioso, esquisito; (village etc) pitoresco

quake [kweɪk] vi (with fear) tremer ▷ n abbr = **earthquake**

qualification [kwɔlɪfɪˈkeɪʃən] n (skill, quality) qualificação f; (reservation) restrição f, ressalva; (modification) modificação f; (often pl: degree, training) título, qualificação

qualified [ˈkwɔlɪfaɪd] adj (trained) habilitado, qualificado; (professionally) diplomado; (fit): **~ to** apto para, capaz de; (limited) limitado

qualify [ˈkwɔlɪfaɪ] vt (modify) modificar ▷ vi (pass examination(s)) formar-se or diplomar-se (em); **to ~ (for)** reunir os requisitos (para)

quality [ˈkwɔlɪtɪ] n qualidade f; **quality (news)papers** (Brit) npl ver nota

● QUALITY (NEWS)PAPERS
●
● Os **quality (news)papers**
● (ou **quality press**) englobam
● os jornais "sérios", diários ou
● semanais, em oposição aos
● jornais populares (**tabloid**
● **press**). Esses jornais visam a um
● público que procura informações
● detalhadas sobre uma grande
● variedade de assuntos e que está
● disposto a dedicar um bom
● tempo à leitura. Geralmente os
● *quality newspapers* são publicados
● em formato grande.

quantify [ˈkwɔntɪfaɪ] vt quantificar

quantity [ˈkwɔntɪtɪ] n quantidade f

quarantine [ˈkwɔrəntiːn] n quarentena

quarrel [ˈkwɔrl] n (argument) discussão f ▷ vi: **to ~ (with)** brigar (com)

quarry [ˈkwɔrɪ] n (for stone) pedreira; (animal) presa, caça

quart [kwɔːt] n quarto de galão (1.136 l)

quarter [ˈkwɔːtəʳ] n quarto, quarta parte f; (of year) trimestre m; (district) bairro; (US: 25 cents) (moeda de) 25 centavos mpl de dólar ▷ vt dividir em quatro; (Mil: lodge) aquartelar; **quarters** npl (Mil) quartel m; (living quarters) alojamento; **a ~ of an hour** um quarto de hora; **quarter final** n quarta de final; **quarterly** adj trimestral ▷ adv trimestralmente

quay [kiː] n (also: **~side**) cais m

queasy ['kwiːzɪ] *adj* (*sickly*) enjoado
queen [kwiːn] *n* rainha; (*also:* ~ **bee**) abelha-mestra, rainha; (*Cards etc*) dama
queer [kwɪər] *adj* (*odd*) esquisito, estranho ▷ *n* (*inf: homosexual*) bicha *m* (*BR*), maricas *m inv* (*PT*)
quench [kwɛntʃ] *vt*: **to ~ one's thirst** matar a sede
query ['kwɪərɪ] *n* pergunta ▷ *vt* questionar
quest [kwɛst] *n* busca
question ['kwɛstʃən] *n* pergunta; (*doubt*) dúvida; (*issue, in test*) questão *f* ▷ *vt* (*doubt*) duvidar; (*interrogate*) interrogar, inquirir; **beyond ~** sem dúvida; **out of the ~** fora de cogitação, impossível; **questionable** *adj* discutível; (*doubtful*) duvidoso; **question mark** *n* ponto de interrogação; **questionnaire** [kwɛstʃəˈnɛər] *n* questionário
queue [kjuː] *n* (*Brit*) fila (*BR*), bicha (*PT*) ▷ *vi* (*also:* ~ **up**) fazer fila (*BR*) or bicha (*PT*)
quick [kwɪk] *adj* rápido; (*agile*) ágil; (*mind*) sagaz, despachado ▷ *n*: **to cut sb to the ~** ferir alguém; **be ~!** ande depressa!, vai rápido!; **quickly** *adv* rapidamente, depressa
quid [kwɪd] (*Brit: inf*) *n inv* libra
quiet ['kwaɪət] *adj* (*voice, music*) baixo; (*peaceful: place*) tranquilo; (*person: calm*) calmo; (*not noisy: place*) silencioso; (*: person*) calado; (*silent*) silencioso; (*ceremony*) discreto ▷ *n* (*peacefulness*) sossego; (*silence*) quietude *f* ▷ *vt*, *vi* (*US*) = **quieten**; **quieten** (*also:* **quieten down**) *vi* (*grow calm*) acalmar-se; (*grow silent*) calar-se ▷ *vt* tranquilizar; fazer calar; **quietly**

adv silenciosamente; (*talk*) baixo
quilt [kwɪlt] *n* acolchoado, colcha; **(continental)** ~ (*Brit*) edredom *m* (*BR*), edredão *m* (*PT*)
quit [kwɪt] (*pt, pp* **quit** *or* **quitted**) *vt* (*smoking etc*) parar; (*job*) deixar; (*premises*) desocupar ▷ *vi* desistir; (*resign*) pedir demissão
quite [kwaɪt] *adv* (*rather*) bastante; (*entirely*) completamente, totalmente; **that's not ~ big enough** não é suficientemente grande; ~ **a few of them** um bom número deles; ~ **(so)!** exatamente!, isso mesmo!
quiver ['kwɪvər] *vi* estremecer
quiz [kwɪz] *n* concurso (de cultura geral) ▷ *vt* interrogar
quota ['kwəʊtə] *n* cota, quota
quotation [kwəʊˈteɪʃən] *n* citação *f*; (*estimate*) orçamento; **quotation marks** *npl* aspas *fpl*
quote [kwəʊt] *n* citação *f*; (*estimate*) orçamento ▷ *vt* citar; (*price*) propor; (*figure, example*) citar, dar; **quotes** *npl* aspas *fpl*

q

r

m; (*dish rack*) secador m de prato
▷ vt: **~ed by** (*pain, anxiety*) tomado
por; **to ~ one's brains** quebrar a
cabeça

racket ['rækɪt] n (*for tennis*) raquete
f (*BR*), raqueta (*PT*); (*noise*)
barulheira, zoeira; (*swindle*)
negócio ilegal, fraude f

racquet ['rækɪt] n raquete f (*BR*),
raqueta (*PT*)

radiation [reɪdɪ'eɪʃən] n radiação f

radiator ['reɪdɪeɪtə'] n radiador m

radical ['rædɪkl] adj radical

radio ['reɪdɪəu] n rádio ▷ vt: **to ~ sb**
comunicar-se por rádio com
alguém

radio... [reɪdɪəu] prefix radio...;
radioactive ['reɪdɪəu'æktɪv] adj
radioativo; **radio station** n
emissora, estação f de rádio

radish ['rædɪʃ] n rabanete m

raffle ['ræfl] n rifa

raft [rɑːft] n balsa

rag [ræg] n (*torn cloth*) trapo; (*pej: newspaper*) jornaleco;
(*University*) atividades estudantis
beneficentes; **rags** npl (*torn clothes*)
trapos mpl, farrapos mpl

rage [reɪdʒ] n (*fury*) raiva, furor m
▷ vi (*person*) estar furioso; (*storm*)
assolar; (*debate*) continuar
calorosamente; **it's all the ~** é a
última moda

ragged ['rægɪd] adj (*edge*) irregular,
desigual; (*clothes*) puído, gasto;
(*appearance*) esfarrapado,
andrajoso

raid [reɪd] n (*Mil*) incursão f;
(*criminal*) assalto; (*attack*) ataque
m; (*by police*) batida ▷ vt invadir,
atacar; assaltar; atacar; fazer uma
batida em

rail [reɪl] n (*on stair*) corrimão m; (*on bridge, balcony*) parapeito,

rabbi ['ræbaɪ] n rabino

rabbit ['ræbɪt] n coelho

rabies ['reɪbiːz] n raiva

RAC (*Brit*) n abbr (= *Royal Automobile Club*) ≈ TCB m (*BR*), ≈ ACP m (*PT*)

race [reɪs] n corrida; (*species*) raça
▷ vt (*horse*) fazer correr ▷ vi
(*compete*) competir; (*run*) correr;
(*pulse*) bater rapidamente; **race
car** (*US*) n = **racing car**;
racecourse n hipódromo;
racehorse n cavalo de corridas;
racetrack n pista de corridas; (*for cars*) autódromo

racing ['reɪsɪŋ] n corrida; **racing
car** (*Brit*) n carro de corrida; **racing
driver** (*Brit*) n piloto(-a) de corrida

racism ['reɪsɪzəm] n racismo;
racist (*pej*) adj, n racista m/f

rack [ræk] n (*also*: **luggage ~**)
bagageiro; (*shelf*) estante f; (*also*:
roof ~) xalmas fpl, porta-bagagem

anteparo; (*of ship*) amurada; **rails**
npl (*for train*) trilhos *mpl*; **by ~** de
trem (*BR*), por caminho de ferro
(*PT*); **railing** *n*, **railings** *npl* grade
f; **railroad** (*US*) *n* = **railway**;
railway *n* estrada (*BR*) *or* caminho
(*PT*) de ferro; **railway line** (*Brit*) *n*
linha de trem (*BR*) *or* de comboio
(*PT*); **railway station** (*Brit*) *n*
estação *f* ferroviária (*BR*) *or* de
caminho de ferro (*PT*)

rain [reɪn] *n* chuva ▷ *vi* chover; **it's
~ing** está chovendo (*BR*), está a
chover (*PT*); **rainbow** *n* arco-íris *m*
inv; **raincoat** *n* impermeável *m*,
capa de chuva; **raindrop** *n* gota de
chuva; **rainfall** *n* chuva;
(*measurement*) pluviosidade *f*;
rainforest *n* floresta tropical;
rainy *adj* chuvoso; **a rainy day** um
dia de chuva

raise [reɪz] *n* aumento ▷ *vt* (*lift*)
levantar; (*salary, production*)
aumentar; (*morale, standards*)
melhorar; (*doubts*) suscitar,
despertar; (*cattle, family*) criar;
(*crop*) cultivar, plantar; (*army*)
recrutar, alistar; (*funds*) angariar;
(*loan*) levantar, obter; **to ~ one's
voice** levantar a voz

raisin ['reɪzn] *n* passa, uva seca

rake [reɪk] *n* ancinho ▷ *vt* (*garden*)
revolver *or* limpar com o ancinho;
(*with machine gun*) varrer

rally ['rælɪ] *n* (*Pol etc*) comício; (*Aut*)
rally *m*, rali *m*; (*Tennis*) rebatida ▷ *vt*
reunir ▷ *vi* reorganizar-se; (*sick
person, stock exchange*) recuperar-se
rally round *vt fus* dar apoio a

RAM [ræm] *n abbr* (*Comput*:
= *random access memory*) RAM *f*

ram [ræm] *n* carneiro ▷ *vt* (*push*)
cravar; (*crash into*) colidir com

ramble ['ræmbl] *n* caminhada,

excursão *f* a pé ▷ *vi* caminhar;
(*talk: also*: **~ on**) divagar; **rambler**
n caminhante *m/f*; (*Bot*) roseira
trepadeira; **rambling** *adj* (*speech*)
desconexo, incoerente; (*house*)
cheio de recantos; (*plant*)
rastejante

ramp [ræmp] *n* (*incline*) rampa;
on/off ~ (*US: Aut*) entrada (para a
rodovia)/saída da rodovia

rampage [ræm'peɪdʒ] *n*: **to be on
the ~** alvoroçar-se

ran [ræn] *pt of* **run**

ranch [rɑːntʃ] *n* rancho, fazenda,
estância

random ['rændəm] *adj* ao acaso,
casual, fortuito; (*Comput, Math*)
aleatório ▷ *n*: **at ~** a esmo,
aleatoriamente

rang [ræŋ] *pt of* **ring**

range [reɪndʒ] *n* (*of mountains*)
cadeia, cordilheira; (*of missile*)
alcance *m*; (*of voice*) extensão *f*;
(*series*) série *f*; (*of products*) gama,
sortimento; (*Mil: also*: **shooting ~**)
estande *m*; (*also*: **kitchen ~**) fogão
m ▷ *vt* (*place*) colocar; (*arrange*)
arrumar, ordenar ▷ *vi*: **to ~ over**
(*extend*) estender-se por; **to ~
from ... to ...** variar de ... a ...,
oscilar entre ... e ...

rank [ræŋk] *n* (*row*) fila, fileira; (*Mil*)
posto; (*status*) categoria, posição *f*;
(*Brit: also*: **taxi ~**) ponto de táxi ▷ *vi*:
to ~ among figurar entre ▷ *adj*
fétido, malcheiroso; **the ~ and file**
(*fig*) a gente comum

ransom ['rænsəm] *n* resgate *m*; **to
hold sb to ~** (*fig*) encostar alguém
contra a parede

rant [rænt] *vi* arengar

rap [ræp] *n*: **~ (music)** rap *m* ▷ *vt*
bater de leve

rape [reɪp] *n* estupro; (*Bot*) colza

▷ vt violentar, estuprar
rapid ['ræpɪd] adj rápido
rapids ['ræpɪdz] npl (Geo) cachoeira
rapist ['reɪpɪst] n estuprador m
rapport [ræ'pɔː'] n harmonia, afinidade f
rare [rɛə'] adj raro; (Culin: steak) mal passado
rascal ['rɑːskl] n maroto, malandro
rash [ræʃ] adj impetuoso, precipitado ▷ n (Med) exantema m, erupção f cutânea; (of events) série f, torrente f
rasher ['ræʃə'] n fatia fina
raspberry ['rɑːzbərɪ] n framboesa
rat [ræt] n rato (BR), ratazana (PT)
rate [reɪt] n (ratio) razão f; (price) preço, taxa; (: of hotel) diária; (of interest, change) taxa; (speed) velocidade f ▷ vt (value) taxar; (estimate) avaliar; **rates** npl (Brit) imposto predial e territorial; (fees) pagamento; **to ~ sb/sth as** considerar alguém/algo como
rather ['rɑːðə'] adv (somewhat) um tanto, meio; (to some extent) até certo ponto; (more accurately): **or ~** ou melhor; **it's ~ expensive** (quite) é meio caro; (too) é caro demais; **there's ~ a lot** há bastante or muito; **I would** or **I'd ~ go** preferiria or preferia ir; **or ~** ou melhor
ratio ['reɪʃɪəʊ] n razão f, proporção f
ration ['ræʃən] n ração f ▷ vt racionar; **rations** npl (Mil) mantimentos mpl, víveres mpl
rational ['ræʃənl] adj lógico; (person) sensato, razoável
rat race n: **the ~** a competição acirrada na vida moderna
rattle ['rætl] n (of door) batida; (of train etc) chocalhada; (of coins) chocalhar m; (object: for baby) chocalho ▷ vi (small objects)

tamborilar; (vehicle): **to ~ along** mover-se ruidosamente ▷ vt sacudir, fazer bater; (unnerve) perturbar
rave [reɪv] vi (in anger) encolerizar-se; (Med) delirar; (with enthusiasm): **to ~ about** vibrar com
raven ['reɪvən] n corvo
ravine [rə'viːn] n ravina, barranco
raw [rɔː] adj (uncooked) cru(a); (not processed) bruto; (sore) vivo; (inexperienced) inexperiente, novato; (weather) muito frio
ray [reɪ] n raio; **~ of hope** fio de esperança
razor ['reɪzə'] n (open) navalha; (safety razor) aparelho de barbear; (electric) aparelho de barbear elétrico; **razor blade** n gilete m (BR), lâmina de barbear (PT)
Rd abbr = **road**
re [riː] prep referente a
reach [riːtʃ] n alcance m; (of river etc) extensão f ▷ vt alcançar; (arrive at: place) chegar em; (: agreement, conclusion) chegar a; (by telephone) conseguir falar com ▷ vi (stretch out) esticar-se; **within ~** ao alcance (da mão); **out of** or **beyond ~** fora de alcance **reach out** vt (hand) esticar ▷ vi: **to ~ out for sth** estender or esticar ã mão para pegar (em) algo
react [riː'ækt] vi reagir; **reaction** n reação f; **reactions** npl (reflexes) reflexos mpl
reactor [riː'æktə'] n (also: **nuclear ~**) reator m nuclear
read [riːd] (pt, pp **read**) [rɛd] vi ler ▷ vt ler; (understand) compreender; (study) estudar **read out** vt ler em voz alta; **reader** n leitor(a) m/f; (book) livro de leituras; (Brit: at university) professor(a) m/f

adjunto(-a)

readily ['rɛdɪlɪ] adv (willingly) de boa vontade; (easily) facilmente; (quickly) sem demora, prontamente

reading ['ri:dɪŋ] n leitura; (on instrument) indicação f, registro (BR), registo (PT)

ready ['rɛdɪ] adj pronto, preparado; (willing) disposto; (available) disponível ▷ n: **at the ~** (Mil) pronto para atirar; **to get ~** vi preparar-se ▷ vt preparar; **ready-made** adj (já) feito; (clothes) pronto

real [rɪəl] adj real; (genuine) verdadeiro, autêntico; **in ~ terms** em termos reais; **real estate** n bens mpl imobiliários or de raiz; **realistic** [rɪə'lɪstɪk] adj realista

reality [ri:'ælɪtɪ] n realidade f; **reality TV** n reality TV f

realization [rɪəlaɪ'zeɪʃən] n (fulfilment) realização f; (understanding) compreensão f; (Comm) conversão f em dinheiro, realização

realize ['rɪəlaɪz] vt (understand) perceber; (fulfil, Comm) realizar

really ['rɪəlɪ] adv (for emphasis) realmente, (actually): **what ~ happened?** o que aconteceu na verdade?; **~?** (interest) é mesmo?; (surprise) verdade!; **~!** (annoyance) realmente!

realm [rɛlm] n reino, (fig) esfera, domínio

realtor ['rɪəltər] (US) n corretor(a) m/f de imóveis (BR), agente m/f imobiliário(-a) (PT)

reappear [ri:ə'pɪər] vi reaparecer

rear [rɪər] adj traseiro, de trás ▷ n traseira ▷ vt criar ▷ vi (also: **~ up**) empinar-se

reason ['ri:zn] n (cause) razão f; (ability to think) raciocínio; (sense) bom-senso ▷ vi: **to ~ with sb** argumentar com alguém, persuadir alguém; **it stands to ~ that** é razoável or lógico que; **reasonable** adj (fair) razoável; (sensible) sensato; **reasonably** adv razoavelmente; (sensibly) sensatamente; **reasoning** n raciocínio

reassurance [ri:ə'ʃuərəns] n garantia

reassure [ri:ə'ʃuər] vt tranquilizar; **to ~ sb of** reafirmar a confiança de alguém acerca de

rebate ['ri:beɪt] n devolução f

rebel [n 'rɛbl, vi rɪ'bɛl] n rebelde m/f ▷ vi rebelar-se; **rebellious** [rɪ'bɛljəs] adj insurreto; (behaviour) rebelde

recall [rɪ'kɔ:l] vt (remember) recordar, lembrar; (parliament) reunir de volta; (ambassador etc) chamar de volta ▷ n (memory) recordação f, lembrança; (of ambassador etc) chamada (de volta)

receipt [rɪ'si:t] n recibo; (act of receiving) recebimento (BR), recepção f (PT); **receipts** npl (Comm) receitas fpl

receive [rɪ'si:v] vt receber; (guest) acolher; (wound, criticism) sofrer; **receiver** n (Tel) fone m (BR), auscultador m (PT); (Radio, TV) receptor m; (of stolen goods) receptador(a) m/f; (Comm) curador(a) m/f síndico(-a) de massa falida

recent ['ri:snt] adj recente; **recently** adv recentemente; (in recent times) ultimamente

reception [rɪ'sɛpʃən] n recepção f; (welcome) acolhida; **reception desk** n (mesa de) recepção f;

r

receptionist n recepcionista m/f
recession [rɪ'sɛʃən] n recessão f
recipe ['rɛsɪpɪ] n receita
recipient [rɪ'sɪpɪənt] n recipiente m/f, recebedor(a) m/f; (of letter) destinatário(-a)
recite [rɪ'saɪt] vt recitar
reckless ['rɛkləs] adj (driver) imprudente; (speed) imprudente, excessivo; (spending) irresponsável
reckon ['rɛkən] vt (calculate) calcular, contar; (think): **I ~ that ...** acho que ... **reckon on** vt fus contar com
reclaim [rɪ'kleɪm] vt (demand back) reivindicar; (land: from sea) aterrar; (waste materials) reaproveitar
recline [rɪ'klaɪn] vi reclinar-se
recognition [rɛkəg'nɪʃən] n reconhecimento
recognize ['rɛkəgnaɪz] vt reconhecer
recommend [rɛkə'mɛnd] vt recomendar
reconcile ['rɛkənsaɪl] vt reconciliar; (two facts) conciliar, harmonizar; **to ~ o.s. to sth** resignar-se a or conformar-se com algo
reconsider [ri:kən'sɪdər] vt reconsiderar
reconstruct [ri:kən'strʌkt] vt reconstruir; (event) reconstituir
record [n, adj 'rɛkɔːd, vt rɪ'kɔːd] n (Mus) disco; (of meeting etc) ata, minuta; (Comput, of attendance) registro (BR), registo (PT); (written) história; (also: **criminal ~**) antecedentes mpl; (Sport) recorde m ▷ vt (write down) anotar; (temperature, speed) registrar (BR), registar (PT); (Mus: song etc) gravar ▷ adj: **in ~ time** num tempo recorde; **off the ~** adj confidencial

▷ adv confidencialmente;
recorder n (Mus) flauta;
recording n (Mus) gravação f;
record player n toca-discos m inv (BR), gira-discos m inv (PT)
recover [rɪ'kʌvər] vt recuperar ▷ vi (from illness) recuperar-se; (from shock) refazer-se; **recovery** n recuperação f; (Med) recuperação, melhora
recreation [rɛkrɪ'eɪʃən] n recreio;
recreational drug n droga recreacional
recruit [rɪ'kru:t] n recruta m/f; (in company) novato(-a) ▷ vt recrutar
rectangle ['rɛktæŋgl] n retângulo
rector ['rɛktər] n (Rel) pároco
recur [rɪ'kə:r] vi repetir-se, ocorrer outra vez; (symptoms) reaparecer
recyclable [ri:'saɪkləbl] adj reciclável; **recycle** vt reciclar; **recycling** n reciclagem f
red [rɛd] n vermelho; (Pol: pej) vermelho(-a) ▷ adj vermelho; (hair) ruivo; (wine) tinto; **to be in the ~** não ter fundos; **Red Cross** n Cruz f Vermelha
redeem [rɪ'di:m] vt (Rel) redimir; (sth in pawn) tirar do prego; (loan, fig: situation) salvar
red: **red-haired** adj ruivo; **redhead** ['rɛdhɛd] n ruivo(-a); **red-hot** adj incandescente; **red-light district** n zona de meretrício
reduce [rɪ'dju:s] vt reduzir; (lower) rebaixar; **"~ speed now"** (Aut) "diminua a velocidade"; **to ~ sb to** (silence, begging) levar alguém a; (tears) reduzir alguém a; **reduction** [rɪ'dʌkʃən] n redução f; (of price) abatimento
redundancy [rɪ'dʌndənsɪ] n (Brit: dismissal) demissão f; (unemployment) desemprego

redundant [rɪ'dʌndənt] *adj* (*Brit: worker*) desempregado; (*detail, object*) redundante, supérfluo; **to be made ~** ficar desempregado *or* sem trabalho

reed [riːd] *n* (*Bot*) junco; (*Mus: of clarinet etc*) palheta

reef [riːf] *n* (*at sea*) recife *m*

reel [riːl] *n* carretel *m*, bobina; (*of film*) rolo, filme *m*; (*on fishing-rod*) carretilha; (*dance*) dança típica da Escócia ▷ *vi* (*sway*) cambalear, oscilar **reel in** *vt* puxar enrolando a linha

ref [rɛf] (*inf*) *n abbr* = **referee**

refectory [rɪ'fɛktərɪ] *n* refeitório

refer [rɪ'fəː*] *vt* (*matter, problem*): **to ~ sth to** submeter algo à apreciação de; (*person, patient*): **to ~ sb to** encaminhar alguém a ▷ *vi*: **to ~ to** referir-se *or* aludir a; (*consult*) recorrer a

referee [rɛfə'riː] *n* árbitro(-a); (*Brit: for job application*) referência ▷ *vt* apitar

reference ['rɛfrəns] *n* referência; (*mention*) menção *f*; **with ~ to** com relação a; (*Comm: in letter*) com referência a; **"please quote this ~"** (*Comm*) "queira citar esta referência"

refill [*vt* riː'fɪl, *n* 'riːfɪl] *vt* reencher; (*lighter etc*) reabastecer ▷ *n* (*for pen*) carga nova

refine [rɪ'faɪn] *vt* refinar; **refined** *adj* refinado, culto

reflect [rɪ'flɛkt] *vt* refletir ▷ *vi* (*think*) refletir, meditar; **it ~s badly/well on him** isso repercute mal/bem para ele; **reflection** *n* reflexo; (*thought, act*) reflexão *f*; (*criticism*): **reflection on** crítica de; **on reflection** pensando bem

reflex ['riːflɛks] *adj, n* reflexo

reform [rɪ'fɔːm] *n* reforma ▷ *vt* reformar

refrain [rɪ'freɪn] *vi*: **to ~ from doing** abster-se de fazer ▷ *n* estribilho, refrão *m*

refresh [rɪ'frɛʃ] *vt* refrescar; **refreshing** *adj* refrescante; (*sleep*) repousante

refreshment [rɪ'frɛʃmənt] *n* (*eating*): **for some ~** para comer alguma coisa; **refreshments** *npl* comes e bebes *mpl*

refrigerator [rɪ'frɪdʒəreɪtə*] *n* refrigerador *m*, geladeira (*BR*), frigorífico (*PT*)

refuel [riː'fjuəl] *vi* reabastecer

refuge ['rɛfjuːdʒ] *n* refúgio; **to take ~ in** refugiar-se em

refugee [rɛfju'dʒiː] *n* refugiado(-a)

refund [*n* 'riːfʌnd, *vt* rɪ'fʌnd] *n* reembolso ▷ *vt* devolver, reembolsar

refurbish [riː'fəːbɪʃ] *vt* renovar

refusal [rɪ'fjuːzəl] *n* recusa, negativa; **first ~** primeira opção

refuse¹ [rɪ'fjuːz] *vt* recusar; (*order*) recusar-se a ▷ *vi* recusar-se, negar-se; (*horse*) recusar-se a pular a cerca

refuse² ['rɛfjuːs] *n* refugo, lixo

regain [rɪ'geɪn] *vt* recuperar, recobrar

regard [rɪ'gɑːd] *n* (*gaze*) olhar *m* firme; (*attention*) atenção *f*; (*esteem*) estima, consideração *f* ▷ *vt* (*consider*) considerar; **to give one's ~s to** dar lembranças a; **"with kindest ~s"** "cordialmente"; **as ~s**, **with ~ to** com relação a, com respeito a, quanto a; **regarding** *prep* com relação a; **regardless** *adv* apesar de tudo; **regardless of** apesar de

regiment ['rɛdʒɪmənt] *n* regimento

r

region ['ri:dʒən] n região f; **in the ~ of** (fig) por volta de, ao redor de; **regional** adj regional

register ['rɛdʒɪstə'] n registro (BR), registo (PT); (Sch) chamada ▷ vt registrar (BR), registar (PT); (subj: instrument) marcar, indicar ▷ vi (at hotel) registrar-se (BR), registar-se (PT); (for work) candidatar-se; (as student) inscrever-se; (make impression) causar impressão; **registered** adj (letter, parcel) registrado (BR), registado (PT)

registrar ['rɛdʒɪstrɑ:'] n oficial m/f de registro (BR) or registo (PT), escrivão(-vã) m/f; (in college) funcionário(-a) administrativo(-a) sênior; (in hospital) médico(-a) sênior

registration [rɛdʒɪs'treɪʃən] n (act) registro (BR), registo (PT); (Aut: also: ~ number) número da placa

regret [rɪ'grɛt] n desgosto, pesar m ▷ vt lamentar; (repent of) arrepender-se de

regular ['rɛgjulə'] adj regular; (frequent) frequente; (usual) habitual; (soldier) de linha ▷ n habitual m/f; **regularly** adv regularmente; (shaped) simetricamente; (often) frequentemente

regulate ['rɛgjuleɪt] vt (speed) regular; (spending) controlar; (Tech) regular, ajustar; **regulation** [rɛgju'leɪʃən] n (rule) regra, regulamento; (adjustment) ajuste m

rehearsal [rɪ'hə:səl] n ensaio
rehearse [rɪ'hə:s] vt ensaiar
reign [reɪn] n reinado; (fig) domínio ▷ vi reinar; imperar
reimburse [ri:ɪm'bə:s] vt reembolsar
rein [reɪn] n (for horse) rédea

reindeer ['reɪndɪə'] n inv rena
reinforce [ri:ɪn'fɔ:s] vt reforçar
reinstate [ri:ɪn'steɪt] vt (worker) readmitir; (tax, law) reintroduzir
reject [n 'ri:dʒɛkt, vt rɪ'dʒɛkt] n (Comm) artigo defeituoso ▷ vt rejeitar; (offer of help) recusar; (goods) refugar; **rejection** n rejeição f; (of offer of help) recusa
rejoice [rɪ'dʒɔɪs] vi: **to ~ at or over** regozijar-se or alegrar-se de
relate [rɪ'leɪt] vt (tell) contar, relatar; (connect): **to ~ sth to** relacionar algo com ▷ vi: **to ~ to** relacionar-se com; **~d to** ligado a, relacionado a
relation [rɪ'leɪʃən] n (person) parente m/f; (link) relação f; **relations** npl (dealings) relações fpl; (relatives) parentes mpl; **relationship** n relacionamento; (between two things) relação f; (also: **family relationship**) parentesco
relative ['rɛlətɪv] n parente m/f ▷ adj relativo; **relatively** adv relativamente
relax [rɪ'læks] vi (unwind) descontrair-se; (muscle) relaxar-se ▷ vt (grip) afrouxar; (control) relaxar; (mind, person) descansar; **relaxation** [ri:læk'seɪʃən] n (rest) descanso; (of muscle, control) relaxamento; (of grip) afrouxamento; (recreation) lazer m; **relaxed** adj relaxado; (tranquil) descontraído
relay ['ri:leɪ] n (race) corrida de revezamento ▷ vt (message) retransmitir
release [rɪ'li:s] n (from prison) libertação f; (from obligation) liberação f; (of gas) escape m; (of water) despejo; (of film, book etc) lançamento ▷ vt (prisoner) pôr em

liberdade; (*book, film*) lançar; (*report, news*) publicar; (*gas etc*) soltar; (*free: from wreckage etc*) soltar; (*Tech: catch, spring etc*) desengatar, desapertar

relegate ['rɛləgeɪt] *vt* relegar; (*Sport*): **to be ~d** ser rebaixado

relent [rɪ'lɛnt] *vi* (*yield*) ceder; **relentless** *adj* (*unceasing*) contínuo; (*determined*) implacável

relevant ['rɛləvənt] *adj* pertinente; **~ to** relacionado com

reliable [rɪ'laɪəbl] *adj* (*person, firm*) de confiança, confiável, sério; (*method, machine*) seguro; (*news*) fidedigno

relic ['rɛlɪk] *n* (*Rel*) relíquia; (*of the past*) vestígio

relief [rɪ'liːf] *n* alívio; (*help, supplies*) ajuda, socorro; (*Art, Geo*) relevo

relieve [rɪ'liːv] *vt* (*pain, fear*) aliviar; (*bring help to*) ajudar, socorrer; (*take over from: gen*) substituir, revezar; (*: guard*) render; **to ~ sb of sth** (*load*) tirar algo de alguém; (*duties*) destituir alguém de algo; **to ~ o.s.** fazer as necessidades

religion [rɪ'lɪdʒən] *n* religião *f*; **religious** *adj* religioso

relish ['rɛlɪʃ] *n* (*Culin*) condimento, tempero; (*enjoyment*) entusiasmo ▷ *vt* (*food etc*) saborear; (*thought*) ver com satisfação

reluctant [rɪ'lʌktənt] *adj* relutante; **reluctantly** *adv* relutantemente, de má vontade

rely on [rɪ'laɪ-] *vt fus* confiar em, contar com; (*be dependent on*) depender de

remain [rɪ'meɪn] *vi* (*survive*) sobreviver; (*stay*) ficar, permanecer; (*be left*) sobrar; (*continue*) continuar; **remainder** *n* resto, restante *m*; **remaining** *adj*

restante; **remains** *npl* (*of body*) restos *mpl*; (*of meal*) sobras *fpl*; (*of building*) ruínas *fpl*

remand [rɪ'mɑːnd] *n*: **on ~** sob prisão preventiva ▷ *vt*: **to be ~ed in custody** continuar sob prisão preventiva, manter sob custódia

remark [rɪ'mɑːk] *n* observação *f*, comentário ▷ *vt* comentar; **remarkable** *adj* (*outstanding*) extraordinário

remarry [riː'mærɪ] *vi* casar-se de novo

remedy ['rɛmədɪ] *n*: **~ (for)** remédio (contra *or* a) ▷ *vt* remediar

remember [rɪ'mɛmbə'] *vt* lembrar-se de, lembrar; (*bear in mind*) ter em mente; (*send greetings*): **~ me to her** dê lembranças a ela

remembrance [rɪ'mɛmbrəns] *n* (*memory*) memória; (*souvenir*) lembrança, recordação *f*; **Remembrance Sunday** *n* ver nota

⊛ **REMEMBRANCE SUNDAY**
⊛
⊛ **Remembrance Sunday** ou
⊛ **Remembrance Day** é o
⊛ domingo mais próximo do dia 11
⊛ de novembro, dia em que a
⊛ Primeira Guerra Mundial
⊛ terminou oficialmente e no qual
⊛ se homenageia as vítimas das
⊛ duas guerras mundiais. Nessa
⊛ ocasião são observados dois
⊛ minutos de silêncio às 11 horas,
⊛ horário da assinatura do
⊛ armistício com a Alemanha em
⊛ 1918. Nos dias anteriores,
⊛ papoulas de papel são vendidas
⊛ por associações de caridade e a
⊛ renda é revertida aos
⊛ ex-combatentes e suas famílias.

remind [rɪ'maɪnd] vt: **to ~ sb to do sth** lembrar a alguém que tem de fazer algo; **to ~ sb of sth** lembrar algo a alguém, lembrar alguém de algo; **reminder** n lembrança; (letter) carta de advertência

remnant ['rɛmnənt] n resto; (of cloth) retalho; **remnants** npl (Comm) retalhos mpl

remorse [rɪ'mɔːs] n remorso

remote [rɪ'məut] adj remoto; (person) reservado, afastado; **remote control** n controle m remoto; **remotely** adv remotamente; (slightly) levemente

removal [rɪ'muːvəl] n (taking away) remoção f; (Brit: from house) mudança; (from office: sacking) afastamento, demissão f; (Med) extração f; **removal van** (Brit) n caminhão m (BR) or camião m (PT) de mudanças

remove [rɪ'muːv] vt tirar, retirar; (clothing) tirar; (stain) remover; (employee) afastar, demitir; (name from list, obstacle) eliminar, remover; (doubt, abuse) afastar; (Med) extrair, extirpar

render ['rɛndəʳ] vt (thanks) trazer; (service) prestar; (make) fazer, tornar

rendezvous ['rɔndɪvuː] n encontro; (place) ponto de encontro

renew [rɪ'njuː] vt retomar, recomeçar; (loan etc) prorrogar; (negotiations, acquaintance) reatar

renovate ['rɛnəveɪt] vt renovar; (house, room) reformar

rent [rɛnt] n aluguel m (BR), aluguer m (PT) ▷ vt (also: ~ out) alugar; **rental** n (for television, car) aluguel m (BR), aluguer m (PT)

rep [rɛp] n abbr (Comm)

= **representative**

repair [rɪ'pɛəʳ] n reparação f, conserto ▷ vt consertar; **in good/bad ~** em bom/mau estado; **repair kit** n caixa de ferramentas

repay [riː'peɪ] irreg vt (money) reembolsar, restituir; (person) pagar de volta; (debt) saldar, liquidar; (sb's efforts) corresponder, retribuir; (favour) retribuir; **repayment** n reembolso; (of debt) pagamento

repeat [rɪ'piːt] n (Radio, TV) repetição f ▷ vt repetir; (Comm: order) renovar ▷ vi repetir-se

repetitive [rɪ'pɛtɪtɪv] adj repetitivo

replace [rɪ'pleɪs] vt (put back) repor, devolver; (take the place of) substituir; **replacement** n (substitution) substituição f; (substitute) substituto(-a)

replay ['riːpleɪ] n (of match) partida decisiva; (TV: also: **action ~**) replay m

replica ['rɛplɪkə] n réplica, cópia, reprodução f

reply [rɪ'plaɪ] n resposta ▷ vi responder

report [rɪ'pɔːt] n relatório; (Press etc) reportagem f; (Brit: also: **school ~**) boletim m escolar; (of gun) estampido, detonação f ▷ vt informar sobre; (Press etc) fazer uma reportagem sobre; (bring to notice) comunicar, anunciar ▷ vi (make a report): **to ~ (on)** apresentar um relatório (sobre); (present o.s.): **to ~ (to sb)** apresentar-se (a alguém); (be responsible to): **to ~ to sb** obedecer as ordens de alguém; **report card** (US, Scotland) n boletim m escolar; **reportedly** adv: **she is reportedly living in Spain** dizem que ela mora na Espanha; **reporter** n repórter m/f

represent [rɛprɪ'zɛnt] vt representar; (*constitute*) constituir; (*Comm*) ser representante de; **representation** [rɛprɪzɛn'teɪʃən] n representação f; (*picture, statue*) representação, retrato; (*petition*) petição f; **representations** npl (*protest*) reclamação f, protesto; **representative** [rɛprɪ'zɛntətɪv] n representante m/f; (*US: Pol*) deputado(-a) ▷ adj: **representative (of)** representativo (de)

repress [rɪ'prɛs] vt reprimir; **repression** n repressão f

reproduce [ri:prə'dju:s] vt reproduzir ▷ vi reproduzir-se

reptile ['rɛptaɪl] n réptil m

republic [rɪ'pʌblɪk] n república; **republican** adj, n republicano(-a); (*US: Pol*): **Republican** membro(-a) do Partido Republicano

reputable ['rɛpjutəbl] adj (*make etc*) bem conceituado, de confiança; (*person*) honrado, respeitável

reputation [rɛpju'teɪʃən] n reputação f

request [rɪ'kwɛst] n pedido; (*formal*) petição f ▷ vt: **to ~ sth of** or **from sb** pedir algo a alguém; (*formally*) solicitar algo a alguém; **request stop** (*Brit*) n (*for bus*) parada não obrigatória

require [rɪ'kwaɪər] vt (*need: subj: person*) precisar de, necessitar; (: *thing, situation*) requerer, exigir; (*want*) pedir; (*order*): **to ~ sb to do sth/sth of sb** exigir que alguém faça algo/algo de alguém; **requirement** n (*need*) necessidade f; (*want*) pedido

rescue ['rɛskju:] n salvamento, resgate m ▷ vt: **to ~ (from)** resgatar (de); (*save, fig*) salvar (de)

research [rɪ'sə:tʃ] n pesquisa ▷ vt pesquisar

resemblance [rɪ'zɛmbləns] n semelhança

resemble [rɪ'zɛmbl] vt parecer-se com

resent [rɪ'zɛnt] vt (*attitude*) ressentir-se de; (*person*) estar ressentido com; **resentful** adj ressentido

reservation [rɛzə'veɪʃən] n reserva

reserve [rɪ'zə:v] n reserva; (*Sport*) suplente m/f, reserva m/f (BR) ▷ vt reservar; **reserves** npl (*Mil*) (tropas fpl da) reserva; (*Comm*) reserva; **in ~** de reserva; **reserved** adj reservado

residence ['rɛzɪdəns] n residência; (*formal: home*) domicílio; **residence permit** (*Brit*) n autorização f de residência

resident ['rɛzɪdənt] n (*of country, town*) habitante m/f; (*in hotel*) hóspede m/f ▷ adj (*population*) permanente; (*doctor*) interno, residente; **residential** [rɛzɪ'dɛnʃəl] adj residencial

residue ['rɛzɪdju:] n resto

resign [rɪ'zaɪn] vt renunciar a, demitir-se de ▷ vi: **to ~ (from)** demitir-se (de); **to ~ o.s. to** resignar-se a; **resignation** [rɛzɪg'neɪʃən] n demissão f; (*state of mind*) resignação f

resist [rɪ'zɪst] vt resistir a

resolution [rɛzə'lu:ʃən] n resolução f; (*of problem*) solução f

resolve [rɪ'zɔlv] n resolução f ▷ vt resolver ▷ vi: **to ~ to do** resolver-se a fazer

resort [rɪ'zɔ:t] n local m turístico,

estação f de veraneio; (*recourse*)
recurso ▷ vi: **to ~ to** recorrer a;
in the last ~ em último caso, em
última instância

resource [rɪˈsɔːs] *n* (*raw material*)
recurso natural; **resources** *npl*
(*coal, money, energy*) recursos *mpl*;
resourceful *adj* engenhoso,
habilidoso

respect [rɪsˈpɛkt] *n* respeito ▷ *vt*
respeitar; **respects** *npl* (*greetings*)
cumprimentos *mpl*; **respectable**
adj respeitável; (*large*)
considerável; (*result, player*)
razoável; **respectful** *adj*
respeitoso

respond [rɪsˈpɔnd] *vi* (*answer*)
responder; (*react*) reagir;
response *n* resposta; (*reaction*)
reação f

responsibility [rɪspɔnsɪˈbɪlɪtɪ] *n*
responsabilidade f; (*duty*) dever *m*

responsible [rɪsˈpɔnsɪbl] *adj* sério,
responsável; (*job*) de
responsabilidade; (*liable*): **~ (for)**
responsável (por)

responsive [rɪsˈpɔnsɪv] *adj*
receptivo

rest [rɛst] *n* descanso, repouso;
(*pause*) pausa, intervalo; (*support*)
apoio; (*remainder*) resto; (*Mus*)
pausa ▷ *vi* descansar; (*stop*) parar;
(*be supported*): **to ~ on** apoiar-se em
▷ *vt* descansar; (*lean*): **to ~ sth on/
against** apoiar algo em or sobre/
contra; **the ~ of them** os outros;
it ~s with him to do it cabe a ele
fazê-lo

restaurant [ˈrɛstərɔn] *n*
restaurante *m*; **restaurant car**
(*Brit*) *n* vagão-restaurante *m*

restless [ˈrɛstlɪs] *adj*
desassossegado, irrequieto

restore [rɪˈstɔːʳ] *vt* (*building, order*)

restaurar; (*sth stolen*) restituir;
(*peace, health*) restabelecer

restrain [rɪsˈtreɪn] *vt* (*feeling*)
reprimir; (*growth, inflation*) refrear;
(*person*): **to ~ (from doing)** impedir
(de fazer); **restraint** *n* (*restriction*)
restrição f; (*moderation*) moderação
f, comedimento; (*of style*)
sobriedade f

restrict [rɪsˈtrɪkt] *vt* restringir,
limitar; (*people, animals*) confinar;
(*activities*) limitar; **restriction** *n*
restrição f, limitação f

rest room (*US*) *n* banheiro (*BR*),
lavabo (*PT*)

result [rɪˈzʌlt] *n* resultado ▷ *vi*:
to ~ in resultar em; **as a ~ of** como
resultado or consequência de

resume [rɪˈzjuːm] *vt* (*work, journey*)
retomar, recomeçar ▷ *vi*
recomeçar

résumé [ˈreɪzjuːmeɪ] *n* (*summary*)
resumo; (*US: curriculum vitae*)
currículum vitae *m*, currículo

resuscitate [rɪˈsʌsɪteɪt] *vt* (*Med*)
ressuscitar, reanimar

retail [ˈriːteɪl] *adj* a varejo (*BR*), a
retalho (*PT*) ▷ *adv* a varejo (*BR*), a
retalho (*PT*); **retailer** *n* varejista
m/f (*BR*), retalhista *m/f* (*PT*)

retain [rɪˈteɪn] *vt* (*keep*) reter,
conservar

retire [rɪˈtaɪəʳ] *vi* aposentar-se;
(*withdraw*) retirar-se; (*go to bed*)
deitar-se; **retired** *adj* aposentado
(*BR*), reformado (*PT*); **retirement**
n aposentadoria (*BR*), reforma (*PT*)

retort [rɪˈtɔːt] *vi* replicar, retrucar

retreat [rɪˈtriːt] *n* (*place*) retiro;
(*act*) retirada ▷ *vi* retirar-se

retrieve [rɪˈtriːv] *vt* (*sth lost*) reaver,
recuperar; (*situation, honour*)
salvar; (*error, loss*) reparar

retrospect [ˈrɛtrəspɛkt] *n*: **in ~**

retrospectivamente, em retrospecto; **retrospective** [rɛtrə'spɛktɪv] adj retrospectivo; (law) retroativo

return [rɪ'tə:n] n regresso, volta; (of sth stolen etc) devolução f; (Finance: from land, shares) rendimento ▷ cpd (journey) de volta; (Brit: ticket) de ida e volta; (match) de revanche ▷ vi voltar, regressar; (symptoms etc) voltar; (regain): **to ~ to** (consciousness) recobrar; (power) retornar a ▷ vt devolver; (favour, love etc) retribuir; (verdict) proferir, anunciar; (Pol: candidate) eleger; **returns** npl (Comm) receita; **in ~ (for)** em troca (de); **many happy ~s (of the day)!** parabéns!; **by ~ (of post)** por volta do correio

reunion [ri:'ju:nɪən] n (family) reunião f; (two people, class) reencontro

reunite [ri:ju:'naɪt] vt reunir; (reconcile) reconciliar

revamp ['ri:'væmp] vt dar um jeito em

reveal [rɪ'vi:l] vt revelar; (make visible) mostrar; **revealing** adj revelador(a)

revel ['rɛvl] vi: **to ~ in sth/in doing sth** deleitar-se com algo/em fazer algo

revenge [rɪ'vɛndʒ] n vingança, desforra; **to take ~ on** vingar-se de

revenue ['rɛvənju:] n receita, renda

reversal [rɪ'və:sl] n (of order) reversão f; (of direction) mudança em sentido contrário; (of decision) revogação f; (of roles) inversão f

reverse [rɪ'və:s] n (opposite) contrário; (of cloth) avesso; (of coin) reverso; (of paper) dorso; (Aut: also: **~ gear**) marcha à ré (BR), marcha atrás (PT); (setback) revés m, derrota ▷ adj (order) inverso, oposto; (direction) contrário; (process) inverso ▷ vt inverter; (position) mudar; (process, decision) revogar; (car) dar ré com ▷ vi (Brit: Aut) dar (marcha à) ré (BR), fazer marcha atrás (PT); **reverse-charge call** (Brit) n (Tel) ligação f a cobrar

revert [rɪ'və:t] vi: **to ~ to** voltar a; (Law) reverter a

review [rɪ'vju:] n (magazine, Mil) revista; (of book, film) crítica, resenha; (examination) recapitulação f, exame m ▷ vt rever, examinar; (Mil) passar em revista; (book, film) fazer a crítica or resenha de

revise [rɪ'vaɪz] vt (manuscript) corrigir; (opinion, procedure) alterar; (price) revisar; **revision** [rɪ'vɪʒən] n correção f; (for exam) revisão f

revival [rɪ'vaɪvəl] n (recovery) restabelecimento; (of interest) renascença, renascimento; (Theatre) reestreia; (of faith) despertar m

revive [rɪ'vaɪv] vt (person) reanimar, ressuscitar; (economy) recuperar; (custom) restabelecer, restaurar; (hope, courage) despertar; (play) reapresentar ▷ vi (person: from faint) voltar a si, recuperar os sentidos; (: from ill-health) recuperar-se; (activity, economy) reativar; (hope, interest) renascer

revolt [rɪ'vəult] n revolta, rebelião f, insurreição f ▷ vi revoltar-se ▷ vt causar aversão a, repugnar; **revolting** adj revoltante, repulsivo

revolution [rɛvə'lu:ʃən] n revolução f; (of wheel, earth) rotação f

revolve [rɪ'vɔlv] vi girar
revolver [rɪ'vɔlvəʳ] n revólver m
reward [rɪ'wɔːd] n recompensa
▷ vt: **to ~ (for)** recompensar or
premiar (por); **rewarding** adj (fig)
gratificante, compensador(a)
rewind [riː'waɪnd] irreg vt (tape)
voltar para trás
rewritable adj regravável
rheumatism ['ruːmətɪzəm] n
reumatismo
rhinoceros [raɪ'nɔsərəs] n
rinoceronte m
rhubarb ['ruːbɑːb] n ruibarbo
rhyme [raɪm] n rima; (verse)
verso(s) m(pl) rimado(s), poesia
rhythm ['rɪðm] n ritmo
rib [rɪb] n (Anat) costela ▷ vt (mock)
zombar de, encarnar em
ribbon ['rɪbən] n fita; **in ~s** (torn) em
tirinhas, esfarrapado
rice [raɪs] n arroz m; **rice pudding**
n arroz m doce
rich [rɪtʃ] adj rico; (clothes) valioso;
(soil) fértil; (food) suculento, forte;
(colour) intenso; (voice) suave,
cheio ▷ npl: **the rich** os ricos;
riches npl (wealth) riquezas fpl
rid [rɪd] (pt, pp **rid**) vt: **to ~ sb of sth**
livrar alguém de algo; **to get ~ of**
livrar-se de; (sth no longer required)
desfazer-se de
riddle ['rɪdl] n (conundrum)
adivinhação f; (mystery) enigma m,
charada ▷ vt: **to be ~d with** estar
cheio de
ride [raɪd] (pt **rode**, pp **ridden**) n
(gen) passeio; (on horse) passeio a
cavalo; (distance covered) percurso,
trajeto ▷ vi (as sport) montar; (go
somewhere: on horse, bicycle) ir (a
cavalo, de bicicleta); (journey: on
bicycle, motorcycle, bus) viajar ▷ vt (a
horse) montar a; (bicycle,

motorcycle) andar de; (distance)
percorrer; **to ~ at anchor** (Naut)
estar ancorado; **to take sb for a ~**
(fig) enganar alguém; **rider** n (on
horse: male) cavaleiro; (: female)
amazona; (on bicycle) ciclista m/f;
(on motorcycle) motociclista m/f
ridge [rɪdʒ] n (of hill) cume m, topo;
(of roof) cumeeira; (wrinkle) ruga
ridicule ['rɪdɪkjuːl] n escárnio,
zombaria, mofa ▷ vt ridicularizar,
zombar de; **ridiculous** adj ridículo
riding ['raɪdɪŋ] n equitação f
rife [raɪf] adj: **to be ~** ser comum; **to
be ~ with** estar repleto de, abundar
em
rifle ['raɪfl] n rifle m, fuzil m ▷ vt
saquear **rifle through** vt fus
vascular
rift [rɪft] n fenda, fratura; (in clouds)
brecha; (fig: between friends)
desentendimento; (: in party)
rompimento, divergência
rig [rɪg] n (also: **oil ~**) torre f de
perfuração ▷ vt adulterar or
falsificar os resultados de **rig out**
(Brit) vt: **to ~ out as/in** ataviar or
vestir como/com **rig up** vt
instalar, montar, improvisar
right [raɪt] adj certo, correto;
(suitable) adequado, conveniente;
(: decision) certo; (just) justo;
(morally good) bom; (not left) direito
▷ n direito; (not left) direita ▷ adv
bem, corretamente; (fairly)
adequadamente, justamente; (not
on the left) à direita; (exactly): **~ now**
agora mesmo ▷ vt colocar em pé;
(correct) corrigir, indireitar ▷ excl
bom!; **to be ~** (person) ter razão;
(answer, clock) estar certo; **by ~s** por
direito; **on the ~** à direita; **to be in
the ~** ter razão; **~ away**
imediatamente, logo, já; **~ in the**

middle bem no meio; **rightful** adj (heir) legítimo; (place) justo, legítimo; **right-handed** adj destro; **rightly** adv (with reason) com razão; **right of way** n prioridade f de passagem; (Aut) preferência; **right-wing** adj de direita

rigid ['rɪdʒɪd] adj rígido; (principle) inflexível

rim [rɪm] n borda, beira; (of spectacles, wheel) aro

rind [raɪnd] n (of bacon) pele f; (of lemon etc) casca; (of cheese) crosta, casca

ring [rɪŋ] (pt **rang**, pp **rung**) n (of metal) aro; (on finger) anel m; (of people, objects) círculo, grupo; (for boxing) ringue m; (of circus) pista, picadeiro; (bullring) picadeiro, arena; (of light, smoke) círculo; (of small bell) toque m; (of large bell) badalada, repique m ▷ vi (on telephone) telefonar; (bell) tocar; (also: **~ out**) soar; (ears) zumbir ▷ vt (Brit: Tel) telefonar a, ligar para; (bell etc) badalar; (doorbell) tocar; **to give sb a ~** (Brit: Tel) dar uma ligada or ligar para alguém **ring back** (Brit) vi (Tel) telefonar or ligar de volta ▷ vt telefonar or ligar de volta para **ring off** (Brit) vi (Tel) desligar **ring up** (Brit) vt (Tel) telefonar a, ligar para; **ringing tone** (Brit) n (Tel) sinal m de chamada; **ringleader** n cabeça m/f, cérebro; **ring road** (Brit) n estrada periférica or perimetral; **ringtone** n (on cellphone) toque m

rink [rɪŋk] n (also: **ice ~**) pista de patinação, rinque m

rinse [rɪns] n enxaguada ▷ vt enxaguar; (also: **~ out**: mouth) bochechar

riot ['raɪət] n distúrbio, motim m, desordem f; (of colour) festival m, profusão f ▷ vi provocar distúrbios, amotinar-se; **to run ~** desenfrear-se

rip [rɪp] n rasgão m ▷ vt rasgar ▷ vi rasgar-se

ripe [raɪp] adj maduro

ripple ['rɪpl] n ondulação f, encrespação f; (of laughter etc) onda ▷ vi encrespar-se

rise [raɪz] (pt **rose**, pp **risen**) n elevação f, ladeira; (hill) colina, rampa; (in wages: Brit) aumento; (in prices, temperature) subida; (to power etc) ascensão f ▷ vi levantar-se, erguer-se; (prices, waters) subir; (sun) nascer; (from bed etc) levantar(-se); (sound, voice) aumentar, erguer-se; (also: **~ up**: building) erguer-se; (: rebel) sublevar-se; (in rank) ascender, subir; **to give ~ to** ocasionar, dar origem a; **to ~ to the occasion** mostrar-se à altura da situação; **rising** adj (prices) em alta; (number) crescente, cada vez maior; (tide) montante; (sun, moon) nascente

risk [rɪsk] n risco, perigo; (Insurance) risco ▷ vt pôr em risco; (chance) arriscar, aventurar; **to take** or **run the ~ of doing** correr o risco de fazer; **at ~** em perigo; **at one's own ~** por sua própria conta e risco; **risky** adj perigoso

rite [raɪt] n rito; **last ~s** últimos sacramentos

ritual ['rɪtjuəl] adj ritual ▷ n ritual m; (of initiation) rito

rival ['raɪvl] adj, n rival m/f; (in business) concorrente m/f ▷ vt competir com; **rivalry** n rivalidade f

river ['rɪvəʳ] n rio ▷ cpd (port, traffic)

r

fluvial; **up/down ~** rio acima/abaixo; **riverbank** n margem f (do rio)

road [rəud] n via; (motorway etc) estrada (de rodagem); (in town) rua ▷ cpd rodoviário; **road accident** n acidente m de trânsito; **roadblock** n barricada; **road map** n mapa m rodoviário; **road rage** n conduta agressiva dos motoristas no trânsito; **roadside** n beira da estrada; **road sign** n placa de sinalização

roam [rəum] vi vagar, perambular, errar

roar [rɔːʳ] n (of animal) rugido, urro; (of crowd) bramido; (of vehicle, storm) estrondo; (of laughter) barulho ▷ vi (animal, engine) rugir; (person, crowd) bradar; **to ~ with laughter** dar gargalhadas

roast [rəust] n carne f assada, assado ▷ vt assar; (coffee) torrar; **roast beef** n rosbife m

rob [rɔb] vt roubar; (bank) assaltar; **to ~ sb of sth** roubar algo de alguém; (fig: deprive) despojar alguém de algo; **robber** n ladrão/ladra m/f; **robbery** n roubo

robe [rəub] n toga, beca; (also: **bath ~**) roupão m (de banho)

robin ['rɔbɪn] n pisco-de-peito-ruivo (BR), pintarroxo (PT)

robot ['rəubɔt] n robô m

robust [rəu'bʌst] adj robusto, forte; (appetite) sadio; (economy) forte

rock [rɔk] n rocha; (boulder) penhasco, rochedo; (US: small stone) cascalho; (Brit: sweet) pirulito ▷ vt (swing gently: cradle) balançar, oscilar; (: child) embalar, acalentar; (shake) sacudir ▷ vi (object) balançar-se; (person) embalar-se; **on the ~s** (drink) com gelo; (marriage etc) arruinado, em

dificuldades; **rock and roll** n rock-and-roll m

rocket ['rɔkɪt] n foguete m

rocky ['rɔkɪ] adj rochoso, bambo, instável; (marriage etc) instável

rod [rɔd] n vara, varinha; (also: **fishing ~**) vara de pescar

rode [rəud] pt of **ride**

rodent ['rəudnt] n roedor m

rogue [rəug] n velhaco, maroto

role [rəul] n papel m; **role model** n modelo

roll [rəul] n rolo; (of banknotes) maço; (also: **bread ~**) pãozinho; (register) rol m, lista; (of drums etc) rufar m ▷ vt rolar; (also: **~ up**: string) enrolar; (: sleeves) arregaçar; (cigarette) enrolar; (eyes) virar; (also: **~ out**: pastry) esticar; (lawn, road etc) aplanar ▷ vi rolar; (drum) rufar; (vehicle: also: **~ along**) rodar; (ship) balançar, jogar **roll about** vi ficar rolando **roll around** vi = **roll about** **roll by** vi (time) passar **roll in** vi (mail, cash) chegar em grande quantidade **roll over** vi dar uma volta **roll up** vi (inf) pintar, chegar, aparecer ▷ vt (carpet etc) enrolar; **roller** n (in machine) rolo, cilindro; (wheel) roda, roldana; (for lawn, road) rolo compressor; (for hair) rolo; **roller coaster** n montanha-russa; **roller skates** npl patins mpl de roda

rolling pin n rolo de pastel

ROM [rɔm] n abbr (Comput: = read-only memory) ROM f

Roman ['rəumən] adj, n romano(-a); **Roman Catholic** adj, n católico(-a) (romano(-a))

romance [rə'mæns] n aventura amorosa, romance m; (book etc) história de amor; (charm) romantismo

Romania [ruːˈmeɪnɪə] *n* Romênia; **Romanian** *adj* romeno ▷ *n* romeno(-a); (*Ling*) romeno

romantic [rəˈmæntɪk] *adj* romântico

Rome [rəʊm] *n* Roma

roof [ruːf] *n* (*of house*) telhado; (*of car*) capota, teto ▷ *vt* telhar, cobrir com telhas; **the ~ of the mouth** o céu da boca; **roof rack** *n* (*Aut*) bagageiro

rook [ruk] *n* (*bird*) gralha; (*Chess*) torre *f*

room [ruːm] *n* (*in house*) quarto, aposento; (*also*: **bed~**) quarto, dormitório; (*in school etc*) sala; (*space*) espaço, lugar *m*; (*scope: for improvement etc*) espaço; **rooms** *npl* (*lodging*) alojamento; **"~s to let"** (*Brit*), **"~s for rent"** (*US*) "alugam-se quartos *or* apartamentos"; **roommate** *n* companheiro(-a) de quarto; **room service** *n* serviço de quarto; **roomy** *adj* espaçoso; (*garment*) folgado

rooster [ˈruːstər] *n* galo

root [ruːt] *n* raiz *f*; (*fig*) origem *f* ▷ *vi* enraizar, arraigar; **roots** *npl* (*family origins*) raízes *fpl* **root about** *vi* (*fig*): **to ~ about in** (*drawer*) vasculhar; (*house*) esquadrinhar **root for** *vt fus* torcer por **root out** *vt* extirpar

rope [rəʊp] *n* corda; (*Naut*) cabo ▷ *vt* (*tie*) amarrar; (*climbers: also*: **~ together**) amarrar *or* atar com uma corda; (*area: also*: **~ off**) isolar; **to know the ~s** (*fig*) estar por dentro (do assunto) **rope in** *vt* (*fig*): **to ~ sb in** persuadir alguém a tomar parte

rose [rəʊz] *pt of* **rise** ▷ *n* rosa; (*also*: **~bush**) roseira; (*on watering can*) crivo

rosé [ˈrəʊzeɪ] *n* rosado, rosé *m*

rosemary [ˈrəʊzmərɪ] *n* alecrim *m*

rosy [ˈrəʊzɪ] *adj* rosado, rosáceo; (*cheeks*) rosado; (*situation*) cor-de-rosa *inv*; **a ~ future** um futuro promissor

rot [rɒt] *n* (*decay*) putrefação *f*, podridão *f*; (*fig: pej*) besteira ▷ *vt, vi* apodrecer

rota [ˈrəʊtə] *n* lista de tarefas, escala de serviço

rotate [rəʊˈteɪt] *vt* fazer girar, dar voltas em; (*jobs*) alternar, revezar ▷ *vi* girar, dar voltas

rotten [ˈrɒtn] *adj* podre; (*wood*) carcomido; (*fig*) corrupto; (*inf: bad*) péssimo; **to feel ~** (*ill*) sentir-se podre

rough [rʌf] *adj* (*skin, surface*) áspero; (*terrain*) acidentado; (*road*) desigual; (*voice*) áspero, rouco; (*person, manner: violent*) violento; (*: brusque*) ríspido; (*weather*) tempestuoso; (*treatment*) brutal, mau/má; (*sea*) agitado; (*district*) violento; (*plan*) preliminar; (*work, cloth*) grosseiro; (*guess*) aproximado ▷ *n* (*Golf*): **in the ~** na grama crescida; **to sleep ~** (*Brit*) dormir na rua; **roughly** *adv* bruscamente; (*make*) toscamente; (*approximately*) aproximadamente

roulette [ruːˈlɛt] *n* roleta

round [raund] *adj* redondo ▷ *n* (*Brit: of toast*) rodela; (*of policeman*) ronda; (*of milkman*) trajeto; (*of doctor*) visitas *fpl*; (*game: of cards, golf, in competition*) partida; (*of ammunition*) cartucho; (*Boxing*) rounde *m*, assalto; (*of talks*) ciclo ▷ *vt* virar, dobrar ▷ *prep* (*surrounding*): **~ his neck/the table** em volta de seu pescoço/ao redor da mesa; (*in a circular movement*):

to go ~ the world dar a volta ao mundo; (in various directions): **to move ~ a house** mover-se por uma casa; (approximately): **~ about** aproximadamente ▷ adv: **all ~** por todos os lados; **the long way ~** o caminho mais comprido; **all the year ~** durante todo o ano; **it's just ~ the corner** (fig) está pertinho; **~ the clock** ininterrupto; **to go ~ the back** passar por detrás; **to go ~ a house** visitar uma casa; **enough to go ~** suficiente para todos; **a ~ of applause** uma salva de palmas; **a ~ of drinks** uma rodada de bebidas; **~ of sandwiches** sanduíche m (BR), sandes f inv (PT)
round off vt terminar, completar
round up vt (cattle) encurralar; (people) reunir; (price, figure) arredondar; **roundabout** n (Brit: Aut) rotatória; (: at fair) carrossel m ▷ adj indireto; **round trip** n viagem f de ida e volta
rouse [rauz] vt (wake up) despertar, acordar; (stir up) suscitar
route [ru:t] n caminho, rota; (of bus) trajeto; (of shipping) rumo, rota; (of procession) rota
routine [ru:'ti:n] adj (work) rotineiro; (procedure) de rotina ▷ n rotina; (Theatre) número
row¹ [rəu] n (line) fila, fileira; (in theatre, boat) fileira; (Knitting) carreira, fileira ▷ vi, vt remar; **in a ~** (fig) a fio, seguido
row² [rau] n barulho, balbúrdia; (dispute) discussão f, briga; (scolding) repreensão f ▷ vi brigar; **to have a ~** ter uma briga
rowboat ['rəubəut] (US) n barco a remo
rowing ['rəuɪŋ] n remo; **rowing boat** (Brit) n barco a remo

royal ['rɔɪəl] adj real
Royal Academy (Brit) n ver nota

⦿ **ROYAL ACADEMY**
⦿
⦿ A **Royal Academy**, ou **Royal**
⦿ **Academy of Arts**, fundada em
⦿ 1768 por George III para
⦿ desenvolver a pintura, a
⦿ escultura e a arquitetura,
⦿ situa-se em Burlington House,
⦿ Piccadilly. A cada verão há uma
⦿ exposição de obras de artistas
⦿ contemporâneos. A **Royal**
⦿ **Academy** também oferece
⦿ cursos de pintura, escultura e
⦿ arquitetura.

royalty n família real, realeza; (payment: to author) direitos mpl autorais
rpm abbr (= revolutions per minute) rpm
rub [rʌb] vt (part of body) esfregar; (object) friccionar ▷ n: **to give sth a ~** dar uma esfregada em algo; **to ~ sb up** (Brit) or **~ sb** (US) **the wrong way** irritar alguém **rub off** vi sair esfregando **rub off on** vt fus transmitir-se para, influir sobre **rub out** vt apagar
rubber ['rʌbər] n borracha; (Brit: eraser) borracha; **rubber band** n elástico, tira elástica
rubbish ['rʌbɪʃ] n (waste) refugo; (from household, in street) lixo; (junk) coisas fpl sem valor; (fig: pej: nonsense) disparates mpl, asneiras fpl; **rubbish bin** (Brit) n lata de lixo; **rubbish dump** n (in town) depósito (de lixo)
rubble ['rʌbl] n (debris) entulho; (Constr) escombros mpl
ruby ['ru:bɪ] n rubi m

rucksack ['rʌksæk] n mochila
rudder ['rʌdə^r] n leme m; (of plane)
leme de direção
rude [ruːd] adj (person) grosso,
mal-educado; (word, manners)
grosseiro; (shocking) obsceno,
chocante
rug [rʌg] n tapete m; (Brit: for knees)
manta (de viagem)
rugby ['rʌgbɪ] n (also: **~ football**)
rúgbi m (BR), râguebi m (PT)
rugged ['rʌgɪd] adj (landscape)
acidentado, irregular; (features)
marcado; (character) severo,
austero
ruin ['ruːɪn] n ruína; (of plans)
destruição f; (downfall) queda;
(bankruptcy) bancarrota ▷ vt
destruir; (future, person) arruinar;
(spoil) estragar; **ruins** npl (of
building) ruínas fpl
rule [ruːl] n (norm) regra;
(regulation) regulamento;
(government) governo, domínio;
(ruler) régua ▷ vt governar ▷ vi
governar; (monarch) reger; (Law):
to ~ in favour of/against decidir
oficialmente a favor de/contra; **as
a ~** por via de regra, geralmente
rule out vt excluir; **ruler** n
(sovereign) soberano(-a); (for
measuring) régua; **ruling** adj (party)
dominante; (class) dirigente ▷ n
(Law) parecer m, decisão f
rum [rʌm] n rum m
rumble ['rʌmbl] n ruído surdo,
barulho; (of thunder) estrondo,
ribombo ▷ vi ribombar, ressoar;
(stomach) roncar; (pipe) fazer
barulho; (thunder) ribombar
rumour ['ruːmə^r], (US) **rumor**
rumor m, boato ▷ vt: **it is ~ed that
...** corre o boato de que ...
rump steak n alcatra

run [rʌn] (pt **ran**, pp **run**) n corrida;
(in car) passeio (de carro); (distance
travelled) trajeto, percurso;
(journey) viagem f; (series) série f;
(Theatre) temporada; (Ski) pista;
(in stockings) fio puxado ▷ vt (race)
correr; (operate: business) dirigir;
(: competition, course) organizar;
(: hotel, house) administrar; (water)
deixar correr; (bath) encher; (Press:
feature) publicar; (Comput) rodar;
(hand, finger) passar ▷ vi correr;
(work: machine) funcionar; (bus,
train: operate) ir; (: travel) ir;
(continue: play) continuar em
cartaz; (: contract) ser válido; (river,
bath) fluir, correr; (colours, washing)
desbotar; (in election)
candidatar-se; (nose) escorrer;
there was a ~ on houve muita
procura de; **in the long ~** no final
das contas, mais cedo ou mais
tarde; **on the ~** em fuga, foragido
run about vi correr por todos os
lados **run across** vt fus encontrar
por acaso, topar com, dar com **run
around** vi = **run about run away**
vi fugir **run down** vt (Aut)
atropelar; (production) reduzir;
(criticize) criticar; **to be ~ down**
estar enfraquecido or exausto **run
in** (Brit) vt (car) rodar **run into** vt
fus (meet: person) dar com, topar
com; (: trouble) esbarrar em; (collide
with) bater em **run off** vi fugir **run
out** vi (person) sair correndo;
(liquid) escorrer, esgotar-se; (lease,
passport) caducar, vencer; (money)
acabar **run out of** vt fus ficar sem
run over vt (Aut) atropelar ▷ vt fus
(revise) recapitular **run through** vt
fus (instructions) recapitular **run up**
vt (debt) acumular ▷ vi: **to ~ up
against** esbarrar em; **runaway**

r

adj (*horse*) desembestado; (*truck*) desgovernado; (*person*) fugitivo

rung [rʌŋ] *pp of* **ring** ▷ *n* (*of ladder*) degrau *m*

runner ['rʌnəʳ] *n* (*in race*) corredor(a) *m/f*; (*horse*) corredor *m*; (*on sledge*) patim *m*, lâmina; (*for drawer*) corrediça; **runner bean** (*Brit*) *n* (*Bot*) vagem *f* (*BR*), feijão *m* verde (*PT*); **runner-up** *n* segundo(-a) colocado(-a)

running ['rʌnɪŋ] *n* (*sport, race*) corrida; (*of business*) direção *f* ▷ *adj* (*water*) corrente; (*commentary*) contínuo, seguido; **6 days ~** 6 dias seguidos *or* consecutivos; **to be in/out of the ~ for sth** disputar algo/estar fora da disputa por algo

runny ['rʌnɪ] *adj* aguado; (*egg*) mole; **to have a ~ nose** estar com coriza, estar com o nariz escorrendo

run-up *n*: **~ to sth** (*election etc*) período que antecede algo; **during** *or* **in the ~ to** nas vésperas de

runway ['rʌnweɪ] *n* (*Aviat*) pista (de decolagem *or* de pouso)

rupture ['rʌptʃəʳ] *n* (*Med*) hérnia

rural ['ruərl] *adj* rural

rush [rʌʃ] *n* (*hurry*) pressa; (*Comm*) grande procura *or* demanda; (*Bot*) junco; (*current*) torrente *f*; (*of emotion*) ímpeto ▷ *vt* apressar ▷ *vi* apressar-se, precipitar-se; **rush hour** *n* rush *m* (*BR*), hora de ponta (*PT*)

Russia ['rʌʃə] *n* Rússia; **Russian** *adj* russo ▷ *n* russo(-a); (*Ling*) russo

rust [rʌst] *n* ferrugem *f* ▷ *vi* enferrujar

rusty ['rʌstɪ] *adj* enferrujado

ruthless ['ru:θlɪs] *adj* implacável, sem piedade

rye [raɪ] *n* centeio

S

S, s [ɛs] *n* S, s *m*

Sabbath ['sæbəθ] *n* (*Christian*) domingo; (*Jewish*) sábado

sabotage ['sæbətɑːʒ] *n* sabotagem *f* ▷ *vt* sabotar

saccharin, saccharine ['sækərɪn] *n* sacarina

sachet ['sæʃeɪ] *n* sachê *m*

sack [sæk] *n* (*bag*) saco, saca ▷ *vt* (*dismiss*) despedir; (*plunder*) saquear; **to get the ~** ser demitido

sacred ['seɪkrɪd] *adj* sagrado

sacrifice ['sækrɪfaɪs] *n* sacrifício ▷ *vt* sacrificar

sad [sæd] *adj* triste; (*deplorable*) deplorável, triste

saddle ['sædl] *n* sela; (*of cycle*) selim *m* ▷ *vt* selar; **to ~ sb with sth** (*inf: task, bill*) pôr algo nas costas de alguém; (: *responsibility*) sobrecarregar alguém com algo

sadistic [sə'dɪstɪk] *adj* sádico

sadly ['sædlɪ] adv tristemente; (regrettably) infelizmente; (mistaken, neglected) gravemente; **~ lacking (in)** muito carente (de)

sadness ['sædnɪs] n tristeza

safe [seɪf] adj seguro; (out of danger) fora de perigo; (unharmed) ileso, incólume ▷ n cofre m, caixa-forte f; **~ from** protegido de; **~ and sound** são e salvo; **(just) to be on the ~ side** por via das dúvidas; **safely** adv com segurança, a salvo; (without mishap) sem perigo

safety ['seɪftɪ] n segurança; **safety belt** n cinto de segurança; **safety pin** n alfinete m de segurança

sag [sæg] vi (breasts) cair; (roof) afundar; (hem) desmanchar

sage [seɪdʒ] n salva; (man) sábio

Sagittarius [sædʒɪ'tɛərɪəs] n Sagitário

Sahara [sə'hɑːrə] n: **the ~ (Desert)** o Saara

said [sɛd] pt, pp of **say**

sail [seɪl] n (on boat) vela; (trip): **to go for a ~** dar um passeio de barco a vela ▷ vt (boat) governar ▷ vi (travel: ship) navegar, velejar; (: passenger) ir de barco; (Sport) velejar; (set off) zarpar; **they ~ed into Rio de Janeiro** entraram no porto do Rio de Janeiro **sail through** vt fus (fig) fazer com facilidade; **sailboat** (US) n barco a vela; **sailing** n (Sport) navegação f a vela, vela; **to go sailing** ir velejar

sailor ['seɪlə[r]] n marinheiro, marujo

saint [seɪnt] n santo(-a)

sake [seɪk] n: **for the ~ of** (cause de), em consideração a; **for sb's/sth's ~** pelo bem de alguém/ algo

salad ['sæləd] n salada; **salad**
cream (Brit) n maionese f; **salad dressing** n tempero or molho da salada

salami [sə'lɑːmɪ] n salame m

salary ['sælərɪ] n salário

sale [seɪl] n venda; (at reduced prices) liquidação f, saldo; (auction) leilão m; **sales** npl (total amount sold) vendas fpl; **"for ~"** "vende-se"; **on ~** à venda; **on ~ or return** em consignação; **sales assistant**, (US) **sales clerk** n vendedor(a) m/f

salmon ['sæmən] n inv salmão m

salon ['sælɒn] n (hairdressing salon) salão m (de cabeleireiro); (beauty salon) salão (de beleza)

saloon [sə'luːn] n (US) bar m, botequim m; (Brit: Aut) sedã m; (ship's lounge) salão m

salt [sɔːlt] n sal m ▷ vt salgar; **saltwater** adj de água salgada; **salty** adj salgado

salute [sə'luːt] n (greeting) saudação f; (of guns) salva; (Mil) continência ▷ vt saudar; (Mil) fazer continência a

salvage ['sælvɪdʒ] n (saving) salvamento, recuperação f; (things saved) salvados mpl ▷ vt salvar

same [seɪm] adj mesmo ▷ pron: **the ~** o mesmo/a mesma; **the ~ book as** o mesmo livro que; **all** or **just the ~** apesar de tudo, mesmo assim; **the ~ to you!** igualmente!

sample ['sɑːmpl] n amostra ▷ vt (food, wine) provar, experimentar

sanction ['sæŋkʃən] n sanção f ▷ vt sancionar

sanctuary ['sæŋktjuərɪ] n (holy place) santuário; (refuge) refúgio, asilo; (for animals) reserva

sand [sænd] n areia; (beach: also: **~s**) praia ▷ vt (also: **~ down**) lixar

sandal ['sændl] n sandália

sand: **sandbox** ['sændbɔks] (US) n (for children) caixa de areia; **sand castle** n castelo de areia; **sandpaper** ['sændpeɪpə^r] n lixa; **sandpit** ['sændpɪt] n (for children) caixa de areia; **sandstone** ['sændstəʊn] n arenito, grés m

sandwich ['sændwɪtʃ] n sanduíche m (BR), sandes f inv (PT) ▷ vt: **~ed between** encaixado entre

sandy ['sændɪ] adj arenoso; (colour) vermelho amarelado

sane [seɪn] adj são/sã do juízo; (sensible) ajuizado, sensato

sang [sæŋ] pt of **sing**

sanity ['sænɪtɪ] n sanidade f, equilíbrio mental; (common sense) juízo, sensatez f

sank [sæŋk] pt of **sink**

Santa Claus [sæntə'klɔːz] n Papai Noel m

sap [sæp] n (of plants) seiva ▷ vt (strength) esgotar, minar

sapphire ['sæfaɪə^r] n safira

sarcasm ['sɑːkæzm] n sarcasmo

sardine [sɑː'diːn] n sardinha

Sardinia [sɑː'dɪnɪə] n Sardenha

sat [sæt] pt, pp of **sit**

satchel ['sætʃl] n sacola

satellite ['sætəlaɪt] n satélite m; **satellite dish** n antena parabólica; **satellite television** n televisão f via satélite

satin ['sætɪn] n cetim m ▷ adj acetinado

satire ['sætaɪə^r] n sátira

satisfaction [sætɪs'fækʃən] n satisfação f; (refund, apology etc) compensação f; **satisfactory** adj satisfatório

satisfy ['sætɪsfaɪ] vt satisfazer; (convince) convencer, persuadir

Saturday ['sætədɪ] n sábado

sauce [sɔːs] n molho; (sweet) calda;

saucepan n panela (BR), caçarola (PT)

saucer ['sɔːsə^r] n pires m inv

Saudi ['saudɪ] adj, n (also: **~ Arabia**) Arábia Saudita; (also: **~ Arabian**) saudita m/f

sauna ['sɔːnə] n sauna

sausage ['sɔsɪdʒ] n salsicha, linguiça; (cold meat) frios mpl; **sausage roll** n folheado de salsicha

savage ['sævɪdʒ] adj (cruel, fierce) cruel, feroz; (primitive) selvagem ▷ n selvagem m/f

save [seɪv] vt (rescue, Comput) salvar; (money) poupar, economizar; (time) ganhar; (Sport) impedir; (avoid: trouble) evitar; (keep: seat) guardar ▷ vi (also: **~ up**) poupar ▷ n (Sport) salvamento ▷ prep salvo, exceto

saw [sɔː] (pt **sawed**, pp **sawed** or **sawn**) pt of **see** ▷ n (tool) serra ▷ vt serrar; **sawdust** n serragem f, pó m de serra

saxophone ['sæksəfəʊn] n saxofone m

say [seɪ] (pt, pp **said**) n: **to have one's ~** exprimir sua opinião, vender seu peixe (inf) ▷ vt dizer, falar; **to have a** or **some ~ in sth** opinar sobre algo, ter que ver com algo; **could you ~ that again?** poderia repetir?; **that is to ~** ou seja; **saying** n ditado, provérbio

scab [skæb] n casca, crosta (de ferida); (pej) fura-greve m/f inv

scald [skɔːld] n escaldadura ▷ vt escaldar, queimar

scale [skeɪl] n escala; (of fish) escama; (of salaries, fees etc) tabela ▷ vt (mountain) escalar; **scales** npl (for weighing) balança; **~ of charges** tarifa, lista de preços **scale down**

vt reduzir

scallop ['skɔləp] n (Zool) vieira, venera; (Sewing) barra, arremate m

scalp [skælp] n couro cabeludo ▷ vt escalpar

scam [skæm] (inf) n maracutaia, falcatrua

scampi ['skæmpɪ] npl camarões mpl fritos

scan [skæn] vt (examine) esquadrinhar, perscrutar; (glance at quickly) passar uma vista de olhos por; (TV, Radar) explorar ▷ n (Med) exame m

scandal ['skændl] n escândalo; (gossip) fofocas fpl; (fig: disgrace) vergonha

Scandinavian [skændɪ'neɪvɪən] adj, n escandinavo(-a)

scanner ['skænəʳ] n (Med, Comput) scanner m

scapegoat ['skeɪpgəut] n bode m expiatório

scar [skɑ:] n cicatriz f ▷ vt marcar (com uma cicatriz)

scarce [skɛəs] adj escasso, raro; **to make o.s. ~** (inf) dar o fora, cair fora; **scarcely** adv mal, quase não; (barely) apenas

scare [skɛəʳ] n susto; (panic) pânico ▷ vt assustar; **to ~ sb stiff** deixar alguém morrendo de medo; **bomb ~** alarme de bomba **scare away** vt espantar **scare off** vt = **scare away**; **scarecrow** n espantalho; **scared** adj: **to be scared** estar assustado or com medo

scarf [skɑ:f] (pl **scarfs** or **scarves**) n cachecol m; (square) lenço (de cabeça)

scarlet ['skɑ:lɪt] adj escarlate

scary ['skɛərɪ] (inf) adj assustador(a)

scatter ['skætəʳ] vt espalhar; (put to flight) dispersar ▷ vi espalhar-se

scene [si:n] n (Theatre, fig) cena; (of crime, accident) cenário; (sight) vista, panorama m; (fuss) escândalo; **scenery** n ['si:nərɪ] n (Theatre) cenário; (landscape) paisagem f; **scenic** adj pitoresco

scent [sɛnt] n perfume m; (smell) aroma; (track, fig) pista, rastro

schedule ['ʃɛdju:l, (US) 'skɛdju:l] n (of trains) horário; (of events) programa m; (list) lista ▷ vt (timetable) planejar; (visit) marcar (a hora de); **on ~** na hora, sem atraso; **to be ahead of/behind ~** estar adiantado/atrasado

scheme [ski:m] n (plan, plot) maquinação f; (pension scheme etc) projeto; (arrangement) arranjo ▷ vi conspirar

scholar ['skɔləʳ] n aluno(-a), estudante m/f; (learned person) sábio(-a), erudito(-a); **scholarship** n erudição f; (grant) bolsa de estudos

school [sku:l] n escola; (secondary school) colégio; (US: university) universidade f ▷ cpd escolar; **schoolboy** n aluno; **schoolchildren** npl alunos mpl; **schoolgirl** n aluna; **schoolteacher** n professor(a) m/f

science ['saɪəns] n ciência; **science fiction** n ficção f científica; **scientific** [saɪən'tɪfɪk] adj científico; **scientist** n cientista m/f

scissors ['sɪzəz] npl tesoura; **a pair of ~** uma tesoura

scold [skəuld] vt ralhar

scone [skɔn] n bolinho de trigo

scoop [sku:p] n colherona; (for flour etc) pá f; (Press) furo (jornalístico) **scoop out** vt escavar **scoop up** vt recolher

S

scooter ['sku:tə^r] n (also: **motor ~**) lambreta; (toy) patinete m

scope [skəup] n liberdade f de ação; (of plan, undertaking) âmbito; (of person) competência; (opportunity) oportunidade f

score [skɔ:^{r}] n (points etc) escore m, contagem f; (Mus) partitura; (twenty) vintena ▷ vt (goal, point) fazer; (mark) marcar, entalhar; (success) alcançar ▷ vi (in game) marcar; (Football) marcar or fazer um gol; (keep score) marcar o escore; **on that ~** a esse respeito, por esse motivo; **~s of** (fig) um monte de; **to ~ 6 out of 10** tirar nota 6 num total de 10 **score out** vt riscar; **scoreboard** n marcador m, placar m

scorn [skɔ:n] n desprezo ▷ vt desprezar, rejeitar

Scorpio ['skɔ:pɪəu] n Escorpião m

Scot [skɔt] n escocês(-esa) m/f

Scotch [skɔtʃ] n uísque m (BR) or whisky m (PT) escocês

Scotland ['skɔtlənd] n Escócia; **Scots** adj escocês(-esa); **Scotsman** irreg n escocês m; **Scotswoman** irreg n escocesa; **Scottish** adj escocês(-esa)

scout [skaut] n (Mil) explorador m, batedor m; (also: **boy ~**) escoteiro; **girl ~** (US) escoteira **scout around** vi explorar

scowl [skaul] vi franzir a testa; **to ~ at sb** olhar de cara feia para alguém

scramble ['skræmbl] n (climb) escalada (difícil); (struggle) luta ▷ vi: **to ~ out/through** conseguir sair com dificuldade; **to ~ for** lutar por; **scrambled eggs** npl ovos mpl mexidos

scrap [skræp] n (of paper) pedacinho; (of material) fragmento; (fig: of truth) mínimo; (fight) rixa, luta; (also: **~ iron**) ferro velho, sucata ▷ vt sucatar, jogar no ferro velho; (fig) descartar, abolir ▷ vi brigar; **scraps** npl (leftovers) sobras fpl, restos mpl; **scrapbook** n álbum m de recortes

scrape [skreɪp] n (fig): **to get into a ~** meter-se numa enrascada ▷ vt raspar; (scrape against: hand, car) arranhar, roçar ▷ vi: **to ~ through** (in exam) passar raspando **scrape together** vt (money) juntar com dificuldade

scrap paper n papel m de rascunho

scratch [skrætʃ] n arranhão m; (from claw) arranhadura ▷ cpd: **~ team** time m improvisado, escrete m ▷ vt (rub) coçar; (with claw, nail) arranhar, unhar; (damage) arranhar ▷ vi coçar(-se); **to start from ~** partir do zero; **to be up to ~** estar à altura (das circunstâncias)

scream [skri:m] n grito ▷ vi gritar

screen [skri:n] n (Cinema, TV, Comput) tela (BR), écran m (PT); (movable) biombo; (fig) cortina ▷ vt (conceal) esconder, tapar; (from the wind etc) proteger; (film) projetar; (candidates etc, Med) examinar; **screenplay** n roteiro; **screensaver** ['skri:nseɪvə^r] n protetor m de tela

screw [skru:] n parafuso ▷ vt aparafusar; (also: **~ in**) apertar, atarraxar **screw up** vt (paper etc) amassar; **to ~ up one's eyes** franzir os olhos; **screwdriver** n chave f de fenda or de parafuso

scribble ['skrɪbl] n garrancho ▷ vt escrevinhar ▷ vi rabiscar

script [skrɪpt] n (Cinema etc) roteiro, script m; (writing) escrita, caligrafia

scroll [skrəul] n rolo de pergaminho

scrub [skrʌb] n mato, cerrado ▷ vt esfregar; (inf) cancelar, eliminar

scruffy ['skrʌfɪ] adj desmazelado

scrutiny ['skru:tɪnɪ] n escrutínio, exame m cuidadoso

sculptor ['skʌlptə^r] n escultor(a) m/f

sculpture ['skʌlptʃə^r] n escultura

scum [skʌm] n (on liquid) espuma; (pej: people) ralé f, gentinha

scurry ['skʌrɪ] vi sair correndo **scurry off** vi sair correndo, dar no pé

sea [si:] n mar m ▷ cpd do mar, marinho; **on the ~** (boat) no mar; (town) junto ao mar; **to go by ~** viajar por mar; **out to** or **at ~** em alto mar; **to be all at ~** (fig) estar confuso or desorientado; **seafood** n mariscos mpl; **seagull** n gaivota

seal [si:l] n (animal) foca; (stamp) selo ▷ vt fechar **seal off** vt fechar

sea level n nível m do mar

seam [si:m] n (of coal) veio, filão m costura; (where edges meet) junta;

search [sə:tʃ] n busca, procura; (Comput) busca; (inspection) exame m, investigação f ▷ vt (look in) procurar em; (examine) examinar; (person, place) revistar ▷ vi: **to ~ for** procurar; **in ~ of** à procura de **search through** vt fus dar busca em; **search engine** n (on internet) site m de busca; **search party** n equipe f de salvamento

sea: **seashore** n praia, beira-mar f, litoral m; **seasick** adj: **to be** or **get seasick** enjoar; **seaside** n praia; **seaside resort** n balneário

season ['si:zn] n (of year) estação f; (sporting etc) temporada; (of films etc) série f ▷ vt (food) temperar; **to be in/out of ~** (fruit) estar na

época/fora de época; **season ticket** n bilhete m de temporada

seat [si:t] n (in bus, train: place) assento; (chair) cadeira; (Pol) lugar m, cadeira; (buttocks) traseiro, nádegas fpl; (of trousers) fundilhos mpl ▷ vt sentar; (have room for) ter capacidade para; **to be ~ed** estar sentado; **seat belt** n cinto de segurança

sea water n água do mar

seaweed ['si:wi:d] n alga marinha

sec. abbr (= second) seg.

secluded [sɪ'klu:dɪd] adj (place) afastado; (life) solitário

second[1] [sɪ'kɔnd] (Brit) vt (employee) transferir temporariamente

second[2] ['sɛkənd] adj segundo ▷ adv (in race etc) em segundo lugar ▷ n segundo; (Aut: also: **~ gear**) segunda; (Comm) artigo defeituoso; (Brit: Sch: degree) uma qualificação boa mas sem distinção ▷ vt (motion) apoiar, secundar; **secondary** adj secundário; **secondary school** n escola secundária, colégio; ver nota

○ **SECONDARY SCHOOL**
○
○ Uma **secondary school** é um
○ estabelecimento de ensino para
○ alunos de 11 a 18 anos, alguns dos
○ quais interrompem os estudos
○ aos 16 anos. A maior parte dessas
○ escolas é formada por
○ comprehensive schools , mas
○ algumas secondary schools ainda
○ têm sistemas rigorosos de
○ seleção.

second ['sɛkənd]: **second-class** adv em segunda classe; **secondhand** adj de (BR) or em (PT) segunda mão, usado; **second hand** n (on clock) ponteiro de segundos; **secondly** adv em segundo lugar; **second-rate** adj de segunda categoria; **second thoughts**, (US) **second thought** npl: **to have second thoughts (about doing sth)** pensar duas vezes (antes de fazer algo); **on second thoughts** pensando bem

secrecy ['si:krəsɪ] n sigilo

secret ['si:krɪt] adj secreto ▷ n segredo

secretary ['sɛkrətərɪ] n secretário(-a); (Brit: Pol): **S~ of State** Ministro(-a) de Estado

secretive ['si:krətɪv] adj sigiloso, reservado

section ['sɛkʃən] n seção f; (part) parte f, porção f; (of document) parágrafo, artigo; (of opinion) setor m; **cross-~** corte m transversal

sector ['sɛktər] n setor m

secular ['sɛkjulər] adj (priest) secular; (music, society) leigo

secure [sɪ'kjuər] adj (safe) seguro; (firmly fixed) firme, rígido ▷ vt (fix) prender; (get) conseguir, obter; **security** n segurança; (for loan) fiança, garantia; **security guard** n segurança m/f

sedate [sɪ'deɪt] adj calmo ▷ vt sedar, tratar com calmantes; **sedative** n calmante m, sedativo

seduce [sɪ'dju:s] vt seduzir; **seductive** adj sedutor(a)

see [si:] (pt **saw**, pp **seen**) vt ver; (understand) entender; (accompany): **to ~ sb to the door** acompanhar or levar alguém até a porta ▷ vi ver; (find out) achar ▷ n sé f, sede f; **to ~ that** (ensure) assegurar que; **~ you soon/later/tomorrow!** até logo/mais tarde/

amanhã! **see about** vt fus tratar de **see off** vt despedir-se de **see through** vt fus enxergar através de ▷ vt levar a cabo **see to** vt fus providenciar

seed [si:d] n semente f; (sperm) esperma m; (fig: gen pl) germe m; (Tennis) pré-selecionado(-a); **to go to ~** produzir sementes; (fig) deteriorar-se

seeing ['si:ɪŋ] conj: **~ (that)** visto (que), considerando (que)

seek [si:k] (pt, pp **sought**) vt procurar; (post) solicitar

seem [si:m] vi parecer; **there ~s to be ...** parece que há ...

seen [si:n] pp of **see**

seesaw ['si:sɔ:] n gangorra, balanço

segment ['sɛgmənt] n segmento; (of orange) gomo

seize [si:z] vt agarrar, pegar; (power, hostage) apoderar-se de, confiscar; (territory) tomar posse de; (opportunity) aproveitar **seize on** vt fus valer-se de **seize up** vi (Tech) gripar **seize upon** vt fus = **seize on**; **seizure** n (Med) ataque m, acesso; (Law, of power) confisco, embargo

seldom ['sɛldəm] adv raramente

select [sɪ'lɛkt] adj seleto, fino ▷ vt escolher, selecionar; (Sport) selecionar, escalar; **selection** n seleção f, escolha; (Comm) sortimento

self [sɛlf] (pl **selves**) pron see **herself**; **himself**; **itself**; **myself**; **oneself**; **ourselves**; **themselves**; **yourself** ▷ n: **the ~** o eu; **self-assured** adj seguro de si; **self-catering** (Brit) adj (flat) com cozinha; (holiday) em casa alugada; **self-centred**, (US) **self-centered**

adj egocêntrico; **self-confidence** *n* autoconfiança, confiança em si; **self-conscious** *adj* inibido, constrangido; **self-control** *n* autocontrole *m*, autodomínio; **self-defence**, (US) **self-defense** *n* legítima defesa, autodefesa; **in self-defence** em legítima defesa; **self-employed** *adj* autônomo; **self-interest** *n* egoísmo; **selfish** *adj* egoísta; **self-pity** *n* pena de si mesmo; **self-respect** *n* amor *m* próprio; **self-service** *adj* de autosserviço

sell [sɛl] (*pt, pp* **sold**) *vt* vender; (*fig*): **to ~ sb an idea** convencer alguém de uma ideia ▷ *vi* vender-se; **to ~ at** or **for £10** vender a or por £10 **sell off** *vt* liquidar **sell out** *vi* vender todo o estoque ▷ *vt*: **the tickets are all sold out** todos os ingressos já foram vendidos; **sell-by date** *n* vencimento; **seller** *n* vendedor(a) *m/f*

selves [sɛlvz] *pl of* **self**

semi... [sɛmɪ] *prefix* semi..., meio...; **semicircle** *n* semicírculo; **semidetached, semidetached house** (*Brit*) *n* (casa) geminada

seminar [ˈsɛmɪnɑːʳ] *n* seminário

senate [ˈsɛnɪt] *n* senado; **senator** *n* senador(a) *m/f*

send [sɛnd] (*pt, pp* **sent**) *vt* mandar, enviar; (*dispatch*) expedir, remeter; (*transmit*) transmitir **send away** *vt* (*letter, goods*) expedir, mandar; (*unwelcome visitor*) mandar embora **send away for** *vt fus* encomendar, pedir pelo correio **send back** *vt* devolver, mandar de volta **send for** *vt fus* mandar buscar; (*by post*) pedir pelo correio, encomendar **send off** *vt* (*goods*) despachar, expedir; (*Brit: Sport: player*)

expulsar **send on** *vt* (*Brit: letter*) remeter; (*luggage etc: in advance*) mandar com antecedência **send out** *vt* (*invitation*) distribuir; (*signal*) emitir **send up** *vt* (*person, price*) fazer subir; (*Brit: parody*) parodiar; **sender** *n* remetente *m/f*; **send-off** *n*: **a good send-off** uma boa despedida

senior [ˈsiːnɪəʳ] *adj* (*older*) mais velho or idoso; (*on staff*) mais antigo; (*of higher rank*) superior; **senior citizen** *n* idoso(-a)

sensation [sɛnˈseɪʃən] *n* sensação *f*; **sensational** *adj* sensacional; (*headlines, result*) sensacionalista

sense [sɛns] *n* sentido; (*feeling*) sensação *f*; (*good sense*) bom senso ▷ *vt* sentir, perceber; **it makes ~** faz sentido; **senseless** *adj* insensato, estúpido; (*unconscious*) sem sentidos, inconsciente; **sensible** *adj* sensato, de bom senso; (*reasonable: price*) razoável; (: *advice, decision*) sensato

sensitive [ˈsɛnsɪtɪv] *adj* sensível; (*fig: touchy*) suscetível

sensual [ˈsɛnsjuəl] *adj* sensual

sensuous [ˈsɛnsjuəs] *adj* sensual

sent [sɛnt] *pt, pp of* **send**

sentence [ˈsɛntəns] *n* (*Ling*) frase *f*, oração *f*; (*Law*) sentença ▷ *vt*: **to ~ sb to death/to 5 years** condenar alguém à morte/a 5 anos de prisão

sentiment [ˈsɛntɪmənt] *n* sentimento; (*opinion: also pl*) opinião *f*; **sentimental** [sɛntɪˈmɛntl] *adj* sentimental

separate [*adj* ˈsɛprɪt, *vt, vi* ˈsɛpəreɪt] *adj* separado; (*distinct*) diferente ▷ *vt* separar; (*part*) dividir ▷ *vi* separar-se; **separately** *adv* separadamente

September [sɛpˈtɛmbəʳ] *n*

setembro
septic ['sɛptɪk] adj sético; (wound) infeccionado
sequel ['si:kwl] n consequência, resultado; (of film, story) continuação f
sequence ['si:kwəns] n série f, sequência; (Cinema) série
sequin ['si:kwɪn] n lantejoula, paetê m
sergeant ['sɑ:dʒənt] n sargento
serial ['sɪərɪəl] n seriado; **serial killer** n assassino(-a) em série, serial killer m/f; **serial number** n número de série
series ['sɪəri:z] n inv série f
serious ['sɪərɪəs] adj sério; (matter) importante; (illness) grave; **seriously** adv a sério, com seriedade; (hurt) gravemente
sermon ['sə:mən] n sermão m
servant ['sə:vənt] n empregado(-a); (fig) servidor(a) m/f
serve [sə:v] vt servir; (customer) atender; (subj: train) passar por; (apprenticeship) fazer; (prison term) cumprir ▷ vi (at table) servir-se; (Tennis) sacar; (be useful): **to ~ as/for/to do** servir como/para/para fazer ▷ n (Tennis) saque m; **it ~s him right** é bem feito para ele **serve out** vt (food) servir **serve up** vt = **serve out**
service ['sə:vɪs] n serviço; (Rel) culto; (Aut) revisão f; (Tennis) saque m; (also: **dinner ~**) aparelho de jantar ▷ vt (car, washing machine) fazer a revisão de, revisar; **the Services** npl (army, navy etc) as Forças Armadas; **to be of ~ to sb** ser útil a alguém; **service area** n (on motorway) posto de gasolina com bar, restaurante etc; **service charge**

(Brit) n serviço; **serviceman** irreg n militar m; **service station** n posto de gasolina (BR), estação f de serviço (PT)
serviette [sə:vɪ'ɛt] (Brit) n guardanapo
session ['sɛʃən] n sessão f; **to be in ~** estar reunido em sessão
set [sɛt] (pt, pp **set**) n (collection of things) jogo; (radio set, TV set) aparelho; (of utensils) bateria de cozinha; (of cutlery) talher m; (of books) coleção f; (group of people) grupo; (Tennis) set m; (Theatre, Cinema) cenário; (Hairdressing) penteado; (Math) conjunto ▷ adj fixo; (ready) pronto ▷ vt pôr, colocar; (table) pôr; (price) fixar; (rules etc) estabelecer, decidir; (record) estabelecer; (time) marcar; (adjust) ajustar; (task, exam) passar ▷ vi (sun) pôr-se; (jam, jelly, concrete) endurecer, solidificar-se; **to be ~ on doing sth** estar decidido a fazer algo; **to ~ to music** musicar, pôr música em; **to ~ on fire** botar fogo em, incendiar; **to ~ free** libertar; **to ~ sth going** pôr algo em movimento **set about** vt fus começar com **set aside** vt deixar de lado **set back** vt (cost): **it ~ me back £50** custou £50; (in time): **to ~ sb back (by)** atrasar alguém (em) **set off** vi partir, ir indo ▷ vt (bomb) fazer explodir; (alarm) disparar; (chain of events) iniciar; (show up well) ressaltar **set out** vi partir ▷ vt (arrange) colocar, dispor; (state) expor, explicar; **to ~ out to do sth** pretender fazer algo **set up** vt fundar, estabelecer; **setback** n revés m, contratempo; **set menu** n refeição f a preço fixo
settee [sɛ'ti:] n sofá m

setting ['sɛtɪŋ] n (background) cenário; (position) posição f; (of sun) pôr(-do-sol) m; (of jewel) engaste m

settle ['sɛtl] vt (argument, matter) resolver, esclarecer; (accounts) ajustar, liquidar; (Med: calm) acalmar, tranquilizar ▷ vi (dust etc) assentar; (calm down: children) acalmar-se; (also: ~ **down**) instalar-se, estabilizar-se; **to ~ for sth** concordar em aceitar algo; **to ~ on sth** optar por algo **settle in** vi instalar-se **settle up** vi: **to ~ up with sb** ajustar as contas com alguém; **settlement** n (payment) liquidação f; (agreement) acordo, convênio; (village etc) povoado, povoação f

setup ['sɛtʌp] n (organization) organização f; (situation) situação f

seven ['sɛvn] num sete; **seventeen** ['sɛvn'tiːn] num dezessete; **seventeenth** [sɛvn'tiːnθ] num décimo sétimo; **seventh** ['sɛvnθ] num sétimo; **seventieth** ['sɛvntɪɪθ] num septuagésimo; **seventy** ['sɛvntɪ] num setenta

sever ['sɛvəʳ] vt cortar; (relations) romper

several ['sɛvərl] adj, pron vários(-as); **~ of us** vários de nós

severe [sɪ'vɪəʳ] adj severo; (serious) grave; (hard) duro; (pain) intenso; (dress) austero

sew [səu] (pt sewed, pp sewn) vt coser, costurar **sew up** vt coser, costurar

sewage ['suːɪdʒ] n detritos mpl

sewer ['suːəʳ] n (cano do) esgoto, bueiro

sewing ['səuɪŋ] n costura; **sewing machine** n máquina de costura

sewn [səun] pp of **sew**

sex [sɛks] n sexo; **sexist** adj sexista

sexual ['sɛksjuəl] adj sexual

sexy ['sɛksɪ] adj sexy

shabby ['ʃæbɪ] adj (person) esfarrapado, maltrapilho; (clothes) usado, surrado; (behaviour) indigno

shack [ʃæk] n choupana, barraca

shade [ʃeɪd] n sombra; (for lamp) quebra-luz m; (of colour) tom m, tonalidade f; (small quantity): **a ~ (more/big)** um pouquinho (mais/grande) ▷ vt dar sombra a; (eyes) sombrear; **in the ~** à sombra

shadow ['ʃædəu] n sombra ▷ vt (follow) seguir de perto (sem ser visto)

shady ['ʃeɪdɪ] adj à sombra; (fig: dishonest: person) suspeito, duvidoso; (: deal) desonesto

shaft [ʃɑːft] n (of arrow, spear) haste f; (Aut, Tech) eixo, manivela; (of mine, of lift) poço; (of light) raio

shake [ʃeɪk] (pt shook, pp shaken) vt sacudir; (building, confidence) abalar; (surprise) surpreender ▷ vi tremer; **to ~ hands with sb** apertar a mão de alguém; **to ~ one's head** (in refusal etc) dizer não com a cabeça; (in dismay) sacudir a cabeça **shake off** vt sacudir; (fig) livrar-se de **shake up** vt sacudir; (fig) reorganizar; **shaky** adj (hand, voice) trêmulo; (table) instável; (building) abalado

shall [ʃæl] aux vb: **I ~ go** irei; **~ I open the door?** posso abrir a porta?; **I'll get some, ~ I?** eu vou pegar algum, está bem?

shallow ['ʃæləu] adj raso; (breathing) fraco; (fig) superficial

sham [ʃæm] n fraude f, fingimento ▷ vt fingir, simular

shambles ['ʃæmblz] n confusão f

shame [ʃeɪm] n vergonha ▷ vt

S

envergonhar; **it is a ~ (that/to do)** é (uma) pena (que/fazer); **what a ~!** que pena!; **shameful** adj vergonhoso; **shameless** adj sem vergonha, descarado

shampoo [ʃæm'pu:] n xampu m (BR), champô m (PT) ▷ vt lavar o cabelo (com xampu or champô)

shandy ['ʃændɪ] n mistura de cerveja com refresco gaseificado

shan't [ʃɑːnt] = **shall not**

shape [ʃeɪp] n forma ▷ vt (form) moldar; (sb's ideas) formar; (sb's life) definir, determinar; **to take ~** tomar forma **shape up** vi (events) desenrolar-se; (person) tomar jeito

share [ʃɛəʳ] n parte f; (contribution) cota; (Comm) ação f ▷ vt dividir; (have in common) compartilhar **share out** vi distribuir; **shareholder** n acionista m/f

shark [ʃɑːk] n tubarão m

sharp [ʃɑːp] adj (razor, knife) afiado; (point, features) pontiagudo; (outline) definido, bem marcado; (pain, voice) agudo; (taste) acre; (Mus) desafinado; (contrast) marcado; (quick-witted) perspicaz; (dishonest) desonesto ▷ n (Mus) sustenido ▷ adv: **at 2 o'clock ~** às 2 (horas) em ponto; **sharpen** vt afiar; (pencil) apontar, fazer a ponta de; (fig) aguçar; **sharpener** n (also: **pencil sharpener**) apontador m (BR), apara-lápis m inv (PT); **sharply** adv (abruptly) bruscamente; (clearly) claramente; (harshly) severamente

shatter ['ʃætəʳ] vt despedaçar, estilhaçar; (fig: ruin) destruir, acabar com; (: upset) arrasar ▷ vi despedaçar-se, estilhaçar-se

shave [ʃeɪv] vt barbear, fazer a barba de ▷ vi fazer a barba,

barbear-se ▷ n: **to have a ~** fazer a barba; **shaver** n barbeador m; **electric shaver** barbeador elétrico; **shaving cream** n creme m de barbear; **shaving foam** n espuma de barbear

shawl [ʃɔːl] n xale m

she [ʃiː] pron ela ▷ prefix: **~-elephant** etc elefante etc fêmea

sheath [ʃiːθ] n bainha; (contraceptive) camisa-de-vênus f, camisinha

shed [ʃɛd] (pt, pp **shed**) n alpendre m, galpão m ▷ vt (skin) mudar; (load, leaves, fur) perder; (tears, blood) derramar; (workers) despedir

she'd [ʃiːd] = **she had**; **she would**

sheep [ʃiːp] n inv ovelha; **sheepdog** n cão m pastor; **sheepskin** n pele f de carneiro, pelego

sheer [ʃɪəʳ] adj (utter) puro, completo; (steep) íngreme, empinado; (almost transparent) fino, translúcido ▷ adv a pique

sheet [ʃiːt] n (on bed) lençol m; (of paper) folha; (of glass, metal) lâmina, chapa; (of ice) camada

sheik, sheikh [ʃeɪk] n xeque m

shelf [ʃɛlf] (pl **shelves**) n prateleira

shell [ʃɛl] n (on beach) concha; (of egg, nut etc) casca; (explosive) obus m; (of building) armação f, esqueleto ▷ vt (peas) descascar; (Mil) bombardear

she'll [ʃiːl] = **she will**; **she shall**

shellfish ['ʃɛlfɪʃ] n inv crustáceo; (as food) frutos mpl do mar, mariscos mpl

shelter ['ʃɛltəʳ] n (building) abrigo; (protection) refúgio ▷ vt (protect) proteger; (give lodging to) abrigar ▷ vi abrigar-se, refugiar-se

shepherd ['ʃɛpəd] n pastor m ▷ vt guiar, conduzir; **shepherd's pie**

(Brit) n empadão m de carne e batata
sheriff ['ʃerɪf] (US) n xerife m
sherry ['ʃerɪ] n (vinho de) Xerez m
she's [ʃi:z] = **she is**; **she has**
Shetland ['ʃetlənd] n (also: **the ~s, the ~ Isles**) as ilhas Shetland
shield [ʃi:ld] n escudo; (Sport) escudo, brasão m; (protection) proteção f ▷ vt: **to ~ (from)** proteger (contra)
shift [ʃɪft] n mudança; (of work) turno; (of workers) turma ▷ vt transferir; (remove) tirar ▷ vi mudar
shin [ʃɪn] n canela (da perna)
shine [ʃaɪn] (pt, pp **shone**) n brilho, lustre m ▷ vi brilhar ▷ vt (shoes: pt, pp **shined**) lustrar; **to ~ a torch on sth** apontar uma lanterna para algo
shingles ['ʃɪŋglz] n (Med) herpes-zoster m
shiny ['ʃaɪnɪ] adj brilhante, lustroso
ship [ʃɪp] n barco ▷ vt (goods) embarcar; (send) transportar or mandar (por via marítima); **shipment** n carregamento; **shipping** n (ships) navios mpl; (cargo) transporte m de mercadorias (por via marítima); (traffic) navegação f; **shipwreck** n (event) malogro; (ship) naufrágio ▷ vt: **to be shipwrecked** naufragar; **shipyard** n estaleiro
shirt [ʃə:t] n (man's) camisa; (woman's) blusa; **in ~ sleeves** em manga de camisa
shit [ʃɪt] (infl) excl merda (!)
shiver ['ʃɪvəʳ] n tremor m, arrepio ▷ vi tremer, estremecer, tiritar
shock [ʃɔk] n (impact) choque m; (Elec) descarga; (emotional) comoção f, abalo; (start) susto, sobressalto; (Med) trauma m ▷ vt

dar um susto em, chocar; (offend) escandalizar; **shocking** adj chocante, lamentável; (outrageous) revoltante, chocante
shoe [ʃu:] (pt, pp **shod**) n sapato; (for horse) ferradura ▷ vt (horse) ferrar; **shoelace** n cadarço, cordão m (de sapato); **shoe polish** n graxa de sapato; **shoeshop** n sapataria
shone [ʃɔn] pt, pp of **shine**
shook [ʃʊk] pt of **shake**
shoot [ʃu:t] (pt, pp **shot**) n (on branch, seedling) broto ▷ vt disparar; (kill) matar à bala, balear; (wound) ferir à bala, balear; (execute) fuzilar; (film) filmar, rodar ▷ vi: **to ~ (at)** atirar (em); (Football) chutar; **shoot down** vt (plane) derrubar, abater **shoot in** vi entrar correndo **shoot out** vi sair correndo **shoot up** vi (fig) subir vertiginosamente
shop [ʃɔp] n loja; (workshop) oficina ▷ vi (also: **go ~ping**) ir fazer compras; **shop assistant** (Brit) n vendedor(a) m/f; **shopkeeper** n lojista m/f; **shoplifting** n furto (em lojas); **shopping** n (goods) compras fpl; **shopping bag** n bolsa (de compras); **shopping centre**, (US) **shopping center** n shopping (center) m; **shop window** n vitrine f (BR), montra (PT)
shore [ʃɔ:ʳ] n (of sea) costa, praia; (of lake) margem f ▷ vt: **to ~ (up)** reforçar, escorar; **on ~** em terra
short [ʃɔ:t] adj curto; (in time) breve, de curta duração; (person) baixo; (curt) seco, brusco; (insufficient) insuficiente, em falta; **to be ~ of sth** estar em falta de algo; **in ~** em resumo; **~ of doing ...**

a não ser fazer ...; **everything ~ of ...** tudo a não ser ...; **it is ~ for** é a abreviatura de; **to cut ~** (*speech, visit*) encurtar; **to fall ~ of** não ser à altura de; **to run ~ of sth** ficar sem algo; **to stop ~** parar de repente; **to stop ~ of** chegar quase a; **shortage** *n* escassez *f*, falta; **shortbread** *n* biscoito amanteigado; **shortcoming** *n* defeito, imperfeição *f*, falha; **shortcrust pastry**, (*Brit*) **short pastry** *n* massa amanteigada; **shortcut** *n* atalho; **shorten** *vt* encurtar; (*visit*) abreviar; **shorthand** (*Brit*) *n* estenografia; **shortly** *adv* em breve, dentro em pouco; **shorts** *npl*: **(a pair of) shorts** um calção (*BR*), um short (*BR*), uns calções (*PT*); **short-sighted** (*Brit*) *adj* míope; (*fig*) imprevidente; **short story** *n* conto; **short-tempered** *adj* irritadiço; **short-term** *adj* a curto prazo

shot [ʃɔt] *pt, pp of* **shoot** ▷ *n* (*of gun*) tiro; (*pellets*) chumbo; (*try, Football*) tentativa; (*injection*) injeção *f*; (*Phot*) fotografia; **to be a good/bad ~** (*person*) ter boa/má pontaria; **like a ~** como um relâmpago, de repente; **shotgun** *n* espingarda

should [ʃud] *aux vb*: **I ~ go now** devo ir embora agora; **he ~ be there now** ele já deve ter chegado; **I ~ go if I were you** se eu fosse você eu iria; **I ~ like to** eu gostaria de

shoulder [ʃəuldər] *n* ombro ▷ *vt* (*fig*) arcar com; **shoulder blade** *n* omoplata *m*

shouldn't [ʃudnt] = **should not**

shout [ʃaut] *n* grito ▷ *vt* gritar ▷ *vi* (*also*: **~ out**) gritar, berrar; **shout**

down *vt* fazer calar com gritos

shove [ʃʌv] *vt* empurrar; (*inf: put*): **to ~ sth in** botar algo em; **shove off** *vi* (*inf*) dar o fora

shovel [ʃʌvl] *n* pá *f*; (*mechanical*) escavadeira ▷ *vt* cavar com pá

show [ʃəu] (*pt* **showed**, *pp* **shown**) *n* (*of emotion*) demonstração *f*; (*semblance*) aparência; (*exhibition*) exibição *f*; (*Theatre*) espetáculo, representação *f*; (*Cinema*) sessão *f* ▷ *vt* mostrar; (*courage etc*) demonstrar, dar prova de; (*exhibit*) exibir, expor; (*depict*) ilustrar; (*film*) exibir ▷ *vi* mostrar-se; (*appear*) aparecer; **to be on ~** estar em exposição **show in** *vt* mandar entrar **show off** *vi* (*pej*) mostrar-se, exibir-se ▷ *vt* (*display*) exibir, mostrar **show out** *vt* levar até a porta **show up** *vi* (*stand out*) destacar-se; (*inf: turn up*) aparecer, pintar ▷ *vt* descobrir; **show business** *n* o mundo do espetáculo

shower [ʃauər] *n* (*rain*) pancada de chuva; (*of stones etc*) chuva, enxurrada; (*also*: **~ bath**) chuveiro ▷ *vi* tomar banho (de chuveiro) ▷ *vt*: **to ~ sb with** (*gifts etc*) cumular alguém de; **to have** *or* **take a ~** tomar banho (de chuveiro)

showing [ʃəuɪŋ] *n* (*of film*) projeção *f*, exibição *f*

show jumping [-ˈdʒʌmpɪŋ] *n* hipismo

shown [ʃəun] *pp of* **show**

show-off (*inf*) *n* (*person*) exibicionista *m/f*, faroleiro(-a)

showpiece [ʃəupiːs] *n* (*of exhibition etc*) obra mais importante

showroom [ʃəurum] *n* sala de exposição

shrank [ʃræŋk] *pt of* **shrink**

shred [ʃrɛd] n (gen pl) tira, pedaço ▷ vt rasgar em tiras, retalhar; (Culin) desfiar, picar

shrewd [ʃruːd] adj perspicaz

shriek [ʃriːk] n grito ▷ vi gritar, berrar

shrimp [ʃrɪmp] n camarão m

shrine [ʃraɪn] n santuário

shrink [ʃrɪŋk] (pt **shrank**, pp **shrunk**) vi encolher; (be reduced) reduzir-se; (also: ~ **away**) encolher-se ▷ vt (cloth) fazer encolher ▷ n (inf: pej) psicanalista m/f; **to ~ from doing sth** não se atrever a fazer algo

shrivel ['ʃrɪvl] vt (also: ~ **up**: dry) secar; (: crease) enrugar ▷ vi secar-se; enrugar-se, murchar

Shrove Tuesday [ʃrəuv-] n terça-feira gorda

shrub [ʃrʌb] n arbusto

shrug [ʃrʌg] n encolhimento dos ombros ▷ vt, vi: **to ~ (one's shoulders)** encolher os ombros, dar de ombros (BR) **shrug off** vt negar a importância de

shrunk [ʃrʌŋk] pp of **shrink**

shudder ['ʃʌdəʳ] n estremecimento, tremor m ▷ vi estremecer, tremer de medo

shuffle ['ʃʌfl] vt (cards) embaralhar ▷ vi: **to ~ (one's feet)** arrastar os pés

shun [ʃʌn] vt evitar, afastar-se de

shut [ʃʌt] (pt, pp **shut**) vt fechar ▷ vi fechar(-se) **shut down** vt, vi fechar **shut off** vt cortar, interromper **shut up** vi (inf: keep quiet) calar-se, calar a boca ▷ vt (close) fechar; (silence) calar; **shutter** n veneziana; (Phot) obturador m

shuttle ['ʃʌtl] n (plane: also: ~ **service**) ponte f aérea; (space shuttle) ônibus m espacial

shuttlecock ['ʃʌtlkɔk] n peteca

shy [ʃaɪ] adj tímido; (reserved) reservado

sick [sɪk] adj (ill) doente; (nauseated) enjoado; (humour) negro; (vomiting): **to be ~** vomitar; **to feel ~** estar enjoado; **to be ~ of** (fig) estar cheio or farto de; **sickening** adj (fig) repugnante; **sick leave** n licença por doença; **sickly** adj doentio; (causing nausea) nauseante; **sickness** n doença, indisposição f; (vomiting) náusea, enjoo

side [saɪd] n lado; (of body) flanco; (of lake) margem f; (aspect) aspecto; (team) time m (BR), equipa (PT); (of hill) declive m ▷ cpd (door, entrance) lateral ▷ vi: **to ~ with sb** tomar o partido de alguém; **by the ~ of** ao lado de; **~ by ~** lado a lado, juntos; **from ~ to ~** para lá e para cá; **to take ~s with** pôr-se ao lado de; **sideboard** n aparador m; **sideboards** npl (Brit) = **sideburns**; **sideburns** npl suíças fpl, costeletas fpl; **side effect** n efeito colateral; **sidelight** n (Aut) luz f lateral; **side order** n acompanhamento; **sidetrack** vt (fig) desviar (do seu propósito); **sidewalk** (US) n calçada; **sideways** adv de lado

siege [siːdʒ] n sítio, assédio

sieve [sɪv] n peneira ▷ vt peneirar

sift [sɪft] vt peneirar; (fig) esquadrinhar, analisar minuciosamente

sigh [saɪ] n suspiro ▷ vi suspirar

sight [saɪt] n (faculty) vista, visão f; (spectacle) espetáculo; (on gun) mira ▷ vt avistar; **in ~** à vista; **on ~** (shoot) no local; **out of ~** longe dos olhos; **sightseeing** n turismo; **to**

go sightseeing fazer turismo, passear

sign [saɪn] n (with hand) sinal m, aceno; (indication) indício; (notice) letreiro, tabuleta; (written, of zodiac) signo ▷ vt assinar; **to ~ sth over to sb** assinar a transferência de algo para alguém **sign on** vi (Mil) alistar-se; (Brit: as unemployed) cadastrar-se para receber auxílio-desemprego; (for course) inscrever-se ▷ vt (Mil) alistar; (employee) efetivar **sign up** vi (Mil) alistar-se; (for course) inscrever-se ▷ vt recrutar

signal ['sɪɡnl] n sinal m, aviso ▷ vi (also: Aut) sinalizar, dar sinal ▷ vt (person) fazer sinais para; (message) transmitir

signature ['sɪɡnətʃəʳ] n assinatura

significance [sɪɡ'nɪfɪkəns] n importância; **significant** adj significativo; (important) importante

sign language n mímica, linguagem f através de sinais

silence ['saɪləns] n silêncio ▷ vt silenciar, impor silêncio a

silent ['saɪlənt] adj silencioso; (not speaking) calado; (film) mudo; **to keep** or **remain ~** manter-se em silêncio

silhouette [sɪluːˈɛt] n silhueta

silicon chip n placa or chip m de silício

silk [sɪlk] n seda ▷ adj de seda

silly ['sɪlɪ] adj (person) bobo, idiota, imbecil; (idea) absurdo, ridículo

silver ['sɪlvəʳ] n prata; (money) moedas fpl; (also: **~ware**) prataria ▷ adj de prata; **silver-plated** adj prateado, banhado a prata

SIM card ['sɪm-] n (Tel) cartão m SIM, chip m

similar ['sɪmɪləʳ] adj **~ to** parecido com, semelhante a

simmer ['sɪməʳ] vi cozer em fogo lento, ferver lentamente

simple ['sɪmpl] adj simples inv; (foolish) ingênuo; **simply** adv de maneira simples; (merely) simplesmente

simultaneous [sɪməl'teɪnɪəs] adj simultâneo

sin [sɪn] n pecado ▷ vi pecar

since [sɪns] adv desde então, depois ▷ prep desde ▷ conj (time) desde que; (because) porque, visto que, já que; **~ then** desde então; **(ever) ~ I arrived** desde que eu cheguei

sincere [sɪn'sɪəʳ] adj sincero; **sincerely** adv: **yours sincerely** (at end of letter) atenciosamente

sing [sɪŋ] (pt **sang**, pp **sung**) vt, vi cantar

Singapore [sɪŋɡəˈpɔːʳ] n Cingapura (no article)

singer ['sɪŋəʳ] n cantor(a) m/f

singing ['sɪŋɪŋ] n canto; (songs) canções fpl

single ['sɪŋɡl] adj único, só; (unmarried) solteiro; (not double) simples inv ▷ n (Brit: also: **~ ticket**) passagem f de ida; (record) compacto **single out** vt (choose) escolher; (distinguish) distinguir; **single file** n: **in single file** em fila indiana; **single-handed** adv sem ajuda, sozinho; **single-minded** adj determinado; **single room** n quarto individual

singular ['sɪŋɡjuləʳ] adj (odd) esquisito; (outstanding) extraordinário, excepcional; (Ling) singular ▷ n (Ling) singular m

sinister ['sɪnɪstəʳ] adj sinistro

sink [sɪŋk] (pt **sank**, pp **sunk**) n pia ▷ vt (ship) afundar; (foundations)

escavar ▷ vi afundar-se; (*heart*)
partir; (*spirits*) ficar deprimido;
(*also:* **~ back, ~ down**) cair or
mergulhar gradativamente; **to ~
sth into** enterrar algo em **sink in**
vi (*fig*) penetrar

sinus ['saɪnəs] n (*Anat*) seio
(paranasal)

sip [sɪp] n gole m ▷ vt sorver,
bebericar

sir [səʳ] n senhor m; **S~ John Smith**
Sir John Smith; **yes, ~** sim, senhor

siren ['saɪərn] n sirena

sirloin ['səːlɔɪn] n lombo de vaca

sister ['sɪstəʳ] n irmã f; (*Brit: nurse*)
enfermeira-chefe f; (*nun*) freira;
sister-in-law n cunhada

sit [sɪt] (*pt, pp* **sat**) vi sentar-se; (*be
sitting*) estar sentado; (*assembly*)
reunir-se; (*for painter*) posar ▷ vt
(*exam*) prestar **sit down** vi
sentar-se **sit in on** vt fus assistir a
sit up vi (*after lying*) levantar-se;
(*straight*) endireitar-se; (*not go to
bed*) aguardar acordado, velar

sitcom ['sɪtkɔm] n abbr (= *situation
comedy*) comédia de costumes

site [saɪt] n local m, sítio; (*also:*
building ~) lote m (de terreno) ▷ vt
situar, localizar

sitting ['sɪtɪŋ] n (*in canteen*) turno;
sitting room n sala de estar

situation [sɪtjuˈeɪʃən] n situação f;
(*job*) posição f; (*location*) local m;
"~s vacant/wanted" (*Brit*)
"empregos oferecem-se/
procurados"

six [sɪks] num seis; **sixteen** num
dezesseis; **sixteenth** [sɪksˈtiːnθ]
num décimo sexto; **sixth** num
sexto; **sixtieth** ['sɪkstɪɪθ] num
sexagésimo; **sixty** num sessenta

size [saɪz] n tamanho; (*extent*)
extensão f; (*of clothing*) tamanho,

medida; (*of shoes*) número **size up**
vt avaliar, formar uma opinião
sobre; **sizeable** adj considerável,
importante

sizzle ['sɪzl] vi chiar

skate [skeɪt] n patim m; (*fish: pl inv*)
arraia ▷ vi patinar; **skateboard** n
skate m, patim-tábua m; **skating** n
patinação f; **skating rink** n rinque
m de patinação

skeleton ['skɛlɪtn] n esqueleto;
(*Tech*) armação f; (*outline*) esquema
m, esboço

sketch [skɛtʃ] n (*drawing*) desenho;
(*outline*) esboço, croqui m; (*Theatre*)
quadro, esquete m ▷ vt desenhar,
esboçar; (*ideas: also:* **~ out**) esboçar

skewer ['skjuːəʳ] n espetinho

ski [skiː] n esqui m ▷ vi esquiar;
ski boot n bota de esquiar

skid [skɪd] n derrapagem f ▷ vi
deslizar; (*Aut*) derrapar

skier ['skiːəʳ] n esquiador(a) m/f

skiing ['skiːɪŋ] n esqui m

skilful ['skɪlful], (*US*) **skillful** adj
habilidoso, jeitoso

ski lift n ski lift m

skill [skɪl] n habilidade f, perícia;
(*for work*) técnica; **skilled** adj hábil,
perito; (*worker*) especializado,
qualificado

skim [skɪm] vt (*milk*) desnatar;
(*glide over*) roçar ▷ vi: **to ~ through**
(*book*) folhear; **skimmed milk** n
leite m desnatado

skin [skɪn] n pele f; (*of fruit,
vegetable*) casca ▷ vt (*fruit etc*)
descascar; (*animal*) tirar a pele de;
skinny adj magro, descarnado

skip [skɪp] n salto, pulo; (*Brit:
container*) balde m ▷ vi saltar; (*with
rope*) pular corda ▷ vt (*pass over*)
omitir, saltar; (*miss*) deixar de

skipper ['skɪpəʳ] n capitão m

S

skipping rope ['skɪpɪŋ-] (Brit) n corda (de pular)

skirt [skə:t] n saia ▷ vt orlar, circundar; **skirting board** (Brit) n rodapé m

skull [skʌl] n caveira; (Anat) crânio

skunk [skʌŋk] n gambá m

sky [skaɪ] n céu m; **skyscraper** n arranha-céu m

slab [slæb] n (stone) bloco; (flat) laje f; (of cake) fatia grossa

slack [slæk] adj (loose) frouxo; (slow) lerdo; (careless) descuidoso, desmazelado; **slacks** npl (trousers) calça (BR), calças fpl (PT)

slam [slæm] vt (door) bater or fechar (com violência); (throw) atirar violentamente; (criticize) malhar, criticar ▷ vi fechar-se (com violência)

slander ['slɑ:ndə'] n calúnia, difamação f

slang [slæŋ] n gíria; (jargon) jargão m

slant [slɑ:nt] n declive m, inclinação f; (fig) ponto de vista

slap [slæp] n tapa m or f ▷ vt dar um(a) tapa em; (paint etc): **to ~ sth on sth** passar algo em algo descuidadamente ▷ adv diretamente, exatamente

slash [slæʃ] vt cortar, talhar; (fig: prices) cortar

slate [sleɪt] n ardósia ▷ vt (fig: criticize) criticar duramente, arrasar

slaughter ['slɔ:tə'] n (of animals) matança; (of people) carnificina ▷ vt abater; matar, massacrar; **slaughterhouse** n matadouro

slave [sleɪv] n escravo(-a) ▷ vi (also: **~ away**) trabalhar como escravo; **slavery** n escravidão f

slay [sleɪ] (pt **slew**, pp **slain**) vt (literary) matar

sleazy ['sli:zɪ] adj sórdido

sledge [slɛdʒ] n trenó m

sleek [sli:k] adj (hair, fur) macio, lustroso; (car, boat) aerodinâmico

sleep [sli:p] (pt, pp **slept**) n sono ▷ vi dormir; **to go to ~** dormir, adormecer **sleep around** vi ser promíscuo sexualmente **sleep in** vi (oversleep) dormir demais; **sleeper** n (Rail: train) vagão-leitos m (BR), carruagem-camas f (PT); **sleeping bag** n saco de dormir; **sleeping car** n vagão-leitos m (BR), carruagem-camas f (PT); **sleeping pill** n pílula para dormir; **sleepy** adj sonolento; (fig) morto

sleet [sli:t] n chuva com neve or granizo

sleeve [sli:v] n manga; (of record) capa

sleigh [sleɪ] n trenó m

slender ['slɛndə'] adj esbelto, delgado; (means) escasso, insuficiente

slept [slɛpt] pt, pp of **sleep**

slice [slaɪs] n (of meat, bread) fatia; (of lemon) rodela; (utensil) pá f or espátula de bolo ▷ vt cortar em fatias

slick [slɪk] adj (skilful) jeitoso, ágil, engenhoso; (clever) esperto, astuto ▷ n (also: **oil ~**) mancha de óleo

slide [slaɪd] (pt, pp **slid**) n deslizamento, escorregão m; (in playground) escorregador m; (Phot) slide m; (Brit: also: **hair ~**) passador m ▷ vt deslizar ▷ vi escorregar; **sliding** adj (door) corrediço

slight [slaɪt] adj (slim) fraco, franzino; (frail) delicado; (error, pain, increase) pequeno; (trivial) insignificante ▷ n desfeita, desconsideração f; **not in the ~est** em absoluto, de maneira alguma;

slightly adv ligeiramente, um pouco

slim [slɪm] adj esbelto, delgado; (chance) pequeno ▷ vi emagrecer

slimming n emagrecimento

sling [slɪŋ] (pt, pp **slung**) n (Med) tipoia; (for baby) bebêbag m; (weapon) estilingue m, funda ▷ vt atirar, arremessar, lançar

slip [slɪp] n (fall) escorregão m; (mistake) erro, lapso; (underskirt) combinação f; (of paper) tira ▷ vt deslizar ▷ vi (slide) deslizar; (lose balance) escorregar; (decline) decair; (move smoothly): **to ~ into/ out of** entrar furtivamente em/ sair furtivamente de; **to ~ sth on/ off** enfiar/tirar algo; **to give sb the ~** esguerar-se de alguém; **a ~ of the tongue** um lapso da língua **slip away** vi escapulir **slip in** vt meter ▷ vi (errors) surgir **slip out** vi (go out) sair (um momento) **slip up** vi cometer um erro

slipper ['slɪpər] n chinelo

slippery ['slɪpərɪ] adj escorregadio

slip-up n equívoco, mancada

slit [slɪt] (pt, pp **slit**) n fenda; (cut) corte m ▷ vt (cut) rachar, cortar; (open) abrir

slog [slɒg] (Brit) vi mourejar ▷ n: **it was a ~** deu um trabalho louco

slogan ['sləugən] n lema m, slogan m

slope [sləup] n ladeira; (side of mountain) encosta, vertente f; (ski slope) pista; (slant) inclinação f, declive m ▷ vi: **to ~ down** estar em declive; **to ~ up** inclinar-se; **sloping** adj inclinado, em declive; (handwriting) torto

sloppy ['slɒpɪ] adj (work) descuidado; (appearance) relaxado

slot [slɒt] n (in machine) fenda ▷ vt:

to ~ into encaixar em

slow [sləu] adj lento; (not clever) bronco, de raciocínio lento; (watch): **to be ~** atrasar ▷ adv lentamente, devagar ▷ vt, vi ir (mais) devagar; **"~"** (road sign) "devagar"; **slowly** adv lentamente, devagar; **slow motion** n: **in slow motion** em câmara lenta

slug [slʌg] n lesma; **sluggish** adj vagaroso; (business) lento

slum [slʌm] n (area) favela; (house) cortiço, barraco

slump [slʌmp] n (economic) depressão f; (Comm) baixa, queda ▷ vi (person) cair; (prices) baixar repentinamente

slung [slʌŋ] pt, pp of **sling**

slur [slə:r] n calúnia ▷ vt pronunciar indistintamente

slush [slʌʃ] n neve f meio derretida

sly [slaɪ] adj (person) astuto; (smile, remark) malicioso, velhaco

smack [smæk] n palmada ▷ vt bater; (child) dar uma palmada em; (on face) dar um tabefe em ▷ vi: **to ~ of** cheirar a, saber a

small [smɔ:l] adj pequeno; **small change** n trocado

smart [smɑ:t] adj elegante; (clever) inteligente, astuto; (quick) vivo, esperto ▷ vi sofrer; **smart phone** n smartphone m

smash [smæʃ] n (also: **~-up**) colisão f, choque m; (smash hit) sucesso de bilheteira ▷ vt (break) escangalhar, despedaçar; (car etc) bater com; (Sport: record) quebrar ▷ vi despedaçar-se; (against wall etc) espatifar-se; **smashing** (inf) adj excelente

smear [smɪər] n mancha, nódoa; (Med) esfregaço ▷ vt untar; (to make dirty) lambuzar

S

smell [smɛl] (*pt*, *pp* **smelt** *or*
smelled) *n* cheiro; (*sense*) olfato
▷ *vt* cheirar ▷ *vi* (*food etc*) cheirar;
(*pej*) cheirar mal; **to ~ of** cheirar a;
smelly (*pej*) *adj* fedorento,
malcheiroso
smile [smaɪl] *n* sorriso ▷ *vi* sorrir
smirk [smə:k] (*pej*) *n* sorriso falso *or*
afetado
smog [smɔg] *n* nevoeiro com
fumaça (*BR*) *or* fumo (*PT*)
smoke [sməuk] *n* fumaça (*BR*),
fumo (*PT*) ▷ *vi* fumar; (*chimney*)
fumegar ▷ *vt* (*cigarettes*) fumar;
smoked *adj* (*bacon*) defumado;
(*glass*) fumée; **smoker** *n* (*person*)
fumante *m/f*; (*Rail*) vagão *m* para
fumantes; **smoking** *n*: **"no
smoking"** (*sign*) "proibido fumar";
he's given up smoking ele deixou
de fumar; **smoky** *adj* enfumaçado;
(*taste*) defumado
smooth [smu:ð] *adj* liso, macio;
(*sauce*) cremoso; (*sea*) tranquilo,
calmo; (*flavour, movement*) suave;
(*person: pej*) meloso ▷ *vt* (*also:* **~
out**) alisar; (: *difficulties*) aplainar
smother ['smʌðəʳ] *vt* (*fire*) abafar;
(*person*) sufocar; (*emotions*)
reprimir
SMS *n abbr* (= *short message service*)
SMS *m*
smudge [smʌdʒ] *n* mancha ▷ *vt*
manchar, sujar
smug [smʌg] (*pej*) *adj* convencido
smuggle ['smʌgl] *vt*
contrabandear; **smuggling** *n*
contrabando
snack [snæk] *n* lanche *m* (*BR*),
merenda *f* (*PT*); **snack bar** *n*
lanchonete *f* (*BR*), snackbar *m* (*PT*)
snag [snæg] *n* dificuldade *f*,
obstáculo
snail [sneɪl] *n* caracol *m*

snake [sneɪk] *n* cobra
snap [snæp] *n* (*sound*) estalo;
(*photograph*) foto *f* ▷ *adj* repentino
▷ *vt* quebrar; (*fingers, whip*) estalar
▷ *vi* quebrar; (*fig: person*) retrucar
asperamente; **to ~ shut** fechar
com um estalo **snap at** *vt fus* (*subj:
dog*) tentar morder **snap off** *vt*
(*break*) partir **snap up** *vt* arrebatar,
comprar rapidamente; **snapshot**
n foto *f* (instantânea)
snarl [snɑ:l] *vi* grunhir
snatch [snætʃ] *n* (*small piece*) trecho
▷ *vt* agarrar; (*fig: look*) roubar
sneak [sni:k] (*pt* **sneaked**) *vi*: **to ~
in/out** entrar/sair furtivamente
▷ *n* (*inf*) dedo-duro; **to ~ up on sb**
chegar de mansinho perto de
alguém; **sneakers** *npl* tênis *m*
(*BR*), sapatos *mpl* de treino (*PT*)
sneer [snɪəʳ] *vi* rir-se com desdém;
(*mock*): **to ~ at** zombar de,
desprezar
sneeze [sni:z] *n* espirro ▷ *vi*
espirrar
sniff [snɪf] *n* fungada; (*of dog*)
farejada; (*of person*) fungadela ▷ *vi*
fungar ▷ *vt* fungar, farejar; (*glue,
drug*) cheirar
snigger ['snɪgəʳ] *vi* rir-se com
dissimulação
snip [snɪp] *n* tesourada; (*Brit: inf*)
pechincha ▷ *vt* cortar com tesoura
sniper ['snaɪpəʳ] *n* franco-
atirador(a) *m/f*
snob [snɔb] *n* esnobe *m/f*
snooker ['snu:kəʳ] *n* sinuca
snoop [snu:p] *vi*: **to ~ about**
bisbilhotar
snooze [snu:z] *n* soneca ▷ *vi* tirar
uma soneca, dormitar
snore [snɔ:ʳ] *vi* roncar ▷ *n* ronco
snorkel ['snɔ:kl] *n* tubo snorkel
snort [snɔ:t] *n* bufo, bufido ▷ *vi* bufar

snow [snəʊ] n neve f ▷ vi nevar;
snowball n bola de neve ▷ vi (fig)
aumentar (como bola de neve);
snowdrift n monte m de neve
(formado pelo vento); **snowman**
irreg n boneco de neve;
snowplough, (US) **snowplow** n
máquina limpa-neve, removedor m
de neve; **snowstorm** n nevasca,
tempestade f de neve

snub [snʌb] vt desdenhar,
menosprezar ▷ n repulsa

snug [snʌg] adj (sheltered) abrigado,
protegido; (fitted) justo, cômodo

◯ KEYWORD

so [səʊ] adv 1 (thus, likewise) assim,
deste modo; **so saying he walked
away** falou isto e foi embora; **if so**
se for assim, se assim é; **I didn't
do it — you did so** não fiz isso —
você fez!; **so do I, so am I** etc eu
também; **so it is!** é verdade!;
I hope/think so espero/acho que
sim; **so far** até aqui
2 (in comparisons etc: to such a degree)
tão; **so big/quickly (that)** tão
grande/rápido (que)
3: **so much** adj, adv tanto; **I've got
so much work** tenho tanto
trabalho; **so many** tantos(-as);
there are so many people to see
tem tanta gente para ver
4 (phrases): **10 or so** uns 10; **so
long!** (inf: goodbye) tchau!
▷ conj 1 (expressing purpose): **so as
to do** para fazer; **we hurried so as
not to be late** nós nos apressamos
para não chegarmos atrasados;
so (that) para que, a fim de que
2 (result) de modo que; **he didn't
arrive so I left** como ele não
chegou, eu fui embora; **so I was**

right after all então eu estava
certo no final das contas

soak [səʊk] vt embeber, ensopar;
(put in water) pôr de molho ▷ vi
estar de molho, impregnar-se **soak
in** vi infiltrar **soak up** vt absorver
soap [səʊp] n sabão m; **soap opera**
n novela; **soap powder** n sabão m
em pó
soar [sɔːʳ] vi (on wings) elevar-se em
voo; (rocket, temperature) subir;
(building etc) levantar-se; (price,
production) disparar
sob [sɒb] n soluço ▷ vi soluçar
sober ['səʊbəʳ] adj (serious) sério;
(not drunk) sóbrio; (colour, style)
discreto **sober up** vi ficar sóbrio
so-called [-kɔːld] adj chamado
soccer ['sɒkəʳ] n futebol m
social ['səʊʃl] adj social ▷ n reunião
f social; **socialism** n socialismo;
socialist adj, n socialista m/f;
socialize vi: **to socialize (with)**
socializar (com); **social
networking** [-'nɛtwəːkɪŋ] n redes
fpl sociais; **social security** (Brit) n
previdência social; **social work** n
assistência social, serviço social;
social worker n assistente m/f
social
society [sə'saɪətɪ] n sociedade f;
(club) associação f; (also: **high ~**)
alta sociedade
sociology [səʊsɪ'ɒlədʒɪ] n
sociologia
sock [sɒk] n meia (BR), peúga (PT)
socket ['sɒkɪt] n bocal m, encaixe m;
(Brit: Elec) tomada
soda ['səʊdə] n (Chem) soda; (also:
~ water) água com gás; (US: also:
~ pop) soda
sofa ['səʊfə] n sofá m
soft [sɒft] adj mole; (voice, music,

S

light) suave; (*kind*) meigo, bondoso; **soft drink** *n* refrigerante *m*; **soften** *vt* amolecer, amaciar; (*effect*) abrandar; (*expression*) suavizar ▷ *vi* amolecer-se; (*voice, expression*) suavizar-se; **softly** *adv* suavemente; (*gently*) delicadamente; **software** *n* software *m*

soggy ['sɔgɪ] *adj* ensopado, encharcado

soil [sɔɪl] *n* terra, solo; (*territory*) território ▷ *vt* sujar, manchar

solar ['səʊləʳ] *adj* solar; **solar power** *n* energia solar

sold [səʊld] *pt, pp de* **sell** ▷ *adj*: **~ out** (*Comm*) esgotado

soldier ['səʊldʒəʳ] *n* soldado; (*army man*) militar *m*

sole [səʊl] *n* (*of foot, shoe*) sola; (*fish: pl inv*) solha, linguado ▷ *adj* único

solicitor [sə'lɪsɪtəʳ] (*Brit*) *n* (*for wills etc*) tabelião(-lioa) *m/f*; (*in court*) ≈ advogado(-a)

solid ['sɔlɪd] *adj* sólido; (*gold etc*) maciço; (*person*) sério ▷ *n* sólido; **solids** *npl* (*food*) comida sólida

solitary ['sɔlɪtərɪ] *adj* solitário, só; (*walk*) só; (*isolated*) isolado, retirado; (*single*) único

solo ['səʊləʊ] *n, adv* solo; **soloist** *n* solista *m/f*

solution [sə'lu:ʃən] *n* solução *f*

solve [sɔlv] *vt* resolver, solucionar

solvent ['sɔlvənt] *adj* (*Comm*) solvente ▷ *n* (*Chem*) solvente *m*

 KEYWORD

some [sʌm] *adj* **1** (*a certain number or amount*): **some tea/water/biscuits** um pouco de chá/água/uns biscoitos; **some children**

came algumas crianças vieram **2** (*certain: in contrasts*) algum(a); **some people say that ...** algumas pessoas dizem que ...

3 (*unspecified*) um pouco de; **some woman was asking for you** uma mulher estava perguntando por você; **some day** um dia

▷ *pron* **1** (*a certain number*) alguns/algumas; **I've got some** (*books etc*) tenho alguns; **some went for a taxi and some walked** alguns foram pegar um táxi e outros foram andando

2 (*a certain amount*) um pouco; **I've got some** (*milk, money etc*) tenho um pouco

▷ *adv*: **some 10 people** umas 10 pessoas

somebody ['sʌmbədɪ] *pron* = **someone**

somehow ['sʌmhaʊ] *adv* de alguma maneira; (*for some reason*) por uma razão ou outra

someone ['sʌmwʌn] *pron* alguém

someplace ['sʌmpleɪs] (*US*) *adv* = **somewhere**

something ['sʌmθɪŋ] *pron* alguma coisa, algo (*BR*)

sometime ['sʌmtaɪm] *adv* (*in future*) algum dia, em outra oportunidade; (*in past*): **~ last month** durante o mês passado

sometimes ['sʌmtaɪmz] *adv* às vezes, de vez em quando

somewhat ['sʌmwɔt] *adv* um tanto

somewhere ['sʌmwɛəʳ] *adv* (*be*) em algum lugar; (*go*) para algum lugar; (*be*) em outro lugar; (*go*) para outro lugar

son [sʌn] *n* filho

song [sɔŋ] *n* canção *f*; (*of bird*) canto

son-in-law ['sʌnɪnlɔ:] n genro
soon [su:n] adv logo, brevemente; (*a short time after*) logo após; (*early*) cedo; ~ **afterwards** pouco depois; *see also* **as**; **sooner** adv antes, mais cedo; (*preference*): **I would sooner do that** preferia fazer isso; **sooner or later** mais cedo ou mais tarde
soothe [su:ð] vt acalmar, sossegar; (*pain*) aliviar, suavizar
soprano [sə'prɑ:nəu] n soprano m/f
sore [sɔ:ʳ] adj dolorido ▷ n chaga, ferida
sorrow ['sɔrəu] n tristeza, mágoa, dor f; **sorrows** npl (*causes of grief*) tristezas fpl
sorry ['sɔrɪ] adj (*regretful*) arrependido; (*condition, excuse*) lamentável; ~! desculpe!, perdão!, sinto muito!; **to feel ~ for sb** sentir pena de alguém
sort [sɔ:t] n tipo ▷ vt (*also*: ~ **out**: *papers*) classificar; (: *problems*) solucionar, resolver
SOS n abbr (= *save our souls*) S.O.S. m
so-so adv mais ou menos, regular
sought [sɔ:t] pt, pp of **seek**
soul [səul] n alma; (*person*) criatura
sound [saund] adj (*healthy*) saudável, sadio; (*safe, not damaged*) sólido, completo; (*secure*) seguro; (*reliable*) confiável; (*sensible*) sensato ▷ adv: ~ **asleep** dormindo profundamente ▷ n (*noise*) som m, ruído, barulho; (*volume: on TV etc*) volume m; (*Geo*) estreito, braço (de mar) ▷ vt (*alarm*) soar ▷ vi soar, tocar; (*fig: seem*) parecer; **to ~ like** parecer **sound out** vi sondar; **soundtrack** n trilha sonora
soup [su:p] n sopa; **in the ~** (*fig*) numa encrenca
sour ['sauəʳ] adj azedo, ácido; (*milk*) talhado; (*fig*) mal-humorado,

rabugento; **it's ~ grapes!** (*fig*) é despeito!
source [sɔ:s] n fonte f
south [sauθ] n sul m ▷ adj do sul, meridional ▷ adv ao or para o sul; **South Africa** n África do Sul; **South African** adj, n sul-africano(-a); **South America** n América do Sul; **South American** adj, n sul-americano(-a); **south-east** n sudeste m; **southern** ['sʌðən] adj (*to the south*) para o sul, em direção do sul; (*from the south*) do sul, sulista; **the southern hemisphere** o Hemisfério Sul; **South Pole** n Pólo Sul; **southward, southwards** adv para o sul; **south-west** n sudoeste m
souvenir [su:və'nɪəʳ] n lembrança
sovereign ['sɔvrɪn] n soberano(-a)
sow[1] [sau] n porca
sow[2] [səu] (*pt* **sowed**, *pp* **sown**) vt semear; (*fig: spread*) disseminar, espalhar
soya ['sɔɪə], **soy** [sɔɪ] (*US*) n soja; **soya bean** n semente f de soja; **soya sauce** n molho de soja
spa [spɑ:] n (*town*) estância hidro-mineral; (*US: also*: **health ~**) estância balnear
space [speɪs] n (*gen*) espaço; (*room*) lugar m; (*cpd*) espacial ▷ vt (*also*: ~ **out**) espaçar; **spacecraft** n nave f espacial; **spaceship** n = **spacecraft**; **spacious** ['speɪʃəs] adj espaçoso
spade [speɪd] n pá f; **spades** npl (*Cards*) espadas fpl
Spain [speɪn] n Espanha
spam ['spæm] n (*junk email*) spam m
span [spæn] n (*also*: **wing~**) envergadura; (*of arch*) vão m; (*in time*) lapso, espaço ▷ vt

estender-se sobre, atravessar; (fig) abarcar

Spaniard ['spænjəd] n espanhol(a) m/f

Spanish ['spænɪʃ] adj espanhol(a) ▷ n (Ling) espanhol m, castelhano m; **the Spanish** npl os espanhóis

spanner ['spænə^r] (Brit) n chave f inglesa

spare [spɛə^r] adj vago, desocupado; (surplus) de sobra, a mais ▷ n = **spare part** ▷ vt dispensar, passar sem; (make available) dispor de; (refrain from hurting) perdoar, poupar; **to ~** de sobra; **spare part** n peça sobressalente; **spare time** n tempo livre; **spare wheel** n estepe m

spark [spɑːk] n chispa, faísca; (fig) centelha

sparkle ['spɑːkl] n cintilação f, brilho ▷ vi (shine) brilhar, faiscar; **sparkling** adj (mineral water) gasoso; (wine) espumante; (conversation) animado; (performance) brilhante

sparrow ['spærəu] n pardal m

sparse [spɑːs] adj escasso; (hair) ralo

spasm ['spæzəm] n (Med) espasmo

spat [spæt] pt, pp of **spit**

speak [spiːk] (pt **spoke**, pp **spoken**) vt (language) falar; (truth) dizer ▷ vi falar; (make a speech) discursar; **~ up!** fale alto!; **speaker** n (in public) orador(a) m/f; (also: **loudspeaker**) alto-falante m; (Pol): **the Speaker** o Presidente da Câmara

spear [spɪə^r] n lança ▷ vt lancear, arpoar

special ['spɛʃl] adj especial; (edition etc) extra; (delivery) rápido; **specialist** n especialista m/f; **speciality** [spɛʃɪ'ælɪtɪ] n especialidade f; **specialize** vi: **to**

specialize (in) especializar-se (em); **specially** adv especialmente; **specialty** ['spɛʃəltɪ] (esp US) n = **speciality**

species ['spiːʃiːz] n inv espécie f

specific [spə'sɪfɪk] adj específico

specimen ['spɛsɪmən] n espécime m, amostra; (for testing, Med) espécime

speck [spɛk] n mancha, pinta

spectacle ['spɛktəkl] n espetáculo; **spectacles** npl (glasses) óculos mpl; **spectacular** [spɛk'tækjulə^r] adj espetacular ▷ n (Cinema etc) superprodução f

spectator [spɛk'teɪtə^r] n espectador(a) m/f

spectrum ['spɛktrəm] (pl **spectra**) n espectro

speech [spiːtʃ] n (faculty, Theatre) fala; (formal talk) discurso; **speechless** adj estupefato, emudecido

speed [spiːd] (pt, pp **sped**) n velocidade f; (rate) rapidez f; (haste) pressa; (promptness) prontidão f; **at full** or **top ~** a toda a velocidade; **speed up** (pt, pp **speeded up**) vt, vi acelerar; **speedboat** n lancha; **speeding** n (Aut) excesso de velocidade; **speed limit** n limite m de velocidade, velocidade f máxima; **speedometer** [spɪ'dɔmɪtə^r] n velocímetro; **speedy** adj veloz, rápido; (prompt) pronto, imediato

spell [spɛl] (pt, pp **spelled** or **spelt**) n (also: **magic ~**) encanto, feitiço; (period of time) período, temporada ▷ vt (also: **~ out**) soletrar; (fig) pressagiar, ser sinal de; **to cast a ~ on sb** enfeitiçar alguém; **he can't ~** não sabe escrever bem, comete erros de ortografia; **spellchecker**

['speltʃekə'] n (Comput) corretor m ortográfico

spend [spɛnd] (pt, pp **spent**) vt (money) gastar; (time) passar

sperm [spə:m] n esperma

sphere [sfɪə'] n esfera

spice [spaɪs] n especiaria ▷ vt condimentar

spicy ['spaɪsɪ] adj condimentado

spider ['spaɪdə'] n aranha

spike [spaɪk] n (point) ponta, espigão m; (Bot) espiga

spill [spɪl] (pt, pp **spilt** or **spilled**) vt entornar, derramar ▷ vi derramar-se

spill over vi transbordar

spin [spɪn] (pt, pp **spun**) n (Aviat) parafuso; (trip in car) volta or passeio de carro; (ball): **to put ~ on** fazer rolar ▷ vt (wool etc) fiar, tecer ▷ vi girar, rodar; (make thread) tecer

spin out vt prolongar; (money) fazer render

spinach ['spɪnɪtʃ] n espinafre m

spinal cord n espinha dorsal

spin doctor (inf) n marqueteiro(-a)

spin-dryer (Brit) n secadora

spine [spaɪn] n espinha dorsal; (thorn) espinho

spiral ['spaɪərl] n espiral f ▷ vi (prices) disparar

spire ['spaɪə'] n flecha, agulha

spirit ['spɪrɪt] n (soul) alma; (ghost) fantasma m; (courage) coragem f, ânimo; (frame of mind) estado de espírito; (sense) sentido; **spirits** npl (drink) álcool m; **in good ~s** alegre, de bom humor; **spiritual** adj espiritual ▷ n (also: **Negro spiritual**) canto religioso dos negros

spit [spɪt] (pt, pp **spat**) n (for roasting) espeto; (saliva) saliva ▷ vi cuspir; (sound) escarrar; (rain) chuviscar

spite [spaɪt] n rancor m,

ressentimento ▷ vt contrariar; **in ~ of** apesar de, a despeito de; **spiteful** adj maldoso, malévolo

splash [splæʃ] n (sound) borrifo, respingo; (of colour) mancha ▷ vt: **to ~ (with)** salpicar (de) ▷ vi (also: **~ about**) borrifar, respingar

splendid ['splɛndɪd] adj esplêndido; (impressive) impressionante

splinter ['splɪntə'] n (of wood, glass) lasca; (in finger) farpa ▷ vi lascar-se, estilhaçar-se, despedaçar-se

split [splɪt] (pt, pp **split**) n fenda, brecha; (fig: division) rompimento; (: difference) diferença; (Pol) divisão f ▷ vt partir, fender; (party, work) dividir; (profits) repartir ▷ vi (divide) dividir-se, repartir-se **split up** vi (couple) separar-se, acabar; (meeting) terminar

spoil [spɔɪl] (pt, pp **spoilt** or **spoiled**) vt (damage) danificar; (mar) estragar, arruinar; (child) mimar

spoke [spəuk] pt of **speak** ▷ n raio

spoken ['spəukn] pp of **speak**

spokesman ['spəuksmən] irreg n porta-voz m

spokeswoman ['spəukswumən] irreg n porta-voz f

sponge [spʌndʒ] n esponja; (cake) pão de ló m ▷ vt lavar com esponja ▷ vi: **to ~ on sb** viver às custas de alguém; **sponge bag** (Brit) n bolsa de toalete

sponsor ['spɔnsə'] n patrocinador(a) m/f ▷ vt patrocinar; apadrinhar; fiar; (applicant, proposal) apoiar, defender; **sponsorship** n patrocínio

spontaneous [spɔn'teɪnɪəs] adj espontâneo

S

spooky ['spu:kɪ] (inf) adj arrepiante
spoon [spu:n] n colher f; **spoonful** n colherada
sport [spɔ:t] n esporte m (BR), desporto (PT); (person) bom perdedor/boa perdedora m/f ▷ vt (wear) exibir; **sport jacket** (US) n = **sports jacket**; **sports car** n carro esporte (BR), carro de sport (PT); **sports jacket** (Brit) n casaco esportivo (BR) or desportivo (PT); **sportsman** irreg n esportista m (BR), desportista m (PT); **sportswear** n roupa esportiva (BR) or desportiva (PT) or esporte; **sportswoman** irreg n esportista (BR), desportista (PT); **sporty** adj esportivo (BR), desportivo (PT)
spot [spɔt] n (mark) marca; (place) lugar m, local m; (dot: on pattern) mancha, ponto; (on skin) espinha; (Radio, TV) hora; (small amount): **a ~ of** um pouquinho de ▷ vt notar; **on the ~** na hora; (there) ali mesmo; (in difficulty) em apuros; **spotless** adj sem mancha, imaculado; **spotlight** n holofote m, refletor m
spouse [spauz] n cônjuge m/f
sprain [spreɪn] n distensão f, torcedura f ▷ vt torcer
sprang [spræŋ] pt of **spring**
sprawl [sprɔ:l] vi esparramar-se
spray [spreɪ] n borrifo; (container) spray m, atomizador m; (garden spray) vaporizador m; (of flowers) ramalhete m ▷ vt pulverizar; (crops) borrifar, regar
spread [sprɛd] (pt, pp **spread**) n extensão f; (distribution) expansão f, difusão f; (Culin) pasta; (inf: food) banquete m ▷ vt espalhar; (butter) untar, passar; (wings, sails) abrir, desdobrar; (workload, wealth) distribuir; (scatter) disseminar ▷ vi

(news, stain) espalhar-se; (disease) alastrar-se **spread out** vi dispersar-se; **spreadsheet** n (Comput) planilha
spree [spri:] n: **to go on a ~** cair na farra
spring [sprɪŋ] (pt **sprang**, pp **sprung**) n salto, pulo; (coiled metal) mola; (season) primavera; (of water) fonte f **spring up** vi aparecer de repente
sprinkle ['sprɪŋkl] vt (liquid) salpicar; (salt, sugar) borrifar; **to ~ water on**, **~ with water** salpicar de água
sprint [sprɪnt] n corrida de pequena distância ▷ vi correr a toda velocidade
sprung [sprʌŋ] pp of **spring**
spun [spʌn] pt, pp of **spin**
spur [spə:ʳ] n espora; (fig) estímulo ▷ vt (also: **~ on**) incitar, estimular; **on the ~ of the moment** de improviso, de repente
spurt [spə:t] n (of energy) acesso; (of blood etc) jorro ▷ vi jorrar
spy [spaɪ] n espião/espiã m/f ▷ vi: **to ~ on** espiar, espionar ▷ vt enxergar, avistar
sq. abbr (Math etc) = **square**
squabble ['skwɔbl] vi brigar, discutir
squad [skwɔd] n (Mil, Police) pelotão m, esquadra; (Football) seleção f
squadron ['skwɔdrən] n (Mil) esquadrão m; (Aviat) esquadrilha; (Naut) esquadra
squander ['skwɔndəʳ] vt esbanjar, dissipar; (chances) desperdiçar
square [skwɛəʳ] n quadrado; (in town) praça; (inf: person) quadrado(-a), careta m/f ▷ adj quadrado; (inf: ideas, tastes) careta,

antiquado ▷ vt (*arrange*) ajustar, acertar; (*Math*) elevar ao quadrado; (*reconcile*) conciliar; **all ~** igual, quite; **a ~ meal** uma refeição substancial; **2 metres ~** um quadrado de dois metros de lado; **2 ~ metres** 2 metros quadrados

squash [skwɔʃ] n (*Brit: drink*): **lemon/orange ~** limonada/laranjada concentrada; (*Sport*) squash m; (*US: vegetable*) abóbora ▷ vt esmagar

squat [skwɔt] adj atarracado ▷ vi (*also: ~ down*) agachar-se, acocorar-se; **squatter** n posseiro(-a)

squeak [skwiːk] vi (*door*) ranger; (*mouse*) guinchar

squeal [skwiːl] vi guinchar, gritar agudamente

squeeze [skwiːz] n (*gen, of hand*) aperto; (*Econ*) arrocho ▷ vt comprimir, socar; (*hand, arm*) apertar **squeeze out** vt espremer; (*fig*) extorquir

squid [skwɪd] (*pl* **squids** *or* **squid**) n lula

squint [skwɪnt] vi olhar *or* ser vesgo ▷ n (*Med*) estrabismo

squirm [skwəːm] vi retorcer-se

squirrel ['skwɪrəl] n esquilo

squirt [skwəːt] vi, vt jorrar, esguichar

Sr *abbr* = **senior**

St *abbr* (= *saint*) S.; = **street**

stab [stæb] n (*with knife etc*) punhalada; (*of pain*) pontada; (*inf: try*): **to have a ~ at (doing) sth** tentar (fazer) algo ▷ vt apunhalar

stable ['steɪbl] adj estável ▷ n estábulo, cavalariça

stack [stæk] n montão m, pilha ▷ vt amontoar, empilhar

stadium ['steɪdɪəm] (*pl* **stadia** *or*

stadiums) n estádio

staff [stɑːf] n (*work force*) pessoal m, quadro; (*Brit: Sch: also:* **teaching ~**) corpo docente ▷ vt prover de pessoal

stag [stæg] n veado, cervo

stage [steɪdʒ] n palco, cena; (*point*) etapa, fase f; (*platform*) plataforma, estrado; (*profession*): **the ~** o palco, o teatro ▷ vt pôr em cena, representar; (*demonstration*) montar, organizar; **in ~s** por etapas

stagger ['stægəʳ] vi cambalear ▷ vt (*amaze*) surpreender, chocar; (*hours, holidays*) escalonar; **staggering** adj (*amazing*) surpreendente, chocante

stain [steɪn] n mancha; (*colouring*) tinta, tintura ▷ vt manchar; (*wood*) tingir

stair [stɛəʳ] n (*step*) degrau m; **stairs** npl (*flight of steps*) escada; **staircase** n escadaria, escada; **stairway** n = **staircase**

stake [steɪk] n estaca, poste m; (*Comm: interest*) interesse m, participação f; (*Betting: gen pl*) aposta ▷ vt apostar; (*claim*) reivindicar; **to be at ~** estar em jogo

stale [steɪl] adj (*bread*) dormido; (*food*) estragado; (*air*) viciado; (*smell*) mofado; (*beer*) velho

stalk [stɔːk] n talo, haste f ▷ vt caçar de tocaia; **to ~ in/out** entrar/sair silenciosamente; **to ~ off** andar com arrogância

stall [stɔːl] n (*Brit: in market*) barraca; (*in stable*) baia ▷ vt (*Aut*) fazer morrer; (*fig: delay*) impedir, atrasar ▷ vi morrer; esquivar-se, ganhar tempo; **stalls** npl (*Brit: in cinema, theatre*) plateia

stamina ['stæmɪnə] n resistência

stammer ['stæməʳ] n gagueira ▷ vi gaguejar, balbuciar

stamp [stæmp] n selo; (rubber stamp) carimbo, timbre m; (mark, also fig) marca, impressão f ▷ vi (also: **~ one's foot**) bater com o pé ▷ vt (letter) selar; (mark) marcar; (with rubber stamp) carimbar

stampede [stæm'piːd] n debandada, estouro (da boiada)

stance [stæns] n postura, posição f

stand [stænd] (pt, pp **stood**) n posição f, postura; (for taxis) ponto; (also: **hall ~**) pedestal m; (also: **music ~**) (Sport) tribuna, palanque m; (stall) barraca ▷ vi (be) estar, encontrar-se; (be on foot) estar em pé; (rise) levantar-se; (remain: decision, offer) estar de pé; (in election) candidatar-se ▷ vt (place) pôr, colocar; (tolerate, withstand) aguentar, suportar; (cost) pagar; **to make a ~** resistir; (fig) ater-se a um princípio; **to ~ for parliament** (Brit) apresentar-se como candidato ao parlamento **stand by** vi estar a postos ▷ vt fus (opinion) aferrar-se a; (person) ficar ao lado de **stand down** vi retirar-se **stand for** vt fus (signify) significar; (represent) representar; (tolerate) tolerar, permitir **stand in for** vt fus substituir **stand out** vi (be prominent) destacar-se **stand up** vi levantar-se **stand up for** vt fus defender **stand up to** vt fus enfrentar

standard ['stændəd] n padrão m, critério; (flag) estandarte m; (level) nível m ▷ adj padronizado, regular, normal; **standards** npl (morals) valores mpl morais; **standard of living** n padrão m de vida (BR), nível m de vida (PT)

stand-by adj de reserva ▷ n: **to be on ~** estar de sobreaviso or de prontidão; **stand-by ticket** n bilhete m de stand-by

standing ['stændɪŋ] adj (on foot) em pé; (permanent) permanente ▷ n posição f, reputação f; **of many years' ~** de muitos anos

standpoint ['stændpɔɪnt] n ponto de vista

standstill ['stændstɪl] n: **at a ~** paralisado, parado; **to come to a ~** (car) parar; (factory, traffic) ficar paralisado

stank [stæŋk] pt of **stink**

staple ['steɪpl] n (for papers) grampo ▷ adj (food etc) básico ▷ vt grampear

star [stɑːʳ] n estrela; (celebrity) astro/estrela ▷ vi: **to ~ in** ser a estrela em, estrelar ▷ vt (Cinema) ser estrelado por; **the stars** npl (horoscope) o horóscopo

starboard ['stɑːbəd] n estibordo

starch [stɑːtʃ] n (in food) amido, fécula; (for clothes) goma

stardom ['stɑːdəm] n estrelato

stare [stɛəʳ] n olhar m fixo ▷ vi: **to ~ at** olhar fixamente, fitar

stark [stɑːk] adj severo, áspero ▷ adv: **~ naked** completamente nu, em pelo

start [stɑːt] n princípio, começo; (departure) partida; (sudden movement) sobressalto, susto; (advantage) vantagem f ▷ vt começar, iniciar; (cause) causar; (found) fundar; (engine) ligar ▷ vi começar, iniciar; (with fright) sobressaltar-se, assustar-se; (train etc) sair **start off** vi começar, principiar; (leave) sair, pôr-se a caminho **start up** vi começar; (car) pegar, pôr-se em marcha ▷ vt começar; (car) ligar; **starter** n (Aut) arranque m; (Sport: official) juiz/juíza m/f da partida; **starting point** n ponto de partida

startle ['stɑːtl] vt assustar, aterrar; **startling** adj surpreendente

starvation [stɑːˈveɪʃən] n fome f

starve ['stɑːv] vi passar fome; (to death) morrer de fome ▷ vt fazer passar fome; (fig): **to ~ (of)** privar (de)

state [steɪt] n estado ▷ vt afirmar, declarar; **the States** npl (Geo) os Estados Unidos; **to be in a ~** estar agitado; **statement** n declaração f; **statesman** irreg n estadista m

static ['stætɪk] n (Radio, TV) interferência ▷ adj estático

station ['steɪʃən] n estação f; (Police) delegacia; (Radio) emissora ▷ vt colocar

stationary ['steɪʃnərɪ] adj estacionário

station wagon (US) n perua (BR), canadiana (PT)

statistic [stəˈtɪstɪk] n estatística; **statistics** [stəˈtɪstɪks] n (science) estatística

statue ['stætjuː] n estátua

status ['steɪtəs] n posição f; (official classification) categoria; (importance) status m

staunch [stɔːntʃ] adj fiel

stay [steɪ] n estadia, estada ▷ vi ficar; (as guest) hospedar-se; (spend some time) demorar-se; **to ~ put** não se mexer; **to ~ the night** pernoitar **stay behind** vi ficar atrás **stay in** vi ficar em casa **stay on** vi ficar **stay out** vi ficar fora de casa **stay up** vi (at night) velar, ficar acordado

steadily ['stedɪlɪ] adv (firmly) firmemente; (unceasingly) sem parar, constantemente; (walk) regularmente

steady ['stedɪ] adj (job, boyfriend) constante; (speed) fixo; (regular) regular; (person, character) sensato; (calm) calmo, sereno ▷ vt (stabilize) estabilizar; (nerves) acalmar

steak [steɪk] n filé m; (beef) bife m

steal [stiːl] (pt **stole**, pp **stolen**) vt roubar ▷ vi mover-se furtivamente

steam [stiːm] n vapor m ▷ vt (Culin) cozinhar no vapor ▷ vi fumegar; **steamy** adj vaporoso; (room) cheio de vapor, úmido (BR), húmido (PT); (heat, atmosphere) vaporoso

steel [stiːl] n aço ▷ adj de aço

steep [stiːp] adj íngreme; (increase) acentuado; (price) exorbitante ▷ vt (food) colocar de molho; (cloth) ensopar, encharcar

steeple ['stiːpl] n campanário, torre f

steer [stɪəʳ] vt (person) guiar; (vehicle) dirigir ▷ vi conduzir; **steering** n (Aut) direção f; **steering wheel** n volante m

stem [stem] n (of plant) caule m, haste f; (of glass) pé m ▷ vt deter, reter; (blood) estancar **stem from** vt fus originar-se de

step [step] n passo; (stair) degrau m ▷ vi: **to ~ forward** dar um passo a frente/atrás; **steps** npl (Brit) = **stepladder**; **to be in ~ (with)** (fig) manter a paridade (com); **to be out of ~ (with)** (fig) estar em disparidade (com) **step down** vi (fig) renunciar **step on** vt fus pisar **step up** vt aumentar; **stepbrother** n meio-irmão m; **stepdaughter** n enteada; **stepfather** n padrasto; **stepladder** (Brit) n escada portátil or de abrir; **stepmother** n madrasta; **stepsister** n meia-irmã f; **stepson** n enteado

stereo ['stɛrɪəu] n estéreo; (record player) (aparelho de) som m ▷ adj (also: ~**phonic**) estereofônico

sterile ['stɛraɪl] adj esterelizado; (barren) estéril; **sterilize** ['stɛrɪlaɪz] vt esterilizar

sterling ['stə:lɪŋ] adj esterlino; (silver) de lei ▷ n (currency) libra esterlina; **one pound ~** uma libra esterlina

stern [stə:n] adj severo, austero ▷ n (Naut) popa, ré f

stew [stju:] n guisado, ensopado ▷ vt guisar, ensopar; (fruit) cozinhar

steward ['stju:əd] n (Aviat) comissário de bordo; **stewardess** n aeromoça (BR), hospedeira de bordo (PT)

stick [stɪk] (pt, pp **stuck**) n pau m; (as weapon) cacete m; (walking stick) bengala, cajado m ▷ vt (glue) colar; (thrust): **to ~ sth into** cravar or enfiar algo em; (inf: put) meter; (: tolerate) aguentar, suportar ▷ vi (become attached) colar-se; (be unmoveable) emperrar; (in mind etc) gravar-se **stick out** vi estar saliente, projetar-se **stick up** vi estar saliente, projetar-se **stick up for** vt fus defender; **sticker** n adesivo; **sticking plaster** n esparadrapo

sticky ['stɪkɪ] adj pegajoso; (label) adesivo; (fig) delicado

stiff [stɪf] adj (strong) forte; (hard) duro; (difficult) difícil; (moving with difficulty: person) teso; (: door, zip) empenado; (formal) formal ▷ adv (bored, worried) extremamente

stigma ['stɪgmə] n estigma m

stiletto [stɪ'lɛtəu] (Brit) n (also: ~

heel) salto alto e fino

still [stɪl] adj parado ▷ adv (up to this time) ainda; (even, yet) ainda; (nonetheless) entretanto, contudo

stimulate ['stɪmjuleɪt] vt estimular

stimulus ['stɪmjuləs] (pl **stimuli**) n estímulo, incentivo

sting [stɪŋ] (pt, pp **stung**) n (wound) picada; (pain) ardência; (of insect) ferrão m ▷ vt arguilhar ▷ vi (insect, animal) picar; (eyes, ointment) queimar

stink [stɪŋk] (pt **stank**, pp **stunk**) n fedor m, catinga ▷ vi feder, cheirar mal

stir [stə:ʳ] n (fig) comoção f, rebuliço ▷ vt mexer; (fig) comover ▷ vi mover-se, remexer-se **stir up** vt excitar; (trouble) provocar

stitch [stɪtʃ] n (Sewing, Knitting, Med) ponto; (pain) pontada ▷ vt costurar; (Med) dar pontos em, suturar

stock [stɔk] n suprimento; (Comm: reserves) estoque m, provisão f; (: selection) sortimento; (Agr) gado; (Culin) caldo; (lineage) estirpe f, linhagem f; (Finance) valores mpl, títulos mpl ▷ adj (reply etc) de sempre, costumeiro ▷ vt ter em estoque, estocar; **in ~** em estoque; **out of ~** esgotado; **to take ~ of** (fig) fazer um balanço de; **~s and shares** valores e títulos mobiliários **stock up** vi: **to ~ up (with)** abastecer-se (de); **stockbroker** n corretor(a) m/f de valores; **stock cube** (Brit) n cubo de caldo; **stock exchange** n Bolsa de Valores

stocking ['stɔkɪŋ] n meia

stock market (Brit) n Bolsa, mercado de valores

stole [stəul] pt of **steal** ▷ n estola

stolen ['stəʊln] pp of **steal**

stomach ['stʌmək] n (Anat) estômago; (belly) barriga, ventre m ▷ vt suportar, tolerar

stone [stəʊn] n pedra; (pebble) pedrinha; (in fruit) caroço; (Med) pedra, cálculo; (Brit: weight) = 6.348kg; 14 pounds ▷ adj de pedra ▷ vt apedrejar; (fruit) tirar o(s) caroço(s) de

stood [stʊd] pt, pp of **stand**

stool [stu:l] n tamborete m, banco

stoop [stu:p] vi (also: **have a ~**) ser corcunda; (also: **~ down**) debruçar-se, curvar-se

stop [stɔp] n parada, interrupção f; (for bus etc) parada (BR), ponto (BR), paragem f (PT); (also: **full ~**) ponto ▷ vt parar, deter; (break off) interromper; (pay, cheque) sustar, suspender; (also: **put a ~ to**) impedir ▷ vi parar, deter-se; (watch, noise) parar; (end) acabar; **to ~ doing sth** deixar de fazer algo **stop dead** vi parar de repente **stop off** vi dar uma parada **stop up** vt tapar; **stopover** n parada rápida; (Aviat) escala

storage ['stɔːrɪdʒ] n armazenagem f

store [stɔːr] n (stock) suprimento; (depot) armazém m; (reserve) estoque m; (Brit: large shop) loja de departamentos; (US: shop) loja ▷ vt armazenar; **stores** npl (provisions) víveres mpl, provisões fpl; **who knows what is in ~ for us?** quem sabe o que nos espera? **store up** vt acumular

storey ['stɔːrɪ], (US) **story** n andar m

storm [stɔːm] n tempestade f; (fig) tumulto ▷ vi (fig) enfurecer-se ▷ vt tomar de assalto, assaltar; **stormy** adj tempestuoso

story ['stɔːrɪ] n história, estória; (lie) mentira; (US) = **storey**

stout [staʊt] adj sólido, forte; (fat) gordo, corpulento; (resolute) decidido, resoluto ▷ n cerveja preta

stove [stəʊv] n (for cooking) fogão m; (for heating) estufa, fogareiro

straight [streɪt] adj reto; (back) esticado; (hair) liso; (honest) honesto; (simple) simples inv ▷ adv reto; (drink) puro; **to put** or **get sth ~** esclarecer algo; **~ away, ~ off** imediatamente; **straighten** vt arrumar; **to straighten things out** arrumar as coisas **straighten out** vt endireitar; (fig) esclarecer; **straightforward** adj (simple) simples inv, direto; (honest) honesto, franco

strain [streɪn] n tensão f; (Tech) esforço; (Med: back strain) distensão f; (: tension) luxação f; (breed) raça, estirpe f ▷ vt forçar, torcer, distender; (stretch) puxar, estirar; (Culin) coar; **strains** npl (Mus) acordes mpl; **strained** adj distendido; (laugh) forçado; (relations) tenso; **strainer** n coador m; (sieve) peneira

strait [streɪt] n estreito; **straits** npl: **to be in dire ~s** estar em apuros

strand [strænd] n (of thread, hair) fio; (of rope) tira; **stranded** adj preso

strange [streɪndʒ] adj (not known) desconhecido; (odd) estranho, esquisito; **strangely** adv estranhamente; **stranger** n desconhecido(-a); (from another area) forasteiro(-a)

strangle ['stræŋgl] vt estrangular; (fig) sufocar

S

strap [stræp] n correia; (of slip, dress) alça

strategic [strə'ti:dʒɪk] adj estratégico

strategy ['strætɪdʒɪ] n estratégia

straw [strɔ:] n palha; (drinking straw) canudo; **that's the last ~!** essa foi a última gota!

strawberry ['strɔ:bərɪ] n morango

stray [streɪ] adj (animal) extraviado; (bullet) perdido; (scattered) espalhado ▷ vi perder-se

streak [stri:k] n listra, traço; (in hair) mecha ▷ vt listrar ▷ vi: **to ~ past** passar como um raio

stream [stri:m] n riacho, córrego; (of people, vehicles) fluxo; (of smoke) rastro; (of questions etc) torrente f ▷ vt (Sch) classificar ▷ vi correr, fluir; **to ~ in/out** entrar/sair em massa

street [stri:t] n rua; **streetcar** (US) n bonde m (BR), eléctrico (PT); **street plan** n mapa m

strength [strɛŋθ] n força; (of girder, knot etc) firmeza, resistência; (fig) poder m; **strengthen** vt fortificar; (fig) fortalecer

strenuous ['strɛnjuəs] adj enérgico; (determined) tenaz

stress [strɛs] n pressão f; (mental strain) tensão f, stress m; (emphasis) ênfase f; (Tech) tensão ▷ vt realçar, dar ênfase a; (syllable) acentuar; **stressed** adj (tense) estressado; (syllable) tônico

stretch [strɛtʃ] n (of sand etc) trecho, extensão f ▷ vi espreguiçar-se; (extend): **to ~ to** or **as far as** estender-se até ▷ vt estirar, esticar; (fig: subj: job, task) exigir o máximo de **stretch out** vi esticar-se ▷ vt (arm etc) esticar; (spread) estirar

stretcher ['strɛtʃəʳ] n maca, padiola

strict [strɪkt] adj (person) severo, rigoroso; (meaning) exato, estrito

stride [straɪd] (pt **strode**, pp **stridden**) n passo largo ▷ vi andar a passos largos

strike [straɪk] (pt, pp **struck**) n greve f; (of oil etc) descoberta; (attack) ataque m ▷ vt bater em; (fig): **the thought** or **it ~s me that ...** me ocorre que ...; (oil etc) descobrir; (deal) fechar, acertar ▷ vi estar em greve; (attack: soldiers, illness) atacar; (: disaster) assolar; (clock) bater; **on ~** em greve; **to ~ a match** acender um fósforo **strike down** vt derrubar **strike up** vt (Mus) começar a tocar; (conversation, friendship) travar; **striker** n grevista m/f; (Sport) atacante m/f; **striking** adj impressionante

string [strɪŋ] (pt, pp **strung**) n (cord) barbante m (BR), cordel m (PT); (of beads) cordão m; (of onions) réstia; (Mus) corda ▷ vt: **to ~ out** esticar; **the strings** npl (Mus) os instrumentos de corda; **to ~ together** (words) unir; (ideas) concatenar; **to get a job by pulling ~s** (fig) usar pistolão

strip [strɪp] n tira; (of land) faixa; (of metal) lâmina, tira ▷ vt despir; (also: **~ down**: machine) desmontar ▷ vi despir-se

stripe [straɪp] n listra; (Mil) galão m; **striped** adj listrado, com listras

strive [straɪv] (pt **strove**, pp **striven**) vi: **to ~ for sth/to do sth** esforçar-se por or batalhar para algo/para fazer algo

strode [strəud] pt of **stride**

stroke [strəuk] n (blow) golpe m;

(*Med*) derrame *m* cerebral; (*of paintbrush*) pincelada; (*Swimming: style*) nado ▷ *vt* acariciar, afagar; **at a ~** de repente, de golpe

stroll [strəul] *n* volta, passeio ▷ *vi* passear, dar uma volta; **stroller** (*US*) *n* carrinho (de criança)

strong [strɔŋ] *adj* forte; (*imagination*) fértil; (*personality*) forte, dominante; (*nerves*) de aço; **they are 50 ~** são em 50 pessoas; **stronghold** *n* fortaleza; (*fig*) baluarte *m*; **strongly** *adv* firmemente; (*push, defend*) vigorosamente; (*believe*) profundamente

strove [strəuv] *pt of* **strive**

struck [strʌk] *pt, pp of* **strike**

structure ['strʌktʃəʳ] *n* estrutura; (*building*) construção *f*

struggle ['strʌgl] *n* luta, contenda ▷ *vi* (*fight*) lutar; (*try hard*) batalhar

strung [strʌŋ] *pt, pp of* **string**

stub [stʌb] *n* (*of ticket etc*) canhoto; (*of cigarette*) toco, ponta; **to ~ one's toe** dar uma topada **stub out** *vt* apagar

stubble ['stʌbl] *n* restolho; (*on chin*) barba por fazer

stubborn ['stʌbən] *adj* teimoso, cabeçudo, obstinado

stuck [stʌk] *pt, pp of* **stick** ▷ *adj* (*jammed*) emperrado

stud [stʌd] *n* (*shirt stud*) botão *m*; (*earring*) tarraxa, rosca; (*of boot*) cravo; (*also*: **~ farm**) fazenda de cavalos; (*also*: **~ horse**) garanhão *m* ▷ *vt* (*fig*): **~ded with** salpicado de

student ['stju:dənt] *n* estudante *m/f* ▷ *adj* estudantil; **student driver** (*US*) *n* aprendiz *m/f*

studio ['stju:dɪəu] *n* estúdio; (*sculptor's*) ateliê *m*

study ['stʌdɪ] *n* estudo; (*room*) sala de leitura *or* estudo ▷ *vt* estudar; (*examine*) examinar, investigar ▷ *vi* estudar; **studies** *npl* (*subjects*) estudos *mpl*, matérias *fpl*

stuff [stʌf] *n* (*substance*) troço; (*things*) troços *mpl*, coisas *fpl* ▷ *vt* (*Culin*) rechear; (*animals*) empalhar; (*inf: push*) enfiar; **~ed toy** brinquedo de pelúcia; **stuffing** *n* recheio; **stuffy** *adj* (*room*) abafado, mal ventilado; (*person*) rabujento, melindroso

stumble ['stʌmbl] *vi* tropeçar; **to ~ across** *or* **on** (*fig*) topar com

stump [stʌmp] *n* (*of tree*) toco; (*of limb*) coto ▷ *vt*: **to be ~ed** ficar perplexo

stun [stʌn] *vt* (*subj: blow*) aturdir; (: *news*) pasmar

stung [stʌŋ] *pt, pp of* **sting**

stunk [stʌŋk] *pp of* **stink**

stunning ['stʌnɪŋ] *adj* (*news*) atordoante; (*appearance*) maravilhoso

stunt [stʌnt] *n* façanha sensacional; (*publicity stunt*) truque *m* publicitário

stupid ['stju:pɪd] *adj* estúpido, idiota

sturdy ['stə:dɪ] *adj* (*person*) robusto, firme; (*thing*) sólido

stutter ['stʌtəʳ] *n* gagueira, gaguez *f* ▷ *vi* gaguejar

style [staɪl] *n* estilo; (*elegance*) elegância; **stylish** *adj* elegante, chique

subconscious [sʌb'kɔnʃəs] *adj* do subconsciente

subject [*n* 'sʌbdʒɪkt, *vt* səb'dʒɛkt] *n* (*of king*) súdito(-a); (*theme*) assunto; (*Sch*) matéria; (*Ling*) sujeito ▷ *vt*: **to ~ sb to sth** submeter alguém a algo; **to be ~ to** estar sujeito a; **subjective** [səb'dʒɛktɪv] adj subjetivo; **subject matter** n assunto; (content) conteúdo

submarine ['sʌbməri:n] n submarino

submission [səb'mɪʃən] n submissão f; (to committee) petição f; (of plan) apresentação f, exposição f

submit [səb'mɪt] vt submeter ▷ vi submeter-se

subordinate [sə'bɔ:dɪnət] adj, n subordinado(-a)

subscribe [səb'skraɪb] vi subscrever; **to ~ to** (opinion) concordar com; (fund) contribuir para; (newspaper) assinar; **subscription** [səb'skrɪpʃən] n assinatura

subsequent ['sʌbsɪkwənt] adj subsequente, posterior; **subsequently** adv posteriormente, depois

subside [səb'saɪd] vi (feeling, wind) acalmar-se; (flood) baixar

subsidiary [səb'sɪdɪərɪ] adj secundário ▷ n (also: **~ company**) subsidiária

subsidize ['sʌbsɪdaɪz] vt subsidiar

subsidy ['sʌbsɪdɪ] n subsídio

substance ['sʌbstəns] n substância

substantial [səb'stænʃl] adj (solid) sólido; (reward, meal) substancial

substitute ['sʌbstɪtju:t] n substituto(-a); (person) suplente m/f ▷ vt: **to ~ A for B** substituir B por A

subtitled ['sʌbtaɪtld] adj (film) legendado

subtle ['sʌtl] adj sutil

subtract [səb'trækt] vt subtrair, deduzir

suburb ['sʌbə:b] n subúrbio; **suburban** [sə'bə:bən] adj

suburbano; (train etc) de subúrbio

subway ['sʌbweɪ] n (Brit) passagem f subterrânea; (US) metrô m (BR), metro(-politano) (PT)

succeed [sək'si:d] vi (person) ser bem sucedido, ter êxito; (plan) sair bem ▷ vt suceder a; **to ~ in doing** conseguir fazer

success [sək'sɛs] n êxito; (hit, person) sucesso; **successful** adj (venture) bem sucedido; (writer) de sucesso, bem sucedido; **to be successful (in doing)** conseguir (fazer); **successfully** adv com sucesso, com êxito

succession [sək'sɛʃən] n sucessão f, série f; (to throne) sucessão

such [sʌtʃ] adj tal, semelhante; (of that kind: singular): **~ a book** um livro parecido, tal livro; (: plural): **~ books** tais livros; (so much): **~ courage** tanta coragem ▷ adv tão; **~ a long trip** uma viagem tão longa; **~ a lot of** tanto; **~ as** tal como; **as ~** como tal; **such-and-such** adj tal e qual

suck [sʌk] vt chupar; (breast) mamar

sudden ['sʌdn] adj (rapid) repentino, súbito; (unexpected) imprevisto; **all of a ~** inesperadamente; **suddenly** adv inesperadamente

sudoku [su'dəuku:] n sudoku m

sue [su:] vt processar

suede [sweɪd] n camurça

suffer ['sʌfər] vt sofrer; (bear) aguentar, suportar ▷ vi sofrer, padecer; **to ~ from** sofrer de, estar com; **suffering** n sofrimento

sufficient [sə'fɪʃənt] adj suficiente, bastante

suffocate ['sʌfəkeɪt] vi sufocar(-se), asfixiar(-se)

sugar ['ʃʊgəʳ] n açúcar m ▷ vt pôr açúcar em, açucarar

suggest [səˈdʒɛst] vt sugerir; (indicate) indicar; **suggestion** n sugestão f; (indication) indicação f

suicide ['suɪsaɪd] n suicídio; (person) suicida m/f; see also **commit**; **suicide attack** n ataque m suicida, atentado suicida; **suicide bomber** n homem-bomba m, mulher-bomba f; **suicide bombing** n ataque m suicida

suit [su:t] n (man's) terno (BR), fato (PT); (woman's) conjunto; (Law) processo; (Cards) naipe m ▷ vt convir a; (clothes) ficar bem a; (adapt): **to ~ sth to** adaptar or acomodar algo a; **they are well ~ed** fazem um bom par; **suitable** adj conveniente; (appropriate) apropriado

suitcase ['su:tkeɪs] n mala

suite [swi:t] n (of rooms) conjunto de salas; (Mus) suite f; **a three-piece ~** um conjunto estofado (sofá e duas poltronas)

sulfur ['sʌlfəʳ] (US) = **sulphur**

sulk [sʌlk] vi ficar emburrado, fazer beicinho or biquinho (inf)

sulphur ['sʌlfəʳ], (US) **sulfur** n enxofre m

sultana [sʌlˈtɑːnə] n passa branca

sum [sʌm] n soma; (calculation) cálculo **sum up** vt, vi resumir

summarize ['sʌməraɪz] vt resumir

summary ['sʌmərɪ] n resumo

summer ['sʌməʳ] n verão m ▷ adj de verão; **in (the) ~** no verão; **summertime** n (season) verão m

summit ['sʌmɪt] n topo, cume m; (also: **~ conference**) (conferência de) cúpula

summon ['sʌmən] vt (person) mandar chamar; (meeting) convocar; (Law: witness) convocar **summon up** vt concentrar

sun [sʌn] n sol m; **sunbathe** vi tomar sol; **sunblock** n bloqueador m solar; **sunburn** n queimadura do sol

Sunday ['sʌndɪ] n domingo

sunflower ['sʌnflauəʳ] n girassol m

sung [sʌŋ] pp of **sing**

sunglasses ['sʌnglɑːsɪz] npl óculos mpl de sol

sunk [sʌŋk] pp of **sink**

sun: **sunlight** n (luz f do) sol m; **sunny** adj cheio de sol; (day) ensolarado, de sol; **sunrise** n nascer m do sol; **sun roof** n (Aut) teto solar; **sunscreen** n protetor m solar; **sunset** n pôr m do sol; **sunshade** n para-sol m; **sunshine** n (luz f do) sol m; **sunstroke** n insolação f; **suntan** n bronzeado; **suntan lotion** n loção f de bronzear

super ['su:pəʳ] (inf) adj bacana (BR), muito giro (PT)

superb [su:ˈpə:b] adj excelente

superintendent [su:pərɪnˈtɛndənt] n superintendente m/f; (Police) chefe m/f de polícia

superior [suˈpɪərɪəʳ] adj superior; (smug) desdenhoso ▷ n superior m

supermarket ['su:pəmɑːkɪt] n supermercado

supernatural [su:pəˈnætʃərəl] adj sobrenatural ▷ n: **the ~** o sobrenatural

superpower ['su:pəpauəʳ] n (Pol) superpotência

superstitious [su:pəˈstɪʃəs] adj supersticioso

supervise ['su:pəvaɪz] vt supervisar, supervisionar; **supervision** [su:pəˈvɪʒən] n supervisão f; **supervisor** n

s

supervisor(a) *m/f*; (*academic*) orientador(a) *m/f*

supper ['sʌpə^r] *n* jantar *m*; (*late evening*) ceia

supple ['sʌpl] *adj* flexível

supplement [*n* 'sʌplɪmənt, *vt* sʌplɪ'mɛnt] *n* suplemento ▷ *vt* suprir, completar

supplier [sə'plaɪə^r] *n* abastecedor(a) *m/f*, fornecedor(a) *m/f*

supply [sə'plaɪ] *vt* (*provide*): **to ~ sth (to sb)** fornecer algo (a alguém); (*equip*): **to ~ (with)** suprir (de) ▷ *n* fornecimento, provisão *f*; (*stock*) estoque *m*; (*supplying*) abastecimento

support [sə'pɔːt] *n* (*moral, financial etc*) apoio; (*Tech*) suporte *m* ▷ *vt* apoiar; (*financially*) manter; (*Tech*: *hold up*) sustentar; (*theory etc*) defender; **supporter** *n* (*Pol etc*) partidário(-a); (*Sport*) torcedor(a) *m/f*

suppose [sə'pəuz] *vt* supor; (*imagine*) imaginar; (*duty*): **to be ~d to do sth** dever fazer algo; **supposedly** [sə'pəuzɪdlɪ] *adv* supostamente, pretensamente; **supposing** *conj* caso, supondo-se que

suppress [sə'prɛs] *vt* (*information*) suprimir; (*feelings, revolt*) reprimir; (*yawn*) conter

supreme [su'priːm] *adj* supremo

surcharge ['səːtʃɑːdʒ] *n* sobretaxa

sure [ʃuə^r] *adj* seguro; (*definite*) certo; (*aim*) certeiro; **to make ~ of sth/that** assegurar-se de algo/que; **~!** claro que sim!; **~ enough** efetivamente; **surely** *adv* (*certainly*: US: also: **sure**) certamente

surf [səːf] *n* (*waves*) ondas *fpl*, arrebentação *f*

surface ['səːfɪs] *n* superfície *f* ▷ *vt* (*road*) revestir ▷ *vi* vir à superfície or à tona; (*fig: news, feeling*) vir à tona

surfboard ['səːfbɔːd] *n* prancha de surfe

surfer ['səːfə^r] *n* surfista *m/f*; (*on the Internet*) internauta *m/f*

surfing ['səːfɪŋ] *n* surfe *m*

surge [səːdʒ] *n* onda ▷ *vi* (*sea*) encapelar-se; (*people, vehicles*) precipitar-se; (*feeling*) aumentar repentinamente

surgeon ['səːdʒən] *n* cirurgião(-giã) *m/f*

surgery ['səːdʒərɪ] *n* cirurgia, (*Brit*: *room*) consultório; (*also*: **~ hours**) horas *fpl* de consulta

surname ['səːneɪm] *n* sobrenome *m* (*BR*), apelido (*PT*)

surplus ['səːpləs] *n* excedente *m*; (*Comm*) superávit *m* ▷ *adj* excedente, de sobra

surprise [sə'praɪz] *n* surpresa ▷ *vt* surpreender; **surprising** *adj* surpreendente

surrender [sə'rɛndə^r] *n* rendição *f*, entrega ▷ *vi* render-se, entregar-se

surround [sə'raund] *vt* circundar, rodear; (*Mil etc*) cercar; **surrounding** *adj* circundante, adjacente; **surroundings** *npl* arredores *mpl*, cercanias *fpl*

surveillance [səː'veɪləns] *n* vigilância

survey [*n* 'səːveɪ, *vt* səː'veɪ] *n* inspeção *f*; (*of habits etc*) pesquisa; (*of house*) inspeção *f*; (*of land*) levantamento ▷ *vt* observar, contemplar; (*land*) fazer um levantamento de; **surveyor** *n* (*of land*) agrimensor(a) *m/f*; (*of building*) inspetor(a) *m/f*

survival [sə'vaɪvl] *n* sobrevivência; (*relic*) remanescente *m*

survive [sə'vaɪv] vi sobreviver; (custom etc) perdurar ▷ vt sobreviver a; **survivor** n sobrevivente m/f

suspect [adj, n 'sʌspɛkt, vt səs'pɛkt] adj, n suspeito(-a) ▷ vt suspeitar, desconfiar

suspend [səs'pɛnd] vt suspender; **suspenders** npl (Brit) ligas fpl; (US) suspensórios mpl

suspense [səs'pɛns] n incerteza, ansiedade f; (in film etc) suspense m; **to keep sb in ~** manter alguém em suspense or na expectativa

suspension [səs'pɛnʃən] n suspensão f; (of driving licence) cassação f

suspicion [səs'pɪʃən] n suspeita; **suspicious** adj (suspecting) suspeitoso; (causing suspicion) suspeito

sustain [səs'teɪn] vt sustentar; (suffer) sofrer; **sustainable** adj sustentável

SUV n abbr (= sports utility vehicle) SUV m

swallow ['swɔləʊ] n (bird) andorinha ▷ vt engolir, tragar; (fig: story) engolir; (pride) pôr de lado; (one's words) retirar **swallow up** vt (savings etc) consumir

swam [swæm] pt of **swim**

swamp [swɔmp] n pântano, brejo ▷ vt atolar, inundar; (fig) assoberbar

swan [swɔn] n cisne m

swap [swɔp] n troca, permuta ▷ vt: **to ~ (for)** trocar (por); (replace (with)) substituir (por)

swarm [swɔːm] n (of bees) enxame m; (of people) multidão f ▷ vi enxamear; aglomerar-se; (place): **to be ~ing with** estar apinhado de

sway [sweɪ] vi balançar-se, oscilar

▷ vt (influence) influenciar

swear [swɛəʳ] (pt **swore**, pp **sworn**) vi (curse) xingar ▷ vt (promise) jurar; **swearword** n palavrão m

sweat [swɛt] n suor m ▷ vi suar

sweater n suéter m or f (BR), camisola (PT)

sweaty adj suado

Swede [swiːd] n sueco(-a)

swede [swiːd] n tipo de nabo

Sweden ['swiːdən] n Suécia; **Swedish** adj sueco ▷ n (Ling) sueco

sweep [swiːp] (pt, pp **swept**) n (act) varredura; (also: **chimney ~**) limpador m de chaminés ▷ vt varrer; (with arm) empurrar; (subj: current) arrastar; (: fashion, craze) espalhar-se por ▷ vi varrer **sweep away** vt varrer **sweep past** vi passar rapidamente **sweep up** vi varrer

sweet [swiːt] n (candy) bala (BR), rebuçado (PT); (Brit: pudding) sobremesa ▷ adj doce; (fig: air) fresco; (: water, smell) doce; (: sound) suave; (: kind) meigo; (baby, kitten) bonitinho; **sweetheart** n namorado(-a)

swell [swɛl] (pt **swelled**, pp **swollen** or **swelled**) n (of sea) vaga, onda ▷ adj (US: inf: excellent) bacana ▷ vi (increase) aumentar; (get stronger) intensificar-se; (also: **~ up**) inchar(-se); **swelling** n (Med) inchação f

swept [swɛpt] pt, pp of **sweep**

swerve [swəːv] vi desviar-se

swift [swɪft] n (bird) andorinhão m ▷ adj rápido

swim [swɪm] (pt **swam**, pp **swum**) n: **to go for a ~** ir nadar ▷ vi nadar; (head, room) rodar ▷ vt atravessar a nado; (distance) percorrer (a nado);

S

swimmer n nadador(a) m/f;
swimming n natação f;
swimming costume (Brit) n (woman's) maiô m (BR), fato de banho (PT); (man's) calção m de banho (BR), calções mpl de banho (PT); **swimming pool** n piscina; **swimming trunks** npl sunga (BR), calções mpl de banho (PT); **swimsuit** n maiô m (BR), fato de banho (PT)

swing [swiŋ] (pt, pp **swung**) n (in playground) balanço; (movement) balanceio, oscilação f; (in opinion) mudança, virada; (rhythm) ritmo ▷ vt balançar; (also: **~ round**) girar, rodar ▷ vi oscilar; (on swing) balançar; (also: **~ round**) voltar-se bruscamente; **to be in full ~** estar a todo vapor

swirl [swəːl] vi redemoinhar
Swiss [swis] adj, n inv suíço(-a)
switch [switʃ] n (for light, radio etc) interruptor m; (change) mudança ▷ vt (change) trocar **switch off** vt apagar; (engine) desligar **switch on** vt acender; ligar; **switchboard** n (Tel) mesa telefônica
Switzerland ['switsələnd] n Suíça
swollen ['swəulən] pp of **swell**
swoop [swuːp] n (by police etc) batida ▷ vi (also: **~ down**) precipitar-se, cair
swop [swɔp] n, vt = **swap**
sword [sɔːd] n espada
swore [swɔːr] pt of **swear**
sworn [swɔːn] pp of **swear** ▷ adj (statement) sob juramento; (enemy) declarado
swum [swʌm] pp of **swim**
swung [swʌŋ] pt, pp of **swing**
syllable ['siləbl] n sílaba
syllabus ['siləbəs] n programa m de estudos

symbol ['simbl] n símbolo
sympathetic [simpə'θεtik] adj (understanding) compreensivo; (likeable) agradável; (supportive): **~ to(wards)** solidário com
sympathize ['simpəθaiz] vi: **to ~ with** (person) compadecer-se de; (sb's feelings) compreender; (cause) simpatizar com
sympathy ['simpəθi] n compaixão f; **sympathies** npl (tendencies) simpatia; **in ~ with** em acordo com; (strike) em solidariedade com; **with our deepest ~** com nossos mais profundos pêsames
symphony ['simfəni] n sinfonia
symptom ['simptəm] n sintoma m; (sign) indício
syndicate ['sindikit] n sindicato; (of newspapers) cadeia
synthetic [sin'θεtik] adj sintético
Syria ['siriə] n Síria
syringe [si'rindʒ] n seringa
syrup ['sirəp] n xarope m; (also: **golden ~**) melaço
system ['sistəm] n sistema m; (method) método; (Anat) organismo; **systematic** [sistə'mætik] adj sistemático

t

muitas fotografias e adotam um estilo bastante conciso. O público-alvo desses jornais é composto por leitores que se interessam pelos fatos do dia que contenham um certo toque de escândalo; veja **quality (news) papers**.

T, t [tiː] n T, t m

tab [tæb] n lingueta, aba; (*label*) etiqueta; **to keep ~s on** (*fig*) vigiar

table ['teɪbl] n mesa ▷ vt (*motion etc*) apresentar; **to lay** or **set the ~** pôr a mesa; **~ of contents** índice m, sumário; **tablecloth** n toalha de mesa; **tablespoon** n colher f de sopa; (*also*: **tablespoonful**: *as measurement*) colherada

tablet ['tæblɪt] n (*Med*) comprimido; (*of stone*) lápide f

table tennis n pingue-pongue m, tênis m de mesa

tabloid ['tæblɔɪd] n tabloide m; **tabloid press** n ver nota

TABLOID PRESS

O termo **tabloid press** refere-se aos jornais populares de formato meio jornal que apresentam

tack [tæk] n (*nail*) tachinha, percevejo ▷ vt prender com tachinha; (*stitch*) alinhavar ▷ vi virar de bordo

tackle ['tækl] n (*gear*) equipamento; (*also*: **fishing ~**) apetrechos mpl; (*for lifting*) guincho; (*Football*) ato de tirar a bola de adversário ▷ vt (*difficulty*) atacar; (*challenge: person*) desafiar; (*grapple with*) atracar-se com; (*Football*) tirar a bola de

tacky ['tækɪ] adj pegajoso, grudento; (*inf: tasteless*) cafona

tact [tækt] n tato, diplomacia; **tactful** adj diplomático

tactics ['tæktɪks] n, npl tática

tactless ['tæktlɪs] adj sem diplomacia

tag [tæg] n (*label*) etiqueta **tag along** vi seguir

tail [teɪl] n rabo; (*of bird, comet, plane*) cauda; (*of shirt, coat*) aba ▷ vt (*follow*) seguir bem de perto; *see also* **head tail away** vi diminuir gradualmente **tail off** vi diminuir gradualmente

tailor ['teɪləʳ] n alfaiate m

take [teɪk] (*pt* **took**, *pp* **taken**) vt tomar; (*photo, holiday*) tirar; (*grab*) pegar (em); (*prize*) ganhar; (*effort, courage*) requerer, exigir; (*tolerate*) aguentar; (*accompany, bring, carry: person*) acompanhar, trazer; (: *thing*) trazer, carregar; (*exam*)

t

fazer; (*passengers etc*): **it ~s 50 people** cabem 50 pessoas; **to ~ sth from** (*drawer etc*) tirar algo de; (*person*) pegar algo de; **I ~ it that ...** suponho que ... **take after** *vt fus* parecer-se com **take apart** *vt* desmontar **take away** *vt* (*extract*) tirar; (*carry off*) levar; (*subtract*) subtrair **take back** *vt* (*return*) devolver; (*one's words*) retirar **take down** *vt* (*building*) demolir; (*dismantle*) desmontar; (*letter etc*) tomar por escrito **take in** *vt* (*deceive*) enganar; (*understand*) compreender; (*include*) abranger; (*lodger*) receber **take off** *vi* (*Aviat*) decolar; (*go away*) ir-se ▷ *vt* (*remove*) tirar **take on** *vt* (*work*) empreender; (*employee*) empregar; (*opponent*) desafiar **take out** *vt* tirar; (*extract*) extrair; (*invite*) acompanhar **take over** *vt* (*business*) assumir; (*country*) tomar posse de ▷ *vi*: **to ~ over from sb** suceder a alguém **take to** *vt fus* (*person*) simpatizar com; (*activity*) afeiçoar-se a; **to ~ to doing sth** criar o hábito de fazer algo **take up** *vt* (*dress*) encurtar; (*time, space*) ocupar; (*hobby etc*) dedicar-se a; (*offer, challenge*) aceitar; **to ~ sb up on a suggestion/offer** aceitar a oferta/sugestão de alguém sobre algo; **takeaway** (*Brit*) *adj* (*food*) para levar; **takeoff** *n* (*Aviat*) decolagem *f*; **takeover** *n* (*Comm*) aquisição *f* de controle; **takings** *npl* (*Comm*) receita, renda

talc [tælk] *n* (*also*: **talcum powder**) talco

tale [teɪl] *n* (*story*) conto; (*account*) narrativa; **to tell ~s** (*fig*: *lie*) dizer mentiras

talent ['tælənt] *n* talento;

talented *adj* talentoso

talk [tɔːk] *n* conversa, fala; (*gossip*) mexerico, fofocas *fpl*; (*conversation*) conversa, conversação *f* ▷ *vi* falar; **talks** *npl* (*Pol etc*) negociações *fpl*; **to ~ about** falar sobre; **to ~ sb into doing sth** convencer alguém a fazer algo; **to ~ sb out of doing sth** dissuadir alguém de fazer algo; **to ~ shop** falar sobre negócios/ questões profissionais **talk over** *vt* discutir

tall [tɔːl] *adj* alto; **to be 6 feet ~** medir 6 pés, ter 6 pés de altura

tame [teɪm] *adj* domesticado; (*fig*: *story, style*) sem graça, insípido

tamper ['tæmpəʳ] *vi*: **to ~ with** mexer em

tampon ['tæmpən] *n* tampão *m*

tan [tæn] *n* (*also*: **sun~**) bronzeado ▷ *vi* bronzear-se ▷ *adj* (*colour*) bronzeado, marrom claro

tangerine [tændʒə'riːn] *n* tangerina, mexerica

tangle ['tæŋgl] *n* emaranhado; **to get in(to) a ~** meter-se num rolo

tank [tæŋk] *n* depósito, tanque *m*; (*for fish*) aquário; (*Mil*) tanque *m*

tanker ['tæŋkəʳ] *n* (*ship*) navio-tanque *m*; (*truck*) caminhão-tanque *m*

tantrum ['tæntrəm] *n* chilique *m*, acesso (de raiva)

tap [tæp] *n* (*on sink etc*) torneira; (*gentle blow*) palmadinha; (*gas tap*) chave *f* ▷ *vt* dar palmadinha em, bater de leve; (*resources*) utilizar, explorar; (*telephone*) grampear; **on ~** disponível

tape [teɪp] *n* fita; (*also*: **magnetic ~**) fita magnética; (*sticky tape*) fita adesiva ▷ *vt* (*record*) gravar (em fita); (*stick with tape*) colar; **tape measure** *n* fita métrica, trena

tar [tɑ:] *n* alcatrão *m*

target ['tɑ:gɪt] *n* alvo

tariff ['tærɪf] *n* tarifa

tarmac ['tɑ:mæk] *n* (*Brit: on road*) macadame *m*; (*Aviat*) pista

tarpaulin [tɑ:'pɔ:lɪn] *n* lona alcatroada

tart [tɑ:t] *n* (*Culin*) torta; (*Brit: inf: pej: woman*) piranha ▷ *adj* (*flavour*) ácido, azedo **tart up** (*inf*) *vt* arrumar, dar um jeito em; **to ~ o.s. up** arrumar-se; (*pej*) empetecar-se

tartan ['tɑ:tn] *n* pano escocês axadrezado, tartan ▷ *adj* axadrezado

tartar ['tɑ:təʳ] *n* (*on teeth*) tártaro

taste [teɪst] *n* gosto *m*; (*also:* **after~**) gosto residual; (*sample, fig*) amostra, ideia ▷ *vt* provar; (*test*) experimentar ▷ *vi*: **to ~ of** *or* **like** ter gosto *or* sabor de; **you can ~ the garlic (in it)** sente-se o gosto de alho; **in good/bad ~** de bom/ mau gosto; **tasteful** *adj* de bom gosto; **tasteless** *adj* insípido, insosso; (*remark*) de mau gosto; **tasty** *adj* saboroso, delicioso

tatters ['tætəz] *npl*: **in ~** (*clothes*) em farrapos; (*papers etc*) em pedaços

tattoo [tə'tu:] *n* tatuagem *f*; (*spectacle*) espetáculo militar ▷ *vt* tatuar

taught [tɔ:t] *pt, pp of* **teach**

taunt [tɔ:nt] *n* zombaria, escárnio ▷ *vt* zombar de, mofar de

Taurus ['tɔ:rəs] *n* Touro

taut [tɔ:t] *adj* esticado

tax [tæks] *n* imposto *m* ▷ *vt* tributar; (*fig: test*) sobrecarregar; (*: patience*) esgotar; **tax-free** *adj* isento de impostos

taxi ['tæksɪ] *n* táxi *m* ▷ *vi* (*Aviat*) taxiar; **taxi driver** *n* motorista *m/f* de táxi; **taxi rank** (*Brit*) *n* ponto de táxi; **taxi stand** *n* ponto de táxi; **tax payer** *n* contribuinte *m/f*; **tax return** *n* declaração *f* de rendimentos

TB *abbr of* **tuberculosis**

tea [ti:] *n* chá *m*; (*Brit: meal*) refeição *f* à noite; **high ~** (*Brit*) ajantarado; **tea bag** *n* saquinho (*BR*) or carteira (*PT*) de chá; **tea break** (*Brit*) *n* pausa (para o chá)

teach [ti:tʃ] (*pt, pp* **taught**) *vt*: **to ~ sb sth, ~ sth to sb** ensinar algo a alguém; (*in school*) lecionar ▷ *vi* ensinar; (*be a teacher*) lecionar; **teacher** *n* professor(a) *m/f*; **teaching** *n* ensino; (*as profession*) magistério

teacup ['ti:kʌp] *n* xícara (*BR*) or chávena (*PT*) de chá

team [ti:m] *n* (*Sport*) time *m* (*BR*), equipa (*PT*); (*group*) equipe *f* (*BR*), equipa (*PT*); (*of animals*) parelha

teapot ['ti:pɔt] *n* bule *m* de chá

tear¹ [tɪəʳ] *n* lágrima; **in ~s** chorando, em lágrimas

tear² [tɛəʳ] (*pt* **tore**, *pp* **torn**) *n* rasgão *m* ▷ *vt* rasgar ▷ *vi* rasgar-se; **tear along** *vi* (*rush*) precipitar-se; **tear up** *vt* rasgar

tearful ['tɪəful] *adj* choroso

tear gas *n* gás *m* lacrimogênio

tearoom ['ti:ru:m] *n* salão *m* de chá

tease [ti:z] *vt* implicar com

teaspoon ['ti:spu:n] *n* colher *f* de chá; (*also:* **~ful**: *as measurement*) (conteúdo de) colher de chá

teatime ['ti:taɪm] *n* hora do chá

tea towel (*Brit*) *n* pano de prato

technical ['tɛknɪkl] *adj* técnico

technician [tɛk'nɪʃn] *n* técnico(-a)

technique [tɛk'ni:k] *n* técnica

technology [tɛk'nɔlədʒɪ] *n* tecnologia

teddy ['tɛdɪ], **teddy bear** *n* ursinho

t

de pelúcia

tedious ['tiːdɪəs] *adj* maçante, chato

teenage ['tiːneɪdʒ] *adj* (*fashions etc*) de *or* para adolescentes; **teenager** *n* adolescente *m/f*, jovem *m/f*

teens [tiːnz] *npl*: **to be in one's ~** estar entre os 13 e 19 anos, estar na adolescência

teeth [tiːθ] *npl of* **tooth**

teetotal ['tiːˈtəutl] *adj* abstêmio

teleconferencing ['tɛlɪkɔnfərənsɪŋ] *n* teleconferência *f*

telegram ['tɛlɪgræm] *n* telegrama *m*

telephone ['tɛlɪfəun] *n* telefone *m* ▷ *vt* (*person*) telefonar para; (*message*) telefonar; **to be on the ~** (*Brit*), **to have a ~** (*subscriber*) ter telefone; **to be on the ~** (*be speaking*) estar falando no telefone; **telephone booth**, (*Brit*) **telephone box** *n* cabine *f* telefônica; **telephone call** *n* telefonema *m*; **telephone directory** *n* lista telefônica, catálogo (*BR*); **telephone number** *n* (número de) telefone *m*

telesales ['tɛlɪseɪlz] *npl* televendas *fpl*

telescope ['tɛlɪskəup] *n* telescópio

television ['tɛlɪvɪʒən] *n* televisão *f*; **on ~** na televisão

tell [tɛl] (*pt, pp* **told**) *vt* dizer; (*relate*: *story*) contar; (*distinguish*): **to ~ sth from** distinguir algo de ▷ *vi* (*have effect*) ter efeito; (*talk*): **to ~ (of)** falar (de *or* em); **to ~ sb to do sth** dizer para alguém fazer algo **tell off** *vt* repreender

telly ['tɛlɪ] (*Brit: inf*) *n abbr* = **television**

temp [tɛmp] (*Brit: inf*) *n* temporário(-a) ▷ *vi* trabalhar como temporário(-a)

temper ['tɛmpəʳ] *n* (*nature*) temperamento; (*mood*) humor *m*; (*fit of anger*) cólera ▷ *vt* (*moderate*) moderar; **to be in a ~** estar de mau humor; **to lose one's ~** perder a paciência *or* a calma, ficar zangado

temperament ['tɛmprəmənt] *n* temperamento; **temperamental** [tɛmprə'mɛntl] *adj* temperamental

temperature ['tɛmprətʃəʳ] *n* temperatura; **to have** *or* **run a ~** ter febre

temple ['tɛmpl] *n* (*building*) templo; (*Anat*) têmpora

temporary ['tɛmpərərɪ] *adj* temporário; (*passing*) transitório

tempt [tɛmpt] *vt* tentar; **tempting** ['tɛmptɪŋ] *adj* tentador(a)

ten [tɛn] *num* dez ▷ *n see also* **five**

tenant ['tɛnənt] *n* inquilino(-a), locatário(-a)

tend [tɛnd] *vt* (*sick etc*) cuidar de ▷ *vi*: **to ~ to do sth** tender a fazer algo

tendency ['tɛndənsɪ] *n* tendência

tender ['tɛndəʳ] *adj* terno; (*age*) tenro; (*sore*) sensível, dolorido; (*meat*) macio ▷ *n* (*Comm: offer*) oferta, proposta; **legal ~** moeda corrente *or* legal ▷ *vt* oferecer; **to ~ one's resignation** pedir demissão

tennis ['tɛnɪs] *n* tênis *m*; **tennis ball** *n* bola de tênis; **tennis court** *n* quadra de tênis; **tennis player** *n* jogador(a) *m/f* de tênis; **tennis racket** *n* raquete *f* de tênis

tenor ['tɛnəʳ] *n* (*Mus*) tenor *m*

tense [tɛns] *adj* tenso; (*muscle*) rígido, teso ▷ *n* (*Ling*) tempo

tension ['tɛnʃən] *n* tensão *f*

tent [tɛnt] *n* tenda, barraca

tentative ['tɛntətɪv] *adj* provisório,

tentativo; (*person*) hesitante, indeciso

tenth [tɛnθ] *num* décimo

tent peg *n* estaca

tent pole *n* pau *m*

tepid ['tɛpɪd] *adj* tépido, morno

term [təːm] *n* (*word, expression*) termo, expressão *f*; (*period*) período; (*Sch*) trimestre *m* ▷ *vt* denominar; **terms** *npl* (*conditions*) condições *fpl*; (*Comm*) cláusulas *fpl*, termos *mpl*; **in the short/long ~** a curto/longo prazo; **to be on good ~s with sb** dar-se bem com alguém; **to come to ~s with** aceitar

terminal ['təːmɪnl] *adj* incurável ▷ *n* (*Elec*) borne *m*; (*Brit: also*: **air ~**) terminal *m*; (*for oil, ore etc, also*: *Comput*) terminal *m*; (*Brit: also*: **coach ~**) estação *f* rodoviária

terminate ['təːmɪneɪt] *vt* terminar; **to ~ a pregnancy** fazer um aborto

terminus ['təːmɪnəs] (*pl* **termini**) *n* terminal *m*

terrace ['tɛrəs] *n* terraço; (*Brit: row of houses*) lance *m* de casas; **the terraces** *npl* (*Brit: Sport*) a arquibancada (BR), a geral (PT); **terraced** *adj* (*house*) ladeado por outras casas; (*garden*) em dois níveis

terrain [tɛˈreɪn] *n* terreno

terrible ['tɛrɪbl] *adj* terrível, horroroso; (*conditions*) precário; (*inf: awful*) terrível; **terribly** *adv* terrivelmente; (*very badly*) pessimamente

terrific [təˈrɪfɪk] *adj* terrível, magnífico; (*wonderful*) maravilhoso, sensacional

terrify ['tɛrɪfaɪ] *vt* apavorar

territory ['tɛrɪtərɪ] *n* território

terror ['tɛrəʳ] *n* terror *m*; **terrorist** *n* terrorista *m/f*

test [tɛst] *n* (*trial, check*) prova, ensaio; (*of courage etc, Chem*) prova; (*Med*) exame *m*; (*exam*) teste *m*, prova; (*also*: **driving ~**) exame de motorista ▷ *vt* testar, pôr à prova

testicle ['tɛstɪkl] *n* testículo

testify ['tɛstɪfaɪ] *vi* (*Law*) depor, testemunhar; **to ~ to sth** atestar algo, testemunhar algo

testimony ['tɛstɪmənɪ] *n* (*Law*) testemunho, depoimento; **to be (a) ~ to** ser uma prova de

test match *n* (*Cricket, Rugby*) jogo internacional

test tube *n* proveta, tubo de ensaio

tetanus ['tɛtənəs] *n* tétano

text [tɛkst] *n* texto; (*also*: **~ message**) mensagem *f* de texto, torpedo (*inf*) ▷ *vt* mandar uma mensagem de texto *ou* (*inf*) um torpedo para; **textbook** *n* livro didático; (*Sch*) livro escolar; **text message** *n* mensagem *f* de texto, torpedo (*inf*)

texture ['tɛkstʃəʳ] *n* textura

Thailand ['taɪlænd] *n* Tailândia

Thames [tɛmz] *n*: **the ~** o Tâmisa (BR), o Tamisa (PT)

than [ðæn, ðən] *conj* (*in comparisons*) do que; **more ~ 10** mais de 10; **I have more/less ~ you** tenho mais/menos do que você; **she has more apples ~ pears** ela tem mais maçãs do que peras; **she is older ~ you think** ela é mais velha do que você pensa

thank [θæŋk] *vt* agradecer; **~ you (very much)** muito obrigado(-a); **thanks** *npl* agradecimentos *mpl* ▷ *excl* obrigado(-a)!

Thanksgiving ['θæŋksgɪvɪŋ], **Thanksgiving Day** *n* Dia *m* de Ação de Graças; *ver nota*

2222

○ **THANKSGIVING DAY**
○
○ O feriado de Ação de graças
○ **Thanksgiving Day** nos Estados
○ Unidos, quarta quinta-feira do
○ mês de novembro, é o dia em que
○ se comemora a boa colheita feita
○ pelos peregrinos originários da
○ Grã-Bretanha em 1621;
○ tradicionalmente, é um dia em
○ que se agradece a Deus e se
○ organiza um grande banquete.
○ Uma festa semelhante é
○ celebrada no Canadá na segunda
○ segunda-feira de outubro.

 KEYWORD

that [ðæt, ðət] (pl **those**) adj (demonstrative) esse/essa; (more remote) aquele/aquela; **that man/woman/book** aquele homem/aquela mulher/aquele livro; **that one** esse/essa
▷ pron **1** (demonstrative) esse/essa, aquele/aquela; (neuter) isso, aquilo; **who's/what's that?** quem é?/o que é isso?; **is that you?** é você?; **I prefer this to that** eu prefiro isto a aquilo; **that's what he said** foi isso o que ele disse; **that is (to say)** isto é, quer dizer
2 (relative: direct: thing, person) que; (: person) quem; (relative: indirect: thing, person) o/a qual sg, os/as quais pl; (: person) quem; **the book (that) I read** o livro que eu li; **the box (that) I put it in** a caixa na qual eu o coloquei; **the man (that) I spoke to** o homem com quem or o qual falei
3 (relative: of time): **on the day that he came** no dia em que ele veio
▷ conj que; **she suggested that I phone you** ela sugeriu que eu telefonasse para você ▷ adv (demonstrative): **I can't work that much** não posso trabalhar tanto; **I didn't realize it was that bad** não pensei que fôsse tão ruim; **that high** dessa altura, até essa altura

thatched [θætʃt] adj (roof) de sapê; **~ cottage** chalé m com telhado de sapê or de colmo
thaw [θɔ:] n degelo ▷ vi (ice) derreter-se; (food) descongelar-se ▷ vt (food) descongelar

 KEYWORD

the [ði:, ðə] def art **1** (gen: singular) o/a; (: plural) os/as; **the books/children are in the library** os livros/as crianças estão na biblioteca; **she put it on the table** ela colocou-o na mesa; **he took it from the drawer** ele tirou isto da gaveta; **to play the piano/violin** tocar piano/violino; **I'm going to the cinema** vou ao cinema
2 (+ adj to form n): **the rich and the poor** os ricos e os pobres; **to attempt the impossible** tentar o impossível
3 (in titles): **Richard the Second** Ricardo II; **Peter the Great** Pedro o Grande
4 (in comparisons: + adv): **the more he works the more he earns** quanto mais ele trabalha, mais ele ganha

theatre ['θɪətər], (US) **theater** n teatro; (Med: also: **operating ~**) sala de operação
theft [θɛft] n roubo

their [ðɛəʳ] *adj* seu/sua, deles/
delas; **theirs** *pron* (o) seu/(a) sua

them [ðɛm, ðəm] *pron* (*direct*) os/
as; (*indirect*) lhes; (*stressed, after
prep*) a eles/a elas

theme [θiːm] *n* tema *m*; **theme
park** *n* parque de diversões em torno
de um único tema

themselves [ðəm'sɛlvz] *pron*
(*subject*) eles mesmos/elas
mesmas, se; (*after prep*) si
(mesmos/as)

then [ðɛn] *adv* (*at that time*) então;
(*next*) em seguida; (*later*) logo,
depois; (*and also*) além disso ▷ *conj*
(*therefore*) então, nesse caso,
portanto ▷ *adj*: **the ~ president** o
então presidente; **by ~** (*past*) até
então; (*future*) até lá; **from ~ on** a
partir de então

theology [θi'ɔlədʒɪ] *n* teologia

theory ['θɪərɪ] *n* teoria; **in ~** em
teoria, teoricamente

therapy ['θɛrəpɪ] *n* terapia

 KEYWORD

there [ðɛəʳ] *adv* **1**: **there is, there
are** há, tem; **there are 3 of them**
são três; **there is no-one here/no
bread left** não tem ninguém aqui/
não tem mais pão; **there has been
an accident** houve um acidente
2 (*referring to place*) aí, ali, lá; **put it
in/on/up/down there** põe isto lá
dentro/cima/em cima/embaixo; **I
want that book there** quero aquele
livro lá; **there he is!** lá está ele!
3: **there, there!** (*esp to child*) calma!

thereabouts ['ðɛərəbauts] *adv* por
aí; (*amount*) aproximadamente

thereafter [ðɛər'ɑːftəʳ] *adv* depois
disso

thereby ['ðɛəbaɪ] *adv* assim, deste
modo

therefore ['ðɛəfɔː] *adv* portanto

there's [ðɛəz] = **there is**; **there has**

thermal ['θəːml] *adj* térmico

thermometer [θə'mɔmɪtəʳ] *n*
termômetro

thermostat ['θəːməustæt] *n*
termostato

these [ðiːz] *pl adj, pron* estes/estas

thesis ['θiːsɪs] (*pl* **theses**) *n* tese *f*

they [ðeɪ] *pl pron* eles/elas; **~ say
that ...** (*it is said that*) diz-se que ...,
dizem que ...; **they'd** = **they had**;
they would; **they'll** = **they shall**;
they will; **they've** = **they have**

thick [θɪk] *adj* espesso; (*mud, fog,
forest*) denso; (*sauce*) grosso;
(*stupid*) burro ▷ *n*: **in the ~ of the
battle** em plena batalha; **it's 20
cm ~** tem 20 cm de espessura;
thicken *vi* (*fog*) adensar-se; (*plot
etc*) complicar-se ▷ *vt* engrossar;
thickness *n* espessura, grossura

thief [θiːf] (*pl* **thieves**) *n* ladrão/
ladra *m/f*

thigh [θaɪ] *n* coxa

thin [θɪn] *adj* magro; (*slice, line,
book*) fino; (*light*) leve; (*hair*) ralo;
(*crowd*) pequeno; (*soup, sauce*)
aguado ▷ *vt* (*also:* **~ down**) diluir

thing [θɪŋ] *n* coisa; (*object*) negócio;
(*matter*) assunto, negócio; (*mania*)
mania; **things** *npl* (*belongings*)
pertences *mpl*; **to have a ~ about
sb/sth** ser vidrado em alguém/
algo; **the best ~ would be to ...** o
melhor seria ...; **how are ~s?** como
vai?, tudo bem?; **she's got a ~
about ...** ela detesta ...; **poor ~!**
coitadinho(-a)!

think [θɪŋk] (*pt, pp* **thought**) *vi*
pensar; (*believe*) achar ▷ *vt* pensar,
achar; (*imagine*) imaginar; **what**

t

did you ~ of them? o que você achou deles?; **to ~ about sth/sb** pensar em algo/alguém; **I'll ~ about it** vou pensar sobre isso; **to ~ of doing sth** pensar em fazer algo; **I ~ so/not** acho que sim/não; **to ~ well of sb** fazer bom juízo de alguém **think over** vt refletir sobre, meditar sobre **think up** vt inventar, bolar

third [θəːd] adj terceiro ▷ n terceiro(-a); (fraction) terço; (Aut) terceira; (Sch: degree) terceira categoria; **thirdly** adv em terceiro lugar; **third party insurance** n seguro contra terceiros; **Third World** n: **the Third World** o Terceiro Mundo

thirst [θəːst] n sede f; **thirsty** adj (person) sedento, com sede; (work) que dá sede; **to be thirsty** estar com sede

thirteen ['θəː'tiːn] num treze

thirty ['θəːtɪ] num trinta

 KEYWORD

this [ðɪs] (pl **these**) adj (demonstrative) este/esta; **this man/woman/book** este homem/esta mulher/este livro; **these people/children/records** estas pessoas/crianças/estes discos; **this one** este aqui ▷ pron (demonstrative) este/esta; (neuter) isto; **who/what is this?** quem é esse?/o que é isso?; **this is where I live** é aqui que eu moro; **this is Mr Brown** este é o Sr Brown; (on phone) aqui é o Sr Brown ▷ adv (demonstrative): **this high** desta altura; **this long** deste comprimento; **we can't stop now we've gone this far** não podemos parar agora que fomos tão longe

thistle ['θɪsl] n cardo

thorn [θɔːn] n espinho

thorough ['θʌrə] adj (search) minucioso; (knowledge, research, person) metódico, profundo; **thoroughly** adv minuciosamente; (search) profundamente; (wash) completamente; (very) muito

those [ðəuz] pl pron, adj esses/essas

though [ðəu] conj embora, se bem que ▷ adv no entanto

thought [θɔːt] pt, pp of **think** ▷ n pensamento; (idea) ideia; (opinion) opinião f; (reflection) reflexão f; **thoughtful** adj pensativo; (serious) sério; (considerate) atencioso; **thoughtless** adj desatencioso; (words, person) inconsequente

thousand ['θauzənd] num mil; **two ~** dois mil; **~s (of)** milhares mpl (de); **thousandth** adj milésimo

thrash [θræʃ] vt surrar, malhar; (defeat) derrotar **thrash about** vi debater-se **thrash out** vt discutir exaustivamente

thread [θrɛd] n fio, linha; (of screw) rosca ▷ vt (needle) enfiar

threat [θrɛt] n ameaça; **threaten** vi ameaçar ▷ vt: **to threaten sb with sth/to do** ameaçar alguém com algo/de fazer

three [θriː] num três; **three-dimensional** adj tridimensional, em três dimensões; **three-piece suit** n terno (3 peças) (BR), fato de 3 peças (PT)

threshold ['θrɛʃhəuld] n limiar m

threw [θruː] pt of **throw**

thrill [θrɪl] n emoção f; (shudder) estremecimento ▷ vt emocionar, vibrar; **to be ~ed** (with gift etc) estar emocionado; **thriller** n romance m or filme m de suspense; **thrilling**

adj emocionante

throat [θrəʊt] *n* garganta; **to have a sore ~** estar com dor de garganta

throb [θrɔb] *n* (*of heart*) batida; (*of engine*) vibração *f*; (*of pain*) latejo ▷ *vi* (*heart*) bater, palpitar; (*pain*) dar pontadas; (*engine*) vibrar

throne [θrəʊn] *n* trono

through [θruː] *prep* por, através de; (*time*) durante; (*by means of*) por meio de, por intermédio de; (*owing to*) devido a ▷ *adj* (*ticket, train*) direto ▷ *adv* através; **to put sb ~ to sb** (*Tel*) ligar alguém com alguém; **to be ~** (*Tel*) estar na linha; (*have finished*) acabar; **"no ~ road"** "rua sem saída"; **I'm halfway ~ the book** estou na metade do livro; **throughout** *prep* (*place*) por todo(-a); (*time*) durante todo(-a) ▷ *adv* por or em todas as partes

throw [θrəʊ] (*pt* **threw**, *pp* **thrown**) *n* arremesso, tiro; (*Sport*) lançamento ▷ *vt* jogar, atirar; (*Sport*) lançar; (*rider*) derrubar; (*fig*) desconcertar; **to ~ a party** dar uma festa **throw away** *vt* (*dispose of*) jogar fora; (*waste*) desperdiçar **throw off** *vt* desfazer-se de; (*habit, cold*) livrar-se **throw out** *vt* expulsar; (*rubbish*) jogar fora; (*idea*) rejeitar **throw up** *vi* vomitar, botar para fora

thru [θruː] (*US*) *prep, adj, adv* = **through**

thrush [θrʌʃ] *n* (*Zool*) tordo

thrust [θrʌst] (*pt, pp* **thrust**) *n* impulso; (*Tech*) empuxo ▷ *vt* empurrar

thud [θʌd] *n* baque *m*, som *m* surdo

thug [θʌg] *n* facínora *m/f*

thumb [θʌm] *n* (*Anat*) polegar *m*; **to ~ a lift** pegar carona (*BR*), arranjar uma boleia (*PT*) **thumb through**

vt fus folhear; **thumbtack** (*US*) *n* percevejo, tachinha

thump [θʌmp] *n* murro, pancada; (*sound*) baque *m* ▷ *vt* dar um murro em ▷ *vi* bater

thunder ['θʌndəʳ] *n* trovão *m* ▷ *vi* trovejar; (*train etc*): **to ~ past** passar como um raio; **thunderstorm** *n* tempestade *f* com trovoada, temporal *m*

Thursday ['θəːzdɪ] *n* quinta-feira

thyme [taɪm] *n* tomilho

tick [tɪk] *n* (*of clock*) tique-taque *m*; (*mark*) tique *m*, marca; (*Zool*) carrapato; (*Brit: inf*): **in a ~** num instante ▷ *vi* fazer tique-taque ▷ *vt* marcar, ticar **tick off** *vt* assinalar, ticar; (*person*) dar uma bronca em **tick over** (*Brit*) *vi* (*engine*) funcionar em marcha lenta; (*fig*) ir indo

ticket ['tɪkɪt] *n* (*for bus, plane*) passagem *f*; (*for theatre, raffle*) bilhete *m*; (*for cinema*) entrada; (*in shop: on goods*) etiqueta; (*parking ticket: fine*) multa; (*for library*) cartão *m*; **to get a (parking) ~** (*Aut*) ganhar uma multa (por estacionamento ilegal); **ticket barrier** (*Brit*) *n* (*Rail*) catraca de embarque/desembarque; **ticket collector** *n* revisor(a) *m/f*; **ticket office** *n* bilheteria (*BR*), bilheteira (*PT*)

tickle ['tɪkl] *vt* fazer cócegas em ▷ *vi* fazer cócegas; **ticklish** *adj* coceguento; (*problem*) delicado

tide [taɪd] *n* maré *f*; (*fig*) curso; **high/low ~** maré alta/baixa; **the ~ of public opinion** a corrente da opinião pública **tide over** *vt* ajudar num período difícil

tidy ['taɪdɪ] *adj* (*room*) arrumado; (*dress, work*) limpo; (*person*) bem arrumado ▷ vt (also: **~ up**) pôr em ordem, arrumar

tie [taɪ] n (string etc) fita, corda; (Brit: also: **neck~**) gravata; (fig: link) vínculo, laço; (Sport: draw) empate m ▷ vt amarrar ▷ vi (Sport) empatar; **to ~ in a bow** dar um laço em; **to ~ a knot in sth** dar um nó em algo **tie down** vt amarrar; (fig: restrict) limitar, restringir; (to date, price etc) obrigar **tie up** vt embrulhar; (dog) prender; (boat, prisoner etc) amarrar; (arrangements) concluir; **to be ~d up** estar ocupado

tier [tɪər] n fileira; (of cake) camada

tiger ['taɪgər] n tigre m

tight [taɪt] adj (rope) esticado, firme; (money) escasso; (clothes, shoes) justo; (bend) fechado; (budget, programme) rigoroso; (inf: drunk) bêbado ▷ adv (squeeze) bem forte; (shut) hermeticamente; (people) estar apinhado; **tighten** vt (rope) esticar; (screw, grip) apertar; (security) aumentar ▷ vi esticar-se, apertar-se; **tightly** adv firmemente

tile [taɪl] n (on roof) telha; (on floor) ladrilho; (on wall) azulejo, ladrilho

till [tɪl] n caixa (registradora) ▷ vt (land) cultivar ▷ prep, conj = **until**

tilt [tɪlt] vt inclinar ▷ vi inclinar-se

timber ['tɪmbər] n (material) madeira; (trees) mata, floresta

time [taɪm] n tempo; (epoch: often pl) época; (by clock) hora; (moment) momento; (occasion) vez f; (Mus) compasso ▷ vt calcular or medir o tempo de; (visit etc) escolher o momento para; **a long ~** muito tempo; **4 at a ~** quatro de uma vez; **for the ~ being** por enquanto; **from ~ to ~** de vez em quando;

at ~s às vezes; **in ~** (soon enough) a tempo; (after some time) com o tempo; (Mus) no compasso; **in a week's ~** dentro de uma semana; **in no ~** num abrir e fechar de olhos; **any ~** a qualquer hora; **on ~** na hora; **5 ~s 5 is 25** 5 vezes 5 são 25; **what ~ is it?** que horas são?; **to have a good ~** divertir-se; **timely** adj oportuno; **timetable** n horário; **time zone** n fuso horário

timid ['tɪmɪd] adj tímido

timing ['taɪmɪŋ] n escolha do momento; (Sport) cronometragem f; **the ~ of his resignation** o momento que escolheu para se demitir

tin [tɪn] n estanho; (also: **~ plate**) folha-de-flandres f; (Brit: can) lata

tingle ['tɪŋgl] vi formigar

tinned [tɪnd] (Brit) adj (food) em lata, em conserva

tin opener (Brit) n abridor m de latas (BR), abre-latas m inv (PT)

tinsel ['tɪnsl] n ouropel m

tint [tɪnt] n matiz m; (for hair) tintura, tinta; **tinted** adj (hair) pintado; (spectacles, glass) fumê inv

tiny ['taɪnɪ] adj pequenininho, minúsculo

tip [tɪp] n ponta; (gratuity) gorjeta; (Brit: for rubbish) depósito; (advice) dica ▷ vt dar uma gorjeta a; (tilt) inclinar; (overturn: also: **~ over**) virar, emborcar; (empty: also: **~ out**) esvaziar, entornar

tiptoe ['tɪptəu] n: **on ~** na ponta dos pés

tire ['taɪər] n (US) = **tyre** ▷ vt cansar ▷ vi cansar-se; (become bored) chatear-se; **tired** adj cansado; **to be tired of sth** estar farto or cheio de algo; **tiring** adj cansativo

tissue ['tɪʃu:] n tecido; (paper

handkerchief) lenço de papel; **tissue paper** n papel m de seda
tit [tɪt] n (*bird*) passarinho; **to give ~ for tat** pagar na mesma moeda
title ['taɪtl] n título
TM n abbr = **trademark**

 KEYWORD

to [tuː, tə] prep **1** (*direction*) a, para; (*towards*) para; **to go to France/ London/school/the station** ir à França/a Londres/ao colégio/à estação; **to go to Lígia's/the doctor's** ir à casa da Lígia/ao médico; **the road to Edinburgh** a estrada para Edinburgo; **to the left/right** à esquerda/direita
2 (*as far as*) até; **to count to 10** contar até 10; **from 40 to 50 people** de 40 a 50 pessoas
3 (*with expressions of time*): **a quarter to 5** quinze para as 5 (BR), 5 menos um quarto (PT)
4 (*for, or*) de, para; **the key to the front door** a chave da porta da frente; **a letter to his wife** uma carta para a sua mulher
5 (*expressing indirect object*): **to give sth to sb** dar algo a alguém; **to talk to sb** falar com alguém; **I sold it to a friend** vendi isto para um amigo; **to cause damage to sth** causar danos em algo
6 (*in relation to*) para; **3 goals to 2** 3 a 2; **8 apples to the kilo** 8 maçãs por quilo
7 (*purpose, result*) para; **to come to sb's aid** prestar ajuda a alguém; **to sentence sb to death** condenar alguém à morte; **to my surprise** para minha surpresa
▷ *with vb* **1** (*simple infin*): **to go/eat** ir/comer

2 (*following another vb*): **to want/ try to do** querer/tentar fazer; **to start to do** começar a fazer
3 (*with vb omitted*): **I don't want to** eu não quero; **you ought to** você deve
4 (*purpose, result*) para
5 (*equivalent to relative clause*) para, a; **I have things to do** eu tenho coisas para fazer; **the main thing is to try** o principal é tentar
6 (*after adj etc*) para; **ready to go** pronto para ir; **too old/young to ...** muito velho/jovem para ...
▷ *adv*: **pull/push the door to** puxar/empurrar a porta

toad [təud] n sapo
toadstool ['təudstuːl] n chapéu-de-cobra m, cogumelo venenoso
toast [təust] n (*Culin*) torradas fpl; (*drink, speech*) brinde m ▷ vt torrar; (*drink to*) brindar; **toaster** n torradeira
tobacco [tə'bækəu] n tabaco, fumo (BR)
today [tə'deɪ] adv, n hoje m
toddler ['tɔdlə'] n criança que começa a andar
toe [təu] n dedo do pé; (*of shoe*) bico ▷ vt: **to ~ the line** (*fig*) conformar-se, cumprir as obrigações
toffee ['tɔfɪ] n puxa-puxa m (BR), caramelo (PT)
together [tə'gɛðə'] adv juntos; (*at same time*) ao mesmo tempo; **~ with** junto com
toilet ['tɔɪlət] n privada, vaso sanitário; (*Brit: lavatory*) banheiro (BR), casa de banho (PT) ▷ cpd de toalete; **toilet paper** n papel m higiênico; **toiletries** npl artigos

t

mpl de toalete; **toilet roll** *n* rolo de papel higiênico

token ['təukən] *n* (*sign*) sinal *m*, símbolo, prova; (*souvenir*) lembrança; (*substitute coin*) ficha ▷ *cpd* simbólico; **book/record ~** (*Brit*) vale para comprar livros/ discos

told [təuld] *pt, pp of* **tell**

tolerant ['tɔlərənt] *adj*: **~ of** tolerante com

tolerate ['tɔləreɪt] *vt* suportar; (*Med, Tech*) tolerar

toll [təul] *n* (*of casualties*) número de baixas; (*tax, charge*) pedágio (*BR*), portagem *f* (*PT*) ▷ *vi* dobrar, tanger

tomato [tə'mɑːtəu] (*pl* **tomatoes**) *n* tomate *m*

tomb [tuːm] *n* tumba

tombstone ['tuːmstəun] *n* lápide *f*

tomorrow [tə'mɔrəu] *adv, n* amanhã *m*; **the day after ~** depois de amanhã; **~ morning** amanhã de manhã

ton [tʌn] *n* tonelada; **~s of** (*inf*) um monte de

tone [təun] *n* tom *m* ▷ *vi* harmonizar **tone down** *vt* (*colour, criticism*) suavizar; (*sound*) baixar; (*Mus*) entoar **tone up** *vt* (*muscles*) tonificar

tongs [tɔŋz] *npl* (*for coal*) tenaz *f*; (*for hair*) ferros *mpl* de frisar cabelo

tongue [tʌŋ] *n* língua; **~ in cheek** ironicamente

tonic ['tɔnɪk] *n* (*Med*) tônico; (*also:* **~ water**) (água) tônica

tonight [tə'naɪt] *adv, n* esta noite, hoje à noite

tonsil ['tɔnsəl] *n* amígdala; **tonsillitis** [tɔnsɪ'laɪtɪs] *n* amigdalite *f*

too [tuː] *adv* (*excessively*) demais, muito; (*also*) também; **~ much**

(*adv*) demais; (*adj*) demasiado; **~ many** demasiados(-as)

took [tuk] *pt of* **take**

tool [tuːl] *n* ferramenta

tooth [tuːθ] (*pl* **teeth**) *n* (*Anat, Tech*) dente *m*; (*molar*) molar *m*; **toothache** *n* dor *f* de dente; **to have toothache** estar com dor de dente; **toothbrush** *n* escova de dentes; **toothpaste** *n* pasta de dentes, creme *m* dental; **toothpick** *n* palito

top [tɔp] *n* (*of mountain*) cume *m*, cimo; (*of tree*) topo; (*of head*) cocuruto; (*of cupboard, table*) superfície *f*, topo; (*of box, jar, bottle*) tampa; (*of ladder, page*) topo; (*toy*) pião *m*; (*blouse etc*) top *m*, blusa ▷ *adj* (*shelf, step*) mais alto; (*marks*) máximo; (*in rank*) principal, superior ▷ *vt* exceder; (*be first in*) estar à cabeça de; **on ~ of** sobre, em cima de; (*in addition to*) além de; **from ~ to toe** (*Brit*) da cabeça aos pés; **from ~ to bottom** de cima abaixo **top up**, (*US*) **top off** *vt* completar; (*mobile phone*) recarregar; **top floor** *n* último andar *m*

topic ['tɔpɪk] *n* tópico, assunto; **topical** *adj* atual

topless ['tɔplɪs] *adj* (*bather etc*) topless *inv*, sem a parte superior do biquíni

topple ['tɔpl] *vt* derrubar ▷ *vi* cair para frente; **top-up card** *n* cartão de recarga (para celular)

torch [tɔːtʃ] *n* (*Brit: electric torch*) lanterna

tore [tɔːʳ] *pt of* **tear**

torment [*n* 'tɔːmɛnt, *vt* tɔː'mɛnt] *n* tormento, suplício ▷ *vt* atormentar; (*fig: annoy*) chatear, aborrecer

torn [tɔːn] *pp of* **tear**

tornado [tɔːˈneɪdəu] (*pl* **tornadoes**) *n* tornado

torrent [ˈtɔrənt] *n* torrente *f*

tortoise [ˈtɔːtəs] *n* tartaruga

torture [ˈtɔːtʃəʳ] *n* tortura ▷ *vt* torturar; (*fig*) atormentar

Tory [ˈtɔːrɪ] (*Brit*) *adj, n* (*Pol*) conservador(a) *m/f*

toss [tɔs] *vt* atirar, arremessar; (*head*) lançar para trás ▷ *vi*: **to ~ and turn in bed** virar de um lado para o outro na cama; **to ~ a coin** tirar cara ou coroa; **to ~ up for sth** (*Brit*) jogar cara ou coroa por algo

total [ˈtəutl] *adj* total ▷ *n* total *m*, soma ▷ *vt* (*add up*) somar; (*amount to*) montar a

touch [tʌtʃ] *n* (*sense*) toque *m*; (*contact*) contato ▷ *vt* tocar (em); (*tamper with*) mexer com; (*make contact with*) fazer contato com; (*emotionally*) comover; **a ~ of** (*fig*) um traço de; **to get in ~ with sb** entrar em contato com alguém; **to lose ~** perder o contato **touch on** *vt fus* (*topic*) tocar em, fazer menção de **touch up** *vt* (*paint*) retocar; **touchdown** *n* aterrissagem *f* (*BR*), aterragem *f* (*PT*); (*on sea*) amerissagem *f* (*BR*), amaragem *f* (*PT*); (*US: Football*) touchdown *m* (*colocação da bola no chão atrás da linha de gol*); **touching** *adj* comovedor(a)

tough [tʌf] *adj* duro; (*difficult*) difícil; (*resistant*) resistente; (*person: physically*) forte; (*: mentally*) tenaz; (*firm*) firme, inflexível

tour [ˈtuəʳ] *n* viagem *f*, excursão *f*; (*also:* **package ~**) excursão organizada; (*of town, museum*) visita; (*by artist*) turnê *f* ▷ *vt* (*country, city*) excursionar por; (*factory*) visitar

tourism [ˈtuərɪzm] *n* turismo

tourist [ˈtuərɪst] *n* turista *m/f* ▷ *cpd* turístico; **tourist office** *n* (*in country*) escritório de turismo; (*in embassy etc*) departamento de turismo

tournament [ˈtuənəmənt] *n* torneio

tow [təu] *vt* rebocar; **"on ~"** (*Brit*), **"in ~"** (*US*) (*Aut*) "rebocado"

toward [təˈwɔːd], **towards** [təˈwɔːdz] *prep* em direção a; (*of attitude*) para com; (*of purpose*) para; **~(s) noon/the end of the year** perto do meio-dia/do fim do ano

towel [ˈtauəl] *n* toalha; **towelling** *n* (*fabric*) tecido para toalhas

tower [ˈtauəʳ] *n* torre *f*; **tower block** (*Brit*) *n* prédio alto, espigão *m*, cortiço (*BR*)

town [taun] *n* cidade *f*; **to go to ~** ir à cidade; (*fig*) pegar com entusiasmo, mandar brasa (*BR*); **town centre** *n* centro (da cidade); **town hall** *n* prefeitura (*BR*), concelho (*PT*)

toy [tɔɪ] *n* brinquedo **toy with** *vt fus* brincar com; (*idea*) contemplar

trace [treɪs] *n* (*sign*) sinal *m*; (*small amount*) traço ▷ *vt* (*draw*) traçar, esboçar; (*follow*) seguir a pista de; (*locate*) encontrar

track [træk] *n* (*mark*) pegada, vestígio; (*path: gen*) caminho, vereda; (*: of bullet etc*) trajetória; (*: of suspect, animal*) pista, rasto; (*Rail*) trilhos (*BR*), carris *mpl* (*PT*); (*on tape*) trilha; (*Sport*) pista; (*on record*) faixa ▷ *vt* seguir a pista de; **to keep ~ of** não perder de vista; (*fig*) manter-se informado sobre **track down** *vt* (*prey*) seguir a pista

de; (*sth lost*) procurar e encontrar
tractor ['træktə^r] *n* trator *m*
trade [treɪd] *n* comércio; (*skill, job*)
ofício ▷ *vi* negociar, comerciar
▷ *vt*: **to ~ sth (for sth)** trocar algo
(por algo) **trade in** *vt* dar como
parte do pagamento; **trademark**
n marca registrada; **trader** *n*
comerciante *m/f*; **tradesman** *irreg*
n lojista *m*; **trade union** *n*
sindicato
tradition [trə'dɪʃən] *n* tradição *f*;
traditional *adj* tradicional
traffic ['træfɪk] *n* trânsito *f*; (*air
traffic etc*) tráfego; (*illegal*) tráfico
▷ *vi*: **to ~ in** (*pej: liquor, drugs*)
traficar com, fazer tráfico com;
traffic circle (*US*) *n* rotatória;
traffic jam *n* engarrafamento,
congestionamento; **traffic lights**
npl sinal *m* luminoso; **traffic
warden** *n* guarda *m/f* de trânsito
tragedy ['trædʒədɪ] *n* tragédia
tragic ['trædʒɪk] *adj* trágico
trail [treɪl] *n* (*tracks*) rasto, pista;
(*path*) caminho, trilha; (*of smoke,
dust*) rasto ▷ *vt* (*drag*) arrastar;
(*follow*) seguir a pista de ▷ *vi*
arrastar-se; (*hang loosely*) pender;
(*in game, contest*) ficar para trás
trail behind *vi* atrasar-se; **trailer**
n (*Aut*) reboque *m*; (*US: caravan*)
trailer *m* (*BR*), rulote *f* (*PT*); (*Cinema*)
trailer
train [treɪn] *n* trem *m* (*BR*),
comboio (*PT*); (*of dress*) cauda ▷ *vt*
formar; (*teach skills to*) instruir;
(*Sport*) treinar; (*dog*) adestrar,
amestrar; (*point: gun etc*): **to ~ on**
apontar para ▷ *vi* (*learn a skill*)
instruir; (*Sport*) treinar; (*be
educated*) ser treinado; **to lose
one's ~ of thought** perder o fio;
trainee [treɪ'niː] *n* estagiário(-a);

trainer *n* (*Sport*) treinador(a) *m/f*;
(*of animals*) adestrador(a) *m/f*;
trainers *npl* (*shoes*) tênis *m*;
training *n* instrução *f*; (*Sport, for
occupation*) treinamento;
(*professional*) formação
trait [treɪt] *n* traço
traitor ['treɪtə^r] *n* traidor(a) *m/f*
tram [træm] (*Brit*) *n* (*also*: **~-car**)
bonde *m* (*BR*), eléctrico (*PT*)
tramp [træmp] *n* (*person*)
vagabundo(-a); (*inf: pej: woman*)
piranha ▷ *vi* caminhar
pesadamente
trample ['træmpl] *vt*: **to ~
(underfoot)** calcar aos pés
trampoline ['træmpəliːn] *n*
trampolim *m*
tranquil ['træŋkwɪl] *adj* tranquilo;
tranquillizer *n* (*Med*)
tranquilizante *m*
transfer [*n* 'trænsfə^r, *vt* træns'fə:^r]
n transferência; (*picture, design*)
decalcomania ▷ *vt* transferir; **to ~
the charges** (*Brit: Tel*) ligar a cobrar
transform [træns'fɔːm] *vt*
transformar
transfusion [træns'fjuːʒən] *n*
(*also*: **blood ~**) transfusão *f* (de
sangue)
transit ['trænzɪt] *n*: **in ~** em
trânsito, de passagem
translate [trænz'leɪt] *vt* traduzir;
translation *n* tradução *f*;
translator *n* tradutor(a) *m/f*
transmission [trænz'mɪʃən] *n*
transmissão *f*
transmit [trænz'mɪt] *vt* transmitir
transparent [træns'pærnt] *adj*
transparente
transplant [*vt* træns'plɑːnt, *n*
'trænsplɑːnt] *vt* transplantar ▷ *n*
(*Med*) transplante *m*
transport [*n* 'trænspɔːt, *vt*

træns'pɔːt] n transporte m ▷ vt
transportar; (carry) acarretar;
transportation [trænspɔːˈteɪʃən]
n transporte m
trap [træp] n (snare) armadilha,
cilada; (trick) cilada; (carriage)
aranha, charrete f ▷ vt (animal,
person) pegar numa armadilha;
(immobilize) bloquear; **to be ~ped**
(in bad marriage, fire) estar preso(-a)
trash [træʃ] n (pej: nonsense)
besteiras fpl; (US: rubbish) lixo;
trash can (US) n lata de lixo
trauma [ˈtrɔːmə] n trauma m
travel [ˈtrævl] n viagem f ▷ vi
viajar; (sound) propagar-se; (news)
levar; (wine): **this wine ~s well**
este vinho não sofre alteração ao
ser transportado ▷ vt percorrer;
travels npl (journeys) viagens fpl;
travel agent n agente m/f de
viagens; **traveller**, (US) **traveler** n
viajante m/f; (Comm) caixeiro(-a)
viajante; **traveller's cheque**, (US)
traveler's check n cheque m de
viagem; **travelling**, (US) **traveling**
n as viagens, viajar m ▷ adj (circus,
exhibition) itinerante; (salesman)
viajante ▷ cpd de viagem; **travel
sickness** n enjoo
tray [treɪ] n bandeja; (on desk) cesta
treacherous [ˈtrɛtʃərəs] adj
traiçoeiro; (ground, tide) perigoso
treacle [ˈtriːkl] n melado
tread [trɛd] (pt **trod**, pp **trodden**) n
(step) passo, pisada; (sound)
passada; (of stair) piso; (of tyre)
banda de rodagem ▷ vi pisar **tread
on** vt fus pisar (em)
treasure [ˈtrɛʒəʳ] n tesouro;
(person) joia ▷ vt (value) apreciar,
estimar; **treasures** npl (art
treasures etc) preciosidades fpl
treasurer [ˈtrɛʒərəʳ] n

tesoureiro(-a)
treasury [ˈtrɛʒərɪ] n tesouraria
treat [triːt] n regalo, deleite m ▷ vt
tratar; **to ~ sb to sth** convidar
alguém para algo
treatment [ˈtriːtmənt] n
tratamento
treaty [ˈtriːtɪ] n tratado, acordo
treble [ˈtrɛbl] adj tríplice ▷ vt
triplicar ▷ vi triplicar(-se)
tree [triː] n árvore f
trek [trɛk] n (long journey) jornada;
(walk) caminhada
tremble [ˈtrɛmbl] vi tremer
tremendous [trɪˈmɛndəs] adj
tremendo; (enormous) enorme;
(excellent) sensacional, fantástico
trench [trɛntʃ] n trincheira
trend [trɛnd] n (tendency)
tendência; (of events) curso;
(fashion) modismo, tendência;
trendy adj (idea) de acordo com a
tendência atual; (clothes) da última
moda
trespass [ˈtrɛspəs] vi: **to ~ on**
invadir; **"no ~ing"** "entrada
proibida"
trial [ˈtraɪəl] n (Law) processo; (test:
of machine etc) prova, teste m; **trials**
npl (unpleasant experiences)
dissabores mpl; **by ~ and error** por
tentativas; **to be on ~** ser julgado;
trial period n período de
experiência
triangle [ˈtraɪæŋgl] n (Math, Mus)
triângulo
tribe [traɪb] n tribo f
tribunal [traɪˈbjuːnl] n tribunal m
tribute [ˈtrɪbjuːt] n homenagem f;
to pay ~ to prestar homenagem a,
homenagear
trick [trɪk] n truque m; (joke) peça,
brincadeira; (skill, knack) habilidade
f; (Cards) vaza ▷ vt enganar; **to play**

t

a ~ on sb pregar uma peça em alguém; **that should do the ~** (inf) isso deveria dar resultado

trickle ['trɪkl] n (of water etc) fio (de água) ▷ vi gotejar, pingar

tricky ['trɪkɪ] adj difícil, complicado

trifle ['traɪfl] n bobagem f, besteira; (Culin) tipo de bolo com fruta e creme ▷ adv: **a ~ long** um pouquinho longo

trigger ['trɪgəʳ] n (of gun) gatilho **trigger off** vt desencadear

trim [trɪm] adj (figure) elegante; (house) arrumado; (garden) bem cuidado ▷ n (haircut etc) aparada; (on car) estofamento ▷ vt aparar, cortar; (decorate): **to ~ (with)** enfeitar (com); (Naut: sail) ajustar

trip [trɪp] n viagem f; (outing) excursão f; (stumble) tropeção m ▷ vi tropeçar; (go lightly) andar com passos ligeiros; **on a ~** de viagem **trip up** vi tropeçar ▷ vt passar uma rasteira em

triple ['trɪpl] adj triplo, tríplice; **triplets** npl trigêmeos(-as) m/fpl

tripod ['traɪpɒd] n tripé m

triumph ['traɪʌmf] n (satisfaction) satisfação f; (great achievement) triunfo ▷ vi: **to ~ (over)** triunfar (sobre)

trivial ['trɪvɪəl] adj insignificante; (commonplace) trivial

trod [trɒd] pt of **tread**; **trodden** pp of **tread**

trolley ['trɒlɪ] n carrinho; (table on wheels) mesa volante

trombone [trɒm'bəun] n trombone m

troop [tru:p] n bando, grupo ▷ vi: **to ~ in/out** entrar/sair em bando; **troops** npl (Mil) tropas fpl; **~ing the colour** (Brit) saudação da bandeira

trophy ['trəufɪ] n troféu m

tropic ['trɒpɪk] n trópico; **tropical** adj tropical

trot [trɒt] n trote m; (fast pace) passo rápido ▷ vi trotar; (person) andar rapidamente; **on the ~** (fig: inf) a fio

trouble ['trʌbl] n problema(s) m(pl), dificuldade(s) f(pl); (worry) preocupação f; (bother, effort) incômodo, trabalho; (Pol) distúrbios mpl; (Med): **stomach ~** etc problemas mpl gástricos etc ▷ vt perturbar; (worry) preocupar, incomodar ▷ vi: **to ~ to do sth** incomodar-se or preocupar-se de fazer algo; **troubles** npl (Pol etc) distúrbios mpl; **to be in ~** estar num aperto; (ship, climber etc) estar em dificuldade; **what's the ~?** qual é o problema?; **troubled** adj preocupado; (epoch, life) agitado; **troublemaker** n criador(a)-de-casos m/f; (child) encrenqueiro(-a); **troublesome** adj importuno; (child: cough) incômodo

trough [trɒf] n (also: **drinking ~**) bebedouro, cocho; (also: **feeding ~**) gamela; (depression) depressão f

trousers ['trauzəz] npl calça (BR), calças fpl (PT)

trout [traut] n inv truta

truant ['truənt] (Brit) n: **to play ~** matar aula (BR), fazer gazeta (PT)

truce [tru:s] n trégua, armistício

truck [trʌk] n caminhão m (BR), camião m (PT); (Rail) vagão m; **truck driver** n caminhoneiro(-a) (BR), camionista m/f (PT)

true [tru:] adj verdadeiro; (accurate) exato; (genuine) autêntico; (faithful) fiel, leal; **to come ~** realizar-se, tornar-se realidade

truly ['tru:lɪ] adv realmente;

(*truthfully*) verdadeiramente; (*faithfully*) fielmente; **yours ~** (*in letter*) atenciosamente

trumpet ['trʌmpɪt] *n* trombeta

trunk [trʌŋk] *n* tronco; (*of elephant*) tromba; (*case*) baú *m*; (*US: Aut*) mala (*BR*), porta-bagagens *m* (*PT*); **trunks** *npl* (*also*: **swimming ~s**) sunga (*BR*), calções *mpl* de banho (*PT*)

trust [trʌst] *n* confiança; (*responsibility*) responsabilidade *f*; (*Law*) fideicomisso ▷ *vt* (*rely on*) confiar em; (*entrust*): **to ~ sth to sb** confiar algo a alguém; (*hope*): **to ~ (that)** esperar que; **to take sth on ~** aceitar algo sem verificação prévia; **trusted** *adj* de confiança; **trustworthy** *adj* digno de confiança

truth [truːθ] *n* verdade *f*; **truthful** *adj* (*person*) sincero, honesto

try [traɪ] *n* tentativa, (*Rugby*) ensaio ▷ *vt* (*Law*) julgar; (*test: sth new*) provar, pôr à prova; (*strain*) cansar ▷ *vi* tentar; **to have a ~** fazer uma tentativa; **to ~ to do sth** tentar fazer algo **try on** *vt* (*clothes*) experimentar, provar; **trying** *adj* exasperante

T-shirt *n* camiseta (*BR*), T-shirt *f* (*PT*)

tub [tʌb] *n* tina; (*bath*) banheira

tube [tjuːb] *n* tubo; (*pipe*) cano; (*Brit: underground*) metrô *m* (*BR*), metro(-politano) (*PT*); (*for tyre*) câmara-de-ar *f*

tuck [tʌk] *vt* (*put*) enfiar, meter **tuck away** *vt* esconder; **to be ~ed away** estar escondido **tuck in** *vt* enfiar para dentro; (*child*) aconchegar ▷ *vi* (*eat*) comer com apetite **tuck up** *vt* (*child*) aconchegar

Tuesday ['tjuːzdɪ] *n* terça-feira

tug [tʌg] *n* (*ship*) rebocador *m* ▷ *vt* puxar

tuition [tjuːˈɪʃən] *n* ensino; (*private tuition*) aulas *fpl* particulares; (*US: fees*) taxas *fpl* escolares

tulip ['tjuːlɪp] *n* tulipa

tumble ['tʌmbl] *n* (*fall*) queda ▷ *vi* cair, tombar; **to ~ to sth** (*inf*) sacar algo

tumbler ['tʌmbləʳ] *n* copo

tummy ['tʌmɪ] (*inf*) *n* (*belly*) barriga; (*stomach*) estômago

tumour ['tjuːməʳ], (*US*) **tumor** *n* tumor *m*

tuna ['tjuːnə] *n inv* (*also*: **~ fish**) atum *m*

tune [tjuːn] *n* melodia ▷ *vt* (*Mus*) afinar; (*Radio, TV*) sintonizar; (*Aut*) regular; **to be in/out of ~** (*instrument*) estar afinado/ desafinado; (*singer*) cantar afinado/desafinar; **to be in/out of ~ with** (*fig*) harmonizar-se com/ destoar de **tune in** *vi* (*Radio, TV*): **to ~ in (to)** sintonizar (com) **tune up** *vi* (*musician*) afinar (seu instrumento)

tunic ['tjuːnɪk] *n* túnica

Tunisia [tjuːˈnɪzɪə] *n* Tunísia

tunnel ['tʌnl] *n* túnel *m*; (*in mine*) galeria ▷ *vi* abrir um túnel (*or* uma galeria)

turbulence ['təːbjuləns] *n* (*Aviat*) turbulência

turf [təːf] *n* torrão *m* ▷ *vt* relvar, gramar **turf out** (*inf*) *vt* (*person*) pôr no olho da rua

Turk [təːk] *n* turco(-a)

Turkey ['təːkɪ] *n* Turquia

turkey ['təːkɪ] *n* peru(a) *m/f*

Turkish ['təːkɪʃ] *adj* turco(-a) ▷ *n* (*Ling*) turco

turmoil ['təːmɔɪl] *n* tumulto, distúrbio, agitação *f*; **in ~** agitado, tumultuado

turn [təːn] *n* volta, turno; (*in road*)

curva; (*of mind, events*) propensão *f*, tendência; (*Theatre*) número; (*Med*) choque *m* ▷ *vt* dar volta a, fazer girar; (*collar*) virar; (*change*): **to ~ sth into** converter algo em ▷ *vi* virar; (*person: look back*) voltar-se; (*reverse direction*) mudar de direção; (*milk*) azedar; (*become*) tornar-se, virar; **to ~ nasty** engrossar; **to ~ forty** fazer quarenta anos; **a good ~** um favor; **it gave me quite a ~** me deu um susto enorme; **"no left ~"** (*Aut*) "proibido virar à esquerda"; **it's your ~** é a sua vez; **in ~** por sua vez; **to take ~s (at)** revezar (em) **turn away** *vi* virar a cabeça ▷ *vt* recusar **turn back** *vi* voltar atrás ▷ *vt* voltar para trás; (*clock*) atrasar **turn down** *vt* (*refuse*) recusar; (*reduce*) baixar; (*fold*) dobrar, virar para baixo **turn in** *vi* (*inf: go to bed*) ir dormir ▷ *vt* (*fold*) dobrar para dentro **turn off** *vi* (*from road*) virar, sair do caminho ▷ *vt* (*light, radio etc*) apagar; (*engine*) desligar **turn on** *vt* (*light*) acender; (*engine, radio*) ligar; (*tap*) abrir **turn out** *vt* (*light, gas*) apagar; (*produce*) produzir ▷ *vi* (*troops*) ser mobilizado; **to ~ out to be ...** revelar-se (ser) ..., resultar (ser) ..., vira a ser ... **turn over** *vi* (*person*) virar-se ▷ *vt* (*object*) virar **turn round** *vi* voltar-se, virar-se **turn up** *vi* (*person*) aparecer, pintar; (*lost object*) aparecer ▷ *vt* (*collar*) subir; (*volume, radio etc*) aumentar; **turning** *n* (*in road*) via lateral

turnip ['tə:nɪp] *n* nabo

turnout ['tə:naut] *n* assistência; (*in election*) comparecimento às urnas

turnover ['tə:nəuvə^r] *n* (*Comm: amount of money*) volume *m* de negócios; (*: of goods*) movimento;

(*of staff*) rotatividade *f*

turn-up (*Brit*) *n* (*on trousers*) volta, dobra

turquoise ['tə:kwɔɪz] *n* (*stone*) turquesa ▷ *adj* azul-turquesa *inv*

turtle ['tə:tl] *n* tartaruga, cágado

tusk [tʌsk] *n* defesa (de elefante)

tutor ['tju:tə^r] *n* professor(a) *m/f*; (*private tutor*) professor(a) *m/f* particular; **tutorial** [tju:'tɔ:rɪəl] *n* (*Sch*) seminário

tuxedo [tʌk'si:dəu] (*US*) *n* smoking *m*

TV *n abbr* (= television) TV *f*

tweed [twi:d] *n* tweed *m*, pano grosso de lã

tweezers ['twi:zəz] *npl* pinça (pequena)

twelfth [twɛlfθ] *num* décimo segundo

twelve [twɛlv] *num* doze; **at ~ (o'clock)** (*midday*) ao meio-dia; (*midnight*) à meia-noite

twentieth ['twɛntɪɪθ] *num* vigésimo

twenty ['twɛntɪ] *num* vinte

twice [twaɪs] *adv* duas vezes; **~ as much** duas vezes mais

twig [twɪg] *n* graveto, varinha ▷ *vi* (*inf*) sacar

twilight ['twaɪlaɪt] *n* crepúsculo, meia-luz *f*

twin [twɪn] *adj* gêmeo(-a); (*beds*) separado ▷ *n* gêmeo(-a) ▷ *vt* irmanar; **twin-bedded room** *n* quarto com duas camas

twinkle ['twɪŋkl] *vi* cintilar; (*eyes*) pestanejar

twist [twɪst] *n* torção *f*; (*in road, coil*) curva; (*in wire, flex*) virada; (*in story*) mudança imprevista ▷ *vt* torcer, retorcer; (*ankle*) torcer; (*weave*) entrelaçar; (*roll around*) enrolar; (*fig*) deturpar ▷ *vi* serpentear

twit [twɪt] (*inf*) *n* idiota *m/f*, bobo(-a)

twitch [twɪtʃ] *n* puxão *m*; (*nervous*) tique *m* nervoso ▷ *vi* contrair-se

two [tuː] *num* dois; **to put ~ and ~ together** (*fig*) tirar conclusões; **two-way** *adj*: **two-way traffic** trânsito em mão dupla

type [taɪp] *n* (*category*) tipo, espécie *f*; (*model*) modelo; (*Typ*) tipo, letra ▷ *vt* (*letter etc*) datilografar, bater (à máquina); **typewriter** *n* máquina de escrever

typhoid ['taɪfɔɪd] *n* febre *f* tifoide

typical ['tɪpɪkl] *adj* típico

typing ['taɪpɪŋ] *n* datilografia

typist ['taɪpɪst] *n* datilógrafo(-a) *m/f*

tyre ['taɪəʳ], (*US*) **tire** *n* pneu *m*

UFO ['juːfəu] *n abbr* (= *unidentified flying object*) óvni *m*

Uganda [juːˈgændə] *n* Uganda (*no article*)

ugly ['ʌglɪ] *adj* feio; (*dangerous*) perigoso

UK *n abbr* = **United Kingdom**

ulcer ['ʌlsəʳ] *n* úlcera; **mouth ~** afta

ultimate ['ʌltɪmət] *adj* último, final; (*authority*) máximo; **ultimately** *adv* (*in the end*) no final, por último; (*fundamentally*) no fundo

ultrasound ['ʌltrəsaund] *n* (*Med*) ultrassom *m*

umbrella [ʌmˈbrɛlə] *n* guarda-chuva *m*; (*for sun*) guarda-sol *m*, barraca (da praia)

umpire ['ʌmpaɪəʳ] *n* árbitro ▷ *vt* arbitrar

UN *n abbr* (= *United Nations*) ONU *f*

unable [ʌnˈeɪbl] *adj*: **to be ~ to do**

sth não poder fazer algo

unanimous [ju:'nænɪməs] adj unânime

unarmed [ʌn'ɑ:md] adj (without a weapon) desarmado; (defenceless) indefeso

unattended [ʌnə'tendɪd] adj (car, luggage) abandonado

unattractive [ʌnə'træktɪv] adj sem atrativos; (building, appearance, idea) pouco atraente

unavoidable [ʌnə'vɔɪdəbl] adj inevitável

unaware [ʌnə'wɛəʳ] adj: **to be ~ of** ignorar, não perceber

unawares [ʌnə'wɛəz] adv improvisamente, de surpresa

unbearable [ʌn'bɛərəbl] adj insuportável

unbeatable [ʌn'bi:təbl] adj (team) invencível; (price) sem igual

unbelievable [ʌnbɪ'li:vəbl] adj inacreditável; (amazing) incrível

unborn [ʌn'bɔ:n] adj por nascer

unbutton [ʌn'bʌtn] vt desabotoar

uncalled-for [ʌn'kɔ:ld-] adj desnecessário, gratuito

uncanny [ʌn'kænɪ] adj estranho; (knack) excepcional

uncertain [ʌn'sə:tn] adj incerto; (character) indeciso; (unsure): **~ about** inseguro sobre; **in no ~ terms** em termos precisos; **uncertainty** n incerteza; (also pl: doubts) dúvidas fpl

uncle ['ʌŋkl] n tio

uncomfortable [ʌn'kʌmfətəbl] adj incômodo; (uneasy) pouco à vontade; (situation) desagradável

uncommon [ʌn'kɔmən] adj raro, incomum, excepcional

unconditional [ʌnkən'dɪʃənl] adj incondicional

unconscious [ʌn'kɔnʃəs] adj sem

sentidos, desacordado; (unaware): **~ of** inconsciente de ▷ n: **the ~** o inconsciente

uncontrollable [ʌnkən'trəʊləbl] adj (temper) ingovernável; (child, animal, laughter) incontrolável

unconventional [ʌnkən'vɛnʃənl] adj inconvencional

uncover [ʌn'kʌvəʳ] vt descobrir; (take lid off) destapar, destampar

undecided [ʌndɪ'saɪdɪd] adj indeciso; (question) não respondido, pendente

under ['ʌndəʳ] prep embaixo de (BR), debaixo de (PT); (fig) sob; (less than) menos de; (according to) segundo, de acordo com ▷ adv embaixo; (movement) por baixo; **~ there** ali embaixo; **~ repair** em conserto; **undercover** adj secreto, clandestino; **underdog** n o mais fraco; **underdone** adj (Culin) mal passado; **underestimate** vt subestimar; **undergo** irreg vt sofrer; (test) passar por; (operation, treatment) ser submetido a; **undergraduate** n universitário(-a); **underground** n (Brit) metrô m (BR), metro(-politano) (PT); (Pol) organização f clandestina ▷ adj subterrâneo; (fig) clandestino ▷ adv (work) embaixo da terra; (fig) na clandestinidade; **undergrowth** n vegetação f rasteira; **underline** vt sublinhar; **undermine** vt minar, solapar; **underneath** adv embaixo, debaixo, por baixo ▷ prep embaixo de (BR), debaixo de (PT); **underpaid** adj mal pago; **underpants** (Brit) npl cueca (BR), cuecas fpl (PT); **underpass** (Brit) n passagem f inferior; **underprivileged** adj menos favorecido

understand [ʌndə'stænd] *irreg vt* entender, compreender ▷ *vi*: **to ~ that** acreditar que; **understandable** *adj* compreensível; **understanding** *adj* compreensivo ▷ *n* compreensão f; (*knowledge*) entendimento; (*agreement*) acordo

understatement [ʌndə'steɪtmənt] *n* (*quality*) subestimação f; (*euphemism*) eufemismo; **it's an ~ to say that ...** é uma subestimação dizer que ...

understood [ʌndə'stud] *pt, pp of* **understand** ▷ *adj* entendido; (*implied*) subentendido, implícito

undertake [ʌndə'teɪk] (*irreg: like* **take**) *vt* incumbir-se de, encarregar-se de; **to ~ to do sth** comprometer-se a fazer algo

undertaking ['ʌndəteɪkɪŋ] *n* empreendimento; (*promise*) promessa

underwater [ʌndə'wɔːtəʳ] *adv* sob a água ▷ *adj* subaquático

underwear ['ʌndəwɛəʳ] *n* roupa de baixo

underworld ['ʌndəwəːld] *n* (*of crime*) submundo

undo [ʌn'duː] (*irreg: like* **do**) *vt* (*unfasten*) desatar; (*spoil*) desmanchar

undress [ʌn'drɛs] *vi* despir-se, tirar a roupa

unearth [ʌn'əːθ] *vt* desenterrar; (*fig*) revelar

uneasy [ʌn'iːzɪ] *adj* (*person*) preocupado; (*feeling*) incômodo; (*peace, truce*) desconfortável

uneducated [ʌn'ɛdjukeɪtɪd] *adj* inculto, sem instrução, não escolarizado

unemployed [ʌnɪm'plɔɪd] *adj* desempregado ▷ *npl*: **the ~** os desempregados

unemployment [ʌnɪm'plɔɪmənt] *n* desemprego

uneven [ʌn'iːvn] *adj* desigual; (*road etc*) irregular, acidentado

unexpected [ʌnɪk'spɛktɪd] *adj* inesperado; **unexpectedly** [ʌnɪk'spɛktɪdlɪ] *adv* inesperadamente

unfair [ʌn'fɛəʳ] *adj*: **~ (to)** injusto (com); **it's ~ that ...** não é justo que ...

unfaithful [ʌn'feɪθful] *adj* infiel

unfamiliar [ʌnfə'mɪlɪəʳ] *adj* pouco familiar, desconhecido; **to be ~ with sth** não estar familiarizado com algo

unfashionable [ʌn'fæʃnəbl] *adj* fora da moda

unfasten [ʌn'fɑːsn] *vt* desatar; (*open*) abrir

unfavourable [ʌn'feɪvərəbl], (*US*) **unfavorable** *adj* desfavorável

unfinished [ʌn'fɪnɪʃt] *adj* incompleto, inacabado

unfit [ʌn'fɪt] *adj* sem preparo físico; (*incompetent*) incompetente, incapaz; **~ for work** inapto para trabalhar

unfold [ʌn'fəuld] *vt* desdobrar ▷ *vi* (*story, situation*) desdobrar-se

unfortunate [ʌn'fɔːtʃənət] *adj* infeliz; (*event, remark*) inoportuno

unfriendly [ʌn'frɛndlɪ] *adj* antipático

unhappiness [ʌn'hæpɪnɪs] *n* infelicidade f

unhappy [ʌn'hæpɪ] *adj* triste; (*unfortunate*) desventurado; (*childhood*) infeliz; (*dissatisfied*): **~ with** descontente com, insatisfeito com

unhealthy [ʌn'hɛlθɪ] *adj* insalubre; (*person*) doentio; (*fig*) anormal

unheard-of [ʌnˈhəːd-] adj insólito

unhurt [ʌnˈhəːt] adj ileso

uniform [ˈjuːnɪfɔːm] n uniforme m ▷ adj uniforme

uninhabited [ʌnɪnˈhæbɪtɪd] adj inabitado

unintentional [ʌnɪnˈtɛnʃənəl] adj involuntário, não intencional

union [ˈjuːnjən] n união f; (also: **trade ~**) sindicato (de trabalhadores) ▷ cpd sindical; **Union Jack** n bandeira britânica

unique [juːˈniːk] adj único, sem igual

unit [ˈjuːnɪt] n unidade f; (of furniture etc) seção f; (team, squad) equipe f; **kitchen ~** armário de cozinha

unite [juːˈnaɪt] vt unir ▷ vi unir-se; **united** adj unido; (effort) conjunto; **United Kingdom** n Reino Unido; **United Nations, United Nations Organization** n (Organização f das) Nações fpl Unidas; **United States, United States of America** n Estados Unidos mpl (da América)

universal [juːnɪˈvəːsl] adj universal

universe [ˈjuːnɪvəːs] n universo

university [juːnɪˈvəːsɪtɪ] n universidade f

unjust [ʌnˈdʒʌst] adj injusto

unkind [ʌnˈkaɪnd] adj maldoso; (comment etc) cruel

unknown [ʌnˈnəun] adj desconhecido

unlawful [ʌnˈlɔːful] adj ilegal

unleaded [ʌnˈlɛdɪd] adj (petrol, fuel) sem chumbo

unleash [ʌnˈliːʃ] vt (fig) desencadear

unless [ʌnˈlɛs] conj a menos que, a não ser que; **~ he comes** a menos que ele venha

unlike [ʌnˈlaɪk] adj diferente ▷ prep diferentemente de, ao contrário de

unlikely [ʌnˈlaɪklɪ] adj (not likely) improvável; (unexpected) inesperado

unlisted [ʌnˈlɪstɪd] adj (US: Tel): **an ~ number** um número que não consta na lista telefônica

unload [ʌnˈləud] vt descarregar

unlock [ʌnˈlɔk] vt destrancar

unlucky [ʌnˈlʌkɪ] adj infeliz; (object, number) de mau agouro; **to be ~** ser azarado, ter azar

unmarried [ʌnˈmærɪd] adj solteiro

unmistakable, unmistakeable [ʌnmɪsˈteɪkəbl] adj inconfundível

unnatural [ʌnˈnætʃrəl] adj antinatural, artificial; (manner) afetado; (habit) depravado

unnecessary [ʌnˈnɛsəsərɪ] adj desnecessário, inútil

UNO [ˈjuːnəu] n abbr (= United Nations Organization) ONU f

unofficial [ʌnəˈfɪʃl] adj não-oficial, informal; (strike) desautorizado

unpack [ʌnˈpæk] vi desembrulhar ▷ vt desfazer

unpleasant [ʌnˈplɛznt] adj desagradável; (person, manner) antipático

unplug [ʌnˈplʌg] vt desligar

unpopular [ʌnˈpɔpjuləʳ] adj impopular

unprecedented [ʌnˈprɛsɪdəntɪd] adj sem precedentes

unpredictable [ʌnprɪˈdɪktəbl] adj imprevisível

unravel [ʌnˈrævl] vt desemaranhar; (mystery) desvendar

unreal [ʌnˈrɪəl] adj irreal, ilusório; (extraordinary) extraordinário

unrealistic [ʌnrɪəˈlɪstɪk] adj pouco realista

unreasonable [ʌn'riːznəbl] *adj* insensato; (*demand*) absurdo

unrelated [ʌnrɪ'leɪtɪd] *adj* sem relação; (*family*) sem parentesco

unreliable [ʌnrɪ'laɪəbl] *adj* (*person*) indigno de confiança; (*machine*) incerto, perigoso

unrest [ʌn'rɛst] *n* inquietação *f*, desassossego; (*Pol*) distúrbios *mpl*

unroll [ʌn'rəul] *vt* desenrolar

unruly [ʌn'ruːlɪ] *adj* indisciplinado; (*hair*) desalinhado

unsafe [ʌn'seɪf] *adj* perigoso

unsatisfactory [ʌnsætɪs'fæktərɪ] *adj* insatisfatório

unscrew [ʌn'skruː] *vt* desparafusar

unsettled [ʌn'sɛtld] *adj* (*weather*) instável; (*person*) inquieto

unsightly [ʌn'saɪtlɪ] *adj* feio, disforme

unskilled [ʌn'skɪld] *adj* não-especializado

unstable [ʌn'steɪbl] *adj* em falso; (*government, mentally*) instável

unsteady [ʌn'stɛdɪ] *adj* (*hand, person*) trêmulo; (*ladder*) instável

unsuccessful [ʌnsək'sɛsful] *adj* (*attempt*) frustrado, vão/vã; (*writer, proposal*) sem êxito; **to be ~** (*in attempting sth*) ser mal sucedido, não conseguir; (*application*) ser recusado

unsuitable [ʌn'suːtəbl] *adj* inadequado; (*time, moment*) inconveniente

unsure [ʌn'ʃuəʳ] *adj* inseguro, incerto; **to be ~ of o.s.** não ser seguro de si

untidy [ʌn'taɪdɪ] *adj* (*room*) desarrumado, desleixado; (*appearance*) desmazelado, desalinhado

untie [ʌn'taɪ] *vt* desatar, desfazer; (*dog, prisoner*) soltar

until [ən'tɪl] *prep* até ▷ *conj* até que; **~ he comes** até que ele venha; **~ now** até agora; **~ then** até então

unused¹ [ʌn'juːzd] *adj* novo, sem uso

unused² [ʌn'juːst] *adj*: **to be ~ to sth/to doing sth** não estar acostumado com algo/a fazer algo

unusual [ʌn'juːʒuəl] *adj* (*strange*) estranho; (*rare*) incomum; (*exceptional*) extraordinário

unveil [ʌn'veɪl] *vt* desvelar, descobrir

unwanted [ʌn'wɔntɪd] *adj* não desejado, indesejável

unwell [ʌn'wɛl] *adj*: **to be ~** estar doente; **to feel ~** estar indisposto

unwilling [ʌn'wɪlɪŋ] *adj*: **to be ~ to do sth** relutar em fazer algo, não querer fazer algo

unwind [ʌn'waɪnd] *irreg vt* desenrolar ▷ *vi* (*relax*) relaxar-se

unwise [ʌn'waɪz] *adj* imprudente

unwrap [ʌn'ræp] *vt* desembrulhar

 KEYWORD

up [ʌp] *prep*: **to go/be up sth** subir algo/estar em cima de algo; **we climbed/walked up the hill** nós subimos/andamos até em cima da colina; **they live further up the street** eles moram mais adiante nesta rua

▷ *adv* **1** (*upwards, higher*) em cima, para cima; **up in the sky/the mountains** lá no céu/nas montanhas; **up there** lá em cima; **up above** em cima

2: **to be up** (*out of bed*) estar de pé; (*prices, level*) estar elevado; (*building, tent*) estar erguido

3: **up to** (*as far as*) até; **up to now** até agora

4: **to be up to** (*depending on*): **it is up to you** você é quem sabe, você decide
5: **to be up to** (*equal to*) estar à altura de; **he's not up to it** (*job, task etc*) ele não é capaz de fazê-lo; **his work is not up to the required standard** seu trabalho não atende aos padrões exigidos
6: **to be up to** (*inf: be doing*) estar fazendo (*BR*) or a fazer (*PT*); **what is he up to?** o que ele está querendo?, o que ele está tramando?
▷ *n*: **ups and downs** altos *mpl* e baixos

upbringing ['ʌpbrɪŋɪŋ] *n* educação *f*, criação *f*
update [ʌp'deɪt] *vt* atualizar, pôr em dia
upgrade [ʌp'greɪd] *vt* (*person*) promover; (*job*) melhorar; (*house*) reformar
upheaval [ʌp'hi:vl] *n* transtorno, (*unrest*) convulsão *f*
uphill [ʌp'hɪl] *adj* ladeira acima; (*fig: task*) trabalhoso, árduo ▷ *adv*: **to go ~** ir morro acima
upon [ə'pɔn] *prep* sobre
upper ['ʌpəʳ] *adj* superior, de cima ▷ *n* (*of shoe*) gáspea, parte *f* superior; **upper-class** *adj* de classe alta
upright ['ʌpraɪt] *adj* vertical; (*straight*) reto; (*fig*) honesto
uprising ['ʌpraɪzɪŋ] *n* revolta, rebelião *f*, sublevação *f*
uproar ['ʌprɔ:ʳ] *n* tumulto, algazarra
upset [*n* 'ʌpsɛt, *vt, adj* ʌp'sɛt] (*irreg: like* **set**) *n* (*to plan etc*) revés *m*, reviravolta; (*stomach upset*) indisposição *f* ▷ *vt* (*glass etc*) virar; (*plan*) perturbar; (*person: annoy*)

aborrecer ▷ *adj* aflito; (*stomach*) indisposto
upside down ['ʌpsaɪd-] *adv* de cabeça para baixo; **to turn a place ~** (*fig*) deixar um lugar de cabeça para baixo
upstairs [ʌp'stɛəz] *adv* (*be*) em cima; (*go*) lá em cima ▷ *adj* (*room*) de cima ▷ *n* andar *m* de cima
up-to-date *adj* (*person*) moderno, atualizado; (*information*) atualizado
upward ['ʌpwəd] *adj* ascendente, para cima ▷ *adv* para cima
upwards ['ʌpwədz] *adv* = **upward**
urban ['ə:bən] *adj* urbano, da cidade
urge [ə:dʒ] *n* desejo ▷ *vt*: **to ~ sb to do sth** incitar alguém a fazer algo
urgent ['ə:dʒənt] *adj* urgente; (*tone, plea*) insistente
urinal ['juərɪnl] (*Brit*) *n* (*vessel*) urinol *m*; (*building*) mictório
urine ['juərɪn] *n* urina
URL *n abbr* (= *uniform resource locator*) URL *m*
Uruguay ['juərəgwaɪ] *n* Uruguai *m*
US *n abbr* (= *United States*) EUA *mpl*
us [ʌs] *pron* nos; (*after prep*) nós; *see also* **me**
USA *n abbr* (= *United States (of America)*) EUA *mpl*
use [*n* ju:s, *vt* ju:z] *n* uso, emprego; (*usefulness*) utilidade *f* ▷ *vt* usar, utilizar; (*phrase*) empregar; **in ~** em uso; **out of ~** fora de uso; **to be of ~** ser útil; **it's no ~** (*pointless*) é inútil; (*not useful*) não serve; **to be ~d to** estar acostumado a; **she ~d to do it** ela costumava fazê-lo **use up** *vt* esgotar, consumir; (*money*) gastar; **used** [ju:zd] *adj* usado; **useful** ['ju:sful] *adj* útil; **useless** ['ju:slɪs] *adj* inútil; (*person*) incapaz; **user**

['ju:zə'] *n* usuário(-a) (*BR*), utente *m/f* (*PT*); **user-friendly** *adj* de fácil utilização

usual ['ju:ʒuəl] *adj* usual, habitual; **as ~** como de hábito, como sempre; **usually** ['ju:ʒuəlɪ] *adv* normalmente

utensil [ju:'tɛnsl] *n* utensílio

utmost ['ʌtməust] *adj* maior ▷ *n*: **to do one's ~** fazer todo o possível

utter ['ʌtə'] *adj* total ▷ *vt* (*sounds*) emitir; (*words*) proferir, pronunciar; **utterly** *adv* completamente, totalmente

U-turn *n* retorno

V, v [vi:] *n* V, v *m*

vacancy ['veɪkənsɪ] *n* (*Brit: job*) vaga; (*room*) quarto livre

vacant ['veɪkənt] *adj* desocupado, livre; (*expression*) distraído

vacate [və'keɪt] *vt* (*house*) desocupar; (*job*) deixar

vacation [və'keɪʃən] (*esp US*) *n* férias *fpl*

vacuum ['vækjum] *n* vácuo *m*; **vacuum cleaner** *n* aspirador *m* de pó

vagina [və'dʒaɪnə] *n* vagina

vague [veɪg] *adj* vago; (*blurred: memory*) fraco

vain [veɪn] *adj* vaidoso; (*useless*) vão/vã, inútil; **in ~** em vão

valentine ['væləntaɪn] *n* (*also:* **~ card**) cartão *m* do Dia dos Namorados; (*person*) namorado

valid ['vælɪd] *adj* válido

valley ['vælɪ] *n* vale *m*

valuable ['væljuəbl] *adj* (*jewel*) de valor; (*time*) valioso; (*help*) precioso; **valuables** *npl* objetos *mpl* de valor

value ['vælju:] *n* valor *m*; (*importance*) importância ▷ *vt* (*fix price of*) avaliar; (*appreciate*) valorizar, estimar; **values** *npl* (*principles*) valores *mpl*

valve [vælv] *n* válvula

van [væn] *n* (*Aut*) camionete *f* (*BR*), camioneta (*PT*)

vandal ['vændl] *n* vândalo(-a); **vandalize** *vt* destruir, depredar

vanilla [və'nɪlə] *n* baunilha

vanish ['vænɪʃ] *vi* desaparecer, sumir

vanity ['vænɪtɪ] *n* vaidade *f*

vapour ['veɪpə'], (*US*) **vapor** *n* vapor *m*

variety [və'raɪətɪ] *n* variedade *f*, diversidade *f*; (*type, quantity*) variedade

various ['vɛərɪəs] *adj* vários(-as), diversos(-as); (*several*) vários(-as)

varnish ['vɑːnɪʃ] *n* verniz *m*; (*nail varnish*) esmalte *m* ▷ *vt* envernizar; (*nails*) pintar (com esmalte)

vary ['vɛərɪ] *vt* mudar ▷ *vi* variar; (*become different*) **to ~ with** *or* **according to** variar de acordo com

vase [vɑːz] *n* vaso

vast [vɑːst] *adj* enorme

VAT [væt] (*Brit*) *n abbr* (= *value added tax*) ≈ ICM *m* (*BR*), IVA *m* (*PT*)

vault [vɔːlt] *n* (*of roof*) abóbada; (*tomb*) sepulcro; (*in bank*) caixa-forte *f* ▷ *vt* (*also*: **~ over**) saltar (por cima de)

VCR *n abbr* = **video cassette recorder**

VDU *n abbr* = **visual display unit**

veal [viːl] *n* carne *f* de vitela

vegan ['viːgən] *n* vegetalista *m/f*

vegetable ['vɛdʒtəbl] *n* (*Bot*) vegetal *m*; (*edible plant*) legume *m*, hortaliça ▷ *adj* vegetal

vegetarian [vɛdʒɪ'tɛərɪən] *adj, n* vegetariano(-a)

vehicle ['viːɪkl] *n* veículo

veil [veɪl] *n* véu *m* ▷ *vt* velar

vein [veɪn] *n* veia; (*of ore etc*) filão *m*; (*on leaf*) nervura

velvet ['vɛlvɪt] *n* veludo ▷ *adj* aveludado

vending machine ['vɛndɪŋ-] *n* vendedor *m* automático

Venezuela [vɛnɛ'zweɪlə] *n* Venezuela

vengeance ['vɛndʒəns] *n* vingança; **with a ~** (*fig*) para valer

venison ['vɛnɪsn] *n* carne *f* de veado

venom ['vɛnəm] *n* veneno; (*bitterness*) malevolência

vent [vɛnt] *n* (*opening, in jacket*) abertura; (*also*: **air ~**) respiradouro ▷ *vt* (*fig: feelings*) desabafar, descarregar

venture ['vɛntʃə'] *n* empreendimento ▷ *vt* (*opinion*) arriscar ▷ *vi* arriscar-se; **business ~** empreendimento comercial

venue ['vɛnjuː] *n* local *m*

verb [vəːb] *n* verbo

verdict ['vəːdɪkt] *n* veredicto, decisão *f*; (*fig*) opinião *f*, parecer *m*

verge [vəːdʒ] *n* beira, margem *f*; (*on road*) acostamento (*BR*), berma (*PT*); **"soft ~s"** (*Brit: Aut*) "acostamento mole"; **to be on the ~ of doing sth** estar a ponto *or* à beira de fazer algo **verge on** *vt fus* beirar em

versatile ['vəːsətaɪl] *adj* (*person*) versátil; (*machine, tool etc*) polivalente

verse [vəːs] *n* verso, poesia; (*stanza*)

estrofe f; (in bible) versículo
version ['vəːʃən] n versão f
versus ['vəːsəs] prep contra, versus
vertical ['vəːtɪkl] adj vertical
very ['vɛrɪ] adv muito ▷ adj: **the ~ book which** o mesmo livro que; **the ~ last** o último (de todos), bem o último; **at the ~ least** no mínimo; **~ much** muitíssimo
vessel ['vɛsl] n (Naut) navio, barco; (container) vaso, vasilha
vest [vɛst] n (Brit) camiseta (BR), camisola interior (PT); (US: waistcoat) colete m
vet [vɛt] n abbr (= veterinary surgeon) veterinário(-a) ▷ vt examinar
veteran ['vɛtərn] n (also: **war ~**) veterano de guerra
veto ['viːtəu] (pl **vetoes**) n veto ▷ vt vetar
via ['vaɪə] prep por, via
vibrate [vaɪ'breɪt] vi vibrar
vicar ['vɪkəʳ] n vigário
vice [vaɪs] n (evil) vício; (Tech) torno mecânico
vice- [vaɪs] prefix vice-
vice versa ['vaɪsɪ'vəːsə] adv vice-versa
vicinity [vɪ'sɪnɪtɪ] n proximidade f; **in the ~ of** nas proximidades de
vicious ['vɪʃəs] adj violento; (cruel) cruel
victim ['vɪktɪm] n vítima f
victor ['vɪktəʳ] n vencedor(a) m/f
Victorian [vɪk'tɔːrɪən] adj vitoriano
victory ['vɪktərɪ] n vitória
video ['vɪdɪəu] n (video film) vídeo; (also: **~ cassette**) videocassete m; (also: **~ cassette recorder**) videocassete m; **video camera** n filmadora; **videophone** n videofone m
Vienna [vɪ'ɛnə] n Viena
Vietnam ['vjɛt'næm] n Vietnã m

(BR), Vietname m (PT);
Vietnamese [vjɛtnə'miːz] adj vietnamita ▷ n inv vietnamita m/f; (Ling) vietnamita m
view [vjuː] n vista; (outlook) perspectiva; (opinion) opinião f, parecer m ▷ vt olhar; **in full ~ (of)** à plena vista (de); **in my ~** na minha opinião; **in ~ of the weather/the fact that** em vista do tempo/do fato de que; **viewer** n telespectador(a) m/f; **viewpoint** n ponto de vista; (place) lugar m
vigorous ['vɪgərəs] adj vigoroso; (plant) vigoso
vile [vaɪl] adj vil, infame; (smell) repugnante, repulsivo; (temper) violento
villa ['vɪlə] n (country house) casa de campo; (suburban house) vila, quinta
village ['vɪlɪdʒ] n aldeia, povoado; **villager** n aldeão/aldeã m/f
villain ['vɪlən] n (scoundrel) patife m; (Brit: in novel etc) vilão m; (criminal) marginal m/f
vine [vaɪn] n planta trepadeira
vinegar ['vɪnɪgəʳ] n vinagre m
vineyard ['vɪnjɑːd] n vinha, vinhedo
vintage ['vɪntɪdʒ] n vindima; (year) safra, colheita ▷ cpd (comedy) de época; (performance) clássico; **the 1970 ~** a safra de 1970
viola [vɪ'əulə] n viola
violate ['vaɪəleɪt] vt violar
violence ['vaɪələns] n violência; (strength) força
violent ['vaɪələnt] adj violento; (intense) intenso
violet ['vaɪələt] adj violeta ▷ n violeta
violin [vaɪə'lɪn] n violino
VIP n abbr (= very important person)

V

VIP m/f

virgin ['vəːdʒɪn] n virgem m/f ▷ adj virgem

Virgo ['vəːgəu] n Virgem f

virtually ['vəːtjuəlɪ] adv praticamente

virtual reality ['vəːtjuəl-] n (Comput) realidade f virtual

virtue ['vəːtjuː] n virtude f; (advantage) vantagem f; **by ~ of** em virtude de

virus ['vaɪərəs] n vírus m

visa ['viːzə] n visto

visible ['vɪzəbl] adj visível

vision ['vɪʒən] n (sight) vista, visão f; (foresight, in dream) visão f

visit ['vɪzɪt] n visita ▷ vt (person: US: also: **~ with**) visitar, fazer uma visita a; (place) ir a, ir conhecer; **visiting hours** npl horário de visita; **visitor** n visitante m/f; (to one's house) visita; (tourist) turista m/f

visual ['vɪzjuəl] adj visual; **visualize** vt visualizar

vital ['vaɪtl] adj essencial, indispensável; (important) de importância vital; (crucial) crucial; (person) vivo; (of life) vital

vitamin ['vɪtəmɪn] n vitamina

vivid ['vɪvɪd] adj (account) vívido; (light) claro, brilhante; (imagination, colour) vivo

V-neck n (also: **~ jumper, ~ pullover**) suéter f com decote em V

vocabulary [vəu'kæbjulərɪ] n vocabulário

vocal ['vəukl] adj vocal; (noisy) clamoroso; (articulate) claro, eloquente

vodka ['vɔdkə] n vodca

vogue [vəug] n voga, moda; **to be in ~** estar na moda

voice [vɔɪs] n voz f ▷ vt expressar;

voice mail n (system) correio m de voz; (device) caixa f postal

void [vɔɪd] n vazio; (hole) oco ▷ adj nulo; (empty): **~ of** destituído de

volatile ['vɔlətaɪl] adj volátil; (situation, person) imprevisível

volcano [vɔl'keɪnəu] (pl **volcanoes**) n vulcão m

volt [vəult] n volt m

volume ['vɔljuːm] n volume m; (of tank) capacidade f

voluntarily ['vɔləntrɪlɪ] adv livremente, voluntariamente

voluntary ['vɔləntərɪ] adj voluntário; (unpaid) (a título) gratuito

volunteer [vɔlən'tɪər] n voluntário(-a) ▷ vt oferecer voluntariamente ▷ vi (Mil) alistar-se voluntariamente; **to ~ to do** oferecer-se voluntariamente para fazer

vomit ['vɔmɪt] n vômito ▷ vt, vi vomitar

vote [vəut] n voto; (votes cast) votação f; (right to vote) direito de votar ▷ vt: **to be ~d chairman** etc ser eleito presidente etc; (propose): **to ~ that** propor que; (in election) votar ▷ vi votar; **voter** n votante m/f, eleitor(a) m/f

voucher ['vautʃər] n (also: **luncheon ~**) vale-refeição m; (with petrol etc) vale m; (gift voucher) vale m para presente

vow [vau] n voto ▷ vt: **to ~ to do/ that** prometer solenemente fazer/ que

vowel ['vauəl] n vogal f

voyage ['vɔɪɪdʒ] n viagem f

vulgar ['vʌlgər] adj grosseiro, ordinário; (in bad taste) vulgar, baixo

vulture ['vʌltʃər] n abutre m, urubu m

W

W, w ['dʌblju:] n W, w m

wade [weɪd] vi: **to ~ through** andar em; (fig: a book) ler com dificuldade

wafer ['weɪfə[r]] n (biscuit) bolacha

waffle ['wɔfl] n (Culin) waffle m; (empty talk) lengalenga ▷ vi encher linguiça

wag [wæg] vt (tail) sacudir; (finger) menear ▷ vi abanar

wage [weɪdʒ] n (also: ~s) salário, ordenado ▷ vt: **to ~ war** empreender or fazer guerra

waggon, wagon ['wægən] n (horse-drawn) carroça; (Brit: Rail) vagão m

wail [weɪl] n lamento, gemido ▷ vi lamentar-se, gemer; (siren) tocar

waist [weɪst] n cintura; **waistcoat** n colete m

wait [weɪt] n espera ▷ vi esperar; **I can't ~ to** (fig) estou morrendo de vontade de; **to ~ for sb/sth**
esperar por alguém/algo **wait behind** vi ficar para trás **wait on** vt fus servir; **waiter** n garçom m (BR), empregado (PT); **waiting list** n lista de espera; **waiting room** n sala de espera; **waitress** n garçonete f (BR), empregada (PT)

waive [weɪv] vt abrir mão de

wake [weɪk] (pt **woke**, pp **woken**) vt (also: **~ up**) acordar ▷ vi acordar ▷ n (for dead person) velório; (Naut) esteira

Wales [weɪlz] n País m de Gales

walk [wɔ:k] n passeio; (hike) excursão f a pé, caminhada; (gait) passo, modo de andar; (in park etc) alameda, passeio ▷ vi andar; (for pleasure, exercise) passear ▷ vt (distance) percorrer a pé, andar; (dog) levar para passear; **it's 10 minutes' ~ from here** daqui são 10 minutos a pé; **people from all ~s of life** pessoas de todos os níveis **walk out** vi sair; (audience) retirar-se; (strike) entrar em greve **walk out on** vt fus abandonar; **walkie-talkie** n transmissor-receptor m portátil, walkie-talkie m; **walking** n o andar; **walking shoes** npl sapatos mpl de caminhada; **walking stick** n bengala; **walkway** n passeio, passadiço

wall [wɔ:l] n parede f; (exterior) muro; (city wall etc) muralha

wallet ['wɔlɪt] n carteira

wallpaper ['wɔ:lpeɪpə[r]] n papel m de parede ▷ vt colocar papel de parede em

walnut ['wɔ:lnʌt] n noz f; (tree, wood) nogueira

walrus ['wɔ:lrəs] (pl **walrus** or **walruses**) n morsa, vaca marinha

waltz [wɔ:lts] n valsa ▷ vi valsar

w

wand [wɒnd] n (also: **magic ~**) varinha de condão

wander ['wɒndəʳ] vi (person) vagar, perambular; (thoughts) divagar ▷ vt perambular

want [wɒnt] vt querer; (demand) exigir; (need) precisar de, necessitar; **wanted** adj (criminal etc) procurado (pela polícia); **"cook wanted"** (in advertisement) "precisa-se cozinheiro"

war [wɔːʳ] n guerra; **to make ~ (on)** fazer guerra (contra)

ward [wɔːd] n (in hospital) ala; (Pol) distrito eleitoral; (Law: child) tutelado(-a), pupilo(-a) **ward off** vt desviar, aparar; (attack) repelir

warden ['wɔːdn] n (Brit: of institution) diretor(a) m/f; (of park, game reserve) administrador(a) m/f; (Brit: also: **traffic ~**) guarda m/f

wardrobe ['wɔːdrəub] n guarda-roupa m

warehouse ['wɛəhaus] n armazém m, depósito

warfare ['wɔːfɛəʳ] n guerra, combate m

warhead ['wɔːhɛd] n ogiva

warm [wɔːm] adj quente; (thanks, welcome) caloroso; **it's ~** está quente; **I'm ~** estou com calor **warm up** vi esquentar ▷ vt esquentar; **warmly** adv calorosamente; **warmth** n calor m; (friendliness) calor humano

warn [wɔːn] vt prevenir, avisar; **to ~ sb that/of/(not) not to do** prevenir alguém de que/de/para (não) fazer

warning ['wɔːnɪŋ] n advertência; (in writing) aviso; (signal) sinal m; (without notice) sem aviso prévio, sem avisar

warrant ['wɔrnt] n (voucher) comprovante m; (Law: to arrest) mandado de prisão; (: to search) mandado de busca; **warranty** n garantia

warrior ['wɒrɪəʳ] n guerreiro(-a)

Warsaw ['wɔːsɔː] n Varsóvia

warship ['wɔːʃɪp] n navio de guerra

wart [wɔːt] n verruga

wartime ['wɔːtaɪm] n: **in ~** em tempo de guerra

wary ['wɛərɪ] adj cauteloso, precavido

was [wɒz] pt of **be**

wash [wɒʃ] vt lavar ▷ vi lavar-se; (sea etc): **to ~ over/against sth** bater/chocar-se contra algo ▷ n (clothes etc) lavagem f; (of ship) esteira; **to have a ~** lavar-se **wash away** vt (stain) tirar ao lavar; (subj: river etc) levar, arrastar **wash off** vt tirar lavando ▷ vi sair ao lavar **wash up** vi (Brit) lavar a louça; (US) lavar-se; **washbasin** n pia (BR), lavatório (PT); **washing** (Brit) n (dirty) roupa suja; (clean) roupa lavada; **washing machine** n máquina de lavar roupa, lavadora; **washing powder** (Brit) n sabão m em pó; **washing-up** n: **to do the washing-up** lavar a louça; **washing-up liquid** n detergente m; **washroom** (US) n banheiro (BR), casa de banho (PT)

wasn't ['wɒznt] = **was not**

wasp [wɒsp] n vespa

waste [weɪst] n desperdício, esbanjamento; (of time) perda; (also: **household ~**) detritos mpl domésticos; (rubbish) lixo ▷ adj (material) de refugo; (left over) de sobra; (land) baldio ▷ vt (squander) esbanjar, desperdiçar; (time, opportunity) perder; **wastes** npl ermos mpl; **to lay ~** devastar

waste away vi definhar
watch [wɔtʃ] n (clock) relógio; (also: **wrist~**) relógio de pulso; (act of watching) vigia; (guard: Mil) sentinela; (Naut: spell of duty) quarto ▷ vt (look at) observar, olhar; (programme, match) assistir a; (television) ver; (spy on, guard) vigiar; (be careful of) tomar cuidado com ▷ vi ver, olhar; (keep guard) montar guarda **watch out** vi ter cuidado; **watchdog** n cão m de guarda; (fig) vigia m/f
water ['wɔːtə⁺] n água ▷ vt (plant) regar ▷ vi (eyes) lacrimejar; (mouth) salivar; **in British ~s** nas águas territoriais britânicas **water down** vt (milk) aguar; (fig) diluir; **watercolour**, (US) **watercolor** n aquarela; **waterfall** n cascata, cachoeira; **watering can** n regador m; **watermelon** n melancia; **waterproof** adj impermeável; **water-skiing** n esqui m aquático
watt [wɔt] n watt m
wave [weɪv] n onda; (of hand) aceno, sinal m; (in hair) onda, ondulação f ▷ vi acenar com a mão; (flag, grass, branches) tremular ▷ vt (hand) acenar; (handkerchief) acenar com; (weapon) brandir; **wavelength** n comprimento de onda; **to be on the same wavelength as** ter os mesmos gostos e atitudes que
waver ['weɪvə⁺] vi vacilar; (voice, eyes, love) hesitar
wavy ['weɪvɪ] adj (hair) ondulado; (line) ondulante
wax [wæks] n cera ▷ vt encerar; (car) polir ▷ vi (moon) crescer
way [weɪ] n caminho; (distance) percurso; (direction) direção f,

sentido; (manner) maneira, modo; (habit) costume m; **which ~? — this ~** por onde? — por aqui; **on the ~ (to)** a caminho (de); **to be on one's ~** estar a caminho; **to be in the ~** atrapalhar; **to go out of one's ~ to do sth** dar-se ao trabalho de fazer algo; **to lose one's ~** perder-se; **to be under ~** estar em andamento; **in a ~** de certo modo, até certo ponto; **in some ~s** a certos respeitos; **by the ~** a propósito; **"~ in"** (Brit) "entrada"; **"~ out"** (Brit) "saída"; **the ~ back** o caminho de volta; **"give ~"** (Brit: Aut) "dê a preferência"; **no ~!** (inf) de jeito nenhum!
WC ['dʌblju'siː] n abbr (= water closet) privada
we [wiː] pl pron nós
weak [wiːk] adj fraco, débil; (morally, currency) fraco; (excuse) pouco convincente; (tea) aguado, ralo; **weaken** vi enfraquecer(-se); (give way) ceder; (influence, power) diminuir ▷ vt enfraquecer; **weakness** n fraqueza; (fault) ponto fraco; **to have a weakness for** ter uma queda por
wealth [wɛlθ] n riqueza; (of details) abundância; **wealthy** adj rico, abastado; (country) rico
weapon ['wɛpən] n arma; **~s of mass destruction** armas de destruição em massa
wear [wɛə⁺] (pt **wore**, pp **worn**) n (use) uso; (deterioration through use) desgaste m; (clothing): **baby/ sports ~** roupa infantil/de esporte ▷ vt (clothes) usar; (shoes) usar, calçar; (put on) vestir; (damage: through use) desgastar ▷ vi (last) durar; (rub through etc) gastar-se; **town/evening ~** traje m de

W

passeio/de gala **wear away** vt gastar ▷ vi desgastar-se **wear down** vt gastar; (strength) esgotar **wear off** vi (pain etc) passar **wear out** vt desgastar; (person, strength) esgotar

weary ['wɪərɪ] adj cansado; (dispirited) deprimido ▷ vi: **to ~ of** cansar-se de

weasel ['wi:zl] n (Zool) doninha

weather ['wɛðəʳ] n tempo ▷ vt (storm, crisis) resistir a; **under the ~** (fig: ill) doente; **weather forecast** n previsão f do tempo

weave [wi:v] (pt, pp **wove** or **woven**) vt tecer

web [wɛb] n (of spider) teia; (on foot) membrana; (network) rede f; **the (World Wide) W~** a (World Wide) Web; **web address** n endereço web; **webcam** ['wɛbkæm] n webcam f; **weblog** n weblog m; **web page** n página (da) web; **website** ['wɛbsaɪt] n site m, website m

wed [wɛd] (pt, pp **wedded**) vt casar ▷ vi casar-se

we'd [wi:d] = **we had**; **we would**

wedding ['wɛdɪŋ] n casamento, núpcias fpl; **wedding dress** n vestido de noiva; **wedding ring** n anel m or aliança de casamento

wedge [wɛdʒ] n (of wood etc) cunha, calço; (of cake) fatia ▷ vt (pack tightly) apinhar; (door) pôr calço em

Wednesday ['wɛdnzdɪ] n quarta-feira

wee [wi:] (Scotland) adj pequeno, pequenino

weed [wi:d] n erva daninha ▷ vt capinar; **weedkiller** n herbicida m

week [wi:k] n semana; **a ~ today** daqui a uma semana; **a ~ on Tuesday** sem ser essa terça-feira, a outra; **every other ~** uma semana sim, uma semana não; **weekday** n dia m de semana; (Comm) dia útil; **weekend** n fim m de semana; **weekly** adv semanalmente ▷ adj semanal ▷ n semanário

weep [wi:p] (pt, pp **wept**) vi (person) chorar

weigh [weɪ] vt, vi pesar; **to ~ anchor** levantar ferro **weigh down** vt sobrecarregar; (fig: with worry) deprimir, acabrunhar **weigh up** vt ponderar, avaliar

weight [weɪt] n peso; **to lose/put on ~** emagrecer/engordar

weird [wɪəd] adj esquisito, estranho

welcome ['wɛlkəm] adj bem-vindo ▷ n acolhimento, recepção f ▷ vt dar as boas-vindas a; (be glad of) saudar; **you're ~** (after thanks) de nada

weld [wɛld] n solda ▷ vt soldar, unir

welfare ['wɛlfɛəʳ] n bem-estar m; (social aid) assistência social; **welfare state** n país auto-financiador da sua assistência social

well [wɛl] n poço ▷ adv bem ▷ adj: **to be ~** estar bem (de saúde) ▷ excl bem!, então!; **as ~** também; **as ~ as** assim como; **~ done!** muito bem!; **get ~ soon!** melhoras!; **to do ~** ir or sair-se bem; (business) ir bem **well up** vi brotar

we'll [wi:l] = **we will**; **we shall**

well: **well-behaved** [-bɪ'heɪvd] adj bem comportado; **well-built** adj robusto; (house) bem construído; **well-dressed** [-drɛst] adj bem vestido

wellingtons ['wɛlɪŋtənz] n (also: **wellington boots**) botas de borracha até os joelhos

well-known adj conhecido

well-off adj próspero, rico

Welsh [wɛlʃ] *adj* galês/galesa
▷ *n* (Ling) galês *m*; **the Welsh** *npl*
(*people*) os galeses; **Welshman**
irreg n galês *m*; **Welshwoman** *irreg*
n galesa

went [wɛnt] *pt of* **go**

wept [wɛpt] *pt, pp of* **weep**

were [wəːʳ] *pt of* **be**

we're [wɪəʳ] = **we are**

weren't [wəːnt] = **were not**

west [wɛst] *n* oeste *m* ▷ *adj*
ocidental, do oeste ▷ *adv* para o
oeste *or* ao oeste; **the W~** (*Pol*) o
Oeste, o Ocidente; **western** *adj*
ocidental ▷ *n* (*Cinema*) western *m*,
bangue-bangue (*BR*) (*inf*); **West
Indian** *adj, n* antilhano(-a); **West
Indies** *npl* Antilhas *fpl*

wet [wɛt] *adj* molhado; (*damp*)
úmido; (*wet through*) encharcado;
(*rainy*) chuvoso ▷ *n* (*Brit: Pol*)
político de tendência moderada;
to get ~ molhar-se; **"~ paint"**
"tinta fresca"; **wetsuit** *n* roupa de
mergulho

we've [wiːv] = **we have**

whale [weɪl] *n* (*Zool*) baleia

wharf [wɔːf] (*pl* **wharves**) *n* cais *m inv*

🅞 KEYWORD

what [wɔt] *adj* **1** (*in direct/indirect
questions*) que, qual; **what size is
it?** que tamanho é este?; **what
colour/shape is it?** qual é a cor/
o formato?; **he asked me what
books I needed** ele me perguntou
de quais os livros eu precisava
2 (*in exclamations*) quê!, como!;
what a mess! que bagunça!
▷ *pron* **1** (*interrogative*) que, o que;
what are you doing? o que é que
você está fazendo?; **what is it
called?** como se chama?; **what**

about me? e eu?; **what about
doing ...?** que tal fazer ...?
2 (*relative*) o que; **I saw what you
did/was on the table** eu vi o que
você fez/estava na mesa; **he asked
me what she had said** ele me
perguntou o que ela tinha dito
▷ *excl* (*disbelieving*): **what, no
coffee?** ué, não tem café?

whatever [wɔtˈɛvəʳ] *adj*: **~ book
you choose** qualquer livro que
você escolha ▷ *pron*: **do ~ is
necessary/you want** faça tudo o
que for preciso/o que você quiser;
~ happens aconteça o que
acontecer; **no reason ~** *or*
whatsoever nenhuma razão seja
qual for *or* em absoluto; **nothing ~**
nada em absoluto

whatsoever [wɔtsəuˈɛvəʳ] *adj*
= **whatever**

wheat [wiːt] *n* trigo

wheel [wiːl] *n* roda; (*also*: **steering
~**) volante *m*; (*Naut*) roda do leme
▷ *vt* (*pram etc*) empurrar ▷ *vi* (*birds*)
dar voltas; (*also*: **~ round**) girar, dar
voltas, virar-se; **wheelbarrow** *n*
carrinho de mão; **wheelchair** *n*
cadeira de rodas; **wheel clamp** *n*
(*Aut*) grampo com que se imobiliza
carros estacionados ilegalmente

wheeze [wiːz] *vi* respirar
ruidosamente

🅞 KEYWORD

when [wɛn] *adv* quando
▷ *conj* **1** (*at, during, after the time that*)
quando; **when you've read it, tell
me what you think** depois que
você tiver lido isto, diga-me o que
acha; **that was when I needed
you** foi quando eu precisei de você

W

2 (*on, at which*) quando, em que; **on the day when I met him** no dia em que o conheci; **one day when it was raining** um dia quando estava chovendo

3 (*whereas*) ao passo que; **you said I was wrong when in fact I was right** você disse que eu estava errado quando, na verdade, eu estava certo

whenever [wɛn'ɛvə˞] *conj* quando, quando quer que; (*every time that*) sempre que ▷ *adv* quando você quiser

where [wɛə˞] *adv* onde ▷ *conj* onde, aonde; **this is ~ ...** aqui é onde ...; **whereabouts** ['wɛərəbauts] *adv* (por) onde ▷ *n*: **nobody knows his whereabouts** ninguém sabe o seu paradeiro; **whereas** [wɛər'æz] *conj* uma vez que, ao passo que; **whereby** *adv* (*formal*) pelo qual (*or* pela qual *etc*); **wherever** [wɛər'ɛvə˞] *conj* onde quer que ▷ *adv* (*interrogative*) onde?

whether ['wɛðə˞] *conj* se; **I don't know ~ to accept or not** não sei se aceito ou não; **~ you go or not** quer você vá quer não; **it's doubtful ~ ...** não é certo que ...

 KEYWORD

which [wɪtʃ] *adj* **1** (*interrogative: direct, indirect*) que, qual; **which picture do you want?** que quadro você quer?; **which books are yours?** quais são os seus livros?; **which one?** qual?

2: **in which case** em cujo caso; **by which time** momento em que ▷ *pron* **1** (*interrogative*) qual; **which (of these) are yours?** quais

(destes) são seus?

2 (*relative*) que, o que, o qual *etc*; **the apple which you ate** a maçã que você comeu; **the chair on which you are sitting** a cadeira na qual você está sentado; **he said he knew, which is true** ele disse que sabia, o que é verdade; **after which** depois do que

whichever [wɪtʃ'ɛvə˞] *adj*: **take ~ book you prefer** pegue o livro que preferir; **~ book you take** qualquer livro que você pegue

while [waɪl] *n* tempo, momento ▷ *conj* enquanto, ao mesmo tempo que; (*as long as*) contanto que; (*although*) embora; **for a ~** durante algum tempo **while away** *vt* (*time*) encher

whim [wɪm] *n* capricho, veneta

whine [waɪn] *n* (*of pain*) gemido; (*of engine, siren*) zunido ▷ *vi* gemer; zunir; (*fig*) lamuriar-se

whip [wɪp] *n* açoite *m*; (*for riding*) chicote *m*; (*Pol*) líder *m/f* da bancada ▷ *vt* chicotear; (*snatch*) apanhar de repente; (*cream, eggs*) bater; (*move quickly*): **to ~ sth out/off/away** *etc* arrancar algo; **whipped cream** [wɪpt-] *n* creme *m* chantilly

whirl [wə:l] *vt* fazer girar ▷ *vi* (*dancers*) rodopiar; (*leaves, water etc*) redemoinhar

whisk [wɪsk] *n* (*Culin*) batedeira ▷ *vt* bater; **to ~ sb away** *or* **off** levar alguém rapidamente

whiskers ['wɪskəz] *npl* (*of animal*) bigodes *mpl*; (*of man*) suíças *fpl*

whisky ['wɪskɪ], (*US, Ireland*) **whiskey** *n* uísque *m* (*BR*), whisky *m* (*PT*)

whisper ['wɪspə˞] *n* sussurro,

murmúrio ▷ *vt, vi* sussurrar
whistle ['wɪsl] *n* (*sound*) assobio;
(*object*) apito ▷ *vt, vi* assobiar
white [waɪt] *adj* branco; (*pale*)
pálido ▷ *n* branco; (*of egg*) clara;
white coffee *n* café *m* com leite;
White House *n* ver nota

○ **WHITE HOUSE**
○
○ A Casa Branca **White House**
○ é um grande edifício branco
○ situado em Washington D.C.
○ onde reside o presidente dos
○ Estados Unidos. Por extensão,
○ o termo se refere também ao
○ poder executivo americano.

whitewash ['waɪtwɔʃ] *n* (*paint*)
cal *f* ▷ *vt* caiar; (*fig*) encobrir
whiting ['waɪtɪŋ] *n inv*
pescada-marlonga
Whitsun ['wɪtsn] *n* Pentecostes *m*
whizz [wɪz] *vi*: **to ~ past** or **by**
passar a toda velocidade

 KEYWORD

who [huː] *pron* **1** (*interrogative*)
quem?; **who is it?** quem é?
2 (*relative*) que, o qual *etc*, quem;
**my cousin, who lives in New
York** meu primo que mora em
Nova Iorque; **the man/woman
who spoke to me** o homem/a
mulher que falou comigo

whole [həʊl] *adj* (*complete*)
todo, inteiro; (*not broken*) intacto
▷ *n* (*all*): **the ~ of the time**
o tempo todo; (*entire unit*)
conjunto; **on the ~**, **as a ~** como
um todo, no conjunto; **wholemeal**
(*Brit*) *adj* integral; **wholesale** *n*

venda por atacado ▷ *adj* por
atacado; (*destruction*) em grande
escala ▷ *adv* por atacado;
wholewheat *adj* = **wholemeal**;
wholly ['həʊlɪ] *adv* totalmente,
completamente

 KEYWORD

whom [huːm] *pron* **1** (*interrogative*)
quem?; **to whom did you give it?**
para quem você deu isto?
2 (*relative*) que, quem; **the man
whom I saw/to whom I spoke**
o homem que eu vi/com quem eu
falei

whore [hɔːr] (*inf: pej*) *n* puta

○ KEYWORD

whose [huːz] *adj* **1** (*possessive:
interrogative*): **whose book is this?**,
whose is this book? de quem é
este livro?; **I don't know whose it
is** eu não sei de quem é isto
2 (*possessive: relative*): **the man
whose son you rescued** o homem
cujo filho você salvou; **the woman
whose car was stolen** a mulher
de quem o carro foi roubado
▷ *pron* de quem

 KEYWORD

why [waɪ] *adv* por que (BR), porque
(PT); (*at end of sentence*) por quê
(BR), porquê (PT)
▷ *conj* por que; **that's not why I'm
here** não é por isso que estou aqui;
the reason why a razão por que
▷ *excl* (*expressing surprise, shock,
annoyance*) ora essa!; (*explaining*)
bem!; **why, it's you!** ora, é você!

W

wicked ['wɪkɪd] *adj* perverso;
(*smile*) malicioso

wicket ['wɪkɪt] *n* (*Cricket*) arco

wide [waɪd] *adj* largo; (*area,
publicity, knowledge*) amplo ▷ *adv*:
to open ~ abrir totalmente; **to
shoot ~** atirar longe do alvo;
widely *adv* extremamente;
(*travelled, spaced*) muito; (*believed,
known*) ampliamente; **widen** *vt*
alargar; (*one's experience*) aumentar
▷ *vi* alargar-se; **wide open** *adj*
(*eyes*) arregalado; (*door*)
escancarado; **widespread** *adj*
(*belief etc*) difundido, comum

widow ['wɪdəu] *n* viúva; **widower**
n viúvo

width [wɪdθ] *n* largura

wield [wi:ld] *vt* (*sword*) brandir,
empunhar; (*power*) exercer

wife [waɪf] (*pl* **wives**) *n* mulher *f*,
esposa

Wi-Fi ['waɪfaɪ] *n* Wi-Fi *m*

wig [wɪg] *n* peruca

wild [waɪld] *adj* (*animal*) selvagem;
(*plant*) silvestre; (*rough*) violento,
furioso; (*idea*) disparatado,
extravagante; (*person*) insensato;
wilderness ['wɪldənɪs] *n* ermo;
wildlife *n* animais *mpl* (e plantas
fpl) selvagens; **wildly** *adv* (*behave*)
freneticamente; (*hit, guess*)
irrefletidamente; (*happy*)
extremamente

 KEYWORD

will [wɪl] (*vt*) (*pt, pp* **willed**) *aux vb*
1 (*forming future tense*): **I will finish
it tomorrow** vou acabar isto
amanhã; **I will have finished it by
tomorrow** até amanhã eu terei
terminado isto; **will you do it? —
yes I will/no I won't** você vai fazer

isto? — sim, vou/não eu não vou
2 (*in conjectures, predictions*): **he will
come** ele virá; **he will** *or* **he'll be
there by now** nesta altura ele está
lá; **that will be the postman** deve
ser o carteiro; **this medicine will/
won't help you** este remédio vai/
não vai fazer efeito em você
3 (*in commands, requests, offers*):
will you be quiet! fique quieto,
por favor!; **will you come?** você
vem?; **will you help me?** você pode
me ajudar?; **will you have a cup of
tea?** você vai querer uma xícara de
chá *or* um chá?; **I won't put up
with it** eu não vou tolerar isto
▷ *vt*: **to will sb to do sth** desejar
que alguém faça algo; **he willed
himself to go on** reuniu grande
força de vontade para continuar
▷ *n* (*volition*) vontade *f*; (*testament*)
testamento

willing ['wɪlɪŋ] *adj* disposto,
pronto; (*enthusiastic*)
entusiasmado; **willingly** *adv* de
bom grado, de boa vontade

willow ['wɪləu] *n* salgueiro

willpower ['wɪlpauəʳ] *n* força de
vontade

wilt [wɪlt] *vi* (*flower*) murchar;
(*plant*) morrer

win [wɪn] (*pt, pp* **won**) *n* vitória ▷ *vt*
ganhar, vencer; (*obtain*) conseguir,
obter; (*support*) alcançar ▷ *vi*
ganhar **win over** *vt* conquistar
win round (*Brit*) *vt* = **win over**

wince [wɪns] *vi* encolher-se,
estremecer

wind¹ [wɪnd] *n* vento; (*Med*) gases
mpl, flatulência; (*breath*) fôlego
▷ *vt* (*take breath away from*) deixar
sem fôlego

wind² [waɪnd] (*pt, pp* **wound**) *vt*

enrolar, bobinar; (*wrap*) envolver;
(*clock, toy*) dar corda a ▷ *vi* (*road,
river*) serpentear **wind up** *vt* (*clock*)
dar corda em; (*debate*) rematar,
concluir

windfall ['wɪndfɔ:l] *n* golpe *m* de
sorte

wind farm *n* parque *m* eólico

winding ['wɪndɪŋ] *adj* (*road*)
sinuoso, tortuoso; (*staircase*) de
caracol, em espiral

windmill ['wɪndmɪl] *n* moinho de
vento

window ['wɪndəu] *n* janela; (*in
shop etc*) vitrine *f* (BR), montra (PT);
window box *n* jardineira (no
peitoril da janela); **window
cleaner** *n* limpador(a) *m/f* de
janelas; **window-shopping** *n*:
to go window-shopping ir ver
vitrines

windscreen ['wɪndskri:n] (*Brit*) *n*
para-brisa *m*; **windscreen wiper**
(*Brit*) *n* limpador *m* de para-brisa

windshield ['wɪndʃi:ld] (US) *n*
= **windscreen**

windy ['wɪndɪ] *adj* com muito
vento, batido pelo vento; **it's ~** está
ventando (BR), faz vento (PT)

wine [waɪn] *n* vinho; **wine bar** *n*
bar *m* para degustação de vinhos;
wine glass *n* cálice *m* (de vinho);
wine list *n* lista de vinhos

wing [wɪŋ] *n* asa; (*of building*) ala;
(*Aut*) aleta, para-lamas *m inv*;
wings *npl* (*Theatre*) bastidores *mpl*

wink [wɪŋk] *n* piscadela ▷ *vi* piscar
o olho; (*light etc*) piscar

winner ['wɪnər] *n* vencedor(a) *m/f*

winning ['wɪnɪŋ] *adj* (*team*)
vencedor(a); (*goal*) decisivo; (*smile*)
sedutor(a)

winter ['wɪntər] *n* inverno; **winter
sports** *npl* esportes *mpl* (BR) or

desportos *mpl* (PT) de inverno

wipe [waɪp] *n*: **to give sth a ~**
limpar algo com um pano; (*rub*)
esfregar; (*erase: tape*) apagar ▷ *vt*
limpar **wipe off** *vt* remover
esfregando **wipe out** *vt* (*debt*)
liquidar; (*memory*) apagar; (*destroy*)
exterminar **wipe up** *vt* limpar

wire ['waɪər] *n* arame *m*; (*Elec*) fio
(elétrico); (*telegram*) telegrama *m*
▷ *vt* (*house*) instalar a rede elétrica
em; (*also*: **~ up**) conectar;
(*telegram*) telegrafar para

wiring ['waɪərɪŋ] *n* instalação *f*
elétrica

wisdom ['wɪzdəm] *n* prudência;
(*of action, remark*) bom-senso,
sabedoria; **wisdom tooth** *irreg n*
dente *m* do siso

wise [waɪz] *adj* prudente; (*action,
remark*) sensato

wish [wɪʃ] *n* desejo ▷ *vt* (*want*)
querer; **best ~es** (*on birthday etc*)
parabéns *mpl*, felicidades *fpl*; **with
best ~es** (*in letter*) cumprimentos;
to ~ sb goodbye despedir-se de
alguém; **he ~ed me well** me
desejou boa sorte; **to ~ to do/sb to
do sth** querer fazer/que alguém
faça algo; **to ~ for** desejar

wistful ['wɪstful] *adj* melancólico

wit [wɪt] *n* (*wittiness*) presença de
espírito, engenho; (*intelligence*:
also: **~s**) entendimento; (*person*)
espirituoso(-a)

witch [wɪtʃ] *n* bruxa

KEYWORD

with [wɪð, wɪθ] *prep*
1 (*accompanying, in the company of*)
com; **I was with him** eu estava
com ele; **to stay overnight with
friends** dormir na casa de amigos;

we'll take the children with us vamos levar as crianças conosco; **I'll be with you in a minute** vou vê-lo num minuto; **I'm with you** (I understand) compreendo; **to be with it** (inf) estar por dentro; (aware) estar a par da situação; (: up-to-date) estar atualizado com **2** (descriptive) com, de; **a room with a view** um quarto com vista; **the man with the grey hat/blue eyes** o homem do chapéu cinza/de olhos azuis

3 (indicating manner, means, cause) com, de; **with tears in her eyes** com os olhos cheios de lágrimas; **to fill sth with water** encher algo de água

withdraw [wɪð'drɔ:] irreg vt tirar, remover; (offer) retirar ▷ vi retirar-se; **to ~ money (from the bank)** retirar dinheiro (do banco); **withdrawal** n retirada; **withdrawal symptoms** npl síndrome f de abstinência; **withdrawn** adj (person) reservado, introvertido

wither ['wɪðə'] vi murchar

withhold [wɪð'həʊld] (irreg: like **hold**) vt (money) reter; (permission) negar; (information) esconder

within [wɪð'ɪn] prep dentro de ▷ adv dentro; **~ reach** ao alcance da mão; **~ sight** à vista; **~ the week** antes do fim da semana; **~ a mile of** a uma milha de

without [wɪð'aʊt] prep sem; **~ anybody knowing** sem ninguém saber; **to go** or **do ~ sth** passar sem algo

withstand [wɪð'stænd] (irreg: like **stand**) vt resistir a

witness ['wɪtnɪs] n testemunha ▷ vt testemunhar, presenciar; (document) legalizar; **to bear ~ to sth** (fig) testemunhar algo

witty ['wɪtɪ] adj espirituoso

wives [waɪvz] npl of **wife**

wizard ['wɪzəd] n feiticeiro, mago

wk abbr = **week**

wobble ['wɔbl] vi oscilar; (chair) balançar

woe [wəʊ] n dor f, mágoa

woke [wəʊk] pt of **wake**; **woken** pp of **wake**

wolf [wulf] (pl **wolves**) n lobo

woman ['wʊmən] (pl **women**) n mulher f; **~ doctor** médica

womb [wu:m] n (Anat) matriz f, útero

women ['wɪmɪn] npl of **woman**

won [wʌn] pt, pp of **win**

wonder ['wʌndə'] n maravilha, prodígio; (feeling) espanto ▷ vi: **to ~ whether/why** perguntar-se a si mesmo se/por quê; **to ~ at** admirar-se de; **to ~ about** pensar sobre or em; **it's no ~ that** não é de admirar que; **wonderful** adj maravilhoso; (miraculous) impressionante

won't [wəʊnt] = **will not**

wood [wʊd] n (timber) madeira; (forest) floresta, bosque m; **wooden** adj de madeira; (fig) inexpressivo; **woodwind** n (Mus) instrumentos mpl de sopro de madeira; **woodwork** n carpintaria

wool [wʊl] n lã f; **to pull the ~ over sb's eyes** (fig) enganar alguém, vender a alguém gato por lebre; **woollen** adj de lã; **woolly**, (US) **wooly** adj de lã; (fig) confuso

word [wə:d] n palavra; (news) notícia ▷ vt (express) redigir; **in other ~s** em outras palavras, ou seja; **to break/keep one's ~** faltar

à palavra/cumprir a promessa;
to have ~s with sb discutir com
alguém; **wording** n fraseado;
word processing n
processamento de textos; **word
processor** n processador m de
textos

wore [wɔːʳ] pt of **wear**

work [wəːk] n trabalho; (job)
emprego, trabalho; (Art, Literature)
obra ▷ vi trabalhar; (mechanism)
funcionar; (medicine etc) surtir
efeito, ser eficaz ▷ vt (clay) moldar;
(wood etc) talhar; (mine etc)
explorar; (machine) fazer trabalhar,
manejar; (effect, miracle) causar; **to
~ loose** (part) soltar-se; (knot)
afrouxar-se **work on** vt fus
trabalhar em, dedicar-se a;
(principle) basear-se em **work out**
vi dar certo, surtir efeito ▷ vt
(problem) resolver; (plan) elaborar,
formular; **it ~s out at £100** dá
£100; **worker** n trabalhador(a)
m/f, operário(-a); **working class** n
proletariado, classe f operária
▷ adj: **working-class** do
proletariado, da classe operária;
workman irreg n operário,
trabalhador m; **worksheet** n (with
exercises) folha de exercícios;
workshop n oficina; (practical
session) aula prática

world [wəːld] n mundo ▷ cpd
mundial; **to think the ~ of sb** (fig)
ter alguém em alto conceito

worm [wəːm] n (also: **earth~**)
minhoca, lombriga

worn [wɔːn] pp of **wear** ▷ adj
gasto; **worn-out** adj (object)
gasto; (person) esgotado, exausto

worry ['wʌrɪ] n preocupação f ▷ vt
preocupar, inquietar ▷ vi
preocupar-se, afligir-se

worse [wəːs] adj, adv pior ▷ n o
pior; **a change for the ~** uma
mudança para pior, uma piora;
worsen vt, vi piorar; **worse off** adj
com menos dinheiro; (fig): **you'll
be worse off this way** assim você
ficará pior que nunca

worship ['wəːʃɪp] n adoração f ▷ vt
adorar, venerar; (person, thing)
adorar; **Your W~** (Brit: to mayor)
vossa Excelência; (: to judge) senhor
Juiz

worst [wəːst] adj (o/a) pior ▷ adv
pior ▷ n o pior; **at ~** na pior das
hipóteses

worth [wəːθ] n valor m, mérito
▷ adj: **to be ~** valer; **it's ~ it** vale a
pena; **to be ~ one's while (to do)**
valer a pena (fazer); **worthless** adj
(person) imprestável; (thing) inútil;
worthwhile adj (activity) que vale
a pena; (cause) de mérito, louvável

worthy ['wəːðɪ] adj (person)
merecedor(a), respeitável; (motive)
justo; **~ of** digno de

 KEYWORD

would [wud] aux vb **1** (conditional
tense): **if you asked him, he would
do it** se você pedisse, ele faria isto;
**if you had asked him, he would
have done it** se você tivesse
pedido, ele teria feito isto
2 (in offers, invitations, requests):
would you like a biscuit? você
quer um biscoito?; **would you ask
him to come in?** pode pedir a ele
para entrar?; **would you close the
door, please?** quer fechar a porta
por favor?
3 (in indirect speech): **I said I would
do it** eu disse que eu faria isto
4 (emphatic): **you WOULD say**

that, wouldn't you? é lógico que você vai dizer isso
5 (*insistence*): **she wouldn't behave** não houve jeito dela se comportar
6 (*conjecture*): **it would have been midnight** devia ser meia-noite; **it would seem so** parece que sim
7 (*indicating habit*): **he would go on Mondays** costumava ir nas segundas-feiras

wouldn't ['wʊdnt] = **would not**
wound[1] [waʊnd] *pt, pp of* **wind**
wound[2] [wuːnd] *n* ferida ▷ *vt* ferir
wove [wəʊv] *pt of* **weave**; **woven** *pp of* **weave**
wrap [ræp] *n* (*stole*) xale *m*; (*cape*) capa ▷ *vt* (*cover*) envolver; (*also:* **~ up**) embrulhar; **wrapper** *n* invólucro; (*Brit: of book*) capa; **wrapping paper** *n* papel *m* de embrulho; (*fancy*) papel de presente
wreath [riːθ] *n* coroa
wreck [rɛk] *n* (*of vehicle*) destroços *mpl*; (*ship*) restos *mpl* do naufrágio; (*pej: person*) caco ▷ *vt* destruir, danificar; (*fig*) arruinar, arrasar; **wreckage** *n* (*of car, plane*) destroços *mpl*; (*of ship*) restos *mpl*; (*of building*) escombros *mpl*
wren [rɛn] *n* (*Zool*) carriça
wrench [rɛntʃ] *n* (*Tech*) chave *f* inglesa; (*tug*) puxão *m*; (*fig*) separação *f* penosa ▷ *vt* torcer com força; **to ~ sth from sb** arrancar algo de alguém
wrestle ['rɛsl] *vi*: **to ~ (with sb)** lutar (com *or* contra alguém); **wrestler** *n* lutador *m*; **wrestling** *n* luta (livre)
wretched ['rɛtʃɪd] *adj* desventurado, infeliz; (*inf*) maldito

wriggle ['rɪgl] *vi* (*also:* **~ about**) retorcer-se, contorcer-se
wring [rɪŋ] (*pt, pp* **wrung**) *vt* (*clothes, neck*) torcer; (*hands*) apertar; (*fig*): **to ~ sth out of sb** arrancar algo de alguém
wrinkle ['rɪŋkl] *n* (*on skin*) ruga; (*on paper*) prega ▷ *vt* franzir ▷ *vi* enrugar-se
wrist [rɪst] *n* pulso
write [raɪt] (*pt* **wrote**, *pp* **written**) *vt* escrever; (*cheque, prescription*) passar ▷ *vi* escrever; **to ~ to sb** escrever para alguém **write down** *vt* (*note*) anotar; (*put on paper*) pôr no papel **write off** *vt* cancelar **write out** *vt* escrever por extenso; (*cheque etc*) passar **write up** *vt* redigir; **write-off** *n* perda total; **writer** *n* escritor(a) *m/f*
writing *n* escrita; (*handwriting*) caligrafia, letra; (*of author*) obra; **in ~** por escrito
wrong [rɔŋ] *adj* (*bad*) errado, mau; (*unfair*) injusto; (*incorrect*) errado, equivocado; (*inappropriate*) impróprio ▷ *adv* mal, errado ▷ *n* injustiça ▷ *vt* ser injusto com; **you are ~ to do it** você se engana ao fazê-lo; **you are ~ about that, you've got it ~** você está enganado sobre isso; **to be in the ~** não ter razão; **what's ~?** o que é que há?; **to go ~** (*person*) desencaminhar-se; (*plan*) dar errado; (*machine*) sofrer uma avaria; **wrongly** *adv* errado
wrote [rəʊt] *pt of* **write**
wrung [rʌŋ] *pt, pp of* **wring**
WWW *n abbr* (= *World Wide Web*): **the ~** a WWW

X, x [ɛks] *n* X, x *m*
Xmas ['ɛksməs] *n abbr* = **Christmas**
X-ray [ɛks'reɪ] *n* radiografia ▷ *vt*
  radiografar, tirar uma chapa de

Y, y [waɪ] *n* Y, y *m*
yacht [jɔt] *n* iate *m*; **yachting** *n*
  iatismo
yard [jɑːd] *n* pátio, quintal *m*;
  (*measure*) jarda (914 *mm*; 3 *feet*)
yarn [jɑːn] *n* fio; (*tale*) história
  inverossímil
yawn [jɔːn] *n* bocejo ▷ *vi* bocejar
yeah [jɛə] (*inf*) *adv* é
year [jɪəʳ] *n* ano; **to be 8 ~s old** ter
  8 anos; **an eight-~-old child** uma
  criança de oito anos (de idade);
  yearly *adj* anual ▷ *adv*
  anualmente
yearn [jəːn] *vi*: **to ~ to do/for sth**
  ansiar fazer/por algo
yeast [jiːst] *n* levedura, fermento
yell [jɛl] *n* grito, berro ▷ *vi* gritar,
  berrar
yellow ['jɛləu] *adj* amarelo; **Yellow**
  Pages® *npl* (*Tel*) Páginas Amarelas
  fpl

yes [jɛs]ˋ *adv, n* sim *m*
yesterday [ˈjɛstədɪ] *adv, n* ontem *m*
yet [jɛt] *adv* ainda ▷ *conj* porém, no entanto; **the best ~** o melhor até agora; **as ~** até agora, ainda
yew [juː] *n* teixo®
yield [jiːld] *n* (*Agr*) colheita; (*Comm*) rendimento ▷ *vt* produzir; (*profit*) render; (*surrender*) ceder ▷ *vi* render-se, ceder; (*US: Aut*) ceder
yoghurt, yogurt [ˈjəʊgət] *n* iogurte *m*
yolk [jəʊk] *n* gema (do ovo)

 KEYWORD

you [juː] *pron* **1** (*subj: singular*) tu, você; (: *plural*) vós, vocês; **you French enjoy your food** vocês franceses gostam de comer; **you and I will go** nós iremos
2 (*direct object: singular*) te, o/a; (: *plural*) vos, os/as; (*indirect object: singular*) te, lhe; (: *plural*) vos, lhes; **I know you** eu lhe conheço; **I gave it to you** dei isto para você
3 (*stressed*) você; **I told YOU to do it** eu disse para você fazer isto
4 (*after prep, in comparisons: singular*) ti, você; (: *plural*) vós, vocês; (*polite form: singular*) o senhor/a senhora; (: *plural*) os senhores/as senhoras; **it's for you** é para você; **with you** contigo, com você; convosco, com vocês; com o senhor *etc*
5 (*impers: one*): **you never know** nunca se sabe; **apples do you good** as maçãs fazem bem à saúde

you'd [juːd] = **you had**; **you would**
you'll [juːl] = **you will**; **you shall**
young [jʌŋ] *adj* jovem ▷ *npl* (*of animal*) filhotes *mpl*, crias *fpl*; (*people*): **the ~** a juventude, os jovens; **younger** *adj* mais novo
your [jɔːʳ] *adj* teu/tua, seu/sua; (*plural*) vosso, seu/sua; (*formal*) do senhor/da senhora; *see also* **my**
you're [juəʳ] = **you are**
yours [jɔːz] *pron* teu/tua, seu/sua; (*plural*) vosso, seu/sua; (*formal*) do senhor/da senhora; **~ sincerely** or **faithfully** atenciosamente; *see also* **mine**
yourself [jɔːˈsɛlf] *pron* (*emphatic*) tu mesmo, você mesmo; (*object, reflexive*) te, se; (*after prep*) ti mesmo, si mesmo; (*formal*) o senhor mesmo/a senhora mesma; **yourselves** *pron* vós mesmos, vocês mesmos; (*object, reflexive*) vos, se; (*after prep*) vós mesmos, vôces mesmos; (*formal*) os senhores mesmos/as senhoras mesmas; *see also* **oneself**
youth [juːθ] *n* mocidade *f*, juventude *f*; (*young man*) jovem *m*; **youth club** *n* associação *f* de juventude; **youthful** *adj* juvenil; **youth hostel** *n* albergue *m* da juventude
you've [juːv] = **you have**

zunindo; **zoom lens** n zoom m,
zum m
zucchini [zuːˈkiːnɪ] (US) npl
abobrinha

Z

Z, z [zɛd, (US) ziː] n Z, z m
zebra [ˈziːbrə] n zebra; **zebra
  crossing** (Brit) n faixa (para
  pedestres) (BR), passadeira (PT)
zero [ˈzɪərəu] n zero
zest [zɛst] n vivacidade f,
  entusiasmo; (of lemon etc) zesto
zigzag [ˈzɪgzæg] n ziguezague m
  ▷ vi ziguezaguear
zinc [zɪŋk] n zinco
zip [zɪp] n (also: ~ **fastener**)
  fecho ecler (BR) or éclair (PT) ▷ vt
  (also: ~ **up**) fechar o fecho ecler de,
  subir o fecho ecler de; **zip code**
  (US) n código postal; **zip file** n
  arquivo zipado; **zipper** (US) n
  = **zip**
zit [zɪt] (inf) n espinha
zodiac [ˈzəudɪæk] n zodíaco
zone [zəun] n zona
zoo [zuː] n (jardim m) zoológico
zoom [zuːm] vi: **to ~ past** passar

Portuguese in Action

Inglês em Ação

Contents   # Indice

Correspondência

▶ Carta pessoal

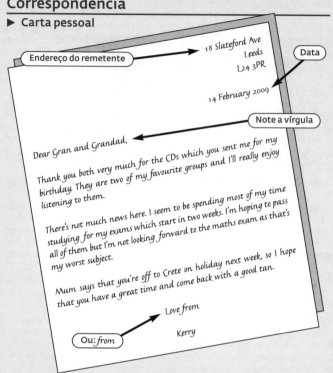

Endereço do remetente →

18 Slateford Ave
Leeds
L24 3PR

Data

14 February 2009

Note a vírgula

Dear Gran and Grandad,

Thank you both very much for the CDs which you sent me for my birthday. They are two of my favourite groups and I'll really enjoy listening to them.

There's not much news here. I seem to be spending most of my time studying for my exams which start in two weeks. I'm hoping to pass all of them but I'm not looking forward to the maths exam as that's my worst subject.

Mum says that you're off to Crete on holiday next week, so I hope that you have a great time and come back with a good tan.

Love from

Ou: *from*

Kerry

A introdução numa carta pessoal

Thank you for your letter.	*Obrigado/da por sua carta.*
It was lovely to hear from you.	*Foi ótimo/Adorei receber notícias suas.*
I'm sorry I didn't write earlier.	*Desculpe por eu não ter te escrito mais cedo.*

A despedida numa carta pessoal

Write soon!	*Escreva em breve!*
Give my love to Vanessa.	*Mande um beijo para a Vanessa.*
Samuel sends his best wishes.	*Samuel manda lembranças/abraços.*

4

Correspondence

▶ Personal letter

Rio de Janeiro, 5 de junho de 2009 ← **Place & Date**

Queridos vovó e vovô,

Muito obrigado pelos CDs que vocês me enviaram de presente de aniversário. São dois dos meus grupos favoritos, e estou gostando muito de escutá-los.

Não há muitas novidades por aqui. Tenho passado a maior parte do tempo estudando para os meus exames, que começam daqui a duas semanas. Espero ser aprovada em todos, mas não estou muito animada com o exame de matemática porque é a matéria em que sou mais fraca.

Mamãe me falou que vocês vão de férias para Fortaleza na semana que vem. Espero que se divirtam bastante e voltem com um belo bronzeado.

Com um beijo da

Mônica.

Starting a personal letter

Obrigado/da por sua carta.	*Thank you for your letter.*
Foi ótimo/Adorei receber notícias suas.	*It was lovely to hear from you.*
Desculpe por eu não ter te escrito mais cedo.	*I'm sorry I didn't write earlier.*

Ending a personal letter

Escreva em breve!	*Write soon!*
Mande um beijo para a Vanessa.	*Give my love to Vanessa.*
Samuel manda lembranças/abraços.	*Samuel sends his best wishes.*

109 Belleview Road
Cumbernauld
CA7 4TX

29th March 2009

Mrs Elaine Harris
Manager
Poppywell Cottage
Devon DV3 8SP

Dear Mrs Harris,

My sister stayed with you last year and has highly recommended your guest house.

I would like to reserve a room for one week from 18th – 24th August of this year. I would be obliged if you would let me know how much this would be for two adults and two children, and whether you have rooms free on those dates.

I hope to hear from you soon,

Yours sincerely,

Correspondence

▶ Letters

Rosalinda Pereira
Rua Barreto, 109
Curitiba, PR
CEP 80000-999

29 de março de 2009

Sra. Eliana Gomes
Gerente
Pousada Acalanto
Mauá

Prezada Sra. Gomes,

Minha irmã hospedou-se em sua pousada no ano passado e a recomendou muito.

Gostaria de fazer a reserva de um quarto por uma semana, de 18 a 24 de agosto deste ano. Agradeceria se pudesse me informar quanto sairia para dois adultos e duas crianças, e se há vaga nessas datas.

No aguardo de um contato seu em breve,

Atenciosamente,

Correspondência

► Cartas

Miss C Sauterelle
Rua Porto Gomes, 262
Catete – 22475-120
Rio de Janeiro, RJ

13th April 2009

Mrs Aileen Fields
Funky Fashions
14 Bracken Lane
Windermere
UK

Dear Mrs Fields,

I am anxious to find a job in Britain during my summer holiday from University and wish to gain experience in the fashion industry. I would be obliged if you could offer me work in any capacity. I can supply references from former employers, if you would like them.

Yours sincerely,

Correspondence

▶ Letters

Ms Eileen Ross
85 Rush Lane
Triptown
Lancs
LC4 2DT
UK

13 de abril de 2009

Srta. Cristina Santos
Rua Porto Gomes, 262
Catete, Rio de Janeiro, RJ
CEP 22475-120

Prezada Srta. Santos,

Quero muito trabalhar no Brasil durante o período de minhas férias universitárias e adquirir experiência na indústria da moda. Ficaria grata por uma posição na empresa, qualquer que fosse ela. Posso fornecer cartas de referência de empregadores anteriores, se desejar.

Atenciosamente,

Correspondência

▶ Cartas

Sra. Maria Antônia Gonçalves
Avenida 20 de Março, apto. 302,
Goiânia, GO
CEP 74000-310

2nd March 2009

Mr Brian Goodman
Human Resources Manager
DTL Thompson Ltd
30 Brownwood Street
Brighton
BR8 4LJ

Dear Mr Goodman,

I am 19 years old and a student of English at São Paulo University. I would like to work in Britain in order to perfect my English. I would be grateful if you would let me know if your agency could offer me work for a period of about ten months from Easter.

Yours in anticipation,

Maria Antônia Gonçalves

Correspondence

► Letters

129 Strathmore Ave
Edinburgh
EH11 2AD

2 de março de 2009

Sr. Carlos Mota
Rua dos Andradas, 29,
Centro, Rio de Janeiro, RJ
CEP 22475-000

Prezado Sr. Mota,

Tenho 19 anos e sou estudante de graduação em Português na Universidade de Edimburgo. Gostaria de trabalhar no Brasil para aperfeiçoar meu português. Agradeceria se pudesse me informar se sua agência me arrumaria trabalho por um período de dez meses, a partir da Páscoa.

Atenciosamente,

Jessica Lister

▶ Carta de apresentação

Rosalind Williamson
11 North Street
Barnton
BN7 2BT

Human Resources Dept
Messrs. J M. Kenyon Ltd.,
Firebrick House
Clifton
MC45 6RB

20th February 2009

Dear Sir or Madam,

With reference to your advertisement in today's Guardian,
I wish to apply for the post of Human Resources Manager.

I enclose my curriculum vitae. Please do not hesitate to
contact me if you require any further details.

Yours faithfully,
Rosalind Williamson

Enc: CV with two references.

Correspondence

▶ **Covering letter**

Rosalinda Pereira
Rua Norte 204
apto 201
São Paulo – SP

20 de fevereiro de 2009

Dept. de Recursos Humanos
Kenyon Ltda.
Rua da Graça, 25
São Paulo - SP

Prezado Senhor/Senhora,

Venho por meio desta me candidatar à posição de Gerente de Recursos Humanos, conforme vaga anunciada no jornal O Globo nesta data.

Envio anexo meu currículo e coloco-me à disposição para fornecer informações adicionais, caso deseje.

Cordialmente,
Rosalinda Pereira

Em anexo: CV e duas cartas de referência.

CURRICULUM VITAE

Name:	Rosalind Anna WILLJAMSON
Address:	11 North Street, Barton, BN7 2BT, England
Telephone:	Barton (01294) 476230
Date of Birth:	6.5.1985
Marital Status:	Single
Nationality:	British
Qualifications:	A Levels (2003): Italian (A), French (B), English (D) GCSEs (2001): 9 subjects B.A. 2nd class Honours degree in Italian with French, University of Newby, England (2007)
Present Post:	Assistant Personnel Officer, Metal Company plc. Barton (since February 2009)
Previous Employment:	Nov. 2007 – Jan 2009: Personnel trainee, Metal Company plc Oct. 2003 – June 2007: Student, University of Newby
Skills, Interests and Experience:	Fluent Italian & French; good working knowledge of German; some Russian; car owner and driver (clean licence); riding & sailing.

The following have agreed to provide references:
Ms Alice Bluegown, Personnel Manager, Metal Company plc, Barnton, NB4 3KL
Dr I.O. Sono, Department of Italian, University of Newby, Newby, SR13 2RR

Correspondence

▶ Curriculum vitae

CURRÍCULO

Nome:	Rosalinda PEREJRA
Endereço:	Rua Norte 204, apto 201, São Paulo – SP
Telefone:	(011) 4762 3081
Data de Nascimento:	6/5/1985
Estado Civil:	Solteira
Nacionalidade:	Brasileira
Qualificações:	Certificado de Conclusão do Ensino Médio (2003) Licenciatura em italiano e francês, USP, São Paulo (2007)
Cargo atual:	Assistente de RH, Companhia Metaldom S/A, São Paulo, SP (desde fevereiro de 2009)
Cargo anterior:	Novembro 2007 – Janeiro 2009: Estagiária na área de RH, Companhia Metaldom S/A Outubro 2003 – Junho 2007: Estudante, USP
Habilidades, Interesses e Experiência	Fluência em italiano e francês; bom conhecimento de alemão; conhecimento rudimentar de russo; proprietária de veículo, carteira de motorista (sem pontuação); hipismo e iatismo.

Referências:
Sra. Alice Amaral, Gerente de Recursos Humanos, Companhia Metaldom S/A, São Paulo, SP
Dr I.O. Sono, Departamento de Italiano, USP, São Paulo, SP

15

Correspondência

▶ Correio eletrônico/e-mail

Em inglês, pronuncia-se o endereço
eletrônico assim:
'gemma at n t net dot co dot u k'

New Message

To:	gemma@ntnet.co.uk
From:	gordon@onemo.net
Subject:	concert next week
cc:	jeremy@bit.com
bcc:	

Attachment   **Send**

Hi guys

I've just bought the new album by Rockstar, and it's brilliant!
I've got two spare tickets to a concert they're giving in
Edinburgh next Wednesday evening, so I hope you can both
make it.

See you soon!

New message	Nova mensagem
To	Para
From	De
Subject	Assunto
cc	Cc
bcc	Cco
Attachment	Anexo
Send	Enviar

16

Correspondence

▶ Email

> To give your email address to someone in Portuguese, say:
> 'isabel ponto costa arroba globanet ponto com ponto b r'

	Nova Mensagem
De:	isabel.costa@globanet.com.br
Para:	su@oneri.com
Assunto:	concerto
Cc:	paulolmuniz@folig.com
Cco:	

Anexo   Enviar

Olá!

Como foi o fim de semana? Sobraram duas entradas para o concerto de amanhã, de uns amigos que não vão poder ir. Se interessar a você, ou se conhecer alguém que queira ir, me avise assim que puder.

Abraços,

Nova mensagem	New message
Para	To
De	From
Assunto	Subject
Cc	cc
Cco	bcc
Anexo	Attachment
Enviar	Send

The telephone

O telefone

▶ **When your number answers**

- Hello! Could I speak to Susana, please?
- Could you ask him/her to call me back, please?
- I'll call back in half an hour.

▶ **Answering the telephone**

- Hello! It's Marcos speaking.
- Speaking.
- Who's speaking?

▶ **When the switchboard answers**

- Who shall I say is calling?
- I'm putting you through.
- Please hold.
- Would you like to leave a message?

▶ **Problems**

- I don't have a signal.
- My battery's low.
- I can't hear you.
- Sorry, I dialled the wrong number.
- This is a very bad line.

▶ **Ao telefonar para alguém**

- Alô! Posso falar com a Susana, por favor?
- Você podia pedir a ele/ela para retornar minha ligação?
- Volto a ligar daqui a meia hora.

▶ **Ao atender o telefone**

- Alô! Aqui é o Marcos.
- É ele/ela.
- Com quem falo?

▶ **Quando a/o telefonista atende**

- Quem gostaria de falar?
- Vou transferir a ligação.
- Aguarde, por favor.
- Gostaria de deixar um recado?

▶ **Problemas**

- Não tenho sinal.
- Estou quase sem bateria.
- Não estou escutando.
- Desculpe, foi engano.
- A ligação está muito ruim.

False friends

English ≠ *Portuguese*

actual ≠ *atual*

The film is based on **actual** events. → O filme se baseia em eventos **reais**.

O filme se baseia em eventos **atuais**. → The film is based on **current** events.

agenda ≠ *agenda*

I've drawn up an **agenda** for the meeting. → Preparei uma **pauta** para a reunião.

Perdi minha **agenda**. → I have lost my **diary**.

beef ≠ *bife*

Did you buy **beef** or pork? → Você comprou **carne de vaca** ou porco?

bife com batatas fritas → **steak** and chips

deception ≠ *decepção*

Katie continued to keep up the **deception**. → Katie continuou a manter a **ilusão**.

Ontem tive uma grande **decepção**. → Yesterday I had a big **disappointment**.

exit ≠ *êxito*

"**Exit**" (sign) → "**Saída**" (placa)

Seu filme obteve grande **êxito**. → Her film was a huge **success**.

False friends   Falsos amigos

expert ≠ *esperto*

She's an **expert** in marine biology. → Ela é **especialista** em biologia marinha.

Meu irmão é muito **esperto**. → My brother is very **smart**.

fabric ≠ *fábrica*

five metres of **fabric** → cinco metros de **tecido**

Ela trabalha em uma **fábrica**. → She works at a **factory**.

intend ≠ *entender*

I didn't **intend** to hurt her feelings. → Eu não **pretendia** ferir seus sentimentos.

Não **entendi** a pergunta. → I didn't **understand** the question.

large ≠ *largo*

a **large** house → uma casa **grande**

A estrada é bastante **larga**. → The road is very **wide**.

library ≠ *livraria*

the public **library** → a **biblioteca** pública

Esta é minha **livraria** preferida. → This is my favourite **bookshop**.

False friends

location ≠ *locação*

The **location** is still to be decided.	→	O **local** ainda precisa ser decidido.
A empresa lida com **locação** de apartamentos.	→	The company deals with apartment **rentals**.

lunch ≠ *lanche*

Let's have **lunch** at one.	→	Vamos **almoçar** à uma da tarde.
Vamos fazer um **lanche** mais tarde.	→	Let's have a **snack** later.

notice ≠ *notícia*

There's a **notice** on the board about the trip.	→	Há um **aviso** no quadro sobre a viagem.
Recebi boas **notícias**.	→	I got some good **news**.

parent ≠ *parente*

My **parents** are Scottish.	→	Meus **pais** são escoceses.
Meus **parentes** vieram me visitar.	→	My **relatives** came to visit me.

pretend ≠ *pretender*

He was just **pretending** to be ill.	→	Ele só estava **fingindo** que estava doente.
Pretendo terminar o trabalho hoje.	→	I **intend** to finish the job today.

push ≠ *puxar*

Push the door to open it.	→	Empurre a porta para abri-la.
O assaltante quase puxou o gatilho.	→	The robber almost pulled the trigger.

record ≠ *recordar*

They've just recorded a new album.	→	Eles acabaram de gravar um novo álbum.
Eu me recordo dessa pessoa.	→	I remember this person.

retired ≠ *retirado*

Is your dad retired yet?	→	Seu pai já é aposentado?
O computador deve ser retirado da caixa com cuidado.	→	The computer must be removed from the box carefully.

sensible ≠ *sensível*

Be sensible!	→	Seja sensato!
Ela é uma pessoa muito sensível.	→	She is a very sensitive person.

sympathetic ≠ *simpático*

She's a sympathetic listener.	→	Ela é uma ouvinte muito compassiva.
Meu amigo é muito simpático.	→	My friend is very nice.

Useful phrases

Frases úteis

Greetings

Hello!
Goodbye!
Bye!
Good morning.
Good afternoon.
Good evening.
Good night.
Welcome!
How are you?
I'm fine, thank you.
Pleased to meet you.
How's life?
See you tomorrow!
See you later!
Good luck!
Congratulations!
Have fun!
Cheers!
Bless you!

Take care!
Enjoy your meal!
Happy Birthday!
Merry Christmas!
Happy New Year!

On the telephone

Hello?
Who's speaking?
It's Laura speaking.
Could I speak to ..., please?
My phone number is ...
My mobile number is ...

Saudações

Oi! *(BR)*, Olá! *(PT)*
Adeus!
Tchau!
Bom dia.
Boa tarde.
Boa noite. *(para saudar)*
Boa noite. *(para despedir-se)*
Bem-vindo!
Como está?
Bem, obrigado.
Prazer em conhecê-lo.
Tudo bem?
Até amanhã!
Até logo!
Boa sorte!
Parabéns!/Felicidades!
Divirta-se!
Saúde! *(brinde)*
Saúde! *(ao espirrar)* *(BR)*,
  Santinho! *(PT)*
Cuide-se!
Bom apetite!
Parabéns!
Feliz Natal!
Feliz Ano Novo!

Ao telefone

Alô? *(BR)*, Estou? *(PT)*
Quem fala?
Aqui fala a Laura.
Posso falar com ...?
O meu (número de) telefone é ...
O meu número de celular *(BR)*
  or telemóvel *(PT)* é ...

Useful phrases

Frases úteis

It's engaged.	Está ocupado.
There's no reply.	Ninguém atende.
Do you speak Portuguese/English?	Fala português/inglês?
Please hold the line.	Não desligue, por favor.
Could you put me through to extension 3395?	Eu gostaria de falar com o ramal 3395?
Would you like to leave a message?	Quer deixar recado?
Could you tell him that I called?	Pode dizer que eu liguei?
I'll call back later.	Volto a ligar mais tarde.
I'm afraid you have the wrong number.	Acho que você ligou para o número errado.

Letter writing

Cartas

Dear Sir/Madam Yours faithfully	Exmo(-a). Senhor(a) Atenciosamente
Dear Mr. Fontes Yours sincerely Best wishes Kind regards	Caro Sr. Fontes Atenciosamente Cordialmente Cumprimentos
Dear Carlota All the best With love from …	Cara Carlota Um abraço Um beijo
Please find enclosed … Thank you for your letter.	Envio anexo … Obrigado(-a) pela sua carta.

Email

Correio eletrônico

Do you have email?	Você tem e-mail/correio eletrônico?
What's your email address?	Qual é o seu endereço de e-mail/correio eletrônico?
My email address is …	Meu endereço de e-mail/correio eletrônico é …
emma@coolmail.com = "emma at coolmail dot com"	emma@coolmail.com = "emma arroba coolmail ponto com"

Verbos irregulares em Inglês

PRESENT	PT	PP	PRESENT	PT	PP
arise	arose	arisen	fight	fought	fought
awake	awoke	awoken	find	found	found
be (am, is, are; being)	was, were	been	fling	flung	flung
			fly	flew	flown
bear	bore	born(e)	forbid	forbad(e)	forbidden
beat	beat	beaten	forecast	forecast	forecast
begin	began	begun	forget	forgot	forgotten
bend	bent	bent	forgive	forgave	forgiven
bet	bet, betted	bet, betted	freeze	froze	frozen
			get	got	got, (US) gotten
bid (at auction)	bid	bid			
bind	bound	bound	give	gave	given
bite	bit	bitten	go (goes)	went	gone
bleed	bled	bled	grind	ground	ground
blow	blew	blown	grow	grew	grown
break	broke	broken	hang	hung	hung
breed	bred	bred	hang (execute)	hanged	hanged
bring	brought	brought	have	had	had
build	built	built	hear	heard	heard
burn	burnt, burned	burnt, burned	hide	hid	hidden
			hit	hit	hit
burst	burst	burst	hold	held	held
buy	bought	bought	hurt	hurt	hurt
can	could	(been able)	keep	kept	kept
cast	cast	cast	kneel	knelt, kneeled	knelt, kneeled
catch	caught	caught			
choose	chose	chosen	know	knew	known
cling	clung	clung	lay	laid	laid
come	came	come	lead	led	led
cost	cost	cost	lean	leant, leaned	leant, leaned
creep	crept	crept			
cut	cut	cut	leap	leapt, leaped	leapt, leaped
deal	dealt	dealt			
dig	dug	dug	learn	learnt, learned	learnt, learned
do (does)	did	done			
draw	drew	drawn	leave	left	left
dream	dreamed, dreamt	dreamed, dreamt	lend	lent	lent
			let	let	let
drink	drank	drunk	lie (lying)	lay	lain
drive	drove	driven	light	lit, lighted	lit, lighted
eat	ate	eaten			
fall	fell	fallen	lose	lost	lost
feed	fed	fed	make	made	made
feel	felt	felt	may	might	–

25

Verbos irregulares em Inglês

PRESENT	PT	PP	PRESENT	PT	PP
mean	meant	meant	speak	spoke	spoken
meet	met	met	speed	sped,	sped,
mistake	mistook	mistaken		speeded	speeded
mow	mowed	mown,	spell	spelt,	spelt,
		mowed		spelled	spelled
must	(had to)	(had to)	spend	spent	spent
pay	paid	paid	spill	spilt,	spilt,
put	put	put		spilled	spilled
quit	quit,	quit,	spin	spun	spun
	quitted	quitted	spit	spat	spat
read	read	read	spoil	spoiled,	spoiled,
rid	rid	rid		spoilt	spoilt
ride	rode	ridden	spread	spread	spread
ring	rang	rung	spring	sprang	sprung
rise	rose	risen	stand	stood	stood
run	ran	run	steal	stole	stolen
saw	sawed	sawed,	stick	stuck	stuck
		sawn	sting	stung	stung
say	said	said	stink	stank	stunk
see	saw	seen	stride	strode	stridden
sell	sold	sold	strike	struck	struck
send	sent	sent	swear	swore	sworn
set	set	set	sweep	swept	swept
sew	sewed	sewn	swell	swelled	swollen,
shake	shook	shaken			swelled
shear	sheared	shorn,	swim	swam	swum
		sheared	swing	swung	swung
shed	shed	shed	take	took	taken
shine	shone	shone	teach	taught	taught
shoot	shot	shot	tear	tore	torn
show	showed	shown	tell	told	told
shrink	shrank	shrunk	think	thought	thought
shut	shut	shut	throw	threw	thrown
sing	sang	sung	thrust	thrust	thrust
sink	sank	sunk	tread	trod	trodden
sit	sat	sat	wake	woke,	woken,
sleep	slept	slept		waked	waked
slide	slid	slid			
sling	slung	slung	wear	wore	worn
slit	slit	slit	weave	wove	woven
smell	smelt,	smelt,	weep	wept	wept
	smelled	smelled	win	won	won
			wind	wound	wound
sow	sowed	sown,	wring	wrung	wrung
		sowed	write	wrote	written

26

Portuguese verb forms

1 Gerund. 2 Imperative. 3 Present. 4 Imperfect. 5 Preterite. 6 Future.
7 Present subjunctive. 8 Imperfect subjunctive. 9 Future subjunctive.
10 Past participle. 11 Pluperfect. 12 Personal infinitive.

etc indicates that the irregular root is used for all persons of the tense,
e.g. **ouvir** 7 ouça ouça, ouças, ouça, ouçamos, ouçais, ouçam.

abrir 10 aberto
acudir 2 acode 3 acudo, acodes,
  acode, acodem
aderir 3 adiro 7 adira
advertir 3 advirto 7 advirta *etc*
agir 3 ajo 7 aja *etc*
agradecer 3 agradeço 7 agradeça *etc*
agredir 2 agride 3 agrido, agrides,
  agride, agridem 7 agrida *etc*
AMAR 1 amando 2 ama, amai
  3 amo, amas, ama, amamos, amais,
  amam 4 amava, amavas, amava,
  amávamos, amáveis, amavam
  5 amei, amaste, amou, amamos
  (*PT*: amámos), amastes, amaram
  6 amarei, amarás, amará,
  amaremos, amareis, amarão
  7 ame, ames, ame, amemos, ameis,
  amem 8 amasse, amasses, amasse,
  amássemos, amásseis, amassem
  9 amar, amares, amar, ámarmos,
  amardes, amarem 10 amado
  11 amara, amaras, amara,
  amáramos, amáreis, amaram
  12 amar, amares, amar, amarmos,
  amardes, amarem
ansiar 2 anseia 3 anseio, anseias,
  anseia, anseiam 7 anseie *etc*
apreçar 7 aprece *etc*
arrancar 7 arranque *etc*
arruinar 2 arruína 3 arruíno, arruínas,
  arruína, arruínam 7 arruíne,
  arruínes, arruíne, arruínem
aspergir 3 aspirjo 7 aspirja *etc*

atribuir 3 atribuo, atribuis, atribui,
  atribuímos, atribuís, atribuem
bulir 2 bole 3 bulo, boles, bole,
  bolem
caber 3 caibo 5 coube *etc* 7 caiba *etc*
  8 coubesse *etc* 9 couber *etc*
cair 2 cai 3 caio, cais, cai, caímos,
  caís, caem 4 caía *etc* 5 caí, caíste
  7 caia *etc* 8 caisse *etc*
cobrir 3 cubro 7 cubra *etc* 10 coberto
colorir 3 coluro 7 colura *etc*
compelir 3 compilo 7 compila *etc*
crer 2 crê 3 creio, crês, crê, cremos,
  credes, creem 5 cri, creste, creu,
  cremos, crestes, creram 7 creia *etc*
cuspir 2 cospe 3 cuspo, cospes, cospe,
  cospem
dar 2 dá 3 dou, dás, dá, damos, dais,
  dão 5 dei, deste, deu, demos,
  destes, deram 7 dê, dês, dê, demos,
  deis, deem 8 desse *etc* 9 der *etc*
  11 dera *etc*
deduzir 2 deduz 3 deduzo, deduzes,
  deduz
denegrir 2 denigre 3 denigro,
  denigres, denigre, denigrem
  7 denigre *etc*
despir 3 dispo 7 dispa *etc*
dizer 2 diz (dize) 3 digo, dizes, diz,
  dizemos, dizeis, dizem 5 disse *etc*
  6 direi *etc* 7 diga *etc* 8 dissesse *etc*
  9 disser *etc* 10 dito
doer 2 dói 3 doo, dóis, dói
dormir 3 durmo 7 durma *etc*

Portuguese verb forms

escrever 10 escrito
ESTAR 2 está 3 estou, estás, está,
  estamos, estais, estão 4 estava *etc*
  5 estive, estiveste, esteve,
  estivemos, estivestes, estiveram
  7 esteja *etc* 8 estivesse *etc*
  9 estiver *etc* 11 estivera *etc*
extorquir 3 exturco 7 exturca *etc*
FAZER 3 faço 5 fiz, fizeste, fez,
  fizemos, fizestes, fizeram 6 farei *etc*
  7 faça *etc* 8 fizesse *etc* 9 fizer *etc*
  10 feito 11 fizera *etc*
ferir 3 firo 7 fira *etc*
fluir 3 fluo, fluis, flui, fluímos, fluís,
  fluem
fugir 2 foge 3 fujo, foges, foge, fogem
  7 fuja *etc*
ganhar 10 ganho
gastar 10 gasto
gerir 3 giro 7 gira *etc*
haver 2 há 3 hei, hás, há, havemos,
  haveis, hão 4 havia *etc* 5 houve,
  houveste, houve, houvemos,
  houvestes, houveram 7 haja *etc*
  8 houvesse *etc* 9 houver *etc*
  11 houvera *etc*
ir 1 indo 2 vai 3 vou, vais, vai, vamos,
  ides, vão 4 ia *etc* 5 fui, foste, foi,
  fomos, fostes, foram 7 vá, vás, vá,
  vamos, vades, vão 8 fosse, fosses,
  fosse, fôssemos, fôsseis, fossem
  9 for *etc* 10 ido 11 fora *etc*
ler 2 lê 3 leio, lês, lê, lemos, ledes,
  leem 5 li, leste, leu, lemos, lestes,
  leram 7 leia *etc*
medir 3 meço, 7 meça *etc*
mentir 3 minto 7 minta *etc*
ouvir 3 ouço 7 ouça *etc*
pagar 10 pago
parir 3 pairo 7 paira *etc*

pecar 7 peque *etc*
pedir 3 peço 7 peça *etc*
perder 3 perco 7 perca *etc*
poder 3 posso 5 pude, pudeste, pôde,
  pudemos, pudestes, puderam
  7 possa *etc* 8 pudesse *etc* 9 puder *etc*
  11 pudera *etc*
polir 2 pule 3 pulo, pules, pule,
  pulem 7 pula *etc*
pôr 1 pondo 2 põe 3 ponho, pões, põe,
  pomos, pondes, põem 4 punha *etc*
  5 pus, puseste, pôs, pusemos,
  pusestes, puseram 6 porei *etc*
  7 ponha *etc* 8 pusesse *etc* 9 puser *etc*
  10 posto 11 pusera *etc*
preferir 3 prefiro 7 prefire *etc*
prevenir 2 previne 3 previno,
  prevines, previne, previnem
  7 previna *etc*
prover 2 provê 3 provejo, provês,
  provê, provemos, provedes,
  proveem 5 provi, proveste, proveu,
  provemos, provestes, proveram
  7 proveja *etc* 8 provesse *etc* 9 prover
  etc
querer 3 quero, queres, quer 5 quis,
  quiseste, quis, quisemos, quisestes,
  quiseram 7 queira *etc* 8 quisesse *etc*
  9 quiser *etc* 11 quisera *etc*
refletir 3 reflito 7 reflita *etc*
repetir 3 repito 7 repita *etc*
requerer 3 requeiro, requeres, requer
  7 requeira *etc*
reunir 2 reúne 3 reúno, reúnes,
  reúne, reúnem 7 reúna *etc*
rir 2 ri 3 rio, ris, ri, rimos, rides,
  ridem 5 ri, riste, riu, rimos, ristes,
  riram 7 ria *etc*
saber 3 sei, sabes, sabe, sabemos,
  sabeis, sabem 5 soube, soubeste,

Portuguese verb forms

soube, soubemos, soubestes,
souberam 7 saiba *etc* 8 soubesse *etc*
9 souber *etc* 11 soubera *etc*
seguir 3 sigo 7 siga *etc*
sentir 3 sinto 7 sinta *etc*
ser 2 sê 3 sou, és, é, somos, sois, são
4 era *etc* 5 fui, foste, foi, fomos,
fostes, foram 7 seja *etc* 8 fosse *etc*
9 for *etc* 11 fora *etc*
servir 3 sirvo 7 sirva *etc*
subir 2 sobe 3 subo, sobes, sobe, sobem
suster 2 sustém 3 sustenho, sustens,
sustém, sustendes, sustêm
5 sustive, sustiveste, susteve,
sustivemos, sustivestes,
sustiveram 7 sustenha *etc*
ter 2 tem 3 tenho, tens, tem, temos,
tendes, têm 4 tinha *etc* 5 tive,
tiveste, teve, tivemos, tivestes,
tiveram 6 terei *etc* 7 tenha *etc*
8 tivesse *etc* 9 tiver *etc* 11 tivera *etc*
torcer 3 torço 7 torça *etc*
tossir 3 tusso 7 tussa *etc*
trair 2 trai 3 traio, trais, trai,
traímos, traís, traem 7 traia *etc*
trazer 2 (traze) traz 3 trago, trazes,
traz, 5 trouxe, trouxeste, trouxe,
trouxemos, trouxestes, trouxeram
6 trarei *etc* 7 traga *etc* 8 trouxesse *etc*
9 trouxer *etc* 11 trouxera *etc*
UNIR 1 unindo 2 une, uni 3 uno,
unes, une, unimos, unis, unem
4 unia, unias, uníamos, uníeis,
uniam 5 uni, uniste, uniu, unimos,
unistes, uniram 6 unirei, unirás,

unirá, uniremos, unireis, unirão
7 una, unas, una, unamos, unais,
unam 8 unisse, unisses, unisse,
uníssemos, unísseis, unissem
9 unir, unires, unir, unirmos,
unirdes, unirem 10 unido 11 unira,
uniras, unira, uníramos, uníreis,
uniram 12 unir, unires, unir,
unirmos, unirdes, unirem
valer 3 valho 7 valha *etc*
ver 2 vê 3 vejo, vês, vê, vemos, vedes,
veem 4 via *etc* 5 vi, viste, viu, vimos,
vistes, viram 7 veja *etc* 8 visse *etc*
9 vir *etc* 10 visto 11 vira
vir 1 vindo, 2 vem 3 venho, vens,
vem, vimos, vindes, vêm 4 vinha *etc*
5 vim, vieste, veio, viemos, viestes,
vieram 7 venha *etc* 8 viesse *etc* 9 vier
etc 10 vindo 11 viera *etc*
VIVER 1 vivendo 2 vive, vivei 3 vivo,
vives, vive, vivemos, viveis, vivem
4 vivia, vivias, vivia, vivíamos,
vivíeis, viviam 5 vivi, viveste,
viveu, vivemos, vivestes, viveram
6 viverei, viverás, viverá,
viveremos, vivereis, viverão 7 viva,
vivas, viva, vivamos, vivais, vivam
8 vivesse, vivesses, vivesse,
vivêssemos, vivêsseis, vivessem
9 viver, viveres, viver, vivermos,
viverdes, viverem 10 vivido
11 vivera, viveras, vivera,
vivêramos, vivêreis, viveram
12 viver, viveres, viver, vivermos,
viverdes, viverem

Dates   Datas

Days of the week   ## Dias da semana
Monday   segunda(-feira)
Tuesday   terça(-feira)
Wednesday   quarta(-feira)
Thursday   quinta(-feira)
Friday   sexta(-feira)
Saturday   sábado
Sunday   domingo

Months   ## Meses
January   janeiro
February   fevereiro
March   março
April   abril
May   maio
June   junho
July   julho
August   agosto
September   setembro
October   outubro
November   novembro
December   dezembro

Useful vocabulary   ## Vocabulário útil
What day is it today?   Que dia é hoje?
Today is the 28th.   Hoje é dia 28.
When?   Quando?
today   hoje
tomorrow   amanhã
yesterday   ontem
this morning/afternoon   hoje de manhã/à tarde
in two weeks *ou* a fortnight em duas semanas
in a week's time   daqui a uma semana
last/next month   o mês passado/que vem

The time

As horas

What time is it?

Que horas são?

É uma e quinze.
É uma e um quarto (PT).
_____

It's one fifteen.

É meio-dia/meia-noite.
_____

It's midday/midnight.

São três e meia.
_____

It's half past three.

Faltam dez para as duas.
São duas menos dez (PT).
_____

It's ten to two.

São nove (horas) da
manhã/da noite.
_____

It's nine o'clock in the
morning/at night.

Faltam vinte para as oito.
São oito menos vinte (PT).
_____

It's twenty to eight.

Numbers   Números

Cardinal numbers   ## Números cardinais

one	1	um (uma)
two	2	dois (duas)
three	3	três
four	4	quatro
five	5	cinco
six	6	seis
seven	7	sete
eight	8	oito
nine	9	nove
ten	10	dez
eleven	11	onze
twelve	12	doze
thirteen	13	treze
fourteen	14	catorze
fifteen	15	quinze
sixteen	16	dezesseis (BR), dezasseis (PT)
seventeen	17	dezessete (BR), dezassete (PT)
eighteen	18	dezoito
nineteen	19	dezenove (BR), dezanove (PT)
twenty	20	vinte
twenty-one	21	vinte e um (uma)
thirty	30	trinta
forty	40	quarenta
fifty	50	cinquenta
sixty	60	sessenta
seventy	70	setenta
eighty	80	oitenta
ninety	90	noventa
a hundred	100	cem
a hundred and one	101	cento e um (uma)
two hundred	200	duzentos(-as)
three hundred	300	trezentos(-as)
five hundred	500	quinhentos(-as)
a thousand	1.000/1,000	mil
a million	1.000.000/1,000,000	um milhão

Numbers   Números

Fractions etc

zero point five	0,5/0.5
three point four	3,4/3.4
ten per cent	10%
a hundred per cent	100%

Ordinal numbers

first	1°/1st
second	2°/2nd
third	3°/3rd
fourth	4°/4th
fifth	5°/5th
sixth	6°/6th
seventh	7°/7th
eighth	8°/8th
ninth	9°/9th
tenth	10°/10th
eleventh	11°/11th
twentieth	20°/20th
thirtieth	30°/30th
fortieth	40°/40th
fiftieth	50°/50th
hundredth	100°/100th
hundred-and-first	101°/101st
thousandth	1000°/1000th

Frações etc

zero vírgula cinco
três vírgula quatro
dez por cento
cem por cento

Números ordinais

primeiro
segundo
terceiro
quarto
quinto
sexto
sétimo
oitavo
nono
décimo
décimo primeiro
vigésimo
trigésimo
quadragésimo
quinquagésimo
centésimo
centésimo primeiro
milésimo

Português – Inglês

Portuguese – English

a

A, a [a] *m* A, a

○ **PALAVRA-CHAVE**

a [a] *art def* the; *ver tb* **o** ▷ *pron (ela)* her; *(você)* you; *(coisa)* it; *ver tb* **o** ▷ *prep (a + o(s) = ao(s); a + a(s) = à(s); a + aquele/a(s) = àquele/a(s))*
1 *(direção)* to; **à direita/esquerda** to *ou* on the right/left
2 *(distância)*: **está a 15 km daqui** it's 15 km from here
3 *(posição)*: **ao lado de** beside, at the side of
4 *(tempo)* at; **a que horas?** at what time?; **às 5 horas** at 5 o'clock; **à noite** at night; **aos 15 anos** at 15 years of age
5 *(maneira)*: **à francesa** in the French way; **a cavalo/pé** on horseback/foot
6 *(meio, instrumento)*: **à força** by force; **a mão** by hand; **a lápis** in pencil; **fogão a gás** gas stove
7 *(razão)*: **a R$10 o quilo** at R$10 a kilo; **a mais de 100 km/h** at over 100 km/h
8 *(depois de certos verbos)*: **começou a nevar** it started snowing *ou* to snow; **passar a fazer** to become
9 *(+ infin)*: **ao vê-lo, reconheci-o imediatamente** when I saw him, I recognized him immediately; **ele ficou muito nervoso ao falar com o professor** he became very nervous while he was talking to the teacher
10 *(PT: + infin: gerúndio)*: **a correr** running; **estou a trabalhar** I'm working

à [a] = **a + a**

(a) *abr (= assinado)* signed

aba ['aba] *f (de chapéu)* brim; *(de casaco)* tail; *(de montanha)* foot

abacate [aba'katʃi] *m* avocado (pear)

abacaxi [abaka'ʃi] *(BR) m* pineapple

abafado, -a [aba'fadu, a] *adj (ar)* stuffy; *(tempo)* humid, close; *(ocupado)* (extremely) busy; *(angustiado)* anxious

abaixar [abaj'ʃar] *vt* to lower; *(luz, som)* to turn down; **abaixar-se** *vr* to stoop

abaixo [a'bajʃu] *adv* down ▷ *prep*: **~ de** below; **~ o governo!** down with the government!; **morro ~** downhill; **rio ~** downstream; **mais ~** further down; **~ e acima** up and down; **~ assinado** undersigned; **abaixo-assinado** [-asi'nadu] *(pl* **abaixo-assinados)** *m* petition

abalado, -a [aba'ladu, a] *adj* unstable, unsteady; *(fig)* shaken

abalar [aba'lar] *vt* to shake; *(fig:*

comover) to affect ▷ *vi* to shake;
abalar-se *vr* to be moved
abalo [a'balu] *m* (*comoção*) shock;
(*ação*) shaking; **~ sísmico** earth
tremor
abanar [aba'nar] *vt* to shake; (*rabo*)
to wag; (*com leque*) to fan
abandonar [abãdo'nar] *vt* to leave;
(*ideia*) to reject; (*esperança*) to give
up; (*descuidar*) to neglect
abarrotado, -a [abaho'tadu, a] *adj*
(*gaveta*) crammed full; (*lugar*)
packed
abastecer [abaste'ser] *vt* to supply;
(*motor*) to fuel; (*Auto*) to fill up;
(*Aer*) to refuel; **abastecer-se** *vr*:
~-se de to stock up with
abastecimento [abastesi'mẽtu] *m*
supply; (*comestíveis*) provisions *pl*;
(*ato*) supplying; **abastecimentos**
mpl (*suprimentos*) supplies
abater [aba'ter] *vt* (*gado*) to
slaughter; (*preço*) to reduce;
(*desalentar*) to upset; **abatido, -a**
[aba'tʃidu, a] *adj* depressed,
downcast; **abatimento**
[abatʃi'mẽtu] *m* (*fraqueza*)
weakness; (*de preço*) reduction;
(*prostração*) depression; **fazer um
abatimento em** to give a discount
on
abdômen [ab'domẽ] *m* abdomen
á-bê-cê [abe'se] *m* alphabet
abecedário [abese'darju] *m*
alphabet, ABC
abelha [a'beʎa] *f* bee
abelhudo, -a [abe'ʎudu, a] *adj*
nosy
abençoar [abẽ'swar] *vt* to bless
aberto, -a [a'bɛrtu, a] *pp de* **abrir**
▷ *adj* open; (*céu*) clear; (*sinal*)
green; (*torneira*) on
abestalhado, -a [abesta'ʎadu, a]
adj stupid

abismado, -a [abiz'madu, a] *adj*
astonished
ABL *abr f* = **Academia Brasileira de
Letras**
abnegado, -a [abne'gadu, a] *adj*
self-sacrificing
abnegar [abne'gar] *vt* to renounce
abóbada [a'bɔbada] *f* vault;
(*telhado*) arched roof
abobalhado, -a [aboba'ʎadu, a]
adj (*criança*) simple
abóbora [a'bɔbora] *f* pumpkin
abobrinha [abo'briɲa] *f* courgette
(*Brit*), zucchini (*US*)
abolir [abo'lir] *vt* to abolish
aborrecer [abohe'ser] *vt* (*chatear*)
to annoy; (*maçar*) to bore;
aborrecer-se *vr* to get upset; to
get bored; **aborrecido, -a**
[abohe'sidu, a] *adj* boring;
(*chateado*) annoyed;
aborrecimento [abohesi'mẽtu] *m*
boredom; (*chateação*) annoyance
abortar [abor'tar] *vi* (*Med*) to have a
miscarriage; (: *de propósito*) to have
an abortion; **aborto** [a'bortu] *m*
miscarriage; (*forçado*) abortion;
fazer/ter um aborto to have an
abortion/a miscarriage
abotoadura [abotwa'dura] *f*
cufflink
abotoar [abo'twar] *vt* to button up
▷ *vi* (*Bot*) to bud
abraçar [abra'sar] *vt* to hug;
(*causa*) to embrace; **abraçar-se** *vr*
to embrace; **ele abraçou-se a
mim** he embraced me; **abraço**
[a'brasu] *m* embrace, hug; **com
um abraço** (*em carta*) with best
wishes
abre-garrafas ['abri-] (*PT*) *m inv*
bottle opener
abre-latas ['abri-] (*PT*) *m inv* tin
(*Brit*) *ou* can opener

abreviar [abre'vjar] *vt* to abbreviate; (*texto*) to abridge; **abreviatura** [abrevja'tura] *f* abbreviation

abridor [abri'dor] (*BR*) *m*: **~ (de lata)** tin (*Brit*) *ou* can opener; **~ de garrafa** bottle opener

abrigar [abri'gar] *vt* to shelter; (*proteger*) to protect; **abrigar-se** *vr* to take shelter

abrigo [a'brigu] *m* shelter, cover; **~ antiaéreo** air-raid shelter; **~ antinuclear** fall-out shelter

abril [a'briw] *m* April; **25 de A~** *see note*

- **25 DE ABRIL**

- On 25 April 1974 in Portugal, the
- MAF (Armed Forces Movement)
- instigated the bloodless
- revolution that was to topple the
- 48-year-old dictatorship presided
- over until 1968 by António de
- Oliveira Salazar. The red
- carnation has come to symbolize
- the coup, as it is said that the
- Armed Forces took to the streets
- with carnations in the barrels of
- their rifles. 25 April is now a
- public holiday in Portugal.

abrir [a'brir] *vt* to open; (*fechadura*) to unlock; (*vestuário*) to unfasten; (*torneira*) to turn on; (*buraco, exceção*) to make ▷ *vi* to open; (*sinal*) to go green; **abrir-se** *vr*: **~-se com alguém** to confide in sb

abrupto, -a [a'bruptu, a] *adj* abrupt; (*repentino*) sudden

absolutamente [absoluta'mētʃi] *adv* absolutely; (*em resposta*) absolutely not, not at all

absoluto, -a [abso'lutu, a] *adj* absolute; **em ~** absolutely not, not at all

absorto, -a [ab'sortu, a] *pp de* **absorver** ▷ *adj* absorbed, engrossed

absorvente [absor'vētʃi] *adj* (*papel etc*) absorbent; (*livro etc*) absorbing

absorver [absor'ver] *vt* to absorb; **absorver-se** *vr*: **~-se em** to concentrate on

abstêmio, -a [abs'temju, a] *adj* abstemious; (*álcool*) teetotal ▷ *m/f* abstainer; teetotaller (*Brit*), teetotaler (*US*)

abster-se [ab'stersi] (*irreg: como* **ter**) *vr*: **~ de** to abstain *ou* refrain from

abstinência [abstʃi'nēsja] *f* abstinence; (*jejum*) fasting

abstrato, -a [abs'tratu, a] *adj* abstract

absurdo, -a [abi'surdu, a] *adj* absurd ▷ *m* nonsense

abundante [abũ'dātʃi] *adj* abundant; **abundar** [abũ'dar] *vi* to abound

abusar [abu'zar] *vi* to go too far; **~ de** to abuse

abuso [a'buzu] *m* abuse; (*Jur*) indecent assault

a.C. *abr* (= *antes de Cristo*) B.C.

a/c *abr* (= *aos cuidados de*) Attn:

acabado, -a [aka'badu, a] *adj* finished; (*esgotado*) worn out

acabamento [akaba'mētu] *m* finish

acabar [aka'bar] *vt* to finish, complete; (*consumir*) to use up; (*rematar*) to finish off ▷ *vi* to finish, end; **acabar-se** *vr* to be over; (*prazo*) to expire; (*esgotar-se*) to run out; **~ com** to put an end to; **~ de chegar** to have just arrived; **~ por fazer** to end up (by) doing;

acabou-se! it's all over!; (*basta!*) that's enough!

academia [akade'mia] *f* academy; **Academia Brasileira de Letras** *see note*

acadêmico, -a [aka'demiku, a] *adj, m/f* academic

açafrão [asa'frãw] *m* saffron

acalmar [akaw'mar] *vt* to calm ▷ *vi* (*vento etc*) to abate; **acalmar-se** *vr* to calm down

acampamento [akãpa'mētu] *m* camping; (*Mil*) camp, encampment

acampar [akã'par] *vi* to camp

acanhado, -a [aka'ɲadu, a] *adj* shy

acanhamento [akaɲa'mētu] *m* shyness

acanhar-se [aka'ɲarsi] *vr* to be shy

ação [a'sãw] (*pl* **-ões**) *f* action; (*ato*) act, deed; (*Mil*) battle; (*enredo*) plot; (*Jur*) lawsuit; (*Com*) share; **~ ordinária/preferencial** (*Com*)

ordinary/preference share

acarajé [akara'ʒɛ] *m* (*Culin*) beans fried in palm oil

acarretar [akahe'tar] *vt* to result in, bring about

acaso [a'kazu] *m* chance; **ao ~** at random; **por ~** by chance

acatar [aka'tar] *vt* to respect; (*lei*) to obey

aceitação [asejta'sãw] *f* acceptance; (*aprovação*) approval

aceitar [asej'tar] *vt* to accept; (*aprovar*) to approve; **aceitável** [asej'tavew] (*pl* **-eis**) *adj* acceptable; **aceito, -a** [a'sejtu, a] *pp de* **aceitar**

acelerador [aselera'dor] *m* accelerator

acelerar [asele'rar] *vt, vi* to accelerate; **~ o passo** to go faster

acenar [ase'nar] *vi* (*com a mão*) to wave; (*com a cabeça*) to nod

acender [asẽ'der] *vt* (*cigarro, fogo*) to light; (*luz*) to switch on; (*fig*) to excite, inflame

acento [a'sẽtu] *m* accent; (*de intensidade*) stress; **acentuar** [asẽ'twar] *vt* to accent; (*salientar*) to stress, emphasize

acepção [asep'sãw] (*pl* **-ões**) *f* (*de uma palavra*) sense

acerca [a'serka] *adv*: **~ de** about, concerning

acertado, -a [aser'tadu, a] *adj* right, correct; (*sensato*) sensible

acertar [aser'tar] *vt* (*ajustar*) to put right; (*relógio*) to set; (*alvo*) to hit; (*acordo*) to reach; (*pergunta*) to get right ▷ *vi* to get it right, be right; **~ o caminho** to find the right way; **~ com** to hit upon

aceso, -a [a'sezu, a] *pp de* **acender** ▷ *adj* (*luz, gás, TV*) on; (*fogo*) alight; (*excitado*) excited; (*furioso*) furious

acessar [ase'sar] *vt* (*Comput*) to access

acessível [ase'sivew] (*pl* **-eis**) *adj* accessible; (*pessoa*) approachable; (*preço*) reasonable, affordable

acesso [a'sɛsu] *m* access; (*Med*) fit, attack

acessório, -a [ase'sɔrju, a] *adj* (*máquina, equipamento*) backup ⊳ *m* accessory

achado [a'ʃadu] *m* find, discovery; (*pechincha*) bargain; (*sorte*) godsend

achar [a'ʃar] *vt* (*descobrir*) to find; (*pensar*) to think; **achar-se** *vr* to think (that) one is; (*encontrar-se*) to be; **~ de fazer** (*resolver*) to decide to do; **o que é que você acha disso?** what do you think of it?; **acho que sim** I think so

achatar [aʃa'tar] *vt* to squash, flatten

acidentado, -a [asidẽ'tadu, a] *adj* (*terreno*) rough; (*estrada*) bumpy; (*viagem*) eventful; (*vida*) difficult ⊳ *m/f* injured person

acidental [asidẽ'taw] (*pl* **-ais**) *adj* accidental

acidente [asi'dẽtʃi] *m* accident; **por ~** by accident; **~ de trânsito** road accident

acidez [asi'dez] *f* acidity

ácido, -a ['asidu, a] *adj* acid; (*azedo*) sour ⊳ *m* acid

acima [a'sima] *adv* above; (*para cima*) up ⊳ *prep*: **~ de** above; (*além de*) beyond; **mais ~** higher up; **rio ~** up river; **passar rua ~** to go up the street; **~ de 1000** more than 1000

acionar [asjo'nar] *vt* to set in motion; (*máquina*) to operate; (*Jur*) to sue

acionista [asjo'nista] *m/f* shareholder

acirrado, -a [asi'hadu, a] *adj* (*luta, competição*) tough

acirrar [asi'har] *vt* to incite, stir up

aclamar [akla'mar] *vt* to acclaim; (*aplaudir*) to applaud

aço ['asu] *m* steel

acocorar-se [akoko'rarsi] *vr* to squat, crouch

acode *etc* [a'kɔdʒi] *vb ver* **acudir**

ações [a'sõjs] *fpl de* **ação**

acolá [ako'la] *adv* over there

acolchoado [akow'ʃwadu] *m* quilt

acolhedor, a [akoʎe'dor(a)] *adj* welcoming; (*hospitaleiro*) hospitable

acolher [ako'ʎer] *vt* to welcome; (*abrigar*) to shelter; (*aceitar*) to accept; **acolher-se** *vr* to shelter; **acolhida** [ako'ʎida] *f* (*recepção*) reception, welcome; (*refúgio*) refuge; **acolhimento** [akoʎi'mẽtu] *m* = **acolhida**

acomodação [akomoda'sãw] (*pl* **-ões**) *f* accommodation; (*arranjo*) arrangement; (*adaptação*) adaptation

acomodar [akomo'dar] *vt* to accommodate; (*arrumar*) to arrange; (*adaptar*) to adapt

acompanhamento [akõpaɲa'mẽtu] *m* attendance; (*cortejo*) procession; (*Mús*) accompaniment; (*Culin*) side dish

acompanhante [akõpa'ɲãtʃi] *m/f* companion; (*Mús*) accompanist; (*de idoso, doente*) carer (*Brit*), caregiver (*US*)

acompanhar [akõpa'ɲar] *vt* to accompany

aconchegante [akõʃe'gãtʃi] *adj* cosy (*Brit*), cozy (*US*)

aconselhar [akõse'ʎar] *vt* to advise; **aconselhar-se** *vr*: **~-se com** to consult

acontecer [akõte'ser] *vi* to happen; **acontecimento** [akõtesi'mẽtu] *m* event

acordar [akor'dar] *vt* to wake (up); (*concordar*) to agree (on) ▷ *vi* to wake up

acorde [a'kɔrdʒi] *m* chord

acordo [a'kordu] *m* agreement; **"de ~!"** "agreed"; **de ~ com** (*pessoa*) in agreement with; (*conforme*) in accordance with; **estar de ~** to agree

Açores [a'soris] *mpl*: **os ~** the Azores; **açoriano, -a** [aso'rjanu, a] *adj, m/f* Azorean

acossar [ako'sar] *vt* (*perseguir*) to pursue; (*atormentar*) to harass

acostamento [akosta'mẽtu] *m* hard shoulder (*Brit*), berm (*US*)

acostumado, -a [akostu'madu, a] *adj* usual, customary; **estar ~ a algo** to be used to sth

acostumar [akostu'mar] *vt* to accustom; **acostumar-se** *vr*: **~-se a** to get used to

açougue [a'sogi] *m* butcher's (shop); **açougueiro** [aso'gejru] *m* butcher

acovardar-se [akovar'darsi] *vr* (*desanimar*) to lose courage; (*amedrontar-se*) to flinch, cower

acreditado, -a [akredʒi'tadu, a] *adj* accredited

acreditar [akredʒi'tar] *vt* to believe; (*Com*) to credit; (*afiançar*) to guarantee ▷ *vi*: **~ em** to believe in

acrescentar [akresẽ'tar] *vt* to add

açúcar [a'sukar] *m* sugar; **açucareiro** [asuka'rejru] *m* sugar bowl

açude [a'sudʒi] *m* dam

acudir [aku'dʒir] *vt* (*ir em socorro*) to help, assist ▷ *vi* (*responder*) to reply, respond; **~ a** to come to the aid of

acumular [akumu'lar] *vt* to accumulate; (*reunir*) to collect; (*funções*) to combine

acusação [akuza'sãw] (*pl* **-ões**) *f* accusation, charge; (*Jur*) prosecution

acusar [aku'zar] *vt* to accuse; (*revelar*) to reveal; (*culpar*) to blame; **~ o recebimento de** to acknowledge receipt of

acústico, -a [a'kustʃiku, a] *adj* acoustic

adaptar [adap'tar] *vt* to adapt; (*acomodar*) to fit; **adaptar-se** *vr*: **~-se a** to adapt to

adega [a'dɛga] *f* cellar

ademais [adʒi'majs] *adv* besides, moreover

adentro [a'dẽtru] *adv* inside, in; **mata ~** into the woods

adequado, -a [ade'kwadu, a] *adj* appropriate

adereço [ade'resu] *m* adornment; **adereços** *mpl* (*Teatro*) stage props

aderente [ade'rẽtʃi] *adj* adhesive, sticky ▷ *m/f* supporter

aderir [ade'rir] *vi* to adhere

adesão [ade'zãw] *f* adhesion; (*patrocínio*) support

adesivo, -a [ade'zivu, a] *adj* adhesive, sticky ▷ *m* adhesive tape; (*Med*) sticking plaster

adestrar [ades'trar] *vt* to train; (*cavalo*) to break in

adeus [a'dews] *excl* goodbye!

adiantado, -a [adʒjã'tadu, a] *adj* advanced; (*relógio*) fast; **chegar ~** to arrive ahead of time; **pagar ~** to pay in advance

adiantamento [adʒjãta'mẽtu] *m* progress; (*dinheiro*) advance (payment)

adiantar [adʒjã'tar] *vt* (*dinheiro, salário*) to advance; (*relógio*) to put forward; **não adianta reclamar/insistir** there's no point ou it's no use complaining/insisting

adiante [a'dʒjãtʃi] adv (na frente) in front; (para a frente) forward; **mais ~** further on; (no futuro) later on

adiar [a'dʒjar] vt to postpone, put off; (sessão) to adjourn

adição [adʒi'sãw] (pl **-ões**) f addition; (Mat) sum; **adicionar** [adʒisjo'nar] vt to add

adido, -a [a'dʒidu, a] m/f attaché

adiro etc [a'diru] vb ver **aderir**

adivinhar [adʒivi'ɲar] vt to guess; (ler a sorte) to foretell ▷ vi to guess; **~ o pensamento de alguém** to read sb's mind; **adivinho, -a** [adʒi'viɲu, a] m/f fortune-teller

adjetivo [adʒe'tʃivu] m adjective

adjudicar [adʒudʒi'kar] vt to award, grant

administração [adʒiministra'sãw] (pl **-ões**) f administration; (direção) management; (comissão) board

administrador, a [adʒiministra'dor(a)] m/f administrator; (diretor) director; (gerente) manager

administrar [adʒiminis'trar] vt to administer, manage; (governar) to govern

admiração [adʒimira'sãw] f wonder; (estima) admiration; **ponto de ~** (PT) exclamation mark

admirado, -a [adʒimi'radu, a] adj astonished, surprised

admirar [adʒimi'rar] vt to admire; **admirar-se** vr: **~-se de** to be astonished ou surprised at; **admirável** [adʒimi'ravew] (pl **-eis**) adj amazing

admissão [adʒimi'sãw] (pl **-ões**) f admission; (consentimento para entrar) admittance; (de escola) intake

admitir [adʒimi'tʃir] vt to admit; (permitir) to allow; (funcionário) to take on

adoção [ado'sãw] f adoption

adoçar [ado'sar] vt to sweeten

adoecer [adoe'ser] vi to fall ill ▷ vt to make ill; **~ de** ou **com** to fall ill with

adoidado, -a [adoj'dadu, a] adj crazy

adolescente [adole'sẽtʃi] adj, m/f adolescent

adorar [ado'rar] vt to adore; (venerar) to worship

adormecer [adorme'ser] vi to fall asleep; (entorpecer-se) to go numb; **adormecido, -a** [adorme'sidu, a] adj sleeping ▷ m/f sleeper

adorno [a'dornu] m adornment

adotar [ado'tar] vt to adopt; **adotivo, -a** [ado'tʃivu, a] adj (filho) adopted

adquirir [adʒiki'rir] vt to acquire

Adriático, -a [a'drjatʃiku, a] adj: **o (mar) ~** the Adriatic (Sea)

adro ['adru] m (church) forecourt; (em volta da igreja) churchyard

adulação [adula'sãw] f flattery

adulterar [aduwte'rar] vt to adulterate; (contas) to falsify ▷ vi to commit adultery

adultério [aduw'tɛrju] m adultery

adulto, -a [a'duwtu, a] adj, m/f adult

advento [ad'vẽtu] m advent; **o A~** Advent

advérbio [adʒi'vɛrbju] m adverb

adverso, -a [adʒi'vɛrsu, a] adj adverse; (oposto): **~ a** opposed to

advertência [adʒiver'tẽsja] f warning

advertir [adʒiver'tʃir] vt to warn; (repreender) to reprimand; (chamar a atenção a) to draw attention to

advogado, -a [adʒivo'gadu, a] *m/f* lawyer

advogar [adʒivo'gar] *vt* to advocate; (*Jur*) to plead ▷ *vi* to practise (*Brit*) *ou* practice (*US*) law

aéreo, -a [a'ɛrju, a] *adj* air atr

aerobarco [aero'barku] *m* jetfoil

aeromoço, -a [aero'mosu, a] (*BR*) *m/f* steward/air hostess

aeronáutica [aero'nawtʃika] *f* air force; (*ciência*) aeronautics *sg*

aeronave [aero'navi] *f* aircraft

aeroporto [aero'portu] *m* airport

aerossol [aero'sɔw] (*pl* **-óis**) *m* aerosol

afã [a'fã] *m* (*entusiasmo*) enthusiasm; (*diligência*) diligence; (*ânsia*) eagerness; (*esforço*) effort

afagar [afa'gar] *vt* to caress; (*cabelo*) to stroke

afastado, -a [afas'tadu, a] *adj* (*distante*) remote; (*isolado*) secluded; **manter-se ~** to keep to o.s.

afastamento [afasta'mẽtu] *m* removal; (*distância*) distance; (*de pessoal*) lay-off

afastar [afas'tar] *vt* to remove; (*separar*) to separate; (*ideia*) to put out of one's mind; (*pessoal*) to lay off; **afastar-se** *vr* to move away

afável [a'favew] (*pl* **-eis**) *adj* friendly

afazeres [afa'zeris] *mpl* business *sg*; (*dever*) duties, tasks; **~ domésticos** household chores

afeição [afej'sãw] *f* affection, fondness; (*dedicação*) devotion; **afeiçoado, -a** [afej'swadu, a] *adj*: **afeiçoado a** (*amoroso*) fond of; (*devotado*) devoted to; **afeiçoar-se** [afej'swarsi] *vr*: **afeiçoar-se a** to take a liking to

afeito, -a [a'fejtu, a] *adj*: **~ a** accustomed to, used to

aferrado, -a [afe'hadu, a] *adj* obstinate, stubborn

afetar [afe'tar] *vt* to affect; (*fingir*) to feign

afetivo, -a [afe'tʃivu, a] *adj* affectionate; (*problema*) emotional

afeto [a'fɛtu] *m* affection; **afetuoso, -a** [afe'twozu, ɔza] *adj* affectionate

afiado, -a [a'fjadu, a] *adj* sharp; (*pessoa*) well-trained

afiar [a'fjar] *vt* to sharpen

aficionado, -a [afisjo'nadu, a] *m/f* enthusiast

afilhado, -a [afi'ʎadu, a] *m/f* godson/goddaughter

afim [a'fĩ] (*pl* **-ns**) *adj* (*semelhante*) similar; (*consanguíneo*) related ▷ *m/f* relative, relation

afinado, -a [afi'nadu, a] *adj* in tune

afinal [afi'naw] *adv* at last, finally; **~ (de contas)** after all

afinar [afi'nar] *vt* (*Mús*) to tune

afinco [a'fĩku] *m* tenacity, persistence

afins [a'fĩs] *pl de* **afim**

afirmação [afirma'sãw] (*pl* **-ões**) *f* affirmation; (*declaração*) statement

afirmar [afir'mar] *vt, vi* to affirm, assert; (*declarar*) to declare

afirmativo, -a [afirma'tʃivu, a] *adj* affirmative

afixar [afik'sar] *vt* (*cartazes*) to stick, post

aflição [afli'sãw] *f* affliction; (*ansiedade*) anxiety; (*angústia*) anguish

afligir [afli'ʒir] *vt* to distress; (*atormentar*) to torment; (*inquietar*) to worry; **afligir-se** *vr*: **~-se com** to worry about; **aflito, -a** [a'flitu, a] *pp de* **afligir** ▷ *adj* distressed, anxious

afluência [a'flwẽsja] *f* affluence; (*corrente copiosa*) flow; (*de pessoas*) stream; **afluente** [a'flwẽtʃi] *adj* copious; (*rico*) affluent ▷ *m* tributary

afobação [afoba'sãw] *f* fluster; (*ansiedade*) panic

afobado, -a [afo'badu, a] *adj* flustered; (*ansioso*) panicky, nervous

afobar [afo'bar] *vt* to fluster; (*deixar ansioso*) to make nervous *ou* panicky ▷ *vi* to get flustered; to panic, get nervous; **afobar-se** *vr* to get flustered

afogar [afo'gar] *vt* to drown ▷ *vi* (*Auto*) to flood; **afogar-se** *vr* to drown

afoito, -a [a'fojtu, a] *adj* bold, daring

afortunado, -a [afortu'nadu, a] *adj* fortunate, lucky

África ['afrika] *f*: **a ~** Africa; **a ~ do Sul** South Africa; **africano, -a** [afri'kanu, a] *adj, m/f* African

afro-brasileiro, -a ['afru-] (*pl* **afro-brasileiros**) *adj* Afro-Brazilian

afronta [a'frõta] *f* insult, affront; **afrontar** [afrõ'tar] *vt* to insult; (*ofender*) to offend

afrouxar [afro'ʃar] *vt* (*desapertar*) to slacken; (*soltar*) to loosen ▷ *vi* to come loose

afta ['afta] *f* (*mouth*) ulcer

afugentar [afuʒẽ'tar] *vt* to drive away, put to flight

afundar [afũ'dar] *vt* to sink; (*cavidade*) to deepen; **afundar-se** *vr* to sink

agachar-se [aga'ʃarsi] *vr* (*acaçapar-se*) to crouch, squat; (*curvar-se*) to stoop

agarrar [aga'har] *vt* to seize, grasp;

agarrar-se *vr*: **~-se a** to cling to, hold on to

agasalhar [agaza'ʎar] *vt* to dress warmly, wrap up; **agasalhar-se** *vr* to wrap o.s. up

agasalho [aga'zaʎu] *m* (*casaco*) coat; (*suéter*) sweater

ágeis ['aʒejs] *pl de* **ágil**

agência [a'ʒẽsja] *f* agency; (*escritório*) office; **~ de correio** (*BR*) post office; **~ de viagens** travel agency

agenda [a'ʒẽda] *f* diary; **~ eletrônica** personal organizer

agente [a'ʒẽtʃi] *m/f* agent; (*de polícia*) policeman/woman

ágil ['aʒiw] (*pl* **-eis**) *adj* agile

agir [a'ʒir] *vi* to act

agitação [aʒita'sãw] (*pl* **-ões**) *f* agitation; (*perturbação*) disturbance; (*inquietação*) restlessness

agitado, -a [aʒi'tadu, a] *adj* agitated, disturbed; (*inquieto*) restless

agitar [aʒi'tar] *vt* to agitate, disturb; (*sacudir*) to shake; (*cauda*) to wag; (*mexer*) to stir; **agitar-se** *vr* to get upset; (*mar*) to get rough

aglomeração [aglomera'sãw] (*pl* **-ões**) *f* gathering; (*multidão*) crowd

aglomerar [aglome'rar] *vt* to heap up, pile up; **aglomerar-se** *vr* (*multidão*) to crowd together

agonia [ago'nia] *f* agony, anguish; (*ânsia da morte*) death throes *pl*; **agonizante** [agoni'zãtʃi] *adj* dying ▷ *m/f* dying person; **agonizar** [agoni'zar] *vi* to be dying; (*afligir-se*) to agonize

agora [a'gɔra] *adv* now; **~ mesmo** right now; (*há pouco*) a moment ago; **até ~** so far, up to now; **por ~**

for now

agosto [a'gostu] *m* August

agouro [a'goru] *m* omen

agraciar [agra'sjar] *vt* to decorate

agradar [agra'dar] *vt* to please; (*fazer agrados a*) to be nice to ▷ *vi* to be pleasing; (*satisfazer*) to go down well

agradável [agra'davew] (*pl* **-eis**) *adj* pleasant

agradecer [agrade'ser] *vt*: ~ **algo a alguém**, ~ **a alguém por algo** to thank sb for sth; **agradecido, -a** [agrade'sidu, a] *adj* grateful; **mal agradecido** ungrateful; **agradecimento** [agradesi'mẽtu] *m* gratitude; **agradecimentos** *mpl* (*gratidão*) thanks

agrado [a'gradu] *m*: **fazer um ~ a alguém** (*afagar*) to be affectionate with sb; (*ser agradável*) to be nice to sb

agrário, -a [a'grarju, a] *adj* agrarian; **reforma agrária** land reform

agravante [agra'vãtʃi] *adj* aggravating ▷ *f* aggravating circumstance

agravar [agra'var] *vt* to aggravate, make worse; **agravar-se** *vr* (*piorar*) to get worse

agredir [agre'dʒir] *vt* to attack; (*insultar*) to insult

agregar [agre'gar] *vt* (*juntar*) to collect; (*acrescentar*) to add

agressão [agre'sãw] (*pl* **-ões**) *f* aggression; (*ataque*) attack; (*assalto*) assault

agressivo, -a [agre'sivu, a] *adj* aggressive

agressões [agre'sõjs] *fpl de* **agressão**

agreste [a'grɛstʃi] *adj* rural, rustic; (*terreno*) wild

agrião [a'grjãw] *m* watercress

agrícola [a'grikola] *adj* agricultural

agricultor [agrikuw'tor] *m* farmer

agricultura [agrikuw'tura] *f* agriculture, farming

agrido *etc* [a'gridu] *vb ver* **agredir**

agridoce [agri'dosi] *adj* bittersweet

agronegócio [agrone'gɔsju] *m* agribusiness

agronomia [agrono'mia] *f* agronomy

agropecuária [agrope'kwarja] *f* farming, agriculture

agrupar [agru'par] *vt* to group; **agrupar-se** *vr* to group together

agrura [a'grura] *f* bitterness

água ['agwa] *f* water; **águas** *fpl* (*mar*) waters; (*chuvas*) rain *sg*; (*maré*) tides; ~ **abaixo/acima** downstream/upstream; **dar ~ na boca** (*comida*) to be mouthwatering; **estar na ~** (*bêbado*) to be drunk; **fazer ~** (*Náut*) to leak; ~ **benta** holy water; ~ **corrente** running water; ~ **de coco** coconut water; ~ **doce** fresh water; ~ **dura/leve** hard/soft water; ~ **mineral** mineral water; ~ **oxigenada** peroxide; ~ **salgada** salt water; ~ **sanitária** household bleach

água-de-colônia (*pl* **águas-de-colônia**) *f* eau-de-cologne

aguado, -a [a'gwadu, a] *adj* watery

aguardar [agwar'dar] *vt* to wait for; (*contar com*) to expect ▷ *vi* to wait

aguardente [agwar'dẽtʃi] *m* spirit (*Brit*), liquor (*US*)

aguçado, -a [agu'sadu, a] *adj* pointed; (*espírito, sentidos*) acute

agudo, -a [a'gudu, a] *adj* sharp,

shrill; (*intenso*) acute
aguentar [agwẽ'tar] *vt* (*muro etc*)
to hold up; (*dor, injustiças*) to stand,
put up with; (*peso*) to withstand
▷ *vi* to last; **aguentar-se** *vr* to
remain, hold on; **~ fazer algo** to
manage to do sth; **não ~ de** not to
be able to stand
águia ['agja] *f* eagle; (*fig*) genius
agulha [a'guʎa] *f* (*de coser, tricô*)
needle; (*Náut*) compass; (*Ferro*)
points *pl* (*Brit*), switch (*US*);
trabalho de ~ needlework
ai [aj] *excl* (*suspiro*) oh!; (*de dor*) ouch!
▷ *m* (*suspiro*) sigh; (*gemido*) groan;
ai de mim! poor me!
aí [a'i] *adv* there; (*então*) then; **por aí**
(*em lugar indeterminado*)
somewhere over there,
thereabouts; **espera aí!** wait!,
hang on a minute!; **está aí!** (*col*)
right!; **e aí?** and then what?
AIDS ['ajdʒs] *f* AIDS
ainda [a'ĩda] *adv* still; (*mesmo*)
even; **~ agora** just now; **~ assim**
even so, nevertheless; **~ bem** just
as well; **~ por cima** on top of all
that, in addition; **~ não** not yet; **~
que** even if; **maior ~** even bigger
aipo ['ajpu] *m* celery
ajeitar [aʒej'tar] *vt* (*adaptar*) to fit,
adjust; (*arranjar*) to arrange;
ajeitar-se *vr* to adapt
ajo *etc* ['aʒu] *vb ver* **agir**
ajoelhar [aʒwe'ʎar] *vi* to kneel
(down); **ajoelhar-se** *vr* to kneel
down
ajuda [a'ʒuda] *f* help; (*subsídio*)
grant, subsidy; **dar ~ a alguém** to
lend *ou* give sb a hand; **~ de custo**
allowance; **ajudante** [aʒu'dãtʃi]
m/f assistant, helper; (*Mil*)
adjutant
ajudar [aʒu'dar] *vt* to help

ajuizado, -a [aʒwi'zadu, a] *adj*
(*sensato*) sensible; (*sábio*) wise;
(*prudente*) discreet
ajuntamento [aʒũta'mẽtu] *m*
gathering
ajustagem [aʒus'taʒẽ] (*BR*) (*pl* **-ns**)
f (*Tec*) adjustment
ajustamento [aʒusta'mẽtu] *m*
adjustment; (*de contas*) settlement
ajustar [aʒus'tar] *vt* to adjust;
(*conta, disputa*) to settle; (*acomodar*)
to fit; (*roupa*) to take in; (*preço*)
to agree on; **ajustar-se** *vr*: **~-se a**
to conform to; (*adaptar-se*)
to adapt to
ajuste [a'ʒustʃi] *m* (*acordo*)
agreement; (*de contas*) settlement;
(*adaptação*) adjustment
ala ['ala] *f* (*fileira*) row; (*passagem*)
aisle; (*de edifício, exército, ave*) wing
alagar [ala'gar] *vt, vi* to flood
alameda [ala'meda] *f* (*avenida*)
avenue; (*arvoredo*) grove
alarde [a'lardʒi] *m* ostentation;
(*jactância*) boasting; **fazer ~ de** to
boast about; **alardear** [alar'dʒar]
vt to show off; (*gabar-se de*) to
boast of ▷ *vi* to boast; **alardear-se**
vr to boast
alargar [alar'gar] *vt* to extend;
(*fazer mais largo*) to widen, broaden;
(*afrouxar*) to loosen, slacken
alarma [a'larma] *f* alarm; (*susto*)
panic; (*tumulto*) tumult; (*vozearia*)
outcry; **dar o sinal de ~** to raise the
alarm; **~ de roubo** burglar alarm;
alarmante [alar'mãtʃi] *adj*
alarming; **alarmar** [alar'mar] *vt*
to alarm; **alarmar-se** *vr* to be
alarmed
alarme [a'larmi] *m* = **alarma**
alastrar [alas'trar] *vt* to scatter;
(*disseminar*) to spread; **alastrar-se**
vr (*epidemia, rumor*) to spread

alavanca [ala'vāka] f lever; (*pé de cabra*) crowbar; **~ de mudanças** gear lever

albergue [aw'bɛrgi] m (*estalagem*) inn; (*refúgio*) hospice, shelter; **~ noturno** hotel; **~ para jovens** youth hostel

álbum ['awbū] (*pl* **-ns**) m album; **~ de recortes** scrapbook

alça ['awsa] f strap; (*asa*) handle; (*de fusil*) sight

alcachofra [awka'ʃofra] f artichoke

alcançar [awkā'sar] vt to reach; (*estender*) to hand, pass; (*obter*) to obtain, get; (*atingir*) to attain; (*compreender*) to understand; (*desfalcar*): **~ uma firma em $1 milhão** to embezzle $1 million from a firm

alcance [aw'kāsi] m reach; (*competência*) power; (*compreensão*) understanding; (*de tiro, visão*) range; **ao ~ de** within reach *ou* range of; **ao ~ da voz** within earshot; **de grande ~** far-reaching; **fora do ~ da mão** out of reach; **fora do ~ de alguém** beyond sb's grasp

alcaparra [awka'paha] f caper

alcatrão [awka'trāw] m tar

álcool ['awkɔw] m alcohol; **alcoólatra** [aw'kɔlatra] m/f alcoholic; **alcoólico, -a** [aw'kɔliku, a] adj, m/f alcoholic

Alcorão [awko'rāw] m Koran

alcova [aw'kova] f bedroom

alcunha [aw'kuɲa] f nickname

aldeão, -deã [aw'dʒjāw, jā] (*pl* **-ões/-s**) m/f villager

aldeia [aw'deja] f village

aldeões [aw'dʒjõjs] mpl de **aldeão**

alecrim [ale'krī] m rosemary

alegar [ale'gar] vt to allege; (*Jur*) to plead

alegoria [alego'ria] f allegory

alegórico, -a [ale'gɔriku, a] adj allegorical; **carro ~** float

alegrar [ale'grar] vt to cheer (up), gladden; (*ambiente*) to brighten up; (*animar*) to liven (up); **alegrar-se** vr to cheer up

alegre [a'lɛgri] adj cheerful; (*contente*) happy, glad; (*cores*) bright; (*embriagado*) merry, tight; **alegria** [ale'gria] f joy, happiness

aleijado, -a [alej'ʒadu, a] adj crippled ▷ m/f cripple

aleijar [alej'ʒar] vt to maim

além [a'lēj] adv (*lá ao longe*) over there; (*mais adiante*) further on ▷ m: **o ~** the hereafter ▷ prep: **~ de** beyond; (*no outro lado de*) on the other side of; (*para mais de*) over; (*ademais de*) apart from, besides; **~ disso** moreover; **mais ~** further

alemã [ale'mā] f de **alemão**

alemães [ale'mãjs] mpl de **alemão**

Alemanha [ale'māɲa] f: **a ~** Germany

alemão, -mã [ale'māw, 'mā] (*pl* **-ães/-s**) adj, m/f German ▷ m (*Ling*) German

alento [a'lētu] m (*fôlego*) breath; (*ânimo*) courage; **dar ~** to encourage; **tomar ~** to draw breath

alergia [aler'ʒia] f: **~ (a)** allergy (to); (*fig*) aversion (to); **alérgico, -a** [a'lɛrʒiku, a] adj: **alérgico (a)** allergic (to)

alerta [a'lɛrta] adj alert ▷ adv on the alert ▷ m alert

alfabetizar [awfabetʃi'zar] vt to teach to read and write; **alfabetizar-se** vr to learn to read and write

alfabeto [awfa'bɛtu] m alphabet

alface [aw'fasi] f lettuce

alfaiate [awfa'jatʃi] m tailor

alfândega [aw'fãdʒiga] f customs pl, customs house; **alfandegário, -a** [awfãde'garju, a] m/f customs officer

alfazema [awfa'zɛma] f lavender

alfinete [awfi'netʃi] m pin; **~ de segurança** safety pin

alga ['awga] f seaweed

Algarve [aw'garvi] m: **o ~** the Algarve

algazarra [awga'zaha] f uproar, racket

álgebra ['awʒebra] f algebra

algemas [aw'ʒɛmas] fpl handcuffs

algo ['awgu] adv somewhat, rather ▷ pron something; (qualquer coisa) anything

algodão [awgo'dãw] m cotton; **~ (hidrófilo)** cotton wool (Brit), absorbent cotton (US)

alguém [aw'gẽj] pron someone, somebody; (em frases interrogativas ou negativas) anyone, anybody

algum, a [aw'gũ, 'guma] adj some; (em frases interrogativas ou negativas) any ▷ pron one; (no plural) some; (negativa): **de modo ~** in no way; **coisa ~a** nothing; **~ dia** one day; **~ tempo** for a while; **~a coisa** something; **~a vez** sometime

alheio, -a [a'ʎeju, a] adj (de outra pessoa) someone else's; (de outras pessoas) other people's; (estranho) alien; (estrangeiro) foreign; (impróprio) irrelevant

alho ['aʎu] m garlic

ali [a'li] adv there; **até ~** up to there; **por ~** around there; (direção) that way; **~ por** (tempo) round about; **de ~ por diante** from then on; **~ dentro** in there

aliado, -a [a'ljadu, a] adj allied ▷ m/f ally

aliança [a'ljãsa] f alliance; (anel) wedding ring

aliar [a'ljar] vt to ally; **aliar-se** vr to form an alliance

aliás [a'ljajs] adv (a propósito) as a matter of fact; (ou seja) rather, that is; (contudo) nevertheless; (diga-se de passagem) incidentally

álibi ['alibi] m alibi

alicate [ali'katʃi] m pliers pl; **~ de unhas** nail clippers pl

alienação [aljena'sãw] f alienation; (de bens) transfer (of property); **~ mental** insanity

alienado, -a [alje'nadu, a] adj alienated; (demente) insane; (bens) transferred ▷ m/f lunatic

alienar [alje'nar] vt (bens) to transfer; (afastar) to alienate

alimentação [alimẽta'sãw] f (alimentos) food; (ação) feeding; (nutrição) nourishment; (Elet) supply

alimentar [alimẽ'tar] vt to feed; (fig) to nurture ▷ adj (produto) food atr; (hábitos) eating atr; **alimentar-se** vr: **~-se de** to feed on

alimento [ali'mẽtu] m food; (nutrição) nourishment

alisar [ali'zar] vt to smooth; (cabelo) to straighten; (acariciar) to stroke

aliviar [ali'vjar] vt to relieve

alívio [a'livju] m relief

alma ['awma] f soul; (entusiasmo) enthusiasm; (caráter) character

almejar [awme'ʒar] vt to long for, yearn for

almirante [awmi'rãtʃi] m admiral

almoçar [awmo'sar] vi to have lunch ▷ vt: **~ peixe** to have fish for lunch

almoço [aw'mosu] m lunch;

pequeno ~ (PT) breakfast
almofada [awmo'fada] f cushion; (PT: travesseiro) pillow
almoxarifado [awmoʃari'fadu] m storeroom
alô [a'lo] excl (BR) (Tel) hello
alocar [alo'kar] vt to allocate
alojamento [aloʒa'mẽtu] m accommodation (Brit), accommodations pl (US); (habitação) housing
alojar [alo'ʒar] vt to lodge; (Mil) to billet; **alojar-se** vr to stay
alongar [alõ'gar] vt to lengthen; (prazo) to extend; (prolongar) to prolong; (braço) to stretch out; **alongar-se** vr (sobre um assunto) to dwell
aloprado, -a [alo'pradu, a] (col) adj nutty
alpendre [aw'pẽdri] m (telheiro) shed; (pórtico) porch
Alpes ['awpis] mpl: **os ~** the Alps
alpinismo [awpi'nizmu] m mountaineering, climbing; **alpinista** [awpi'nista] m/f mountaineer, climber
alta ['awta] f (de preços) rise; (de hospital) discharge
altar [aw'tar] m altar
alterado, -a [awte'radu, a] adj bad-tempered, irritated
alterar [awte'rar] vt to alter; (falsificar) to falsify; **alterar-se** vr (mudar-se) to change; (enfurecer-se) to lose one's temper
alternar [awter'nar] vt, vi to alternate; **alternar-se** vr to alternate; (por turnos) to take turns
alternativa [awterna'tʃiva] f alternative
alternativo, -a [awterna'tʃivu, a] adj alternative; (Elet) alternating
alteza [aw'teza] f highness

altitude [awtʃi'tudʒi] f altitude
alto, -a ['awtu, a] adj high; (pessoa) tall; (som) loud; (Geo) upper ▷ adv (falar) loudly, loud; (voar) high ▷ excl halt! ▷ m top, summit; **do ~** from above; **por ~** superficially; **alta fidelidade** high fidelity, hi-fi; **alta noite** dead of night
alto-falante (pl **alto-falantes**) m loudspeaker
altura [aw'tura] f height; (momento) point, juncture; (altitude) altitude; (de um som) pitch; **em que ~ da Rio Branco fica a livraria?** whereabouts in Rio Branco is the bookshop?; **nesta ~** at this juncture; **estar à ~ de** (ser capaz de) to be up to; **ter 1.80 metros de ~** to be 1.80 metres (Brit) ou meters (US) tall
alucinado, -a [alusi'nadu, a] adj crazy
alugar [alu'gar] vt (tomar de aluguel) to rent, hire; (dar de aluguel) to let, rent out; **alugar-se** vr to let; **aluguel** [alu'gɛw] (pl **-éis**) (BR) m rent; (ação) renting; **aluguel de carro** car hire (Brit) ou rental (US); **aluguer** [alu'gɛr] (PT) m = **aluguel**
alumínio [alu'minju] m aluminium (Brit), aluminum (US)
aluno, -a [a'lunu, a] m/f pupil, student
alvejar [awve'ʒar] vt (tomar como alvo) to aim at; (branquear) bleach
alvenaria [awvena'ria] f masonry; **de ~** brick atr, brick-built
alvéolo [aw'vɛolu] m cavity
alvo, -a ['awvu, a] adj white ▷ m target
alvorada [awvo'rada] f dawn
alvorecer [awvore'ser] vi to dawn
alvoroço [awvo'rosu] m commotion; (entusiasmo) enthusiasm

amabilidade [amabili'dadʒi] f
kindness; (simpatia) friendliness

amaciante [ama'sjãtʃi] m: **~ (de
roupa)** fabric conditioner

amaciar [ama'sjar] vt (tornar
macio) to soften; (carro) to run in

amado, -a [a'madu, a] m/f
beloved, sweetheart

amador, a [ama'dor(a)] adj, m/f
amateur

amadurecer [amadure'ser] vt, vi
(frutos) to ripen; (fig) to mature

âmago ['amagu] m (centro) heart,
core; (medula) pith; (essência)
essence

amalgamar [amawga'mar] vt to
amalgamate; (combinar) to fuse
(Brit), fuze (US), blend

amalucado, -a [amalu'kadu, a]
adj crazy, whacky

amamentar [amamē'tar] vt, vi to
breast-feed

amanhã [ama'ɲã] adv, m tomorrow

amanhecer [amaɲe'ser] vi
(alvorecer) to dawn; (encontrar-se
pela manhã): **amanhecemos em
Paris** we were in Paris at daybreak
▷ m dawn; **ao ~** at daybreak

amansar [amã'sar] vt (animais) to
tame; (cavalos) to break in;
(aplacar) to placate

amante [a'mãtʃi] m/f lover

amar [a'mar] vt to love; **eu te amo** I
love you

amarelo, -a [ama'rɛlu, a] adj
yellow ▷ m yellow

amargar [amar'gar] vt to make
bitter; (fig) to embitter

amargo, -a [a'margu, a] adj bitter;
amargura [amar'gura] f
bitterness

amarrar [ama'har] vt to tie (up);
(Náut) to moor; **~ a cara** to frown,
scowl

amarrotar [amaho'tar] vt to
crease

amassar [ama'sar] vt (pão) to
knead; (misturar) to mix; (papel) to
screw up; (roupa) to crease; (carro)
to dent

amável [a'mavew] (pl **-eis**) adj kind

Amazonas [ama'zɔnas] m: **o ~** the
Amazon

Amazônia [ama'zonja] f: **a ~** the
Amazon region

○ **AMAZÔNIA**
○
○ **Amazônia** is the region formed
○ by the basin of the river Amazon
○ (the river with the largest volume
○ of water in the world) and its
○ tributaries. With a total area of
○ almost 7 million square
○ kilometres, it stretches from the
○ Atlantic to the Andes. Most of
○ **Amazônia** is in Brazilian
○ territory, although it also
○ extends into Peru, Colombia,
○ Venezuela and Bolivia. It
○ contains the richest biodiversity
○ and largest area of tropical
○ rainforest in the world.

ambição [ambi'sãw] (pl **-ões**) f
ambition; **ambicionar**
[ãbisjo'nar] vt to aspire to;
ambicioso, -a [ãbi'sjozu, ɔza] adj
ambitious

ambidestro, -a [ãbi'destru, a] adj
ambidextrous

ambientar [ãbjē'tar] vt (filme etc)
to set; (adaptar): **~ alguém a algo**
to get sb used to sth;
ambientar-se vr to fit in

ambiente [ã'bjētʃi] m atmosphere;
(meio, Comput) environment; **meio
~** environment; **temperatura ~**

room temperature

ambíguo, -a [ã'bigwu, a] *adj* ambiguous

âmbito ['ãbitu] *m* extent; (*campo de ação*) scope, range

ambos, ambas ['ãbus, as] *adj pl* both

ambulância [ãbu'lãsja] *f* ambulance

ambulante [ãbu'lãtʃi] *adj* walking; (*errante*) wandering; (*biblioteca*) mobile

ambulatório [ãbula'tɔrju] *m* outpatient department

ameaça [ame'asa] *f* threat; **~ de bomba** bomb scare; **ameaçar** [amea'sar] *vt* to threaten

amedrontar [amedrõ'tar] *vt* to scare, intimidate; **amedrontar-se** *vr* to be frightened

ameixa [a'mejʃa] *f* plum; (*passa*) prune

amém [a'mẽj] *excl* amen

amêndoa [a'mẽdwa] *f* almond; **amendoeira** [amẽ'dwejra] *f* almond tree

amendoim [amẽdo'ĩ] (*pl* **-ns**) *m* peanut

amenidade [ameni'dadʒi] *f* wellbeing; **amenidades** *fpl* (*assuntos superficiais*) small talk *sg*

amenizar [ameni'zar] *vt* (*abrandar*) to soften; (*tornar agradável*) to make pleasant; (*facilitar*) to ease

ameno, -a [a'mɛnu, a] *adj* pleasant; (*clima*) mild

América [a'mɛrika] *f*: **a ~** America; **a ~ do Norte/do Sul** North/South America; **a ~ Central/Latina** Central/Latin America; **americano, -a** [ameri'kanu, a] *adj, m/f* American

amestrar [ames'trar] *vt* to train

amianto [a'mjãtu] *m* asbestos

amido [a'midu] *m* starch

amigável [ami'gavew] (*pl* **-eis**) *adj* amicable

amígdala [a'migdala] *f* tonsil; **amigdalite** [amigda'litʃi] *f* tonsillitis

amigo, -a [a'migu, a] *adj* friendly ▷ *m/f* friend; **ser ~ de** to be friends with

amistoso, -a [amis'tozu, ɔza] *adj* friendly, cordial ▷ *m* (*jogo*) friendly

amiúde [a'mjudʒi] *adv* often, frequently

amizade [ami'zadʒi] *f* (*relação*) friendship; (*simpatia*) friendliness

amnistia [amnis'tia] (*PT*) *f* = **anistia**

amolação [amola'sãw] (*pl* **-ões**) *f* bother, annoyance

amolar [amo'lar] *vt* to sharpen; (*aborrecer*) to annoy, bother ▷ *vi* to be annoying

amolecer [amole'ser] *vt* to soften ▷ *vi* to soften; (*abrandar-se*) to relent

amônia [a'monja] *f* ammonia

amoníaco [amo'niaku] *m* ammonia

amontoar [amõ'twar] *vt* to pile up, accumulate; **~ riquezas** to amass a fortune

amor [a'mor] *m* love; **por ~ de** for the sake of; **fazer ~** to make love

amora [a'mɔra] *f* (*amora-preta*) blackberry; **~ silvestre** blackberry

amordaçar [amorda'sar] *vt* to gag

amoroso, -a [amo'rozu, ɔza] *adj* loving, affectionate

amor-perfeito (*pl* **amores-perfeitos**) *m* pansy

amortização [amortʃiza'sãw] *f* payment in instalments (*Brit*) *ou* installments (*US*)

amortizar [amortʃi'zar] *vt* to pay

in instalments (*Brit*) *ou* installments (*US*)

amostra [a'mɔstra] *f* sample

amparar [ãpa'rar] *vt* to support; (*ajudar*) to assist; **amparar-se** *vr*: **~-se em/contra** to lean on/against

amparo [ã'paru] *m* support; (*auxílio*) help, assistance

ampliação [amplja'sãw] (*pl* **-ões**) *f* enlargement; (*extensão*) extension

ampliar [ã'pljar] *vt* to enlarge; (*conhecimento*) to broaden

amplificador [ãplifika'dor] *m* amplifier

amplificar [ãplifi'kar] *vt* to amplify

amplitude [ãpli'tudʒi] *f* (*espaço*) spaciousness; (*fig: extensão*) extent

amplo, -a ['ãplu, a] *adj* (*sala*) spacious; (*conhecimento, sentido*) broad; (*possibilidade*) ample

amputar [ãpu'tar] *vt* to amputate

Amsterdã [amister'dã] (*BR*) *n* Amsterdam

Amsterdão [amister'dãw] (*PT*) *n* = **Amsterdã**

amuado, -a [a'mwadu, a] *adj* sulky

anã [a'nã] *f de* **anão**

anais [a'najs] *mpl* annals

analfabeto, -a [anawfa'bɛtu, a] *adj, m/f* illiterate

analgésico, -a [anaw'ʒɛziku, a] *adj* analgesic ▷ *m* painkiller

analisar [anali'zar] *vt* to analyse; **análise** [a'nalizi] *f* analysis; **analista** [ana'lista] *m/f* analyst

ananás [ana'nas] (*pl* **ananases**) *m* (*BR*) variety of pineapple; (*PT*) pineapple

anão, anã [a'nãw, a'nã] (*pl* **-ões/-s**) *m/f* dwarf

anarquia [anar'kia] *f* anarchy; **anarquista** [anar'kista] *m/f* anarchist

anatomia [anato'mia] *f* anatomy

anca ['ãka] *f* (*de pessoa*) hip; (*de animal*) rump

ancião, anciã [ã'sjãw, ã'sjã] (*pl* **-ões/anciãs**) *adj* old ▷ *m/f* old man/woman; (*de uma tribo*) elder

anciões [a'sjõjs] *mpl de* **ancião**

âncora ['ãkora] *f* anchor; **ancorar** [ãko'rar] *vt, vi* to anchor

andaime [ã'dajmi] *m* (*Arq*) scaffolding

andamento [ãda'mẽtu] *m* (*progresso*) progress; (*rumo*) course; (*Mús*) tempo; **em ~** in progress

andar [ã'dar] *vi* to walk; (*máquina*) to work; (*progredir*) to progress; (*estar*): **ela anda triste** she's been sad lately ▷ *m* gait; (*pavimento*) floor, storey (*Brit*), story (*US*); **anda!** hurry up!; **~ a cavalo** to ride; **~ de trem/avião/bicicleta** to travel by train/fly/ride a bike

Andes ['ãdʒis] *mpl*: **os ~** the Andes

andorinha [ãdo'riɲa] *f* (*pássaro*) swallow

anedota [ane'dɔta] *f* anecdote

anel [a'nɛw] (*pl* **-éis**) *m* ring; (*elo*) link; (*de cabelo*) curl; **~ de casamento** wedding ring

anestesia [aneste'zia] *f* anaesthesia (*Brit*), anesthesia (*US*); (*anestésico*) anaesthetic (*Brit*), anesthetic (*US*)

anexar [anek'sar] *vt* to annex; (*juntar*) to attach; (*documento*) to enclose; **anexo, -a** [a'nɛksu, a] *adj* attached ▷ *m* annexe; (*em carta*) enclosure; (*em e-mail*) attachment; **segue em anexo** please find enclosed

anfitrião, -triã [ãfi'trjãw, 'trjã] (*pl* **-ões/-s**) *m/f* host/hostess

angina [ã'ʒina] *f*: **~ do peito** angina (pectoris)

Angola [ã'gɔla] *f* Angola

angu [ã'gu] *m* corn-meal purée

ângulo ['ãgulu] *m* angle; (*canto*) corner

angústia [ã'guʃtʃja] *f* anguish, distress

animado, -a [ani'madu, a] *adj* lively; (*alegre*) cheerful; **~ com** enthusiastic about

animador, a [anima'dor(a)] *adj* encouraging ▷ *m/f* (BR: TV) presenter; (*de festa*) entertainer; **~a de torcida** cheerleader

animal [ani'maw] (*pl* **-ais**) *adj, m* animal; **~ de estimação** pet (animal)

animar [ani'mar] *vt* to liven up; (*encorajar*) to encourage; **animar-se** *vr* to cheer up; (*festa etc*) to liven up; **~-se a** to bring o.s. to

ânimo ['animu] *m* (*coragem*) courage; **~!** cheer up!; **perder o ~** to lose heart; **recobrar o ~** to pluck up courage; (*alegrar-se*) to cheer up

aninhar [ani'ɲar] *vt* to nestle; **aninhar-se** *vr* to nestle

anis [a'nis] *m* aniseed

anistia [anis'tʃia] *f* amnesty

aniversário [aniver'sarju] *m* anniversary; (*de nascimento*) birthday; (: *festa*) birthday party

anjo ['ãʒu] *m* angel; **~ da guarda** guardian angel

ano ['anu] *m* year; **Feliz A~ Novo!** Happy New Year!; **o ~ que vem** next year; **por ~** per annum; **fazer ~s** to have a birthday; **ter dez ~s** to be ten (years old); **dia de ~s** (PT) birthday; **~ letivo** academic year; (*da escola*) school year

anões [a'nõjs] *mpl de* **anão**

anoitecer [anojte'ser] *vi* to grow dark ▷ *m* nightfall

anomalia [anoma'lia] *f* anomaly

anônimo, -a [a'nonimu, a] *adj* anonymous

anoraque [ano'raki] *m* anorak

anormal [anor'maw] (*pl* **-ais**) *adj* abnormal; (*excepcional*) handicapped; **anormalidade** [anormali'dadʒi] *f* abnormality

anotação [anota'sãw] (*pl* **-ões**) *f* annotation; (*nota*) note

anotar [ano'tar] *vt* (*tomar nota*) to note down; (*esclarecer*) to annotate

anseio *etc* [ã'seju] *vb ver* **ansiar**

ânsia ['ãsja] *f* anxiety; (*desejo*): **~ (de)** longing (for); **ter ~s (de vômito)** to feel sick

ansiar [ã'sjar] *vi*: **~ por** (*desejar*) to yearn for; **~ por fazer** to long to do

ansiedade [ãsje'dadʒi] *f* anxiety; (*desejo*) eagerness

ansioso, -a [ã'sjozu, ɔza] *adj* anxious; (*desejoso*) eager

antártico, -a [ã'tartʃiku, a] *adj* antarctic ▷ *m*: **o A~** the Antarctic

ante ['ãtʃi] *prep* (*na presença de*) before; (*em vista de*) in view of, faced with

antecedência [ãtese'dẽsja] *f*: **com ~** in advance; **3 dias de ~** three days' notice

antecedente [ãtese'dẽtʃi] *adj* preceding ▷ *m* antecedent; **antecedentes** *mpl* (*registro*) record *sg*; (*passado*) background *sg*

anteceder [ãtese'der] *vt* to precede

antecipação [ãtesipa'sãw] *f* anticipation; **com um mês de ~** a month in advance; **~ de pagamento** advance (payment)

antecipadamente [ãtesipada'mẽtʃi] *adv* in advance, beforehand

antecipado, -a [ãtesi'padu, a] *adj* (*pagamento*) (in) advance

antecipar [ãtesi'par] *vt* to

anticipate, forestall; (*adiantar*) to bring forward

antemão [ante'mãw] *adv*: **de ~** beforehand

antena [ã'tɛna] *f* (*Bio*) antenna, feeler; (*Radio, TV*) aerial

anteontem [ãtʃi'õtẽ] *adv* the day before yesterday

antepassado [ãtʃipa'sadu] *m* ancestor

anterior [ãte'rjor] *adj* previous; (*antigo*) former; (*de posição*) front

antes ['ãtʃis] *adv* before; (*antigamente*) formerly; (*ao contrário*) rather ▷ *prep*: **~ de** before; **o quanto ~** as soon as possible; **~ de partir** before leaving; **~ de tudo** above all; **~ que** before

anti- [ãtʃi] *prefixo* anti-

antiácido, -a [ã'tʃjasidu, a] *adj, m* antacid

antibiótico, -a [ãtʃi'bjɔtʃiku, a] *adj, m* antibiotic

anticaspa [ãtʃi'kaspa] *adj inv* anti-dandruff

anticlímax [ãtʃi'klimaks] *m* anticlimax

anticoncepcional [ãtʃikõsepsjo'naw] (*pl* **-ais**) *adj, m* contraceptive

antidepressivo, -a [ãtʃidepre'sivu, a] *adj, m* anti-depressant

antigamente [ãtʃiga'mẽtʃi] *adv* formerly; (*no passado*) in the past

antiglobalização [ãtʃiglobaliza'sãw] *f* antiglobalization

antigo, -a [ã'tʃigu, a] *adj* old; (*histórico*) ancient; (*de estilo*) antique; (*chefe etc*) former

antiguidade [ãtʃigwi'dadʒi] *f* antiquity, ancient times *pl*; (*de

emprego) seniority; **antiguidades** *fpl* (*monumentos*) ancient monuments; (*artigos*) antiques

anti-horário, -a *adj* anticlockwise

antilhano, -a [ãtʃi'ʎanu, a] *adj, m/f* West Indian

Antilhas [ã'tʃiʎas] *fpl*: **as ~** the West Indies

antipatia [ãtʃipa'tʃia] *f* dislike; **antipático, -a** [ãtʃi'patʃiku, a] *adj* unpleasant, unfriendly

antipatizar [ãtʃipatʃi'zar] *vi*: **~ com alguém** to dislike sb

antiquado, -a [ãtʃi'kwadu, a] *adj* antiquated; (*fora de moda*) out of date, old-fashioned

antiquário, -a [ãtʃi'kwarju, a] *m/f* antique dealer ▷ *m* (*loja*) antique shop

antissemita *adj* anti-Semitic

antisséptico, -a *adj, m* antiseptic

antissocial (*pl* **-ais**) *adj* antisocial

antivírus [ãtʃi'virus] *m inv* (*Comput*) antivirus

antologia [ãtolo'ʒia] *f* anthology

anual [a'nwaw] (*pl* **-ais**) *adj* annual, yearly

anulação [anula'sãw] (*pl* **-ões**) *f* cancellation; (*de contrato, casamento*) annulment

anunciante [anũ'sjãtʃi] *m* (*Com*) advertiser

anunciar [anũ'sjar] *vt* to announce; (*Com*) to advertise

anúncio [a'nũsju] *m* announcement; (*Com*) advertisement; (*cartaz*) notice; **~s classificados** small *ou* classified ads

ânus ['anus] *m inv* anus

anzol [ã'zɔw] (*pl* **-óis**) *m* fish-hook

ao [aw] = **a + o**; *ver* **a**

aonde [a'õdʒi] *adv* where; **~ quer que** wherever

aos [aws] = **a** + **os**; *ver* **a**

Ap. *abr* = **apartamento**

apagado, -a [apa'gadu, a] *adj*
(*fogo*) out; (*luz elétrica*) off

apagão [apa'gãw] (*pl* **-ões**) *m*
power cut (*Brit*), power outage (*US*)

apagar [apa'gar] *vt* to put out; (*luz
elétrica*) to switch off; (*vela*) to blow
out; (*com borracha*) to rub out,
erase; **apagar-se** *vr* to go out

apaixonado, -a [apajʃo'nadu, a]
adj (*discurso*) impassioned;
(*pessoa*): **ele está ~ por ela** he is in
love with her; **ele é ~ por tênis** he's
mad about tennis

apaixonar-se [apajʃo'narsi] *vr*:
~ por to fall in love with

apalpar [apaw'par] *vt* to touch,
feel; (*Med*) to examine

apanhado [apa'ɲadu] *m* (*de flores*)
bunch; (*resumo*) summary

apanhar [apa'ɲar] *vt* to catch;
(*algo à mão, do chão*) to pick up; (*ir
buscar, surra, táxi*) to get; (*flores,
frutas*) to pick; (*agarrar*) to grab ▷ *vi*
to get a beating; **~ sol/chuva** to
sunbathe/get soaked

aparador [apara'dor] *m* sideboard

apara-lápis [apara'lapis] (*PT*) *m inv*
pencil sharpener

aparar [apa'rar] *vt* (*cabelo*) to trim;
(*lápis*) to sharpen; (*algo
arremessado*) to catch

aparato [apa'ratu] *m* pomp;
(*coleção*) array

aparecer [apare'ser] *vi* to appear;
(*apresentar-se*) to turn up; (*ser
publicado*) to be published; **~ em
casa de alguém** to call on sb;
aparecimento [aparesi'mẽtu] *m*
appearance; (*publicação*) publication

aparelho [apa'reʎu] *m* apparatus;
(*equipamento*) equipment; (*Pesca*)
tackle; (*máquina*) machine; (*BR:

fone*) telephone; **~ de barbear**
electric shaver; **~ de chá** tea set;
~ de rádio/TV radio/TV set;
~ doméstico domestic appliance

aparência [apa'rẽsja] *f*
appearance; **na ~** apparently; **sob
a ~ de** under the guise of; **ter ~ de**
to look like, seem

aparentar [aparẽ'tar] *vt* (*fingir*) to
feign; (*parecer*) to give the
appearance of

aparente [apa'rẽtʃi] *adj* apparent

aparição [apari'sãw] (*pl* **-ões**) *f*
(*visão*) apparition; (*fantasma*) ghost

apartamento [aparta'mẽtu] *m*
apartment, flat (*Brit*)

apartar [apar'tar] *vt* to separate;
apartar-se *vr* to separate

apatia [apa'tʃia] *f* apathy

apático, -a [a'patʃiku, a] *adj*
apathetic

apavorado, -a [apavo'radu, a] *adj*
terrified

apavorante [apavo'rãtʃi] *adj*
terrifying

apavorar [apavo'rar] *vt* to terrify
▷ *vi* to be terrifying; **apavorar-se**
vr to be terrified

apear-se [a'pjarsi] *vr*: **~ de** (*cavalo*)
to dismount from

apegado, -a [ape'gadu, a] *adj*:
ser ~ a (*gostar de*) to be attached to

apegar-se [ape'garsi] *vr*: **~ a**
(*afeiçoar-se*) to become attached to

apego [a'pegu] *m* (*afeição*)
attachment

apelar [ape'lar] *vi* to appeal; **~ da
sentença** (*Jur*) to appeal against
the sentence; **~ para** to appeal to;
~ para a ignorância/violência to
resort to abuse/violence

apelido [ape'lidu] *m* (*PT: nome de
família*) surname; (*BR: alcunha*)
nickname

apelo [a'pelu] *m* appeal
apenas [a'penas] *adv* only
apendicite [apēdʒi'sitʃi] *f* appendicitis
aperfeiçoar [aperfej'swar] *vt* to perfect; *(melhorar)* to improve
apertado, -a [aper'tadu, a] *adj* tight; *(estreito)* narrow; *(sem dinheiro)* hard-up; *(vida)* hard
apertar [aper'tar] *vt (agarrar)* to hold tight; *(roupa)* to take in; *(esponja)* to squeeze; *(botão)* to press; *(despesas)* to limit; *(vigilância)* to step up; *(coração)* to break; ▷ *vi (sapatos)* to pinch; *(chuva, frio)* to get worse; *(estrada)* to narrow; **~ em** *(insistir)* to insist on; **~ a mão de alguém** to shake hands with sb
aperto [a'pertu] *m (pressão)* pressure; *(situação difícil)* spot of bother, jam; **um ~ de mãos** a handshake
apesar [ape'zar] *prep*: **~ de** in spite of, despite; **~ disso** nevertheless; **~ de que** even though
apetecer [apete'ser] *vi (comida)* to be appetizing
apetite [ape'tʃitʃi] *m* appetite; **bom ~!** enjoy your meal!
apetrechos [ape'treʃus] *mpl* gear *sg*; *(Pesca)* tackle *sg*
apinhado, -a [api'ɲadu, a] *adj* crowded
apitar [api'tar] *vi* to whistle; **apito** [a'pitu] *m* whistle
aplacar [apla'kar] *vt* to placate ▷ *vi* to calm down; **aplacar-se** *vr* to calm down
aplaudir [aplaw'dʒir] *vt* to applaud
aplauso [a'plawzu] *m* applause; *(apoio)* support; *(elogio)* praise; *(aprovação)* approval

aplicação [aplika'sãw] *(pl* **-ões)** *f* application; *(esforço)* effort; *(da lei)* enforcement; *(de dinheiro)* investment
aplicado, -a [apli'kadu, a] *adj* hard-working
aplicar [apli'kar] *vt* to apply; *(lei)* to enforce; *(dinheiro)* to invest; **aplicar-se** *vr*: **~-se a** to devote o.s. to
apoderar-se [apode'rarsi] *vr*: **~ de** to seize, take possession of
apodrecer [apodre'ser] *vt* to rot; *(dente)* to decay ▷ *vi* to rot; to decay
apogeu [apo'ʒew] *m (fig)* height, peak
apoiar [apo'jar] *vt* to support; *(basear)* to base; *(moção)* to second; **apoiar-se** *vr*: **~-se em** to rest on
apoio [a'poju] *m* support; *(financeiro)* backing
apólice [a'polisi] *f (certificado)* policy, certificate; *(ação)* share, bond; **~ de seguro** insurance policy
apontamento [apōta'mētu] *m (nota)* note
apontar [apō'tar] *vt (fusil)* to aim; *(erro)* to point out; *(com o dedo)* to point at *ou* to; *(razão)* to put forward ▷ *vi* to begin to appear; *(brotar)* to sprout; *(com o dedo)* to point; **~ para** to point to; *(com arma)* to aim at
após [a'pojs] *prep* after
aposentado, -a [apozē'tadu, a] *adj* retired ▷ *m/f* retired person, pensioner; **ser ~** to be retired; **aposentadoria** [apozētado'ria] *f* retirement; *(dinheiro)* pension
aposentar [apozē'tar] *vt* to retire; **aposentar-se** *vr* to retire
aposento [apo'zētu] *m* room
apossar-se [apo'sarsi] *vr*: **~ de** to take possession of, seize

apostar [apos'tar] *vt* to bet ▷ *vi*:
~ **em** to bet on

apóstrofo [a'pɔstrofu] *m*
apostrophe

apreciar [apre'sjar] *vt* to
appreciate; (*gostar de*) to enjoy

apreço [a'presu] *m* esteem, regard;
(*consideração*) consideration; **em ~**
in question

apreender [aprjē'der] *vt* to
apprehend; (*tomar*) to seize;
(*entender*) to grasp

apreensão [aprjē'sãw] (*pl* -**ões**) *f*
(*percepção*) perception; (*tomada*)
seizure; (*receio*) apprehension

apreensivo, -a [aprjē'sivu, a] *adj*
apprehensive

apreensões [aprjē'sõjs] *fpl de*
apreensão

apregoar [apre'gwar] *vt* to
proclaim, announce; (*mercadorias*)
to cry

aprender [aprē'der] *vt*, *vi* to learn;
~ **a ler** to learn to read; ~ **de cor** to
learn by heart

aprendizagem [aprēdʒi'zaʒē] *f*
(*num ofício*) apprenticeship; (*numa
profissão*) training; (*escolar*)
learning

apresentação [aprezēta'sãw] (*pl*
-**ões**) *f* presentation; (*de peça,
filme*) performance; (*de pessoas*)
introduction; (*porte pessoal*)
appearance

apresentador, a [aprezēta'dor(a)]
m/f presenter

apresentar [aprezē'tar] *vt* to
present; (*pessoas*) to introduce;
apresentar-se *vr* to
introduce o.s.; (*problema*) to
present itself; (*à polícia etc*) to
report; **quero ~-lhe ...** may I
introduce you to ...

apressado, -a [apre'sadu, a] *adj*
hurried, hasty; **estar ~** to be in a
hurry

apressar [apre'sar] *vt* to hurry;
apressar-se *vr* to hurry (up)

aprisionar [aprizjo'nar] *vt* (*cativar*)
to capture; (*encarcerar*) to imprison

aprontar [aprõ'tar] *vt* to get ready,
prepare; **aprontar-se** *vr* to get
ready

apropriado, -a [apro'prjadu, a] *adj*
appropriate, suitable

aprovado, -a [apro'vadu, a] *adj*
approved; **ser ~ num exame** to
pass an exam

aprovar [apro'var] *vt* to approve of;
(*exame*) to pass ▷ *vi* to make the
grade

aproveitador, a [aprovejta'dor(a)]
m/f opportunist

aproveitamento
[aprovejta'mētu] *m* use,
utilization; (*nos estudos*) progress

aproveitar [aprovej'tar] *vt* to take
advantage of; (*utilizar*) to use;
(*oportunidade*) to take ▷ *vi* to make
the most of it; (*PT*) to be of use;
aproveite! enjoy yourself!

aproximação [aprosima'sãw] (*pl*
-**ões**) *f* approximation; (*chegada*)
approach; (*proximidade*) nearness

aproximar [aprosi'mar] *vt* to bring
near; (*aliar*) to bring together;
aproximar-se *vr*: **~-se de**
(*acercar-se*) to approach

aptidão [aptʃi'dãw] *f* aptitude;
(*jeito*) knack; ~ **física** physical fitness

apto, -a ['aptu, a] *adj* apt; (*capaz*)
capable

apto. *abr* = **apartamento**

apunhalar [apuɲa'lar] *vt* to stab

apurado, -a [apu'radu, a] *adj*
refined

apurar [apu'rar] *vt* to perfect;
(*averiguar*) to investigate; (*dinheiro*)

to raise, get; (*votos*) to count;
apurar-se *vr* to dress up
aquarela [akwaˈrɛla] *f* watercolour
(*Brit*), watercolor (*US*)
aquário [aˈkwarju] *m* aquarium;
A~ (*Astrologia*) Aquarius
aquático, -a [aˈkwatʃiku, a] *adj*
aquatic, water *atr*
aquecer [akeˈser] *vt* to heat ▷ *vi* to
heat up; **aquecer-se** *vr* to heat up;
aquecido, -a [akeˈsidu, a] *adj*
heated; **aquecimento**
[akesiˈmẽtu] *m* heating;
aquecimento central central
heating; **aquecimento global**
global warming
aquele, aquela [aˈkeli, ɛla] *adj* (*sg*)
that; (*pl*) those ▷ *pron* (*sg*) that
one; (*pl*) those
àquele, àquela [aˈkeli, ɛla] = **a +
aquele**
aquém [aˈkẽj] *adv* on this side; **~ de**
on this side of
aqui [aˈki] *adv* here; **eis ~** here is/
are; **~ mesmo** right here; **até ~** up
to here; **por ~** hereabouts; (*nesta
direção*) this way
aquilo [aˈkilu] *pron* that; **~ que**
what
àquilo [aˈkilu] = **a + aquilo**
aquisição [akiziˈsãw] (*pl* **-ões**) *f*
acquisition
ar [ar] *m* air; (*aspecto*) look; (*brisa*)
breeze; (*PT: Auto*) choke; **ares** *mpl*
(*atitude*) airs; (*clima*) climate *sg*; **ao
ar livre** in the open air; **no ar** (*TV,
Rádio*) on air; (*fig: planos*) up in the
air; **dar-se ares** to put on airs
árabe [ˈarabi] *adj, m/f* Arab ▷ *m*
(*Ling*) Arabic
Arábia [aˈrabja] *f*: **a ~ Saudita**
Saudi Arabia
arame [aˈrami] *m* wire
aranha [aˈraɲa] *f* spider

arara [aˈrara] *f* macaw
arbitragem [arbiˈtraʒẽ] *f*
arbitration
arbitrar [arbiˈtrar] *vt* to arbitrate;
(*Esporte*) to referee
arbitrário, -a [arbiˈtrarju, a] *adj*
arbitrary
arbítrio [arˈbitrju] *m* decision; **ao ~
de** at the discretion of
árbitro [ˈarbitru] *m* (*juiz*) arbiter;
(*Jur*) arbitrator; (*Futebol*) referee;
(*Tênis*) umpire
arbusto [arˈbustu] *m* shrub, bush
arca [ˈarka] *f* chest, trunk; **~ de Noé**
Noah's Ark
arcar [arˈkar] *vt*: **~ com**
(*responsabilidades*) to shoulder;
(*despesas*) to handle;
(*consequencias*) to take
arcebispo [arseˈbispu] *m*
archbishop
arco [ˈarku] *m* (*Arq*) arch; (*Mil, Mús*)
bow; (*Elet, Mat*) arc
arco-íris (*pl* **arcos-íris**) *m* rainbow
ar-condicionado (*pl* **ares-
condicionados**) *m* (*aparelho*) air
conditioner; (*sistema*) air
conditioning
arder [arˈder] *vi* to burn; (*pele, olhos*)
to sting; **~ de raiva** to seethe (with
rage)
ardiloso, -a [ardʒiˈlozu, ɔza] *adj*
cunning
ardor [arˈdor] *m* ardour (*Brit*), ardor
(*US*); **ardoroso, -a** [ardoˈrozu,
ɔza] *adj* ardent
árduo, -a [ˈardwu, a] *adj* arduous;
(*difícil*) hard, difficult
área [ˈarja] *f* area; (*Esporte*) penalty
area; (*fig*) field; **~ (de serviço)**
balcony (*for hanging washing etc*)
areia [aˈreja] *f* sand; **~ movediça**
quicksand
arejar [areˈʒar] *vt* to air ▷ *vi* to get

some air; (*descansar*) to have a breather; **arejar-se** *vr* to get some air; to have a break

arena [a'rɛna] *f* arena; (*de circo*) ring

Argélia [ar'ʒɛlja] *f*: **a ~** Algeria

Argentina [arʒē'tʃina] *f*: **a ~** Argentina

argila [ar'ʒila] *f* clay

argola [ar'gɔla] *f* ring; **argolas** *fpl* (*brincos*) hooped earrings; **~ (de porta)** door-knocker

argumentação [argumēta'sãw] *f* line of argument

argumentar [argumē'tar] *vt, vi* to argue

argumento [argu'mētu] *m* argument; (*de obra*) theme

aridez [ari'deʒ] *f* dryness; (*esterilidade*) barrenness; (*falta de interesse*) dullness

árido, -a ['aridu, a] *adj* arid, dry; (*estéril*) barren; (*maçante*) dull

Áries ['aris] *f* Aries

aritmética [aritʃ'metʃika] *f* arithmetic

arma ['arma] *f* weapon; **armas** *fpl* (*nucleares etc*) arms; (*brasão*) coat *sg* of arms; **passar pelas ~s** to shoot, execute; **~ convencional/nuclear** conventional/nuclear weapon; **~s de destruição em massa** weapons of mass destruction; **~ de fogo** firearm

armação [arma'sãw] (*pl* **-ões**) *f* (*armadura*) frame; (*Pesca*) tackle; (*Náut*) rigging; (*de óculos*) frames *pl*

armado, -a [ar'madu, a] *adj* armed

armar [ar'mar] *vt* to arm; (*montar*) to assemble; (*barraca*) to pitch; (*um aparelho*) to set up; (*armadilha*) to set; (*Náut*) to fit out; **armar-se** *vr* to arm o.s.; **~ uma briga com** to pick a quarrel with

armarinho [arma'riɲu] *m* haberdashery (*Brit*), notions *pl* (*US*)

armário [ar'marju] *m* cupboard; (*de roupa*) wardrobe

armazém [arma'zēj] (*pl* **-ns**) *m* (*depósito*) warehouse; (*loja*) grocery store; **armazenar** [armaze'nar] *vt* to store; (*provisões*) to stock

aro ['aru] *m* (*argola*) ring; (*de óculos, roda*) rim; (*de porta*) frame

aroma [a'rɔma] *m* aroma; **aromático, -a** [aro'matʃiku, a] *adj* (*comida*) aromatic; (*perfume*) fragrant

arpão [ar'pãw] (*pl* **-ões**) *m* harpoon

arqueiro, -a [ar'kejru, a] *m/f* archer; (*goleiro*) goalkeeper

arqueologia [arkjolo'ʒia] *f* archaeology (*Brit*), archeology (*US*); **arqueólogo, -a** [ar'kjɔlogu, a] *m/f* archaeologist (*Brit*), archeologist (*US*)

arquiteto, -a [arki'tɛtu, a] *m/f* architect; **arquitetônico, -a** [arkite'toniku, a] *adj* architectural; **arquitetura** [arkite'tura] *f* architecture

arquivar [arki'var] *vt* to file; (*projeto*) to shelve

arquivo [ar'kivu] *m* (*ger, Comput*) file; (*lugar*) archive; (*de empresa*) files *pl*; (*móvel*) filing cabinet; **~ zipado** (*Comput*) zip file

arraial [aha'jaw] (*pl* **-ais**) *m* (*PT: festa*) fair

arrancada [ahã'kada] *f* (*puxão*) jerk; **dar uma ~** (*em carro*) to pull away (suddenly)

arrancar [ahã'kar] *vt* to pull out; (*botão etc*) to pull off; (*arrebatar*) to snatch (away); (*fig: confissão*) to extract ▷ *vi* to start (off); **arrancar-se** *vr* to leave; (*fugir*) to run off

arranha-céu [a'haɲa-] (pl **-s**) m
skyscraper

arranhão [ahaˈɲãw] (pl **-ões**) m
scratch

arranhar [ahaˈɲar] vt to scratch

arranjar [ahãˈʒar] vt to arrange;
(emprego etc) to get, find; (doença)
to get, catch; (questão) to settle;
arranjar-se vr to manage;
(conseguir emprego) to get a job;
~-se sem to do without

arranjo [aˈhãʒu] m arrangement

arrasar [ahaˈzar] vt to devastate;
(demolir) to demolish; (estragar) to
ruin; **arrasar-se** vr to be
devastated; (destruir-se) to destroy
o.s.; (arruinar-se) to lose everything

arrastão [ahasˈtãw] (pl **-ões**) m
tug; (rede) dragnet

arrastar [ahasˈtar] vt to drag;
(atrair) to draw ▷ vi to trail;
arrastar-se vr to crawl; (tempo) to
drag; (processo) to drag on

arrebatado, -a [ahebaˈtadu, a] adj
rash, impetuous

arrebatar [ahebaˈtar] vt to snatch
(away); (levar) to carry off; (enlevar)
to entrance; (enfurecer) to enrage;
arrebatar-se vr to be entranced

arrebentado, -a [ahebẽˈtadu, a]
adj broken; (estafado) worn out

arrebentar [ahebẽˈtar] vt to break;
(porta) to break down; (corda) to
snap ▷ vi to break; to snap; (guerra)
to break out

arrebitado, -a [ahebiˈtadu, a] adj
turned-up; (nariz) snub

arrecadar [ahekaˈdar] vt (impostos
etc) to collect

arredondado, -a [ahedõˈdadu, a]
adj round, rounded

arredondar [ahedõˈdar] vt to
round (off); (conta) to round up

arredores [aheˈdɔris] mpl suburbs;
(cercanias) outskirts

arrefecer [ahefeˈser] vt to cool;
(febre) to lower; (desanimar) to
discourage ▷ vi to cool (off); to get
discouraged

arregaçar [ahegaˈsar] vt to roll up

arregalado, -a [ahegaˈladu, a] adj
(olhos) wide

arregalar [ahegaˈlar] vt: **~ os
olhos** to stare in amazement

arrematar [ahemaˈtar] vt (dizer
concluindo) to conclude; (comprar)
to buy by auction; (vender) to sell by
auction; (Costura) to finish off

arremessar [ahemeˈsar] vt to
throw, hurl; **arremesso**
[aheˈmesu] m throw

arremeter [ahemeˈter] vi to lunge;
~ contra (acometer) to attack,
assail

arrendar [ahẽˈdar] vt to lease

arrepender-se [ahepẽˈdersi] vr to
repent; (mudar de opinião) to
change one's mind; **~ de** to regret,
be sorry for; **arrependido, -a**
[ahepẽˈdʒidu, a] adj (pessoa)
sorry; **arrependimento**
[ahepẽdʒiˈmẽtu] m regret; (Rel, de
crime) repentance

arrepiar [aheˈpjar] vt (amedrontar)
to horrify; (cabelo) to cause to
stand on end; **arrepiar-se** vr to
shiver; (cabelo) to stand on end;
(ser) de arrepiar os cabelos (to
be) hair-raising

arrepio [aheˈpiu] m shiver; (de frio)
chill; **isso me dá ~s** it gives me the
creeps

arriar [aˈhjar] vt to lower; (depor) to
lay down ▷ vi to drop; (vergar) to
sag; (desistir) to give up; (fig) to
collapse

arriscado, -a [ahisˈkadu, a] adj
risky; (audacioso) daring

arriscar [ahis'kar] vt to risk; (pôr em perigo) to endanger, jeopardize; **arriscar-se** vr to take a risk; **~-se a fazer** to risk doing

arrogante [aho'gãtʃi] adj arrogant

arrojado, -a [aho'ʒadu, a] adj (design) bold; (temerário) rash; (ousado) daring

arrolar [aho'lar] vt to list

arrombar [ahõ'bar] vt (porta) to break down; (cofre) to crack

arrotar [aho'tar] vi to belch ▷ vt (alardear) to boast of

arroz [a'hoz] m rice; **~ doce** rice pudding

arruinar [ahwi'nar] vt to ruin; (destruir) to destroy; **arruinar-se** vr to be ruined; (perder a saúde) to ruin one's health

arrumação [ahuma'sãw] f arrangement; (de um quarto etc) tidying up; (de malas) packing

arrumadeira [ahuma'dejra] f cleaning lady; (num hotel) chambermaid

arrumar [ahu'mar] vt to put in order, arrange; (quarto etc) to tidy up; (malas) to pack; (emprego) to get; (vestir) to dress up; (desculpa) to make up, find; (vida) to sort out; **arrumar-se** vr (aprontar-se) to get dressed, get ready; (na vida) to sort o.s. out; (virar-se) to manage

arte ['artʃi] f art; (habilidade) skill; (ofício) trade, craft

artefato [artʃi'fatu], (PT) **artefacto** m (manufactured) article

artéria [ar'tɛrja] f (Anat) artery

artesão, -sã [arte'zãw, zã] (pl -s/-s) m/f artisan, craftsman/woman

ártico, -a ['artʃiku, a] adj Arctic ▷ m: **o Á~** the Arctic

artificial [artʃifi'sjaw] (pl -ais) adj artificial

artifício [artʃi'fisju] m stratagem, trick

artigo [ar'tʃigu] m article; (Com) item; **artigos** mpl (produtos) goods

artista [ar'tʃista] m/f artist; **artístico, -a** [ar'tʃistʃiku, a] adj artistic

artrite [ar'tritʃi] f (Med) arthritis

árvore ['arvori] f tree; (Tec) shaft; **~ de Natal** Christmas tree

as [as] art def ver **a**

ás [ajs] m ace

às [as] = **a** + **as**

asa ['aza] f wing; (de xícara etc) handle

ascendência [asẽ'dẽsja] f (antepassados) ancestry; (domínio) ascendancy, sway; **ascendente** [asẽ'dẽtʃi] adj rising, upward

ascender [asẽ'der] vi to rise, ascend

ascensão [asẽ'sãw] (pl -ões) f ascent; (Rel): **dia da A~** Ascension Day

asco ['asku] m loathing, revulsion; **dar ~ a** to revolt, disgust

asfalto [as'fawtu] m asphalt

asfixia [asfik'sia] f asphyxia, suffocation

Ásia ['azja] f: **a ~** Asia

asiático, -a [a'zjatʃiku, a] adj, m/f Asian

asilo [a'zilu] m (refúgio) refuge; (estabelecimento) home; **~ político** political asylum

asma ['azma] f asthma

asneira [az'nejra] f (tolice) stupidity; (ato, dito) stupid thing

asno ['aznu] m donkey; (fig) ass

aspas ['aspas] fpl inverted commas

aspecto [as'pɛktu] m aspect; (aparência) look, appearance;

(*característica*) feature; (*ponto de vista*) point of view

aspereza [aspe'reza] *f* roughness; (*severidade*) harshness; (*rudeza*) rudeness

áspero, -a ['asperu, a] *adj* rough; (*severo*) harsh; (*rude*) rude

aspiração [aspira'sãw] (*pl* **-ões**) *f* aspiration; (*inalação*) inhalation

aspirador [aspira'dor] *m*: **~ (de pó)** vacuum cleaner; **passar o ~ (em)** to vacuum

aspirante [aspi'rãtʃi] *adj* aspiring ▷ *m/f* candidate

aspirar [aspi'rar] *vt* to breathe in; (*bombear*) to suck up ▷ *vi* to breathe; (*soprar*) to blow; (*desejar*): **~ a algo** to aspire to sth

aspirina [aspi'rina] *f* aspirin

asqueroso, -a [aske'rozu, ɔza] *adj* disgusting, revolting

assado, -a [a'sadu, a] *adj* roasted; (*Culin*) roast ▷ *m* roast; **carne assada** roast beef

assaltante [asaw'tãtʃi] *m/f* assailant; (*de banco*) robber; (*de casa*) burglar; (*na rua*) mugger

assaltar [asaw'tar] *vt* to attack; (*casa*) to break into; (*banco*) to rob; (*pessoa na rua*) to mug; **assalto** [a'sawtu] *m* attack, raid, robbery; (*a uma casa*) burglary, break-in; (*a uma pessoa na rua*) mugging; (*Boxe*) round

assar [a'sar] *vt* to roast; (*na grelha*) to grill

assassinar [asasi'nar] *vt* to murder, kill; (*Pol*) to assassinate; **assassinato** [asasi'natu] *m* murder, killing; (*Pol*) assassination; **assassino, -a** [asa'sinu, a] *m/f* murderer; (*Pol*) assassin; **assassino em série** serial killer

assaz [a'saz] *adv* (*suficientemente*)

sufficiently; (*muito*) rather

assediar [ase'dʒjar] *vt* (*sitiar*) to besiege; (*importunar*) to pester; **assédio** [a'sɛdʒu] *m* siege; (*insistência*) insistence

assegurar [asegu'rar] *vt* to secure; (*garantir*) to ensure; (*afirmar*) to assure; **assegurar-se** *vr*: **~-se de** to make sure of

asseio [a'seju] *m* cleanliness

assembleia [asẽ'bleja] *f* assembly; (*reunião*) meeting; **~ geral (ordinária)** annual general meeting

assentar [asẽ'tar] *vt* (*fazer sentar*) to seat; (*colocar*) to place; (*estabelecer*) to establish; (*decidir*) to decide upon ▷ *vi* (*pó etc*) to settle; **assentar-se** *vr* to sit down; **~ em** *ou* **a** (*roupa*) to suit

assentir [asẽ'tʃir] *vi*: **~ (em)** to consent *ou* agree (to)

assento [a'sẽtu] *m* seat; (*base*) base

assíduo, -a [a'sidwu, a] *adj* (*aluno*) who attends regularly; (*diligente*) assiduous; (*constante*) constant; **ser ~ num lugar** to be a regular visitor to a place

assim [a'sĩ] *adv* (*deste modo*) like this, in this way, thus; (*portanto*) therefore; (*igualmente*) likewise; **~ ~** so-so; **~ mesmo** in any case; **e ~ por diante** and so on; **~ como** as well as; **como ~?** how do you mean?; **~ que** (*logo que*) as soon as

assimilar [asimi'lar] *vt* to assimilate; (*apreender*) to take in; (*assemelhar*) to compare

assinante [asi'nãtʃi] *m/f* (*de jornal etc*) subscriber

assinar [asi'nar] *vt* to sign

assinatura [asina'tura] *f* (*nome*) signature; (*de jornal etc*) subscription; (*Teatro*) season ticket

assinto etc [a'sĩtu] vb ver **assentir**

assistência [asis'tẽsja] f (presença) presence; (público) audience; (auxílio) aid; **~ social** social work

assistente [asis'tẽtʃi] adj assistant ▷ m/f spectator, onlooker; (ajudante) assistant; **~ social** social worker

assistir [asis'tʃir] vt, vi: **~ (a)** (Med) to attend (to); **~ a** to assist; (TV, filme, jogo) to watch; (reunião) to attend

assoar [aso'ar] vt: **~ o nariz** to blow one's nose; **assoar-se** vr (PT) to blow one's nose

assobiar [aso'bjar] vi to whistle

assobio [aso'biu] m whistle

associação [asosja'sãw] (pl **-ões**) f association; (organização) society; (parceria) partnership

associado, -a [aso'sjadu, a] adj associate ▷ m/f associate, member; (Com) associate; (sócio) partner

associar [aso'sjar] vt to associate; **associar-se** vr: **~-se a** to associate with

assombração [asõbra'sãw] (pl **-ões**) f ghost

assombro [a'sõbru] m amazement, astonishment; (maravilha) marvel; **assombroso, -a** [asõ'brozu, ɔza] adj astonishing, amazing

assoviar [aso'vjar] vt = **assobiar**

assovio [aso'viu] m = **assobio**

assumir [asu'mir] vt to assume, take on; (reconhecer) to accept

assunto [a'sũtu] m subject, matter; (enredo) plot

assustador, a [asusta'dor(a)] adj (alarmante) startling; (amedrontador) frightening

assustar [asus'tar] vt to frighten, startle; **assustar-se** vr to be frightened

asteca [as'tɛka] adj, m/f Aztec

astral [as'traw] (pl **-ais**) m mood; **bom ~** good vibe; **alto ~** upbeat mood; **baixo ~** gloom; **estar de baixo ~** to be feeling glum

astrologia [astrolo'ʒia] f astrology

astronauta [astro'nawta] m/f astronaut

astronave [astro'navi] f spaceship

astronomia [astrono'mia] f astronomy

astúcia [as'tusja] f cunning

ata ['ata] f (de reunião) minutes pl

atacado, -a [ata'kadu, a] adj (col: pessoa) in a bad mood ▷ m: **por ~** wholesale

atacante [ata'kãtʃi] adj attacking ▷ m/f attacker, assailant ▷ m (Futebol) forward

atacar [ata'kar] vt to attack; (problema etc) to tackle

atado, -a [a'tadu, a] adj (desajeitado) clumsy, awkward; (perplexo) puzzled

atalho [a'taʎu] m (caminho) short cut

ataque [a'taki] m attack; **~ aéreo** air raid; **~ suicida** suicide attack

atar [a'tar] vt to tie (up), fasten; **não ~ nem desatar** (pessoa) to waver; (negócio) to be in the air

atarefado, -a [atare'fadu, a] adj busy

atarracado, -a [ataha'kadu, a] adj stocky

até [a'tɛ] prep (PT: + a: lugar) up to, as far as; (tempo etc) until, till ▷ adv (tb: **~ mesmo**) even; **~ certo ponto** to a certain extent; **~ em cima** to the top; **~ já** see you soon; **~ logo** bye!; **~ onde** as far as; **~ que** until; **~ que enfim!** at last!

atear [ate'ar] vt (fogo) to kindle; (fig) to incite, inflame; **atear-se** vr to blaze; (paixões) to flare up

ateia [a'tɛja] *f de* **ateu**

atemorizar [atemori'zar] *vt* to frighten; (*intimidar*) to intimidate

Atenas [a'tenas] *n* Athens

atenção [atẽ'sãw] (*pl* **-ões**) *f* attention; (*cortesia*) courtesy; (*bondade*) kindness; **~!** be careful!; **chamar a ~** to attract attention; **atencioso, -a** [atẽ'sjozu, ɔza] *adj* considerate

atender [atẽ'der] *vt*: **~ (a)** to attend to; (*receber*) to receive; (*deferir*) to grant; (*telefone etc*) to answer; (*paciente*) to see ▷ *vi* to answer; (*dar atenção*) to pay attention; **atendimento** [atẽdʒi'mẽtu] *m* service; (*recepção*) reception; **horário de atendimento** opening hours; (*em consultório*) surgery (*Brit*) *ou* office (*US*) hours

atentado [atẽ'tadu] *m* attack; (*crime*) crime; (*contra a vida de alguém*) attempt on sb's life; **~ suicida** suicide attack

atento, -a [a'tẽtu, a] *adj* attentive; **estar ~ a** to be aware *ou* mindful of

atenuante [ate'nwãtʃi] *adj* extenuating ▷ *m* extenuating circumstance

atenuar [ate'nwar] *vt* to reduce, lessen

aterragem [ate'haʒẽj] (*PT*) (*pl* **-ns**) *f* (*Aer*) landing

aterrar [ate'har] (*PT*) *vi* (*Aer*) to land

aterrissagem [atehi'saʒẽ] (*BR*) (*pl* **-ns**) *f* (*Aer*) landing

aterrissar [atehi'sar] (*BR*) *vi* (*Aer*) to land

aterrorizante [atehori'zãtʃi] *adj* terrifying

aterrorizar [atehori'zar] *vt* to terrorize

atestado, -a [ates'tadu, a] *adj* certified ▷ *m* certificate; (*prova*)

proof; (*Jur*) testimony

ateu, ateia [a'tew, a'tɛja] *adj, m/f* atheist

atinar [atʃi'nar] *vt* (*acertar*) to guess correctly ▷ *vi*: **~ com** (*solução*) to find; **~ em** to notice; **~ a fazer algo** to succeed in doing sth

atingir [atʃĩ'ʒir] *vt* to reach; (*acertar*) to hit; (*afetar*) to affect; (*objetivo*) to achieve; (*compreender*) to grasp

atirador, a [atʃira'dor(a)] *m/f* marksman/woman; **~ de tocaia** sniper

atirar [atʃi'rar] *vt* to throw, fling ▷ *vi* (*arma*) to shoot; **atirar-se** *vr*: **~-se a** to hurl o.s. at

atitude [atʃi'tudʒi] *f* attitude; (*postura*) posture

atividade [atʃivi'dadʒi] *f* activity

ativo, -a [a'tʃivu, a] *adj* active ▷ *m* (*Com*) assets *pl*

atlântico, -a [at'lãtʃiku, a] *adj* Atlantic ▷ *m*: **o (Oceano) A~** the Atlantic (Ocean)

atlas ['atlas] *m inv* atlas

atleta [at'lɛta] *m/f* athlete; **atlético, -a** [at'lɛtʃiku, a] *adj* athletic; **atletismo** [atle'tʃizmu] *m* athletics *sg*

atmosfera [atmos'fɛra] *f* atmosphere

ato ['atu] *m* act, action; (*cerimônia*) ceremony; (*Teatro*) act; **em ~ contínuo** straight after; **no ~** on the spot; **no mesmo ~** at the same time

atômico, -a [a'tomiku, a] *adj* atomic

átomo ['atomu] *m* atom

atônito, -a [a'tonitu, a] *adj* astonished, amazed

ator [a'tor] *m* actor

atordoado, -a [ator'dwadu, a] *adj* dazed

atordoar [ator'dwar] vt to daze, stun

atormentar [atormē'tar] vt to torment

atração [atra'sãw] (pl **-ões**) f attraction

atracar [atra'kar] vt, vi (Náut) to moor; **atracar-se** vr to grapple

atrações [atra'sõjs] fpl de **atração**

atraente [atra'ētʃi] adj attractive

atrair [atra'ir] vt to attract; (fascinar) to fascinate

atrapalhar [atrapa'ʎar] vt to confuse; (perturbar) to disturb; (dificultar) to hinder ▷ vi to be a nuisance

atrás [a'trajs] adv behind; (no fundo) at the back ▷ prep: **~ de** behind; (no tempo) after; **dois meses ~** two months ago

atrasado, -a [atra'zadu, a] adj late; (país etc) backward; (relógio etc) slow; (pagamento) overdue; **atrasados** [atra'zadus] mpl (Com) arrears

atrasar [atra'zar] vt to delay; (progresso, desenvolvimento) to hold back; (relógio) to put back; (pagamento) to be late with ▷ vi (relógio etc) to be slow; (avião, pessoa) to be late; **atrasar-se** vr to be late; (num trabalho) to fall behind; (num pagamento) to get into arrears

atraso [a'trazu] m delay; (de país etc) backwardness; **atrasos** mpl (Com) arrears; **com 20 minutos de ~** 20 minutes late

atrativo, -a [atra'tʃivu, a] adj attractive ▷ m attraction; (incentivo) incentive; **atrativos** mpl (encantos) charms

através [atra'vɛs] adv across; **~ de** across; (pelo centro de) through

atravessar [atrave'sar] vt to cross; (pôr ao través) to put ou lay across; (traspassar) to pass through

atrever-se [atre'versi] vr: **~ a** to dare to; **atrevido, -a** [atre'vidu, a] adj cheeky; (corajoso) bold; **atrevimento** [atrevi'mētu] m (ousadia) boldness; (insolência) cheek

atribuir [atri'bwir] vt: **~ algo a** to attribute sth to; (prêmios, regalias) to confer sth on

atributo [atri'butu] m attribute

átrio ['atrju] m hall; (pátio) courtyard

atrito [a'tritu] m (fricção) friction; (desentendimento) disagreement

atriz [a'triz] f actress

atropelamento [atropela'mētu] m (de pedestre) accident involving a pedestrian

atropelar [atrope'lar] vt to knock down, run over; (empurrar) to jostle

atuação [atwa'sãw] (pl **-ões**) f acting; (de ator etc) performance

atual [a'twaw] (pl **-ais**) adj current; (pessoa, carro) modern; **atualidade** [atwali'dadʒi] f present (time); **atualidades** fpl (notícias) news sg; **atualizar** [atwali'zar] vt to update; **atualmente** [atwaw'mētʃi] adv at present, currently; (hoje em dia) nowadays

atuante [a'twãtʃi] adj active

atuar [a'twar] vi to act; **~ para** to contribute to; **~ sobre** to influence

atum [a'tũ] (pl **-ns**) m tuna (fish)

aturdido, -a [atur'dʒidu, a] adj stunned; (com barulho) deafened; (com confusão, movimento) bewildered

audácia [aw'dasja] f boldness; (insolência) insolence; **audacioso, -a** [awda'sjozu, ɔza] adj daring;

(*insolente*) insolent

audição [awdʒi'sãw] (*pl* **-ões**) *f* audition

audiência [aw'dʒjẽsja] *f* audience; (*de tribunal*) session, hearing

auditar [awdʒi'tar] *vt* to audit

auditor, a [awdʒi'tor(a)] *m/f* auditor; (*juiz*) judge; (*ouvinte*) listener

auditoria [awdʒito'ria] *f*: **fazer a ~ de** to audit

auditório [awdʒi'tɔrju] *m* audience; (*recinto*) auditorium

auge ['awʒi] *m* height, peak

aula ['awla] *f* (*PT*: *sala*) classroom; (*lição*) lesson, class; **dar ~** to teach

aumentar [awmẽ'tar] *vt* to increase; (*salários, preços*) to raise; (*sala, casa*) to expand, extend; (*suj*: *lente*) to magnify; (*acrescentar*) to add ▷ *vi* to increase; (*preço, salário*) to rise, go up

aumento [aw'mẽtu] *m* increase; (*de preços*) rise; (*ampliação*) enlargement; (*crescimento*) growth

ausência [aw'zẽsja] *f* absence

ausentar-se [awzẽ'tarsi] *vr* (*ir-se*) to go away; (*afastar-se*) to stay away

ausente [aw'zẽtʃi] *adj* absent

austral [aws'traw] (*pl* **-ais**) *adj* southern

Austrália [aws'tralja] *f*: **a ~** Australia; **australiano, -a** [awstra'ljanu, a] *adj, m/f* Australian

Áustria ['awstrja] *f*: **a ~** Austria; **austríaco, -a** [aws'triaku, a] *adj, m/f* Austrian

autêntico, -a [aw'tẽtʃiku, a] *adj* authentic; (*pessoa*) genuine; (*verdadeiro*) true, real

auto ['awtu] *m* car; **autos** *mpl* (*Jur*: *processo*) legal proceedings;

(*documentos*) legal papers

autobiografia [awtobjogra'fia] *f* autobiography

autobronzeador [awtobrõzja'dor] *adj* self-tanning

autocarro [awto'kahu] (*PT*) *m* bus

autodefesa [awtode'feza] *f* self-defence (*Brit*), self-defense (*US*)

autódromo [aw'tɔdromu] *m* race track

autoestrada [awtois'trada] *f* motorway (*Brit*), expressway (*US*)

autografar [awtogra'far] *vt* to autograph

autógrafo [aw'tɔgrafu] *m* autograph

automático, -a [awto'matʃiku, a] *adj* automatic

automobilismo [awtomobi'lizmu] *m* motoring; (*Esporte*) motor car racing

automóvel [awto'mɔvew] (*pl* **-eis**) *m* motor car (*Brit*), automobile (*US*)

autonomia [awtono'mia] *f* autonomy

autor, a [aw'tor(a)] *m/f* author; (*de um crime*) perpetrator; (*Jur*) plaintiff

autoral [awto'raw] (*pl* **-ais**) *adj*: **direitos autorais** copyright *sg*

autoridade [awtori'dadʒi] *f* authority

autorização [awtoriza'sãw] (*pl* **-ões**) *f* permission, authorization; **dar ~ a alguém para** to authorize sb to

autorizar [awtori'zar] *vt* to authorize

autosserviço [awtoser'visu] *m* self-service

auxiliar [awsi'ljar] *adj* auxiliary ▷ *m/f* assistant ▷ *vt* to help; **auxílio** [aw'silju] *m* help, assistance

Av. *abr* (= *avenida*) Ave

aval [a'vaw] (pl **-ais**) m guarantee

avalancha [ava'lãʃa] f avalanche

avaliar [ava'ljar] vt to value; to assess

avançado, -a [avã'sadu, a] adj advanced; (ideias, pessoa) progressive

avançar [avã'sar] vt to move forward ▷ vi to advance; **avanço** [a'vãsu] m advancement; (progresso) progress

avaria [ava'ria] f (Tec) breakdown; **avariado, -a** [ava'rjadu, a] adj (máquina) out of order; (carro) broken down; **avariar** [ava'rjar] vt to damage ▷ vi to suffer damage; (Tec) to break down

ave ['avi] f bird

aveia [a'veja] f oats pl

avelã [ave'lã] f hazelnut

avenida [ave'nida] f avenue

avental [avẽ'taw] (pl **-ais**) m apron; (vestido) pinafore dress (Brit), jumper (US)

averiguar [averi'gwar] vt to investigate; (verificar) to verify

avermelhado, -a [averme'ʎadu, a] adj reddish

avesso, -a [a'vesu, a] adj (lado) opposite, reverse ▷ m wrong side, reverse; **ao ~** inside out; **às avessas** (inverso) upside down; (oposto) the wrong way round

avestruz [aves'truz] m ostrich

aviação [avja'sãw] f aviation, flying

aviador, a [avja'dor(a)] m/f aviator, airman/woman

avião [a'vjãw] (pl **-ões**) m aeroplane; **~ a jato** jet

ávido, -a ['avidu, a] adj greedy; (desejoso) eager

aviões [a'vjõjs] mpl de **avião**

avisar [avi'zar] vt to warn; (informar) to tell, let know; **aviso** [a'vizu] m (comunicação) notice

avistar [avis'tar] vt to catch sight of

avô, avó [a'vo, a'vɔ] m/f grandfather/mother; **avós** mpl grandparents

avulso, -a [a'vuwsu, a] adj separate, detached

axila [ak'sila] f armpit

azar [a'zar] m bad luck; **~!** too bad, bad luck!; **estar com ~, ter ~** to be unlucky; **azarento, -a** [aza'rẽtu, a] adj unlucky

azedar [aze'dar] vt to turn sour ▷ vi to turn sour; (leite) to go off; **azedo, -a** [a'zedu, a] adj sour; (leite) off; (fig) grumpy

azeite [a'zejtʃi] m oil; (de oliva) olive oil

azeitona [azej'tɔna] f olive

azia [a'zia] f heartburn

azougue [a'zogi] m (Quím) mercury

azul [a'zuw] (pl **-uis**) adj blue

azulejo [azu'leʒu] m (glazed) tile

azul-marinho adj inv navy blue

azul-turquesa adj inv turquoise

b

B, b [be] *m* B, b

baba ['baba] *f* dribble

babá [ba'ba] *f* nanny

babado [ba'badu] *m* frill; (*col*) piece of gossip

babador [baba'dor] *m* bib

babar [ba'bar] *vi* to dribble; **babar-se** *vr* to dribble

baby-sitter ['bejbisiter] (*pl* **baby-sitters**) *m/f* baby-sitter

bacalhau [baka'ʎaw] *m* (dried) cod

bacana [ba'kana] (*col*) *adj* great

bacharel [baʃa'rɛw] (*pl* **-éis**) *m* graduate

bacia [ba'sia] *f* basin; (*Anat*) pelvis

backup [ba'kapi] (*pl* **backups**) *m* (*Comput*) back-up; **fazer um ~ de** to back up

bactéria [bak'tɛrja] *f* germ, bacterium; **bactérias** *mpl* bacteria *pl*

badalar [bada'lar] *vt, vi* to ring

baderna [ba'dɛrna] *f* commotion

bafo ['bafu] *m* (bad) breath

bagaço [ba'gasu] *m* (*de frutos*) pulp; (*PT: cachaça*) brandy; **estar/ficar um ~** (*fig: pessoa*) to be/get run down.

bagageiro [baga'ʒejru] *m* (*Auto*) roof rack; (*PT*) porter

bagagem [ba'gaʒē] *f* luggage; (*fig*) baggage; **recebimento de ~** (*Aer*) baggage reclaim

bagulho [ba'guʎu] *m* (*objeto*) piece of junk

bagunça [ba'gūsa] *f* mess, shambles *sg*; **bagunçado, -a** [bagū'sadu, a] *adj* messy; **bagunçar** [bagū'sar] *vt* to mess up; **bagunceiro, -a** [bagū'sejru, a] *adj* messy

baía [ba'ia] *f* bay

bailado [baj'ladu] *m* dance; (*balé*) ballet

bailarino, -a [bajla'rinu, a] *m/f* ballet dancer

baile ['bajli] *m* dance; (*formal*) ball; **~ à fantasia** fancy-dress ball

bainha [ba'ina] *f* (*de arma*) sheath; (*de costura*) hem

bairro ['bajhu] *m* district

baixa ['bajʃa] *f* decrease; (*de preço*) reduction, fall, drop; (*em combate*) casualty; (*do serviço*) discharge

baixar [baj'ʃar] *vt* to lower; (*ordem*) to issue; (*lei*) to pass; (*Comput*) to download ▷ *vi* to go (*ou* come) down; (*temperatura, preço*) to drop, fall

baixinho [baj'ʃiɲu] *adv* (*falar*) softly, quietly; (*em segredo*) secretly

baixo, -a ['bajʃu, a] *adj* low; (*pessoa*) short, small; (*rio*) shallow; (*linguagem*) common; (*olhos*) lowered; (*atitude*) mean; (*metal*) base ▷ *adv* low; (*em posição baixa*) low down; (*falar*) softly ▷ *m* (*Mús*) bass; **em ~** below; (em casa) downstairs; **em voz baixa** in a quiet voice; **para ~** down, downwards; (em casa) downstairs; **por ~ de** under, underneath

bala ['bala] f bullet; (BR: doce) sweet

balança [ba'lãsa] f scales pl; **B~** (Astrologia) Libra; **~ comercial** balance of trade; **~ de pagamentos** balance of payments

balançar [balã'sar] vt to swing; (pesar) to weigh (up) ▷ vi to swing; (carro, avião) to shake; (em cadeira) to rock; **balançar-se** vr to swing; **balanço** [ba'lãsu] m (movimento) swinging; (brinquedo) swing; (de carro, avião) shaking; (Com: registro) balance (sheet); (: verificação) audit; **fazer um balanço de** (fig) to take stock of

balão [ba'lãw] (pl -ões) m balloon

balbúrdia [baw'burdʒja] f uproar, bedlam

balcão [baw'kãw] (pl -ões) m balcony; (de loja) counter; (Teatro) circle; **balconista** [bawko'nista] m/f shop assistant

balde ['bawdʒi] m bucket, pail

balé [ba'lɛ] m ballet

baleia [ba'leja] f whale

baliza [ba'liza] f (estaca) post; (boia) buoy; (luminosa) beacon; (Esporte) goal

balneário [baw'njarju] m bathing resort

balões [ba'lõjs] mpl de **balão**

baloiço [ba'lojsu] (PT) m (de criança) swing; (ação) swinging

balsa ['bawsa] f raft; (barca) ferry

bamba ['bãba] adj, m/f expert

bambo, -a ['bãbu, a] adj slack, loose

banana [ba'nana] f banana; **bananeira** [bana'nejra] f banana tree

banca ['bãka] f bench; (escritório) office; (em jogo) bank; **~ (de jornais)** newsstand; **bancada** [bã'kada] f (banco, Pol) bench; (de cozinha) worktop

bancar [bã'kar] vt to finance ▷ vi (fingir): **~ que** to pretend that; **bancário, -a** [bã'karju, a] adj bank atr ▷ m/f bank employee

bancarrota [bãka'hota] f bankruptcy; **ir à ~** to go bankrupt

banco ['bãku] m (assento) bench; (Com) bank; **~ de areia** sandbank; **~ de dados** (Comput) database

banda ['bãda] f band; (lado) side; (cinto) sash; **de ~** sideways; **pôr de ~** to put aside; **~ desenhada** (PT) cartoon; **~ larga** (Tel) broadband

bandeira [bã'dejra] f flag; (estandarte, fig) banner; **bandeirinha** [bãdej'riɲa] m (Esporte) linesman

bandeja [bã'deʒa] f tray

bandido [bã'dʒidu, a] m bandit

bando ['bãdu] m band; (grupo) group; (de malfeitores) gang; (de ovelhas) flock; (de gado) herd; (de livros etc) pile

banha ['baɲa] f fat; (de porco) lard

banhar [ba'ɲar] vt to wet; (mergulhar) to dip; (lavar) to wash; **banhar-se** vr to bathe

banheira [ba'ɲejra] f bath

banheiro [ba'ɲejru] m bathroom

banho ['baɲu] m bath; (mergulho) dip; **tomar ~** to have a bath; (de chuveiro) to have a shower; **~ de chuveiro** shower; **~ de sol** sunbathing

banir [ba'nir] vt to banish

banqueiro, -a [bã'kejru, a] m/f banker

banquete [bã'ketʃi] m banquet

bar [bar] m bar

baralho [ba'raʎu] *m* pack of cards
barata [ba'rata] *f* cockroach
barateiro, -a [bara'tejru, a] *adj* cheap
barato, -a [ba'ratu, a] *adj* cheap
▷ *adv* cheaply
barba ['barba] *f* beard; **fazer a ~** to shave
bárbaro, -a ['barbaru, a] *adj* barbaric; (*dor, calor*) terrible; (*maravilhoso*) great
barbeador [barbja'dor] *m* razor; (*tb: ~ elétrico*) shaver
barbear [bar'bjar] *vt* to shave; **barbear-se** *vr* to shave; **barbearia** [barbja'ria] *f* barber's (shop)
barbeiro [bar'bejru] *m* barber; (*loja*) barber's
barca ['barka] *f* barge; (*de travessia*) ferry
barco ['barku] *m* boat; **~ a motor** motorboat; **~ a remo** rowing boat; **~ a vela** sailing boat
barganha [bar'gaɲa] *f* bargain; **barganhar** [barga'ɲar] *vt, vi* to negotiate
barman [bar'mã] (*pl* **-men**) *m* barman
barra ['baha] *f* bar; (*faixa*) strip; (*traço*) stroke; (*alavanca*) lever; (*em endereço web*) forward slash
barraca [ba'haka] *f* (*tenda*) tent; (*de feira*) stall; (*de madeira*) hut; (*de praia*) sunshade; **barracão** [baha'kãw] (*pl* **-ões**) *m* shed; **barraco** [ba'haku] *m* shack, shanty; (*col: confusão*) scene
barragem [ba'haʒẽ] (*pl* **-ns**) *f* dam; (*impedimento*) barrier
barrar [ba'har] *vt* to bar
barreira [ba'hejra] *f* barrier; (*cerca*) fence; (*Esporte*) hurdle
barricada [bahi'kada] *f* barricade
barriga [ba'higa] *f* belly; **estar de ~**

to be pregnant; **~ da perna** calf; **barrigudo, -a** [bahi'gudu, a] *adj* paunchy, pot-bellied
barril [ba'hiw] (*pl* **-is**) *m* barrel, cask
barro ['bahu] *m* clay; (*lama*) mud
barulhento, -a [baru'ʎẽtu, a] *adj* noisy
barulho [ba'ruʎu] *m* (*ruído*) noise; (*tumulto*) din
base ['bazi] *f* base; (*fig*) basis; **sem ~** groundless; **com ~ em** based on; **na ~ de** by means of
basear [ba'zjar] *vt* to base; **basear-se** *vr*: **~-se em** to be based on
básico, -a ['baziku, a] *adj* basic
basquete [bas'ketʃi] *m* = **basquetebol**
basquetebol [baskete'bɔw] *m* basketball
basta ['basta] *m*: **dar um ~ em** to call a halt to
bastante [bas'tãtʃi] *adj* (*suficiente*) enough; (*muito*) quite a lot (of) ▷ *adv* enough; a lot
bastão [bas'tãw] (*pl* **-ões**) *m* stick
bastar [bas'tar] *vi* to be enough, be sufficient; **bastar-se** *vr* to be self-sufficient; **basta!** (that's) enough!; **~ para** to be enough to
bastardo, -a [bas'tardu, a] *adj, m/f* bastard
bastões [bas'tõjs] *mpl de* **bastão**
bata ['bata] *f* (*de mulher*) smock; (*de médico*) overall
batalha [ba'taʎa] *f* battle; **batalhador, a** [bataʎa'dor(a)] *adj* struggling ▷ *m/f* fighter; **batalhão** [bata'ʎãw] (*pl* **-ões**) *m* battalion; **batalhar** [bata'ʎar] *vi* to battle, fight; (*esforçar-se*) to make an effort, try hard ▷ *vt* (*emprego*) to go after
batata [ba'tata] *f* potato; **~ doce**

sweet potato; **~ frita** chips pl (Brit), French fries pl; (de pacote) crisps pl (Brit), (potato) chips pl (US)

bate-boca ['batʃi-] (pl **bate-bocas**) m row, quarrel

batedeira [bate'dejra] f beater; (de manteiga) churn; **~ elétrica** mixer

batente [ba'tẽtʃi] m doorpost

bate-papo ['batʃi-] (pl **bate-papos**) (BR) m chat

bater [ba'ter] vt to beat, to strike; (pé) to stamp; (foto) to take; (porta) to slam; (asas) to flap; (recorde) to break; (roupa) to wear all the time ▷ vi to slam; (sino) to ring; (janela) to bang; (coração) to beat; (sol) to beat down; **bater-se** vr: **~-se para fazer/por** to fight to do/for; **~ (à porta)** to knock (at the door); **~ à máquina** to type; **~ em** to hit; **~ com o carro** to crash one's car; **~ com a cabeça** to bang one's head; **~ com o pé (em)** to kick

bateria [bate'ria] f battery; (Mús) drums pl; **~ de cozinha** kitchen utensils pl; **baterista** [bate'rista] m/f drummer

batida [ba'tʃida] f beat; (da porta) slam; (à porta) knock; (da polícia) raid; (Auto) crash; (bebida) cocktail of cachaça, fruit and sugar

batido, -a [ba'tʃidu, a] adj beaten; (roupa) worn ▷ m: **~ de leite** (PT) milk shake

batina [ba'tʃina] f (Rel) cassock

batismo [ba'tʃizmu] m baptism, christening

batizar [batʃi'zar] vt to baptize, christen

batom [ba'tõ] (pl **-ns**) m lipstick

batucada [batu'kada] f dance percussion group

batucar [batu'kar] vt, vi to drum

baú [ba'u] m trunk

baunilha [baw'niʎa] f vanilla

bazar [ba'zar] m bazaar; (loja) shop

bêbado, -a ['bebadu, a] adj, m/f drunk

bebê [be'be] m baby

bebedeira [bebe'dejra] f drunkenness; **tomar uma ~** to get drunk

bêbedo, -a ['bebedu, a] adj, m/f = **bêbado**

bebedouro [bebe'douru] m drinking fountain

beber [be'ber] vt to drink; (absorver) to soak up ▷ vi to drink; **bebida** [be'bida] f drink (pl **-ns**

beça ['bɛsa] (col) f: **à ~** (com vb) a lot; (com n) a lot of

beco ['beku] m alley, lane; **~ sem saída** cul-de-sac

bege ['bɛʒi] adj inv beige

beija-flor [bejʒa'flɔr] (pl **beija-flores**) m hummingbird

beijar [bej'ʒar] vt to kiss; **beijar-se** vr to kiss (one another); **beijo** ['bejʒu] m kiss; **dar beijos em alguém** to kiss sb

beira ['bejra] f edge; (de rio) bank; (orla) border; **à ~ de** on the edge of; (ao lado de) beside, by; (fig) on the verge of; **~ do telhado** eaves pl; **beira-mar** f seaside

belas-artes fpl fine arts

beldade [bew'dadʒi] f beauty

beleza [be'leza] f beauty; **que ~!** how lovely!

belga ['bɛwga] adj, m/f Belgian

Bélgica ['bɛwʒika] f: **a ~** Belgium

beliche [be'liʃi] m bunk

beliscão [belis'kãw] (pl **-ões**) m pinch; **beliscar** [belis'kar] vt to pinch, nip; (comida) to nibble

Belize [be'lizi] m Belize

belo, -a ['bɛlu, a] adj beautiful

○ PALAVRA-CHAVE

bem [bẽj] adv 1 (de maneira satisfatória, correta etc) well; **trabalha/come bem** she works/eats well; **respondeu bem** he answered correctly; **me sinto/não me sinto bem** I feel fine/I don't feel very well; **tudo bem?—tudo bem** how's it going? — fine
2 (valor intensivo) very; **um quarto bem quente** a nice warm room; **bem se vê que ...** it's clear that ...
3 (bastante) quite, fairly; **a casa é bem grande** the house is quite big
4 (exatamente): **bem ali** right there; **não é bem assim** it's not quite like that
5 (estar bem): **estou muito bem aqui** I feel very happy here; **está bem!** vou fazê-lo oh all right, I'll do it!
6 (de bom grado): **eu bem que iria mas ...** I'd gladly go but ...
7 (cheirar) good, nice
▷ m 1 (bem-estar) good; **estou dizendo isso para o seu bem** I'm telling you for your own good; **o bem e o mal** good and evil
2 (posses): **bens** goods, property sg; **bens de consumo** consumer goods; **bens de família** family possessions; **bens móveis/imóveis** moveable property sg/real estate sg
▷ excl 1 (aprovação): **bem!** OK!; **muito bem!** well done!
2 (desaprovação): **bem feito!** it serves you right!
▷ adj inv (tom depreciativo): **gente bem** posh people
▷ conj 1: **nem bem** as soon as, no sooner than; **nem bem ela chegou começou a dar ordens** as soon as she arrived she started to give

orders, no sooner had she arrived than she started to give orders
2: **se bem que** though; **gostaria de ir se bem que não tenho dinheiro** I'd like to go even though I've got no money
3: **bem como** as well as; **o livro bem como a peça foram escritos por ele** the book as well as the play was written by him

bem-conceituado, -a [-kõsej'twadu, a] adj highly regarded
bem-disposto, -a [-dʒis'postu, 'pɔsta] adj well, in good form
bem-me-quer (pl **bem-me-queres**) m daisy
bem-vindo, -a adj welcome
bênção ['bẽsãw] (pl **bênçãos**) f blessing
beneficência [benefi'sẽsja] f kindness; (caridade) charity
beneficiar [benefi'sjar] vt to benefit; (melhorar) to improve; **beneficiar-se** vr to benefit
benefício [bene'fisju] m benefit, profit; (favor) favour (Brit), favor (US); **em ~ de** in aid of; **benéfico, -a** [be'nɛfiku, a] adj beneficial; (generoso) generous
bengala [bẽ'gala] f walking stick
benigno, -a [be'nignu, a] adj kind; (agradável) pleasant; (Med) benign
bens [bẽjs] mpl de **bem**
bento, -a ['bẽtu, a] pp de **benzer** ▷ adj blessed; (água) holy
benzer [bẽ'zer] vt to bless; **benzer-se** vr to cross o.s.
berço ['bersu] m cradle; (cama) cot; (origem) birthplace
Berlim [ber'lĩ] n Berlin
berma ['bɛrma] (PT) f hard shoulder (Brit), berm (US)

berrar [be'har] *vi* to bellow; (*criança*) to bawl; **berreiro** [be'hejru] *m*: **abrir o berreiro** to burst out crying; **berro** ['bɛhu] *m* yell

besta ['bɛsta] *adj* stupid; (*convencido*) full of oneself; **~ de carga** beast of burden; **besteira** [bes'tejra] *f* foolishness; **dizer besteiras** to talk nonsense; **fazer uma besteira** to do something silly; **bestial** [bes'tʃjaw] (*pl* **-ais**) *adj* bestial; (*repugnante*) repulsive

best-seller [bɛst'sɛler] (*pl* **best-sellers**) *m* best seller

betão [be'tãw] (*PT*) *m* concrete

beterraba [bete'haba] *f* beetroot

bexiga [be'ʃiga] *f* bladder

bezerro, -a [be'zehu, a] *m/f* calf

BI *abr m see note*

- **BI**
-
-
- All Portuguese citizens are
- required to carry an identity card,
- known as the **BI** or *bilhete de*
- *identidade*. The photocard, which
- gives the holder's name, date of
- birth, marital status, height and
- a fingerprint, can be used instead
- of a passport for travel within the
- European Union. Failure to
- produce a valid identity card
- when stopped by the police
- can result in a fine.

Bíblia ['biblja] *f* Bible

bibliografia [bibljogra'fia] *f* bibliography

biblioteca [bibljo'tɛka] *f* library; (*estante*) bookcase; **bibliotecário, -a** [bibljote'karju, a] *m/f* librarian

bica ['bika] *f* tap; (*PT*) black coffee, expresso

bicha ['biʃa] *f* (*lombriga*) worm; (*PT*: *fila*) queue

bicho ['biʃu] *m* animal; (*inseto*) insect, bug

bicicleta [bisi'klɛta] *f* bicycle; (*col*) bike; **andar de ~** to cycle

bico ['biku] *m* (*de ave*) beak; (*ponta*) point; (*de chaleira*) spout; (*boca*) mouth; (*de pena*) nib; (*do peito*) nipple; (*de gás*) jet; (*col: emprego*) casual job; (*chupeta*) dummy; **calar o ~** to shut up

bidê [bi'de] *m* bidet

bife ['bifi] *m* (beef) steak; **~ a cavalo** steak with fried eggs; **~ à milanesa** beef escalope; **~ de panela** beef stew

bifurcação [bifurka'sãw] (*pl* **-ões**) *f* fork

bifurcar-se [bifur'karsi] *vr* to fork, divide

bigode [bi'gɔdʒi] *m* moustache

bijuteria [biʒute'ria] *f* (*costume*) jewellery (*Brit*) *ou* jewelry (*US*)

bilhão [bi'ʎãw] (*pl* **-ões**) *m* billion

bilhar [bi'ʎar] *m* (*jogo*) billiards *sg*

bilhete [bi'ʎetʃi] *m* ticket; (*cartinha*) note; **~ eletrônico** e-ticket; **~ de ida** single (*Brit*) *ou* one-way ticket; **~ de ida e volta** return (*Brit*) *ou* round-trip (*US*) ticket; **bilheteira** [biʎe'tejra] (*PT*) *f* ticket office; (*Teatro*) box office; **bilheteiro, -a** [biʎe'tejru, a] *m/f* ticket seller; **bilheteria** [biʎete'ria] *f* ticket office

bilhões [bi'ʎõjs] *mpl de* **bilhão**

bilíngue [bi'lĩgwi] *adj* bilingual

binóculo [bi'nɔkulu] *m* binoculars *pl*; (*para teatro*) opera glasses *pl*

biocombustível [bjokõbus'tʃivew] (*pl* **-eis**) *m* biofuel

biodiversidade [bjodʒiversi'dadʒi] *f* biodiversity

biografia [bjogra'fia] *f* biography

biologia [bjolo'ʒia] *f* biology

biombo ['bjõbu] *m* screen

bioterrorismo [bjoteho'rizmu] *m* bioterrorism

bip [bip] *n* pager

biquíni [bi'kini] *m* bikini

birita [bi'rita] *(col) f* drink

biruta [bi'ruta] *adj* crazy ▷ *f* windsock

bis [bis] *excl* encore!

bisavô, -vó [biza'vo, vɔ] *m/f* great-grandfather/great-grandmother; **bisavós** [biza'vɔs] *mpl* great-grandparents

biscate [bis'katʃi] *m* odd job

biscoito [bis'kojtu] *m* biscuit *(Brit)*, cookie *(US)*

bispo ['bispu] *m* bishop

bissexto, -a [bi'sestu, a] *adj:* **ano ~** leap year

bit ['bitʃi] *m (Comput)* bit

bizarro, -a [bi'zahu, a] *adj* bizarre

blasfemar [blasfe'mar] *vt* to curse ▷ *vi* to blaspheme; **blasfêmia** [blas'femja] *f* blasphemy

blazer ['blejzer] *(pl* **blazers)** *m* blazer

blecaute [ble'kawtʃi] *m* power cut

blindado, -a [blĩ'dadu, a] *adj* armoured *(Brit)*, armored *(US)*

blitz [blits] *f* police road block

bloco ['blɔku] *m* block; *(Pol)* bloc; *(de escrever)* writing pad; **~ de carnaval** carnival troupe

blog ['blɔgi] *m* blog; **blogueiro, -a** [blo'gejru, a] *m/f* blogger

bloqueador [blokja'dor] *m:* **~ solar** sunblock

bloquear [blo'kjar] *vt* to blockade; *(obstruir)* to block; **bloqueio** [blo'keju] *m (Mil)* blockade; *(obstrução)* blockage

blusa ['bluza] *f (de mulher)* blouse; *(de homem)* shirt; **~ de lã** jumper; **blusão** [blu'zãw] *(pl* **-ões)** *m* jacket

boa ['boa] *adj f de* **bom** ▷ *f* boa constrictor

boate ['bwatʃi] *f* nightclub

boato ['bwatu] *m* rumour *(Brit)*, rumor *(US)*

bobagem [bo'baʒẽ] *(pl* **-ns)** *f* silliness, nonsense; *(dito, ato)* silly thing

bobo, -a ['bobu, a] *adj* silly, daft ▷ *m/f* fool ▷ *m (de corte)* jester; **fazer-se de ~** to act the fool

bobó [bo'bɔ] *m* beans, palm oil and manioc

boca ['boka] *f* mouth; *(entrada)* entrance; *(de fogão)* ring; **de ~ aberta** amazed; **bater ~** to argue

bocadinho [boka'dʒiɲu] *m:* **um ~** *(pouco tempo)* a little while; *(pouquinho)* a little bit

bocado [bo'kadu] *m* mouthful, bite; *(pedaço)* piece, bit; **um ~ de tempo** quite some time

boçal [bo'saw] *(pl* **-ais)** *adj* ignorant; *(grosseiro)* uncouth

bocejar [bose'ʒar] *vi* to yawn; **bocejo** [bo'seʒu] *m* yawn

bochecha [bo'ʃeʃa] *f* cheek; **bochecho** [bo'ʃeʃu] *m* mouthwash

boda ['boda] *f* wedding; **bodas** *fpl* *(aniversário de casamento)* wedding anniversary *sg*

bode ['bɔdʒi] *m* goat; **~ expiatório** scapegoat

bofetada [bofe'tada] *f* slap

bofetão [bofe'tãw] *(pl* **-ões)** *m* punch

boi [boj] *m* ox

boia ['bɔja] *f* buoy; *(col)* grub; *(de braço)* armband, water wing

boiar [bo'jar] *vt, vi* to float

boi-bumbá [-bũ'ba] *n see note*

BOI-BUMBÁ

The **boi-bumbá**, or *bumba-meu-boi*, is a traditional folk dance from north-eastern Brazil, which brings together human, animal and mythological characters in a theatrical performance. The ox, which the dance is named after, is played by a dancer wearing an iron frame covered in pieces of colourful fabric. Eventually the beast is "killed" and its meat is symbolically shared out before it comes back to life in the finale.

boicotar [bojko'tar] *vt* to boycott; **boicote** [boj'kɔtʃi] *m* boycott
bola ['bɔla] *f* ball; **dar ~ para** (*flertar*) to flirt with; **ela não dá a menor ~ (para isso)** she couldn't care less (about it); **não ser certo da ~** (*col*) not to be right in the head
bolacha [bo'laʃa] *f* biscuit (*Brit*), cookie (*US*); (*col: bofetada*) wallop; (*para chope*) beer mat
boleia [bo'leja] *f* (*de caminhão*) cab; (*PT: carona*) lift; **dar uma ~ a alguém** (*PT*) to give sb a lift
boletim [bole'tʃĩ] (*pl* **-ns**) *m* report; (*publicação*) newsletter; **~ meteorológico** weather forecast
bolha ['boʎa] *f* (*na pele*) blister; (*de ar, sabão*) bubble
boliche [bo'liʃi] *m* bowling, skittles *sg*
bolinho [bo'liɲu] *m*: **~ de carne** meat ball; **~ de arroz/bacalhau** rice/dry cod cake
Bolívia [bo'livja] *f*: **a ~** Bolivia
bolo ['bolu] *m* cake; (*monte: de gente*) bunch; (: *de papéis*) bundle; **dar o ~ em alguém** to stand sb up;

vai dar ~ (*col*) there's going to be trouble
bolor [bo'lor] *m* mould (*Brit*), mold (*US*); (*nas plantas*) mildew; (*bafio*) mustiness
bolota [bo'lɔta] *f* acorn
bolsa ['bowsa] *f* bag; (*Com: tb:* **~ de valores**) stock exchange; **~ (de estudos)** scholarship
bolso ['bowsu] *m* pocket; **de ~** pocket *atr*

 PALAVRA-CHAVE

bom, boa [bõ, 'boa] (*pl* **bons/boas**) *adj* **1** (*ótimo*) good; **é um livro bom ou um bom livro** it's a good book; **a comida está boa** the food is delicious; **o tempo está bom** the weather's fine; **ele foi muito bom comigo** he was very nice *ou* kind to me
2 (*apropriado*): **ser bom para** to be good for; **acho bom você não ir** I think it's better if you don't go
3 (*irônico*): **um bom quarto de hora** a good quarter of an hour; **que bom motorista você é!** a fine *ou* some driver you are!; **seria bom que ...!** a fine thing it would be if ...!; **essa é boa!** what a cheek!
4 (*saudação*): **bom dia!** good morning!; **boa tarde!** good afternoon!; **boa noite!** good evening!; (*ao deitar-se*) good night!; **tudo bom?** how's it going?
5 (*outras frases*): **está bom?** OK? ▷ *excl*: **bom!** all right!; **bom, ...** right, ...

bomba ['bõba] *f* bomb; (*Tec*) pump; (*fig*) bombshell; **~ atômica/relógio/de fumaça** atomic/time/smoke bomb; **~ de gasolina** petrol

bombardear [bõbarˈdʒjar] vt to bomb; (fig) to bombard; **bombardeio** [bõbarˈdeju] m bombing, bombardment; **bombardeio suicida** suicide bombing

bombeiro [bõˈbejru] m fireman; (BR: encanador) plumber; **o corpo de ~s** fire brigade

bombom [bõˈbõ] (pl **-ns**) m chocolate

bondade [bõˈdadʒi] f goodness, kindness; **tenha a ~ de vir** would you please come

bonde [ˈbõdʒi] (BR) m tram

bondoso, -a [bõˈdozu, ɔza] adj kind, good

boné [boˈnɛ] m cap

boneca [boˈnɛka] f doll

boneco [boˈnɛku] m dummy

bonito, -a [boˈnitu, a] adj pretty; (gesto, dia) nice ▷ m (peixe) tuna (fish), tunny

bônus [ˈbonus] m inv bonus

boquiaberto, -a [bokjaˈbɛrtu, a] adj dumbfounded, astonished

borboleta [borboˈleta] f butterfly; (BR: roleta) turnstile

borbotão [borboˈtãw] (pl **-ões**) m gush, spurt; **sair aos borbotões** to gush out

borbulhar [borbuˈʎar] vi to bubble

borda [ˈbɔrda] f edge; (do rio) bank; **à ~ de** on the edge of

bordado [borˈdadu] m embroidery

bordar [borˈdar] vt to embroider

bordo [ˈbɔrdu] m (de navio) side; **a ~** on board

borra [ˈboha] f dregs pl

borracha [boˈhaʃa] f rubber; **borracheiro** [bohaˈʃejru] m tyre (Brit) ou tire (US) specialist

borrão [boˈhãw] (pl **-ões**) m (rascunho) rough draft; (mancha) blot

borrifar [bohiˈfar] vt to sprinkle; **borrifo** [boˈhifu] m spray

borrões [boˈhõjs] mpl de **borrão**

bosque [ˈbɔski] m wood, forest

bossa [ˈbɔsa] f charm; (inchaço) swelling; **Bossa nova** (Mús) see note

BOSSA NOVA

Bossa nova is a type of music invented by young, middle-class inhabitants of Rio de Janeiro at the end of the 1950s. It has an obvious jazz influence, an unusual, rhythmic beat and lyrics praising beauty and love. **Bossa nova** became known around the world through the work of the conductor and composer Antônio Carlos Jobim whose compositions, working with the poet Vinícius de Morais, include the famous song "The Girl from Ipanema".

bota [ˈbɔta] f boot; **~s de borracha** wellingtons

botânica [boˈtanika] f botany

botão [boˈtãw] (pl **-ões**) m button; (flor) bud

botar [boˈtar] vt to put; (roupa, sapatos) to put on; (mesa) to set; (defeito) to find; (ovos) to lay

bote [ˈbɔtʃi] m boat; (com arma) thrust; (salto) spring

botequim [botʃiˈkĩ] (pl **-ns**) m bar

botija [boˈtʃiʒa] f (earthenware) jug

botões [boˈtõjs] mpl de **botão**

boxe [ˈbɔksi] m boxing

brabo, -a [ˈbrabu, a] adj fierce;

(*zangado*) angry; (*ruim*) bad; (*calor*) unbearable

braçada [bra'sada] *f* armful; (*Natação*) stroke

bracelete [brase'letʃi] *m* bracelet

braço ['brasu] *m* arm; **de ~s cruzados** with arms folded; (*fig*) without lifting a finger; **de ~ dado** arm-in-arm

bradar [bra'dar] *vt, vi* to shout, yell; **brado** ['bradu] *m* shout, yell

braguilha [bra'giʎa] *f* flies *pl*

branco, -a ['brãku, a] *adj* white ▷ *m/f* white man/woman ▷ *m* (*espaço*) blank; **em ~** blank; **noite em ~** sleepless night; **brancura** [brã'kura] *f* whiteness

brando, -a ['brãdu, a] *adj* gentle; (*mole*) soft

brasão [bra'zãw] (*pl* -**ões**) *m* coat of arms

braseiro [bra'zejru] *m* brazier

Brasil [bra'ziw] *m*: **o ~** Brazil; **brasileiro, -a** [brazi'lejru, a] *adj, m/f* Brazilian

Brasília [bra'zilja] *n* Brasília

brasões [bra'zõjs] *mpl de* **brasão**

bravata [bra'vata] *f* bravado, boasting

bravio, -a [bra'viu, a] *adj* (*selvagem*) wild; (*feroz*) ferocious

bravo, -a ['bravu, a] *adj* brave; (*furioso*) angry; (*mar*) rough ▷ *m* brave man; **~!** bravo!; **bravura** [bra'vura] *f* courage, bravery

brecar [bre'kar] *vt* (*carro*) to stop; (*reprimir*) to curb ▷ *vi* to brake

breu [brew] *m* tar, pitch

breve ['brɛvi] *adj* short; (*conciso, rápido*) brief ▷ *adv* soon; **em ~** soon, shortly; **até ~** see you soon

bridge ['bridʒi] *m* bridge

briga ['briga] *f* fight; (*verbal*) quarrel

brigada [bri'gada] *f* brigade

brigão, -gona [bri'gãw, ɔna] (*pl* -**ões/-s**) *adj* quarrelsome ▷ *m/f* troublemaker

brigar [bri'gar] *vi* to fight; (*altercar*) to quarrel

brigões [bri'gõjs] *mpl de* **brigão**

brigona [bri'gona] *f de* **brigão**

brilhante [bri'ʎãtʃi] *adj* brilliant ▷ *m* diamond

brilhar [bri'ʎar] *vi* to shine

brincadeira [brĩka'dejra] *f* fun; (*gracejo*) joke; (*de criança*) game; **deixe de ~s!** stop fooling!; **de ~** for fun

brincalhão, -lhona [brĩka'ʎãw, ɔna] (*pl* -**ões/-s**) *adj* playful ▷ *m/f* joker, teaser

brincar [brĩ'kar] *vi* to play; (*gracejar*) to joke; **estou brincando** I'm only kidding; **~ de soldados** to play (at) soldiers; **~ com alguém** to tease sb

brinco ['brĩku] *m* (*joia*) earring

brindar [brĩ'dar] *vt* to drink to; (*presentear*) to give a present to; **brinde** ['brĩdʒi] *m* toast; (*presente*) free gift

brinquedo [brĩ'kedu] *m* toy

brio ['briu] *m* self-respect, dignity

brisa ['briza] *f* breeze

britânico, -a [bri'taniku, a] *adj* British ▷ *m/f* Briton

broche ['brɔʃi] *m* brooch

brochura [bro'ʃura] *f* (*livro*) paperback; (*folheto*) brochure, pamphlet

brócolis ['brɔkolis] *mpl* broccoli *sg*

bronca ['brõka] (*col*) *f* telling off; **dar uma ~ em** to tell off; **levar uma ~** to get told off

bronco, -a ['brõku, a] *adj* (*rude*) coarse; (*burro*) thick

bronquite [brõ'kitʃi] *f* bronchitis

bronze ['brõzi] *m* bronze;

bronzear [brõ'zjar] *vt* to tan; **bronzear-se** *vr* to get a tan

broto ['brotu] *m* bud; (*fig*) youngster

broxa ['brɔʃa] *f* (large) paint brush

bruços ['brusus] *mpl*: **de ~** face down

bruma ['bruma] *f* mist, haze

brusco, -a ['brusku, a] *adj* brusque; (*súbito*) sudden

brutal [bru'taw] (*pl* **-ais**) *adj* brutal

bruto, -a ['brutu, a] *adj* brutish; (*grosseiro*) coarse; (*móvel*) heavy; (*petróleo*) crude; (*peso, Com*) gross ▷ *m* brute; **em ~** raw, unworked

bruxa ['bruʃa] *f* witch; **bruxaria** [bruʃa'ria] *f* witchcraft

Bruxelas [bru'ʃelas] *n* Brussels

bruxo ['bruʃu] *m* wizard

budismo [bu'dʒizmu] *m* Buddhism

bufar [bu'far] *vi* to puff, pant; (*com raiva*) to snort; (*reclamar*) to moan, grumble

bufê [bu'fe] *m* sideboard; (*comida*) buffet

buffer ['bafer] (*pl* **buffers**) *m* (*Comput*) buffer

bula ['bula] *f* (*Med*) directions *pl* for use

bule ['buli] *m* (*de chá*) teapot; (*de café*) coffeepot

Bulgária [buw'garja] *f*: **a ~** Bulgaria; **búlgaro, -a** ['buwgaru, a] *adj, m/f* Bulgarian ▷ *m* (*Ling*) Bulgarian

bunda ['bũda] (*col*) *f* bottom, backside

buquê [bu'ke] *m* bouquet

buraco [bu'raku] *m* hole; (*de agulha*) eye; **ser um ~** to be tough; **~ da fechadura** keyhole

burguês, -guesa [bur'ges, 'geza] *adj* middle-class, bourgeois; **burguesia** [burge'zia] *f* middle

class, bourgeoisie

burocracia [burokra'sia] *f* bureaucracy

burro, -a ['buhu, a] *adj* stupid ▷ *m/f* (*Zool*) donkey; (*pessoa*) fool, idiot; **pra ~** (*col*) a lot; (*com adj*) really; **~ de carga** (*fig*) hard worker

busca ['buska] *f* search; **em ~ de** in search of; **dar ~ a** to search for

buscador [buska'dor] *m* search engine

buscar [bus'kar] *vt* to fetch; (*procurar*) to look *ou* search for; **ir ~** to fetch, go for; **mandar ~** to send for

bússola ['busola] *f* compass

busto ['bustu] *m* bust

buzina [bu'zina] *f* horn; **buzinar** [buzi'nar] *vi* to sound one's horn, toot the horn ▷ *vt* to hoot

búzio ['buzju] *m* conch

C, c [se] *m* C, c

c/ *abr* = **com**

cá [ka] *adv* here; **de cá** on this side; **para cá** here, over here; **para lá e para cá** back and forth; **de lá para cá** since then

caatinga [ka'tʃĩga] (*BR*) *f* scrub(-land)

cabana [ka'bana] *f* hut

cabeça [ka'besa] *f* head; (*inteligência*) brain; (*de uma lista*) top ▷ *m/f* leader; **de ~** off the top of one's head; (*calcular*) in one's head; **de ~ para baixo** upside down; **por ~** per person, per head; **cabeçada** [kabe'sada] *f* (*pancada com cabeça*) butt; (*Futebol*) header; (*asneira*) blunder; **cabeçalho** [kabe'saʎu] *m* (*de livro*) title page; (*de página, capítulo*) heading

cabeceira [kabe'sejra] *f* (*de cama*) head

cabeçudo, -a [kabe'sudu, a] *adj* with a big head; (*teimoso*) headstrong

cabeleira [kabe'lejra] *f* head of hair; (*postiça*) wig; **cabeleireiro, -a** [kabelej'rejru, a] *m/f* hairdresser

cabelo [ka'belu] *m* hair; **cortar/ fazer o ~** to have one's hair cut/ done; **cabeludo, -a** [kabe'ludu, a] *adj* hairy

caber [ka'ber] *vi*: **~ (em)** to fit; (*ser compatível*) to be appropriate (in); **~ a** (*em partilha*) to fall to; **cabe a alguém fazer** it is up to sb to do; **não cabe aqui fazer comentários** this is not the time or place to comment

cabide [ka'bidʒi] *m* (*coat*) hanger; (*móvel*) hat stand; (*fixo à parede*) coat rack

cabine [ka'bini] *f* cabin; (*em loja*) fitting room; **~ do piloto** (*Aer*) cockpit; **~ telefônica** telephone box (*Brit*) *ou* booth

cabo ['kabu] *m* (*extremidade*) end; (*de faca, vassoura etc*) handle; (*corda*) rope; (*elétrico etc*) cable; (*Geo*) cape; (*Mil*) corporal; **ao ~ de** at the end of; **de ~ a rabo** from beginning to end; **levar a ~** to carry out; **dar ~ de** to do away with

caboclo, -a [ka'boklu, a] (*BR*) *m/f* mestizo

cabra ['kabra] *f* goat

cabreiro, -a [ka'brejru, a] (*col*) *adj* suspicious

cabrito [ka'britu] *m* kid

caça ['kasa] *f* hunting; (*busca*) hunt; (*animal*) quarry, game ▷ *m* (*Aer*) fighter (plane); **caçador, a** [kasa'dor(a)] *m/f* hunter

cação [ka'sãw] *m* (*pl* **-ões**) *m* shark

caçar [ka'sar] *vt* to hunt; (*com espingarda*) to shoot; (*procurar*) to

seek ▷ *vi* to hunt, go hunting
caçarola [kasaˈrola] *f* (sauce)pan
cacau [kaˈkaw] *m* cocoa; (*Bot*) cacao
cacetada [kaseˈtada] *f* blow (with a stick)
cachaça [kaˈʃasa] *f* (white) rum
cachaceiro, -a [kaʃaˈsejru, a] *adj* drunk ▷ *m/f* drunkard
cachê [kaˈʃe] *m* fee
cachecol [kaʃeˈkɔw] (*pl* **-óis**) *m* scarf
cachimbo [kaˈʃĩbu] *m* pipe
cacho [ˈkaʃu] *m* bunch; (*de cabelo*) curl; (*longo*) ringlet
cachoeira [kaʃˈwejra] *f* waterfall
cachorra [kaˈʃoha] *f* bitch, (female) puppy
cachorrinho, -a [kaʃoˈhiɲu, a] *m/f* puppy
cachorro [kaˈʃohu] *m* dog, puppy; **cachorro-quente** (*pl* **cachorros-quentes**) *m* hot dog
cacique [kaˈsiki] *m* (Indian) chief; (*mandachuva*) local boss
caco [ˈkaku] *m* bit, fragment; (*pessoa velha*) old relic
caçoar [kaˈswar] *vt, vi* to mock
cacoete [kaˈkwetʃi] *m* twitch, tic
cacto [ˈkaktu] *m* cactus
cada [ˈkada] *adj inv* each; (*todo*) every; **~ um** each one; **~ semana** each week; **a ~ 3 horas** every 3 hours; **~ vez mais** more and more
cadastrar [kadasˈtrar] *vt* to register; **cadastrar-se** *vr* ro register
cadastro [kaˈdastru] *m* register; (*ato*) registration; (*de criminosos*) criminal record
cadáver [kaˈdaver] *m* corpse, (dead) body
cadê [kaˈde] (*col*) *adv*: **~ ...?** where's/where are ...?, what's happened to ...?

cadeado [kaˈdʒjadu] *m* padlock
cadeia [kaˈdeja] *f* chain; (*prisão*) prison; (*rede*) network
cadeira [kaˈdejra] *f* chair; (*disciplina*) subject; (*Teatro*) stall; (*função*) post; **cadeiras** *fpl* (*Anat*) hips; **~ de balanço** rocking chair; **~ de rodas** wheelchair
cadela [kaˈdɛla] *f* (*cão*) bitch
caderneta [kaderˈneta] *f* notebook; **~ de poupança** savings account
caderno [kaˈdɛrnu] *m* exercise book; (*de notas*) notebook; (*de jornal*) section
caducar [kaduˈkar] *vi* to lapse, expire; **caduco, -a** [kaˈduku, a] *adj* invalid, expired; (*senil*) senile; (*Bot*) deciduous
cães [kãjs] *mpl de* **cão**
cafajeste [kafaˈʒɛstʃi] (*col*) *adj* roguish; (*vulgar*) vulgar, coarse ▷ *m/f* rogue; rough customer
café [kaˈfɛ] *m* coffee; (*estabelecimento*) café; **~ com leite** white coffee (*Brit*), coffee with cream (*US*); **~ preto** black coffee; **~ da manhã** (*BR*) breakfast
cafeteira [kafeˈtejra] *f* coffeepot; (*máquina*) percolator; **cafezal** [kafeˈzaw] (*pl* **-ais**) *m* coffee plantation; **cafezinho** [kafeˈziɲu] *m small black coffee*
cagada [kaˈgada] (*col!*) *f* shit (!)
cágado [ˈkagadu] *m* turtle
cagar [kaˈgar] (*col!*) *vi* to (have a) shit (!)
caguetar [kagweˈtar] *vt* to inform on; **caguete** [kaˈgwetʃi] *m* informer
caiba *etc* [ˈkajba] *vb ver* **caber**
cãibra [ˈkãjbra] *f* (*Med*) cramp
caída [kaˈida] *f* = **queda**
caído, -a [kaˈidu, a] *adj* dejected;

(*derrubado*) fallen; (*pendente*) droopy; **~ por** (*apaixonado*) in love with

câimbra ['kãjbra] *f* = **cãibra**

caipirinha [kajpi'riɲa] *f* cocktail of cachaça, lemon and sugar

cair [ka'ir] *vi* to fall; **~ bem/mal** (*roupa*) to fit well/badly; (*col: pessoa*) to look good/bad; **~ em si** to come to one's senses; **ao ~ da noite** at nightfall; **essa comida me caiu mal** that food did not agree with me

Cairo ['kajru] *m:* **o ~** Cairo

cais [kajs] *m* (*Náut*) quay; (*PT: Ferro*) platform

caixa ['kajʃa] *f* box; (*cofre*) safe; (*de uma loja*) cash desk ▷ *m/f* (*pessoa*) cashier; **~ automático** *ou* **eletrônico** cash machine; **pequena ~** petty cash; **~ de correio** letter box; **~ de mudanças** (*BR*) *ou* **de velocidades** gear box; **~ econômica** savings bank; **~ postal** P.O. box; **~ registradora** cash register; **caixa-forte** (*pl* **caixas-fortes**) *f* vault

caixão [kaj'ʃãw] (*pl* **-ões**) *m* (*ataúde*) coffin; (*caixa grande*) large box

caixeiro-viajante, caixeira-viajante (*pl* **caixeiros/-as-viajantes**) *m/f* commercial traveller (*Brit*) *ou* traveler (*US*)

caixilho [kaj'ʃiʎu] *m* (*moldura*) frame

caixões [kaj'ʃõjs] *mpl de* **caixão**

caixote [kaj'ʃɔtʃi] *m* packing case; **~ do lixo** (*PT*) dustbin (*Brit*), garbage can (*US*)

caju [ka'ʒu] *m* cashew fruit

cal [kaw] *f* lime; (*na água*) chalk; (*para caiar*) whitewash

calabouço [kala'bosu] *m* dungeon

calado, -a [ka'ladu, a] *adj* quiet

calafrio [kala'friu] *m* shiver; **ter ~s** to shiver

calamidade [kalami'dadʒi] *f* calamity, disaster

calão [ka'lãw] *m:* **(baixo) ~** slang

calar [ka'lar] *vt* (*não dizer*) to keep quiet about; (*impor silêncio a*) to silence ▷ *vi* to go quiet; (*manter-se calado*) to keep quiet; **calar-se** *vr* to go quiet; to keep quiet; **cala a boca!** shut up!

calça ['kawsa] *f* (*tb:* **~s**) trousers *pl* (*Brit*), pants *pl* (*US*)

calçada [kaw'sada] *f* (*PT: rua*) roadway; (*BR: passeio*) pavement (*Brit*), sidewalk (*US*)

calçadão [kawsa'dãw] (*pl* **-ões**) *m* pedestrian precinct (*Brit*)

calçado, -a [kaw'sadu, a] *adj* (*rua*) paved ▷ *m* shoe; **calçados** *mpl* (*para os pés*) footwear *sg*

calçadões [kawsa'dõjs] *mpl de* **calçadão**

calçamento [kawsa'mẽtu] *m* paving

calcanhar [kawka'ɲar] *m* (*Anat*) heel

calção [kaw'sãw] (*pl* **-ões**) *m* shorts *pl*; **~ de banho** swimming trunks *pl*

calcar [kaw'kar] *vt* to tread on; (*espezinhar*) to trample (on)

calçar [kaw'sar] *vt* (*sapatos, luvas*) to put on; (*pavimentar*) to pave; **calçar-se** *vr* to put on one's shoes; **ela calça (número) 28** she takes size 28 (in shoes)

calcário, -a [kaw'karju, a] *adj* (*água*) hard ▷ *m* limestone

calcinha [kaw'siɲa] *f* panties *pl*

calço ['kawsu] *m* wedge

calções [kaw'sõjs] *mpl de* **calção**

calculador [kawkula'dor] *m* = **calculadora**

calculadora [kawkula'dora] *f* calculator

calcular [kawku'lar] vt to calculate; (imaginar) to imagine; **~ que** to reckon that

cálculo ['kawkulu] m calculation; (Mat) calculus; (Med) stone

calda ['kawda] f (de doce) syrup; **caldas** fpl (águas termais) hot springs

caldeirada [kawdej'rada] (PT) f (guisado) fish stew

caldo ['kawdu] m broth; (de fruta) juice; **~ de carne/galinha** beef/ chicken stock; **~ verde** potato and cabbage broth

calendário [kalē'darju] m calendar

calhar [ka'ʎar] vi: **calhou viajarmos no mesmo avião** we happened to travel on the same plane; **calhou que** it so happened that; **~ a** (cair bem) to suit; **se ~** (PT) perhaps, maybe

calibre [ka'libri] m calibre (Brit), caliber (US)

cálice ['kalisi] m wine glass; (Rel) chalice

calista [ka'lista] m/f chiropodist (Brit), podiatrist (US)

calma ['kawma] f calm

calmante [kaw'mãtʃi] adj soothing ▷ m (Med) tranquillizer

calmo, -a ['kawmu, a] adj calm

calo ['kalu] m callus; (no pé) corn

calor [ka'lor] m heat; (agradável: fig) warmth; **está** ou **faz ~** it is hot; **estar com ~** to be hot

calorento, -a [kalo'rētu, a] adj (pessoa) sensitive to heat; (lugar) hot

caloria [calo'ria] f calorie

caloroso, -a [kalo'rozu, ɔza] adj warm; (entusiástico) enthusiastic

calouro, -a [ka'loru, a] m/f (Educ) fresher (Brit), freshman (US)

calúnia [ka'lunja] f slander

calvo, -a ['kawvu, a] adj bald

cama ['kama] f bed; **~ de casal** double bed; **~ de solteiro** single bed; **de ~** (doente) ill (in bed)

camada [ka'mada] f layer; (de tinta) coat

câmara ['kamara] f chamber; (PT: Foto) camera; **~ de ar** inner tube; **~ municipal** (BR) town council; (PT) town hall

camarão [kama'rãw] (pl **-ões**) m shrimp; (graúdo) prawn

camarões [kama'rõjs] mpl de **camarão**

camarote [kama'rɔtʃi] m (Náut) cabin; (Teatro) box

cambaleante [kãba'ljãtʃi] adj unsteady (on one's feet)

cambalhota [kãba'ʎɔta] f somersault

câmbio ['kãbju] m (dinheiro etc) exchange; (preço de câmbio) rate of exchange; **~ livre** free trade; **~ oficial/paralelo** official/black market

cambista [kã'bista] m money changer

Camboja [kã'bɔja] m: **o ~** Cambodia

camelo [ka'melu] m camel

câmera ['kamera] (BR) f camera; **em ~ lenta** in slow motion; **~ digital** digital camera

camião [ka'mjãw] (pl **-ões**) (PT) m lorry (Brit), truck (US)

caminhada [kami'nada] f walk

caminhão [kami'nãw] (pl **-ões**) (BR) m lorry (Brit), truck (US)

caminhar [kami'nar] vi to walk; (processo) to get under way; (negócios) to progress

caminho [ka'minu] m way; (vereda) road, path; **~ de ferro** (PT) railway (Brit), railroad (US); **a ~** on the way, en route; **cortar ~** to take a short cut; **pôr-se a ~** to set off

caminhões [kami'nõjs] *mpl de* **caminhão**

caminhoneiro, -a [kamiɲo'nejru, a] *m/f* lorry driver (*Brit*), truck driver (*US*)

camiões [ka'mjõjs] *mpl de* **camião**

camioneta [kamjo'neta] (*PT*) *f* (*para passageiros*) coach; (*comercial*) van

camionista [kamjo'nista] (*PT*) *m/f* lorry driver (*Brit*), truck driver (*US*)

camisa [ka'miza] *f* shirt; **~ de dormir** nightshirt; **~ de força** straitjacket; **~ esporte/polo/social** sports/polo/dress shirt

camiseta [kami'zɛta] (*BR*) *f* T-shirt; (*interior*) vest

camisinha [kami'ziɲa] (*col*) *f* condom

camisola [kami'zɔla] *f* (*BR*) nightdress; (*PT: pulôver*) sweater; **~ interior** (*PT*) vest

campainha [kampa'iɲa] *f* bell

campanário [kãpa'narju] *m* church tower, steeple

campeão, -peã [kã'pjãw, 'pjã] (*pl* **-ões/-s**) *m/f* champion; **campeonato** [kãpjo'natu] *m* championship

campestre [kã'pɛstri] *adj* rural, rustic

camping ['kãpĩŋ] (*BR*) (*pl* **-s**) *m* camping; (*lugar*) campsite

campismo [kã'pizmu] *m* camping; **parque de ~** campsite

campista [kã'pista] *m/f* camper

campo [kãpu] *m* field; (*fora da cidade*) countryside; (*Esporte*) ground; (*acampamento*) camp; (*Tênis*) court

camponês, -esa [kãpo'nes, eza] *m/f* countryman/woman;

(*agricultor*) farmer

campus ['kãpus] *m inv* campus

camuflagem [kamu'flaʒẽ] *f* camouflage

camundongo [kamũ'dõgu] (*BR*) *m* mouse

camurça [ka'mursa] *f* suede

cana ['kana] *f* cane; (*col: cadeia*) nick; (*de açúcar*) sugar cane

Canadá [kana'da] *m*: **o ~** Canada; **canadense** [kana'dẽsi] *adj, m/f* Canadian

canal [ka'naw] (*pl* **-ais**) *m* channel; (*de navegação*) canal; (*Anat*) duct

canalização [kanaliza'sãw] *f* plumbing

canalizador, a [kanaliza'dor(a)] (*PT*) *m/f* plumber

canário [ka'narju] *m* canary

canastra [ka'nastra] *f* (big) basket

canção [kã'sãw] (*pl* **-ões**) *f* song; **~ de ninar** lullaby

cancela [kã'sɛla] *f* gate

cancelamento [kãsela'mẽtu] *m* cancellation

cancelar [kãse'lar] *vt* to cancel; (*riscar*) to cross out

câncer ['kãser] *m* cancer; **C~** (*Astrologia*) Cancer

canções [kã'sõjs] *fpl de* **canção**

cancro ['kãkru] (*PT*) *m* cancer

candelabro [kãde'labru] *m* candlestick; (*lustre*) chandelier

candidato, -a [kãdʒi'datu, a] *m/f* candidate; (*a cargo*) applicant

cândido, -a ['kãdʒidu, a] *adj* naive; (*inocente*) innocent

candomblé [kãdõ'blɛ] *m see note*

- **CANDOMBLÉ**
-
- **Candomblé** is Brazil's most
- influential Afro-Brazilian
- religion. Practised mainly in

Bahia, it mixes catholicism and Yoruba tradition. According to **candomblé**, believers become possessed by spirits and thus become an instrument of communication between divine and mortal forces. **Candomblé** ceremonies are great spectacles of African rhythm and dance held in *terreiros*.

caneca [ka'nɛka] f mug

canela [ka'nɛla] f cinnamon; (*Anat*) shin

caneta [ka'neta] f pen; **~ esferográfica** ballpoint pen; **~ pilot** felt-tip pen

cangaceiro [kãga'sejru] (*BR*) m bandit

canguru [kãgu'ru] m kangaroo

canhão [ka'nãw] (*pl* **-ões**) m cannon; (*Geo*) canyon

canhoto, -a [ka'ɲotu, a] *adj* left-handed ▷ m/f left-handed person ▷ m (*de cheque*) stub

canibal [kani'baw] (*pl* **-ais**) m/f cannibal

canil [ka'niw] (*pl* **-is**) m kennel

canja ['kãʒa] f chicken broth; (*col*) cinch, pushover

canjica [kã'ʒika] f maize porridge

cano ['kanu] m pipe; (*tubo*) tube; (*de arma de fogo*) barrel; (*de bota*) top; **~ de esgoto** sewer

canoa [ka'noa] f canoe

cansaço [kã'sasu] m tiredness

cansado, -a [kã'sadu, a] *adj* tired

cansar [kã'sar] *vt* to tire; (*entediar*) to bore ▷ *vi* to get tired; **cansar-se** *vr* to get tired; **cansativo, -a** [kãsa'tʃivu, a] *adj* tiring; (*tedioso*) tedious

cantar [kã'tar] *vt, vi* to sing ▷ m song

canteiro [kã'tejru] m stonemason; (*de flores*) flower bed

cantiga [kã'tʃiga] f ballad; **~ de ninar** lullaby

cantil [kã'tʃiw] (*pl* **-is**) m canteen

cantina [kã'tʃina] f canteen

cantis [kã'tʃis] *mpl de* **cantil**

canto ['kãtu] m corner; (*lugar*) place; (*canção*) song

cantor, a [kã'tor(a)] m/f singer

cão [kãw] (*pl* **cães**) m dog

caolho, -a [ka'oʎu, a] *adj* cross-eyed

caos ['kaos] m chaos

capa ['kapa] f cape; (*cobertura*) cover; **livro de ~ dura/mole** hardback/paperback (book)

capacete [kapa'setʃi] m helmet

capacidade [kapasi'dadʒi] f capacity; (*aptidão*) ability, competence

capaz [ka'paz] *adj* able, capable; **ser ~ de** to be able to (*ou* capable of); **sou ~ de ...** (*talvez*) I might ...; **é ~ de chover hoje** it might rain today

capela [ka'pɛla] f chapel

capim [ka'pĩ] m grass

capitães [kapi'tãjs] *mpl de* **capitão**

capital [kapi'taw] (*pl* **-ais**) *adj, m* capital ▷ f (*cidade*) capital; **~ (em) ações** (*Com*) share capital

capitalismo [kapita'lizmu] m capitalism; **capitalista** [kapita'lista] m/f capitalist

capitalizar [kapitali'zar] *vt* to capitalize on; (*Com*) to capitalize

capitão [kapi'tãw] (*pl* **-ães**) m captain

capítulo [ka'pitulu] m chapter

capô [ka'po] m (*Auto*) bonnet (*Brit*), hood (*US*)

capoeira [ka'pwejra] f (*PT*) hencoop; (*dança*) see note

○ **CAPOEIRA**
○
○ **Capoeira** is a fusion of martial
○ arts and dance which originated
○ among African slaves in colonial
○ Brazil. It is danced in a circle to
○ the sound of the *berimbau*, a
○ percussion instrument of African
○ origin. Opposed by the Brazilian
○ authorities until the beginning of
○ the twentieth century, today
○ **capoeira** is regarded as a
○ national sport.

capota [ka'pɔta] *f* (*Auto*) hood, top
capotar [kapo'tar] *vi* to overturn
capricho [ka'priʃu] *m* whim,
  caprice; (*teimosia*) obstinacy;
  (*apuro*) care; **caprichoso, -a**
  [kapri'ʃozu, ɔza] *adj* capricious;
  (*com apuro*) meticulous
Capricórnio [kapri'kɔrnju] *m*
  Capricorn
cápsula ['kapsula] *f* capsule
captar [kap'tar] *vt* (*atrair*) to win;
  (*Rádio*) to pick up
captura [kap'tura] *f* capture;
  capturar [kaptu'rar] *vt* to capture
capuz [ka'puz] *m* hood
cáqui ['kaki] *adj* khaki
cara ['kara] *f* face; (*aspecto*)
  appearance ▷ *m* (*col*) guy; **~ ou
  coroa?** heads or tails?; **de ~**
  straightaway; **dar de ~ com** to
  bump into; **ser a ~ de** (*col*) to be the
  spitting image of; **ter ~ de** to look
  (like)
caracol [kara'kɔw] (*pl* **-óis**) *m* snail;
  (*de cabelo*) curl; **escada em ~** spiral
  staircase
caracteres [karak'tɛris] *mpl de*
  caráter
característica [karakte'ristʃika] *f*
  characteristic, feature

característico, -a
  [karakte'ristʃiku, a] *adj*
  characteristic
cara de pau *f* cheek ▷ *adj inv*
  brazen
caramelo [kara'mɛlu] *m* caramel;
  (*bala*) toffee
caranguejo [karã'geʒu] *m* crab
caratê [kara'te] *m* karate
caráter [ka'rater] (*pl* **caracteres**) *m*
  character
caravana [kara'vana] *f* caravan
cardápio [kar'dapju] (*BR*) *m* menu
cardeal [kar'dʒjaw] (*pl* **-ais**) *adj, m*
  cardinal
cardigã [kardʒi'gã] *m* cardigan
careca [ka'rɛka] *adj* bald
carecer [kare'ser] *vi*: **~ de** to lack;
  (*precisar*) to need
carência [ka'rẽsja] *f* lack;
  (*necessidade*) need; (*privação*)
  deprivation; **carente** [ka'rẽtʃi] *adj*
  wanting; (*pessoa*) needy, deprived
carga ['karga] *f* load; (*de navio,
  avião*) cargo; (*ato de carregar*)
  loading; (*Elet*) charge; (*fig: peso*)
  burden; (*Mil*) attack, charge
cargo ['kargu] *m* responsibility;
  (*função*) post; **a ~ de** in charge of;
  ter a ~ to be in charge of; **tomar a
  ~** to take charge of
Caribe [ka'ribi] *m*: **o ~** the
  Caribbean (Sea)
caridade [kari'dadʒi] *f* charity;
  obra de ~ charity
cárie ['kari] *f* tooth decay
carimbar [karĩ'bar] *vt* to stamp;
  (*no correio*) to postmark
carimbo [ka'rĩbu] *m* stamp;
  (*postal*) postmark
carinho [ka'riɲu] *m* affection,
  fondness; (*carícia*) caress; **fazer ~**
  to caress; **com ~** affectionately;
  (*com cuidado*) with care;

carinhoso, -a [kari'nozu, ɔza] *adj*
affectionate
carioca [ka'rjɔka] *adj* of Rio de
Janeiro ▷ *m/f* native of Rio de
Janeiro ▷ *m* (*café*) type of weak coffee
carnal [kar'naw] (*pl* **-ais**) *adj* carnal;
primo ~ first cousin
carnaval [karna'vaw] (*pl* **-ais**) *m*
carnival

○ **CARNAVAL**
○
○ In Brazil, **Carnaval** is the popular
○ festival held each year in the four
○ days before Lent. It is celebrated
○ in very different ways in different
○ parts of the country. In Rio de
○ Janeiro, for example, the big
○ attraction is the parades of the
○ *escolas de samba*, in Salvador the
○ *trios elétricos*, in Recife the *frevo*
○ and, in Olinda, the giant figures,
○ such as the **Homen da
○ meia-noite** and **Mulher do
○ meio-dia**. In Portugal, **Carnaval**
○ is celebrated on Shrove Tuesday,
○ with street parties and
○ processions taking place
○ throughout the country.

carne ['karni] *f* flesh; (*Culin*) meat;
em ~ e osso in the flesh
carnê [kar'ne] *m* (*para compras*)
payment book
carneiro [kar'nejru] *m* sheep;
(*macho*) ram; **perna/costeleta de
~** leg of lamb/lamb chop
carnificina [karnifi'sina] *f*
slaughter
caro, -a ['karu, a] *adj* dear; **cobrar/
pagar ~** to charge a lot/pay dearly
carochinha [karo'ʃiɲa] *f*: **conto da
~** fairy tale
caroço [ka'rosu] *m* (*de frutos*) stone;

(*endurecimento*) lump
carona [ka'rona] *f* lift; **viajar de ~**
to hitchhike; **pegar uma ~** to get a
lift
carpete [kar'pɛtʃi] *m* (fitted) carpet
carpinteiro [karpĩ'tejru] *m*
carpenter
carrapato [kaha'patu] *m* (*inseto*)
tick
carrasco [ka'hasku] *m*
executioner; (*fig*) tyrant
carregado, -a [kahe'gadu, a] *adj*
loaded; (*semblante*) sullen; (*céu*)
dark; (*ambiente*) tense
carregador [kahega'dor] *m* porter
carregamento [kahega'mẽtu] *m*
(*ação*) loading; (*carga*) load, cargo
carregar [kahe'gar] *vt* to load;
(*levar*) to carry; (*bateria*) to charge;
(*PT: apertar*) to press; (*levar para
longe*) to take away ▷ *vi*: **~ em** to
overdo; (*pôr enfase*) to bring out
carreira [ka'hejra] *f* run, running;
(*profissão*) career; (*Turfe*) race;
(*Náut*) slipway; (*fileira*) row; **às ~s**
in a hurry
carretel [kahe'tɛw] (*pl* **-éis**) *m*
spool, reel
carrinho [ka'hiɲu] *m* trolley;
(*brinquedo*) toy car; **~ de criança)**
pram; **~ de mão** wheelbarrow
carro ['kahu] *m* car; (*de bois*) cart;
(*de mão*) barrow; (*de máquina de
escrever*) carriage; **~ de corrida**
racing car; **~ de passeio** saloon
car; **~ de praça** cab; **~ de
bombeiro** fire engine; **~ esporte**
sports car
carroça [ka'hɔsa] *f* cart, wagon
carroçeria [kahose'ria] *f* (*Auto*)
bodywork
carro-chefe (*pl* **carros-chefe(s)**) *m*
(*de desfile*) main float; (*fig*) flagship,
centrepiece (*Brit*), centerpiece (*US*)

carrossel [kahoˈsɛw] (pl **-éis**) m
merry-go-round

carruagem [kaˈhwaʒẽ] (pl **-ns**) f
carriage, coach

carta [ˈkarta] f letter; (de jogar)
card; (mapa) chart; **~ aérea** airmail
letter; **~ registrada** registered
letter; **~ de condução** (PT) driving
licence (Brit), driver's license (US);
dar as ~s to deal

cartão [karˈtãw] (pl **-ões**) m card;
(PT: material) cardboard; **~ de
débito** debit card; **~ de crédito**
credit card; **~ de memória** memory
card; **~ telefônico** phone card; **~ de
recarga** (para celular) top-up card;
cartão-postal (pl **cartões-
postais**) m postcard; (lugar
turístico) sight

cartaz [karˈtaz] m poster, bill (US);
(estar) em ~ (Teatro, Cinema) (to
be) showing

carteira [karˈtejra] f desk; (para
dinheiro) wallet; (de ações) portfolio;
~ de identidade identity card; **~ de
motorista** driving licence (Brit),
driver's license (US)

carteiro [karˈtejru] m postman
(Brit), mailman (US)

cartões [karˈtõjs] mpl de **cartão**

cartola [karˈtɔla] f top hat

cartolina [kartoˈlina] f card

cartório [karˈtɔrju] m registry
office

cartucho [karˈtuʃu] m cartridge;
(saco de papel) packet

cartum [karˈtũ] (pl **-ns**) m cartoon

carvalho [karˈvaʎu] m oak

carvão [karˈvãw] (pl **-ões**) m coal;
(de madeira) charcoal

casa [ˈkaza] f house; (lar) home;
(Com) firm; (Mat: decimal) place;
em/para ~ (at) home/home; **~ de
saúde** hospital; **~ da moeda** mint;

~ de banho (PT) bathroom; **~ e
comida** board and lodging; **~ de
cômodos** tenement; **~ de repouso**
old people's home (BRIT),
retirement home (US); **~ popular**
≈ council house

casacão [kazaˈkãw] (pl **-ões**) m
overcoat

casaco [kaˈzaku] m coat; (paletó)
jacket

casacões [kazaˈkõjs] mpl de
casacão

casado, -a [kaˈzadu, a] adj married

casal [kaˈzaw] (pl **-ais**) m couple

casamento [kazaˈmẽtu] m
marriage; (boda) wedding

casar [kaˈzar] vt to marry;
(combinar) to match (up); **casar-se**
vr to get married; (harmonizar-se)
to combine well

casarão [kazaˈrãw] (pl **-ões**) m
mansion

casca [ˈkaska] f (de árvore) bark; (de
banana) skin; (de ferida) scab; (de
laranja) peel; (de nozes, ovos) shell;
(de milho etc) husk; (de pão) crust

cascata [kasˈkata] f waterfall

casco [ˈkasku] m skull; (de animal)
hoof; (de navio) hull; (para bebidas)
empty bottle; (de tartaruga) shell

caseiro, -a [kaˈzejru, a] adj
home-made; (pessoa, vida)
domestic ▷ m/f housekeeper

caso [ˈkazu] m case; (tb: **~
amoroso**) affair; (estória) story
▷ conj in case, if; **no ~ de** in case
(of); **em todo ~** in any case; **neste
~** in that case; **~ necessário** if
necessary; **criar ~** to cause trouble;
não fazer ~ de to ignore; **~ de
emergência** emergency

caspa [ˈkaspa] f dandruff

casquinha [kasˈkiɲa] f (de sorvete)
cone; (pele) skin

cassar [ka'sar] vt (direitos, licença) to cancel, withhold; (políticos) to ban

cassete [ka'sɛtʃi] m cassette

cassino [ka'sinu] m casino

castanha [kas'taɲa] f chestnut; **~ de caju** cashew nut; **castanha-do-pará** [-pa'ra] (pl **castanhas-do-pará**) f Brazil nut

castanheiro [kasta'neɪru] m chestnut tree

castanho, -a [kas'taɲu, a] adj brown

castelo [kas'tɛlu] m castle

castiçal [kastʃi'saw] (pl **-ais**) m candlestick

castiço, -a [kas'tʃisu, a] adj pure

castidade [kastʃi'dadʒi] f chastity

castigar [kastʃi'gar] vt to punish; **castigo** [kas'tʃigu] m punishment; (fig: mortificação) pain

casto, -a ['kastu, a] adj chaste

casual [ka'zwaw] (pl **-ais**) adj chance atr, accidental; (fortuito) fortuitous; **casualidade** [kazwali'dadʒi] f chance; (acidente) accident

cata ['kata] f: **à ~ de** in search of

catalizador, a [kataliza'dor(a)] adj catalytic ▷ m catalyst

catalogar [katalo'gar] vt to catalogue (Brit), catalog (US)

catálogo [ka'talogu] m catalogue (Brit), catalog (US); **~ (telefônico)** telephone directory

catapora [kata'pora] (BR) f chickenpox

catar [ka'tar] vt to pick (up); (procurar) to look for, search for; (recolher) to collect, gather

catarata [kata'rata] f waterfall; (Med) cataract

catarro [ka'tahu] m catarrh

catástrofe [ka'tastrofi] f catastrophe

cata-vento m weathercock

catedral [kate'draw] (pl **-ais**) f cathedral

categoria [katego'ria] f category; (social) rank; (qualidade) quality; **de alta ~** first-rate

cativar [katʃi'var] vt to enslave; (fascinar) to captivate; (atrair) to charm

cativeiro [katʃi'veɪru] m captivity; (escravidão) slavery; (cadeia) prison

católico, -a [ka'tɔliku, a] adj, m/f Catholic

catorze [ka'torzi] num fourteen

catraca [ka'traka] f turnstile; **~ de embarque/desembarque** (em estação) ticket barrier

caução [kaw'sãw] (pl **-ões**) f security, guarantee; (Jur) bail; **sob ~** on bail

caule ['kauli] m stalk, stem

causa ['kawza] f cause; (motivo) motive, reason; (Jur) lawsuit, case; **por ~ de** because of; **causador, a** [kawza'dor(a)] adj which caused ▷ m cause; **causar** [kaw'zar] vt to cause, bring about

cautela [kaw'tɛla] f caution; (senha) ticket; **~ (de penhor)** pawn ticket; **cauteloso, -a** [kawte'lozu, ɔza] adj cautious, wary

cavado, -a [ka'vadu, a] adj (olhos) sunken; (roupa) low-cut

cavala [ka'vala] f mackerel

cavaleiro [kava'leɪru] m rider, horseman; (medieval) knight

cavalheiro, -a [kava'ʎeɪru, a] adj courteous, gallant ▷ m gentleman

cavalo [ka'valu] m horse; (Xadrez) knight; **a ~** on horseback; **50 ~s(-vapor)**, **50 ~s de força** 50 horsepower; **~ de corrida** racehorse

cavaquinho [kava'kiɲu] m small guitar

cavar [ka'var] vt to dig; (esforçar-se para obter) to try to get ▷ vi to dig; (fig) to delve; (animal) to burrow

cave ['kavi] (PT) f wine-cellar

caveira [ka'vejra] f skull

cavidade [kavi'dadʒi] f cavity

caxumba [ka'ʃũba] f mumps sg

CD abr m CD

cê [se] (col) pron = **você**

cear [sjar] vt to have for supper ▷ vi to dine

cebola [se'bola] f onion; **cebolinha** [sebo'liɲa] f spring onion

ceder [se'der] vt to give up; (dar) to hand over; (emprestar) to lend ▷ vi to give in, yield; (porta etc) to give (way)

cedilha [se'dʒiʎa] f cedilla

cedo ['sedu] adv early; (em breve) soon

cedro ['sɛdru] m cedar

cédula ['sɛdula] f banknote; (eleitoral) ballot paper

CEE abr f (= Comunidade Econômica Europeia) EEC

cegar [se'gar] vt to blind; (ofuscar) to dazzle ▷ vi to be dazzling

cego, -a ['sɛgu, a] adj blind; (total) complete, total; (tesoura) blunt ▷ m/f blind man/woman; **às cegas** blindly

ceia ['seja] f supper

cela ['sɛla] f cell

celebração [selebra'sãw] (pl **-ões**) f celebration

celebrar [sele'brar] vt to celebrate; (exaltar) to praise; (acordo) to seal

celeiro [se'lejru] m granary; (depósito) barn

celeste [se'lɛstʃi] adj celestial, heavenly

celibatário, -a [seliba'tarju, a] adj unmarried, single ▷ m/f bachelor/spinster

celofane [selo'fani] m cellophane; **papel ~** cling film

célula ['sɛlula] f (Bio, Elet) cell; **celular** [selu'lar] adj cellular ▷ n: **(telefone) celular** mobile (phone), cellphone (US); **celular com câmera** camera phone

cem [sẽ] num hundred

cemitério [semi'tɛrju] m cemetery, graveyard

cena ['sena] f scene; (palco) stage

cenário [se'narju] m scenery; (Cinema) scenario; (de um acontecimento) setting

cenoura [se'nora] f carrot

censo ['sẽsu] m census

censor, a [sẽ'sor(a)] m/f censor

censura [sẽ'sura] f censorship; (reprovação) censure, criticism; **censurar** [sẽsu'rar] vt to censure; (filme, livro etc) to censor

centavo [sẽ'tavu] m cent; **estar sem um ~** to be penniless

centeio [sẽ'teju] m rye

centelha [sẽ'teʎa] f spark

centena [sẽ'tɛna] f hundred; **às ~s** in hundreds

centenário, -a [sẽte'narju, a] adj centenary ▷ m centenary

centígrado [sẽ'tʃigradu] m centigrade

centímetro [sẽ'tʃimetru] m centimetre (Brit), centimeter (US)

cento ['sẽtu] m: **~ e um** one hundred and one; **por ~** per cent

centopeia [sẽto'peja] f centipede

central [sẽ'traw] (pl **-ais**) adj central ▷ f (de polícia etc) head office; **~ elétrica** (electric) power station; **~ telefônica** telephone exchange; **centralizar** [sẽtrali'zar] vt to centralize

centrar [sẽ'trar] *vt* to centre (*Brit*), center (*US*)

centro ['sẽtru] *m* centre (*Brit*), center (*US*); (*de uma cidade*) town centre; **centroavante** [sẽtroa'vãtʃi] *m* (*Futebol*) centre forward

CEP ['sɛpi] (*BR*) *abr m* (= *Código de Endereçamento Postal*) postcode (*Brit*), zip code (*US*)

cera ['sera] *f* wax

cerâmica [se'ramika] *f* pottery

cerca ['serka] *f* fence ▷ *prep*: **~ de** (*aproximadamente*) around, about; **~ viva** hedge

cercado, -a [ser'kadu, a] *adj* surrounded ▷ *m* enclosure; (*para animais*) pen; (*para crianças*) playpen

cercanias [serka'nias] *fpl* outskirts; (*vizinhança*) neighbourhood *sg* (*Brit*), neighborhood *sg* (*US*)

cerco ['serku] *m* siege; **pôr ~ a** to besiege

cereal [se'rjaw] (*pl* **-ais**) *m* cereal

cérebro ['serebru] *m* brain; (*fig*) brains *pl*

cereja [se'reʒa] *f* cherry

cerimônia [seri'monja] *f* ceremony

cerração [seha'sãw] *f* fog

cerrado, -a [se'hadu, a] *adj* shut, closed; (*denso*) thick ▷ *m* scrub(land)

certeza [ser'teza] *f* certainty; **com ~** certainly, surely; (*provavelmente*) probably; **ter ~ de** to be certain *ou* sure of; **ter ~ de que** to be sure that

certidão [sertʃi'dãw] (*pl* **-ões**) *f* certificate

certificado [sertʃifi'kadu] *m* certificate

certificar [sertʃifi'kar] *vt* to certify; (*assegurar*) to assure; **certificar-se** *vr*: **~-se de** to make sure of

certo, -a ['sertu, a] *adj* certain, sure; (*exato, direito*) right; (*um, algum*) a certain ▷ *adv* correctly; **na certa** certainly; **ao ~** for certain; **está ~** okay, all right

cerveja [ser'veʒa] *f* beer; **cervejaria** [serveʒa'ria] *f* (*fábrica*) brewery; (*bar*) bar, public house

cervical [servi'kaw] (*pl* **-ais**) *adj* cervical

cessação [sesa'sãw] *f* halting, ceasing

cessão [se'sãw] (*pl* **-ões**) *f* surrender

cessar [se'sar] *vi* to cease, stop; **sem ~** continually; **cessar-fogo** *m inv* cease-fire

cessões [se'sõjs] *fpl de* **cessão**

cesta ['sesta] *f* basket; **cesta básica** food parcel

cesto ['sestu] *m* basket; (*com tampa*) hamper

cético, -a ['sɛtʃiku, a] *m/f* sceptic (*Brit*), skeptic (*US*)

cetim [se'tʃĩ] *m* satin

céu [sɛw] *m* sky; (*Rel*) heaven; (*da boca*) roof

cevada [se'vada] *f* barley

chá [ʃa] *m* tea

chácara ['ʃakara] *f* farm; (*casa de campo*) country house

chacina [ʃa'sina] *f* slaughter; **chacinar** [ʃasi'nar] *vt* (*matar*) to slaughter

chacota [ʃa'kɔta] *f* mockery

chafariz [ʃafa'riz] *m* fountain

chalé [ʃa'lɛ] *m* chalet

chaleira [ʃa'lejra] *f* kettle; (*bajulador*) crawler, toady

chama ['ʃama] *f* flame

chamada [ʃa'mada] *f* call; (*Mil*) roll call; (*Educ*) register; (*no jornal*) headline; **dar uma ~ em alguém**

to tell sb off

chamar [ʃaˈmar] vt to call;
(convidar) to invite; (atenção) to
attract ▷ vi to call; (telefone) to
ring; **chamar-se** vr to be called;
chamo-me João my name is John;
~ alguém de idiota/Dudu to call
sb an idiot/Dudu; **mandar ~** to
summon, send for

chamariz [ʃamaˈriz] m decoy

chamativo, -a [ʃamaˈtʃivu, a] adj
showy, flashy

chaminé [ʃamiˈnɛ] f chimney; (de
navio) funnel

champanha [ʃãˈpaɲa] m ou f
champagne

champanhe [ʃãˈpaɲi] m ou f
= **champanha**

champu [ʃãˈpu] (PT) m shampoo

chance [ˈʃãsi] f chance

chantagear [ʃãtaˈʒjar] vt to
blackmail

chantagem [ʃãˈtaʒẽ] f blackmail

chão [ʃãw] (pl **chãos**) m ground;
(terra) soil; (piso) floor

chapa [ˈʃapa] f (placa) plate;
(eleitoral) list; **~ de matrícula** (PT:
Auto) number (Brit) ou license (US)
plate; **oi, meu ~!** hi, mate!

chapéu [ʃaˈpɛw] m hat

charco [ˈʃarku] m marsh, bog

charme [ˈʃarmi] m charm; **fazer ~**
to be nice, use one's charm;
charmoso, -a [ʃarˈmozu, ɔza] adj
charming

charrete [ʃaˈhɛtʃi] f cart

charuto [ʃaˈrutu] m cigar

chassi [ʃaˈsi] m (Auto, Elet) chassis

chata [ˈʃata] f barge; ver tb **chato**

chateação [ʃatʃjaˈsãw] (pl **-ões**) f
bother, hassle; (maçada) bore

chatear [ʃaˈtʃjar] vt to bother,
upset; (importunar) to pester; (irritar) to annoy

▷ vi to be upsetting; to be boring;
to be annoying; **chatear-se** vr to
get upset; to get bored; to get
annoyed

chatice [ʃaˈtʃisi] f nuisance

chato, -a [ˈʃatu, a] adj flat; (tedioso)
boring; (irritante) annoying; (que
fica mal) rude ▷ m/f bore; (quem
irrita) pain

chauvinista [ʃawviˈnista] adj
chauvinistic ▷ m/f chauvinist

chavão [ʃaˈvãw] (pl **-ões**) m cliché

chave [ˈʃavi] f key; (Elet) switch;
~ de porcas spanner; **~ inglesa**
(monkey) wrench; **~ de fenda**
screwdriver

chávena [ˈʃavena] (PT) f cup

checar [ʃeˈkar] vt to check

check-up [tʃeˈkapi] (pl **-s**) m
check-up

chefe [ˈʃɛfi] m/f head, chief; (patrão)
boss; **~ de estação** stationmaster;
chefia [ʃeˈfia] f leadership;
(direção) management; (repartição)
headquarters sg; **chefiar** [ʃeˈfjar]
vt to lead

chegada [ʃeˈgada] f arrival

chegado, -a [ʃeˈgadu, a] adj near;
(íntimo) close

chegar [ʃeˈgar] vt to bring near ▷ vi
to arrive; (ser suficiente) to be
enough; **chegar-se** vr: **~-se a** to
approach; **chega!** that's enough!;
~ a (atingir) to reach; (conseguir) to
manage to

cheio, -a [ˈʃeju, a] adj full; (repleto)
full up; (col: farto) fed up; (inibido)
awkward

cheirar [ʃejˈrar] vt, vi to smell; **~ a**
to smell of; **cheiro** [ˈʃejru] m smell;
ter cheiro de to smell of;
cheiroso, -a [ʃejˈrozu, ɔza] adj:
ser ou estar cheiroso to smell nice

cheque [ˈʃɛki] m cheque (Brit),

check (US); **~ de viagem** traveller's cheque (Brit), traveler's check (US)

chiar [ʃjar] vi to squeak; (porta) to creak; (vapor) to hiss; (col: reclamar) to grumble

chiclete [ʃi'klɛtʃi] m chewing gum

chicória [ʃi'kɔrja] f chicory

chicote [ʃi'kɔtʃi] m whip

chifre ['ʃifri] m horn

Chile ['ʃili] m: **o ~** Chile

chimarrão [ʃimaˈhãw] (pl **-ões**) m mate tea without sugar taken from a pipe-like cup

chimpanzé [ʃĩpã'zɛ] m chimpanzee

China ['ʃina] f: **a ~** China

chinelo [ʃi'nɛlu] m slipper; **~ (de dedo)** flip-flops pl

chinês, -esa [ʃi'nes, eza] adj, m/f Chinese ▷ m (Ling) Chinese

chip ['ʃipi] m (Comput) chip

Chipre ['ʃipri] f Cyprus

chique ['ʃiki] adj stylish, chic

chocalho [ʃo'kaʎu] m (Mús, brinquedo) rattle; (para animais) bell

chocante [ʃo'kãtʃi] adj shocking; (col) amazing

chocar [ʃo'kar] vt to hatch, incubate; (ofender) to shock, offend ▷ vi to shock; **chocar-se** vr to crash, collide; to be shocked

chocho, -a ['ʃoʃu, a] adj hollow, empty; (fraco) weak; (sem graça) dull

chocolate [ʃoko'latʃi] m chocolate

chofer [ʃo'fer] m driver

chope ['ʃopi] m draught beer

choque¹ ['ʃɔki] m shock; (colisão) collision; (impacto) impact; (conflito) clash

choque² ['ʃɔki] vb ver **chocar**

choramingar [ʃoramĩ'gar] vi to whine, whimper

chorão, -rona [ʃo'rãw, rɔna] (pl **-ões/-s**) adj tearful ▷ m/f crybaby

▷ m (Bot) weeping willow

chorar [ʃo'rar] vt, vi to weep, cry

chorinho [ʃo'riɲu] m type of Brazilian music

choro ['ʃoru] m crying; (Mús) type of Brazilian music

choupana [ʃo'pana] f shack, hut

chouriço [ʃo'risu] m (BR) black pudding; (PT) spicy sausage

chover [ʃo'ver] vi to rain; **~ a cântaros** to rain cats and dogs

chulé [ʃu'lɛ] m foot odour (Brit) ou odor (US)

chulo, -a ['ʃulu, a] adj vulgar

chumbo ['ʃũbu] m lead; (de caça) gunshot; (PT: de dente) filling; **sem ~ (gasolina)** unleaded

chupar [ʃu'par] vt to suck

chupeta [ʃu'peta] f dummy (Brit), pacifier (US)

churrasco [ʃu'hasku] m barbecue; **churrasqueira** [ʃuhas'kejra] f barbecue

churrasquinho [ʃuhas'kiɲu] m kebab

chutar [ʃu'tar] vt to kick; (col: adivinhar) to guess at; (: dar o fora em) to dump ▷ vi to kick; to guess; (col: mentir) to lie

chute ['ʃutʃi] m kick; (col: mentira) lie; **dar o ~ em alguém** (col) to give sb the boot

chuteira [ʃu'tejra] f football boot

chuva ['ʃuva] f rain; **chuveiro** [ʃu'vejru] m shower

chuviscar [ʃuvis'kar] vi to drizzle; **chuvisco** [ʃu'visku] m drizzle

chuvoso, -a [ʃu'vozu, ɔza] adj rainy

Cia. abr (= companhia) Co

cibercafé [siberka'fɛ] m cybercafé

ciberespaço [siberis'pasu] m cyberspace

cicatriz [sika'triz] f scar; **cicatrizar** [sikatri'zar] vi to heal;

(*rosto*) to scar
cicerone [sise'roni] *m* tourist guide
ciclismo [si'klizmu] *m* cycling
ciclista [si'klista] *m/f* cyclist
ciclo ['siklu] *m* cycle
ciclovia [siklo'via] *f* cycle path
cidadã [sida'dã] *f de* **cidadão**
cidadania [sidada'nia] *f*
citizenship
cidadão, cidadã [sida'dãw] (*pl*
-s/-s) *m/f* citizen
cidade [si'dadʒi] *f* town; (*grande*)
city
ciência ['sjẽsja] *f* science
ciente ['sjẽtʃi] *adj* aware
científico, -a [sjẽ'tʃifiku, a] *adj*
scientific
cientista [sjẽ'tʃista] *m/f* scientist
cifra ['sifra] *f* cipher; (*algarismo*)
number, figure; (*total*) sum
cigano, -a [si'ganu, a] *adj, m/f*
gypsy
cigarra [si'gaha] *f* cicada; (*Elet*)
buzzer
cigarrilha [siga'hiʎa] *f* cheroot
cigarro [si'gahu] *m* cigarette
cilada [si'lada] *f* ambush;
(*armadilha*) trap; (*embuste*) trick
cilindro [si'lĩdru] *m* cylinder; (*rolo*)
roller
cima ['sima] *f*: **de ~ para baixo**
from top to bottom; **para ~** up; **em
~ de** on, on top of; **por ~ de** over;
de ~ from above; **lá em ~** up there;
(*em casa*) upstairs; **ainda por ~** on
top of that
cimento [si'mẽtu] *m* cement; (*fig*)
foundation
cimo ['simu] *m* top, summit
cinco ['sĩku] *num* five
cineasta [sine'asta] *m/f* film maker
cinema [si'nɛma] *f* cinema
Cingapura [sĩga'pura] *f* Singapore
cinquenta [sĩ'kwẽta] *num* fifty

cinta ['sĩta] *f* sash; (*de mulher*) girdle
cinto ['sĩtu] *m* belt; **~ de
segurança** safety belt; (*Auto*) seat
belt
cintura [sĩ'tura] *f* waist; (*linha*)
waistline
cinza ['sĩza] *adj inv* grey (*Brit*), gray
(*US*) ▷ *f* ash, ashes *pl*
cinzeiro [sĩ'zejru] *m* ashtray
cinzento, -a [sĩ'zẽtu, a] *adj* grey
(*Brit*), gray (*US*)
cio [siu] *m*: **no ~** on heat, in season
cipreste [si'prɛstʃi] *m* cypress (tree)
cipriota [si'prjɔta] *adj, m/f* Cypriot
circo ['sirku] *m* circus
circuito [sir'kwitu] *m* circuit
circulação [sirkula'sãw] *f*
circulation
circular [sirku'lar] *adj* circular ▷ *f*
(*carta*) circular ▷ *vi* to circulate;
(*girar, andar*) to go round ▷ *vt* to
circulate; (*estar em volta de*) to
surround; (*percorrer em roda*) to go
round
círculo ['sirkulu] *m* circle
circundar [sirkũ'dar] *vt* to
surround
circunferência [sirkũfe'rẽsja] *f*
circumference
circunflexo, -a [sirkũ'flɛksu, a] *adj*
circumflex ▷ *m* circumflex (accent)
circunstância [sirkũ'stãsja] *f*
circumstance; **~s atenuantes**
mitigating circumstances
cirurgia [sirur'ʒia] *f* surgery;
~ plástica/estética plastic/
cosmetic surgery
cirurgião, -giã [sirur'ʒjãw, 'ʒjã] (*pl*
cirurgões/cirurgiãs) *m/f* surgeon
cisco ['sisku] *m* speck
cismado, -a [siz'madu, a] *adj* with
fixed ideas
cismar [siz'mar] *vi* (*pensar*): **~ em** to
brood over; (*antipatizar*): **~ com** to

take a dislike to ▷ *vt*: **~ que** to be convinced that; **~ de** *ou* **em fazer** (*meter na cabeça*) to get into one's head to do; (*insistir*) to insist on doing

cisne ['sizni] *m* swan

cisterna [sis'tɛrna] *f* cistern, tank

citação [sita'sãw] (*pl* **-ões**) *f* quotation; (*Jur*) summons *sg*

citar [si'tar] *vt* to quote; (*Jur*) to summon

ciúme ['sjumi] *m* jealousy; **ter ~s de** to be jealous of; **ciumento, -a** [sju'mẽtu, a] *adj* jealous

cívico, -a ['siviku, a] *adj* civic

civil [si'viw] (*pl* **-is**) *adj* civil ▷ *m/f* civilian; **civilidade** [sivili'dadʒi] *f* politeness

civilização [siviliza'sãw] (*pl* **-ões**) *f* civilization

civis [si'vis] *pl de* **civil**

clamar [kla'mar] *vt* to clamour (*Brit*) *ou* clamor (*US*) for ▷ *vi* to cry out, clamo(u)r

clamor [kla'mor] *m* outcry, uproar

clandestino, -a [klãdes'tʃinu, a] *adj* clandestine; (*ilegal*) underground

clara ['klara] *f* egg white

clarão [kla'rãw] (*pl* **-ões**) *m* (*cintilação*) flash; (*claridade*) gleam

clarear [kla'rjar] *vi* (*dia*) to dawn; (*tempo*) to clear up, brighten up ▷ *vt* to clarify

claridade [klari'dadʒi] *f* brightness

clarim [kla'rĩ] (*pl* **-ns**) *m* bugle

clarinete [klari'netʃi] *m* clarinet

clarins [kla'rĩs] *mpl de* **clarim**

claro, -a ['klaru, a] *adj* clear; (*luminoso*) bright; (*cor*) light; (*evidente*) clear, evident ▷ *m* (*na escrita*) space; (*clareira*) clearing ▷ *adv* clearly; **~!** of course!; **~ que sim!/não!** of course!/of course

not!; **às claras** openly

classe ['klasi] *f* class; **~ econômica/executiva** economy/business class

clássico, -a ['klasiku, a] *adj* classical; (*fig*) classic; (*habitual*) usual ▷ *m* classic

classificação [klasifika'sãw] (*pl* **-ões**) *f* classification; (*Esporte*) place, placing

classificado, -a [klasifi'kadu, a] *adj* (*em exame*) successful; (*anúncio*) classified; (*Esporte*) placed ▷ *m* classified ad

classificar [klasifi'kar] *vt* to classify; **classificar-se** *vr*: **~-se de algo** to call o.s. sth, describe o.s. as sth

cláusula ['klawzula] *f* clause

clausura [klaw'zura] *f* enclosure

clavícula [kla'vikula] *f* collar bone

clemência [kle'mẽsja] *f* mercy

clero ['klɛru] *m* clergy

clicar [kli'kar] *vi* (*Comput*) to click; **~ duas vezes em** to double-click on

cliente ['kljẽtʃi] *m* client, customer; (*de médico*) patient; **clientela** [kljẽ'tɛla] *f* clientele; (*de loja*) customers *pl*

clima ['klima] *m* climate

clímax ['klimaks] *m inv* climax

clipe ['klipi] *m* clip; (*para papéis*) paper clip

clique ['kliki] *m* (*Comput*) click

cloro ['kloru] *m* chlorine

close ['klozi] *m* close-up

clube ['klubi] *m* club

coadjuvante [koadʒu'vãtʃi] *adj* supporting ▷ *m/f* (*num crime*) accomplice; (*Teatro, Cinema*) co-star

coador [koa'dor] *m* strainer; (*de café*) filter bag; (*para legumes*) colander

coalhada [koa'ʎada] f curd
coalizão [koali'zãw] (pl **-ões**) f coalition
coar [ko'ar] vt (líquido) to strain
coberta [ko'bɛrta] f cover, covering; (Náut) deck
cobertor [kober'tor] m blanket
cobertura [kober'tura] f covering; (telhado) roof; (apartamento) penthouse; (TV, Rádio, Jornalismo) coverage; (Seguros) cover; (Tel) network coverage; **aqui não tem ~** there's no network coverage here
cobiça [ko'bisa] f greed
cobra ['kɔbra] f snake
cobrador, a [kobra'dor(a)] m/f collector; (em transporte) conductor; **~ de ônibus** bus conductor
cobrança [ko'brãsa] f collection; (ato de cobrar) charging
cobrar [ko'brar] vt to collect; (preço) to charge
cobre ['kɔbri] m copper; **cobres** mpl (dinheiro) money sg
cobrir [ko'brir] vt to cover
cocada [ko'kada] f coconut sweet
cocaína [koka'ina] f cocaine
coçar [ko'sar] vt to scratch ⊳ vi to itch; **coçar-se** vr to scratch o.s.
cócegas ['kɔsegas] fpl: **fazer ~ em** to tickle; **tenho ~ nos pés** my feet tickle; **sentir ~** to be ticklish
coceira [ko'sejra] f itch; (qualidade) itchiness
cochichar [koʃi'ʃar] vi to whisper; **cochicho** [ko'ʃiʃu] m whispering
cochilar [koʃi'lar] vi to snooze, doze; **cochilo** [ko'ʃilu] m nap
coco ['koku] m coconut
cócoras ['kɔkoras] fpl: **de ~** squatting; **ficar de ~** to squat (down)
código ['kɔdʒigu] m code; **~ de**

barras bar code
coelho [ko'eʎu] m rabbit
coerente [koe'rẽtʃi] adj coherent; (consequente) consistent
cofre ['kɔfri] m safe; (caixa) strongbox; **os ~s públicos** public funds
cogitar [koʒi'tar] vt, vi to contemplate
cogumelo [kogu'mɛlu] m mushroom; **~ venenoso** toadstool
coice ['kojsi] m kick; (de arma) recoil; **dar ~s em** to kick
coincidência [koĩsi'dẽsja] f coincidence
coincidir [koĩsi'dʒir] vi to coincide; (concordar) to agree
coisa ['kojza] f thing; (assunto) matter; **~ de** about
coitado, -a [koj'tadu, a] adj poor, wretched
cola ['kɔla] f glue
colaborador, a [kolabora'dor(a)] m/f collaborator; (em jornal) contributor
colaborar [kolabo'rar] vi to collaborate; (ajudar) to help; (escrever artigos etc) to contribute
colante [ko'lãtʃi] adj (roupa) skin-tight
colapso [ko'lapsu] m collapse; **~ cardíaco** heart failure
colar [ko'lar] vt to stick, glue; (BR: copiar) to crib ⊳ vi to stick; to cheat ⊳ m necklace
colarinho [kola'riɲu] m collar
colarinho-branco (pl **colarinhos-brancos**) m white-collar worker
colcha ['kowʃa] f bedspread
colchão [kow'ʃãw] (pl **-ões**) m mattress
colchete [kow'ʃetʃi] m clasp, fastening; (parêntese) square

bracket; **~ de gancho** hook and eye; **~ de pressão** press stud, popper

colchões [kowˈʃõjs] *mpl de* **colchão**

coleção [koleˈsãw] (*pl* **coleções**) *f* collection; **colecionador, a** [kolesjonaˈdor(a)] *m/f* collector; **colecionar** [kolesjoˈnar] *vt* to collect

colega [koˈlɛga] *m/f* colleague; (*de escola*) classmate

colegial [koleˈʒjaw] (*pl* **-ais**) *m/f* schoolboy/girl

colégio [koˈlɛʒu] *m* school

coleira [koˈlejra] *f* collar

cólera [ˈkɔlera] *f* anger ▷ *m ou f* (*Med*) cholera

colesterol [kolesteˈrɔw] *m* cholesterol

colete [koˈletʃi] *m* waistcoat (*Brit*), vest (*US*); **~ salva-vidas** life jacket (*Brit*), life preserver (*US*)

coletivo, -a [koleˈtʃivu, a] *adj* collective; (*transportes*) public ▷ *m* bus

colheita [koˈʎejta] *f* harvest

colher [koˈʎer] *vt* to gather, pick; (*dados*) to gather ▷ *f* spoon; **~ de chá/sopa** teaspoon/tablespoon

colidir [koliˈdʒir] *vi*: **~ com** to collide with, crash into

coligação [koligaˈsãw] (*pl* **-ões**) *f* coalition

colina [koˈlina] *f* hill

colisão [koliˈzãw] (*pl* **-ões**) *f* collision

collant [koˈlã] (*pl* **collants**) *m* tights *pl* (*Brit*), pantihose (*US*); (*blusa*) leotard

colmeia [kowˈmeja] *f* beehive

colo [ˈkɔlu] *m* neck; (*regaço*) lap

colocar [koloˈkar] *vt* to put, place; (*empregar*) to find a job for, place; (*Com*) to market; (*pneus, tapetes*) to

fit; (*questão, ideia*) to put forward

Colômbia [koˈlõbja] *f*: **a ~** Colombia

colônia [koˈlonja] *f* colony; (*perfume*) cologne; **colonial** [koloˈnjaw] (*pl* **-ais**) *adj* colonial

colonizador, a [kolonizaˈdor(a)] *m/f* colonist, settler

coloquial [koloˈkjaw] (*pl* **-ais**) *adj* colloquial

colóquio [koˈlɔkju] *m* conversation; (*congresso*) conference

colorido, -a [koloˈridu, a] *adj* colourful (*Brit*), colorful (*US*) ▷ *m* colouring (*Brit*), coloring (*US*)

colorir [koloˈrir] *vt* to colour (*Brit*), color (*US*)

coluna [koˈluna] *f* column; (*pilar*) pillar; **~ dorsal** *ou* **vertebral** spine; **colunável** [koluˈnavew] (*pl* **-eis**) *adj* famous ▷ *m/f* celebrity; **colunista** [koluˈnista] *m/f* columnist

com [kõ] *prep* with; **estar ~ fome** to be hungry; **~ cuidado** carefully; **estar ~ dinheiro/câncer** to have some money on one/have cancer

coma [ˈkɔma] *f* coma

comandante [komãˈdãtʃi] *m* commander; (*Mil*) commandant; (*Náut*) captain

comandar [komãˈdar] *vt* to command

comando [koˈmãdu] *m* command

combate [kõˈbatʃi] *m* combat; **combater** [kõbaˈter] *vt* to fight; (*opor-se a*) to oppose ▷ *vi* to fight; **combater-se** *vr* to fight

combinação [kõbinaˈsãw] (*pl* **-ões**) *f* combination; (*Quím*) compound; (*acordo*) arrangement; (*plano*) scheme; (*roupa*) slip

combinar [kõbiˈnar] *vt* to

combine; (*jantar etc*) to arrange; (*fuga etc*) to plan ▷ vi (*roupas etc*) to go together; **combinar-se** vr to combine; (*pessoas*) to get on well together; **~ com** (*harmonizar-se*) to go with; **~ de fazer** to arrange to do; **combinado!** agreed!

comboio [kõ'boju] m (*PT*) train; (*de navios, carros*) convoy

combustível [kõbus'tʃivew] m fuel

começar [kome'sar] vt, vi to begin, start; **~ a fazer** to begin ou start to do

começo [ko'mesu] m beginning, start

comédia [ko'mɛdʒja] f comedy

comemorar [komemo'rar] vt to commemorate, to celebrate

comentar [komẽ'tar] vt to comment on; (*maliciosamente*) to make comments about

comentário [komẽ'tarju] m comment, remark; (*análise*) commentary

comer [ko'mer] vt to eat; (*Damas, Xadrez*) to take, capture ▷ vi to eat; **dar de ~ a** to feed

comercial [komer'sjaw] (*pl* **-ais**) adj commercial; (*relativo ao negócio*) business atr ▷ m commercial

comercializar [komersjali'zar] vt to market

comerciante [komer'sjãtʃi] m/f trader

comércio [ko'mɛrsju] m commerce; (*tráfico*) trade; (*negócio*) business; (*lojas*) shops pl; **~ eletrônico** e-commerce

comes ['kɔmis] mpl: **~ e bebes** food and drink

comestíveis [komes'tʃiveis] mpl foodstuffs, food sg

comestível [komes'tʃivew] (*pl* **-eis**) adj edible

cometer [kome'ter] vt to commit

comício [ko'misju] m (*Pol*) rally, meeting; (*assembleia*) assembly

cômico, -a ['komiku, a] adj comic(al) ▷ m comedian; (*de teatro*) actor

comida [ko'mida] f (*alimento*) food; (*refeição*) meal; **comida pronta** ready meal (*Brit*), TV dinner (*US*)

comigo [ko'migu] pron with me

comilão, -lona [komi'lãw] (*pl* **-ões/-s**) adj greedy ▷ m/f glutton

comiserar [komize'rar] vt to move to pity; **comiserar-se** vr: **~-se (de)** to sympathize (with)

comissão [komi'sãw] (*pl* **-ões**) f commission; (*comitê*) committee

comissário [komi'sarju] m commissioner; (*Com*) agent; **~ de bordo** (*Aer*) steward; (*Náut*) purser

comissões [komi'sõjs] fpl de **comissão**

comitê [komi'te] m committee

 PALAVRA-CHAVE

como ['kɔmu] adv **1** (*modo*) as; **ela fez como eu pedi** she did as I asked; **como se** as if; **como quiser** as you wish; **seja como for** be that as it may

2 (*assim como*) like; **ela tem olhos azuis como o pai** she has blue eyes like her father's; **ela trabalha numa loja, como a mãe** she works in a shop, as does her mother

3 (*de que maneira*) how; **como?** pardon?; **como!** what!; **como assim?** what do you mean?; **como não!** of course!

▷ conj (*porque*) as, since; **como estava tarde ele dormiu aqui** since it was late he slept here

comoção [komo'sãw] (pl **-ões**) f
distress; (revolta) commotion

cômoda ['komoda] f chest of
drawers (Brit), bureau (US)

comodidade [komodʒi'dadʒi] f
comfort; (conveniência)
convenience

comodismo [komo'dʒizmu] m
complacency

cômodo, -a ['komodu, a] adj
comfortable; (conveniente)
convenient ▷ m room

comovente [komo'vẽtʃi] adj
moving, touching

comover [komo'ver] vt to move
▷ vi to be moving; **comover-se** vr
to be moved

compacto, -a [kõ'paktu, a] adj
compact; (espesso) thick; (sólido)
solid ▷ m (disco) single

compadecer-se [kõpade'sersi] vr:
~ de to pity

compadre [kõ'padri] m (col:
companheiro) buddy, pal

compaixão [kõpaj'ʃãw] m
compassion; (misericórdia) mercy

companheiro, -a [kõpa'ɲejru, a]
m/f companion; (colega) friend;
(col) buddy, mate

companhia [kõpa'ɲia] f company

comparação [kõpara'sãw] (pl **-ões**)
f comparison

comparar [kõpa'rar] vt to
compare; **~ a** to liken to; **~ com**
compare with

comparecer [kõpare'ser] vi to
appear, make an appearance; **~ a
uma reunião** to attend a meeting

comparsa [kõ'parsa] m/f (Teatro)
extra; (cúmplice) accomplice

compartilhar [kõpartʃi'ʎar] vt to
share ▷ vi: **~ de** to share in,
participate in

compartimento [kõpartʃi'mẽtu]

m compartment; (aposento) room

compasso [kõ'pasu] m
(instrumento) pair of compasses;
(Mús) time; (ritmo) beat

compatível [kõpa'tʃivew] (pl **-eis**)
adj compatible

compensar [kõpẽ'sar] vt to make
up for, compensate for; (equilibrar)
to offset; (cheque) to clear

competência [kõpe'tẽsja] f
competence, ability;
(responsabilidade) responsibility;
competente [kõpe'tẽtʃi] adj
competent; (apropriado)
appropriate; (responsável)
responsible

competição [kõpetʃi'sãw] (pl **-ões**)
f competition

competidor, a [kõpetʃi'dor(a)] m/f
competitor

competir [kõpe'tʃir] vi to compete;
~ a alguém to be sb's
responsibility; (caber) to be up to sb

competitivo, -a [kõpetʃi'tʃivu, a]
adj competitive

compito etc [kõ'pitu] vb ver
competir

complementar [kõplemẽ'tar] adj
complementary ▷ vt to
supplement

complemento [kõple'mẽtu] m
complement

completamente [kõpleta'mẽtʃi]
adv completely, quite

completar [kõple'tar] vt to
complete, to fill up; **~ dez anos** to
be ten

completo, -a [kõ'plɛtu, a] adj
complete; (cheio) full (up); **por ~**
completely

complexo, -a [kõ'plɛksu, a] adj
complex ▷ m complex

complicação [kõplika'sãw] (pl
-ões) f complication

complicado, -a [kõpli'kadu, a] *adj*
complicated

complicar [kõpli'kar] *vt* to
complicate

complô [kõ'plo] *m* plot, conspiracy

componente [kõpo'nẽtʃi] *adj, m*
component

compor [kõ'por] (*irreg: como* **pôr**) *vt*
to compose; (*discurso, livro*) to
write; (*arranjar*) to arrange ▷ *vi* to
compose; **compor-se** *vr*
(*controlar-se*) to compose o.s.; **~-se
de** to consist of

comportamento [kõporta'mẽtu]
m behaviour (*Brit*), behavior (*US*)

comportar [kõpor'tar] *vt* to put up
with; **comportar-se** *vr* (*portar-se*)
to behave; **~-se mal** to misbehave,
behave badly

composição [kõpozi'sãw] (*pl* **-ões**)
f composition; (*Tip*) typesetting

compositor, a [kõpozi'tor(a)] *m/f*
composer; (*Tip*) typesetter

compota [kõ'pɔta] *f* fruit in syrup

compra ['kõpra] *f* purchase; **fazer
~s** to go shopping; **comprador, a**
[kõpra'dor(a)] *m/f* buyer,
purchaser

comprar [kõ'prar] *vt* to buy

compreender [kõprjen'der] *vt* to
understand; (*constar de*) to be
comprised of, consist of; (*abranger*)
to cover

compreensão [kõprjẽ'sãw] *f*
understanding, comprehension;
compreensivo, -a [kõprjẽ'sivu, a]
adj understanding

compressa [kõ'prɛsa] *f* compress

comprido, -a [kõ'pridu, a] *adj*
long; (*alto*) tall; **ao ~** lengthways

comprimento [kõpri'mẽtu] *m*
length

comprimido, -a [kõpri'midu, a]
adj compressed ▷ *m* pill, tablet

comprimir [kõpri'mir] *vt* to
compress

comprometer [kõprome'ter] *vt* to
compromise; (*envolver*) to involve;
(*arriscar*) to jeopardize; (*empenhar*)
to pledge; **comprometer-se** *vr*:
~-se a to undertake to, promise to

compromisso [kõpro'misu] *m*
promise; (*obrigação*) commitment;
(*hora marcada*) appointment;
(*acordo*) agreement

comprovante [kõpro'vãtʃi] *m*
receipt; **comprovante de
residência** proof of address

comprovar [kõpro'var] *vt* to prove;
(*confirmar*) to confirm;
compulsivo, -a [kõpuw'sivu, a]
adj compulsive; **compulsório, -a**
[kõpuw'sɔrju, a] *adj* compulsory

computação [kõputa'sãw] *f*
computer science, computing

computador [kõputa'dor] *m*
computer

computar [kõpu'tar] *vt* (*calcular*) to
calculate; (*contar*) to count

comum [ko'mũ] (*pl* **-ns**) *adj*
ordinary, common; (*habitual*)
usual; **em ~** in common

comungar [komũ'gar] *vi* to take
communion

comunhão [komu'ɲãw] (*pl* **-ões**) *f*
communion

comunicação [komunika'sãw] (*pl*
-ões) *f* communication;
(*mensagem*) message; (*acesso*)
access

comunicado [komuni'kadu] *m*
notice

comunicar [komuni'kar] *vt, vi* to
communicate; **comunicar-se** *vr*
to communicate; **~-se com** (*entrar
em contato*) to get in touch with

comunidade [komuni'dadʒi] *f*
community; **C~ (Econômica)**

Europeia European (Economic) Community

comunismo [komu'nizmu] *m* communism; **comunista** [komu'nista] *adj, m/f* communist

comuns [ko'mũs] *pl de* **comum**

conceber [kõse'ber] *vt, vi* to conceive

conceder [kõse'der] *vt* to allow; (*outorgar*) to grant; (*dar*) to give ▷ *vi*: **~ em** to agree to

conceito [kõ'sejtu] *m* concept, idea; (*fama*) reputation; (*opinião*) opinion; **conceituado, -a** [kõsej'twadu, a] *adj* well thought of, highly regarded

concentração [kõsẽtra'sãw] (*pl* **-ões**) *f* concentration

concepção [kõsep'sãw] (*pl* **-ões**) *f* (*geração*) conception; (*noção*) idea, concept; (*opinião*) opinion

concerto [kõ'sertu] *m* concert

concessão [kõse'sãw] (*pl* **-ões**) *f* concession; (*permissão*) permission

concha ['kõʃa] *f* shell; (*para líquidos*) ladle

conchavo [kõ'ʃavu] *m* conspiracy

conciliar [kõsi'ljar] *vt* to reconcile

concluir [kõ'klwir] *vt, vi* to conclude

conclusão [kõklu'zãw] (*pl* **-ões**) *f* end; (*dedução*) conclusion

conclusões [kõklu'zõjs] *fpl de* **conclusão**

concordância [kõkor'dãsja] *f* agreement

concordar [kõkor'dar] *vi, vt* to agree

concorrência [kõko'hẽsja] *f* competition; (*a um cargo*) application

concorrente [kõko'hẽtʃi] *m/f* contestant; (*candidato*) candidate

concorrer [kõko'her] *vi* to

compete; **~ a** to apply for

concretizar [kõkretʃi'zar] *vt* to make real; **concretizar-se** *vr* (*sonho*) to come true; (*ambições*) to be realized

concreto, -a [kõ'krɛtu, a] *adj* concrete ▷ *m* concrete

concurso [kõ'kursu] *m* contest; (*exame*) competition

conde ['kõdʒi] *m* count

condenar [kõde'nar] *vt* to condemn; (*Jur: sentenciar*) to sentence; (: *declarar culpado*) to convict

condensar [kõdẽ'sar] *vt* to condense; **condensar-se** *vr* to condense

condessa [kõ'desa] *f* countess

condimento [kõdʒi'mẽtu] *m* seasoning

condomínio [kõdo'minju] *m* condominium

condução [kõdu'sãw] *f* driving; (*transporte*) transport; (*ônibus*) bus

condutor, a [kõdu'tor(a)] *m/f* (*de veículo*) driver ▷ *m* (*Elet*) conductor

conduzir [kõdu'zir] *vt* (*levar*) to lead; (*Fís*) to conduct; **conduzir-se** *vr* to behave; **~ a** to lead to

cone ['kɔni] *m* cone

conectar [konek'tar] *vt* to connect

conexão [konek'sãw] (*pl* **-ões**) *f* connection; (*voo*) connecting flight

confecção [kõfek'sãw] (*pl* **-ões**) *f* making; (*de um boletim*) production; (*roupa*) ready-to-wear clothes *pl*; (*negócio*) *business selling ready-to-wear clothes*

confeccionar [kõfeksjo'nar] *vt* to make; (*fabricar*) to manufacture

confecções [kõfek'sõjs] *fpl de* **confecção**

confeitaria [kõfejta'ria] *f* patisserie

conferência [kõfe'rēsja] f
conference; (*discurso*) lecture

conferir [kõfe'rir] vt to check;
(*comparar*) to compare; (*outorgar*)
to grant ▷ vi to tally

confessar [kõfe'sar] vt, vi to
confess; **confessar-se** vr to
confess

confiança [kõ'fjãsa] f confidence;
(*fé*) trust; **de ~** reliable; **ter ~ em
alguém** to trust sb

confiar [kõ'fjar] vt to entrust;
(*segredo*) to confide ▷ vi: **~ em** to
trust; (*ter fé*) to have faith in

confiável [kõ'fjavew] (*pl* -**eis**) adj
reliable

confidência [kõfi'dēsja] f secret;
em ~ in confidence; **confidencial**
[kõfidē'sjaw] (*pl* -**ais**) adj
confidential

confirmação [kõfirma'sãw] (*pl*
-**ões**) f confirmation

confirmar [kõfir'mar] vt to
confirm

confiro *etc* [kõ'firu] vb ver **conferir**

confissão [kõfi'sãw] (*pl* -**ões**) f
confession

conformar [kõfor'mar] vt to form
▷ vi: **~ com** to conform to;
conformar-se vr: **~-se com** to
resign o.s. to; (*acomodar-se*) to
conform to

conforme [kõ'fɔrmi] prep
according to; (*dependendo de*)
depending on ▷ conj (*logo que*) as
soon as; (*como*) as, according to
what; (*à medida que*) as; **você vai?
— ~** are you going? — it depends

conformidade [kõformi'dadʒi] f
agreement; **em ~ com** in
accordance with

confortar [kõfor'tar] vt to comfort,
console

confortável [kõfor'tavew] (*pl* -**eis**)

adj comfortable

conforto [kõ'fortu] m comfort

confrontar [kõfrõ'tar] vt to
confront; (*comparar*) to compare

confronto [kõ'frõtu] m
confrontation; (*comparação*)
comparison

confusão [kõfu'zãw] (*pl* -**ões**) f
confusion; (*tumulto*) uproar;
(*problemas*) trouble

confuso, -a [kõ'fuzu, a] adj
confused; (*problema*) confusing

confusões [kõfu'zõjs] fpl de
confusão

congelador [kõʒela'dor] m freezer,
deep freeze

congelamento [kõʒela'mētu] m
freezing; (Econ) freeze

congelar [kõʒe'lar] vt to freeze;
congelar-se vr to freeze

congestão [kõʒes'tãw] f
congestion; **congestionado, -a**
[kõʒestʃjo'nadu, a] adj congested;
(*olhos*) bloodshot; (*rosto*) flushed;
congestionamento
[kõʒestʃjona'mētu] m congestion;
**um congestionamento (de
tráfego)** a traffic jam

congestionar [kõʒestʃjo'nar] vt
to congest; **congestionar-se** vr
(*rosto*) to go red

congressista [kõgre'sista] m/f
congressman/woman

congresso [kõ'grɛsu] m congress,
conference

conhaque [ko'ɲaki] m cognac,
brandy

conhecedor, a [koɲese'dor(a)] adj
knowing ▷ m/f connoisseur,
expert

conhecer [koɲe'ser] vt to know;
(*travar conhecimento com*) to meet;
(*descobrir*) to discover;
conhecer-se vr to meet; (*ter*

conhecimento) to know each other
conhecido, -a [koɲe'sidu, a] *adj*
known; (*célebre*) well-known ▷ *m/f*
acquaintance
conhecimento [koɲesi'mẽtu] *m*
knowledge; (*ideia*) idea; (*conhecido*)
acquaintance; (*Com*) bill of lading;
conhecimentos *mpl* (*informações*)
knowledge *sg*; **levar ao ~ de**
alguém to bring to sb's notice
conjugado [kõʒu'gadu] *m* studio
cônjuge ['kõʒuʒi] *m* spouse
conjunção [kõʒũ'sãw] (*pl* **-ões**) *f*
union; (*Ling*) conjunction
conjuntivo [kõʒũ'tʃivu] (*PT*) *m*
(*Ling*) subjunctive
conosco [ko'nosku] *pron* with us
conquista [kõ'kista] *f* conquest;
conquistador, a [kõkista'dor(a)]
adj conquering ▷ *m* conqueror;
conquistar [kõkis'tar] *vt* to
conquer; (*alcançar*) to achieve;
(*ganhar*) to win
consciência [kõ'sjẽsja] *f*
conscience; (*percepção*) awareness;
(*senso de responsabilidade*)
conscientiousness
consciente [kõ'sjẽtʃi] *adj*
conscious
conseguinte [kõse'gĩtʃi] *adj*: **por ~**
consequently
conseguir [kõse'gir] *vt* to get,
obtain; **~ fazer** to manage to do,
succeed in doing
conselho [kõ'seʎu] *m* piece of
advice; (*corporação*) council;
conselhos *mpl* (*advertência*) advice
sg; **~ de guerra** court martial; **C~**
de ministros (*Pol*) Cabinet
consentimento [kõsẽtʃi'mẽtu] *m*
consent
consentir [kõsẽ'tʃir] *vt* to allow,
permit; (*aprovar*) to agree to ▷ *vi*:
~ em to agree to

consequência [kõse'kwẽsja] *f*
consequence; **por ~** consequently
consertar [kõser'tar] *vt* to mend,
repair; (*remediar*) to put right;
conserto [kõ'sertu] *m* repair
conserva [kõ'serva] *f* pickle; **em ~**
pickled
conservação [kõserva'sãw] *f*
conservation; (*de vida, alimentos*)
preservation
conservador, a [kõserva'dor(a)]
adj conservative ▷ *m/f* (*Pol*)
conservative
conservante [kõser'vãtʃi] *m*
preservative
conservar [kõser'var] *vt* to
preserve, maintain; (*reter, manter*)
to keep, retain; **conservar-se** *vr*
to keep
conservatório [kõserva'tɔrju] *m*
conservatory
consideração [kõsidera'sãw] (*pl*
-ões) *f* consideration; (*estima*)
respect, esteem; **levar em ~** to
take into account
considerar [kõside'rar] *vt* to
consider; (*prezar*) to respect ▷ *vi*
to consider
considerável [kõside'ravew] (*pl*
-eis) *adj* considerable
consigo¹ [kõ'sigu] *pron* (*m*) with
him; (*f*) with her; (*pl*) with them;
(*com você*) with you
consigo² *vb ver* **conseguir**
consinto [kõ'sĩtu] *vb ver* **consentir**
consistente [kõsis'tẽtʃi] *adj* solid;
(*espesso*) thick
consistir [kõsis'tʃir] *vi*: **~ em** to be
made up of, consist of
consoante [kõso'ãtʃi] *f* consonant
▷ *prep* according to ▷ *conj*: **~**
prometera as he had promised
consolação [kõsola'sãw] (*pl* **-ões**) *f*
consolation

consolar [kõso'lar] *vt* to console
consolidar [kõsoli'dar] *vt* to consolidate; *(fratura)* to knit ▷ *vi* to become solid; to knit together
consolo [kõ'solu] *m* consolation
consome *etc* [kõ'somi] *vb ver* **consumir**
consórcio [kõ'sɔrsju] *m (união)* partnership; *(Com)* consortium
conspiração [kõspira'sãw] *(pl -ões)* *f* plot, conspiracy
conspirar [kõspi'rar] *vt, vi* to plot
constante [kõs'tãtʃi] *adj* constant
constar [kõs'tar] *vi* to be in; **ao que me consta** as far as I know
constatar [kõsta'tar] *vt* to establish; *(notar)* to notice; *(evidenciar)* to show up
consternado, -a [kõster'nadu, a] *adj* depressed; *(desolado)* distressed
constipação [kõstʃipa'sãw] *(pl -ões)* *f (PT)* cold
constipado, -a [kõstʃi'padu, a] *(PT) adj*: **estar ~** to have a cold
constituição [kõstʃitwi'sãw] *(pl -ões)* *f* constitution
constituinte [kõstʃi'twĩtʃi] *m/f (deputado)* member ▷ *f*: **a C~** the Constituent Assembly
constituir [kõstʃi'twir] *vt* to constitute; *(formar)* to form; *(estabelecer)* to establish; *(nomear)* to appoint
constrangimento [kõstrãʒi'mẽtu] *m* constraint; *(acanhamento)* embarrassment
construção [kõstru'sãw] *(pl -ões)* *f* building, construction
construir [kõs'trwir] *vt* to build, construct
construtivo, -a [kõstru'tʃivu, a] *adj* constructive
construtor, a [kõstru'tor(a)] *m/f* builder

cônsul ['kõsuw] *(pl* **cônsules***)* *m* consul; **consulado** [kõsu'ladu] *m* consulate
consulta [kõ'suwta] *f* consultation; **livro de ~** reference book; **horário de ~** surgery hours *pl (Brit)*, office hours *pl (US)*; **consultar** [kõsuw'tar] *vt* to consult; **consultor, a** [kõsuw'tor(a)] *m/f* consultant
consultório [kõsuw'tɔrju] *m* surgery
consumidor, a [kõsumi'dor(a)] *adj* consumer *atr* ▷ *m/f* consumer
consumir [kõsu'mir] *vt* to consume; *(gastar)* to use up; **consumir-se** *vr* to waste away
consumo [kõ'sumu] *m* consumption; **artigos de ~** consumer goods
conta ['kõta] *f* count; *(em restaurante)* bill; *(fatura)* invoice; *(bancária)* account; *(de colar)* bead; **contas** *fpl (Com)* accounts; **levar** *ou* **ter em ~** to take into account; **tomar ~ de** to take care of; *(dominar)* to take hold of; **afinal de ~s** after all; **dar-se ~ de** to realize; *(notar)* to notice; **~ corrente** current account; **~ de e-mail** *ou* **de correio eletrônico** email account
contabilista [kõtabi'lista] *(PT) m/f* accountant
contabilizar [kõtabili'zar] *vt* to write up, book
contacto [kõ'tatu] *(PT) =* **contato**
contador, a [kõta'dor(a)] *m/f (Com)* accountant ▷ *m (Tec: medidor)* meter
contagiante [kõta'ʒjãtʃi] *adj (alegria)* contagious
contagiar [kõta'ʒjar] *vt* to infect
contágio [kõ'taʒju] *m* infection
contagioso, -a [kõta'ʒjozu, ɔza]

adj (*doença*) contagious

contaminar [kõtami'nar] *vt* to contaminate

contanto que [kõ'tãtu ki] *conj* provided that

conta-quilómetros (*PT*) *m inv* speedometer

contar [kõ'tar] *vt* to count; (*narrar*) to tell; (*pretender*) to intend ▷ *vi* to count; **~ com** to count on; (*esperar*) to expect; **~ em fazer** to count on doing, expect to do

contatar [kõta'tar] *vt* to contact; **contato** [kõ'tatu] *m* contact; **entrar em contato com** to get in touch with, contact

contemplar [kõtẽ'plar] *vt* to contemplate; (*olhar*) to gaze at

contemplativo, -a [kõtẽpla'tʃivu, a] *adj* (*pessoa*) thoughtful

contemporâneo, -a [kõtẽpo'ranju, a] *adj, m/f* contemporary

contentamento [kõtẽta'mẽtu] *m* (*felicidade*) happiness; (*satisfação*) contentment

contente [kõ'tẽtʃi] *adj* happy; (*satisfeito*) pleased, satisfied

contento [kõ'tẽtu] *m*: **a ~** satisfactorily

conter [kõ'ter] (*irreg: como* **ter**) *vt* to contain, hold; (*refrear*) to restrain, hold back; (*gastos*) to curb

contestação [kõtesta'sãw] (*pl* **-ões**) *f* challenge; (*negação*) denial

contestar [kõtes'tar] *vt* to dispute, contest; (*impugnar*) to challenge

conteúdo [kõte'udu] *m* contents *pl*; (*de um texto*) content

contexto [kõ'testu] *m* context

contigo [kõ'tʃigu] *pron* with you

contíguo, -a [kõ'tʃigwu, a] *adj*: **~ a** next to

continental [kõtʃinẽ'taw] (*pl* **-ais**)

adj continental

continente [kõtʃi'nẽtʃi] *m* continent

continuação [kõtʃinwa'sãw] *f* continuation

continuar [kõtʃi'nwar] *vt, vi* to continue; **~ falando** *ou* **a falar** to go on talking; **ela continua doente** she is still sick

continuidade [kõtʃinwi'dadʒi] *f* continuity

conto ['kõtu] *m* story, tale; (*PT: dinheiro*) 1000 escudos

contorcer [kõtor'ser] *vt* to twist; **contorcer-se** *vr* to writhe

contornar [kõtor'nar] *vt* (*rodear*) to go round; (*ladear*) to skirt; (*fig: problema*) to get round

contorno [kõ'tornu] *m* outline; (*da terra*) contour; (*do rosto*) profile

contra ['kõtra] *prep* against ▷ *m*: **os prós e os ~s** the pros and cons; **dar o ~ (a)** to be opposed (to)

contra-ataque *m* counterattack

contrabandear [kõtrabã'dʒjar] *vt* to smuggle; **contrabandista** [kõtrabã'dʒista] *m/f* smuggler; **contrabando** [kõtra'bãdu] *m* smuggling; (*artigos*) contraband

contraceptivo, -a [kõtrasep'tʃivu, a] *adj* contraceptive ▷ *m* contraceptive

contracheque [kõtra'ʃɛki] *m* pay slip (*Brit*), check stub (*US*)

contradição [kõtradʒi'sãw] (*pl* **-ões**) *f* contradiction

contraditório, -a [kõtradʒi'tɔrju, a] *adj* contradictory

contradizer [kõtradʒi'zer] (*irreg: como* **dizer**) *vt* to contradict

contragosto [kõtra'gostu] *m*: **a ~** against one's will, unwillingly

contrair [kõtra'ir] *vt* to contract; (*hábito*) to form

contramão [kõtra'mãw] adj
one-way ▷ f: **na ~** the wrong way
down a one-way street
contraproducente
[kõtraprodu'sẽtʃi] adj
counterproductive
contrário, -a [kõ'trarju, a] adj
(oposto) opposite; (pessoa)
opposed; (desfavorável)
unfavourable (Brit), unfavorable
(US), adverse ▷ m opposite; **do ~**
otherwise; **pelo** ou **ao ~** on the
contrary; **ao ~** the other way round
contrassenso m nonsense
contrastar [kõtras'tar] vt to
contrast; **contraste** [kõ'trastʃi] m
contrast
contratação [kõtrata'sãw] f (de
pessoal) employment
contratar [kõtra'tar] vt (serviços) to
contract; (pessoal) to employ, take
on
contratempo [kõtra'tẽpu] m
setback; (aborrecimento) upset;
(dificuldade) difficulty
contrato [kõ'tratu] m contract;
(acordo) agreement
contribuição [kõtribwi'sãw] (pl
-ões) f contribution; (imposto) tax
contribuinte [kõtri'bwĩtʃi] m/f
contributor; (que paga impostos)
taxpayer
contribuir [kõtri'bwir] vt to
contribute ▷ vi to contribute;
(pagar impostos) to pay taxes
controlar [kõtro'lar] vt to control
controle [kõ'troli] m control;
~ remoto remote control; **~ de
crédito** (Com) credit control; **~ de
qualidade** (Com) quality control
controvérsia [kõtro'vɛrsja] f
controversy; (discussão) debate;
controverso, -a [kõtro'vɛrsu, a]
adj controversial

contudo [kõ'tudu] conj
nevertheless, however
contumaz [kõtu'majz] adj
obstinate, stubborn
contusão [kõtu'zãw] (pl **-ões**) f
bruise
convenção [kõvẽ'sãw] (pl **-ões**) f
convention; (acordo) agreement
convencer [kõvẽ'ser] vt to
convince; (persuadir) to persuade;
convencer-se vr: **~-se de** to be
convinced about; **convencido, -a**
[kõvẽ'sidu, a] adj convinced; (col:
imodesto) conceited, smug
convencional [kõvẽsjo'naw] (pl
-ais) adj conventional
convenções [kõvẽ'sõjs] fpl de
convenção
conveniência [kõve'njẽsja] f
convenience
conveniente [kõve'njẽtʃi] adj
convenient, suitable; (vantajoso)
advantageous
convênio [kõ'venju] m (reunião)
convention; (acordo) agreement
convento [kõ'vẽtu] m convent
conversa [kõ'vɛrsa] f conversation;
~ fiada idle talk; (promessa falsa)
hot air
conversão [kõver'sãw] (pl **-ões**) f
conversion
conversar [kõver'sar] vi to talk, to
chat
conversões [kõver'sõjs] fpl de
conversão
converter [kõver'ter] vt to convert
convés [kõ'vɛs] (pl **-eses**) m (Náut)
deck
convexo, -a [kõ'vɛksu, a] adj
convex
convicção [kõvik'sãw] (pl **-ões**) f
conviction
convidado, -a [kõvi'dadu, a] m/f
guest

convidar [kõvi'dar] *vt* to invite

convincente [kõvĩ'sẽtʃi] *adj* convincing

convir [kõ'vir] (*irreg: como* **vir**) *vi* to suit, be convenient; (*ficar bem*) to be appropriate; (*concordar*) to agree; **convém fazer isso o mais rápido possível** we must do this as soon as possible

convite [kõ'vitʃi] *m* invitation

convivência [kõvi'vẽsja] *f* living together; (*familiaridade*) familiarity, intimacy

conviver [kõvi'ver] *vi*: **~ com** (*viver em comum*) to live with; (*ter familiaridade*) to get on with; **convívio** [kõ'vivju] *m* living together; (*familiaridade*) familiarity

convocar [kõvo'kar] *vt* to summon, call upon; (*reunião, eleições*) to call; (*para o serviço militar*) to call up

convosco [kõ'vosku] *adv* with you

convulsão [kõvuw'sãw] (*pl* **-ões**) *f* convulsion

cooper ['kuper] *m* jogging; **fazer ~** to go jogging *ou* running

cooperação [koopera'sãw] *f* cooperation

cooperar [koope'rar] *vi* to cooperate

coordenada [koorde'nada] *f* coordinate

copa ['kɔpa] *f* (*de árvore*) top; (*torneio*) cup; **copas** *fpl* (*Cartas*) hearts

cópia ['kɔpja] *f* copy; **tirar ~ de** to copy; **copiadora** [kopja'dora] *f* duplicating machine

copiar [ko'pjar] *vt* to copy

copo ['kɔpu] *m* glass

coque ['kɔki] *m* (*penteado*) bun

coqueiro [ko'kejru] *m* (*Bot*) coconut palm

coquetel [koke'tɛw] (*pl* **-éis**) *m* cocktail; (*festa*) cocktail party

cor¹ [kɔr] *m*: **de ~** by heart

cor² [kor] *f* colour (*Brit*), color (*US*); **de ~** colo(u)red

coração [kora'sãw] (*pl* **-ões**) *m* heart; **de bom ~** kind-hearted; **de todo o ~** wholeheartedly

corado, -a [ko'radu, a] *adj* ruddy

coragem [ko'raʒẽ] *f* courage; (*atrevimento*) nerve

corais [ko'rajs] *mpl de* **coral**

corajoso, -a [kora'ʒozu, ɔza] *adj* courageous

coral [ko'raw] (*pl* **-ais**) *m* (*Mús*) choir; (*Zool*) coral

corar [ko'rar] *vt* (*roupa*) to bleach (in the sun) ▷ *vi* to blush; (*tornar-se branco*) to bleach

corda ['kɔrda] *f* rope, line; (*Mús*) string; (*varal*) clothes line; (*de relógio*) spring; **dar ~ em** to wind up; **~s vocais** vocal chords

cordão [kor'dãw] (*pl* **-ões**) *m* string, twine; (*joia*) chain; (*no carnaval*) group; (*Elet*) lead; (*fileira*) row

cordeiro [kor'dejru] *m* lamb

cordel [kor'dɛw] (*pl* **-éis**) *m* string; **literatura de ~** pamphlet literature

cor-de-rosa *adj inv* pink

cordões [kor'dõjs] *mpl de* **cordão**

coreano, -a [ko'rjanu, a] *adj* Korean ▷ *m/f* Korean ▷ *m* (*Ling*) Korean

Coreia [ko'rɛja] *f*: **a ~** Korea

coreto [ko'retu] *m* bandstand

córner ['kɔrner] *m* (*Futebol*) corner

coro ['koru] *m* chorus; (*conjunto de cantores*) choir

coroa [ko'roa] *f* crown; (*de flores*) garland ▷ *m/f* (*BR: col*) old timer

coroar [koro'ar] *vt* to crown; (*premiar*) to reward

coronel [koro'nɛw] (pl **-éis**) m
colonel; (político) local political
boss

corpo ['korpu] m body; (aparência
física) figure; (: de homem) build; (de
vestido) bodice; (Mil) corps sg; **de ~
e alma** (fig) wholeheartedly; **~
diplomático** diplomatic corps sg

corpulento, -a [korpu'lētu, a] adj
stout

correção [kohe'sãw] (pl **-ões**) f
correction; (exatidão) correctness;
casa de ~ reformatory

corre-corre [kɔhi'kɔhi] (pl
corre-corres) m (pressa) scramble;
(de muitas pessoas) stampede

corredor, a [kohe'dor(a)] m/f
runner ▷ m corridor; (em avião etc)
aisle; (cavalo) racehorse

correia [ko'heja] f strap; (de
máquina) belt; (para cachorro) leash

correio [ko'heju] m mail, post;
(local) post office; (carteiro)
postman (Brit), mailman (US);
~ aéreo air mail; **pôr no ~** to post;
~ eletrônico email; **~ de voz** voice
mail

corrente [ko'hētʃi] adj (atual)
current; (águas) running; (comum)
usual, common ▷ f current;
(cadeia, joia) chain; **~ de ar** draught
(Brit), draft (US); **correnteza**
[kohē'teza] f (de ar) draught (Brit),
draft (US); (de rio) current

correr [ko'her] vt to run; (viajar por)
to travel across ▷ vi to run; (em
carro) to drive fast, speed; (o tempo)
to elapse; (boato) to go round;
(atuar com rapidez) to rush; **correria**
[kohe'ria] f rush

correspondência [kohespõ'dēsja]
f correspondence;
correspondente [kohespõ'dētʃi]
adj corresponding ▷ m

correspondent

corresponder [kohespõ'der] vi:
~ a to correspond to; (ser igual) to
match (up to); **corresponder-se**
vr: **~-se com** to correspond with

correto, -a [ko'hɛtu, a] adj correct;
(conduta) right; (pessoa) straight,
honest

corretor, a [kohe'tor(a)] m/f
broker; **~ de fundos** ou **da bolsa**
stockbroker; **~ de imóveis** estate
agent (Brit), realtor (US); **~
ortográfico** spellchecker

corrida [ko'hida] f running;
(certame) race; (de taxi) fare;
~ de cavalos horse race

corrido, -a [ko'hidu, a] adj quick;
(expulso) driven out ▷ adv quickly

corrigir [kohi'ʒir] vt to correct

corriqueiro, -a [kohi'kejru, a] adj
common; (problema) trivial

corromper [kohõ'per] vt to
corrupt; (subornar) to bribe;
corromper-se vr to be corrupted

corrosão [koho'zãw] f corrosion;
(fig) erosion

corrosivo, -a [koho'zivu, a] adj
corrosive

corrupção [kohup'sãw] f
corruption

corrupto, -a [ko'huptu, a] adj
corrupt

Córsega ['kɔrsega] f: **a ~** Corsica

cortada [kor'tada] f: **dar uma ~
em alguém** (fig) to cut sb short

cortante [kor'tãtʃi] adj cutting

cortar [kor'tar] vt to cut; (eliminar)
to cut out; (água, telefone etc) to cut
off; (efeito) to stop ▷ vi to cut;
(encurtar caminho) to take a short
cut; **~ o cabelo** (no cabeleireiro) to
have one's hair cut; **~ a palavra de
alguém** to interrupt sb

corte¹ ['kɔrtʃi] m cut; (de luz) power

cut; **sem ~** (*tesoura etc*) blunt;
~ de cabelo haircut

corte² ['kɔrtʃi] *f* court; **cortes** *fpl*
(*PT*) parliament *sg*

cortejo [kor'teʒu] *m* procession

cortesia [korte'zia] *f* politeness;
(*de empresa*) free offer

cortiça [kor'tʃisa] *f* cork

cortiço [kor'tʃisu] *m* slum
tenement

cortina [kor'tʃina] *f* curtain

coruja [ko'ruʒa] *f* owl

corvo ['korvu] *m* crow

coser [ko'zer] *vt, vi* to sew

cosmético, -a [koz'mɛtʃiku, a] *adj*
cosmetic ▷ *m* cosmetic

cospe *etc* ['kɔspi] *vb ver* **cuspir**

costa ['kɔsta] *f* coast; **costas** *fpl*
(*dorso*) back *sg*; **dar as ~s a** to turn
one's back on

Costa Rica *f*: **a ~** Costa Rica

costela [kos'tɛla] *f* rib

costeleta [koste'leta] *f* chop,
cutlet; **costeletas** *fpl* (*suíças*)
side-whiskers

costumar [kostu'mar] *vt* (*habituar*)
to accustom ▷ *vi*: **ele costuma
chegar às 6.00** he usually arrives
at 6.00; **costumava dizer ...** he
used to say ...

costume [kos'tumi] *m* custom,
habit; (*traje*) costume; **costumes**
mpl (*comportamento*) behaviour *sg*
(*Brit*), behavior *sg* (*US*); (*conduta*)
conduct *sg*; (*de um povo*) customs;
de ~ usual; **como de ~** as usual

costura [kos'tura] *f* sewing;
(*sutura*) seam; **costurar**
[kostu'rar] *vt, vi* to sew;
costureira [kostu'rejra] *f*
dressmaker

cota ['kɔta] *f* quota, share

cotação [kota'sãw] (*pl* **-ões**) *f* (*de
preços*) list, quotation; (*Bolsa*) price;

(*consideração*) esteem; **~ bancária**
bank rate

cotado, -a [ko'tadu, a] *adj* (*Com:
ação*) quoted; (*bem-conceituado*)
well thought of; (*num concurso*)
fancied

cotar [ko'tar] *vt* (*ações*) to quote;
~ algo em to value sth at

cotejar [kote'ʒar] *vt* to compare

cotidiano, -a [kotʃi'dʒianu, a] *adj*
daily, everyday ▷ *m*: **o ~** daily life

cotonete® [koto'nɛtʃi] *m* cotton
bud (*Brit*)

cotovelada [kotove'lada] *f* shove;
(*cutucada*) nudge

cotovelo [koto'velu] *m* (*Anat*)
elbow; (*curva*) bend; **falar pelos ~s**
to talk non-stop

coube *etc* ['kobi] *vb ver* **caber**

couro ['koru] *m* leather; (*de um
animal*) hide

couve ['kovi] *f* spring greens *pl*;
couve-flor (*pl* **couves-flor(es)**) *f*
cauliflower

couvert [ku'vɛr] *m* cover charge

cova ['kɔva] *f* pit; (*caverna*) cavern;
(*sepultura*) grave

covarde [ko'vardʒi] *adj* cowardly
▷ *m/f* coward; **covardia**
[kovar'dʒia] *f* cowardice

covil [ko'viw] (*pl* **-is**) *m* den, lair

covis [ko'vis] *mpl de* **covil**

coxa ['kɔʃa] *f* thigh

coxear [ko'ʃjar] *vi* to limp

coxia [ko'ʃia] *f* aisle, gangway

coxo, -a ['kɔʃu, a] *adj* lame

cozer [ko'zer] *vt, vi* to cook

cozido [ko'zidu] *m* stew

cozinha [ko'ziɲa] *f* kitchen; (*arte*)
cookery; **~ planejada** fitted
kitchen

cozinhar [kozi'ɲar] *vt, vi* to cook

cozinheiro, -a [kozi'ɲejru, a] *m/f*
cook

CP *abr* = **Caminhos de Ferro Portugueses**

CPF (*BR*) *abr m* (= *Cadastro de Pessoa Física*) identification number

CPLP *abr f see note*

○ **CPLP**
○
○ The *Comunidade de Países de*
○ *Língua Portuguesa* was set up in
○ 1996 to establish economic and
○ diplomatic links between all
○ countries where the official
○ language is Portuguese. The
○ members are Brazil, Portugal,
○ Angola, Mozambique,
○ Guinea-Bissau, Cape Verde and
○ São Tomé e Príncipe. Portuguese
○ is spoken by around 170 million
○ people around the world today.

crachá [kra'ʃa] *m* badge

crânio ['kranju] *m* skull

craque ['kraki] *m/f* ace, expert

crasso, -a ['krasu, a] *adj* crass

cratera [kra'tɛra] *f* crater

cravar [kra'var] *vt* (*prego etc*) to drive (in); (*com os olhos*) to stare at; **cravar-se** *vr* to penetrate

cravo ['kravu] *m* carnation; (*Mús*) harpsichord; (*especiaria*) clove; (*na pele*) blackhead; (*prego*) nail

creche ['krɛʃi] *f* crèche, day-care centre

credenciais [kredẽ'sjajs] *fpl* credentials

creditar [kredʒi'tar] *vt* to guarantee; (*Com*) to credit; **~ algo a alguém** to credit sb with sth; (*garantir*) to assure sb of sth

crédito ['krɛdʒitu] *m* credit; **digno de ~** reliable

creme ['krɛmi] *adj inv* cream ⊳ *m* cream; (*Culin: doce*) custard;

~ dental toothpaste; **cremoso, -a** [kre'mozu, ɔza] *adj* creamy

crença ['krẽsa] *f* belief

crente ['krẽtʃi] *m/f* believer

crepúsculo [kre'puskulu] *m* dusk, twilight

crer [krer] *vt, vi* to believe; **crer-se** *vr* to believe o.s. to be; **~ em** to believe in; **creio que sim** I think so

crescer [kre'ser] *vi* to grow; **crescimento** [kresi'mẽtu] *m* growth

crespo, -a ['krespu, a] *adj* (*cabelo*) curly

cretinice [kretʃi'nisi] *f* stupidity; (*ato, dito*) stupid thing

cretino [kre'tʃinu] *m* cretin, imbecile

cria ['kria] *f* (*animal: sg*) baby animal; (: *pl*) young *pl*

criação [krja'sãw] (*pl* -ões) *f* creation; (*de animais*) raising, breeding; (*educação*) upbringing; (*animais domésticos*) livestock *pl*; **filho de ~** adopted child

criado, -a [kri'jadu, a] *m/f* servant

criador, a [krja'dor(a)] *m/f* creator; **~ de gado** cattle breeder

criança ['krjãsa] *adj* childish ⊳ *f* child; **criançada** [krjã'sada] *f*: **a criançada** the kids

criar [krjar] *vt* to create; (*crianças*) to bring up; (*animais*) to raise; (*amamentar*) to suckle, nurse; (*planta*) to grow; **criar-se** *vr*: **~-se (com)** to grow up (with); **~ caso** to make trouble

criatura [kria'tura] *f* creature; (*indivíduo*) individual

crime ['krimi] *m* crime; **criminal** [krimi'naw] (*pl* -ais) *adj* criminal; **criminalidade** [kriminali'dadʒi] *f* crime; **criminoso, -a** [krimi'nozu, ɔza] *adj, m/f* criminal

crina ['krina] f mane

crioulo, -a ['krjolu, a] adj creole ▷ m/f creole; (BR: negro) Black (person)

crise ['krizi] f crisis; (escassez) shortage; (Med) attack, fit

crista ['krista] f (de serra, onda) crest; (de galo) cock's comb

cristal [kris'taw] (pl -ais) m crystal; (vidro) glass; **cristais** mpl (copos) glassware sg; **cristalino, -a** [krista'linu, a] adj crystal-clear

cristão, -tã [kris'tãw, 'tã] (pl -s/-s) adj, m/f Christian

cristianismo [kristʃja'nizmu] m Christianity

Cristo ['kristu] m Christ

critério [kri'terju] m criterion; (juízo) discretion, judgement; **criterioso, -a** [krite'rjozu, ɔza] adj thoughtful, careful

crítica ['kritʃika] f criticism; ver tb **crítico**

criticar [kritʃi'kar] vt to criticize; (um livro) to review

crítico, -a ['kritʃiku, a] adj critical ▷ m/f critic

crivar [kri'var] vt (com balas etc) to riddle

crivo ['krivu] m sieve

crocante [kro'kãtʃi] adj (pão, alface) crispy; (nozes, chocolate) crunchy

crônica ['kronika] f chronicle; (coluna de jornal) newspaper column; (texto jornalístico) feature; (conto) short story

crônico, -a ['kroniku, a] adj chronic

cronológico, -a [krono'lɔʒiku, a] adj chronological

croquete [kro'ketʃi] m croquette

cru, a [kru, 'krua] adj raw; (não refinado) crude

crucial [kru'sjaw] (pl -ais) adj crucial

crucificar [krusifi'kar] vt to crucify

crucifixo [krusi'fiksu] m crucifix

cruel [kru'ɛw] (pl -éis) adj cruel; **crueldade** [kruew'dadʒi] f cruelty

cruz [kruz] f cross; **C~ Vermelha** Red Cross

cruzado, -a [kru'zadu, a] adj crossed ▷ m (moeda) cruzado

cruzamento [kruza'mẽtu] m crossroads

cruzar [kru'zar] vt to cross ▷ vi (Náut) to cruise; (pessoas) to pass each other by; **~ com** to meet

cruzeiro [kru'zejru] m (cruz) (monumental) cross; (moeda) cruzeiro; (viagem de navio) cruise

cu [ku] (col!) m arse (!); **vai tomar no cu** fuck off (!)

Cuba ['kuba] f Cuba

cubro etc ['kubru] vb ver **cobrir**

cuca ['kuka] f (col) m head; **fundir a ~** (quebrar a cabeça) to rack one's brain; (baratinar) to boggle the mind; (perturbar) to drive crazy

cuco ['kuku] m cuckoo

cueca ['kwɛka] f (BR) underpants pl; **~s** (PT) underpants pl; (: para mulheres) panties pl

cuíca ['kwika] f kind of musical instrument

cuidado [kwi'dadu] m care; **aos ~s de** in the care of; **ter ~** to be careful; **~!** watch out!, be careful!; **tomar ~ (de)** to be careful (of); **cuidadoso, -a** [kwida'dozu, ɔza] adj careful

cuidar [kwi'dar] vi: **~ de** to take care of, look after; **cuidar-se** vr to look after o.s.

cujo, -a ['kuʒu, a] pron (de quem) whose; (de que) of which

culinária [kuli'narja] f cookery

culpa ['kuwpa] f fault; (Jur) guilt; **ter ~ de** to be to blame for; **por ~ de** because of; **culpado, -a**

[kuw'padu, a] *adj* guilty ▷ *m/f*
culprit; **culpar** [kuw'par] *vt* to
blame; (*acusar*) to accuse;
culpar-se *vr* to take the blame;
culpável [kuw'pavew] (*pl* **-eis**) *adj*
guilty

cultivar [kuwtʃi'var] *vt* to
cultivate; (*plantas*) to grow;
cultivo [kuw'tʃivu] *m* cultivation

culto, -a ['kuwtu, a] *adj* cultured
▷ *m* (*homenagem*) worship;
(*religião*) cult

cultura [kuw'tura] *f* culture; (*da
terra*) cultivation; **cultural**
[kuwtu'raw] (*pl* **culturais**) *adj*
cultural

cume ['kumi] *m* top, summit; (*fig*)
climax

cúmplice ['kũplisi] *m/f* accomplice

cumprimentar [kũprimẽ'tar] *vt* to
greet; (*dar parabéns*) to
congratulate

cumprimento [kũpri'mẽtu] *m*
fulfilment; (*saudação*) greeting;
(*elogio*) compliment;
cumprimentos *mpl* (*saudações*)
best wishes; **~ de uma lei/ordem**
compliance with a law/an order

cumprir [kũ'prir] *vt* (*desempenhar*)
to carry out; (*promessa*) to keep;
(*lei*) to obey; (*pena*) to serve ▷ *vi* to
be necessary; **~ a palavra** to keep
one's word; **fazer ~** to enforce

cúmulo ['kumulu] *m* height; **é o ~!**
that's the limit!

cunha ['kuɲa] *f* wedge

cunhado, -a [ku'ɲadu, a] *m/f*
brother-in-law/sister-in-law

cunho ['kuɲu] *m* (*marca*) hallmark;
(*caráter*) nature

cupim [ku'pĩ] (*pl* **-ns**) *m* termite

cupins [ku'pĩs] *mpl de* **cupim**

cúpula ['kupula] *f* dome; (*de abajur*)
shade; (*de partido etc*) leadership;

(reunião de) ~ summit (meeting)

cura ['kura] *f* cure; (*tratamento*)
treatment; (*de carnes etc*) curing,
preservation ▷ *m* priest

curar [ku'rar] *vt* (*doença*) to cure;
(*ferida*) to treat; **curar-se** *vr* to get
well

curativo [kura'tʃivu] *m* dressing

curiosidade [kurjozi'dadʒi] *f*
curiosity; (*objeto raro*) curio

curioso, -a [ku'rjozu, ɔza] *adj*
curious ▷ *m/f* snooper, inquisitive
person; **curiosos** *mpl*
(*espectadores*) onlookers

curral [ku'haw] (*pl* **-ais**) *m* pen,
enclosure

currículo [ku'hikulu] *m*
(*curriculum*) curriculum vitae

cursar [kur'sar] *vt* (*aulas, escola*) to
attend; (*cursos*) to follow; **ele está
cursando História** he's studying
ou doing History

curso ['kursu] *m* course; (*direção*)
direction; **em ~** (*ano etc*) current;
(*processo*) in progress

cursor [kur'sor] *m* (*Comput*) cursor

curtição [kurtʃi'sãw] *f* fun

curtir [kur'tʃir] *vt* (*couro*) to tan;
(*tornar rijo*) to toughen up; (*padecer*)
to suffer, endure; (*col*) to enjoy

curto, -a ['kurtu, a] *adj* short ▷ *m*
(*Elet*) short (circuit); **curto-
circuito** (*pl* **curtos-circuitos**) *m*
short circuit

curva ['kurva] *f* curve; (*de estrada,
rio*) bend; **~ fechada** hairpin bend

curvo, -a ['kurvu, a] *adj* curved;
(*estrada*) winding

cuscuz [kus'kuz] *m* couscous

cuspe ['kuspi] *m* spit, spittle

cuspir [kus'pir] *vt, vi* to spit

custa ['kusta] *f*: **à ~ de** at the
expense of; **custas** *fpl* (*Jur*) costs

custar [kus'tar] *vi* to cost; (*ser*

difícil): **~ a fazer** to have trouble doing; (*demorar*) to take a long time to do
custo ['kustu] *m* cost; **a ~** with difficulty; **a todo ~** at all costs
cutelo [ku'tɛlu] *m* cleaver
cutícula [ku'tʃikula] *f* cuticle
cutucar [kutu'kar] *vt* (*com o dedo*) to prod, poke; (*com o cotovelo*) to nudge

d

D, d [de] *m* D, d ▷ *abr* = **Dom**; **Dona**; (= *direito*) r; (= *deve*) d
d/ *abr* = **dia**
da [da] = **de + a**
dá [da] *vb ver* **dar**
dactilografar *etc* [datilogra'far] (*PT*) = **datilografar** *etc*
dado, -a ['dadu, a] *adj* given; (*sociável*) sociable ▷ *m* (*em jogo*) die; (*fato*) fact; **dados** *mpl* dice; (*fatos*, *Comput*) data *sg*; **~ que** supposing that; (*uma vez que*) given that
daí [da'ji] *adv* = **de + aí**; (*desse lugar*) from there; (*desse momento*) from then; **~ a um mês** a month later
dali [da'li] *adv* = **de + ali**
daltônico, -a [daw'toniku, a] *adj* colour-blind (*Brit*), color-blind (*US*)
dama ['dama] *f* lady; (*Xadrez*, *Cartas*) queen; **damas** *fpl* (*jogo*) draughts (*Brit*), checkers (*US*); **~ de honra** bridesmaid

damasco [da'masku] *m* apricot
danado, -a [da'nadu, a] *adj*
damned; (*zangado*) furious;
(*menino*) mischievous
dança ['dãsa] *f* dance; **dançar**
[dã'sar] *vi* to dance
danificar [danifi'kar] *vt* to damage
dano ['danu] *m* (*tb:* **~s**) damage,
harm; (*a uma pessoa*) injury
dantes ['dãtʃis] *adv* before, formerly
daquele, -a [da'kele, 'kɛla] = **de +
aquele**
daqui [da'ki] *adv* = **de + aqui**; (*deste
lugar*) from here; **~ a pouco** soon, in
a little while; **~ a uma semana** a
week from now; **~ em diante** from
now on
daquilo [da'kilu] = **de + aquilo**

 PALAVRA-CHAVE

dar [dar] *vt* **1** (*ger*) to give; (*festa*)
to hold; (*problemas*) to cause; **dar
algo a alguém** to give sb sth, give
sth to sb; **dar de beber a alguém**
to give sb a drink; **dar aula de
francês** to teach French
2 (*produzir: fruta etc*) to produce
3 (*notícias no jornal*) to publish
4 (*cartas*) to deal
5 (+ *n: perífrase de vb*): **me dá medo/
pena** it frightens/upsets me
▷ *vi* **1**: **dar com** (*coisa*) to find;
(*pessoa*) to meet
2: **dar em** (*bater*) to hit; (*resultar*)
to lead to; (*lugar*) to come to
3: **dá no mesmo** it's all the same
4: **dar de si** (*sapatos etc*) to stretch,
give
5: **dar para** (*impess: ser possível*):
dá para trocar dinheiro aqui?
can I change money here?; **vai dar
para eu ir amanhã** I'll be able to go
tomorrow; **dá para você vir**

**amanhã? — não, amanhã não
vai dar** can you come tomorrow?
— no, I can't
6: **dar para** (*ser suficiente*): **dar
para/para fazer** to be enough for/
to do; **dá para todo mundo?** is
there enough for everyone?
dar-se *vr* **1** (*sair-se*): **dar-se bem/
mal** to do well/badly
2: **dar-se (com alguém)** to be
acquainted (with sb); **dar-se bem
(com alguém)** to get on well
(with sb)
3: **dar-se por vencido** to give up

das [das] = **de + as**
data ['data] *f* date; (*época*) time;
datar [da'tar] *vt* to date ▷ *vi*:
datar de to date from
datilografar [datʃilogra'far] *vt* to
type; **datilografia** [datʃilogra'fia]
f typing; **datilógrafo, -a**
[datʃi'lɔgrafu, a] *m/f* typist (*Brit*),
stenographer (*US*)
d.C. *abr* (= *depois de Cristo*) A.D.
DDD *abr f* (= *discagem direta a
distância*) direct long-distance dialling
▷ *abr m* (*código*) dialling code (*Brit*),
area code (*US*)
DDI *abr f* (= *discagem direta
internacional*) IDD ▷ *abr m* (*código de
país*) country code

 PALAVRA-CHAVE

de [dʒi] (*de + o(s)/a(s) = do(s)/da(s);
+ ele(s)/a(s) = dele(s)/a(s);
+ esse(s)/a(s) = desse(s)/a(s);
+ isso = disso; + este(s)/a(s) =
deste(s)/a(s); + isto = disto;
+ aquele(s)/a(s) = daquele(s)/a(s);
+ aquilo = daquilo*) *prep* **1** (*posse*) of;
a casa de João/da irmã João's/
my sister's house; **é dele** it's his;

um romance de a novel by **2** (*origem, distância, com números*) from; **sou de São Paulo** I'm from São Paulo; **de 8 a 20** from 8 to 20; **sair do cinema** to leave the cinema; **de dois em dois** two by two, two at a time

3 (*valor descritivo*): **um copo de vinho** a glass of wine; **um homem de cabelo comprido** a man with long hair; **o infeliz do homem** (*col*) the poor man; **um bilhete de avião** an air ticket; **uma criança de três anos** a three-year-old (child); **uma máquina de costurar** a sewing machine; **aulas de inglês** English lessons; **feito de madeira** made of wood; **vestido de branco** dressed in white

4 (*modo*): **de trem/avião** by train/plane; **de lado** sideways

5 (*hora, tempo*): **às 8 da manhã** at 8 o'clock in the morning; **de dia/noite** by day/night; **de hoje a oito dias** a week from now; **de dois em dois dias** every other day

6 (*comparações*): **mais/menos de cem pessoas** more/less than a hundred people; **é o mais caro da loja** it's the most expensive in the shop; **ela é mais bonita do que sua irmã** she's prettier than her sister; **gastei mais do que pretendia** I spent more than I intended

7 (*causa*): **estou morto de calor** I'm boiling hot; **ela morreu de câncer** she died of cancer

8 (*adj + de + infin*): **fácil de entender** easy to understand

dê *etc* [de] *vb ver* **dar**
debaixo [de'bajʃu] *adv* below, underneath ▷ *prep*: **~ de** under, beneath

debate [de'batʃi] *m* discussion, debate; (*disputa*) argument; **debater** [deba'ter] *vt* to debate; (*discutir*) to discuss; **debater-se** *vr* to struggle

débil ['debiw] (*pl* -**eis**) *adj* weak, feeble ▷ *m*: **~ mental** mentally handicapped person; **debilidade** [debili'dadʒi] *f* weakness; **debilidade mental** mental handicap; **debilitar** [debili'tar] *vt* to weaken; **debilitar-se** *vr* to become weak, weaken; **debiloide** [debi'lɔjdʒi] (*col*) *adj* idiotic ▷ *m/f* idiot

debitar [debi'tar] *vt*: **~ $40 à** *ou* **na conta de alguém** to debit $40 to sb's account; **débito** ['dɛbitu] *m* debit

debochado, -a [debo'ʃadu, a] *adj* (*pessoa*) sardonic; (*jeito, tom*) mocking

década ['dɛkada] *f* decade

decadência [deka'dẽsja] *f* decadence

decair [deka'ir] *vi* to decline

decente [de'sẽtʃi] *adj* decent; (*apropriado*) proper; (*honrado*) honourable (*Brit*), honorable (*US*); (*trabalho*) neat; **decentemente** [desẽtʃi'mẽtʃi] *adv* decently; (*apropriadamente*) properly; (*honradamente*) honourably (*Brit*), honorably (*US*)

decepção [desep'sãw] (*pl* -**ões**) *f* disappointment; **decepcionar** [desepsjo'nar] *vt* to disappoint; (*desiludir*) to disillusion; **decepcionar-se** *vr* to be disappointed; to be disillusioned

decidir [desi'dʒir] *vt* to decide; (*solucionar*) to resolve; **decidir-se** *vr*: **~-se a** to make up one's mind

d

to; **~-se por** to decide on, go for

decifrar [desi'frar] *vt* to decipher; (*futuro*) to foretell; (*compreender*) to understand

decimal [desi'maw] (*pl* **-ais**) *adj, m* decimal

décimo, -a ['dɛsimu, a] *adj* tenth ▷ *m* tenth; *ver tb* **quinto**

decisão [desi'zãw] (*pl* **-ões**) *f* decision; **decisivo, -a** [desi'zivu, a] *adj* (*fator*) decisive; (*jogo*) deciding

declaração [deklara'sãw] (*pl* **-ões**) *f* declaration; (*depoimento*) statement

declarado, -a [dekla'radu, a] *adj* (*intenção*) declared; (*opinião*) professed; (*inimigo*) sworn; (*alcoólatra*) self-confessed; (*cristão etc*) avowed

declarar [dekla'rar] *vt* to declare; (*confessar*) to confess

declinar [dekli'nar] *vt* to decline ▷ *vi* (*sol*) to go down; (*terreno*) to slope down; **declínio** [de'klinju] *m* decline

declive [de'klivi] *m* slope, incline

decolagem [deko'laʒē] (*pl* **-ns**) *f* (*Aer*) take-off

decolar [deko'lar] *vi* (*Aer*) to take off

decompor [dekõ'por] (*irreg: como* **pôr**) *vt* to analyse; (*apodrecer*) to rot; **decompor-se** *vr* to rot, decompose

decomposição [dekõpozi'sãw] (*pl* **-ões**) *f* decomposition; (*análise*) dissection

decorar [deko'rar] *vt* to decorate; (*aprender*) to learn by heart; **decorativo, -a** [dekora'tʃivu, a] *adj* decorative

decoro [de'koru] *m* decency; (*dignidade*) decorum

decorrente [deko'hētʃi] *adj*: **~ de** resulting from

decorrer [deko'her] *vi* (*tempo*) to pass; (*acontecer*) to take place, happen ▷ *m*: **no ~ de** in the course of; **~ de** to result from

decrescer [dekre'ser] *vi* to decrease, diminish

decretar [dekre'tar] *vt* to decree, order; **decreto** [de'kretu] *m* decree, order; **decreto-lei** (*pl* **decretos-leis**) *m* act, law

dedetizar [dedetʃi'zar] *vt* to spray with insecticide

dedicação [dedʒika'sãw] *f* dedication; (*devotamento*) devotion

dedicar [dedʒi'kar] *vt* to dedicate; (*tempo, atenção*) to devote; **dedicar-se** *vr*: **~-se a** to devote o.s to; **dedicatória** [dedʒika'tɔrja] *f* (*de obra*) dedication

dedo ['dedu] *m* finger; (*do pé*) toe; **~ anular** ring finger; **~ indicador** index finger; **~ mínimo** *ou* **mindinho** little finger

dedução [dedu'sãw] (*pl* **-ões**) *f* deduction

deduzir [dedu'zir] *vt* to deduct; (*concluir*) to deduce, infer

defasagem [defa'zaʒē] (*pl* **-ns**) *f* discrepancy

defeito [de'fejtu] *m* defect, flaw; **pôr ~s em** to find fault with; **com ~** broken, out of order; **para ninguém botar ~** (*col*) perfect; **defeituoso, -a** [defej'twozu, ɔza] *adj* defective, faulty

defender [defē'der] *vt* to defend; **defender-se** *vr* to stand up for o.s. (*numa língua*) to get by

defensiva [defē'siva] *f*: **estar** *ou* **ficar na ~** to be on the defensive

defensor, a [defē'sor(a)] *m/f* defender; (*Jur*) defending counsel

defesa [de'feza] f defence (Brit), defense (US); (Jur) counsel for the defence ▷ m (Futebol) back

deficiente [defi'sjētʃi] adj (imperfeito) defective; (carente): **~ (em)** deficient (in)

déficit ['dɛfisitʃi] (pl **déficits**) m deficit

definição [defini'sãw] (pl **-ões**) f definition

definir [defi'nir] vt to define; **definir-se** vr to make a decision; (explicar-se) to make one's position clear; **~-se a favor de/contra algo** to come out in favo(u)r of/against sth

definitivamente [definitʃiva'mētʃi] adv definitively; (permanentemente) for good; (sem dúvida) definitely

definitivo, -a [defini'tʃivu, a] adj final, definitive; (permanente) permanent; (resposta, data) definite

defronte [de'frõtʃi] adv opposite ▷ prep: **~ de** opposite

defumar [defu'mar] vt (presunto) to smoke; (perfumar) to perfume

defunto, -a [de'fūtu, a] adj dead ▷ m/f dead person

degelar [deʒe'lar] vt to thaw; (geladeira) to defrost ▷ vi to thaw out; to defrost

degradar [degra'dar] vt to degrade, debase; **degradar-se** vr to demean o.s.

degrau [de'graw] m step; (de escada de mão) rung

degustação [degusta'sãw] (pl **-ões**) f tasting, sampling; (saborear) savouring (Brit), savoring (US)

degustar [degus'tar] vt (provar) to taste; (saborear) to savour (Brit), savor (US)

dei etc [dej] vb ver **dar**

deitada [dej'tada] (col) f: **dar uma ~** to have a lie-down

deitado, -a [dej'tadu, a] adj (estendido) lying down; (na cama) in bed

deitar [dej'tar] vt to lay down; (na cama) to put to bed; (colocar) to put, place; (lançar) to cast; (PT: líquido) to pour; **deitar-se** vr to lie down; to go to bed; **~ sangue** (PT) to bleed; **~ abaixo** to knock down, flatten; **~ a fazer algo** to start doing sth; **~ uma carta** (PT) to post a letter; **~ fora** (PT) to throw away ou out; **~ e rolar** (col) to do as one likes

deixa ['dejʃa] f clue, hint; (Teatro) cue; (chance) chance

deixar [dej'ʃar] vt to leave; (abandonar) to abandon; (permitir) to let, allow ▷ vi: **~ de** (parar) to stop; (não fazer) to fail to; **não posso ~ de ir** I must go; **~ cair** to drop; **~ alguém louco** to drive sb crazy ou mad; **~ alguém cansado/ nervoso** etc to make sb tired/ nervous etc; **deixa disso!** (col) come off it!; **deixa para lá!** (col) forget it!

dela ['dɛla] = **de + ela**

delatar [dela'tar] vt (pessoa) to inform on; (abusos) to reveal; (à polícia) to report; **delator, a** [dela'tor(a)] m/f informer

dele ['deli] = **de + ele**

delegacia [delega'sia] f office; **~ de polícia** police station

delegado, -a [dele'gadu, a] m/f delegate, representative; **~ de polícia** police chief

delegar [dele'gar] vt to delegate

deleitar [delej'tar] vt to delight; **deleitar-se** vr: **~-se com** to delight in

delgado, -a [dew'gadu, a] *adj* thin; (*esbelto*) slim; (*fino*) fine

deliberação [delibera'sãw] (*pl* **-ões**) *f* deliberation; (*decisão*) decision

deliberar [delibe'rar] *vt* to decide, resolve ▷ *vi* to deliberate

delicadeza [delika'deza] *f* delicacy; (*cortesia*) kindness

delicado, -a [deli'kadu, a] *adj* delicate; (*frágil*) fragile; (*cortês*) polite; (*sensível*) sensitive

delícia [de'lisja] *f* delight; (*prazer*) pleasure; **que ~!** how lovely!; **deliciar** [deli'sjar] *vt* to delight; **deliciar-se** *vr*: **deliciar-se com algo** to take delight in sth

delicioso, -a [deli'sjozu, ɔza] *adj* lovely; (*comida, bebida*) delicious

delinear [deli'njar] *vt* to outline

delinquente [delĩ'kwẽtʃi] *adj, m/f* delinquent, criminal

delirar [deli'rar] *vi* (*com febre*) to be delirious; (*de ódio, prazer*) to go mad, go wild

delírio [de'lirju] *m* (*Med*) delirium; (*êxtase*) ecstasy; (*excitação*) excitement

delito [de'litu] *m* (*crime*) crime; (*falta*) offence (*Brit*), offense (*US*)

demais [dʒi'majs] *adv* (*em demasia*) too much; (*muitíssimo*) a lot, very much ▷ *pron*: **os/as ~** the rest (of them); **já é ~!** this is too much!; **é bom ~** it's really good; **foi ~** (*col*: *bacana*) it was great

demanda [de'mãda] *f* lawsuit; (*disputa*) claim; (*requisição*) request; (*Econ*) demand; **em ~ de** in search of; **demandar** [demã'dar] *vt* (*Jur*) to sue; (*exigir, reclamar*) to demand

demasia [dema'zia] *f* excess, surplus; (*imoderação*) lack of moderation; **em ~** (*dinheiro, comida*

etc) too much; (*cartas, problemas etc*) too many

demasiadamente [demazjada'mẽtʃi] *adv* too much; (*com adj*) too

demasiado, -a [dema'zjadu, a] *adj* too much; (*pl*) too many ▷ *adv* too much; (*com adj*) too

demitir [demi'tʃir] *vt* to dismiss; (*col*) to sack, fire; **demitir-se** *vr* to resign

democracia [demokra'sia] *f* democracy

democrático, -a [demo'kratʃiku, a] *adj* democratic

demolir [demo'lir] *vt* to demolish, knock down; (*fig*) to destroy

demonstração [demõstra'sãw] (*pl* **-ões**) *f* demonstration; (*de amizade*) show, display; (*prova*) proof

demonstrar [demõs'trar] *vt* to demonstrate; (*provar*) to prove; (*amizade etc*) to show

demora [de'mɔra] *f* delay; (*parada*) stop; **sem ~** at once, without delay; **qual é a ~ disso?** how long will this take?; **demorado, -a** [demo'radu, a] *adj* slow; **demorar** [demo'rar] *vt* to delay, slow down ▷ *vi* (*permanecer*) to stay; (*tardar a vir*) to be late; (*conserto*) to take (a long) time; **demorar-se** *vr* to stay for a long time, linger; **demorar a chegar** to be a long time coming; **vai demorar muito?** will it take long?; **não vou demorar** I won't be long

dendê [dẽ'de] *m* (*Culin*: *óleo*) palm oil; (*Bot*) oil palm

dengoso, -a [dẽ'gozu, ɔza] *adj* coy; (*criança*: *choraminguento*): **ser ~** to be a crybaby

dengue ['dẽgi] *f* (*Med*) dengue

denominar [denomi'nar] *vt*:
~ **algo/alguém** ... to call sth/sb ...;
denominar-se *vr* to be called; (*a si mesmo*) to call o.s.

denotar [deno'tar] *vt* (*indicar*) to show, indicate; (*significar*) to signify

densidade [dẽsi'dadʒi] *f* density

denso, -a [dẽsu, a] *adj* dense; (*espesso*) thick; (*compacto*) compact

dentada [dẽ'tada] *f* bite

dentadura [dẽta'dura] *f* teeth *pl*, set of teeth; (*artificial*) dentures *pl*

dente ['dẽtʃi] *m* tooth; (*de animal*) fang; (*de elefante*) tusk; (*de alho*) clove; **falar entre os ~s** to mutter, mumble; **~ de leite/do siso** milk/wisdom tooth; **~s postiços** false teeth

dentista [dẽ'tʃista] *m/f* dentist

dentre ['dẽtri] *prep* (from) among

dentro ['dẽtru] *adv* inside ▷ *prep*:
~ **de** inside; (*tempo*) (with)in; **de ~ para fora** inside out; **dar uma ~** (*col*) to get it right; **aí ~** in there; **por ~** on the inside; **estar por ~** (*col: fig*) to be in the know

denúncia [de'nũsja] *f* denunciation; (*acusação*) accusation; (*de roubo*) report

denunciar [denũ'sjar] *vt* (*acusar*) to denounce; (*delatar*) to inform on; (*revelar*) to reveal

deparar [depa'rar] *vt* to reveal; (*fazer aparecer*) to present ▷ *vi*:
~ **com** to come across, meet;
deparar-se *vr*: **~-se com** to come across, meet

departamento [departa'mẽtu] *m* department

dependência [depẽ'dẽsja] *f* dependence; (*edificação*) annexe (*Brit*), annex (*US*); (*colonial*) dependency; (*cômodo*) room

dependente [depẽ'dẽtʃi] *m/f* dependant

depender [depẽ'der] *vi*: ~ **de** to depend on

depilar [depi'lar] *vt* to wax;
depilatório [depila'tɔrju] *m* hair-remover

deplorável [deplo'ravew] (*pl* **-eis**) *adj* deplorable; (*lamentável*) regrettable

depoimento [depoj'mẽtu] *m* testimony, evidence; (*na polícia*) statement

depois [de'pojs] *adv* afterwards ▷ *prep*: ~ **de** after; ~ **de comer** after eating; ~ **que** after

depor [de'por] (*irreg: como* **pôr**) *vt* (*pôr*) to place; (*indicar*) to indicate; (*rei*) to depose; (*governo*) to overthrow ▷ *vi* (*Jur*) to testify, give evidence; (*na polícia*) to give a statement

depositar [depozi'tar] *vt* to deposit; (*voto*) to cast; (*colocar*) to place

depósito [de'pɔzitu] *m* deposit; (*armazém*) warehouse, depot; (*de lixo*) dump; (*reservatório*) tank;
~ **de bagagens** left-luggage office (*Brit*), checkroom (*US*)

depreciação [depresja'sãw] *f* depreciation

depredar [depre'dar] *vt* to wreck

depressa [dʒi'prɛsa] *adv* fast, quickly; **vamos ~** let's get a move on!

depressão [depre'sãw] (*pl* **-ões**) *f* depression

deprimente [depri'mẽtʃi] *adj* depressing

deprimido, -a [depri'midu, a] *adj* depressed

deprimir [depri'mir] *vt* to depress;
deprimir-se *vr* to get depressed

deputado, -a [depu'tadu, a] *m/f*
deputy; (*agente*) agent; (*Pol*)
≈ Member of Parliament (*Brit*),
≈ Representative (*US*)

der *etc* [der] *vb ver* **dar**

deriva [de'riva] *f* drift; **ir à ~** to drift;
ficar à ~ to be adrift

derivar [deri'var] *vt* to divert; (*Ling*)
to derive ▷ *vi* to drift; **derivar-se**
vr to be derived; (*ir à deriva*) to drift;
(*provir*) **~(-se) (de)** to derive *ou* be
derived (from)

derradeiro, -a [deha'dejru, a] *adj*
last, final

derramamento [dehama'mētu]
m spilling; (*de sangue, lágrimas*)
shedding

derramar [deha'mar] *vt* to spill;
(*entornar*) to pour; (*sangue,
lágrimas*) to shed; **derramar-se** *vr*
to pour out

derrame [de'hami] *m*
haemorrhage (*Brit*), hemorrhage
(*US*)

derrapar [deha'par] *vi* to skid

derreter [dehe'ter] *vt* to melt;
derreter-se *vr* to melt; (*coisa
congelada*) to thaw; (*enternecer-se*)
to be touched

derrota [de'hɔta] *f* defeat, rout;
(*Náut*) route; **derrotar** [deho'tar]
vt (*vencer*) to defeat; (*em jogo*) to
beat

derrubar [dehu'bar] *vt* to knock
down; (*governo*) to bring down;
(*suj: doença*) to lay low; (*col:
prejudicar*) to put down

desabafar [dʒizaba'far] *vt*
(*sentimentos*) to give vent to ▷ *vi*: **~
(com)** to unburden o.s. (to);
desabafar-se *vr*: **~-se (com)** to
unburden o.s. (to); **desabafo**
[dʒiza'bafu] *m* confession

desabamento [dʒizaba'mētu] *m*
collapse

desabar [dʒiza'bar] *vi* (*edifício,
ponte*) to collapse; (*chuva*) to pour
down; (*tempestade*) to break

desabitado, -a [dʒizabi'tadu, a]
adj uninhabited

desabotoar [dʒizabo'twar] *vt* to
unbutton

desabrigado, -a [dʒizabri'gadu, a]
adj (*sem casa*) homeless; (*exposto*)
exposed

desabrochar [dʒizabro'ʃar] *vi*
(*flores, fig*) to blossom

desacatar [dʒizaka'tar] *vt*
(*desrespeitar*) to have *ou* show no
respect for; (*afrontar*) to defy;
(*desprezar*) to scorn; **desacato**
[dʒiza'katu] *m* disrespect;
(*desprezo*) disregard

desaconselhar [dʒizakōse'ʎar] *vt*:
~ algo (a alguém) to advise (sb)
against sth

desacordado, -a [dʒizakor'dadu,
a] *adj* unconscious

desacordo [dʒiza'kordu] *m*
disagreement; (*desarmonia*)
discord

desacostumado, -a
[dʒizakostumadu, a] *adj*: **~ (a)**
unaccustomed (to)

desacreditar [dʒizakredʒi'tar] *vt*
to discredit; **desacreditar-se** *vr* to
lose one's reputation

desafiador, a [dʒizafja'dor(a)] *adj*
challenging; (*pessoa*) defiant ▷ *m/f*
challenger

desafiar [dʒiza'fjar] *vt* to
challenge; (*afrontar*) to defy

desafinado, -a [dʒizafi'nadu, a]
adj out of tune

desafio [dʒiza'fiu] *m* challenge;
(*PT: Esporte*) match, game

desaforado, -a [dʒizafo'radu, a]
adj rude, insolent

desaforo [dʒiza'foru] *m* insolence, abuse

desafortunado, -a [dʒizafortu'nadu, a] *adj* unfortunate, unlucky

desagradar [dʒizagra'dar] *vt* to displease ▷ *vi:* **~ a alguém** to displease sb; **desagradável** [dʒizagra'davew] (*pl* **-eis**) *adj* unpleasant; **desagrado** [dʒiza'gradu] *m* displeasure

desaguar [dʒiza'gwar] *vt* to drain ▷ *vi:* **~ (em)** to flow *ou* empty (into)

desajeitado, -a [dʒizaʒej'tadu, a] *adj* clumsy, awkward

desalentado, -a [dʒizalẽ'tadu, a] *adj* disheartened

desalentar [dʒizalẽ'tar] *vt* to discourage; (*deprimir*) to depress; **desalento** [dʒiza'lẽtu] *m* discouragement

desalmado, -a [dʒizaw'madu, a] *adj* cruel, inhuman

desalojar [dʒizalo'ʒar] *vt* (*expulsar*) to oust; **desalojar-se** *vr* to move out

desamarrar [dʒizama'har] *vt* to untie ▷ *vi* (*Náut*) to cast off

desamor [dʒiza'mor] *m* dislike

desamparado, -a [dʒizãpa'radu, a] *adj* abandoned; (*sem apoio*) helpless

desanimação [dʒizanima'sãw] *f* dejection

desanimado, -a [dʒizani'madu, a] *adj* (*pessoa*) fed up, dispirited; (*festa*) dull; **ser ~** (*pessoa*) to be apathetic

desanuviar [dʒizanu'vjar] *vt* (*céu*) to clear; **desanuviar-se** *vr* to clear; (*fig*) to stop; **~ alguém** to put sb's mind at rest

desaparafusar [dʒizaparafu'zar] *vt* to unscrew

desaparecer [dʒizapare'ser] *vi* to disappear, vanish; **desaparecido, -a** [dʒizapare'sidu, a] *adj* lost, missing ▷ *m/f* missing person; **desaparecimento** [dʒizaparesi'mẽtu] *m* disappearance; (*falecimento*) death

desapego [dʒiza'pegu] *m* indifference, detachment

desapercebido, -a [dʒizaperse'bidu, a] *adj* unnoticed

desapertar [dʒizaper'tar] *vt* to loosen; (*livrar*) to free

desapontamento [dʒizapõta'mẽtu] *m* disappointment

desapontar [dʒizapõ'tar] *vt* to disappoint

desapropriar [dʒizapro'prjar] *vt* (*bens*) to expropriate; (*pessoa*) to dispossess

desaprovar [dʒizapro'var] *vt* to disapprove of; (*censurar*) to object to

desarmamento [dʒizarma'mẽtu] *m* disarmament

desarmar [dʒizar'mar] *vt* to disarm; (*desmontar*) to dismantle; (*bomba*) to defuse

desarmonia [dʒizarmo'nia] *f* discord

desarranjo [dʒiza'hãʒu] *m* disorder; (*enguiço*) breakdown; (*diarreia*) diarrhoea (*Brit*), diarrhea (*US*)

desarrumado, -a [dʒizahu'madu, a] *adj* untidy, messy

desarrumar [dʒizahu'mar] *vt* to mess up; (*mala*) to unpack

desassossego [dʒizaso'segu] *m* (*inquietação*) disquiet; (*perturbação*) restlessness

desastrado, -a [dʒizas'tradu, a] *adj* clumsy

desastre [dʒi'zastri] *m* disaster;

(*acidente*) accident; (*de avião*) crash

desatar [dʒiza'tar] *vt* (*nó*) to undo, untie ▷ *vi*: **~ a fazer** to begin to do; **~ a chorar** to burst into tears; **~ a rir** to burst out laughing

desatento, -a [dʒiza'tẽtu, a] *adj* inattentive

desatinado, -a [dʒizatʃi'nadu, a] *adj* crazy, wild ▷ *m/f* lunatic

desatino [dʒiza'tʃinu] *m* madness; (*ato*) folly

desativar [dʒizatʃi'var] *vt* (*firma, usina*) to shut down; (*veículos*) to withdraw from service; (*bomba*) to deactivate, defuse

desatualizado, -a [dʒizatwali'zadu, a] *adj* out of date; (*pessoa*) out of touch

desavença [dʒiza'vẽsa] *f* (*briga*) quarrel; (*discórdia*) disagreement; **em ~** at loggerheads

desavergonhado, -a [dʒizavergo'ɲadu, a] *adj* shameless

desavisado, -a [dʒizavi'zadu, a] *adj* careless

desbastar [dʒizbas'tar] *vt* (*cabelo, plantas*) to thin (out); (*vegetação*) to trim

desbocado, -a [dʒizbo'kadu, a] *adj* foul-mouthed

desbotar [dʒizbo'tar] *vt* to discolour (*Brit*), discolor (*US*) ▷ *vi* to fade

desbragadamente [dʒizbragada'mẽtʃi] *adv* (*beber*) to excess; (*mentir*) blatantly

desbravar [dʒizbra'var] *vt* (*terras desconhecidas*) to explore

descabelar [dʒiskabe'lar] *vt*: **~ alguém** to mess up sb's hair; **descabelar-se** *vr* to get one's hair messed up

descabido, -a [dʒiska'bidu, a] *adj*

improper; (*inoportuno*) inappropriate

descafeinado [dʒiskafej'nadu] *adj* decaffeinated ▷ *n* decaff

descalçar [dʒiskaw'sar] *vt* (*sapatos*) to take off; **descalçar-se** *vr* to take off one's shoes

descalço, -a [dʒis'kawsu, a] *adj* barefoot

descansado, -a [dʒiskã'sadu, a] *adj* calm, quiet; (*vagaroso*) slow; **fique ~** don't worry; **pode ficar ~ que ...** you can rest assured that ...

descansar [dʒiskã'sar] *vt* to rest; (*apoiar*) to lean ▷ *vi* to rest; to lean; **descanso** [dʒis'kãsu] *m* rest; (*folga*) break; (*para prato*) mat

descarregamento [dʒiskahega'mẽtu] *m* (*de carga*) unloading; (*Elet*) discharge

descarregar [dʒiskahe'gar] *vt* (*carga*) to unload; (*Elet*) to discharge; (*aliviar*) to relieve; (*raiva*) to vent, give vent to; (*arma*) to fire ▷ *vi* to unload; (*bateria*) to run out; **~ a raiva em alguém** to take it out on sb

descartar [dʒiskar'tar] *vt* to discard; **descartar-se** *vr*: **~-se de** to get rid of; **descartável** [dʒiskar'tavew] (*pl* **-eis**) *adj* disposable

descascar [dʒiskas'kar] *vt* (*fruta*) to peel; (*ervilhas*) to shell ▷ *vi* (*depois do sol*) to peel; (*cobra*) to shed its skin

descaso [dʒis'kazu] *m* disregard

descendência [desẽ'dẽsja] *f* descendants *pl*, offspring *pl*

descendente [desẽ'dẽtʃi] *adj* descending, going down ▷ *m/f* descendant

descer [de'ser] *vt* (*escada*) to go (*ou* come) down; (*bagagem*) to take down ▷ vi (*saltar*) to get off; (*baixar*) to go (*ou* come) down; **descida** [de'sida] *f* descent; (*declive*) slope; (*abaixamento*) fall, drop

desclassificar [dʒisklasifi'kar] *vt* to disqualify; (*desacreditar*) to discredit

descoberta [dʒisko'bɛrta] *f* discovery; (*invenção*) invention

descoberto, -a [dʒisko'bɛrtu, a] *pp de* **descobrir** ▷ *adj* bare, naked; (*exposto*) exposed ▷ *m* overdraft; **a ~** openly; **conta a ~** overdrawn account; **pôr** *ou* **sacar a ~** (*conta*) to overdraw

descobridor, a [dʒiskobri'dor(a)] *m/f* discoverer; (*explorador*) explorer

descobrimento [dʒiskobri'mẽtu] *m* discovery; **Descobrimentos** *mpl see note*

○ **DESCOBRIMENTOS**
○
○ Mainly due to the seafaring
○ expertise of Henry the Navigator,
○ Portugal enjoyed a period of
○ unrivalled overseas expansion
○ during the 15th century. He
○ organized and financed several
○ voyages to Africa, which
○ eventually led to the rounding of
○ the Cape of Good Hope in 1488 by
○ Bartolomeu Dias. In 1497, Vasco
○ da Gama became the first
○ European to travel by sea to
○ India, where he established a
○ lucrative spice trade, and a few
○ years later, in 1500, Pedro Álvares
○ Cabral reached Brazil, which he
○ claimed for Portugal. Brazil
○ remained under Portuguese rule
○ until 1822.

descobrir [dʒisko'brir] *vt* to discover; (*tirar a cobertura de*) to uncover; (*panela*) to take the lid off; (*averiguar*) to find out; (*enigma*) to solve

descolar [dʒisko'lar] *vt* to unstick ▷ *vi*: **a criança não descola da mãe** the child won't leave its mother's side

descolorante [dʒiskolo'rãtʃi] *m* bleach

descolorir [dʒiskolo'rir] *vt* to discolour (*Brit*), discolor (*US*); (*cabelo*) to bleach ▷ *vi* to fade

descompostura [dʒiskõpos'tura] *f* (*repreensão*) dressing-down; (*insulto*) abuse; **passar uma ~ em alguém** to give sb a dressing-down; to hurl abuse at sb

desconcentrar [dʒiskõsẽ'trar] *vt* to distract; **desconcentrar-se** *vr* to lose one's concentration

desconfiado, -a [dʒiskõ'fjadu, a] *adj* suspicious, distrustful ▷ *m/f* suspicious person

desconfiança [dʒiskõ'fjãsa] *f* suspicion, distrust

desconfiar [dʒiskõ'fjar] *vi* to be suspicious; **~ de alguém** (*não ter confiança em*) to distrust sb; (*suspeitar*) to suspect sb; **~ que ...** to have the feeling that ...

desconfortável [dʒiskõfor'tavew] (*pl* **-eis**) *adj* uncomfortable

desconforto [dʒiskõ'fortu] *m* discomfort

desconhecer [dʒiskoɲe'ser] *vt* (*ignorar*) not to know; (*não reconhecer*) not to recognize; (*um benefício*) not to acknowledge; (*não admitir*) not to accept; **desconhecido, -a** [dʒiskoɲe'sidu, a] *adj* unknown ▷ *m/f* stranger; **desconhecimento**

[dʒiskoɲesi'mẽtu] *m* ignorance

desconsolado, -a [dʒiskõso'ladu, a] *adj* miserable, disconsolate

descontar [dʒiskõ'tar] *vt* to deduct; (*não levar em conta*) to discount; (*não fazer caso de*) to make light of

descontentamento [dʒiskõtẽta'mẽtu] *m* discontent; (*desprazer*) displeasure

desconto [dʒis'kõtu] *m* discount; **com ~** at a discount; **dar um ~ (para)** (*fig*) to make allowances (for)

descontraído, -a [dʒiskõtra'idu, a] *adj* casual, relaxed

descontrair [dʒiskõtra'ir] *vt* to relax; **descontrair-se** *vr* to relax

descontrolar-se [dʒiskõtro'larsi] *vr* (*situação*) to get out of control; (*pessoa*) to lose one's self-control

desconversar [dʒiskõver'sar] *vi* to change the subject

descortesia [dʒiskorte'zia] *f* rudeness, impoliteness

descoser [dʒisko'zer] *vt* (*descosturar*) to unstitch; (*rasgar*) to rip apart; **descoser-se** *vr* to come apart at the seams

descrença [dʒis'krẽsa] *f* disbelief, incredulity

descrente [dʒis'krẽtʃi] *adj* sceptical (*Brit*), skeptical (*US*) ⊳ *m/f* sceptic (*Brit*), skeptic (*US*)

descrever [dʒiskre'ver] *vt* to describe

descrição [dʒiskri'sãw] (*pl* **-ões**) *f* description

descritivo, -a [dʒiskri'tʃivu, a] *adj* descriptive

descrito, -a [dʒis'kritu, a] *pp de* **descrever**

descubro *etc* [dʒis'kubru] *vb ver* **descobrir**

descuidar [dʒiskwi'dar] *vt* to neglect ⊳ *vi*: **~ de** to neglect, disregard; **descuido** [dʒis'kwidu] *m* carelessness; (*negligência*) neglect; (*erro*) oversight, slip; **por descuido** inadvertently

desculpa [dʒis'kuwpa] *f* excuse; (*perdão*) pardon; **pedir ~s a alguém por** *ou* **de algo** to apologise to sb for sth; **desculpar** [dʒiskuw'par] *vt* to excuse; (*perdoar*) to pardon, forgive; **desculpar-se** *vr* to apologize; **desculpar algo a alguém** to forgive sb for sth; **desculpe!** (I'm) sorry, I beg your pardon; **desculpável** [dʒiskuw'pavew] (*pl* **-eis**) *adj* forgivable

 PALAVRA-CHAVE

desde ['dezdʒi] *prep* **1** (*lugar*): **desde ... até ...** from ... to ...; **andamos desde a praia até o restaurante** we walked from the beach to the restaurant

2 (*tempo*: + *adv, n*): **desde então** from then on, ever since; **desde já** (*de agora*) from now on; (*imediatamente*) at once, right now; **desde o casamento** since the wedding

3 (*tempo*: + *vb*) since; for; **conhecemo-nos desde 1978/há 20 anos** we've known each other since 1978/for 20 years; **não o vejo desde 1983** I haven't seen him since 1983

4 (*variedade*): **desde os mais baratos até os mais luxuosos** from the cheapest to the most luxurious

⊳ *conj*: **desde que** since; **desde que comecei a trabalhar não o vi**

mais I haven't seen him since I started work; **não saiu de casa desde que chegou** he hasn't been out since he arrived

desdizer [dʒizdʒi'zer] (*irreg: como* **dizer**) *vt* to contradict; **desdizer-se** *vr* to go back on one's word

desdobrar [dʒizdo'brar] *vt* (*abrir*) to unfold; (*esforços*) to increase, redouble; (*tropas*) to deploy; (*bandeira*) to unfurl; (*dividir em grupos*) to split up; **desdobrar-se** *vr* to unfold; (*empenhar-se*) to work hard, make a big effort

desejar [dese'ʒar] *vt* to want, desire

desejo [de'zeʒu] *m* wish, desire; **desejoso, -a** [deze'ʒozu, ɔza] *adj*: **desejoso de algo** wishing for sth; **desejoso de fazer** keen to do

desembaraçar [dʒizẽbara'sar] *vt* (*livrar*) to free; (*cabelo*) to untangle; **desembaraçar-se** *vr* (*desinibir-se*) to lose one's inhibitions; **~-se de** to get rid of

desembaraço [dʒizẽba'rasu] *m* liveliness; (*facilidade*) ease; (*confiança*) self-assurance

desembarcar [dʒizẽbar'kar] *vt* (*carga*) to unload; (*passageiros*) to let off ▷ *vi* to disembark; **desembarque** [dʒizẽ'barki] *m* landing, disembarkation; **"desembarque"** (*no aeroporto*) "arrivals"

desembolsar [dʒizẽbow'sar] *vt* to spend

desembrulhar [dʒizẽbru'ʎar] *vt* to unwrap

desempacotar [dʒizẽpako'tar] *vt* to unpack

desempatar [dʒizẽpa'tar] *vt* to decide ▷ *vi* to decide the match (*ou* race *etc*); **desempate** [dʒizẽ'patʃi] *m*: **partida de desempate** (*jogo*) play-off, decider

desempenhar [dʒizẽpe'ɲar] *vt* (*cumprir*) to carry out, fulfil (Brit), fulfill (US); (*papel*) to play; **desempenho** [dʒizẽ'peɲu] *m* performance; (*de obrigações etc*) fulfilment (Brit), fulfillment (US)

desempregado, -a [dʒizẽpre'gadu, a] *adj* unemployed ▷ *m/f* unemployed person

desempregar-se [dʒizẽpre'garsi] *vr* to lose one's job

desemprego [dʒizẽ'pregu] *m* unemployment

desencadear [dʒizẽka'dʒjar] *vt* to unleash; (*despertar*) to provoke, trigger off ▷ *vi* (*chuva*) to pour; **desencadear-se** *vr* to break loose; (*tempestade*) to break

desencaixar [dʒizẽkaj'ʃar] *vt* to put out of joint; (*deslocar*) to dislodge; **desencaixar-se** *vr* to become dislodged

desencaixotar [dʒizẽkajʃo'tar] *vt* to unpack

desencarregar-se [dʒizẽkahe'garsi] *vr* (*de obrigação*) to discharge o.s.

desencontrar [dʒizẽkõ'trar] *vt* to keep apart; **desencontrar-se** *vr* (*não se encontrar*) to miss each other; (*perder-se um do outro*) to lose each other; **~-se de** to miss; to get separated from

desencorajar [dʒizẽkora'ʒar] *vt* to discourage

desencostar [dʒizẽkos'tar] *vt* to move away; **desencostar-se** *vr*: **~-se de** to move away from

desenfreado, -a [dʒizẽ'frjadu, a] *adj* wild

desenganado, -a [dʒizẽga'nadu, a] *adj* incurable; (*desiludido*) disillusioned

desenganar [dʒizẽga'nar] *vt*: **~ alguém** to disillusion sb; (*de falsas crenças*) to open sb's eyes; (*doente*) to give up hope of curing; **desenganar-se** *vr* to become disillusioned; (*sair de erro*) to realize the truth; **desengano** [dʒizẽ'ganu] *m* disillusionment; (*desapontamento*) disappointment

desengonçado, -a [dʒizẽgõ'sadu, a] *adj* (*malseguro*) rickety; (*pessoa*) ungainly

desenhar [deze'ɲar] *vt* to draw; (*Tec*) to design; **desenhar-se** *vr* (*destacar-se*) to stand out; (*figurar-se*) to take shape; **desenhista** [deze'ɲista] *m/f* (*Tec*) designer

desenho [de'zeɲu] *m* drawing; (*modelo*) design; (*esboço*) sketch; (*plano*) plan; **~ animado** cartoon

desenlace [dʒizẽ'lasi] *m* outcome

desenrolar [dʒizẽɦo'lar] *vt* to unroll; (*narrativa*) to develop; **desenrolar-se** *vr* to unfold

desentender [dʒizẽtẽ'der] *vt* to misunderstand; **desentender-se** *vr*: **~-se com** to have a disagreement with; **desentendido, -a** [dʒizẽtẽ'dʒidu, a] *adj*: **fazer-se de desentendido** to pretend not to understand; **desentendimento** [dʒizẽtẽdʒi'mẽtu] *m* misunderstanding

desenterrar [dʒizẽte'har] *vt* (*cadáver*) to exhume; (*tesouro*) to dig up; (*descobrir*) to bring to light

desentupir [dʒizẽtu'pir] *vt* to unblock

desenvoltura [dʒizẽvow'tura] *f* self-confidence

desenvolver [dʒizẽvow'ver] *vt* to develop; **desenvolver-se** *vr* to develop; **desenvolvimento** [dʒizẽvowvi'mẽtu] *m* development; (*crescimento*) growth; **país em desenvolvimento** developing country

deserção [dezer'sãw] *f* desertion

desertar [deser'tar] *vt* to desert, abandon ▷ *vi* to desert; **deserto, -a** [de'zɛrtu, a] *adj* deserted ▷ *m* desert; **desertor, a** [dezer'tor(a)] *m/f* deserter

desesperado, -a [dʒizespe'radu, a] *adj* desperate; (*furioso*) furious

desesperador, a [dʒizespera'dor(a)] *adj* desperate; (*enfurecedor*) maddening

desesperança [dʒizespe'rãsa] *f* despair

desesperar [dʒizespe'rar] *vt* to drive to despair; (*enfurecer*) to infuriate; **desesperar-se** *vr* to despair; (*enfurecer-se*) to become infuriated; **desespero** [dʒizes'peru] *m* despair, desperation; (*raiva*) fury

desestimular [dʒizestʃimu'lar] *vt* to discourage

desfalcar [dʒisfaw'kar] *vt* (*dinheiro*) to embezzle; (*reduzir*): **~ (de)** to reduce (by); **o jogo está desfalcado** the game is incomplete

desfalecer [dʒisfale'ser] *vt* (*enfraquecer*) to weaken ▷ *vi* (*enfraquecer*) to weaken; (*desmaiar*) to faint

desfalque [dʒis'fawki] *m* (*de dinheiro*) embezzlement; (*diminuição*) reduction

desfavorável [dʒisfavo'ravew] (*pl* **-eis**) *adj* unfavourable (*Brit*), unfavorable (*US*)

desfazer [dʒisfa'zer] (*irreg: como* **fazer**) *vt* (*costura*) to undo; (*dúvidas*) to dispel; (*agravo*) to redress; (*grupo*) to break up; (*contrato*) to dissolve; (*noivado*) to break off ▷ *vi*: **~ de alguém** to belittle sb; **desfazer-se** *vr* to vanish; (*tecido*) to come to pieces; (*grupo*) to break up; (*vaso*) to break; **~-se de** (*livrar-se*) to get rid of; **~-se em lágrimas/gentilezas** to burst into tears/go out of one's way to please

desfecho [dʒis'feʃu] *m* ending, outcome

desfeito, -a [dʒis'fejtu, a] *adj* undone; (*cama*) unmade; (*contrato*) broken

desfilar [dʒisfi'lar] *vi* to parade; **desfile** [dʒis'fili] *m* parade, procession

desforra [dʒis'fɔha] *f* revenge; (*reparação*) redress; **tirar ~** to get even

desfrutar [dʒisfru'tar] *vt* to enjoy ▷ *vi*: **~ de** to enjoy

desgarrado, -a [dʒizga'hadu, a] *adj* stray; (*navio*) off course

desgastante [dʒizgas'tãtʃi] *adj* (*fig*) stressful

desgrudar [dʒizgru'dar] *vt* to unstick ▷ *vi*: **~ de** to tear o.s. away from; **~ algo de algo** to take sth off sth

desidratar [dʒizidra'tar] *vt* to dehydrate

design [dʒi'zãjn] *m* design

designar [dezig'nar] *vt* to designate; (*nomear*) to name, appoint; (*dia, data*) to fix

desigual [dezi'gwaw] (*pl* **-ais**) *adj* unequal; (*terreno*) uneven; **desigualdade** [dʒizigwaw'dadʒi]

f inequality

desiludir [dʒizilu'dʒir] *vt* to disillusion; (*causar decepção a*) to disappoint; **desiludir-se** *vr* to lose one's illusions

desimpedido, -a [dʒizĩpe'dʒidu, a] *adj* free

desinfetante [dʒizĩfe'tãtʃi] *adj, m* disinfectant

desinfetar [dʒizĩfe'tar] *vt* to disinfect

desintegração [dʒizĩtegra'sãw] *f* disintegration, break-up

desintegrar [dʒizĩte'grar] *vt* to separate; **desintegrar-se** *vr* to disintegrate, fall to pieces

desistir [dezis'tʃir] *vi* to give up; **~ de fumar** to stop smoking; **ele ia, mas no final desistiu** he was going, but in the end he gave up the idea *ou* he decided not to

desjejum [dʒizʒe'ʒũ] *m* breakfast

deslavado, -a [dʒizla'vadu, a] *adj* (*pessoa, atitude*) shameless; (*mentira*) blatant

desleal [dʒizle'aw] (*pl* **-ais**) *adj* disloyal

desleixo [dʒiz'lejʃu] *m* sloppiness

desligado, -a [dʒizli'gadu, a] *adj* (*eletricidade*) off; (*pessoa*) absent-minded; **estar ~** to be miles away

desligar [dʒizli'gar] *vt* (*Tec*) to disconnect; (*luz, TV, motor*) to switch off; (*telefone*) to hang up; **desligar-se** *vr*: **~-se de algo** (*afastar-se*) to leave sth; (*problemas etc*) to turn one's back on sth; **não desligue** (*Tel*) hold the line

deslizar [dʒizli'zar] *vi* to slide; (*por acidente*) to slip; (*passar de leve*) to glide; **deslize** [dʒiz'lizi] *m* lapse; (*escorregadela*) slip

deslocado, -a [dʒizlo'kadu, a] *adj*

(*membro*) dislocated; (*desambientado*) out of place

deslumbramento [dʒizlũbra'mẽtu] *m* dazzle; (*fascinação*) fascination

deslumbrante [dʒizlũ'brãtʃi] *adj* dazzling; (*casa, festa*) amazing

deslumbrar [dʒizlũ'brar] *vt* to dazzle; (*maravilhar*) to amaze; (*fascinar*) to fascinate ▷ *vi* to be dazzling; to be amazing; **deslumbrar-se** *vr*: **~-se com** to be fascinated by

desmaiado, -a [dʒizma'jadu, a] *adj* unconscious; (*cor*) pale

desmaiar [dʒizma'jar] *vi* to faint; **desmaio** [dʒiz'maju] *m* faint

desmanchar [dʒizman'ʃar] *vt* (*costura*) to undo; (*contrato*) to break; (*noivado*) to break off; (*penteado*) to mess up; **desmanchar-se** *vr* (*costura*) to come undone

desmarcar [dʒizmar'kar] *vt* (*compromisso*) to cancel

desmascarar [dʒizmaska'rar] *vt* to unmask

desmazelado, -a [dʒizmaze'ladu, a] *adj* slovenly, untidy

desmedido, -a [dʒizme'dʒidu, a] *adj* excessive

desmentido [dʒizmẽ'tʃidu] *m* (*negação*) denial; (*contradição*) contradiction

desmentir [dʒizmẽ'tʃir] *vt* (*contradizer*) to contradict; (*negar*) to deny

desmiolado, -a [dʒizmjo'ladu, a] *adj* brainless; (*esquecido*) forgetful

desmoronamento [dʒizmorona'mẽtu] *m* collapse

desmoronar [dʒizmoro'nar] *vt* to knock down ▷ *vi* to collapse

desnatado, -a [dʒizna'tadu, a] *adj* (*leite*) skimmed

desnaturado, -a [dʒiznatu'radu, a] *adj* inhumane ▷ *m/f* monster

desnecessário, -a [dʒiznese'sarju, a] *adj* unnecessary

desnutrição [dʒiznutri'sãw] *f* malnutrition

desobedecer [dʒizobede'ser] *vt* to disobey; **desobediência** [dʒizobe'dʒjẽsja] *f* disobedience; **desobediente** [dʒizobe'dʒjẽtʃi] *adj* disobedient

desobstruir [dʒizobis'trwir] *vt* to unblock

desocupado, -a [dʒizoku'padu, a] *adj* (*casa*) empty, vacant; (*disponível*) free; (*sem trabalho*) unemployed

desocupar [dʒizoku'par] *vt* (*casa*) to vacate; (*liberar*) to free

desodorante [dʒizodo'rãtʃi], (*PT*) **desodorizante** *m* deodorant

desolação [dezola'sãw] *f* (*consternação*) grief; (*de um lugar*) desolation; **desolado, -a** [dezo'ladu, a] *adj* distressed; (*lugar*) desolate

desonesto, -a [dezo'nɛstu, a] *adj* dishonest

desordem [dʒi'zordẽ] *f* disorder, confusion; **em ~** (*casa*) untidy

desorganizar [dʒizorgani'zar] *vt* to disorganize; (*dissolver*) to break up; **desorganizar-se** *vr* to become disorganized; to break up

desorientação [dʒizorjẽta'sãw] *f* bewilderment, confusion

desorientar [dʒizorjẽ'tar] *vt* (*desnortear*) to throw off course; (*perturbar*) to confuse; (*desvairar*) to unhinge; **desorientar-se** *vr* to lose one's way; to get confused; to go mad

desovar [dʒizo'var] *vt* to lay; (*peixe*)

to spawn

despachado, -a [dʒispa'ʃadu, a] *adj* (*pessoa*) efficient

despachar [dʒispa'ʃar] *vt* to dispatch, send off; (*atender, resolver*) to deal with; (*despedir*) to sack; **despachar-se** *vr* to hurry (up); **despacho** [dʒis'paʃu] *m* dispatch; (*de negócios*) handling; (*nota em requerimento*) ruling; (*reunião*) consultation; (*macumba*) witchcraft

despeço *etc* [dʒis'pɛsu] *vb ver* **despedir**

despedaçar [dʒispeda'sar] *vt* (*quebrar*) to smash; (*rasgar*) to tear apart; **despedaçar-se** *vr* to smash; to tear

despedida [dʒispe'dʒida] *f* farewell; (*de trabalhador*) dismissal

despedir [dʒispe'dʒir] *vt* (*de emprego*) to dismiss, sack; **despedir-se** *vr*: **~-se (de)** to say goodbye (to)

despeitado, -a [dʒispej'tadu, a] *adj* spiteful; (*ressentido*) resentful

despeito [dʒis'pejtu] *m* spite; **a ~ de** in spite of, despite

despejar [dʒispe'ʒar] *vt* (*água*) to pour; (*esvaziar*) to empty; (*inquilino*) to evict; **despejo** [dʒis'peʒu] *m* eviction; **quarto de despejo** junk room

despencar [dʒispẽ'kar] *vi* to fall down, tumble down

despentear [dʒispẽ'tʃjar] *vt* (*cabelo: sem querer*) to mess up; (*: de propósito*) to let down; **despentear-se** *vr* to mess one's hair up; to let one's hair down

despercebido, -a [dʒisperse'bidu, a] *adj* unnoticed

desperdiçar [dʒisperdʒi'sar] *vt* to waste; (*dinheiro*) to squander; **desperdício** [dʒisper'dʒisju] *m*

waste

despertador [dʒisperta'dor] *m* (*tb*: **relógio ~**) alarm clock

despertar [dʒisper'tar] *vt* to wake; (*suspeitas, interesse*) to arouse; (*reminiscências*) to revive; (*apetite*) to whet ▷ *vi* to wake up ▷ *m* awakening; **desperto, -a** [dʒis'pɛrtu, a] *adj* awake

despesa [dʒis'peza] *f* expense; **despesas** *fpl* (*de uma empresa*) expenses, costs; **~s gerais** (*Com*) overheads

despido, -a [dʒis'pidu, a] *adj* naked, bare; (*livre*) free

despir [dʒis'pir] *vt* (*roupa*) to take off; (*pessoa*) to undress; (*despojar*) to strip; **despir-se** *vr* to undress

despojar [dʒispo'ʒar] *vt* (*casas*) to loot, sack; (*pessoas*) to rob

despontar [dʒispõ'tar] *vi* to emerge; (*sol*) to come out; (*: ao amanhecer*) to come up; **ao ~ do dia** at daybreak

desporto [dʒis'portu] *m* sport

desprender [dʒisprẽ'der] *vt* to loosen; (*desatar*) to unfasten; (*emitir*) to emit; **desprender-se** *vr* (*botão*) to come off; (*cheiro*) to be given off

desprezar [dʒispre'zar] *vt* to despise, disdain; (*não dar importância a*) to disregard, ignore; **desprezível** [dʒispre'zivew] (*pl* **-eis**) *adj* despicable; **desprezo** [dʒis'prezu] *m* scorn, contempt; **dar ao desprezo** to ignore

desproporcional [dʒisproporsjo'naw] *adj* disproportionate

despropósito [dʒispro'pɔzitu] *m* nonsense

desprovido, -a [dʒispro'vidu, a] *adj* deprived; **~ de** without

desqualificar [dʒiskwalifi'kar] vt (Esporte etc) to disqualify; (tornar indigno) to disgrace, lower

desregrado, -a [dʒizhe'gradu, a] adj disorderly, unruly; (devasso) immoderate

desrespeito [dʒizhe'spejtu] m disrespect

desse¹ ['desi] = **de** + **esse**

desse² vb ver **dar**

destacar [dʒista'kar] vt (Mil) to detail; (separar) to detach; (enfatizar) to emphasize ▷ vi to stand out; **destacar-se** vr to stand out; (pessoa) to be outstanding

destampar [dʒistã'par] vt to take the lid off

destapar [dʒista'par] vt to uncover

destaque [dʒis'taki] m distinction; (pessoa, coisa) highlight

deste ['destʃi] = **de** + **este**

destemido, -a [deste'midu, a] adj fearless, intrepid

destilar [destʃi'lar] vt to distil (Brit), distill (US)

destinação [destʃina'sãw] (pl **-ões**) f destination

destinar [des'tʃinar] vt to destine; (dinheiro): **~ (para)** to set aside (for); **destinar-se** vr: **~-se a** to be intended for; (carta) to be addressed to

destinatário, -a [destʃina'tarju, a] m/f addressee

destino [des'tʃinu] m destiny, fate; (lugar) destination; **com ~ a** bound for

destituir [destʃi'twir] vt to dismiss; **~ de** (privar de) to deprive of

destrancar [dʒistrã'kar] vt to unlock

destratar [dʒistra'tar] vt to abuse, insult

destreza [des'treza] f skill; (agilidade) dexterity

destro, -a ['dɛstru, a] adj skilful (Brit), skillful (US); (ágil) agile; (não canhoto) right-handed

destrocar [dʒistro'kar] vt to give back, return

destroçar [dʒistro'sar] vt to destroy; (quebrar) to smash, break; **destroços** [dʒis'trɔsus] mpl wreckage sg

destruição [dʒistrwi'sãw] f destruction

destruir [dʒis'trwir] vt to destroy

desvairado, -a [dʒizvaj'radu, a] adj (louco) crazy, demented; (desorientado) bewildered

desvalorizar [dʒizvalori'zar] vt to devalue

desvantagem [dʒizvã'taʒẽ] (pl **-ns**) f disadvantage

desvão [dʒiz'vãw] (pl **-s**) m loft

desventura [dʒizvẽ'tura] f misfortune; (infelicidade) unhappiness

desvio [dʒiz'viu] m diversion, detour; (curva) bend; (fig) deviation; (de dinheiro) embezzlement

detalhadamente [detaʎada'mẽtʃi] adv in detail

detalhado, -a [deta'ʎadu, a] adj detailed

detalhe [de'taʎi] m detail

detectar [detek'tar] vt to detect

detector [detek'tor] m detector

detenção [detẽ'sãw] (pl **-ões**) f detention

deter [de'ter] (irreg: como **ter**) vt to stop; (prender) to arrest, detain; (reter) to keep; (conter: riso) to contain; **deter-se** vr to stop; (ficar) to stay; (conter-se) to restrain o.s.

detergente [deter'ʒẽtʃi] m detergent

deteriorar [deterjo'rar] *vt* to spoil, damage; **deteriorar-se** *vr* to deteriorate; (*relações*) to worsen

determinação [determina'sãw] *f* determination; (*decisão*) decision; (*ordem*) order

determinado, -a [determi'nadu, a] *adj* determined; (*certo*) certain, given

determinar [determi'nar] *vt* to determine; (*decretar*) to order; (*resolver*) to decide (on); (*causar*) to cause

detestar [detes'tar] *vt* to hate; **detestável** [detes'tavew] (*pl* **-eis**) *adj* horrible, hateful

detetive [dete'tʃivi] *m/f* detective

detido, -a [de'tʃidu, a] *adj* (*preso*) under arrest; (*minucioso*) thorough ▷ *m/f* person under arrest, prisoner

detonação [detona'sãw] (*pl* **-ões**) *f* explosion

detonar [deto'nar] *vi, vt* to detonate

detrás [de'trajs] *adv* behind ▷ *prep*: **~ de** behind

detrimento [detri'mētu] *m*: **em ~ de** to the detriment of

detrito [de'tritu] *m* debris *sg*; (*de comida*) remains *pl*; (*resíduo*) dregs *pl*

deturpação [deturpa'sãw] *f* corruption; (*de palavras*) distortion

deturpar [detur'par] *vt* to corrupt; (*desfigurar*) to disfigure; (*palavras*) to twist

deu [dew] *vb ver* **dar**

deus, a [dews, 'dewza] *m/f* god/goddess; **D~ me livre!** God forbid!; **graças a D~** thank goodness; **meu D~!** good Lord!

devagar [dʒiva'gar] *adv* slowly

devaneio [deva'neju] *m* daydream

devassa [de'vasa] *f* investigation, inquiry

devassidão [devasi'dãw] *f* debauchery

devasso, -a [de'vasu, a] *adj* dissolute

deve ['dɛvi] *m* debit

dever [de'ver] *m* duty ▷ *vt* to owe ▷ *vi* (*suposição*): **deve (de) estar doente** he must be ill; (*obrigação*): **devo partir às oito** I must go at eight; **você devia ir ao médico** you should go to the doctor; **que devo fazer?** what shall I do?

devido, -a [de'vidu, a] *adj* (*maneira*) proper; (*respeito*) due; **~ a** due to, owing to; **no ~ tempo** in due course

devoção [devo'sãw] *f* devotion

devolução [devolu'sãw] *f* devolution; (*restituição*) return; (*reembolso*) refund; **~ de impostos** tax rebate

devolver [devow'ver] *vt* to give back, return; (*Com*) to refund

devorar [devo'rar] *vt* to devour; (*destruir*) to destroy

devotar [devo'tar] *vt* to devote

dez [dɛz] *num* ten

dezanove [deza'nɔvə] (*PT*) *num* = **dezenove**

dezasseis [deza'sejs] (*PT*) *num* = **dezesseis**

dezassete [deza'setə] (*PT*) *num* = **dezessete**

dezembro [de'zēbru] *m* December

dezena [de'zena] *f*: **uma ~** ten

dezenove [deze'nɔvi] *num* nineteen

dezesseis [deze'sejs] *num* sixteen

dezessete [dezi'setʃi] *num* seventeen

dezoito [dʒi'zojtu] *num* eighteen

dia ['dʒia] *m* day; (*claridade*) daylight; **~ a ~** day by day; **~ santo**

holy day; **~ útil** weekday; **estar** *ou* **andar em ~ (com)** to be up to date (with); **de ~** in the daytime, by day; **mais ~ menos ~** sooner or later; **~ sim, ~ não** every other day; **no ~ seguinte** the next day; **bom ~** good morning; **um ~ desses** one of these days; **~s a fio** days on end; **~ cheio/morto** busy/quiet *ou* slow day; **todo santo ~** *(col)* every single day, day after day; **recebo por ~** I'm paid by the day; **um bebê de ~s** a newborn baby; **ele está com os ~s contados** his days are numbered; **dia a dia** *m* daily life, everyday life

diabete, diabetes [dʒjaˈbɛtʃi(s)] *f* diabetes *sg*; **diabético, -a** [dʒjaˈbɛtʃiku, a] *adj, m/f* diabetic

diabo [ˈdʒjabu] *m* devil; **que ~!** *(col)* damn it!

diabrura [dʒjaˈbrura] *f* prank; **diabruras** *fpl* *(travessura)* mischief *sg*

diagnóstico [dʒjagˈnɔstʃiku] *m* diagnosis

diagonal [dʒjagoˈnaw] *(pl -ais) adj, f* diagonal

diagrama [dʒjaˈgrama] *m* diagram

dialeto [dʒjaˈlɛtu] *m* dialect

dialogar [dʒjaloˈgar] *vi:* **~ (com alguém)** to talk (to sb); *(Pol)* to have *ou* hold talks (with sb)

diálogo [ˈdʒjalogu] *m* dialogue; *(conversa)* talk, conversation

diamante [dʒjaˈmãtʃi] *m* diamond

diâmetro [ˈdʒjametru] *m* diameter

diante [ˈdʒjãtʃi] *prep:* **~ de** before; *(na frente de)* in front of; *(problemas etc)* in the face of; **e assim por ~** and so on; **para ~** forward

dianteira [dʒjãˈtejra] *f* front, vanguard; **tomar a ~** to get ahead

dianteiro, -a [dʒjãˈtejru, a] *adj* front

diapositivo [dʒjapoziˈtʃivu] *m* *(Foto)* slide

diária [ˈdʒjarja] *f (de hotel)* daily rate

diário, -a [ˈdʒjarju, a] *adj* daily ▷ *m* diary; *(jornal)* (daily) newspaper; **~ de bordo** *(Aer)* logbook

diarreia [dʒjaˈhɛja] *f* diarrhoea *(Brit)*, diarrhea *(US)*

dica [ˈdʒika] *(col) f* hint

dicionário [dʒisjoˈnarju] *m* dictionary

dieta [ˈdʒjɛta] *f* diet; **fazer ~** to go on a diet

diferença [dʒifeˈrẽsa] *f* difference; **ela tem uma ~ comigo** she's got something against me

diferenciar [dʒiferẽˈsjar] *vt* to differentiate

diferente [dʒifeˈrẽtʃi] *adj* different; **estar ~ com alguém** to be at odds with sb

difícil [dʒiˈfisiw] *(pl -eis) adj* difficult; *(improvável)* unlikely; **o ~ é ...** the difficult thing is ...; **acho ~ ela aceitar nossa proposta** I think it's unlikely she will accept our proposal; **dificilmente** [dʒifisiwˈmẽtʃi] *adv* with difficulty; *(mal)* hardly; *(raramente)* hardly ever

dificuldade [dʒifikuwˈdadʒi] *f* difficulty; *(aperto):* **em ~s** in trouble

dificultar [dʒifikuwˈtar] *vt* to make difficult; *(complicar)* to complicate

difundir [dʒifũˈdʒir] *vt* to diffuse; *(boato, rumor)* to spread

digerir [dʒiʒeˈrir] *vt, vi* to digest

digestão [dʒiʒesˈtãw] *f* digestion

digital [dʒiʒiˈtaw] *(pl -ais) adj:* **impressão ~** fingerprint

digitar [dʒiʒiˈtar] *vt (Comput: dados)* to key (in)

dígito [ˈdʒiʒitu] *m* digit

dignidade [dʒigni'dadʒi] f dignity

digno, -a ['dʒignu, a] adj (merecedor) worthy; (nobre) dignified

digo etc ['dʒigu] vb ver **dizer**

dilatar [dʒila'tar] vt to dilate, expand; (prolongar) to prolong; (retardar) to delay

dilema [dʒi'lɛma] m dilemma

diluir [dʒi'lwir] vt to dilute

dilúvio [dʒi'luvju] m flood

dimensão [dʒimē'sãw] (pl -ões) f dimension; **dimensões** fpl (medidas) measurements

diminuição [dʒiminwi'sãw] f reduction

diminuir [dʒimi'nwir] vt to reduce; (som) to turn down; (interesse) to lessen ▷ vi to lessen, diminish; (preço) to go down; (dor) to wear off; (barulho) to die down

diminutivo, -a [dʒiminu'tʃivu, a] adj diminutive ▷ m (Ling) diminutive

Dinamarca [dʒina'marka] f Denmark; **dinamarquês, -quesa** [dʒinamar'kes, 'keza] adj Danish ▷ m/f Dane ▷ m (Ling) Danish

dinâmico, -a [dʒi'namiku, a] adj dynamic

dínamo ['dʒinamu] m dynamo

dinheirão [dʒiɲej'rãw] m: **um ~** loads pl of money

dinheiro [dʒi'ɲejru] m money; **~ à vista** cash for paying in cash; **~ em caixa** money in the till; **~ em espécie** cash

dinossauro [dʒino'sawru] m dinosaur

diploma [dʒip'lɔma] m diploma

diplomacia [dʒiploma'sia] f diplomacy; (fig) tact

diplomata [dʒiplo'mata] m/f diplomat; **diplomático, -a**

[dʒiplo'matʃiku, a] adj diplomatic

dique ['dʒiki] m dam; (Geo) dyke

direção [dʒire'sãw] (pl -ões) f direction; (endereço) address; (Auto) steering; (administração) management; (comando) leadership; (diretoria) board of directors; **em ~ a** towards

direi etc [dʒi'rej] vb ver **dizer**

direita [dʒi'rejta] f (mão) right hand; (lado) right-hand side; (Pol) right wing; **à ~** on the right

direito, -a [dʒi'rejtu, a] adj (lado) right-hand; (mão) right; (honesto) honest; (devido) proper; (justo) right, just ▷ m right; (Jur) law ▷ adv straight; (bem) right; (de maneira certa) properly; **direitos** mpl (humanos) rights; (alfandegários) duty sg

direto, -a [dʒi'rɛtu, a] adj direct ▷ adv straight; **transmissão direta** (TV) live broadcast

diretor, a [dʒire'tor(a)] adj directing, guiding ▷ m/f director; (de jornal) editor; (de escola) head teacher; **diretoria** [dʒireto'ria] f (Com) management

dirigente [dʒiri'ʒētʃi] m/f (de país, partido) leader; (diretor) director; (gerente) manager

dirigir [dʒiri'ʒir] vt to direct; (Com) to manage; (veículo) to drive ▷ vi to drive; **dirigir-se** vr: **~-se a** (falar com) to speak to; (ir, recorrer) to go to; (esforços) to be directed towards

discagem [dʒis'kaʒē] f (Tel) dialling

discar [dʒis'kar] vt to dial

disciplina [dʒisi'plina] f discipline; **disciplinar** [dʒisipli'nar] vt to discipline

discípulo, -a [dʒi'sipulu, a] m/f disciple; (aluno) pupil

disco ['dʒisku] m disc; (Comput)

disk; (*Mús*) record; (*de telefone*) dial;
~ rígido (*Comput*) hard disk; **~ do**
sistema system disk; **~ voador**
flying saucer

discordar [dʒiskor'dar] *vi*: **~ de**
alguém em algo to disagree with
sb on sth

discórdia [dʒis'kɔrdʒja] *f* discord,
strife

discoteca [dʒisko'tɛka] *f*
discotheque, disco (*col*)

discrepância [dʒiskre'pãsja] *f*
discrepancy; (*desacordo*)
disagreement; **discrepante**
[dʒiskre'pãtʃi] *adj* conflicting

discreto, -a [dʒis'krɛtu, a] *adj*
discreet; (*modesto*) modest;
(*prudente*) shrewd; (*roupa*) plain;
discrição [dʒiskri'sãw] *f*
discretion

discriminação [dʒiskrimina'sãw]
f discrimination

discriminar [dʒiskrimi'nar] *vt* to
distinguish ▷ *vi*: **~ entre** to
discriminate between

discurso [dʒis'kursu] *m* speech

discussão [dʒisku'sãw] (*pl* **-ões**) *f*
discussion; (*contenda*) argument

discutir [dʒisku'tʃir] *vt* to discuss
▷ *vi*: **~ (sobre algo)** to talk (about
sth); (*contender*) to argue (about
sth)

disenteria [dʒizẽte'ria] *f* dysentery

disfarçar [dʒisfar'sar] *vt* to
disguise ▷ *vi* to pretend;
disfarçar-se *vr*: **~-se em** *ou* **de**
algo to disguise o.s. as sth;
disfarce [dʒis'farsi] *m* disguise;
(*máscara*) mask

dislexia [dʒizlek'sia] *f* dyslexia

disparar [dʒispa'rar] *vt* to shoot,
fire ▷ *vi* to fire; (*arma*) to go off;
(*correr*) to shoot off, bolt

disparatado, -a [dʒispara'tadu, a]
adj silly, absurd

disparate [dʒispa'ratʃi] *m*
nonsense, rubbish

disparidade [dʒispari'dadʒi] *f*
disparity

dispensar [dʒispẽ'sar] *vt* to excuse;
(*prescindir de*) to do without;
(*conferir*) to grant; **dispensável**
[dʒispẽ'savew] (*pl* **-eis**) *adj*
expendable

dispersar [dʒisper'sar] *vt, vi* to
disperse; **disperso, -a** [dʒis'pɛrsu,
a] *adj* scattered

displicência [dʒispli'sensja] (*BR*) *f*
negligence, carelessness;
displicente [dʒispli'sẽtʃi] *adj*
careless

dispo *etc* ['dʒispu] *vb ver* **despir**

disponível [dʒispo'nivɛw] (*pl* **-eis**)
adj available

dispor [dʒis'por] (*irreg: como* **pôr**) *vt*
to arrange ▷ *vi*: **~ de** to have the
use of; (*ter*) to have, own; (*pessoas*)
to have at one's disposal;
dispor-se *vr*: **~-se a** (*estar pronto a*)
to be prepared to; be willing to;
(*decidir*) to decide to; **~ sobre** to talk
about; **disponha!** feel free!

disposição [dʒispozi'sãw] (*pl* **-ões**) *f*
arrangement; (*humor*) disposition;
(*inclinação*) inclination; **à sua ~** at
your disposal

dispositivo [dʒispozi'tʃivu] *m*
gadget, device; (*determinação de lei*)
provision

disputa [dʒis'puta] *f* dispute,
argument; (*competição*) contest;
disputar [dʒispu'tar] *vt* to
dispute; (*concorrer a*) to compete
for; (*lutar por*) to fight over ▷ *vi* to
quarrel, argue; to compete;
disputar uma corrida to run a
race

disquete [dʒis'ketʃi] *m* (*Comput*)

diskette

disse etc ['dʒisi] vb ver **dizer**

disseminar [dʒisemi'nar] vt to disseminate; (espalhar) to spread

dissertar [dʒiser'tar] vi to speak

dissidência [dʒisi'dẽsja] f (cisão) difference of opinion

disso ['dʒisu] = **de + isso**

dissolução [dʒisolu'sãw] f (libertinagem) debauchery; (de casamento) dissolution

dissolver [dʒisow'ver] vt to dissolve; (dispersar) to disperse; (motim) to break up

dissuadir [dʒiswa'dʒir] vt to dissuade; **~ alguém de fazer algo** to talk sb out of doing sth, dissuade sb from doing sth

distância [dʒis'tãsja] f distance; **a 3 quilômetros de ~** 3 kilometres (Brit) ou kilometers (US) away

distanciar [dʒistã'sjar] vt to distance, set apart; (colocar por intervalos) to space out; **distanciar-se** vr to move away; (fig) to distance o.s.

distante [dʒis'tãtʃi] adj distant

distender [dʒistẽ'der] vt to expand; (estirar) to stretch; (dilatar) to distend; (músculo) to pull; **distender-se** vr to expand; to distend

distinção [dʒistʃĩ'sãw] (pl -ões) f distinction; **fazer ~** to make a distinction

distinguir [dʒistʃĩ'gir] vt to distinguish; (avistar, ouvir) to make out; **distinguir-se** vr to stand out

distinto, -a [dʒis'tʃĩtu, a] adj different; (eminente) distinguished; (claro) distinct; (refinado) refined

disto ['dʒistu] = **de + isto**

distorcer [dʒistor'ser] vt to distort

distração [dʒistra'sãw] (pl -ões) f (alheamento) absent-mindedness; (divertimento) pastime; (descuido) oversight

distraído, -a [dʒistra'idu, a] adj absent-minded; (não atento) inattentive

distrair [dʒistra'ir] vt to distract; (divertir) to amuse

distribuição [dʒistribwi'sãw] f distribution; (de cartas) delivery

distribuidor, a [dʒistribwi'dor(a)] m/f distributor ▷ m (Auto) distributor ▷ f (Com) distribution company, distributor

distribuir [dʒistri'bwir] vt to distribute; (repartir) to share out; (cartas) to deliver

distrito [dʒis'tritu] m district; (delegacia) police station; **~ eleitoral** constituency; **~ federal** federal area

distúrbio [dʒis'turbju] m disturbance

ditado [dʒi'tadu] m dictation; (provérbio) saying

ditador [dʒita'dor] m dictator; **ditadura** [dʒita'dura] f dictatorship

ditar [dʒi'tar] vt to dictate; (impor) to impose

dito, -a ['dʒitu, a] pp de **dizer**; **~ e feito** no sooner said than done

diurno, -a ['dʒjurnu, a] adj daytime atr

divã [dʒi'vã] m couch, divan

divergir [dʒiver'ʒir] vi to diverge; (discordar): **~ (de alguém)** to disagree (with sb)

diversão [dʒiver'sãw] (pl -ões) f amusement; (passatempo) pastime

diverso, -a [dʒi'versu, a] adj different; (pl) various

diversões [diver'sõjs] fpl de **diversão**

diversos [dʒiˈvɛrsuʃ] *mpl* sundries
divertido, -a [dʒiverˈtʃidu, a] *adj*
amusing, funny
divertimento [dʒivertʃiˈmẽtu] *m*
amusement, entertainment
divertir [dʒiverˈtʃir] *vt* to amuse,
entertain; **divertir-se** *vr* to enjoy
o.s., have a good time
dívida [ˈdʒivida] *f* debt; **contrair ~s**
to run into debt; **~ externa** foreign
debt
dividir [dʒiviˈdʒir] *vt* to divide;
(*despesas, lucro, comida etc*) to share;
(*separar*) to separate ▷ *vi* (*Mat*) to
divide; **dividir-se** *vr* to divide, split
up
divino, -a [dʒiˈvinu, a] *adj* divine
▷ *m* Holy Ghost
divirjo *etc* [dʒiˈvirʒu] *vb ver* **divergir**
divisa [dʒiˈviza] *f* emblem; (*frase*)
slogan; (*fronteira*) border; (*Mil*)
stripe; **divisas** *fpl* (*câmbio*) foreign
exchange *sg*
divisão [dʒiviˈzãw] (*pl* **-ões**) *f*
division; (*discórdia*) split; (*partilha*)
sharing
divisões [dʒiviˈzõjʃ] *fpl de* **divisão**
divisória [dʒiviˈzɔrja] *f* partition
divorciado, -a [dʒivorˈsjadu, a] *adj*
divorced ▷ *m/f* divorcé(e)
divorciar [dʒivorˈsjar] *vt* to
divorce; **divorciar-se** *vr* to get
divorced; **divórcio** [dʒiˈvɔrsju] *m*
divorce
divulgar [dʒivuwˈgar] *vt* (*notícias*)
to spread; (*segredo*) to divulge;
(*produto*) to market; (*livro*) to
publish; **divulgar-se** *vr* to leak out
dizer [dʒiˈzer] *vt* to say ▷ *m* saying;
dizer-se *vr* to claim to be; **diz-se**
ou **dizem que ...** it is said that ...; **~
algo a alguém** to tell sb sth; (*falar*)
to say sth to sb; **~ a alguém que ...**
to tell sb that ...; **o que você diz da**

minha sugestão? what do you
think of my suggestion?; **querer ~**
to mean; **quer ~** that is to say; **digo**
(*ou seja*) I mean; **não diga!** you
don't say!; **por assim ~** so to speak;
até ~ chega as much as possible
do [du] = **de + o**
doação [doaˈsãw] (*pl* **-ões**) *f*
donation
doador, a [doaˈdor(a)] *m/f* donor
doar [doˈar] *vt* to donate, give
dobra [ˈdɔbra] *f* fold; (*prega*) pleat;
(*de calças*) turn-up
dobradiça [dobraˈdʒisa] *f* hinge
dobradinha [dobraˈdʒiɲa] *f* (*Culin*)
tripe stew
dobrar [doˈbrar] *vt* to double;
(*papel*) to fold; (*joelho*) to bend;
(*esquina*) to turn, go round; (*fazer
ceder*): **~ alguém** to talk sb round
▷ *vi* to double; (*sino*) to toll; (*vergar*)
to bend; **dobrar-se** *vr* to double
(up)
dobro [ˈdobru] *m* double
doce [ˈdosi] *adj* sweet; (*terno*)
gentle ▷ *m* sweet
dóceis [ˈdɔsejʃ] *adj pl de* **dócil**
dócil [ˈdɔsiw] (*pl* **-eis**) *adj* docile
documentação [dokumẽtaˈsãw] *f*
documentation; (*documentos*)
papers *pl*
documentário, -a [dokumẽˈtarju,
a] *adj* documentary ▷ *m*
documentary
documento [dokuˈmẽtu] *m*
document
doçura [doˈsura] *f* sweetness;
(*brandura*) gentleness
doença [doˈẽsa] *f* illness
doente [doˈẽtʃi] *adj* ill, sick ▷ *m/f*
sick person; (*cliente*) patient
doentio, -a [doẽˈtʃiu, a] *adj*
(*pessoa*) sickly; (*clima*) unhealthy;
(*curiosidade*) morbid

doer [do'er] *vi* to hurt, ache; **~ a alguém** (*pesar*) to grieve sb

doido, -a ['dojdu, a] *adj* mad, crazy ▷ *m/f* madman/woman

doído, -a [do'idu, a] *adj* painful; (*moralmente*) hurt; (*que causa dor*) painful

dois, duas [dojs, 'duas] *num* two; **conversa a ~** tête-à-tête

dólar ['dɔlar] *m* dollar; **~ oficial** dollar at the official rate; **~ turismo** dollar at the special tourist rate; **doleiro, -a** [do'lejru, a] *m/f* (black market) dollar dealer

dolorido, -a [dolo'ridu, a] *adj* painful, sore

dom [dõ] *m* gift; (*aptidão*) knack

domar [do'mar] *vt* to tame

doméstica [do'mɛstʃika] *f* maid

domesticar [domestʃi'kar] *vt* to domesticate; (*povo*) to tame

doméstico, -a [do'mɛstʃiku, a] *adj* domestic; (*vida*) home *atr*

domicílio [domi'silju] *m* home, residence; **"entregamos a ~"** "we deliver"

dominador, a [domina'dor(a)] *adj* (*pessoa*) domineering; (*olhar*) imposing ▷ *m/f* ruler

dominar [domi'nar] *vt* to dominate; (*reprimir*) to overcome ▷ *vi* to dominate; **dominar-se** *vr* to control o.s.

domingo [do'mĩgu] *m* Sunday

domínio [do'minju] *m* power; (*dominação*) control; (*território*) domain; (*esfera*) sphere; **~ próprio** self-control

dona ['dɔna] *f* owner; (*col: mulher*) lady; **~ de casa** housewife; **D~ Lígia** Lígia; **D~ Luísa Souza** Mrs Luísa Souza

donde ['dõdə] (*PT*) *adv* from where; (*daí*) thus

dono ['donu] *m* owner

dopar [do'par] *vt* (*cavalo*) to dope

dor [dor] *f* ache; (*aguda*) pain; (*fig*) grief, sorrow; **~ de cabeça** headache; **~ de dentes** toothache; **~ de estômago** stomachache

dormente [dor'mẽtʃi] *adj* numb ▷ *m* (*Ferro*) sleeper

dormir [dor'mir] *vi* to sleep; **~ fora** to spend the night away

dormitório [dormi'tɔrju] *m* bedroom; (*coletivo*) dormitory

dorso ['dorsu] *m* back

dos [dus] = **de + os**

dosagem [do'zaʒẽ] *m* dosage

dose ['dɔzi] *f* dose

dossiê [do'sje] *m* dossier, file

dotado, -a [do'tadu, a] *adj* gifted; **~ de** endowed with

dotar [do'tar] *vt* to endow

dou [do] *vb ver* **dar**

dourado, -a [do'radu, a] *adj* golden; (*com camada de ouro*) gilt ▷ *m* gilt

doutor, a [do'tor(a)] *m/f* doctor; **D~** (*forma de tratamento*) Sir; **D~ Eduardo Souza** Mr Eduardo Souza

doutrina [do'trina] *f* doctrine

doze ['dozi] *num* twelve

Dr. *abr* (= *Doutor*) Dr

Dra. *abr* (= *Doutora*) Dr

dragão [dra'gãw] (*pl* **-ões**) *m* dragon

dragões [dra'gõjs] *mpl de* **dragão**

drama ['drama] *m* drama; **dramático, -a** [dra'matʃiku, a] *adj* dramatic; **dramatizar** [dramatʃi'zar] *vt, vi* to dramatize

drástico, -a ['drastʃiku, a] *adj* drastic

dreno ['drɛnu] *m* drain

driblar [dri'blar] *vt* (*Futebol*) to dribble

drinque ['drĩki] *m* drink

droga ['drɔga] f drug; (fig) rubbish;
  drogado, -a [dro'gadu, a] m/f
  drug addict; **drogar** [dro'gar] vt to
  drug; **drogar-se** vr to take drugs
drogaria [droga'ria] f chemist's
  shop (Brit), drugstore (US)
duas ['duas] f de **dois**
ducha ['duʃa] f shower
dueto ['dwetu] m duet
duna ['duna] f dune
dupla ['dupla] f pair; (Esporte):
  ~ masculina/feminina/mista
  men's/women's/mixed doubles
duplicar [dupli'kar] vt to duplicate
  ▷ vi to double; **duplicata**
  [dupli'kata] f duplicate; (título)
  trade note, bill
duplo, -a ['duplu, a] adj double
  ▷ m double
duque ['duki] m duke
duração [dura'sãw] f duration;
  de pouca ~ short-lived
durante [du'rãtʃi] prep during;
  ~ uma hora for an hour
durar [du'rar] vi to last
durável [du'ravew] (pl **-eis**) adj
  lasting
durex® [du'rɛks] adj: **fita ~**
  adhesive tape, Sellotape® (Brit),
  Scotch tape® (US)
durmo etc ['durmu] vb ver **dormir**
duro, -a ['duru, a] adj hard; (severo)
  harsh; (resistente, fig) tough; **estar
  ~** (col) to be broke
dúvida ['duvida] f doubt; **sem ~**
  undoubtedly, without a doubt;
  duvidar [duvi'dar] vt to doubt ▷ vi
  to have one's doubts; **duvidar de
  alguém/algo** to doubt sb/sth;
  duvidar que ... to doubt that ...;
  duvido! I doubt it!; **duvidoso, -a**
  [duvi'dozu, ɔza] adj doubtful;
  (suspeito) dubious
duzentos, -as [du'zẽtus, as] num

two hundred
dúzia ['duzja] f dozen; **meia ~** half a
  dozen
DVD abr m (= disco digital versátil)
  DVD
dz. abr = **dúzia**

E, e [ε] *m* E, e

e [i] *conj* and; **e a bagagem?** what about the luggage?

é [ε] *vb ver* **ser**

eclipse [e'klipsi] *m* eclipse

eco ['εku] *m* echo; **ter ~** to catch on; **ecoar** [e'kwar] *vt* to echo ▷ *vi* (*ressoar*) to echo

ecologia [ekolo'ʒia] *f* ecology

ecológico, -a [eko'lɔʒiku, a] *adj* ecological, eco-friendly

economia [ekono'mia] *f* economy; (*ciência*) economics *sg*; **economias** *fpl* (*poupanças*) savings; **fazer ~ (de)** to economize (with)

econômico, -a [eko'nomiku, a] *adj* economical; (*pessoa*) thrifty; (*Com*) economic

economizar [ekonomi'zar] *vt* (*gastar com economia*) to economize on; (*poupar*) to save (up) ▷ *vi* to economize; to save up

écran ['εkrã] (*PT*) *m* screen

edição [edʒi'sãw] (*pl* **-ões**) *f* publication; (*conjunto de exemplares*) edition; (*TV, Cinema*) editing

edifício [edʒi'fisju] *m* building; **~ garagem** multistorey car park (*Brit*), multistory parking lot (*US*)

Edimburgo [edʒĩ'burgu] *n* Edinburgh

editar [edʒi'tar] *vt* to publish; (*Comput etc*) to edit

editor, a [edʒi'tor(a)] *adj* publishing *atr* ▷ *m/f* publisher; (*redator*) editor ▷ *f* publishing company; **casa ~a** publishing house

editoração [edʒitora'sãw] *f*: **~ eletrônica** desktop publishing; **editorial** [edʒito'rjaw] (*pl* **-ais**) *adj* publishing *atr* ▷ *m* editorial

edredão [ədrə'dãw] (*pl* **-ões**) (*PT*) *m* = **edredom**

edredom [edre'dõ] (*pl* **-ns**) *m* eiderdown

educação [eduka'sãw] *f* education; (*criação*) upbringing; (*de animais*) training; (*maneiras*) good manners *pl*; **educacional** [edukasjo'naw] (*pl* **-ais**) *adj* education *atr*

educar [edu'kar] *vt* to educate; (*criar*) to bring up; (*animal*) to train

efeito [e'fejtu] *m* effect; **fazer ~** to work; **levar a ~** to put into effect; **com ~** indeed

efeminado, -a [efemi'nadu] *adj* effeminate

efervescente [eferve'sẽtʃi] *adj* fizzy

efetivamente [efetʃiva'mẽtʃi] *adv* effectively; (*realmente*) really, in fact

efetivo, -a [efe'tʃivu, a] *adj* effective; (*real*) actual, real; (*cargo, funcionário*) permanent

efetuar [efe'twar] vt to carry out; (soma) to do, perform

eficaz [efi'kaz] adj (pessoa) efficient; (tratamento) effective

eficiência [efi'sjēsja] f efficiency; **eficiente** [efi'sjētʃi] adj efficient

egípcio, -a [e'ʒipsju, a] adj, m/f Egyptian

Egito [e'ʒitu] m: **o ~** Egypt

egoísmo [ego'izmu] m selfishness, egoism; **egoísta** [ego'ista] adj selfish, egoistic ▷ m/f egoist

égua ['ɛgwa] f mare

ei [ej] excl hey!

ei-lo = **eis + o**

eis [ejs] adv (sg) here is; (pl) here are; **~ aí** there is; there are

ejacular [eʒaku'lar] vt (sêmen) to ejaculate; (líquido) to spurt ▷ vi to ejaculate

ela ['ɛla] pron (pessoa) she; (coisa) it; (com prep) her; it; **elas** fpl they; (com prep) them; **~s por ~s** (col) tit for tat

elaboração [elabora'sãw] (pl **-ões**) f (de uma teoria) working out; (preparo) preparation

elaborar [elabo'rar] vt to prepare; (fazer) to make

elástico, -a [e'lastʃiku, a] adj elastic; (flexível) flexible; (colchão) springy ▷ m elastic band

ele ['eli] pron he; (coisa) it; (com prep) him; it; **eles** mpl they; (com prep) them

elefante, -ta [ele'fãtʃi, ta] m/f elephant

elegante [ele'gãtʃi] adj elegant; (da moda) fashionable

eleger [ele'ʒer] vt to elect; (escolher) to choose

eleição [elej'sãw] (pl **-ões**) f election; (escolha) choice

eleito, -a [e'lejtu, a] pp de **eleger** ▷ adj elected; (escolhido) chosen

eleitor, a [elej'tor(a)] m/f voter

elejo etc [e'leʒu] vb ver **eleger**

elementar [elemē'tar] adj elementary; (fundamental) basic, fundamental

elemento [ele'mētu] m element; (parte) component; (recurso) means; (informação) grounds pl; **elementos** mpl (rudimentos) rudiments

elenco [e'lēku] m list; (de atores) cast

eletricidade [eletrisi'dadʒi] f electricity

eletricista [eletri'sista] m/f electrician

elétrico, -a [e'lɛtriku, a] adj electric; (fig: agitado) worked up ▷ m tram (Brit), streetcar (US)

eletrificar [eletrifi'kar] vt to electrify

eletrizar [eletri'zar] vt to electrify; (fig) to thrill

eletro... [eletru] prefixo electro...; **eletrocutar** [eletroku'tar] vt to electrocute; **eletrodo** [ele'trodu], (PT) **elétrodo** m electrode; **eletrodomésticos** [eletrodo'mɛstʃikus] (BR) mpl (electrical) household appliances

eletrônica [ele'tronika] f electronics sg

eletrônico, -a [ele'troniku, a] adj electronic

elevação [eleva'sãw] (pl **-ões**) f (Arq) elevation; (aumento) rise; (ato) raising; (altura) height; (promoção) promotion; (ponto elevado) bump

elevador [eleva'dor] m lift (Brit), elevator (US)

elevar [ele'var] vt to lift up; (voz, preço) to raise; (exaltar) to exalt; (promover) to promote; **elevar-se**

vr to rise

eliminar [elimi'nar] *vt* to remove; (*suprimir*) to delete; (*possibilidade*) to rule out; (*Med, banir*) to expel; (*Esporte*) to eliminate; **eliminatória** [elimina'tɔrja] *f* (*Esporte*) heat, preliminary round; (*exame*) test

elite [e'litʃi] *f* elite

elogiar [elo'ʒjar] *vt* to praise; **elogio** [elo'ʒiu] *m* praise; (*cumprimento*) compliment

El Salvador [ew-] *n* El Salvador

 PALAVRA-CHAVE

em [ẽ] (*em + o(s)/a(s) = no(s)/na(s); + ele(s)/a(s) = nele(s)/a(s); + esse(s)/a(s) = nesse(s)/a(s); + isso = nisso; + este(s)/a(s) = neste(s)/a(s); + isto = nisto; + aquele(s)/a(s) = naquele(s)/a(s); + aquilo = naquilo*) *prep* **1** (*posição*) in; (: *sobre*) on; **está na gaveta/no bolso** it's in the drawer/pocket; **está na mesa/no chão** it's on the table/floor

2 (*lugar*) in; (: *casa, escritório etc*) at; (: *andar, meio de transporte*) on; **no Brasil/em São Paulo** in Brazil/São Paulo; **em casa/no dentista** at home/the dentist; **no avião** on the plane; **no quinto andar** on the fifth floor

3 (*ação*) into; **ela entrou na sala de aula** she went into the classroom; **colocar algo na bolsa** to put sth into one's bag

4 (*tempo*) in; on; **em 1962/3 semanas** in 1962/3 weeks; **no inverno** in the winter; **em janeiro, no mês de janeiro** in January; **nessa ocasião/altura** on that occasion/at that time; **em breve** soon

5 (*diferença*): **reduzir/aumentar em 20%** to reduce/increase by 20%

6 (*modo*): **escrito em inglês** written in English

7 (*após vb que indica gastar etc*) on; **a metade do seu salário vai em comida** he spends half his salary on food

8 (*tema, ocupação*): **especialista no assunto** expert on the subject; **ele trabalha na construção civil** he works in the building industry

emagrecer [imagre'ser] *vt* to make thin ▷ *vi* to grow thin; (*mediante regime*) to slim; **emagrecimento** [imagresi'mẽtu] *m* (*mediante regime*) slimming

e-mail [i'mew] *m* email; **mandar um ~ para alguém** to email sb; **mandar algo por ~** to email sth

emaranhado, -a [imara'ɲadu, a] *adj* tangled ▷ *m* tangle

embaixada [ẽbaj'ʃada] *f* embassy

embaixador, a [ẽbajʃa'dor(a)] *m/f* ambassador

embaixatriz [ẽbajʃa'triz] *f* ambassador; (*mulher de embaixador*) ambassador's wife

embaixo [ẽ'bajʃu] *adv* below, underneath ▷ *prep*: **~ de** under, underneath; **(lá) ~** (*em andar inferior*) downstairs

embalagem [ẽba'laʒẽ] *f* packing; (*de produto: caixa etc*) packaging

embalar [ẽba'lar] *vt* to pack; (*balançar*) to rock

embaraçar [ẽbara'sar] *vt* to hinder; (*complicar*) to complicate; (*encabular*) to embarrass; (*confundir*) to confuse; (*obstruir*) to block; **embaraçar-se** *vr* to become embarrassed

embaraço [ẽba'rasu] *m* hindrance;

e

(*cábula*) embarrassment;
embaraçoso, -a [ẽbara'sozu, ɔza] *adj* embarrassing

embarcação [ẽbarka'sãw] (*pl* **-ões**) *f* vessel

embarcar [ẽbar'kar] *vt* to embark, put on board; (*mercadorias*) to ship, stow ▷ *vi* to go on board, embark

embarque [ẽ'barkı] *m* (*de pessoas*) boarding, embarkation; (*de mercadorias*) shipment

embebedar [ẽbebe'dar] *vt* to make drunk ▷ *vi*: **o vinho embebeda** wine makes you drunk;
embebedar-se *vr* to get drunk

emblema [ẽ'blɛma] *m* emblem; (*na roupa*) badge

êmbolo ['ẽbolu] *m* piston

embolsar [ẽbow'sar] *vt* to pocket; (*herança etc*) to come into

embora [ẽ'bɔra] *conj* though, although ▷ *excl* even so; **ir(-se) ~** to go away

emboscada [ẽbos'kada] *f* ambush

embriagar [ẽbrja'gar] *vt* to make drunk, intoxicate; **embriagar-se** *vr* to get drunk; **embriaguez** [ẽbrja'gez] *f* drunkenness; (*fig*) rapture

embrião [e'brjãw] (*pl* **-ões**) *m* embryo

embromar [ẽbro'mar] *vt* (*adiar*) to put off; (*enganar*) to cheat ▷ *vi* (*prometer e não cumprir*) to make empty promises, be all talk (and no action); (*protelar*) to stall; (*falar em rodeios*) to beat about the bush

embrulhar [ẽbru'ʎar] *vt* (*pacote*) to wrap; (*enrolar*) to roll up; (*confundir*) to muddle up; (*enganar*) to cheat; (*estômago*) to upset;
embrulhar-se *vr* to get into a muddle

embrulho [ẽ'bruʎu] *m* package,

parcel; (*confusão*) mix-up

emburrar [ẽbu'har] *vi* to sulk

embutido, -a [ẽbu'tʃidu, a] *adj* (*armário*) built-in, fitted

emenda [e'mẽda] *f* correction; (*Jur*) amendment; (*de uma pessoa*) improvement; (*ligação*) join; (*sambladura*) joint; (*Costura*) seam

emendar [emẽ'dar] *vt* to correct; (*reparar*) to mend; (*injustiças*) to make amends for; (*Jur*) to amend; (*ajuntar*) to put together;
emendar-se *vr* to mend one's ways

ementa [e'mẽta] (*PT*) *f* menu

emergência [imer'ʒẽsja] *f* emergence; (*crise*) emergency

emigrado, -a [emi'gradu, a] *adj* emigrant

emigrante [emi'grãtʃi] *m/f* emigrant

emigrar [emi'grar] *vi* to emigrate; (*aves*) to migrate

eminência [emi'nẽsja] *f* eminence; (*altura*) height; **eminente** [emi'nẽtʃi] *adj* eminent, distinguished; (*Geo*) high

emissão [emi'sãw] (*pl* **-ões**) *f* emission; (*Rádio*) broadcast; (*de moeda, ações*) issue

emissor, a [emi'sor(a)] *adj* (*de moeda-papel*) issuing ▷ *m* (*Rádio*) transmitter ▷ *f* (*estação*) broadcasting station; (*empresa*) broadcasting company

emitir [emi'tʃir] *vt* (*som*) to give out; (*cheiro*) to give off; (*moeda, ações*) to issue; (*Rádio*) to broadcast; (*opinião*) to express ▷ *vi* (*emitir moeda*) to print money

emoção [emo'sãw] (*pl* **-ões**) *f* emotion; (*excitação*) excitement; **emocional** [imosjo'naw] (*pl* **-ais**) *adj* emotional; **emocionante**

[imosjo'nãtʃi] *adj* moving;
(*excitante*) exciting; **emocionar**
[imosjo'nar] *vt* to move;
(*perturbar*) to upset; (*excitar*) to
excite, thrill ▷ *vi* to be exciting;
(*comover*) to be moving;
emocionar-se *vr* to get emotional
emotivo, -a [emo'tʃivu, a] *adj*
emotional
empacotar [ẽpako'tar] *vt* to pack,
wrap up
empada [ẽ'pada] *f* pie
empadão [ẽpa'dãw] (*pl* **-ões**) *m* pie
empalidecer [ẽpalide'ser] *vi* to
turn pale
empanturrar [ẽpãtu'har] *vt*: **~
alguém de algo** to stuff sb full of
sth
empatar [ẽpa'tar] *vt* to hinder;
(*dinheiro*) to tie up; (*no jogo*) to
draw; (*tempo*) to take up ▷ *vi* (*no
jogo*): **~ (com)** to draw (with);
empate [ẽ'patʃi] *m* draw; (*numa
corrida etc*) tie; (*Xadrez*) stalemate;
(*em negociações*) deadlock
empecilho [ẽpe'siʎu] *m* obstacle;
(*col*) snag
empenhar [ẽpe'ɲar] *vt* (*objeto*) to
pawn; (*palavra*) to pledge;
(*empregar*) to exert; (*compelir*) to
oblige; **empenhar-se** *vr*: **~-se em
fazer** to strive to do, do one's
utmost to do; **empenho** [ẽ'peɲu]
m pawning; (*palavra*) pledge;
(*insistência*): **empenho (em)**
commitment (to)
empilhar [ẽpi'ʎar] *vt* to pile up
empinado, -a [ẽpi'nadu, a] *adj*
upright; (*cavalo*) rearing; (*colina*)
steep
empinar [ẽpi'nar] *vt* to raise, uplift
empobrecer [ẽpobre'ser] *vt* to
impoverish ▷ *vi* to become poor;
empobrecimento [ẽpobresi'mẽtu]

m impoverishment
empolgação [ẽpowga'sãw] *f*
excitement; (*entusiasmo*)
enthusiasm
empolgante [ẽpow'gãtʃi] *adj*
exciting
empolgar [ẽpow'gar] *vt* to
stimulate, fill with enthusiasm;
(*prender a atenção de*): **~ alguém** to
keep sb riveted
empossar [ẽpo'sar] *vt* to appoint
empreendedor, a [ẽprjẽde'dor(a)]
adj enterprising ▷ *m/f*
entrepreneur
empreender [ẽprjẽ'der] *vt* to
undertake; **empreendimento**
[ẽprjẽdʒi'mẽtu] *m* undertaking
empregada [ẽpre'gada] *f* (*BR*:
doméstica) maid; (*PT*: *de restaurante*)
waitress; *ver tb* **empregado**
empregado, -a [ẽpre'gadu, a] *m/f*
employee; (*em escritório*) clerk ▷ *m*
(*PT*: *de restaurante*) waiter
empregador, a [ẽprega'dor(a)] *m/f*
employer
empregar [ẽpre'gar] *vt* (*pessoa*) to
employ; (*coisa*) to use;
empregar-se *vr* to get a job
emprego [ẽ'pregu] *m* job; (*uso*) use
empreiteiro [ẽprej'tejru] *m*
contractor
empresa [ẽ'preza] *f* undertaking;
(*Com*) enterprise, firm; **~
pontocom** dotcom; **empresário,
-a** [ẽpre'zarju, a] *m/f*
businessman/woman; (*de cantor,
boxeador etc*) manager
emprestado, -a [ẽpres'tadu, a] *adj*
on loan; **pedir ~** to borrow; **tomar
algo ~** to borrow sth
emprestar [ẽpres'tar] *vt* to lend;
empréstimo [ẽ'prestʃimu] *m* loan
empunhar [ẽpu'ɲar] *vt* to grasp,
seize

e

empurrão [ēpu'hãw] (pl -ões) m
push, shove; **aos empurrões**
jostling

empurrar [ēpu'har] vt to push

empurrões [ēpu'hõjs] mpl de
empurrão

emudecer [emude'ser] vt to
silence ▷ vi to fall silent, go quiet

enamorado, -a [enamo'radu, a]
adj enchanted; (apaixonado) in love

encabulado, -a [ēkabu'ladu, a] adj
shy

encadernação [ēkaderna'sãw] (pl
-ões) f (de livro) binding

encadernado, -a [ēkader'nadu, a]
adj bound; (de capa dura) hardback

encadernar [ēkader'nar] vt to bind

encaixar [ēkaj'ʃar] vt (colocar) to fit
in; (inserir) to insert ▷ vi to fit;
encaixe [ē'kajʃi] m (ato) fitting;
(ranhura) groove; (buraco) socket

encalço [ē'kawsu] m pursuit; **ir no
~ de** to pursue

encaminhar [ēkami'nar] vt to
direct; (no bom caminho) to put on
the right path; (processo) to set in
motion; **encaminhar-se** vr: **~-se
para/a** to set out for/to

encanar [ēka'nar] vt to channel

encantado, -a [ēkã'tadu, a] adj
delighted; (castelo etc) enchanted;
(fascinado): **~ (por alguém/algo)**
smitten (with sb/sth)

encantamento [ēkãta'mẽtu] m
(magia) spell; (fascinação) charm

encanto [ē'kãtu] m delight;
(fascinação) charm

encarar [ēka'rar] vt to face; (olhar)
to look at; (considerar) to consider

encargo [ē'kargu] m responsibility;
(ocupação) job, assignment;
(oneroso) burden

encarnação [ēkarna'sãw] (pl -ões)
f incarnation

encarnado, -a [ēkar'nadu, a] adj
red, scarlet

encarnar [ēkar'nar] vt to embody,
personify; (Teatro) to play

encarregado, -a [ēkahe'gadu, a]
adj: **~ de** in charge of ▷ m/f person
in charge ▷ m (de operários)
foreman

encarregar [ēkahe'gar] vt: **~
alguém de algo** to put sb in charge
of sth; **encarregar-se** vr: **~-se de
fazer** to undertake to do

encenação [ēsena'sãw] (pl -ões) f
(de peça) staging, putting on;
(produção) production; (fingimento)
playacting; (atitude fingida) put-on

encerar [ēse'rar] vt to wax

encerramento [ēseha'mẽtu] m
close, end

encerrar [ēse'har] vt to shut in,
lock up; (conter) to contain;
(concluir) to close

encharcar [ēʃar'kar] vt to flood;
(ensopar) to soak, drench;
encharcar-se vr to get soaked ou
drenched

enchente [ē'ʃẽtʃi] f flood

encher [ē'ʃer] vt to fill (up); (balão)
to blow up; (tempo) to fill, take up
▷ vi (col) to be annoying;
encher-se vr to fill up; **~-se (de)**
(col) to get fed up (with);
enchimento [ēʃi'mẽtu] m filling

enciclopédia [ēsiklo'pɛdʒa] f
encyclopedia, encyclopaedia (Brit)

encoberto, -a [ēko'bɛrtu, a] pp de
encobrir ▷ adj concealed; (tempo)
overcast

encobrir [ēko'brir] vt to conceal,
hide

encolher [ēko'ʎer] vt (pernas) to
draw up; (os ombros) to shrug;
(roupa) to shrink ▷ vi to shrink;
encolher-se vr (de frio) to huddle

encomenda [ēko'mēda] f order;
feito de ~ made to order,
custom-made; **encomendar**
[ēkomē'dar] vt: **encomendar
algo a alguém** to order sth from sb
encontrar [ēkõ'trar] vt to find;
(*inesperadamente*) to come across,
meet; (*dar com*) to bump into ▷ vi:
~ com to bump into; **encontrar-se**
vr (*achar-se*) to be; (*ter encontro*):
~-se (com alguém) to meet (sb)
encontro [ē'kõtru] m (*de pessoas*)
meeting; (*Mil*) encounter; **~
marcado** appointment; **ir/vir ao ~
de** to go/come and meet
encorajar [ēkora'ʒar] vt to
encourage
encosta [ē'kɔsta] f slope
encostar [ēkos'tar] vt (*cabeça*) to
put down; (*carro*) to park; (*pôr de
lado*) to put to one side; (*pôr junto*)
to put side by side; (*porta*) to leave
ajar ▷ vi to pull in; **encostar-se** vr:
~-se em to lean against; (*deitar-se*)
to lie down on; **~ em** to lean
against; **~ a mão em** (*bater*) to hit
encosto [ē'kostu] m (*arrimo*)
support; (*de cadeira*) back
encrencar [ēkrē'kar] (*col*) vt
(*situação*) to complicate; (*pessoa*) to
get into trouble ▷ vi to get
complicated; (*carro*) to break
down; **encrencar-se** vr to get
complicated; to get into trouble
encruzilhada [ēkruzi'ʎada] f
crossroads sg
encurtar [ēkur'tar] vt to shorten
endereçar [ēdere'sar] vt (*carta*) to
address; (*encaminhar*) to direct
endereço [ēde'resu] m address;
~ de e-mail email address; **~ web**
web address
endiabrado, -a [ēdʒia'bradu, a]
adj devilish; (*travesso*) mischievous

endinheirado, -a [ēdʒiɲej'radu, a]
adj rich, wealthy
endireitar [ēdʒirej'tar] vt (*objeto*)
to straighten; (*retificar*) to put
right; **endireitar-se** vr to
straighten up
endividar [ēdʒivi'dar] vt to put
into debt; **endividar-se** vr to run
into debt
endossar [ēdo'sar] vt to endorse
endurecer [ēdure'ser] vt, vi to
harden
energia [enɛr'ʒia] f energy, drive;
(*Tec*) power, energy; **~ solar** solar
power; **enérgico, -a** [e'nɛrʒiku, a]
adj energetic, vigorous
enervante [enɛr'vãtʃi] adj
annoying
enevoado, -a [ene'vwadu, a] adj
misty, hazy
enfado [ē'fadu] m annoyance
ênfase ['ēfazi] f emphasis, stress
enfastiado, -a [ēfas'tʃjadu, a] adj
bored
enfático, -a [ē'fatʃiku, a] adj
emphatic
enfatizar [ēfatʃi'zar] vt to
emphasize
enfeitar [ēfej'tar] vt to decorate;
enfeitar-se vr to dress up; **enfeite**
[ē'fejtʃi] m decoration
enfermeiro, -a [ēfɛr'mejru, a] m/f
nurse
enfermidade [ēfɛrmi'dadʒi] f
illness
enfermo, -a [ē'fɛrmu, a] adj ill,
sick ▷ m/f sick person, patient
enferrujar [ēfɛhu'ʒar] vt to rust,
corrode ▷ vi to go rusty
enfiar [ē'fjar] vt (*meter*) to put;
(*agulha*) to thread; (*vestir*) to slip
on; **enfiar-se** vr: **~-se em** to slip
into
enfim [ē'fĩ] adv finally, at last; (*em*

suma) in short; **até que ~!** at last!
enfoque [ē'fɔki] *m* approach
enforcar [ēfor'kar] *vt* to hang;
(trabalho, aulas) to skip;
enforcar-se *vr* to hang o.s.
enfraquecer [ēfrake'ser] *vt* to
weaken ▷ *vi* to grow weak
enfrentar [ēfrē'tar] *vt* to face;
(confrontar) to confront;
(problemas) to face up to
enfurecer [ēfure'ser] *vt* to
infuriate; **enfurecer-se** *vr* to get
furious
enganado, -a [ēga'nadu, a] *adj*
mistaken; *(traído)* deceived
enganar [ēga'nar] *vt* to deceive;
(desonrar) to seduce; *(cônjuge)* to be
unfaithful to; *(fome)* to stave off;
enganar-se *vr* to be wrong, be
mistaken; *(iludir-se)* to deceive o.s.
engano [ē'gãnu] *m* mistake;
(ilusão) deception; *(logro)* trick; **é ~**
(Tel) I've *(ou* you've) got the wrong
number
engarrafamento [ēgahafa'mẽtu]
m bottling; *(de trânsito)* traffic jam
engarrafar [ēgaha'far] *vt* to
bottle; *(trânsito)* to block
engasgar [ēgaz'gar] *vt* to choke
▷ *vi* to choke; *(máquina)* to
splutter; **engasgar-se** *vr* to choke
engatinhar [ēgatʃi'ɲar] *vi* to crawl
engenharia [ēʒeɲa'ria] *f*
engineering; **engenheiro, -a**
[ēʒe'ɲejru, a] *m/f* engineer
engenhoso, -a [ēʒe'ɲozu, ɔza] *adj*
clever, ingenious
engessar [ēʒe'sar] *vt* *(perna)* to put
in plaster; *(parede)* to plaster
englobar [ēglo'bar] *vt* to include
engodo [ē'godu] *m* bait
engolir [ēgo'lir] *vt* to swallow
engordar [ēgor'dar] *vt* to fatten
▷ *vi* to put on weight

engraçado, -a [ēgra'sadu, a] *adj*
funny, amusing
engradado [ēgra'dadu] *m* crate
engraxador [ēgraʃa'dor] *(PT)* *m*
shoe shiner
engraxar [ēgra'ʃar] *vt* to polish
engrenagem [ēgre'naʒē] *(pl* **-ns)** *f*
(Auto) gear
engrenar [ēgre'nar] *vt* to put into
gear; *(fig: conversa)* to strike up ▷ *vi*:
~ com alguém to get on with sb
engrossar [ēgro'sar] *vt* *(sopa)* to
thicken; *(aumentar)* to swell; *(voz)*
to raise ▷ *vi* to thicken; to swell; to
rise; *(col: pessoa, conversa)* to turn
nasty
enguia [ē'gia] *f* eel
enguiçar [ēgi'sar] *vi* *(máquina)* to
break down ▷ *vt* to cause to break
down; **enguiço** [ē'gisu] *m* snag;
(desarranjo) breakdown
enigma [e'nigma] *m* enigma;
(mistério) mystery
enjeitado, -a [ēʒej'tadu, a] *m/f*
foundling, waif
enjoado, -a [ē'ʒwadu, a] *adj* sick;
(enfastiado) bored; *(enfadonho)*
boring; *(mal-humorado)* in a bad
mood
enjoar [ē'ʒwar] *vt* to make sick;
(enfastiar) to bore ▷ *vi* *(pessoa)* to be
sick; *(remédio, comida)* to cause
nausea; **enjoar-se** *vr*: **~-se de** to
get sick of
enjoo [ē'ʒou] *m* sickness; *(em carro)*
travel sickness; *(em navio)*
seasickness; *(aborrecimento)*
boredom
enlatado, -a [ēla'tadu, a] *adj*
tinned *(Brit)*, canned ▷ *m* *(pej: filme)*
foreign import; **enlatados** *mpl*
(comida) tinned *(Brit)* *ou* canned
foods
enlouquecer [ēloke'ser] *vt* to drive

mad ▷ *vi* to go mad

enlutado, -a [ēlu'tadu, a] *adj* in mourning

enorme [e'nɔrmi] *adj* enormous, huge; **enormidade** [enormi'dadʒi] *f* enormity; **uma enormidade (de)** (*col*) a hell of a lot (of)

enquanto [ē'kwãtu] *conj* while; (*considerado como*) as; **~ isso** meanwhile; **por ~** for the time being; **~ ele não vem** until he comes; **~ que** whereas

enquete [ē'kɛtʃi] *f* survey

enraivecer [ēhajve'ser] *vt* to enrage

enredo [ē'hedu] *m* (*de uma obra*) plot; (*intriga*) intrigue

enriquecer [ēhike'ser] *vt* to make rich; (*fig*) to enrich ▷ *vi* to get rich; **enriquecer-se** *vr* to get rich

enrolar [ēho'lar] *vt* to roll up; (*agasalhar*) to wrap up; (*col: enganar*) to con ▷ *vi* (*col*) to waffle; **enrolar-se** *vr* to roll up; to wrap up; (*col: confundir-se*) to get mixed *ou* muddled up

enroscar [ēhos'kar] *vt* (*torcer*) to twist, wind (round); **enroscar-se** *vr* to coil up

enrugar [ēhu'gar] *vt* (*pele*) to wrinkle; (*testa*) to furrow; (*tecido*) to crease ▷ *vi* (*pele, mãos*) to go wrinkly; (*pessoa*) to get wrinkles

ensaiar [ēsa'jar] *vt* to test, try out; (*treinar*) to practise (*Brit*), practice (*US*); (*Teatro*) to rehearse

ensaio [ē'saju] *m* test; (*tentativa*) attempt; (*treino*) practice; (*Teatro*) rehearsal; (*literário*) essay

enseada [ē'sjada] *f* inlet, cove; (*baía*) bay

ensejo [ē'seʒu] *m* chance, opportunity

ensinamento [ēsina'mētu] *m* teaching; (*exemplo*) lesson

ensinar [ēsi'nar] *vt, vi* to teach

ensino [ē'sinu] *m* teaching, tuition; (*educação*) education; **~ fundamental** primary education; **~ médio** secondary education

ensopado, -a [ēso'padu, a] *adj* soaked ▷ *m* stew

ensurdecer [ēsurde'ser] *vt* to deafen ▷ *vi* to go deaf

entalar [ēta'lar] *vt* to wedge, jam; (*encher*): **ela me entalou de comida** she stuffed me full of food

entalhar [ēta'ʎar] *vt* to carve; **entalhe** [ē'taʎi] *m* groove, notch

entanto [ē'tãtu] *adv*: **no ~** yet, however

então [ē'tãw] *adv* then; **até ~** up to that time; **desde ~** ever since; **e ~?** well then?; **para ~** so that; **pois ~** in that case; **~, você vai ou não?** so, are you going or not?

entardecer [ētarde'ser] *vi* to get late ▷ *m* sunset

ente [ˈētʃi] *m* being

enteado, -a [ē'tʃjadu, a] *m/f* stepson/stepdaughter

entediar [ēte'dʒjar] *vt* to bore; **entediar-se** *vr* to get bored

entender [ētē'der] *vt* to understand; (*pensar*) to think; (*ouvir*) to hear; **entender-se** *vr* to understand one another; **dar a ~** to imply; **no meu ~** in my opinion; **~ de música** to know about music; **~ de fazer** to decide to do; **~-se por** to be meant by; **~-se com alguém** to get along with sb; (*dialogar*) to sort things out with sb

entendimento [ētēdʒi'mētu] *m* understanding

enterrar [ēte'har] *vt* to bury; (*faca*) to plunge; (*lever à ruina*) to ruin; (*assunto*) to close

enterro [ē'teɦu] *m* burial; *(funeral)* funeral

entidade [ētʃi'dadʒi] *f (ser)* being; *(corporação)* body; *(coisa que existe)* entity

entornar [ētor'nar] *vt* to spill; *(fig: copo)* to drink ▷ *vi* to drink a lot

entorpecente [ētorpe'sētʃi] *m* narcotic

entorpecimento [ētorpesi'mētu] *m* numbness; *(torpor)* lethargy

entorse [ē'tɔrsi] *f* sprain

entortar [ētor'tar] *vt (curvar)* to bend; *(empenar)* to warp; **~ os olhos** to squint

entrada [ē'trada] *f (ato)* entry; *(lugar)* entrance; *(Tec)* inlet; *(de casa)* doorway; *(começo)* beginning; *(bilhete)* ticket; *(Culin)* starter, entrée; *(Comput)* input; *(pagamento inicial)* down payment; *(corredor de casa)* hall; **entradas** *fpl (no cabelo)* receding hairline; **~ gratuita** admission free; **"~ proibida"** "no entry", "no admittance"; **meia ~** half-price ticket

entra e sai ['ētrai'saj] *m* comings and goings *pl*

entranhado, -a [ētra'ɲadu, a] *adj* deep-rooted

entranhas [ē'traɲas] *fpl* bowels, entrails; *(sentimentos)* feelings; *(centro)* heart *sg*

entrar [ē'trar] *vi* to go *(ou* come) in, enter; **~ com** *(Comput: dados etc)* to enter; **eu entrei com £100** I put in £100; **~ de férias/licença** to start one's holiday *(Brit) ou* vacation *(US)*/leave; **~ em** to go *(ou* come) into, enter; *(assunto)* to get onto; *(comida, bebida)* to start in on

entrave [ē'travi] *m (fig)* impediment

entre ['ētri] *prep (dois)* between; *(mais de dois)* among(st); **~ si** amongst themselves

entreaberto, -a [ētrja'bɛrtu, a] *adj* half-open; *(porta)* ajar

entrega [ē'trɛga] *f (de mercadorias)* delivery; *(a alguém)* handing over; *(rendição)* surrender; **~ rápida** special delivery

entregar [ētre'gar] *vt* to hand over; *(mercadorias)* to deliver; *(confiar)* to entrust; *(devolver)* to return; **entregar-se** *vr (render-se)* to give o.s. up; *(dedicar-se)* to devote o.s.

entregue [ē'trɛgi] *pp de* **entregar**

entrelinha [ētre'liɲa] *f* line space; **ler nas ~s** to read between the lines

entreolhar-se [ētrio'ʎarsi] *vr* to exchange glances

entretanto [ētri'tãtu] *conj* however

entretenimento [ētriteni'mētu] *m* entertainment; *(distração)* pastime

entreter [ētri'ter] *(irreg: como* **ter**) *vt* to entertain, amuse; *(ocupar)* to occupy; *(manter)* to keep up; *(esperanças)* to cherish; **entreter-se** *vr* to amuse o.s.; to occupy o.s.

entrevista [ētre'vista] *f* interview; **~ coletiva (à imprensa)** press conference; **entrevistar** [ētrevis'tar] *vt* to interview; **entrevistar-se** *vr* to have an interview

entristecer [ētriste'ser] *vt* to sadden, grieve ▷ *vi* to feel sad; **entristecer-se** *vr* to feel sad

entroncamento [ētrõka'mētu] *m* junction

entrudo [ē'trudu] *(PT) m* carnival; *(Rel)* Shrovetide

entulhar [ētu'ʎar] *vt* to cram full;

(*suj: multidão*) to pack

entupido, -a [ẽtu'pidu, a] *adj* blocked; **estar ~** (*col: congestionado*) to have a blocked-up nose; (*de comida*) to be fit to burst, be full up

entupimento [ẽtupi'mẽtu] *m* blockage

entupir [ẽtu'pir] *vt* to block, clog; **entupir-se** *vr* to become blocked; (*de comida*) to stuff o.s.

entusiasmar [ẽtuzjaz'mar] *vt* to fill with enthusiasm; (*animar*) to excite; **entusiasmar-se** *vr* to get excited

entusiasmo [ẽtu'zjazmu] *m* enthusiasm; (*júbilo*) excitement

entusiasta [ẽtu'zjasta] *adj* enthusiastic ▷ *m/f* enthusiast

enumerar [enume'rar] *vt* to enumerate; (*com números*) to number

envelhecer [ẽveʎe'ser] *vt* to age ▷ *vi* to grow old, age

envelope [ẽve'lɔpi] *m* envelope

envenenamento [ẽvenena'mẽtu] *m* poisoning; **~ do sangue** blood poisoning

envenenar [ẽvene'nar] *vt* to poison; (*fig*) to corrupt; (: *declaração, palavras*) to distort, twist; (*tornar amargo*) to sour ▷ *vi* to be poisonous; **envenenar-se** *vr* to poison o.s.

envergonhado, -a [ẽvergo'ɲadu, a] *adj* ashamed; (*tímido*) shy

envergonhar [ẽvergo'ɲar] *vt* to shame; (*degradar*) to disgrace; **envergonhar-se** *vr* to be ashamed

enviado, -a [ẽ'vjadu, a] *m/f* envoy, messenger

enviar [ẽ'vjar] *vt* to send

envio [ẽ'viu] *m* sending; (*expedição*) dispatch; (*remessa*) remittance; (*de mercadorias*) consignment

enviuvar [ẽvju'var] *vi* to be widowed

envolver [ẽvow'ver] *vt* to wrap (up); (*cobrir*) to cover; (*comprometer, acarretar*) to involve; (*nos braços*) to embrace; **envolver-se** *vr* (*intrometer-se*) to become involved; (*cobrir-se*) to wrap o.s. up; **envolvimento** [ẽvowvi'mẽtu] *m* involvement

enxada [ẽ'ʃada] *f* hoe

enxaguar [ẽʃa'gwar] *vt* to rinse

enxame [ẽ'ʃami] *m* swarm

enxaqueca [ẽʃa'keka] *f* migraine

enxergar [ẽʃer'gar] *vt* (*avistar*) to catch sight of; (*divisar*) to make out; (*notar*) to observe, see

enxofre [ẽ'ʃofri] *m* sulphur (*Brit*), sulfur (*US*)

enxotar [ẽʃo'tar] *vt* to drive out

enxoval [ẽʃo'vaw] (*pl* **-ais**) *m* (*de noiva*) trousseau; (*de recém-nascido*) layette

enxugar [ẽʃu'gar] *vt* to dry; (*fig: texto*) to tidy up

enxurrada [ẽʃu'hada] *f* (*de água*) torrent; (*fig*) spate

enxuto, -a [ẽ'ʃutu, a] *adj* dry; (*corpo*) shapely; (*bonito*) good-looking

épico, -a ['ɛpiku, a] *adj* epic ▷ *m* epic poet

epidemia [epide'mia] *f* epidemic

epilepsia [epile'psia] *f* epilepsy

episódio [epi'zɔdʒu] *m* episode

época ['ɛpoka] *f* time, period; (*da história*) age, epoch; **naquela ~** at that time; **fazer ~** to be epoch-making

equação [ekwa'sãw] (*pl* **-ões**) *f* equation

Equador [ekwa'dor] *m*: **o ~** Ecuador

equador [ekwa'dor] *m* equator

equilibrar [ekili'brar] *vt* to

balance; **equilibrar-se** vr to balance; **equilíbrio** [eki'librju] m balance

equipa [e'kipa] (PT) f team

equipamento [ekipa'mẽtu] m equipment, kit

equipar [eki'par] vt (navio) to fit out; (prover) to equip

equipe [e'kipi] (BR) f team

equitação [ekita'sãw] f (ato) riding; (arte) horsemanship

equivalente [ekiva'lẽtʃi] adj, m equivalent

equivaler [ekiva'ler] vi: **~ a** to be the same as, equal

equivocado, -a [ekivo'kadu, a] adj mistaken, wrong

equivocar-se [ekivo'karsi] vr to make a mistake, be wrong

era¹ ['ɛra] f era, age

era² vb ver **ser**

erário [e'rarju] m exchequer

ereto, -a [e'rɛtu, a] adj upright, erect

erguer [er'ger] vt to raise, lift; (edificar) to build, erect; **erguer-se** vr to rise; (pessoa) to stand up

eriçar [eri'sar] vt: **~ o cabelo de alguém** to make sb's hair stand on end; **eriçar-se** vr to bristle; (cabelos) to stand on end

erigir [eri'ʒir] vt to erect

erosão [ero'zãw] f erosion

erótico, -a [e'rɔtʃiku, a] adj erotic

errado, -a [e'hadu, a] adj wrong; **dar ~** to go wrong

errar [e'har] vt (alvo) to miss; (conta) to get wrong ▷ vi to wander, roam; (enganar-se) to be wrong, make a mistake; **~ o caminho** to lose one's way

erro ['ehu] m mistake; **salvo ~** unless I am mistaken; **~ de imprensa** misprint

errôneo, -a [e'honju, a] adj wrong, mistaken; (falso) false, untrue

erva ['ɛrva] f herb; **~ daninha** weed; (col: dinheiro) dosh; (: maconha) dope

erva-mate (pl **ervas-mate(s)**) f mate

ervilha [er'viʎa] f pea

esbanjar [izbã'ʒar] vt to squander, waste

esbarrar [izba'har] vi: **~ em** to bump into; (obstáculo, problema) to come up against

esbelto, -a [iz'bɛwtu, a] adj slim, slender

esboçar [izbo'sar] vt to sketch; (delinear) to outline; (plano) to draw up; **esboço** [iz'bosu] m sketch; (primeira versão) draft; (fig: resumo) outline

esbofetear [izbofe'tʃjar] vt to slap, hit

esburacar [izbura'kar] vt to make holes (ou a hole) in

esc (PT) abr = **escudo**

escabroso, -a [iska'brozu, ɔza] adj (difícil) tough; (indecoroso) indecent

escada [is'kada] f (dentro da casa) staircase, stairs pl; (fora da casa) steps pl; (de mão) ladder; **~ de incêndio** fire escape; **~ rolante** escalator; **escadaria** [iskada'ria] f staircase

escala [is'kala] f scale; (Náut) port of call; (parada) stop; **fazer ~ em** to call at; **sem ~** non-stop

escalada [iska'lada] f (de guerra) escalation

escalão [iska'lãw] (pl **-ões**) m step; (Mil) echelon

escalar [iska'lar] vt (montanha) to climb; (muro) to scale; (designar) to select

escaldar [iskaw'dar] vt to scald;

escaldar-se vr to scald o.s.

escalões [ɛskaˈlõjs] mpl de **escalão**

escama [isˈkama] f (de peixe) scale; (de pele) flake

escancarado, -a [iskãkaˈradu, a] adj wide open

escandalizar [iskãdaliˈzar] vt to shock; **escandalizar-se** vr to be shocked; (ofender-se) to be offended

escândalo [isˈkãdalu] m scandal; (indignação) outrage; **fazer** ou **dar um ~** to make a scene; **escandaloso, -a** [iskãdaˈlozu, ɔza] adj shocking, scandalous

Escandinávia [iskãdʒiˈnavja] f: **a ~** Scandinavia; **escandinavo, -a** [iskãdʒiˈnavu, a] adj, m/f Scandinavian

escangalhar [iskãgaˈʎar] vt to break, smash (up); **escangalhar-se** vr: **~-se de rir** to split one's sides laughing

escapar [iskaˈpar] vi: **~ a** ou **de** to escape from; (fugir) to run away from; **escapar-se** vr to run away, flee; **deixar ~** (uma oportunidade) to miss; (palavras) to blurt out; **~ de boa** (col) to have a close shave

escapatória [iskapaˈtɔrja] f way out; (desculpa) excuse

escape [isˈkapi] m (de gás) leak; (Auto) exhaust

escapulir [iskapuˈlir] vi: **~ (de)** to get away (from); (suj: coisa) to slip (from)

escarrar [iskaˈhar] vt to spit, cough up ▷ vi to spit

escarro [isˈkahu] m phlegm, spit

escassear [iskaˈsjar] vt to skimp on ▷ vi to become scarce

escassez [iskaˈsez] f (falta) shortage

escavar [iskaˈvar] vt to excavate

esclarecer [isklareˈser] vt (situação) to explain; (mistério) to clear up, explain; **esclarecer-se** vr: **~-se (sobre algo)** to find out (about sth); **esclarecimento** [isklaresiˈmẽtu] m explanation; (informação) information

escoadouro [iskoaˈdoru] m drain; (cano) drainpipe

escocês, -esa [iskoˈses, seza] adj Scottish, Scots ▷ m/f Scot, Scotsman/woman

Escócia [isˈkɔsja] f Scotland

escola [isˈkɔla] f school; **~ de línguas** language school; **~ naval** naval college; **~ primária/ secundária** primary (Brit) ou elementary (US) /secondary (Brit) ou high (US) school; **~ particular/ pública** private/state (Brit) ou public (US) school; **~ superior** college

Escola de samba see note

● **ESCOLA DE SAMBA**
●
● **Escolas de samba** are musical
● and recreational associations
● made up, among others, of
● samba dancers, percussionists
● and carnival dancers. Although
● they exist throughout Brazil, the
● most famous schools are in Rio
● de Janeiro. The schools in Rio
● rehearse all year long for the
● **carnaval**, when they parade
● along the Sambódromo, a
● purpose-built avenue flanked by
● stands for spectators, and
● compete for the samba school
● championship. Characterised by
● their extravagance, the biggest
● schools have up to 4,000
● members and are one of Brazil's
● major tourist attractions.

escolar [isko'lar] *adj* school *atr*
▷ *m/f* schoolboy/girl

escolha [is'koʎa] *f* choice

escolher [isko'ʎer] *vt* to choose,
select

escolho [is'koʎu] *m* (*recife*) reef;
(*rocha*) rock

escolta [is'kɔwta] *f* escort;
escoltar [iskow'tar] *vt* to escort

escombros [is'kõbrus] *mpl* ruins,
debris *sg*

esconde-esconde [iskõdʒis'kõdʒi]
m hide-and-seek

esconder [iskõ'der] *vt* to hide,
conceal; **esconder-se** *vr* to hide

escondidas [iskõ'dʒidas] *fpl*: **às ~**
secretly

escopo [is'kopu] *m* aim, purpose

escorar [isko'rar] *vt* to prop (up);
(*amparar*) to support; (*esperar de
espreita*) to lie in wait for ▷ *vi* to lie
in wait; **escorar-se** *vr*: **~-se em**
(*fundamentar-se*) to go by;
(*amparar-se*) to live off

escore [is'kɔri] *m* score

escoriação [iskorja'sãw] (*pl* **-ões**) *f*
abrasion, scratch

escorpião [iskorpi'ãw] (*pl* **-ões**) *m*
scorpion; **E~** (*Astrologia*) Scorpio

escorrega [isko'hɛga] *f* slide;
escorregadela [iskohega'dɛla] *f*
slip; **escorregadio, -a**
[iskohega'dʒiu, a] *adj* slippery;
escorregão [iskohe'gãw] (*pl* **-ões**)
m slip; (*fig*) slip(-up); **escorregar**
[iskohe'gar] *vi* to slip; (*errar*) to slip
up

escorrer [isko'her] *vt* to drain (off);
(*verter*) to pour out ▷ *vi* (*pingar*) to
drip; (*correr em fio*) to trickle

escoteiro [isko'tejru] *m* scout

escova [is'kova] *f* brush; (*penteado*)
blow-dry; **~ de dentes** toothbrush;
~ progressiva keratin

straightening; **escovar** [isko'var]
vt to brush

escravatura [iskrava'tura] *f*
(*tráfico*) slave trade; (*escravidão*)
slavery

escravidão [iskravi'dãw] *f* slavery

escravizar [iskravi'zar] *vt* to
enslave; (*cativar*) to captivate

escravo, -a [is'kravu, a] *adj*
captive ▷ *m/f* slave

escrever [iskre'ver] *vt, vi* to write;
escrever-se *vr* to write to each
other; **~ à máquina** to type

escrita [es'krita] *f* writing; (*pessoal*)
handwriting

escrito, -a [es'kritu, a] *pp de*
escrever ▷ *adj* written ▷ *m* piece
of writing; **~ à mão** handwritten;
dar por ~ to put in writing

escritor, a [iskri'tor(a)] *m/f* writer;
(*autor*) author

escritório [iskri'tɔrju] *m* office;
(*em casa*) study

escritura [iskri'tura] *f* (*Jur*) deed;
(*na compra de imóveis*) ≈ exchange of
contracts; **as Sagradas E~s** the
Scriptures

escrivã [iskri'vã] *f de* **escrivão**

escrivaninha [iskriva'niɲa] *f*
writing desk

escrivão, -vã [iskri'vãw, vã] (*pl*
-ões/-s) *m/f* registrar, recorder

escrupuloso, -a [iskrupu'lozu,
ɔza] *adj* scrupulous; (*cuidadoso*)
careful

escudo [is'kudu] *m* shield; (*moeda*)
escudo

esculhambado, -a [iskuʎã'badu,
a] (*col!*) *adj* shabby, slovenly;
(*estragado*) knackered

esculhambar [iskuʎã'bar] (*col!*) *vt*
to mess up, fuck up (!); **~ alguém**
(*criticar*) to give sb stick;
(*descompor*) to give sb a bollocking (!)

esculpir [iskuw'pir] *vt* to carve, sculpt; (*gravar*) to engrave

escultor, a [iskuw'tor(a)] *m/f* sculptor

escultura [iskuw'tura] *f* sculpture

escuras [is'kuras] *fpl*: **às ~** in the dark

escurecer [iskure'ser] *vt* to darken ▷ *vi* to get dark; **ao ~** at dusk

escuridão [iskuri'dãw] *f* (*trevas*) darkness

escuro, -a [is'kuru, a] *adj* dark; (*dia*) overcast; (*pessoa*) swarthy ▷ *m* dark

escuso, -a [is'kuzu, a] *adj* shady

escuta [is'kuta] *f* listening; **à ~** listening out; **ficar na ~** to stand by

escutar [isku'tar] *vt* to listen to; (*sem prestar atenção*) to hear ▷ *vi* to listen; to hear

esfacelar [isfase'lar] *vt* to destroy

esfaquear [isfaki'ar] *vt* to stab

esfarrapado, -a [isfaha'padu, a] *adj* (*roupa*) ragged, tattered; (*desculpa*) lame

esfera [is'fɛra] *f* sphere; (*globo*) globe; (*Tip*) golfball

esfolar [isfo'lar] *vt* to skin; (*arranhar*) to graze; (*cobrar demais a*) to overcharge, fleece

esfomeado, -a [isfo'mjadu, a] *adj* famished, starving

esforçado, -a [isfor'sadu, a] *adj* committed, dedicated

esforçar-se [isfor'sarsi] *vr*: **~ para** to try hard to, strive to

esforço [is'forsu] *m* effort

esfregar [isfre'gar] *vt* to rub; (*com água*) to scrub

esfriar [is'frjar] *vt* to cool, chill ▷ *vi* to get cold; (*fig*) to cool off

esganar [izga'nar] *vt* to strangle, choke

esgotado, -a [izgo'tadu, a] *adj* exhausted; (*consumido*) used up; (*livros*) out of print; **os ingressos estão ~s** the tickets are sold out

esgotamento [izgota'mẽtu] *m* exhaustion

esgotar [izgo'tar] *vt* to drain, empty; (*recursos*) to use up; (*pessoa, assunto*) to exhaust; **esgotar-se** *vr* to become exhausted; (*mercadorias, edição*) to be sold out; (*recursos*) to run out

esgoto [iz'gotu] *m* drain; (*público*) sewer

esgrima [iz'grima] *f* (*Esporte*) fencing

esgueirar-se [izgej'rarsi] *vr* to slip away, sneak off

esguelha [iz'geʎa] *f* slant; **olhar alguém de ~** to look at sb out of the corner of one's eye

esguio, -a [ez'giu, a] *adj* slender

esmagador, a [izmaga'dor(a)] *adj* crushing; (*provas*) irrefutable; (*maioria*) overwhelming

esmalte [iz'mawtʃi] *m* enamel; (*de unhas*) nail polish

esmeralda [izme'rawda] *f* emerald

esmerar-se [izme'rarsi] *vr*: **~ em** to take great care to

esmigalhar [izmiga'ʎar] *vt* to crumble; (*despedaçar*) to shatter; (*esmagar*) to crush; **esmigalhar-se** *vr* to crumble; (*vaso*) to smash, shatter

esmo ['ezmu] *m*: **a ~** at random; **falar a ~** to prattle

esmola [iz'mɔla] *f* alms *pl*; **pedir ~s** to beg

esmurrar [izmu'har] *vt* to punch

esoterismo [ezote'rizmu] *m* New Age

espacial [ispa'sjaw] (*pl* **-ais**) *adj* space *atr*; **nave ~** spaceship

espaço [is'pasu] *m* space; (*tempo*)

period; **~ para 3 pessoas** room for 3 people; **a ~s** from time to time; **espaçoso, -a** [ispa'sozu, ɔza] *adj* spacious, roomy

espada [is'pada] *f* sword; **espadas** *fpl* (*Cartas*) spades

espadarte [ispa'dartʃi] *m* swordfish

espairecer [ispajre'ser] *vt* to amuse, entertain ▷ *vi* to relax; **espairecer-se** *vr* to relax

espaldar [ispaw'dar] *m* (chair) back

espalhafato [ispaʎa'fatu] *m* din, commotion

espalhar [ispa'ʎar] *vt* to scatter; (*boato, medo*) to spread; (*luz*) to shed; **espalhar-se** *vr* to spread; (*refestelar-se*) to lounge

espanador [ispana'dor] *m* duster

espancar [ispã'kar] *vt* to beat up

Espanha [is'paɲa] *f*: **a ~** Spain; **espanhol, a** [ispa'ɲɔw, ɔla] (*pl* **-óis/-s**) *adj* Spanish ▷ *m/f* Spaniard ▷ *m* (*Ling*) Spanish; **os espanhóis** *mpl* the Spanish

espantado, -a [ispã'tadu, a] *adj* astonished

espantalho [ispã'taʎu] *m* scarecrow

espantar [ispã'tar] *vt* to frighten; (*admirar*) to amaze, astonish; (*afugentar*) to frighten away ▷ *vi* to be amazing; **espantar-se** *vr* to be amazed; (*assustar-se*) to be frightened

espanto [is'pãtu] *m* fright, fear; (*admiração*) amazement; **espantoso, -a** [ispã'tozu, ɔza] *adj* amazing

esparadrapo [ispara'drapu] *m* (sticking) plaster (*Brit*), bandaid® (*US*)

esparramar [ispaha'mar] *vt* to splash; (*espalhar*) to scatter

esparso, -a [is'parsu, a] *adj* scattered; (*solto*) loose

espasmo [is'pazmu] *m* spasm, convulsion

espatifar [ispatʃi'far] *vt* to smash; **espatifar-se** *vr* to smash; (*avião*) to crash

especial [ispe'sjaw] (*pl* **-ais**) *adj* special; **em ~** especially; **especialidade** [ispesjali'dadʒi] *f* speciality (*Brit*), specialty (*US*); (*ramo de atividades*) specialization; **especialista** [ispesja'lista] *m/f* specialist; (*perito*) expert; **especializar-se** [ispesjali'zarsi] *vr*: **especializar-se (em)** to specialize (in)

espécie [is'pɛsi] *f* (*Bio*) species; (*tipo*) sort, kind; **causar ~** to be surprising; **pagar em ~** to pay in cash

especificar [ispesifi'kar] *vt* to specify; **específico, -a** [ispe'sifiku, a] *adj* specific

espécime [is'pɛsimi] *m* specimen

espécimen [is'pɛsimẽ] (*pl* **espécimens**) *m* = **espécime**

espectador, a [ispekta'dor(a)] *m/f* onlooker; (*TV*) viewer; (*Esporte*) spectator; (*Teatro*) member of the audience; **espectadores** *mpl* audience *sg*

especular [ispeku'lar] *vi*: **~ (sobre)** to speculate (on)

espelho [is'peʎu] *m* mirror; (*fig*) model; **~ retrovisor** (*Auto*) rear-view mirror

espera [is'pera] *f* (*demora*) wait; (*expectativa*) expectation; **à ~ de** waiting for; **à minha ~** waiting for me

esperança [ispe'rãsa] *f* hope; (*expectativa*) expectation; **dar ~s a alguém** to get sb's hopes up;

esperançoso, -a [isperã'sozu, ɔza] *adj* hopeful

esperar [ispe'rar] *vt* to wait for; (*desejar*) to hope for; (*contar com, bebê*) to expect ▷ *vi* to wait; to hope; to expect

esperma [is'pɛrma] *m* sperm

espertalhão, -lhona [isperta'ʎãw, ʎona] (*pl* **-ões/-s**) *adj* crafty, shrewd

esperteza [isper'teza] *f* cleverness; (*astúcia*) cunning

esperto, -a [is'pɛrtu, a] *adj* clever; (*espertalhão*) crafty

espetacular [ispetaku'lar] *adj* spectacular

espetáculo [ispe'takulu] *m* (*Teatro*) show; (*vista*) sight; (*cena ridícula*) spectacle; **dar ~** to make a spectacle of o.s.

espetar [ispe'tar] *vt* (*carne*) to put on a spit; (*cravar*) to stick; **espetar-se** *vr* to prick o.s.; **~ algo em algo** to pin sth to sth

espeto [is'petu] *m* spit; (*pau*) pointed stick; **ser um ~** (*ser difícil*) to be awkward

espevitado, -a [ispevi'tadu, a] *adj* (*fig: vivo*) lively

espiã [is'pjã] *f de* **espião**

espiada [is'pjada] *f*: **dar uma ~** to have a look

espião, -piã [is'pjãw, 'pjã] (*pl* -**ões/-s**) *m/f* spy

espiar [is'pjar] *vt* to spy on; (*uma ocasião*) to watch out for; (*olhar*) to watch ▷ *vi* to spy; (*olhar*) to peer

espiga [is'piga] *f* (*de milho*) ear

espinafre [ispi'nafri] *m* spinach

espingarda [ispĩ'garda] *f* shotgun, rifle

espinha [is'piɲa] *f* (*de peixe*) bone; (*na pele*) spot, zit (*col*); (*coluna vertebral*) spine

espinho [is'piɲu] *m* thorn; (*de animal*) spine; (*fig: dificuldade*) snag; **espinhoso, -a** [ispi'ɲozu, ɔza] *adj* (*planta*) prickly, thorny; (*fig: difícil*) difficult; (: *problema*) thorny

espiões [is'pjõjs] *mpl de* **espião**

espionar [ispjo'nar] *vt* to spy on ▷ *vi* to spy, snoop

espírito [is'piritu] *m* spirit; (*pensamento*) mind; **~ esportivo** sense of humo(u)r; **E~ Santo** Holy Spirit

espiritual [ispiri'twaw] (*pl* -**ais**) *adj* spiritual

espirituoso, -a [ispiri'twozu, ɔza] *adj* witty

espirrar [ispi'har] *vi* to sneeze; (*jorrar*) to spurt out ▷ *vt* (*água*) to spurt; **espirro** [is'pihu] *m* sneeze

esplêndido, -a [is'plẽdʒidu, a] *adj* splendid

esplendor [isplẽ'dor] *m* splendour (*Brit*), splendor (*US*)

esponja [is'põʒa] *f* sponge

espontâneo, -a [ispõ'tanju, a] *adj* spontaneous; (*pessoa*) straightforward

esporádico, -a [ispo'radʒiku, a] *adj* sporadic

esporte [is'pɔrtʃi] (*BR*) *m* sport; **esportista** [ispor'tʃista] *adj* sporting ▷ *m/f* sportsman/woman; **esportivo, -a** [ispor'tʃivu, a] *adj* sporting

esposa [is'poza] *f* wife

esposo [is'pozu] *m* husband

espreguiçadeira [ispregisa'dejra] *f* deck chair; (*com lugar para as pernas*) lounger

espreguiçar-se [ispregi'sarsi] *vr* to stretch

espreita [is'prejta] *f*: **ficar à ~** to keep watch

espreitar [isprej'tar] *vt* to spy on;

(*observar*) to observe, watch

espremer [ispre'mer] *vt* (*fruta*) to squeeze; (*roupa molhada*) to wring out; (*pessoas*) to squash; **espremer-se** *vr* (*multidão*) to be squashed together; (*uma pessoa*) to squash up

espuma [is'puma] *f* foam; (*de cerveja*) froth, head; (*de sabão*) lather; (*de ondas*) surf; **~ de borracha** foam rubber; **espumante** [ispu'mãtʃi] *adj* frothy, foamy; (*vinho*) sparkling

esq. *abr* (= *esquerdo*) l.; = **esquina**

esquadra [is'kwadra] *f* (*Náut*) fleet; (*PT: da polícia*) police station

esquadrão [iskwa'drãw] (*pl* **-ões**) *m* squadron

esquadrilha [iskwa'driʎa] *f* squadron

esquadrões [iskwa'drõjs] *mpl de* **esquadrão**

esquartejar [iskwarte'ʒar] *vt* to quarter

esquecer [iske'ser] *vt, vi* to forget; **esquecer-se** *vr*: **~-se de** to forget; **esquecido, -a** [iske'sidu, a] *adj* forgotten; (*pessoa*) forgetful

esqueleto [iske'letu] *m* skeleton; (*arcabouço*) framework

esquema [is'kema] *m* outline; (*plano*) scheme; (*diagrama*) diagram, plan

esquentar [iskẽ'tar] *vt* to heat (up), warm (up); (*fig: irritar*) to annoy ▷ *vi* to warm up; (*casaco*) to be warm; **esquentar-se** *vr* to get annoyed

esquerda [is'kerda] *f* (*tb: Pol*) left; **à ~** on the left

esquerdista [isker'dʃista] *adj* left-wing ▷ *m/f* left-winger

esquerdo, -a [is'kerdu, a] *adj* left

esqui [is'ki] *m* (*patim*) ski; (*esporte*) skiing; **~ aquático** water skiing; **fazer ~** to go skiing; **esquiar** [is'kjar] *vi* to ski

esquilo [is'kilu] *m* squirrel

esquina [is'kina] *f* corner

esquisito, -a [iski'zitu, a] *adj* strange, odd

esquivar-se [iski'varsi] *vr*: **~ de** to escape from, get away from; (*deveres*) to get out of

esquivo, -a [is'kivu, a] *adj* aloof, standoffish

essa ['ɛsa] *pron*: **~ é/foi boa** that is/ was a good one; **~ não, sem ~** come off it!; **vamos n~** let's go!; **ainda mais ~!** that's all I need!; **corta ~!** cut it out!; **por ~s e outras** for these and other reasons; **~ de fazer ...** this business of doing ...

esse ['esi] *adj* (*sg*) that; (*pl*) those; (*BR: este: sg*) this; (*: pl*) these ▷ *pron* (*sg*) that one; (*pl*) those; (*BR: este: sg*) this one; (*: pl*) these

essência [e'sẽsja] *f* essence; **essencial** [esẽ'sjaw] (*pl* **-ais**) *adj* essential; (*principal*) main ▷ *m*: **o essencial** the main thing

esta ['ɛsta] *f de* **este**

estabelecer [istabele'ser] *vt* to establish; (*fundar*) to set up

estabelecimento [istabelesi'mẽtu] *m* establishment; (*casa comercial*) business

estábulo [is'tabulu] *m* cow-shed

estaca [is'taka] *f* post, stake; (*de barraca*) peg

estação [ista'sãw] (*pl* **-ões**) *f* station; (*do ano*) season; **~ de águas** spa; **~ balneária** seaside resort; **~ emissora** broadcasting station

estacionamento [istasjona'mẽtu] *m* (*ato*) parking; (*lugar*) car park

(Brit), parking lot (US)

estacionar [istasjo'nar] vt to park
▷ vi to park; (não mover) to remain
stationary

estacionário, -a [istasjo'narju, a]
adj (veículo) stationary; (Com) slack

estações [ista'sõjs] fpl de **estação**

estada [is'tada] f stay

estadia [ista'dʒia] f = **estada**

estádio [is'tadʒu] m stadium

estadista [ista'dʒista] m/f
statesman/woman

estado [i'stadu] m state; **E~s
Unidos (da América)** United
States (of America); **~ civil** marital
status; **~ de espírito** state of mind;
~ maior staff; **estadual**
[ista'dwaw] (pl **-ais**) adj state atr

estafa [is'tafa] f fatigue;
(esgotamento) nervous exhaustion

estagiário, -a [ista'ʒjarju, a] m/f
probationer, trainee; (professor)
student teacher; (médico) junior
doctor

estágio [is'taʒu] m (aprendizado)
traineeship; (fase) stage

estagnado, -a [istag'nadu, a] adj
stagnant

estalar [ista'lar] vt to break; (os
dedos) to snap; ▷ vi to split, crack;
(crepitar) to crackle

estalido [ista'lidu] m pop

estalo [is'talu] m (do chicote) crack;
(dos dedos) snap; (dos lábios) smack;
(de foguete) bang; **~ de trovão**
thunderclap; **de ~** suddenly

estampa [is'tãpa] f (figura impressa)
print; (ilustração) picture

estampado, -a [istã'padu, a] adj
printed ▷ m (tecido) print; (num
tecido) pattern

estampar [istã'par] vt to print;
(marcar) to stamp

estancar [istã'kar] vt to staunch;

(fazer cessar) to stop; **estancar-se**
vr to stop

estância [is'tãsja] f ranch, farm

estandarte [istã'dartʃi] m
standard, banner

estanho [is'tanu] m (metal) tin

estante [is'tãtʃi] f bookcase;
(suporte) stand

 PALAVRA-CHAVE

estar [is'tar] vi **1** (lugar) to be; (em
casa) to be in; (no telefone): **a Lúcia
está? — não, ela não está** is Lúcia
there? — no, she's not in
2 (estado) to be; **estar doente** to be
ill; **estar bem** (de saúde) to be well;
(financeiramente) to be well off;
estar calor/frio to be hot/cold;
estar com fome/sede/medo to
be hungry/thirsty/afraid
3 (ação contínua): **estar fazendo**
(BR) ou **a fazer** (PT) to be doing
4 (+ pp: = adj): **estar sentado/
cansado** to be sitting down/tired
5 (+ pp: uso passivo): **está
condenado à morte** he's been
condemned to death; **o livro está
emprestado** the book's been
borrowed
6: **estar de férias/licença** to be on
holiday (Brit) ou vacation (US)/
leave; **ela estava de chapéu** she
had a hat on, she was wearing a
hat
7: **estar para fazer** to be about to
do; **ele está para chegar a
qualquer momento** he'll be here
any minute; **não estar para
conversas** not to be in the mood
for talking
8: **estar por fazer** to be still to be
done
9: **estar sem dinheiro** to have no

money; **estar sem dormir** not to have slept; **estou sem dormir há três dias** I haven't slept for three days; **está sem terminar** it isn't finished yet

10 (*frases*): **tá (bem)** (*col*) OK; **estar bem com** to be on good terms with

estardalhaço [istarda'ʎasu] *m* fuss; (*ostentação*) ostentation

estas ['ɛstas] *fpl de* **este**

estatal [ista'taw] (*pl* **-ais**) *adj* nationalized, state-owned ▷ *f* state-owned company

estático, -a [is'tatʃiku, a] *adj* static

estatística [ista'tʃistʃika] *f* statistic; (*ciência*) statistics *sg*

estatizar [istatʃi'zar] *vt* to nationalize

estátua [is'tatwa] *f* statue

estatura [ista'tura] *f* stature

estável [is'tavew] (*pl* **-eis**) *adj* stable

este ['ɛstʃi] *m* east ▷ *adj inv* (*região*) eastern; (*vento, direção*) easterly

este, esta ['estʃi, 'ɛsta] *adj* (*sg*) this; (*pl*) these ▷ *pron* this one; (*pl*) these; (*a quem/que se referiu por último*) the latter; **esta noite** (*noite passada*) last night; (*noite de hoje*) tonight

esteira [is'tejra] *f* mat; (*de navio*) wake; (*rumo*) path

esteja *etc* [is'teʒa] *vb ver* **estar**

estelionato [isteljo'natu] *m* fraud

estender [istẽ'der] *vt* to extend; (*mapa*) to spread out; (*pernas*) to stretch; (*massa*) to roll out; (*conversa*) to draw out; (*corda*) to pull tight; (*roupa molhada*) to hang out; **estender-se** *vr* to lie down; (*fila, terreno*) to stretch, extend; **~-se sobre algo** to dwell on sth, expand on sth; **~ a mão** to hold out

one's hand

estéreis [is'tɛrejs] *adj pl de* **estéril**

estereo... [isterju] *prefixo* stereo...; **estereofônico, -a** [isterjo'foniku, a] *adj* stereo(phonic); **estereótipo** [iste'rjɔtʃipu] *m* stereotype

estéril [is'tɛriw] (*pl* **-eis**) *adj* sterile; (*terra*) infertile; (*fig*) futile; **esterilizar** [isterili'zar] *vt* to sterilize

esteve [is'tevi] *vb ver* **estar**

esticar [istʃi'kar] *vt* to stretch; **esticar-se** *vr* to stretch out

estigma [is'tʃigima] *m* mark, scar; (*fig*) stigma

estilhaçar [istʃiʎa'sar] *vt* to splinter; (*despedaçar*) to shatter; **estilhaçar-se** *vr* to shatter; **estilhaço** [istʃi'ʎasu] *m* fragment; (*de pedra*) chip; (*de madeira, metal*) splinter

estilo [is'tʃilu] *m* style; (*Tec*) stylus; **~ de vida** way of life

estima [is'tʃima] *f* esteem; (*afeto*) affection

estimação [istʃima'sãw] *f*: **... de ~** favourite (*Brit*) ..., favorite (*US*) ...

estimado, -a [istʃi'madu, a] *adj* respected; (*em cartas*): **E~ Senhor** Dear Sir

estimar [istʃi'mar] *vt* to appreciate; (*avaliar*) to value; (*ter estima a*) to have a high regard for; (*calcular aproximadamente*) to estimate

estimativa [istʃima'tʃiva] *f* estimate

estimulante [istʃimu'lãtʃi] *adj* stimulating ▷ *m* stimulant

estimular [istʃimu'lar] *vt* to stimulate; (*incentivar*) to encourage; **estímulo** [is'tʃimulu] *m* stimulus; (*ânimo*) encouragement

estipular [istʃipuˈlar] vt to stipulate

estirar [istʃiˈrar] vt to stretch (out); **estirar-se** vr to stretch

estive etc [isˈtʃivi] vb ver **estar**

estocada [istoˈkada] f stab, thrust

estocar [istoˈkar] vt to stock

estofo [isˈtofu] m (tecido) material; (para acolchoar) padding, stuffing

estojo [isˈtoʒu] m case; **~ de ferramentas** tool kit; **~ de unhas** manicure set

estômago [isˈtomagu] m stomach; **ter ~ para (fazer) algo** to be up to (doing) sth

estontear [istõˈtʃjar] vt to stun, daze

estoque [isˈtɔki] m (Com) stock

estourado, -a [istoˈradu, a] adj (temperamental) explosive; (col: cansado) knackered, worn out

estourar [istoˈrar] vi to explode; (pneu) to burst; (escândalo) to blow up; (guerra) to break out; (BR: chegar) to turn up, arrive; **~ (com alguém)** (zangar-se) to blow up (at sb)

estouro [isˈtoru] m explosion; **dar o ~** (fig: zangar-se) to blow up, blow one's top

estrábico, -a [isˈtrabiku, a] adj cross-eyed

estraçalhar [istrasaˈʎar] vt (livro, objeto) to pull to pieces; (pessoa) to tear to pieces

estrada [isˈtrada] f road; **~ de ferro** (BR) railway (Brit), railroad (US); **~ principal** main road (Brit), state highway (US)

estrado [isˈtradu] m (tablado) platform; (de cama) base

estragado, -a [istraˈgadu, a] adj ruined; (fruta) rotten; (muito mimado) spoiled, spoilt (Brit)

estraga-prazeres [istraga-] m/f inv spoilsport

estragar [istraˈgar] vt to spoil; (arruinar) to ruin, wreck; (desperdiçar) to waste; (saúde) to damage; (mimar) to spoil; **estrago** [isˈtragu] m destruction; (desperdício) waste; (dano) damage; **os estragos da guerra** the ravages of war

estrangeiro, -a [istrãˈʒejru, a] adj foreign ▷ m/f foreigner; **no ~** abroad

estrangular [istrãguˈlar] vt to strangle

estranhar [istraˈɲar] vt to be surprised at; (achar estranho): **~ algo** to find sth strange; **estranhei o clima** the climate did not agree with me; **não é de se ~** it's not surprising

estranho, -a [isˈtraɲu, a] adj strange, odd; (influências) outside ▷ m/f (desconhecido) stranger; (de fora) outsider

estratégia [istraˈtɛʒa] f strategy

estrear [isˈtrjar] vt (vestido) to wear for the first time; (peça de teatro) to perform for the first time; (veículo) to use for the first time; (filme) to show for the first time, première; (iniciar): **~ uma carreira** to embark on ou begin a career ▷ vi (ator, jogador) to make one's first appearance; (filme, peça) to open

estrebaria [istrebaˈria] f stable

estreia [isˈtreja] f (de artista) debut; (de uma peça) first night; (de um filme) première, opening

estreitar [istrejˈtar] vt to narrow; (roupa) to take in; (abraçar) to hug; (laços de amizade) to strengthen ▷ vi (estrada) to narrow

estreito, -a [isˈtrejtu, a] adj

narrow; (*saia*) straight; (*vínculo, relação*) close; (*medida*) strict ▷ *m* strait

estrela [is'trela] *f* star; **~ cadente** falling star; **estrelado, -a** [istre'ladu, a] *adj* (*céu*) starry; (*ovo*) fried

estremecer [istreme'ser] *vt* to shake; (*amizade*) to strain; (*fazer tremer*) to make sb shudder ▷ *vi* to shake; (*tremer*) to tremble; (*horrorizar-se*) to shudder; (*amizade*) to be strained

estremecimento [istremesi'mẽtu] *m* shaking, trembling; (*tremor*) tremor; (*numa amizade*) tension

estresse [is'tresi] *m* stress

estribeira [istri'bejra] *f*: **perder as ~s** (*col*) to fly off the handle, lose one's temper

estridente [istri'dẽtʃi] *adj* shrill, piercing

estrofe [is'trɔfi] *f* stanza

estrondo [is'trõdu] *m* (*de trovão*) rumble; (*de armas*) din

estrutura [istru'tura] *f* structure; (*armação*) framework; (*de edifício*) fabric

estudante [istu'dãtʃi] *m/f* student; **estudantil** [istudã'tʃiw] (*pl* **-is**) *adj* student *atr*

estudar [istu'dar] *vt, vi* to study

estúdio [is'tudʒu] *m* studio

estudo [is'tudu] *m* study

estufa [is'tufa] *f* (*fogão*) stove; (*de plantas*) greenhouse; (*de fogão*) plate warmer; **efeito ~** greenhouse effect

estufado [istu'fadu] (*PT*) *m* stew

estupefato, -a [istupe'fatu, a], (*PT*) **estupefacto** *adj* dumbfounded

estupendo, -a [istu'pẽdu, a] *adj* wonderful, terrific

estupidez [istupi'dez] *f* stupidity; (*ato, dito*) stupid thing; (*grosseria*) rudeness

estúpido, -a [is'tupidu, a] *adj* stupid; (*grosseiro*) rude, churlish ▷ *m/f* idiot; (*grosseiro*) oaf

estuprar [istu'prar] *vt* to rape; **estupro** [is'tupru] *m* rape

esvaziar [izva'zjar] *vt* to empty; **esvaziar-se** *vr* to empty

etapa [e'tapa] *f* stage

etc. *abr* (= *et cetera*) etc

eternidade [eterni'dadʒi] *f* eternity

ética ['ɛtʃika] *f* ethics *pl*

ético, -a ['ɛtʃiku, a] *adj* ethical

Etiópia [e'tʃjɔpja] *f*: **a ~** Ethiopia

etiqueta [etʃi'keta] *f* etiquette; (*rótulo, em roupa*) label; (*que se amarra*) tag

étnico, -a ['ɛtʃniku, a] *adj* ethnic

etos ['ɛtus] *m inv* ethos

eu [ew] *pron* I ▷ *m* self; **sou eu** it's me

EUA *abr mpl* (= *Estados Unidos da América*) USA

eucaristia [ewkaris'tʃia] *f* Holy Communion

euro ['ewru] *m* (*moeda*) euro

Europa [ew'rɔpa] *f*: **a ~** Europe; **europeu, -peia** [ewro'peu, 'pɛja] *adj, m/f* European

evacuar [eva'kwar] *vt* to evacuate; (*sair de*) to leave; (*Med*) to discharge ▷ *vi* to defecate

evadir [eva'dʒir] *vt* to evade; **evadir-se** *vr* to escape

evangelho [evã'ʒeʎu] *m* gospel

evaporar [evapo'rar] *vt, vi* to evaporate; **evaporar-se** *vr* to evaporate; (*desaparecer*) to vanish

evasão [eva'zãw] (*pl* **-ões**) *f* escape, flight; (*fig*) evasion

evasiva [eva'ziva] *f* excuse

evasivo, -a [eva'zivu, a] *adj* evasive

evasões [eva'zõjs] *fpl de* **evasão**

evento [e'vẽtu] *m* event; (*eventualidade*) eventuality

eventual [evẽ'tuaw] (*pl* **-ais**) *adj* fortuitous, accidental; **eventualidade** [evẽtwali'dadʒi] *f* eventuality

evidência [evi'dẽsja] *f* evidence, proof; **evidenciar** [evidẽ'sjar] *vt* to prove; (*mostrar*) to show; **evidenciar-se** *vr* to be evident, be obvious

evidente [evi'dẽtʃi] *adj* obvious, evident

evitar [evi'tar] *vt* to avoid; **~ de fazer algo** to avoid doing sth

evocar [evo'kar] *vt* to evoke; (*espíritos*) to invoke

evolução [evolu'sãw] (*pl* **-ões**) *f* development; (*Mil*) manoeuvre (*Brit*), maneuver (*US*); (*movimento*) movement; (*Bio*) evolution

evoluir [evo'lwir] *vi* to evolve; **~ para** to evolve into

Ex.a *abr* = **Excelência**

exagerar [ezaʒe'rar] *vt* to exaggerate ▷ *vi* to exaggerate; (*agir com exagero*) to overdo it; **exagero** [eza'ʒeru] *m* exaggeration

exalar [eza'lar] *vt* (*odor*) to give off

exaltado, -a [ezaw'tadu, a] *adj* fanatical; (*apaixonado*) overexcited

exaltar [ezaw'tar] *vt* (*elevar: pessoa, virtude*) to exalt; (*louvar*) to praise; (*excitar*) to excite; (*irritar*) to annoy; **exaltar-se** *vr* (*irritar-se*) to get worked up; (*arrebatar-se*) to get carried away

exame [e'zami] *m* (*Educ*) examination, exam; (*Med etc*) examination; **fazer um ~** (*Educ*) to take an exam; (*Med*) to have an examination

examinar [ezami'nar] *vt* to examine

exatidão [ezatʃi'dãw] *f* accuracy; (*perfeição*) correctness

exato, -a [e'zatu, a] *adj* right, correct; (*preciso*) exact; **~!** exactly!

exaustão [ezaw'stãw] *f* exhaustion; **exausto, -a** [e'zawstu, a] *adj* exhausted

exaustor [ezaw'stor] *m* extractor fan

exceção [ese'sãw] (*pl* **-ões**) *f* exception; **com ~ de** with the exception of; **abrir ~** to make an exception

excecional (*PT*) = **excepcional**

excedente [ese'dẽtʃi] *adj* excess; (*Com*) surplus ▷ *m* (*Com*) surplus

exceder [ese'der] *vt* to exceed; (*superar*) to surpass; **exceder-se** *vr* (*cometer excessos*) to go too far; (*cansar-se*) to overdo things

excelência [ese'lẽsja] *f* excellence; **por ~** par excellence; **Vossa E~** Your Excellency; **excelente** [ese'lẽtʃi] *adj* excellent

excêntrico, -a [e'sẽtriku, a] *adj*, *m/f* eccentric

excepcional [esepsjo'naw] (*pl* **-ais**) *adj* exceptional; (*especial*) special; (*Med*) handicapped

excesso [e'sɛsu] *m* excess; (*Com*) surplus

exceto [e'sɛtu] *prep* except (for), apart from

excitação [esita'sãw] *f* excitement

excitado, -a [esi'tadu, a] *adj* excited; (*estimulado*) aroused

excitante [esi'tãtʃi] *adj* exciting

exclamação [isklama'sãw] (*pl* **-ões**) *f* exclamation

exclamar [iskla'mar] *vi* to exclaim

e

excluir [isˈklwir] vt to exclude, leave out; (*eliminar*) to rule out; (*ser incompatível com*) to preclude; **exclusão** [iskluˈzãw] f exclusion; **exclusivo, -a** [iskluˈzivu, a] adj exclusive

excursão [iskurˈsãw] (pl **-ões**) f outing, excursion; **~ a pé** hike; **excursionista** [iskursjoˈnista] m/f tourist; (*para o dia*) day-tripper; (*a pé*) hiker

execução [ezekuˈsãw] (pl **-ões**) f execution; (*de música*) performance

executar [ezekuˈtar] vt to execute; (*Mús*) to perform; (*plano*) to carry out; (*papel teatral*) to play

executivo, -a [ezekuˈtʃivu, a] adj, m/f executive

exemplar [ezẽˈplar] adj exemplary ▷ m model, example; (*Bio*) specimen; (*livro*) copy; (*peça*) piece

exemplo [eˈzẽplu] m example; **por ~** for example

exercer [ezerˈser] vt to exercise; (*influência, pressão*) to exert; (*função*) to perform; (*profissão*) to practise (*Brit*), practice (*US*); (*obrigações*) to carry out

exercício [ezerˈsisju] m exercise; (*de medicina*) practice; (*Mil*) drill; (*Com*) financial year

exercitar [ezersiˈtar] vt (*profissão*) to practise (*Brit*), practice (*US*); (*direitos, músculos*) to exercise; (*adestrar*) to train

exército [eˈzɛrsitu] m army

exibição [ezibiˈsãw] (pl **-ões**) f show, display; (*de filme*) showing

exibir [eziˈbir] vt to show, display; (*alardear*) to show off; (*filme*) to show, screen; **exibir-se** vr to show off; (*indecentemente*) to expose o.s.

exigência [eziˈʒẽsja] f demand; (*o necessário*) requirement; **exigente** [eziˈʒẽtʃi] adj demanding

exigir [eziˈʒir] vt to demand

exíguo, -a [eˈzigwu, a] adj (*diminuto*) small; (*escasso*) scanty

exilado, -a [eziˈladu, a] m/f exile

exilar [eziˈlar] vt to exile; **exilar-se** vr to go into exile; **exílio** [eˈzilju] m exile; (*forçado*) deportation

existência [ezisˈtẽsja] f existence; (*vida*) life

existir [ezisˈtʃir] vi to exist; **existe/ existem ...** (*há*) there is/are ...

êxito [ˈezitu] m result; (*sucesso*) success; (*música, filme etc*) hit; **ter ~ (em)** to succeed (in), be successful (in)

Exmo, -a (pl **Exmos/Exmas**) abr (= *Excelentíssimo*) Dear

êxodo [ˈezodu] m exodus

exorcista [ezorˈsista] m/f exorcist

exótico, -a [eˈzɔtʃiku, a] adj exotic

expandir [ispãˈdʒir] vt to expand; (*espalhar*) to spread; **expandir-se** vr to expand; **~-se com alguém** to be frank with sb

expansão [ispãˈsãw] f expansion, spread; (*de alegria*) effusiveness

expansivo, -a [ispãˈsivu, a] adj (*pessoa*) outgoing

expeça etc [isˈpɛsa] vb ver **expedir**

expectativa [ispektaˈtʃiva] f expectation

expedição [ispedʒiˈsãw] (pl **-ões**) f (*viagem*) expedition; (*de mercadorias*) despatch; (*por navio*) shipment; (*de passaporte etc*) issue

expediente [ispeˈdʒjẽtʃi] m means; (*serviço*) working day; (*correspondência*) correspondence ▷ adj expedient; **~ bancário** banking hours pl; **~ do escritório** office hours pl

expedir [ispeˈdʒir] vt to send, despatch; (*bilhete, passaporte,*

decreto) to issue
expelir [ispe'lir] *vt* to expel;
(*sangue*) to spit
experiência [ispe'rjẽsja] *f*
experience; (*prova*) experiment,
test; **em ~** on trial
experimentar [isperimẽ'tar] *vt*
(*comida*) to taste; (*vestido*) to try on;
(*pôr à prova*) to try out, test;
(*conhecer pela experiência*) to
experience; (*sofrer*) to suffer,
undergo; **experimento**
[isperi'mẽtu] *m* experiment
expilo *etc* [is'pilu] *vb ver* **expelir**
expirar [ispi'rar] *vt* to exhale,
breathe out ▷ *vi* to die; (*terminar*)
to end
explicação [isplika'sāw] (*pl* **-ões**) *f*
explanation
explicar [ispli'kar] *vt, vi* to explain;
explicar-se *vr* to explain o.s.
explícito, -a [is'plisitu, a] *adj*
explicit, clear
explodir [isplo'dʒir] *vt, vi* to
explode
exploração [isplora'sāw] *f*
exploration; (*abuso*) exploitation;
(*de uma mina*) running
explorador, a [isplora'dor(a)] *m/f*
explorer; (*de outros*) exploiter
explorar [isplo'rar] *vt* (*região*) to
explore; (*mina*) to work, run;
(*ferida*) to probe; (*trabalhadores etc*)
to exploit
explosão [isplo'zāw] (*pl* **-ões**) *f*
explosion; (*fig*) outburst;
explosivo, -a [isplo'zivu, a] *adj*
explosive; (*pessoa*) hot-headed ▷ *m*
explosive
expor [is'por] (*irreg: como* **pôr**) *vt* to
expose; (*a vida*) to risk; (*teoria*) to
explain; (*revelar*) to reveal;
(*mercadorias*) to display; (*quadros*)
to exhibit; **expor-se** *vr* to expose o.s.

exportação [isporta'sāw] *f* (*ato*)
export(ing); (*mercadorias*) exports *pl*
exportador, a [isporta'dor(a)] *adj*
exporting ▷ *m/f* exporter
exportar [ispor'tar] *vt* to export
exposição [ispozi'sāw] (*pl* **-ões**) *f*
exhibition; (*explicação*)
explanation; (*declaração*)
statement; (*narração*) account;
(*Foto*) exposure
exposto, -a [is'postu, 'pɔsta] *adj*
(*lugar*) exposed; (*quadro,
mercadoria*) on show *ou* display ▷ *m*:
o acima ~ the above
expressão [ispre'sāw] (*pl* **-ões**) *f*
expression
expressar [ispre'sar] *vt* to express;
expressivo, -a [ispre'sivu, a] *adj*
expressive; (*pessoa*) demonstrative
expresso, -a [is'prɛsu, a] *pp de*
exprimir ▷ *adj* definite, clear;
(*trem, ordem, carta*) express ▷ *m*
express
expressões [ispre'sōjs] *fpl de*
expressão
exprimir [ispri'mir] *vt* to express
expulsão [ispul'sāw] (*pl* **-ões**) *f*
expulsion; (*Esporte*) sending off
expulsar [ispuw'sar] *vt* to expel;
(*de uma festa, clube etc*) to throw
out; (*inimigo*) to drive out;
(*estrangeiro*) to expel, deport;
(*jogador*) to send off
expulso, -a [is'puwsu, a] *pp de*
expulsar
expulsões [ispul'sōjs] *fpl de*
expulsão
êxtase ['estazi] *m* ecstasy
extenso, -a [is'tẽsu, a] *adj*
extensive; (*comprido*) long; (*artigo*)
full, comprehensive; **por ~** in full
extenuante [iste'nwātʃi] *adj*
exhausting; (*debilitante*)
debilitating

e

exterior [iste'rjor] *adj* (*de fora*) outside, exterior; (*aparência*) outward; (*comércio*) foreign ▷ *m* (*da casa*) outside; (*aspecto*) outward appearance; **do ~** (*do estrangeiro*) from abroad; **no ~** abroad

exterminar [istermi'nar] *vt* (*inimigo*) to wipe out, exterminate; (*acabar com*) to do away with

externo, -a [is'tɛrnu, a] *adj* external; (*aparente*) outward; **aluno ~** day pupil

extinguir [istʃĩ'gir] *vt* (*fogo*) to put out, extinguish; (*um povo*) to wipe out; **extinguir-se** *vr* (*fogo, luz*) to go out; (*Bio*) to become extinct

extinto, -a [is'tʃĩtu, a] *adj* (*fogo*) extinguished; (*língua*) dead; (*animal, vulcão*) extinct; (*associação etc*) defunct; **extintor** [istĩ'tor] *m* (fire) extinguisher

extorsão [istor'sãw] *f* extortion

extra ['ɛstra] *adj* extra ▷ *m/f* extra person; (*Teatro*) extra

extração [istra'sãw] (*pl* **-ões**) *f* extraction; (*de loteria*) draw

extrair [istra'jir] *vt* to extract, take out

extraordinário, -a [istraordʒi'narju, a] *adj* extraordinary; (*despesa*) extra; (*reunião*) special

extrato [is'tratu] *m* extract; (*resumo*) summary; **~ (bancário)** (bank) statement

extravagância [istrava'gãsja] *f* extravagance; **extravagante** [istrava'gãtʃi] *adj* extravagant; (*roupa*) outlandish; (*conduta*) wild

extravasar [istrava'zar] *vi* to overflow

extraviado, -a [istra'vjadu, a] *adj* lost, missing

extraviar [istra'vjar] *vt* to mislay; (*pessoa*) to lead astray; (*dinheiro*) to embezzle; **extraviar-se** *vr* to get lost; **extravio** [istra'viu] *m* loss; (*roubo*) embezzlement; (*fig*) deviation

extremado, -a [istre'madu, a] *adj* extreme

extremidade [istremi'dadʒi] *f* extremity; (*do dedo*) tip; (*ponta*) end; (*beira*) edge

extremo, -a [is'trɛmu, a] *adj* extreme ▷ *m* extreme; **ao ~** extremely

extrovertido, -a [estrover'tʃidu, a] *adj* extrovert, outgoing ▷ *m/f* extrovert

exultante [ezuw'tãtʃi] *adj* jubilant, exultant

F, f [ˈɛfi] *m* F, f

fã [fã] (*col*) *m/f* fan

fábrica [ˈfabrika] *f* factory; **~ de cerveja** brewery; **a preço de ~** wholesale

fabricação [fabrikaˈsãw] *f* manufacture; **~ em série** mass production

fabuloso, -a [fabuˈlozu, ɔza] *adj* fabulous

faca [ˈfaka] *f* knife; **facada** [faˈkada] *f* stab, cut

façanha [faˈsaɲa] *f* exploit, deed

facção [fakˈsãw] (*pl* **-ões**) *f* faction

face [ˈfasi] *f* face; (*bochecha*) cheek; **em ~ de** in view of; **fazer ~ a** to face up to

fáceis [ˈfasejs] *adj pl de* **fácil**

faceta [faˈseta] *f* facet

fachada [faˈʃada] *f* façade, front

fácil [ˈfasiw] (*pl* **-eis**) *adj* easy; (*temperamento, pessoa*) easy-going

▷ *adv* easily; **facilidade** [fasiliˈdadʒi] *f* ease; (*jeito*) facility; **facilidades** *fpl* (*recursos*) facilities; **ter facilidade para algo** to have a talent *ou* a facility for sth

facilitar [fasiliˈtar] *vt* to facilitate, make easy; (*fornecer*): **~ algo a alguém** to provide sb with sth

fã-clube [fãˈklubi] (*pl* **fã-clubes**) *m* fan club

faço *etc* [ˈfasu] *vb ver* **fazer**

facto [ˈfaktu] (*PT*) *m* = **fato**

factual [fakˈtwaw] (*pl* **-ais**) *adj* factual

faculdade [fakuwˈdadʒi] *f* faculty; (*poder*) power

facultativo, -a [fakuwtaˈtʃivu, a] *adj* optional ▷ *m/f* doctor

fadado, -a [faˈdadu, a] *adj* destined

fadiga [faˈdʒiga] *f* fatigue

fadista [faˈdʒista] *m/f* "fado" singer ▷ *m* (*PT*) ruffian

fado [ˈfadu] *m* fate; (*canção*) traditional song of Portugal

◉ FADO

The best-known musical form in Portugal is the melancholic **fado**, which is traditionally sung by a soloist (known as a *fadista*) accompanied by the Portuguese *guitarra*. There are two main types of Fado: Coimbra **fado** is traditionally sung by men, and is considered to be more cerebral than the fado from Lisbon, which is sung by both men and women. The theme is nearly always one of deep nostalgia known as *saudade*, and the harsh reality of life.

faia [ˈfaja] *f* beech (tree)

faisão [fajˈzãw] (*pl* **-ões**) *m* pheasant

faísca [fa'iska] f spark; (*brilho*) flash
faisões [faj'zõjs] mpl de **faisão**
faixa ['fajʃa] f (*cinto, Judô*) belt; (*tira*) strip; (*área*) zone; (*Auto: pista*) lane; (*BR: para pedestres*) zebra crossing (*Brit*), crosswalk (*US*); (*Med*) bandage; (*num disco*) track
fala ['fala] f speech; **chamar às ~s** to call to account; **sem ~** speechless
falante [fa'lãtʃi] adj talkative
falar [fa'lar] vt (*língua*) to speak; (*besteira etc*) to talk; (*dizer*) to say; (*verdade, mentira*) to tell ▷ vi to speak; **~ algo a alguém** to tell sb sth; **~ de** ou **em algo** to talk about sth; **~ com alguém** to talk to sb; **por ~ em** speaking of; **sem ~ em** not to mention; **falou!**, **'tá falado!** (*col*) OK!
falcão [faw'kãw] (pl -**ões**) m falcon
falcatrua [fawka'trua] f (*col*) scam
falecer [fale'ser] vi to die; **falecimento** [falesi'mētu] m death
falência [fa'lēsja] f bankruptcy; **abrir ~** to declare o.s. bankrupt; **ir à ~** to go bankrupt; **levar à ~** to bankrupt
falésia [fa'lɛzja] f cliff
falha ['faʎa] f fault; (*lacuna*) omission; (*de caráter*) flaw
falhar [fa'ʎar] vi to fail; (*não acertar*) to miss; (*errar*) to be wrong; **sua voz está falhando** you're breaking up
falho, -a ['faʎu, a] adj faulty; (*deficiente*) wanting
falido, -a [fa'lidu, a] adj, m/f bankrupt
falir [fa'lir] vi to fail; (*Com*) to go bankrupt
falsário, -a [faw'sarju, a] m/f forger
falsidade [fawsi'dadʒi] f

falsehood; (*fingimento*) pretence (*Brit*), pretense (*US*)
falsificar [fawsifi'kar] vt (*forjar*) to forge; (*falsear*) to falsify; (*adulterar*) to adulterate; (*desvirtuar*) to misrepresent
falso, -a ['fawsu, a] adj false; (*fraudulento*) dishonest; (*errôneo*) wrong; (*joia, moeda, quadro*) fake; **pisar em ~** to blunder
falta ['fawta] f (*carência*) lack; (*ausência*) absence; (*defeito, culpa*) fault; (*Futebol*) foul; **por** ou **na ~ de** for lack of; **sem ~** without fail; **fazer ~** to be lacking, be needed; **sentir ~ de alguém/algo** to miss sb/sth; **ter ~ de** to lack, be in need of
faltar [faw'tar] vi to be lacking, be wanting; (*pessoa*) to be absent; (*falhar*) to fail; **~ ao trabalho** to be absent from work; **~ à palavra** to break one's word; **falta pouco para ...** it won't be long until ...
fama ['fama] f (*renome*) fame; (*reputação*) reputation
família [fa'milja] f family
familiar [fami'ljar] adj (*da família*) family atr; (*conhecido*) familiar ▷ m/f relation, relative; **familiaridade** [familjari'dadʒi] f familiarity; (*sem-cerimônia*) informality
famoso, -a [fa'mozu, ɔza] adj famous
fanático, -a [fa'natʃiku, a] adj fanatical ▷ m/f fanatic
fantasia [fãta'zia] f fantasy; (*imaginação*) imagination; (*capricho*) fancy; (*traje*) fancy dress
fantasiar [fãta'zjar] vt to imagine ▷ vi to daydream; **fantasiar-se** vr to dress up (in fancy dress)
fantasma [fã'tazma] m ghost; (*alucinação*) illusion

fantástico, -a [fã'tastʃiku, a] *adj*
fantastic; (*ilusório*) imaginary;
(*incrível*) unbelievable

fantoche [fã'tɔʃi] *m* puppet

farda ['farda] *f* uniform

farei *etc* [fa'rej] *vb ver* **fazer**

farinha [fa'riɲa] *f*: **~ (de mesa)**
(manioc) flour; **~ de rosca**
breadcrumbs *pl*; **~ de trigo** plain
flour

farmacêutico, -a
[farma'sewtʃiku, a] *adj*
pharmaceutical ▷ *m/f* pharmacist,
chemist (*Brit*)

farmácia [far'masja] *f* pharmacy,
chemist's (shop) (*Brit*)

faro ['faru] *m* sense of smell; (*fig*)
flair

farofa [fa'rɔfa] *f* (*Culin*) side dish
based on manioc flour

farol [fa'rɔw] (*pl* **-óis**) *m* lighthouse;
(*Auto*) headlight; **~ alto** (*Auto*) full
(*Brit*) *ou* high (*US*) beam; **~ baixo**
dipped headlights *pl* (*Brit*), dimmed
beam (*US*)

farra ['faha] *f* binge, spree

farrapo [fa'hapu] *m* rag

farsa ['farsa] *f* farce; **farsante**
[far'sãtʃi] *m/f* joker

fartar [far'tar] *vt* to satiate;
(*encher*) to fill up; **fartar-se** *vr* to
gorge o.s.

farto, -a ['fartu, a] *adj* full,
satiated; (*abundante*) plentiful;
(*aborrecido*) fed up

fartura [far'tura] *f* abundance

fascinante [fasi'nãtʃi] *adj*
fascinating

fascinar [fasi'nar] *vt* to fascinate;
(*encantar*) to charm; **fascínio**
[fa'sinju] *m* fascination

fase ['fazi] *f* phase

fashion ['fɛʃjõ] (*col*) *adj* trendy

fatal [fa'taw] (*pl* **-ais**) *adj* (*mortal*)
fatal; (*inevitável*) fateful;
fatalidade [fatali'dadʒi] *f* fate;
(*desgraça*) disaster

fatia [fa'tʃia] *f* slice

fatigante [fatʃi'gãtʃi] *adj* tiring;
(*aborrecido*) tiresome

fatigar [fatʃi'gar] *vt* to tire;
(*aborrecer*) to bore; **fatigar-se** *vr*
to get tired

Fátima ['fatima] *f see note*

f

fato ['fatu] *m* fact; (*acontecimento*)
event; (*PT: traje*) suit; **~ de banho**
(*PT*) swimming costume (*Brit*),
bathing suit (*US*); **de ~** in fact, really

fator [fa'tor] *m* factor

fatura [fa'tura] *f* bill, invoice;
faturar [fatu'rar] *vt* to invoice;
(*dinheiro*) to make ▷ *vi* (*col: ganhar
dinheiro*): **faturar (alto)** to rake it in

fava ['fava] *f* broad bean; **mandar
alguém às ~s** to send sb packing

favela [fa'vɛla] *f* slum

favor [fa'vor] *m* favour (*Brit*), favor
(*US*); **a ~ de** in favo(u)r of; **por ~**
please; **faça** *ou* **faz o ~ de ...** would
you be so good as to ..., kindly ...;
favorável [favo'ravew] (*pl* **-eis**)
adj: **favorável (a)** favourable (*Brit*)
ou favorable (*US*) (to); **favorecer**
[favore'ser] *vt* to favour (*Brit*),
favor (*US*); (*beneficiar*) to benefit;
(*suj: vestido*) to suit; (*: retrato*) to

flatter; **favorito, -a** [favo'ritu, a] *adj, m/f (tb Comput)* favourite *(Brit)*, favorite *(US)*

fax [faks] *m* fax; **enviar por ~** to fax

faxina [fa'ʃina] *f*: **fazer ~** to clean up; **faxineiro, -a** [faʃi'nejru, a] *m/f* cleaner

fazenda [fa'zẽda] *f* farm; *(de café)* plantation; *(de gado)* ranch; *(pano)* cloth, fabric; *(Econ)* treasury; **fazendeiro** [fazẽ'dejru] *m* farmer; *(de café)* plantation-owner; *(de gado)* rancher, ranch-owner

 PALAVRA-CHAVE

fazer [fa'zer] *vt* **1** *(fabricar, produzir)* to make; *(construir)* to build; *(pergunta)* to ask; *(poema, música)* to write; **fazer um filme/ruído** to make a film/noise

2 *(executar)* to do; **o que você está fazendo?** what are you doing?; **fazer a comida** to do the cooking; **fazer o papel de** *(Teatro)* to play

3 *(estudos, alguns esportes)* to do; **fazer medicina/direito** to do *ou* study medicine/law; **fazer ioga/ginástica** to do yoga/keep-fit

4 *(transformar, tornar)*: **sair o fará sentir melhor** going out will make him feel better; **sua partida fará o trabalho mais difícil** his departure will make work more difficult

5 *(como sustituto de vb)*: **ele bebeu e eu fiz o mesmo** he drank and I did likewise

6: **ele faz anos hoje** it's his birthday today; **fiz 30 anos ontem** I was 30 yesterday

▷ *vi* **1** *(portar-se)* to act, behave; **fazer bem/mal** to do the right/wrong thing; **não fiz por mal** I didn't mean it; **faz como quem não sabe** act as if you don't know anything

2: **fazer com que alguém faça algo** to make sb do sth

▷ *vb impess* **1**: **faz calor/frio** it's hot/cold

2 *(tempo)*: **faz um ano** a year ago; **faz dois anos que ele se formou** it's two years since he graduated; **faz três meses que ele está aqui** he's been here for three months

3: **não faz mal** never mind; **tanto faz** it's all the same

fazer-se *vr* **1**: **fazer-se de desentendido** to pretend not to understand

2: **faz-se com ovos e leite** it's made with eggs and milk; **isso não se faz** that's not done

fé [fɛ] *f* faith; *(crença)* belief; *(confiança)* trust; **de boa/má fé** in good/bad faith

febre ['fɛbri] *f* fever; *(fig)* excitement; **~ do feno** hay fever; **febril** [fe'briw] *(pl* **-is)** *adj* feverish

fechado, -a [fe'ʃadu, a] *adj* shut, closed; *(pessoa)* reserved; *(sinal)* red; *(luz, torneira)* off; *(tempo)* overcast; *(cara)* stern

fechadura [feʃa'dura] *f* lock

fechar [fe'ʃar] *vt* to close, shut; *(concluir)* to finish, conclude; *(luz, torneira)* to turn off; *(rua)* to close off; *(ferida)* to close up; *(bar, loja)* to close down ▷ *vi* to close (up), shut; to close down; *(tempo)* to cloud over; **fechar-se** *vr* to close, shut; *(pessoa)* to withdraw; **~ à chave** to lock

fecho ['feʃu] *m* fastening; *(trinco)* latch; *(término)* close; **~ ecler** zip fastener *(Brit)*, zipper *(US)*

fécula ['fɛkula] *f* starch

feder [fe'der] *vi* to stink

federação [federa'sãw] (pl **-ões**) f
federation

federal [fede'raw] (pl **-ais**) adj
federal; (col: grande) huge

fedor [fe'dor] m stench

feijão [fej'ʒãw] (pl **-ões**) m bean(s)
(pl); (preto) black bean(s) (pl);
feijoada [fej'ʒwada] f (Culin)
meat, rice and black beans

feio, -a ['feju, a] adj ugly; (situação)
grim; (atitude) bad; (tempo)
horrible ▷ adv (perder) badly

feira ['fejra] f fair; (mercado) market

feiticeira [fejtʃi'sejra] f witch

feiticeiro, -a [fejtʃi'sejru, a] adj
bewitching, enchanting ▷ m
wizard

feitiço [fej'tʃisu] m charm, spell

feitio [fej'tʃiu] m shape, pattern;
(caráter) nature, manner; (Tec)
workmanship

feito, -a ['fejtu, a] pp de **fazer** ▷ adj
finished, ready ▷ m act, deed;
(façanha) feat ▷ conj like; **~ a mão**
hand-made; **homem ~** grown man

feiura [fe'jura] f ugliness

felicidade [felisi'dadʒi] f
happiness; (sorte) good luck; (êxito)
success; **felicidades** fpl
(congratulações) congratulations

felicitações [felisita'sõjs] fpl
congratulations, best wishes

feliz [fe'liz] adj happy; (afortunado)
lucky; **felizmente** [feliz'mẽtʃi] adv
fortunately

feltro ['fewtru] m felt

fêmea ['femja] f female

feminino, -a [femi'ninu, a] adj
feminine; (sexo) female; (equipe,
roupa) women's ▷ m (Ling) feminine

feminista [femi'nista] adj, m/f
feminist

feno ['fenu] m hay

fenomenal [fenome'naw] (pl **-ais**)

adj phenomenal; (espantoso)
amazing; (pessoa) brilliant

fenômeno [fe'nomenu] m
phenomenon

fera ['fɛra] f wild animal

feriado [fe'rjadu] m (public)
holiday (Brit), vacation (US)

férias ['fɛrjas] fpl holiday(s) (Brit),
vacation sg (US); **de ~** on holiday;
tirar ~ to have ou take a holiday

ferida [fe'rida] f wound, injury; ver
tb **ferido**

ferido, -a [fe'ridu, a] adj injured;
(em batalha) wounded; (magoado)
hurt ▷ m/f casualty

ferimento [feri'mẽtu] m injury;
(em batalha) wound

ferir [fe'rir] vt to injure; (tb fig) to
hurt; (em batalha) to wound;
(ofender) to offend

fermentar [fermẽ'tar] vi to
ferment

fermento [fer'mẽtu] m yeast; **~ em
pó** baking powder

feroz [fe'roz] adj fierce, ferocious;
(cruel) cruel

ferragem [fe'haʒẽ] (pl **-ns**) f (peças)
hardware; (guarnição) metalwork;
loja de ferragens ironmonger's
(Brit), hardware store

ferramenta [feha'mẽta] f tool;
(caixa de ferramentas) tool kit

ferrão [fe'hãw] (pl **-ões**) m goad;
(de inseto) sting

ferrenho, -a [fe'heɲu, a] adj
(vontade) iron

ferro ['fɛhu] m iron; **ferros** mpl
(algemas) shackles, chains; **~
batido** wrought iron; **~ de passar**
iron; **~ fundido** cast iron; **~
ondulado** corrugated iron

ferrões [fe'hõjs] mpl de **ferrão**

ferrolho [fe'hoʎu] m (trinco) bolt

ferrovia [feho'via] f railway (Brit),

railroad (US); **ferroviário, -a**
[feho'vjarju, a] adj railway atr
(Brit), railroad atr (US) ▷ m/f
railway ou railroad worker
ferrugem [fe'huʒẽ] f rust
fértil ['fɛrtfiw] (pl -**eis**) adj fertile;
fertilizante [fertfili'zãtfi] m
fertilizer; **fertilizar** [fertfili'zar] vt
to fertilize
ferver [fer'ver] vt, vi to boil; ~ **de
raiva/indignação** to seethe with
rage/indignation; ~ **em fogo
baixo** (Culin) to simmer
fervilhar [fervi'ʎar] vi to simmer;
(com atividade) to hum; (pulular): ~
de to swarm with
fervor [fer'vor] m fervour (Brit),
fervor (US)
festa ['fɛsta] f (reunião) party;
(conjunto de ceremônias) festival;
festas fpl (carícia) embrace; **boas
~s** Merry Christmas and a Happy
New Year; **dia de ~** public holiday
festejar [feste'ʒar] vt to celebrate;
(acolher) to welcome, greet;
festejo [fes'teʒu] m festivity; (ato)
celebration
festival [festfi'vaw] (pl -**ais**) m
festival
festividade [festfivi'dadʒi] f
festivity
festivo, -a [fes'tfivu, a] adj festive
fetiche [fe'tfiʃi] m fetish
feto ['fɛtu] m (Med) foetus (Brit),
fetus (US)
fevereiro [feve'rejru] m February
fez [fez] vb ver **fazer**
fezes ['fɛzis] fpl faeces (Brit), feces
(US)
fiado, -a ['fjadu, a] adv: **comprar/
vender ~** to buy/sell on credit
fiador, a [fja'dor(a)] m/f (Jur)
guarantor; (Com) backer
fiambre ['fjãbri] m cold meat;

(presunto) ham
fiança ['fjãsa] f guarantee; (Jur)
bail; **prestar ~ por** to stand bail for;
sob ~ on bail
fiar ['fjar] vt (algodão etc) to spin;
(confiar) to entrust; (vender a
crédito) to sell on credit; **fiar-se** vr:
~-**se em** to trust
fibra ['fibra] f fibre (Brit), fiber (US)

PALAVRA-CHAVE

ficar [fi'kar] vi 1 (permanecer) to stay;
(sobrar) to be left; **ficar
perguntando/olhando** etc to
keep asking/looking etc; **ficar por
fazer** to have still to be done; **ficar
para trás** to be left behind
2 (tornar-se) to become; **ficar cego/
surdo/louco** to go blind/deaf/
mad; **fiquei contente ao saber da
notícia** I was happy when I heard
the news; **ficar com raiva/medo**
to get angry/frightened; **ficar de
bem/mal com alguém** (col) to
make up/fall out with sb
3 (posição) to be; **a casa fica ao
lado da igreja** the house is next to
the church; **ficar sentado/
deitado** to be sitting down/lying
down
4 (tempo: durar): **ele ficou duas
horas para resolver** he took two
hours to decide; (: ser adiado): **a
reunião ficou para amanhã** the
meeting has been postponed until
tomorrow
5: **ficar bem** (comportamento): **sua
atitude não ficou bem** his (ou her
etc) behaviour was inappropriate;
(cor): **você fica bem em azul** blue
suits you, you look good in blue;
(roupa): **ficar bem para** to suit
6: **ficar bom** (de saúde) to be cured;

(*trabalho, foto etc*) to turn out well

7: **ficar de fazer algo** (*combinar*) to arrange to do sth; (*prometer*) to promise to do sth

8: **ficar de pé** to stand up

ficção [fik'sãw] *f* fiction

ficha ['fiʃa] *f* (*tb*: **~ de telefone**) token; (*tb*: **~ de jogo**) chip; (*de fichário*) (index) card; (*Polícia*) record; (*PT*: *Elet*) plug; (*em loja, lanchonete*) ticket

fichário [fi'ʃarju] *m* filing cabinet; (*caixa*) card index; (*caderno*) file

ficheiro [fi'ʃejru] (*PT*) *m* = **fichário**

fidelidade [fideli'dadʒi] *f* fidelity, loyalty; (*exatidão*) accuracy

fiel [fjɛw] (*pl* **-éis**) *adj* (*leal*) faithful, loyal; (*acurado*) accurate; (*que não falha*) reliable

figa ['figa] *f* talisman; **fazer uma ~** to make a *figa*, ≈ cross one's fingers; **de uma ~** (*col*) damned

fígado ['figadu] *m* liver

figo ['figu] *m* fig; **figueira** [fi'gejra] *f* fig tree

figura [fi'gura] *f* figure; (*forma*) form, shape; (*Ling*) figure of speech; (*aspecto*) appearance

figurino [figu'rinu] *m* model; (*revista*) fashion magazine

fila ['fila] *f* row, line; (*BR*: *fileira de pessoas*) queue (*Brit*), line (*US*); (*num teatro, cinema*) row; **em ~** in a row; **fazer ~** to form a line, queue; **~ indiana** single file

filé [fi'lɛ] *m* (*bife*) steak; (*peixe*) fillet

fileira [fi'lejra] *f* row, line; **fileiras** *fpl* (*serviço militar*) military service *sg*

filho, -a ['fiʎu, a] *m/f* son/ daughter; **filhos** *mpl* children; (*de animais*) young; **~ da mãe, ~ da puta** (*col!*) bastard (!)

filhote [fi'ʎɔtʃi] *m* (*de leão, urso etc*) cub; (*cachorro*) pup(py)

filial [fi'ljaw] (*pl* **-ais**) *f* (*sucursal*) branch

filipeta [fili'peta] *f* flyer

Filipinas [fili'pinas] *fpl*: **as ~** the Philippines

filmadora [fiwma'dora] *f* video camera

filmar [fiw'mar] *vt, vi* to film

filme ['fiwmi] *m* film (*Brit*), movie (*US*)

filosofia [filozo'fia] *f* philosophy; **filósofo, -a** [fi'lɔzofu, a] *m/f* philosopher

filtrar [fiw'trar] *vt* to filter; **filtrar-se** *vr* to filter; (*infiltrar-se*) to infiltrate

filtro ['fiwtru] *m* (*Tec*) filter

fim [fĩ] (*pl* **-ns**) *m* end; (*motivo*) aim, purpose; (*de história, filme*) ending; **a ~ de** in order to; **no ~ das contas** after all; **por ~** finally; **sem ~** endless; **levar ao ~** to carry through; **pôr** *ou* **dar ~ a** to put an end to; **ter ~** to come to an end; **~ de semana** weekend

finado, -a [fi'nadu, a] *adj, m/f* deceased

⬤ **FINADOS**

⬤
⬤ The day of **Finados**, 2 November,
⬤ a holiday throughout Brazil, is
⬤ dedicated to remembering the
⬤ dead. On this day, people usually
⬤ gather in cemeteries to remember
⬤ their family dead, and also to
⬤ worship at the graves of popular
⬤ figures from Brazilian culture
⬤ and society, such as singers,
⬤ actors and other personalities.
⬤ It is popularly believed that these
⬤ people can work miracles.

final [fi'naw] (*pl* **-ais**) *adj* final, last

▷ *m* end; (*Mús*) finale ▷ *f* (*Esporte*) final; **finalista** [fina'lista] *m/f* finalist; **finalizar** [finali'zar] *vt* to finish, conclude

finanças [fi'nãsas] *fpl* finance *sg*; **financeiro, -a** [finã'sejru, a] *adj* financial ▷ *m/f* financier; **financiar** [finã'sjar] *vt* to finance

fingimento [fĩʒi'mẽtu] *m* pretence (*Brit*), pretense (*US*)

fingir [fĩ'ʒir] *vt* to feign ▷ *vi* to pretend; **fingir-se** *vr*: **~-se de** to pretend to be

finito, -a [fi'nitu, a] *adj* finite

finlandês, -esa [fĩlã'des, eza] *adj* Finnish ▷ *m/f* Finn ▷ *m* (*Ling*) Finnish

Finlândia [fĩ'lãdʒja] *f*: **a ~** Finland

fino, -a ['finu, a] *adj* fine; (*delgado*) slender; (*educado*) polite; (*som, voz*) shrill; (*elegante*) refined ▷ *adv*: **falar ~** to talk in a high voice

fins [fĩs] *mpl de* **fim**

fio ['fiu] *m* thread; (*Bot*) fibre (*Brit*), fiber (*US*); (*Elet*) wire; (*Tel*) line; (*de líquido*) trickle; (*gume*) edge; (*encadeamento*) series; **horas/dias a ~** hours/days on end; **sem ~** (*Comput*) wireless

firewall [fajau'aw] *m* firewall

firma ['firma] *f* signature; (*Com*) firm, company

firmar [fir'mar] *vt* to secure, make firm; (*assinar*) to sign; (*estabelecer*) to establish; (*basear*) to base ▷ *vi* (*tempo*) to settle; **firmar-se** *vr*: **~-se em** (*basear-se*) to rest on, be based on

firme ['firmi] *adj* firm; (*estável*) stable; (*sólido*) solid; (*tempo*) settled ▷ *adv* firmly; **firmeza** [fir'meza] *f* firmness; (*estabilidade*) stability; (*solidez*) solidity

fiscal [fis'kaw] (*pl* **-ais**) *m/f*

supervisor; (*aduaneiro*) customs officer; (*de impostos*) tax inspector; **fiscalizar** [fiskali'zar] *vt* to supervise; (*examinar*) to inspect, check

fisco ['fisku] *m*: **o ~** ≈ the Inland Revenue (*Brit*), ≈ the Internal Revenue Service (*US*)

física ['fizika] *f* physics *sg*; *ver tb* **físico**

físico, -a ['fiziku, a] *adj* physical ▷ *m/f* (*cientista*) physicist ▷ *m* (*corpo*) physique

fisionomia [fizjono'mia] *f* (*rosto*) face; (*ar*) expression, look; (*aspecto de algo*) appearance

fissura [fi'sura] *f* crack

fita ['fita] *f* (*tira*) strip, band; (*filme*) film; (*para máquina de escrever*) ribbon; (*magnética, adesiva*) tape; **~ durex®** adhesive tape, Sellotape® (*Brit*), Scotch tape® (*US*); **~ métrica** tape measure

fitar [fi'tar] *vt* to stare at, gaze at

fivela [fi'vɛla] *f* buckle

fixar [fik'sar] *vt* to fix; (*colar, prender*) to stick; (*data, prazo, regras*) to set; (*atenção*) to concentrate; **fixar-se** *vr*: **~-se em** (*assunto*) to concentrate on; (*detalhe*) to fix on; (*apegar-se a*) to be attached to; **~ os olhos em** to stare at; **~ residência** to set up house

fixo, -a ['fiksu, a] *adj* fixed; (*firme*) firm; (*permanente*) permanent; (*cor*) fast

fiz *etc* [fiz] *vb ver* **fazer**

flagelado, -a [flaʒe'ladu, a] *m/f*: **os ~s** the afflicted, the victims

flagrante [fla'grãtʃi] *adj* flagrant; **apanhar em ~ (delito)** to catch red-handed *ou* in the act

flagrar [fla'grar] *vt* to catch

flanela [fla'nɛla] *f* flannel

flash [flaʃ] m (Foto) flash

flauta ['flawta] f flute

flecha ['flɛʃa] f arrow

fleuma ['flewma] f phlegm

floco ['flɔku] m flake; **~ de milho** cornflake; **~ de neve** snowflake

flor [flor] f flower; (o melhor) cream, pick; **em ~** in bloom; **à ~ da pele** on edge

florescente [flore'sẽtʃi] adj (Bot) in flower; (próspero) flourishing

florescer [flore'ser] vi (Bot) to flower; (prosperar) to flourish

floresta [flo'rɛsta] f forest; **florestal** [flores'taw] (pl **florestais**) adj forest atr

florido, -a [flo'ridu, a] adj (jardim) in flower

fluente [flu'ẽtʃi] adj fluent

fluido, -a ['flwidu, a] adj fluid ⊳ m fluid

fluir [flwir] vi to flow

fluminense [flumi'nẽsi] adj from the state of Rio de Janeiro ⊳ m/f native ou inhabitant of the state of Rio de Janeiro

flutuar [flu'twar] vi to float; (bandeira) to flutter; (fig: vacilar) to waver

fluvial [flu'vjaw] (pl **-ais**) adj river atr

fluxo ['fluksu] m (corrente) flow; (Elet) flux; **~ de caixa** (Com) cash flow

fobia [fo'bia] f phobia

foca ['fɔka] f seal

foco ['fɔku] m focus; (Med, fig) seat, centre (Brit), center (US); **fora de ~** out of focus

fofo, -a ['fofu, a] adj soft; (col: pessoa) cute

fofoca [fo'fɔka] f piece of gossip; **fofocas** fpl (mexericos) gossip sg; **fofocar** [fofo'kar] vi to gossip

fogão [fo'gãw] (pl **-ões**) m stove, cooker

fogareiro [foga'rejru] m stove

foge etc ['fɔʒi] vb ver **fugir**

fogo ['fogu] m fire; (fig) ardour (Brit), ardor (US); **você tem ~?** have you got a light?; **~s de artifício** fireworks; **pôr ~ a** to set fire to

fogões [fo'gõjs] mpl de **fogão**

fogueira [fo'gejra] f bonfire

foguete [fo'getʃi] m rocket

foi [foj] vb ver **ir**; **ser**

folclore [fowk'lɔri] m folklore

folclórico, -a [fowk'lɔriku, a] adj (música etc) folk atr; (comida, roupa) ethnic

fôlego ['folegu] m breath; (folga) breathing space; **perder o ~** to get out of breath

folga ['fɔwga] f rest, break; (espaço livre) clearance; (ócio) inactivity; (col: atrevimento) cheek; **dia de ~** day off; **folgado, -a** [fow'gadu, a] adj (roupa) loose; (vida) leisurely; (col: atrevido) cheeky; **folgar** [fow'gar] vt to loosen ⊳ vi (descansar) to rest; (divertir-se) to have fun

folha ['foʎa] f leaf; (de papel, de metal) sheet; (página) page; (de faca) blade; (jornal) paper; **novo em ~** brand new; **~ de estanho** tinfoil (Brit), aluminum foil (US); **~ de exercícios** worksheet

folhagem [fo'ʎaʒẽ] f foliage

folheto [fo'ʎetu] m booklet, pamphlet

fome ['fɔmi] f hunger; (escassez) famine; (fig: avidez) longing; **passar ~** to go hungry; **estar com** ou **ter ~** to be hungry

fone ['fɔni] m telephone, phone; (peça do telefone) receiver

fonte ['fõtʃi] f (nascente) spring; (chafariz) fountain; (origem) source; (Anat) temple

for [for] *vb ver* **ir**; **ser**
fora¹ ['fɔra] *adv* out, outside ▷ *prep*
(*além de*) apart from ▷ *m*: **dar o ~**
(*bateria, radio*) to give out; (*pessoa*)
to leave, be off; **dar um ~** to slip up;
dar um ~ em alguém (*namorado*)
to chuck sb, dump sb; (*esnobar*) to
snub sb; **levar um ~** (*de namorado*)
to be given the boot; (*ser esnobado*)
to get the brush-off; **~ de** outside; **~
de si** beside o.s.; **estar ~** (*viajando*)
to be away; **estar ~ (de casa)** to be
out; **lá ~** outside; (*no exterior*)
abroad; **jantar ~** to eat out; **com
os braços de ~** with bare arms; **ser
de ~** to be from out of town; **ficar
de ~** not to join in; **lá para ~**
outside; **ir para ~** (*viajar*) to go out
of town; **com a cabeça para ~ da
janela** with one's head sticking out
of the window; **costurar/
cozinhar para ~** to do sewing/
cooking for other people; **por ~** on
the outside; **cobrar por ~** to charge
extra; **~ de dúvida** beyond doubt;
~ de propósito irrelevant
fora² *vb ver* **ir**; **ser**
foragido, -a [fora'ʒidu, a] *adj, m/f*
fugitive; **estar ~** to be on the run
forasteiro, -a [foras'tejru, a] *m/f*
outsider, stranger; (*de outro país*)
foreigner
força ['forsa] *f* strength; (*Tec, Elet*)
power; (*esforço*) effort; (*coerção*)
force; **à ~** by force; **à ~ de** by dint of;
com ~ hard; **por ~** of necessity;
fazer ~ to try (hard); **~ de trabalho**
workforce
forçado, -a [for'sadu, a] *adj* forced;
(*afetado*) false
forçar [for'sar] *vt* to force; (*olhos,
voz*) to strain
forma ['fɔrma] *f* form; (*de um
objeto*) shape; (*físico*) figure;
(*maneira*) way; (*Med*) fitness; **desta
~** in this way; **de qualquer ~**
anyway; **manter a ~** to keep fit
fôrma ['forma] *f* (*Culin*) cake tin;
(*molde*) mould (*Brit*), mold (*US*)
formação [forma'sãw] (*pl* **-ões**) *f*
formation; (*antecedentes*)
background; (*caráter*) make-up;
(*profissional*) training
formado, -a [for'madu, a] *adj*
(*modelado*): **ser ~ de** to consist of
▷ *m/f* graduate
formal [for'maw] (*pl* **-ais**) *adj*
formal; **formalidade**
[formali'dadʒi] *f* formality
formar [for'mar] *vt* to form;
(*constituir*) to constitute, make up;
(*educar*) to train; **formar-se** *vr* to
form; (*Educ*) to graduate
formatar [forma'tar] *vt* (*Comput*)
to format
formidável [formi'davew] (*pl* **-eis**)
adj tremendous, great
formiga [for'miga] *f* ant
formigar [formi'gar] *vi* to abound;
(*sentir comichão*) to itch
formoso, -a [for'mozu, ɔza] *adj*
beautiful; (*esplêndido*) superb
fórmula ['fɔrmula] *f* formula
formular [formu'lar] *vt* to
formulate; (*queixas*) to voice
formulário [formu'larju] *m* form;
formulários *mpl*: **~s contínuos**
(*Comput*) continuous stationery *sg*
fornecedor, a [fornese'dor(a)] *m/f*
supplier ▷ *f* (*empresa*) supplier
fornecer [forne'ser] *vt* to supply,
provide; **fornecimento**
[fornesi'mẽtu] *m* supply
forno ['fornu] *m* (*Culin*) oven; (*Tec*)
furnace; (*para cerâmica*) kiln; **alto ~**
blast furnace
foro ['foru] *m* forum; (*Jur*) Court of
Justice; **foros** *mpl* (*privilégios*)

privileges
forro ['fohu] *m* covering; *(interior)* lining
forró [fo'hɔ] *m see note*

○ **FORRÓ**
○
○ **Forró** is a style of popular music
○ and dance that originated in the
○ north-east of Brazil, but which is
○ now popular all over the country.
○ The instruments which feature
○ in **forró** are the accordion, the
○ bass drum and the triangle, and
○ it is danced with a partner. There
○ are a number of different styles
○ of **forró**, such as the faster-paced
○ *forró universitário*, which has
○ attracted a considerable
○ following among the younger
○ generation in Brazil's cities.

fortalecer [fortale'ser] *vt* to strengthen
fortaleza [forta'leza] *f* fortress; *(força)* strength; *(moral)* fortitude
forte ['fɔrtʃi] *adj* strong; *(pancada)* hard; *(chuva)* heavy; *(som)* loud; *(dor)* sharp ▷ *adv* strongly; *(som)* loud(ly) ▷ *m* fort; *(talento)* strength; **ser ~ em algo** *(versado)* to be good at sth *ou* strong in sth
fortuito, -a [for'twitu, a] *adj* accidental
fortuna [for'tuna] *f* fortune, (good) luck; *(riqueza)* fortune, wealth
fosco, -a ['fosku, a] *adj* dull; *(opaco)* opaque
fósforo ['fɔsforu] *m* match
fossa ['fɔsa] *f* pit
fosse ['fɔsi] *vb ver* **ir**; **ser**
fóssil ['fɔsiw] *(pl* **-eis***)* *m* fossil
fosso ['fosu] *m* trench, ditch
foto ['fɔtu] *f* photo

fotocópia [foto'kɔpja] *f* photocopy; **fotocopiadora** [fotokopja'dora] *f* photocopier; **fotocopiar** [fotoko'pjar] *vt* to photocopy
fotografar [fotogra'far] *vt* to photograph
fotografia [fotogra'fia] *f* photography; *(uma foto)* photograph
fotógrafo, -a [fo'tɔgrafu, a] *m/f* photographer
foz [fɔz] *f* mouth *(of river)*
fração [fra'sãw] *(pl* **-ões***)* *f* fraction
fracassar [fraka'sar] *vi* to fail; **fracasso** [fra'kasu] *m* failure
fraco, -a ['fraku, a] *adj* weak; *(sol, som)* faint
frágil ['fraʒiw] *(pl* **-eis***)* *adj* *(débil)* fragile; *(Com)* breakable; *(pessoa)* frail; *(saúde)* delicate, poor
fragmento [frag'mẽtu] *m* fragment
fragrância [fra'grãsja] *f* fragrance, perfume
fralda ['frawda] *f* *(da camisa)* shirt tail; *(para bebê)* nappy *(Brit)*, diaper *(US)*; *(de montanha)* foot
framboesa [frãbo'eza] *f* raspberry
França ['frãsa] *f* France
francamente [frãka'mẽtʃi] *adv* *(abertamente)* frankly; *(realmente)* really
francês, -esa [frã'ses, eza] *adj* French ▷ *m/f* Frenchman/woman ▷ *m* *(Ling)* French
franco, -a ['frãku, a] *adj* frank; *(isento de pagamento)* free; *(óbvio)* clear ▷ *m* franc; **entrada franca** free admission
frango ['frãgu] *m* chicken
franja ['frãʒa] *f* fringe *(Brit)*, bangs *pl (US)*
franquia [frã'kia] *f* *(Com)* franchise; *(isenção)* exemption

franzino, -a [frã'zinu, a] *adj* skinny
fraqueza [fra'keza] *f* weakness
frasco ['frasku] *m* bottle
frase ['frazi] *f* sentence; **~ feita** set phrase
fratura [fra'tura] *f* fracture, break; **fraturar** [fratu'rar] *vt* to fracture
freada [fre'ada] (*BR*) *f*: **dar uma ~** to slam on the brakes
frear [fre'ar] (*BR*) *vt* to curb, restrain; (*veículo*) to stop ▷ *vi* (*veículo*) to brake
freezer ['frizer] *m* freezer
freguês, -guesa [fre'ges, 'geza] *m/f* customer; (*PT*) parishioner; **freguesia** [frege'zia] *f* customers *pl*; (*PT*) parish
freio ['freju] *m* (*BR: veículo*) brake; (*de cavalo*) bridle; (*bocado do freio*) bit; **~ de mão** handbrake
freira ['frejra] *f* nun
frenesi [frene'zi] *m* frenzy; **frenético, -a** [fre'nɛtʃiku, a] *adj* frantic, frenzied
frente ['frɛtʃi] *f* front; (*rosto*) face; (*fachada*) façade; **~ a ~** face to face; **de ~ para** facing; **em ~ de** in front of; (*de fronte a*) opposite; **para a ~** ahead, forward; **porta da ~** front door; **seguir em ~** to go straight on; **na minha** (*ou* **sua** *etc*) **~** in front of me (*ou* you *etc*); **sair da ~** to get out of the way; **pra ~** (*col*) fashionable, trendy
frequência [fre'kwɛsja] *f* frequency; **com ~** often, frequently
frequentar [frekwẽ'tar] *vt* to frequent
frequente [fre'kwẽtʃi] *adj* frequent
fresco, -a ['fresku, a] *adj* fresh; (*vento, tempo*) cool; (*col: efeminado*) camp; (*: afetado*) pretentious; (*: cheio de luxo*) fussy ▷ *m* (*ar*) fresh air

frescobol [fresko'bɔw] *m* (kind of) racketball (*played mainly on the beach*)
frescura [fres'kura] *f* freshness; (*frialdade*) coolness; (*col: luxo*) fussiness; (*: afetaçao*) pretentiousness
frete ['frɛtʃi] *m* (*carregamento*) freight, cargo; (*tarifa*) freightage
frevo ['frevu] *m* improvised Carnival dance
fria ['fria] *f*: **dar uma ~ em alguém** to give sb the cold shoulder; **estar/entrar numa ~** (*col*) to be in/get into a mess
fricção [frik'sãw] *f* friction; (*ato*) rubbing; (*Med*) massage; **friccionar** [friksjo'nar] *vt* to rub
frieza ['frjeza] *f* coldness; (*indiferença*) coolness
frigideira [friʒi'dejra] *f* frying pan
frigorífico [frigo'rifiku] *m* refrigerator; (*congelador*) freezer
frio, -a ['friu, a] *adj* cold ▷ *m* coldness; **frios** *mpl* (*Culin*) cold meats; **estou com ~** I'm cold; **faz** *ou* **está ~** it's cold
frisar [fri'zar] *vt* (*encrespar*) to curl; (*salientar*) to emphasize
fritar [fri'tar] *vt* to fry
fritas ['fritas] *fpl* chips (*Brit*), French fries (*US*)
frito, -a ['fritu, a] *adj* fried; (*col*): **estar ~** to be done for
frívolo, -a ['frivolu, a] *adj* frivolous
fronha ['froɲa] *f* pillowcase
fronteira [frõ'tejra] *f* frontier, border
frota ['frɔta] *f* fleet
frouxo, -a ['froʃu, a] *adj* loose; (*corda*) slack; (*fraco*) weak; (*col: condescendente*) soft
frustrar [frus'trar] *vt* to frustrate
fruta ['fruta] *f* fruit; **frutífero, -a**

[fru'tʃiferu, a] *adj* (*proveitoso*) fruitful; (*árvore*) fruit-bearing

fruto ['frutu] *m* (*Bot*) fruit; (*resultado*) result, product; **dar ~** (*fig*) to bear fruit

fubá [fu'ba] *m* corn meal

fugir [fu'ʒir] *vi* to flee, escape; (*prisioneiro*) to escape

fui [fuj] *vb ver* **ir**; **ser**

fulano, -a [fu'lanu, a] *m/f* so-and-so

fulminante [fuwmi'nãtʃi] *adj* devastating; (*palavras*) scathing

fulo, -a ['fulu, a] *adj*: **estar** *ou* **ficar ~ de raiva** to be furious

fumaça [fu'masa] (*BR*) *f* (*de fogo*) smoke; (*de gás*) fumes *pl*

fumador, a [fuma'dor(a)] (*PT*) *m/f* smoker

fumante [fu'mãtʃi] *m/f* smoker

fumar [fu'mar] *vt, vi* to smoke

fumo ['fumu] *m* (*PT: de fogo*) smoke; (: *de gás*) fumes *pl*; (*BR: tabaco*) tobacco; (*fumar*) smoking

função [fũ'sãw] (*pl* **-ões**) *f* function; (*ofício*) duty; (*papel*) role; (*espetáculo*) performance

funcionalismo [fũsjona'lizmu] *m*: **~ público** civil service

funcionamento [fũsjona'mẽtu] *m* functioning, working; **pôr em ~** to set going, start

funcionar [fũsjo'nar] *vi* to function; (*máquina*) to work, run; (*dar bom resultado*) to work

funcionário, -a [fũsjo'narju, a] *m/f* official; **~ (público)** civil servant

funções [fũ'sõjs] *fpl de* **função**

fundação [fũda'sãw] (*pl* **-ões**) *f* foundation

fundamental [fũdamẽ'taw] (*pl* **-ais**) *adj* fundamental, basic

fundamento [fũda'mẽtu] *m* (*fig*) foundation, basis; (*motivo*) motive

fundar [fũ'dar] *vt* to establish, found; (*basear*) to base; **fundar-se** *vr*: **~-se em** to be based on

fundir [fũ'dʒir] *vt* to fuse; (*metal*) to smelt, melt down; (*Com: empresas*) to merge; (*em molde*) to cast; **fundir-se** *vr* to melt; (*juntar-se*) to merge

fundo, -a ['fũdu, a] *adj* deep; (*fig*) profound ▷ *m* (*do mar, jardim*) bottom; (*profundidade*) depth; (*base*) basis; (*da loja, casa, do papel*) back; (*de quadro*) background; (*de dinheiro*) fund ▷ *adv* deeply; **fundos** *mpl* (*Com*) funds; (*da casa etc*) back *sg*; **a ~** thoroughly; **no ~** at the bottom; (*da casa etc*) at the back; (*fig*) basically

fúnebre ['funebri] *adj* funeral *atr*, funereal; (*fig*) gloomy

funeral [fune'raw] (*pl* **-ais**) *m* funeral

funil [fu'niw] (*pl* **-is**) *m* funnel

furacão [fura'kãw] (*pl* **-ões**) *m* hurricane

furado, -a [fu'radu, a] *adj* perforated; (*pneu*) flat; (*orelha*) pierced

furão, -rona [fu'rãw, 'rona] (*pl* **-ões/-s**) *m* ferret ▷ *m/f* (*col*) go-getter ▷ *adj* (*col*) hard-working, dynamic

furar [fu'rar] *vt* to perforate; (*penetrar*) to penetrate; (*frustrar*) to foil; (*fila*) to jump ▷ *vi* (*col: programa*) to fall through

fúria ['furja] *f* fury, rage; **furioso, -a** [fu'rjozu, ɔza] *adj* furious

furo ['furu] *m* hole; (*num pneu*) puncture

furões [fu'rõjs] *mpl de* **furão**

furona [fu'rona] *f de* **furão**

furor [fu'ror] *m* fury, rage; **fazer ~**

to be all the rage
furtar [fur'tar] *vt, vi* to steal;
  furtar-se *vr*: **~-se a** to avoid
furtivo, -a [fur'tʃivu, a] *adj* furtive,
stealthy
furto ['furtu] *m* theft
fusível [fu'zivew] (*pl* **-eis**) *m* (*Elet*)
fuse
fuso ['fuzu] *m* (*Tec*) spindle; **~
horário** time zone
futebol [futʃi'bɔw] *m* football; **~ de
salão** indoor football
futevôlei [futʃi'volej] *m see note*

○ **FUTEVÔLEI**
○
○ **Futevôlei** is a type of volleyball
○ in which the ball is allowed to
○ touch only the feet, legs, trunk
○ and head of the players. It is very
○ popular on the beaches of Rio de
○ Janeiro, where tournaments
○ take place during the summer, in
○ which many famous footballers
○ take part.

fútil ['futʃiw] (*pl* **-eis**) *adj* (*pessoa*)
shallow; (*insignificante*) trivial
futilidade [futʃili'dadʒi] *f* (*de
pessoa*) shallowness;
(*insignificância*) triviality; (*coisa
fútil*) trivial thing
futuro, -a [fu'turu, a] *adj* future
  ▷ *m* future; **no ~** in the future
fuzil [fu'ziw] (*pl* **-is**) *m* rifle; **fuzilar**
[fuzi'lar] *vt* to shoot
fuzis [fu'zis] *mpl de* **fuzil**

g

G, g [ʒe] *m* G, g
g. *abr* (= *grama*) gr.
gabar [ga'bar] *vt* to praise;
  gabar-se *vr*: **~-se de** to boast
about
gabinete [gabi'netʃi] *m* (*Com*)
office; (*escritório*) study; (*Pol*)
cabinet
gado ['gadu] *m* livestock; (*bovino*)
cattle; **~ leiteiro** dairy cattle; **~
suíno** pigs *pl*
gafanhoto [gafa'ɲotu] *m*
grasshopper
gafe ['gafi] *f* gaffe, faux pas
gagueira [ga'gejra] *f* stutter
gaguejar [gage'ʒar] *vi* to stammer,
stutter
gaiato, -a [ga'jatu, a] *adj* funny
gaiola [ga'jɔla] *f* cage; (*cadeia*) jail
  ▷ *m* (*barco*) riverboat
gaita ['gajta] *f* harmonica; **~ de
foles** bagpipes *pl*

gaivota [gaj'vɔta] f seagull

gajo ['gaʒu] (PT: col) m guy, fellow

gala ['gala] f: **traje de ~** evening dress; **festa de ~** gala

galão [ga'lãw] (pl -ões) m (Mil) stripe; (medida) gallon; (PT: café) white coffee; (passamanaria) braid

Galápagos [ga'lapagus] n: **(as) Ilhas ~** (the) Galapagos Islands

galáxia [ga'laksja] m galaxy

galera [ga'lɛra] f (Náut) galley; (col: pessoas, público) crowd

galeria [gale'ria] f gallery; (Teatro) circle

Gales ['galis] m: **País de ~** Wales

galho ['gaʎu] m (de árvore) branch

galinha [ga'liɲa] f hen; (Culin) chicken; **galinheiro** [gali'ɲejru] m hen-house

galo ['galu] m cock, rooster; (inchação) bump; **missa do ~** midnight mass

galões [ga'lõjs] mpl de **galão**

galopar [galo'par] vi to gallop; **galope** [ga'lɔpi] m gallop

gama ['gama] f (Mús) scale; (fig) range; (Zool) doe

gambá [gã'ba] m (Zool) opossum

game ['geimi] m computer game

Gana ['gana] f Ghana

gana ['gana] f craving, desire; (ódio) hate; **ter ~s de (fazer) algo** to feel like (doing) sth; **ter ~ de alguém** to hate sb

ganância [ga'nãsja] f greed; **ganancioso, -a** [ganã'sjozu, ɔza] adj greedy

gancho ['gãʃu] m hook; (de calça) crotch

gangue ['gãgi] (col) f gang

ganhador, a [gaɲa'dor(a)] adj winning ▷ m/f winner

ganha-pão ['gaɲa-] (pl -pães) m living, livelihood

ganhar [ga'ɲar] vt to win; (salário) to earn; (adquirir) to get; (lugar) to reach; (lucrar) to gain ▷ vi to win; **~ de alguém** (num jogo) to beat sb; **ganho, -a** ['gaɲu, a] pp de **ganhar** ▷ m profit, gain; **ganhos** mpl (ao jogo) winnings

ganso, -a ['gãsu, a] m/f goose

garagem [ga'raʒẽ] (pl -ns) f garage

garantia [garã'tʃia] f guarantee; (de dívida) surety

garçom [gar'sõ] (BR) (pl -ns) m waiter

garçonete [garso'netʃi] (BR) f waitress

garçons [gar'sõs] mpl de **garçom**

garfo ['garfu] m fork

gargalhada [garga'ʎada] f burst of laughter; **rir às ~s** to roar with laughter; **dar** ou **soltar uma ~** to burst out laughing

gargalo [gar'galu] m (tb fig) bottleneck

garganta [gar'gãta] f throat; (Geo) gorge, ravine

gargarejo [garga'reʒu] m (ato) gargling; (líquido) gargle

gari [ga'ri] m/f (na rua) road sweeper (Brit), street sweeper (US); (lixeiro) dustman (Brit), garbage man (US)

garoa [ga'roa] f drizzle; **garoar** [ga'rwar] vi to drizzle

garotada [garo'tada] f: **a ~** the kids pl

garoto, -a [ga'rotu, a] m/f boy/girl ▷ m (BR: chope) small beer; (PT: café) coffee with milk

garoupa [ga'ropa] f (peixe) grouper

garrafa [ga'hafa] f bottle

garupa [ga'rupa] f (de cavalo) hindquarters pl; (de moto) back seat; **andar na ~** (de moto) to ride pillion

gás [gajs] m gas; **gases** mpl (do

intestino) wind *sg*; **~ natural** natural gas; **~ de efeito estufa** greenhouse gas

gasóleo [ga'zɔlju] *m* diesel oil

gasolina [gazo'lina] *f* petrol (*Brit*), gas(oline) (*US*)

gasosa [ga'zɔza] *f* fizzy drink

gasoso, -a [ga'zozu, ɔza] *adj* (*água*) sparkling; (*bebida*) fizzy

gastador, -deira [gasta'dor, 'dejra] *adj, m/f* spendthrift

gastar [gas'tar] *vt* to spend; (*gasolina, electricidade*) to use; (*roupa, sapato*) to wear out; (*salto, piso etc*) to wear down; (*saúde*) to damage; (*desperdiçar*) to waste ▷ *vi* to spend; to wear out; to wear down; **gastar-se** *vr* to wear out; to wear down

gata ['gata] *f* (she-)cat

gatilho [ga'tʃiʎu] *m* trigger

gato ['gatu] *m* cat; **~ montês** wild cat

gatuno, -a [ga'tunu, a] *adj* thieving ▷ *m/f* thief

gaveta [ga'veta] *f* drawer

geada ['ʒjada] *f* frost

geladeira [ʒela'dejra] (*BR*) *f* refrigerator, icebox (*US*)

gelado, -a [ʒe'ladu, a] *adj* frozen ▷ *m* (*PT: sorvete*) ice cream

gelar [ʒe'lar] *vt* to freeze; (*vinho etc*) to chill ▷ *vi* to freeze

gelatina [ʒela'tʃina] *f* gelatine; (*sobremesa*) jelly (*Brit*), jello (*US*)

geleia [ʒe'leja] *f* jam

gélido, -a ['ʒɛlidu, a] *adj* chill, icy

gelo ['ʒelu] *adj inv* light grey (*Brit*) *ou* gray (*US*) ▷ *m* ice; (*cor*) light grey (*Brit*) *ou* gray (*US*)

gema ['ʒɛma] *f* yolk; (*pedra preciosa*) gem

gêmeo, -a ['ʒemju, a] *adj, m/f* twin; **Gêmeos** *mpl* (*Astrologia*) Gemini *sg*

gemer [ʒe'mer] *vi* (*de dor*) to groan, moan; (*lamentar-se*) to wail; (*animal*) to whine; (*vento*) to howl;

gemido [ʒe'midu] *m* groan, moan; (*lamento*) wail; (*de animal*) whine

gene ['ʒɛni] *m* gene

Genebra [ʒe'nɛbra] *n* Geneva

general [ʒene'raw] (*pl* **-ais**) *m* general

generalizar [ʒenerali'zar] *vt* to propagate ▷ *vi* to generalize; **generalizar-se** *vr* to become general, spread

gênero ['ʒeneru] *m* type, kind; (*Bio*) genus; (*Ling*) gender; **gêneros** *mpl* (*produtos*) goods; **~s alimentícios** foodstuffs; **~ humano** humankind, human race

generosidade [ʒenerozi'dadʒi] *f* generosity

generoso, -a [ʒene'rozu, ɔza] *adj* generous

genética [ʒe'nɛtʃika] *f* genetics *sg*

gengibre [ʒẽ'ʒibri] *m* ginger

gengiva [ʒẽ'ʒiva] *f* (*Anat*) gum

genial [ʒe'njaw] (*pl* **-ais**) *adj* inspired, brilliant; (*col*) terrific, fantastic

gênio ['ʒenju] *m* (*temperamento*) nature; (*irascibilidade*) temper; (*talento, pessoa*) genius; **de bom ~** good-natured; **de mau ~** bad-tempered

genital [ʒeni'taw] (*pl* **-ais**) *adj*: **órgãos genitais** genitals *pl*

genro ['ʒẽhu] *m* son-in-law

gente ['ʒẽtʃi] *f* people *pl*; (*col*) folks *pl*, family; (*col: alguém*): **tem ~ batendo à porta** there's somebody knocking at the door; **a ~** (*nós: suj*) we; (*: obj*) us; **a casa da ~** our house; **toda a ~** everybody; **~ grande** grown-ups *pl*

gentil [ʒēˈtʃiw] (pl **-is**) adj kind;
gentileza [ʒētʃiˈleza] f kindness;
por gentileza if you please; **tenha
a gentileza de fazer ...** would you
be so kind as to do ...?
genuíno, -a [ʒeˈnwinu, a] adj
genuine
geografia [ʒeograˈfia] f geography
geometria [ʒeomeˈtria] f
geometry
geração [ʒeraˈsāw] (pl **-ões**) f
generation
gerador, a [ʒeraˈdor(a)] m/f
(produtor) creator ▷ m (Tec)
generator
geral [ʒeˈraw] (pl **-ais**) adj general
▷ f (Teatro) gallery; **em ~** in general,
generally; **de um modo ~** on the
whole; **geralmente** [ʒerawˈmētʃi]
adv generally, usually
gerânio [ʒeˈranju] m geranium
gerar [ʒeˈrar] vt to produce;
(eletricidade) to generate
gerência [ʒeˈrēsja] f management;
gerenciar [ʒerēˈsjar] vt, vi to
manage
gerente [ʒeˈrētʃi] adj managing
▷ m/f manager
gerir [ʒeˈrir] vt to manage, run
germe [ˈʒɛrmi] m (embrião) embryo;
(micróbio) germ
gesso [ˈʒesu] m plaster (of Paris)
gesticular [ʒestʃikuˈlar] vi to make
gestures, gesture
gesto [ˈʒɛstu] m gesture
Gibraltar [ʒibrawˈtar] f Gibraltar
gigante, -a [ʒiˈgātʃi] adj gigantic,
huge ▷ m giant; **gigantesco, -a**
[ʒigāˈtesku, a] adj gigantic
gim [ʒī] (pl **-ns**) m gin
ginásio [ʒiˈnazju] m gymnasium;
(escola) secondary (Brit) ou high (US)
school
ginástica [ʒiˈnastʃika] f

gymnastics sg; (para fortalecer o
corpo) keep-fit
ginecologia [ʒinekoloˈʒia] f
gynaecology (Brit), gynecology (US)
ginecologista [ʒinekoloˈʒista] m/f
gynaecologist (Brit), gynecologist
(US)
ginjinha [ʒīˈʒiɲa] (PT) f cherry
brandy
gira-discos (PT) m inv record-player
girafa [ʒiˈrafa] f giraffe
girar [ʒiˈrar] vt to turn, rotate;
(como pião) to spin ▷ vi to go round;
to spin; (vaguear) to wander
girassol [ʒiraˈsɔw] (pl **-óis**) m
sunflower
gíria [ˈʒirja] f (calão) slang; (jargão)
jargon
giro¹ [ˈʒiru] m turn; **dar um ~** to go
for a wander; (em veículo) to go for a
spin; **que ~!** (PT) great!
giro² vb ver **gerir**
giz [ʒiz] m chalk
glacê [glaˈse] m icing
glacial [glaˈsjaw] (pl **-ais**) adj icy
glamouroso, -a [glamuˈrozu, ɔza]
adj glamorous
glândula [ˈglādula] f gland
global [gloˈbaw] (pl **-ais**) adj global;
(total) overall; **quantia ~** lump
sum; **globalização**
[globalizaˈsāw] f globalization
globo [ˈglobu] m globe; **~ ocular**
eyeball
glória [ˈglɔrja] f glory; **glorificar**
[glorifiˈkar] vt to glorify;
glorioso, -a [gloˈrjozu, ɔza] adj
glorious
glossário [gloˈsarju] m glossary
gnomo [ˈgnomu] m gnome
goiaba [goˈjaba] f guava;
goiabada [gojaˈbada] f guava jelly
gol [gow] (pl **gols**) m goal
gola [ˈgɔla] f collar

g

gole ['gɔli] *m* gulp, swallow; (*pequeno*) sip; **dar um ~** to have a sip

goleiro [go'lejru] (*BR*) *m* goalkeeper; (*inf*) goalie

golfe ['gowfi] *m* golf; **campo de ~** golf course

golfinho [gow'fiɲu] *m* (*Zool*) dolphin

golfo ['gowfu] *m* gulf

golinho [go'liɲu] *m* sip; **beber algo aos ~s** to sip sth

golo ['golu] (*PT*) *m* = **gol**

golpe ['gɔwpi] *m* (*tb fig*) blow; (*de mão*) smack; (*de punho*) punch; (*manobra*) ploy; (*de vento*) gust; **de um só ~** at a stroke; **dar um ~ em alguém** to hit sb; (*fig: trapacear*) to trick sb; **~ (de estado)** coup (d'état); **~ de mestre** masterstroke; **golpear** [gow'pjar] *vt* to hit; (*com navalha*) to stab; (*com o punho*) to punch

goma ['gɔma] *f* gum, glue; (*de roupa*) starch; **~ de mascar** chewing gum

gomo ['gomu] *m* (*de laranja*) slice

gordo, -a ['gordu, a] *adj* fat; (*gordurento*) greasy; (*carne*) fatty; (*fig: quantia*) considerable, ample ▷ *m/f* fat man/woman

gordura [gor'dura] *f* fat; (*derretida*) grease; (*obesidade*) fatness; **gorduroso, -a** [gordu'rozu, ɔza] *adj* (*pele*) greasy; (*comida*) fatty

gorila [go'rila] *m* gorilla

gorjeta [gor'ʒeta] *f* tip, gratuity

gorro ['gohu] *m* cap; (*de lã*) hat

gosma ['gɔzma] *f* spittle; (*fig*) slime

gostar [gos'tar] *vi*: **~ de** to like; (*férias, viagem etc*) to enjoy; **gostar-se** *vr* to like each other; **~ mais de ...** to prefer ..., to like ... better

gosto ['gostu] *m* taste; (*prazer*) pleasure; **a seu ~** to your liking; **com ~** willingly; (*vestir-se*) tastefully; (*comer*) heartily; **de bom/mau ~** in good/bad taste; **ter ~ de** to taste of; **gostoso, -a** [gos'tozu, ɔza] *adj* tasty; (*agradável*) pleasant; (*cheiro*) lovely; (*risada*) good; (*col: pessoa*) gorgeous

gota ['gota] *f* drop; (*de suor*) bead; (*Med*) gout; **~ a ~** drop by drop

goteira [go'tejra] *f* (*cano*) gutter; (*buraco*) leak

gourmet [gur'me] (*pl* **gourmets**) *m/f* gourmet

governador, a [governador(a)] *m/f* governor

governamental [governamẽ'taw] (*pl* **-ais**) *adj* government *atr*

governante [gover'nãtʃi] *adj* ruling ▷ *m/f* ruler ▷ *f* governess

governar [gover'nar] *vt* to govern, rule; (*barco*) to steer

governo [go'vernu] *m* government; (*controle*) control

gozação [goza'sãw] (*pl* **-ões**) *f* enjoyment; (*zombaria*) teasing; (*uma gozação*) joke

gozado, -a [go'zadu, a] *adj* funny; (*estranho*) strange, odd

gozar [go'zar] *vt* to enjoy; (*col: rir de*) to make fun of ▷ *vi* to enjoy o.s.; **~ de** to enjoy; to make fun of; **gozo** ['gozu] *m* (*prazer*) pleasure; (*uso*) enjoyment, use; (*orgasmo*) orgasm

Grã-Bretanha [grã-bre'taɲa] *f* Great Britain

graça ['grasa] *f* (*Rel*) grace; (*charme*) charm; (*gracejo*) joke; (*Jur*) pardon; **de ~** (*grátis*) for nothing; (*sem motivo*) for no reason; **sem ~** dull, boring; **fazer** *ou* **ter ~** to be funny; **ficar sem ~** to be embarrassed; **~s a** thanks to

gracejar [grase'ʒar] vi to joke; **gracejo** [gra'seʒu] m joke

gracioso, -a [gra'sjozu, ɔza] adj (*pessoa*) charming; (*gestos*) gracious

grade ['gradʒi] f (*no chão*) grating; (*grelha*) grill; (*na janela*) bars pl; (*col: cadeia*) prison

gradear [gra'dʒar] vt (*janela*) to put bars up at; (*jardim*) to fence off

graduação [gradwa'sãw] (pl **-ões**) f (*classificação*) grading; (*Educ*) graduation; (*Mil*) rank

gradual [gra'dwaw] (pl **-ais**) adj gradual

graduar [gra'dwar] vt (*classificar*) to grade; (*luz, fogo*) to regulate; **graduar-se** vr to graduate

gráfica ['grafika] f graphics sg; ver tb **gráfico**

gráfico, -a ['grafiku, a] adj graphic ⊳ m/f printer ⊳ m (*Mat*) graph; (*diagrama*) diagram, chart; **gráficos** mpl (*Comput*) graphics; **~ de barras** bar chart

grã-fino, -a [grã'finu, a] (*col*) adj posh ⊳ m/f nob, toff

grama ['grama] m gramme ⊳ f (BR: *capim*) grass

gramado [gra'madu] (BR) m lawn; (*Futebol*) pitch

gramática [gra'matʃika] f grammar

grampear [grã'pjar] vt to staple

grampo ['grãpu] m staple; (*no cabelo*) hairgrip; (*de carpinteiro*) clamp; (*de chapéu*) hatpin

grande ['grãdʒi] adj big, large; (*alto*) tall; (*notável, intenso*) great; (*longo*) long; (*adulto*) grown-up; **mulher ~** big woman; **~ mulher** great woman; **grandeza** [grã'deza] f size; (*fig*) greatness; (*ostentação*) grandeur

grandioso, -a [grã'dʒjozu, ɔza] adj magnificent, grand

granito [gra'nitu] m granite

granizo [gra'nizu] m hailstone; **chover ~** to hail; **chuva de ~** hailstorm

granulado, -a [granu'ladu, a] adj grainy; (*açúcar*) granulated

grão ['grãw] (pl **grãos**) m grain; (*semente*) seed; (*de café*) bean; **grão-de-bico** (pl **grãos-de-bico**) m chickpea

gratidão [gratʃi'dãw] f gratitude

gratificar [gratʃifi'kar] vt to tip; (*dar bônus a*) to give a bonus to; (*recompensar*) to reward

grátis ['gratʃis] adj free

grato, -a ['gratu, a] adj grateful; (*agradável*) pleasant

gratuito, -a [gra'twitu, a] adj (*grátis*) free; (*infundado*) gratuitous

grau [graw] m degree; (*nível*) level; (*Educ*) class; **em alto ~** to a high degree; **ensino de primeiro/ segundo ~** primary (*Brit*) ou elementary (*US*)/secondary education

gravação [grava'sãw] f (*em madeira*) carving; (*em disco, fita*) recording

gravador, a [grava'dor(a)] m tape recorder ⊳ m/f engraver; **~ de CD/ DVD** CD/DVD burner, CD/DVD writer

gravar [gra'var] vt to carve; (*metal, pedra*) to engrave; (*na memória*) to fix; (*disco, fita*) to record

gravata [gra'vata] f tie; **~ borboleta** bow tie

grave ['gravi] adj serious; (*tom*) deep; **gravemente** [grave'mētʃi] adv (*doente, ferido*) seriously

grávida ['gravida] adj pregnant

gravidade [gravi'dadʒi] f gravity

g

gravidez [gravi'deʒ] f pregnancy

gravura [gra'vura] f (em madeira) engraving; (estampa) print

graxa ['graʃa] f (para sapatos) polish; (lubrificante) grease

Grécia ['grɛsja] f: **a ~** Greece; **grego, -a** ['gregu, a] adj, m/f Greek ▷ m (Ling) Greek

grelha ['grɛʎa] f grill; (de fornalha) grate; **bife na ~** grilled steak; **grelhado, -a** [gre'ʎadu, a] adj grilled ▷ m (prato) grill

grêmio ['gremju] m (associação) guild; (clube) club

grená [gre'na] adj, m dark red

greve ['grɛvi] f strike; **fazer ~** to go on strike; **~ branca** go-slow; **grevista** [gre'vista] m/f striker

grilo ['grilu] m cricket; (Auto) squeak; (col: de pessoa) hang-up; **qual é o ~?** what's the matter?; **não tem ~!** (col) (there's) no problem!

gringo, -a ['grĩgu, a] (col: pej) m/f foreigner

gripado, -a [gri'padu, a] adj: **estar/ficar ~** to have/get a cold

gripe ['gripi] f flu, influenza

grisalho, -a [gri'zaʎu, a] adj (cabelo) grey (Brit), gray (US)

gritante [gri'tãtʃi] adj (hipocrisia) glaring; (desigualdade) gross; (mentira) blatant; (cor) loud, garish

gritar [gri'tar] vt to shout, yell ▷ vi to shout; (de dor, medo) to scream; **~ com alguém** to shout at sb; **gritaria** [grita'ria] f shouting, din; **grito** ['gritu] m shout; (de medo) scream; (de dor) cry; (de animal) call; **dar um grito** to cry out; **falar/protestar aos gritos** to shout/shout protests

Groenlândia [grwẽ'lãdʒja] f: **a ~** Greenland

grosseiro, -a [gro'sejru, a] adj rude; (piada) crude; (modos) coarse; **grosseria** [grose'ria] f rudeness; (ato): **fazer uma grosseria** to be rude; (dito): **dizer uma grosseria** to be rude, say something rude

grosso, -a ['grosu, 'grɔsa] adj thick; (áspero) rough; (voz) deep; (col: pessoa, piada) rude ▷ m: **o ~ de** the bulk of; **grossura** [gro'sura] f thickness

grotesco, -a [gro'tesku, a] adj grotesque

grudar [gru'dar] vt to glue, stick ▷ vi to stick

grude ['grudʒi] f glue; **grudento, -a** [gru'dẽtu, a] adj sticky

grunhir [gru'ɲir] vi (porco) to grunt; (tigre) to growl; (resmungar) to grumble

grupo ['grupu] m group

guarda ['gwarda] m/f policeman/woman ▷ f (vigilância) guarding; (de objeto) safekeeping ▷ m (Mil) guard; **estar de ~** to be on guard; **pôr-se em ~** to be on one's guard; **a G~ Civil** the Civil Guard; **guarda-chuva** (pl **guarda-chuvas**) m umbrella; **guarda-costas** m inv (Náut) coastguard boat; (capanga) bodyguard; **guardados** [gwar'dadus] mpl keepsakes, valuables; **guarda-fogo** (pl **guarda-fogos**) m fireguard; **guarda-louça** [gwarda'losa] (pl **guarda-louças**) m sideboard; **guardanapo** [gwarda'napu] m napkin; **guarda-noturno** (pl **guardas-noturnos**) m night watchman; **guardar** [gwar'dar] vt to put away; (zelar por) to guard; (lembrança, segredo) to keep;

guardar-se *vr* (*defender-se*) to protect o.s.; **guardar-se de** (*acautelar-se*) to guard against; **guarda-redes** (*PT*) *m inv* goalkeeper; **guarda-roupa** (*pl* **guarda-roupas**) *m* wardrobe; **guarda-sol** (*pl* **guarda-sóis**) *m* sunshade, parasol

guardião, -diã [gwar'dʒjãw, 'dʒjã] (*pl* **-ães/-s**) *m/f* guardian

guarnição [gwarni'sãw] (*pl* **-ões**) *f* (*Mil*) garrison; (*Náut*) crew; (*Culin*) garnish

Guatemala [gwate'mala] *f*: **a ~** Guatemala

gude ['gudʒi] *m*: **bola de ~** marble; (*jogo*) marbles *pl*

guerra ['gɛha] *f* war; **em ~** at war; **fazer ~** to wage war; **~ civil** civil war; **~ mundial** world war; **guerreiro, -a** [ge'hejru, a] *adj* (*espírito*) fighting; (*belicoso*) warlike ▷ *m* warrior

guerrilha [ge'hiʎa] *f* (*luta*) guerrilla warfare; (*tropa*) guerrilla band; **guerrilheiro, -a** [gehi'ʎejru, a] *m/f* guerrilla

guia ['gia] *f* guidance; (*Com*) permit, bill of lading; (*formulário*) advice slip ▷ *m* (*livro*) guide(book) ▷ *m/f* (*pessoa*) guide

Guiana ['gjana] *f*: **a ~** Guyana

guiar [gjar] *vt* to guide; (*Auto*) to drive ▷ *vi* to drive; **guiar-se** *vr*: **~-se por** to go by

guichê [gi'ʃe] *m* ticket window; (*em banco, repartição*) window, counter

guinada [gi'nada] *f*: **dar uma ~** (*com o carro*) to swerve

guindaste [gĩ'dastʃi] *m* hoist, crane

guisado [gi'zadu] *m* stew

guitarra [gi'taha] *f* (electric) guitar

guloso, -a [gu'lozu, ɔza] *adj* greedy

h

H, h [a'ga] *m* H, h

há [a] *vb ver* **haver**

hábil ['abiw] (*pl* **-eis**) *adj* competent, capable; (*astucioso, esperto*) clever; (*sutil*) diplomatic; **em tempo ~** in reasonable time; **habilidade** [abili'dadʒi] *f* skill, ability; (*astúcia, esperteza*) shrewdness; (*tato*) discretion; **habilidoso, -a** [abili'dozu, ɔza] *adj* skilful (*Brit*), skillful (*US*), clever

habilitação [abilita'sãw] (*pl* **-ões**) *f* competence; (*ato*) qualification; **habilitações** *fpl* (*conhecimentos*) qualifications

habilitar [abili'tar] *vt* to enable; (*dar direito a*) to qualify, entitle; (*preparar*) to prepare

habitação [abita'sãw] (*pl* **-ões**) *f* dwelling, residence; (*alojamento*) housing

habitante [abi'tãtʃi] *m/f*

inhabitant

habitar [abi'tar] *vt* to live in; (*povoar*) to inhabit ▷ *vi* to live

hábito ['abitu] *m* habit; (*social*) custom; (*Rel: traje*) habit

habituado, -a [abi'twadu, a] *adj*: **~ a (fazer) algo** used to (doing) sth

habituar [abi'twar] *vt*: **~ alguém a** to get sb used to, accustom sb to; **habituar-se** *vr*: **~-se a** to get used to

hacker ['haker] (*pl* **hackers**) *m* (*Comput*) hacker

Haia ['aja] *n* the Hague

haja *etc* ['aʒa] *vb ver* **haver**

hálito ['alitu] *m* breath

hall [hɔw] (*pl* **halls**) *m* hall; (*de teatro, hotel*) foyer; **~ de entrada** entrance hall

hambúrguer [ã'burger] *m* hamburger

hão [ãw] *vb ver* **haver**

hardware ['hadwer] *m* (*Comput*) hardware

harmonia [armo'nia] *f* harmony

harmonioso, -a [armo'njozu, ɔza] *adj* harmonious

harmonizar [armoni'zar] *vt* (*Mús*) to harmonize; (*conciliar*): **~ algo (com algo)** to reconcile sth (with sth); **harmonizar-se** *vr*: **~(-se) (com algo)** (*ideias etc*) to coincide (with sth); (*pessoas*) to be in agreement (with sth)

harpa ['arpa] *f* harp

Havaí [avaj'i] *m*: **o ~** Hawaii

PALAVRA-CHAVE

haver [a'ver] *vb aux* **1** (*ter*) to have; **ele havia saído/comido** he had left/eaten

2: **quem haveria de dizer que ...** who would have thought that ... ▷ *vb impess* **1** (*existência*): **há** (*sg*) there is; (*pl*) there are; **o que é que há?** what's the matter?; **o que é que houve?** what happened?, what was that?; **não há de quê** don't mention it, you're welcome; **haja o que houver** come what may

2 (*tempo*): **há séculos/cinco dias que não o vejo** I haven't seen him for ages/five days; **há um ano que ela chegou** it's a year since she arrived; **há cinco dias (atrás)** five days ago

haver-se *vr*: **haver-se com alguém** to sort things out with sb ▷ *m* (*Com*) credit; **haveres** *mpl* (*pertences*) property *sg*, possessions; (*riqueza*) wealth *sg*

haxixe [a'ʃiʃi] *m* hashish

hebraico, -a [e'brajku, a] *adj* Hebrew ▷ *m* (*Ling*) Hebrew

Hébridas ['ɛbridas] *fpl*: **as (ilhas) ~** the Hebrides

hediondo, -a [e'dʒjõdu, a] *adj* vile, revolting; (*crime*) heinous

hei [ej] *vb ver* **haver**

hélice ['ɛlisi] *f* propeller

helicóptero [eli'kɔpteru] *m* helicopter

hematoma [ema'tɔma] *m* bruise

hemorragia [emoa'ʒia] *f* haemorrhage (*Brit*), hemorrhage (*US*); **~ nasal** nosebleed

hemorróidas [emo'hɔjdas] *fpl* haemorrhoids (*Brit*), hemorrhoids (*US*), piles

hepatite [epa'tʃitʃi] *f* hepatitis

hera ['ɛra] *f* ivy

herança [e'rãsa] *f* inheritance; (*fig*) heritage

herdar [er'dar] *vt*: **~ algo (de)** to inherit sth (from); **~ a** to bequeath to

herdeiro, -a [er'dejru, a] *m/f* heir(ess)

herói [e'rɔj] *m* hero

heroína [ero'ina] *f* heroine; *(droga)* heroin

hesitação [ezita'sãw] *f(pl* **-ões)** hesitation

hesitante [ezi'tãtʃi] *adj* hesitant

hesitar [ezi'tar] *vi* to hesitate

heterossexual [eterosek'swaw] *(pl* **-ais)** *adj, m/f* heterosexual

híbrido, -a ['ibridu, a] *adj* hybrid

hidratante [idra'tãtʃi] *m* moisturizer

hidráulico, -a [i'drawliku, a] *adj* hydraulic

hidrelétrico, -a [idre'lɛtriku, a] *adj* hydroelectric

hidro... [idru] *prefixo* hydro..., water... *atr*

hidrogênio [idro'ʒenju] *m* hydrogen

hidroginástica [idroʒi'nastʃika] *f* aquaerobics

hífen ['ifẽ] *(pl* **hífens)** *m* hyphen

higiene [i'ʒjeni] *f* hygiene; **higiênico, -a** [i'ʒjeniku, a] *adj* hygienic; *(pessoa)* clean; **papel higiênico** toilet paper

hindu [ĩ'du] *adj, m/f* Hindu

hino ['inu] *m* hymn; **~ nacional** national anthem

hipermercado [ipermer'kadu] *m* hypermarket

hipertensão [ipertẽ'sãw] *f* high blood pressure

hipismo [i'pizmu] *m (turfe)* horse racing; *(equitação)* (horse) riding

hipocrisia [ipokri'zia] *f* hypocrisy; **hipócrita** [i'pɔkrita] *adj* hypocritical ▷ *m/f* hypocrite

hipódromo [i'pɔdromu] *m* racecourse

hipopótamo [ipo'pɔtamu] *m* hippopotamus

hipoteca [ipo'tɛka] *f* mortgage; **hipotecar** [ipote'kar] *vt* to mortgage

hipótese [i'pɔtezi] *f* hypothesis; **na ~ de** in the event of; **em ~ alguma** under no circumstances; **na melhor/pior das ~s** at best/worst

hispânico, -a [is'paniku, a] *adj* Hispanic

histeria [iste'ria] *f* hysteria; **histérico, -a** [is'tɛriku, a] *adj* hysterical

história [is'tɔrja] *f* history; *(conto)* story; **histórias** *fpl (chateação)* bother *sg*, fuss *sg*; **isso é outra ~** that's a different matter; **que ~ é essa?** what's going on?; **historiador, a** [istɔrja'dor(a)] *m/f* historian; **histórico, -a** [is'tɔriku, a] *adj* historical; *(fig: notável)* historic ▷ *m* history

hobby ['hɔbi] *(pl* **-bies)** *m* hobby

hoje ['oʒi] *adv* today; *(atualmente)* now(adays); **~ à noite** tonight

Holanda [o'lãda] *f*: **a ~** Holland; **holandês, -esa** [olã'des, eza] *adj* Dutch ▷ *m/f* Dutchman/woman ▷ *m (Ling)* Dutch

holocausto [olo'kawstu] *m* holocaust

homem ['omẽ] *(pl* **-ns)** *m* man; *(a humanidade)* mankind; **~ de empresa** *ou* **negócios** businessman; **~ de estado** statesman; **homem-bomba** *(pl* **homens-bomba)** *m* suicide bomber

homenagear [omena'ʒjar] *vt (pessoa)* to pay tribute to, honour *(Brit)*, honor *(US)*

homenagem [ome'naʒẽ] *f* tribute; *(Rel)* homage; **prestar ~ a alguém** to pay tribute to sb

homens ['omẽs] *mpl de* **homem**

homeopático, -a [omjo'patʃiku, a] *adj* homoeopathic (*Brit*), homeopathic (*US*)

homicida [omi'sida] *adj* homicidal ▷ *m/f* murderer; **homicídio** [omi'sidʒju] *m* murder; **homicídio involuntário** manslaughter

homologar [omolo'gar] *vt* to ratify

homólogo, -a [o'mɔlogu, a] *adj* homologous; (*fig*) equivalent ▷ *m/f* opposite number

homossexual [omosek'swaw] (*pl* **-ais**) *adj, m/f* homosexual

Honduras [õ'duras] *f* Honduras

honestidade [onestʃi'dadʒi] *f* honesty; (*decência*) decency; (*justeza*) fairness

honesto, -a [o'nɛstu, a] *adj* honest; (*decente*) decent; (*justo*) fair, just

honorário, -a [ono'rarju, a] *adj* honorary; **honorários** [ono'rarjus] *mpl* fees

honra ['õha] *f* honour (*Brit*), honor (*US*); **em ~ de** in hono(u)r of

honrado, -a [õ'hadu, a] *adj* honest; (*respeitado*) honourable (*Brit*), honorable (*US*)

honrar [õ'har] *vt* to honour (*Brit*), honor (*US*)

honroso, -a [õ'hozu, ɔza] *adj* honourable (*Brit*), honorable (*US*)

hóquei ['hɔkej] *m* hockey; **~ sobre gelo** ice hockey

hora ['ɔra] *f* (*60 minutos*) hour; (*momento*) time; **a que ~s?** (at) what time?; **que ~s são?** what time is it?; **são duas ~s** it's two o'clock; **você tem as ~s?** have you got the time?; **fazer ~** to kill time; **de ~ em ~** every hour; **na ~** on the spot; **chegar na ~** to be on time; **de última ~** *adj* last-minute ▷ *adv* at

the last minute; **~ do almoço** lunch hour; **meia ~** half an hour; **~s extras** overtime *sg*; **horário, -a** [o'rarju, a] *adj*: **100 km horários** 100 km an hour ▷ *m* timetable; (*hora*) time; **horário de expediente** working hours *pl*; (*de um escritório*) office hours *pl*

horizontal [orizõ'taw] (*pl* **-ais**) *adj* horizontal

horizonte [ori'zõtʃi] *m* horizon

horóscopo [o'rɔskopu] *m* horoscope

horrível [o'hivew] (*pl* **-eis**) *adj* awful, horrible

horror [o'hor] *m* horror; **que ~!** how awful!; **ter ~ a algo** to hate sth; **horrorizar** [ohori'zar] *vt* to horrify, frighten; **horroroso, -a** [oho'rozu, ɔza] *adj* horrible, ghastly

hortaliças [orta'lisas] *fpl* vegetables

hortelã [orte'lã] *f* mint; **~ pimenta** peppermint

horticultor, a [ortʃikuw'tor(a)] *m/f* market gardener (*Brit*), truck farmer (*US*)

hortifrutigranjeiros [ortʃifrutʃigrã'ʒejrus] *mpl* fruit and vegetables

horto ['ortu] *m* market garden (*Brit*), truck farm (*US*)

hospedagem [ospe'daʒẽ] *f* guest house

hospedar [ospe'dar] *vt* to put up; **hospedar-se** *vr* to stay, lodge; **hospedaria** [ospeda'ria] *f* guest house

hóspede ['ɔspedʒi] *m* (*amigo*) guest; (*estranho*) lodger

hospedeira [ospe'dejra] *f* landlady; (*PT: de bordo*) stewardess, air hostess (*Brit*)

hospício [os'pisju] *m* mental hospital
hospital [ospi'taw] (*pl* **-ais**) *m* hospital
hospitalidade [ospitali'dadʒi] *f* hospitality
hostil [os'tʃiw] (*pl* **-is**) *adj* hostile; **hostilizar** [ostʃili'zar] *vt* to antagonize; (*Mil*) to wage war on
hotel [o'tɛw] (*pl* **-éis**) *m* hotel; **hoteleiro, -a** [ote'lejru, a] *m/f* hotelier
houve *etc* ['ovi] *vb ver* **haver**
humanidade [umani'dadʒi] *f* (*os homens*) man(kind); (*compaixão*) humanity
humanitário, -a [umani'tarju, a] *adj* humane
humano, -a [u'manu, a] *adj* human; (*bondoso*) humane
humildade [umiw'dadʒi] *f* humility; (*pobreza*) poverty
humilde [u'miwdʒi] *adj* humble; (*pobre*) poor
humilhar [umi'ʎar] *vt* to humiliate
humor [u'mor] *m* mood, temper; (*graça*) humour (*Brit*), humor (*US*); **de bom/mau ~** in a good/bad mood; **humorista** [umo'rista] *m/f* comedian; **humorístico, -a** [umo'ristʃiku, a] *adj* humorous
húngaro, -a ['ũgaru, a] *adj, m/f* Hungarian
Hungria [ũ'gria] *f*: **a ~** Hungary
hurra ['uha] *m* cheer ▷ *excl* hurrah!

I, i [i:] *m* I, i
ia *etc* ['ia] *vb ver* **ir**
iate ['jatʃi] *m* yacht; **~ clube** yacht club
ibérico, -a [i'bɛriku, a] *adj, m/f* Iberian
ibero-americano, -a [iberu-] *adj, m/f* Ibero-American
ICMS (*BR*) *abr m* (= *Imposto sobre Circulação de Mercadorias e Prestação de Serviços*) ≈ VAT
ícone ['ikoni] *m* (*ger, Comput*) icon
ida ['ida] *f* going, departure; **~ e volta** round trip, return; **a (viagem de) ~** the outward journey; **na ~** on the way there
idade [i'dadʒi] *f* age; **ter cinco anos de ~** to be five (years old); **de meia ~** middle-aged; **qual é a ~ dele?** how old is he?; **na minha ~** at my age; **ser menor/maior de ~** to be under/of age; **pessoa de ~**

elderly person; **l~ Média** Middle
Ages pl
ideal [ide'jaw] (pl **-ais**) adj, m ideal;
idealista [idea'lista] adj idealistic
▷ m/f idealist
ideia [i'dɛja] f idea; (mente) mind;
mudar de ~ to change one's mind;
não ter a mínima ~ to have no
idea; **não faço ~** I can't imagine;
estar com ~ de fazer to plan to do
idem ['idẽ] pron ditto
idêntico, -a [i'dẽtʃiku, a] adj
identical
identidade [idẽtʃi'dadʒi] f identity
identificação [idẽtʃifika'sãw] f
identification
identificar [idẽtʃifi'kar] vt to
identify; **identificar-se** vr: **~-se
com** to identify with
idioma [i'dʒɔma] m language
idiota [i'dʒɔta] adj idiotic ▷ m/f
idiot
ido, -a ['idu, a] adj past
ídolo ['idolu] m idol
idoso, -a [i'dozu, ɔza] adj elderly,
old
ignorado, -a [igno'radu, a] adj
unknown
ignorância [igno'rãsja] f
ignorance; **ignorante** [igno'rãtʃi]
adj ignorant, uneducated ▷ m/f
ignoramus
ignorar [igno'rar] vt not to know;
(não dar atenção a) to ignore
igreja [i'greʒa] f church
igual [i'gwaw] (pl **-ais**) adj equal;
(superfície) even ▷ m/f equal
igualar [igwa'lar] vt to equal; (fazer
igual) to make equal; (nivelar) to
level ▷ vi: **~ a ou com** to be equal
to, be the same as; (ficar no mesmo
nível) to be level with; **igualar-se**
vr: **~-se a alguém** to be sb's equal
igualdade [igwaw'dadʒi] f

equality; (uniformidade) uniformity
igualmente [igwaw'mẽtʃi] adv
equally; (também) likewise, also; **~!**
(saudação) the same to you!
ilegal [ile'gaw] (pl **-ais**) adj illegal
ilegítimo, -a [ile'ʒitʃimu, a] adj
illegitimate; (ilegal) unlawful
ilegível [ile'ʒivew] (pl **-eis**) adj
illegible
iletrado, -a [ile'tradu, a] adj
illiterate
ilha ['iʎa] f island; **ilhéu, ilhoa**
[i'ʎɛw, i'ʎoa] m/f islander
ilícito, -a [i'lisitu, a] adj illicit
ilimitado, -a [ilimi'tadu, a] adj
unlimited
iluminar [ilumi'nar] vt to light up;
(estádio etc) to floodlight; (fig) to
enlighten
ilusão [ilu'zãw] (pl **-ões**) f illusion;
(quimera) delusion; **ilusório, -a**
[ilu'zɔrju, a] adj deceptive
ilustração [ilustra'sãw] (pl **-ões**) f
illustration
ilustrado, -a [ilus'tradu, a] adj
illustrated; (instruído) learned
ilustrar [ilus'trar] vt to illustrate;
(instruir) to instruct
ilustre [i'lustri] adj illustrious; **um
~ desconhecido** a complete
stranger
ímã ['imã] m magnet
imagem [i'maʒẽ] (pl **-ns**) f image;
(semelhança) likeness; (TV) picture;
imagens fpl (Literatura) imagery sg
imaginação [imaʒina'sãw] (pl
-ões) f imagination
imaginar [imaʒi'nar] vt to
imagine; (supor) to suppose;
imaginar-se vr to imagine o.s.;
imagine só! just imagine!;
imaginário, -a [imaʒi'narju, a]
adj imaginary
imaturo, -a [ima'turu, a] adj

immature

imbatível [ĩba'tʃivew] (pl **-eis**) adj invincible

imbecil [ĩbe'siw] (pl **-is**) adj stupid ▷ m/f imbecile; **imbecilidade** [ĩbesili'daʒi] f stupidity

imediações [imedʒa'sõjs] fpl vicinity sg, neighbourhood sg (Brit), neighborhood sg (US)

imediatamente [imedʒata'mẽtʃi] adv immediately, right away

imediato, -a [ime'dʒatu, a] adj immediate; (seguinte) next; **~ a** next to; **de ~** straight away

imenso, -a [i'mẽsu, a] adj immense, huge; (ódio, amor) great

imigração [imigra'sãw] (pl **-ões**) f immigration

imigrante [imi'grãtʃi] adj, m/f immigrant

iminente [imi'nẽtʃi] adj imminent

imitação [imita'sãw] (pl **-ões**) f imitation

imitar [imi'tar] vt to imitate; (assinatura) to copy

imobiliária [imobi'ljarja] f estate agent's (Brit), real estate broker's (US)

imobiliário, -a [imobi'ljarju, a] adj property atr

imobilizar [imobili'zar] vt to immobilize; (fig) to bring to a standstill

imoral [imo'raw] (pl **-ais**) adj immoral

imortal [imor'taw] (pl **-ais**) adj immortal

imóvel [i'mɔvew] (pl **-eis**) adj motionless, still; (não movediço) immovable ▷ m property; (edifício) building; **imóveis** mpl (propriedade) real estate sg, property sg

impaciência [ĩpa'sjẽsja] f impatience; **impacientar-se**

[ĩpasjẽ'tarsi] vr to lose one's patience; **impaciente** [ĩpa'sjẽtʃi] adj impatient

impacto [ĩ'paktu], (PT) **impacte** m impact

ímpar ['ĩpar] adj (número) odd; (sem igual) unique, unequalled

imparcial [ĩpar'sjaw] (pl **-ais**) adj fair, impartial

impecável [ĩpe'kavew] (pl **-eis**) adj perfect, impeccable

impeço etc [ĩ'pesu] vb ver **impedir**

impedido, -a [ĩpe'dʒidu, a] adj (Futebol) offside; (PT: Tel) engaged (Brit), busy (US)

impedimento [ĩpedʒi'mẽtu] m impediment

impedir [ĩpe'dʒir] vt to obstruct; (estrada, passagem, tráfego) to block; (movimento, execução, progresso) to impede; **~ alguém de fazer algo** to prevent sb from doing sth; (proibir) to forbid sb to do sth; **~ (que aconteça) algo** to prevent sth (happening)

impenetrável [ĩpene'travew] (pl **-eis**) adj impenetrable

impensado, -a [ĩpẽ'sadu, a] adj thoughtless; (não calculado) unpremeditated; (imprevisto) unforeseen

imperador [ĩpera'dor] m emperor

imperativo, -a [ĩpera'tʃivu, a] adj imperative ▷ m imperative

imperatriz [ĩpera'triz] f empress

imperdoável [ĩper'dwavew] (pl **-eis**) adj unforgivable, inexcusable

imperfeito, -a [ĩper'fejtu, a] adj imperfect ▷ m (Ling) imperfect (tense)

imperial [ĩpe'rjaw] (pl **-ais**) adj imperial

imperícia [ĩpe'risja] f inability; (inexperiência) inexperience

império [ĩ'pɛrju] *m* empire
impermeável [ĩper'mjavew] (*pl
-eis*) *adj*: **~ a** (*tb fig*) impervious to;
(*à água*) waterproof ▷ *m* raincoat
impessoal [ĩpe'swaw] (*pl -ais*) *adj*
impersonal
ímpeto ['ĩpetu] *m* (*Tec*) impetus;
(*movimento súbito*) start; (*de cólera*)
fit; (*de emoção*) surge; (*de chamas*)
fury; **agir com ~** to act on impulse;
levantar-se num ~ to get up with
a start
impiedoso, -a [ĩpje'dozu, ɔza] *adj*
merciless, cruel
implacável [ĩpla'kavew] (*pl -eis*)
adj (*pessoa*) unforgiving
implantação [ĩplãta'sãw] (*pl -ões*)
f introduction; (*Med*) implant
implementar [ĩplemẽ'tar] *vt* to
implement
implicar [ĩpli'kar] *vt* (*envolver*) to
implicate; (*pressupor*) to imply ▷ *vi*:
~ com alguém (*chatear*) to tease
sb, pick on sb; **implicar-se** *vr* to
get involved; **~ (em) algo** to
involve sth
implícito, -a [ĩ'plisitu, a] *adj*
implicit
implorar [ĩplo'rar] *vt*: **~ (algo a
alguém)** to beg *ou* implore (sb for
sth)
impopular [ĩpopu'lar] *adj*
unpopular; **impopularidade**
[ĩpopulari'dadʒi] *f* unpopularity
impor [ĩ'por] (*irreg: como* **pôr**) *vt* to
impose; (*respeito*) to command;
impor-se *vr* to assert o.s.; **~ algo a
alguém** to impose sth on sb
importação [importa'sãw] (*pl
-ões*) *f* (*ato*) importing;
(*mercadoria*) import
importador, a [ĩporta'dor(a)] *adj*
import *atr* ▷ *m/f* importer
importância [ĩpor'tãsja] *f*

importance; (*de dinheiro*) sum,
amount; **não tem ~** it doesn't
matter, never mind; **ter ~** to be
important; **sem ~** unimportant;
importante [ĩpor'tãtʃi] *adj*
important ▷ *m*: **o (mais)
importante** the (most) important
thing
importar [ĩpor'tar] *vt* (*Com*) to
import; (*trazer*) to bring in; (*causar:
prejuízos etc*) to cause; (*implicar*) to
imply, involve ▷ *vi* to matter, be
important; **importar-se** *vr*: **~-se
com algo** to mind sth; **não me
importo** I don't care
importunar [ĩportu'nar] *vt* to
bother, annoy
importuno, -a [ĩpor'tunu, a] *adj*
annoying; (*inoportuno*)
inopportune ▷ *m/f* nuisance
impossibilitado, -a
[ĩposibili'tadu, a] *adj*: **~ de fazer**
unable to do
impossibilitar [ĩposibili'tar] *vt*: **~
algo** to make sth impossible; **~
alguém de fazer, ~ a alguém
fazer** to prevent sb doing; **~ algo a
alguém, ~ alguém para algo** to
make sth impossible for sb
impossível [ĩpo'sivew] (*pl -eis*) *adj*
impossible; (*insuportável: pessoa*)
insufferable; (*incrível*) incredible
imposto [ĩ'postu] *m* tax; **antes/
depois de ~s** before/after tax; **~ de
renda** (*BR*) income tax; **~ predial**
rates *pl*; **I~ sobre Circulação de
Mercadorias (e Serviços)** (*BR*), **~
sobre valor agregado** value
added tax (*Brit*), sales tax (*US*)
impotente [ĩpo'tẽtʃi] *adj*
powerless; (*Med*) impotent
impraticável [ĩpratʃi'kavew] (*pl
-eis*) *adj* impracticable; (*rua, rio etc*)
impassable

impreciso, -a [ĩpre'sizu, a] *adj*
vague; (*falto de rigor*) inaccurate

imprensa [ĩ'prẽsa] *f* printing;
(*máquina, jornais*) press

imprescindível [ĩpresĩ'dʒivew] (*pl*
-eis) *adj* essential, indispensable

impressão [impre'sãw] (*pl* **-ões**) *f*
impression; (*de livros*) printing;
(*marca*) imprint; **causar boa ~** to
make a good impression; **ficar
com/ter a ~ (de) que** to get/have
the impression that

impressionante [ĩpresjo'nãtʃi] *adj*
impressive

impressionar [ĩpresjo'nar] *vt* to
affect ▷ *vi* to be impressive;
(*pessoa*) to make an impression;
impressionar-se *vr*: **~-se (com
algo)** (*comover-se*) to be moved (by
sth)

impresso, -a [ĩ'prɛsu, a] *pp de*
imprimir ▷ *adj* printed ▷ *m* (*para
preencher*) form; (*folheto*) leaflet;
impressos *mpl* (*formulário*) printed
matter *sg*

impressões [impre'sõjs] *fpl de*
impressão

impressora [ĩpre'sora] *f* (*Comput*)
printer; **~ jato de tinta** ink-jet
printer

imprestável [ĩpres'tavew] (*pl* **-eis**)
adj (*inútil*) useless; (*pessoa*)
unhelpful

imprevisível [ĩprevi'zivew] (*pl* **-eis**)
adj unforeseeable

imprevisto, -a [ĩpre'vistu, a] *adj*
unexpected, unforeseen ▷ *m*: **um ~**
something unexpected

imprimir [ĩpri'mir] *vt* to print;
(*marca*) to stamp; (*infundir*) to instil
(*Brit*), instill (*US*)

impróprio, -a [ĩ'prɔprju, a] *adj*
inappropriate; (*indecente*) improper

improvável [ĩpro'vavew] (*pl* **-eis**)

adj unlikely

improviso [ĩpro'vizu] *m*: **de ~** (*de
repente*) suddenly; (*sem preparação*)
without preparation

imprudente [ĩpru'dẽtʃi] *adj*
(*irrefletido*) rash; (*motorista*)
careless

impulsivo, -a [ĩpuw'sivu, a] *adj*
impulsive

impulso [ĩ'puwsu] *m* impulse; (*fig:
estímulo*) urge, impulse

impune [ĩ'puni] *adj* unpunished;
impunidade [ĩpuni'dadʒi] *f*
impunity

imundície [imũ'dʒisji] *f* filth;
imundo, -a [i'mũdu, a] *adj* filthy;
(*obsceno*) dirty

imune [i'muni] *adj*: **~ a** immune to;
imunidade [imuni'dadʒi] *f*
immunity

inábil [i'nabiw] (*pl* **-eis**) *adj*
incapable; (*desajeitado*) clumsy

inabitado, -a [inabi'tadu, a] *adj*
uninhabited

inacabado, -a [inaka'badu, a] *adj*
unfinished

inacreditável [inakredʒi'tavew]
(*pl* **-eis**) *adj* unbelievable,
incredible

inadequado, -a [inade'kwadu, a]
adj inadequate; (*impróprio*)
unsuitable

inadiável [ina'dʒjavew] (*pl* **-eis**) *adj*
pressing

inadimplência [inadʒĩ'plẽsja] *f*
(*Jur*) breach of contract, default

inaptidão [inaptʃi'dãw] (*pl* **-ões**) *f*
inability

inatingível [inatʃĩ'ʒivew] (*pl* **-eis**)
adj unattainable

inativo, -a [ina'tʃivu, a] *adj*
inactive; (*aposentado, reformado*)
retired

inauguração [inawgura'sãw] (*pl*

-ões) f inauguration; (de exposição) opening; **inaugural** [inawguˈraw] (pl -**ais**) adj inaugural; **inaugurar** [inawguˈrar] vt to inaugurate; (exposição) to open

incapacidade [ĩkapasiˈdadʒi] f incapacity; (incompetência) incompetence

incapacitado, -a [ĩkapasiˈtadu, a] adj (inválido) disabled, handicapped ▷ m/f handicapped person; **estar ~ de fazer** to be unable to do

incapaz [ĩkaˈpajʃ] adj, m/f incompetent; ~ **de fazer** incapable of doing; ~ **para** unfit for

incendiar [ĩsẽˈdʒjar] vt to set fire to; (fig) to inflame; **incendiar-se** vr to catch fire

incêndio [ĩˈsẽdʒju] m fire; ~ **criminoso** ou **premeditado** arson

incenso [ĩˈsẽsu] m incense

incentivar [ĩsẽtʃiˈvar] vt to stimulate, encourage

incentivo [ĩsẽˈtʃivu] m incentive; ~ **fiscal** tax incentive

incerteza [ĩserˈteza] f uncertainty

incerto, -a [ĩˈsɛrtu, a] adj uncertain

incesto [ĩˈsɛstu] m incest

inchado, -a [ĩˈʃadu, a] adj swollen; (fig) conceited

inchar [ĩˈʃar] vt, vi to swell

incidência [ĩsiˈdẽsja] f incidence, occurrence

incidente [ĩsiˈdẽtʃi] m incident

incisivo, -a [ĩsiˈzivu, a] adj cutting, sharp; (fig) incisive

incitar [ĩsiˈtar] vt to incite; (pessoa, animal) to drive on

inclinação [ĩklinaˈsãw] (pl -**ões**) f inclination; ~ **da cabeça** nod

inclinar [ĩkliˈnar] vt to tilt; (cabeça) to nod ▷ vi to slope; (objeto) to tilt; **inclinar-se** vr to tilt; (dobrar o corpo) to bow, stoop; ~-**se sobre algo** to lean over sth

incluir [ĩˈklwir] vt to include; (em carta) to enclose; **incluir-se** vr to be included

inclusão [ĩkluˈzãw] f inclusion; **inclusive** [ĩkluˈzivi] prep including ▷ adv inclusive; (até mesmo) even

incoerente [ĩkoeˈrẽtʃi] adj incoherent; (contraditório) inconsistent

incógnita [ĩˈkɔgnita] f (Mat) unknown; (fato incógnito) mystery; **incógnito, -a** [ĩˈkɔgnitu, a] adj unknown ▷ adv incognito

incolor [ĩkoˈlor] adj colourless (Brit), colorless (US)

incomodar [ĩkomoˈdar] vt to bother, trouble; (aborrecer) to annoy ▷ vi to be bothersome; **incomodar-se** vr to bother, put o.s. out; ~-**se com algo** to be bothered by sth, mind sth; **não se incomode!** don't worry!

incômodo, -a [ĩˈkomodu, a] adj uncomfortable; (incomodativo) troublesome; (inoportuno) inconvenient

incompetente [ĩkõpeˈtẽtʃi] adj, m/f incompetent

incompreendido, -a [ĩkõprjẽˈdʒidu, a] adj misunderstood

incomum [ĩkoˈmũ] adj uncommon

incomunicável [ĩkomuniˈkavew] (pl -**eis**) adj cut off; (privado de comunicação, fig) incommunicado; (preso) in solitary confinement

inconformado, -a [ĩkõforˈmadu, a] adj bitter; ~ **com** unreconciled to

inconfundível [ĩkõfũˈdʒivew] (pl -**eis**) adj unmistakeable

inconsciência [ĩkõˈsjẽsja] f (Med)

unconsciousness; (*irreflexão*)
thoughtlessness
inconsciente [ĩkõ'sjẽtʃi] *adj*
unconscious ▷ *m* unconscious
inconsequente [ĩkõse'kwẽtʃi] *adj*
inconsistent; (*contraditório*)
illogical; (*irresponsável*)
irresponsible
inconsistente [ĩkõsis'tẽtʃi] *adj*
inconsistent; (*sem solidez*) runny
inconstante [ĩkõs'tãtʃi] *adj* fickle;
(*tempo*) changeable
incontrolável [ĩkõtro'lavew] (*pl*
-eis) *adj* uncontrollable
inconveniência [ĩkõve'njẽsja] *f*
inconvenience; (*impropriedade*)
inappropriateness
inconveniente [ĩkõve'njẽtʃi] *adj*
inconvenient; (*inoportuno*)
awkward; (*grosseiro*) rude;
(*importuno*) annoying ▷ *m*
disadvantage; (*obstáculo*) difficulty,
problem
incorreto, -a [ĩko'hɛtu, a] *adj*
incorrect; (*desonesto*) dishonest
incrédulo, -a [ĩ'krɛdulu, a] *adj*
incredulous; (*cético*) sceptical
(*Brit*), skeptical (*US*) ▷ *m/f* sceptic
(*Brit*), skeptic (*US*)
incrível [ĩ'krivew] (*pl* **-eis**) *adj*
incredible
incumbência [ĩkũ'bẽsja] *f* task,
duty
incumbir [ĩkũ'bir] *vt*: **~ alguém de**
algo *ou* **algo a alguém** to put sb in
charge of sth ▷ *vi*: **~ a alguém** to
be sb's duty; **incumbir-se** *vr*: **~-se**
de to undertake, take charge of
indagação [ĩdaga'sãw] (*pl* **-ões**) *f*
investigation; (*pergunta*) inquiry,
question
indagar [ĩda'gar] *vt* to investigate
▷ *vi* to inquire; **indagar-se** *vr*: **~-se**
a si mesmo to ask o.s.; **~ algo de**

alguém to ask sb about sth
indecente [ĩde'sẽtʃi] *adj* indecent,
improper; (*obsceno*) rude, vulgar
indecoroso, -a [ĩdeko'rozu, ɔza]
adj indecent, improper
indefinido, -a [ĩdefi'nidu, a] *adj*
indefinite; (*vago*) vague,
undefined; **por tempo ~**
indefinitely
indelicado, -a [ĩdeli'kadu, a] *adj*
impolite, rude
indenização [indeniza'sãw], (*PT*)
indemnização (*pl* **-ões**) *f*
compensation; (*Com*) indemnity
indenizar [ĩdeni'zar], (*PT*)
indemnizar *vt*: **~ alguém por** *ou*
de algo (*compensar*) to compensate
sb for sth; (*por gastos*) to reimburse
sb for sth
independência [ĩdepẽ'dẽsja] *f*
independence; **independente**
[ĩdepẽ'dẽtʃi] *adj* independent
indesejável [ĩdeze'ʒavew] (*pl* **-eis**)
adj undesirable
indevido, -a [ĩde'vidu, a] *adj*
(*imerecido*) unjust; (*impróprio*)
inappropriate
Índia [ĩdʒa] *f*: **a ~** India; **as ~s**
Ocidentais the West Indies;
indiano, -a [ĩ'dʒanu, a] *adj*, *m/f*
Indian
indicação [indʒika'sãw] (*pl* **-ões**) *f*
indication; (*de termômetro*) reading;
(*para um cargo, prêmio*) nomination;
(*recomendação*) recommendation;
(*de um caminho*) directions *pl*
indicado, -a [ĩdʒi'kadu, a] *adj*
appropriate
indicador, a [ĩdʒika'dor(a)] *adj*:
~ de indicative of ▷ *m* indicator;
(*Tec*) gauge; (*dedo*) index finger;
(*ponteiro*) pointer
indicar [ĩdʒi'kar] *vt* to indicate;
(*apontar*) to point to; (*temperatura*)

to register; (*recomendar*) to recommend; (*para um cargo*) to nominate; (*determinar*) to determine; **~ o caminho a alguém** to give sb directions

índice ['ĩdʒisi] *m* (*de livro*) index; (*taxa*) rate

indício [in'dʒisju] *m* (*sinal*) sign; (*vestígio*) trace; (*Jur*) clue

indiferença [ĩdʒife'rẽsa] *f* indifference; **indiferente** [ĩdʒife'rẽtʃi] *adj*: **indiferente (a)** indifferent (to); **isso me é indiferente** it's all the same to me

indígena [ĩ'dʒiʒena] *adj, m/f* native; (*índio: da América*) Indian

indigência [ĩdʒi'ʒẽsja] *f* poverty; (*fig*) lack, need

indigestão [ĩdʒiʒes'tãw] *f* indigestion

indigesto, -a [ĩdʒi'ʒɛstu, a] *adj* indigestible

indignação [ĩdʒigna'sãw] *f* indignation; **indignado, -a** [ĩdʒig'nadu, a] *adj* indignant

indignar [ĩdʒig'nar] *vt* to anger, incense; **indignar-se** *vr* to get angry

índio, -a ['ĩdʒju, a] *adj, m/f* (*da América*) Indian; **o Oceano Í~** the Indian Ocean

indireto, -a [ĩdʒi'rɛtu, a] *adj* indirect

indiscreto, -a [ĩdʒis'krɛtu, a] *adj* indiscreet

indiscutível [ĩdʒisku'tʃivew] (*pl* **-eis**) *adj* indisputable

indispensável [ĩdʒispẽ'savew] (*pl* **-eis**) *adj* essential, vital ▷ *m*: **o ~** the essentials *pl*

indispor [ĩdʒis'por] (*irreg: como* **pôr**) *vt* (*de saúde*) to make ill; (*aborrecer*) to upset; **indisposto, -a** [ĩdʒis'postu, 'pɔsta] *adj* unwell, poorly

indistinto, -a [ĩdʒis'tʃĩtu, a] *adj* indistinct

individual [ĩdʒivi'dwaw] (*pl* **-ais**) *adj* individual

indivíduo [ĩdʒi'vidwu] *m* individual; (*col: sujeito*) person

indócil [ĩ'dɔsiw] (*pl* **-eis**) *adj* unruly, wayward; (*impaciente*) restless

índole ['ĩdoli] *f* (*temperamento*) nature; (*tipo*) sort, type

indolor [ĩdo'lor] *adj* painless

Indonésia [ĩdo'nɛzja] *f*: **a ~** Indonesia

indústria [ĩ'dustrja] *f* industry; **industrial** [ĩdus'trjaw] (*pl* **-ais**) *adj* industrial ▷ *m/f* industrialist; **industrializar** [ĩdustrjali'zar] *vt* (*país*) to industrialize; (*aproveitar*) to process

induzir [ĩdu'zir] *vt* to induce; (*persuadir*): **~ alguém a fazer** to persuade sb to do

inédito, -a [i'nɛdʒitu, a] *adj* (*livro*) unpublished; (*incomum*) unheard-of, rare

inegável [ine'gavew] (*pl* **-eis**) *adj* undeniable

inelutável [inelu'tavew] (*pl* **-eis**) *adj* inescapable

inepto, -a [i'nɛptu, a] *adj* inept, incompetent

inequívoco, -a [ine'kivoku, a] *adj* (*evidente*) clear; (*inconfundível*) unmistakeable

inércia [i'nɛrsja] *f* lethargy; (*Fís*) inertia

inerente [ine'rẽtʃi] *adj*: **~ a** inherent in *ou* to

inerte [i'nɛrtʃi] *adj* lethargic; (*Fís*) inert

inesgotável [inezgo'tavew] (*pl* **-eis**) *adj* inexhaustible; (*superabundante*) boundless

inesperado, -a [inespe'radu, a] *adj* unexpected, unforeseen ▷ *m*: **o ~** the unexpected

inesquecível [ineske'sivew] (*pl* **-eis**) *adj* unforgettable

inestimável [inestʃi'mavew] (*pl* **-eis**) *adj* invaluable

inexato, -a [ine'zatu, a] *adj* inaccurate

inexistência [inezis'tẽsja] *f* lack

inexperiência [inespe'rjẽsja] *f* inexperience; **inexperiente** [inespe'rjẽtʃi] *adj* inexperienced; (*ingênuo*) naive

inexpressivo, -a [inespre'sivu, a] *adj* expressionless

infância [ĩ'fãsja] *f* childhood

infantil [ĩfã'tʃiw] (*pl* **-is**) *adj* (*ingênuo*) childlike; (*pueril*) childish; (*para crianças*) children's

infarto [ĩ'fartu] *m* heart attack

infecção [ĩfek'sãw] (*pl* **-ões**) *f* infection; **infeccionar** [ĩfeksjo'nar] *vt* (*ferida*) to infect; **infeccioso, -a** [ĩfek'sjozu, ɔza] *adj* infectious

infelicidade [ĩfelisi'dadʒi] *f* unhappiness; (*desgraça*) misfortune

infeliz [ĩfe'liz] *adj* unhappy; (*infausto*) unlucky; (*ação, medida*) unfortunate; (*sugestão, ideia*) inappropriate ▷ *m/f* unhappy person; **infelizmente** [ĩfeliz'mẽtʃi] *adv* unfortunately

inferior [ĩfe'rjor] *adj*: **~ (a)** (*em valor, qualidade*) inferior (to); (*mais baixo*) lower (than) ▷ *m/f* inferior, subordinate; **inferioridade** [ĩferjori'dadʒi] *f* inferiority

infernal [ĩfer'naw] (*pl* **-ais**) *adj* infernal

inferno [ĩ'fɛrnu] *m* hell; **vá pro ~!** (*col*) piss off!

infetar [ĩfe'tar] *vt* to infect

infiel [ĩ'fjɛw] (*pl* **-éis**) *adj* disloyal; (*marido*) unfaithful; (*texto*) inaccurate ▷ *m/f* (*Rel*) non-believer

ínfimo, -a ['ĩfimu, a] *adj* lowest; (*qualidade*) poorest

infindável [ĩfĩ'davew] (*pl* **-eis**) *adj* unending, constant

infinidade [ĩfini'dadʒi] *f* infinity; **uma ~ de** countless

infinitivo, -a [ĩfini'tʃivu, a] *adj, m* (*Ling*) infinitive

inflação [ĩfla'sãw] *f* inflation; **inflacionário, -a** [ĩflasjo'narju, a] *adj* inflationary

inflamação [ĩflama'sãw] (*pl* **-ões**) *f* inflammation; **inflamado, -a** [ĩfla'madu, a] *adj* (*Med*) inflamed; (*discurso*) heated

inflamar [ĩfla'mar] *vt* (*madeira, pólvora*) to set fire to; (*Med, fig*) to inflame; **inflamar-se** *vr* to catch fire; (*fig*) to get worked up; **~-se de algo** to be consumed with sth

inflamável [ĩfla'mavew] (*pl* **-eis**) *adj* inflammable

inflar [ĩ'flar] *vt* to inflate, blow up; **inflar-se** *vr* to swell (up)

inflexível [ĩflek'sivew] (*pl* **-eis**) *adj* stiff, rigid; (*fig*) unyielding

influência [ĩ'flwẽsja] *f* influence; **sob a ~ de** under the influence of; **influenciar** [ĩflwẽ'sjar] *vt* to influence ▷ *vi*: **influenciar em algo** to influence sth, have an influence on sth; **influenciar-se** *vr*: **influenciar-se por** to be influenced by; **influente** [ĩ'flwẽtʃi] *adj* influential; **influir** [ĩ'flwir] *vi* to matter, be important; **influir em** *ou* **sobre** to influence, have an influence on

informação [ĩforma'sãw] (*pl* **-ões**) *f* (piece of) information; (*notícia*) news; **informações** fpl (detalhes) information sg; **Informações** (Tel) directory enquiries (Brit), information (US); **pedir informações sobre** to ask about, inquire about

informal [ĩfor'maw] (pl -ais) adj informal

informar [ĩfor'mar] vt: **~ alguém (de/sobre algo)** to inform sb (of/ about sth) ▷ vi to inform, be informative; **informar-se** vr: **~-se de** to find out about, inquire about; **~ de** to report on

informática [ĩfor'matʃika] f IT, information technology

informativo, -a [ĩforma'tʃivu, a] adj informative

informatizar [ĩformatʃi'zar] vt to computerize

infortúnio [ĩfor'tunju] m misfortune

infração [ĩfra'sãw] (pl -ões) f breach, infringement; (Esporte) foul

infrator, a [ĩfra'tor(a)] m/f offender

infrutífero, -a [ĩfru'tʃiferu, a] adj fruitless

ingênuo, -a [ĩ'ʒenwu, a] adj ingenuous, naïve; (comentário) harmless ▷ m/f naïve person

ingerir [ĩʒe'rir] vt to ingest; (engolir) to swallow

Inglaterra [ĩgla'tɛha] f: **a ~** England; **inglês, -esa** [ĩ'gles, eza] adj English ▷ m/f Englishman/ woman ▷ m (Ling) English; **os ingleses** mpl the English

ingrediente [ĩgre'dʒjẽtʃi] m ingredient

íngreme ['ĩgremi] adj steep

ingressar [ĩgre'sar] vi: **~ em** to enter, go into; (um clube) to join

ingresso [ĩ'grɛsu] m (entrada) entry; (admissão) admission; (bilhete) ticket

inibição [inibi'sãw] (pl -ões) f inhibition

inibido, -a [ini'bidu, a] adj inhibited

inibir [ini'bir] vt to inhibit

inicial [ini'sjaw] (pl -ais) adj, f initial

iniciar [ini'sjar] vt, vi (começar) to begin, start; **~ alguém em algo** (arte, seita) to initiate sb into sth

iniciativa [inisja'tʃiva] f initiative; **a ~ privada** (Econ) private enterprise

início [i'nisju] m beginning, start; **no ~** at the start

inimigo, -a [ini'migu, a] adj, m/f enemy

injeção [ĩʒe'sãw] (pl -ões) f injection

injetar [ĩʒe'tar] vt to inject

injúria [ĩ'ʒurja] f insult

injustiça [ĩʒus'tʃisa] f injustice

inocência [ino'sẽsja] f innocence

inocentar [inosẽ'tar] vt: **~ alguém (de algo)** to clear sb (of sth)

inocente [ino'sẽtʃi] adj innocent ▷ m/f innocent man/woman

inofensivo, -a [inofẽ'sivu, a] adj harmless, inoffensive

inovação [inova'sãw] (pl -ões) f innovation

inquérito [ĩ'kɛritu] m inquiry; (Jur) inquest

inquietação [ĩkjeta'sãw] f anxiety, uneasiness; (agitação) restlessness

inquietante [ĩkje'tãtʃi] adj worrying, disturbing

inquietar [ĩkje'tar] vt to worry, disturb; **inquietar-se** vr to worry, bother; **inquieto, -a** [ĩ'kjɛtu, a] adj anxious, worried; (agitado) restless

inquilino, -a [ĩki'linu, a] *m/f*
tenant

insalubre [ĩsa'lubri] *adj* unhealthy

insanidade [ĩsani'dadʒi] *f*
madness, insanity; **insano, -a**
[ĩ'sanu, a] *adj* insane

insatisfatório, -a [ĩsatʃisfa'tɔrju,
a] *adj* unsatisfactory

insatisfeito, -a [ĩsatʃis'fejtu, a]
adj dissatisfied, unhappy

inscrever [ĩskre'ver] *vt* to inscribe;
(*aluno*) to enrol (*Brit*), enroll (*US*);
(*em registro*) to register

inscrito, -a [ĩ'skritu, a] *pp de*
inscrever

insegurança [ĩsegu'rãsa] *f*
insecurity; **inseguro, -a** [ĩse'guru,
a] *adj* insecure; **insensato, -a**
[ĩsẽ'satu, a] *adj* unreasonable,
foolish

inserir [ĩse'rir] *vt* to insert, put in;
(*Comput: dados*) to enter

inseticida [ĩsetʃi'sida] *m*
insecticide

inseto [ĩ'setu] *m* insect

insípido, -a [ĩ'sipidu, a] *adj* insipid

insiro *etc* [ĩ'siru] *vb ver* **inserir**

insistência [ĩsis'tẽsja] *f*: **~ (em)**
insistence (on); (*obstinação*)
persistence (in); **insistente**
[ĩsis'tẽtʃi] *adj* (*pessoa*) insistent;
(*apelo*) urgent

insistir [ĩsis'tʃir] *vi*: **~ (em)** to insist
(on); (*perseverar*) to persist (in);
~ (em) que to insist that

insolação [ĩsola'sãw] *f* sunstroke;
pegar uma ~ to get sunstroke

insólito, -a [ĩ'sɔlitu, a] *adj* unusual

insônia [ĩ'sonja] *f* insomnia

insosso, -a [ĩ'sosu, a] *adj* unsalted;
(*sem sabor*) tasteless; (*pessoa*)
uninteresting, dull

inspeção [ĩspe'sãw] (*pl* **-ões**) *f*
inspection, check; **inspecionar**

[ĩspesjo'nar] *vt* to inspect

inspetor, a [ĩspe'tor(a)] *m/f*
inspector

inspirar [ĩspi'rar] *vt* to inspire;
(*Med*) to inhale; **inspirar-se** *vr* to
be inspired

INSS (*BR*) *abr m* (= *Instituto Nacional
do Seguro Social*) ≈ DSS (*Brit*),
≈ Welfare Dept (*US*)

instalação [ĩstala'sãw] (*pl* **-ões**) *f*
installation; **~ elétrica** (*de casa*)
wiring

instalar [ĩsta'lar] *vt* to install;
(*estabelecer*) to set up; **instalar-se**
vr (*numa cadeira*) to settle down

instantâneo, -a [ĩstã'tanju, a] *adj*
instant, instantaneous ▷ *m* (*Foto*)
snap

instante [ĩs'tãtʃi] *adj* urgent ▷ *m*
moment; **num ~** in an instant,
quickly; **só um ~!** just a moment!

instável [ĩs'tavew] (*pl* **-eis**) *adj*
unstable; (*tempo*) unsettled

instintivo, -a [ĩstʃĩ'tʃivu, a] *adj*
instinctive

instinto [ĩs'tʃĩtu] *m* instinct; **por ~**
instinctively

instituição [ĩstʃitwi'sãw] (*pl* **-ões**) *f*
institution

instituto [ĩstʃi'tutu] *m* (*escola*)
institute; (*instituição*) institution;
~ de beleza beauty salon

instrução [ĩstru'sãw] (*pl* **-ões**) *f*
education; (*erudição*) learning;
(*diretriz*) instruction; (*Mil*) training;
instruções *fpl* (*para o uso*)
instructions (for use)

instruído, -a [ĩs'trwidu, a] *adj*
educated

instruir [ĩs'trwir] *vt* to instruct;
(*Mil*) to train; **instruir-se** *vr*: **~-se
em algo** to learn sth; **~ alguém de
ou sobre algo** to inform sb about
sth

instrumento [ĩstru'mẽtu] *m*
instrument; (*ferramenta*)
implement; (*Jur*) deed, document;
~ de cordas/percussão/sopro
stringed/percussion/wind
instrument; **~ de trabalho** tool
instrutivo, -a [ĩstru'tʃivu, a] *adj*
instructive
instrutor, a [ĩstru'tor(a)] *m/f*
instructor; (*Esporte*) coach
insubordinação
[ĩsubordʒina'sãw] *f* rebellion;
(*Mil*) insubordination
insubstituível [ĩsubistʃi'twivew]
(*pl* **-eis**) *adj* irreplaceable
insuficiência [ĩsufi'sjẽsja] *f*
inadequacy; (*carência*) shortage;
(*Med*) deficiency; **~ cardíaca** heart
failure; **insuficiente** [ĩsufi'sjẽtʃi]
adj insufficient; (*Educ: nota*) ≈ fail;
(*pessoa*) incompetent
insulina [ĩsu'lina] *f* insulin
insultar [ĩsuw'tar] *vt* to insult;
insulto [ĩ'suwtu] *m* insult
insuportável [ĩsupor'tavew] (*pl*
-eis) *adj* unbearable
insurgir-se [ĩsur'ʒirsi] *vr* to rebel,
revolt
insurreição [ĩsuhej'sãw] (*pl* **-ões**) *f*
rebellion, insurrection
intato, -a [ĩ'tatu, a] *adj* intact
íntegra ['ĩtegra] *f*: **na ~** in full
integral [ĩte'graw] (*pl* **-ais**) *adj*
whole ▷ *f* (*Mat*) integral; **pão ~**
wholemeal (*Brit*) *ou* wholewheat
(*US*) bread; **integralmente**
[ĩtegraw'mẽtʃi] *adv* in full, fully
integrar [ĩte'grar] *vt* to unite,
combine; (*completar*) to form,
make up; (*Mat, raças*) to integrate;
integrar-se *vr* to become
complete; **~-se em** *ou* **a algo** to
join sth; (*adaptar-se*) to integrate
into sth

integridade [ĩtegri'dadʒi] *f*
entirety; (*fig: de pessoa*) integrity
íntegro, -a ['ĩtegru, a] *adj* entire;
(*honesto*) upright, honest
inteiramente [ĩtejra'mẽtʃi] *adv*
completely
inteirar [ĩtej'rar] *vt* (*completar*) to
complete; **inteirar-se** *vr*: **~-se de**
to find out about; **~ alguém de** to
inform sb of
inteiro, -a [ĩ'tejru, a] *adj* whole,
entire; (*ileso*) unharmed; (*não
quebrado*) undamaged
intelecto [ĩte'lɛktu] *m* intellect;
intelectual [ĩtelek'twaw] (*pl* **-ais**)
adj, m/f intellectual
inteligência [ĩteli'ʒẽsja] *f*
intelligence; **inteligente**
[ĩteli'ʒẽtʃi] *adj* intelligent, clever
inteligível [ĩteli'ʒivew] (*pl* **-eis**) *adj*
intelligible
intenção [ĩtẽ'sãw] (*pl* **-ões**) *f*
intention; **segundas intenções**
ulterior motives; **ter a ~ de** to
intend to; **intencionado, -a**
[ĩtẽsjo'nadu, a] *adj*: **bem
intencionado** well-meaning; **mal
intencionado** spiteful;
intencional [ĩtẽsjo'naw] (*pl* **-ais**)
adj intentional, deliberate;
intencionar [ĩtẽsjo'nar] *vt* to
intend
intensificar [ĩtẽsifi'kar] *vt* to
intensify; **intensificar-se** *vr* to
intensify
intensivo, -a [ĩtẽ'sivu, a] *adj*
intensive
intenso, -a [ĩ'tẽsu, a] *adj* intense;
(*emoção*) deep; (*impressão*) vivid;
(*vida social*) full
interação [ĩtera'sãw] *f* interaction
interativo, -a [ĩtera'tʃivu, a] *adj*
(*Comput*) interactive
intercâmbio [ĩter'kãbju] *m*

exchange

interdição [ĩterdʒi'sãw] (pl **-ões**) f (de estrada, porta) closure; (Jur) injunction

interditar [ĩterdʒi'tar] vt (importação etc) to ban; (estrada, praia) to close off; (cinema etc) to close down

interessado, -a [ĩtere'sadu, a] adj interested; (amizade) self-seeking

interessante [ĩtere'sãtʃi] adj interesting

interessar [ĩtere'sar] vt to interest ▷ vi to be interesting; **interessar-se** vr: **~-se em** ou **por** to take an interest in, be interested in; **a quem possa ~** to whom it may concern

interesse [ĩte'resi] m interest; (próprio) self-interest; (proveito) advantage; **no ~ de** for the sake of; **por ~ (próprio)** for one's own ends; **interesseiro, -a** [ĩtere'sejru, a] adj self-seeking

interface [ĩter'fasi] f (Comput) interface

interferência [ĩterfe'rēsja] f interference

interferir [ĩterfe'rir] vi: **~ em** to interfere in; (rádio) to jam

interfone [ĩter'fɔni] m intercom

interior [ĩte'rjor] adj inner, inside; (Com) domestic, internal ▷ m inside, interior; (do país): **no ~** inland; **Ministério do I~** ≈ Home Office (Brit), ≈ Department of the Interior (US)

interjeição [ĩterʒej'sãw] (pl **-ões**) f interjection

interlocutor, a [ĩterloku'tor(a)] m/f speaker; **meu ~** the person I was speaking to

intermediário, -a [ĩterme'dʒjarju, a] adj intermediary ▷ m/f (Com)

middleman; (mediador) intermediary, mediator

intermédio [ĩter'mɛdʒu] m: **por ~ de** through

internação [ĩterna'sãw] (pl **-ões**) f (de doente) admission

internacional [ĩternasjo'naw] (pl **-ais**) adj international

internações [ĩterna'sõjs] fpl de **internação**

internar [ĩter'nar] vt (aluno) to put into boarding school; (doente) to take into hospital; (Mil, Pol) to intern

internauta [ĩter'nawta] m/f internet user, web ou net surfer (col)

Internet [ĩter'nɛtʃi] f internet

interno, -a [ĩ'tɛrnu, a] adj internal; (Pol) domestic ▷ m/f (tb: **aluno ~**) boarder; (Med: estudante) houseman (Brit), intern (US); **de uso ~** (Med) for internal use

interpretação [ĩterpreta'sãw] (pl **-ões**) f interpretation; (Teatro) performance

interpretar [ĩterpre'tar] vt to interpret; (um papel) to play; **intérprete** [ĩ'tɛrpretʃi] m/f interpreter; (Teatro) performer, artist

interrogação [ĩterhoga'sãw] (pl **-ões**) f interrogation; **ponto de ~** question mark

interrogar [ĩterho'gar] vt to question, interrogate; (Jur) to cross-examine

interromper [ĩterhõ'per] vt to interrupt; (parar) to stop; (Elet) to cut off

interruptor [ĩterhup'tor] m (Elet) switch

interseção [ĩterse'sãw] (pl **-ões**) f intersection

interurbano, -a [ĩterur'banu, a] *adj* (*Tel*) long-distance ▷ *m* long-distance *ou* trunk call

intervalo [ĩter'valu] *m* interval; (*descanso*) break; **a ~s** every now and then

intervir [ĩter'vir] (*irreg*: *como* **vir**) *vi* to intervene; (*sobrevir*) to come up

intimação [ĩtʃima'sãw] (*pl* **-ões**) *f* (*ordem*) order; (*Jur*) summons

intimar [ĩtʃi'mar] *vt* (*Jur*) to summon; **~ alguém a fazer** *ou* **a alguém que faça** to order sb to do

íntimo, -a ['ĩtʃimu, a] *adj* intimate; (*sentimentos*) innermost; (*amigo*) close; (*vida*) private ▷ *m/f* close friend; **no ~** at heart

intolerante [ĩtole'rãtʃi] *adj* intolerant

intolerável [ĩtole'ravew] (*pl* **-eis**) *adj* intolerable, unbearable

intoxicação [ĩtoksika'sãw] *f* poisoning; **~ alimentar** food poisoning

intoxicar [ĩtoksi'kar] *vt* to poison

intranet [ĩtra'nɛtʃi] *f* intranet

intransitável [ĩtrãsi'tavew] (*pl* **-eis**) *adj* impassable

intratável [ĩtra'tavew] (*pl* **-eis**) *adj* (*pessoa*) contrary, awkward; (*doença*) untreatable; (*problema*) insurmountable

intriga [ĩ'triga] *f* intrigue; (*enredo*) plot; (*fofoca*) piece of gossip; **intrigas** (*fofocas*) gossip *sg*; **~ amorosa** (*PT*) love affair; **intrigante** [ĩtri'gãtʃi] *m/f* troublemaker ▷ *adj* intriguing; **intrigar** [ĩtri'gar] *vt* to intrigue ▷ *vi* to be intriguing

introdução [ĩtrodu'sãw] (*pl* **-ões**) *f* introduction

introduzir [ĩtrodu'zir] *vt* to introduce

intrometer-se [ĩtrome'tersi] *vr* to interfere, meddle; **intrometido, -a** [ĩtrome'tʃidu, a] *adj* interfering; (*col*) nosey ▷ *m/f* busybody

introvertido, -a [ĩtrover'tʃidu, a] *adj* introverted ▷ *m/f* introvert

intruso, -a [ĩ'truzu, a] *m/f* intruder

intuição [ĩtwi'sãw] (*pl* **-ões**) *f* intuition

intuito [ĩ'tuito] *m* intention, aim

inúmero, -a [i'numeru, a] *adj* countless, innumerable

inundação [inũda'sãw] (*pl* **-ões**) *f* (*enchente*) flood; (*ato*) flooding

inundar [inũ'dar] *vt* to flood; (*fig*) to inundate ▷ *vi* to flood

inusitado, -a [inuzi'tadu, a] *adj* unusual

inútil [i'nutʃiw] (*pl* **-eis**) *adj* useless; (*esforço*) futile; (*desnecessário*) pointless; **inutilizar** [inutʃili'zar] *vt* to make useless, render useless; (*incapacitar*) to put out of action; (*danificar*) to ruin; (*esforços*) to thwart; **inutilmente** [inutʃiw'mẽtʃi] *adv* in vain

invadir [ĩva'dʒir] *vt* to invade; (*suj*: *água*) to overrun; (: *sentimento*) to overcome

inválido, -a [ĩ'validu, a] *adj*, *m/f* invalid

invasão [ĩva'zãw] (*pl* **-ões**) *f* invasion

inveja [ĩ'vɛʒa] *f* envy; **invejar** [ĩve'ʒar] *vt* to envy; (*cobiçar*) to covet ▷ *vi* to be envious; **invejoso, -a** [ĩve'ʒozu, ɔza] *adj* envious

invenção [ĩvẽ'sãw] (*pl* **-ões**) *f* invention

inventado, -a [[ĩi]vẽ'tadu, a] *adj* (*história, personagem*) made-up

inventar [ĩvẽ'tar] *vt* to invent

inventivo, -a [ĩvẽ'tʃivu, a] *adj* inventive

inventor, a [ĩvẽ'tor(a)] *m/f*
inventor

inverno [ĩ'vɛrnu] *m* winter

inverossímil [ĩvero'simiw], *(PT)*
inverosímil *(pl* **-eis)** *adj* unlikely,
improbable; *(inacreditável)*
implausible

invés [ĩ'vɛs] *m*: **ao ~ de** instead of

investigação [ĩvestʃiga'sãw] *(pl*
-ões) *f* investigation; *(pesquisa)*
research

investigar [ĩvestʃi'gar] *vt* to
investigate; *(examinar)* to examine

investimento [ĩvestʃi'mẽtu] *m*
investment

investir [ĩves'tʃir] *vt* *(dinheiro)* to
invest

inviável [ĩ'vjavew] *(pl* **-eis)** *adj*
impracticable

invisível [ĩvi'zivew] *(pl* **-eis)** *adj*
invisible

invisto *etc* [ĩ'vistu] *vb ver* **investir**

invocar [ĩvo'kar] *vt* to invoke

ioga ['jɔga] *f* yoga

iogurte [jo'gurtʃi] *m* yogurt

IR *(BR)* *abr m* = **Imposto de Renda**

PALAVRA-CHAVE

ir [ir] *vi* **1** to go; *(a pé)* to walk; *(a
cavalo)* to ride; *(viajar)* to travel; **ir
caminhando** to walk; **fui de trem**
I went *ou* travelled by train; **vamos
(embora)!**, **vamos nessa!** *(col)*
let's go!; **já vou!** I'm coming!; **ir
atrás de alguém** *(seguir)* to follow
sb; *(confiar)* to take sb's word for it
2 *(progredir: pessoa, coisa)* to go; **o
trabalho vai muito bem** work is
going very well; **como vão as
coisas?** how are things going?; **vou
muito bem** I'm very well; *(na escola
etc)* I'm getting on very well
▷ *vb aux* **1** (+ *infin*): **vou fazer** I will

do, I am going to do
2 (+ *gerúndio*): **ir fazendo** to keep
on doing
ir-se *vr* to go away, leave

ira ['ira] *f* anger, rage

Irã [i'rã] *m*: **o ~** Iran

iraniano, -a [ira'njanu, a] *adj, m/f*
Iranian

Irão [i'rãw] *(PT)* *m* = **Irã**

Iraque [i'raki] *m*: **o ~** Iraq;
iraquiano, -a [ira'kjanu, a] *adj,
m/f* Iraqi

ir e vir *m inv* comings and goings *pl*

Irlanda [ir'lãda] *f*: **a ~** Ireland; **a ~
do Norte** Northern Ireland;
irlandês, -esa [irlã'des, eza] *adj*
Irish ▷ *m/f* Irishman/woman ▷ *m*
(Ling) Irish

irmã [ir'mã] *f* sister; **~ gêmea** twin
sister; **~ de criação** adoptive sister

irmão [ir'mãw] *(pl* **irmãos)** *m*
brother; *(fig: similar)* twin; *(col:
companheiro)* mate; **~ de criação**
adoptive brother; **~ gêmeo** twin
brother

ironia [iro'nia] *f* irony

irra! ['iha] *(PT)* *excl* damn!

irracional [ihasjo'naw] *(pl* **-ais)** *adj*
irrational

irreal [ihe'aw] *(pl* **-ais)** *adj* unreal

irregular [ihegu'lar] *adj* irregular;
(vida) unconventional; *(feições)*
unusual; *(aluno, gênio)* erratic

irremediável [iheme'dʒjavew] *(pl*
-eis) *adj* irremediable; *(sem
remédio)* incurable

irrequieto, -a [ihe'kjɛtu, a] *adj*
restless

irresistível [ihezis'tʃivew] *(pl* **-eis)**
adj irresistible

irresponsável [ihespõ'savew] *(pl*
-eis) *adj* irresponsible

irrigar [ihi'gar] *vt* to irrigate

irritação [ihita'sãw] (pl **-ões**) f
irritation
irritadiço, -a [ihita'dʒisu, a] adj
irritable
irritante [ihi'tãtʃi] adj irritating,
annoying
irritar [ihi'tar] vt to irritate;
irritar-se vr to get angry, get
annoyed
irromper [ihõ'per] vi (entrar
subitamente): **~ (em)** to burst in(to)
isca ['iska] f (Pesca) bait; (fig) lure,
bait
isenção [izẽ'sãw] (pl **-ões**) f
exemption
isentar [izẽ'tar] vt to exempt;
(livrar) to free
Islã [iz'lã] m Islam
Islândia [iz'lãdʒa] f: **a ~** Iceland
isolado, -a [izo'ladu, a] adj
isolated; (solitário) lonely
isolamento [izola'mẽtu] m
isolation; (Elet) insulation
isqueiro [is'kejru] m (cigarette)
lighter
Israel [izha'ɛw] m Israel;
israelense [izhae'lẽsi] adj, m/f
Israeli
isso ['isu] pron that; (col: isto) this;
~ mesmo exactly; **por ~** therefore,
so; **por ~ mesmo** for that very
reason; **só ~?** is that all?
isto ['istu] pron this; **~ é** that is,
namely
Itália [i'talja] f: **a ~** Italy; **italiano,
-a** [ita'ljanu, a] adj, m/f Italian
▷ m (Ling) Italian
Itamarati [itamara'tʃi] m: **o ~** the
Brazilian Foreign Ministry

- **ITAMARATI**
-
- The Palace of Itamarati was built
- in 1855 in Rio de Janeiro. It

- became the seat of government
- when Brazil became a republic in
- 1889, and was later the Foreign
- Ministry. It ceased to be this
- when the Brazilian capital was
- transferred to Brasília, but
- **Itamarati** is still used to refer to
- the Foreign Ministry.

item ['itẽ] (pl **-ns**) m item
itinerário [itʃine'rarju] m itinerary;
(caminho) route

J, j ['ʒɔta] *m* J, j

já [ʒa] *adv* already; (*em perguntas*) yet; (*agora*) now; (*imediatamente*) right away; (*agora mesmo*) right now ▷ *conj* on the other hand; **até já** bye; **desde já** from now on; **já não** no longer; **já que** as, since; **já se vê** of course; **já vou** I'm coming; **já até** even; **já, já** right away

jabuti [ʒabu'tʃi] *m* giant tortoise

jabuticaba [ʒabutʃi'kaba] *f* jaboticaba (*type of berry*)

jaca ['ʒaka] *f* jack fruit

jacaré [ʒaka'rɛ] (BR) *m* alligator

jaguar [ʒa'gwar] *m* jaguar

jaguatirica [ʒagwatʃi'rika] *f* leopard cat

Jamaica [ʒa'majka] *f*: **a ~** Jamaica

jamais [ʒa'majs] *adv* never; (*com palavra negativa*) ever

janeiro [ʒa'nejru] *m* January

janela [ʒa'nɛla] *f* window

jangada [ʒã'gada] *f* raft

jantar [ʒã'tar] *m* dinner ▷ *vt* to have for dinner ▷ *vi* to have dinner

Japão [ʒa'pãw] *m*: **o ~** Japan; **japonês, -esa** [ʒapo'nes, eza] *adj, m/f* Japanese ▷ *m* (*Ling*) Japanese

jararaca [ʒara'raka] *f* jararaca (*snake*)

jardim [ʒar'dʒĩ] (*pl* **-ns**) *m* garden; **~ de infância** kindergarten; **~ zoológico** zoo; **jardinagem** [ʒardʒi'naʒẽ] *f* gardening

jardineira [ʒardʒi'nejra] *f* (*caixa*) trough; (*calça*) dungarees *pl*; *ver tb* **jardineiro**

jardineiro, -a [ʒardʒi'nejru, a] *m/f* gardener

jardins [ʒar'dʒĩs] *mpl de* **jardim**

jargão [ʒar'gãw] *m* jargon

jarra ['ʒaha] *f* pot

jarro ['ʒahu] *m* jug

jasmim [ʒaz'mĩ] *m* jasmine

jato ['ʒatu] *m* jet; (*de luz*) flash; (*de ar*) blast; **a ~** at top speed

jaula ['ʒawla] *f* cage

jazigo [ʒa'zigu] *m* grave; (*monumento*) tomb

jazz [dʒɛz] *m* jazz

jeito ['ʒejtu] *m* (*maneira*) way; (*aspecto*) appearance; (*aptidão, habilidade*) skill, knack; (*modos pessoais*) manner; **ter ~ de** to look like; **não ter ~** (*pessoa*) to be awkward; (*situação*) to be hopeless; **dar um ~ em algo** (*pé*) to twist sth; (*quarto, casa, papéis*) to tidy sth up; (*consertar*) to fix sth; **dar um ~** to find a way; **o ~ é ...** the thing to do is ...; **é o ~** it's the best way; **ao ~ de** in the style of; **com ~** tactfully; **daquele ~** (in) that way; (*col: em desordem, mal*) anyhow; **de qualquer ~** anyway; **de ~ nenhum!** no way!

jejuar [ʒe'ʒwar] *vi* to fast

jejum [ʒe'ʒũ] (*pl* **-ns**) *m* fast; **em ~** fasting

Jesus [ʒe'zus] *m* Jesus ▷ *excl* heavens!

jiboia [ʒi'bɔja] *f* boa (constrictor)

jiló [ʒi'lɔ] *m* kind of vegetable

jingle ['dʒĩgew] *m* jingle

joalheria [ʒoaʎe'ria] *f* jeweller's (shop) (*Brit*), jewelry store (*US*)

joaninha [ʒwa'niɲa] *f* ladybird (*Brit*), ladybug (*US*)

joelho [ʒo'eʎu] *m* knee; **de ~s** kneeling; **ficar de ~s** to kneel down

jogada [ʒo'gada] *f* move; (*lanço*) throw; (*negócio*) scheme, move

jogador, a [ʒoga'dor(a)] *m/f* player; (*de jogo de azar*) gambler

jogar [ʒo'gar] *vt* to play; (*em jogo de azar*) to gamble; (*atirar*) to throw; (*indiretas*) to drop ▷ *vi* to play; to gamble; (*barco*) to pitch; **~ fora** to throw away

jogging ['ʒɔgĩ] *m* jogging; (*roupa*) track suit; **fazer ~** to go jogging, jog

jogo ['ʒogu] *m* game; (*jogar*) play; (*de azar*) gambling; (*conjunto*) set; (*artimanha*) trick; **J~s Olímpicos** Olympic Games

joia ['ʒɔja] *f* jewel

Jordânia [ʒor'danja] *f*: **a ~** Jordan; **Jordão** [ʒor'dãw] *m*: **o (rio) Jordão** the Jordan (River)

jornada [ʒor'nada] *f* journey; **~ de trabalho** working day

jornal [ʒor'naw] (*pl* **-ais**) *m* newspaper; (*TV, Rádio*) news *sg*; **jornaleiro, -a** [ʒorna'lejru, a] *m/f* newsagent (*Brit*), newsdealer (*US*)

jornalismo [ʒorna'lizmu] *m* journalism; **jornalista** [ʒorna'lista] *m/f* journalist

jovem ['ʒovẽ] (*pl* **-ns**) *adj* young

▷ *m/f* young person

jovial [ʒo'vjaw] (*pl* **-ais**) *adj* jovial, cheerful

Jr *abr* = **Júnior**

judaico, -a [ʒu'dajku, a] *adj* Jewish

judeu, judia [ʒu'dew, ʒu'dʒia] *adj* Jewish ▷ *m/f* Jew

judiar [ʒu'dʒjar] *vi*: **~ de alguém/ algo** to ill-treat sb/sth

judicial [ʒudʒi'sjaw] (*pl* **-ais**) *adj* judicial

judiciário, -a [ʒudʒi'sjarju, a] *adj* judicial; **o (poder) ~** the judiciary

judô [ʒu'do] *m* judo

juiz, juíza [ʒwiz, -'iza] *m/f* judge; (*em jogos*) referee; **~ de paz** justice of the peace; **juizado** [ʒwi'zado] *m* court

juízo ['ʒwizu] *m* judgement; (*parecer*) opinion; (*siso*) common sense; (*foro*) court; **perder o ~** to lose one's mind; **não ter ~** to be foolish; **tomar** *ou* **criar ~** to come to one's senses; **chamar/levar a ~** to summon/take to court; **~!** behave yourself!

julgamento [ʒuwga'mẽtu] *m* judgement; (*audiência*) trial; (*sentença*) sentence

julgar [ʒuw'gar] *vt* to judge; (*achar*) to think; (*Jur: sentenciar*) to sentence; **julgar-se** *vr*: **~-se algo** to consider o.s. sth, think of o.s. as sth

julho ['ʒuʎu] *m* July

jumento, -a [ʒu'mẽtu, a] *m/f* donkey

junção [ʒũ'sãw] (*pl* **-ões**) *f* (*ato*) joining; (*junta*) join

junco ['ʒũku] *m* reed, rush

junções [ʒũ'sõjs] *fpl de* **junção**

junho ['ʒuɲu] *m* June

júnior ['ʒunjor] (*pl* **juniores**) *adj* younger, junior ▷ *m/f* (*Esporte*)

junior; **Eduardo Autran J~**
Eduardo Autran Junior

juntar [ʒũ'tar] *vt* to join; (*reunir*) to
bring together; (*aglomerar*) to
gather together; (*recolher*) to
collect up; (*acrescentar*) to add;
(*dinheiro*) to save up ▷ *vi* to gather;
juntar-se *vr* to gather;
(*associar-se*) to join up; **~-se a
alguém** to join sb

junto, -a ['ʒũtu, a] *adj* joined;
(*chegado*) near; **ir ~s** to go together;
~ a/de near/next to; **segue ~** (*Com*)
please find enclosed

jura ['ʒura] *f* vow

jurado, -a [ʒu'radu, a] *adj* sworn
▷ *m/f* juror

juramento [ʒura'mẽtu] *m* oath

jurar [ʒu'rar] *vt, vi* to swear; **jura?**
really?

júri ['ʒuri] *m* jury

jurídico, -a [ʒu'ridʒiku, a] *adj* legal

juros ['ʒurus] *mpl* (*Econ*) interest *sg*;
~ simples/compostos simple/
compound interest

justamente [ʒusta'mẽtʃi] *adv*
fairly, justly; (*precisamente*) exactly

justiça [ʒus'tʃisa] *f* justice; (*poder
judiciário*) judiciary; (*equidade*)
fairness; (*tribunal*) court; **com ~**
justly, fairly; **ir à ~** to go to court

justificar [ʒustʃifi'kar] *vt* to justify

justo, -a ['ʒustu, a] *adj* just, fair;
(*legítimo: queixa*) legitimate,
justified; (*exato*) exact; (*apertado*)
tight ▷ *adv* just

juvenil [ʒuve'niw] (*pl* **-is**) *adj*
youthful; (*roupa*) young; (*livro*) for
young people; (*Esporte: equipe,
campeonato*) youth *atr*, junior

juventude [ʒuvẽ'tudʒi] *f* youth;
(*jovialidade*) youthfulness; (*jovens*)
young people *pl*, youth

K, k [ka] *m* K, k

kg *abr* (= *quilograma*) kg

kit ['kitʃi] (*pl* **kits**) *m* kit

kitchenette [kitʃe'nɛtʃi] *f* studio
flat

km *abr* (= *quilômetro*) km

km/h *abr* (= *quilômetros por hora*)
km/h

omission; (espaço em branco) blank

ladeira [la'dejra] f slope

lado ['ladu] m side; (Mil) flank; (rumo) direction; **ao ~** (perto) close by; **a casa ao ~** the house next door; **ao ~ de** beside; **deixar de ~** to set aside; (fig) to leave out; **de um ~ para outro** back and forth

ladra ['ladra] f thief, robber; (picareta) crook

ladrão, -ona [la'drãw, 'ɔna] (pl **-ões/-s**) adj thieving ▷ m/f thief, robber; (picareta) crook

ladrilho [la'driʎu] m tile; (chão) tiled floor, tiles pl

ladrões [la'drõjs] mpl de **ladrão**

lagarta [la'garta] f caterpillar

lagartixa [lagar'tʃiʃa] f gecko

lagarto [la'gartu] m lizard

lago ['lagu] m lake; (de jardim) pond

lagoa [la'goa] f pool, pond; (lago) lake

-la [la] pron her; (você) you; (coisa) it

lá [la] adv there ▷ m (Mús) A; **lá fora** outside; **lá em baixo** down there; **por lá** (direção) that way; (situação) over there; **até lá** (no espaço) there; (no tempo) until then

lã [lã] f wool

labia ['labja] f (astúcia) cunning; **ter ~** to have the gift of the gab

lábio ['labju] m lip

labirinto [labi'rĩtu] m labyrinth, maze

laboratório [labora'tɔrju] m laboratory

laca ['laka] f lacquer

laçar [la'sar] vt to bind, tie

laço ['lasu] m bow; (de gravata) knot; (armadilha) snare; (fig) bond, tie; **dar um ~** to tie a bow

lacrar [la'krar] vt to seal (with wax); **lacre** ['lakri] m sealing wax

lacuna [la'kuna] f gap; (omissão)

lagosta [la'gosta] f lobster

lagostim [lagos'tʃĩ] (pl **-ns**) m crayfish

lágrima ['lagrima] f tear

lama ['lama] f mud

lamaçal [lama'saw] (pl **-ais**) m quagmire; (pântano) bog, marsh

lamber [lã'ber] vt to lick; **lambida** [lã'bida] f: **dar uma lambida em algo** to lick sth

lambuzar [lãbu'zar] vt to smear

lamentar [lamẽ'tar] vt to lament; (sentir) to regret; **lamentar-se** vr: **~-se (de algo)** to lament (sth); **~ (que)** to be sorry (that); **lamentável** [lamẽ'tavew] (pl **-eis**) adj regrettable; (deplorável) deplorable; **lamento** [la'mẽtu] m lament; (gemido) moan

lâmina ['lamina] f (chapa) sheet; (placa) plate; (de faca) blade; (de persiana) slat

lâmpada ['lãpada] *f* lamp; (*tb:* ~ **elétrica**) light bulb; ~ **de mesa** table lamp

lançar [lã'sar] *vt* to throw; (*navio, produto, campanha*) to launch; (*disco, filme*) to release; (*Com: em livro*) to enter; (*em leilão*) to bid

lancha ['lãʃa] *f* launch; ~ **torpedeira** torpedo boat

lanchar [lã'ʃar] *vi* to have a snack ▷ *vt* to have as a snack; **lanche** ['lãʃi] *m* snack

lanchonete [lãʃo'nɛtʃi] (*BR*) *f* snack bar

LAN house [lã'hawzi] *f* internet café

lanterna [lã'tɛrna] *f* lantern; (*portátil*) torch (*Brit*), flashlight (*US*)

lápide ['lapidʒi] *f* (*tumular*) tombstone; (*comemorativa*) memorial stone

lápis ['lapis] *m inv* pencil; ~ **de cor** coloured (*Brit*) *ou* colored (*US*) pencil, crayon; ~ **de olho** eyebrow pencil; **lapiseira** [lapi'zejra] *f* propelling (*Brit*) *ou* mechanical (*US*) pencil; (*caixa*) pencil case

lapso ['lapsu] *m* lapse; (*de tempo*) interval; (*erro*) slip

lar [lar] *m* home

laranja [la'rãʒa] *adj inv* orange ▷ *f* orange ▷ *m* (*cor*) orange; **laranjada** [larã'ʒada] *f* orangeade; **laranjeira** [larã'ʒejra] *f* orange tree

lareira [la'rejra] *f* hearth, fireside

larga ['larga] *f*: **à** ~ lavishly; **dar** ~**s a** to give free rein to; **viver à** ~ to lead a lavish life

largada [lar'gada] *f* start; **dar a** ~ to start; (*fig*) to make a start

largar [lar'gar] *vt* to let go of, release; (*deixar*) to leave; (*deixar cair*) to drop; (*risada*) to let out;

(*velas*) to unfurl; (*piada*) to tell; (*pôr em liberdade*) to let go ▷ *vi* (*Náut*) to set sail; **largar-se** *vr* (*desprender-se*) to free o.s.; (*ir-se*) to go off; (*pôr-se*) to proceed

largo, -a ['largu, a] *adj* wide, broad; (*amplo*) extensive; (*roupa*) loose, baggy; (*conversa*) long ▷ *m* (*praça*) square; (*alto-mar*) open sea; **ao** ~ at a distance, far off; **passar de** ~ **sobre um assunto** to gloss over a subject; **passar ao** ~ **de algo** (*fig*) to sidestep sth; **largura** [lar'gura] *f* width, breadth

laringite [larĩ'ʒitʃi] *f* laryngitis

lasanha [la'zaɲa] *f* lasagna

laser ['lejzer] *m* laser; **raio** ~ laser beam

lástima ['lastʃima] *f* pity, compassion; (*infortúnio*) misfortune; **é uma** ~ **(que)** it's a shame (that); **lastimar** [lastʃi'mar] *vt* to lament; **lastimar-se** *vr* to complain, feel sorry for o.s.

lata ['lata] *f* can, tin (*Brit*); (*material*) tin-plate; ~ **de lixo** rubbish bin (*Brit*), garbage can (*US*); ~ **velha** (*col: carro*) old banger (*Brit*) *ou* clunker (*US*)

latão [la'tãw] *m* brass

lataria [lata'ria] *f* (*Auto*) bodywork; (*enlatados*) canned food

latejar [late'ʒar] *vi* to throb

latente [la'tẽtʃi] *adj* latent

lateral [late'raw] (*pl* -**ais**) *adj* side, lateral ▷ *f* (*Futebol*) sideline ▷ *m* (*Futebol*) throw-in

latido [la'tʃidu] *m* bark(ing), yelp(ing)

latifundiário, -a [latʃifũ'dʒjarju, a] *m/f* landowner

latifúndio [latʃi'fũdʒju] *m* large estate

latim [la'tʃĩ] m (Ling) Latin; **gastar o seu ~** to waste one's breath

latino, -a [la'tʃinu, a] adj Latin; **latino-americano, -a** adj, m/f Latin-American

latir [la'tʃir] vi to bark, yelp

latitude [latʃi'tudʒi] f latitude; (largura) breadth; (fig) scope

latrocínio [latro'sinju] m armed robbery

laudo ['lawdu] m (Jur) decision; (resultados) findings pl; (peça escrita) report

lava ['lava] f lava

lavabo [la'vabu] m toilet

lavadeira [lava'dejra] f washerwoman

lavagem [la'vaʒẽ] f washing; **~ a seco** dry cleaning; **~ cerebral** brainwashing

lavanda [la'vãda] f (Bot) lavender; (colônia) lavender water; (para lavar os dedos) finger bowl

lavar [la'var] vt to wash; (culpa) to wash away; **~ a seco** to dry clean

lavatório [lava'tɔrju] m washbasin; (aposento) toilet

lavoura [la'vora] f tilling; (agricultura) farming; (terreno) plantation

laxativo, -a [laʃa'tʃivu, a] adj, m laxative

lazer [la'zer] m leisure

leal [le'aw] (pl -**ais**) adj loyal; **lealdade** [leaw'dadʒi] f loyalty

leão [le'ãw] (pl -**ões**) m lion; **L~** (Astrologia) Leo

lebre ['lɛbri] f hare

lecionar [lesjo'nar] vt, vi to teach

legal [le'gaw] (pl -**ais**) adj legal, lawful; (col) fine; (: pessoa) nice ▷ adv (col) well; **(tá) ~!** OK!; **legalidade** [legali'dadʒi] f legality, lawfulness; **legalizar** [legali'zar] vt to legalize; (documento) to authenticate

legendado, -a [leʒẽ'dadu, a] adj (filme) subtitled

legendário, -a [leʒẽ'darju, a] adj legendary

legislação [leʒizla'sãw] f legislation

legislar [leʒiz'lar] vi to legislate ▷ vt to pass

legislativo, -a [leʒizla'tʃivu, a] adj legislative ▷ m legislature

legitimar [leʒitʃi'mar] vt to legitimize; (justificar) to legitimate

legume [le'gumi] m vegetable

lei [lej] f law; (regra) rule; (metal) standard

leigo, -a ['lejgu, a] adj (Rel) lay, secular ▷ m layman; **ser ~ em algo** (fig) to be no expert at sth, be unversed in sth

leilão [lej'lãw] (pl -**ões**) m auction; **vender em ~** to sell by auction, auction off; **leiloar** [lej'lwar] vt to auction

leio etc ['leju] vb ver **ler**

leitão, -toa [lej'tãw, 'toa] (pl -**ões/-s**) m/f sucking (Brit) ou suckling (US) pig

leite ['lejtʃi] m milk; **~ em pó** powdered milk; **~ desnatado** ou **magro** skimmed milk; **~ de magnésia** milk of magnesia; **~ semidesnatado** semi-skimmed milk; **leiteira** [lej'tejra] f (para ferver) milk pan; (para servir) milk jug; **leiteiro, -a** [lej'tejru, a] adj (vaca, gado) dairy ▷ m/f milkman/woman

leitões [lej'tõjs] mpl de **leitão**

leitor, a [lej'tor(a)] m/f reader; (professor) lector

leitura [lej'tura] f reading; (livro etc) reading matter

lema ['lɛma] m motto; (Pol) slogan

lembrança [lẽ'brãsa] f recollection, memory; (presente) souvenir; **lembranças** fpl (recomendações): **~s a sua mãe!** regards to your mother!

lembrar [lẽ'brar] vt, vi to remember; **lembrar-se** vr: **~(-se) de** to remember; **~(-se) (de) que** to remember that; **~ algo a alguém, ~ alguém de algo** to remind sb of sth; **~ alguém de que, ~ a alguém que** to remind sb that; **ele lembra meu irmão** he reminds me of my brother, he is like my brother; **lembrete** [lẽ'bretʃi] m reminder

leme ['lɛmi] m rudder; (Náut) helm; (fig) control

lenço ['lẽsu] m handkerchief; (de pescoço) scarf; (de cabeça) headscarf; **~ de papel** tissue; **~ umedecido** baby wipe

lençol [lẽ'sɔw] (pl **-óis**) m sheet; **estar em maus lençóis** to be in a fix

lenda ['lẽda] f legend; (fig: mentira) lie; **lendário, -a** [lẽ'darju, a] adj legendary

lenha ['lɛɲa] f firewood

lente ['lẽtʃi] f lens sg; **~ de aumento** magnifying glass; **~s de contato** contact lenses

lentidão [lẽtʃi'dãw] f slowness

lento, -a ['lẽtu, a] adj slow

leoa [le'oa] f lioness

leões [le'õjs] mpl de **leão**

leopardo [ljo'pardu] m leopard

lepra ['lɛpra] f leprosy

leque ['lɛki] m fan; (fig) array

ler [ler] vt, vi to read

lesão [le'zãw] (pl **-ões**) f harm, injury; (Jur) violation; (Med) lesion; **~ corporal** (Jur) bodily harm

lesar [le'zar] vt to harm, damage; (direitos) to violate

lésbica ['lɛzbika] f lesbian

lesma ['lezma] f slug; (fig: pessoa) slowcoach

lesões [le'zõjs] fpl de **lesão**

lesse etc ['lesi] vb ver **ler**

leste ['lɛstʃi] m east

letal [le'taw] (pl **-ais**) adj lethal

letargia [letar'ʒia] f lethargy

letivo, -a [le'tʃivu, a] adj school atr; **ano ~** academic year

letra ['letra] f letter; (caligrafia) handwriting; (de canção) lyrics pl; **Letras** fpl (curso) language and literature; **à ~** literally; **ao pé da ~** literally, word for word; **~ de câmbio** (Com) bill of exchange; **~ de imprensa** print; **letrado, -a** [le'tradu, a] adj learned, erudite ▷ m/f scholar; **letreiro** [le'trejru] m sign, notice; (inscrição) inscription; (Cinema) subtitle

leu etc [lew] vb ver **ler**

léu [lɛw] m: **ao ~** (à toa) aimlessly; (à mostra) uncovered

leucemia [lewse'mia] f leukaemia (Brit), leukemia (US)

levado, -a [le'vadu, a] adj mischievous; (criança) naughty

levantador, a [levãta'dor(a)] adj lifting ▷ m/f: **~ de pesos** weightlifter

levantamento [levãta'mẽtu] m lifting, raising; (revolta) uprising, rebellion; (arrolamento) survey

levantar [levã'tar] vt to lift, raise; (voz, capital) to raise; (apanhar) to pick up; (suscitar) to arouse; (ambiente) to brighten up ▷ vi to stand up; (da cama) to get up; (dar vida) to brighten; **levantar-se** vr to stand up; (da cama) to get up; (rebelar-se) to rebel

levar [le'var] vt to take; (portar) to carry; (tempo) to pass, spend; (roupa) to wear; (lidar com) to handle; (induzir) to lead; (filme) to show; (peça teatral) to do, put on; (vida) to lead ▷ vi to get a beating; **~ a** to lead to; **~ a mal** to take amiss

leve ['lɛvi] adj light; (insignificante) slight; **de ~** lightly, softly

leviandade [levjã'dadʒi] f frivolity

leviano, -a [le'vjanu, a] adj frivolous

lha [ʎa] = **lhe + a**

lhas [ʎas] = **lhe + as**

lhe [ʎi] pron (a ele) to him; (a ela) to her; (a você) to you

lhes [ʎis] pron pl (a eles/elas) to them; (a vocês) to you

lho [ʎu] = **lhe + o**

lhos [ʎus] = **lhe + os**

li etc [li] vb ver **ler**

Líbano ['libanu] m: **o ~** Lebanon

libélula [li'bɛlula] f dragonfly

liberação [libera'sãw] f liberation

liberal [libe'raw] (pl **-ais**) adj, m/f liberal

liberar [libe'rar] vt to release; (permitir) to allow

liberdade [liber'dadʒi] f freedom; **liberdades** fpl (direitos) liberties; **pôr alguém em ~** to set sb free; **~ condicional** probation; **~ de palavra** freedom of speech; **~ sob palavra** parole

libertação [liberta'sãw] f release

libertino, -a [liber'tʃinu, a] adj loose-living ▷ m/f libertine

Líbia ['libja] f: **a ~** Libya

libidinoso, -a [libidʒi'nozu, ɔza] adj lecherous, lustful

líbio, -a ['libju, a] adj, m/f Libyan

libra ['libra] f pound; **L~** (Astrologia) Libra

lição [li'sãw] (pl **-ões**) f lesson

licença [li'sẽsa] f licence (Brit), license (US); (permissão) permission; (Mil: do trabalho) leave; **com ~** excuse me; **estar de ~** to be on leave; **dá ~?** may I?

licenciado, -a [lisẽ'sjadu, a] m/f graduate

licenciar [lisẽ'sjar] vt to license; **licenciar-se** vr (Educ) to graduate; (ficar de licença) to take leave; **licenciatura** [lisẽsja'tura] f (título) degree; (curso) degree course

liceu [li'sew] (PT) m secondary (Brit) ou high (US) school

lições [li'sõjs] fpl de **lição**

licor [li'kor] m liqueur

lidar [li'dar] vi: **~ com** (ocupar-se) to deal with; (combater) to struggle against; **~ em algo** to work in sth

líder ['lider] m/f leader; **liderança** [lide'rãsa] f leadership; (Esporte) lead; **liderar** [lide'rar] vt to lead

ligado, -a [li'gadu, a] adj (Tec) connected; (luz, rádio etc) on; (metal) alloy

ligadura [liga'dura] f bandage

ligamento [liga'mẽtu] m ligament

ligar [li'gar] vt to tie, bind; (unir) to join, connect; (luz, TV) to switch on; (afetivamente) to bind together; (carro) to start (up) ▷ vi (telefonar) to ring; **ligar-se** vr to join; **~-se com alguém** to join with sb; **~-se a algo** to be connected with sth; **~ para alguém** to ring sb up; **~ para ou a algo** (dar atenção) to take notice of sth; (dar importância) to care about sth; **eu nem ligo** it doesn't bother me; **não ligo a mínima (para)** I couldn't care less (about)

ligeiro, -a [li'ʒejru, a] adj light; (ferimento) slight; (referência) passing; (*conhecimentos*) scant; (*rápido*) quick, swift; (*ágil*) nimble ▷ *adv* swiftly, nimbly

lilás [li'las] *adj, m* lilac

lima ['lima] *f* (*laranja*) type of orange; (*ferramenta*) file; **~ de unhas** nailfile

limão [li'mãw] (*pl* **-ões**) *m* lime; (*tb*: **~-galego**) lemon

limão-galego (*pl* **limões-galegos**) *m* lemon

limiar [li'mjar] *m* threshold

limitação [limita'sãw] (*pl* **-ões**) *f* limitation, restriction

limitar [limi'tar] *vt* to limit, restrict; **limitar-se** *vr*: **~-se a** to limit o.s. to; **~(-se) com** to border on; **limite** [li'mitʃi] *m* limit, boundary; (*fig*) limit; **passar dos limites** to go too far

limo ['limu] *m* (*Bot*) water weed; (*lodo*) slime

limoeiro [li'mwejru] *m* lemon tree

limões [li'mõjs] *mpl de* **limão**

limonada [limo'nada] *f* lemonade (*Brit*), lemon soda (*US*)

limpar [lĩ'par] *vt* to clean; (*lágrimas, suor*) to wipe away; (*polir*) to shine, polish; (*fig*) to clean up; (*roubar*) to rob

limpo, -a ['lĩpu, a] *pp de* **limpar** ▷ *adj* clean; (*céu, consciência*) clear; (*Com*) net; (*fig*) pure; (*col: pronto*) ready; **passar a ~** to make a fair copy; **tirar a ~** to find out the truth about, clear up; **estar ~ com alguém** (*col*) to be in with sb

linchar [lĩ'ʃar] *vt* to lynch

lindo, -a ['lĩdu, a] *adj* lovely

lingerie [lĩʒe'ri] *m* lingerie

língua ['lĩgwa] *f* tongue; (*linguagem*) language; **botar a ~ para fora** to stick out one's tongue; **dar com a ~ nos dentes** to let the cat out of the bag; **estar na ponta da ~** to be on the tip of one's tongue

linguado [lĩ'gwadu] *m* (*peixe*) sole

linguagem [lĩ'gwaʒẽ] (*pl* **-ns**) *f* (*tb*: *Comput*) language; **~ de máquina** (*Comput*) machine language

linguarudo, -a [lĩgwa'rudu, a] *adj* gossiping ▷ *m/f* gossip

linguiça [lĩ'gwisa] *f* sausage

linha ['liɲa] *f* line; (*para costura*) thread; (*barbante*) string, cord; **linhas** *fpl* (*carta*) letter *sg*; **em ~** in line, in a row; (*Comput*) on line; **fora de ~** out of production; **manter/perder a ~** to keep/lose one's cool; **o telefone não deu ~** the line was dead; **~ aérea** airline; **~ de mira** sights *pl*; **~ de montagem** assembly line; **~ férrea** railway (*Brit*), railroad (*US*)

linho ['liɲu] *m* linen; (*planta*) flax

liquidação [likida'sãw] (*pl* **-ões**) *f* liquidation; (*em loja*) (clearance) sale; (*de conta*) settlement; **em ~** on sale

liquidar [liki'dar] *vt* to liquidate; (*conta*) to settle; (*mercadoria*) to sell off; (*assunto*) to lay to rest ▷ *vi* (*loja*) to have a sale; **liquidar-se** *vr* (*destruir-se*) to be destroyed; **~ (com) alguém** (*fig*: *arrasar*) to destroy sb; (: *matar*) to do away with sb

liquidificador [likwidʒifika'dor] *m* liquidizer

líquido, -a ['likidu, a] *adj* liquid, fluid; (*Com*) net ▷ *m* liquid

lira ['lira] *f* lyre; (*moeda*) lira

lírio ['lirju] *m* lily

Lisboa [liz'boa] *n* Lisbon; **lisboeta** [liz'bweta] *adj* Lisbon *atr* ▷ *m/f* inhabitant *ou* native of Lisbon

liso, -a ['lizu, a] *adj* smooth; (*tecido*) plain; (*cabelo*) straight; (*col: sem dinheiro*) broke

lisonjear [lizõ'ʒjar] *vt* to flatter

lista ['lista] *f* list; (*listra*) stripe; (*PT: menu*) menu; ~ **negra** blacklist; ~ **telefônica** telephone directory; **listar** [lis'tar] *vt* to list

listra ['listra] *f* stripe; **listrado, -a** [lis'tradu, a] *adj* striped

literal [lite'raw] (*pl* -**ais**) *adj* literal

literário, -a [lite'rarju, a] *adj* literary

literatura [litera'tura] *f* literature

Literatura de cordel *see note*

○ **LITERATURA DE CORDEL**
○
○ **Literatura de cordel** is a type
○ of literature typical of the
○ north-east of Brazil, and
○ published in the form of cheaply
○ printed booklets. Their authors
○ hang these booklets from wires
○ attached to walls in the street so
○ that people can look at them.
○ While they do this, the authors
○ sing their stories aloud.
○ **Literatura de cordel** deals both
○ with local events and people,
○ and with everyday public life,
○ almost always in an irreverent
○ manner.

litoral [lito'raw] (*pl* -**ais**) *adj* coastal ▷ *m* coast, seaboard

litro ['litru] *m* litre (*Brit*), liter (*US*)

livrar [li'vrar] *vt* to release, liberate; (*salvar*) to save; **livrar-se** *vr* to escape; ~-**se de** to get rid of; (*compromisso*) to get out of; **Deus me livre!** Heaven forbid!

livraria [livra'ria] *f* bookshop (*Brit*), bookstore (*US*)

livre ['livri] *adj* free; (*lugar*) unoccupied; (*desimpedido*) clear, open; ~ **de impostos** tax-free;

livre-arbítrio *m* free will

livro ['livru] *m* book; ~ **brochado** paperback; ~ **de bolso** pocket-sized book; ~ **de cheques** cheque book (*Brit*), check book (*US*); ~ **de consulta** reference book; ~ **encadernado** *ou* **de capa dura** hardback

lixa ['liʃa] *f* sandpaper; (*de unhas*) nailfile; (*peixe*) dogfish; **lixar** [li'ʃar] *vt* to sand

lixeira [li'ʃejra] *f* dustbin (*Brit*), garbage can (*US*)

lixeiro [li'ʃejru] *m* dustman (*Brit*), garbage man (*US*)

lixo ['liʃu] *m* rubbish, garbage (*US*); **ser um** ~ (*col*) to be rubbish; ~ **atômico** nuclear waste

-lo [lu] *pron* him; (*você*) you; (*coisa*) it

lobo ['lobu] *m* wolf

locação [loka'sãw] (*pl* -**ões**) *f* lease; (*de vídeo etc*) rental

locador, a [loka'dor(a)] *m/f* (*de casa*) landlord; (*de carro, filme*) rental agent ▷ *f* rental company; ~**a de vídeo** video rental shop

local [lo'kaw] (*pl* -**ais**) *adj* local ▷ *m* site, place ▷ *f* (*notícia*) story; **localidade** [lokali'dadʒi] *f* (*lugar*) locality; (*povoação*) town; **localização** [lokaliza'sãw] (*pl* -**ões**) *f* location; **localizar** [lokali'zar] *vt* to locate; (*situar*) to place; **localizar-se** *vr* to be located; (*orientar-se*) to get one's bearings

loção [lo'sãw] (*pl* -**ões**) *f* lotion; ~ **após-barba** aftershave (lotion)

locatário, -a [loka'tarju, a] *m/f* (*de casa*) tenant; (*de carro, filme*) hirer

loções [lo'sõjs] *fpl de* **loção**

locomotiva [lokomo'tʃiva] *f* railway (*Brit*) *ou* railroad (*US*) engine, locomotive

locomover-se [lokomo'versi] *vr* to move around

locutor, a [loku'tor(a)] *m/f (TV, Rádio)* announcer

lógica ['lɔʒika] *f* logic; **lógico, -a** ['lɔʒiku, a] *adj* logical; **(é) lógico!** of course!

logo ['lɔgu] *adv (imediatamente)* right away, at once; *(em breve)* soon; *(justamente)* just, right; *(mais tarde)* later; **~, ~** in no time; **~ mais** later; **~ no começo** right at the start; **~ que, tão ~** as soon as; **até ~!** bye!; **~ antes/depois** just before/shortly afterwards; **~ de saída** *ou* **de cara** straightaway, right away

logotipo [logo'tʃipu] *m* logo

lograr [lo'grar] *vt (alcançar)* to achieve; *(obter)* to get, obtain; *(enganar)* to cheat; **~ fazer** to manage to do

loiro, -a ['lojru, a] *adj* = **louro**

loja ['lɔʒa] *f* shop; **~ de presentes** gift shop *(Brit)*, gift store *(US)*; **lojista** [lo'ʒista] *m/f* shopkeeper

lombo ['lõbu] *m* back; *(carne)* loin

lona ['lɔna] *f* canvas

Londres ['lõdris] *n* London; **londrino, -a** [lõ'drinu, a] *adj* London *atr* ▷ *m/f* Londoner

longa-metragem *(pl* **longas-metragens)** *m:* **(filme de) ~** feature (film)

longe ['lõʒi] *adv* far, far away ▷ *adj* distant; **ao ~** in the distance; **de ~** from far away; *(sem dúvida)* by a long way; **~ de** a long way *ou* far from; **~ disso** far from it; **ir ~ demais** *(fig)* to go too far

longínquo, -a [lõ'ʒĩkwu, a] *adj* distant, remote

longitude [lõʒi'tudʒi] *f (Geo)* longitude

longo, -a ['lõgu, a] *adj* long ▷ *m (vestido)* long dress, evening dress; **ao ~ de** along, alongside

lotação [lota'sãw] *f* capacity; *(de funcionários)* complement; *(BR: ônibus)* bus; **~ completa** *ou* **esgotada** *(Teatro)* sold out

lotado, -a [lo'tadu, a] *adj (Teatro)* full; *(ônibus)* full up; *(bar, praia)* packed, crowded

lotar [lo'tar] *vt* to fill, pack; *(funcionário)* to place ▷ *vi* to fill up

lote ['lɔtʃi] *m* portion, share; *(em leilão)* lot; *(terreno)* plot; *(de ações)* parcel, batch

loteria [lote'ria] *f* lottery; **~ esportiva** football pools *pl (Brit)*, lottery *(US)*

louça ['losa] *f* china; *(conjunto)* crockery; *(tb:* **~ sanitária)** bathroom suite; **de ~** china *atr*; **~ de barro** earthenware; **~ de jantar** dinner service; **lavar a ~** to do the washing up *(Brit) ou* the dishes

louco, -a ['loku, a] *adj* crazy, mad; *(sucesso)* runaway; *(frio)* freezing ▷ *m/f* lunatic; **~ varrido** raving mad; **~ de fome/raiva** ravenous/hopping mad; **~ por** crazy about; **deixar alguém ~** to drive sb crazy; **loucura** [lo'kura] *f* madness; *(ato)* crazy thing; **ser loucura (fazer)** to be crazy (to do); **ser uma loucura** to be crazy; *(col: ser muito bom)* to be fantastic

louro, -a ['loru, a] *adj* blond, fair ▷ *m* laurel; *(Culin)* bay leaf; *(papagaio)* parrot; **louros** *mpl (fig)* laurels

louva-a-deus ['lova-] *m inv* praying mantis

louvar [lo'var] *vt, vi:* **~ (a)** to praise; **louvável** [lo'vavew] *(pl* **-eis)** *adj* praiseworthy

louvor [lo'vor] *m* praise
LP *abr m* LP (record)
Ltda. *abr* (= *Limitada*) Ltd
lua ['lua] *f* moon; **estar ou viver no mundo da ~** to have one's head in the clouds; **estar de ~** (*col*) to be in a mood; **ser de ~** (*col*) to be moody; **~ cheia/nova** full/new moon; **~ de mel** honeymoon
luar ['lwar] *m* moonlight
lubrificante [lubrifi'kãtʃi] *m* lubricant
lúcido, -a ['lusidu, a] *adj* lucid
lúcio ['lusju] *m* (*peixe*) pike
lucrar [lu'krar] *vt* (*tirar proveito*) to profit from *ou* by; (*dinheiro*) to make; (*gozar*) to enjoy ▷ *vi* to make a profit; **~ com** *ou* **em** to profit by
lucrativo, -a [lukra'tʃivu, a] *adj* lucrative, profitable
lucro ['lukru] *m* gain; (*Com*) profit; **~s e perdas** (*Com*) profit and loss
lugar [lu'gar] *m* place; (*espaço*) space, room; (*para sentar*) seat; (*emprego*) job; (*ocasião*) opportunity; **em ~ de** instead of; **dar ~ a** (*causar*) to give rise to; **~ comum** commonplace; **em primeiro ~** in the first place; **em algum/ nenhum/todo ~** somewhere/ nowhere/everywhere; **em outro ~** somewhere else, elsewhere; **ter ~** (*acontecer*) to take place; **~ de nascimento** place of birth;
lugarejo [luga'reʒu] *m* village
lula ['lula] *f* squid
lume ['lumi] *m* fire; (*luz*) light
luminária [lumi'narja] *f* lamp; **luminárias** *fpl* (*iluminações*) illuminations
luminosidade [luminozi'dadʒi] *f* brightness
luminoso, -a [lumi'nozu, ɔza] *adj* luminous; (*fig: raciocínio*) clear; (*: ideia, talento*) brilliant; (*letreiro*) illuminated

lunar [lu'nar] *adj* lunar ▷ *m* (*na pele*) mole
lunático, -a [lu'natʃiku, a] *adj* mad
lusitano, -a [luzi'tanu, a] *adj* Portuguese, Lusitanian
luso, -a ['luzu, a] *adj* Portuguese; **luso-brasileiro, -a** (*pl* **luso-brasileiros**) *adj* Luso-Brazilian
lustre ['lustri] *m* gloss, sheen; (*fig*) lustre (*Brit*), luster (*US*); (*luminária*) chandelier
luta ['luta] *f* fight, struggle; **~ de boxe** boxing; **~ livre** wrestling; **lutador, a** [luta'dor(a)] *m/f* fighter; (*atleta*) wrestler; **lutar** [lu'tar] *vi* to fight, struggle; (*luta livre*) to wrestle ▷ *vt* (*caratê, judô*) to do; **lutar contra/por algo** to fight against/for sth; **lutar para fazer algo** to fight *ou* struggle to do sth; **lutar com** (*dificuldades*) to struggle against; (*competir*) to fight with
luto ['lutu] *m* mourning; (*tristeza*) grief; **de ~** in mourning; **pôr ~** to go into mourning
luva ['luva] *f* glove; **luvas** *fpl* (*pagamento*) payment *sg*; (*ao locador*) fee *sg*
Luxemburgo [luʃẽ'burgu] *m*: **o ~** Luxembourg
luxo ['luʃu] *m* luxury; **de ~** luxury *atr*; **dar-se ao ~ de** to allow o.s. to; **luxuoso, -a** [lu'ʃwozu, ɔza] *adj* luxurious
luxúria [lu'ʃurja] *f* lust
luz [luz] *f* light; (*eletricidade*) electricity; **à ~ de** by the light of; (*fig*) in the light of; **a meia ~** with subdued lighting; **dar à ~ (um filho)** to give birth (to a son); **deu-me uma ~** I had an idea

m

ma [ma] *pron* = **me** + **a**

má [ma] *adj f de* **mau**

maca ['maka] *f* stretcher

maçã [ma'sã] *f* apple; **~ do rosto** cheekbone

macabro, -a [ma'kabru, a] *adj* macabre

macacão [maka'kãw] (*pl* **-ões**) *m* (*de trabalhador*) overalls *pl* (*Brit*), coveralls *pl* (*US*); (*da moda*) jump-suit

macaco, -a [ma'kaku, a] *m/f* monkey ▷ *m* (*Mecânica*) jack; **(fato) ~** (*PT*) overalls *pl* (*Brit*), coveralls *pl* (*US*); **~ velho** (*fig*) old hand

macacões [maka'kõjs] *mpl de* **macacão**

maçador, a [masa'dor(a)] (*PT*) *adj* boring

maçaneta [masa'neta] *f* knob

maçante [ma'sãtʃi] (*BR*) *adj* boring

macarrão [maka'hãw] *m* pasta;

(*em forma de canudo*) spaghetti; **macarronada** [makaho'nada] *f* pasta with cheese and tomato sauce

macete [ma'setʃi] *m* mallet

machado [ma'ʃadu] *m* axe (*Brit*), ax (*US*)

machista [ma'ʃista] *adj* chauvinistic, macho ▷ *m* male chauvinist

macho ['maʃu] *adj* male; (*fig*) virile, manly; (*valentão*) tough ▷ *m* male; (*Tec*) tap

machucado, -a [maʃu'kadu, a] *adj* hurt; (*pé, braço*) bad ▷ *m* injury; (*área machucada*) sore patch

machucar [maʃu'kar] *vt* to hurt; (*produzir contusão*) to bruise ▷ *vi* to hurt; **machucar-se** *vr* to hurt o.s.

maciço, -a [ma'sisu, a] *adj* solid; (*espesso*) thick; (*quantidade*) massive

macio, -a [ma'siu, a] *adj* soft; (*liso*) smooth

maço ['masu] *m* (*de folhas, notas*) bundle; (*de cigarros*) packet

maçom [ma'sõ] (*pl* **-ns**) *m* (free) mason

maconha [ma'kõɲa] *f* dope; **cigarro de ~** joint

maçons [ma'sõs] *mpl de* **maçom**

má-criação (*pl* **-ões**) *f* rudeness; (*ato, dito*) rude thing

mácula ['makula] *f* stain, blemish

macumba [ma'kũba] *f* ≈ voodoo; (*despacho*) macumba offering; **macumbeiro, -a** [makũ'bejru, a] *adj* ≈ voodoo *atr* ▷ *m/f* follower of macumba

madama [ma'dama] *f* = **madame**

madame [ma'dami] *f* (*senhora*) lady; (*col: dona de casa*) lady of the house

madeira [ma'dejra] *f* wood ▷ *m*

m

Madeira (wine); **de ~** wooden;
bater na ~ (*fig*) to touch (*Brit*) *ou*
knock on (*US*) wood; **~
compensada** plywood

madeirense [madej'rẽsi] *adj, m/f*
Madeiran

madeixa [ma'dejʃa] *f* (*de cabelo*)
lock

madrasta [ma'drasta] *f*
stepmother

madrepérola [madre'pɛrola] *f*
mother of pearl

Madri [ma'dri] *n* Madrid

Madrid [ma'drid] (*PT*) *n* Madrid

madrinha [ma'driɲa] *f* godmother

madrugada [madru'gada] *f* (early)
morning; (*alvorada*) dawn,
daybreak

madrugar [madru'gar] *vi* to get up
early; (*aparecer cedo*) to be early

maduro, -a [ma'duro, a] *adj* ripe;
(*fig*) mature; (*: prudente*) prudent

mãe [mãj] *f* mother; **~ adotiva** *ou*
de criação adoptive mother

maestro, -trina [ma'ɛstru, 'trina]
m/f conductor

má-fé *f* malicious intent

magia [ma'ʒia] *f* magic

mágica ['maʒika] *f* magic; (*truque*)
magic trick; *ver tb* **mágico**

mágico, -a ['maʒiku, a] *adj* magic
▷ *m/f* magician

magistério [maʒis'tɛrju] *m*
(*ensino*) teaching; (*profissão*)
teaching profession; (*professorado*)
teachers *pl*

magnético, -a [mag'nɛtʃiku, a]
adj magnetic

magnífico, -a [mag'nifiku, a] *adj*
splendid, magnificent

mago ['magu] *m* magician; **os reis
~s** the Three Wise Men, the Three
Kings

mágoa ['magwa] *f* (*tristeza*) sorrow,
grief; (*fig*: *desagrado*) hurt

magoado, -a [ma'gwadu, a] *adj*
hurt

magoar [ma'gwar] *vt, vi* to hurt;
magoar-se *vr*: **~-se com algo** to
be hurt by sth

magro, -a ['magru, a] *adj* (*pessoa*)
slim; (*carne*) lean; (*fig*: *parco*)
meagre (*Brit*), meager (*US*); (*leite*)
skimmed

maio ['maju] *m* May

maiô [ma'jo] (*BR*) *m* swimsuit

maionese [majo'nɛzi] *f*
mayonnaise

maior [ma'jɔr] *adj* (*compar*: *de
tamanho*) bigger; (*: de importância*)
greater; (*superl*: *de tamanho*)
biggest; (*: de importância*) greatest
▷ *m/f* adult; **~ de idade** of age,
adult; **~ de 21 anos** over 21;

maioria [majo'ria] *f* majority; **a
maioria de** most of; **maioridade**
[majori'dadʒi] *f* adulthood

 PALAVRA-CHAVE

mais [majs] *adv* **1** (*compar*): **mais
magro/inteligente (do que)**
thinner/more intelligent (than);
ele trabalha mais (do que eu) he
works more (than me)
2 (*superl*): **o mais ...** the most ...;
o mais magro/inteligente the
thinnest/most intelligent
3 (*negativo*): **ele não trabalha
mais aqui** he doesn't work here
any more; **nunca mais** never again
4 (+ *adj*: *valor intensivo*): **que livro
mais chato!** what a boring book!
5: **por mais que** however much;
por mais que se esforce ... no
matter how hard you try ...; **por
mais que eu quisesse ...** much as I
should like to ...

6: **a mais: temos um a mais** we've got one extra

7 (*tempo*): **mais cedo ou mais tarde** sooner or later; **a mais tempo** sooner; **logo mais** later on; **no mais tardar** at the latest

8 (*frases*): **mais ou menos** more or less; **mais uma vez** once more; **cada vez mais** more and more; **sem mais nem menos** out of the blue

▷ *adj* **1** (*compar*): **mais (do que)** more (than); **ele tem mais dinheiro (do que o irmão)** he's got more money (than his brother)

2 (*superl*): **ele é quem tem mais dinheiro** he's got most money

3 (+ *números*): **ela tem mais de dez bolsas** she's got more than ten bags

4 (*negativo*): **não tenho mais dinheiro** I haven't got any more money

5 (*adicional*) else; **mais alguma coisa?** anything else?; **nada/ ninguém mais** nothing/no-one else

▷ *prep*: **2 mais 2 são 4** 2 and 2 *ou* plus 2 is 4

▷ *m*: **o mais** the rest

maisena [majˈzena] *f* cornflower (*Brit*), corn starch (*US*)

maiúscula [maˈjuskula] *f* capital letter

majestade [maʒesˈtadʒi] *f* majesty; **majestoso, -a** [maʒesˈtozu, ɔza] *adj* majestic

major [maˈʒɔr] *m* (*Mil*) major

majoritário, -a [maʒoriˈtarju, a] *adj* majority *atr*

mal [maw] (*pl* **males**) *m* harm; (*Med*) illness ▷ *adv* badly; (*quase não*) hardly ▷ *conj* hardly; **~ desliguei o fone, a campainha tocou** I had hardly put the phone

down when the doorbell rang; **falar ~ de alguém** to speak ill of sb, run sb down; **não faz ~** never mind; **estar ~** (*doente*) to be ill; **passar ~** to be sick; **estar de ~ com alguém** not to be speaking to sb; **~ de Alzheimer** Alzheimer's

mal- [maw] *prefixo* badly, mis-

mala [ˈmala] *f* suitcase; (*BR: Auto*) boot, trunk (*US*); **malas** *fpl* (*bagagem*) luggage *sg*; **fazer as ~s** to pack

malabarismo [malabaˈrizmu] *m* juggling; **malabarista** [malabaˈrista] *m/f* juggler

mal-acabado, -a *adj* badly finished; (*pessoa*) deformed

malagueta [malaˈgeta] *f* chilli (*Brit*) *ou* chili (*US*) pepper

Malaísia [malaˈizja] *f*: **a ~** Malaysia

malandragem [malãˈdraʒẽ] *f* (*patifaria*) double-dealing; (*preguiça*) idleness; (*esperteza*) cunning

malária [maˈlarja] *f* malaria

mal-arrumado, -a [-ahuˈmadu, a] *adj* untidy

malcomportado, -a [mawkõporˈtadu, a] *adj* badly behaved

malcriado, -a [mawˈkrjadu, a] *adj* rude ▷ *m/f* slob

maldade [mawˈdadʒi] *f* cruelty; (*malícia*) malice

maldição [mawdʒiˈsãw] (*pl* **-ões**) *f* curse

maldizer [mawdʒiˈzer] (*irreg: como* **dizer**) *vt* to curse

maldoso, -a [mawˈdozu, ɔza] *adj* wicked; (*malicioso*) malicious

maledicência [maledʒiˈsẽsja] *f* slander

mal-educado, -a *adj* rude ▷ *m/f* slob

malefício [maleˈfisju] *m* harm;

m

maléfico, -a [ma'lɛfiku, a] *adj* (*pessoa*) malicious; (*prejudicial*) harmful

mal-entendido, -a *adj* misunderstood ▷ *m* misunderstanding

mal-estar *m* indisposition; (*embaraço*) awkward situation

malfeito, -a [maw'fejtu, a] *adj* (*roupa*) poorly made; (*corpo*) misshapen

malfeitor, -a [mawfej'tor(a)] *m/f* wrongdoer

malha ['maʎa] *f* (*de rede*) mesh; (*tecido*) jersey; (*suéter*) sweater; (*de ginástica*) leotard; **fazer ~** (*PT*) to knit; **artigos de ~** knitwear; **vestido de ~** jersey dress

malhar [ma'ʎar] *vt* (*bater*) to beat; (*cereais*) to thresh; (*col: criticar*) to knock, run down

mal-humorado, -a [-umo'radu, a] *adj* grumpy, sullen

maligno, -a [ma'lignu, a] *adj* evil, malicious; (*danoso*) harmful; (*Med*) malignant

malograr [malo'grar] *vt* (*planos*) to upset; (*frustrar*) to thwart, frustrate ▷ *vi* (*planos*) to fall through; (*fracassar*) to fail; **malograr-se** *vr* to fall through; to fail

malpassado, -a [mawpa'sadu,a] *adj* underdone; (*bife*) rare

malsucedido, -a [mawsuse'dʒidu, a] *adj* unsuccessful

Malta ['mawta] *f* Malta

malta ['mawta] (*PT*) *f* gang, mob

maltrapilho, -a [mawtra'piʎu, a] *adj* in rags, ragged ▷ *m/f* ragamuffin

maluco, -a [ma'luku, a] *adj* crazy, daft ▷ *m/f* madman/woman

malvadeza [mawva'deza] *f* wickedness; (*ato*) wicked thing

malvado, -a [maw'vadu, a] *adj* wicked

Malvinas [maw'vinas] *fpl*: **as (ilhas) ~** the Falklands, the Falkland Islands

mama ['mama] *f* breast

mamadeira [mama'dejra] (*BR*) *f* feeding bottle

mamãe [ma'mãj] *f* mum, mummy

mamão [ma'mãw] (*pl* **-ões**) *m* papaya

mamar [ma'mar] *vt* to suck; (*dinheiro*) to extort ▷ *vi* to be breastfed; **dar de ~ a um bebê** to (breast)feed a baby

mamífero [ma'miferu] *m* mammal

mamilo [ma'milu] *m* nipple

mamões [ma'mõjs] *mpl de* **mamão**

manada [ma'nada] *f* herd, drove

mancada [mã'kada] *f* (*erro*) mistake; (*gafe*) blunder; **dar uma ~** to blunder

mancar [mã'kar] *vt* to cripple ▷ *vi* to limp; **mancar-se** *vr* (*col*) to get the message, take the hint

Mancha ['mãʃa] *f*: **o canal da ~** the English Channel

mancha ['mãʃa] *f* stain; (*na pele*) mark, spot; **sem ~s** (*reputação*) spotless; **manchado, -a** [mã'ʃadu, a] *adj* soiled; (*malhado*) mottled, spotted; **manchar** [mã'ʃar] *vt* to stain, mark; (*reputação*) to soil

manchete [mã'ʃetʃi] *f* headline

manco, -a ['mãku, a] *adj* crippled, lame ▷ *m/f* cripple

mandado [mã'dadu] *m* order; (*Jur*) writ; (*: tb:* **~ de segurança**) injunction; **~ de prisão/busca** arrest/search warrant; **~ de segurança** injunction

mandão, -dona [mã'dãw, 'dɔna] (*pl* **-ões/-s**) *adj* bossy, domineering

mandar [mã'dar] *vt* (*ordenar*) to order; (*enviar*) to send ▷ *vi* to be in charge; **mandar-se** *vr* (*col: partir*) to make tracks, get going; (*fugir*) to take off; **~ buscar** *ou* **chamar** to send for; **~ fazer um vestido** to have a dress made; **~ que alguém faça, ~ alguém fazer** to tell sb to do; **o que é que você manda?** (*col*) what can I do for you?; **~ em alguém** to boss sb around

mandato [mã'datu] *m* mandate; (*ordem*) order; (*Pol*) term of office

mandioca [mã'dʒjɔka] *f* cassava, manioc

mandões [mã'dõjs] *mpl de* **mandão**

mandona [mã'dɔna] *f de* **mandão**

maneira [ma'nejra] *f* (*modo*) way; (*estilo*) style, manner; **maneiras** *fpl* (*modos*) manners; **à ~ de** like; **de ~ que** so that; **de ~ alguma** *ou* **nenhuma** not at all; **desta ~** in this way; **de qualquer ~** anyway; **não houve ~ de convencê-lo** it was impossible to convince him

maneiro, -a [ma'nejru, a] *adj* (*ferramenta*) easy to use; (*roupa*) attractive; (*trabalho*) easy; (*pessoa*) capable; (*col: bacana*) great, brilliant

manejar [mane'ʒar] *vt* (*instrumento*) to handle; (*máquina*) to work; **manejo** [ma'neʒu] *m* handling

manequim [mane'kĩ] (*pl* **-ns**) *m* (*boneco*) dummy ▷ *m/f* model

manga ['mãga] *f* sleeve; (*fruta*) mango; **em ~s de camisa** in (one's) shirt sleeves

mangueira [mã'gejra] *f* hose(pipe); (*árvore*) mango tree

manha ['maɲa] *f* guile, craftiness; (*destreza*) skill; (*ardil*) trick; (*birra*) tantrum; **fazer ~** to have a tantrum

manhã [ma'ɲã] *f* morning; **de** *ou* **pela ~** in the morning; **amanhã/ hoje de ~** tomorrow/this morning

manhoso, -a [ma'ɲozu, ɔza] *adj* crafty, sly; (*criança*) whining

mania [ma'nia] *f* (*Med*) mania; (*obsessão*) craze; **estar com ~ de ...** to have a thing about ...; **maníaco, -a** [ma'niaku, a] *adj* manic ▷ *m/f* maniac

manicômio [mani'komju] *m* asylum, mental hospital

manifestação [manifesta'sãw] (*pl* **-ões**) *f* show, display; (*expressão*) expression, declaration; (*política*) demonstration

manifestante [manifes'tãtʃi] *m/f* demonstrator

manifestar [manifes'tar] *vt* to show, display; (*declarar*) to express, declare

manifesto, -a [mani'fɛstu, a] *adj* obvious, clear ▷ *m* manifesto

manipulação [manipula'sãw] *f* handling; (*fig*) manipulation

manipular [manipu'lar] *vt* to manipulate; (*manejar*) to handle

manjericão [mãʒeri'kãw] *m* basil

manobra [ma'nɔbra] *f* manoeuvre (*Brit*), maneuver (*US*); (*de mecanismo*) operation; (*de trens*) shunting; **manobrar** [mano'brar] *vt* to manoeuvre (*Brit*), maneuver (*US*); (*mecanismo*) to operate, work; (*governar*) to take charge of; (*manipular*) to manipulate ▷ *vi* to manoeuvre *ou* maneuver

manso, -a ['mãsu, a] *adj* gentle; (*mar*) calm; (*animal*) tame

manta ['mãta] *f* blanket; (*xale*) shawl; (*agasalho*) cloak

manteiga [mã'tejga] *f* butter; **~ de cacau** cocoa butter

manter [mã'ter] (*irreg: como* **ter**) *vt* to maintain; (*num lugar*) to keep; (*uma família*) to support; (*a palavra*) to keep; (*princípios*) to abide by; **manter-se** *vr* to support o.s.; (*permanecer*) to remain;

mantimento [mãtʃi'mẽtu] *m* maintenance; **mantimentos** *mpl* (*alimentos*) provisions

manual [ma'nwaw] (*pl* **-ais**) *adj* manual ▷ *m* handbook, manual

manufatura [manufa'tura] *f* manufacture; **manufaturar** [manufatu'rar] *vt* to manufacture

manusear [manu'zjar] *vt* to handle; (*livro*) to leaf through

mão [mãw] (*pl* **mãos**) *f* hand; (*de animal*) paw; (*de pintura*) coat; (*de direção*) flow of traffic; **à ~** by hand; (*perto*) at hand; **de segunda ~** second-hand; **em ~** by hand; **dar a ~ a alguém** to hold sb's hand; (*cumprimentar*) to shake hands with sb; **dar uma ~ a alguém** to give sb a hand, help sb out; **~ única/dupla** one-way/two-way traffic; **rua de duas ~s** two-way street; **~ de obra** labour (*Brit*), labor (*US*)

mapa ['mapa] *m* map; (*gráfico*) chart

maquiagem [ma'kjaʒẽ] *f* = **maquilagem**

maquiar [ma'kjar] *vt* to make up; **maquiar-se** *vr* to make o.s. up, put on one's make-up

maquilagem [maki'laʒẽ], (*PT*) **maquilhagem** *f* make-up; (*ato*) making up

máquina ['makina] *f* machine; (*de trem*) engine; (*fig*) machinery; **~ de costura** sewing machine; **~ fotográfica** camera; **~ de lavar (roupa)** washing machine; **~ de lavar louça** dishwasher; **escrito à ~** typewritten

maquinar [maki'nar] *vt* to plot ▷ *vi* to conspire

maquinista [maki'nista] *m* (*Ferro*) engine driver; (*Náut*) engineer

mar [mar] *m* sea; **por ~** by sea; **fazer-se ao ~** to set sail; **pleno ~**, **~ alto** high sea; **o ~ Morto** the Dead Sea; **o ~ Negro** the Black Sea

maracujá [maraku'ʒa] *m* passion fruit; **pé de ~** passion flower

maratona [mara'tona] *f* marathon

maravilha [mara'viʎa] *f* marvel, wonder; **maravilhoso, -a** [maravi'ʎozu, ɔza] *adj* wonderful

marca ['marka] *f* mark; (*Com*) make, brand; (*carimbo*) stamp; **~ de fábrica** trademark; **~ registrada** registered trademark

marcação [marka'sãw] (*pl* **-ões**) *f* marking; (*em jogo*) scoring; (*de instrumento*) reading; (*Teatro*) action; (*PT: Tel*) dialling

marcador [marka'dor] *m* marker; (*de livro*) bookmark; (*Esporte: quadro*) scoreboard; (*: jogador*) scorer

marca-passo [marka'pasu] (*pl* **-s**) *m* (*Med*) pacemaker

marcar [mar'kar] *vt* to mark; (*hora, data*) to fix, set; (*PT: Tel*) to dial; (*gol, ponto*) to score ▷ *vi* to make one's mark; **~ uma consulta, ~ hora** to make an appointment; **~ um encontro com alguém** to arrange to meet sb

marcha ['marʃa] *f* march; (*de acontecimento*) course; (*passo*) pace; (*Auto*) gear; (*progresso*) progress; **~ à ré** (*BR*), **~ atrás** (*PT*) reverse (gear); **pôr-se em ~** to set off

marchar [mar'ʃar] *vi* to go; (*andar a pé*) to walk; (*Mil*) to march

marco ['marku] *m* landmark; (*de janela*) frame; (*fig*) frontier; (*moeda*) mark

março ['marsu] *m* March
maré [ma'rɛ] *f* tide
marechal [mare'ʃaw] (*pl* **-ais**) *m* marshal
maremoto [mare'mɔtu] *m* tidal wave
marfim [mar'fĩ] *m* ivory
margarida [marga'rida] *f* daisy
margarina [marga'rina] *f* margarine
margem ['marʒẽ] (*pl* **-ns**) *f* (*borda*) edge; (*de rio*) bank; (*litoral*) shore; (*de impresso*) margin; (*fig: tempo*) time; (*: lugar*) space; **à ~ de** alongside
marginal [marʒi'naw] (*pl* **-ais**) *adj* marginal ▷ *m/f* delinquent
marido [ma'ridu] *m* husband
marimbondo [marĩ'bõdu] *m* hornet
marinha [ma'riɲa] *f* (*tb*: **~ de guerra**) navy; **~ mercante** merchant navy; **marinheiro** [mari'ɲejru] *m* seaman, sailor
marinho, -a [ma'riɲu, a] *adj* sea *atr*, marine
mariposa [mari'poza] *f* moth
marítimo, -a [ma'ritʃimu, a] *adj* sea *atr*
marketing ['marketʃĩŋ] *m* marketing
marmelada [marme'lada] *f* quince jam
marmelo [mar'mɛlu] *m* quince
marmita [mar'mita] *f* (*vasilha*) pot
mármore [mar'mori] *m* marble
marquês, -quesa [mar'kes, 'keza] *m/f* marquis/marchioness
marqueteiro, -a [marke'tejru, a] *m/f* (*col*) spin doctor
marquise [mar'kizi] *f* awning, canopy
Marrocos [ma'hɔkus] *m*: **o ~** Morocco

marrom [ma'hõ] (*pl* **-ns**) *adj, m* brown
martelar [marte'lar] *vt* to hammer; (*amolar*) to bother ▷ *vi* to hammer; (*insistir*): **~ (em algo)** to keep *ou* harp on (about sth); **martelo** [mar'tɛlu] *m* hammer
mártir ['martʃir] *m/f* martyr; **martírio** [mar'tʃirju] *m* martyrdom; (*fig*) torment
marxista [mar'ksista] *adj, m/f* Marxist
mas [ma(j)s] *conj* but ▷ *pron* = **me + as**
mascar [mas'kar] *vt* to chew
máscara ['maskara] *f* mask; (*para limpeza de pele*) face pack; **sob a ~ de** under the guise of; **mascarar** [maska'rar] *vt* to mask; (*disfarçar*) to disguise; (*encobrir*) to cover up
mascote [mas'kɔtʃi] *f* mascot
masculino, -a [masku'linu, a] *adj* masculine; (*Bio*) male
massa ['masa] *f* (*Fís: fig*) mass; (*de tomate*) paste; (*Culin: de pão*) dough; (*: macarrão etc*) pasta
massacrar [masa'krar] *vt* to massacre; **massacre** [ma'sakri] *f* massacre
massagear [masa'ʒjar] *vt* to massage; **massagem** [ma'saʒẽ] (*pl* **-ns**) *f* massage
mastigar [mastʃi'gar] *vt* to chew
mastro ['mastru] *m* (*Náut*) mast; (*para bandeira*) flagpole
masturbar-se [mastur'barsi] *vr* to masturbate
mata ['mata] *f* forest, wood
matadouro [mata'doru] *m* slaughterhouse
matança [ma'tãsa] *f* massacre; (*de reses*) slaughter(ing)
matar [ma'tar] *vt* to kill; (*sede*) to quench; (*fome*) to satisfy; (*aula*) to

m

skip; (*trabalho: não aparecer*) to skive off; (*: fazer rápido*) to dash off; (*adivinhar*) to guess ▷ *vi* to kill; **matar-se** *vr* to kill o.s.; (*esfalfar-se*) to wear o.s. out; **um calor/uma dor de ~** stifling heat/excruciating pain

mate ['matʃi] *adj* matt ▷ *m* (*chá*) maté tea; (*xeque-mate*) checkmate

matemática [mate'matʃika] *f* mathematics *sg*, maths *sg* (*Brit*), math (*US*); **matemático, -a** [mate'matʃiku, a] *adj* mathematical ▷ *m/f* mathematician

matéria [ma'tɛrja] *f* matter; (*Tec*) material; (*Educ: assunto*) subject; (*tema*) topic; (*jornalística*) story, article; **em ~ de** on the subject of

material [mate'rjaw] (*pl* **-ais**) *adj* material; (*físico*) physical ▷ *m* material; (*Tec*) equipment; **materialista** [materja'lista] *adj* materialistic; **materializar** [materjali'zar] *vt* to materialize; **materializar-se** *vr* to materialize

maternal [mater'naw] (*pl* **-ais**) *adj* motherly, maternal; **escola ~** nursery (school); **maternidade** [materni'dadʒi] *f* motherhood, maternity; (*hospital*) maternity hospital

materno, -a [ma'tɛrnu, a] *adj* motherly, maternal; (*língua*) native

matinê [matʃi'ne] *f* matinée

matiz [ma'tʃiz] *m* (*de cor*) shade

mato ['matu] *m* scrubland, bush; (*plantas agrestes*) scrub; (*o campo*) country

matraca [ma'traka] *f* rattle

matrícula [ma'trikula] *f* (*lista*) register; (*inscrição*) registration; (*pagamento*) enrolment (*Brit*) *ou* enrollment (*US*) fee; (*PT: Auto*)

registration number (*Brit*), license number (*US*); **fazer a ~** to enrol (*Brit*), enroll (*US*)

matrimonial [matrimo'njaw] (*pl* **-ais**) *adj* marriage *atr*, matrimonial

matrimônio [matri'monju] *m* marriage

matriz [ma'triz] *f* (*Med*) womb; (*fonte*) source; (*molde*) mould (*Brit*), mold (*US*); (*Com*) head office

maturidade [maturi'dadʒi] *f* maturity

mau, má [maw, ma] *adj* bad; (*malvado*) evil, wicked ▷ *m* bad; (*Rel*) evil; **os ~s** bad people; (*num filme*) the baddies

maus-tratos *mpl* ill-treatment *sg*

maxila [mak'sila] *f* jawbone

maxilar [maksi'lar] *m* jawbone

máxima ['masima] *f* maxim

máximo, -a ['masimu, a] *adj* (*maior que todos*) greatest; (*o maior possível*) maximum ▷ *m* maximum; (*o cúmulo*) peak; (*temperature*) high; **no ~** at most; **ao ~** to the utmost

me [mi] *pron* (*direto*) me; (*indireto*) (to) me; (*reflexivo*) (to) myself

meado ['mjadu] *m* middle; **em** *ou* **nos ~s de julho** in mid-July

Meca ['mɛka] *n* Mecca

mecânica [me'kanika] *f* (*ciência*) mechanics *sg*; (*mecanismo*) mechanism; *ver tb* **mecânico**

mecânico, -a [me'kaniku, a] *adj* mechanical ▷ *m/f* mechanic

mecanismo [meka'nizmu] *m* mechanism

meço *etc* ['mɛsu] *vb ver* **medir**

medalha [me'daʎa] *f* medal; **medalhão** [meda'ʎãw] (*pl* **-ões**) *m* medallion

média ['mɛdja] *f* average; (*café*) coffee with milk; **em ~** on average

mediano, -a [me'dʒjanu, a] *adj*

medium; (*médio*) average;
(*medíocre*) mediocre
mediante [me'dʒjãtʃi] *prep* by
(means of), through; (*a troco de*) in
return for
medicamento [medʒika'mẽtu] *m*
medicine
medicina [medʒi'sina] *f* medicine
médico, -a ['medʒiku, a] *adj*
medical ▷ *m/f* doctor; **receita
médica** prescription
medida [me'dʒida] *f* measure;
(*providência*) step; (*medição*)
measurement; (*moderação*)
prudence; **à ~ que** while, as; **na ~
em que** in so far as; **feito sob ~**
made to measure; **ir além da ~** to
go too far; **tirar as ~s de alguém**
to take sb's measurements; **tomar
~s** to take steps; **tomar as ~s de** to
measure
medieval [medʒje'vaw] (*pl* **-ais**) *adj*
medieval
médio, -a ['medʒju, a] *adj* (*dedo,
classe*) middle; (*tamanho, estatura*)
medium; (*mediano*) average;
ensino ~ secondary education
medir [me'dʒir] *vt* to measure;
(*atos, palavras*) to weigh; (*avaliar:
consequências, distâncias*) to weigh
up ▷ *vi* to measure; **quanto você
mede? — meço 1.60 m** how tall
are you? — I'm 1.60 m (tall)
meditar [medʒi'tar] *vi* to meditate;
~ sobre algo to ponder (on) sth
mediterrâneo, -a [medʒite'hanju,
a] *adj* Mediterranean ▷ *m*: **o M~**
the Mediterranean
medo ['medu] *m* fear; **com ~** afraid;
meter ~ em alguém to frighten
sb; **ter ~ de** to be afraid of
medonho, -a [me'doɲu, a] *adj*
terrible, awful
medroso, -a [me'drozu, ɔza] *adj*

(*com medo*) frightened; (*tímido*)
timid
megabyte [mega'bajtʃi] *m*
megabyte
meia ['meja] *f* stocking; (*curta*)
sock; (*meia-entrada*) half-price
ticket ▷ *num* six; **meia-idade** *f*
middle age; **pessoa de
meia-idade** middle-aged person;
meia-noite *f* midnight
meigo, -a ['mejgu, a] *adj* sweet
meio, -a ['meju, a] *adj* half ▷ *adv* a
bit, rather ▷ *m* middle; (*recurso*)
means; (*social, profissional*)
environment; (*tb*: **~ ambiente**)
environment; **meios** *mpl* (*recursos*)
means *pl*; **~ quilo** half a kilo; **um
mês e ~** one and a half months;
cortar ao ~ to cut in half; **dividir
algo ao ~** to divide sth in half *ou*
fifty-fifty; **em ~ a** amid; **no ~ (de)** in
the middle (of); **~s de
comunicação (de massa)** (mass)
media *pl*; **por ~ de** through;
meio-dia *m* midday, noon;
meio-fio *m* kerb (*Brit*), curb (*US*);
meio-termo (*pl* **meios-termos**) *m*
(*fig*) compromise
mel [mɛw] *m* honey
melaço [me'lasu] *m* treacle (*Brit*),
molasses *pl* (*US*)
melancia [melã'sia] *f* watermelon
melancolia [melãko'lia] *f*
melancholy, sadness;
melancólico, -a [melã'kɔliku, a]
adj melancholy, sad
melão [me'lãw] (*pl* **-ões**) *m* melon
melhor [me'ʎɔr] *adj, adv* (*compar*)
better; (*superl*) best; **~ que nunca**
better than ever; **quanto mais ~**
the more the better; **seria ~
começarmos** we had better begin;
tanto ~ so much the better; **ou ~ ...**
(*ou antes*) or rather ...; **melhora**

m

[meˈʎɔɾa] f improvement;
melhoras! get well soon!;
melhorar [meʎoˈɾar] vt to
improve, make better; (doente) to
cure ▷ vi to improve, get better
melodia [meloˈdʒia] f melody;
(composição) tune
melões [meˈlõjs] mpl de **melão**
melro [ˈmɛwhu] m blackbird
membro [ˈmẽbɾu] m member;
(Anat: braço, perna) limb
memória [meˈmɔɾja] f memory;
memórias fpl (de autor) memoirs;
de ~ by heart
memorizar [memoɾiˈzar] vt to
memorize
mencionar [mẽsjoˈnar] vt to
mention
mendigar [mẽdʒiˈgar] vt to beg for
▷ vi to beg; **mendigo, -a**
[mẽˈdʒigu, a] m/f beggar
menina [meˈnina] f: **~ do olho**
pupil; **ser a ~ dos olhos de
alguém** (fig) to be the apple of sb's
eye; ver tb **menino**
meninada [meniˈnada] f kids pl
menino, -a [meˈninu, a] m/f boy/
girl
menopausa [menoˈpawza] f
menopause
menor [meˈnɔr] adj (mais pequeno:
compar) smaller; (: superl) smallest;
(mais jovem: compar) younger;
(: superl) youngest; (o mínimo) least,
slightest; (tb: **~ de idade**) under
age ▷ m/f juvenile, young person;
(Jur) minor; **não tenho a ~ ideia** I
haven't the slightest idea

PALAVRA-CHAVE

menos [ˈmenus] adj **1** (compar):
menos (do que) (quantidade) less
(than); (número) fewer (than); **com**

menos entusiasmo with less
enthusiasm; **menos gente** fewer
people
2 (superl) least; **é o que tem menos
culpa** he is the least to blame
▷ adv **1** (compar): **menos (do que)**
less (than); **gostei menos do que
do outro** I liked it less than the
other one
2 (superl): **é o menos inteligente
da classe** he is the least bright in
his class; **de todas elas é a que
menos me agrada** out of all of
them she's the one I like least; **pelo
menos** at (the very) least
3 (frases): **temos sete a menos** we
are seven short; **não é para
menos** it's no wonder; **isso é o de
menos** that's nothing
▷ prep (exceção) except; (números)
minus; **todos menos eu** everyone
except (for) me; **5 menos 2** 5 minus 2
▷ conj: **a menos que** unless; **a
menos que ele venha amanhã**
unless he comes tomorrow
▷ m: **o menos** the least

menosprezar [menuspɾeˈzar] vt
(subestimar) to underrate;
(desprezar) to despise, scorn
mensageiro, -a [mẽsaˈʒejru, a]
m/f messenger
mensagem [mẽˈsaʒẽ] (pl **-ns**) f
message; **~ de texto** text
(message); **mandar uma ~ de
texto para alguém** to text sb
mensal [mẽˈsaw] (pl **-ais**) adj
monthly; **ele ganha £2000
mensais** he earns £2000 a month;
mensalidade [mẽsaliˈdadʒi] f
monthly payment; **mensalmente**
[mẽsawˈmẽtʃi] adv monthly
menstruação [mẽstrwaˈsãw] f
period; (Med) menstruation

menta ['mẽta] f mint
mental [mẽ'taw] (pl **-ais**) adj mental; **mentalidade** [mẽtali'dadʒi] f mentality
mente ['mẽtʃi] f mind; **de boa ~** willingly; **ter em ~** to bear in mind
mentir [mẽ'tʃir] vi to lie
mentira [mẽ'tʃira] f lie; (ato) lying; **parece ~ que** it seems incredible that; **de ~** not for real; **~!** (acusação) that's a lie!, you're lying; (de surpresa) you don't say!, no!; **mentiroso, -a** [mẽtʃi'rozu, ɔza] adj lying ▷ m/f liar
menu [me'nu] m (tb: Comput) menu
mercado [mer'kadu] m market; **M~ Comum** Common Market; **~ negro** ou **paralelo** black market
mercadoria [merkado'ria] f commodity; **mercadorias** fpl (produtos) goods
mercearia [mersja'ria] f grocer's (shop) (Brit), grocery store
mercúrio [mer'kurju] m mercury
merda ['mɛrda] f (col!) shit (!) ▷ m/f (pessoa) jerk; **a ~ do carro** the bloody (Brit) ou goddamn (US) car (!)
merecer [mere'ser] vt to deserve; (consideração) to merit; (valer) to be worth ▷ vi to be worthy; **merecido, -a** [mere'sidu, a] adj deserved; (castigo, prêmio) just
merenda [me'rẽda] f packed lunch
merengue [me'rẽgi] m meringue
mergulhador, a [merguʎa'dor(a)] m/f diver
mergulhar [mergu'ʎar] vi to dive; (penetrar) to plunge ▷ vt: **~ algo em algo** (num líquido) to dip sth into sth; (na terra etc) to plunge sth into sth; **mergulho** [mer'guʎu] m dip(ping), (em natação) dive; **dar um mergulho** (na praia) to go for a dip

mérito ['mɛritu] m merit
mero, -a ['mɛru, a] adj mere
mês [mes] m month
mesa ['meza] f table; (de trabalho) desk; (comitê) board; (numa reunião) panel; **pôr/tirar a ~** to lay/clear the table; **à ~** at the table; **~ de cabeceira** bedside table; **~ de toalete** dressing table; **~ telefônica** switchboard
mesada [me'zada] f monthly allowance; (de criança) pocket money
mesmo, -a ['mezmu, a] adj same; (enfático) very ▷ adv (exatamente) right; (até) even; (realmente) really ▷ m/f: **o ~/a mesma** the same (one); **o ~** (a mesma coisa) the same (thing); **este ~ homem** this very man; **ele ~ o fez** he did it himself; **dá no ~** ou **na mesma** it's all the same; **aqui/agora/hoje ~** right here/right now/this very day; **~ que** even if; **é ~** it's true; **é ~?** really?; **(é) isso ~!** exactly!; **por isso ~** that's why; **nem ~** not even; **só ~** only; **por si ~** by oneself
mesquinho, -a [mes'kiɲu, a] adj mean
mesquita [mes'kita] f mosque
mestre, -a ['mɛstri, a] adj (chave, viga) master; (linha, estrada) main ▷ m/f master/mistress; (professor) teacher; **obra mestra** masterpiece
meta ['mɛta] f (em corrida) finishing post; (gol) goal; (objetivo) aim
metade [me'tadʒi] f half; (meio) middle
metáfora [me'tafora] f metaphor
metal [me'taw] (pl **-ais**) m metal; **metais** mpl (Mús) brass sg; **metálico, -a** [me'taliku, a] adj metallic; (de metal) metal atr
meteorologia [meteorolo'ʒia] f

meteorology; **meteorologista** [meteorolo'ʒista] *m/f* meteorologist; (*TV, Rádio*) weather forecaster

meter [me'ter] *vt* (*colocar*) to put; (*envolver*) to involve; (*introduzir*) to introduce; **meter-se** *vr* (*esconder-se*) to hide; **~-se a fazer algo** to decide to have a go at sth; **~-se com** (*provocar*) to pick a quarrel with; (*associar-se*) to get involved with; **~-se em** to get involved in; (*intrometer-se*) to interfere in

meticuloso, -a [metʃiku'lozu, ɔza] *adj* meticulous

metido, -a [me'tʃidu, a] *adj* (*envolvido*) involved; (*intrometido*) meddling; **~ (a besta)** snobbish

metódico, -a [me'tɔdʒiku, a] *adj* methodical

método ['mɛtodu] *m* method

metralhadora [metraʎa'dora] *f* machine gun

métrico, -a ['mɛtriku, a] *adj* metric

metro ['mɛtru] *m* metre (*Brit*), meter (*US*); (*PT: metropolitano*) underground (*Brit*), subway (*US*)

metrô [me'tro] (*BR*) *m* underground (*Brit*), subway (*US*)

metrópole [me'trɔpoli] *f* metropolis; (*capital*) capital

meu, minha [mew, 'miɲa] *adj* my ▷ *pron* mine; **os meus** *mpl* (*minha família*) my family ou folks (*col*); **um amigo ~** a friend of mine

mexer [me'ʃer] *vt* to move; (*cabeça: dizendo sim*) to nod; (: *dizendo não*) to shake; (*misturar*) to stir; (*ovos*) to scramble ▷ *vi* to move; **mexer-se** *vr* to move; (*apressar-se*) to get a move on; **~ em algo** to touch sth; **mexa-se!** get going!, move

yourself!

mexerico [meʃe'riku] *m* piece of gossip; **mexericos** *mpl* (*fofocas*) gossip *sg*

México, - ['mɛʃiku] *m*: **o ~** Mexico

mexido, -a [me'ʃidu, a] *adj* (*papéis*) mixed up; (*ovos*) scrambled

mexilhão [meʃi'ʎãw] (*pl* -**ões**) *m* mussel

mi [mi] *m* (*Mús*) E

miau [mjaw] *m* miaow

micro... [mikru] *prefixo* micro...; **microfone** [mikro'foni] *m* microphone; **micro-ondas** [mikro'õdas] *m inv* microwave; **microprocessador** [mikroprosesa'dor] *m* microprocessor; **microscópio** [mikro'skɔpju] *m* microscope

mídia ['midʒja] *f* media *pl*

migalha [mi'gaʎa] *f* crumb; **migalhas** *fpl* (*restos, sobras*) scraps

migrar [mi'grar] *vi* to migrate

mijar [mi'ʒar] (*col*) *vi* to pee; **mijar-se** *vr* to wet o.s.

mil [miw] *num* thousand; **dois ~** two thousand

milagre [mi'lagri] *m* miracle; **por ~** miraculously; **milagroso, -a** [mila'grozu, ɔza] *adj* miraculous

milhão [mi'ʎãw] (*pl* -**ões**) *m* million; **um ~ de vezes** hundreds of times

milhar [mi'ʎar] *m* thousand; **turistas aos ~es** tourists in their thousands

milho ['miʎu] *m* maize (*Brit*), corn (*US*)

milhões [mi'ʎõjs] *mpl de* **milhão**

miligrama [mili'grama] *m* milligram(me)

milionário, -a [miljo'narju, a] *m/f* millionaire

milionésimo, -a [miljo'nɛzimu, a]

num millionth

militar [mili'tar] *adj* military ▷ *m*
soldier ▷ *vi* to fight; **~ em** (*Mil: regimento*) to serve in; (*Pol: partido*)
to belong to, be active in;
(*profissão*) to work in

mim [mĩ] *pron* me; (*reflexivo*)
myself; **de ~ para ~** to myself

mímica ['mimika] *f* mime

mimo ['mimu] *m* gift; (*pessoa, coisa encantadora*) delight; (*carinho*)
tenderness; (*gentileza*) kindness;
cheio de ~s (*criança*) spoiled, spoilt
(*Brit*); **mimoso, -a** [mi'mozu, ɔza]
adj (*delicado*) delicate; (*carinhoso*)
tender, loving; (*encantador*)
delightful

mina ['mina] *f* mine

mindinho [mĩ'dʒiɲu] *m* (*tb:* **dedo ~**)
little finger

mineiro, -a [mi'nejru, a] *adj*
mining *atr* ▷ *m/f* miner

mineral [mine'raw] (*pl* **-ais**) *adj, m*
mineral

minério [mi'nɛrju] *m* ore

míngua ['mĩgwa] *f* lack; **à ~ de** for
want of; **viver à ~** to live in poverty;
minguado, -a [mĩ'gwadu, a] *adj*
scant; (*criança*) stunted;
minguado de algo short of sth

minguar [mĩ'gwar] *vi* (*diminuir*) to
decrease, dwindle; (*faltar*) to run
short

minha ['miɲa] *f de* **meu**

minhoca [mi'ɲɔka] *f* (earth)worm

mini... [mini] *prefixo* mini...

miniatura [minja'tura] *adj, f*
miniature

mínima ['minima] *f* (*temperatura*)
low; (*Mús*) minim

mínimo, -a ['minimu, a] *adj*
minimum ▷ *m* minimum; (*tb:*
dedo ~) little finger; **não dou** *ou*
ligo a mínima para isso I couldn't

care less about it; **a mínima
importância/ideia** the slightest
importance/idea; **no ~** at least

minissaia [mini'saja] *f* miniskirt

ministério [mini'stɛrju] *m*
ministry; **~ da Fazenda** ≈ Treasury
(*Brit*), ≈ Treasury Department (*US*);
M~ das Relações Exteriores
≈ Foreign Office (*Brit*), ≈ State
Department (*US*)

ministro, -a [mi'nistru, a] *m/f*
minister

minoria [mino'ria] *f* minority

minto *etc* ['mĩtu] *vb ver* **mentir**

minucioso, -a [minu'sjozu, ɔza]
adj (*indivíduo, busca*) thorough;
(*explicação*) detailed

minúsculo, -a [mi'nuskulu, a] *adj*
minute, tiny; **letra minúscula**
lower case

minuta [mi'nuta] *f* draft

minuto [mi'nutu] *m* minute

miolo ['mjolu] *m* inside; (*polpa*)
pulp; (*de maçã*) core; **miolos** *mpl*
(*cérebro, inteligência*) brains

míope ['miopi] *adj* short-sighted

mira ['mira] *f* (*de fuzil*) sight;
(*pontaria*) aim; (*fig*) aim, purpose; **à
~ de** on the lookout for; **ter em ~** to
have one's eye on

miragem [mi'raʒẽ] (*pl* **-ns**) *f* mirage

miserável [mize'ravew] (*pl* **-eis**) *adj*
(*digno de compaixão*) wretched;
(*pobre*) impoverished; (*avaro*)
stingy, mean; (*insignificante*) paltry;
(*lugar*) squalid; (*infame*) despicable
▷ *m* wretch; (*coitado*) poor thing;
(*pessoa infame*) rotter

miséria [mi'zɛrja] *f* misery;
(*pobreza*) poverty; (*avareza*)
stinginess

misericórdia [mizeri'kɔrdʒja] *f*
(*compaixão*) pity, compassion;
(*graça*) mercy

m

missa ['misa] f (Rel) mass
missão [mi'sãw] (pl **-ões**) f mission; (dever) duty
míssil ['misiw] (pl **-eis**) m missile
missionário, -a [misjo'narju, a] m/f missionary
missões [mi'sõjs] fpl de **missão**
mistério [mis'tɛrju] m mystery; **misterioso, -a** [miste'rjozu, ɔza] adj mysterious
mistificar [mistʃifi'kar] vt, vi to fool
misto, -a ['mistu, a] adj mixed; (confuso) mixed up ▷ m mixture; **misto-quente** (pl **mistos-quentes**) m toasted cheese and ham sandwich
mistura [mis'tura] f mixture; (ato) mixing; **misturar** [mistu'rar] vt to mix; (confundir) to mix up; **misturar-se** vr: **misturar-se com** to mingle with
mito ['mitu] m myth
miudezas [mju'dezas] fpl minutiae; (bugigangas) odds and ends; (objetos pequenos) trinkets
miúdo, -a ['mjudu, a] adj tiny, minute ▷ m/f (PT: criança) youngster, kid; **miúdos** mpl (dinheiro) change sg; (de aves) giblets; **dinheiro ~** small change
mm abr (= milímetro) mm
mo [mu] pron = **me + o**
moa etc ['mɔa] vb ver **moer**
móbil ['mɔbiw] (pl **-eis**) adj = **móvel**
móbile ['mɔbili] m mobile
mobília [mo'bilja] f furniture; **mobiliar** [mobi'ljar] (BR) vt to furnish; **mobiliário** [mobi'ljarju] m furnishings pl
moça ['mosa] f girl, young woman
Moçambique [mosã'biki] m Mozambique
moção [mo'sãw] (pl **-ões**) f motion

mochila [mo'ʃila] f rucksack
mochilão [moʃi'lãw] m backpacking trip
mocidade [mosi'dadʒi] f youth; (os moços) young people pl
moço, -a ['mosu, a] adj young ▷ m young man, lad
moções [mo'sõjs] fpl de **moção**
moda ['mɔda] f fashion; **estar na ~** to be in fashion, be all the rage; **fora da ~** old-fashioned; **sair da** ou **cair de ~** to go out of fashion
modalidade [modali'dadʒi] f kind; (Esporte) event
modelo [mo'delu] m model; (criação de estilista) design; (pessoa admirada) role-model ▷ m/f (manequim) model
moderar [mode'rar] vt to moderate; (violência) to control, restrain; (velocidade) to reduce; (voz) to lower; (gastos) to cut down
modernizar [moderni'zar] vt to modernize; **modernizar-se** vr to modernize
moderno, -a [mo'dɛrnu, a] adj modern; (atual) present-day
modéstia [mo'dɛstʃja] f modesty
módico, -a ['mɔdʒiku, a] adj moderate; (preço) reasonable; (bens) scant
modificar [modʒifi'kar] vt to modify, alter
modista [mo'dʒista] f dressmaker
modo ['mɔdu] m (maneira) way, manner; (método) way; (Mús) mode; **modos** mpl (comportamento) manners; **de (tal) ~ que** so (that); **de ~ nenhum** in no way; **de qualquer ~** anyway, anyhow; **~ de emprego** instructions pl for use
módulo ['mɔdulu] m module
moeda ['mwɛda] f (uma moeda)

coin; (*dinheiro*) currency; **uma ~ de 50p** a 50p piece; **~ corrente** currency; **Casa da M~** ≈ the Mint (*Brit*), ≈ the (*US*) Mint (*US*)

moedor [moe'dor] *m* (*de café*) grinder; (*de carne*) mincer

moer [mwer] *vt* (*café*) to grind; (*cana*) to crush

mofado, -a [mo'fadu, a] *adj* mouldy (*Brit*), moldy (*US*)

mofo ['mofu] *m* (*Bot*) mould (*Brit*), mold (*US*); **cheiro de ~** musty smell

mogno ['mɔgnu] *m* mahogany

mói *etc* [mɔj] *vb ver* **moer**

moía *etc* [mo'ia] *vb ver* **moer**

moído, -a [mo'idu, a] *adj* (*café*) ground; (*carne*) minced; (*cansado*) tired out; (*corpo*) aching

moinho ['mwiɲu] *m* mill; (*de café*) grinder; **~ de vento** windmill

mola ['mɔla] *f* (*Tec*) spring; (*fig*) motive, motivation

moldar [mow'dar] *vt* to mould (*Brit*), mold (*US*); (*metal*) to cast; **molde** ['mɔwdʒi] *m* mould (*Brit*), mold (*US*); (*de papel*) pattern; (*fig*) model; **molde de vestido** dress pattern

moldura [mow'dura] *f* (*de pintura*) frame

mole ['mɔli] *adj* soft; (*sem energia*) listless; (*carnes*) flabby; (*col: fácil*) easy; (*lento*) slow; (*preguiçoso*) sluggish ▷ *adv* (*lentamente*) slowly

moleque [mo'lɛki] *m* (*de rua*) urchin; (*menino*) youngster; (*pessoa sem palavra*) unreliable person; (*canalha*) scoundrel ▷ *adj* (*levado*) mischievous; (*brincalhão*) funny

molestar [moles'tar] *vt* to upset; (*enfadar*) to annoy; (*importunar*) to bother

moléstia [mo'lɛstʃja] *f* illness

moleza [mo'leza] *f* softness; (*falta de energia*) listlessness; (*falta de força*) weakness; **ser (uma) ~** (*col*) to be easy; **na ~** without exerting oneself

molhado, -a [mo'ʎadu, a] *adj* wet, damp

molhar [mo'ʎar] *vt* to wet; (*de leve*) to moisten, dampen; (*mergulhar*) to dip; **molhar-se** *vr* to get wet

molho¹ ['mɔʎu] *m* (*de chaves*) bunch; (*de trigo*) sheaf

molho² ['moʎu] *m* (*Culin*) sauce; (: *de salada*) dressing; (: *de carne*) gravy; **pôr de ~** to soak; **estar/deixar de ~** (*roupa etc*) to be/leave to soak

momentâneo, -a [momẽ'tanju, a] *adj* momentary

momento [mo'mẽtu] *m* moment; (*Tec*) momentum; **a todo ~** constantly; **de um ~ para outro** suddenly; **no ~ em que** just as

Mônaco ['monaku] *m* Monaco

monarquia [monar'kia] *f* monarchy

monitor [moni'tor] *m* monitor

monopólio [mono'pɔlju] *m* monopoly; **monopolizar** [monopoli'zar] *vt* to monopolize

monotonia [monoto'nia] *f* monotony; **monótono, -a** [mo'nɔtonu, a] *adj* monotonous

monstro, -a ['mõstru, a] *adj inv* giant ▷ *m* (*tb fig*) monster; **monstruoso, -a** [mõs'trwozu, ɔza] *adj* monstrous; (*enorme*) gigantic, huge

montagem [mõ'taʒẽ] (*pl* **-ns**) *f* assembly; (*Arq*) erection; (*Cinema*) editing; (*Teatro*) production

montanha [mõ'taɲa] *f* mountain; **montanha-russa** *f* roller coaster

montante [mõ'tãtʃi] *m* amount, sum; **a ~** (*nadar*) upstream

m

montar [mõ'tar] *vt* (*cavalo*) to mount, get on; (*colocar em*) to put on; (*cavalgar*) to ride; (*peças*) to assemble, put together; (*loja, máquina*) to set up; (*casa*) to put up; (*peça teatral*) to put on ▷ *vi* to ride; **~ a** *ou* **em** (*animal*) to get on; (*cavalgar*) to ride; (*despesa*) to come to

monte ['mõtʃi] *m* hill; (*pilha*) heap, pile; **um ~ de** (*muitos*) a lot of, lots of; **gente aos ~s** loads of people

montra ['mõtra] (*PT*) *f* shop window

monumento [monu'mẽtu] *m* monument

moqueca [mo'kɛka] *f* fish or seafood simmered in coconut cream and palm oil; **~ de camarão** prawn *moqueca*

morada [mo'rada] *f* home, residence; (*PT: endereço*) address; **moradia** [mora'dʒia] *f* home, dwelling; **morador, a** [mora'dor(a)] *m/f* resident; (*de casa alugada*) tenant

moral [mo'raw] (*pl* **-ais**) *adj* moral ▷ *f* (*ética*) ethics *pl*; (*conclusão*) moral ▷ *m* (*de pessoa*) sense of morality; (*ânimo*) morale; **moralidade** [morali'dadʒi] *f* morality

morango [mo'rãgu] *m* strawberry

morar [mo'rar] *vi* to live, reside

mórbido, -a ['mɔrbidu, a] *adj* morbid

morcego [mor'segu] *m* (*Bio*) bat

mordaça [mor'dasa] *f* (*de animal*) muzzle; (*fig*) gag

morder [mor'der] *vt* to bite; (*corroer*) to corrode; **mordida** [mor'dʒida] *f* bite

mordomia [mordo'mia] *f* (*de executivos*) perk; (*col: regalia*) luxury, comfort

mordomo [mor'dɔmu] *m* butler

moreno, -a [mo'renu, a] *adj* dark(-skinned); (*de cabelos*) dark(-haired); (*de tomar sol*) brown ▷ *m/f* dark person

mormaço [mor'masu] *m* sultry weather

morno, -a ['mornu, 'mɔrna] *adj* lukewarm, tepid

morrer [mo'her] *vi* to die; (*luz, cor*) to fade; (*fogo*) to die down; (*Auto*) to stall

morro ['mohu] *m* hill; (*favela*) slum

mortadela [morta'dɛla] *f* salami

mortal [mor'taw] (*pl* **-ais**) *adj* mortal; (*letal, insuportável*) deadly ▷ *m* mortal

mortalidade [mortali'dadʒi] *f* mortality

morte ['mɔrtʃi] *f* death

mortífero, -a [mor'tʃiferu, a] *adj* deadly, lethal

morto, -a ['mortu, 'mɔrta] *pp de* **matar**; **morrer** ▷ *adj* dead; (*cor*) dull; (*exausto*) exhausted; (*inexpressivo*) lifeless ▷ *m/f* dead man/woman; **estar ~** to be dead; **ser ~** to be killed; **estar ~ de inveja** to be green with envy; **estar ~ de vontade de** to be dying to

mos [mus] *pron* = **me + os**

mosca ['moska] *f* fly; **estar às ~s** (*bar etc*) to be deserted

Moscou [mos'kow] (*BR*) *n* Moscow

Moscovo [mos'kovu] (*PT*) *n* Moscow

mosquito [mos'kitu] *m* mosquito

mostarda [mos'tarda] *f* mustard

mosteiro [mos'tejru] *m* monastery; (*de monjas*) convent

mostrador [mostra'dor] *m* (*de relógio*) face, dial

mostrar [mos'trar] *vt* to show; (*mercadorias*) to display; (*provar*) to demonstrate, prove; **mostrar-se** vr to show o.s. to be; (*exibir-se*) to show off

motel [mo'tɛw] (*pl* **-éis**) *m* motel

motivar [motʃi'var] *vt* (*causar*) to cause, bring about; (*estimular*) to motivate; **motivo** [mo'tʃivu] *m* (*causa*): **motivo (de ou para)** cause (of), reason (for); (*fim*) motive; (*Arte, Mús*) motif; **por motivo de** because of, owing to

moto ['mɔtu] *f* motorbike ▷ *m* (*lema*) motto

motoboy [moto'bɔj] *m* motorcycle courier

motocicleta [motosi'kleta] *f* motorcycle, motorbike

motociclista [motosi'klista] *m/f* motorcyclist

motociclo [moto'siklu] (*PT*) *m* = **motocicleta**

motor, motriz [mo'tor, mo'triz] *adj*: **força motriz** driving force ▷ *m* motor; (*de carro, avião*) engine; **~ de explosão** internal combustion engine; **~ diesel** diesel engine; **~ de pesquisa** (*PT: Comput*) search engine

motorista [moto'rista] *m/f* driver

móvel ['mɔvew] (*pl* **-eis**) *adj* movable ▷ *m* piece of furniture; **móveis** *mpl* (*mobília*) furniture *sg*

mover [mo'ver] *vt* to move; (*cabeça*) to shake; (*mecanismo*) to drive; (*campanha*) to start (up); **mover-se** vr to move

movimentado, -a [movimẽ'tadu, a] *adj* (*rua, lugar*) busy; (*pessoa*) active; (*show, música*) up-tempo

movimentar [movimẽ'tar] *vt* to move; (*animar*) to liven up

movimento [movi'mẽtu] *m* movement; (*Tec*) motion; (*na rua*) activity, bustle; **de muito ~** busy

pressure group for land reform

muamba ['mwãba] (*col*) *f* (*contrabando*) contraband; (*objetos roubados*) loot

muçulmano, -a [musuw'manu, a] *adj, m/f* Moslem

muda ['muda] *f* (*planta*) seedling; (*vestuário*) outfit; **~ de roupa** change of clothes

mudança [mu'dãsa] *f* change; (*de casa*) move; (*Auto*) gear; **~s climáticas** climate change

mudar [mu'dar] *vt* to change; (*deslocar*) to move ▷ *vi* to change; (*ave*) to moult (*Brit*), molt (*US*); **mudar-se** vr (*de casa*) to move (away); **~ de roupa/de assunto** to change clothes/the subject; **~ de casa** to move (house); **~ de ideia** to change one's mind

mudo, -a ['mudu, a] *adj* dumb; (*calado, filme*) silent; (*telefone*) dead ▷ *m/f* mute

 PALAVRA-CHAVE

muito, -a ['mwĩtu, a] *adj* (*quantidade*) a lot of; (: *em frase negativa ou interrogativa*) much; (*número*) lots of, a lot of, many; **muito esforço** a lot of effort; **faz muito calor** it's very hot; **muito tempo** a long time; **muitas amigas** lots *ou* a lot of friends; **muitas vezes** often ▷ *pron* a lot; (*em frase negativa ou interrogativa: sg*) much; (: *pl*) many; **tenho muito que fazer** I've got a lot to do; **muitos dizem que ...** a lot of people say that ... ▷ *adv* **1** a lot; (+ *adj*) very; (+ *compar*): **muito melhor** much *ou* far *ou* a lot better; **gosto muito disto** I like it a lot; **sinto muito** I'm very sorry; **muito interessante** very interesting **2** (*resposta*) very; **está cansado? — muito** are you tired? — very **3** (*tempo*): **muito depois** long after; **há muito** a long time ago; **não demorou muito** it didn't take long

mula ['mula] *f* mule

mulato, -a [mu'latu, a] *adj, m/f* mulatto

muleta [mu'leta] *f* crutch; (*fig*) support

mulher [mu'ʎer] *f* woman; (*esposa*) wife; **mulher-bomba** (*pl* **mulheres-bomba**) *f* suicide bomber

multa ['muwta] *f* fine; **levar uma ~** to be fined; **multar** [muw'tar] *vt* to fine; **multar alguém em $1000** to fine sb $1000

multi... [muwtʃi] *prefixo* multi...

multidão [muwtʃi'dãw] (*pl* **-ões**) *f* crowd; **uma ~ de** (*muitos*) lots of

multimídia [muwtʃi'midʒja] *adj* multimedia

multinacional [muwtʃinasjo'naw] (*pl* **-ais**) *adj, f* multinational

multiplicar [muwtʃipli'kar] *vt* to multiply; (*aumentar*) to increase

múltiplo, -a ['muwtʃiplu, a] *adj, m* multiple

múmia ['mumja] *f* mummy

mundial [mũ'dʒjaw] (*pl* **-ais**) *adj* worldwide; (*guerra, recorde*) world *atr* ▷ *m* world championship

mundo ['mũdu] *m* world; **todo o ~** everybody; **um ~ de** lots of, a great many

munição [muni'sãw] (*pl* **-ões**) *f* (*de armas*) ammunition; (*chumbo*) shot; (*Mil*) munitions *pl*, supplies *pl*

municipal [munisi'paw] (*pl* **-ais**) *adj* municipal

município [muni'sipju] *m* local authority; (*cidade*) town; (*condado*) county

munições [muni'sõjs] *fpl de* **munição**

munir [mu'nir] *vt*: **~ de** to provide with, supply with; **munir-se** *vr*: **~-se de** (*provisões*) to equip o.s. with

muralha [mu'raʎa] *f* (*de fortaleza*) rampart; (*muro*) wall

murchar [mur'ʃar] *vt* (*Bot*) to wither; (*sentimentos*) to dull; (*pessoa*) to sadden ▷ *vi* to wither, wilt; (*fig*) to fade

murmurar [murmu'rar] *vi* to murmur, whisper; (*queixar-se*) to mutter, grumble; (*água*) to ripple; (*folhagem*) to rustle ▷ *vt* to murmur; **murmúrio** [mur'murju] *m* murmuring, whispering; (*queixa*) grumbling; (*de água*) rippling; (*de folhagem*) rustling

muro ['muru] *m* wall

murro ['muhu] *m* punch; **dar um ~ em alguém** to punch sb

musa ['muza] *f* muse

musculação [muskula'sãw] *f* weight training

músculo ['muskulu] *m* muscle; **musculoso, -a** [musku'lozu, ɔza] *adj* muscular

museu [mu'zew] *m* museum; (*de pintura*) gallery

musgo ['muzgu] *m* moss

música ['muzika] *f* music; (*canção*) song; *ver tb* **músico**; **músico, -a** ['muziku, a] *adj* musical ▷ *m/f* musician

mútuo, -a ['mutwu, a] *adj* mutual

n

N abr (= norte) N

na [na] = **em + a**

-na [na] pron her; (coisa) it

nabo ['nabu] m turnip

nação [na'sãw] (pl -ões) f nation

nacional [nasjo'naw] (pl -ais) adj national; (carro, vinho etc) domestic, home-produced; **nacionalidade** [nasjonali'dadʒi] f nationality; **nacionalismo** [nasjona'lizmu] m nationalism; **nacionalista** [nasjona'lista] adj, m/f nationalist

nações [na'sõjs] fpl de **nação**

nada ['nada] pron nothing ▷ adv at all; **antes de mais ~** first of all; **não é ~ difícil** it's not at all hard, it's not hard at all; **~ mais** nothing else; **~ de novo** nothing new; **obrigado -- de ~** thank you -- not at all ou don't mention it

nadador, a [nada'dor(a)] m/f swimmer

nadar [na'dar] vi to swim

nádegas ['nadegas] fpl buttocks

nado ['nadu] m: **atravessar a ~** to swim across; **~ borboleta** butterfly (stroke); **~ de costas** backstroke; **~ de peito** breaststroke

naipe ['najpi] m (cartas) suit

namorado, -a [namo'radu, a] m/f boyfriend/girlfriend

namorar [namo'rar] vt (ser namorado de) to be going out with

namoro [na'moru] m relationship

não [nãw] adv not; (resposta) no ▷ m no; **~ sei** I don't know; **~ muito** not much; **~ só ... mas também** not only ... but also; **agora ~** not now; **~ tem de quê** don't mention it; **~ é?** isn't it?, won't you?; **eles são brasileiros, ~ é?** they're Brazilian, aren't they?

não... [nãw] prefixo non-

naquele(s), naquela(s) [na'keli(s), na'kɛla(s)] = **em + aquele(s)/aquela(s)**

naquilo [na'kilu] = **em + aquilo**

narina [na'rina] f nostril

nariz [na'riz] m nose

narração [naha'sãw] (pl -ões) f narration; (relato) account

narrar [na'har] vt to narrate

narrativa [naha'tʃiva] f narrative; (história) story

nas [nas] = **em + as**

-nas [nas] pron them

nascença [na'sẽsa] f birth; **de ~** by birth; **ele é surdo de ~** he was born deaf

nascente [na'sẽtʃi] m East, Orient ▷ f (fonte) spring

nascer [na'ser] vi to be born; (plantas) to sprout; (o sol) to rise; (ave) to hatch; (fig: ter origem) to come into being ▷ m: **~ do sol** sunrise; **ele nasceu para médico**

etc he was born to be a doctor *etc*;
nascimento [nasi'mẽtu] *m* birth;
(fig) origin; *(estirpe)* descent
nata ['nata] *f* cream
natação [nata'sãw] *f* swimming
natais [na'tajs] *adj pl de* **natal**
Natal [na'taw] *m* Christmas; **Feliz
~!** Merry Christmas!
natal [na'taw] *(pl* **-ais)** *adj (relativo
ao nascimento)* natal; *(país)* native;
cidade ~ home town
natalino, -a [nata'linu, a] *adj*
Christmas *atr*
nativo, -a [na'tʃivu, a] *adj, m/f*
native
natural [natu'raw] *(pl* **-ais)** *adj*
natural; *(nativo)* native ▷ *m/f*
native; **ao ~** *(Culin)* fresh,
uncooked; **naturalidade**
[naturali'dadʒi] *f* naturalness; **de
naturalidade paulista** *etc* born in
São Paulo *etc*; **naturalizar**
[naturali'zar] *vt* to naturalize;
naturalizar-se *vr* to become
naturalized; **naturalmente**
[naturaw'mẽtʃi] *adv* naturally;
naturalmente! of course!
natureza [natu'reza] *f* nature;
(espécie) kind, type
nau [naw] *f (literário)* ship
náusea ['nawzea] *f* nausea; **dar ~s
a alguém** to make sb feel sick;
sentir ~s to feel sick
náutico, -a ['nawtʃiku, a] *adj*
nautical
naval [na'vaw] *(pl* **-ais)** *adj* naval;
construção ~ shipbuilding
navalha [na'vaʎa] *f (de barba)*
razor; *(faca)* knife
nave ['navi] *f (de igreja)* nave
navegação [navega'sãw] *f*
navigation, sailing; **~ aérea** air
traffic; **companhia de ~** shipping
line

navegar [nave'gar] *vt* to navigate;
(mares) to sail ▷ *vi* to sail; *(dirigir o
rumo)* to navigate
navio [na'viu] *m* ship; **~ cargueiro**
cargo ship, freighter; **~ de guerra**
warship; **~ petroleiro** oil tanker
nazi [na'zi] *(PT) adj, m/f* = **nazista**
nazista [na'zista] *(BR) adj, m/f* Nazi
NB *abr* (= *note bem*) NB
neblina [ne'blina] *f* fog, mist
nebuloso, -a [nebu'lozu, ɔza] *adj*
foggy, misty; *(céu)* cloudy; *(fig)*
vague
necessário, -a [nese'sarju, a] *adj*
necessary ▷ *m:* **o ~** the necessities
pl
necessidade [nesesi'dadʒi] *f* need,
necessity; *(o que se necessita)* need;
(pobreza) poverty, need; **ter ~ de** to
need; **em caso de ~** if need be
necessitado, -a [nesesi'tadu, a]
adj needy, poor; **~ de** in need of
necessitar [nesesi'tar] *vt* to need,
require ▷ *vi:* **~ de** to need
neerlandês, -esa [neerlã'des, eza]
adj Dutch ▷ *m/f* Dutchman/
woman
Neerlândia [neer'lãdʒa] *f* the
Netherlands *pl*
negar [ne'gar] *vt* to deny; *(recusar)*
to refuse; **negar-se** *vr:* **~-se a** to
refuse to
negativa [nega'tʃiva] *f (Ling)*
negative; *(recusa)* denial
negativo, -a [nega'tʃivu, a] *adj*
negative ▷ *m (Tec, Foto)* negative
▷ *excl (col)* nope!
negligência [negli'ʒẽsja] *f*
negligence, carelessness;
negligente [negli'ʒẽtʃi] *adj*
negligent, careless
negociação [negosja'sãw] *(pl* **-ões)**
f negotiation
negociante [nego'sjãtʃi] *m/f*

businessman/woman

negociar [nego'sjar] *vt* to negotiate; (*Com*) to trade ▷ *vi*: ~ **(com)** to trade *ou* deal (in); to negotiate (with)

negócio [ne'gɔsju] *m* (*Com*) business; (*transação*) deal; (*questão*) matter; (*col: troço*) thing; (*assunto*) affair, business; **homem de ~** businessman; **a ~s** on business; **fechar um ~** to make a deal

negro, -a ['negru, a] *adj* black; (*raça*) Black; (*fig: lúgubre*) black, gloomy ▷ *m/f* Black man/woman

nele(s), nela(s) ['neli(s), 'nɛla(s)] = **em + ele(s)/ela(s)**

nem [nẽj] *conj* nor, neither; ~ **(sequer)** not even; ~ **que** even if; ~ **bem** hardly; ~ **um só** not a single one; ~ **estuda ~ trabalha** he neither studies nor works; ~ **eu** nor me; **sem ~** without even; ~ **todos** not all; ~ **tanto** not so much; ~ **sempre** not always

nenê [ne'ne] *m/f* baby

neném [ne'nẽj] (*pl* **-ns**) *m/f* = **nenê**

nenhum, a [ne'ɲũ, 'numa] *adj* no, not any ▷ *pron* (*nem um só*) none, not one; (*de dois*) neither; ~ **lugar** nowhere

nervo ['nervu] *m* (*Anat*) nerve; (*fig*) energy, strength; (*em carne*) sinew; **nervosismo** [nervo'zizmu] *m* (*nervosidade*) nervousness; (*irritabilidade*) irritability; **nervoso, -a** [ner'vozu, ɔza] *adj* nervous; (*irritável*) touchy, on edge; (*exaltado*) worked up; **isso/ele me deixa nervoso** he gets on my nerves

nesse(s), nessa(s) ['nesi(s), 'nɛsa(s)] = **em + esse(s)/essa(s)**

neste(s), nesta(s) ['nestʃi(s), 'nɛsta(s)] = **em + este(s)/esta(s)**

neto, -a ['nɛtu, a] *m/f* grandson/daughter; **netos** *mpl* grandchildren

neurose [new'rɔzi] *f* neurosis; **neurótico, -a** [new'rɔtʃiku, a] *adj, m/f* neurotic

neutro, -a ['newtru, a] *adj* (*Ling*) neuter; (*imparcial*) neutral

nevar [ne'var] *vi* to snow; **nevasca** [ne'vaska] *f* snowstorm; **neve** ['nɛvi] *f* snow

névoa ['nɛvoa] *f* fog; **nevoeiro** [nevo'ejru] *m* thick fog

nexo ['nɛksu] *m* connection, link; **sem ~** disconnected, incoherent

Nicarágua [nika'ragwa] *f*: **a ~** Nicaragua

nicotina [niko'tʃina] *f* nicotine

Nigéria [ni'ʒɛrja] *f*: **a ~** Nigeria

Nilo ['nilu] *m*: **o ~** the Nile

ninguém [nĩ'gẽj] *pron* nobody, no-one

ninho ['niɲu] *m* nest; (*toca*) lair; (*lar*) home

nisso ['nisu] = **em + isso**

nisto ['nistu] = **em + isto**

nitidez [nitʃi'dez] *f* (*clareza*) clarity; (*brilho*) brightness; (*imagem*) sharpness

nítido, -a ['nitʃidu, a] *adj* clear, distinct; (*brilhante*) bright; (*imagem*) sharp, clear

nível ['nivew] (*pl* **-eis**) *m* level; (*fig: padrão*) standard; (*: ponto*) point, pitch; ~ **de vida** standard of living

no [nu] = **em + o**

-no [nu] *pron* him; (*coisa*) it

n° *abr* (= *número*) no.

nó [nɔ] *m* knot; (*de uma questão*) crux; **nós dos dedos** knuckles; **dar um nó** to tie a knot

nobre ['nɔbri] *adj, m/f* noble; **horário ~** prime time; **nobreza**

n

[no'breza] f nobility

noção [no'sãw] (pl **-ões**) f notion; **noções** fpl (rudimentos) rudiments, basics; **~ vaga** inkling; **não ter a menor ~ de algo** not to have the slightest idea about sth

nocaute [no'kawtʃi] m knockout ▷ adv: **pôr alguém ~** to knock sb out

nocivo, -a [no'sivu, a] adj harmful

noções [no'sõjs] fpl de **noção**

nódoa ['nɔdwa] f spot; (mancha) stain

nogueira [no'gejra] f (árvore) walnut tree; (madeira) walnut

noite ['nojtʃi] f night; **à** ou **de ~** at night, in the evening; **boa ~** good evening; (despedida) good night; **da ~ para o dia** overnight; **tarde da ~** late at night

noivado [noj'vadu] m engagement

noivo, -a ['nojvu, a] m/f (prometido) fiancé/fiancée; (no casamento) bridegroom/bride; **os noivos** mpl (prometidos) the engaged couple; (no casamento) the bride and groom; (recém-casados) the newly-weds

nojento, -a [no'ʒẽtu, a] adj disgusting

nojo ['noʒu] m nausea; (repulsão) disgust, loathing; **ela é um ~** she's horrible; **este trabalho está um ~** this work is messy

no-la(s) = nos + a(s)

no-lo(s) = nos + o(s)

nome ['nɔmi] m name; (fama) fame; **de ~** by name; **escritor de ~** famous writer; **um restaurante de ~** a restaurant with a good reputation; **em ~ de** in the name of; **~ de batismo** Christian name

nomear [no'mjar] vt to nominate; (conferir um cargo a) to appoint; (dar nome a) to name

nono, -a ['nonu, a] num ninth

nora ['nɔra] f daughter-in-law

nordeste [nor'dɛstʃi] m, adj northeast

norma ['nɔrma] f standard, norm; (regra) rule; **como ~** as a rule

normal [nor'maw] (pl **-ais**) adj normal; (habitual) usual; **normalizar** [normali'zar] vt to bring back to normal; **normalizar-se** vr to return to normal

noroeste [nor'wɛstʃi] adj northwest, northwestern ▷ m northwest

norte ['nɔrtʃi] adj northern, north; (vento, direção) northerly ▷ m north; **norte-americano, -a** adj, m/f (North) American

Noruega [nor'wega] f Norway; **norueguês, -esa** [norwe'ges, geza] adj, m/f Norwegian ▷ m (Ling) Norwegian

nos¹ [nus] = **em + os**

nos² [nus] pron (direto) us; (indireto) us, to us, for us; (reflexivo) (to) ourselves; (recíproco) (to) each other

-nos [nus] pron them

nós [nɔs] pron we; (depois de prep) us; **~ mesmos** we ourselves

nosso, -a ['nɔsu, a] adj our ▷ pron ours; **um amigo ~** a friend of ours; **Nossa Senhora** (Rel) Our Lady

nostalgia [nostaw'ʒia] f nostalgia; **nostálgico, -a** [nos'tawʒiku, a] adj nostalgic

nota ['nɔta] f note; (Educ) mark; (conta) bill; (cédula) banknote; **~ de venda** sales receipt; **~ fiscal** receipt

notar [no'tar] vt to notice, note; **notar-se** vr to be obvious; **fazer ~**

to call attention to; **notável** [no'tavew] (pl **-eis**) adj notable, remarkable

notícia [no'tʃisja] f (uma notícia) piece of news; (TV etc) news item; **notícias** fpl (informações) news sg; **pedir ~s de** to inquire about; **ter ~s de** to hear from; **noticiário** [notʃi'sjarju] m (de jornal) news section; (Cinema) newsreel; (TV, Rádio) news bulletin

notório, -a [no'tɔrju, a] adj well-known

noturno, -a [no'turnu, a] adj nocturnal, nightly; (trabalho) night atr ▷ m (trem) night train

nova ['nɔva] f piece of news; **novas** fpl (novidades) news sg

novamente [nova'mẽtʃi] adv again

novato, -a [no'vatu, a] adj inexperienced, raw ▷ m/f beginner, novice; (Educ) fresher

nove ['nɔvi] num nine

novela [no'vɛla] f short novel, novella; (Rádio, TV) soap opera

novelo [no'velu] m ball of thread

novembro [no'vẽbru] m November

noventa [no'vẽta] num ninety

novidade [novi'dadʒi] f novelty; (notícia) piece of news; **novidades** fpl (notícias) news sg

novilho, -a [no'viʎu, a] m/f young bull/heifer

novo, -a ['novu, 'nɔva] adj new; (jovem) young; (adicional) further; **de ~** again

noz [nɔz] f nut; (da nogueira) walnut; **~ moscada** nutmeg

nu, a [nu, 'nua] adj naked; (braço, arvore, sala, parede) bare ▷ m nude

nublado, -a [nu'bladu, a] adj cloudy, overcast

nuclear [nu'kljar] adj nuclear

núcleo ['nuklju] m nucleus sg; (centro) centre (Brit), center (US)

nudez [nu'dez] f nakedness, nudity; (de paredes etc) bareness

nudista [nu'dʒista] adj, m/f nudist

nulo, -a ['nulu, a] adj (Jur) null, void; (nenhum) non-existent; (sem valor) worthless; (esforço) vain, useless

num [nũ] = **em** + **um**

numa(s) ['numa(s)] = **em** + **uma(s)**

numeral [nume'raw] (pl **-ais**) m numeral

numerar [nume'rar] vt to number

numérico, -a [nu'mɛriku, a] adj numerical

número ['numeru] m number; (de jornal) issue; (Teatro etc) act; (de sapatos, roupa) size; **sem ~** countless; **~ de matrícula** registration (Brit) ou license plate (US) number; **numeroso, -a** [nume'rozu, ɔza] adj numerous

nunca ['nũka] adv never; **~ mais** never again; **quase ~** hardly ever; **mais que ~** more than ever

nuns [nũs] = **em** + **uns**

núpcias ['nupsjas] fpl nuptials, wedding sg

nutrição [nutri'sãw] f nutrition

nuvem ['nuvẽj] (pl **-ns**) f cloud; (de insetos) swarm

n

O

▷ *pron relativo*: **o que** *etc* 1 (*indef*):
os que quiserem podem sair
anyone who wants to can leave;
leve o que mais gostar take the
one you like best
2 (*def*): **o que comprei ontem** the
one I bought yesterday; **os que
sairam** those who left
3: **o que** what; **o que eu acho/
mais gosto** what I think/like most
▷ *pron pessoal* 1 (*pessoa*: *m*) him; (: *f*)
her; (: *pl*) them; **não consigo
vê-lo(s)** I can't see him/them;
vemo-la todas as semanas we
see her every week
2 (*animal, coisa*: *sg*) it; (: *pl*) them;
não consigo vê-lo(s) I can't see it/
them; **acharam-nos na praia** they
found them on the beach

PALAVRA-CHAVE

o, a [u, a] *art def* 1 the; **o livro/a
mesa/os estudantes** the book/
table/students
2 (*com n abstrato: não se traduz*):
o amor/a juventude love/youth
3 (*posse: traduz-se muitas vezes por
adj possessivo*): **quebrar o braço** to
break one's arm; **ele levantou a
mão** he put his hand up; **ela colocou
o chapéu** she put her hat on
4 (*valor descritivo*): **ter a boca
grande/os olhos azuis** to have a
big mouth/blue eyes
▷ *pron demonstrativo*: **meu livro e o
seu** my book and yours; **as de
Pedro são melhores** Pedro's are
better; **não a(s) branca(s) mas
a(s) verde(s)** not the white one(s)
but the green one(s)

obedecer [obede'ser] *vi*: **~ a** to
obey; **obediência** [obe'dʒẽsja] *f*
obedience; **obediente** [obe'dʒẽtʃi]
adj obedient
óbito ['ɔbitu] *m* death; **atestado
de ~** death certificate
objeção [obʒe'sãw] (*pl* **-ões**) *f*
objection; **fazer** *ou* **pôr objeções a**
to object to
objetivo, -a [obʒe'tʃivu, a] *adj*
objective ▷ *m* objective
objeto [ob'ʒɛtu] *m* object
obra ['ɔbra] *f* work; (*Arq*) building,
construction; (*Teatro*) play; **em ~s**
under repair; **ser ~ de alguém** to
be the work of sb; **~ de arte** work
of art; **~s públicas** public works;
obra-prima (*pl* **obras-primas**) *f*
masterpiece
obrigação [obriga'sãw] (*pl* **-ões**) *f*
obligation; (*Com*) bond
obrigado, -a [obri'gadu, a] *adj*
obliged, compelled ▷ *excl* thank
you; (*recusa*) no, thank you

obrigar [obri'gar] *vt* to oblige, compel; **obrigar-se** *vr*: **~-se a fazer algo** to undertake to do sth; **obrigatório, -a** [obriga'tɔrju, a] *adj* compulsory, obligatory

obsceno, -a [obi'sɛnu, a] *adj* obscene

obscurecer [obiskure'ser] *vt* to darken; (*entendimento, verdade etc*) to obscure ▷ *vi* to get dark

obscuro, -a [obi'skuru, a] *adj* dark; (*fig*) obscure

observação [obiserva'sãw] (*pl* **-ões**) *f* observation; (*comentário*) remark, comment; (*de leis, regras*) observance

observador, a [obiserva'dor(a)] *m/f* observer

observar [obiser'var] *vt* to observe; (*notar*) to notice; **~ algo a alguém** to point sth out to sb

observatório [obiserva'tɔrju] *m* observatory

obsessão [obise'sãw] (*pl* **-ões**) *f* obsession; **obsessivo, -a** [obise'sivu, a] *adj* obsessive

obsoleto, -a [obiso'lɛtu, a] *adj* obsolete

obstinado, -a [obistʃi'nadu, a] *adj* obstinate, stubborn

obstrução [obistru'sãw] (*pl* **-ões**) *f* obstruction; **obstruir** [obi'strwir] *vt* to obstruct; (*impedir*) to impede

obter [obi'ter] (*irreg: como* **ter**) *vt* to obtain, get; (*alcançar*) to gain

obturação [obitura'sãw] (*pl* **-ões**) *f* (*de dente*) filling

obtuso, -a [obi'tuzu, a] *adj* (*ger*) obtuse; (*fig: pessoa*) thick

óbvio, -a ['ɔbvju, a] *adj* obvious; **(é) ~!** of course!

ocasião [oka'zjãw] (*pl* **-ões**) *f* opportunity, chance; (*momento, tempo*) occasion; **ocasionar**

[okazjo'nar] *vt* to cause, bring about

oceano [o'sjanu] *m* ocean

ocidental [oside'taw] (*pl* **-ais**) *adj* western ▷ *m/f* westerner

ocidente [osi'dẽtʃi] *m* west

ócio ['ɔsju] *m* (*lazer*) leisure; (*inação*) idleness; **ocioso, -a** [o'sjozu, ɔza] *adj* idle; (*vaga*) unfilled

oco, -a ['oku, a] *adj* hollow, empty

ocorrência [oko'hẽsja] *f* incident, event; (*circunstância*) circumstance

ocorrer [oko'her] *vi* to happen, occur; (*vir ao pensamento*) to come to mind; **~ a alguém** to happen to sb; (*vir ao pensamento*) to occur to sb

octogésimo, -a [okto'ʒɛzimu, a] *num* eightieth

oculista [oku'lista] *m/f* optician

óculo ['ɔkulu] *m* spyglass; **óculos** *mpl* glasses, spectacles; **~s de proteção** goggles

ocultar [okuw'tar] *vt* to hide, conceal; **oculto, -a** [o'kuwtu, a] *adj* hidden; (*desconhecido*) unknown; (*secreto*) secret; (*sobrenatural*) occult

ocupação [okupa'sãw] (*pl* **-ões**) *f* occupation

ocupado, -a [oku'padu, a] *adj* (*pessoa*) busy; (*lugar*) taken, occupied; (*BR: telefone*) engaged (*Brit*), busy (*US*); **sinal de ~** (*BR: Tel*) engaged tone (*Brit*), busy signal (*US*)

ocupar [oku'par] *vt* to occupy; (*tempo*) to take up; (*pessoa*) to keep busy; **ocupar-se** *vr*: **~-se com** *ou* **de** *ou* **em algo** (*cuidar de*) to look after sth; (*passar seu tempo com*) to occupy o.s. with sth

odiar [o'dʒjar] *vt* to hate; **ódio** ['ɔdʒju] *m* hate, hatred; **odioso, -a**

o

[o'dʒozu, ɔza] *adj* hateful
odor [o'dor] *m* smell
oeste ['wɛstʃi] *m* west ▷ *adj inv*
(*região*) western; (*direção, vento*)
westerly
ofegante [ofe'gãtʃi] *adj* breathless,
panting
ofender [ofẽ'der] *vt* to offend;
ofender-se *vr* to take offence (*Brit*)
ou offense (*US*)
ofensa [o'fẽsa] *f* insult; (*à lei, moral*)
offence (*Brit*), offense (*US*);
ofensiva [ofẽ'siva] *f* offensive;
ofensivo, -a [ofẽ'sivu, a] *adj*
offensive
oferecer [ofere'ser] *vt* to offer; (*dar*)
to give; (*jantar*) to give; (*propor*) to
propose; (*dedicar*) to dedicate;
oferecer-se *vr* (*pessoa*) to
offer o.s., volunteer; (*oportunidade*)
to present itself, arise; **~-se para
fazer** to offer to do; **oferecimento**
[oferesi'mẽtu] *m* offer; **oferta**
[o'fɛrta] *f* offer; (*dádiva*) gift; (*Com*)
bid; (*em loja*) special offer
oficial [ofi'sjaw] (*pl* **-ais**) *adj* official
▷ *m/f* official; (*Mil*) officer; **~ de
justiça** bailiff
oficina [ofi'sina] *f* workshop;
~ mecânica garage
ofício [o'fisju] *m* trade; (*Rel*)
service; (*carta*) official letter;
(*função*) function; (*encargo*) job,
task
oitavo, -a [oj'tavu, a] *num* eighth
oitenta [oj'tẽta] *num* eighty
oito ['ojtu] *num* eight
olá [o'la] *excl* hello!
olaria [ola'ria] *f* (*fábrica: de louças de
barro*) pottery; (: *de tijolos*)
brickworks *sg*
óleo ['ɔlju] *m* (*lubricante*) oil; **~ de
bronzear** suntan oil; **~ diesel**
diesel oil; **oleoso, -a** [o'ljozu, ɔza]

adj oily; (*gorduroso*) greasy
olfato [ow'fatu] *m* sense of smell
olhada [o'ʎada] *f* glance, look;
dar uma ~ to have a look
olhadela [oʎa'dɛla] *f* peep
olhar [o'ʎar] *vt* to look at; (*observar*)
to watch; (*ponderar*) to consider;
(*cuidar de*) to look after ▷ *vi* to look
▷ *m* look; **olhar-se** *vr* to look at
o.s.; (*duas pessoas*) to look at each
other; **~ fixamente** to stare at; **~
para** to look at; **~ por** to look after;
~ fixo stare
olho ['oʎu] *m* (*Anat, de agulha*) eye;
(*vista*) eyesight; **~ nele!** watch
him!; **~ vivo!** keep your eyes open!;
a ~ (*medir, calcular etc*) by eye; **~
mágico** (*na porta*) peephole; **~ roxo**
black eye; **num abrir e fechar de
~s** in a flash
olimpíada [olĩ'piada] *f*: **as O~s** the
Olympics
oliveira [oli'vejra] *f* olive tree
ombro ['õbru] *m* shoulder;
encolher os ~s, dar os ~s to shrug
one's shoulders
omeleta [ome'leta] (*PT*) *f*
= **omelete**
omelete [ome'letʃi] (*BR*) *f* omelette
(*Brit*), omelet (*US*)
omissão [omi'sãw] (*pl* **-ões**) *f*
omission; (*negligência*) negligence
omitir [omi'tʃir] *vt* to omit
omoplata [omo'plata] *f* shoulder
blade
onça ['õsa] *f* ounce; (*animal*) jaguar
onda ['õda] *f* wave; (*moda*) fashion;
~ curta/média/longa short/
medium/long wave; **~ de calor**
heat wave
onde ['õdʒi] *adv* where ▷ *conj*
where, in which; **de ~ você é?**
where are you from?; **por ~** through
which; **por ~?** which way?; **~ quer**

que wherever

ondulado, -a [õdu'ladu, a] *adj* wavy

ônibus ['onibus] *(BR)* *m inv* bus; **ponto de ~** bus-stop

ontem ['õtẽ] *adv* yesterday; **~ à noite** last night

ONU ['onu] *abr f (= Organização das Nações Unidas)* UNO

ônus ['onus] *m inv* onus; *(obrigação)* obligation; *(Com)* charge; *(encargo desagradável)* burden

onze ['õzi] *num* eleven

opaco, -a [o'paku, a] *adj* opaque; *(obscuro)* dark

opção [op'sãw] *(pl -ões)* f option, choice; *(preferência)* first claim, right

ópera ['ɔpera] f opera

operação [opera'sãw] *(pl -ões)* f operation; *(Com)* transaction

operador, a [opera'dor(a)] *m/f* operator; *(cirurgião)* surgeon; *(num cinema)* projectionist

operar [ope'rar] *vt* to operate; *(produzir)* to effect, bring about; *(Med)* to operate on ▷ *vi* to operate; *(agir)* to act, function; **operar-se** *vr (suceder)* to take place; *(Med)* to have an operation

operário, -a [ope'rarju, a] *adj* working ▷ *m/f* worker; **classe operária** working class

opinar [opi'nar] *vt* to think ▷ *vi* to give one's opinion

opinião [opi'njãw] *(pl -ões)* f opinion; **mudar de ~** to change one's mind

oponente [opo'nẽtʃi] *adj* opposing ▷ *m/f* opponent

opor [o'por] *(irreg: como pôr)* *vt* to oppose; *(resistência)* to put up, offer; *(objeção, dificuldade)* to raise; **opor-se** *vr*: **~-se a** to object to;

(resistir) to oppose

oportunidade [oportuni'dadʒi] f opportunity

oportunista [oportu'nista] *adj*, *m/f* opportunist

oportuno, -a [opor'tunu, a] *adj (momento)* opportune, right; *(oferta de ajuda)* well-timed; *(conveniente)* convenient, suitable

oposição [opozi'sãw] f opposition; **em ~ a** against; **fazer ~ a** to oppose

opressão [opre'sãw] *(pl -ões)* f oppression; **opressivo, -a** [opre'sivu, a] *adj* oppressive

oprimir [opri'mir] *vt* to oppress; *(comprimir)* to press

optar [op'tar] *vi* to choose; **~ por** to opt for; **~ por fazer** to opt to do

ora ['ɔra] *adv* now ▷ *conj* well; **por ~** for the time being; **~ ..., ~ ...** one moment ..., the next ...; **~ bem** now then

oração [ora'sãw] *(pl -ões)* f prayer; *(discurso)* speech; *(Ling)* clause

oral [o'raw] *(pl -ais)* *adj* oral ▷ f oral (exam)

orar [o'rar] *vi (Rel)* to pray

órbita ['ɔrbita] f orbit; *(do olho)* socket

Órcades ['ɔrkadʒis] *fpl*: **as ~** the Orkneys

orçamento [orsa'mẽtu] *m (do estado etc)* budget; *(avaliação)* estimate

orçar [or'sar] *vt* to value, estimate ▷ *vi*: **~ em** *(gastos etc)* to be valued at, be put at

ordem ['ordẽ] *(pl -ns)* f order; **até nova ~** until further notice; **de primeira ~** first-rate; **estar em ~** to be tidy; **por ~** in order, in turn; **~ do dia** agenda; **~ pública** public order, law and order

ordenado, -a [orde'nadu, a] *adj*

o

(*posto em ordem*) in order; (*metódico*) orderly ▷ *m* salary, wages *pl*
ordens ['ordẽs] *fpl de* **ordem**
ordinário, -a [ordʒi'narju, a] *adj* ordinary; (*comum*) usual; (*medíocre*) mediocre; (*grosseiro*) coarse, vulgar; (*de má qualidade*) inferior; **de ~** usually
orelha [o'reʎa] *f* ear; (*aba*) flap
orelhão [ore'ʎãw] (*pl* -**ões**) *m* payphone
órfão, -fã ['ɔrfãw, fã] (*pl* -**s/-s**) *adj*, *m/f* orphan
orgânico, -a [or'ganiku, a] *adj* organic
organismo [orga'nizmu] *m* organism; (*entidade*) organization
organização [organiza'sãw] (*pl* -**ões**) *f* organization; **organizar** [organi'zar] *vt* to organize
órgão ['ɔrgãw] (*pl* -**s**) *m* organ; (*governamental etc*) institution, body
orgasmo [or'gazmu] *m* orgasm
orgia [or'ʒia] *f* orgy
orgulho [or'guʎu] *m* pride; **orgulhoso, -a** [orgu'ʎozu, ɔza] *adj* proud
orientação [orjẽta'sãw] *f* guidance; (*posição*) position; **~ educacional** training, guidance
oriental [orjẽ'taw] (*pl* -**ais**) *adj* eastern; (*do Extremo Oriente*) oriental
orientar [orjẽ'tar] *vt* to orientate; (*indicar o rumo*) to direct; (*aconselhar*) to guide; **orientar-se** *vr* to get one's bearings; **~-se por algo** to follow sth
oriente [o'rjẽtʃi] *m*: **o O~** the East; **Extremo O~** Far East; **O~ Médio** Middle East
origem [o'riʒẽ] (*pl* -**ns**) *f* origin; (*ascendência*) lineage, descent;

lugar de ~ birthplace
original [oriʒi'naw] (*pl* -**ais**) *adj* original; (*estranho*) strange, odd ▷ *m* original; **originalidade** [oriʒinali'dadʒi] *f* originality; (*excentricidade*) eccentricity
originar [oriʒi'nar] *vt* to give rise to, start; **originar-se** *vr* to arise; **~-se de** to originate from
oriundo, -a [o'rjũdu, a] *adj*: **~ de** arising from; (*natural*) native of
orla ['ɔrla] *f*: **~ marítima** seafront
ornamento [orna'mẽtu] *m* adornment, decoration
orquestra [or'kɛstra], (*PT*) **orquesta** *f* orchestra
orquídea [or'kidʒja] *f* orchid
ortodoxo, -a [orto'dɔksu, a] *adj* orthodox
ortografia [ortogra'fia] *f* spelling
orvalho [or'vaʎu] *m* dew
os [us] *art def ver* **o**
osso ['osu] *m* bone
ostensivo, -a [ostẽ'sivu, a] *adj* ostensible
ostentar [ostẽ'tar] *vt* to show; (*alardear*) to show off, flaunt
ostra ['ostra] *f* oyster
OTAN ['otã] *abr f* (= *Organização do Tratado do Atlântico Norte*) NATO
ótica ['ɔtʃika] *f* optics *sg*; (*loja*) optician's; (*fig: ponto de vista*) viewpoint; *ver tb* **ótico**
ótico, -a ['ɔtʃiku, a] *adj* optical ▷ *m/f* optician
otimista [otʃi'mista] *adj* optimistic ▷ *m/f* optimist
ótimo, -a ['ɔtʃimu, a] *adj* excellent, splendid ▷ *excl* great!, super!
ou [o] *conj* or; **ou este ou aquele** either this one or that one; **ou seja** in other words
ouço *etc* ['osu] *vb ver* **ouvir**
ouriço [o'risu] *m* (*europeu*)

hedgehog; (*casca*) shell
ouro ['oru] *m* gold; **ouros** *mpl*
(*Cartas*) diamonds
ousadia [oza'dʒia] *f* daring;
ousado, -a [o'zadu, a] *adj* daring,
bold
ousar [o'zar] *vt, vi* to dare
outono [o'tɔnu] *m* autumn

 PALAVRA-CHAVE

outro, -a ['otru, a] *adj* **1** (*distinto: sg*)
another; (: *pl*) other; **outra coisa**
something else; **de outro modo,
de outra maneira** otherwise; **no
outro dia** the next day; **ela está
outra** (*mudada*) she's changed
2 (*adicional*): **quer outro café?**
would you like another coffee?;
outra vez again
▷ *pron* **1**: **o outro** the other one;
(os) outros (the) others; **de outro**
somebody else's
2 (*recíproco*): **odeiam-se uns aos
outros** they hate one another *ou*
each other
3: **outro tanto** the same again;
comer outro tanto to eat the
same *ou* as much again; **ele
recebeu uma dezena de
telegramas e outras tantas
chamadas** he got about ten
telegrams and as many calls

outubro [o'tubru] *m* October
ouvido [o'vidu] *m* (*Anat*) ear;
(*sentido*) hearing; **de ~** by ear;
dar ~s a to listen to
ouvinte [o'vĩtʃi] *m/f* listener;
(*estudante*) auditor
ouvir [o'vir] *vt* to hear; (*com
atenção*) to listen to; (*missa*) to
attend ▷ *vi* to hear; to listen;
~ dizer que ... to hear that ...;

~ falar de to hear of
ova ['ɔva] *f* roe
oval [o'vaw] (*pl* **-ais**) *adj, f* oval
ovário [o'varju] *m* ovary
ovelha [o'veʎa] *f* sheep
óvni ['ɔvni] *m* UFO
ovo ['ovu] *m* egg; **~ pochê** (*BR*) *ou*
escalfado (*PT*) poached egg; **~
estrelado** *ou* **frito** fried egg; **~s
mexidos** scrambled eggs; **~ cozido**
ou **quente** boiled egg; **~s de granja**
free-range eggs
oxidar [oksi'dar] *vt* to rust;
oxidar-se *vr* to rust, go rusty
oxigenado, -a [oksiʒe'nadu, a] *adj*
(*cabelo*) bleached; **água
oxigenada** peroxide
oxigênio [oksi'ʒenju] *m* oxygen
ozônio [o'zonju] *m* ozone; **camada
de ~** ozone layer

O

P

P. *abr* (= *Praça*) Sq.

pá [pa] *f* shovel; (*de remo, hélice*) blade ▷ *m* (*PT*) pal, mate; **pá de lixo** dustpan

paca ['paka] *f* (*Zool*) paca

pacato, -a [pa'katu, a] *adj* (*pessoa*) quiet; (*lugar*) peaceful

paciência [pa'sjẽsja] *f* patience; **paciente** [pa'sjẽtʃi] *adj, m/f* patient

pacífico, -a [pa'sifiku, a] *adj* (*pessoa*) peace-loving; (*aceito sem discussão*) undisputed; (*sossegado*) peaceful; **o (Oceano) P~** the Pacific (Ocean)

pacote [pa'kɔtʃi] *m* packet; (*embrulho*) parcel; (*Econ, Comput, Turismo*) package

pacto ['paktu] *m* pact; (*ajuste*) agreement

padaria [pada'ria] *f* bakery, baker's (shop)

padeiro [pa'dejru] *m* baker

padiola [pa'dʒjɔla] *f* stretcher

padrão [pa'drãw] (*pl* -**ões**) *m* standard; (*medida*) gauge; (*desenho*) pattern; (*fig: modelo*) model; **~ de vida** standard of living

padrasto [pa'drastu] *m* stepfather

padre ['padri] *m* priest

padrinho [pa'driɲu] *m* godfather; (*de noivo*) best man; (*patrono*) sponsor

padroeiro, -a [pa'drwejru, a] *m/f* patron; (*santo*) patron saint

padrões [pa'drõjs] *mpl de* **padrão**

pães [pãjs] *mpl de* **pão**

pagador, a [paga'dor(a)] *adj* paying ▷ *m/f* payer; (*de salário*) pay clerk; (*de banco*) teller

pagamento [paga'mẽtu] *m* payment; **~ a prazo** *ou* **em prestações** payment in instal(l)ments; **~ à vista** cash payment; **~ contra entrega** (*Com*) COD, cash on delivery

pagar [pa'gar] *vt* to pay; (*compras, pecados*) to pay for; (*o que devia*) to pay back; (*retribuir*) to repay ▷ *vi* to pay; **~ por algo** (*tb fig*) to pay for sth; **~ a prestações** to pay in instal(l)ments; **~ de contado** (*PT*) to pay cash

página ['paʒina] *f* page; **~ (da) web** web page; **~ inicial** home page; **P~s Amarelas** Yellow Pages®

pago, -a ['pagu, a] *pp de* **pagar** ▷ *adj* paid; (*fig*) even ▷ *m* pay

pai [paj] *m* father; **pais** *mpl* parents

painel [paj'nɛw] (*pl* -**éis**) *m* panel; (*quadro*) picture; (*Auto*) dashboard; (*de avião*) instrument panel

país [pa'jis] *m* country; (*região*) land; **~ natal** native land

paisagem [paj'zaʒẽ] (*pl* -**ns**) *f* scenery, landscape

paisano, -a [paj'zanu, a] *adj*
civilian ▷ *m/f* (*não militar*) civilian;
(*compatriota*) fellow countryman
Países Baixos *mpl*: **os ~** the
Netherlands
paixão [paj'ʃãw] (*pl* **-ões**) *f* passion
palácio [pa'lasju] *m* palace; **~ da
justiça** courthouse; **Palácio do
Planalto** *see note*

- **PALÁCIO DO PLANALTO**
-
- **Palácio de Planalto** is the seat
- of the Brazilian government, in
- Brasília. The name comes from
- the fact that the Brazilian capital
- is situated on a plateau. It has
- come to be a byword for central
- government.

paladar [pala'dar] *m* taste; (*Anat*)
palate
palafita [pala'fita] *f* (*estacaria*)
stilts *pl*; (*habitação*) stilt house
palavra [pa'lavra] *f* word; (*fala*)
speech; (*promessa*) promise;
(*direito de falar*) right to speak; **dar a
~ a alguém** to give sb the chance
to speak; **ter ~** (*pessoa*) to be
reliable; **~s cruzadas** crossword
(puzzle) *sg*; **palavrão** [pala'vrãw]
(*pl* **-ões**) *m* swearword
palco ['pawku] *m* (*Teatro*) stage;
(*fig: local*) scene
Palestina [pales'tʃina] *f*: **a ~**
Palestine; **palestino, -a**
[pales'tʃinu, a] *adj, m/f*
Palestinian
palestra [pa'lɛstra] *f* chat, talk;
(*conferência*) lecture
paletó [pale'tɔ] *m* jacket
palha ['paʎa] *f* straw
palhaço [pa'ʎasu] *m* clown
pálido, -a ['palidu, a] *adj* pale

palito [pa'litu] *m* stick; (*para os
dentes*) toothpick
palma ['pawma] *f* (*folha*) palm leaf;
(*da mão*) palm; **bater ~s** to clap;
palmada [paw'mada] *f* slap
palmeira [paw'mejra] *f* palm tree
palmo ['pawmu] *m* span; **~ a ~** inch
by inch
palpável [paw'pavew] (*pl* **-eis**) *adj*
tangible; (*fig*) obvious
pálpebra ['pawpebra] *f* eyelid
palpitação [pawpita'sãw] (*pl* **-ões**)
f beating, throbbing; **palpitações**
fpl (*batimentos cardíacos*)
palpitations
palpitante [pawpi'tãtʃi] *adj*
beating, throbbing; (*fig:
emocionante*) thrilling; (: *de interesse
atual*) sensational
palpitar [pawpi'tar] *vi* (*coração*) to
beat
palpite [paw'pitʃi] *m* (*intuição*)
hunch; (*Jogo, Turfe*) tip; (*opinião*)
opinion
pampa ['pãpa] *f* pampas
Panamá [pana'ma] *m*: **o ~**
Panama; **o canal do ~** the Panama
Canal
pancada [pã'kada] *f* (*no corpo*)
blow, hit; (*choque*) knock; (*de
relógio*) stroke; **dar ~ em alguém** to
hit sb; **pancadaria** [pãkada'ria] *f*
(*surra*) beating; (*tumulto*) fight
pandeiro [pã'dejru] *m* tambourine
pane ['pani] *f* breakdown
panela [pa'nɛla] *f* (*de barro*) pot; (*de
metal*) pan; (*de cozinhar*) saucepan;
(*no dente*) hole; **~ de pressão**
pressure cooker
panfleto [pã'fletu] *m* pamphlet
pânico ['paniku] *m* panic; **entrar
em ~** to panic
pano ['panu] *m* cloth; (*Teatro*)
curtain; (*vela*) sheet, sail; **~ de**

p

pratos tea towel; **~ de pó** duster; **~ de fundo** (tb fig) backdrop

panorama [pano'rama] m view

panqueca [pã'kɛka] f pancake

pantanal [pãta'naw] (pl **-ais**) m swampland

pântano ['pãtanu] m marsh, swamp

pantera [pã'tɛra] f panther

pão [pãw] (pl **pães**) m bread; **o P~ de Açúcar** (no Rio) Sugarloaf Mountain; **~ árabe** pitta (Brit) or pita (US) bread; **~ torrado** toast; **pão-duro** (pl **pães-duros**) (col) adj mean, stingy ▷ m/f miser; **pãozinho** [pãw'ziɲu] m roll

papa ['papa] m Pope; (mingau) porridge

papagaio [papa'gaju] m parrot; (pipa) kite

papai [pa'paj] m dad, daddy; **P~ Noel** Santa Claus, Father Christmas

papel [pa'pɛw] (pl **-éis**) m paper; (Teatro) part; (função) role; **~ de embrulho** wrapping paper; **~ de escrever/de alumínio** writing paper/tinfoil; **~ de parede** wallpaper; **~ de seda/ transparente** tissue paper/tracing paper; **~ filme** Clingfilm® (Brit), Saran Wrap® (US); **~ higiênico** toilet paper; **papelada** [pape'lada] f pile of papers; (burocracia) paperwork, red tape; **papelão** [pape'lãw] m cardboard; (fig) fiasco; **papelaria** [papela'ria] f stationer's (shop); **papel-carbono** m carbon paper

papinha [pa'piɲa] f: **~ de bebê** baby food

papo ['papu] m (col) double chin; (: conversa) chat; (: papo furado) hot air; **bater** ou **levar um ~** (col) to have a chat; **bater ~** (col) to chat (also internet); **ficar de ~ para o ar** (fig) to laze around

paquerar [pake'rar] (col) vi to flirt ▷ vt to chat up

paquistanês, -esa [pakista'nes, eza] adj, m/f Pakistani

Paquistão [pakis'tãw] m: **o ~** Pakistan

par [par] adj (igual) equal; (número) even ▷ m pair; (casal) couple; (pessoa na dança) partner; **~ a ~** side by side, level; **sem ~** incomparable

para ['para] prep for; (direção) to, towards; **~ que** so that, in order that; **~ quê?** what for?, why?; **ir ~ casa** to go home; **~ com** (atitude) towards; **de lá ~ cá** since then; **~ a semana** next week; **estar ~** to be about to; **é ~ nós ficarmos aqui?** should we stay here?

parabéns [para'bẽjs] mpl congratulations; (no aniversário) happy birthday; **dar ~ a** to congratulate

para-brisa ['para-] (pl **-s**) m windscreen (Brit), windshield (US)

para-choque ['para-] (pl **-s**) m (Auto) bumper

parada [pa'rada] f stop; (Com) stoppage; (militar, colegial) parade

parado, -a [pa'radu, a] adj (imóvel) standing still; (sem vida) lifeless; (carro) stationary; (máquina) out of action; (olhar) fixed; (trabalhador, fábrica) idle

paradoxo [para'dɔksu] m paradox

parafuso [para'fuzu] m screw

paragem [pa'raʒẽ] (pl **-ns**) f (PT) stop; **~ de elétrico** (PT) tram (Brit) ou streetcar (US) stop; **paragens** fpl (lugares) parts

parágrafo [pa'ragrafu] m paragraph

Paraguai [para'gwaj] m: **o ~**
Paraguay; **paraguaio, -a**
[para'gwaju, a] adj, m/f
Paraguayan

paraíso [para'izu] m paradise

para-lama ['para-] (pl **-s**) m wing
(Brit), fender (US); (de bicicleta)
mudguard

paralelepípedo [paralele'pipedu]
m cobblestone

paralelo, -a [para'lɛlu, a] adj
parallel

parapeito [para'pejtu] m wall,
parapet; (da janela) windowsill

parapente [para'pẽjtʃi] m (Esporte)
paragliding; (equipamento)
paraglider

paraquedas [para'kɛdas] m inv
parachute

parar [pa'rar] vi to stop; (ficar) to
stay ▷ vt to stop; **fazer ~** (deter) to
stop; **~ na cadeia** to end up in jail; **~
de fazer** to stop doing

para-raios ['para-] m inv lightning
conductor

parasita [para'zita] m parasite

parceiro, -a [par'sejru, a] adj
matching ▷ m/f partner

parcela [par'sɛla] f piece, bit; (de
pagamento) instalment (Brit),
installment (US); (de terra) plot; (do
eleitorado etc) section; (Mat) item

parceria [parse'ria] f partnership

parcial [par'sjaw] (pl **-ais**) adj
partial; (feito por partes) in parts;
(pessoa) biased; (Pol) partisan;
parcialidade [parsjali'dadʒi] f
bias, partiality

pardal [par'daw] (pl **-ais**) m
sparrow

pardieiro [par'dʒjejru] m ruin,
heap

pardo, -a ['pardu, a] adj (cinzento)
grey (Brit), gray (US); (castanho)
brown; (mulato) mulatto

parecer [pare'ser] vi (ter a aparência
de) to look, seem; **parecer-se** vr:
~-se com alguém to look like sb;
~ alguém/algo to look like sb/sth;
ao que parece apparently;
parece-me que I think that, it
seems to me that; **que lhe parece?**
what do you think?; **parece que**
(pelo visto) it looks as if; (segundo
dizem) apparently

parecido, -a [pare'sidu, a] adj
alike, similar; **~ com** like

parede [pa'redʒi] f wall

parente, -a [pa'rẽtʃi] m/f relative,
relation; **parentesco** [parẽ'tesku]
m relationship; (fig) connection

parêntese [pa'rẽtezi] m
parenthesis; (na escrita) bracket;
(fig: digressão) digression

páreo ['parju] m race; (fig)
competition

parir [pa'rir] vt to give birth to
▷ vi to give birth; (mulher) to have a
baby

Paris [pa'ris] n Paris; **parisiense**
[pari'zjẽsi] adj, m/f Parisian

parlamentar [parlamẽ'tar] adj
parliamentary ▷ m/f member of
parliament

parlamento [parla'mẽtu] m
parliament

paróquia [pa'rɔkja] f (Rel) parish

parque ['parki] m park; **~
industrial** industrial estate;
~ nacional national park; **~ de
diversões** amusement park

parte ['partʃi] f part; (quinhão)
share; (lado) side; (ponto) point;
(Jur) party; (papel) role; **a maior ~
de** most of; **à ~** aside; (separado)
separate; (separadamente)
separately; (além de) apart from;
da ~ de alguém on sb's part; **em**

P

alguma/qualquer ~ somewhere/anywhere; **em ~ alguma** nowhere; **por toda (a) ~** everywhere; **pôr de ~** to set aside; **tomar ~ em** to take part in; **dar ~ de alguém à polícia** to report sb to the police

participar [partʃisi'par] *vt* to announce, notify of ▷ *vi*: **~ de** *ou* **em** to participate in, take part in; *(compartilhar)* to share in

particípio [partʃi'sipju] *m* participle

particular [partʃiku'lar] *adj* particular, special; *(privativo, pessoal)* private ▷ *m* particular; *(indivíduo)* individual; **particulares** *mpl* *(pormenores)* details; **em ~** in private; **particularmente** [partʃikular'mẽtʃi] *adv* privately; *(especialmente)* particularly

partida [par'tʃida] *f* *(saída)* departure; *(Esporte)* game, match

partidário, -a [partʃi'darju, a] *adj* supporting ▷ *m/f* supporter, follower

partido, -a [par'tʃidu, a] *adj* broken ▷ *m* *(Pol)* party; **tirar ~ de** to profit from; **tomar o ~ de** to side with

partilhar [partʃi'ʎar] *vt* to share; *(distribuir)* to share out

partir [par'tʃir] *vt* to break; *(dividir)* to split ▷ *vi* *(pôr-se a caminho)* to set off, set out; *(ir-se embora)* to leave, depart; **partir-se** *vr* to break; **a ~ de** *(starting)* from; **~ para outra** *(col)* to move on

parto ['partu] *m* (child)birth; **estar em trabalho de ~** to be in labour *(Brit)* *ou* labor *(US)*

Páscoa ['paskwa] *f* Easter; *(dos judeus)* Passover

pasmo, -a ['pazmu, a] *adj* astonished ▷ *m* amazement

passa ['pasa] *f* raisin

passadeira [pasa'dejra] *f* *(tapete)* stair carpet; *(mulher)* ironing lady; *(PT: para peões)* zebra crossing *(Brit)*, crosswalk *(US)*

passado, -a [pa'sadu, a] *adj* past; *(antiquado)* old-fashioned; *(fruta)* bad; *(peixe)* off ▷ *m* past; **o ano ~** last year; **bem ~** *(carne)* well done

passageiro, -a [pasa'ʒejru, a] *adj* passing ▷ *m/f* passenger

passagem [pa'saʒẽ] *(pl* **-ns)** *f* passage; *(preço de condução)* fare; *(bilhete)* ticket; **~ de ida e volta** return ticket, round trip ticket *(US)*; **~ de nível** level *(Brit)* *ou* grade *(US)* crossing; **~ de pedestres** pedestrian crossing *(Brit)*, crosswalk *(US)*; **~ subterrânea** underpass, subway *(Brit)*

passaporte [pasa'portʃi] *m* passport

passar [pa'sar] *vt* to pass; *(exceder)* to go beyond, exceed; *(a ferro)* to iron; *(o tempo)* to spend; *(a outra pessoa)* to pass on; *(pomada)* to put on ▷ *vi* to pass; *(na rua)* to go past; *(tempo)* to go by; *(dor)* to wear off; *(terminar)* to be over; **passar-se** *vr* *(acontecer)* to go on, happen; **~ bem** *(de saúde)* to be well; **passava das dez horas** it was past ten o' clock; **~ alguém para trás** to con sb; *(cônjuge)* to cheat on sb; **~ por algo** *(sofrer)* to go through sth; *(transitar: estrada)* to go along sth; *(ser considerado como)* to be thought of as sth; **~ sem** to do without

passarela [pasa'rɛla] *f* footbridge

pássaro ['pasaru] *m* bird

passatempo [pasa'tẽpu] *m* pastime

passe ['pasi] *m* pass

passear [pa'sjar] *vt* to take for a

walk ▷ *vi* (*a pé*) to go for a walk; (*sair*) to go out; **~ a cavalo/de carro** to go for a ride/a drive; **passeata** [pa'sjata] *f* (*marcha coletiva*) protest march; **passeio** [pa'seju] *m* walk; (*de carro*) drive, ride; (*excursão*) outing; (*calçada*) pavement (*Brit*), sidewalk (*US*); **dar um passeio** to go for a walk; (*de carro*) to go for a drive *ou* ride

passível [pa'sivew] (*pl* -**eis**) *adj*: **~ de** (*dor etc*) susceptible to; (*pena, multa*) subject to

passivo, -a [pa'sivu, a] *adj* passive ▷ *m* (*Com*) liabilities *pl*

passo ['pasu] *m* step; (*medida*) pace; (*modo de andar*) walk; (*ruído dos passos*) footstep; (*sinal de pé*) footprint; **ao ~ que** while; **ceder o ~ a** to give way to

pasta ['pasta] *f* paste; (*de couro*) briefcase; (*de cartolina*) folder; (*de ministro*) portfolio; **~ dentifrícia** *ou* **de dentes** toothpaste

pastar [pas'tar] *vt* to graze on ▷ *vi* to graze

pastel [pas'tɛw] (*pl* -**éis**) *adj inv* (*cor*) pastel ▷ *m* samosa

pastelão [paste'lãw] *m* slapstick

pastelaria [pastela'ria] *f* cake shop; (*comida*) pastry

pasteurizado, -a [pastewri'zadu, a] *adj* pasteurized

pastilha [pas'tʃiʎa] *f* (*Med*) tablet; (*doce*) pastille

pastor, a [pas'tor(a)] *m/f* shepherd(ess) ▷ *m* (*Rel*) clergyman, pastor

pata ['pata] *f* (*pé de animal*) foot, paw; (*ave*) duck; (*col: pé*) foot

patamar [pata'mar] *m* (*de escada*) landing; (*fig*) level

pateta [pa'tɛta] *adj* stupid, daft ▷ *m/f* idiot

patético, -a [pa'tɛtʃiku, a] *adj* pathetic, moving

patife [pa'tʃifi] *m* scoundrel, rogue

patim [pa'tʃĩ] (*pl* -**ns**) *m* skate; **~ de rodas** roller skate; **patins em linha** Rollerblades®; **patinar** [patʃi'nar] *vi* to skate; (*Auto: derrapar*) to skid

patins [pa'tʃĩs] *mpl de* **patim**

pátio ['patʃju] *m* (*de uma casa*) patio, backyard; (*espaço cercado de edifícios*) courtyard; (*tb*: **~ de recreio**) playground; (*Mil*) parade ground

pato ['patu] *m* duck; (*macho*) drake

patologia [patolo'ʒia] *f* pathology; **patológico, -a** [pato'lɔʒiku, a] *adj* pathological

patrão [pa'trãw] (*pl* -**ões**) *m* (*Com*) boss; (*dono de casa*) master; (*proprietário*) landlord; (*Náut*) skipper

pátria ['patrja] *f* homeland

patrimônio [patri'monju] *m* (*herança*) inheritance; (*fig*) heritage; (*bens*) property

patriota [pa'trjɔta] *m/f* patriot

patrocinar [patrosi'nar] *vt* to sponsor; (*proteger*) to support; **patrocínio** [patro'sinju] *m* sponsorship, backing; (*proteção*) support

patrões [pa'trõjs] *mpl de* **patrão**

patrulha [pa'truʎa] *f* patrol; **patrulhar** [patru'ʎar] *vt, vi* to patrol

pau [paw] *m* (*madeira*) wood; (*vara*) stick; **paus** *mpl* (*Cartas*) clubs; **~ a ~** neck and neck; **~ de bandeira** flagpole

pausa ['pawza] *f* pause; (*intervalo*) break; (*descanso*) rest

pauta ['pawta] *f* (*linha*) (guide)line; (*ordem do dia*) agenda; (*indicações*)

P

guidelines pl; **sem ~** (papel) plain;
em ~ on the agenda

pavão, -voa [pa'vãw, 'voa] (pl
-ões/-s) m/f peacock/peahen

pavilhão [pavi'ʎãw] (pl -ões) m
tent; (de madeira) hut; (no jardim)
summerhouse; (em exposição)
pavilion; (bandeira) flag

pavimento [pavi'mẽtu] m (chão,
andar) floor; (da rua) road surface

pavões [pa'võjs] mpl de **pavão**

pavor [pa'vor] m dread, terror; **ter ~
de** to be terrified of; **pavoroso, -a**
[pavo'rozu, ɔza] adj dreadful,
terrible

paz [pajz] f peace; **fazer as ~es** to
make up, be friends again

PC abr m PC

Pça. abr (= Praça) Sq.

pé [pɛ] m foot; (da mesa) leg; (fig:
base) footing; (de milho, café) plant;
ir a pé to walk, go on foot; **ao pé
de** near, by; **ao pé da letra** literally;
estar de pé (festa etc) to be on; **em
ou de pé** standing (up); **dar no pé**
(col) to run away, take off; **não ter
pé nem cabeça** (fig) to make no
sense

peão [pjãw] (pl -ões) m (PT)
pedestrian

peça ['pɛsa] f piece; (Auto) part;
(aposento) room; (Teatro) play; **~ de
reposição** spare part; **~ de roupa**
garment

pecado [pe'kadu] m sin

pecar [pe'kar] vi to sin; **~ por
excesso de zelo** to be over-zealous

pechincha [pe'ʃĩʃa] f (vantagem)
godsend; (coisa barata) bargain;
pechinchar [peʃĩ'ʃar] vi to
bargain, haggle

peço etc ['pɛsu] vb ver **pedir**

peculiar [peku'ljar] adj special,
peculiar; (particular) particular;

peculiaridade [pekuljari'dadʒi] f
peculiarity

pedaço [pe'dasu] m piece; (fig:
trecho) bit; **aos ~s** in pieces

pedágio [pe'daʒju] (BR) m
(pagamento) toll

pedal [pe'daw] (pl -ais) m pedal;
pedalar [peda'lar] vt, vi to pedal

pedante [pe'dãtʃi] adj pretentious
▷ m/f pseud

pedestre [pe'dɛstri] (BR) m
pedestrian

pedicuro, -a [pedʒi'kuru, a] m/f
chiropodist (Brit), podiatrist (US)

pedido [pe'dʒidu] m request; (Com)
order; **~ de demissão** resignation;
~ de desculpa apology

pedinte [pe'dʒĩtʃi] m/f beggar

pedir [pe'dʒir] vt to ask for; (Com,
comida) to order; (exigir) to demand
▷ vi to ask; (num restaurante) to
order; **~ algo a alguém** to ask sb
for sth; **~ a alguém que faça, ~
para alguém fazer** to ask sb to do

pedófilo, -a [pe'dɔfilu, a] m/f
paedophile (Brit), pedophile (US)

pedra ['pɛdra] f stone; (rochedo)
rock; (de granizo) hailstone; (de
açúcar) lump; (quadro-negro) slate;
~ de gelo ice cube; **pedreiro**
[pe'drejru] m stonemason

pegada [pe'gada] f (de pé) footprint;
(Futebol) save

pegado, -a [pe'gadu, a] adj stuck;
(unido) together

pegajoso, -a [pega'ʒozu, ɔza] adj
sticky

pegar [pe'gar] vt to catch; (selos) to
stick (on); (segurar) to take hold of;
(hábito, mania) to get into;
(compreender) to take in; (trabalho)
to take on; (estação de rádio) to pick
up, get ▷ vi to stick; (planta) to
take; (moda) to catch on; (doença)

to be catching; (*motor*) to start; **~ em** (*segurar*) to grab, pick up; **ir ~** (*buscar*) to go and get; **~ um emprego** to get a job; **~ fogo a algo** to set fire to sth; **~ no sono** to get to sleep

pego, -a ['pɛgu, a] *pp de* **pegar**
peito ['pejtu] *m* (*Anat*) chest; (*de ave, mulher*) breast; (*fig*) courage
peitoril [pejto'riw] (*pl* **-is**) *m* windowsill
peixada [pej'ʃada] *f* fish cooked in a seafood sauce
peixaria [pejʃa'ria] *f* fish shop, fishmonger's (*Brit*)
peixe ['pejʃi] *m* fish; **Peixes** *mpl* (*Astrologia*) Pisces *sg*
pela ['pɛla] = **por + a**
pelada [pe'lada] *f* football game

○ **PELADA**
○
○ **Pelada** is an improvised,
○ generally short, game of
○ football, which in the past was
○ played with a ball made out of
○ socks, or an inflatable rubber
○ ball. It is still played today on any
○ piece of open land, or even in the
○ street.

pelado, -a [pe'ladu, a] *adj* (*sem pele*) skinned; (*sem pelo, cabelo*) shorn; (*nu*) naked, in the nude; (*sem dinheiro*) broke
pelar [pe'lar] *vt* (*tirar a pele*) to skin; (*tirar o pelo*) to shear
pelas ['pɛlas] = **por + as**
pele ['pɛli] *f* skin; (*couro*) leather; (*como agasalho*) fur; (*de animal*) hide
película [pe'likula] *f* film
pelo¹ ['pɛlu] = **por + o**
pelo² ['pelu] *m* hair; (*de animal*) fur, coat; **nu em ~** stark naked

pelos ['pɛlus] = **por + os**
peludo, -a [pe'ludu, a] *adj* hairy; (*animal*) furry
pena ['pena] *f* feather; (*de caneta*) nib; (*escrita*) writing; (*Jur*) penalty, punishment; (*sofrimento*) suffering; (*piedade*) pity; **que ~!** what a shame!; **dar ~** to be upsetting; **ter ~ de** to feel sorry for; **~ de morte** death penalty
pênalti ['penawtʃi] *m* (*Futebol*) penalty (kick)
penar [pe'nar] *vt* to grieve ▷ *vi* to suffer
pendência [pē'dēsja] *f* dispute, quarrel
pendente [pē'dētʃi] *adj* hanging; (*por decidir*) pending; (*inclinado*) sloping; (*dependent*): **~ de** dependent on ▷ *m* pendant
pêndulo ['pēdulu] *m* pendulum
pendurar [pēdu'rar] *vt* to hang
penedo [pe'nedu] *m* rock, boulder
peneira [pe'nejra] *f* sieve; **peneirar** [penej'rar] *vt* to sift, sieve ▷ *vi* (*chover*) to drizzle
penetrar [pene'trar] *vt* to get into, penetrate; (*compreender*) to understand ▷ *vi*: **~ em** *ou* **por** *ou* **entre** to penetrate
penhasco [pe'ɲasku] *m* cliff, crag
penhorar [peɲo'rar] *vt* (*dar em penhor*) to pledge, pawn
penicilina [penisi'lina] *f* penicillin
península [pe'nīsula] *f* peninsula
pênis ['penis] *m inv* penis
penitência [peni'tēsja] *f* penitence; (*expiação*) penance; **penitenciária** [penitē'sjarja] *f* prison
penoso, -a [pe'nozu, ɔza] *adj* (*assunto, tratamento*) painful; (*trabalho*) hard
pensamento [pēsa'mētu] *m*

P

thought; (*mente*) mind; (*opinião*) way of thinking; (*ideia*) idea

pensão [pẽ'sãw] (*pl* **-ões**) *f* (*tb*: **casa de ~**) boarding house; (*comida*) board; **~ completa** full board; **~ de aposentadoria** (retirement) pension

pensar [pẽ'sar] *vi* to think; (*imaginar*) to imagine; **~ em** to think of *ou* about; **~ fazer** to intend to do; **pensativo, -a** [pẽsa'tʃivu, a] *adj* thoughtful, pensive

pensionista [pẽsjo'nista] *m/f* pensioner

pensões [pẽ'sõjs] *fpl de* **pensão**

pente ['pẽtʃi] *m* comb; **penteado, -a** [pẽ'tʃjadu, a] *adj* (*cabelo*) in place; (*pessoa*) smart ▷ *m* hairdo, hairstyle; **pentear** [pẽ'tʃjar] *vt* to comb; (*arranjar o cabelo*) to do, style; **pentear-se** *vr* to comb one's hair; to do one's hair

penúltimo, -a [pe'nuwtʃimu, a] *adj* last but one, penultimate

penumbra [pe'nũbra] *f* twilight, dusk; (*sombra*) shadow; (*meia-luz*) half-light

penúria [pe'nurja] *f* poverty

peões [pjõjs] *mpl de* **peão**

pepino [pe'pinu] *m* cucumber

pequeno, -a [pe'kenu, a] *adj* small; (*mesquinho*) petty ▷ *m* boy

Pequim [pe'kĩ] *n* Beijing

pera ['pera] *f* pear

perambular [perãbu'lar] *vi* to wander

perante [pe'rãtʃi] *prep* before, in the presence of

per capita [pɛr'kapita] *adv, adj* per capita

perceber [perse'ber] *vt* to realize; (*por meio dos sentidos*) to perceive; (*compreender*) to understand; (*ver*) to see; (*ouvir*) to hear; (*ver ao longe*) to make out; (*dinheiro: receber*) to receive

percentagem [persẽ'taʒẽ] *f* percentage

percepção [persep'sãw] *f* perception; **perceptível** [persep'tʃivew] (*pl* **-eis**) *adj* perceptible, noticeable; (*som*) audible

percevejo [perse'veʒu] *m* (*inseto*) bug; (*prego*) drawing pin (*Brit*), thumbtack (*US*)

perco *etc* ['perku] *vb ver* **perder**

percorrer [perko'her] *vt* (*viajar por*) to travel (across *ou* over); (*passar por*) to go through, traverse; (*investigar*) to search through

percurso [per'kursu] *m* (*espaço percorrido*) distance (covered); (*trajeto*) route; (*viagem*) journey

percussão [perku'sãw] *f* (*Mús*) percussion

perda ['perda] *f* loss; (*desperdício*) waste; **~s e danos** damages, losses

perdão [per'dãw] *m* pardon, forgiveness; **~!** sorry!, I beg your pardon!

perder [per'der] *vt* to lose; (*tempo*) to waste; (*trem, show, oportunidade*) to miss ▷ *vi* to lose; **perder-se** *vr* to get lost; (*arruinar-se*) to be ruined; (*desaparecer*) to disappear; **~-se de alguém** to lose sb

perdido, -a [per'dʒidu, a] *adj* lost; **~s e achados** lost and found, lost property

perdiz [per'dʒiz] *f* partridge

perdoar [per'dwar] *vt* to forgive

perdurar [perdu'rar] *vi* to last a long time; (*continuar a existir*) to still exist

perecível [pere'sivew] (*pl* **-eis**) *adj* perishable

peregrinação [peregrina'sãw] (*pl*

-ões) f (viagem) travels pl; (Rel) pilgrimage

peregrino, -a [pere'grinu, a] m/f pilgrim

peremptório, -a [perēp'tɔrju, a] adj final; (decisivo) decisive

perene [pe'reni] adj everlasting; (Bot) perennial

perfeição [perfej'sãw] f perfection

perfeitamente [perfejta'mētʃi] adv perfectly ▷ excl exactly!

perfeito, -a [per'fejtu, a] adj perfect ▷ m (Ling) perfect

perfil [per'fiw] (pl **-is**) m profile; (silueta) silhouette, outline; (Arq) (cross) section

perfume [per'fumi] m perfume, scent

perfurar [perfu'rar] vt (o chão) to drill a hole in; (papel) to punch (a hole in)

pergunta [per'gũta] f question; **fazer uma ~ a alguém** to ask sb a question; **perguntar** [pergũ'tar] vt to ask; (interrogar) to question ▷ vi: **perguntar por alguém** to ask after sb; **perguntar-se** vr to wonder; **perguntar algo a alguém** to ask sb sth

perícia [pe'risja] f expertise; (destreza) skill; (exame) investigation

periferia [perife'ria] f periphery; (da cidade) outskirts pl

perigo [pe'rigu] m danger; **perigoso, -a** [peri'gozu, ɔza] adj dangerous; (arriscado) risky

período [pe'riodu] m period; (estação) season

periquito [peri'kitu] m parakeet

perito, -a [pe'ritu, a] adj expert ▷ m/f expert; (quem faz perícia) investigator

permanecer [permane'ser] vi to

remain; (num lugar) to stay; (continuar a ser) to remain, keep; **~ parado** to keep still

permanência [perma'nēsja] f permanence; (estada) stay; **permanente** [perma'nētʃi] adj (dor) constant; (cor) fast; (residência, pregas) permanent ▷ m (cartão) pass ▷ f perm

permissão [permi'sãw] f permission, consent; **permissivo, -a** [permi'sivu, a] adj permissive

permitir [permi'tʃir] vt to allow, permit

perna ['pɛrna] f leg; **~s tortas** bow legs

pernil [per'niw] (pl **-is**) m (de animal) haunch; (Culin) leg

pernilongo [perni'lõgu] m mosquito

pernis [per'nis] mpl de **pernil**

pernoitar [pernoj'tar] vi to spend the night

pérola ['pɛrola] f pearl

perpendicular [perpēdʒiku'lar] adj, f perpendicular

perpetuar [perpe'twar] vt to perpetuate; **perpétuo, -a** [per'pɛtwu, a] adj perpetual

persa ['pɛrsa] adj, m/f Persian

perseguição [persegi'sãw] f pursuit; (Rel, Pol) persecution

perseguir [perse'gir] vt to pursue; (correr atrás) to chase (after); (Rel, Pol) to persecute; (importunar) to harass, pester

perseverante [perseve'rātʃi] adj persistent

perseverar [perseve'rar] vi to persevere

Pérsia ['pɛrsja] f: **a ~** Persia

persiana [per'sjana] f blind

Pérsico, -a ['pɛrsiku, a] adj: **o golfo ~** the Persian Gulf

p

persigo etc [per'sigu] vb ver
  perseguir
persistir [persis'tʃir] vi to persist
personagem [perso'naʒẽ] (pl **-ns**)
  m/f famous person, celebrity; (num
  livro, filme) character
personalidade [personali'dadʒi] f
  personality
perspectiva [perspek'tʃiva] f
  perspective; (panorama) view;
  (probabilidade) prospect
perspicácia [perspi'kasja] f
  insight, perceptiveness; **perspicaz**
  [perspi'kajz] adj perceptive;
  (sagaz) shrewd
persuadir [perswa'dʒir] vt to
  persuade; **persuadir-se** vr to
  convince o.s.; **persuasão**
  [perswa'zãw] f persuasion;
  persuasivo, -a [perswa'zivu, a]
  adj persuasive
pertencente [pertẽ'sẽtʃi] adj: **~ a**
  pertaining to
pertencer [pertẽ'ser] vi: **~ a** to
  belong to; (referir-se) to concern
pertences [per'tẽsis] mpl (de uma
  pessoa) belongings
pertinência [pertʃi'nẽsja] f
  relevance; **pertinente**
  [pertʃi'nẽtʃi] adj relevant;
  (apropriado) appropriate
perto, -a ['pɛrtu, a] adj nearby
  ▷ adv near; **~ de** near to; (em
  comparação com) next to; **de ~**
  closely; (ver) close up; (conhecer)
  very well
perturbar [pertur'bar] vt to
  disturb; (abalar) to upset, trouble;
  (atrapalhar) to put off; (andamento,
  trânsito) to disrupt; (envergonhar) to
  embarrass; (alterar) to affect
Peru [pe'ru] m: **o ~** Peru
peru, a [pe'ru(a)] m/f turkey
peruca [pe'ruka] f wig

perverso, -a [per'vɛrsu, a] adj
  perverse; (malvado) wicked
perverter [perver'ter] vt to
  corrupt, pervert; **pervertido, -a**
  [perver'tʃidu, a] adj perverted
  ▷ m/f pervert
pesadelo [peza'delu] m nightmare
pesado, -a [pe'zadu, a] adj heavy;
  (ambiente) tense; (trabalho) hard;
  (estilo) dull, boring; (andar) slow;
  (piada) coarse; (comida) stodgy;
  (tempo) sultry ▷ adv heavily
pêsames ['pezamis] mpl
  condolences, sympathy sg
pesar [pe'zar] vt to weigh; (fig) to
  weigh up ▷ vi to weigh; (ser pesado)
  to be heavy; (influir) to carry
  weight; (causar mágoa): **~ a** to hurt,
  grieve ▷ m grief; **~ sobre** (recair) to
  fall upon
pesaroso, -a [peza'rozu, ɔza] adj
  sorrowful, sad; (arrependido)
  regretful, sorry
pesca ['pɛska] f fishing; (os peixes)
  catch; **ir à ~** to go fishing
pescada [pes'kada] f whiting
pescado [pes'kadu] m fish
pescador, a [peska'dor(a)] m/f
  fisherman/woman; **~ à linha**
  angler
pescar [pes'kar] vt (peixe) to catch;
  (tentar apanhar) to fish for; (retirar
  da água) to fish out ▷ vi to fish
pescoço [pes'kosu] m neck
peso ['pezu] m weight; (fig: ônus)
  burden; (importância) importance;
  ~ bruto/líquido gross/net weight
pesquisa [pes'kiza] f research;
  uma ~ a study; **pesquisar**
  [peski'zar] vt, vi to research
pêssego ['pesegu] m peach
pessimista [pesi'mista] adj
  pessimistic ▷ m/f pessimist
péssimo, -a ['pɛsimu, a] adj very

bad, awful

pessoa [pe'soa] f person; **pessoas** fpl people; **pessoal** [pe'swaw] (pl **pessoais**) adj personal ▷ m personnel pl, staff pl; (col) people pl, folks pl

pestana [pes'tana] f eyelash

peste ['pɛstʃi] f epidemic; (bubônica) plague; (fig) pest, nuisance

pétala ['pɛtala] f petal

petição [petʃi'sãw] (pl -ões) f request; (documento) petition

petisco [pe'tʃisku] m savoury (Brit), savory (US), titbit (Brit), tidbit (US)

petróleo [pe'trɔlju] m oil, petroleum; **~ bruto** crude oil

peúga ['pjuga] (PT) f sock

pevide [pe'vidʒi] (PT) f (de melão) seed; (de maçã) pip

p. ex. abr (= por exemplo) e.g.

pia ['pia] f wash basin; (da cozinha) sink; **~ batismal** font

piada ['pjada] f joke

pianista [pja'nista] m/f pianist

piano ['pjanu] m piano

piar [pjar] vi (pinto) to cheep; (coruja) to hoot

picada [pi'kada] f (de agulha etc) prick; (de abelha) sting; (de mosquito, cobra) bite; (de avião) dive; (de navalha) stab; (atalho) path, trail

picante [pi'kãtʃi] adj (tempero) hot

picar [pi'kar] vt to prick; (suj: abelha) to sting; (: mosquito) to bite; (: pássaro) to peck; (um animal) to goad; (carne) to mince; (papel) to shred; (fruta) to chop up ▷ vi (comichar) to prickle

picareta [pika'reta] f pickaxe (Brit), pickax (US) ▷ m/f crook

pico ['piku] m (cume) peak; (ponta aguda) sharp point; (PT: um pouco) a bit; **mil e ~** just over a thousand

picolé [piko'lɛ] m lolly

picotar [piko'tar] vt to perforate; (bilhete) to punch

piedade [pje'dadʒi] f piety; (compaixão) pity; **ter ~ de** to have pity on; **piedoso, -a** [pje'dozu, ɔza] adj pious; (compassivo) merciful

piercing ['pirsĩ] (pl -s) m piercing

pifar [pi'far] (col) vi (carro) to break down; (rádio etc) to go wrong; (plano, programa) to fall through

pijama [pi'ʒama] m pyjamas pl (Brit), pajamas pl (US)

pilantra [pi'lãtra] (col) m/f crook

pilar [pi'lar] vt to pound, crush ▷ m pillar

pilha ['piʎa] f (Elet) battery; (monte) pile, heap

pilhar [pi'ʎar] vt to plunder, pillage; (roubar) to rob; (surpreender) to catch

pilotar [pilo'tar] vt (avião) to fly

piloto [pi'lotu] m pilot; (motorista) (racing) driver; (bico de gás) pilot light ▷ adj inv (usina, plano) pilot; (peça) sample atr

pílula ['pilula] f pill; **a ~ (anticoncepcional)** the pill

pimenta [pi'mẽta] f (Culin) pepper; **~ de Caiena** cayenne pepper; **pimenta-do-reino** f black pepper; **pimenta-malagueta** (pl **pimentas-malagueta**) f chilli (Brit) ou chili (US) pepper; **pimentão** [pimẽ'tãw] (pl -ões) m (Bot) pepper

pinça ['pĩsa] f (de sobrancelhas) tweezers pl; (de casa) tongs pl; (Med) callipers pl (Brit), calipers pl (US)

pincel [pĩ'sɛw] (pl -éis) m brush; (para pintar) paintbrush; **pincelar** [pĩse'lar] vt to paint

pinga ['pĩga] f (cachaça) rum; (PT: trago) drink

pingar [pĩ'gar] vi to drip

pingo ['pĩgu] m (gota) drop

pingue-pongue [pĩgi-'põgi] m ping-pong

pinguim [pĩ'gwĩ] (pl -ns) m penguin

pinheiro [pi'ɲejru] m pine (tree)

pinho ['piɲu] m pine

pino ['pinu] m (peça) pin; (Auto: na porta) lock; **a ~** upright

pinta ['pĩta] f (mancha) spot

pintar [pĩ'tar] vt to paint; (cabelo) to dye; (rosto) to make up; (descrever) to describe; (imaginar) to picture ▷ vi to paint; **pintar-se** vr to make o.s. up

pintarroxo [pĩta'hoʃu] m (BR) linnet; (PT) robin

pinto ['pĩtu] m chick; (col!) prick (!)

pintor, a [pĩ'tor(a)] m/f painter

pintura [pĩ'tura] f painting; (maquiagem) make-up

piolho ['pjoʎu] m louse

pioneiro, -a [pjo'nejru, a] m/f pioneer

pior ['pjor] adj, adv (compar) worse; (superl) worst ▷ m: **o ~** worst of all; **piorar** [pjo'rar] vt to make worse, worsen ▷ vi to get worse

pipa ['pipa] f barrel, cask; (de papel) kite

pipi [pi'pi] (col) m pee; **fazer ~** to have a pee

pipoca [pi'pɔka] f popcorn

pipocar [pipo'kar] vi to pop up, pop

piquenique [piki'niki] m picnic

pirâmide [pi'ramidʒi] f pyramid

piranha [pi'raɲa] f piranha (fish)

pirata [pi'rata] m pirate

pires ['piris] m inv saucer

Pirineus [piri'news] mpl: **os ~** the Pyrenees

pirulito [piru'litu] (BR) m lollipop

pisar [pi'zar] vt to tread on; (esmagar, subjugar) to crush ▷ vi to step, tread

pisca-pisca [piska-'piska] (pl -s) m (Auto) indicator

piscar [pis'kar] vt to blink; (dar sinal) to wink; (estrelas) to twinkle ▷ m: **num ~ de olhos** in a flash

piscina [pi'sina] f swimming pool

piso ['pizu] m floor

pisotear [pizo'tʃjar] vt to trample (on)

pista ['pista] f (vestígio) trace; (indicação) clue; (de corridas) track; (Aviat) runway; (de estrada) lane; (de dança) (dance) floor

pistola [pis'tola] f pistol

pitada [pi'tada] f (porção) pinch

pivete [pi'vetʃi] m child thief

pivô [pi'vo] m pivot; (fig) central figure, prime mover

pizza ['pitsa] f pizza

placa ['plaka] f plate; (Auto) number plate (Brit), license plate (US); (comemorativa) plaque; (na pele) blotch; **~ de sinalização** road sign

placar [pla'kar] m scoreboard

plácido, -a ['plasidu, a] adj calm; (manso) placid

plágio ['plaʒu] m plagiarism

planalto [pla'nawtu] m tableland, plateau

planar [pla'nar] vi to glide

planear [pla'njar] (PT) vt = **planejar**

planejamento [planeʒa'mẽtu] m planning; **~ familiar** family planning

planejar [plane'ʒar] (BR) vt to plan; (edifício) to design

planeta [pla'neta] m planet

planície [pla'nisi] f plain

planilha [plaˈniʎa] f spreadsheet
plano, -a [ˈplanu, a] adj flat, level; (liso) smooth ▷ m plan; **em primeiro/em último ~** in the foreground/background; **plano de saúde** health insurance
planta [ˈplãta] f plant; (de pé) sole; (Arq) plan
plantação [plãtaˈsãw] f (ato) planting; (terreno) planted land; (safra) crops pl
plantão [plãˈtãw] (pl -ões) m duty; (noturno) night duty; (plantonista) person on duty; (Mil: serviço) sentry duty; (: pessoa) sentry; **estar de ~** to be on duty
plantar [plãˈtar] vt to plant; (estaca) to drive in; (estabelecer) to set up
plantões [plãˈtõjs] mpl de **plantão**
plástico, -a [ˈplastʃiku, a] adj, m plastic
plataforma [plataˈfɔrma] f platform; **~ de exploração de petróleo** oil rig; **~ de lançamento** launch pad
plateia [plaˈtɛja] f (Teatro etc) stalls pl (Brit), orchestra (US); (espectadores) audience
platina [plaˈtʃina] f platinum
platinados [platʃiˈnadus] mpl (Auto) points
plausível [plawˈzivew] (pl -eis) adj credible, plausible
playground [plejˈgrãwdʒi] (pl -s) m play area
plenamente [plenaˈmẽtʃi] adv fully, completely
pleno, -a [ˈplenu, a] adj full; (completo) complete; **em ~ dia** in broad daylight; **em ~ inverno** in the middle ou depths of winter
plural [pluˈraw] (pl -ais) adj, m plural

pneu [ˈpnew] m tyre (Brit), tire (US)
pneumonia [pnewmoˈnia] f pneumonia
pó [pɔ] m powder; (sujeira) dust; **pó de arroz** face powder; **sabão em pó** soap powder; **tirar o pó (de algo)** to dust (sth)
pobre [ˈpɔbri] adj poor ▷ m/f poor person; **pobreza** [poˈbreza] f poverty
poça [ˈpɔsa] f puddle, pool
poção [poˈsãw] (pl -ões) f potion
poço [ˈposu] m well; (de mina, elevador) shaft
poções [poˈsõjs] fpl de **poção**
pôde etc [ˈpodʒi] vb ver **poder**

 PALAVRA-CHAVE

poder [poˈder] vi **1** (capacidade) can, be able to; **não posso fazê-lo** I can't do it, I'm unable to do it **2** (ter o direito de) can, may, be allowed to; **posso fumar aqui?** can I smoke here?; **pode entrar?** (posso?) can I come in? **3** (possibilidade) may, might, could; **pode ser** maybe; **pode ser que** it may be that; **ele poderá vir amanhã** he might come tomorrow **4**: **não poder com: não posso com ele** I cannot cope with him **5** (col: indignação): **pudera!** no wonder!; **como é que pode?** you're joking!
▷ m power; (autoridade) authority; **poder aquisitivo** purchasing power; **estar no poder** to be in power; **em poder de alguém** in sb's hands

poderoso, -a [podeˈrozu, ɔza] adj powerful
podre [ˈpodri] adj rotten; **podridão**

[podri'dãw] f decay, rottenness; (fig) corruption

põe etc [põj] vb ver **pôr**

poeira ['pwejra] f dust; **~ radioativa** fall-out; **poeirento, -a** [pwej'rẽtu, a] adj dusty

poema ['pwɛma] m poem

poesia [poe'zia] f poetry; (poema) poem

poeta ['pwɛta] m poet; **poético, -a** ['pwɛtʃiku, a] adj poetic; **poetisa** [pwe'tʃiza] f (woman) poet

pois [pojs] adv (portanto) so; (PT: assentimento) yes ▷ conj as, since; (mas) but; **~ bem** well then; **~ é** that's right; **~ não!** (BR) of course!; **~ não?** (BR: numa loja) can I help you?; (PT) isn't it?, aren't you?, didn't they? etc; **~ sim!** certainly not!; **~ (então)** then

polaco, -a [po'laku, a] adj Polish ▷ m/f Pole ▷ m (Ling) Polish

polar [po'lar] adj polar

polegada [pole'gada] f inch

polegar [pole'gar] m (tb: **dedo ~**) thumb

polêmica [po'lemika] f controversy; **polêmico, -a** [po'lemiku, a] adj controversial

pólen ['pɔlẽ] m pollen

polícia [po'lisja] f police, police force ▷ m/f policeman/woman; **policial** [poli'sjaw] (pl **-ais**) adj police atr ▷ m/f (BR) policeman/woman; **novela** ou **romance policial** detective novel; **policiar** [poli'sjar] vt to police; (instintos, modos) to control, keep in check

polidez [poli'dez] f good manners pl, politeness

polido, -a [po'lidu, a] adj polished, shiny; (cortês) well-mannered, polite

pólio ['pɔlju] f polio

polir [po'lir] vt to polish

política [po'litʃika] f politics sg; (programa) policy; **político, -a** [po'litʃiku, a] adj political ▷ m/f politician

polo ['pɔlu] m pole; (Esporte) polo **P~ Norte/Sul** North/South Pole

polonês, -esa [polo'nes, eza] adj Polish ▷ m/f Pole ▷ m (Ling) Polish

Polônia [po'lonja] f: **a ~** Poland

polpa ['powpa] f pulp

poltrona [pow'trɔna] f armchair

poluição [polwi'sãw] f pollution; **poluir** [po'lwir] vt to pollute

polvo ['powvu] m octopus

pólvora ['pɔwvora] f gunpowder

pomada [po'mada] f ointment

pomar [po'mar] m orchard

pomba ['põba] f dove

pombo ['põbu] m pigeon

ponderação [põdera'sãw] f consideration, meditation; (prudência) prudence

ponderado, -a [põde'radu, a] adj prudent

ponderar [põde'rar] vt to consider, weigh up ▷ vi to meditate, muse

ponho etc ['poɲu] vb ver **pôr**

ponta ['põta] f tip; (de faca) point; (de sapato) toe; (extremidade) end; (Futebol: posição) wing; (: jogador) winger; **uma ~ de** (um pouco) a touch of; **~ do dedo** fingertip

pontapé [põta'pɛ] m kick; **dar ~s em alguém** to kick sb

pontaria [põta'ria] f aim; **fazer ~** to take aim

ponte ['põtʃi] f bridge; **~ aérea** air shuttle, airlift; **~ de safena** (heart) bypass operation

ponteiro [põ'tejru] m (indicador) pointer; (de relógio) hand

pontiagudo, -a [põtʃja'gudu, a] adj sharp, pointed

ponto ['põtu] m point; (Med,

Costura, Tricô) stitch; (*pequeno sinal, do i*) dot; (*na pontuação*) full stop (Brit), period (US); (*na pele*) spot; (*de ônibus*) stop; (*de táxi*) rank (Brit), stand (US); (*matéria escolar*) subject; **estar a ~ de fazer** to be on the point of doing; **às cinco em ~** at five o'clock on the dot; **dois ~s** colon *sg*; **~ de admiração** (PT) exclamation mark; **~ de exclamação/interrogação** exclamation/question mark; **~ de vista** point of view, viewpoint; **~ e vírgula** semicolon

pontuação [põtwa'sãw] *f* punctuation

pontual [põ'twaw] (*pl* **-ais**) *adj* punctual

pontudo, -a [põ'tudu, a] *adj* pointed

popa ['popa] *f* stern

população [popula'sãw] (*pl* **-ões**) *f* population

popular [popu'lar] *adj* popular; **popularidade** [populari'dadʒi] *f* popularity

pôquer ['poker] *m* poker

PALAVRA-CHAVE

por [por] (*por + o(s)/a(s) = pelo(s)/a(s)*) *prep* **1** (*objetivo*) for; **lutar pela pátria** to fight for one's country
2 (+ *infin*): **está por acontecer** it is about to happen, it is yet to happen; **está por fazer** it is still to be done
3 (*causa*) out of, because of; **por falta de fundos** through lack of funds; **por hábito/natureza** out of habit/by nature; **faço isso por ela** I do it for her; **por isso** therefore; **a razão pela qual ...** the reason why ...; **pelo amor de Deus!** for Heaven's sake!
4 (*tempo*): **pela manhã** in the morning; **por volta das duas horas** at about two o'clock; **ele vai ficar por uma semana** he's staying for a week
5 (*lugar*): **por aqui** this way; **viemos pelo parque** we came through the park; **passar por São Paulo** to pass through São Paulo; **por fora/dentro** outside/inside
6 (*troca, preço*) for; **trocar o velho pelo novo** to change old for new; **comprei o livro por dez libras** I bought the book for ten pounds
7 (*valor proporcional*): **por cento** per cent; **por hora/dia/semana/mês/ano** hourly/daily/weekly/monthly/yearly; **por cabeça** a ou per head; **por mais difícil** *etc* **que seja** however difficult *etc* it is
8 (*modo, meio*) by; **por correio/avião** by post/air; **por si** by o.s.; **por escrito** in writing; **entrar pela entrada principal** to go in through the main entrance
9: **por que** why; **por quê?** why?
10: **por mim tudo bem** as far as I'm concerned that's OK

PALAVRA-CHAVE

pôr [por] *vt* **1** (*colocar*) to put; (*roupas*) to put on; (*objeções, dúvidas*) to raise; (*ovos, mesa*) to lay; (*defeito*) to find; **põe mais forte** turn it up; **você põe açúcar?** do you take sugar?; **pôr de lado** to set aside
2 (+ *adj*) to make; **você está me pondo nervoso** you're making me nervous

pôr-se *vr* **1** (*sol*) to set
2 (*colocar-se*): **pôr-se de pé** to stand

up; **ponha-se no meu lugar** put yourself in my position
3: **pôr-se a** to start to; **ela pôs-se a chorar** she started crying
▷ *m*: **o pôr do sol** sunset

porão [po'rãw] (*pl* **-ões**) *m* (*de casa*) basement; (: *armazém*) cellar

porca ['pɔrka] *f* (*animal*) sow

porção [por'sãw] (*pl* **-ões**) *f* portion, piece; **uma ~ de** a lot of

porcaria [porka'ria] *f* filth; (*dito sujo*) obscenity; (*coisa ruim*) piece of junk

porcelana [porse'lana] *f* porcelain

porcentagem [porsẽ'taʒẽ] (*pl* **-ns**) *f* percentage

porco, -a ['porku, 'pɔrka] *adj* filthy
▷ *m* (*animal*) pig; (*carne*) pork

porções [por'sõjs] *fpl de* **porção**

porém [po'rẽ] *conj* however

pormenor [porme'nor] *m* detail

pornografia [pornogra'fia] *f* pornography

poro ['pɔru] *m* pore

porões [po'rõjs] *mpl de* **porão**

porque [por'ke] *conj* because; (*interrogativo*: *PT*) why

porquê [por'ke] *adv* (*PT*) why ▷ *m* reason, motive; **~?** (*PT*) why?

porrete [po'hetʃi] *m* club

porta ['pɔrta] *f* door; (*vão da porta*) doorway; (*de um jardim*) gate

portador, a [porta'dor(a)] *m/f* bearer

portagem [por'taʒẽ] (*PT*) (*pl* **-ns**) *f* toll

portal [por'taw] (*pl* **-ais**) *m* doorway

porta-luvas *m inv* (*Auto*) glove compartment

porta-malas *m inv* (*Auto*) boot (*Brit*), trunk (*US*)

porta-níqueis *m inv* purse

portanto [por'tãtu] *conj* so, therefore

portão [por'tãw] (*pl* **-ões**) *m* gate

portar [por'tar] *vt* to carry; **portar-se** *vr* to behave

portaria [porta'ria] *f* (*de um edifício*) entrance hall; (*recepção*) reception desk; (*do governo*) edict, decree

portátil [por'tatʃiw] (*pl* **-eis**) *adj* portable

porta-voz (*pl* **-es**) *m/f* (*pessoa*) spokesman, spokesperson

porte ['pɔrtʃi] *m* transport; (*custo*) freight charge, carriage; **~ pago** post paid; **de grande ~** far-reaching, important

porteiro, -a [por'tejru, a] *m/f* caretaker; **~ eletrônico** entry phone

pórtico ['pɔrtʃiku] *m* porch, portico

porto ['portu] *m* (*do mar*) port, harbour (*Brit*), harbor (*US*); (*vinho*) port; **o P~** Oporto

portões [por'tõjs] *mpl de* **portão**

Portugal [portu'gaw] *m* Portugal;

português, -guesa [portu'ges, 'geza] *adj* Portuguese ▷ *m/f* Portuguese *inv* ▷ *m* (*Ling*) Portuguese

porventura [porvẽ'tura] *adj* by chance; **se ~ você ...** if you happen to ...

pôs [pos] *vb ver* **pôr**

posar [po'zar] *vi* (*Foto*) to pose

posição [pozi'sãw] (*pl* **-ões**) *f* position; (*social*) standing, status; **posicionar** [pozisjo'nar] *vt* to position

positivo, -a [pozi'tʃivu, a] *adj* positive

possante [po'sãtʃi] *adj* powerful, strong; (*carro*) flashy

possessão [pose'sãw] *f* possession;

possessivo, -a [pose'sivu, a] *adj* possessive

possibilidade [posibili'dadʒi] *f* possibility; **possibilidades** *fpl* (*recursos*) means

possibilitar [posibili'tar] *vt* to make possible, permit

possível [po'sivew] (*pl* **-eis**) *adj* possible; **fazer todo o ~** to do one's best

posso *etc* ['posu] *vb ver* **poder**

possuidor, a [poswi'dor(a)] *m/f* owner

possuir [po'swir] *vt* (*casa, livro etc*) to own; (*dinheiro, talento*) to possess

postal [pos'taw] (*pl* **-ais**) *adj* postal ▷ *m* postcard

poste ['pɔstʃi] *m* pole, post

posterior [poste'rjor] *adj* (*mais tarde*) subsequent, later; (*traseiro*) rear, back; **posteriormente** [posterjor'mẽtʃi] *adv* later, subsequently

postiço, -a [pos'tʃisu, a] *adj* false, artificial

posto, -a ['postu, 'pɔsta] *pp de* **pôr** ▷ *m* post, position; (*emprego*) job; **~ de gasolina** service *ou* petrol station; **~ que** although; **~ de saúde** health centre *ou* center

póstumo, -a ['pɔstumu, a] *adj* posthumous

postura [pos'tura] *f* posture; (*aspecto físico*) appearance

potável [po'tavew] (*pl* **-eis**) *adj* drinkable; **água ~** drinking water

pote ['pɔtʃi] *m* jug, pitcher; (*de geleia*) jar; (*de creme*) pot; **chover a ~s** (*PT*) to rain cats and dogs

potência [po'tẽsja] *f* power

potencial [potẽ'sjaw] (*pl* **-ais**) *adj, m* potential

potente [po'tẽtʃi] *adj* powerful, potent

 PALAVRA-CHAVE

pouco, -a ['poku, a] *adj* **1** (*sg*) little, not much; **pouco tempo** little *ou* not much time; **de pouco interesse** of little interest, not very interesting; **pouca coisa** not much **2** (*pl*) few, not many; **uns poucos** a few, some; **poucas vezes** rarely; **poucas crianças comem o que devem** few children eat what they should

▷ *adv* **1** little, not much; **custa pouco** it doesn't cost much; **dentro em pouco, daqui a pouco** shortly; **pouco antes** shortly before **2** (+ *adj: = negativo*): **ela é pouco inteligente/simpática** she's not very bright/friendly

3: **por pouco eu não morri** I almost died

4: **pouco a pouco** little by little

5: **aos poucos** gradually

▷ *m*: **um pouco** a little, a bit; **nem um pouco** not at all

poupador, a [popa'dor(a)] *adj* thrifty

poupança [po'pãsa] *f* thrift; (*economias*) savings *pl*; (*tb*: **caderneta de ~**) savings bank

poupar [po'par] *vt* to save; (*vida*) to spare

pousada [po'zada] *f* (*hospedagem*) lodging; (*hospedaria*) inn

pousar [po'zar] *vt* to place; (*mão*) to rest ▷ *vi* (*avião, pássaro*) to land; (*pernoitar*) to spend the night

povo ['povu] *m* people; (*raça*) people *pl*, race; (*plebe*) common people *pl*; (*multidão*) crowd

povoação [povwa'sãw] (*pl* **-ões**) *f* (*aldeia*) village, settlement; (*habitantes*) population

povoado [po'vwadu] *m* village

P

povoar [po'vwar] *vt* (*de habitantes*) to people, populate; (*de animais etc*) to stock

pra [pra] (*col*) *prep* = **para a**

praça ['prasa] *f* (*largo*) square; (*mercado*) marketplace; (*soldado*) soldier; **~ de touros** bullring

praga ['praga] *f* nuisance; (*maldição*) curse; (*desgraça*) misfortune; (*erva daninha*) weed

pragmático, -a [prag'matʃiku, a] *adj* pragmatic

praia ['praja] *f* beach

prancha ['prãʃa] *f* plank; (*de surfe*) board

prata ['prata] *f* silver; (*col: cruzeiro*) ≈ quid (*Brit*), ≈ buck (*US*)

prateleira [prate'lejra] *f* shelf

prática ['pratʃika] *f* practice; (*experiência*) experience, know-how; (*costume*) habit, custom; *ver tb* **prático**

praticante [pratʃi'kãtʃi] *adj* practising (*Brit*), practicing (*US*) ▷ *m/f* apprentice; (*de esporte*) practitioner

praticar [pratʃi'kar] *vt* to practise (*Brit*), practice (*US*); (*roubo, operação*) to carry out; **prático, -a** ['pratʃiku, a] *adj* practical ▷ *m/f* expert

prato ['pratu] *m* plate; (*comida*) dish; (*de uma refeição*) course; (*de toca-discos*) turntable; **pratos** *mpl* (*Mús*) cymbals

praxe ['praʃi] *f* custom, usage; **de ~** usually; **ser de ~** to be the norm

- **PRAXE**
-
- Student life in Portugal follows
- the traditions set out in a written
- set of rules known as the 'código
- da praxe'. It begins in freshers'
- week, where freshers are jeered
- at by their seniors, and are
- subjected to a number of
- humiliating practical jokes, such
- as having their hair cut against
- their will and being made to walk
- around town in fancy dress.

prazer [pra'zer] *m* pleasure; **muito ~ em conhecê-lo** pleased to meet you

prazo ['prazu] *m* term, period; (*vencimento*) expiry date, time limit; **a curto/médio/longo ~** in the short/medium/long term; **comprar a ~** to buy on hire purchase (*Brit*) *ou* on the installment plan (*US*)

precário, -a [pre'karju, a] *adj* precarious; (*escasso*) failing

precaução [prekaw'sãw] (*pl* **-ões**) *f* precaution

precaver-se [preka'versi] *vr*: **~ (contra** *ou* **de)** to be on one's guard (against); **precavido, -a** [preka'vidu, a] *adj* cautious

prece ['presi] *f* prayer; (*súplica*) entreaty

precedente [prese'dẽtʃi] *adj* preceding ▷ *m* precedent

preceder [prese'der] *vt, vi* to precede; **~ a algo** to precede sth; (*ter primazia*) to take precedence over sth

precioso, -a [pre'sjozu, ɔza] *adj* precious

precipício [presi'pisju] *m* precipice; (*fig*) abyss

precipitação [presipita'sãw] *f* haste; (*imprudência*) rashness

precipitado, -a [presipi'tadu, a] *adj* hasty; (*imprudente*) rash

precisamente [preziza'mẽtʃi] *adv* precisely

precisar [presi'zar] *vt* to need; (*especificar*) to specify; **precisar-se** *vr*: **"precisa-se"** "needed"; **~ de** to need; (*uso impess*): **não precisa você se preocupar** you needn't worry

preciso, -a [pre'sizu, a] *adj* precise, accurate; (*necessário*) necessary; (*claro*) concise; **é ~ você ir** you must go

preço ['presu] *m* price; (*custo*) cost; (*valor*) value; **a ~ de banana** (*BR*) *ou* **de chuva** (*PT*) dirt cheap

preconceito [prekõ'sejtu] *m* prejudice

predador [preda'dor] *m* predator

predileto, -a [predʒi'lɛtu, a] *adj* favourite (*Brit*), favorite (*US*)

prédio ['prɛdʒju] *m* building; **~ de apartamentos** block of flats (*Brit*), apartment house (*US*)

predispor [predʒis'por] (*irreg: como* **pôr**) *vt*: **~ alguém contra** to prejudice sb against; **predispor-se** *vr*: **~-se a/para** to get o.s. in the mood to/for

predominar [predomi'nar] *vi* to predominate, prevail

preencher [preẽ'ʃer] *vt* (*formulário*) to fill in (*Brit*) *ou* out, complete; (*requisitos*) to fulfil (*Brit*), fulfill (*US*), meet; (*espaço, vaga, tempo, cargo*) to fill

prefácio [pre'fasju] *m* preface

prefeito, -a [pre'fejtu, a] *m/f* mayor; **prefeitura** [prefej'tura] *f* town hall

preferencial [preferẽ'sjaw] (*pl* **-ais**) *adj* (*rua*) main ▷ *f* main road (*with priority*)

preferido, -a [prefe'ridu, a] *adj* favourite (*Brit*), favorite (*US*)

preferir [prefe'rir] *vt* to prefer

prefiro *etc* [pre'firu] *vb ver* **preferir**

prefixo [pre'fiksu] *m* (*Ling*) prefix; (*Tel*) code

prega ['prɛga] *f* pleat, fold

pregar¹ [pre'gar] *vt, vi* to preach

pregar² [pre'gar] *vt* (*com prego*) to nail; (*fixar*) to pin, fasten; (*cosendo*) to sew on; **~ uma peça** to play a trick; **~ um susto em alguém** to give sb a fright

prego ['prɛgu] *m* nail; (*col: casa de penhor*) pawn shop

preguiça [pre'gisa] *f* laziness; (*animal*) sloth; **estar com ~** to feel lazy; **preguiçoso, -a** [pregi'sozu, ɔza] *adj* lazy

pré-histórico, -a *adj* prehistoric

preia-mar (*PT*) *f* high tide

prejuízo [pre'ʒwizu] *m* damage, harm; (*em dinheiro*) loss; **em ~ de** to the detriment of

prematuro, -a [prema'turu, a] *adj* premature

premiado, -a [pre'mjadu, a] *adj* prize-winning; (*bilhete*) winning ▷ *m/f* prize-winner

premiar [pre'mjar] *vt* to award a prize to; (*recompensar*) to reward

prêmio ['premju] *m* prize; (*recompensa*) reward; (*Seguros*) premium

prenda ['prẽda] *f* gift, present; (*em jogo*) forfeit; **~s domésticas** housework *sg*

prendedor [prẽde'dor] *m* fastener; (*de cabelo, gravata*) clip; **~ de roupa** clothes peg; **~ de papéis** paper clip

prender [prẽ'der] *vt* to fasten, fix; (*roupa*) to pin; (*cabelo*) to tie back; (*capturar*) to arrest; (*atar, ligar*) to tie; (*atenção*) to catch; (*afetivamente*) to tie, bind; (*reter: doença, compromisso*) to keep; (*movimentos*) to restrict; **prender-se** *vr* to get caught, stick;

P

~-se a alguém (*por amizade*) to be attached to sb

preocupação [preokupa'sãw] (*pl* **-ões**) *f* preoccupation; (*inquietação*) worry, concern

preocupar [preoku'par] *vt* to preoccupy; (*inquietar*) to worry; **preocupar-se** *vr*: **~-se com** to worry about, be worried about

preparação [prepara'sãw] (*pl* **-ões**) *f* preparation

preparar [prepa'rar] *vt* to prepare; **preparar-se** *vr* to get ready; **preparativos** [prepara'tʃivus] *mpl* preparations, arrangements

preponderante [prepõde'rãtʃi] *adj* predominant

preposição [prepozi'sãw] (*pl* **-ões**) *f* preposition

prepotente [prepo'tētʃi] *adj* predominant; (*despótico*) despotic; (*atitude*) overbearing

prescrever [preskre'ver] *vt* to prescribe; (*prazo*) to set

presença [pre'zēsa] *f* presence; (*frequência*) attendance; **ter boa ~** to be presentable; **presenciar** [prezē'sjar] *vt* to be present at; (*testemunhar*) to witness

presente [pre'zētʃi] *adj* present; (*fig: interessado*) present; (*: evidente*) clear, obvious ▷ *m* present ▷ *f* (*Com: carta*): **a ~** this letter; **os presentes** *mpl* (*pessoas*) those present; **presentear** [prezē'tʃjar] *vt*: **presentear alguém (com algo)** to give sb (sth as) a present

preservação [prezerva'sãw] *f* preservation

presidente, -a [prezi'dētʃi, ta] *m/f* president

presidiário, -a [prezi'dʒjarju, a] *m/f* convict

presídio [pre'zidʒju] *m* prison

presidir [prezi'dʒir] *vt, vi*: **~ (a)** to preside over; (*reunião*) to chair; (*suj: leis, critérios*) to govern

preso, -a ['prezu, a] *adj* imprisoned; (*capturado*) under arrest; (*atado*) tied ▷ *m/f* prisoner; **estar ~ a alguém** to be attached to sb

pressa ['prɛsa] *f* haste, hurry; (*rapidez*) speed; (*urgência*) urgency; **às ~s** hurriedly; **estar com ~** to be in a hurry; **ter ~ de** *ou* **em fazer** to be in a hurry to do

presságio [pre'saʒu] *m* omen, sign; (*pressentimento*) premonition

pressão [pre'sãw] (*pl* **-ões**) *f* pressure; **(colchete de) ~** press stud, popper

pressentimento [presētʃi'mētu] *m* premonition

pressentir [presē'tʃir] *vt* to foresee; (*suspeitar*) to sense

pressionar [presjo'nar] *vt* (*botão*) to press; (*coagir*) to pressure ▷ *vi* to press, put on pressure

pressões [pre'sõjs] *fpl de* **pressão**

pressupor [presu'por] (*irreg: como* **pôr**) *vt* to presuppose

prestação [presta'sãw] (*pl* **-ões**) *f* instalment (*Brit*), installment (*US*); (*por uma casa*) repayment

prestar [pres'tar] *vt* (*cuidados*) to give; (*favores, serviços*) to do; (*contas*) to render; (*informações*) to supply; (*uma qualidade a algo*) to lend ▷ *vi*: **~ a alguém para algo** to be of use to sb for sth; **prestar-se** *vr*: **~-se a** to be suitable for; (*admitir*) to lend o.s. to; (*dispor-se*) to be willing to; **~ atenção** to pay attention

prestes ['prɛstʃis] *adj inv* ready; (*a ponto de*): **~ a partir** about to leave

prestígio [preʃ'tʃiʒu] *m* prestige

presunção [prezũ'sãw] (*pl* **-ões**) *f* presumption; (*vaidade*) conceit, self-importance; **presunçoso, -a** [prezũ'sozu, ɔza] *adj* vain, self-important

presunto [pre'zũtu] *m* ham

pretender [pretẽ'der] *vt* to claim; (*cargo, emprego*) to go for; **~ fazer** to intend to do

pretensão [pretẽ'sãw] (*pl* **-ões**) *f* claim; (*vaidade*) pretension; (*propósito*) aim; (*aspiração*) aspiration; **pretensioso, -a** [pretẽ'sjozu, ɔza] *adj* pretentious

pretérito, -a [pre'tɛritu, a] *m* (*Ling*) preterite

pretexto [pre'teʃtu] *m* pretext

preto, -a ['pretu, a] *adj* black

prevalecer [prevale'ser] *vi* to prevail; **prevalecer-se** *vr*: **~-se de** (*aproveitar-se*) to take advantage of

prevenção [prevẽ'sãw] (*pl* **-ões**) *f* prevention; (*preconceito*) prejudice; (*cautela*) caution; **estar de ~ com** *ou* **contra alguém** to be bias(s)ed against sb

prevenido, -a [preve'nidu, a] *adj* cautious, wary

prevenir [preve'nir] *vt* to prevent; (*avisar*) to warn; (*preparar*) to prepare

prever [pre'ver] (*irreg: como* **ver**) *vt* to predict, foresee; (*pressupor*) to presuppose

prévio, -a ['prɛvju, a] *adj* prior; (*preliminar*) preliminary

previsão [previ'zãw] (*pl* **-ões**) *f* foresight; (*prognóstico*) prediction, forecast; **~ do tempo** weather forecast

previsível [previ'zivew] (*pl* **-eis**) *adj* predictable

previsões [previ'zõjs] *fpl de* **previsão**

prezado, -a [pre'zadu, a] *adj* esteemed; (*numa carta*) dear

prezar [pre'zar] *vt* (*amigos*) to value highly; (*autoridade*) to respect; (*gostar de*) to appreciate

primário, -a [pri'marju, a] *adj* primary; (*elementar*) basic, rudimentary; (*primitivo*) primitive ▷ *m* (*curso*) elementary education

primavera [prima'vɛra] *f* spring; (*planta*) primrose

primeira [pri'mejra] *f* (*Auto*) first (gear)

primeiro, -a [pri'mejru, a] *adj, adv* first; **de primeira** first-class

primo, -a ['primu, a] *m/f* cousin; **~ irmão** first cousin

princesa [prĩ'seza] *f* princess

principal [prĩsi'paw] (*pl* **-ais**) *adj* principal; (*entrada, razão, rua*) main ▷ *m* head, principal; (*essencial, de dívida*) principal

príncipe ['prĩsipi] *m* prince

principiante [prĩsi'pjãtʃi] *m/f* beginner

principiar [prĩsi'pjar] *vt, vi* to begin

princípio [prĩ'sipju] *m* beginning, start; (*origem*) origin; (*legal, moral*) principle; **princípios** *mpl* (*de matéria*) rudiments

prioridade [prjori'dadʒi] *f* priority

prisão [pri'zãw] (*pl* **-ões**) *f* imprisonment; (*cadeia*) prison, jail; (*detenção*) arrest; **~ de ventre** constipation; **prisioneiro, -a** [prizjo'nejru, a] *m/f* prisoner

privacidade [privasi'dadʒi] *f* privacy

privada [pri'vada] *f* toilet

privado, -a [pri'vadu, a] *adj* private; (*carente*) deprived

privar [pri'var] *vt* to deprive

privativo, -a [priva'tʃivu, a] *adj* (*particular*) private; **~ de** peculiar to

privilegiado, -a [privile'ʒjadu, a] *adj* privileged; (*excepcional*) unique, exceptional

privilegiar [privile'ʒjar] *vt* to privilege; (*favorecer*) to favour (*Brit*), favor (*US*)

privilégio [privi'lɛʒu] *m* privilege

pró [prɔ] *adv* for, in favour (*Brit*) ou favor (*US*) ▷ *m* advantage; **os ~s e os contras** the pros and cons; **em ~ de** in favo(u)r of

pró- [prɔ] *prefixo* pro-

proa ['proa] *f* prow, bow

probabilidade [probabili'dadʒi] *f* probability; **probabilidades** *fpl* (*chances*) odds

problema [prob'lema] *m* problem

procedência [prose'dẽsja] *f* origin, source; (*lugar de saída*) point of departure

proceder [prose'der] *vi* to proceed; (*comportar-se*) to behave; (*agir*) to act ▷ *m* conduct; **procedimento** [prosedʒi'mẽtu] *m* conduct, behaviour (*Brit*), behavior (*US*); (*processo*) procedure; (*Jur*) proceedings *pl*

processamento [prosesa'mẽtu] *m* processing; (*Jur*) prosecution; (*verificação*) verification; **~ de texto** word processing

processar [prose'sar] *vt* (*Jur*) to take proceedings against, prosecute; (*requerimentos, dados*) to process

processo [pro'sɛsu] *m* process; (*procedimento*) procedure; (*Jur*) lawsuit, legal proceedings *pl*; (: *autos*) record; (*conjunto de documentos*) documents *pl*

procissão [prosi'sãw] (*pl* **-ões**) *f* procession

Proclamação da República *see note*

○ **PROCLAMAÇÃO DA REPÚBLICA**
○
○ Commemorated on 15
○ November, which is a public
○ holiday, the proclamation of the
○ republic in 1889 was a military
○ coup, led by Marshal Deodoro
○ da Fonseca. It brought down
○ the empire which had been
○ established after independence
○ and installed a federal republic
○ in Brazil.

proclamar [prokla'mar] *vt* to proclaim

procura [pro'kura] *f* search; (*Com*) demand

procuração [prokura'sãw] (*pl* **-ões**) *f*: **por ~** by proxy

procurador, a [prokura'dor(a)] *m/f* attorney; **P~ Geral da República** Attorney General

procurar [proku'rar] *vt* to look for, seek; (*emprego*) to apply for; (*ir visitar*) to call on; (*contatar*) to get in touch with; **~ fazer** to try to do

produção [produ'sãw] (*pl* **-ões**) *f* production; (*volume de produção*) output; (*produto*) product; **~ em massa** *ou* **série** mass production

produtivo, -a [produ'tʃivu, a] *adj* productive; (*rendoso*) profitable

produto [pro'dutu] *m* product; (*renda*) proceeds *pl*, profit

produtor, a [produ'tor(a)] *adj* producing ▷ *m/f* producer

produzir [produ'zir] *vt* to produce; (*ocasionar*) to cause, bring about; (*render*) to bring in

proeminente [proemi'nẽtʃi] *adj* prominent

proeza [pro'eza] *f* achievement, feat

profanar [profa'nar] *vt* to

desecrate, profane; **profano, -a**
[pro'fanu, a] adj profane ▷ m/f
layman/woman
profecia [profe'sia] f prophecy
professor, a [profe'sor(a)] m/f
teacher; (universitário) lecturer
profeta, -tisa [pro'fɛta,
profe'tʃiza] m/f prophet;
profetizar [profetʃi'zar] vt, vi to
prophesy, predict
profissão [profi'sãw] (pl **-ões**) f
profession; **profissional**
[profisjo'naw] (pl **-ais**) adj, m/f
professional; **profissionalizante**
[profisjonali'zãtʃi] adj (ensino)
vocational
profundidade [profũdʒi'dadʒi] f
depth
profundo, -a [pro'fũdu, a] adj
deep; (fig) profound
profusão [profu'zãw] f profusion,
abundance
prognóstico [prog'nɔstʃiku] m
prediction, forecast
programa [pro'grama] m
programme (Brit), program (US);
(Comput) program; (plano) plan;
(diversão) thing to do; (de um curso)
syllabus; **programação**
[programa'sãw] f planning; (TV,
Rádio, Comput) programming;
programador, a
[programa'dor(a)] m/f
programmer; **programar**
[progra'mar] vt to plan; (Comput)
to program
progredir [progre'dʒir] vi to
progress; (avançar) to move
forward; (infecção) to progress
progressista [progre'sista] adj, m/f
progressive
progressivo, -a [progre'sivu, a]
adj progressive; (gradual) gradual
progresso [pro'grɛsu] m progress

progrido etc [pro'gridu] vb ver
progredir
proibição [proibi'sãw] (pl **-ões**) f
prohibition, ban
proibir [proi'bir] vt to prohibit;
(livro, espetáculo) to ban; **"é
proibido fumar"** "no smoking"; **~
alguém de fazer, ~ que alguém
faça** to forbid sb to do
projeção [proʒe'sãw] (pl **-ões**) f
projection
projetar [proʒe'tar] vt to project
projétil [pro'ʒɛtʃiw] (pl **-eis**) m
projectile, missile
projeto [pro'ʒetu] m project;
(plano) plan; (Tec) design; **~ de lei**
bill
projetor [proʒe'tor] m (Cinema)
projector
proliferar [prolife'rar] vi to
proliferate
prolongação [prolõga'sãw] f
extension
prolongado, -a [prolõ'gadu, a] adj
prolonged; (alongado) extended
prolongar [prolõ'gar] vt to extend,
lengthen; (decisão etc) to postpone;
(vida) to prolong; **prolongar-se** vr
to extend; (durar) to last
promessa [pro'mɛsa] f promise
prometer [prome'ter] vt, vi to
promise
promíscuo, -a [pro'miskwu, a] adj
disorderly, mixed up;
(comportamento sexual)
promiscuous
promissor, a [promi'sor(a)] adj
promising
promoção [promo'sãw] (pl **-ões**) f
promotion; **fazer ~ de alguém/
algo** to promote sb/sth
promotor, a [promo'tor(a)] m/f
promoter; (Jur) prosecutor
promover [promo'ver] vt to

p

promote; (*causar*) to bring about
pronome [pro'nɔmi] *m* pronoun
pronto, -a [prõtu, a] *adj* ready;
(*rápido*) quick, speedy; (*imediato*)
prompt ⊳ *adv* promptly; **de ~**
promptly; **estar ~ a ...** to be
prepared *ou* willing to ...;
pronto-socorro (*pl* **prontos-
socorros**) *m* (*BR*) casualty (*Brit*),
emergency room (*US*); (*PT: reboque*)
tow truck
pronúncia [pro'nũsja] *f*
pronunciation; (*Jur*) indictment
pronunciar [pronũ'sjar] *vt* to
pronounce; (*discurso*) to make,
deliver; (*Jur: réu*) to indict;
(: *sentença*) to pass
propaganda [propa'gãda] *f* (*Pol*)
propaganda; (*Com*) advertising;
(: *uma propaganda*) advert,
advertisement; **fazer ~ de** to
advertise
propagar [propa'gar] *vt* to
propagate; (*fig: difundir*) to
disseminate
propensão [propẽ'sãw] (*pl* **-ões**) *f*
inclination, tendency; **propenso,
-a** [pro'pẽsu, a] *adj*: **propenso a**
inclined to; **ser propenso a** to be
inclined to, have a tendency to
propina [pro'pina] *f* (*gorjeta*) tip;
(*PT: cota*) fee
propor [pro'por] (*irreg: como* **pôr**) *vt*
to propose; (*oferecer*) to offer; (*um
problema*) to pose; **propor-se** *vr*:
~-se (a) fazer (*pretender*) to intend
to do; (*visar*) to aim to do;
(*dispor-se*) to decide to do;
(*oferecer-se*) to offer to do
proporção [propor'sãw] (*pl* **-ões**) *f*
proportion; **proporções** *fpl*
(*dimensões*) dimensions;
proporcional [proporsjo'naw] (*pl*
-ais) *adj* proportional;

proporcionar [proporsjo'nar] *vt*
to provide, give; (*adaptar*) to
adjust, adapt
proposição [propozi'sãw] (*pl* **-ões**)
f proposition, proposal
proposital [propozi'taw] (*pl* **-ais**)
adj intentional
propósito [pro'pɔzitu] *m* (*intenção*)
purpose; (*objetivo*) aim; **a ~** by the
way; **a ~ de** with regard to; **de ~** on
purpose
proposta [pro'pɔsta] *f* proposal;
(*oferecimento*) offer
propriamente [proprja'mẽtʃi] *adv*
properly, exactly; **~ falando** *ou* **dito**
strictly speaking
propriedade [proprje'dadʒi] *f*
property; (*direito de proprietário*)
ownership; (*o que é apropriado*)
propriety
proprietário, -a [proprje'tarju, a]
m/f owner, proprietor
próprio, -a ['prɔprju, a] *adj* own, of
one's own; (*mesmo*) very, selfsame;
(*hora, momento*) opportune, right;
(*nome*) proper; (*característico*)
characteristic; (*sentido*) proper,
true; (*depois de pronome*) -self; **~
(para)** suitable (for); **eu ~** I myself;
por si ~ of one's own accord; **ele é
o ~ inglês** he's a typical
Englishman; **é o ~** it's him himself
prorrogação [prohoga'sãw] (*pl*
-ões) *f* extension
prosa ['prɔza] *f* prose; (*conversa*)
chatter; (*fanfarrice*) boasting,
bragging ⊳ *adj* full of oneself
prospecto [pros'pɛktu] *m* leaflet;
(*em forma de livro*) brochure
prosperar [prospe'rar] *vi* to
prosper, thrive; **prosperidade**
[prosperi'dadʒi] *f* prosperity; (*bom
êxito*) success; **próspero, -a**
['prɔsperu, a] *adj* prosperous;

(*bem sucedido*) successful; (*favorável*) favourable (*Brit*), favorable (*US*)

prosseguir [prose'gir] *vt, vi* to continue; **~ em** to continue (with)

prostíbulo [pros'tʃibulu] *m* brothel

prostituta [prostʃi'tuta] *f* prostitute

prostrado, -a [pros'tradu, a] *adj* prostrate

protagonista [protago'nista] *m/f* protagonist

proteção [prote'sãw] *f* protection

proteger [prote'ʒer] *vt* to protect; **protegido, -a** [prote'ʒidu, a] *m/f* protégé(e)

proteína [prote'ina] *f* protein

protejo *etc* [pro'teʒu] *vb ver* **proteger**

protestante [protes'tãtʃi] *adj, m/f* Protestant

protestar [protes'tar] *vt, vi* to protest; **protesto** [pro'tɛstu] *m* protest

protetor, a [prote'tor(a)] *adj* protective ▷ *m/f* protector; **~ solar** sunscreen; **~ de tela** (*Comput*) screensaver

protuberância [protube'rãsja] *f* bump; **protuberante** [protube'rãtʃi] *adj* sticking out

prova ['prɔva] *f* proof; (*Tec: teste*) test, trial; (*Educ: exame*) examination; (*sinal*) sign; (*de comida, bebida*) taste; (*de roupa*) fitting; (*Esporte*) competition; (*Tip*) proof; **prova(s)** *f(pl)* (*Jur*) evidence *sg*; **à ~ de bala/fogo/água** bulletproof/fireproof/waterproof; **pôr à ~** to put to the test

provar [pro'var] *vt* to prove; (*comida*) to taste, try; (*roupa*) to try on ▷ *vi* to try

provável [pro'vavew] (*pl* **-eis**) *adj* probable, likely

provedor, a [prove'dor(a)] *m/f* provider; **~ de acesso à Internet** internet service provider

proveito [pro'vejtu] *m* advantage; (*ganho*) profit; **em ~ de** for the benefit of; **fazer ~ de** to make use of; **proveitoso, -a** [provej'tozu, ɔza] *adj* profitable, advantageous; (*útil*) useful

proveniente [prove'njẽtʃi] *adj*: **~ de** originating from; (*que resulta de*) arising from

prover [pro'ver] (*irreg: como* **ver**) *vt* to provide, supply; (*vaga*) to fill ▷ *vi*: **~ a** to take care of, see to

provérbio [pro'vɛrbju] *m* proverb

providência [provi'dẽsja] *f* providence; **providências** *fpl* (*medidas*) measures, steps; **providencial** [providẽ'sjaw] (*pl* **-ais**) *adj* opportune; **providenciar** [providẽ'sjar] *vt* to provide; (*tomar providências*) to arrange ▷ *vi* to make arrangements, take steps; **providenciar para que** to see to it that

província [pro'vĩsja] *f* province; **provinciano, -a** [provĩ'sjanu, a] *adj* provincial

provisório, -a [provi'zɔrju, a] *adj* provisional, temporary

provocador, a [provoka'dor(a)] *adj* provocative

provocante [provo'kãtʃi] *adj* provocative

provocar [provo'kar] *vt* to provoke; (*ocasionar*) to cause; (*atrair*) to tempt, attract; (*estimular*) to rouse, stimulate

próximo, -a ['prɔsimu, a] *adj* (*no espaço*) near, close; (*no tempo*) close; (*seguinte*) next; (*amigo, parente*) close; (*vizinho*)

P

neighbouring (*Brit*), neighboring (*US*) ▷ *adv* near ▷ *m* fellow man; **~ a** *ou* **de** near (to), close to; **até a próxima!** see you again soon!

prudência [pru'dēsja] *f* care, prudence; **prudente** [pru'dẽtʃi] *adj* prudent

prurido [pru'ridu] *m* itch

psicanálise [psika'nalizi] *f* psychoanalysis

psicologia [psikolo'ʒia] *f* psychology; **psicológico, -a** [psiko'lɔʒiku, a] *adj* psychological; **psicólogo, -a** [psi'kɔlogu, a] *m/f* psychologist

psique ['psiki] *f* psyche

psiquiatra [psi'kjatra] *m/f* psychiatrist

psiquiatria [psikja'tria] *f* psychiatry

psíquico, -a ['psikiku, a] *adj* psychological

puberdade [puber'dadʒi] *f* puberty

publicação [publika'sãw] *f* publication

publicar [publi'kar] *vt* to publish; (*divulgar*) to divulge; (*proclamar*) to announce

publicidade [publisi'dadʒi] *f* publicity; (*Com*) advertising; **publicitário, -a** [publisi'tarju, a] *adj* publicity *atr*; (*Com*) advertising *atr*

público, -a ['publiku, a] *adj* public ▷ *m* public; (*Cinema, Teatro etc*) audience

pude *etc* ['pudʒi] *vb ver* **poder**

pudera *etc* [pu'dɛra] *vb ver* **poder**

pudim [pu'dʒĩ] (*pl* **-ns**) *m* pudding

pudor [pu'dor] *m* bashfulness, modesty; (*moral*) decency

pular [pu'lar] *vi* to jump; (*no Carnaval*) to celebrate ▷ *vt* to jump (over); (*páginas, trechos*) to skip; **~**

Carnaval to celebrate Carnival; **~ corda** to skip

pulga ['puwga] *f* flea

pulmão [puw'mãw] (*pl* **-ões**) *m* lung

pulo¹ ['pulu] *m* jump; **dar um ~ em** to stop off at

pulo² *etc vb ver* **polir**

pulôver [pu'lover] (*BR*) *m* pullover

pulsação [puwsa'sãw] *f* pulsation, beating; (*Med*) pulse

pulseira [puw'sejra] *f* bracelet; (*de sapato*) strap

pulso ['puwsu] *m* (*Anat*) wrist; (*Med*) pulse; (*fig*) vigour (*Brit*), vigor (*US*), energy

punha *etc* ['puɲa] *vb ver* **pôr**

punhado [pu'ɲadu] *m* handful

punhal [pu'ɲaw] (*pl* **-ais**) *m* dagger

punho ['puɲu] *m* fist; (*de manga*) cuff; (*de espada*) hilt

punição [puni'sãw] (*pl* **-ões**) *f* punishment

punir [pu'nir] *vt* to punish

pupila [pu'pila] *f* (*Anat*) pupil

purê [pu're] *m* purée; **~ de batatas** mashed potatoes

pureza [pu'reza] *f* purity

purificar [purifi'kar] *vt* to purify

puritano, -a [puri'tanu, a] *adj* puritanical; (*seita*) puritan ▷ *m/f* puritan

puro, -a ['puru, a] *adj* pure; (*uísque etc*) neat; (*verdade*) plain; (*intenções*) honourable (*Brit*), honorable (*US*); (*estilo*) clear

pus¹ [pus] *m* pus

pus² *etc* [pujs] *vb ver* **pôr**

puser *etc* [pu'zer] *vb ver* **pôr**

puta ['puta] (*col!*) *f* whore; *ver tb* **puto**

puto, -a ['putu, a] (*col!*) *m/f* (*sem-vergonha*) bastard ▷ *adj* (*zangado*) furious; (*incrível*): **um ~ ...**

a hell of a ...; **o ~ de ...** the bloody ...

pútrido, -a ['putridu, a] *adj* putrid, rotten

puxador [puʃa'dor] *m* handle, knob

puxão [pu'ʃãw] (*pl* **-ões**) *m* tug, jerk

puxar [pu'ʃar] *vt* to pull; (*sacar*) to pull out; (*assunto*) to bring up; (*conversa*) to strike up; (*briga*) to pick ▷ *vi*: **~ de uma perna** to limp; **~ a** to take after

puxões [pu'ʃõjs] *mpl de* **puxão**

q

QG *abr m* (= *Quartel-General*) HQ

QI *abr m* (= *Quociente de Inteligência*) IQ

quadra ['kwadra] *f* (*quarteirão*) block; (*de tênis etc*) court; (*período*) time, period

quadrado, -a [kwa'dradu, a] *adj* square ▷ *m* square ▷ *m/f* (*col*) square

quadril [kwa'driw] (*pl* **-is**) *m* hip

quadrinho [kwa'driɲu] *m*: **história em ~s** (*BR*) cartoon, comic strip

quadris [kwa'dris] *mpl de* **quadril**

quadro ['kwadru] *m* painting; (*gravura, foto*) picture; (*lista*) list; (*tabela*) chart, table; (*Tec: painel*) panel; (*pessoal*) staff; (*time*) team; (*Teatro, fig*) scene; **quadro-negro** (*pl* **quadros-negros**) *m* blackboard

quadruplicar [kwadrupli'kar] *vt*,

vi to quadruple

qual [kwaw] (*pl* **-ais**) *pron* which ▷ *conj* as, like ▷ *excl* what!; **o ~** which; (*pessoa: suj*) who; (: *objeto*) whom; **seja ~ for** whatever *ou* whichever it may be; **cada ~** each one

qualidade [kwali'dadʒi] *f* quality

qualificação [kwalifika'sãw] (*pl* **-ões**) *f* qualification

qualificado, -a [kwalifi'kadu, a] *adj* qualified

qualificar [kwalifi'kar] *vt* to qualify; (*avaliar*) to evaluate; **qualificar-se** *vr* to qualify; **~ de** *ou* **como** to classify as

qualquer [kwaw'ker] (*pl* **quaisquer**) *adj, pron* any; **~ pessoa** anyone, anybody; **~ um dos dois** either; **~ que seja** whichever it may be; **a ~ momento** at any moment

quando [ˈkwãdu] *adv* when ▷ *conj* when; (*interrogativo*) when?; (*ao passo que*) whilst; **~ muito** at most

quantia [kwã'tʃia] *f* sum, amount

quantidade [kwãtʃi'dadʒi] *f* quantity, amount

quanto, -a [ˈkwãtu, a] *adj*
1 (*interrogativo: sg*) how much?; (: *pl*) how many?; **quanto tempo?** how long?

2 (*o que for necessário*) all that, as much as; **daremos quantos exemplares ele precisar** we'll give him as many copies as *ou* all the copies he needs

3: **tanto/tantos ... quanto** as much/many ... as
▷ *pron* **1** how much?; how many?; **quanto custa?** how much?; **a quanto está o jogo?** what's the score?

2: **tudo quanto** everything that, as much as

3: **tanto/tantos quanto ...** as much/as many as ...

4: **um tanto quanto** somewhat, rather
▷ *adv* **1**: **quanto a** as regards; **quanto a mim** as for me

2: **quanto antes** as soon as possible

3: **quanto mais** (*principalmente*) especially; (*muito menos*) let alone; **quanto mais cedo melhor** the sooner the better

4: **tanto quanto possível** as much as possible; **tão ... quanto ...** as ... as ...
▷ *conj*: **quanto mais trabalha, mais ele ganha** the more he works, the more he earns; **quanto mais, (tanto) melhor** the more, the better

quarenta [kwa'rẽta] *num* forty

quarentena [kwarẽ'tɛna] *f* quarantine

quaresma [kwa'rezma] *f* Lent

quarta [ˈkwarta] *f* (*tb*: **~-feira**) Wednesday; (*parte*) quarter; (*Auto*) fourth (gear); **quarta-feira** (*pl* **quartas-feiras**) *f* Wednesday; **quarta-feira de cinzas** Ash Wednesday

quarteirão [kwartej'rãw] (*pl* **-ões**) *m* (*de casas*) block

quartel [kwar'tɛw] (*pl* **-éis**) *m* barracks *sg*; **quartel-general** *m* headquarters *pl*

quarteto [kwar'tetu] *m* quartet(te)

quarto, -a [ˈkwartu, a] *num* fourth ▷ *m* quarter; (*aposento*) bedroom; **~ de banho** bathroom; **~ de dormir** bedroom; **três ~s de hora** three quarters of an hour

quase ['kwazi] *adv* almost, nearly; **~ nunca** hardly ever

quatorze [kwa'torzi] *num* fourteen

quatro ['kwatru] *num* four

 PALAVRA-CHAVE

que [ki] *conj* **1** (*com oração subordinada: muitas vezes não se traduz*) that; **ele disse que viria** he said (that) he would come; **não há nada que fazer** there's nothing to be done; **espero que sim/não** I hope so/not; **dizer que sim/não** to say yes/no

2 (*consecutivo: muitas vezes não se traduz*) that; **é tão pesado que não consigo levantá-lo** it's so heavy (that) I can't lift it

3 (*comparações*): **(do) que** than; *ver tb* **mais**; **menos**; **mesmo** ▷ *pron* **1** (*coisa*) which, that; (+ *prep*) which; **o chapéu que você comprou** the hat (that *ou* which) you bought

2 (*pessoa: suj*) who, that; (: *complemento*) whom, that; **o amigo que me levou ao museu** the friend who took me to the museum; **a moça que eu convidei** the girl (that *ou* whom) I invited

3 (*interrogativo*) what?; **o que você disse?** what did you say?

4 (*exclamação*) what!; **que pena!** what a pity!; **que lindo!** how lovely!

quê [ke] *m* (*col*) something ▷ *pron* what; **~!** what!; **não tem de ~** don't mention it; **para ~?** what for?; **por ~?** why?

quebra ['kɛbra] *f* break, rupture; (*falência*) bankruptcy; (*de energia elétrica*) cut; **de ~** in addition; **quebra-cabeça** (*pl* **quebra-cabeças**) *m* puzzle, problem; (*jogo*) jigsaw puzzle

quebrado, -a [ke'bradu, a] *adj* broken; (*cansado*) exhausted; (*falido*) bankrupt; (*carro, máquina*) broken down; (*telefone*) out of order

quebrar [ke'brar] *vt* to break ▷ *vi* to break; (*carro*) to break down; (*Com*) to go bankrupt; (*ficar sem dinheiro*) to go broke

queda ['kɛda] *f* fall; (*fig*) downfall; **ter ~ para algo** to have a bent for sth; **~ de barreira** landslide; **queda-d'água** (*pl* **quedas-d'água**) *f* waterfall

queijo ['kejʒu] *m* cheese

queimado, -a [kej'madu, a] *adj* burnt; (*de sol: machucado*) sunburnt; (: *bronzeado*) brown, tanned; (*plantas, folhas*) dried up

queimadura [kejma'dura] *f* burn; (*de sol*) sunburn

queimar [kej'mar] *vt* to burn; (*roupa*) to scorch; (*com líquido*) to scald; (*bronzear a pele*) to tan; (*planta, folha*) to wither ▷ *vi* to burn; **queimar-se** *vr* (*pessoa*) to burn o.s.; (*bronzear-se*) to tan

queima-roupa *f*: **à ~** point-blank, at point-blank range

queira *etc* ['kejra] *vb ver* **querer**

queixa ['kejʃa] *f* complaint; (*lamentação*) lament; **fazer ~ de alguém** to complain about sb

queixar-se [kej'ʃarsi] *vr* to complain; **~ de** to complain about; (*dores etc*) to complain of

queixo ['kejʃu] *m* chin; (*maxilar*) jaw; **bater o ~** to shiver

quem [kẽj] *pron* who; (*como objeto*) who(m); **de ~ é isto?** whose is this?; **~ diria!** who would have thought (it)!; **~ sabe** (*talvez*) perhaps

q

Quênia ['kenja] m: **o ~** Kenya
quente ['kẽtʃi] adj hot; (roupa) warm
quentinha [kẽ'tʃiɲa] f heatproof
carton (for food); (de restaurante)
doggy bag
quer [ker] conj: **~ ... ~ ...** whether ...
or ...; **~ chova ~ não** whether it
rains or not; **onde/quando/quem
~ que** wherever/whenever/
whoever; **o que ~ que seja**
whatever it is

⬤ **PALAVRA-CHAVE**

querer [ke'rer] vt **1** (desejar) to want;
quero mais dinheiro I want more
money; **queria um chá** I'd like a
cup of tea; **quero ajudar/que vá**
I want to help/you to go; **você vai
querer sair amanhã?** do you want
to go out tomorrow?; **eu vou
querer uma cerveja** (num bar etc)
I'd like a beer; **por/sem querer**
intentionally/unintentionally;
como queira as you wish
2 (perguntas para pedir algo): **você
quer fechar a janela?** will you
shut the window?; **quer me dar
uma mão?** can you give me a hand?
3 (amar) to love
4 (convite): **quer entrar/sentar** do
come in/sit down
5: **querer dizer** (significar) to mean;
(pretender dizer) to mean to say;
quero dizer I mean; **quer dizer**
(com outras palavras) in other words
▷ vi: **querer bem a** to be fond of
querer-se vr to love one another
▷ m (vontade) wish; (afeto)
affection

querido, -a [ke'ridu, a] adj dear
▷ m/f darling; **Q~ João** Dear John
querosene [kero'zɛni] m kerosene

questão [kes'tãw] (pl **-ões**) f
question; (problema) issue,
question; (Jur) case; (contenda)
dispute, quarrel; **fazer ~ (de)** to
insist (on); **em ~** in question; **há ~
de um ano** about a year ago;
questionar [kestʃjo'nar] vi to
question ▷ vt to question, call into
question; **questionário**
[kestʃjo'narju] m questionnaire;
questionável [kestʃjo'navew] (pl
-eis) adj questionable
quicar [ki'kar] vt, vi to bounce
quieto, -a ['kjɛtu, a] adj quiet;
(imóvel) still; **quietude** [kje'tudʒi]
f calm, tranquillity
quilate [ki'latʃi] m carat
quilo ['kilu] m kilo; **quilobyte**
[kilo'bajtʃi] m kilobyte;
quilograma [kilo'grama] m
kilogram; **quilometragem**
[kilome'traʒẽ] f number of
kilometres ou kilometers travelled,
≈ mileage; **quilômetro**
[ki'lometru] m kilometre (Brit),
kilometer (US); **quilowatt**
[kilo'watʃi] m kilowatt
química ['kimika] f chemistry
químico, -a ['kimiku, a] adj
chemical ▷ m/f chemist
quina ['kina] f corner; (de mesa etc)
edge; **de ~** edgeways (Brit),
edgewise (US)
quindim [kĩ'dʒĩ] m sweet made of
egg yolks, coconut and sugar
quinhão [ki'ɲãw] (pl **-ões**) m share,
portion
quinhentos, -as [ki'ɲẽtus, as]
num five hundred
quinhões [ki'ɲõjs] mpl de **quinhão**
quinquilharias [kĩkiʎa'rias] fpl
odds and ends; (miudezas)
knick-knacks, trinkets
quinta ['kĩta] f (tb: **~-feira**)

Thursday; (*propriedade*) estate; (*PT*) farm; **quinta-feira** ['kĩta-'fejra] (*pl* **quintas-feiras**) *f* Thursday

quintal [kĩ'taw] (*pl* **-ais**) *m* back yard

quinteto [kĩ'tetu] *m* quintet(te)

quinto, -a ['kĩtu, a] *num* fifth

quinze ['kĩzɪ] *num* fifteen; **duas e ~** a quarter past (*Brit*) *ou* after (*US*) two; **~ para as sete** a quarter to (*Brit*) *ou* of (*US*) seven

quinzena [kĩ'zɛna] *f* two weeks, fortnight (*Brit*); **quinzenal** [kĩze'naw] (*pl* **-ais**) *adj* fortnightly; **quinzenalmente** [kĩzenaw'mẽtʃi] *adv* fortnightly

quiosque ['kjɔski] *m* kiosk

quis *etc* [kiz] *vb ver* **querer**

quiser *etc* [ki'zer] *vb ver* **querer**

quisto ['kistu] *m* cyst

quitanda [ki'tãda] *f* grocer's (shop) (*Brit*), grocery store (*US*)

quitar [ki'tar] *vt* (*dívida: pagar*) to pay off; (: *perdoar*) to cancel; (*devedor*) to release

quite ['kitʃi] *adj* (*livre*) free; (*com um credor*) squared up; (*igualado*) even; **estar ~ (com alguém)** to be quits (with sb)

quitute [ki'tutʃi] *m* titbit (*Brit*), tidbit (*US*)

quota ['kwɔta] *f* quota; (*porção*) share, portion

quotidiano, -a [kwotʃi'dʒjanu, a] *adj* everyday

r

R *abr* (= *rua*) St

R$ *abr* = **real**

rã [hã] *f* frog

rabanete [haba'netʃi] *m* radish

rabiscar [habis'kar] *vt* to scribble; (*papel*) to scribble on ▷ *vi* to scribble; (*desenhar*) to doodle; **rabisco** [ha'bisku] *m* scribble

rabo ['habu] *m* tail

rabugento, -a [habu'ʒẽtu, a] *adj* grumpy

raça ['hasa] *f* breed; (*grupo étnico*) race; **cão/cavalo de ~** pedigree dog/thoroughbred horse

racha ['haʃa] *f* (*fenda*) split; (*greta*) crack; **rachadura** [haʃa'dura] *f* crack; **rachar** [ha'ʃar] *vt* to crack; (*objeto, despesas*) to split; (*lenha*) to chop ▷ *vi* to split; (*cristal*) to crack; **rachar-se** *vr* to split; to crack

racial [ha'sjaw] (*pl* **-ais**) *adj* racial

raciocínio [hasjo'sinju] *m*

reasoning

racional [hasjo'naw] (*pl* **-ais**) *adj*
rational; **racionalizar**
[hasjonali'zar] *vt* to rationalize

racionamento [hasjona'mētu] *m*
rationing

racismo [ha'sizmu] *m* racism;
racista [ha'sista] *adj, m/f* racist

radar [ha'dar] *m* radar

radiação [hadʒja'sãw] *f* radiation

radiador [hadʒja'dor] *m* radiator

radical [hadʒi'kaw] (*pl* **-ais**) *adj*
radical

radicar-se [hadʒi'karsi] *vr* to take
root; (*fixar residência*) to settle

rádio ['hadʒju] *m* radio; (*Quím*)
radium; **radioativo, -a**
[hadʒjua'tʃivu, a] *adj* radioactive;
radiodifusão [hadʒjodʒifu'zãw] *f*
broadcasting; **radiografar**
[hadʒjogra'far] *vt* to X-ray;
radiografia [hadʒjogra'fia] *f*
X-ray

raia ['haja] *f* (*risca*) line; (*fronteira*)
boundary; (*limite*) limit; (*de corrida*)
lane; (*peixe*) ray

raiar [ha'jar] *vi* to shine

rainha [ha'iɲa] *f* queen

raio ['haju] *m* (*de sol*) ray; (*de luz*)
beam; (*de roda*) spoke; (*relâmpago*)
flash of lightning; (*distância*) range;
(*Mat*) radius; **~s X** X-rays

raiva ['hajva] *f* rage, fury; (*Med*)
rabies *sg*; **estar/ficar com ~ (de)**
to be/get angry (with); **ter ~ de** to
hate; **raivoso, -a** [haj'vozu, ɔza]
adj furious

raiz [ha'iz] *f* root; (*origem*) source;
~ quadrada square root

rajada [ha'ʒada] *f* (*vento*) gust

ralado, -a [ha'ladu, a] *adj* grated;
ralador [hala'dor] *m* grater

ralar [ha'lar] *vt* to grate

ralhar [ha'ʎar] *vi* to scold; **~ com**

alguém to tell sb off

rali [ha'li] *m* rally

ralo, -a ['halu, a] *adj* (*cabelo*)
thinning; (*tecido*) flimsy;
(*vegetação*) sparse; (*sopa*) thin,
watery; (*café*) weak ▷ *m* (*de
regador*) rose, nozzle; (*de pia,
banheiro*) drain

rama ['hama] *f* branches *pl*, foliage;
pela ~ superficially; **ramagem**
[ha'maʒē] *f* branches *pl*, foliage;
ramal [ha'maw] (*pl* **-ais**) *m* (*Ferro*)
branch line; (*Tel*) extension; (*Auto*)
side road

ramificar-se [hamifi'karsi] *vr* to
branch out

ramo ['hamu] *m* branch; (*profissão,
negócios*) line; (*de flores*) bunch;
Domingo de R~s Palm Sunday

rampa ['hãpa] *f* ramp; (*ladeira*)
slope

ranger [hã'ʒer] *vi* to creak ▷ *vt*: **~ os
dentes** to grind one's teeth

ranhura [ha'ɲura] *f* groove; (*para
moeda*) slot

rapar [ha'par] *vt* to scrape; (*a
barba*) to shave; (*o cabelo*) to shave
off

rapariga [hapa'riga] *f* girl

rapaz [ha'pajz] *m* boy; (*col*) lad

rapidez [hapi'dez] *f* speed

rápido, -a ['hapidu, a] *adj* quick,
fast ▷ *adv* fast, quickly ▷ *m* (*trem*)
express

rapina [ha'pina] *f* robbery; **ave de
~** bird of prey

raptar [hap'tar] *vt* to kidnap;
rapto ['haptu] *m* kidnapping;
raptor [hap'tor] *m* kidnapper

raquete [ha'ketʃi] *f* racquet

raquítico, -a [ha'kitʃiku, a] *adj*
(*franzino*) puny; (*vegetação*) poor

raramente [hara'mētʃi] *adv* rarely,
seldom

raro, -a ['haru, a] *adj* rare ▷ *adv* rarely, seldom

rasgado, -a [haz'gadu, a] *adj* (*roupa*) torn, ripped

rasgão [haz'gãw] (*pl* **-ões**) *m* tear, rip

rasgar [haz'gar] *vt* to tear, rip; (*destruir*) to tear up, rip up; **rasgar-se** *vr* to split; **rasgo** ['hazgu] *m* tear, rip

rasgões [haz'gõjs] *mpl de* **rasgão**

raso, -a ['hazu, a] *adj* (*liso*) flat, level; (*não fundo*) shallow; (*baixo*) low; **soldado ~** private

raspa ['haspa] *f* (*de madeira*) shaving; (*de metal*) filing

raspão [has'pãw] (*pl* **-ões**) *m* scratch, graze

raspar [has'par] *vt* to scrape; (*alisar*) to file; (*tocar de raspão*) to graze; (*arranhar*) to scratch; (*pelos, cabeça*) to shave; (*apagar*) to rub out ▷ *vi*: **~ em** to scrape

raspões [has'põjs] *mpl de* **raspão**

rasteira [has'tejra] *f*: **dar uma ~ em alguém** to trip sb up

rasteiro, -a [has'tejru, a] *adj* crawling; (*planta*) creeping

rastejar [haste'ʒar] *vi* to crawl; (*furtivamente*) to creep; (*fig: rebaixar-se*) to grovel ▷ *vt* (*fugitivo etc*) to track

rasto ['hastu] *m* (*pegada*) track; (*de veículo*) trail; (*fig*) sign, trace; **andar de ~s** to crawl

rastro ['hastru] *m* = **rasto**

rata ['hata] *f* rat; (*pequena*) mouse

ratificar [hatʃifi'kar] *vt* to ratify

rato ['hatu] *m* rat; (*rato pequeno*) mouse; **~ de hotel/praia** hotel/ beach thief; **ratoeira** [ha'twejra] *f* rat trap, mousetrap

ravina [ha'vina] *f* ravine

razão [ha'zãw] (*pl* **-ões**) *f* reason; (*argumento*) reasoning; (*Mat*) ratio ▷ *m* (*Com*) ledger; **à ~ de** at the rate of; **em ~ de** on account of; **dar ~ a alguém** to support sb; **ter/não ter ~** to be right/wrong; **razoável** [ha'zwavew] (*pl* **-eis**) *adj* reasonable

r/c (*PT*) *abr* = **rés do chão**

ré [hɛ] *f* (*Auto*) reverse (gear); **dar (marcha à) ré** to reverse, back up; *ver tb* **réu**

reabastecer [heabaste'ser] *vt* (*avião*) to refuel; (*carro*) to fill up; **reabastecer-se** *vr*: **~-se de** to replenish one's supply of

reação [hea'sãw] (*pl* **-ões**) *f* reaction

reagir [hea'ʒir] *vi* to react; (*doente, time perdedor*) to fight back; **~ a** (*resistir*) to resist; (*protestar*) to rebel against

reais [he'ajs] *adj pl de* **real**

reaja *etc* [he'aʒa] *vb ver* **reagir**; **reaver**

reajuste [hea'ʒustʃi] *m* adjustment

real [he'aw] (*pl* **-ais**) *adj* real; (*relativo à realeza*) royal ▷ *m* (*moeda*) real

r

● REAL

● The Brazilian currency, the **real**, was introduced in 1994 as part of a comprehensive economic stabilization package known as the **Plano Real**. This brought an end to some thirty years of hyperinflation which saw successive devaluations and name-changes to the Brazilian currency, from *cruzeiro* to *cruzado* (1986), to *cruzado novo* (1989), back to *cruzeiro* (1990), to *cruzeiro real* (1993) and finally to *real* (1994).

- The *real* is subdivided into 100
- *centavos*. The currency symbol is
- R$ and a comma is used to
- separate *reais* and *centavos*, e.g.
- R$ 2,40 (two *reais* and forty
- *centavos*).

realçar [heaw'sar] *vt* to highlight;
realce [he'awsi] *m* emphasis;
(*mais brilho*) highlight; **dar realce a**
to enhance

realeza [hea'leza] *f* royalty

realidade [heali'dadʒi] *f* reality; **na
~** actually, in fact; **~ virtual** virtual
reality

realista [hea'lista] *adj* realistic
▷ *m/f* realist

realização [healiza'sãw] *f*
fulfilment (*Brit*), fulfillment (*US*),
realization; (*de projeto*) execution,
carrying out

realizador, a [healiza'dor(a)] *adj*
enterprising

realizar [heali'zar] *vt* to achieve;
(*projeto*) to carry out; (*ambições,
sonho*) to fulfil (*Brit*), fulfill (*US*),
realize; (*negócios*) to transact;
(*perceber, convertir en dinheiro*) to
realize; **realizar-se** *vr* to take
place; (*ambições*) to be realized;
(*sonhos*) to come true

realmente [heaw'mẽtʃi] *adv* really;
(*de fato*) actually

reanimar [heani'mar] *vt* to revive;
(*encorajar*) to encourage;
reanimar-se *vr* to cheer up

reatar [hea'tar] *vt* to resume, take
up again

reaver [hea'ver] *vt* to recover, get
back

rebaixar [hebaj'ʃar] *vt* to lower;
(*reduzir*) to reduce; (*time*) to
relegate; (*funcionário*) to demote;
(*humilhar*) to put down ▷ *vi* to drop;

rebaixar-se *vr* to demean o.s.

rebanho [he'baɲu] *m* (*de carneiros,
fig*) flock; (*de gado, elefantes*) herd

rebelar-se [hebe'larsi] *vr* to rebel;
rebelde [he'bɛwdʒi] *adj*
rebellious; (*indisciplinado*) unruly,
wild ▷ *m/f* rebel; **rebeldia**
[hebew'dʒia] *f* rebelliousness; (*fig*:
obstinação) stubbornness;
(: *oposição*) defiance

rebelião [hebe'ljãw] (*pl* **-ões**) *f*
rebellion

rebentar [hebẽ'tar] *vi* (*guerra*) to
break out; (*louça*) to smash; (*corda*)
to snap; (*represa*) to burst; (*ondas*)
to break ▷ *vt* to smash, to snap;
(*porta, ponte*) to break down

rebocador [heboka'dor] *m*
tug(boat)

rebocar [hebo'kar] *vt* (*paredes*) to
plaster; (*dar reboque a*) to tow

rebolar [hebo'lar] *vt* to swing ▷ *vi*
to sway

reboque [he'bɔki] *m* tow; (*veículo:
tb*: **carro ~**) trailer; (*cabo*) towrope;
(*BR: de socorro*) tow truck; **a ~** on *ou*
in (*US*) tow

reboque *etc vb ver* **rebocar**

rebuçado [hebu'sadu] (*PT*) *m*
sweet, candy (*US*)

recado [he'kadu] *m* message;
deixar ~ to leave a message

recair [heka'ir] *vi* (*doente*) to relapse

recalcar [hekaw'kar] *vt* to repress

recalque *etc vb ver* **recalcar**

recanto [he'kãtu] *m* corner, nook

recapitular [hekapitu'lar] *vt* to
sum up, recapitulate; (*fatos*) to
review; (*matéria escolar*) to revise

recarga [he'karga] *f* (*de celular*)
top-up; **preciso fazer a ~ do meu
celular** I need to top up my mobile

recarregar [hekahe'gar] *vt* (*celular*)
to top up; (*bateria*) recharge;

(*cartucho*) refill

recatado, -a [heka'tadu, a] *adj*
(*modesto*) modest; (*reservado*)
reserved

recauchutado, -a [hekawʃu'tadu,
a] *adj*: **pneu ~** (*Auto*) retread,
remould (*Brit*)

recear [he'sjar] *vt* to fear ▷ *vi*:
~ por to fear for; **~ fazer/que** to be
afraid to do/that

receber [hese'ber] *vt* to receive;
(*ganhar*) to earn, get; (*hóspedes*) to
take in; (*convidados*) to entertain;
(*acolher bem*) to welcome ▷ *vi*
(*receber convidados*) to entertain;
recebimento [hesebi'mẽtu] (*BR*)
m reception; (*de uma carta*) receipt;
acusar o recebimento de to
acknowledge receipt of

receio [he'seju] *m* fear; **ter ~ de
que** to fear that

receita [he'sejta] *f* income; (*do
Estado*) revenue; (*Med*)
prescription; (*culinária*) recipe; **R~
Federal** ≈ Inland Revenue (*Brit*),
≈ IRS (*US*); **receitar** [hesej'tar] *vt*
to prescribe

recém [he'sẽ] *adv* recently, newly;
recém-casado, -a *adj*: **os
recém-casados** the newlyweds;
recém-chegado, -a *m/f*
newcomer; **recém-nascido, -a**
m/f newborn child

recente [he'sẽtʃi] *adj* recent; (*novo*)
new ▷ *adv* recently;
recentemente [hesẽtʃi'mẽtʃi] *adv*
recently

receoso, -a [he'sjozu, ɔza] *adj*
frightened, fearful; **estar ~ de
(fazer)** to be afraid of (doing)

recepção [hesep'sãw] (*pl* -**ões**) *f*
reception; (*PT*: *de uma carta*)
receipt; **acusar a ~ de** (*PT*) to
acknowledge receipt of;

recepcionista [hesepsjo'nista]
m/f receptionist

receptivo, -a [hesep'tʃivu, a] *adj*
receptive; (*acolhedor*) welcoming

receptor [hesep'tor] *m* receiver

recessão [hese'sãw] (*pl* -**ões**) *f*
recession

recessões [hese'sõjs] *fpl de*
recessão

recheado, -a [he'ʃjadu, a] *adj* (*ave,
carne*) stuffed; (*empada, bolo*) filled;
(*cheio*) full, crammed

rechear [he'ʃjar] *vt* to fill; (*ave,
carne*) to stuff; **recheio** [he'ʃeju] *m*
stuffing; (*de empada, de bolo*) filling;
(*o conteúdo*) contents *pl*

rechonchudo, -a [heʃõ'ʃudu, a] *adj*
chubby, plump

recibo [he'sibu] *m* receipt

reciclar [hesi'klar] *vt* to recycle

reciclável [hesi'klavew] (*pl* -**eis**) *adj*
recyclable

recinto [he'sĩtu] *m* enclosure;
(*lugar*) area

recipiente [hesi'pjẽtʃi] *m*
container, receptacle

recíproco, -a [he'siproku, a] *adj*
reciprocal

recitar [hesi'tar] *vt* to recite

reclamação [heklama'sãw] (*pl*
-**ões**) *f* complaint

reclamar [hekla'mar] *vt* to
demand; (*herança*) to claim ▷ *vi*:
~ (de) (*comida etc*) to complain
(about)

reclinar [hekli'nar] *vt* to rest, lean;
reclinar-se *vr* to lie back;
(*deitar-se*) to lie down

recobrar [heko'brar] *vt* to recover,
get back; **recobrar-se** *vr* to
recover

recolher [heko'ʎer] *vt* to collect;
(*gado, roupa do varal*) to bring in;
(*juntar*) to collect up; **recolhido, -a**

[heko'ʎidu, a] *adj* (*lugar*) secluded; (*pessoa*) withdrawn;
recolhimento [hekoʎi'mẽtu] *m* retirement; (*arrecadação*) collection; (*ato de levar*) taking
recomeçar [hekome'sar] *vt, vi* to restart
recomendação [hekomẽda'sãw] (*pl* **-ões**) *f* recommendation; **recomendações** *fpl* (*cumprimentos*) regards
recomendar [hekomẽ'dar] *vt* to recommend; **recomendável** [hekomẽ'davew] (*pl* **-eis**) *adj* advisable
recompensa [hekõ'pẽsa] *f* reward; **recompensar** [hekõpẽ'sar] *vt* to reward
recompor [hekõ'por] (*irreg: como* **pôr**) *vt* to reorganize; (*restabelecer*) to restore
reconciliar [hekõsi'ljar] *vt* to reconcile
reconhecer [hekoɲe'ser] *vt* to recognize; (*Mil*) to reconnoitre (*Brit*), reconnoiter (*US*); **reconhecido, -a** [hekoɲe'sidu, a] *adj* recognized; (*agradecido*) grateful, thankful; **reconhecimento** [hekoɲesi'mẽtu] *m* recognition; (*admissão*) admission; (*gratidão*) gratitude; (*Mil*) reconnaissance; **reconhecível** [hekoɲe'sivew] (*pl* **-eis**) *adj* recognizable
reconstruir [hekõs'trwir] *vt* to rebuild
recordação [hekorda'sãw] (*pl* **-ões**) *f* (*reminiscência*) memory; (*objeto*) memento
recordar [hekor'dar] *vt* to remember; **recordar-se** *vr*: **~-se de** to remember; **~ algo a alguém** to remind sb of sth

recorde [he'kɔrdʒi] *adj inv* record *atr* ▷ *m* record
recorrer [heko'her] *vi*: **~ a** to turn to; (*valer-se de*) to resort to
recortar [hekor'tar] *vt* to cut out; **recorte** [he'kɔrtʃi] *m* (*ato*) cutting out; (*de jornal*) cutting, clipping
recreação [hekrja'sãw] *f* recreation
recreio [he'kreju] *m* recreation
recriminar [hekrimi'nar] *vt* to reproach, reprove
recrutamento [hekruta'mẽtu] *m* recruitment
recrutar [hekru'tar] *vt* to recruit
recuar [he'kwar] *vt* to move back ▷ *vi* to move back; (*exército*) to retreat
recuperar [hekupe'rar] *vt* to recover; (*tempo perdido*) to make up for; (*reabilitar*) to rehabilitate; **recuperar-se** *vr* to recover
recurso [he'kursu] *m* resource; (*Jur*) appeal; **recursos** *mpl* (*financeiros*) resources
recusa [he'kuza] *f* refusal; (*negação*) denial; **recusar** [heku'zar] *vt* to refuse, to deny; **recusar-se** *vr*: **recusar-se a** to refuse to
redação [heda'sãw] (*pl* **-ões**) *f* (*ato*) writing; (*Educ*) composition, essay; (*redatores*) editorial staff
redator, a [heda'tor(a)] *m/f* editor
rede ['hedʒi] *f* net; (*de dormir*) hammock; (*Ferro, Tec, Comput, TV, fig*) network; **a ~** (*a Internet*) the web; **~ de área local** local area network; **~ sem fio** wireless network
rédea ['hɛdʒja] *f* rein
redentor, a [hedẽ'tor(a)] *adj* redeeming
redigir [hedʒi'ʒir] *vt, vi* to write

redobrar [hedo'brar] *vt* (*aumentar*) to increase; (*esforços*) to redouble

redondamente [hedõda'mẽtʃi] *adv* (*completamente*) completely

redondeza [hedõ'deza] *f* roundness; **redondezas** *fpl* surroundings

redondo, -a [he'dõdu, a] *adj* round

redor [he'dor] *m*: **ao** *ou* **em ~ (de)** around, round about

redução [hedu'sãw] (*pl* **-ões**) *f* reduction

redundância [hedũ'dãsja] *f* redundancy; **redundante** [hedũ'dãtʃi] *adj* redundant

reduzido, -a [hedu'zidu, a] *adj* reduced; (*limitado*) limited; (*pequeno*) small

reduzir [hedu'zir] *vt* to reduce; **reduzir-se** *vr*: **~-se a** to be reduced to; (*fig: resumir-se em*) to come down to

reembolsar [heẽbow'sar] *vt* to recover; (*restituir*) to reimburse; (*depósito*) to refund; **reembolso** [heẽ'bowsu] *m* (*de depósito*) refund; (*de despesa*) reimbursement

reencontro [heẽ'kõtru] *m* reunion

refeição [hefej'sãw] (*pl* **-ões**) *f* meal; **refeitório** [hefej'tɔrju] *m* refectory

refém [he'fẽ] (*pl* **-ns**) *m* hostage

referência [hefe'rẽsja] *f* reference; **referências** *fpl* (*informaçoes para emprego*) references; **fazer ~ a** to make reference to, refer to

referente [hefe'rẽtʃi] *adj*: **~ a** concerning, regarding

referir [hefe'rir] *vt* to relate, tell; **referir-se** *vr*: **~-se a** to refer to

REFESA *f* (= *Rede Ferroviária SA*) Brazilian rail network

refinamento [hefina'mẽtu] *m* refinement

refinaria [hefina'ria] *f* refinery

refiro *etc* [he'firu] *vb ver* **referir**

refletir [hefle'tʃir] *vt* to reflect ▷ *vi*: **~ em** *ou* **sobre** to consider, think about

reflexão [heflek'sãw] (*pl* **-ões**) *f* reflection

reflexo, -a [he'flɛksu, a] *adj* (*luz*) reflected; (*ação*) reflex ▷ *m* reflection; (*Anat*) reflex; (*no cabelo*) streak

reflexões [heflek'sõjs] *fpl de* **reflexão**

reflito *etc* [he'flitu] *vb ver* **refletir**

reforçado, -a [hefor'sadu, a] *adj* reinforced; (*pessoa*) strong; (*café da manhã, jantar*) hearty

reforçar [hefor'sar] *vt* to reinforce; (*revigorar*) to invigorate; **reforço** [he'forsu] *m* reinforcement

reforma [he'fɔrma] *f* reform; (*Arq*) renovation; **reformado, -a** [hefor'madu, a] *adj* reformed, renovated; (*Mil*) retired; **reformar** [hefor'mar] *vt* to reform, to renovate; **reformar-se** *vr* to reform

refrão [he'frãw] (*pl* **-ões**) *m* chorus, refrain; (*provérbio*) saying

refratário, -a [hefra'tarju, a] *adj* (*Tec*) heat-resistant; (*Culin*) ovenproof

refrear [hefre'ar] *vt* (*cavalo*) to rein in; (*inimigo*) to contain, check; (*paixões, raiva*) to control; **refrear-se** *vr* to restrain o.s.

refrescante [hefres'kãtʃi] *adj* refreshing

refrescar [hefres'kar] *vt* (*ar, ambiente*) to cool; (*pessoa*) to refresh ▷ *vi* to cool down

refresco [he'fresku] *m* cool fruit drink, squash; **refrescos** *mpl* (*refrigerantes*) refreshments

r

refrigerador [hefrize'radox] *m* refrigerator, fridge (*Brit*)

refrigerante [hefrize'rãtʃi] *m* soft drink

refugiado, -a [hefu'ʒjadu, a] *adj, m/f* refugee

refugiar-se [hefu'ʒjarsi] *vr* to take refuge; **refúgio** [he'fuʒju] *m* refuge

refugo [he'fugu] *m* rubbish, garbage (*US*); (*mercadoria*) reject

rega ['hɛga] *f* (*PT*) irrigation

regador [hega'dox] *m* watering can

regalia [hega'lia] *f* privilege

regar [he'gax] *vt* (*plantas, jardim*) to water; (*umedecer*) to sprinkle

regatear [hega'tʃjax] *vt* (*o preço*) to haggle over, bargain for ▷ *vi* to haggle

regenerar [heʒene'rax] *vt* to regenerate

reger [he'ʒex] *vt* to govern; (*orquestra*) to conduct; (*empresa*) to run ▷ *vi* to rule; (*maestro*) to conduct

região [he'ʒjãw] (*pl* **-ões**) *f* region, area

regime [he'ʒimi] *m* (*Pol*) regime; (*dieta*) diet; (*maneira*) way; **estar de ~** to be on a diet

regimento [heʒi'mẽtu] *m* regiment

regiões [he'ʒjõjs] *fpl de* **região**

regional [heʒjo'naw] (*pl* **-ais**) *adj* regional

registrar [heʒis'trax], (*PT*) **registar** *vt* to register; (*anotar*) to record

registro [he'ʒistru], (*PT*) **registo** *m* registration; (*anotação*) recording; (*livro, Ling*) register; (*histórico, Comput*) record; **~ civil** registry office

regra ['hɛgra] *f* rule; **regras** *fpl* (*Med*) periods

regravável [hegra'vavew] (*pl* **-eis**) *adj* rewritable

regressar [hegre'sax] *vi* to come (*ou* go) back, return; **regresso** [he'grɛsu] *m* return

régua ['hɛgwa] *f* ruler; **~ de calcular** slide rule

regulador, a [hegula'dox(a)] *m* regulator

regulamento [hegula'mẽtu] *m* rules *pl*, regulations *pl*

regular [hegu'lax] *adj* regular; (*estatura*) average, medium; (*tamanho*) normal; (*razoável*) not bad ▷ *vt* to regulate; (*reger*) to govern; (*máquina*) to adjust; (*carro, motor*) to tune ▷ *vi* to work, function; **regularidade** [hegulari'dadʒi] *f* regularity

rei [hej] *m* king; **Dia de R~s** Epiphany; **R~ Momo** carnival king

reinado [hej'nadu] *m* reign

reinar [hej'nax] *vi* to reign

reino ['hejnu] *m* kingdom; (*fig*) realm; **o R~ Unido** the United Kingdom

reivindicação [hejvĩdʒika'sãw] (*pl* **-ões**) *f* claim, demand

reivindicar [rejvĩdʒi'kax] *vt* to claim; (*aumento salarial, direitos*) to demand

rejeição [heʒej'sãw] (*pl* **-ões**) *f* rejection

rejeitar [heʒej'tax] *vt* to reject; (*recusar*) to refuse

rejo *etc* ['heʒu] *vb ver* **reger**

rejuvenescer [heʒuvene'sex] *vt* to rejuvenate

relação [hela'sãw] (*pl* **-ões**) *f* relation; (*conexão*) connection; (*relacionamento*) relationship; (*Mat*) ratio; (*lista*) list; **com** *ou* **em ~ a** regarding, with reference to; **relações públicas** public relations;

relacionamento
[helasjona'mētu] *m* relationship;
relacionar [helasjo'nar] *vt* to
make a list of; (*ligar*): **relacionar
algo com algo** to connect sth with
sth, relate sth to sth;
relacionar-se *vr* to be connected
ou related

relâmpago [he'lãpagu] *m* flash of
lightning; **relâmpagos** *mpl*
(*clarões*) lightning *sg*

relance [he'lãsi] *m* glance; **olhar
de ~** to glance at

relapso, -a [he'lapsu, a] *adj*
(*negligente*) negligent

relatar [hela'tar] *vt* to give an
account of

relativo, -a [hela'tʃivu, a] *adj*
relative

relato [he'latu] *m* account

relatório [hela'tɔrju] *m* report

relaxado, -a [hela'ʃadu, a] *adj*
relaxed; (*desleixado*) slovenly,
sloppy; (*relapso*) negligent

relaxante [hela'ʃãtʃi] *adj* relaxing

relaxar [hela'ʃar] *vt, vi* to relax

relegar [hele'gar] *vt* to relegate

relembrar [helē'brar] *vt* to recall

relevante [hele'vãtʃi] *adj* relevant

relevo [he'levu] *m* relief

religião [heli'ʒãw] (*pl* **-ões**) *f*
religion; **religioso, -a** [heli'ʒozu,
ɔza] *adj* religious ▷ *m/f* religious
person; (*frade/freira*) monk/nun

relíquia [he'likja] *f* relic; **~ de
família** family heirloom

relógio [he'lɔʒu] *m* clock; (*de gás*)
meter; **~ (de pulso)** (wrist)watch;
~ de sol sundial

relutante [helu'tãtʃi] *adj* reluctant

relva ['hɛwva] *f* grass; (*terreno
gramado*) lawn

relvado [hew'vadu] (*PT*) *m* lawn

remar [he'mar] *vt, vi* to row

rematar [hema'tar] *vt* to finish off;
remate [he'matʃi] *m* (*fim*) end;
(*acabamento*) finishing touch

remediar [heme'dʒjar] *vt* to put
right, remedy

remédio [he'mɛdʒju] *m*
(*medicamento*) medicine; (*recurso,
solução*) remedy; (*Jur*) recourse;
não tem ~ there's no way

remendar [hemē'dar] *vt* to mend;
(*com pano*) to patch; **remendo**
[he'mēdu] *m* repair, patch

remessa [he'mɛsa] *f* shipment; (*de
dinheiro*) remittance

remetente [heme'tētʃi] *m/f* sender

remexer [heme'ʃer] *vt* (*papéis*) to
shuffle; (*sacudir: braços*) to wave;
(*folhas*) to shake; (*revolver: areia,
lama*) to stir up ▷ *vi*: **~ em** to
rummage through

reminiscência [hemini'sēsja] *f*
reminiscence

remo ['hɛmu] *m* oar; (*Esporte*)
rowing

remoção [hemo'sãw] *f* removal

remorso [he'mɔrsu] *m* remorse

remover [hemo'ver] *vt* to move;
(*transferir*) to transfer; (*demitir*) to
dismiss; (*retirar, afastar*) to remove;
(*terra*) to churn up

renal [he'naw] (*pl* **-ais**) *adj* renal,
kidney *atr*

Renascença [hena'sēsa] *f*: **a ~** the
Renaissance

renascer [hena'ser] *vi* to be reborn;
(*fig*) to revive

renascimento [henasi'mētu] *m*
rebirth; (*fig*) revival; **o R~** the
Renaissance

renda ['hēda] *f* income; (*nacional*)
revenue; (*de aplicação, locação*)
yield; (*tecido*) lace

render [hē'der] *vt* (*lucro, dinheiro*) to
bring in, yield; (*preço*) to fetch;

r

(*homenagem*) to pay; (*graças*) to give; (*serviços*) to render; (*armas*) to surrender; (*guarda*) to relieve; (*causar*) to bring ▷ *vi* (*dar lucro*) to pay; **render-se** *vr* to surrender; **rendição** [hẽdʒi'sãw] *f* surrender

rendimento [hẽdʒi'mẽtu] *m* income; (*lucro*) profit; (*juro*) yield, interest

renegar [hene'gar] *vt* (*crença*) to renounce; (*detestar*) to hate; (*trair*) to betray; (*negar*) to deny; (*desprezar*) to reject

renomado, -a [heno'madu, a] *adj* renowned

renovar [heno'var] *vt* to renew; (*Arq*) to renovate

rentabilidade [hẽtabili'dadʒi] *f* profitability

rentável [hẽ'tavew] (*pl* **-eis**) *adj* profitable

renúncia [he'nũsja] *f* resignation

renunciar [henũ'sjar] *vt* to give up, renounce ▷ *vi* to resign; (*abandonar*): **~ a algo** to give up sth up

reouve *etc* [he'ovi] *vb ver* **reaver**

reouver *etc* [heo'ver] *vb ver* **reaver**

reparação [hepara'sãw] (*pl* **-ões**) *f* mending, repairing; (*de mal, erros*) remedying; (*fig*) amends *pl*, reparation

reparar [hepa'rar] *vt* to repair; (*forças*) to restore; (*mal, erros*) to remedy; (*prejuízo, danos, ofensa*) to make amends for; (*notar*) to notice ▷ *vi*: **~ em** to notice; **reparo** [he'paru] *m* repair; (*crítica*) criticism; (*observação*) observation

repartição [hepartʃi'sãw] (*pl* **-ões**) *f* distribution

repartir [hepar'tʃir] *vt* (*distribuir*) to distribute; (*dividir entre vários*) to share out; (*dividir em várias porções*) to divide up

repelente [hepe'lẽtʃi] *adj, m* repellent

repente [he'pẽtʃi] *m* outburst; **de ~** suddenly; (*col: talvez*) maybe

repentino, -a [hepẽ'tʃinu, a] *adj* sudden

repercussão [heperku'sãw] (*pl* **-ões**) *f* repercussion

repercutir [heperku'tʃir] *vt* to echo ▷ *vi* to reverberate, echo; (*fig*): **~ (em)** to have repercussions (on)

repertório [heper'tɔrju] *m* list; (*coleção*) collection; (*Mús*) repertoire

repetidamente [hepetʃida'mẽtʃi] *adv* repeatedly

repetir [hepe'tʃir] *vt* to repeat ▷ *vi* (*ao comer*) to have seconds; **repetir-se** *vr* to happen again; (*pessoa*) to repeat o.s.; **repetitivo, -a** [hepetʃi'tʃivu, a] *adj* repetitive

repito *etc* [he'pitu] *vb ver* **repetir**

repleto, -a [he'plɛtu, a] *adj* replete, full up

réplica ['hɛplika] *f* replica; (*contestação*) reply, retort

replicar [hepli'kar] *vt* to answer, reply to ▷ *vi* to reply, answer back

repolho [he'poʎu] *m* cabbage

repor [he'por] (*irreg: como* **pôr**) *vt* to put back, replace; (*restituir*) to return; **repor-se** *vr* to recover

reportagem [hepor'taʒẽ] (*pl* **-ns**) *f* reporting; (*notícia*) report

repórter [he'pɔrter] *m/f* reporter

repousar [hepo'zar] *vi* to rest; **repouso** [he'pozu] *m* rest

representação [heprezẽta'sãw] (*pl* **-ões**) *f* representation; (*Teatro*) performance; **representante** [heprezẽ'tãtʃi] *m/f* representative

representar [heprezẽ'tar] *vt* to represent; (*Teatro: papel*) to play ▷ *vi* to act; **representativo, -a**

[heprezēta'tʃivu, a] *adj*
representative

repressão [hepre'sãw] (*pl* **-ões**) *f*
repression

reprimir [hepri'mir] *vt* to repress

reprodução [heprodu'sãw] (*pl*
-ões) *f* reproduction

reproduzir [heprodu'zir] *vt* to
reproduce; (*repetir*) to repeat;
reproduzir-se *vr* to breed

reprovar [hepro'var] *vt* to
disapprove of; (*aluno*) to fail

réptil ['hɛptʃiw] (*pl* **-eis**) *m* reptile

república [he'publika] *f* republic;
republicano, -a [hepubli'kanu,
a] *adj, m/f* republican

repudiar [hepu'dʒjar] *vt* to
repudiate; **repúdio** [he'pudʒju] *m*
repudiation; **repulsivo, -a**
[hepuw'sivu, a] *adj* repulsive

reputação [reputa'sãw] (*pl* **-ões**) *f*
reputation

requeijão [hekej'ʒãw] *m* cheese
spread

requerer [heke'rer] *vt* (*emprego*) to
apply for; (*pedir*) to request; (*exigir*)
to require; **requerimento**
[hekeri'mētu] *m* application,
request; (*petição*) petition

requintado, -a [hekī'tadu, a] *adj*
refined, elegant

requinte [he'kītʃi] *m* refinement,
elegance; (*cúmulo*) height

requisito [heki'zitu] *m*
requirement

rés do chão [hɛzdu'ʃãw] (*PT*) *m inv*
ground floor (*Brit*), first floor (*US*)

reserva [he'zɛrva] *f* reserve; (*para
hotel, fig*) reservation ▷ *m/f*
(*Esporte*) reserve

reservado, -a [hezer'vadu, a] *adj*
reserved

reservar [hezer'var] *vt* to reserve;
(*guardar de reserva*) to keep; (*forças*)

to conserve; **reservar-se** *vr* to
save o.s.

reservatório [hezerva'tɔrju] *m*
reservoir

resfriado, -a [hes'frjadu, a] (*BR*)
adj: **estar ~** to have a cold ▷ *m*
cold, chill; **ficar ~** to catch (a) cold

resgatar [hezga'tar] *vt* (*salvar*) to
rescue; (*retomar*) to get back,
recover; **resgate** [hez'gatʃi] *m*
rescue, ransom, recovery

residência [hezi'dēsja] *f* residence;
residencial [hezidē'sjaw] (*pl* **-ais**)
adj residential; (*computador,
telefone etc*) home *atr*; **residente**
[hezi'dētʃi] *adj, m/f* resident

residir [hezi'dʒir] *vi* to live, reside

resíduo [he'zidwu] *m* residue

resignação [hezigna'sãw] (*pl* **-ões**)
f resignation

resignar-se [hezig'narsi] *vr*: **~ com**
to resign o.s. to

resina [he'zina] *f* resin

resistente [hezis'tētʃi] *adj*
resistant; (*material, objeto*)
hard-wearing, strong

resistir [hezis'tʃir] *vi* to hold;
(*pessoa*) to hold out; **~ a** to resist;
(*sobreviver*) to survive

resmungar [hezmũ'gar] *vt, vi* to
mutter, mumble

resolução [hezolu'sãw] (*pl* **-ões**) *f*
resolution; (*de um problema*)
solution; **resoluto, -a** [hezo'lutu,
a] *adj* decisive

resolver [hezow'ver] *vt* to sort out;
(*problema*) to solve; (*questão*) to
resolve; (*decidir*) to decide;
resolver-se *vr*: **~-se (a fazer)** to
make up one's mind (to do), decide
(to do)

respectivo, -a [hespek'tʃivu, a] *adj*
respective

respeitar [hespej'tar] *vt* to respect;

r

respeitável [hespej'tavew] (*pl* **-eis**) *adj* respectable; (*considerável*) considerable

respeito [hes'pejtu] *m*: **~ (a *ou* por)** respect (for); **respeitos** *mpl* (*cumprimentos*) regards; **a ~ de, com ~ a** as to, as regards; (*sobre*) about; **dizer ~ a** to concern; **em ~ a** with respect to

respiração [hespira'sãw] *f* breathing

respirar [hespi'rar] *vt, vi* to breathe

respiro [hes'piru] *m* breath

resplandecente [hesplãde'sẽtʃi] *adj* resplendent

responder [hespõ'der] *vt* to answer ▷ *vi* to answer; (*ser respondão*) to answer back; **~ por** to be responsible for, answer for

responsabilidade [hespõsabili'dadʒi] *f* responsibility

responsabilizar [hespõsabili'zar] *vt*: **~ alguém (por algo)** to hold sb responsible (for sth); **responsabilizar-se** *vr*: **~-se por** to take responsibility for

responsável [hespõ'savew] (*pl* **-eis**) *adj*: **~ (por)** responsible (for); **~ a** answerable to, accountable to

resposta [hes'pɔsta] *f* answer, reply

resquício [hes'kisju] *m* (*vestígio*) trace

ressabiado, -a [hesa'bjadu, a] *adj* wary; (*ressentido*) resentful

ressaca [he'saka] *f* undertow; (*mar bravo*) rough sea; (*fig: de quem bebeu*) hangover

ressalva [he'sawva] *f* safeguard

ressentido, -a [hesẽ'tʃidu, a] *adj* resentful

ressentimento [hesẽtʃi'mẽtu] *m* resentment

ressentir-se [hesẽ'tʃirsi] *vr*: **~ de** (*ofender-se*) to resent; (*magoar-se*) to be hurt by; (*sofrer*) to suffer from, feel the effects of

ressurgimento [hesurʒi'mẽtu] *m* resurgence, revival

ressuscitar [hesusi'tar] *vt, vi* to revive

restabelecer [hestabele'ser] *vt* to re-establish, to restore; **restabelecer-se** *vr* to recover, recuperate; **restabelecimento** [hestabelesi'mẽtu] *m* re-establishment, restoration, recovery

restante [hes'tãtʃi] *adj* remaining ▷ *m* rest

restar [hes'tar] *vi* to remain, be left

restauração [hestawra'sãw] (*pl* **-ões**) *f* restoration; (*de costumes, usos*) revival

restaurante [hestaw'rãtʃi] *m* restaurant

restaurar [hestaw'rar] *vt* to restore

restituição [hestʃitwi'sãw] (*pl* **-ões**) *f* restitution, return; (*de dinheiro*) repayment

restituir [hestʃi'twir] *vt* to return; (*dinheiro*) to repay; (*forças, saúde*) to restore; (*usos*) to revive; (*reempossar*) to reinstate

resto ['hɛstu] *m* rest; (*Mat*) remainder; **restos** *mpl* (*sobras*) remains; (*de comida*) scraps

restrição [hestri'sãw] (*pl* **-ões**) *f* restriction

resultado [hezuw'tadu] *m* result

resultante [hezuw'tãtʃi] *adj* resultant; **~ de** resulting from

resultar [hezuw'tar] *vi*: **~ (de/em)** to result (from/in) ▷ *vi* (*vir a ser*) to turn out to be

resumir [hezu'mir] *vt* to

summarize; (*livro*) to abridge; (*reduzir*) to reduce; (*conter em resumo*) to sum up; **resumo** [he'zumu] *m* summary, résumé; **em resumo** in short, briefly

retaguarda [heta'gwarda] *f* rearguard; (*posição*) rear

retaliação [hetalja'sãw] (*pl* -**ões**) *f* retaliation

retângulo [he'tãgulu] *m* rectangle

retardar [hetar'dar] *vt* to hold up, delay; (*adiar*) to postpone

reter [he'ter] (*irreg: como* **ter**) *vt* (*guardar, manter*) to keep; (*deter*) to stop; (*segurar*) to hold; (*ladrão, suspeito*) to detain; (*na memória*) to retain; (*lágrimas, impulsos*) to hold back; (*impedir de sair*) to keep back

reticente [hetʃi'sẽtʃi] *adj* reticent

retificar [hetʃifi'kar] *vt* to rectify

retirada [hetʃi'rada] *f* (*Mil*) retreat; (*salário, saque*) withdrawal

reto, -a ['hɛtu, a] *adj* straight; (*fig: justo*) fair; (: *honesto*) honest, upright ▷ *m* (*Anat*) rectum

retorcer [hetor'ser] *vt* to twist; **retorcer-se** *vr* to wriggle, writhe

retornar [hetor'nar] *vi* to return, go back; **retorno** [he'tornu] *m* return; **dar retorno** to do a U-turn; **retorno (do carro)** (*Comput*) (carriage) return

retraído, -a [hetra'idu, a] *adj* (*tímido*) reserved, timid

retrair [hetra'ir] *vt* to withdraw; (*contrair*) to contract; (*pessoa*) to make reserved

retrato [he'tratu] *m* portrait; (*Foto*) photo; (*fig: efígie*) likeness; (: *representação*) portrayal; **~ falado** Identikit® picture

retribuir [hetri'bwir] *vt* to reward, recompense; (*pagar*) to remunerate; (*hospitalidade, favor,*

sentimento, visita) to return

retroceder [hetrose'der] *vi* to retreat, fall back; **retrocesso** [hetro'sɛsu] *m* retreat; (*ao passado*) return

retrógrado, -a [he'trɔgradu, a] *adj* retrograde; (*reacionário*) reactionary

retrospecto [hetro'spɛktu] *m*: **em ~** in retrospect

retrovisor [hetrovi'zor] *adj, m*: **(espelho) ~** rear-view mirror

réu, ré [hɛw, hɛ] *m/f* defendant; (*culpado*) culprit, criminal

reumatismo [hewma'tʃizmu] *m* rheumatism

reunião [heu'njãw] (*pl* -**ões**) *f* meeting; (*ato, reencontro*) reunion; (*festa*) get-together, party; **~ de cúpula** summit (meeting)

revanche [he'vãʃi] *f* revenge

reveillon [heve'jõ] *m* New Year's Eve

revelação [hevela'sãw] (*pl* -**ões**) *f* revelation

revelar [heve'lar] *vt* to reveal; (*Foto*) to develop; **revelar-se** *vr* to turn out to be

revelia [heve'lia] *f* default; **à ~** by default; **à ~ de** without the knowledge *ou* consent of

revendedor, a [hevẽde'dor(a)] *m/f* dealer

rever [he'ver] (*irreg: como* **ver**) *vt* to see again; (*examinar*) to check; (*revisar*) to revise

reverência [heve'rẽsja] *f* reverence, respect; (*ato*) bow; (: *de mulher*) curtsey; **fazer uma ~** to bow; to curtsey

reverso [he'vɛrsu] *m* reverse

reverter [hever'ter] *vt* to revert

revestir [heves'tʃir] *vt* (*paredes etc*) to cover; (*interior de uma caixa etc*) to line

revezar [heve'zar] *vt* to take turns with ▷ *vi* to take turns; **revezar-se** *vr* to take it in turns

revidar [hevi'dar] *vt* (*soco, insulto*) to return; (*retrucar*) to answer; (*crítica*) to rise to, respond to ▷ *vi* to hit back; (*retrucar*) to respond

revirar [hevi'rar] *vt* to turn round; (*gaveta*) to turn out, go through

revisão [hevi'zãw] (*pl* **-ões**) *f* revision; (*de máquina*) overhaul; (*de carro*) service; (*Jur*) appeal

revisar [hevi'zar] *vt* to revise

revisões [hevi'zõjs] *fpl de* **revisão**

revista [he'vista] *f* (*busca*) search; (*Mil, exame*) inspection; (*publicação*) magazine; (: *profissional, erudita*) journal; (*Teatro*) revue

revisto *etc* [he'vistu] *vb ver* **revestir**

revogar [hevo'gar] *vt* to revoke

revolta [he'vɔwta] *f* revolt; (*fig: indignação*) disgust; **revoltado, -a** [hevow'tadu, a] *adj* in revolt; (*indignado*) disgusted; (*amargo*) bitter; **revoltante** [hevow'tãtʃi] *adj* disgusting, revolting

revoltar [hevow'tar] *vt* to disgust; **revoltar-se** *vr* to rebel, revolt; (*indignar-se*) to be disgusted

revolto, -a [he'vowtu, a] *pp de* **revolver** ▷ *adj* (*década*) turbulent; (*mundo*) troubled; (*cabelo*) dishevelled; (*mar*) rough; (*desarrumado*) untidy

revolução [hevolu'sãw] (*pl* **-ões**) *f* revolution; **revolucionar** [hevolusjo'nar] *vt* to revolutionize; **revolucionário, -a** [hevolusjo'narju, a] *adj, m/f* revolutionary

revolver [hevow'ver] *vi* to revolve, rotate

revólver [he'vɔwver] *m* revolver

reza ['hɛza] *f* prayer; **rezar** [he'zar] *vi* to pray

riacho ['hjaʃu] *m* stream, brook

ribeiro [hi'bejru] *m* brook, stream

rico, -a ['hiku, a] *adj* rich; (*PT: lindo*) beautiful; (: *excelente*) splendid ▷ *m/f* rich man/woman

ridicularizar [hidʒikulari'zar] *vt* to ridicule

ridículo, -a [hi'dʒikulu, a] *adj* ridiculous

rifa ['hifa] *f* raffle

rifle ['hifli] *m* rifle

rigidez [hiʒi'dez] *f* rigidity, stiffness; (*austeridade*) severity, strictness

rígido, -a ['hiʒidu, a] *adj* rigid, stiff; (*fig*) strict

rigor [hi'gor] *m* rigidity; (*meticulosidade*) rigour (*Brit*), rigor (*US*); (*severidade*) harshness, severity; (*exatidão*) precision; **ser de ~** to be essential *ou* obligatory; **rigoroso, -a** [higo'rozu, ɔza] *adj* rigorous; (*severo*) strict; (*exigente*) demanding; (*minucioso*) precise, accurate; (*inverno*) hard, harsh

rijo, -a ['hiʒu, a] *adj* tough, hard; (*severo*) harsh, severe

rim [hĩ] (*pl* **-ns**) *m* kidney; **rins** *mpl* (*parte inferior das costas*) small *sg* of the back

rima ['hima] *f* rhyme; (*poema*) verse, poem; **rimar** [hi'mar] *vt, vi* to rhyme

rímel® ['himew] (*pl* **-eis**) *m* mascara

ringue ['hĩgi] *m* ring

rins [hĩs] *mpl de* **rim**

Rio ['hiu] *m*: **o ~ (de Janeiro)** Rio (de Janeiro)

rio ['hiu] *m* river

riqueza [hi'keza] *f* wealth, riches *pl*; (*qualidade*) richness

rir [hiʁ] vi to laugh; **~ de** to laugh at
risada [hiˈzada] f laughter
risca [ˈhiska] f stroke; (*listra*) stripe; (*no cabelo*) parting
riscar [hisˈkaʁ] vt (*marcar*) to mark; (*apagar*) to cross out; (*desenhar*) to outline
risco [ˈhisku] m (*marca*) mark, scratch; (*traço*) stroke; (*desenho*) drawing, sketch; (*perigo*) risk; **correr o ~ de** to run the risk of
riso [ˈhizu] m laughter; **risonho, -a** [hiˈzoɲu, a] adj smiling; (*contente*) cheerful
ríspido, -a [ˈhispidu, a] adj brusque; (*áspero*) harsh
ritmo [ˈhitʃmu] m rhythm
rito [ˈhitu] m rite
ritual [hiˈtwaw] (pl **-ais**) adj, m ritual
rival [hiˈvaw] (pl **-ais**) adj, m/f rival; **rivalidade** [hivaliˈdadʒi] f rivalry; **rivalizar** [hivaliˈzaʁ] vt to rival ▷ vi: **rivalizar com** to compete with, vie with
roa etc [ˈhoa] vb ver **roer**
robô [hoˈbo] m robot
roça [ˈhɔsa] f plantation; (*no mato*) clearing; (*campo*) country
rocha [ˈhɔʃa] f rock; (*penedo*) crag
rochedo [hoˈʃedu] m crag, cliff
rock-and-roll [-ãˈhɔw] m rock and roll
roda [ˈhɔda] f wheel; (*círculo, grupo de pessoas*) circle; **~ dentada** cog(wheel); **em** ou **à ~ de** round, around
rodada [hoˈdada] f (*de bebidas, Esporte*) round
rodar [hoˈdaʁ] vt to turn, spin; (*viajar por*) to tour, travel round; (*quilômetros*) to do; (*filme*) to make; (*imprimir*) to print; (*Comput: programa*) to run ▷ vi to turn round;

(*Auto*) to drive around; **~ por** (*a pé*) to wander around; (*de carro*) to drive around
rodela [hoˈdɛla] f (*pedaço*) slice
rodízio [hoˈdʒizju] m rota; **em ~** on a rota basis
rodopiar [hodoˈpjaʁ] vi to whirl around, swirl
rodovia [hodoˈvia] f highway, ≈ motorway (*Brit*), ≈ interstate (*US*)
rodoviária [hodoˈvjarja] f (*tb:* **estação ~**) bus station; *ver tb* **rodoviário**
rodoviário, -a [hodoˈvjarju, a] adj road atr; (*polícia*) traffic atr
roer [hweʁ] vt to gnaw, nibble; (*enferrujar*) to corrode; (*afligir*) to eat away
rogar [hoˈgaʁ] vi to ask, request; **~ a alguém que faça** to beg sb to do
rói [hɔj] vb ver **roer**
roía etc [hoˈia] vb ver **roer**
rolar [hoˈlaʁ] vt, vi to roll
roleta [hoˈleta] f roulette; (*borboleta*) turnstile
rolha [ˈhoʎa] f cork
roliço, -a [hoˈlisu, a] adj (*pessoa*) plump, chubby; (*objeto*) round, cylindrical
rolo [ˈholu] m (*de papel etc*) roll; (*para nivelar o solo, para pintura*) roller; (*para cabelo*) curler; (*col: briga*) brawl, fight; **cortina de ~** roller blind; **~ compressor** steamroller
Roma [ˈhoma] n Rome
romã [hoˈmã] f pomegranate
romance [hoˈmãsi] m novel; (*caso amoroso*) romance; **~ policial** detective story
romano, -a [hoˈmanu, a] adj, m/f Roman
romântico, -a [hoˈmãtʃiku, a] adj romantic

rombo ['hõbu] *m* (*buraco*) hole; (*fig*: *desfalque*) embezzlement; (: *prejuízo*) loss, shortfall

Romênia [ho'menja] *f*: **a ~** Romania; **romeno, -a** [ho'mɛnu, a] *adj*, *m/f* Rumanian ▷ *m* (*Ling*) Rumanian

romper [hõ'per] *vt* to break; (*rasgar*) to tear; (*relações*) to break off ▷ *vi*: **~ em pranto** *ou* **lágrimas** to burst into tears; **rompimento** [hõpi'mẽtu] *m* breakage; (*fenda*) break; (*de relações*) breaking off

roncar [hõ'kar] *vi* to snore; **ronco** ['hõku] *m* snore

ronda ['hõda] *f* patrol, beat; **fazer a ~** to go the rounds; **rondar** [hõ'dar] *vt* to patrol; (*espreitar*) to prowl ▷ *vi* to prowl, lurk; (*fazer a ronda*) to patrol; **a inflação ronda os 10% ao ano** inflation is in the region of 10% a year

rosa ['hɔza] *adj inv* pink ▷ *f* rose; **rosado, -a** [ho'zadu, a] *adj* rosy, pink

rosário [ho'zarju] *m* rosary

rosbife [hoz'bifi] *m* roast beef

roseira [ho'zejra] *f* rosebush

rosnar [hoz'nar] *vi* (*cão*) to growl, snarl; (*murmurar*) to mutter, mumble

rosto ['hostu] *m* face

rota ['hɔta] *f* route, course

roteiro [ho'tejru] *m* itinerary; (*ordem*) schedule; (*guia*) guidebook; (*de filme*) script

rotina [ho'tʃina] *f* routine; **rotineiro, -a** [hotʃi'nejru, a] *adj* routine

roto, -a ['hotu, a] *adj* broken; (*rasgado*) torn

rotular [hotu'lar] *vt* to label; **rótulo** ['hɔtulu] *m* label

roubar [ho'bar] *vt* to steal; (*loja,* *casa, pessoa*) to rob ▷ *vi* to steal; (*em jogo, no preço*) to cheat; **~ algo a alguém** to steal sth from sb; **roubo** ['hobu] *m* theft, robbery

rouco, -a ['roku, a] *adj* hoarse

round ['hãwdʒi] (*pl* **-s**) *m* (*Boxe*) round

roupa ['hopa] *f* clothes *pl*, clothing; **~ de baixo** underwear; **~ de cama** bedclothes *pl*, bed linen

roupão [ho'pãw] (*pl* **-ões**) *m* dressing gown

rouxinol [hoʃi'nɔw] (*pl* **-óis**) *m* nightingale

roxo, -a ['hoʃu, a] *adj* purple, violet

royalty ['hɔjawtʃi] (*pl* **-ies**) *m* royalty

rua ['hua] *f* street; **~ principal** main street; **~ sem saída** no through road, cul-de-sac

rubéola [hu'bɛola] *f* (*Med*) German measles

rubi [hu'bi] *m* ruby

rubor [hu'bor] *m* blush; (*fig*) shyness, bashfulness

ruborizar-se [hubori'zarsi] *vr* to blush

rubrica [hu'brika] *f* (*signed*) initials *pl*

rubro, -a ['hubru, a] *adj* (*faces*) rosy, ruddy

ruço, -a ['husu, a] *adj* grey (*Brit*), gray (*US*), dun; (*desbotado*) faded

rúcula ['hukula] rocket (*Brit*), arugula (*US*)

ruela ['hwɛla] *f* lane, alley

ruga ['huga] *f* (*na pele*) wrinkle; (*na roupa*) crease

ruge ['huʒi] *m* rouge

rugido [hu'ʒidu] *m* roar

rugir [hu'ʒir] *vi* to roar

ruído [hu'widu] *m* noise; **ruidoso, -a** [hwi'dozu, ɔza] *adj* noisy

ruim [hu'ĩ] (*pl* **-ns**) *adj* bad;

(*defeituoso*) defective
ruína ['hwina] *f* ruin; (*decadência*)
downfall
ruins [hu'ĩs] *adj pl de* **ruim**
ruir ['hwir] *vi* to collapse, go to ruin
ruivo, -a ['hwivu, a] *adj* red-haired
▷ *m/f* redhead
rum [hũ] *m* rum
rumo ['humu] *m* course, bearing;
(*fig*) course; **~ a** bound for; **sem ~**
adrift
rumor [hu'mor] *m* noise; (*notícia*)
rumour (*Brit*), rumor (*US*), report
ruptura [hup'tura] *f* break, rupture
rural [hu'raw] (*pl* **-ais**) *adj* rural
rush [hʌʃ] *m* rush; **(a hora do) ~**
rush hour
Rússia ['husja] *f*: **a ~** Russia; **russo,
-a** ['husu, a] *adj, m/f* Russian ▷ *m*
(*Ling*) Russian

S

S. *abr* (= *Santo/a ou São*) St
SA *abr* (= *Sociedade Anônima*) plc
(*Brit*), Inc. (*US*)
sã [sã] *f de* **são**
Saara [sa'ara] *m*: **o ~** the Sahara
sábado ['sabadu] *m* Saturday
sabão [sa'bãw] (*pl* **-ões**) *m* soap
sabedoria [sabedo'ria] *f* wisdom;
(*erudição*) learning
saber [sa'ber] *vt, vi* to know;
(*descobrir*) to find out ▷ *m*
knowledge; **a ~** namely; **~ fazer**
to know how to do, be able to do;
que eu saiba as far as I know
sabiá [sa'bja] *m/f* thrush
sabido, -a [sa'bidu, a] *adj*
knowledgeable; (*esperto*) shrewd
sabões [sa'bõjs] *mpl de* **sabão**
sabonete [sabo'netʃi] *m* toilet soap
sabor [sa'bor] *m* taste, flavour
(*Brit*), flavor (*US*); **saborear**
[sabo'rjar] *vt* to taste, savour

(Brit), savor (US); **saboroso, -a**
[sabo'rozu, ɔza] adj tasty,
delicious

sabotagem [sabo'taʒẽ] f sabotage

sabotar [sabo'tar] vt to sabotage

SAC ['saki] abr m (= serviço de
atendimento ao cliente) customer
service

saca ['saka] f sack

sacar [sa'kar] vt to take out;
(dinheiro) to withdraw; (arma,
cheque) to draw; (Esporte) to serve;
(col: entender) to understand ▷ vi
(col: entender) to understand

saca-rolhas m inv corkscrew

sacerdote [saser'dɔtʃi] m priest

saciar [sa'sjar] vt (fome etc) to
satisfy; (sede) to quench

saco ['saku] m bag; (enseada) inlet;
~ de café coffee filter; **~ de dormir**
sleeping bag

sacode etc [sa'kɔdʒi] vb ver **sacudir**

sacola [sa'kɔla] f bag

sacramento [sakra'mẽtu] m
sacrament

sacrificar [sakrifi'kar] vt to
sacrifice; **sacrificar-se** vr to
sacrifice o.s.; **sacrifício**
[sakri'fisju] m sacrifice

sacrilégio [sakri'lɛʒju] m sacrilege

sacro, -a ['sakru, a] adj sacred

sacudida [saku'dʒida] f shake

sacudir [saku'dʒir] vt to shake;
sacudir-se vr to shake

sádico, -a ['sadʒiku, a] adj sadistic

sadio, -a [sa'dʒiu, a] adj healthy

safado, -a [sa'fadu, a] adj
shameless; (imoral) dirty; (travesso)
mischievous ▷ m rogue

safira [sa'fira] f sapphire

safra ['safra] f harvest

Sagitário [saʒi'tarju] m Sagittarius

sagrado, -a [sa'gradu, a] adj
sacred, holy

saia ['saja] f skirt

saiba etc ['sajba] vb ver **saber**

saída [sa'ida] f exit, way out;
(partida) departure; (ato: de pessoa)
going out; (fig: solução) way out;
(Comput: de programa) exit; (: de
dados) output; **~ de emergência**
emergency exit

sair [sa'ir] vi to go (ou come) out;
(partir) to leave; (realizar-se) to turn
out; (Comput) to exit; **sair-se** vr:
~-se bem/mal de to be successful/
unsuccessful in

sal [saw] (pl **sais**) m salt; **sem ~**
(comida) salt-free; (pessoa)
lacklustre (Brit), lackluster (US)

sala ['sala] f room; (num edifício
público) hall; (classe, turma) class;
~ (de aula) classroom; **~ de
bate-papo** (Internet) chatroom;
~ de espera waiting room; **~ (de
estar)** living room; **~ de jantar**
dining room; **~ de operação** (Med)
operating theatre (Brit) ou theater
(US)

salada [sa'lada] f salad; (fig)
confusion, jumble

sala e quarto m (pl **sala e quartos**)
two-room flat (Brit) ou apartment
(US)

salão [sa'lãw] (pl **-ões**) m large
room, hall; (exposição) show; **~ de
beleza** beauty salon

salário [sa'larju] m wages pl, salary

saldo ['sawdu] m balance; (sobra)
surplus

saleiro [sa'lejru] m salt cellar

salgadinho [sawga'dʒiɲu] m
savoury (Brit), savory (US), snack

salgado, -a [saw'gadu, a] adj salty,
salted

salgueiro [saw'gejru] m willow;
~ chorão weeping willow

salientar [saljẽ'tar] vt to point out;

(*acentuar*) to stress, emphasize;
saliente [sa'ljẽtʃi] *adj* prominent;
(*evidente*) clear, conspicuous;
(*importante*) outstanding;
(*assanhado*) forward
saliva [sa'liva] *f* saliva
salmão [saw'mãw] (*pl* -**ões**) *m* salmon
salmoura [saw'mora] *f* brine
salões [sa'lõjs] *mpl de* **salão**
salsa ['sawsa] *f* parsley
salsicha [saw'siʃa] *f* sausage;
salsichão [sawsi'ʃãw] (*pl* -**ões**) *m* sausage
saltar [saw'tar] *vt* to jump (over), leap (over); (*omitir*) to skip ▷ *vi* to jump, leap; (*sangue*) to spurt out; (*de ônibus, cavalo*) **~ de** to get off
salto ['sawtu] *m* jump, leap; (*de calçado*) heel; **~ de vara** pole vault; **~ em altura** high jump; **~ em distância** long jump
salubre [sa'lubri] *adj* healthy, salubrious
salvamento [sawva'mẽtu] *m* rescue; (*de naufrágio*) salvage
salvar [saw'var] *vt* to save; (*resgatar*) to rescue; (*objetos, de ruína*) to salvage; (*honra*) to defend; **salvar-se** *vr* to escape
salva-vidas *m inv* (*boia*) lifebuoy ▷ *m/f inv* (*pessoa*) lifeguard; **barco ~** lifeboat
salvo, -a ['sawvu, a] *adj* safe ▷ *prep* except, save; **a ~** in safety
samba ['sãba] *m* samba

- **SAMBA**
-
- The greatest form of musical
- expression of the Brazilian
- people, the **samba** is a type of
- music and dance of African
- origin. It embraces a number of
- rhythmic styles, such as *samba*
- *de breque*, *samba-enredo*,
- *samba-canção* and *pagode*, among
- others. Officially, the first samba,
- entitled *Pelo telefone*, was written
- in Rio in 1917.

SAMU (*BR*) *abr m* (= *Serviço de Atendimento Móvel de Urgência*) emergency ambulance service
sanar [sa'nar] *vt* to cure; (*remediar*) to remedy
sanção [sã'sãw] (*pl* -**ões**) *f* sanction;
sancionar [sansjo'nar] *vt* to sanction
sandália [sã'dalja] *f* sandal
sandes ['sãdəs] (*PT*) *f inv* sandwich
sanduíche [sand'wiʃi] (*BR*) *m* sandwich
saneamento [sanja'mẽtu] *m* sanitation
sanear [sa'njar] *vt* to clean up
sangrar [sã'grar] *vt, vi* to bleed;
sangrento, -a [sã'grẽtu, a] *adj* bloody; (*Culin: carne*) rare
sangue ['sãgi] *m* blood
sanguinário, -a [sãgi'narju, a] *adj* bloodthirsty
sanguíneo, -a [sã'ginju, a] *adj*: **grupo ~** blood group; **pressão sanguínea** blood pressure; **vaso ~** blood vessel
sanidade [sani'dadʒi] *f* (*saúde*) health; (*mental*) sanity
sanita [sa'nita] (*PT*) *f* toilet, lavatory
sanitário, -a [sani'tarju, a] *adj* sanitary; **vaso ~** toilet, lavatory (bowl); **sanitários** [sani'tarjus] *mpl* toilets
santo, -a ['sãtu, a] *adj* holy ▷ *m/f* saint
santuário [sã'twarju] *m* shrine, sanctuary

São [sãw] *m* Saint

são, sã [sãw, sã] (*pl* **sãos/sãs**) *adj*
healthy; (*conselho*) sound;
(*mentalmente*) sane; **~ e salvo** safe
and sound

São Paulo [-'pawlu] *n* São Paulo

sapataria [sapata'ria] *f* shoe shop

sapateiro [sapa'tejru] *m*
shoemaker; (*vendedor*) shoe
salesman; (*que conserta*) shoe
repairer; (*loja*) shoe repairer's

sapatilha [sapa'tʃiʎa] *f* (*de balé*)
shoe; (*sapato*) pump; (*de atleta*)
running shoe

sapato [sa'patu] *m* shoe

sapo ['sapu] *m* toad

saque ['saki] *m* (*de dinheiro*)
withdrawal; (*Com*) draft, bill;
(*Esporte*) serve; (*pilhagem*) plunder,
pillage; **~ a descoberto** (*Com*)
overdraft

saque *etc vb ver* **sacar**

saquear [sa'kjar] *vt* to pillage,
plunder

sarampo [sa'rãpu] *m* measles *sg*

sarar [sa'rar] *vt* to cure; (*ferida*) to
heal ▷ *vi* to recover

sarcasmo [sar'kazmu] *m* sarcasm

sarda ['sarda] *f* freckle

Sardenha [sar'dɜɲa] *f*: **a ~** Sardinia

sardinha [sar'dʒiɲa] *f* sardine

sargento [sar'ʒẽtu] *m* sergeant

sarjeta [sar'ʒeta] *f* gutter

Satã [sa'tã] *m* Satan

Satanás [sata'nas] *m* Satan

satélite [sa'tɛlitʃi] *m* satellite

sátira ['satʃira] *f* satire

satisfazer [satʃisfa'zer] (*irreg: como*
fazer) *vt* to satisfy ▷ *vi* to be
satisfactory; **satisfazer-se** *vr* to
be satisfied; (*saciar-se*) to fill o.s. up;
~ a to satisfy; **satisfeito, -a**
[satʃis'fejtu, a] *adj* satisfied;
(*saciado*) full; **dar-se por satisfeito**

com algo to be content with sth

saudação [sawda'sãw] (*pl* **-ões**) *f*
greeting

saudade [saw'dadʒi] *f* longing,
yearning; (*lembrança nostálgica*)
nostalgia; **deixar ~s** to be greatly
missed; **ter ~s de** (*desejar*) to long
for; (*sentir falta de*) to miss; **~s (de
casa** *ou* **da família** *ou* **da pátria)**
homesickness *sg*

saudar [saw'dar] *vt* to greet; (*dar as
boas vindas*) to welcome; (*aclamar*)
to acclaim

saudável [saw'davew] (*pl* **-eis**) *adj*
healthy; (*moralmente*) wholesome

saúde [sa'udʒi] *f* health; (*brinde*)
toast; **~!** (*brindando*) cheers!;
(*quando se espirra*) bless you!; **beber
à ~ de** to drink to, toast; **estar
bem/mal de ~** to be well/ill

saudosismo [sawdo'zizmu] *m*
nostalgia

saudoso, -a [saw'dozu, ɔza] *adj*
(*nostálgico*) nostalgic; (*da família ou
terra natal*) homesick; (*de uma
pessoa*) longing; (*que causa
saudades*) much-missed

sauna ['sawna] *f* sauna

saxofone [sakso'fɔni] *m*
saxophone

sazonal [sazo'naw] (*pl* **-ais**) *adj*
seasonal

scanner ['skaner] *m* scanner

 PALAVRA-CHAVE

se [si] *pron* **1** (*reflexivo: impess*)
oneself; (: *m*) himself; (: *f*) herself;
(: *coisa*) itself; (: *você*) yourself; (: *pl*)
themselves; (: *vocês*) yourselves;
ela está se vestindo she's getting
dressed; (*usos léxicos del pron*) *ver o
vb em questão p. ex.* **arrepender-se**
2 (*uso recíproco*) each other, one

another; **olharam-se** they looked at each other

3 (*impess*): **come-se bem aqui** you can eat well here; **sabe-se que ...** it is known that ...; **vende(m)-se jornais naquela loja** they sell newspapers in that shop
▷ *conj* if; (*em pergunta indireta*) whether; **se bem que** even though

sê [se] *vb ver* **ser**

sebe ['sɛbi] (*PT*) *f* fence; **~ viva** hedge

sebo ['sebu] *m* tallow; **seboso, -a** [se'bozu, ɔza] *adj* greasy; (*sujo*) dirty

seca ['seka] *f* drought

secador [seka'dor] *m*: **~ de cabelo/roupa** hairdryer/clothes horse

seção [se'sãw] (*pl* **-ões**) *f* section; (*em loja, repartição*) department

secar [se'kar] *vt* to dry; (*planta*) to parch ▷ *vi* to dry; to wither; (*fonte*) to dry up

seco, -a ['seku, a] *adj* dry; (*ríspido*) curt, brusque; (*magro*) thin; (*pessoa: frio*) cold; (: *sério*) serious

seções [se'sõjs] *fpl de* **seção**

secretaria [sekreta'ria] *f* general office; (*de secretário*) secretary's office; (*ministério*) ministry

secretária [sekre'tarja] *f* writing desk; **~ eletrônica** answering machine; *ver tb* **secretário**

secretário, -a [sekre'tarju, a] *m/f* secretary; **S~ de Estado de ...** Secretary of State for ...

século ['sɛkulu] *m* century; (*época*) age

secundário, -a [sekũ'darju, a] *adj* secondary

seda ['seda] *f* silk

sedativo [seda'tʃivu] *m* sedative

sede¹ ['sɛdʒi] *f* (*de empresa,* *instituição*) headquarters *sg*; (*de governo*) seat; (*Rel*) see, diocese

sede² ['sedʒi] *f* thirst; **estar com** *ou* **ter ~** to be thirsty; **sedento, -a** [se'dẽtu, a] *adj* thirsty

sediar [se'dʒjar] *vt* to base

sedução [sedu'sãw] (*pl* **-ões**) *f* seduction

sedutor, a [sedu'tor(a)] *adj* seductive; (*oferta etc*) tempting

seduzir [sedu'zir] *vt* to seduce; (*fascinar*) to fascinate

segmento [seg'mẽtu] *m* segment

segredo [se'gredu] *m* secret; (*sigilo*) secrecy; (*de fechadura*) combination

segregar [segre'gar] *vt* to segregate

seguidamente [segida'mẽtʃi] *adv* (*sem parar*) continuously; (*logo depois*) soon afterwards

seguido, -a [se'gidu, a] *adj* following; (*contínuo*) continuous, consecutive; **~ de** *ou* **por** followed by; **três dias ~s** three days running; **horas seguidas** for hours on end; **em seguida** next; (*logo depois*) soon afterwards; (*imediatamente*) immediately, right away

seguimento [segi'mẽtu] *m* continuation; **dar ~ a** to proceed with; **em ~ de** after

seguinte [se'gĩtʃi] *adj* following, next; **eu lhe disse o ~** this is what I said to him

seguir [se'gir] *vt* to follow; (*continuar*) to continue ▷ *vi* to follow; (*continuar*) to continue, carry on; (*ir*) to go; **seguir-se** *vr*: **~-se (a)** to follow; **logo a ~** next; **~-se (de)** to result (from)

segunda [se'gũda] *f* (*tb*: **~-feira**) Monday; (*Auto*) second (gear); **de ~** second-rate; **segunda-feira** (*pl*

segundas-feiras) f Monday

segundo, -a [se'gũdu, a] adj second ▷ prep according to ▷ conj as, from what ▷ adv secondly ▷ m second; **de segunda mão** second-hand; **de segunda (classe)** second-class; **~ ele disse** according to what he said; **~ dizem** apparently; **~ me consta** as far as I know; **segundas intenções** ulterior motives

seguramente [segura'mẽtʃi] adv certainly; (muito provavelmente) surely

segurança [segu'rãsa] f security; (ausência de perigo) safety; (confiança) confidence ▷ m/f security guard; **com ~** assuredly

segurar [segu'rar] vt to hold; (amparar) to hold up; (Com: bens) to insure ▷ vi: **~ em** to hold; **segurar-se** vr: **~-se em** to hold on to

seguro, -a [se'guru, a] adj safe; (livre de risco, firme) secure; (certo) certain, assured; (confiável) reliable; (de si mesmo) confident; (tempo) settled ▷ adv confidently ▷ m (Com) insurance; **estar ~ de/ de que** to be sure of/that; **fazer ~** to take out an insurance policy; **~ contra acidentes/incêndio** accident/fire insurance; **seguro-saúde** (pl **seguros-saúde**) m health insurance

sei [sej] vb ver **saber**

seio ['seju] m breast, bosom; (âmago) heart; **~ paranasal** sinus

seis [sejs] num six

seita ['sejta] f sect

seixo ['sejʃu] m pebble

seja etc ['seʒa] vb ver **ser**

sela ['sɛla] f saddle

selar [se'lar] vt (carta) to stamp; (documento oficial, pacto) to seal; (cavalo) to saddle

seleção [sele'sãw] (pl **-ões**) f selection; (Esporte) team

selecionar [selesjo'nar] vt to select

seleções [sele'sõjs] fpl de **seleção**

seleto, -a [se'lɛtu, a] adj select

selim [se'lĩ] (pl **-ns**) m saddle

selo ['selu] m stamp; (carimbo, sinete) seal

selva ['sɛwva] f jungle

selvagem [sew'vaʒẽ] (pl **-ns**) adj wild; (feroz) fierce; (povo) savage; **selvageria** [sewvaʒe'ria] f savagery

sem [sẽ] prep without ▷ conj: **~ que eu peça** without my asking; **estar/ ficar ~ dinheiro/gasolina** to have no/have run out of money/petrol

semáforo [se'mafuru] m (Auto) traffic lights pl; (Ferro) signal

semana [se'mana] f week; **semanal** [sema'naw] (pl **-ais**) adj weekly; **semanário** [sema'narju] m weekly (publication)

semear [se'mjar] vt to sow; **semelhante** [seme'ʎãtʃi] adj similar; (tal) such ▷ m fellow creature

sêmen ['semẽ] m semen

semente [se'mẽtʃi] f seed

semestral [semes'traw] (pl **-ais**) adj half-yearly, bi-annual

semestre [se'mɛstri] m six months; (Educ) semester

semi... [semi] prefixo semi..., half...; **semicírculo** [semi'sirkulu] m semicircle; **semifinal** [semi'finaw] (pl **-ais**) f semi-final

seminário [semi'narju] m seminar; (Rel) seminary

sem-número m: **um ~ de coisas** loads of things

sempre ['sẽpri] adv always; **você ~**

vai? (PT) are you still going?; **~ que** whenever; **como ~** as usual; **a comida/hora** etc **de ~** the usual food/time etc

sem-terra adj inv landless ▷ m/f inv landless labourer (Brit) ou laborer (US)

sem-teto adj inv homeless ▷ m/f inv homeless person; **os ~** the homeless

sem-vergonha adj inv shameless ▷ m/f inv (pessoa) rogue

senado [se'nadu] m senate; **senador, a** [sena'dor(a)] m/f senator

senão [se'nãw] (pl **-ões**) conj otherwise; (mas sim) but, but rather ▷ prep except ▷ m flaw, defect

senha ['sɛɲa] f sign; (palavra de passe, Comput) password; (de caixa eletrônico) PIN number; (recibo) receipt; (passe) pass

senhor, a [se'ɲor(a)] m (homem) man; (formal) gentleman; (homem idoso) elderly man; (Rel) lord; (dono) owner; (tratamento) Mr(.); (tratamento respeitoso) sir ▷ f (mulher) lady; (esposa) wife; (mulher idosa) elderly lady; (dona) owner; (tratamento) Mrs(.), Ms(.); (tratamento respeitoso) madam; **o ~/a ~a** (você) you; **nossa ~a!** (col) gosh; **sim, ~(a)!** yes indeed

senhorita [seɲo'rita] f young lady; (tratamento) Miss, Ms(.); **a ~** (você) you

senil [se'niw] (pl **-is**) adj senile

senões [se'nõjs] mpl de **senão**

sensação [sẽsa'sãw] (pl **-ões**) f sensation; **sensacional** [sẽsasjo'naw] (pl **-ais**) adj sensational

sensível [sẽ'sivew] (pl **-eis**) adj sensitive; (visível) noticeable; (considerável) considerable; (dolorido) tender

senso ['sẽsu] m sense; (juízo) judgement

sensual [sẽ'swaw] (pl **-ais**) adj sensual

sentado, -a [sẽ'tadu, a] adj sitting

sentar [sẽ'tar] vt to seat ▷ vi to sit; **sentar-se** vr to sit down

sentença [sẽ'tẽsa] f (Jur) sentence; **sentenciar** [sẽtẽ'sjar] vt (julgar) to pass judgement on; (condenar por sentença) to sentence

sentido, -a [sẽ'tʃidu, a] adj (magoado) hurt; (choro, queixa) heartfelt ▷ m sense; (direção) direction; (atenção) attention; (aspecto) respect; **~!** (Mil) attention!; **em certo ~** in a sense; **"~ único"** (PT: sinal) "one-way"

sentimental [sẽ'tʃimẽ'taw] (pl **-ais**) adj sentimental; **vida ~** love life

sentimento [sẽtʃi'mẽtu] m feeling; (senso) sense; **sentimentos** mpl (pêsames) condolences

sentinela [sẽtʃi'nɛla] f sentry, guard

sentir [sẽ'tʃir] vt to feel; (perceber, pressentir) to sense; (ser afetado por) to be affected by; (magoar-se) to be upset by ▷ vi to feel; (sofrer) to suffer; **sentir-se** vr to feel; (julgar-se) to consider o.s. (to be); **~ (a) falta de** to miss; **~ cheiro/ gosto (de)** to smell/taste; **~ vontade de** to feel like; **sinto muito** I am very sorry

separação [separa'sãw] (pl **-ões**) f separation

separado, -a [sepa'radu, a] adj separate; **em ~** separately, apart

separar [sepa'rar] vt to separate; (dividir) to divide; (pôr de lado) to

put aside; **separar-se** vr to
separate; to be divided
sepultamento [sepuwta'mẽtu] m
burial
sepultar [sepuw'tar] vt to bury;
sepultura [sepuw'tura] f grave,
tomb
sequência [se'kwẽsja] f sequence
sequer [se'kɛr] adv at least; **(nem)
~** not even
sequestrar [sekwes'trar] vt (bens)
to seize, confiscate; (raptar) to
kidnap; (avião etc) to hijack;
sequestro [se'kwɛstru] m seizure;
(rapto) abduction, kidnapping; (de
avião etc) hijack

PALAVRA-CHAVE

ser [ser] vi **1** (descrição) to be; **ela é
médica/muito alta** she's a
doctor/very tall; **é Ana** (Tel) Ana
speaking ou here; **ela é de uma
bondade incrível** she's incredibly
kind; **ele está é danado** he's really
angry; **ser de mentir/briga** to be
the sort to lie/fight
2 (horas, datas, números): **é uma
hora** it's one o'clock; **são seis e
meia** it's half past six; **é dia 1° de
junho** it's the first of June; **somos/
são seis** there are six of us/them
3 (origem, material): **ser de** to be ou
come from; (feito de) to be made of;
(pertencer) to belong to; **sua
família é da Bahia** his (ou her etc)
family is from Bahia; **a mesa é de
mármore** the table is made of
marble; **é de Pedro** it's Pedro's, it
belongs to Pedro
4 (em orações passivas): **já foi
descoberto** it had already been
discovered
5 (locuções com subjun): **ou seja** that

is to say; **seja quem for** whoever it
may be; **se eu fosse você** if I were
you; **se não fosse você, ...** if it
hadn't been for you ...
6 (locuções): **a não ser** except; **a
não ser que** unless; **é** (resposta
afirmativa) yes; **..., não é?** isn't it?,
don't you? etc; **ah, é?** really?; **que
foi?** (o que aconteceu?) what
happened?; (qual é o problema?)
what's the problem?; **será que ...?**
I wonder if ...?
▷ m being; **seres** mpl (criaturas)
creatures

sereia [se'reja] f mermaid
série ['sɛri] f series; (sequência)
sequence, succession; (Educ) grade;
(categoria) category; **fora de ~** out of
order; (fig) extraordinary
seriedade [serje'dadʒi] f
seriousness; (honestidade) honesty
seringa [se'rĩga] f syringe
sério, -a ['sɛrju, a] adj serious;
(honesto) honest, decent;
(responsável) responsible; (confiável)
reliable; (roupa) sober ▷ adv
seriously; **a ~** seriously; **~?** really?
sermão [ser'mãw] (pl **-ões**) m
sermon; (fig) telling-off
serpente [ser'pẽtʃi] f snake
serra ['sɛha] f (montanhas)
mountains pl; (Tec) saw
serralheiro, -a [seha'ʎejru, a] m/f
locksmith
serrano, -a [se'hanu, a] adj
highland atr ▷ m/f highlander
serrar [se'har] vt to saw
sertanejo, -a [serta'neʒu, a] adj
rustic, country ▷ m/f inhabitant of
the "sertão"
sertão [ser'tãw] (pl **-ões**) m
backwoods pl, bush (country)
servente [ser'vẽtʃi] m/f servant;

(*operário*) labourer (*Brit*), laborer (*US*)

serviçal [servi'saw] (*pl* **-ais**) *adj* obliging, helpful ▷ *m/f* servant; (*trabalhador*) wage earner

serviço [ser'visu] *m* service; (*de chá etc*) set; **estar de ~** to be on duty; **prestar ~** to help

servidor, a [servi'dor(a)] *m/f* servant; (*funcionário*) employee; **~ público** civil servant

servil [ser'viw] (*pl* **-is**) *adj* servile

servir [ser'vir] *vt* to serve ▷ *vi* to serve; (*ser útil*) to be useful; (*ajudar*) to help; (*roupa: caber*) to fit; **servir-se** *vr*: **~-se (de)** (*comida, café*) to help o.s. (to); **~-se de** (*meios*) to use, make use of; **~ de** (*prover*) to supply with, provide with; **você está servido?** (*num bar*) are you all right for a drink?; **~ de algo** to serve as sth; **qualquer ônibus serve** any bus will do

servis [ser'vis] *adj pl de* **servil**

sessão [se'sãw] (*pl* **-ões**) *f* (*do parlamento etc*) session; (*reunião*) meeting; (*de cinema*) showing

sessenta [se'sẽta] *num* sixty

sessões [se'sõjs] *fpl de* **sessão**

sesta ['sɛsta] *f* siesta, nap

seta ['sɛta] *f* arrow

sete ['sɛtʃi] *num* seven

setembro [se'tẽbru] *m* September; **7 de ~** *see note*

7 DE SETEMBRO

Brazil's independence from Portugal is commemmorated on 7 September. Independence was declared in 1822 by the Portuguese prince regent, Dom Pedro, who rebelled against several orders from the Portuguese crown, among them the order to swear loyalty to the Portuguese constitution. It is a national holiday and the occasion for processions and military parades through the main cities.

setenta [se'tẽta] *num* seventy

sétimo, -a ['sɛtʃimu, a] *num* seventh

setor [se'tor] *m* sector

seu, sua [sew, 'sua] *adj* (*dele*) his; (*dela*) her; (*de coisa*) its; (*deles, delas*) their; (*de você, vocês*) your ▷ *pron* (*dele*) his; (*dela*) hers; (*deles, delas*) theirs; (*de você, vocês*) yours ▷ *m* (*senhor*) Mr(.)

severidade [severi'dadʒi] *f* severity

severo, -a [se'vɛru, a] *adj* severe

sexo ['sɛksu] *m* sex

sexta ['sesta] *f* (*tb*: **~-feira**) Friday; **sexta-feira** (*pl* **sextas-feiras**) *f* Friday; **Sexta-feira Santa** Good Friday

sexto, -a ['sestu, a] *num* sixth

sexual [se'kswaw] (*pl* **-ais**) *adj* sexual; (*vida, ato*) sex *atr*

sexy ['sɛksi] (*pl* **-s**) *adj* sexy

s.f.f. (*PT*) *abr* = **se faz favor**

short ['ʃortʃi] *m* (pair of) shorts *pl*

si [si] *pron* oneself; (*ele*) himself; (*ela*) herself; (*coisa*) itself; (*PT*: *você*) yourself, you; (*: vocês*) yourselves; (*eles, elas*) themselves

SIDA ['sida] (*PT*) *abr f* (= *síndrome de deficiência imunológica adquirida*) AIDS

siderúrgica [side'rurʒika] *f* steel industry

sigilo [si'ʒilu] *m* secrecy

sigla ['sigla] *f* acronym; (*abreviação*) abbreviation

S

significado [signifi'kadu] *m* meaning

significar [signifi'kar] *vt* to mean, signify; **significativo, -a** [signifika'tʃivu, a] *adj* significant

signo ['signu] *m* sign

sigo *etc* ['sigu] *vb ver* **seguir**

sílaba ['silaba] *f* syllable

silenciar [silẽ'sjar] *vt* to silence

silêncio [si'lẽsju] *m* silence, quiet; **silencioso, -a** [silẽ'sjozu, ɔza] *adj* silent, quiet ▷ *m* (*Auto*) silencer (*Brit*), muffler (*US*)

silhueta [si'ʎweta] *f* silhouette

silvestre [siw'vɛstri] *adj* wild

sim [sĩ] *adv* yes; **creio que ~** I think so

símbolo ['sĩbolu] *m* symbol

simetria [sime'tria] *f* symmetry

similar [simi'lar] *adj* similar

simpatia [sĩpa'tʃia] *f* liking; (*afeto*) affection; (*afinidade, solidariedade*) sympathy; **simpatias** *fpl* (*inclinações*) sympathies; **simpático, -a** [sĩ'patʃiku, a] *adj* (*pessoa, decoração etc*) nice; (*lugar*) pleasant, nice; (*amável*) friendly; **simpatizante** [sĩpatʃi'zãtʃi] *adj* sympathetic ▷ *m/f* sympathizer; **simpatizar** [sĩpatʃi'zar] *vi*: **simpatizar com** (*pessoa*) to like; (*causa*) to sympathize with

simples ['sĩplis] *adj inv* simple; (*único*) single; (*fácil*) easy; (*mero*) mere; (*ingênuo*) naïve ▷ *adv* simply; **simplicidade** [sĩplisi'dadʒi] *f* simplicity; **simplificar** [sĩplifi'kar] *vt* to simplify

simular [simu'lar] *vt* to simulate

simultaneamente [simuwtanja'mẽtʃi] *adv* simultaneously

simultâneo, -a [simuw'tanju, a] *adj* simultaneous

sinagoga [sina'gɔga] *f* synagogue

sinal [si'naw] (*pl* **-ais**) *m* sign; (*gesto, Tel*) signal; (*na pele*) mole; (: *de nascença*) birthmark; (*depósito*) deposit; (*tb:* **~ de tráfego luminoso**) traffic light; **por ~** (*por falar nisso*) by the way; (*aliás*) as a matter of fact; **~ de chamada** (*Tel*) ringing tone; **~ de discar** (*BR*) *ou* **de marcar** (*PT*) dialling tone (*Brit*), dial tone (*US*); **~ de ocupado** (*BR*) *ou* **de impedido** (*PT*) engaged tone (*Brit*), busy signal (*US*); **sinalização** [sinaliza'sãw] *f* (*ato*) signalling; (*para motoristas*) traffic signs *pl*

sincero, -a [sĩ'sɛru, a] *adj* sincere

sindicalista [sĩdʒika'lista] *m/f* trade unionist

sindicato [sĩdʒi'katu] *m* trade union; (*financeiro*) syndicate

síndrome ['sĩdromi] *f* syndrome; **~ de Down** Down's syndrome

sinfonia [sĩfo'nia] *f* symphony

singular [sĩgu'lar] *adj* singular; (*extraordinário*) exceptional; (*bizarro*) odd, peculiar

sino ['sinu] *m* bell

sintaxe [sĩ'tasi] *f* syntax

síntese ['sĩtezi] *f* synthesis; **sintético, -a** [sĩ'tɛtʃiku, a] *adj* synthetic; **sintetizar** [sĩtetʃi'zar] *vt* to synthesize

sinto *etc* ['sĩtu] *vb ver* **sentir**

sintoma [sĩ'tɔma] *m* symptom

sinuca [si'nuka] *f* snooker

sinuoso, -a [si'nwozu, ɔza] *adj* (*caminho*) winding; (*linha*) wavy

siri [si'ri] *m* crab

sirvo *etc* ['sirvu] *vb ver* **servir**

sistema [sis'tema] *m* system; (*método*) method; **~ imunológico** immune system

site ['sajtʃi] *m* (*na Internet*) website; **site de relacionamentos** social networking site

sítio ['sitʃju] m (Mil) siege; (propriedade rural) small farm; (PT: lugar) place

situação [sitwa'sãw] (pl **-ões**) f situation; (posição) position

situado, -a [si'twadu, a] adj situated

situar [si'twar] vt to place, put; (edifício) to situate, locate; **situar-se** vr to position o.s.; (estar situado) to be situated

slogan [iz'lɔɡã] (pl **-s**) m slogan

smoking [iz'mokĩs] (pl **-s**) m dinner jacket (Brit), tuxedo (US)

só [sɔ] adj alone; (único) single; (solitário) solitary ▷ adv only; **a sós** alone

soar [swar] vi to sound ▷ vt (horas) to strike; (instrumento) to play; **~ a** to sound like; **~ bem/mal** (fig) to go down well/badly

sob [sob] prep under; **~ juramento** on oath; **~ medida** (roupa) made to measure

sobe etc ['sɔbi] vb ver **subir**

soberano, -a [sobe'ranu, a] adj sovereign; (fig: supremo) supreme ▷ m/f sovereign

sobra ['sɔbra] f surplus, remnant; **sobras** fpl remains; (de tecido) remnants; (de comida) leftovers; **ter algo de ~** to have sth extra; (tempo, comida, motivos) to have plenty of sth; **ficar de ~** to be left over

sobrado [so'bradu] m (andar) floor; (casa) house (of two or more storeys)

sobrancelha [sobrã'seʎa] f eyebrow

sobrar [so'brar] vi to be left; (dúvidas) to remain

sobre ['sobri] prep on; (por cima de) over; (acima de) above; (a respeito de) about

sobrecarregar [sobrikahe'gar] vt to overload

sobremesa [sobri'meza] f dessert

sobrenatural [sobrinatu'raw] (pl **-ais**) adj supernatural

sobrenome [sobri'nɔmi] (BR) m surname, family name

sobrepor [sobri'por] (irreg: como **pôr**) vt: **~ algo a algo** to put sth on top of sth

sobressair [sobrisa'ir] vi to stand out; **sobressair-se** vr to stand out

sobressalente [sobrisa'lẽtʃi] adj, m spare

sobressalto [sobri'sawtu] m start; (temor) trepidation; **de ~** suddenly

sobretaxa [sobri'taʃa] f surcharge

sobretudo [sobri'tudu] m overcoat ▷ adv above all, especially

sobrevivência [sobrivi'vẽsja] f survival; **sobrevivente** [sobrivi'vẽtʃi] adj surviving ▷ m/f survivor

sobreviver [sobrivi'ver] vi: **~ (a)** to survive

sobrinho, -a [so'briɲu, a] m/f nephew/niece

sóbrio, -a ['sɔbrju, a] adj sober; (moderado) moderate, restrained

socar [so'kar] vt (esmurrar) to hit, strike; (calcar) to crush, pound; (massa de pão) to knead

social [so'sjaw] (pl **-ais**) adj social; **socialista** [sosja'lista] adj, m/f socialist

sociedade [sosje'dadʒi] f society; (Com: empresa) company; (associação) association; **~ anônima** limited company (Brit), incorporated company (US)

sócio, -a ['sɔsju, a] m/f (Com) partner; (de clube) member

soco ['soku] m punch; **dar um ~ em** to punch

socorrer [soko'her] vt to help, assist; (salvar) to rescue; **socorrer-se** vr: **~-se de** to resort to, have recourse to; **socorro** [so'kohu] m help, assistance; (reboque) breakdown (Brit) ou tow (US) truck; **socorro!** help!; **primeiros socorros** first aid sg

soda ['sɔda] f soda (water)

sofá [so'fa] m sofa, settee; **sofá-cama** (pl **sofás-camas**) m sofa-bed

sofisticado, -a [sofist∫i'kadu, a] adj sophisticated; (afetado) pretentious

sofrer [so'frer] vt to suffer; (acidente) to have; (aguentar) to bear, put up with; (experimentar) to undergo ▷ vi to suffer; **sofrido, -a** [so'fridu, a] adj long-suffering; **sofrimento** [sofri'mẽtu] m suffering

software [sof'twer] m (Comput) software

sogro, -a ['sogru, 'sɔgra] m/f father-in-law/mother-in-law

sóis [sɔjs] mpl de **sol**

soja ['sɔʒa] f soya (Brit), soy (US)

sol [sɔw] (pl **sóis**) m sun; (luz) sunshine, sunlight; **fazer ~** to be sunny; **pegar ~** to get the sun

sola ['sɔla] f sole

solar [so'lar] adj solar; **energia/painel ~** solar energy/panel

soldado [sow'dadu] m soldier

soleira [so'lejra] f doorstep

solene [so'lɛni] adj solemn; **solenidade** [soleni'dadʒi] f solemnity; (cerimônia) ceremony

soletrar [sole'trar] vt to spell

solicitar [solisi'tar] vt to ask for; (emprego etc) to apply for; (amizade, atenção) to seek; **~ algo a alguém** to ask sb for sth

solícito, -a [so'lisitu, a] adj helpful

solidão [soli'dãw] f solitude; (sensação) loneliness

solidariedade [solidarje'dadʒi] f solidarity

solidário, -a [soli'darju, a] adj (pessoa) supportive; **ser ~ ou com** (pessoa) to stand by; (causa) to be sympathetic to, sympathize with

sólido, -a ['sɔlidu, a] adj solid

solitário, -a [soli'tarju, a] adj lonely, solitary ▷ m hermit

solo ['sɔlu] m ground, earth; (Mús) solo

soltar [sow'tar] vt to set free; (desatar) to loosen; (largar) to let go of; (emitir) to emit; (grito, risada) to let out; (cabelo) to let down; (freio, animais) to release; **soltar-se** vr to come loose; (desinibir-se) to let o.s. go

solteirão, -rona [sowtej'rãw, rɔna] (pl **-ões/-onas**) adj unmarried ▷ m/f bachelor/spinster

solteiro, -a [sow'tejru, a] adj single ▷ m/f single man/woman

solteirões [sowtej'rõjs] mpl de **solteirão**

solto, -a ['sowtu, a] pp de **soltar** ▷ adj loose; (livre) free; (sozinho) alone

solução [solu'sãw] (pl **-ões**) f solution

soluçar [solu'sar] vi (chorar) to sob; (Med) to hiccup

solucionar [solusjo'nar] vt to solve; (decidir) to resolve

soluço [so'lusu] m sob; (Med) hiccup

soluções [solu'sõjs] fpl de **solução**

som [sõ] (pl **-ns**) m sound; **~ cd** compact disc player

soma ['sɔma] f sum; **somar**

[so'mar] *vt* (*adicionar*) to add (up); (*chegar a*) to add up to, amount to ▷ *vi* to add up

sombra ['sõbra] *f* shadow; (*proteção*) shade; (*indício*) trace, sign

sombrinha [sõ'briɲa] *f* parasol, sunshade

some *etc* ['sɔmi] *vb ver* **sumir**

somente [sɔ'mẽtʃi] *adv* only

somos ['somos] *vb ver* **ser**

sonâmbulo, -a [so'nãbulu, a] *m/f* sleepwalker

sondar [sõ'dar] *vt* to probe; (*opinião etc*) to sound out

soneca [so'nɛka] *f* nap, snooze

sonegar [sone'gar] *vt* (*dinheiro, valores*) to conceal, withhold; (*furtar*) to steal, pilfer; (*impostos*) to dodge, evade; (*informações, dados*) to withhold

soneto [so'netu] *m* sonnet

sonhar [so'ɲar] *vt, vi* to dream; ~ **com** to dream about; **sonho** ['sɔɲu] *m* dream; (*Culin*) doughnut

sono ['sonu] *m* sleep; **estar com** *ou* **ter ~** to be sleepy

sonolento, -a [sono'lẽtu, a] *adj* sleepy, drowsy

sonoro, -a [so'nɔru, a] *adj* resonant

sons [sõs] *mpl de* **som**

sonso, -a ['sõsu, a] *adj* sly, artful

sopa ['sopa] *f* soup

soporífero, -a [sopo'riferu, a] *adj* soporific ▷ *m* sleeping drug

soprar [so'prar] *vt* to blow; (*balão*) to blow up; (*vela*) to blow out; (*dizer em voz baixa*) to whisper ▷ *vi* to blow; **sopro** ['sopru] *m* blow, puff; (*de vento*) gust

sórdido, -a ['sɔrdʒidu, a] *adj* sordid; (*imundo*) squalid

soro ['soru] *m* (*Med*) serum

sorridente [sohi'dẽtʃi] *adj* smiling

sorrir [so'hir] *vi* to smile; **sorriso** [so'hizu] *m* smile

sorte ['sɔrtʃi] *f* luck; (*casualidade*) chance; (*destino*) fate, destiny; (*condição*) lot; (*espécie*) sort, kind; **de ~ que** so that; **dar ~** (*trazer sorte*) to bring good luck; (*ter sorte*) to be lucky; **estar com** *ou* **ter ~** to be lucky

sortear [sor'tʃjar] *vt* to draw lots for; (*rifar*) to raffle; (*Mil*) to draft; **sorteio** [sor'teju] *m* draw; (*rifa*) raffle; (*Mil*) draft

sortido, -a [sor'tʃidu, a] *adj* (*abastecido*) supplied, stocked; (*variado*) assorted; (*loja*) well-stocked

sortudo, -a [sor'tudu, a] (*col*) *adj* lucky

sorvete [sor'vetʃi] (*BR*) *m* ice cream

SOS *abr* SOS

sossegado, -a [sose'gadu, a] *adj* peaceful, calm

sossegar [sose'gar] *vt* to calm, quieten ▷ *vi* to quieten down

sossego [so'segu] *m* peace (and quiet)

sótão ['sɔtãw] (*pl* **-s**) *m* attic, loft

sotaque [so'taki] *m* accent

soterrar [sote'har] *vt* to bury

sou [so] *vb ver* **ser**

soube *etc* ['sobi] *vb ver* **saber**

soutien [su'tʃjã] *m* = **sutiã**

sova ['sɔva] *f* beating, thrashing

sovaco [so'vaku] *m* armpit

sovina [so'vina] *adj* mean, stingy ▷ *m/f* miser

sozinho, -a [sɔ'ziɲu, a] *adj* (all) alone, by oneself; (*por si mesmo*) by oneself

spam [is'pã] (*pl* **-s**) *m* (*Comput*) spam

squash [is'kwɛʃ] *m* squash

Sr. *abr* (= *senhor*) Mr

S

Sra. (BR), **Sr.a** (PT) abr (= senhora) Mrs

Srta. (BR), **Sr.ta** (PT) abr (= senhorita) Miss

sua ['sua] f de **seu**

suar [swar] vt, vi to sweat

suave ['swavi] adj gentle; (música, voz) soft; (sabor, vinho) smooth; (cheiro) delicate; (dor) mild; (trabalho) light; **suavidade** [suavi'dadʒi] f gentleness, softness

subalterno, -a [subaw'tɛrnu, a] adj, m/f subordinate

subconsciente [subkõ'sjẽtʃi] adj, m subconscious

subdesenvolvido, -a [subdʒizẽvow'vidu, a] adj underdeveloped

subentender [subẽtẽ'der] vt to understand, assume; **subentendido, -a** [subẽtẽ'dʒidu, a] adj implied ▷ m implication

subestimar [subestʃi'mar] vt to underestimate

subida [su'bida] f ascent, climb; (ladeira) slope; (de preços) rise

subir [su'bir] vi to go up; (preço, de posto etc) to rise ▷ vt to raise; (ladeira, escada, rio) to climb, go up; **~ em** to climb, go up; (cadeira, palanque) to climb onto, get up onto; (ônibus) to get on

súbito, -a ['subitu, a] adj sudden ▷ adv (tb: **de ~**) suddenly

subjetivo, -a [subʒe'tʃivu, a] adj subjective

subjuntivo, -a [subʒũ'tʃivu, a] adj, m subjunctive

sublime [su'blimi] adj sublime

sublinhar [subli'ɲar] vt to underline; (destacar) to emphasize, stress

submarino, -a [subma'rinu, a] adj underwater ▷ m submarine

submeter [subme'ter] vt to subdue; (plano) to submit; (sujeitar): **~ a** to subject to; **submeter-se** vr: **~-se a** to submit to; (operação) to undergo

submisso, -a [sub'misu, a] adj submissive

subnutrição [subnutri'sãw] f malnutrition

subornar [subor'nar] vt to bribe; **suborno** [su'bornu] m bribery

subsequente [subse'kwẽtʃi] adj subsequent

subserviente [subser'vjẽtʃi] adj obsequious, servile

subsidiária [subsi'dʒjarja] f (Com) subsidiary (company)

subsidiário, -a [subsi'dʒjarju, a] adj subsidiary

subsídio [sub'sidʒu] m subsidy; (ajuda) aid

subsistência [subsis'tẽsja] f subsistence

subsistir [subsis'tʃir] vi to exist; (viver) to subsist

subsolo [sub'sɔlu] m (de prédio) basement

substância [sub'stãsja] f substance; **substancial** [substã'sjaw] (pl **-ais**) adj substantial

substantivo, -a [substã'tʃivu, a] adj substantive ▷ m noun

substituir [substʃi'twir] vt to substitute

subtil etc [sub'tiw] (PT) = **sutil** etc

subtrair [subtra'ir] vt to steal; (deduzir) to subtract ▷ vi to subtract

subumano, -a [subu'manu, a] adj subhuman; (desumano) inhuman

suburbano, -a [subur'banu, a] adj suburban

subúrbio [su'burbju] *m* suburb

subvenção [subvẽ'sãw] (*pl* **-ões**) *f* subsidy, grant

subversivo, -a [subver'sivu, a] *adj, m/f* subversive

sucata [su'kata] *f* scrap metal

sucção [suk'sãw] *f* suction

suceder [suse'der] *vi* to happen ▷ *vt* to succeed; **~ a** (*num cargo*) to succeed; (*seguir*) to follow

sucessão [suse'sãw] (*pl* **-ões**) *f* succession; **sucessivo, -a** [suse'sivu, a] *adj* successive

sucesso [su'sɛsu] *m* success; (*música, filme*) hit; **fazer** *ou* **ter ~** to be successful

sucinto, -a [su'sĩtu, a] *adj* succinct

suco ['suku] (*BR*) *m* juice

suculento, -a [suku'lẽtu, a] *adj* succulent

sucumbir [sukũ'bir] *vi* to succumb; (*morrer*) to die, perish

sucursal [sukur'saw] (*pl* **-ais**) *f* (*Com*) branch

Sudão [su'dãw] *m*: **o ~** (the) Sudan

sudeste [su'dɛstʃi] *m* south-east

súdito ['sudʒitu] *m* (*de rei etc*) subject

sudoeste [sud'wɛstʃi] *m* south-west

Suécia ['swɛsja] *f*: **a ~** Sweden; **sueco, -a** ['swɛku, a] *adj* Swedish ▷ *m/f* Swede ▷ *m* (*Ling*) Swedish

suéter ['swɛter] (*BR*) *m ou f* sweater

suficiente [sufi'sjẽtʃi] *adj* sufficient, enough

sufixo [su'fiksu] *m* suffix

sufocar [sufo'kar] *vt, vi* to suffocate

sugar [su'gar] *vt* to suck

sugerir [suʒe'rir] *vt* to suggest

sugestão [suʒes'tãw] (*pl* **-ões**) *f* suggestion; **dar uma ~** to make a suggestion; **sugestivo, -a** [suʒes'tʃivu, a] *adj* suggestive

sugiro *etc* [su'ʒiru] *vb ver* **sugerir**

Suíça ['swisa] *f*: **a ~** Switzerland

suíças ['swisas] *fpl* sideburns; *ver tb* **suíço**

suicida [swi'sida] *adj* suicidal ▷ *m/f* suicidal person; (*morto*) suicide; **suicidar-se** [swisi'darsi] *vr* to commit suicide; **suicídio** [swi'sidʒju] *m* suicide

suíço, -a ['swisu, a] *adj, m/f* Swiss

suíte ['switʃi] *f* (*Mús, em hotel*) suite

sujar [su'ʒar] *vt* to dirty ▷ *vi* to make a mess; **sujar-se** *vr* to get dirty

sujeira [su'ʒejra] *f* dirt; (*estado*) dirtiness; (*col*) dirty trick

sujeito, -a [su'ʒejtu, a] *adj*: **~ a** subject to ▷ *m* (*Ling*) subject ▷ *m/f* man/woman

sujo, -a ['suʒu, a] *adj* dirty; (*fig: desonesto*) dishonest ▷ *m* dirt

sul [suw] *adj inv* south, southern ▷ *m*: **o ~** the south; **sul-africano, -a** *adj, m/f* South African; **sul-americano, -a** *adj, m/f* South American; **sulco** [suw'ku] *m* furrow

suma ['suma] *f*: **em ~** in short

sumário, -a [su'marju, a] *adj* (*breve*) brief, concise; (*Jur*) summary; (*biquíni*) skimpy ▷ *m* summary

sumiço [su'misu] *m* disappearance

sumir [su'mir] *vi* to disappear, vanish

sumo, -a ['sumu, a] *adj* (*importância*) extreme; (*qualidade*) supreme ▷ *m* (*PT*) juice

sunga ['sũga] *f* swimming trunks *pl*

suor [swɔr] *m* sweat

super... [super-] *prefixo* super-, over-

superado, -a [supe'radu, a] *adj* (*ideias*) outmoded

S

superar [supe'rar] vt (rival) to surpass; (inimigo, dificuldade) to overcome; (expectativa) to exceed

superfície [super'fisi] f surface; (extensão) area; (fig: aparência) appearance

supérfluo, -a [su'pɛrflwu, a] adj superfluous

superior [supe'rjor] adj superior; (mais elevado) higher; (quantidade) greater; (mais acima) upper ▷ m superior; **superioridade** [superjori'dadʒi] f superiority

superlotado, -a [superlo'tadu, a] adj crowded; (excessivamente cheio) overcrowded

supermercado [supermer'kadu] m supermarket

superpotência [superpo'tẽsja] f superpower

superstição [superstʃi'sãw] (pl -ões) f superstition; **supersticioso, -a** [superstʃi'sjozu, ɔza] adj superstitious

supervisão [supervi'zãw] f supervision; **supervisionar** [supervizjo'nar] vt to supervise; **supervisor, a** [supervi'zor(a)] m/f supervisor

suplemento [suple'mẽtu] m supplement

súplica ['suplika] f supplication, plea; **suplicar** [supli'kar] vt, vi to plead, beg

suplício [su'plisju] m torture

supor [su'por] (irreg: como **pôr**) vt to suppose; (julgar) to think

suportar [supor'tar] vt to hold up, support; (tolerar) to bear, tolerate; **suportável** [supor'tavew] (pl -eis) adj bearable; **suporte** [su'pɔrtʃi] m support

suposto, -a [su'postu, 'pɔsta] adj supposed ▷ m assumption, supposition

supremo, -a [su'prɛmu, a] adj supreme

suprimir [supri'mir] vt to suppress

surdo, -a ['surdu, a] adj deaf; (som) muffled, dull ▷ m/f deaf person; **surdo-mudo, surda-muda** adj deaf and dumb ▷ m/f deaf-mute

surfe ['surfi] m surfing

surfista [sur'fista] m/f surfer

surgir [sur'ʒir] vi to appear; (problema, dificuldade) to arise

surjo etc [su'ʒu] vb ver **surgir**

surpreendente [surprjẽ'dẽtʃi] adj surprising

surpreender [surprjẽ'der] vt to surprise; **surpreender-se** vr: **~-se (de)** to be surprised (at); **surpresa** [sur'preza] f surprise; **surpreso, -a** [sur'prezu, a] pp de **surpreender** ▷ adj surprised

surra ['suha] f (ger, Esporte): **dar uma ~ em** to thrash; **levar uma ~ (de)** to get thrashed (by); **surrar** [su'har] vt to beat, thrash

surtar [sur'tar] to freak out

surtir [sur'tʃir] vt to produce, bring about

surto ['surtu] m (de doença) outbreak; (ataque) outburst

SUS [sus] (BR) abr m (= Sistema Único de Saúde) national health service

suspeita [sus'pejta] f suspicion; **suspeitar** [suspej'tar] vt to suspect ▷ vi: **suspeitar de algo** to suspect sth; **suspeito, -a** [sus'pejtu, a] adj, m/f suspect

suspender [suspẽ'der] vt (levantar) to lift; (pendurar) to hang; (trabalho, pagamento etc) to suspend; (encomenda) to cancel; (sessão) to adjourn, defer; (viagem) to put off; **suspensão** [suspẽ'sãw] (pl -ões) f (ger, Auto) suspension; (de trabalho, pagamento) stoppage; (de viagem, sessão) deferment; (de encomenda) cancellation; **suspense** [sus'pēsi] m suspense; **filme de suspense** thriller; **suspenso, -a** [sus'pēsu, a] pp de **suspender**

suspensórios [suspē'sɔrjus] mpl braces (Brit), suspenders (US)

suspirar [suspi'rar] vi to sigh; **suspiro** [sus'piru] m sigh; (doce) meringue

sussurrar [susu'har] vt, vi to whisper; **sussurro** [su'suhu] m whisper

sustentar [sustē'tar] vt to sustain; (prédio) to hold up; (padrão) to maintain; (financeiramente, acusação) to support; **sustentável** [sustē'tavew] (pl -**eis**) adj sustainable; **sustento** [sus'tētu] m sustenance; (subsistência) livelihood; (amparo) support

susto ['sustu] m fright, scare

sutiã [su'tʃjã] m bra(ssiere)

sutil [su'tʃiw] (pl -**is**) adj subtle; **sutileza** [sutʃi'leza] f subtlety

t

ta [ta] = **te + a**

tabacaria [tabaka'ria] f tobacconist's (shop)

tabaco [ta'baku] m tobacco

tabela [ta'bɛla] f table, chart; (lista) list; **por ~** indirectly

taberna [ta'bɛrna] f tavern, bar

tablete [ta'blɛtʃi] m (de chocolate) bar

tabu [ta'bu] adj, m taboo

tábua ['tabwa] f plank, board; (Mat) table; **~ de passar roupa** ironing board

tabuleiro [tabu'lejru] m tray; (Xadrez) board

tabuleta [tabu'leta] f (letreiro) sign, signboard

taça ['tasa] f cup

tacha ['taʃa] f tack

tachinha [ta'ʃiɲa] f drawing pin (Brit), thumb tack (US)

taco ['taku] m (Bilhar) cue; (Golfe) club

t

tagarela [taga'rɛla] *adj* talkative ▷ *m/f* chatterbox; **tagarelar** [tagare'lar] *vi* to chatter

Tailândia [taj'lãdʒja] *f*: **a ~** Thailand

tal [taw] (*pl* **tais**) *adj* such; **~ e coisa** this and that; **um ~ de Sr. X** a certain Mr. X; **que ~?** what do you think?; (*PT*) how are things?; **que ~ um cafezinho?** what about a coffee?; **que ~ nós irmos ao cinema?** what about (us) going to the cinema?; **~ pai, ~ filho** like father, like son; **~ como** such as; (*da maneira que*) just as; **~ qual** just like; **o ~ professor** that teacher; **a ~ ponto** to such an extent; **de ~ maneira** in such a way; **e ~** and so on; **o/a ~** (*col*) the greatest; **o Pedro de ~** Peter what's-his-name; **na rua ~** in such and such a street; **foi um ~ de gente ligar lá para casa** there were people ringing home non-stop

talão [ta'lãw] (*pl* **-ões**) *m* (*de recibo*) stub; **~ de cheques** cheque book (*Brit*), check book (*US*)

talco ['tawku] *m* talcum powder; **pó de ~** (*PT*) talcum powder

talento [ta'lẽtu] *m* talent; (*aptidão*) ability

talha ['taʎa] *f* carving; (*vaso*) pitcher; (*Náut*) tackle

talher [ta'ʎer] *m* set of cutlery; **talheres** *mpl* cutlery *sg*

talo ['talu] *m* stalk, stem

talões [ta'lõjs] *mpl de* **talão**

talvez [taw'vez] *adv* perhaps, maybe

tamanco [ta'mãku] *m* clog, wooden shoe

tamanduá [tamã'dwa] *m* anteater

tamanho, -a [ta'maɲu, a] *adj* such (a) great ▷ *m* size

tâmara ['tamara] *f* date

também [tã'bẽj] *adv* also, too, as well; (*além disso*) besides; **~ não** not ... either, nor

tambor [tã'bor] *m* drum

tamborim [tãbo'rĩ] (*pl* **-ns**) *m* tambourine

Tâmisa ['tamiza] *m*: **o ~** the Thames

tampa ['tãpa] *f* lid; (*de garrafa*) cap

tampão [tã'pãw] (*pl* **-ões**) *m* tampon

tampar [tã'par] *vt* (*lata, garrafa*) to put the lid on; (*cobrir*) to cover

tampinha [tã'piɲa] *f* lid, top

tampo ['tãpu] *m* lid

tampões [tã'põjs] *mpl de* **tampão**

tampouco [tã'poku] *adv* nor, neither

tangerina [tãʒe'rina] *f* tangerine

tanque ['tãki] *m* tank; (*de lavar roupa*) sink

tanto, -a ['tãtu, a] *adj, pron* (*sg*) so much; (: + *interrogativa/negativa*) as much; (*pl*) so many; (: + *interrogativa/negativa*) as many ▷ *adv* so much; **~ ... como ...** both ... and ...; **~ ... quanto ...** as much ... as ...; **~ tempo** so long; **quarenta e ~s anos** forty-odd years; **~ faz** it's all the same to me, I don't mind; **um ~ (quanto)** (*como adv*) rather, somewhat; **~ (assim) que** so much so that

tão [tãw] *adv* so; **~ rico quanto** as rich as; **~ só** only

tapa ['tapa] *m* slap

tapar [ta'par] *vt* to cover; (*garrafa*) to cork; (*caixa*) to put the lid on; (*orifício*) to block up; (*encobrir*) to block out

tapear [ta'pjar] *vt, vi* to cheat

tapeçaria [tapesa'ria] *f* tapestry

tapete [ta'petʃi] *m* carpet, rug

tardar [tar'dar] *vi* to delay; (*chegar tarde*) to be late ▷ *vt* to delay; **sem mais ~** without delay; **~ a ou em fazer** to take a long time to do; **o mais ~** at the latest

tarde ['tardʒi] *f* afternoon ▷ *adv* late; **mais cedo ou mais ~** sooner or later; **antes ~ do que nunca** better late than never; **boa ~!** good afternoon!; **à ou de ~** in the afternoon

tardio, -a [tar'dʒiu, a] *adj* late

tarefa [ta'rɛfa] *f* task, job; (*faina*) chore

tarifa [ta'rifa] *f* tariff; (*para transportes*) fare; (*lista de preços*) price list; **~ alfandegária** customs duty

tartaruga [tarta'ruga] *f* turtle

tasca ['taska] (*PT*) *f* cheap eating place

tática ['tatʃika] *f* tactics *pl*

tático, -a ['tatʃiku, a] *adj* tactical

tato ['tatu] *m* touch; (*fig: diplomacia*) tact

tatu [ta'tu] *m* armadillo

tatuagem [ta'twaʒẽ] (*pl* **-ns**) *f* tattoo

taxa ['taʃa] *f* (*imposto*) tax; (*preço*) fee; (*índice*) rate; **~ de câmbio** exchange rate; **~ de juros** interest rate; **taxação** [taʃa'sãw] *f* taxation; **taxar** [ta'ʃar] *vt* (*fixar o preço de*) to fix the price of; (*lançar impostos sobre*) to tax

táxi ['taksi] *m* taxi

taxista [tak'sista] *m/f* taxi driver

tchau [tʃaw] *excl* bye!

tcheco, -a ['tʃɛku, a] *adj, m/f* Czech; **a República Tcheca** the Czech Republic

te [tʃi] *pron* you; (*para você*) (to) you

teatro ['tʃiatru] *m* theatre (*Brit*), theater (*US*); (*obras*) plays *pl*, dramatic works *pl*; (*gênero, curso*) drama; **peça de ~** play

tecer [te'ser] *vt, vi* to weave; **tecido** [te'sidu] *m* cloth, material; (*Anat*) tissue

tecla ['tɛkla] *f* key; **teclado** [tek'ladu] *m* keyboard

técnica ['tɛknika] *f* technique; *ver tb* **técnico**

técnico, -a ['tɛkniku, a] *adj* technical ▷ *m/f* technician; (*especialista*) expert

tecnologia [teknolo'ʒia] *f* technology; **tecnológico, -a** [tekno'lɔʒiku, a] *adj* technological

tédio ['tɛdʒiu] *m* tedium, boredom; **tedioso, -a** [te'dʒiozu, ɔza] *adj* tedious, boring

teia ['teja] *f* web; **~ de aranha** cobweb

teimar [tej'mar] *vi* to insist, keep on; **~ em** to insist on

teimosia [tejmo'zia] *f* stubbornness; **~ em fazer** insistence on doing

teimoso, -a [tej'mozu, ɔza] *adj* obstinate; (*criança*) wilful (*Brit*), willful (*US*)

Tejo ['teʒu] *m*: **o (rio) ~** the (river) Tagus

tela ['tɛla] *f* fabric, material; (*de pintar*) canvas; (*Cinema, TV*) screen

tele... ['tele] *prefixo* tele..; **telecomunicações** [telekomunika'sõjs] *fpl* telecommunications; **teleconferência** [telekõfe'rẽsja] *f* teleconference

teleférico [tele'fɛriku] *m* cable car

telefonar [telefo'nar] *vi*: **~ para alguém** to (tele)phone sb

telefone [tele'foni] *m* phone, telephone; (*número*) (tele)phone number; (*telefonema*) phone call;

~ celular cellphone, mobile phone; **~ de carro** carphone; **telefonema** [telefo'nɛma] *m* phone call; **dar um telefonema** to make a phone call; **telefônico, -a** [tele'foniku, a] *adj* telephone *atr*; **telefonista** [telefo'nista] *m/f* telephonist; *(na companhia telefônica)* operator

telegrama [tele'grama] *m* telegram, cable; **passar um ~** to send a telegram; **telejornal** [teleʒor'naw] *(pl* **-ais)** *m* television news *sg*

telemóvel [tɛle'mɔvel] *(pl* **-eis)** *m (PT)* mobile (phone) *(Brit)*, cell phone *(US)*; **telenovela** [teleno'vɛla] *f (TV)* soap opera; **telescópio** [tele'skɔpju] *m* telescope; **telespectador, a** [telespekta'dor(a)] *m/f* viewer

televendas [tele'vẽdas] *fpl* telesales

televisão [televi'zãw] *f* television; **~ por assinatura** pay television; **~ a cabo** cable television; **~ a cores** colo(u)r television; **~ digital** digital television; **~ via satélite** satellite television; **aparelho de ~** television set; **televisionar** [televizjo'nar] *vt* to televise; **televisivo, -a** [televi'zivu, a] *adj* television *atr*

televisor [televi'zor] *m (aparelho)* television (set), TV (set)

telha ['teʎa] *f* tile; *(col: cabeça)* head; **ter uma ~ de menos** to have a screw loose

telhado [te'ʎadu] *m* roof

tema ['tɛma] *m* theme; *(assunto)* subject; **temática** [te'matʃika] *f* theme

temer [te'mer] *vt* to fear, be afraid of ▷ *vi* to be afraid

temeroso, -a [teme'rozu, ɔza] *adj* fearful, afraid; *(pavoroso)* dreadful

temido, -a [te'midu, a] *adj* fearsome, frightening

temível [te'mivew] *(pl* **-eis)** *adj* = **temido**

temor [te'mor] *m* fear

temperado, -a [tẽpe'radu, a] *adj (clima)* temperate; *(comida)* seasoned

temperamento [tẽpera'mẽtu] *m* temperament, nature

temperar [tẽpe'rar] *vt* to season

temperatura [tẽpera'tura] *f* temperature

tempero [tẽ'peru] *m* seasoning, flavouring *(Brit)*, flavoring *(US)*

tempestade [tẽpes'tadʒi] *f* storm; **tempestuoso, -a** [tẽpes'twozu, ɔza] *adj* stormy

templo ['tẽplu] *m* temple; *(igreja)* church

tempo ['tẽpu] *m* time; *(meteorológico)* weather; *(Ling)* tense; **o ~ todo** the whole time; **a ~** on time; **ao mesmo ~** at the same time; **a um ~** at once; **com ~** in good time; **de ~ em ~** from time to time; **nesse meio ~** in the meantime; **quanto ~?** how long?; **mais ~** longer; **há ~s** for ages; *(atrás)* ages ago; **~ livre** spare time; **primeiro/segundo ~** *(Esporte)* first/second half

temporada [tẽpo'rada] *f* season; *(tempo)* spell

temporal [tẽpo'raw] *(pl* **-ais)** *m* storm, gale

temporário, -a [tẽpo'rarju, a] *adj* temporary, provisional

tenacidade [tenasi'dadʒi] *f* tenacity

tencionar [tẽsjo'nar] *vt* to intend, plan

tenda ['tẽda] *f* tent

tendão [tẽ'dãw] (pl **-ões**) m tendon
tendões [tẽ'dõjs] mpl de **tendão**
tenebroso, -a [tene'brozu, ɔza] adj dark, gloomy; (fig) horrible
tenho etc ['teɲu] vb ver **ter**
tênis ['tenis] m inv tennis; (sapatos) training shoes pl; (um sapato) training shoe; **~ de mesa** table tennis; **tenista** [te'nista] m/f tennis player
tenor [te'nor] m (Mús) tenor
tenro, -a ['tẽhu, a] adj tender; (macio) soft; (delicado) delicate; (novo) young
tensão [tẽ'sãw] f tension; (pressão) pressure, strain; (rigidez) tightness; (Elet: voltagem) voltage
tenso, -a ['tẽsu, a] adj tense; (sob pressão) under stress, strained
tentação [tẽta'sãw] f temptation
tentáculo [tẽ'takulu] m tentacle
tentar [tẽ'tar] vt to try; (seduzir) to tempt ▷ vi to try; **tentativa** [tẽta'tʃiva] f attempt; **tentativa de homicídio/suicídio/roubo** attempted murder/suicide/robbery; **por tentativas** by trial and error
tênue ['tenwi] adj tenuous; (fino) thin; (delicado) delicate; (luz, voz) faint; (pequeníssimo) minute
teor [te'or] m (conteúdo) tenor; (sentido) meaning, drift
teoria [teo'ria] f theory; **teoricamente** [teorika'mẽtʃi] adv theoretically, in theory; **teórico, -a** [te'ɔriku, a] adj theoretical ▷ m/f theoretician
tépido, -a ['tɛpidu, a] adj tepid

PALAVRA-CHAVE

ter [ter] vt **1** (possuir, ger) to have; (na mão) to hold; **você tem uma caneta?** have you got a pen?; **ela vai ter neném** she is going to have a baby
2 (idade, medidas, estado) to be; **ela tem 7 anos** she's 7 (years old); **a mesa tem 1 metro de comprimento** the table is 1 metre long; **ter fome/sorte** to be hungry/lucky; **ter frio/calor** to be cold/hot
3 (conter) to hold, contain; **a caixa tem um quilo de chocolates** the box holds one kilo of chocolates
4: **ter que** ou **de fazer** to have to do
5: **ter a ver com** to have to do with
6: **ir ter com** to (go and) meet
▷ vb impess **1**: **tem** (sg) there is; (pl) there are; **tem 3 dias que não saio de casa** I haven't been out for 3 days
2: **não tem de quê** don't mention it

terapeuta [tera'pewta] m/f therapist
terapia [tera'pia] f therapy
terça ['tersa] f (tb: **~-feira**) Tuesday; **terça-feira** (pl **terças-feiras**) f Tuesday; **terça-feira gorda** Shrove Tuesday
terceiro, -a [ter'sejru, a] num third; **terceiros** mpl (os outros) outsiders; ver tb **quinto**
terço ['tersu] m third (part)
termas ['termas] fpl bathhouse sg
térmico, -a ['termiku, a] adj thermal; **garrafa térmica** (Thermos®) flask
terminal [termi'naw] (pl **-ais**) adj terminal ▷ m (de rede, Elet, Comput) terminal ▷ f terminal; **~ (de vídeo)** monitor, visual display unit
terminar [termi'nar] vt to finish ▷ vi (pessoa) to finish; (coisa) to end; **~ de fazer** to finish doing; (ter feito

t

há pouco) to have just done; **~ por algo/fazer algo** to end with sth/ end up doing sth

término ['tɛrminu] *m* end, termination

termo ['tɛrmu] *m* term; (*fim*) end, termination; (*limite*) limit, boundary; (*prazo*) period; (*PT: garrafa*) (Thermos®) flask; **meio ~** compromise; **em ~s (de)** in terms (of)

termômetro [ter'mometru] *m* thermometer

terno, -a ['tɛrnu, a] *adj* gentle, tender ▷ *m* (*BR: roupa*) suit; **ternura** [ter'nura] *f* gentleness, tenderness

terra ['tɛʀa] *f* earth, world; (*Agr, propriedade*) land; (*pátria*) country; (*chão*) ground; (*Geo*) soil; (*pó*) dirt

terraço [te'ʀasu] *m* terrace

terramoto [teʀa'mɔtu] (*PT*) *m* = **terremoto**

terreiro [te'ʀejru] *m* yard, square

terremoto [teʀe'mɔtu] *m* earthquake

terreno, -a [te'ʀɛnu, a] *m* ground, land; (*porção de terra*) plot of land ▷ *adj* earthly

térreo, -a ['tɛʀju, a] *adj*: **andar ~** (*BR*) ground floor (*Brit*), first floor (*US*)

terrestre [te'ʀɛstri] *adj* land *atr*

território [teʀi'tɔrju] *m* territory

terrível [te'ʀivew] (*pl* **-eis**) *adj* terrible, dreadful

terror [te'ʀoʀ] *m* terror, dread; **terrorista** [teʀo'rista] *adj, m/f* terrorist; **terrorista suicida** suicide bomber

tese ['tɛzi] *f* proposition, theory; (*Educ*) thesis; **em ~** in theory

teso, -a ['tɛzu, a] *adj* (*cabo*) taut; (*rígido*) stiff

tesouraria [tezora'ria] *f* treasury

tesouro [te'zoru] *m* treasure; (*erário*) treasury, exchequer; (*livro*) thesaurus

testa ['tɛsta] *f* brow, forehead

testar [tes'tar] *vt* to test; (*deixar em testamento*) to bequeath

teste ['tɛstʃi] *m* test

testemunha [teste'muɲa] *f* witness; **testemunhar** [testemu'ɲar] *vi* to testify ▷ *vt* to give evidence about; (*presenciar*) to witness; (*confirmar*) to demonstrate; **testemunho** [teste'muɲu] *m* evidence

testículo [tes'tʃikulu] *m* testicle

teta ['tɛta] *f* teat, nipple

tétano ['tɛtanu] *m* tetanus

teto ['tɛtu] *m* ceiling; (*telhado*) roof; (*habitação*) home

teu, tua [tew, 'tua] *adj* your ▷ *pron* yours

teve ['tevi] *vb ver* **ter**

têxtil ['tɛstʃiw] (*pl* **-eis**) *m* textile

texto ['tɛstu] *m* text

textura [tes'tura] *f* texture

thriller ['triler] (*pl* **-s**) *m* thriller

ti [tʃi] *pron* you

tia ['tʃia] *f* aunt

Tibete [tʃi'bɛtʃi] *m*: **o ~** Tibet

tido, -a ['tʃidu, a] *pp de* **ter** ▷ *adj*: **~ como** *ou* **por** considered to be

tigela [tʃi'ʒɛla] *f* bowl

tigre ['tʃigri] *m* tiger

tijolo [tʃi'ʒolu] *m* brick

til [tʃiw] (*pl* **tis**) *m* tilde

timbre ['tʃĩbri] *m* insignia, emblem; (*selo*) stamp; (*Mús*) tone, timbre; (*de voz*) tone; (*em papel de carta*) heading

time ['tʃimi] (*BR*) *m* team; **de segundo ~** (*fig*) second-rate

tímido, -a ['tʃimidu, a] *adj* shy, timid

tímpano ['tʃĩpanu] m eardrum; (Mús) kettledrum

tingir [tʃĩ'ʒir] vt to dye; (fig) to tinge

tinha etc ['tʃiɲa] vb ver **ter**

tinja ['tʃĩʒa] vb ver **ter**

tinjo etc ['tʃĩʒu] vb ver **tingir**

tinta ['tʃĩta] f (de pintar) paint; (de escrever) ink; (para tingir) dye; (fig: vestígio) shade, tinge

tinto, -a ['tʃĩtu, a] adj dyed; (fig) stained; **vinho ~** red wine

tintura [tʃĩ'tura] f dye; (ato) dyeing; (fig) tinge, hint

tinturaria [tʃĩtura'ria] f dry-cleaner's

tio ['tʃiu] m uncle

típico, -a ['tʃipiku, a] adj typical

tipo ['tʃipu] m type; (de imprensa) print; (de impressora) typeface; (col: sujeito) guy, chap; (pessoa) person

tipografia [tʃipogra'fia] f printing; (estabelecimento) printer's

tíquete ['tʃiketʃi] m ticket

tira ['tʃira] f strip ▷ m (BR: col) cop

tira-gosto (pl **-s**) m snack, savoury (Brit)

tirano, -a [tʃi'ranu, a] adj tyrannical ▷ m/f tyrant

tirar [tʃi'rar] vt to take away; (de dentro) to take out; (de cima) to take off; (roupa, sapatos) to take off; (arrancar) to pull out; (férias) to take, have; (boas notas) to get; (salário) earn; (curso) to do, take; (mancha) to remove; (foto, cópia) to take; (mesa) to clear; **~ algo a alguém** to take sth from sb

tiritar [tʃiri'tar] vi to shiver

tiro ['tʃiru] m shot; (ato de disparar) shooting; **~ ao alvo** target practice; **trocar ~s** to fire at one another

tiroteio [tʃiro'teju] m shooting, exchange of shots

tis [tʃis] mpl de **til**

titular [tʃitu'lar] adj titular ▷ m/f holder

título ['tʃitulu] m title; (Com) bond; (universitário) degree; **~ de propriedade** title deed

tive etc ['tʃivi] vb ver **ter**

to [tu] = **te + o**

toa ['toa] f towrope; **à ~** at random; (sem motivo) for no reason; (inutilmente) for nothing

toalete [twa'letʃi] m (banheiro) toilet ▷ f: **fazer a ~** to have a wash

toalha [to'aʎa] f towel

toca ['tɔka] f burrow, hole

toca-discos (BR) m inv record-player

tocador [toka'dor] m player; **~ MP3** MP3 player

toca-fitas m inv cassette player

tocaia [to'kaja] f ambush

tocante [to'kãtʃi] adj moving, touching; **no ~** regarding, concerning

tocar [to'kar] vt to touch; (Mús) to play ▷ vi to touch, to play; (campainha, sino, telefone) to ring; **tocar-se** vr to touch (each other); **~ a** (dizer respeito a) to concern, affect; **~ em** (assunto) to touch upon, to call at; **~ para alguém** (telefonar) to ring sb (up), call sb (up); **pelo que me toca** as far as I am concerned

tocha ['tɔʃa] f torch

todavia [toda'via] adv yet, still, however

PALAVRA-CHAVE

todo, -a ['todu, 'tɔda] adj **1** (com artigo sg) all; **toda a carne** all the meat; **toda a noite** all night, the whole night; **todo o Brasil** the whole of Brazil; **a toda**

t

(velocidade) at full speed; **todo o mundo** (BR), **toda a gente** (PT) everybody, everyone; **em toda (a) parte** everywhere **2** (*com artigo pl*) all; (: *cada*) every; **todos os livros** all the books; **todos os dias/todas as noites** every day/night; **todos os que querem sair** all those who want to leave; **todos nós** all of us ▷ *adv*: **ao todo** altogether; (*no total*) in all; **de todo** completely ▷ *pron*: **todos** everybody *sg*, everyone *sg*

todo-poderoso, -a *adj* all-powerful ▷ *m*: **o T~** the Almighty
toicinho [toj'siɲu] *m* bacon fat
tolerância [tole'rãsja] *f* tolerance; **tolerante** [tole'rãtʃi] *adj* tolerant
tolerar [tole'rar] *vt* to tolerate; **tolerável** [tole'ravew] (*pl* **-eis**) *adj* tolerable, bearable; (*satisfatório*) passable; (*falta*) excusable
tolice [to'lisi] *f* stupidity, foolishness; (*ato, dito*) stupid thing
tom [tõ] (*pl* **-ns**) *m* tone; (*Mús: altura*) pitch; (: *escala*) key; (*cor*) shade
tomada [to'mada] *f* capture; (*Elet*) socket
tomar [to'mar] *vt* to take; (*capturar*) to capture, seize; (*decisão*) to make; (*bebida*) to drink; **~ café** (*de manhã*) to have breakfast
tomara [to'mara] *excl*: **~!** if only!; **~ que venha hoje** I hope he comes today
tomate [to'matʃi] *m* tomato
tombadilho [tõba'dʒiʎu] *m* deck
tombar [tõ'bar] *vi* to fall down, tumble down ▷ *vt* to knock down, knock over; **tombo** ['tõbu] *m* tumble, fall

tomilho [to'miʎu] *m* thyme
tona ['tɔna] *f* surface; **vir à ~** to come to the surface; (*fig*) to emerge; **trazer à ~** to bring up; (*recordações*) to bring back
tonalidade [tonali'dadʒi] *f* (*de cor*) shade; (*Mús: tom*) key
tonelada [tone'lada] *f* ton
tônica ['tonika] *f* (*água*) tonic (water); (*fig*) keynote
tônico, -a ['toniku, a] *adj* tonic ▷ *m* tonic; **acento ~** stress
tons [tõs] *mpl de* **tom**
tonteira [tõ'tejra] *f* dizziness
tonto, -a ['tõtu, a] *adj* stupid, silly; (*zonzo*) dizzy, lightheaded; (*atarantado*) flustered
topar [to'par] *vt* to agree to ▷ *vi*: **~ com** to come across; **topar-se** *vr* (*duas pessoas*) to run into one another; **~ em** (*tropeçar*) to stub one's toe on; (*esbarrar*) to run into; (*tocar*) to touch
tópico, -a ['tɔpiku, a] *adj* topical ▷ *m* topic
topless ['tɔp'lɛs] *adj inv* topless
topo ['topu] *m* top; (*extremidade*) end, extremity
toque *etc vb ver* **tocar**
Tóquio ['tɔkju] *n* Tokyo
tora ['tɔra] *f* (*pedaço*) piece; (*de madeira*) log; (*sesta*) nap
toranja [to'rãʒa] *f* grapefruit
torção [tor'sãw] (*pl* **-ões**) *m* twist; (*Med*) sprain
torcedor, a [torse'dor(a)] *m/f* supporter, fan
torcer [tor'ser] *vt* to twist; (*Med*) to sprain; (*desvirtuar*) to distort, misconstrue; (*roupa: espremer*) to wring; (: *na máquina*) to spin; (*vergar*) to bend ▷ *vi*: **~ por** (*time*) to support; **torcer-se** *vr* to squirm, writhe

torcicolo [torsi'kɔlu] *m* stiff neck

torcida [tor'sida] *f* (*pavio*) wick; (*Esporte: ato de torcer*) cheering; (*: torcedores*) supporters *pl*

torções [tor'sõjs] *mpl de* **torção**

tormenta [tor'mẽta] *f* storm

tormento [tor'mẽtu] *m* torment; (*angústia*) anguish

tornar [tor'nar] *vi* to return, go back ▷ *vt*: **~ algo em algo** to turn *ou* make sth into sth; **tornar-se** *vr* to become; **~ a fazer algo** to do sth again

torneio [tor'neju] *m* tournament

torneira [tor'nejra] *f* tap (*Brit*), faucet (*US*)

tornozelo [torno'zelu] *m* ankle

torpedo [tor'pedu] *m* (*bomba*) torpedo; (*col: mensagem*) text (message)

torrada [to'hada] *f* toast; **uma ~** a piece of toast; **torradeira** [toha'dejra] *f* toaster

torrão [to'hãw] (*pl* **-ões**) *m* turf, sod; (*terra*) soil, land; (*de açúcar*) lump

torrar [to'har] *vt* to toast; (*café*) to roast

torre ['tohi] *f* tower; (*Xadrez*) castle, rook; (*Elet*) pylon; **~ de controle** (*Aer*) control tower

tórrido, -a ['tɔhidu, a] *adj* torrid

torrões [to'hõjs] *mpl de* **torrão**

torso ['torsu] *m* torso

torta ['tɔrta] *f* pie, tart

torto, -a ['tortu, 'tɔrta] *adj* twisted, crooked; **a ~ e a direito** indiscriminately

tortuoso, -a [tor'twozu, ɔza] *adj* winding

tortura [tor'tura] *f* torture; (*fig*) anguish; **torturar** [tortu'rar] *vt* to torture, to torment

tos [tus] = **te** + **os**

tosco, -a ['tosku, a] *adj* rough, unpolished; (*grosseiro*) coarse, crude

tosse ['tɔsi] *f* cough; **~ de cachorro** whooping cough; **tossir** [to'sir] *vi* to cough

tosta ['tɔsta] (*PT*) *f* toast; **~ mista** toasted cheese and ham sandwich

tostão [tos'tãw] *m* cash

tostar [tos'tar] *vt* to toast; (*pele, pessoa*) to tan; **tostar-se** *vr* to get tanned

total [to'taw] (*pl* **-ais**) *adj, m* total

touca ['toka] *f* bonnet; **~ de banho** bathing cap

tourada [to'rada] *f* bullfight; **toureiro** [to'rejru] *m* bullfighter

touro ['toru] *m* bull; **T~** (*Astrologia*) Taurus

tóxico, -a ['tɔksiku, a] *adj* toxic ▷ *m* poison; (*droga*) drug; **toxicômano, -a** [toksi'komanu, a] *m/f* drug addict

TPM *abr f* (= *tensão pré-menstrual*) PMT

trabalhador, a [trabaʎa'dor(a)] *adj* hard-working, industrious; (*Pol: classe*) working ▷ *m/f* worker

trabalhar [traba'ʎar] *vi* to work ▷ *vt* (*terra*) to till; (*madeira, metal*) to work; (*texto*) to work on; **~ com** (*comercial*) to deal in; **~ de** *ou* **como** to work as; **trabalhista** [traba'ʎista] *adj* labour *atr* (*Brit*), labor *atr* (*US*); **trabalho** [tra'baʎu] *m* work; (*emprego, tarefa*) job; (*Educ: tarefa*) assignment; **trabalho braçal** manual work; **trabalho doméstico** housework; **trabalhoso, -a** [traba'ʎozu, ɔza] *adj* laborious, arduous

traça ['trasa] *f* moth

traçado [tra'sadu] *m* sketch, plan

tração [tra'sãw] *f* traction

traçar [tra'sar] *vt* to draw; (*determinar*) to set out, outline;

t

(*planos*) to draw up; (*escrever*) to compose

tradição [tradʒi'sãw] (*pl* **-ões**) *f* tradition; **tradicional** [tradʒisjo'naw] (*pl* **-ais**) *adj* traditional

tradução [tradu'sãw] (*pl* **-ões**) *f* translation

tradutor, a [tradu'tor(a)] *m/f* translator

traduzir [tradu'zir] *vt* to translate

trafegar [trafe'gar] *vi* to move, go

tráfego ['trafegu] *m* traffic

traficante [trafi'kãtʃi] *m/f* trafficker, dealer

traficar [trafi'kar] *vi*: **~ (com)** to deal (in)

tráfico ['trafiku] *m* traffic

tragar [tra'gar] *vt* to swallow; (*fumaça*) to inhale; (*suportar*) to tolerate ▷ *vi* to inhale

tragédia [tra'ʒɛdʒja] *f* tragedy; **trágico, -a** ['traʒiku, a] *adj* tragic

trago¹ ['tragu] *m* mouthful

trago² *etc vb ver* **trazer**

traiçoeiro, -a [traj'swejru, a] *adj* treacherous, disloyal

traidor, a [traj'dor(a)] *m/f* traitor

trailer ['trejler] (*pl* **-s**) *m* trailer; (*tipo casa*) caravan (*Brit*), trailer (*US*)

trair [tra'ir] *vt* to betray; (*mulher, marido*) to be unfaithful to; (*esperanças*) not to live up to; **trair-se** *vr* to give o.s. away

trajar [tra'ʒar] *vt* to wear

traje ['traʒi] *m* dress, clothes *pl*; **~ de banho** swimsuit

trajeto [tra'ʒɛtu] *m* course, path

trajetória [traʒe'tɔrja] *f* trajectory, path; (*fig*) course

tralha ['traʎa] *f* fishing net

trama ['trama] *f* (*tecido*) weft (*Brit*), woof (*US*); (*enredo, conspiração*) plot

tramar [tra'mar] *vt* (*tecer*) to

weave; (*maquinar*) to plot ▷ *vi*: **~ contra** to conspire against

trâmites ['tramitʃis] *mpl* procedure *sg*, channels

trampolim [trãpo'lĩ] (*pl* **-ns**) *m* trampoline; (*de piscina*) diving board; (*fig*) springboard

tranca ['trãka] *f* (*de porta*) bolt; (*de carro*) lock

trança ['trãsa] *f* (*cabelo*) plait; (*galão*) braid

trancar [trã'kar] *vt* to lock

tranquilidade [trãkwili'dadʒi] *f* tranquillity; (*paz*) peace

tranquilizante [trãkwili'zãtʃi] *m* (*Med*) tranquillizer

tranquilizar [trãkwili'zar] *vt* to calm, quieten; (*despreocupar*): **~ alguém** to reassure sb, put sb's mind at rest; **tranquilizar-se** *vr* to calm down

tranquilo, -a [trã'kwilu, a] *adj* peaceful; (*mar, pessoa*) calm; (*criança*) quiet; (*consciência*) clear; (*seguro*) sure, certain

transação [trãza'sãw] (*pl* **-ões**) *f* transaction

transar [trã'zar] (*BR*: *col*) *vi* (*ter relação sexual*) to have sex

transbordar [trãzbor'dar] *vi* to overflow

transbordo [trãz'bordu] *m* (*de viajantes*) change, transfer

transe ['trãzi] *m* ordeal; (*lance*) plight; (*hipnótico*) trance

transeunte [trã'zjũtʃi] *m/f* passer-by

transferência [trãsfe'rẽsja] *f* transfer

transferir [trãsfe'rir] *vt* to transfer; (*adiar*) to postpone

transformação [trãsforma'sãw] (*pl* **-ões**) *f* transformation

transformador [trãsforma'dor] *m*

(*Elet*) transformer

transformar [trãsfor'mar] *vt* to transform; **transformar-se** *vr* to turn

transfusão [trãsfu'zãw] (*pl* **-ões**) *f* transfusion

transgênico, -a [trãz'ʒeniku, a] (*planta, alimento*) genetically modified, GM

transição [trãzi'sãw] (*pl* **-ões**) *f* transition

transitivo, -a [trãzi'tʃivu, a] *adj* (*Ling*) transitive

trânsito ['trãzitu] *m* transit, passage; (*na rua: veículos*) traffic; (: *pessoas*) flow; **transitório, -a** [trãzi'tɔrju, a] *adj* transitory; (*período*) transitional

transmissão [trãzmi'sãw] (*pl* **-ões**) *f* transmission; (*transferência*) transfer; **~ ao vivo** live broadcast

transmissor, a [trãzmi'sor(a)] *adj* transmitting ▷ *m* transmitter

transmitir [trãzmi'tʃir] *vt* to transmit; (*Rádio, TV*) to broadcast; (*transferir*) to transfer; (*recado, notícia*) to pass on; **transparente** [trãspa'rẽtʃi] *adj* transparent; (*roupa*) see-through; (*água*) clear

transpirar [trãspi'rar] *vi* to perspire; (*divulgar-se*) to become known; (*verdade*) to come out ▷ *vt* to exude

transplante [trãs'plãtʃi] *m* transplant

transportar [trãspor'tar] *vt* to transport; (*levar*) to carry; (*enlevar*) to entrance, enrapture

transporte [trãs'pɔrtʃi] *m* transport; (*Com*) haulage

transtorno [trãs'tornu] *m* upset, disruption

trapalhão, -lhona [trapa'ʎãw, 'ʎɔna] (*pl* **-ões/-onas**) *m/f* bungler, blunderer

trapo ['trapu] *m* rag

trarei *etc* [tra'rej] *vb ver* **trazer**

trás [trajs] *prep, adv*: **para ~** backwards; **por ~ de** behind; **de ~** from behind

traseira [tra'zejra] *f* rear; (*Anat*) bottom

traste ['trastʃi] *m* thing; (*coisa sem valor*) piece of junk

tratado [tra'tadu] *m* treaty

tratamento [trata'mẽtu] *m* treatment

tratar [tra'tar] *vt* to treat; (*tema*) to deal with; (*combinar*) to agree ▷ *vi*: **~ com** to deal with; (*combinar*) to agree with; **~ de** to deal with; **de que se trata?** what is it about?

trato ['tratu] *m* treatment; (*contrato*) agreement, contract; **tratos** *mpl* (*relações*) dealings

trator [tra'tor] *m* tractor

trauma ['trawma] *m* trauma

travão [tra'vãw] (*PT*) (*pl* **-ões**) *m* brake

travar [tra'var] *vt* (*roda*) to lock; (*iniciar*) to engage in; (*conversa*) to strike up; (*luta*) to wage; (*carro*) to stop; (*passagem*) to block; (*movimentos*) to hinder ▷ *vi* (*PT*) to brake

trave ['travi] *f* beam; (*Esporte*) crossbar

través [tra'vɛs] *m* slant, incline; **de ~** across, sideways

travessa [tra'vɛsa] *f* crossbeam, crossbar; (*rua*) lane, alley; (*prato*) dish; (*para o cabelo*) comb, slide

travessão [trave'sãw] (*pl* **-ões**) *m* (*de balança*) bar, beam; (*pontuação*) dash

travesseiro [trave'sejru] *m* pillow

travessia [trave'sia] *f* (*viagem*) journey, crossing

t

travessões [trave'sõjs] *mpl de* **travessão**

travessura [trave'sura] *f* mischief, prank

travões [tra'võjs] *mpl de* **travão**

trazer [tra'zer] *vt* to bring

trecho ['treʃu] *m* passage; (*de rua, caminho*) stretch; (*espaço*) space

trégua ['trɛgwa] *f* truce; (*descanso*) respite

treinador, a [trejna'dor(a)] *m/f* trainer

treinamento [trejna'mẽtu] *m* training

treinar [trej'nar] *vt* to train; **treinar-se** *vr* to train; **treino** ['trejnu] *m* training

trejeito [tre'ʒejtu] *m* gesture; (*careta*) grimace, face

trem [trẽj] (*pl* **-ns**) *m* train; **~ de aterrissagem** (*avião*) landing gear

tremendo, -a [tre'mẽdu, a] *adj* tremendous; (*terrível*) terrible, awful

tremer [tre'mer] *vi* to shudder, quake; (*terra*) to shake; (*de frio, medo*) to shiver

trêmulo, -a ['tremulu, a] *adj* shaky, trembling

trenó [tre'nɔ] *m* sledge, sleigh (*Brit*), sled (*US*)

trens [trẽjs] *mpl de* **trem**

trepar [tre'par] *vt* to climb ▷ *vi*: **~ em** to climb

trepidar [trepi'dar] *vi* to tremble, shake

três [tres] *num* three; *ver tb* **cinco**

trevas ['trɛvas] *fpl* darkness *sg*

treze ['trezi] *num* thirteen

triângulo ['trjãgulu] *m* triangle

tribal [tri'baw] (*pl* **-ais**) *adj* tribal

tribo ['tribu] *f* tribe

tribuna [tri'buna] *f* platform, rostrum; (*Rel*) pulpit

tribunal [tribu'naw] (*pl* **-ais**) *m* court; (*comissão*) tribunal

tributo [tri'butu] *m* tribute; (*imposto*) tax

tricô [tri'ko] *m* knitting; **tricotar** [triko'tar] *vt, vi* to knit

trigo ['trigu] *m* wheat

trilha ['triʎa] *f* (*caminho*) path; (*rasto*) track, trail; **~ sonora** soundtrack

trilhão [tri'ʎãw] (*pl* **-ões**) *m* billion (*Brit*), trillion (*US*)

trilho ['triʎu] *m* (*BR: Ferro*) rail; (*vereda*) path, track

trilhões [tri'ʎõjs] *mpl de* **trilhão**

trimestral [trimes'traw] (*pl* **-ais**) *adj* quarterly; **trimestralmente** [trimestraw'mẽtʃi] *adv* quarterly

trimestre [tri'mɛstri] *m* (*Educ*) term; (*Com*) quarter

trincar [trĩ'kar] *vt* to crunch; (*morder*) to bite; (*dentes*) to grit ▷ *vi* to crunch

trinco ['trĩku] *m* latch

trinta ['trĩta] *num* thirty

trio ['triu] *m* trio; **trio elétrico** *see note*

● **TRIO ELÉTRICO**
●
● **Trios elétricos** are lorries,
● carrying floats equipped for
● sound and/or live music, which
● parade through the streets
● during *carnaval*, especially in
● Bahia. Bands and popular
● performers on the floats draw
● crowds by giving frenzied
● performances of various types of
● music.

tripa ['tripa] *f* gut, intestine; **tripas** *fpl* (*intestinos*) bowels; (*vísceras*) guts; (*Culin*) tripe *sg*

tripé [tri'pɛ] *m* tripod
triplicar [tripli'kar] *vt, vi* to treble; **triplicar-se** *vr* to treble
tripulação [tripula'sãw] (*pl* **-ões**) *f* crew
tripulante [tripu'lãtʃi] *m/f* crew member
triste ['tristʃi] *adj* sad; (*lugar*) depressing
tristeza [tris'teza] *f* sadness, gloominess
triturar [tritu'rar] *vt* to grind
triunfar [trjũ'far] *vi* to triumph; **triunfo** ['trjũfu] *m* triumph
trivial [tri'vjaw] (*pl* **-ais**) *adj* common(place), ordinary; (*insignificante*) trivial
triz [triz] *m*: **por um ~** by a hair's breadth
troca ['trɔka] *f* exchange, swap
trocadilho [troka'dʒiʎu] *m* pun, play on words
trocado [tro'kadu] *m*: **~(s)** (small) change
trocador, a [troka'dor(a)] *m/f* (*em ônibus*) conductor
trocar [tro'kar] *vt* to exchange, swap; (*mudar*) to change; (*inverter*) to change *ou* swap round; (*confundir*) to mix up; **trocar-se** *vr* to change; **~ dinheiro** to change money
troco ['trɔku] *m* (*dinheiro*) change; (*revide*) retort, rejoinder
troféu [tro'fɛw] *m* trophy
tromba ['trõba] *f* (*do elefante*) trunk; (*de outro animal*) snout
trombeta [trõ'beta] *f* trumpet
trombone [trõ'bɔni] *m* trombone
trombose [trõ'bɔzi] *f* thrombosis
tronco ['trõku] *m* trunk; (*ramo*) branch; (*de corpo*) torso, trunk
trono ['trɔnu] *m* throne
tropa ['trɔpa] *f* troop; (*exército*)

army; **ir para a ~** (*PT*) to join the army
tropeçar [trope'sar] *vi* to stumble, trip; (*fig*) to blunder
tropical [tropi'kaw] (*pl* **-ais**) *adj* tropical
trotar [tro'tar] *vi* to trot; **trote** ['trɔtʃi] *m* trot; (*por telefone etc*) hoax call
trouxe *etc* ['trosi] *vb ver* **trazer**
trovão [tro'vãw] (*pl* **-ões**) *m* clap of thunder; (*trovoada*) thunder; **trovejar** [trove'ʒar] *vi* to thunder; **trovoada** [tro'vwada] *f* thunderstorm
truque ['truki] *m* trick; (*publicitário*) gimmick
truta ['truta] *f* trout
tu [tu] *pron* you
tua ['tua] *f de* **teu**
tuba ['tuba] *f* tuba
tubarão [tuba'rãw] (*pl* **-ões**) *m* shark
tuberculose [tuberku'lɔzi] *f* tuberculosis
tubo ['tubu] *m* tube, pipe; **~ de ensaio** test tube
tucano [tu'kanu] *m* toucan
tudo ['tudu] *pron* everything; **~ quanto** everything that; **antes de ~** first of all; **acima de ~** above all
tufão [tu'fãw] (*pl* **-ões**) *m* typhoon
tulipa [tu'lipa] *f* tulip
tumba ['tũba] *f* tomb; (*lápide*) tombstone
tumor [tu'mor] *m* tumour (*Brit*), tumor (*US*)
túmulo ['tumulu] *m* tomb; (*sepultura*) burial
tumulto [tu'muwtu] *m* uproar, trouble; (*grande movimento*) bustle; (*balbúrdia*) hubbub; (*motim*) riot; **tumultuado, -a** [tumuw'twadu, a] *adj* riotous, heated; **tumultuar**

[tumuw'twar] *vt* to disrupt;
(*amotinar*) to rouse, incite
túnel ['tunew] (*pl* **-eis**) *m* tunnel
túnica ['tunika] *f* tunic
Tunísia [tu'nizja] *f*: **a ~** Tunisia
tupi [tu'pi] *m* Tupi (tribe); (*Ling*)
Tupi ▷ *m/f* Tupi Indian
tupi-guarani [-gwara'ni] *m* (*Ling*)
see note

○ **TUPI-GUARANI**
○
○ This is an important branch of
○ indigenous languages from the
○ tropical region of South America.
○ It takes in thirty indigenous
○ peoples and includes Tupi,
○ Guarani, and other languages.
○ Before Brazil was discovered by
○ the Portuguese it had 1,300
○ indigenous languages, 87% of
○ which are now extinct due to the
○ extermination of indigenous
○ peoples and the loss of territory.

tupiniquim [tupini'kĩ] (*pej*) (*pl* **-ns**)
adj Brazilian (Indian)
turbilhão [turbi'ʎãw] (*pl* **-ões**) *m*
(*de vento*) whirlwind; (*de água*)
whirlpool
turbulência [turbu'lẽsja] *f*
turbulence; **turbulento, -a**
[turbu'lẽtu, a] *adj* turbulent
turco, -a ['turku, a] *adj* Turkish
▷ *m/f* Turk ▷ *m* (*Ling*) Turkish
turismo [tu'rizmu] *m* tourism;
turista [tu'rista] *m/f* tourist ▷ *adj*
(*classe*) tourist *atr*
turma ['turma] *f* group; (*Educ*)
class
turquesa [tur'keza] *adj inv*
turquoise
Turquia [tur'kia] *f*: **a ~** Turkey
tusso *etc* ['tusu] *vb ver* **tossir**

tutela [tu'tɛla] *f* protection; (*Jur*)
guardianship
tutor, a [tu'tor(a)] *m/f* guardian
tutu [tu'tu] *m* (*Culin*) beans, bacon
and manioc flour
TV [te've] *abr f* (= *televisão*) TV

UE *abr f* (= *União Europeia*) EU

Uganda [u'gãda] *m* Uganda

uísque ['wiski] *m* whisky (*Brit*), whiskey (*US*)

uivar [wi'var] *vi* to howl; (*berrar*) to yell; **uivo** ['wivu] *m* howl; (*fig*) yell

úlcera ['uwsera] *f* ulcer

ultimamente [uwtʃima'mẽtʃi] *adv* lately

ultimato [uwtʃi'matu] *m* ultimatum

último, -a ['uwtʃimu, a] *adj* last; (*mais recente*) latest; (*qualidade*) lowest; (*fig*) final; **por ~** finally; **nos ~s anos** in recent years; **a última** (*notícia*) the latest (news)

ultra... [uwtra-] *prefixo* ultra-

ultrajar [uwtra'ʒar] *vt* to outrage; (*insultar*) to insult, offend; **ultraje** [uw'traʒi] *m* outrage; (*insulto*) insult, offence (*Brit*), offense (*US*)

ultramar [uwtra'mar] *m* overseas

ultrapassado, -a [uwtrapa'sadu, a] *adj* (*ideias etc*) outmoded

ultrapassar [uwtrapa'sar] *vt* (*atravessar*) to cross, go beyond; (*ir além de*) to exceed; (*transgredir*) to overstep; (*Auto*) to overtake (*Brit*), pass (*US*); (*ser superior a*) to surpass ▷ *vi* (*Auto*) to overtake (*Brit*), pass (*US*)

ultrassom [uwtra'sõ] *m* ultrasound

ultravioleta [uwtravjo'leta] *adj* ultraviolet

 PALAVRA-CHAVE

um, a [ũ, 'uma] (*pl* **uns/umas**) *num* one; **um e outro** both; **um a um** one by one; **à uma (hora)** at one (o'clock)
▷ *adj*: **uns cinco** about five; **uns poucos** a few
▷ *art indef* **1** (*sg*) a; (: *antes de vogal ou 'h' mudo*) an; (*pl*) some; **ela é de uma beleza incrível** she's incredibly beautiful
2 (*dando ênfase*): **estou com uma fome!** I'm so hungry!
3: **um ao outro** one another; (*entre dois*) each other

umbigo [ũ'bigu] *m* navel

umbilical [ũbili'kaw] (*pl* **-ais**) *adj*: **cordão ~** umbilical cord

umedecer [umede'ser] *vt* to moisten, wet; **umedecer-se** *vr* to get wet

umidade [umi'dadʒi] *f* dampness; (*clima*) humidity

úmido, -a ['umidu, a] *adj* wet, moist; (*roupa*) damp; (*clima*) humid

unânime [u'nanimi] *adj* unanimous

unha ['uɲa] *f* nail; (*garra*) claw;

unhada [u'ɲada] f scratch
união [u'njãw] (pl **-ões**) f union;
(ato) joining; (unidade, solidariedade)
unity; (casamento) marriage; (Tec)
joint; **a U~ Europeia** the European
Union
unicamente [unika'mẽtʃi] adv
only
único, -a ['uniku, a] adj only; (sem
igual) unique; (um só) single
unidade [uni'dadʒi] f unity; (Tec,
Com) unit; **~ central de
processamento** (Comput) central
processing unit; **~ de disco**
(Comput) disk drive
unido, -a [u'nidu, a] adj joined,
linked; (fig) united
unificar [unifi'kar] vt to unite;
unificar-se vr to join together
uniforme [uni'fɔrmi] adj uniform;
(semelhante) alike, similar;
(superfície) even ▷ m uniform;
uniformizado, -a
[uniformi'zadu, a] adj uniform,
standardized; (vestido de uniforme)
in uniform; **uniformizar**
[uniformi'zar] vt to standardize
uniões [u'njõjs] fpl de **união**
unir [u'nir] vt to join together;
(ligar) to link; (pessoas, fig) to unite;
(misturar) to mix together; **unir-se**
vr to come together; (povos etc) to
unite
uníssono [u'nisonu] m: **em ~** in
unison
universal [univer'saw] (pl **-ais**) adj
universal; (mundial) worldwide
universidade [universi'dadʒi] f
university; **universitário, -a**
[universi'tarju, a] adj university
atr ▷ m/f (professor) lecturer;
(aluno) university student
universo [uni'vɛrsu] m universe;
(mundo) world

uns [ũs] mpl de **um**
untar [ũ'tar] vt (esfregar) to rub;
(com óleo, manteiga) to grease
urbanismo [urba'nizmu] m town
planning
urbano, -a [ur'banu, a] adj (da
cidade) urban; (fig) urbane
urgência [ur'ʒẽsja] f urgency; **com
toda ~** as quickly as possible;
urgente [ur'ʒẽtʃi] adj urgent
urina [u'rina] f urine; **urinar**
[uri'nar] vi to urinate ▷ vt (sangue)
to pass; (cama) to wet; **urinar-se**
vr to wet o.s.; **urinol** [uri'nɔw] (pl
-óis) m chamber pot
urna ['urna] f urn; **~ eleitoral** ballot
box
urrar [u'har] vt, vi to roar; (de dor) to
yell
ursa ['ursa] f bear
urso ['ursu] m bear
urtiga [ur'tʃiga] f nettle
Uruguai [uru'gwaj] m: **o ~** Uruguay
urze ['urzi] m heather
usado, -a [u'zadu, a] adj used;
(comum) common; (roupa) worn;
(gasto) worn out; (de segunda mão)
second-hand
usar [u'zar] vt (servir-se de) to use;
(vestir) to wear; (gastar com o uso) to
wear out; (barba, cabelo curto) to
have, wear ▷ vi: **~ de** to use; **modo
de ~** directions pl
usina [u'zina] f (fábrica) factory;
(de energia) plant
uso ['uzu] m use; (utilização) usage;
(prática) practice
usual [u'zwaw] (pl **-ais**) adj usual;
(comum) common
usuário, -a [u'zwarju, a] m/f user
usufruir [uzu'frwir] vt to enjoy
▷ vi: **~ de** to enjoy
úteis ['utejs] pl de **útil**
utensílio [utẽ'silju] m utensil

útero ['uteru] *m* womb, uterus
útil ['utʃiw] (*pl* **-eis**) *adj* useful;
  (*vantajoso*) profitable, worthwhile;
  utilidade [utʃili'dadʒi] *f*
  usefulness; **utilização**
  [utʃiliza'sãw] *f* use; **utilizar**
  [utʃili'zar] *vt* to use; **utilizar-se**
  vr: **utilizar-se de** to make use of
uva ['uva] *f* grape

V

v *abr* (= *volt*) v
vá *etc* [va] *vb ver* **ir**
vã [vã] *f de* **vão**
vaca ['vaka] *f* cow; **carne de ~** beef
vacina [va'sina] *f* vaccine; **vacinar**
  [vasi'nar] *vt* to vaccinate
vácuo ['vakwu] *m* vacuum; (*fig*)
  void; (*espaço*) space
vaga ['vaga] *f* wave; (*em hotel,
  trabalho*) vacancy
vagão [va'gãw] (*pl* **-ões**) *m* (*de
  passageiros*) carriage; (*de cargas*)
  wagon; **vagão-leito** (*pl*
  vagões-leitos) (*PT*) *m* sleeping
  car; **vagão-restaurante** (*pl*
  vagões-restaurantes) *m* buffet
  car
vagar [va'gar] *vi* to wander about;
  (*barco*) to drift; (*ficar vago*) to be
  vacant
vagaroso, -a [vaga'rozu, ɔza] *adj*
  slow

vagina [va'ʒina] f vagina
vago, -a ['vagu, a] adj vague; (desocupado) vacant, free
vagões [va'gõjs] mpl de **vagão**
vai etc [vaj] vb ver **ir**
vaia ['vaja] f booing; **vaiar** [va'jar] vt, vi to boo, hiss
vaidade [vaj'dadʒi] f vanity; (futilidade) futility
vaidoso, -a [vaj'dozu, ɔza] adj vain
vaivém [vaj'vẽj] m to-ing and fro-ing
vala ['vala] f ditch
vale ['vali] m valley; (escrito) voucher; **~ postal** postal order
valer [va'ler] vi to be worth; (ser válido) to be valid; (ter influência) to carry weight; (servir) to serve; (ser proveitoso) to be useful; **valer-se** vr: **~-se de** to use, make use of; **~ a pena** to be worthwhile; **~ por** (equivaler) to be worth the same as; **para ~** (muito) very much, a lot; (realmente) for real, properly; **vale dizer** in other words; **mais vale ... (do que ...)** it would be better to ... (than ...)
valeta [va'leta] f gutter
valha etc ['vaʎa] vb ver **valer**
validade [vali'dadʒi] f validity; (de cartão de crédito) expiry date (Brit), expiration date (US); (de alimento) best-before date
validar [vali'dar] vt to validate; **válido, -a** ['validu, a] adj valid
valioso, -a [va'ljozu, ɔza] adj valuable
valise [va'lizi] f case, grip
valor [va'lor] m value; (mérito) merit; (coragem) courage; (preço) price; (importância) importance; **valores** mpl (morais) values; (num exame) marks; (Com) securities; **dar ~ a** to value; **valorizar** [valori'zar]

vt to value
valsa ['vawsa] f waltz
válvula ['vawvula] f valve
vampiro, -a [vã'piru, a] m/f vampire
vandalismo [vãda'lizmu] m vandalism
vândalo, -a ['vãdalu, a] m/f vandal
vangloriar-se [vãglo'rjarsi] vr: **~ de** to boast of ou about
vanguarda [vã'gwarda] f vanguard; (arte) avant-garde
vantagem [vã'taʒẽ] (pl **-ns**) f advantage; (ganho) profit, benefit; **tirar ~ de** to take advantage of; **vantajoso, -a** [vãta'ʒozu, ɔza] adj advantageous; (lucrativo) profitable; (proveitoso) beneficial
vão¹ [vãw] vb ver **ir**
vão², vã [vãw, vã] (pl **-s/-s**) adj vain; (fútil) futile ▷ m (intervalo) space; (de porta etc) opening
vaqueiro [va'kejru] m cowboy
vara ['vara] f stick; (Tec) rod; (Jur) jurisdiction; (de porcos) herd; **salto de ~** pole vault; **~ de condão** magic wand
varal [va'raw] (pl **-ais**) m clothes line
varanda [va'rãda] f verandah; (balcão) balcony
varar [va'rar] vt to pierce; (passar) to cross
varejista [vare'ʒista] (BR) m/f retailer ▷ adj (mercado) retail
varejo [va'reʒu] (BR) m (Com) retail trade; **a ~** retail
variação [varja'sãw] (pl **-ões**) f variation
variado, -a [va'rjadu, a] adj varied; (sortido) assorted
variar [va'rjar] vt, vi to vary; **variável** [va'rjavew] (pl **-eis**) adj variable; (tempo, humor)

changeable

varicela [vari'sɛla] f chickenpox

variedade [varje'dadʒi] f variety

varinha [va'riɲa] f wand; **~ de condão** magic wand

vário, -a ['varju, a] adj (diverso) varied; (pl) various, several; (Com) sundry

varizes [va'rizis] fpl varicose veins

varrer [va'her] vt to sweep; (fig) to sweep away

vaselina® [vaze'lina] f Vaseline®

vasilha [va'ziʎa] f (para líquidos) jug; (para alimentos) dish; (barril) barrel

vaso ['vazu] m pot; (para flores) vase

vassoura [va'sora] f broom

vasto, -a ['vastu, a] adj vast

vatapá [vata'pa] m fish or chicken with coconut milk, shrimps, peanuts, palm oil and spices

Vaticano [vatʃi'kanu] m: **o ~** the Vatican

vazamento [vaza'mẽtu] m leak

vazão [va'zãw] (pl **-ões**) f flow; (venda) sale; **dar ~ a** (expressar) to give vent to; (atender) to deal with; (resolver) to attend to

vazar [va'zar] vt to empty; (derramar) to spill; (verter) to pour out ▷ vi to leak

vazio, -a [va'ziu, a] adj empty; (pessoa) empty-headed, frivolous; (cidade) deserted ▷ m emptiness; (deixado por alguém/algo) void

vazões [va'zõjs] fpl de **vazão**

vê etc [ve] vb ver **ver**

veado ['vjadu] m deer; **carne de ~** venison

vedado, -a [ve'dadu, a] adj (proibido) forbidden; (fechado) enclosed

vedar [ve'dar] vt to ban, prohibit; (buraco) to stop up; (entrada,

passagem) to block; (terreno) to close off

vegetação [veʒeta'sãw] f vegetation

vegetal [veʒe'taw] (pl **-ais**) adj vegetable atr; (reino, vida) plant atr ▷ m vegetable

vegetalista [veʒeta'lista] adj, m/f vegan

vegetariano, -a [veʒeta'rjanu, a] adj, m/f vegetarian

veia ['veja] f vein

veículo [ve'ikulu] m (tb: fig) vehicle

veio¹ ['veju] m (de rocha) vein; (na mina) seam; (de madeira) grain

veio² vb ver **vir**

vejo etc ['veʒu] vb ver **ver**

vela ['vɛla] f candle; (Auto) spark plug; (Náut) sail; **barco à ~** sailing boat

velar [ve'lar] vt to veil; (ocultar) to hide; (vigiar) to keep watch over; (um doente) to sit up with ▷ vi (não dormir) to stay up; (vigiar) to keep watch; **~ por** to look after

veleiro [ve'lejru] m sailing boat

velejar [vele'ʒar] vi to sail

velhaco, -a [ve'ʎaku, a] adj crooked ▷ m/f crook

velhice [ve'ʎisi] f old age

velho, -a ['vɛʎu, a] adj old ▷ m/f old man/woman

velocidade [velosi'dadʒi] f speed, velocity; (PT: Auto) gear

velório [ve'lɔrju] m wake

veloz [ve'lɔz] adj fast

vem [vẽj] vb ver **vir**

vêm [vẽj] vb ver **vir**

vencedor, a [vẽse'dor(a)] adj winning ▷ m/f winner

vencer [vẽ'ser] vt (num jogo) to beat; (competição) to win; (inimigo) to defeat; (exceder) to surpass; (obstáculos) to overcome;

(percorrer) to pass ▷ *vi (num jogo)* to win; **vencido, -a** [vẽ'sidu, a] *adj*: **dar-se por vencido** to give in; **vencimento** [vẽsi'mẽtu] *m (Com)* expiry; *(data)* expiry date; *(salário)* salary; *(de gêneros alimentícios etc)* sell-by date; **vencimentos** *mpl (ganhos)* earnings

venda ['vẽda] *f* sale; *(pano)* blindfold; *(mercearia)* general store; **à ~** on sale, for sale

vendaval [vẽda'vaw] *(pl* **-ais)** *m* gale

vendedor, a [vẽde'dor(a)] *m/f* seller; *(em loja)* sales assistant; *(de imóvel)* vendor; **~ ambulante** street vendor

vender [vẽ'der] *vt, vi* to sell; **~ por atacado/a varejo** to sell wholesale/retail

veneno [ve'nɛnu] *m* poison; **venenoso, -a** [vene'nozu, ɔza] *adj* poisonous

venerar [vene'rar] *vt* to revere; *(Rel)* to worship

venéreo, -a [ve'nɛrju, a] *adj*: **doença venérea** venereal disease

Venezuela [vene'zwɛla] *f*: **a ~** Venezuela

venha *etc* ['veɲa] *vb ver* **vir**

ventania [vẽta'nia] *f* gale

ventar [vẽ'tar] *vi*: **está ventando** it is windy

ventilação [vẽtʃila'sãw] *f* ventilation

ventilador [vẽtʃila'dor] *m* ventilator; *(elétrico)* fan

vento ['vẽtu] *m* wind; *(brisa)* breeze; **ventoinha** [vẽ'twiɲa] *f* weathercock, weather vane; *(PT: Auto)* fan

ventre ['vẽtri] *m* belly

ver [ver] *vt* to see; *(olhar para, examinar)* to look at; *(televisão)* to watch ▷ *vi* to see ▷ *m*: **a meu ~** in my opinion; **vai ~ que ...** maybe ...; **não tem nada a ~ (com)** it has nothing to do (with)

veracidade [verasi'dadʒi] *f* truthfulness

veraneio [vera'neju] *m* summer holidays *pl (Brit) ou* vacation *(US)*

verão [ve'rãw] *(pl* **-ões)** *m* summer

verba ['vɛrba] *f* allowance; **verba(s)** *fpl (recursos)* funds *pl*

verbal [ver'baw] *(pl* **-ais)** *adj* verbal

verbete [ver'betʃi] *m (num dicionário)* entry

verbo ['vɛrbu] *m* verb

verdade [ver'dadʒi] *f* truth; **na ~** in fact; **de ~** *(falar)* truthfully; *(ameaçar etc)* really; **para falar a ~** to tell the truth; **verdadeiro, -a** [verda'dejru, a] *adj* true; *(genuíno)* real; *(pessoa)* truthful

verde ['verdʒi] *adj* green; *(fruta)* unripe ▷ *m* green; *(plantas etc)* greenery

verdura [ver'dura] *f (hortaliça)* greens *pl*; *(Bot)* greenery; *(cor verde)* greenness

verdureiro, -a [verdu'rejru, a] *m/f* greengrocer *(Brit)*, produce dealer *(US)*

vereador, a [verja'dor(a)] *m/f* councillor *(Brit)*, councilor *(US)*

veredicto [vere'dʒiktu] *m* verdict

verga ['verga] *f (vara)* stick; *(de metal)* rod

vergonha [ver'goɲa] *f* shame; *(timidez)* embarrassment; *(humilhação)* humiliation; *(ato indecoroso)* indecency; *(brio)* self-respect; **ter ~** to be ashamed; *(tímido)* to be shy; **vergonhoso, -a** [vergo'ɲozu, ɔza] *adj* shameful; *(indecoroso)* disgraceful

verídico, -a [ve'ridʒiku, a] *adj* true, truthful

verificar [verifi'kar] vt to check; (confirmar, Comput) to verify

verme ['vɛrmi] m worm

vermelho, -a [ver'meʎu, a] adj red ▷ m red

verniz [ver'niz] m varnish; (couro) patent leather

verões [ve'rõjs] mpl de **verão**

verossímil [vero'simiw], (PT) **verosímil** (pl **-eis**) adj likely, probable; (crível) credible

verruga [ve'huga] f wart

versão [ver'sãw] (pl **-ões**) f version; (tradução) translation

versátil [ver'satʃiw] (pl **-eis**) adj versatile

verso ['vɛrsu] m verse; (linha) line of poetry

versões [ver'sõjs] fpl de **versão**

verter [ver'ter] vt to pour; (por acaso) to spill; (traduzir) to translate; (lágrimas, sangue) to shed ▷ vi: **~ de** to spring from; **~ em** (rio) to flow into

vertical [vertʃi'kaw] (pl **-ais**) adj vertical; (de pé) upright, standing ▷ f vertical

vespa ['vespa] f wasp

véspera ['vɛspera] f: **a ~ (de)** the day before; **a ~ de Natal** Christmas Eve

vestiário [ves'tʃjarju] m (em casa, teatro) cloakroom; (Esporte) changing room (Brit), locker-room (US); (de ator) dressing room

vestíbulo [ves'tʃibulu] m hall(way), vestibule; (Teatro) foyer

vestido, -a [ves'tʃidu, a] adj: **~ de branco** etc dressed in white etc ▷ m dress

vestígio [ves'tʃiʒju] m (rastro) track; (fig) sign, trace

vestimenta [vestʃi'mẽta] f garment

vestir [ves'tʃir] vt (uma criança) to dress; (pôr sobre si) to put on; (trajar) to wear; (comprar, dar roupa para) to clothe; (fazer roupa para) to make clothes for; **vestir-se** vr to get dressed

vestuário [ves'twarju] m clothing

veterano, -a [vete'ranu, a] adj, m/f veteran

veterinário, -a [veteri'narju, a] m/f vet(erinary surgeon)

veto ['vɛtu] m veto

véu [vɛw] m veil

vexame [ve'ʃami] f shame, disgrace; (tormento) affliction; (humilhação) humiliation; (afronta) insult

vez [vez] f time; (turno) turn; **uma ~** once; **algumas ~es, às ~es** sometimes; **~ por outra** sometimes; **cada ~ (que)** every time; **de ~ em quando** from time to time; **em ~ de** instead of; **uma ~ que** since; **3 ~es 6** 3 times 6; **de uma ~ por todas** once and for all; **muitas ~es** many times; (frequentemente) often; **toda ~ que** every time; **um de cada ~** one at a time; **uma ~ ou outra** once in a while

vi [vi] vb ver **ver**

via¹ ['via] f road, route; (meio) way; (documento) copy; (conduto) channel ▷ prep via, by way of; **em ~s de** in the process of; **por ~ terrestre/marítima** by land/sea

via² etc vb ver **ver**

viaduto [vja'dutu] m viaduct

viagem ['vjaʒẽ] (pl **-ns**) f journey, trip; (o viajar) travel; (Náut) voyage; **viagens** fpl (jornadas) travels; **~ de ida e volta** return trip, round trip

viajante [vja'ʒãtʃi] adj travelling (Brit), traveling (US) ▷ m traveller

(*Brit*), traveler (*US*)
viajar [vja'ʒar] *vi* to travel
viável ['vjavew] (*pl* **-eis**) *adj*
feasible, viable
víbora ['vibora] *f* viper
vibração [vibra'sãw] (*pl* **-ões**) *f*
vibration; (*fig*) thrill
vibrante [vi'brãtʃi] *adj* vibrant;
(*discurso*) stirring
vibrar [vi'brar] *vt* to brandish;
(*fazer estremecer*) to vibrate; (*cordas*)
to strike ▷ *vi* to vibrate; (*som*) to
echo
vice ['visi] *m/f* deputy
vice- [visi-] *prefixo* vice-;
vice-presidente, -a *m/f* vice
president; **vice-versa** [-'vɛrsa] *adv*
vice versa
viciado, -a [vi'sjadu, a] *adj*
addicted; (*ar*) foul ▷ *m/f* addict;
~ em algo addicted to sth
viciar [vi'sjar] *vt* (*falsificar*) to
falsify; **viciar-se** *vr*: **~-se em algo**
become addicted to sth
vício ['visju] *m* vice; (*defeito*) failing;
(*costume*) bad habit; (*em
entorpecentes*) addiction
viço ['visu] *m* vigour (*Brit*), vigor
(*US*); (*da pele*) freshness
vida ['vida] *f* life; (*duração*) lifetime;
(*fig*) vitality; **com ~** alive; **ganhar a
~** to earn one's living; **modo de ~**
way of life; **dar a ~ por algo/por
fazer algo** to give one's right arm
for sth/to do sth; **estar bem de ~**
to be well off
videira [vi'dejra] *f* grapevine
vidente [vi'dẽtʃi] *m/f* clairvoyant
vídeo ['vidʒju] *m* video;
videocassete [vidʒjuka'sɛtʃi] *m*
video cassette *ou* tape; (*aparelho*)
video (recorder); **videoteipe**
[vidʒju'tejpi] *m* video tape
vidraça [vi'drasa] *f* window pane

vidrado, -a [vi'dradu, a] *adj*
glazed; (*porta*) glass *atr*; (*olhos*)
glassy
vidro ['vidru] *m* glass; (*frasco*)
bottle; **fibra de ~** fibreglass (*Brit*),
fiberglass (*US*); **~ de aumento**
magnifying glass
vier *etc* [vjer] *vb ver* **vir**
viés [vjɛs] *m* slant; **ao** *ou* **de ~**
diagonally
vieste ['vjestʃi] *vb ver* **vir**
Vietnã [vjet'nã] *m*: **o ~** Vietnam;
vietnamita [vjetna'mita] *adj, m/f*
Vietnamese
vigiar [vi'ʒjar] *vt* to watch;
(*ocultamente*) to spy on; (*presos,
fronteira*) to guard ▷ *vi* to be on the
lookout
vigilância [viʒi'lãsja] *f* vigilance;
vigilante [viʒi'lãtʃi] *adj* vigilant;
(*atento*) alert
vigor [vi'gor] *m* energy; **em ~** in
force; **entrar/pôr em ~** to take
effect/put into effect; **vigoroso, -a**
[vigo'rozu, ɔza] *adj* vigorous
vil [viw] (*pl* **vis**) *adj* vile
vila ['vila] *f* town; (*casa*) villa
vilão, -lã [vi'lãw, 'lã] (*pl* **-ões/-s**)
m/f villain
vilarejo [vila'reʒu] *m* village
vim [vĩ] *vb ver* **vir**
vime ['vimi] *m* wicker
vinagre [vi'nagri] *m* vinegar
vinco ['vĩku] *m* crease; (*sulco*)
furrow; (*no rosto*) line
vincular [vĩku'lar] *vt* to link, tie;
vínculo ['vĩkulu] *m* bond, tie;
(*relação*) link
vinda ['vĩda] *f* arrival; (*regresso*)
return; **dar as boas ~s a** to
welcome
vingança [vĩ'gãsa] *f* vengeance,
revenge; **vingar** [vĩ'gar] *vt* to
avenge; **vingar-se** *vr*: **vingar-se**

de to take revenge on; **vingativo, -a** [vĩga'tʃivu, a] *adj* vindictive

vinha[1] ['viɲa] *f* vineyard; (*planta*) vine

vinha[2] *etc vb ver* **vir**

vinho ['viɲu] *m* wine; **~ branco/ rosado/tinto** white/rosé/red wine; **~ seco/doce** dry/sweet wine; **~ do Porto** port

vinte ['vĩtʃi] *num* twenty

viola ['vjɔla] *f* viola

violão [vjo'lãw] (*pl* **-ões**) *m* guitar

violar [vjo'lar] *vt* to violate; (*a lei*) to break

violência [vjo'lẽsja] *f* violence; **violentar** [vjolẽ'tar] *vt* to force; (*mulher*) to rape; **violento, -a** [vjo'lẽtu, a] *adj* violent

violeta [vjo'leta] *f* violet

violino [vjo'linu] *m* violin

violões [vjo'lõjs] *mpl de* **violão**

violoncelo [vjolõ'sɛlu] *m* 'cello

vir[1] [vir] *vi* to come; **~ a ser** to turn out to be; **a semana que vem** next week

vir[2] *etc vb ver* **ver**

vira-lata ['vira-] (*pl* **vira-latas**) *m* (*cão*) mongrel

virar [vi'rar] *vt* to turn; (*página, disco, barco*) to turn over; (*copo*) to empty; (*transformar-se em*) to become ▷ *vi* to turn; (*barco*) to capsize; (*mudar*) to change; **virar-se** *vr* to turn; (*voltar-se*) to turn round; (*defender-se*) to fend for o.s.

virgem ['virʒẽ] (*pl* **-ns**) *f* virgin; **V~** (*Astrologia*) Virgo

vírgula ['virgula] *f* comma; (*decimal*) point

viril [vi'riw] (*pl* **-is**) *adj* virile

virilha [vi'riʎa] *f* groin

viris [vi'ris] *adj pl de* **viril**

virtual [vir'twaw] (*pl* **-ais**) *adj* virtual; (*potencial*) potential

virtude [vir'tudʒi] *f* virtue; **em ~ de** owing to, because of; **virtuoso, -a** [vir'twozu, ɔza] *adj* virtuous

virulento, -a [viru'lẽtu, a] *adj* virulent

vírus ['virus] *m inv* virus

vis [vis] *adj pl de* **vil**

visão [vi'zãw] (*pl* **-ões**) *f* vision; (*Anat*) eyesight; (*vista*) sight; (*maneira de perceber*) view

visar [vi'zar] *vt* (*alvo*) to aim at; (*ter em vista*) to have in view; (*ter como objetivo*) to aim for

vísceras ['viseras] *fpl* innards, bowels

visita [vi'zita] *f* visit, call; (*pessoa*) visitor; (*na Internet*) hit; **fazer uma ~ a** to visit; **~ guiada** guided tour; **visitante** [vizi'tãtʃi] *adj* visiting ▷ *m/f* visitor; **visitar** [vizi'tar] *vt* to visit

visível [vi'zivew] (*pl* **-eis**) *adj* visible

vislumbrar [vizlũ'brar] *vt* to glimpse, catch a glimpse of; **vislumbre** [viz'lũbri] *m* glimpse

visões [vi'zõjs] *fpl de* **visão**

visse *etc* ['visi] *vb ver* **ver**

vista ['vista] *f* sight; (*Med*) eyesight; (*panorama*) view; **à** *ou* **em ~ de** in view of; **dar na ~** to attract attention; **dar uma ~ de olhos em** to glance at; **fazer ~ grossa (a)** to turn a blind eye (to); **ter em ~** to have in mind; **à ~** visible, showing; (*Com*) in cash; **até a ~!** see you!

visto[1], **-a** ['vistu, a] *pp de* **ver** ▷ *adj* seen ▷ *m* (*em passaporte*) visa; (*em documento*) stamp; **pelo ~** by the looks of things

visto[2] *vb ver* **vestir**

vistoria [visto'ria] *f* inspection

vistoso, -a [vis'tozu, ɔza] *adj* eye-catching

visual [vi'zwaw] (pl **-ais**) adj visual;
  visualizar [vizwali'zar] vt to
  visualize
vital [vi'taw] (pl **-ais**) adj vital;
  vitalício, -a [vita'lisju, a] adj for
  life
vitamina [vita'mina] f vitamin;
  (para beber) fruit crush
vitela [vi'tɛla] f calf; (carne) veal
vítima ['vitʃima] f victim
vitória [vi'tɔrja] f victory;
  vitorioso, -a [vito'rjozu, ɔza] adj
  victorious
vitrina [vi'trina] f = **vitrine**
vitrine [vi'trini] f shop window;
  (armário) display case
viúvo, -a ['vjuvu, a] m/f widower/
  widow
viva ['viva] m cheer; **~!** hurray!
viva-voz [viva'vɔz] m (BR: Tel: em
  telefone) speakerphone; (para
  celular) hands-free kit
viveiro [vi'vejru] m nursery
vivência [vi'vẽsja] f existence;
  (experiência) experience
vivenda [vi'vẽda] f (casa) residence
viver [vi'ver] vi, vt to live ▷ m life;
  ~ de to live on
vívido, -a ['vividu, a] adj vivid
vivo, -a ['vivu, a] adj living;
  (esperto) clever; (cor) bright;
  (criança, debate) lively ▷ m: **os ~s**
  the living
vizinhança [vizi'ɲãsa] f
  neighbourhood (Brit),
  neighborhood (US)
vizinho, -a [vi'ziɲu, a] adj
  neighbouring (Brit), neighboring
  (US); (perto) nearby ▷ m/f
  neighbour (Brit), neighbor (US)
vó [vɔ] (col) f gran
vô [vo] (col) m grandad (Brit),
  grandpa (US)
voar [vo'ar] vi to fly; (explodir) to

blow up, explode
vocabulário [vokabu'larju] m
  vocabulary
vocábulo [vo'kabulu] m word
vocal [vo'kaw] (pl **-ais**) adj vocal
você [vo'se] pron you
vocês [vo'ses] pron pl you
vodca ['vɔdʒka] f vodka
vogal [vo'gaw] (pl **-ais**) f (Ling)
  vowel
vol. abr (= volume) vol
volante [vo'lãtʃi] m steering wheel
vôlei ['volej] m volleyball
voleibol [volej'bɔw] m = **vôlei**
volt ['vɔwtʃi] (pl **-s**) m volt
volta ['vɔwta] f turn; (regresso)
  return; (curva) bend, curve;
  (circuito) lap; (resposta) retort;
  dar uma ~ (a pé) to go for a walk;
  (de carro) to go for a drive; **estar de
  ~** to be back; **na ~ do correio** by
  return (post); **por ~ de** about,
  around; **à** ou **em ~ de** around;
  na ~ (no caminho de volta) on the
  way back
voltagem [vow'taʒẽ] f voltage
voltar [vow'tar] vt to turn ▷ vi to
  return, go (ou come) back;
  voltar-se vr to turn round; **~ a
  fazer** to do again; **~ a si** to come to;
  ~-se para to turn to; **~-se contra**
  to turn against
volume [vo'lumi] m volume;
  (pacote) package; **volumoso, -a**
  [volu'mozu, ɔza] adj bulky, big
voluntário, -a [volũ'tarju, a] adj
  voluntary ▷ m/f volunteer
volúvel [vo'luvew] (pl **-eis**) adj
  fickle
vomitar [vomi'tar] vt, vi to vomit;
  vômito ['vomitu] m (ato)
  vomiting; (efeito) vomit
vontade [võ'tadʒi] f will; (desejo)
  wish; **com ~** (com prazer) with

pleasure; (com gana) with gusto; **estar com** ou **ter ~ de fazer** to feel like doing

voo ['vou] m flight; **levantar ~** to take off; **~ livre** (Esporte) hang-gliding

voraz [vo'rajz] adj voracious

vos [vus] pron you

vós [vɔs] pron you

vosso, -a ['vɔsu, a] adj your ▷ pron: **(o) ~** yours

votação [vota'sãw] (pl **-ões**) f vote, ballot; (ato) voting

votar [vo'tar] vt (eleger) to vote for; (aprovar) to pass; (submeter a votação) to vote on ▷ vi to vote; **voto** ['vɔtu] m vote; (promessa) vow; **votos** mpl (desejos) wishes

vou [vo] vb ver **ir**

vovó [vo'vɔ] f grandma

vovô [vo'vo] m grandad

voz [vɔz] f voice; (clamor) cry; **a meia ~** in a whisper; **de viva ~** orally; **ter ~ ativa** to have a say; **em ~ baixa** in a low voice; **em ~ alta** aloud; **~ de comando** command

vulcão [vuw'kãw] (pl **-ões**) m volcano

vulgar [vuw'gar] adj common; (pej: pessoa etc) vulgar

vulnerável [vuwne'ravew] (pl **-eis**) adj vulnerable

vulto ['vuwtu] m figure; (volume) mass; (fig) importance; (pessoa importante) important person

walkie-talkie [wɔki'tɔki] (pl **-s**) m walkie-talkie

watt ['wɔtʃi] (pl **-s**) m watt

web ['wɛbi] f, adj (Comput) web

webcam [wɛb'cã] f webcam

windsurfe m windsurfing

X

government and directed by the
brothers Orlando and Cláudio
Vilasboas, who were known
internationally for their efforts
to preserve Brazil's indigenous
people. Situated in the north of
the state of Mato Grosso, it aims
to preserve indigenous culture.
It brings together sixteen
communities, a total of two
thousand Indians.

xadrez [ʃa'drez] *m* chess; (*tabuleiro*)
chessboard; (*tecido*) checked cloth
xampu [ʃã'pu] *m* shampoo
xarope [ʃa'rɔpi] *m* syrup; (*para a
tosse*) cough syrup
xeque ['ʃɛki] *m* (*soberano*) sheikh;
pôr em ~ (*fig*) to call into question;
xeque-mate (*pl* **xeques-mate**) *m*
checkmate
xerocar [ʃero'kar] *vt* to photocopy,
Xerox®
xerox® [ʃe'rɔks] *m* (*copia*)
photocopy; (*máquina*) photocopier
xícara ['ʃikara] (*BR*) *f* cup
xingar [ʃĩ'gar] *vt* to swear at ▷ *vi*
to swear
Xingu [ʃĩ'gu] *m see note*

● **XINGU**
●
● The **Xingu** National Park was
● created in 1961 by the federal

Z

ziguezague [zigi'zagi] *m* zigzag
Zimbábue [zī'babwi] *m*: **o ~** Zimbabwe
-zinho, -a [-'ziɲu, a] *sufixo* little; **florzinha** little flower
zíper ['ziper] *m* zip (*Brit*), zipper (*US*)
zodíaco [zo'dʒiaku] *m* zodiac
zoeira ['zwejra] *f* din
zombar [zõ'bar] *vi* to mock; **~ de** to make fun of; **zombaria** [zõba'ria] *f* mockery, ridicule
zona ['zɔna] *f* area; (*de cidade*) district; (*Geo*) zone; (*col: local de meretrício*) red-light district; (*: confusão*) mess; (*: tumulto*) free-for-all; **~ eleitoral** electoral district, constituency
zonzo, -a ['zõzu, a] *adj* dizzy
zoo ['zou] *m* zoo
zoológico, -a [zo'lɔʒiku, a] *adj* zoological; **jardim ~** zoo
zumbido [zũ'bidu] *m* buzz(ing); (*de tráfego*) hum
zunzum [zũ'zũ] *m* buzz(ing)

zagueiro [za'gejru] *m* (*Futebol*) fullback
Zâmbia ['zãbja] *f* Zambia
zangado, -a [zã'gadu, a] *adj* angry, annoyed; (*irritadiço*) bad-tempered
zangar [zã'gar] *vt* to annoy, irritate ▷ *vi* to get angry; **zangar-se** *vr* (*aborrecer-se*) to get annoyed; **~-se com** to get cross with
zarpar [zar'par] *vi* (*navio*) to set sail; (*ir-se*) to set off; (*fugir*) to run away
zebra ['zebra] *f* zebra
zelador, a [zela'dor(a)] *m/f* caretaker
zelar [ze'lar] *vt, vi*: **~ (por)** to look after
zerar [ze'rar] *vt* (*conta, inflação*) to reduce to zero; (*déficit*) to pay off, wipe out
zero ['zɛru] *m* zero; (*Esporte*) nil; **zero-quilômetro** *adj inv* brand new